2007–2008 Edition

Mass Media Law

2007–2008 Edition

Mass Media Law

Don R. Pember
University of Washington

Clay Calvert
Pennsylvania State University

Mc Graw Hill **Higher Education**

Boston   Burr Ridge, IL   Dubuque, IA   Madison, WI   New York   San Francisco   St. Louis
Bangkok   Bogotá   Caracas   Kuala Lumpur   Lisbon   London   Madrid   Mexico City
Milan   Montreal   New Delhi   Santiago   Seoul   Singapore   Sydney   Taipei   Toronto

Higher Education

MASS MEDIA LAW 2007/2008

Published by McGraw-Hill, a business unit of The McGraw-Hill Companies, Inc., 1221 Avenue of the Americas, New York, NY, 10020. Copyright © 2007, by The McGraw-Hill Companies, Inc.

2 3 4 5 6 7 8 9 0 DOC/DOC 0 9 8 7

ISBN-13: 978-0-07-312685-2
ISBN-10: 0-07-312685-3

Vice President and Editor-in-Chief: *Emily Barrosse*
Publisher: *Phillip A. Butcher*
Sponsoring Editor: *Phillip A. Butcher*
Freelance Developmental Editor: *Craig S. Leonard*
Senior Marketing Manager: *Leslie Oberhuber*
Project Manager: *Roger Geissler*
Designer: *Srdjan Savanovic*
Cover Designer: *George Kokkonas*
Manager, Photo Research: *Brian J. Pecko*
Production Supervisor: *Jason I. Huls*
Media Producer: *Christie Ling*
Composition: *10/12 Times Roman, by Interactive Composition Corporation*
Printing: *45# New Era Matte Plus, R. R. Donnelley & Sons*
Cover: *Capitol building: Mel Curtis, Getty Images; TVs: GoodShoot/SuperStock*

www.mhhe.com

CONTENTS

Contents

Contents

10 Protection of News Sources/Contempt Power — 413

11 Free Press/Fair Trial: Trial Level Remedies and Restrictive Orders — 467

PREFACE

Many people view the law as something that is stationary, something that rarely changes. But that is not necessarily true—especially as it relates to mass media law. Certainly some areas of this kind of law haven't changed much in decades, even centuries. The definition of what is libelous is about the same now as it was 100 years ago. But in many other areas of the law changes have occurred rapidly, subject to the whims of government officials, the winds of public opinion and the growth of legal theory. This edition of Mass Media Law contains numerous examples of this kind of change.

Chapter Two includes new material on the recent spate of laws targeting video games such as "Grand Theft Auto: San Andreas." Government agencies at both the state and local levels proposed a slew of laws in 2004 and 2005 designed to restrict the access of minors to games that they argued fostered violent behavior. Such legislation, of course, does little to reduce real-world violence, but gives the politicians the opportunity to stake out the moral high ground (giving short shrift to freedom of speech in the process) and take popular and self-righteous stands against both virtual and actual violence. In addition to video-game legislation, many public officials and members of the Federal Communications Commission called for cleaning what they called indecent content off the public airwaves to ostensibly protect children from the impact of such matter. Chapter 16 includes substantial new material on these battles.

There were calls for greater media responsibility in the past two years as some elements of the press and the "infotainment industry" demonstrated a new: aggressiveness. California cracked down on the gadfly photographers called paparazzi with several new laws. And the press was pushed by some to pay more attention to what is ethically or morally correct, not simply what is legally possible. There is new material on privacy and ethics in Chapter Eight.

Access to government information in a post 9/11 nation waging a war on terrorism continued to be a major problem for journalists and the public. "[In] the four years since September 11, an astonishing amount of information has been taken away from the American people," wrote Lucy Dalglish, head of the Reporter's Committee on Freedom of the Press in 2005. About the only good news on the access front occurred in December 2005 when President Bush signed an executive order designed to improve and expedite requests for information under the federal Freedom of Information Act. Chapter Nine contains new material on access to information matters.

There were several major battles in the past two years over reporters' efforts to keep the identity of their sources confidential in the face of subpoenas from special prosecutors and others. In one case, journalist Judith Miller spent much of the summer of 2005 in a Virginia detention facility after she chose not to reveal the name of a source who leaked to her the name of a covert CIA agent. And veteran Rhode Island television reporter Jim Taricani was sentenced to home confinement after he refused to reveal the identity of the person who gave him a copy of a secret government surveillance videotape showing an FBI informant handing an envelope, that law enforcement officials said contained a cash bribe, to a Providence, R.I., city official. These incidents and others raised a new call in 2005 for a federal law to shield journalists who are called upon to reveal the identity of their confidential sources, but Congress had taken no action on such proposals as this book went to press. These stories and others are recounted in Chapter 10.

Finally, the legal skirmishing over music file sharing reached at least tentative closure with a unanimous Supreme Court ruling that said the music industry could successfully sue software manufacturers like Grokster if it could show that a company induced copyright infringement in the marketing of its software, even of the product also had lawful uses. While the legal battles diminished and lawful downloading of recorded music increased, illegal file sharing continued as well. This ruling is detailed in Chapter 14.

As in previous editions, a full list of new material contained in this edition follows this short preface. But we have added something new. There is also a list that indicates the location of major segments of the book that relate directly to particular problems of how the law applies to the Internet.

The authors want to thank the following reviewers for their help in putting together this 2007–2008 edition.

Diana Huffman, University of Maryland

Bob Carey, Gardner-Webb University

Steve Craig, University of North Texas

Eric Freedman, Michigan State University

Alisa White, University of Texas at Arlington

Mary P. Arnold, Ph.D., South Dakota State University

Lyombe (Leo) Eko, University of Iowa

Charles Sterin, Ph.D., University of Maryland University College

Eric Ellis, Florida State University

For the record, Don Pember is responsible for Chapters One, Four, Five, Six, Seven, Eight, 11, 12, 13 and 14. He would like to thank Jerry Baldasty and other faculty members at the University of Washington, for continued support for this book. He would also like to thank his wife Diann, for her technical support at he struggled with a new iMac computer. Clay Calvert is responsible for Chapters Two, Three, Nine, 10, 15 and 16. And he wants to thank Penn State students Rachel Frankel and Lesley O'Connor for reviewing early drafts of revised materials for this edition.

Don Pember
Seattle, Washington
February 1, 2006

Clay Calvert
University Park, Pennsylvania
February 1, 2006

IMPORTANT NEW, EXPANDED AND UPDATED MATERIAL

Expanded section on community censorship, including "heckler's veto;" pages 39–41

Expanded discussion of First Amendment theories; pages 45–50

New material on regulation of minor's access to violent video games; pages 64–66

New discussion of prior restraint and Kobe Bryant trial; pages 80–84

Updated discussion of coverage of the war in Iraq; pages 94–100

Revised and updated discussion of First Amendment in public schools; pages 101–100

Revised and expanded discussion of censorship of college press; pages 114–121

Updated information on hate speech; pages 143–147

New introduction to libel chapters; pages 158–163

New material on defamatory opinions; pages 179–180

Updated discussion on defamation by implication; pages 188–189

New material on who is a public official; pages 198–202

Updated material on criminal libel; pages 271–273

New introduction to right to privacy chapters; pages 276–277

New material on intrusion and the Internet; pages 309–312

Expanded discussion on ethics and privacy; pages 330–332

New section on the journalist's right to interview; pages 351–353

Updated and new material on battles over FOIA document requests; pages 365–368

Expanded discussion of *National Archives and Records Admin. v. Favish;* pages 387–389

New section on HIPPA and access to medical records; pages 404–406

New material on reporter/source battles involving Judith Miller and Matthew Cooper; pages 415–418, and Jim Taricani; pages 439–441

New material on breach of promise and source confidentiality; page 427

New material on whether bloggers are journalists; pages 445–447

New material on calls for new federal and state shield laws; pages 418–419 and 448–449

New introduction to free press/fair trial chapters; pages 467–470

Revised material on gag orders aimed at trial participants; pages 486–488

Revised material on access to military tribunals; pages 502–503

New material on access to juror records and deliberations; page 510

Updated material on cameras in the courtroom; pages 516–517

New material on media self-censorship of indecency; pages 527–528

Discussion of *Extreme Associates* case; page 535

New material on Child Online Protection Act; pages 554–555

New material on trademark protection; pages 563–568

Updated and revised section on file sharing; pages 605–609

New material on free-lancing and copyright protection; page 611

New cases on defining what is commercial speech; pages 621–623

INTERNET AND WORLD WIDE WEB-RELATED MATERIAL

2007–2008 Edition

Mass Media Law

THE AMERICAN LEGAL SYSTEM

Before a physician can study surgery, he or she needs to study anatomy. So it is with the study of mass media law. Before a study of this narrow aspect of American law is undertaken, a student must first have a general background in the law and in the operation of the judicial system. That is the purpose of this short chapter.

Probably no nation is more closely tied to the law than is the American Republic. From the 1770s, when at the beginning of a war of revolution we attempted to legally justify our separation from the motherland, to the 21st century, when citizens of the nation attempt to resolve weighty moral, political, social and environmental problems through the judicial process, and during the more than 200 years between, the American people have showed a remarkable faith in the law. One could write a surprisingly accurate history of this nation using reports of court decisions as the only source. Not that what happens in the courts reflects everything that happens in the nation; but as has been observed by 19th-century French political scientist and historian Alexis de Tocqueville and others, political and sometimes moral issues in the United States often end up as legal disputes. Beginning with the sedition cases in the late

1790s, which reflected the political turmoil of that era, one could chart the history of the United States from adolescence to maturity. As the frontier expanded in the 19th century, citizens used the courts to argue land claims and boundary problems. Civil rights litigation in both the mid-19th and mid-20th centuries reflects a people attempting to cope with racial and ethnic diversity. Industrialization brought labor unions, workers' compensation laws and child labor laws, all of which resulted in controversies that found their way into the courts. As mass production developed and large manufacturers began to create most of the consumer goods used, judges and juries had to cope with new laws on product safety, honesty in advertising and consumer complaints. In recent years Americans have gone to court to try to resolve disputes over abortion, gay rights, press coverage of wars and other military operations, university admission policies, the legal rights of persons suspected of terrorism, and even state and national elections.

Americans have protested every war the nation has fought—from the Revolutionary War to the invasion of Iraq. The record of these protests is contained in scores of court decisions. The prohibition and crime of the 1920s and the economic woes of the 1930s both left residue in the law. In the United States, as in most other societies, law is a basic part of existence, as necessary for the survival of civilization as are economic systems, political systems, mass communication systems, cultural achievement and the family.

This chapter has two purposes: to acquaint readers with the law and to present a brief outline of the legal system in the United States. While this is not designed to be a comprehensive course in law and the judicial system—such material can better be studied in depth in an undergraduate political science course—it does provide sufficient introduction to understand the remaining 15 chapters of the book.

The chapter opens with a discussion of the law, giving consideration to the most important sources of the law in the United States, and moves on to the judicial system, including both the federal and state court systems. A summary of judicial review and a brief outline of how both criminal and civil lawsuits are started and proceed through the courts are included in the discussion of the judicial system.

SOURCES OF THE LAW

There are almost as many definitions of law as there are people who study the law. Some people say that law is any social norm or any organized or ritualized method of settling disputes. Most writers on the subject insist that it is a bit more complex, that some system of sanctions is required for a genuine legal system. John Austin, a 19th-century English jurist, defined law as definite rules of human conduct with appropriate sanctions for their enforcement. He added that both the rules and the sanctions must be prescribed by duly constituted human authority.[1] Roscoe Pound, an American legal scholar, has suggested that law is really social engineering—the attempt to order the way people behave. For the purposes of this book, it is probably more helpful to consider the law to be a set of rules that attempt to guide human conduct and a set of formal, governmental sanctions that are applied when those rules are violated.

---

1. Abraham, *Judicial Process.*

Scholars still debate the genesis of "the law." A question that is more meaningful and easier to answer is, What is the source of American law? There are several major sources of the law in the United States: the Constitution; the common law; the law of equity; the statutory law; and the rulings of various executives, such as the president and mayors and governors, and administrative bodies and agencies. Historically, we can trace American law to Great Britain. As colonizers of much of the North American continent, the British supplied Americans with an outline for both a legal system and a judicial system. In fact, because of the many similarities between British and American law, many people consider the Anglo-American legal system to be a single entity. Today in the United States, our federal Constitution is the supreme law of the land. Yet when each of these sources of law is considered separately, it is more useful to begin with the earliest source of Anglo-American law, the common law.

THE COMMON LAW

The **common law,*** which developed in England during the 200 years after the Norman Conquest in the 11th century, is one of the great legacies of the British people to colonial America. During those two centuries, the crude mosaic of Anglo-Saxon customs was replaced by a single system of law worked out by jurists and judges. The system of law became common throughout England; it became the common law. It was also called the common law to distinguish it from the ecclesiastical (church) law prevalent at the time. Initially, the customs of the people were used by the king's courts as the foundation of the law, disputes were resolved according to community custom, and governmental sanction was applied to enforce the resolution. As such, the common law was, and still is, considered "discovered law." When a problem arose, the court's task was to find or discover the proper solution, to seek the common custom of the people. The judge didn't create the law; he or she merely found it, much like a miner finds gold or silver.

This, at least, is the theory of the common law. Perhaps at one point judges themselves believed that they were merely discovering the law when they handed down decisions. As legal problems became more complex and as the law began to be professionally administered (the first lawyers appeared during this era, and eventually professional judges), it became clear that the common law reflected not so much the custom of the land as the custom of the court—or more properly, the custom of the judges. While judges continued to look to the past to discover how other courts decided a case when given similar facts (precedent is discussed in a moment), many times judges were forced to create the law themselves.

This common-law system was the perfect system for the American colonies. It was a very pragmatic system aimed at settling real problems, not at expounding abstract and intellectually satisfying theories. The common law is an inductive system of law in which a legal rule is arrived at after consideration of a great number of cases. (In a deductive system of law, which is common in many other nations, the rules are expounded first and then the court decides the legal situation under the existing rule.) Colonial America was a land of new problems for British and other settlers. The old law frequently did not work. But the common law

*Terms that are in boldface type are defined in the glossary, which begins on page 725.

Stare decisis is the key phrase: Let the decision stand.

easily accommodated the new environment. The ability of the common law to adapt to change is directly responsible for its longevity.

Fundamental to the common law is the concept that judges should look to the past and follow court precedents.* The Latin expression for the concept is this: "Stare decisis et non quieta movere" (to stand by past decisions and not disturb things at rest). **Stare decisis** is the key phrase: Let the decision stand. A judge should resolve current problems in the same manner as similar problems were resolved in the past. When high school wrestling coach Mike Milkovich sued the Lorain (Ohio) Journal Company in the mid-1970s for publishing the claim that Milkovich had lied during a hearing, the judge most certainly looked to past decisions to discover whether in previous cases such a charge had been considered defamatory or libelous. There are ample precedents for ruling that a published charge that a person lied is libelous, and Milkovich won his lawsuit.[2]

The Role of Precedent

At first glance one would think that the law can never change in a system that continually looks to the past. What if the first few rulings in a line of cases were bad decisions? Are the courts saddled with bad law forever? Fortunately, the law does not operate quite in this way. While following **precedent** is the desired state of affairs (many people say that certainty in the law is more important than justice), it is not always the proper way to proceed. To protect the integrity of the common law, judges developed several means of coping with bad law and with new situations in which the application of old law would result in injustice.

Imagine for a moment that the newspaper in your hometown publishes a picture and story about a 12-year-old girl who gave birth to a 7-pound son in a local hospital. The mother and father do not like the publicity and sue the newspaper for invasion of privacy. The attorney for the parents finds a precedent, *Barber* v. *Time,*[3] in which a Missouri court ruled that to photograph a patient in a hospital room against her will and then to publish that picture in a newsmagazine is an **invasion of privacy.**

Does the existence of this precedent mean that the young couple will automatically win this lawsuit? that the court will follow the decision? No, it does not. For one thing, there may be other cases in which courts have ruled that publishing such a picture is not an invasion of privacy. In fact in 1956 in the case of *Meetze* v. *AP,*[4] a South Carolina court made just such a ruling. But for the moment assume that *Barber* v. *Time* is the only precedent. Is the court bound by this precedent? No. The court has several options concerning the 1942 decision.

---

*Appellate courts (see page 16) often render decisions that decide only the particular case and do not establish binding precedent. Courts refer to these as "unpublished decisions." In some parts of the country it is even unlawful for a lawyer to mention these onetime rulings in legal papers submitted in later cases. But change may be in the wind. In early 2003, the U.S. Court of Appeals for the District of Columbia and the Texas Supreme Court reversed their restrictions on citing these unpublished decisions. Courts in other jurisdictions may follow this pattern as well.

2. *Milkovich* v. *Lorain Journal Co.,* 110 S. Ct. 2695 (1991).
3. 159 S.W. 2d 291 (1942).
4. 95 S.E. 2d 606 (1956).

First, it can *accept* the precedent as law and rule that the newspaper has invaded the privacy of the couple by publishing the picture and story about the birth of their child. Second, the court can *modify,* or change, the 1942 precedent by arguing that *Barber* v. *Time* was decided more than 60 years ago when people were more sensitive about going to a hospital, since a stay there was often considered to reflect badly on a patient. Today hospitalization is no longer a sensitive matter to most people. Therefore, a rule of law restricting the publication of a picture of a hospital patient is unrealistic, unless the picture is in bad taste or needlessly embarrasses the patient. Then the publication may be an invasion of privacy. In our imaginary case, then, the decision turns on what kind of picture and story the newspaper published: a pleasant picture that flattered the couple? or one that mocked and embarrassed them? If the court rules in this manner, it *modifies* the 1942 precedent, making it correspond to what the judge perceives to be contemporary sensibilities.

As a third option the court can decide that *Barber* v. *Time* provides an important precedent for a plaintiff hospitalized because of an unusual disease—as Dorothy Barber was—but that in the case before the court, the plaintiff was hospitalized to give birth to a baby, a different situation: giving birth is a voluntary status; catching a disease is not. Because the two cases present different problems, they are really different cases. Hence, the *Barber* v. *Time* precedent does not apply. This practice is called *distinguishing the precedent from the current case,* a very common action.

Finally, the court can *overrule* the precedent. In 1941 the Supreme Court of the United States overruled a decision made by the Supreme Court in 1918 regarding the right of a judge to use what is called the **summary contempt power** (*Toledo Newspaper Co.* v. *U.S.*).[5] This is the power of a judge to charge someone with being in contempt of court, to find that person guilty of contempt, and then to punish him or her for the contempt—all without a jury trial. In *Nye* v. *U.S.*[6] the high court said that in 1918 it had been improperly informed as to the intent of a measure passed by Congress in 1831 that authorized the use of the summary power by federal judges. The 1918 ruling was therefore bad, was wrong, and was reversed. (Fuller explanation of summary contempt as it applies to the mass media is given in Chapter 10.) The only courts that can effectively overrule the 1942 decision by the Missouri Supreme Court in *Barber* v. *Time* are the Missouri Supreme Court and the U.S. Supreme Court.

Obviously, the preceding discussion oversimplifies the judicial process. Rarely is a court confronted with only a single precedent. And whether or not precedent is binding on a court is often an issue. For example, decisions by the Supreme Court of the United States regarding the U.S. Constitution and federal laws are binding on all federal and state courts. Decisions by the U.S. Court of Appeals on federal matters are binding only on other lower federal and state courts in that circuit or region. (See pages 24–25 for a discussion of the circuits.) The supreme court of any state is the final authority on the meaning of the constitution and laws of that state, and its rulings on these matters are binding on all state and *federal* courts in that state. Matters are more complicated when federal courts interpret state laws. State courts can accept or reject these interpretations in most instances. Because mass media

5. 242 U.S. 402 (1918).
6. 313 U.S. 33 (1941).

law is so heavily affected by the First Amendment, state judges are frequently forced to look outside their borders to precedents developed by the federal courts. A state court ruling on a question involving the First Amendment guarantees of freedom of speech and freedom of the press will be substantially guided by federal court precedents on the same subject.

Lawyers and law professors often debate just how important precedent really is when a court makes a decision. Some persons have suggested what is called the "hunch theory" of jurisprudence. Under this theory a judge or justice decides a case based on instinct or a feeling of what is right and wrong and then seeks out precedents to support the decision.

The imaginary invasion-of-privacy case just discussed demonstrates that the common law can have vitality, that despite the rule of precedent a judge is rarely bound tightly by the past. There is a saying: Every age should be the mistress of its own law. This saying applies to the common law as well as to all other aspects of the legal system.

Finding Common-Law Cases

It must be clear at this point that the common law is not specifically written down someplace for all to see and use. It is instead contained in the hundreds of thousands of decisions handed down by courts over the centuries. Many attempts have been made to summarize the law. Sir Edward Coke compiled and analyzed the precedents of common law in the early 17th century. Sir William Blackstone later expanded Coke's work in the monumental "Commentaries on the Law of England." More recently, in such works as the massive "Restatement of Torts," the task was again undertaken, but on a narrower scale.

Courts began to keep records of their decisions centuries ago. In the 13th century unofficial reports of cases began to appear in yearbooks, but they were records of court proceedings in which procedural points were clarified for the benefit of legal practitioners rather than collections of court decisions. The modern concept of fully reporting the written decisions of all courts probably began in 1785 with the publication of the first British Term Reports.

While scholars and lawyers still uncover the common law using the case-by-case method, it is fairly easy today to locate the appropriate cases through a simple system of citation. The cases of a single court (such as the U.S. Supreme Court or the federal district courts) are collected in a single **case reporter** (such as the "United States Reports" or the "Federal Supplement"). The cases are collected chronologically and fill many volumes. Each case collected has its individual **citation,** or identification number, which reflects the name of the reporter in which the case can be found, the volume of that reporter, and the page on which the case begins (Figure 1.1). For example, the citation for the decision in *Adderly* v. *Florida* (a freedom-of-speech case) is 385 U.S. 39 (1966). The letters in the middle (U.S.) indicate that the case is in the "United States Reports," the official government reporter for cases decided by the Supreme Court of the United States. The number 385 refers to the specific volume of the "United States Reports" in which the case is found. The second number (39) gives the page on which the case appears. Finally, 1966 provides the year in which the case was decided. So, *Adderly* v. *Florida* can be found on page 39 of volume 385 of the "United States Reports."

The coming of the computer age has affected the legal community in many ways. Court opinions are now available to lawyers and others via a variety of computer-mediated communication systems. In many jurisdictions, lawyers are permitted to file documents

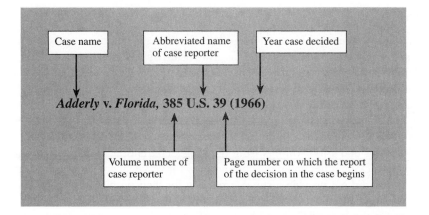

electronically with the court so long as they back these documents up with hard copies soon thereafter. Some legal authorities have argued that a new system of citations is needed, one that is suitable for printed case reporters—which will remain the standard in the judicial system at least in the early years of the 21st century—and for cases transmitted electronically. And new systems have been proposed, including an elaborate modification recommended for adoption in 1996 by the House of Delegates of the American Bar Association. But no scheme has received widespread or enthusiastic support from the judges, lawyers and court administrators who would use it.

If you have the correct citation, you can easily find any case you seek. Locating all citations of the cases apropos to a particular problem—such as a libel suit—is a different matter and is a technique taught in law schools. A great many legal encyclopedias, digests, compilations of the common law, books and articles are used by lawyers to track down the names and citations of the appropriate cases.

There is no better way to sum up the common law than to quote Oliver Wendell Holmes ("The Common Law," published in 1881):[7]

> The life of the law has not been logic; it has been experience. The felt necessities of the time, the prevalent moral and political theories, intuitions of public policy, avowed or unconscious, even the prejudices which judges share with their fellowmen, have had a good deal more to do than syllogism in determining the rules by which men should be governed. The law embodies the story of a nation's development through many centuries, and it cannot be dealt with as if it contained only the axioms and corollaries of a book of mathematics. In order to know what it is, we must know what it has been, and what it tends to become. . . . The very considerations which judges most rarely mention, and always with an apology, are the secret root from which the law draws all the juices of life. I mean, of course, considerations of what is expedient for the community concerned.

"The life of the law has not been logic; it has been experience."

7. Holmes, *Common Law.*

THE LAW OF EQUITY

The law of **equity** is another kind of judge-made law. The distinction today between the common law and equity law has blurred. The cases are heard by the same judges in the same courtrooms. Differences in procedures and remedies are all that is left to distinguish these two categories of the law. Separate consideration of the common law and equity leads to a better understanding of both, however. The law of equity, as developed in Britain beginning in the 14th and 15th centuries, is the second basic source of the law in the United States. Equity was originally a supplement to the common law and developed side by side with the common law. During the 1300s and 1400s rulings from the king's courts often became rigid and narrow. Many persons seeking relief under the common law for very real grievances were turned away because the law did not provide a suitable remedy for their problems. In such instances the disappointed litigant could take the problem to the king for resolution, petitioning the king to "do right for the love of God and by way of charity." According to legal scholar Henry Abraham, "The king was empowered to mold the law for the sake of 'justice,' to grant the relief prayed for as an act of grace."[8] Soon the chancellor, the king's secretary or assistant, set up a special office or court to resolve the problems that the king's common-law courts could not handle. At the outset of the hearing, the aggrieved party had to establish that there was no adequate remedy under the common law and that a special court was needed to hear the case. The office of the chancellor soon became known as the Court of Chancery. Decisions were made on the basis of conscience or fairness or "equity." In the early years of this republic many states established similar Courts of Chancery.

British common law and equity law were American law until the Revolution in 1776. After independence was won, the basic principles of common law in existence before the Revolution were kept because the cases remained acceptable precedent. After some hesitation, equity was accepted in much the same way.

The rules and procedures under equity are far more flexible than those under the common law. Equity really begins where the common law leaves off. Equity suits are never tried before a jury. Rulings come in the form of **judicial decrees,** not in judgments of yes or no. Decisions in equity are (and were) discretionary on the part of judges. And despite the fact that precedents are also relied upon in the law of equity, judges are free to do what they think is right and fair in a specific case.

Equity provides another advantage for troubled litigants—the restraining order. A judge sitting in equity can order preventive measures as well as remedial ones. Individuals who can demonstrate that they are in peril or are about to suffer a serious irremediable wrong can usually gain a legal writ such as an injunction or a restraining order to stop someone from doing something. Generally, a court issues a temporary restraining order until it can hear arguments from both parties in the dispute and decide whether an injunction should be made permanent. Under the common law the court can only provide a remedy (usually money damages) after the harm has occurred.

In 1971 the federal government asked the federal courts to restrain The New York Times and the Washington Post from publishing what have now become known as the Pentagon Papers (this case is discussed in greater detail in Chapter 2). This case is a good example of

8. Abraham, *Judicial Process.*

Source: © Bettmann/CORBIS

Oliver Wendell Holmes, the author of The Common Law, *and an associate justice of the Supreme Court of the United States from 1902 until 1932.*

equity law in action. The government argued that if the purloined documents were published by the two newspapers the nation would suffer irremediable damage; that foreign governments would be reluctant to entrust the United States with their secrets if those secrets might someday be published in the public press; that the enemy would gain valuable defense secrets. The federal government argued further that it would do little good to punish the newspapers after the material had been published since there would be no way to repair the damage. Both newspapers were initially restrained from publishing the material while the case was argued—all the way to the Supreme Court of the United States. After two weeks of hearings, the high court finally ruled that publication could continue, that the government had failed to prove that the nation would be damaged.[9]

STATUTORY LAW

Statutory law, or legislation, is the third great source of U.S. law. Today there are legislative bodies of all shapes and sizes. The common traits they share are that they are popularly elected and that they have the authority to pass laws. In the beginning of our nation, legislation really did not play a very significant role in the legal system. Certainly many laws were passed, but the bulk of our legal rules were developed from the common law and from equity law. After 1825 statutory law began to play an important role in our legal system, and it was

9. *New York Times Co.* v. *United States,* 403 U.S. 713 (1971).

between 1850 and 1900 that a greater percentage of law began to come from legislative acts than from common-law court decisions.

Several important characteristics of statutory law can best be understood by contrasting them with common law. First, **statutes** tend to deal with problems affecting society or large groups of people, in contrast to common law, which usually deals with smaller, individual problems. (Some common-law rulings affect large groups of people, but this occurrence is rare.) It should also be noted in this connection the importance of not confusing common law with constitutional law. Certainly when judges interpret a constitution, they make policy that affects us all. However, it should be kept in mind that a constitution is a legislative document voted on by the people and is not "discovered law" or "judge-made law."

Second, statutory law can anticipate problems, and common law cannot. For example, a state legislature can pass a statute that prohibits publication of the school records of a student without prior consent of the student. Under the common law the problem cannot be resolved until a student's record has been published in a newspaper or transmitted over the Internet and the student brings action against the publisher to recover damages for the injury incurred.

The criminal laws in the United States are all statutory laws.

Third, the criminal laws in the United States are all statutory laws—common-law crimes no longer exist in this country and have not since 1812. Common-law rules are not precise enough to provide the kind of notice needed to protect a criminal defendant's right to due process of law.

Fourth, statutory law is collected in codes and law books, instead of in reports as is the common law. When a proposal or bill is adopted by the legislative branch and approved by the executive branch, it becomes law and is integrated into the proper section of a municipal code, a state code, or whatever. However, this does not mean that some very important statutory law cannot be found in the case reporters.

Passage of a law is rarely the final word on the subject. Courts become involved in the process of determining what that law means. While a properly constructed statute sometimes needs little interpretation by the courts, judges are frequently called upon to rule on the exact meaning of ambiguous phrases and words. The resulting process is called **statutory construction** and is a very important part of the law. Even the simplest kind of statement often needs interpretation. For example, a prohibition stating "it is illegal to distribute an obscene newspaper" is filled with ambiguity. What does *distribution* mean? Can an obscene document be sent through the mail? distributed from house to house? passed out on street corners? transmitted on the Internet? Are all of these actions prohibited? What constitutes a newspaper? Is any printed matter a newspaper? Is any printed matter regularly published a newspaper? Are mimeographed sheets and photocopied newsletters considered newspapers? Should a Web site be considered a newspaper? Of course, implicit is the classic question with which courts have wrestled in this country for more than a century: What is obscenity?

Usually a legislature tries to leave some kind of trail to help a judge find out what the law means. For when judges rule on the meaning of a statute, they are supposed to determine what the legislature meant when it passed the law (the legislative intent), not what they think the law should mean. Minutes of committee hearings in which the law was discussed, legislative staff reports, and reports of debate on the floor can all be used to help a judge determine the legislative intent. Therefore, when lawyers deal with statutes, they frequently are forced to search the case reporters to find out how the courts interpreted a law in which they are interested.

CONSTITUTIONAL LAW

Great Britain does not have a written **constitution.** The United States does have a written constitution, and it is an important source of our law. In fact, there are many constitutions in this country: the federal Constitution, state constitutions, city charters and so forth. All these documents accomplish the same ends. First, they provide the plan for the establishment and organization of the government. Next, they outline the duties, responsibilities and powers of the various elements of government. Finally, they usually guarantee certain basic rights to the people, such as freedom of speech and freedom to peaceably assemble.

Legislative bodies may enact statutes rather easily by a majority vote. It is far more difficult to adopt or change a constitution. State constitutions are approved or changed by a direct vote of the people. It is even more difficult to change the federal Constitution. An amendment may be proposed by a vote of two-thirds of the members of both the U.S. House of Representatives and the Senate. Alternatively, two-thirds of the state legislatures can call for a constitutional convention for proposing amendments. Once proposed, the amendments must be approved either by three-fourths of the state legislatures or by three-fourths of the constitutional conventions called in all the states. Congress decides which method of ratification or approval is to be used. Because the people have an unusually direct voice in the approval and change of a constitution, constitutions are considered the most important source of U.S. law.

One Supreme Court justice described a constitution as a kind of yardstick against which all the other actions of government must be measured to determine whether the actions are permissible. The U.S. Constitution is the supreme law of the land. Any law or other constitution that conflicts with the U.S. Constitution is unenforceable. A state constitution plays the same role for a state: A statute passed by the Michigan legislature and signed by the governor of that state is clearly unenforceable if it conflicts with the Michigan Constitution. And so it goes for all levels of constitutions.

Constitutions tend to be short and, at the federal level and in most states, infrequently amended. Consequently, changes in the language of a constitution are uncommon. But a considerable amount of constitutional law is nevertheless developed by the courts, which are asked to determine the meaning of provisions in the documents and to decide whether other laws or government actions violate constitutional provisions. Hence, the case reporters are repositories for the constitutional law that governs the nation.

Twenty-seven amendments are appended to the U.S. Constitution. The first 10 of these are known as the Bill of Rights and provide a guarantee of certain basic human rights to all citizens. Included are freedom of speech and freedom of the press, rights you will come to understand more fully in future chapters.

The federal Constitution and the 50 state constitutions are very important when considering mass-media law problems. All 51 of these charters contain provisions, in one form or another, that guarantee freedom of speech and freedom of the press. Consequently, any government action that affects in any way the freedom of individuals or mass media to speak or publish or broadcast must be measured against the constitutional guarantees of freedom of expression. There are several reasons why a law limiting speaking or publishing might be declared unconstitutional. The law might be a direct restriction on speech or press that is protected by the First Amendment. For example, an order by a Nebraska judge that prohibited the press from publishing certain information about a pending murder trial was considered a direct restriction on freedom of the press (see *Nebraska Press Association* v. *Stuart,*[10] Chapter 11). A criminal obscenity statute or another kind of criminal law might be declared unconstitutional because it is too vague. A law must provide adequate notice to a person of ordinary intelligence that his or her contemplated conduct is prohibited by the law. An Indianapolis pornography ordinance that made it a crime to publish pornographic material was declared void, at least in part, because the law's definition of pornography was not specific enough. The law defined pornography as including depictions of "the subordination of women." It is almost impossible to settle in one's own mind upon a single meaning or understanding of that term, noted Judge Sarah Barker (see *American Booksellers Association* v. *Hudnut,*[11] Chapter 13). A statute might also be declared to be unconstitutional because it violates what is known as the overbreadth doctrine. A law is overbroad, the Supreme Court said many years ago, if it does not aim specifically at evils within the allowable area of government control but sweeps within its ambit other activities that constitute an exercise of protected expression. Struthers, Ohio, an industrial community where many people worked at night and slept during the day, passed an ordinance that forbade knocking on the door or ringing the doorbell at a residence in order to deliver a handbill. The Supreme Court ruled that the ordinance was overbroad. The city's objective could be obtained by passing an ordinance making it an offense for any person to ring a doorbell of a householder who had, through a sign or some other means, indicated that he or she did not wish to be disturbed, the court noted. As written, however, the law prohibited persons from distributing handbills to all persons—to those who wanted to see and read them as well as those who did not (see *Martin* v. *City of Struthers,*[12] Chapter 3). So there are many reasons why a court might declare a law to be an unconstitutional infringement upon the guarantees of freedom of speech and press.

EXECUTIVE ORDERS, ADMINISTRATIVE RULES

The final source of American law has two streams that have been combined here for the purposes of this discussion. First are the orders issued by duly elected officers of the government, often called executive orders. Second are the myriad of rules that are generated by the administrative agencies of government, at the federal, state and local levels.

Government executives—the U.S. president, governors, mayors, county executives, village presidents—all have more or less power to issue rules of law, sometimes referred to as executive orders or declarations. This power is normally defined by the constitution or the charter that establishes the office, and it varies widely from city to city or state to state. In some instances the individual has fairly broad powers; in others the power is sharply confined. For example, President Bill Clinton, before he left office in 2001, issued a wide array of executive orders aimed at protecting the environment. And President George W. Bush has issued numerous executive orders related to the nation's war on terrorism. Such declarations are possible so long as they are properly within the delegated powers held by the executive. An order from an executive who exceeds his or her power can be overturned by the legislature (the

10. 427 U.S. 539 (1976).
11. 598 F. Supp. 1316 (1985).
12. 319 U.S. 141 (1943).

mayor's order can be changed or vacated by the city council, for example) or by a court. A debate erupted in early 2006 over whether President George Bush had the authority or legal power to order the National Security Agency to eavesdrop on domestic and transnational telephone conversations as a part of the war on terrorists. While such orders are not a large part of the American law, they can nevertheless be important in some circumstances.

A more substantial part of U.S. law is generated by the myriad of administrative agencies that exist in the nation today, agencies that first began to develop in the latter part of the 19th century. By that time in the country's history the job of governing had become much more complex. Congress was being asked to resolve questions going far beyond such matters as budgets, wars, treaties and the like. Technology created new kinds of problems for Congress to resolve. Many such issues were complex and required specialized knowledge and expertise that the representatives and senators lacked and could not easily acquire, had they wanted to. Specialized federal administrative agencies were therefore created to deal with these problems.

For example, regulation of the railroads that traversed the nation created numerous problems in the late 19th century. Since questions concerning use of these railroads fell within the commerce power of Congress, that body was given the task of resolving this complex issue. To deal with these problems, Congress created the first **administrative agency,** the Interstate Commerce Commission (ICC). This agency was established by legislation and funded by Congress. Its members were appointed by the president and approved by Congress. Each member served a fixed term in office. The agency was independent of Congress, the president and the courts. Its task was (and is) to regulate commerce between the states, a matter that concerned pipelines, shipping and transportation. The members of the board presumably were somewhat expert in the area before appointment and of course became more so during the course of their term.

Hundreds of such agencies now exist at both federal and state levels. In fact, many people speculate that the rules generated by these agencies comprise the bulk of American law today. Each agency undertakes to deal with a specific set of problems too technical or too large for the legislative branch to handle. Typical is the Federal Communications Commission (FCC), which was created by Congress in 1934. Its task is to regulate broadcasting and other telecommunication in the United States, a job that Congress has attempted only sporadically. Its members must be citizens of the United States and are appointed by the president. The single stipulation is that at any one time no more than three of the five individuals on the commission can be from the same political party. The Senate must confirm the appointments.

Congress has sketched the framework for the regulation of broadcasting in the Federal Communications Act of 1934 and subsequent amendments to this statute. This legislation is used by the FCC as its basic regulatory guidelines. But the agency generates much law on its own as it interprets the congressional mandates, and uses its considerable authority to generate rules and regulations. The philosophies of its members often dictate the concerns that generate rule making. For example, beginning in 2003 the commission, led by its conservative chairman Michael K. Powell, initiated a controversial campaign to eliminate what some of its members regarded as indecent radio and television programming. (See Chapter 16 for a full discussion of these efforts.)

Persons dissatisfied with an action by an agency can attempt to have it modified by asking the legislative body that created and funds the agency—Congress, for example, when considering the FCC—to change or overturn the action. In the 1980s when the Federal Trade

But courts have limited power to review decisions made by administrative agencies.

Commission made several aggressive pro-consumer rulings, Congress voided these actions because members disagreed with the extent of the rulings. More commonly the actions of an agency will be challenged in the courts. But courts have limited power to review decisions made by administrative agencies and can overturn such a ruling in only these limited circumstances:

1. If the original act that established the commission or agency is unconstitutional.
2. If the commission or agency exceeds its authority.
3. If the commission or agency violates its own rules.
4. If there is no evidentiary basis whatsoever to support the ruling.

The reason for these limitations is simple: These agencies were created to bring expert knowledge to bear on complex problems, and the entire purpose for their creation would be defeated if judges with no special expertise in a given area could reverse an agency ruling merely because they had a different solution to a problem.

The case reporters contain some law created by the administrative agencies, but the reports that these agencies themselves publish contain much more such law. These reports are also arranged on a case-by-case basis in chronological order. A citation system similar to that used for the case reporters is used in these reports.

There are other sources of American law but the sources just discussed—common law, law of equity, statutory law, constitutional law, executive orders and rules and regulations by administrative agencies—are the most important and are of most concern in this book. First Amendment problems fall under the purview of constitutional law. Libel and invasion of privacy are matters generally dealt with by the common law and the law of equity. Obscenity laws in this country are statutory provisions (although this fact is frequently obscured by the hundreds of court cases in which judges attempt to define the meaning of obscenity). And of course the regulation of broadcasting and advertising falls primarily under the jurisdiction of administrative agencies.

While this section provides a basic outline of the law and is not comprehensive, the information is sufficient to make upcoming material on mass media law understandable.

SUMMARY

There are several important sources of American law. The common law is the oldest source of our law, having developed in England more than 700 years ago. The law became common throughout Great Britain and reflected the customs of the people. It was easily transported to the New World, and its pragmatic philosophy was highly useful on the rapidly developing North American continent. Fundamental to the common law is the concept that judges should look to the past and follow earlier court rulings, called precedents. Stare decisis (let the decision stand) is a key concept. But judges have developed the means to change or adapt the common law by modifying, distinguishing or overruling precedent case law. The common law is not written down in a law book but is collected in volumes that contain the reports of legal decisions. Each case is given its own legal identity through a system of numbered citations.

Equity law, the second source of American law, developed because in some instances the common law was simply too rigid to fairly resolve the real grievances of British subjects.

The rules and procedures of equity are far more flexible than those of the common law and permit a judge (equity cases are never heard before a jury) to fashion a solution to unique or unusual problems. A court is permitted under equity law to restrain an individual or a corporation or even a government from taking an action. Under the common law a court can only attempt to compensate the injured party for the damage that results from the action.

Today a great volume of American law is generated by Congress, legislatures, city and county councils, and myriad other legislative bodies. This legislation, called statutory law, is the third important source of American law. All criminal laws are statutes. Statutes usually deal with problems that affect great numbers of people, and statutes can anticipate problems, whereas the common law cannot. All statutes are collected in codes or statute books. Courts become involved in the development of statutes when they are called on to interpret the meaning of the words and phrases contained in a statute.

Constitutions, the fourth source of our law, take precedence over all other American law. The U.S. Constitution is the supreme law of the land. Other laws, whether they spring from common law, equity, legislative bodies, or administrative agencies, cannot conflict with the provisions of the Constitution. Courts are often called upon to interpret the meaning of the provisions of our constitutions (one federal and 50 state constitutions) and through this process can often make these seemingly rigid legal prescriptions adaptable to contemporary problems.

Executives such as presidents and governors can issue orders that carry the force of law. And there are thousands of administrative agencies, boards and commissions in the nation that produce rules and regulations. This administrative law usually deals with technical and complicated matters requiring levels of expertise that members of traditional legislative bodies do not normally possess. Members of these agencies and commissions are usually appointed by presidents or by governors or mayors, and the agencies are supervised and funded by legislative bodies. Their tasks are narrowly defined and their rulings, while they carry the force of law, can always be appealed.

THE JUDICIAL SYSTEM

This section provides an introduction to the court system in the United States. Since the judicial branch of our three-part government is the field on which most of the battles involving communications law are fought, an understanding of the judicial system is essential.

It is technically improper to talk about the American judicial system. There are 52 different judicial systems in the United States, one for the federal government and one for each of the 50 states, plus the District of Columbia. While each of these systems is somewhat different from all the others, the similarities among the 52 systems are much more important than the differences. Each of the systems is divided into two distinct sets of courts—trial courts and appellate courts. Each judicial system is established by a constitution, federal or state. In each system the courts act as the third branch of a common triumvirate of government: a legislative branch, which makes the law; an executive branch, which enforces the law; and a judicial branch, which interprets the law.

FACTS VERSUS THE LAW

Common to all judicial systems is the distinction between trial courts and appellate courts, and it is important to understand this distinction. Each level of court has its own function: basically, **trial courts** are fact-finding courts and **appellate courts** are law-reviewing courts. Trial courts are the courts of first instance, the place where nearly all cases begin. Juries sit in trial courts, but never in appellate courts. Trial courts are empowered to consider both the facts and the law in a case. Appellate courts normally consider only the law. The difference between facts and law is significant. The facts are what happened. The law is what should be done because of the facts.

The difference between facts and law can be emphasized by looking at an imaginary libel suit that might result if the River City Sentinel published a story about costs at the Sandridge Hospital, a privately owned medical facility.

Ineffective Medications Given to Ill, Injured

SANDRIDGE HOSPITAL OVERCHARGING PATIENTS ON PHARMACY COSTS

Scores of patients at the Sandridge Hospital have been given ineffective medications, a three-week investigation at the hospital has revealed. In addition, many of those patients were overcharged for the medicine they received.

The Sentinel has learned that many of the prescription drugs sold to patients at the hospital had been kept beyond the manufacturer's recommended storage period.

Many drugs stored in the pharmacy (as late as Friday) had expiration dates as old as six months ago. Drug manufacturers have told the Sentinel that medication used beyond the expiration date, which is stamped clearly on most packages, may not have the potency or curative effects that fresher pharmaceuticals have.

Hospital representatives deny giving patients any of the expired drugs, but sources at the hospital say it is impossible for administrators to guarantee that none of the dated drugs were sold to patients.

In addition, the investigation by the Sentinel revealed that patients who were sold medications manufactured by Chaos Pharmaceuticals were charged on the basis of 2005 price lists despite the fact that the company lowered prices significantly in 2006.

The Sandridge Hospital sues the newspaper for libel. When the case gets to court, the first thing that has to be done is to establish what the facts are—what happened. The hospital and the newspaper each will present evidence, witnesses and arguments to support its version of the facts. Several issues have to be resolved. In addition to the general questions of whether the story has been published and whether the hospital has been identified in the story, the hospital will have to supply evidence that its reputation has been injured, that the story is false, and that the newspaper staff has been extremely careless or negligent in the publication of the report. The newspaper will seek to defend itself by attempting to document the story or raise the defense that the report was privileged in some way. Or the newspaper may argue that even if the story is mistaken, it was the result of an innocent error; the newspaper staff was not negligent when it wrote and published the story.

All this testimony and evidence establishes the factual record—what actually took place at the hospital and in preparation of the story. When there is conflicting evidence, the jury decides whom to believe (in the absence of a jury, the judge makes the decision). Suppose the hospital is able to prove by documents that pharmacists in fact had removed the dated medicine from their shelves and stored it to return to the manufacturers. Further, the hospital can show that while it did accidentally overcharge some patients for Chaos products, it quickly refunded the excess charge to these patients. Finally, attorneys for the hospital demonstrate that the story was prepared by an untrained stringer for the newspaper who used but a single source—a pharmacist who had been fired by Sandridge for using drugs while on the job—to prepare the story and failed to relate to readers the substance of the evidence (which the reporter had when the story was published) presented by the hospital in court. In such a case, a court would likely rule that the hospital had carried its burden of proof and that no legitimate defense exists for the newspaper. Therefore, the hospital wins the suit. If the newspaper is unhappy with the verdict, it can appeal.

In an appeal, the appellate court does not establish a new factual record. No more testimony is taken. No more witnesses are called. The factual record established by the jury or judge at the trial stands. The appellate court has the power in some kinds of cases (libel suits that involve constitutional issues, for example) to examine whether the trial court properly considered the facts in the case. But normally it is the task of the appellate court to determine whether the law has been applied properly in light of the facts established at the trial. Perhaps the appellate court might rule that even with the documentary evidence the hospital presented in court, this evidence failed to prove that the news story was false. Perhaps the judge erred in allowing certain testimony into evidence or refused to allow a certain witness to testify. Nevertheless, in reaching an opinion the appellate court considers only the law; the factual record established at the trial stands.

What if new evidence is found or a previously unknown witness comes forth to testify? If the appellate court believes that the new evidence is important, it can order a new trial. However, the court itself does not hear the evidence. These facts are developed at a new trial.

There are other differences between the roles and procedures of trial and appellate courts. Juries are never used by appellate courts; a jury may be used in a trial court proceeding. The judge normally sits alone at a trial; appeals are heard by a panel of judges, usually three or more. Cases always begin at the trial level and then proceed to the appellate level. Although the appellate courts appear to have the last word in a legal dispute, that is not always the case. Usually cases are returned to the trial court for resolution with instructions from the appeals court to the trial judge to decide the case, keeping this or that factor in mind. This is called remanding the case to the trial court. In such a case the trial judge can often do what he or she wants.

In the discussion that follows, the federal court system and its methods of operating are considered first, and then some general observations about state court systems are given, based on the discussion of the federal system.

THE FEDERAL COURT SYSTEM

Congress has the authority to abolish every federal court in the land, save the Supreme Court of the United States. The U.S. Constitution calls for but a single federal court, the Supreme Court. Article III, Section 1 states: "The judicial power of the United States shall be vested in one Supreme Court." The Constitution also gives Congress the right to establish inferior courts if it deems these courts to be necessary. And Congress has, of course, established a fairly complex system of courts to complement the Supreme Court.

The jurisdiction of the federal courts is also outlined in Article III of the Constitution. The jurisdiction of a court is its legal right to exercise its authority. Briefly, federal courts can hear the following cases:

1. Cases that arise under the U.S. Constitution, U.S. law and U.S. treaties
2. Cases that involve ambassadors and ministers, duly accredited, of foreign countries
3. Cases that involve admiralty and maritime law
4. Cases that involve controversies when the United States is a party to the suit
5. Cases that involve controversies between two or more states
6. Cases that involve controversies between a state and a citizen of another state (remember that the 11th Amendment to the Constitution requires that a state give its permission before it can be sued)
7. Cases that involve controversies between citizens of different states

While special federal courts have jurisdiction that goes beyond this broad outline, these are the circumstances in which a federal court may normally exercise its authority. Of the seven categories of cases just listed, Categories 1 and 7 account for most of the cases tried in federal court. For example, disputes that involve violations of the myriad federal laws and disputes that involve constitutional rights such as the First Amendment are heard in federal courts. Also, disputes between citizens of different states—what is known as a diversity of citizenship matter—are heard in federal courts. It is very common, for example, for libel suits and invasion-of-privacy suits against publishing companies to start in federal courts rather than in state courts. If a citizen of Arizona is libeled by the Los Angeles Times, the case will very likely be tried in a federal court in the state of Arizona rather than in a state court in either Arizona or California. Arizona law will be applied. The case will most often be heard where the legal wrong, in this case the injury to reputation by libel, occurs. Congress has limited federal trial courts to hearing only those diversity cases in which the damages sought exceeded $75,000.

The Supreme Court

The Supreme Court of the United States is the oldest federal court, having been in operation since 1789. The Constitution does not establish the number of justices who sit on the high court. That task is left to Congress. In 1789 Congress passed the first judiciary act and established the membership of the high court at six: a chief justice and five associate justices. This number was increased to seven in 1807, to nine in 1837, and to 10 in 1863. The Supreme Court had 10 members until 1866, when Congress ruled that only seven justices would sit on the high tribunal. Since 1869 the Supreme Court has comprised the chief justice of the United States and eight associate justices. (Note the title: not chief justice of the Supreme Court, but chief justice of the United States.)

The Supreme Court exercises both original and appellate jurisdictions. Under its **original jurisdiction,** which is established in the Constitution, the Supreme Court is the first

Since 1869 the Supreme Court has comprised the chief justice of the United States and eight associate justices.

court to hear a case and acts much like a trial court. Sometimes the justices will hold a hearing to ascertain the facts; more commonly they will appoint what is called a special master to discern the facts and make recommendations. For example, in the fall of 2003, the Supreme Court heard arguments in a dispute between Maryland and Virginia over which state controlled the use of water from the Potomac River, which forms most of the boundary between the two states. Maryland claimed that it controls the use of the river by virtue of a charter granted to Lord Baltimore by King Charles I in 1632. Lawyers for the state argued that Virginia violated Maryland's sovereignty when it constructed a 725-foot-long pipe to take water from the river to satisfy the needs of the residents of Fairfax County, a fast-growing suburb of Washington, D.C. A special master appointed by the Supreme Court issued a report that endorsed Virginia's position in the matter. The high court accepted this report in December 2003, and ruled in favor of Virginia.[13] But such jurisdiction is rarely exercised. The Potomac River ruling is one of fewer than 200 decisions the court has made in exercising its original jurisdiction since 1789. Because the high court is strictly limited by the Constitution to exercise its original jurisdiction in a few specific instances, and because Congress has given the lower federal courts concurrent jurisdiction with the Supreme Court in those specific instances, few persons begin their lawsuits at the Supreme Court.

The primary task of the Supreme Court is as an appellate tribunal, hearing cases already decided by lower federal courts and state courts of last resort. The appellate jurisdiction of the Supreme Court is established by Congress, not by the Constitution. A case will come before the Supreme Court of the United States for review in one of two principal ways: on a direct appeal or by way of a writ of certiorari. The certification process is a third way for a case to get to the high court, but this process is rarely used today.

In some instances a litigant has an apparent right, guaranteed by federal statute, to appeal a case to the Supreme Court. This is called **direct appeal.** For example, if a federal appeals court declares that a state statute violates the U.S. Constitution or conflicts with a federal law, the state has a right to appeal this decision to the Supreme Court. But this is only an apparent right, because since 1928 the Supreme Court has had the right to reject such an appeal "for want of a substantial federal question." This is another way of the court saying, "We think this is a trivial matter." Almost 90 percent of all appeals that come to the Supreme Court via the direct appeal process are rejected.

The much more common way for a case to reach the nation's high court is via a **writ of certiorari.** No one has the right to such a writ. It is a discretionary order issued by the court when it feels that an important legal question has been raised. Litigants using both the federal court system and the various state court systems can seek a writ of certiorari. The most important requirement that must be met before the court will even consider issuing a writ is that a petitioner first exhaust all other legal remedies. While there are a few exceptions, this generally means that if a case begins in a federal district court (the trial level court) the **petitioner** must first seek a review by a U.S. Court of Appeals before bidding for a writ of certiorari. The writ can be sought if the Court of Appeals refuses to hear the case or sustains the verdict against the petitioner. All other legal remedies have then been exhausted. In state court systems every legal appeal possible must be made within the state before seeking a review by the

---

13. Greenhouse, "Justices Consider Dispute."

The U.S. Supreme Court, Autumn 2005. Associate Justices Ruth Bader Ginsburg, David Souter, Antonin Scalia, John Paul Stevens, Chief Justice John Roberts, Associate Justices Sandra Day O'Connor, Anthony Kennedy, Clarence Thomas and Stephen Breyer. Samuel Alito Jr. replaced Sandra Day O'Connor in early 2006.

U.S. Supreme Court. This usually means going through a trial court, an intermediate appeals court, and finally the state supreme court.

When the Supreme Court grants a writ of certiorari, it is ordering the lower court to send the records to the high court for review. Any litigant can petition the court to grant a writ, and the high court usually receives about 5,000 such requests each year. Each request is considered by the entire nine-member court. If four justices think the petition has merit, the writ will be granted. But the court rejects the vast majority of petitions it receives. In the 1990s the court heard about 100 cases a year. More recently only 80 or 90 cases a year have been accepted. Workload is the key factor. Certain important issues must be decided each term, and the justices do not have the time to consider thoroughly most cases for which an appeal is sought. Term after term, suggestions to reduce the court's workload are made, but most are not popular with Congress or the people in the nation. All citizens believe that they should have the right to appeal to the Supreme Court, even if the appeal will probably be rejected, even if the court may never hear the case.

One final point needs to be made. The Supreme Court of the United States is not as interested in making certain that justice has been served as it is in making certain that the law is developing properly. A petitioner seeking redress through the high court may have a completely valid argument that a lower court has ignored an important precedent in ruling against him or her. But if the law on this point has been established, the Supreme Court is very likely to reject the petition and instead use this time to examine and decide a new or emerging legal issue.

Hearing a Case

The operation of the Supreme Court is unique in many ways, but by gaining an understanding of how the high court does its business, a reader will also gain an understanding of how most appellate courts function.

Once the Supreme Court agrees to hear a case the heaviest burden falls upon the attorneys for the competing parties. The oral argument—the presentation made by the attorneys to the members of the court—will be scheduled. The parties (their attorneys) are expected to submit what are called **legal briefs**—their written legal arguments—for the members of the court to study before the oral hearing. The party that has taken the appeal to the Supreme Court—the **appellant**—must provide the high court with a complete record of the lower-court proceedings: the transcripts from the trial, the rulings by the lower courts, and other relevant material.

Arguing a matter all the way to the Supreme Court takes a long time, often as long as five years (sometimes longer) from initiation of the suit until the court gives its ruling. James Hill brought suit in New York in 1953 against Time Inc. for invasion of privacy. The U.S. Supreme Court made the final ruling in the case in 1967 (*Time, Inc.* v. *Hill*).[14] Even at that the matter would not have ended had Hill decided to go back to trial, which the Supreme Court said he must do if he wanted to collect damages. He chose not to.

After the nine justices study the briefs (or at least the summaries provided by their law clerks), the **oral argument** is held. For a generation schooled on television courtroom dramas like "Law and Order," oral argument before the Supreme Court (or indeed before any appellate court) must certainly seem strange. For one thing, the attorneys are strictly limited as to how much they may say. Each side is given a brief amount of time, usually no more than 30 minutes to an hour, to present its arguments. In important cases, "friends of the court" (**amici curiae**) are allowed to present briefs and to participate for 30 minutes in the oral arguments. For example, the American Civil Liberties Union often seeks the friend status in important civil rights cases.

Deciding a Case

After the oral argument (which of course is given in open court with visitors welcome) is over, the members of the high court move behind closed doors to undertake their deliberations. No one is allowed in the discussion room except members of the court itself—no clerks, no bailiffs, no secretaries. The discussion, which often is held several days after the arguments are completed, is opened by the chief justice. Discussion time is limited, and by being the first speaker the chief justice is in a position to set the agenda, so to speak, for each case—to raise what he or she thinks are the key issues. Next to speak is the justice with the most seniority, and after him or her, the next most senior justice. The court will have many items or cases to dispose of during one conference or discussion day; consequently, brevity is valued. Each justice has just a few moments to state his or her thoughts on the matter. After discussion a tentative vote is taken and recorded by each justice in a small, hinged, lockable docket book. In the voting procedure the junior justice votes first; the chief justice, last.

---

14. 385 U.S. 374 (1967).

Under the United States legal system, which is based so heavily on the concept of court participation in developing and interpreting the law, a simple yes-or-no answer to any legal question is hardly sufficient. More important than the vote, for the law if not for the **litigant,** are the reasons for the decision. Therefore the Supreme Court and all courts that deal with questions of law prepare what are called **opinions,** in which the reasons, or rationale, for the decision are given. One of the justices voting in the majority is asked to write what is called the **court's opinion.** If the chief justice is in the majority, he or she selects the author of the opinion. If not, the senior associate justice in the majority makes the assignment. Self-selection is always an option.

Opinion writing is a difficult task. Getting five or six or seven people to agree to yes or no is one thing; getting them to agree on why they say yes or no is something else. The opinion must therefore be carefully constructed. After it is drafted, it is circulated among all court members, who make suggestions or even draft their own opinions. The opinion writer may incorporate as many of these ideas as possible into the opinion to retain its majority backing. Although all this is done in secret, historians have learned that rarely do court opinions reflect solely the work of the writer. They are more often a conglomeration of paragraphs and pages and sentences from the opinions of several justices.

A justice in agreement with the majority who cannot be convinced to join in backing the court's opinion has the option of writing what is called a **concurring opinion.** A justice who writes a concurring opinion may agree with the outcome of the decision, but does so for reasons different from those expressed in the majority opinion. Or the concurring justice may want to emphasize a specific point not addressed in the majority opinion.

Justices who disagree with the majority can also write an opinion, either individually or as a group, called a **dissenting opinion.** Dissenting opinions are very important. Sometimes, after the court has made a decision, it becomes clear that the decision was not the proper one. The issue is often litigated again by other parties who use the arguments in the dissenting opinion as the basis for a legal claim. If enough time passes, if the composition of the court changes sufficiently, or if the court members change their minds, the high court can swing to the views of the original dissenters. This is what happened in the case of *Nye* v. *U.S.*[15] (noted earlier) when the high court repudiated a stand it had taken in 1918 and supported instead the opinion of Justice Oliver Wendell Holmes, who had vigorously dissented in the earlier decision.

Finally, it is possible for a justice to concur with the majority in part and to dissent in part as well. That is, the justice may agree with some of the things the majority says but disagree with other aspects of the ruling. This kind of stand by a justice, as well as an ordinary concurrence, frequently fractures the court in such a way that in a 6-3 ruling only three persons subscribe to the court's opinion, two others concur, the sixth concurs in part and dissents in part, and three others dissent. Such splits by the members of the court have become more common in recent years. While these kinds of decisions give each justice the satisfaction of knowing that he or she has put his or her own thoughts on paper for posterity, such splits thwart the orderly development of the law. They often leave lawyers and other interested parties at a loss when trying to predict how the court might respond in the next similar case that

---

15. 313 U.S. 33 (1941).

comes along. Some chief justices, such as William Howard Taft and Earl Warren, aggressively plied their colleagues to try to gain consensus for a single opinion.

The Supreme Court can dispose of a case in two other ways. A **per curiam** (by the court) **opinion** can be prepared. This is an unsigned opinion drafted by one or more members of the majority and published as the court's opinion. Per curiam opinions are not common, but neither are they rare.

Finally, the high court can dispose of a case with a **memorandum order**—that is, it just announces the vote without giving an opinion. Or the order cites an earlier Supreme Court decision as the reason for affirming or reversing a lower-court ruling. In cases with little legal importance and in cases in which the issues were really resolved earlier, the court saves a good deal of time by just announcing its decision.

One final matter in regard to voting remains for consideration: What happens in case of a tie vote? When all nine members of the court are present, a tie vote is technically impossible. However, if there is a vacancy on the court, only eight justices hear a case. Even when the court is full, a particular justice may disqualify himself or herself from hearing a case. When a vote ends in a tie, the decision of the lower court is affirmed. No opinion is written. It is as if the Supreme Court had never heard the case.

During the circulation of an opinion, justices have the opportunity to change their vote. The number and membership in the majority may shift. It is not impossible for the majority to become the minority if one of the dissenters writes a particularly powerful dissent that attracts support from members originally opposed to his or her opinion. This event is probably very rare. Nevertheless, a vote of the court is not final until it is announced on decision day, or opinion day. The authors of the various opinions—court opinions, concurrences and dissents—publicly read or summarize their views. Printed copies of these documents are handed out to the parties involved and to the press, and are quickly available online.

Courts have no real way to enforce decisions and must depend on other government agencies for enforcement of their rulings. The job normally falls to the executive branch. If perchance the president decides not to enforce a Supreme Court ruling, no legal force exists to compel the president to do so. If former President Nixon, for example, had chosen to refuse to turn over the infamous Watergate tapes after the court ruled against his arguments of executive privilege, no other agency could have forced him to give up those tapes.

At the same time, there is one force that usually works to see that court decisions are carried out: It is that vague force called public opinion or what political scientists call "legitimacy." Most people believe in the judicial process; they have faith that what the courts do is probably right. This does not mean that they always agree with court decisions, but they do agree that the proper way to settle disputes is through the judicial process. Jurists help engender this spirit or philosophy by acting in a temperate manner. The Supreme Court, for example, has developed means that permit it to avoid having to answer highly controversial questions in which an unpopular decision could weaken its perceived legitimacy. The justices might call the dispute a political question, a **nonjusticiable matter,** or they may refuse to hear a case on other grounds. When the members of the court sense that the public is ready to accept a ruling, they may take on a controversial issue. School desegregation is a good example. In 1954 the Supreme Court ruled in *Brown* v. *Board of Education*[16] that segregated

People believe in the judicial process; they have faith that what the courts do is probably right.

16. 347 U.S. 483 (1954).

23

public schools violated the U.S. Constitution. The foundation for this ruling had been laid by a decade of less momentous desegregation decisions and executive actions. By 1954 the nation was prepared for the ruling, and it was generally accepted, even in many parts of the South. The legitimacy of a court's decisions, then, often rests upon prudent use of the judicial power.

Other Federal Courts

The Supreme Court of the United States is the most visible, perhaps the most glamorous (if that word is appropriate), of the federal courts. But it is not the only federal court nor even the busiest. There are two lower echelons of federal courts, plus various special courts, within the federal system. These special courts, such as the U.S. Court of Military Appeals, U.S. Tax Court, and so forth, were created by Congress to handle special kinds of problems.

Most business in the federal system begins and ends in a district court. This court was created by Congress in the Federal Judiciary Act of 1789, and today in the United States there are 94 such courts staffed by about 650 judges. Every state has at least one U.S. District Court. Some states are divided into two districts or more: an eastern and western district or a northern, central, and southern district. Individual districts often have more than one judge, sometimes many more than one. The southern district of the U.S. District Court in New York has about 30 judges.

When there is a jury trial, the case is heard in a district court. It has been estimated that about half the cases in U.S. District Courts are heard by a jury.

At the intermediate level in the federal judiciary are the 13 circuits of the U.S. Court of Appeals, staffed by about 170 judges. These courts were also created by the Federal Judiciary Act of 1789. Until 1948 these courts were called Circuit Courts of Appeal, a reflection of the early years of the republic when the justices of the Supreme Court "rode the circuit" and presided at the courts-of-appeal hearings. While the title Circuit Courts of Appeal is officially gone, the nation is still divided into 11 numbered circuits, each of which is served by one court (see Figure 1.2).

The 12th and 13th circuits are unnumbered. One is the Court of Appeals for the District of Columbia. This is a very busy court because it hears most of the appeals from decisions made by federal administrative agencies. The 13th is the Court of Appeals for the Federal Circuit, a court created by Congress in 1982 to handle special kinds of appeals. This court is specially empowered to hear appeals from patent and trademark decisions of U.S. District Courts and other federal agencies such as the Board of Patent Appeals. It also hears appeals from rulings by the U.S. Claims Court, the U.S. Court of International Trade, the U.S. International Trade Commission, the Merit Systems Protection Board, and from a handful of other special kinds of rulings. Congress established this court to try to develop a uniform, reliable, and predictable body of law in each of these very special fields.

The Courts of Appeals are appellate courts, which means that they hear appeals only from lower courts and other agencies. These courts are the last stop for 95 percent of all cases in the federal system. The number of judges in each circuit varies, depending upon the size of the circuit and number of cases that are heard. The 9th U.S. Circuit Court of Appeals, which has jurisdiction in nine western states and the territories of Guam and the Northern

4th Circuit: Maryland, North Carolina, South Carolina, Virginia and West Virginia
5th Circuit: Texas, Mississippi and Louisiana
6th Circuit: Kentucky, Michigan, Ohio and Tennessee
7th Circuit: Illinois, Indiana and Wisconsin
8th Circuit: Arkansas, Iowa, Minnesota, Missouri, Nebraska, North Dakota and South Dakota
9th Circuit: Alaska, Arizona, California, Hawaii, Idaho, Montana, Nevada, Oregon, Washington, Guam and Northern Mariana Islands
10th Circuit: Colorado, Kansas, New Mexico, Utah, Oklahoma and Wyoming
11th Circuit: Alabama, Florida, Georgia and the Canal Zone

1st Circuit: Maine, Massachusetts, New Hampshire, Rhode Island and Puerto Rico
2nd Circuit: Connecticut, New York and Vermont
3rd Circuit: Delaware, New Jersey, Pennsylvania and Virgin Islands

▼ FIGURE 1.2

Circuits 1 through 11 comprise the 50 states and the multiple U.S. territories.

Mariana Islands, in 2006 had 51 judgeships, twice as many as any of the other Courts of Appeals* Other circuits had as few as six judges and as many as 18. Typically, a panel of three judges will hear a case. In unusual cases, a larger panel of judges, usually 11, will hear the appeal. When this happens the court is said to be **sitting en banc.** A litigant who loses an appeal heard by a three-judge panel can ask for a rehearing by the entire court. This request is not often granted.

*Since the nineties there have been attempts made by members of Congress to break this circuit into two or more parts. In public the proponents of the division argue that the circuit—which has 20 percent of the nation's population—is simply too big. Few would deny that. Privately, many conservative members of Congress say they believe that the judges on the circuit are too liberal, and its decisions impact far too many citizens. The most recent plan would be to make three separate circuits out of the 9th. California and Hawaii would be lumped with Guam and the Mariana Islands into one circuit. Alaska, Washington and Oregon would be included in the second court; and Nevada, Arizona, Idaho and Montana would make up the third. Opponents of this scheme point out that two-thirds of the circuit's caseload comes from California, so creating two additional circuit courts for other states wouldn't accomplish much. Putting half of California into one circuit, and the other half into another would accomplish a more even division, but this is something most people oppose.

Federal Judges

All federal judges are appointed by the president and must be confirmed by the Senate. The appointment is for life. The only way a federal judge can be removed is by **impeachment.** Eleven federal judges have been impeached: Seven were found guilty by the Senate, and the other four were acquitted. Impeachment and trial is a long process and one rarely undertaken.

Political affiliation plays a distinct part in the appointment of federal judges. Democratic presidents usually appoint Democratic judges, and Republican presidents appoint Republican judges. Nevertheless, it is expected that nominees to the federal bench be competent jurists. This is especially true for appointees to the Courts of Appeals and to the Supreme Court. The Senate must confirm all appointments to the federal courts, a normally perfunctory act in the case of lower-court judges. More careful scrutiny is given nominees to the appellate courts. The Senate has refused to confirm 30 of the 144 persons nominated to serve on the Supreme Court. Nineteen were voted down and 11 were simply not acted upon. Another 16 either declined the nomination or withdrew, as Harriet Miers did in 2005. Most recently, President Ronald Reagan's nomination of Judge Robert Bork to the Supreme Court was rejected.

The appointment of associate justices to the Supreme Court of the United States became a topic of substantial public interest during the last few decades. The high court had manifested a distinctly liberal political philosophy from the late 1930s through the 1960s, and the history of the court during this era is marked by substantial enlargement of both civil rights and civil liberties via constitutional interpretation. But the presidency of Richard Nixon marked the beginning of the end of this era. Since the 1960s the judicial temperament of appointees to the high court has been mixed, with individuals with moderate to conservative views filling most of the seats. In 2006 the members of the court were split along many ideological lines, giving the Supreme Court a rather fine balance on some controversial issues. Liberal advocacy groups outside the court feared a new appointment could shift this balance in such a way that decisions like the 1973 abortion ruling, *Roe* v. *Wade,*[17] might ultimately be reversed. Conservatives, on the other hand, worried that a slight change in the court's makeup would affect issues like affirmative action, school prayer or gun control.

The president appoints the members of the high court with the "advice and consent" of the U.S. Senate. When the White House and the Senate are both in the hands of the same party, Republicans or Democrats, this appointment process will usually proceed smoothly. President Clinton had few problems in winning the appointment of Ruth Bader Ginsburg and Stephen Breyer while Democrats controlled Congress. On the other hand, Richard Nixon and Ronald Reagan, both conservative Republicans, had more difficulty getting their nominees on the court when the Senate was controlled by Democrats. Some argue that the Senate's only function is to ensure that competent jurists sit on the Supreme Court. Others take a more expansive view of the term "advice and consent" and argue that the Senate is obliged to consider judicial and political philosophy as well when evaluating the presidential nominees. This debate heated up once again in 2005–06 as President George W. Bush appointed John Roberts as the 17th Chief Justice, and Samuel L. Alito Jr. to replace Justice Sandra Day O'Connor.

Presidents and senators alike have discovered that the individual who is nominated is not always the one who spends the remainder of his or her lifetime on the court. Justices and

---

17. 410 U.S. 113 (1973).

judges appointed to the bench for life sometimes change. Perhaps they are affected by their colleagues. Or maybe it is because they are largely removed from the pressures faced by others in public life. For whatever reasons, men and women appointed to the bench sometimes drastically modify their philosophy. It is doubtful that President Herbert Hoover expected the man he appointed chief justice, Charles Evans Hughes, to become the leader of the court that sustained much of the liberal and even radical legislation of the New Deal. Republican Dwight Eisenhower appointed Chief Justice Earl Warren and Associate Justice William Brennan, two of the great liberal members of the court during the past 100 years. Liberal president John Kennedy's appointment to the high court, Justice Byron White, developed strong conservative leanings after he was confirmed. It is surely true, as writer Finley Peter Dunne's fictional bartender, Mr. Dooley, once remarked, "Th' Supreme Court follows th' iliction returns." But justices also sometimes follow a deeper set of beliefs as well, beliefs that aren't as obvious during the confirmation process.

THE STATE COURT SYSTEM

The constitution of every one of the 50 states either establishes a court system in that state or authorizes the legislature to do so. The court system in each of the 50 states is somewhat different from the court system in all the other states. There are, however, more similarities than differences among the 50 states.

The trial courts (or court) are the base of each judicial system. At the lowest level are usually what are called courts of limited jurisdiction. Some of these courts have special functions, such as a traffic court, which is set up to hear cases involving violations of the motor-vehicle code. Some of these courts are limited to hearing cases of relative unimportance, such as trials of persons charged with misdemeanors, or minor crimes, or civil suits in which the damages sought fall below $1,000. The court may be a municipal court set up to hear cases involving violations of the city code. Whatever the court, the judges in these courts have limited jurisdiction and deal with a limited category of problems.

Above the lower-level courts normally exist trial courts of general jurisdiction similar to the federal district courts. These courts are sometimes county courts and sometimes state courts, but whichever they are, they handle nearly all criminal and civil matters. They are primarily courts of original jurisdiction; that is, they are the first courts to hear a case. However, on occasion they act as a kind of appellate court when the decisions of the courts of limited jurisdiction are challenged. When that happens, the case is retried in the trial court—the court does not simply review the law. This proceeding is called hearing a case **de novo.**

A **jury** is most likely to be found in the trial court of general jurisdiction. It is also the court in which most civil suits for libel and invasion of privacy are commenced (provided the state court has jurisdiction), in which prosecution for violating state obscenity laws starts, and in which many other media-related matters begin.

Above this court may be one or two levels of appellate courts. Every state has a supreme court, although some states do not call it that. In New York, for example, it is called the Court of Appeals, but it is the high court in the state, the court of last resort.* Formerly, a supreme

---

*To further confuse matters, the trial court of general jurisdiction in New York is called the Supreme Court.

court was the only appellate court in most states. As legal business increased and the number of appeals mounted, the need for an intermediate appellate court became evident. Therefore, in nearly all states there is an intermediate court, usually called the court of appeals. This is the court where most appeals end. In some states it is a single court with three or more judges. More often, numerous divisions within the appellate court serve various geographic regions, each division having three or more judges. Since every litigant is normally guaranteed at least one appeal, this intermediate court takes much of the pressure off the high court of the state. Rarely do individuals appeal beyond the intermediate level.

State courts of appeals tend to operate in much the same fashion as the U.S. Courts of Appeals, with cases being heard by small groups of judges, usually three at a time.

Cases not involving federal questions go no further than the high court in a state, usually called the supreme court. This court—usually a seven- or nine-member body—is the final authority regarding the construction of state laws and interpretation of the state constitution. Not even the Supreme Court of the United States can tell a state supreme court what that state's constitution means. For example, in 1976 the U.S. Supreme Court ruled that the protection of the First Amendment did not include the right to distribute materials, demonstrate, or solicit petition signatures at privately owned shopping centers (*Hudgens* v. *NLRB*[18]—this case is discussed fully on page 137). In 1980, however, the Supreme Court refused to overturn a decision by the California Supreme Court that declared that students had the right *under the California constitution* to solicit signatures for a pro-Israeli petition at a private shopping center in Campbell, Calif. Justice William Rehnquist wrote for the unanimous U.S. Supreme Court that perhaps the free-speech guarantee in the California constitution is broader than the First Amendment. In any case, the California high court was the final authority on the state's constitution (*Pruneyard Shopping Center* v. *Robins*).[19]

State court judges are frequently elected. Normally the process is nonpartisan, but because they are elected and must stand for re-election periodically, state court judges are generally a bit more politically active than their federal counterparts. Nearly half the states in the nation use a kind of compromise system that includes both appointment and election. The compromise is designed to minimize political influence and initially select qualified candidates but still retain an element of popular control. The plans are named after the states that pioneered them, the **California Plan** and the **Missouri Plan.** Typically either the governor nominates a candidate to be approved by a judicial commission, or a judicial commission nominates a slate of candidates, one of which will be chosen by the governor. These jurists serve on the bench until the next general election, at which time the people of the state vote to retain or reject a particular judge. If retained, the judge serves until the next general election, when he or she again must attain voter approval. If the jurist is rejected, the appointment process begins again.

JUDICIAL REVIEW

One of the most important powers of courts (and at one time one of the most controversial) is the power of **judicial review**—that is, the right of any court to declare any law or official

Not even the Supreme Court of the United States can tell a state supreme court what that state's constitution means.

---

18. 424 U.S. 507 (1976).
19. 447 U.S. 74 (1980).

governmental action invalid because it violates a constitutional provision. We usually think of this right in terms of the U.S. Constitution. However, a state court can declare an act of its legislature to be invalid because the act conflicts with a provision of the state constitution. Theoretically, any court can exercise this power. The Circuit Court of Lapeer County, Mich., can rule that the Environmental Protection Act of 1972 is unconstitutional because it deprives citizens of their property without due process of law, something guaranteed by the Fifth Amendment to the federal Constitution. But this action isn't likely to happen, because a higher court would quickly overturn such a ruling. In fact, it is rather unusual for any court—even the U.S. Supreme Court—to invalidate a state or federal law on grounds that it violates the Constitution. Only about 200 federal statutes have been overturned by the courts in the 217-year history of the United States. During the same period, about 1,500 state laws and state constitutional provisions have been declared invalid. Judicial review is therefore not a power that the courts use excessively. In fact, a judicial maxim states: When a court has a choice of two or more ways in which to interpret a statute, the court should always interpret the statute in such a way that it is constitutional.

Judicial review is extremely important when matters concerning regulations of the mass media are considered. Because the First Amendment prohibits laws that abridge freedom of the press and freedom of speech, each new measure passed by Congress, by state legislatures, and even by city councils and township boards must be measured by the yardstick of the First Amendment. Courts have the right, in fact have the duty, to nullify laws and executive actions and administrative rulings that do not meet the standards of the First Amendment. While many lawyers and legal scholars rarely consider constitutional principles in their work and rarely seek judicial review of a statute, attorneys who represent newspapers, magazines, broadcasting stations, and motion-picture theaters constantly deal with constitutional issues, primarily those of the First Amendment. The remainder of this book will illustrate the obvious fact that judicial review, a concept at the very heart of American democracy, plays an important role in maintaining the freedom of the American press, even though the power is not explicitly included in the Constitution.

SUMMARY

There are 52 different judicial systems in the nation: one federal system, one for the District of Columbia, and one for each of the 50 states. Courts within each of these systems are divided into two general classes—trial courts and appellate courts. In any lawsuit both the facts and the law must be considered. The facts or the factual record is an account of what happened to prompt the dispute. The law is what should be done to resolve the dispute. Trial courts determine the facts in the case; then the judge applies the law. Appellate courts, using the factual record established by the trial court, determine whether the law was properly applied by the lower court and whether proper judicial procedures were followed. Trial courts exercise original jurisdiction almost exclusively; that is, they are the first courts to hear a case. Trial courts have very little discretion over which cases they will and will not hear. Appellate courts exercise appellate jurisdiction almost exclusively; that is, they review the work done by the lower courts when decisions are appealed. While the intermediate appellate courts (i.e., courts of appeals; the appellate division) have limited discretion in the selection of cases, the high courts (supreme courts) in the states and the nation generally have the power to select the cases they wish to review.

Federal courts include the Supreme Court of the United States, the U.S. Courts of Appeals, the U.S. District Courts, and several specialized tribunals. These courts have jurisdiction in all cases that involve the U.S. Constitution, U.S. law, and U.S. treaties; in disputes between citizens of different states; and in several less important instances. In each state there are trial-level courts and a court of last resort, usually called the supreme court. In about half the states there are intermediate appellate courts as well. State courts generally have jurisdiction in all disputes between citizens of their state that involve the state constitution or state law.

Judicial review is the power of a court to declare a statute, regulation or executive action to be a violation of the Constitution and thus invalid. Because the First Amendment to the U.S. Constitution guarantees the rights of freedom of speech and freedom of the press, all government actions that relate to the communication of ideas and information face potential scrutiny by the courts to determine their validity.

LAWSUITS

The final topic that needs to be discussed is lawsuits. To the layperson, and even those who work in the legal system, the United States appears to be awash in a sea of lawsuits. Lawyer bashing has become a popular leisure-time activity. The notion that there appears to be a lawsuit around every corner in every city can probably be blamed on the increased attention the press has given legal matters. Courts are fairly easy to cover and stories about lawsuits are commonly published and broadcast. There is even a cable television network dedicated to legal issues, Court TV. Also, some sensational cases are given saturation coverage, and this kind of coverage leaves the impression in the mind of the casual media consumer that the country is being swamped in a sea of legal briefs and writs.

This is not to say that we are not a highly litigious people. The backlogs in the courts are evidence of this. Going to court today is no longer a novelty but a common business or personal practice for a growing number of Americans. And too many of these lawsuits involve silly or trivial legal claims. In the end, the public pays a substantial price for all this litigation, through higher federal and state taxes to build and maintain courthouses and money to pay the salaries of those who work in the judiciary, and through higher insurance costs on everything from automobiles to protection from libel suits.

The material that follows is a simplified description of how a lawsuit proceeds. The picture is stripped of a great deal of the procedural activity that so often lengthens the lawsuit and keeps attorneys busy.

The party who commences a civil action is called the **plaintiff,** the person who brings the suit. The party against whom the suit is brought is called the **defendant.** In a libel suit the person who has been libeled is the plaintiff and is the one who starts the suit against the defendant—the newspaper, the magazine, the television station, or whatever. A civil suit is usually a dispute between two private parties. The government offers its good offices—the courts—to settle the matter. A government can bring a civil suit such as an antitrust action against someone, and an individual can bring a civil action against the government. But normally a civil suit is between private parties. (In a criminal action, the government always initiates the action.)

To start a civil suit the plaintiff first picks the proper court, one that has jurisdiction in the case. Then the plaintiff files a **civil complaint** with the court clerk. This complaint, or **pleading,** is a statement of the charges against the defendant and the remedy that is sought, typically money damages. The plaintiff also summons the defendant to appear in court to answer these charges. While the plaintiff may later amend his or her pleadings in the case, usually the initial complaint is the only pleading filed. After the complaint is filed, a hearing is scheduled by the court.

If the defendant fails to answer the charges, he or she normally loses the suit by default. Usually, however, the defendant will answer the summons and prepare his or her own set of pleadings, which constitute an answer to the plaintiff's charges. If there is little disagreement at this point about the facts—what happened—and that a wrong has been committed, the plaintiff and the defendant might settle their differences out of court. The defendant might say, "I guess I did libel you in this article, and I really don't have a very good defense. You asked for $100,000 in damages; would you settle for $50,000 and keep this out of court?" The plaintiff might very well answer yes, because a court trial is costly and takes a long time, and the plaintiff can also end up losing the case. Smart lawyers try to keep their clients out of court and settle matters in somebody's office.

Smart lawyers try to keep their clients out of court and settle matters in somebody's office.

If there is disagreement, the case is likely to continue. A common move for the defendant to make at this point is to file a motion to dismiss, or a **demurrer.** In such a motion the defendant says this to the court: "I admit that I did everything the plaintiff says I did. On June 5, 2005, I did publish an article in which she was called a socialist. But, Your Honor, it is not libelous to call someone a socialist." The plea made then is that even if everything the plaintiff asserts is true, the defendant did nothing that was legally wrong. The law cannot help the plaintiff. The court might grant the motion, in which case the plaintiff can appeal. Or the court might refuse to grant the motion, in which case the defendant can appeal. If the motion to dismiss is ultimately rejected by all the courts up and down the line, a trial is then held. It is fair play for the defendant at that time to dispute the plaintiff's statement of the facts; in other words to deny, for example, that his newspaper published the article containing the alleged libel.

Before the trial is held, the judge may schedule a conference between both parties in an effort to settle the matter or at least to narrow the issues so that the trial can be shorter and less costly. If the effort to settle the dispute fails, the trial goes forward. If the facts are agreed upon by both sides and the question is merely one of law, a judge hears the case without a jury. There are no witnesses and no testimony; only legal arguments are brought before the court. If the facts are disputed, the case can be tried before either a jury or, again, only a judge. Note that both sides must waive the right to a jury trial. In this event, the judge becomes both the fact finder and the lawgiver. Now, suppose that the case is heard by a jury. After all the testimony is given, all the evidence is presented, and all the arguments are made, the judge instructs the jury in the law. Instructions are often long and complex, despite attempts by judges to simplify them. **Judicial instructions** guide the jury in determining guilt or innocence if certain facts are found to be true. The judge will say that if the jury finds that *X* is true and *Y* is true and *Z* is true, then it must find for the plaintiff, but if the jury finds that *X* is not true, but that *R* is true, then it must find for the defendant.

After deliberation the jury presents its **verdict,** the action by the jury. The judge then announces the **judgment of the court.** This is the decision of the court. The judge is not always bound by the jury verdict. If he or she feels that the jury verdict is unfair or unreasonable, the judge can reverse it and rule for the other party. This rarely happens.

If either party is unhappy with the decision, an appeal can be taken. At that time the legal designations may change. The person seeking the appeal becomes the **appellant,** or petitioner. The other party becomes the **appellee,** or **respondent.** The name of the party initiating the action is usually listed first in the name of the case. For example: Smith sues Jones for libel. The case name is *Smith* v. *Jones.* Jones loses and takes an appeal. At that point in most jurisdictions Jones becomes the party initiating the action and the case becomes *Jones* v. *Smith.* This change in designations often confuses novices in their attempt to trace a case from trial to final appeal. If Jones wins the appeal and Smith decides to appeal to a higher court, the case again becomes *Smith* v. *Jones.* In more and more jurisdictions today, however, the case name remains the same throughout the appeal process. This is an effort by the judiciary to relieve some of the confusion wrought by this constant shifting of party names within the case name. In California, for example, the case of *Smith* v. *Jones* remains *Smith* v. *Jones* through the entire life of that case.

The end result of a successful civil suit is usually the awarding of money **damages.** Sometimes the amount of damages is guided by the law, as in a suit for infringement of copyright in which the law provides that a losing defendant pay the plaintiff the amount of money he or she might have made if the infringement had not occurred, or at least a set number of dollars. But most of the time the damages are determined by how much the plaintiff seeks, how much the plaintiff can prove he or she lost, and how much the jury thinks the plaintiff deserves. It is not a very scientific means of determining the dollar amount.

A **criminal prosecution,** or **criminal action,** is like a civil suit in many ways. The procedures are more formal, are more elaborate, and involve the machinery of the state to a greater extent. The state brings the charges, usually through the county or state prosecutor. The defendant can be apprehended either before or after the charges are brought. In the federal system persons must be **indicted** by a **grand jury,** a panel of from 16 to 23 citizens, before they can be charged with a serious crime. But most states do not use grand juries in that fashion, and the law provides that it is sufficient that the prosecutor issue an **information,** a formal accusation. After being charged, the defendant is arraigned. An **arraignment** is the formal reading of the charge. It is at the arraignment that the defendant makes a formal plea of guilty or not guilty. If the plea is guilty, the judge gives the verdict of the court and passes sentence, but usually not immediately, for presentencing reports and other procedures must be undertaken. If the plea is not guilty, a trial is scheduled.

Some state judicial systems have an intermediate step called a preliminary hearing or preliminary examination. The preliminary hearing is held in a court below the trial court, such as a municipal court, and the state has the responsibility of presenting enough evidence to convince the court—only a judge—that a crime has been committed and that there is sufficient evidence to believe that the defendant might possibly be involved. Today it is also not uncommon that **pretrial hearings** on a variety of matters precede the trial.

In both a civil suit and a criminal case, the result of the trial is not enforced until the final appeal is exhausted. That is, a money judgment is not paid in civil suits until defendants exhaust all their appeals. The same is true in a criminal case. Imprisonment or payment of a fine is not always required until the final appeal. If the defendant is dangerous or if there is some question that the defendant might not surrender when the final appeal is completed, bail can be required. Bail is money given to the court to ensure appearance in court.

SUMMARY

There are two basic kinds of lawsuits—civil suits and criminal prosecutions or actions. A civil suit is normally a dispute between two private parties in which the government offers its good offices (the courts) to resolve the dispute. The person who initiates the civil suit is called the plaintiff; the person at whom the suit is aimed is called the defendant. A plaintiff who wins a civil suit is normally awarded money damages.

A criminal case is normally an action in which the state brings charges against a private individual, who is called the defendant. A defendant who loses a criminal case can be assessed a fine, jailed or, in extreme cases, executed. A jury can be used in both civil and criminal cases. The jury becomes the fact finder and renders a verdict in a case. But the judge issues the judgment in the case. In a civil suit a judge can reject any jury verdict and rule in exactly the opposite fashion, finding for either plaintiff or defendant if the judge feels the jury has made a serious error in judgment. Either side can appeal the judgment of the court. In a criminal case the judge can take the case away from the jury and order a dismissal, but nothing can be done about an acquittal, even an incredible acquittal. While a guilty defendant may appeal the judgment, the state is prohibited from appealing an acquittal.

As stated at the outset, this chapter is designed to provide a glimpse, only a glimpse, of both our legal system and our judicial system. The discussion is in no way comprehensive, but it provides enough information to make the remaining 15 chapters meaningful. This chapter is not intended to be a substitute for a good political science course in the legal process. Students of communications law are at a distinct disadvantage if they do not have some grasp of how the systems work and what their origins are.

The United States legal and judicial systems are old and tradition-bound. But they have worked fairly well for these last 217 years. In the final analysis the job of both the law and the men and women who administer it is to balance the competing interests of society. How this balancing act is undertaken comprises the remainder of this book. The process is not always easy, but it is usually interesting.

BIBLIOGRAPHY ————————————————————————————➤

Abraham, Henry J. *The Judicial Process.* 7th ed. New York: Oxford University Press, 1998.

_____. *The Judiciary: The Supreme Court in the Government Process.* 3rd ed. Boston: Allyn & Bacon, 1973.

Cohn, Bob. "The Lawsuit Cha-Cha." *Newsweek,* 26 August 1991, 58.

Franklin, Marc A. *The Dynamics of American Law.* Mineola, N.Y.: Foundation Press, 1969.

Greenhouse, Linda. "Justices Consider Dispute on Use of Potomac River." *The New York Times,* 8 October 2003, A16.

Holmes, Oliver Wendell. *The Common Law.* Boston: Little, Brown & Co., 1881.

Pound, Roscoe. *The Development of the Constitutional Guarantees of Liberty.* New Haven: Yale University Press, 1957.

Rembar, Charles. *The Law of the Land.* New York: Simon & Schuster, 1980.

Roche, John P. *Courts and Rights.* 2nd ed. New York: Random House, 1966.

THE FIRST AMENDMENT
The Meaning of Freedom

The First Amendment is the wellspring from which flow nearly all U.S. laws on freedom of speech and freedom of the press. The amendment, adopted in 1791 as a part of the Bill of Rights, comprises only 45 words. But court decisions during the past two-plus centuries have added substantial meaning to this basic outline. In this chapter we explore the evolution of the centuries-old notion of freedom of expression, outline the adoption of the First Amendment, and examine the development of some elements of the fundamental meaning of freedom of speech and press.

HISTORICAL DEVELOPMENT

Freedom of expression is not exclusively an American idea. It grew from crude beginnings traced back to Socrates and Plato. The concept developed more fully during the past 400 years. The modern history of freedom of the press began in England during the 16th and 17th centuries as printing developed. Today the most indelible embodiment of the concept is the First Amendment to the U.S. Constitution, forged in the last half of the 18th century by individuals who built upon their memory of earlier experiences and unchanged in its wording for more than 215 years. To understand the meaning of freedom of the press and freedom of speech, it is necessary to understand the meaning of censorship, for viewed from a negative position freedom of expression can be simply defined as the absence of censorship or a freedom from government control.

FREEDOM OF THE PRESS IN ENGLAND

When William Caxton set up the first British printing press in Westminster in 1476, his printing pursuits were restricted only by his imagination and ability. There were no laws governing what he could or could not print—he was completely free. For more than five centuries, the British and Americans have attempted to regain the freedom that Caxton enjoyed, for shortly after he started publishing, the British Crown began to regulate the printing presses in England. Printing developed during a period of great religious struggle in Europe, and it soon became an important tool in that struggle. Printing presses made communication with hundreds of people fairly easy and in doing so gave considerable power to small groups or individuals who owned or could use a printing press.

    The British government soon realized that unrestricted publication and printing could seriously dilute its own power. Information is a potent tool in any society, and those who control the flow and content of information exercise considerable power. The printing press broke the Crown's monopoly of the flow of information, and therefore control of printing was essential.

    Between 1476 and 1776 the British devised and used several means to limit or restrict the press in England. **Seditious libel** laws were used to punish those who criticized the government or the Crown, and it did not matter whether the criticism was truthful or not. The press also suffered under **licensing** or **prior restraint** laws, which required printers to obtain prior approval from the government or the church before printing their handbills, pamphlets or newspapers. Printers were often required to deposit with the government large sums of money called **bonds.** This money was forfeited if material appeared that the government felt should not have been published. And the printer was forced to post another bond before printing could be resumed. The British also granted special patents and monopolies to certain printers in exchange for their cooperation in printing only acceptable works and in helping the Crown ferret out other printers who broke the publication laws.

    British control of the press during these 300 years was generally successful, but did not go unchallenged. As ideas about democracy spread throughout Europe, it became harder and harder for the government to limit freedom of expression. The power of the printing press in spreading ideas quickly to masses of people greatly helped foster the democratic spirit. Although British law regulated American printers as well during the colonial era, regulation of the press in North America was never as successful as it was in Great Britain.

As ideas about democracy spread throughout Europe, it became harder and harder for the government to limit freedom of expression.

FREEDOM OF THE PRESS IN COLONIAL AMERICA

There were laws in the United States restricting freedom of the press for almost 30 years before the first newspaper was published. As early as 1662, statutes in Massachusetts made it a crime to publish anything without first getting prior approval from the government, 28 years before Benjamin Harris published the first—and last—edition of Publick Occurrences. The second and all subsequent issues of the paper were banned because Harris had failed to get permission to publish the first edition, which contained material construed to be criticism of British policy in the colonies, as well as a report that scandalized the Massachusetts clergy because it said the French king took immoral liberties with a married woman (not his wife).

Despite this inauspicious beginning, American colonists had a much easier time getting their views into print (and staying out of jail) than did their counterparts in England. There was censorship, but American juries were reluctant to convict printers prosecuted by the colonial authorities. The colonial governments were less efficient than the government in England. Also, the British had only limited control over the administration of government in many of the colonies.

The British attempted to use licensing, taxes, and sedition laws to control American printers and publishers. Licensing, which ended in England in 1695, lasted until the mid-1720s in the American colonies. Benjamin Franklin's older brother James was jailed in 1722 for failing to get prior government approval for publishing his New England Courant. The unpopular government move failed to daunt the older Franklin, and licensing eventually ended in the colonies as well. The taxes levied against the press, most of which were genuine attempts to raise revenues, were nevertheless seen as censorship by American printers and resulted in growing hostility toward Parliament and the Crown. Most publishers refused to buy the tax stamps, and there was little retribution by the British.

Undoubtedly, the most famous case of government censorship in the American colonies was the seditious libel trial of immigrant printer John Peter Zenger, who found himself involved in a vicious political battle between leading colonial politicians in New York. Zenger published the *New York Weekly Journal,* a newspaper sponsored by Lewis Morris and James Alexander, political opponents of the unpopular colonial governor, William Cosby. Zenger was jailed in November 1734 after his newspaper published several stinging attacks on Cosby, who surmised that by jailing the printer—one of only two working in New York—he could silence his critics. There is little doubt that Zenger was guilty under 18th-century British sedition law. But his attorneys, including the renowned criminal lawyer Andrew Hamilton, were able to convince the jury that no man should be imprisoned or fined for publishing criticism of the government that was both truthful and fair. Jurors simply ignored the law and acquitted the German printer. It was an early example of what today is called **jury nullification**—the power of a jury in a criminal case to ignore (and thereby to "nullify") a law and to return a verdict (typically a not guilty verdict) according to its conscience. While certainly controversial and relatively rare, jury nullification can be seen as an essential part of the legislative process because a law that is repeatedly nullified by juries probably should be revised or discarded by the legislative body that created it.

The verdict in the Zenger case was a great political triumph but did nothing to change the law of seditious libel. In other words, the case did not set an important legal precedent. But the revolt of the American jurors did force colonial authorities to reconsider the use of

Source: © Bettmann/CORBIS

The trial of John Peter Zenger in New York in 1734. The printer was defended by attorney Andrew Hamilton and the acquittal of the printer put the British Crown on notice that American jurors were not inclined to convict those who criticized British officials.

sedition law as a means of controlling the press. While a few sedition prosecutions were initiated after 1735, there is no record of a successful prosecution in the colonial courts after the Zenger case. The case received widespread publicity both in North America and in England, and the outcome of the trial played an important role in galvanizing public sentiment against this kind of government censorship.

The Zenger trial today is an accepted part of American journalism mythology, but it doesn't represent the end of British attempts to control the press in the American colonies. Other means were substituted for sedition. Rather than haul printers and editors before jurors hostile to the state, the government instead hauled them before colonial legislatures and assemblies that were usually hostile to journalists. The charge was not sedition, but breach of parliamentary privilege or contempt of the assembly. There was no distinct separation of powers then, and the legislative body could order printers to appear, question them, convict them and punish them. Printers and publishers were thus still being jailed and fined for publications previously considered seditious. Only the means of exacting this punishment had changed.

Yet despite these potent sanctions occasionally levied against publishers and printers, the press of this era was remarkably robust. Researchers who have painstakingly read the newspapers and pamphlets and handbills produced in the last half of the 18th century are struck by the seeming lack of concern for government censorship. Historian Leonard Levy notes in his book "Emergence of a Free Press" the seeming paradox uncovered by scholars who seek to understand the meaning of freedom of expression during that era.[1] "To one [a scholar] whose prime concern was law and theory, a legacy of suppression [of the press] came

1. Levy, *Emergence of a Free Press.*

into focus; to one who looks at newspaper judgments on public men and measures, the revolutionary controversy spurred an expanding legacy of liberty," he wrote. What Levy suggests is that while the law and legal pronouncements from jurists and legislatures suggest a fairly rigid control of the press, in fact journalists and other publishers tended to ignore the law and suffered little retribution.

But the appearance of such freedom can be deceptive, as political scientist John Roche points out in his book "Shadow and Substance,"[2] for the community often exerted tremendous, and sometimes extralegal, pressure on anyone who expressed an unpopular idea. The belief of many people that freedom was the hallmark of society in America ignores history, Roche argues. In colonial America the people simply did not understand that freedom of thought and expression meant freedom for the other person also, particularly for the person with hated ideas. Roche points out that colonial America was an open society dotted with closed enclaves—villages and towns and cities—in which citizens generally shared similar beliefs about religion and government and so forth. Citizens could hold any belief they chose and could espouse that belief, but personal safety depended on the people in a community agreeing with a speaker or writer. If they didn't, the speaker then kept quiet—an early example of self-censorship or what scholars today call a "chilling effect" on speech—or moved to another enclave where the people shared those ideas. While there was much diversity of thought in the colonies, there was often little diversity of belief within individual towns and cities, according to Roche.

The belief of many people that freedom was the hallmark of society in America ignores history.

The propaganda war that preceded the Revolution is a classic example of the situation. In Boston, the patriots argued vigorously for the right to print what they wanted in their newspapers, even criticism of the government. Freedom of expression was their right, a God-given right, a natural right, a right of all British subjects. Many people, however, did not favor revolution or even separation from England. Yet it was extremely difficult for them to publish such pro-British sentiments in many American cities after 1770. Printers who published such ideas in newspapers and handbills did so at their peril. In cities like Boston the printers were attacked, their shops were wrecked, and their papers were destroyed. Freedom of the press was a concept with limited utility in many communities for colonists who opposed revolution once the patriots had moved the populace to their side.

Community Censorship Then and Now

The plight of the pro-British printer in Boston in the 1770s is not a unique chapter in American history. Today such community censorship still exists—and in some instances is growing. In recent years extreme pressure has been exerted on many retailers, for example, to exclude so-called men's magazines like Playboy from their newsstands. Students at some universities have attempted to block the appearances of right-wing speakers with whom they disagree. For instance, in March 2004, after word had spread on campus that President George W. Bush would welcome the chance to be the commencement speaker at the University of Arizona, "it was faculty, staff and graduate students who raised a ruckus, with nearly 400 signing a letter arguing that his appearance would be inappropriate in an election year. The White House later

2. Roche, *Shadow and Substance.*

Source: © AP/Wide World Photos

Filmmaker Michael
Moore was a
controversial speaker on
college campuses during
the presidential election
year of 2004. He is shown
here criticizing a heckler
during an on-campus
speech.

said Bush would be unavailable."[3] But such instances of nongovernmental community censorship also run in the opposite political direction, as when The New York Times' Chris Hedges, "a war correspondent who sharply criticized the war in Iraq, had to cut his speech short after he was repeatedly interrupted by boos and his microphone was unplugged twice" during a commencement address at Rockford College in Illinois.[4] This is an example of what attorneys sometimes call a **heckler's veto**—when a crowd or audience's reaction to a speech or message is allowed to control and silence that speech or message. In an ideal world, of course, speakers from *both* the right and the left would be allowed to speak freely on college campuses in order to expose students to competing viewpoints. This was the case, for instance, when Pennsylvania State University played host on the same day shortly before the presidential election of 2004 to both liberal filmmaker Michael Moore of "Fahrenheit 9/11" fame and conservative talk-radio host Michael Gallagher, who made his own rebuttal movie, cleverly called "Fahrenhype 9/11."[5] Unfortunately, such instances in which universities live up to the ideal of a diverse marketplace of ideas are rare; indeed, California State University San Marcos president Karen Haynes revoked an invitation in September 2004 to the left-leaning Moore to speak on campus, purportedly because Moore's speech would create a partisan appearance on the state-funded campus in a presidential election year.[6] But community censorship is not just a problem on college campuses; it was famously present when radio stations across the country, in response to outraged conservatives, stopped playing songs by the

3. Marklein, "It's Not Easy."
4. Young, "The Tyranny of Hecklers."
5. O'Connor, "Packed Crowd Gets First Look."
6. Vargo, "Speaking Tonight." In an interesting side note, after Haynes revoked Moore's invitation, students at Cal State San Marcos raised $45,000 to sponsor an appearance by Moore off campus at the nearby Del Mar Fairgrounds in October 2004. Moore ended up speaking there to a crowd of 10,000 (he drew about 7,350 people during his appearance at Penn State mentioned in the text above) as part of his Slacker Uprising Tour—"10 times the audience he would have had if he had not been banned from Cal State San Marcos." Petrillo and Burge, "Slacker Tour."

Dixie Chicks, a Dallas-based country music trio, in early 2003 after lead singer Natalie Maines told an audience in London, England, that "we're ashamed the President of the United States is from Texas."[7] In 2006, a Utah theater refused to show the movie "Brokeback Mountain."

Libraries continue to be the target of those who seek to ban books that they find objectionable. For instance, the American Library Association announced in 2005 that Robert Cormier's book "The Chocolate War" was the most challenged book of 2004 due to its sexual content and offensive language. In many of these instances the general public finds little cause for concern about such censorship. Public malaise about such conditions is dangerous. No individual's freedom is secure unless the freedom of all is ensured. This last point—that the freedom of speech must be ensured for *all* people, not simply those on one side of the political spectrum—is critical. As Nadine Strossen, president of the American Civil Liberties Union, told one of the authors of this textbook, "the notion of neutrality is key. You cannot have freedom of speech only for ideas that you like and people that you like."[8] Those who would engage in community censorship because they don't like what someone has to say would be wise to remember this principle of viewpoint neutrality embodied in the freedom of speech.

SUMMARY

Freedom of the press is part of the great Anglo-American legal tradition, but it is a right that has been won only through many hard-fought battles. The British discovered the power of the press in the early 16th century and devised numerous schemes to restrict publication. Criticism of the government, called seditious libel, was outlawed. Licensing or prior censorship was also common. In addition, the Crown for many years used an elaborate system of patents and monopolies to control printing in England.

While under British law for more than 100 years, American colonists enjoyed somewhat more freedom of expression than did their counterparts in England. Censorship laws existed before the first printing press arrived in North America, but they were enforced erratically or not at all. Licensing ended in the United States colonies in the 1720s. There were several trials for sedition in the colonies, but the acquittal of John Peter Zenger in 1735 by a recalcitrant jury ended that threat. Colonial legislatures and assemblies then attempted to punish dissident printers by using their contempt power. By the time the American colonists began to build their own governments in the 1770s and 1780s, they had the history of a 300-year struggle for freedom of expression on which to build.

THE FIRST AMENDMENT

In 1781, even before the end of the Revolutionary War, the new nation adopted its first constitution, the Articles of Confederation. The Articles provided for a loose-knit confederation of the 13 colonies, or states, in which the central or federal government had little power. The Articles reflected the spirit of the Declaration of Independence, adopted five years earlier,

---

7. Parks, "Chicks Face 'Landslide.'"
8. Richards and Calvert, "Nadine Strossen and Freedom of Expression," 202.

which ranked the rights of individuals in the society higher than the needs of a government to organize and operate a cohesive community. The Articles of Confederation did not contain a guarantee of freedom of expression. In fact, it had no bill of rights of any kind. The individuals who drafted this constitution did not believe such guarantees were necessary. Guarantees of freedom of expression were already a part of the constitutions of most of the 13 states. Virginia, for example, had adopted a new constitution that contained a declaration of rights in June 1776, five years before the Articles of Confederation were written. Freedom of the press was guaranteed as a part of that declaration of rights. Other states soon followed Virginia's lead.

But the system of government created by the Articles of Confederation did not work very well. In the hot summer of 1787, 12 of the 13 states sent a total of 55 delegates to Philadelphia to revise or amend the Articles, to make fundamental changes in the structure of the government.

THE NEW CONSTITUTION

It was a remarkable group of men; perhaps no such group has gathered before or since. The members were merchants and planters and professionals, and none were full-time politicians. As a group these men were by fact or inclination members of the economic, social and intellectual aristocracy of their respective states. They shared a common education centered on history, political philosophy and science. Some of them spent months preparing for the meeting—studying the governments of past nations. While some members came to modify the Articles of Confederation, many others knew from the start that a new constitution was needed. In the end that is what they produced, a new governmental charter. The charter was far different from the Articles in that it gave vast powers to a central government. The states remained supreme in some matters, but in other matters they were forced to relinquish their sovereignty to the new federal government.

No official record of the convention was kept. The delegates deliberated behind closed doors as they drafted the new charter. However, some personal records remain. We do know, for example, that inclusion of a bill of rights in the new charter was not discussed until the last days of the convention. The Constitution was drafted in such a way as not to infringe on state bills of rights. When the meeting was in its final week, George Mason of Virginia indicated his desire that "the plan be prefaced with a Bill of Rights. . . . It would give great quiet to the people," he said, "and with the aid of the state declarations, a bill might be prepared in a few hours." Few joined Mason's call. Only one delegate, Roger Sherman of Connecticut, spoke against the suggestion. He said he favored protecting the rights of the people when it was necessary, but in this case there was no need. "The state declarations of rights are not repealed by this Constitution; and being in force are sufficient." He said that where the rights of the people are involved Congress could be trusted to preserve the rights. The states, voting as units, unanimously opposed Mason's plan. While the Virginian later attempted to add a bill of rights in a piecemeal fashion, the Constitution emerged from the convention and was placed before the people for ratification without a bill of rights.

The new Constitution was not without opposition. The struggle for its adoption was hard fought. The failure to include a bill of rights in the document was a telling complaint raised against the new document. Even Thomas Jefferson, who was in France, lamented, in a letter to his friend James Madison, the lack of a guarantee of political rights in the charter. When the states finally voted on the new Constitution, it was approved, but only after supporters in several states had promised to petition the First Congress to add a bill of rights.

James Madison was elected from Virginia to the House of Representatives, defeating James Monroe only after promising his constituents to work in the First Congress toward adoption of a declaration of human rights. When Congress convened, Madison worked to keep his promise. He first proposed that the new legislature incorporate a bill of rights into the body of the Constitution, but the idea was later dropped. That the Congress would adopt the declaration was not a foregone conclusion. There was much opposition, but after several months, 12 amendments were finally approved by both houses and sent to the states for ratification. Madison's original amendment dealing with freedom of expression states: "The people shall not be deprived or abridged of their right to speak, to write or to publish their sentiments and freedom of the press, as one of the great bulwarks of liberty, shall be inviolable." Congressional committees changed the wording several times, and the section guaranteeing freedom of expression was merged with the amendment guaranteeing freedom of religion and freedom of assembly. The final version is the one we know today:

> *Congress shall make no law respecting an establishment of religion, or prohibiting the free exercise thereof; or abridging the freedom of speech, or of the press; or the right of the people peaceably to assemble, and to petition the Government for a redress of grievances.*

The concept of the "first freedom" is discussed often. Historical myth tells us that because the amendment occurs first in the Bill of Rights it was considered the most important right. In fact, in the Bill of Rights presented to the states for ratification, the amendment was listed third. Amendments 1 and 2 were defeated and did not become part of the Constitution. The original First Amendment called for a fixed schedule that apportioned seats in the House of Representatives on a ratio many people thought unfair. The Second Amendment prohibited senators and representatives from altering their salaries until after a subsequent election of representatives. Both amendments were rejected, and Amendment 3 became the First Amendment. In 1992, the economy-minded legislatures in three-fourths of the United States finally approved the original Second Amendment, and it became the 27th amendment to the Constitution.

Passage of Amendments 3 through 12 did not occur without struggle. Not until two years after being transmitted to the states for approval did a sufficient number of states adopt the amendments for them to become part of the Constitution. Connecticut, Georgia, and Massachusetts did not ratify the Bill of Rights until 1941, a kind of token gesture on the 150th anniversary of its constitutional adoption. In 1791 approval by these states was not needed, since only three-fourths of the former colonies needed to agree to the measures.

FREEDOM OF EXPRESSION IN THE 18TH CENTURY

What did the First Amendment mean to the people who supported its ratification? Technically, the definition of freedom of the press approved by the nation when the First Amendment was ratified in 1791 is what is guaranteed today. To enlarge or narrow that definition requires another vote of the people, a constitutional amendment. This notion is referred to today as "original intent" of the Constitution; that is, if we knew the meaning intended by the framers of the First Amendment, then we would know what it means today.

Most people today consider this notion so much legalistic poppycock. The nation has changed dramatically in 215 years. Television, radio, film and the Internet did not exist in 1791, for example. Does this mean that the guarantees of the First Amendment should not apply to these mass media? Of course not. Our Constitution has survived more than two centuries because it has been somewhat elastic. The Supreme Court of the United States, our final arbiter on the meaning of the Constitution, has helped adapt the document to changing times.

Still, it is important that we respect the document that was adopted more than two centuries ago. If we stray too far from its original meaning, the document may become meaningless; there will be no rules of government. The Constitution will mean only what those in power say it means. Thus the judicial philosophy of historicism, despite what law professor Rodney Smolla correctly calls "the obstinate illusiveness of original intent in the free speech area,"[9] remains an important consideration for some judges and justices. "The experience of the framers will never give us precise answers to modern conflicts," Smolla writes, "but it will give us a sense of how deeply free speech was cherished, at least as an abstract value."[10]

What was the legal or judicial definition of the First Amendment in 1791? Surprisingly, that is not an easy question to answer. The records of the period carry mixed messages. There was really no authoritative definition of freedom of the press and freedom of speech rendered by a body like the Supreme Court. And even the words used by people of that era may have meant something different than they mean in the 21st century. Most everyone agrees that freedom of expression meant at least the right to be free from prior restraint or licensing. Sir William Blackstone, a British legal scholar, published a major four-volume summary of the common law between 1765 and 1769. In this summary, "Commentaries on the Law of England," Blackstone defined freedom of expression as "laying no previous restraints upon publication." Today we call this no prior censorship. Many scholars argue that freedom of expression surely meant more than simply no prior censorship, that it also protected persons from punishment *after publication* or, as First Amendment Scholars might put it, from subsequent punishments. In other words, the First Amendment also precluded prosecutions for seditious libel. After all, they argue, one of the reasons for the American Revolution was to rid the nation of the hated British sedition laws.

Most everyone agrees that freedom of expression meant at least the right to be free from prior restraint or licensing.

The truth is that we probably don't know what freedom of the press meant to American citizens in the 1790s. The written residue of the period reveals only a partial story. It's very likely that it meant something a little different to different people, just as it does today. Even those individuals who drafted the Bill of Rights probably held somewhat different views on the meaning of the First Amendment.

Has the meaning of freedom of expression changed over the past two centuries? Surely, in many small and fairly obvious ways. But some scholars today suggest that a more subtle but profound change has taken place as well. They argue persuasively that many persons see a difference in the values that should be protected by the First Amendment. In the late 18th century freedom of expression was designed to protect the rights of the speaker; the value of the First Amendment was to allow individuals the fullest possible right to say or publish what

9. Smolla, *Free Speech in an Open Society,* 28.
10. Ibid., 39.

they wished. Scholars like Steven Helle at the University of Illinois argue that it is the protection of the public's right to know, or society's right to be informed, that today is the central value in the First Amendment.[11] This subtle shift in what is being protected manifests a different interpretation of what and how much speech is protected under the Constitution. Only serious harm to other individuals or to the community will justify an interference with First Amendment freedoms if the rights of the speaker or publisher are paramount. But when societal interests are put ahead of those of the speaker or publisher, substantially more censorship will be tolerated in order to preserve the wider rights of the community. Those who advocate tougher sanctions on obscenity because it demeans women, or stricter limits on racially or ethnically insulting speech because it denigrates members of racial or ethnic minority groups, do so from the position of this latter interpretation of the First Amendment. We will encounter instances of the advocacy of this new proposition throughout this book.

FREEDOM OF EXPRESSION TODAY

If we are not certain what the First Amendment meant in 1791, do we know what it means today? More or less. The First Amendment means today what the Supreme Court of the United States says it means. The Supreme Court and, occasionally, lower courts define the meaning of the First Amendment to the Constitution.

The First Amendment means today what the Supreme Court of the United States says it means.

The Supreme Court is a collection of nine justices, not a single individual. Consequently, at any given time there can be nine different definitions of freedom of expression. This has never happened—at least not on important issues. What has happened is that groups of justices have subscribed to various theoretical positions regarding the meaning of the First Amendment. These ideas on the meaning of the First Amendment help justices shape their vote on a question regarding freedom of expression. These ideas have changed during the past 85 years, from the point at which the First Amendment first came under serious scrutiny by the Supreme Court.

Legal theories are sometimes difficult to handle. Judge Learned Hand, a distinguished American jurist known as the most important judge *never* to have served on the U.S. Supreme Court, referred to the propagation of legal theory as "shoveling smoke." With such cautions in mind, here are seven important First Amendment theories or strategies that have been used or are used today to help judges develop a practical definition of freedom of expression.

SEVEN FIRST AMENDMENT THEORIES
1. Absolutist theory
2. Ad hoc balancing theory
3. Preferred position balancing theory
4. Meiklejohnian theory
5. Marketplace of ideas
6. Access theory
7. Self-realization

11. Helle, "Public's Right," 1077.

Absolutist theory: Some people have argued that the First Amendment presents an absolute or complete barrier to government censorship of speech or press. When the First Amendment declares that "no law" shall abridge freedom of expression, the framers of the Constitution meant *no law.* This is the essence of the **absolutist theory.** The government cannot censor the press for any reason. There are no exceptions, no caveats, no qualifications.

Few have subscribed to this notion wholeheartedly. Supreme Court justices Hugo Black, who sat on the high court from 1937 to 1971, and William O. Douglas, whose term lasted from 1939 to 1975, claimed adherence to this philosophy, but they were unable to persuade their brethren that this idea had much merit. A majority of the Supreme Court *never* has adopted an absolutist position. In fact, as this book later illustrates, the Supreme Court has held that there are several types of speech that fall outside the scope of First Amendment protection and thus can be abridged without violating the freedoms of speech or press. As Justice Anthony Kennedy wrote for the court in 2002, when striking down a federal law prohibiting virtual child pornography, "[t]he freedom of speech has its limits; it does not embrace certain categories of speech, including defamation, incitement, obscenity, and pornography produced with real children."[12] Other categories of speech also fall outside the ambit of First Amendment protection, including fighting words (see pages 143–147) and true threats of violence.[13]

Ad hoc balancing theory: Freedom of speech and press are two of a number of important human rights we value in this nation. These rights often conflict. When conflict occurs, it is the responsibility of the court to balance the freedom of expression with other values. For example, the government must maintain the military to protect the security of the nation. To function, the military must maintain secrecy about many of its weapons, plans and movements. Imagine that the press seeks to publish information about a secret weapons system. The right to freedom of expression must be balanced with the need for secrecy in the military.

This theory is called *ad hoc* balancing because the scales are erected anew in every case; the meaning of the freedom of expression is determined solely on a case-by-case basis. Freedom of the press might outweigh the need for the government to keep secret the design of its new rifle, but the need for secrecy about a new fighter plane might take precedence over freedom of expression.

Ad hoc balancing is really not a theory; it is a strategy. Developing a definition of freedom of expression on a case-by-case basis leads to uncertainty. Under ad hoc balancing we will never know what the First Amendment means except as it relates to a specific, narrow problem (e.g., the right to publish information about a new army rifle). If citizens cannot reasonably predict whether a particular kind of expression might be protected or prohibited, they will have the tendency to play it safe and keep silent. This is known as a "chilling effect" on speech. This will limit the rights of expression of all persons. Also, ad hoc balancing relies too heavily in its final determination on the personal biases of the judge or justices who decide a case. Ad hoc balancing is rarely invoked as a strategy these days except by judges unfamiliar with First Amendment law.

Preferred position balancing theory: The Supreme Court has held in numerous rulings that some constitutional freedoms, principally those guaranteed by the First Amendment, are

---

12. *Ashcroft* v. *Free Speech Coalition,* 535 U.S. 234, 245–46 (2002).
13. *Watts* v. *United States,* 394 U.S. 705, 708 (1969).

fundamental to a free society and consequently are entitled to more judicial protection than other constitutional values are.[14] Freedom of expression is essential to permit the operation of the political process and to permit citizens to protest when government infringes on their constitutionally protected prerogatives. The Fourth Amendment guarantee of freedom from illegal search and seizure surely has diminished value if citizens who suffer from such unconstitutional searches cannot protest such actions. Freedom of expression does not trump all other rights. Courts, for example, have attempted to balance the rights of free speech and press with the constitutionally guaranteed right of a fair trial. On the other hand, courts have consistently ruled that freedom of expression takes precedence over the right to personal privacy and the right to reputation, neither of which is explicitly guaranteed by the Bill of Rights.

Giving freedom of expression a preferred position *presumes* that government action that limits free speech and free press to protect other interests is usually unconstitutional. This presumption forces the government to bear the burden of proof in any legal action challenging the censorship. The city, county, state or federal government must prove to the court that its censorship is, in fact, justified and is not a violation of the First Amendment. In most instances the government must only prove that the accused violated the law, not that the law itself is constitutional. Were it not for this presumption, the persons whose expression was limited would be forced to convince a court that they had a constitutional right to speak or publish. This difference sounds minor, but in a lawsuit this presumption means a great deal.

While this theory retains some of the negative features of ad hoc balancing, by tilting the scales in favor of freedom of expression, it adds somewhat more certainty to our definition of freedom of expression. By basing this balancing strategy on a philosophical foundation (the maintenance of all rights is dependent on free exercise of speech and press), it becomes easier to build a case in favor of the broad interpretation of freedom of expression under the First Amendment.

Meiklejohnian theory: Philosopher and educator Alexander Meiklejohn presented the legal community with a rather complex set of ideas about freedom of expression in the late 1940s.[15] Meiklejohn looked at the First Amendment in a pragmatic manner and argued that freedom of expression is worth little as an abstract concept; that its primary value is as a means to an end. That end is successful self-government or, as Meiklejohn himself put it, "the voting of wise decisions." Freedom of speech and press are protected in the Constitution so that our system of democracy can function, and that is the only reason they are protected. Expression that relates to the self-governing process must be protected absolutely by the First Amendment. There can be no government interference with such expression. Expression that does not relate to the self-governing process is not protected absolutely by the First Amendment. The value or worth of such speech must be balanced by the courts against other rights and values. Meiklejohnian theory thus represents a hierarchical approach to First Amendment theory, with political speech placed at the top of this hierarchy.

Expression that relates to the self-governing process must be protected absolutely by the First Amendment.

---

14. See *United States* v. *Carolene Products,* 304 U.S. 144 (1938) and *Palko* v. *Connecticut,* 302 U.S. 319 (1937). See also Justice Holmes' opinions in both *Lochner* v. *New York,* 198 U.S. 45 (1905) and *Abrams* v. *United States,* 250 U.S. 616 (1919).
15. Meiklejohn, *Free Speech.*

Critics of this theory argue in a telling fashion that it is not always clear whether expression pertains to self-government (public speech) or to other interests (private speech). While not providing the specific definition sought by critics, Meiklejohn argued that a broad range of speech is essential to successful self-government. He included speech-related education (history, political science, geography, etc.), science, literature and many other topics. This theory has been embraced by some members of the Supreme Court of the United States, most notably former justice William Brennan. American libel law was radically changed when Brennan led the Supreme Court to give First Amendment protection to persons who have defamed government officials or others who attempt to lead public policy, a purely Meiklejohnian approach to the problem.

Marketplace of ideas theory: The marketplace of ideas theory, writes professor Matthew Bunker, "represents one of the most powerful images of free speech, both for legal thinkers and for laypersons."[16] It embodies what First Amendment scholar Daniel Farber calls "the truth-seeking rationale for free expression."[17] Although the theory itself can be traced back to the work of poet John Milton and John Stuart Mill, it was U.S. Supreme Court Justice Oliver Wendell Holmes Jr. who introduced the marketplace rationale for protecting speech to First Amendment case law more than 85 years ago. In his dissent in *Abrams* v. *United States,*[18] Holmes famously wrote:

> But when men have realized that time has upset many fighting faiths, they may come to believe even more than they believe the very foundations of their own conduct that the ultimate good desired is better reached by free trade in ideas—that the best test of truth is the power of the thought to get itself accepted in the competition of the market, and that truth is the only ground upon which their wishes safely can be carried out.[19]

Today, the economics-based marketplace metaphor "consistently dominates the Supreme Court's discussion of freedom of speech."[20] For instance, in writing for a unanimous Supreme Court in 2003 in *Virginia* v. *Hicks,* Justice Antonin Scalia described how overbroad laws—laws that are drafted so broadly that they punish a substantial amount of protected free speech along with unprotected speech—are unconstitutional because they harm "society as a whole, which is deprived of an *uninhibited marketplace of ideas.*"[21]

The marketplace theory, however, is often criticized by scholars. Common condemnations are that much shoddy speech, such as hate speech (see pages 143–147), circulates in the marketplace of ideas despite its lack of value and that access to the marketplace is *not* equal for everyone. In particular, those having the most economic resources (today, large conglomerates such as Viacom, News Corp. and Clear Channel) are able to own and to control the mass media and, in turn, to dominate the marketplace of ideas. Nonetheless, law professor Martin Redish observes that "over the years, it has not been uncommon for scholars or jurists

---

16. Bunker, *Critiquing Free Speech,* 2.
17. Farber, *The First Amendment,* 4.
18. 250 U.S. 616 (1919).
19. 250 U.S. 616, 630 (Holmes, J., dissenting).
20. Baker, *Human Liberty,* 7.
21. 539 U.S. 113, 119 (2003).

to analogize the right of free expression to a marketplace in which contrasting ideas compete for acceptance among a consuming public."[22] The premise of this idealistically free and fair competition of ideas is that truth will be discovered or, at the very least, conceptions of the truth will be tested and challenged.[23]

Access theory. Essayist and social critic H. L. Mencken wrote that freedom of the press belonged to the man who owned one. What the iconoclast meant was that a constitutional guarantee of freedom of expression had little meaning if a citizen did not have the economic means to exercise this right. Owners of magazines, newspapers and broadcasting stations could take advantage of the promises of the First Amendment, whereas the average man or woman lacked this ability. Put differently, access to the metaphorical marketplace of ideas is *not* equal for all, but is skewed in favor of those with the most economic resources. What Mencken wrote more than half a century ago is still true today, although the evolution of the Internet has at least given millions more Americans the opportunity to share their ideas as "bloggers" with a wider audience than was accessible in the past. Still, the audience for the vast majority of Web sites is small in comparison with the number of people reached by a television network or a national magazine or even a metropolitan newspaper.

In the mid-1960s some legal scholars, most notably Professor Jerome Barron, former dean of the National Law Center at George Washington University, argued that the promise of the First Amendment was unfulfilled for most Americans because they lacked the means to exercise their right to freedom of the press.[24] To make the guarantees of the First Amendment meaningful, newspapers, magazines and broadcasting stations should open their pages and studios to the ideas and opinions of their readers and listeners and viewers. Only in this way will all citizens have the opportunity to be heard by more than the few persons they can talk with in a conversation or at a meeting hall. If the press will not do this voluntarily, the obligation falls upon the government to force such access to the press. The access theory thus can be seen as a remedy to correct some of the flaws of the marketplace of ideas theory described earlier. These ideas received a wide and generally welcome hearing in academic circles. Needless to say, the owners and editors of the press were not as enthusiastic. And the courts tended to echo these sentiments.

The Supreme Court unanimously rejected this notion in 1974 in *Miami Herald* v. *Tornillo.*[25] Chief Justice Warren Burger, writing for the court, said that the choice of material to go into a newspaper and the decisions made as to limitations on the size of the paper and to content and treatment of public issues and public officials are decisions that must be made by the editors. The First Amendment does not give the government the right to force a newspaper to publish the views or ideas of a citizen. The *Tornillo* case sounded the legal death knell for this access theory for print media. (See *South Wind Motel* v. *Lashutka*[26] for an example of how courts have rejected the access theory since the *Tornillo* ruling.)

At the same time that federal courts were rejecting the access theory as it applied to the printed press, many courts were embracing these notions to justify the regulation of American

22. Redish and Kaludis, *The Right of Expressive Access,* 1083.
23. Chemerinsky, *Constitutional Law,* 753.
24. Barron, "Access to the Press."
25. 418 U.S. 241 (1974).
26. 9 M.L.R. 1661 (1983).

radio and television. In 1969 the Supreme Court ruled in the famous case of *Red Lion Broadcasting* v. *FCC*[27] that "It is the right of the public to receive suitable access to social, political, esthetic, moral, and other ideas and experiences, which is crucial here." The apparent contradiction in accepting the access theory for broadcast media but rejecting its application to the printed press was based on what many broadcasters regarded as an ill-conceived notion of differences in the two media forms. There could be an unlimited number of voices in the printed press, it was argued, but technological limits in the electromagnetic broadcast spectrum controlled the number of radio and television stations that could broadcast, and the government was required to protect the public interest in the case of the latter. The flaw in this assumption, they argued, was that it failed to take into account 20th-century economic limits that sharply curtailed the number of printing presses.

The regulation of broadcasting by the government has been turned on its head in the past three decades with the emergence of technologies such as cable and direct broadcast and, indirectly at least, the Internet. Little remains of the comprehensive set of rules that were developed in the last half of the 20th century (see Chapter 16). Hence, the access theory has substantially diminished resonance even in relation to telecommunications regulation. At the same time, however, the proponents of this view of the meaning of the First Amendment argue that with the ever-increasing collapse of mass media ownership into fewer hands,* now, more than ever, the courts should be defining freedom of expression in such a way as to protect the voice of the individual as opposed to the voice of the corporate owner.

Self-realization/self-fulfillment theory: While the primary goal of Meiklejohnian theory is successful self-government and the main objective of the marketplace theory is discovery of the truth, it may be that speech is important to an individual *regardless* of its impact on politics or its benefit to society at large. For instance, the act of transcribing one's thoughts in a private diary or a personal journal can be beneficial to the writer, even though no one else ever will (at least the writer hopes!) read them. Speech, in other words, can be inherently valuable to a person regardless of its effect on others—it can be an end in itself. An individual who wears a shirt with the name of his or her favorite political candidate on it may not change anyone else's vote or influence the discovery of the truth, yet the shirt-wearer is realizing and expressing his or her own identity through speech. As law professor C. Edwin Baker writes, "to engage in a speech act is to engage in self-definition."[28]

The seven theories or strategies just outlined guide jurists across the nation as they attempt to fathom the meaning of these seemingly simple 13 words: "Congress shall make no law abridging freedom of speech or of the press." In the remainder of this book, an attempt will be made to outline what the courts—using these theories—say the First Amendment means.

Speech is important to an individual regardless of its impact on politics or its benefit to society at large.

---

*The most recent example of this took place in 2003 when the Federal Communications Commission altered rules on the ownership of broadcast properties permitting an even greater concentration of media voices into fewer hands. Although many of those rules were later enjoined by a federal appellate court, the FCC continues to consider similar deregulatory measures. See Chapter 16.

27. 395 U.S. 367 (1969).

28. Baker, *Human Liberty,* 53.

SUMMARY

The nation's first constitution, the Articles of Confederation, did not contain a guarantee of freedom of speech and press, but nearly all state constitutions provided for a guarantee of such rights. Citizens insisted that a written declaration of rights be included in the Constitution of 1787, and a guarantee of freedom of expression was a part of the Bill of Rights that was added to the national charter in 1791.

There is a debate within the legal-historical community over the meaning of the First Amendment when it was drafted and approved in the late 18th century. Some people argue that it was intended to block both prior censorship and prosecution for seditious libel. Others argue that it was intended to prohibit only prior censorship. We will never know what the guarantee of freedom of expression meant to the persons who drafted it, but it is a good bet that citizens had a wide variety of interpretations of the First Amendment when they voted to approve it.

The meaning of the First Amendment today is largely determined through interpretation by the Supreme Court of the United States. Jurists use legal theories to guide them in determining the meaning of the constitutional guarantee that "Congress shall make no law abridging freedom of speech or of the press." Seven such theories are (1) absolutist theory, (2) ad hoc balancing theory, (3) preferred position balancing theory, (4) Meiklejohnian theory, (5) marketplace of ideas, (6) access theory, and (7) self-realization. Theories 2, 3 and 5 have the most supporters on the Supreme Court, and all the theories have assisted members of the high court to shape the meaning of the First Amendment.

THE MEANING OF FREEDOM

The struggle since 1791 to define the meaning of freedom of expression has involved a variety of issues. Three topics are at the heart of this struggle: the power of the state to limit criticism or published attacks on the government; the power of the state to use taxation to censor the press; and the power of the government to forbid the publication of ideas or information it believes to be harmful. Each of these classic battles will be considered in the remainder of this chapter.

SEDITIOUS LIBEL AND THE RIGHT TO CRITICIZE THE GOVERNMENT

The essence of a democracy is participation by citizens in the process of government. At its most basic level, this participation involves selecting leaders for the nation, the state and the various local governments through the electoral process. Popular participation also includes examination of government and public officials to determine their fitness for serving the people. Discussion, criticism and suggestion all play a part in the orderly transition of governments and elected leaders. The right to speak and print, then, is inherent in a nation governed by popularly elected rulers.

Whether or not the rights of free expression as defined in 1791 included a broad right to criticize the government, this kind of political speech has emerged as a central element of our modern understanding of the First Amendment.

The right to discuss, criticize and oppose the government is at the center of our political philosophy today. This is certainly not the case everywhere in the world, even in so-called free countries. Not long ago the New York Times Co. and the Washington Post Co., co-publishers of the Paris-based International Herald Tribune, were forced to pay nearly $700,000 in damages for publishing comments supposedly critical of the government of Singapore. The Asian printing plant for the Herald Tribune is located in this small independent republic located on the Malay Peninsula. Failure to pay the damages would have forced the relocation of this printing plant and eliminated the opportunity for the newspaper to continue to do business in Singapore.

Even in the United States it is not always possible to criticize the government or advocate political change without suffering reprisals from the government.

Even in the United States it is not always possible to criticize the government or advocate political change without suffering reprisals from the government. For instance, in February 2003, a public high school junior in Dearborn, Mich., named Bretton Barber was prohibited from wearing a T-shirt to school that displayed a photograph of President George W. Bush with the caption "International Terrorist." In this case, the public school principal was the government actor who stopped speech critical of another government actor, President Bush. Fortunately for young Mr. Barber, a federal judge ruled later that same year that his unpopular dissenting political speech—he attempted to wear the shirt to school shortly before the United States invaded Iraq in order, he said, to express his feelings about President Bush's foreign policies—was protected by the First Amendment (see pages 102–104).[29] And in 2004, during the presidential election season, Jeff and Nicole Rank were arrested, handcuffed and jailed on trespassing charges for peacefully wearing anti-Bush T-shirts (one shirt carried the message "Love America, Hate Bush" and the other read "Regime Change Starts at Home") to a rally for President Bush at the West Virginia State Capitol grounds.[30] Although the charges were later dropped, the Ranks filed a lawsuit, with the help of the American Civil Liberties Union, alleging a violation of their fundamental First Amendment right to engage in dissenting political expression. Neither Barber nor the Ranks, it should be noted, yelled, screamed or heckled; they each merely engaged in passive (nonspoken) expression. Many Americans are troubled today when asked to support a broad definition of freedom of expression in light of the growing militancy by right-wing hate groups and radical Islamic terrorists. Can the use of force or violence be advocated as a means of changing the government? Can a citizen use the essence of democracy, free expression, to advocate the violent abolition of democracy and the establishment of a repressive state in which the rights of free speech and free press would be denied? Americans familiar with the history of the past 215 years know that these are more than academic questions. Some of the fiercest First Amendment battles have been fought over exactly these issues.

29. *Barber* v. *Dearborn Public Schools,* 286 F. Supp. 2d 847 (E.D. Mich. 2003).
30. Herman, "Suit Alleges Protesters Are Muzzled."

**CRITICAL DATES IN THE HISTORY OF SEDITION LAW
IN THE UNITED STATES**

1735   Acquittal of John Peter Zenger

1791   Adoption of First Amendment

1798   Alien and Sedition Acts of 1798

1917   Espionage Act

1918   Sedition Act

1919   Clear and present danger test enunciated

1927   Brandeis sedition test in *Whitney* v. *California*

1940   Smith Act adopted

1951   Smith Act ruled constitutional

1957   Scope of Smith Act greatly narrowed

1969   Sedition test in *Brandenburg* v. *Ohio* substantially curbs
        sedition prosecutions

ALIEN AND SEDITION ACTS

The United States wasn't even 10 years old when the nation's resolve in protecting freedom of expression was first tested. Intense rivalry between President John Adams' Federalist party and Thomas Jefferson's Republican* or Jeffersonian party, coupled with the fear that the growing violence in the French Revolution might spread to this country, led to the adoption by the Federalist-dominated Congress of a series of highly repressive measures known as the **Alien and Sedition Acts of 1798.**[31] Three laws dealt with aliens, extending the period of residence prior to naturalization and giving the president extraordinary powers to detain and deport these noncitizen residents of the United States. A sedition law forbade false, scandalous and malicious publications against the U.S. government, Congress and the president. The new law also punished persons who sought to stir up sedition or urged resistance to federal laws. Punishment was a fine of as much as $2,000 and a jail term of up to two years. This latter statute was aimed squarely at the Jeffersonian political newspapers, many of which were relentless in their attacks on President Adams and his government.

There were 15 prosecutions under this law. This doesn't sound like many, but among those prosecuted were editors of eight Jeffersonian newspapers, including some of the leading papers in the nation. Imagine the federal government bringing sedition charges today against the editors of The New York Times, Washington Post, Miami Herald, and Chicago Tribune. Also prosecuted was a Republican member of Congress, Matthew Lyon. The so-called

*This Republican political party was not the forerunner of the contemporary Republican party, which was formed in 1854.

31. Smith, *Freedom's Fetters.*

seditious libel that was the basis for the criminal charges was usually petty and hardly threatened our admittedly youthful government. But Federalist judges heard most of the cases and convictions were common.

Far from inhibiting dissent, the laws succeeded only in provoking dissension among many of President Adams' supporters. Many argue that Adams lost his bid for re-election in 1800 largely because of public dissatisfaction with his attempt to muzzle his critics. The constitutionality of the laws was never tested before the full Supreme Court, but three members of the court heard Sedition Act cases while they were on the circuit. The constitutionality of the provisions was sustained by these justices. The Sedition Act expired in 1801 and newly elected President Thomas Jefferson pardoned all persons convicted under it, while Congress eventually repaid most of the fines. This was the nation's first peacetime sedition law and it left such a bad taste that another peacetime sedition law was not passed until 1940.

Most historians of freedom of expression in the United States focus on two eras in the 19th century during which censorship was not uncommon: the abolitionist period and the Civil War. A wide range of government actions, especially in the South, were aimed at shutting down the abolitionist press in the years between 1830 and 1860. And both the U.S. government and the Confederate States government censored the press during the Civil War. But in his book, "Free Speech in Its Forgotten Years," author David M. Rabban argues that there were also extensive censorship efforts in the latter half of the 19th century against radical labor unionists, anarchists, birth control advocates and other so-called freethinkers. And there was little meaningful public debate about such activities. "In the decades before World War I," Rabban wrote, "Americans generally needed to experience repression of views they shared before formulating a theory of free speech that extended to ideas they opposed."[32]

The issue of political dissent did not enter the national debate again until the end of the 1800s, when hundreds of thousands of Americans began to understand that democracy and capitalism were not going to bring them the prosperity promised as an American birthright. The advancing rush of the new industrial society left many Americans behind and unhappy. Tens of thousands were attracted to radical political movements such as socialism and anarchism, movements that were considered by most in the mainstream to be foreign to the United States. Labor unrest in the late 19th century often turned violent; radical protests turned bloody. President William McKinley was assassinated in 1901, shot by a man most historians describe as an anarchist. Revolution, clearly unlikely, nevertheless arose as a specter in the minds of millions of Americans. Hundreds of laws were passed by states and cities across the nation to try to limit this kind of political dissent. War broke out in Europe in 1914; the United States joined the conflict three years later. This pushed the nation over the edge and anything that remained of our national tolerance toward political dissent and criticism of the government and economic system vanished. At both the state and the federal level, government struck out at those who sought to criticize or suggest radical change.

32. Rabban, *Free Speech.*

SEDITION IN WORLD WAR I

World War I is probably the most unpopular war this nation has fought, easily rivaling the Vietnam conflict in terms of public protest. The war was a replay of the imperial wars of the 18th and 19th centuries in Europe, except that it was fought with deadly new weapons. Industrialists and farmers saw the opportunity for vast economic gains in supplying war goods, and superpatriots were thrilled that the United States was actually going to have the opportunity to fight in a real war on the Continent. But to millions of immigrants in this nation, the war was being fought in their homelands. Their families were dying; their relatives were now our enemies. The economically dispossessed rightly feared as well that the outbreak of war signaled the beginning of a period of internal political repression for those with little power.

Suppression of freedom of expression reached a higher level during World War I than at any other time in our history.[33] Government prosecutions during the Vietnam War, for example, were minor compared with government action between 1918 and 1920. Vigilante groups were active as well, persecuting when the government failed to prosecute.

Suppression of freedom of expression reached a higher level during World War I than at any other time in our history.

Two federal laws were passed to deal with persons who opposed the war and U.S. participation in it. In 1917 the **Espionage Act** was approved by Congress and signed by President Woodrow Wilson. The measure dealt primarily with espionage problems, but some parts were aimed expressly at dissent and opposition to the war. The law provided that it was a crime to willfully convey a false report with the intent to interfere with the war effort. It was a crime to cause or attempt to cause insubordination, disloyalty, mutiny or refusal of duty in the armed forces. It also was a crime to willfully obstruct the recruiting or enlistment service of the United States. Punishment was a fine of not more than $10,000 or a jail term of not more than 20 years. The law also provided that material violating the law could not be mailed.

In 1918 the **Sedition Act,** an amendment to the Espionage Act, was passed, making it a crime to attempt to obstruct the recruiting service. It was criminal to utter or print or write or publish disloyal or profane language that was intended to cause contempt of, or scorn for, the federal government, the Constitution, the flag or the uniform of the armed forces. Penalties for violation of the law were imprisonment for as long as 20 years or a fine of $10,000 or both. Approximately 2,000 people were prosecuted under these espionage and sedition laws, and nearly 900 were convicted. Persons who found themselves in the government's dragnet were usually aliens, radicals, publishers of foreign-language publications and other persons who opposed the war.

In addition the U.S. Post Office Department censored thousands of newspapers, books and pamphlets. Some publications lost their right to the government-subsidized second-class mailing rates and were forced to use the costly first-class rates or find other means of distribution. Entire issues of magazines were held up and never delivered, on the grounds that they violated the law (or what the postmaster general believed to be the law). Finally, the states were not content with allowing the federal government to deal with dissenters, and most adopted sedition statutes, laws against **criminal syndicalism,** laws that prohibited the display of a red flag or a black flag, and so forth.

Political repression in the United States did not end with the termination of fighting in Europe. The government was still suspicious of the millions of European immigrants in the

---

33. See Peterson and Fite, *Opponents of War.*

nation and frightened by the organized political efforts of socialist and communist groups. As the Depression hit the nation, first in the farm belt in the 1920s, and then in the rest of the nation by the next decade, labor unrest mushroomed. Hundreds of so-called agitators were arrested and charged under state and federal laws. Demonstrations were broken up; aliens were detained and threatened with deportation.

But what about the First Amendment? What happened to the rights of freedom of expression? The constitutional guarantees of freedom of speech and freedom of the press were of limited value during this era. The important legal meaning of freedom of expression had developed little in the preceding 125 years. There had been few cases and almost no important rulings before 1920. You will note as we proceed through this book that the words of the First Amendment—"Congress shall make no law"—are not nearly as important as the meaning attached to those words. And that meaning was only then beginning to develop through court rulings that resulted from the thousands of prosecutions for sedition and other such crimes between 1917 and the mid-1930s.

THE SMITH ACT

Congress adopted the nation's second peacetime sedition law in 1940 when it ratified the **Smith Act,** a measure making it a crime to advocate the violent overthrow of the government, to conspire to advocate the violent overthrow of the government, to organize a group that advocated the violent overthrow of the government, or to be a member of a group that advocated the violent overthrow of the government.[34] The law was aimed directly at the Communist party of the United States. While a small group of Trotskyites (members of the Socialist Workers party) were prosecuted and convicted under the Smith Act in 1943, no Communist was indicted under the law until 1948 when many of the nation's top Communist party leaders were charged with advocating the violent overthrow of the government. All were convicted after a nine-month trial and their appeals were denied. In a 7-2 ruling in 1951, the Supreme Court of the United States rejected the defendants' arguments that the Smith Act violated the First Amendment.[35]

Government prosecutions persisted during the early 1950s. But then, in a surprising reversal of its earlier position, the Supreme Court in 1957 overturned the convictions of West Coast Communist party leaders.[36] Justice John Marshall Harlan wrote for the 5-2 majority that government evidence showed that the defendants had advocated the violent overthrow of the government but only as an abstract doctrine, and this was not sufficient to sustain a conviction. Instead there must be evidence that proves the defendants advocated actual *action* aimed at the forcible overthrow of the government. This added burden of proof levied against the government prosecutors made it extremely difficult to use the Smith Act against the Communists, and prosecutions dwindled. The number of prosecutions diminished for other reasons as well, however. The times had changed. The cold war was not as intense. Americans looked at the Soviet Union and the Communists with a bit less fear. The Communist party of the United States had failed to generate any public support. Its membership had fallen precipitously. In

34. Pember, "The Smith Act," 1.
35. *Dennis* v. *U.S.,* 341 U.S. 494 (1951).
36. *Yates* v. *U.S.,* 354 U.S. 298 (1957).

fact, political scientist John Roche has remarked with only a slight wink that it was the dues paid to the party by FBI undercover agents that kept the organization economically solvent in the mid-to-late 1950s.

With the practical demise of the Smith Act, sedition has not been a serious threat against dissent for more than 45 years. No sedition cases were filed against Vietnam War protesters, and the last time the Supreme Court heard an appeal in a sedition case was in 1969 when it overturned the conviction of a Ku Klux Klan leader (*Brandenburg* v. *Ohio*).[37] The federal government has filed sedition charges several times in recent years against alleged white supremacists, neo-Nazis and others on the fringe of the right wing. While juries have been willing to convict such individuals of bombing, bank robbery and even racketeering, the defendants have been acquitted of sedition. The federal government had greater success in the 1990s using a Civil War–era sedition statute to prosecute Muslim militants who bombed the World Trade Center in New York City in 1993. Sheikh Omar Abdel Rahman and nine of his followers were found guilty of violating a 140-year-old law that makes it a crime to "conspire to overthrow, or put down, or to destroy by force the Government of the United States." Although the government could not prove that Abdel Rahman actually participated in the bombing, federal prosecutors argued that his exhortations to his followers amounted to directing a violent conspiracy. The sheikh's attorneys argued that his pronouncements were protected by the First Amendment. In August 1999 the 2nd U.S. Circuit Court of Appeals disagreed, noting that the Bill of Rights does not protect an individual who uses a public speech to commit crimes. Abdel Rahman's speeches were not simply the expression of ideas; "in some instances they constituted the crime of conspiracy to wage war against the United States," the court ruled. "Words of this nature," the three-judge panel wrote, "ones that instruct, solicit, or persuade others to commit crimes of violence—violate the law and may be properly prosecuted regardless of whether they are uttered in private, or in a public place."[38] In the wake of the terror attacks on September 11, 2001, federal prosecutors in New York said they were looking into the possibility that the attacks included a seditious conspiracy to levy war against the United States. This accusation means that individuals suspected of playing a part in the attacks could be charged under the same seditious conspiracy statute that was used against the previously convicted Trade Center bombers. No such charges were filed. Also, the USA Patriot Act, which was passed as a part of the anti-terrorism bill adopted in 2001, defines terrorism as any "attempt to intimidate or coerce a civilian population" or change "the policy of the government by intimidation or coercion." Some civil libertarians argue that this definition could include some kinds of political dissent and that it closely resembles what traditionally has been called sedition.

Another controversial section of the Patriot Act that pits free speech against the war on terrorism makes it a crime to provide "expert advice or assistance" to terrorists. In June 2004, a federal jury acquitted a Saudi-born computer doctoral student at the University of Moscow, Sami Omar Al-Hussayen, of charges under this provision that he spread terrorism by "designing websites and posting messages on the Internet to recruit and raise funds for terrorist missions in Chechnya and Israel. His attorneys argued that he was being prosecuted for expressing views protected by the First Amendment."[39] Georgetown University law professor

37. 395 U.S. 444 (1969).
38. *U.S.* v. *Rahman,* 189 F. 3d 88 (1999).
39. Schmitt, "Acquittal in Internet Terrorism Case."

David Cole remarked after the verdict that it was a "case where the government sought to criminalize pure speech and was resoundingly defeated."[40] And David Nevin, lead attorney for Al-Hussayen, told the Associated Press that "the message is that the First Amendment is important and meaningful in this country."[41]

This brief narrative does not begin to tell the story of the struggle for the right of political dissent in this nation. Books listed in the bibliography at the end of this chapter help to fill in many holes for students seeking a better understanding of the battles to exercise the right of free expression fought by Americans for two centuries. Historian David Shannon's reminder that the present is only the cutting edge of the past is especially apt when looking at American law. What has happened has a great impact on what will happen.

DEFINING THE LIMITS OF FREEDOM OF EXPRESSION

Remarkable as it may seem, the first time the Supreme Court of the United States seriously considered whether a prosecution for sedition violated the First Amendment was in 1919. The Philadelphia Socialist party authorized Charles Schenck, the general secretary of the organization, to publish 15,000 leaflets protesting against U.S. involvement in World War I. The pamphlet described the war as a cold-blooded and ruthless adventure propagated in the interest of the chosen few of Wall Street and urged young men to resist the draft. Schenck and other party members were arrested, tried and convicted of violating the Espionage Act (see page 55). The case was appealed all the way to the Supreme Court, with the Socialists asserting that they had been denied their First Amendment rights of freedom of speech and press. Justice Oliver Wendell Holmes penned the opinion for the court and rejected the First Amendment argument. In ordinary times, he said, such pamphlets might have been harmless and protected by the First Amendment. "But the character of every act depends upon the circumstances in which it is done. . . . The question in every case is whether the words used, are used in such circumstances and are of such a nature as to create a clear and present danger that they will bring about the substantive evils that Congress has a right to prevent. It is a question of proximity and degree."[42]

"The question in every case is whether the words used . . . create a clear and present danger that they will bring about the substantive evils that Congress has a right to prevent."

How can prosecutions for sedition be reconciled with freedom of expression? According to the Holmes test, Congress has the right to outlaw certain kinds of conduct that might be harmful to the nation. In some instances words, through speeches or pamphlets, can push people to undertake acts that violate the laws passed by Congress. In such cases publishers or speakers can be punished without infringing on their First Amendment freedoms. How close must the connection be between the advocacy of the speaker or publisher and the forbidden conduct? Holmes said that the words must create a "clear" (unmistakable? certain?) and "present" (immediate? close?) danger.

Holmes' test means less in the abstract than it does when connected to the facts of the *Schenck* case. In the abstract, an endless debate might be conducted over whether a speech or book presented the requisite clear and present danger. But in rejecting Schenck's appeal, the high court ruled that these 15,000 seemingly innocuous pamphlets posed a real threat to the

---

40. Ibid.
41. Fick, "Jury Acquits Saudi Graduate Student."
42. *Schenck* v. *U.S.,* 249 U.S. 47 (1919).

legitimate right of Congress to successfully conduct the war. To many American liberals this notion seemed farfetched, and Holmes was publicly criticized for the ruling. But the magic words "clear and present danger" stuck like glue on American sedition law, and for more than 30 years American jurists had to work their way around this standard. Holmes changed his mind about his test in less than six months and broke with the majority of the high court to outline a somewhat more liberal definition of freedom of expression in a ruling on the Sedition Act in the fall of 1919.[43] But the majority of the court continued to use the Holmes test to reject First Amendment appeals.

Justice Louis Brandeis attempted to fashion a more useful application of the clear and present danger test in 1927, but his definition of "clear and present danger" was confined to a concurring opinion in the case of *Whitney* v. *California*.[44] The state of California prosecuted Anita Whitney, a 64-year-old philanthropist who was the niece of Justice Stephen J. Field, a member of the Supreme Court from 1863 to 1897. She was charged with violating the state's Criminal Syndicalism Act after she attended a meeting of the Communist Labor party. She was not an active member in the party and during the convention had worked against proposals made by others that the party dedicate itself to gaining power through revolution and general strikes in which workers would seize power by violent means. But the state contended that the Communist Labor party was formed to teach criminal syndicalism, and as a member to the party she participated in the crime. After her conviction she appealed to the Supreme Court.

Justice Edward Sanford wrote the court's opinion and ruled that California had not violated Miss Whitney's First Amendment rights. The jurist said it was inappropriate to even apply the clear and present danger test. He noted that in *Schenck* and other previous cases, the statutes under which prosecution occurred forbade specific actions, such as interference with the draft. The clear and present danger test was then used to judge whether the words used by the defendant presented a clear and present danger that the forbidden action might occur. In this case, Sanford noted, the state of California law forbade specific words—the advocacy of violence to bring about political change. The Holmes test was therefore inapplicable. In addition, the California law was neither unreasonable nor unwarranted.

Justice Brandeis concurred with the majority, but only, he said, because the constitutional issue of freedom of expression had not been raised sufficiently at the trial to make it an issue in the appeal. (If a legal issue is not raised during a trial it is often impossible for an appellate court to later consider the matter.) In his concurring opinion, Brandeis disagreed sharply with the majority regarding the limits of free expression. In doing so he added flesh and bones to Holmes' clear and present danger test. Looking to the *Schenck* decision, the justice noted that the court had agreed that there must be a clear and imminent danger of a substantive evil that the state has the right to prevent before an interference with speech can be allowed. Then he went on to describe what he believed to be the requisite danger:

> To justify suppression of free speech there must be reasonable ground to
> fear that serious evil will result if free speech is practiced. There must be
> reasonable ground to believe that the danger apprehended is imminent.
> There must be reasonable ground to believe that the evil to be prevented is

43. *Abrams* v. *U.S.*, 250 U.S. 616 (1919).
44. 274 U.S. 357 (1927).

Source: © Bettmann/CORBIS

Justice Louis Brandeis, author of an important concurring opinion in Whitney v. California *and other First Amendment rulings.*

a serious one. Every denunciation of existing law tends in some measure to increase the probability that there will be violation of it. Condonation of a breach enhances the probability. Expressions of approval add to the probability. Propagation of the criminal state of mind by teaching syndicalism increases it. Advocacy of law-breaking heightens it further. But even advocacy of violation, however reprehensible morally, is not a justification for denying free speech where the advocacy falls short of incitement, and there is nothing to indicate that the advocacy would be immediately acted on. The wide difference between advocacy and incitement, between preparation and attempt, between assembling and conspiracy, must be borne in mind. In order to support a finding of clear and present danger it must be shown either that immediate serious violence was to be expected or was advocated, or that the past conduct furnished reason to believe that such advocacy was then contemplated.[45]

Brandeis concluded that if there is time to expose through discussion the falsehoods and fallacies, to avert the evil by the process of education, the remedy to be applied is more speech,

45. *Whitney* v. *California,* 274 U.S. 357 (1927).

not enforced silence. Put differently, Brandeis believed that counterspeech is the ideal, self-help remedy (i.e., adding more speech to the marketplace of ideas in order to counterargue), not censorship.

The next major ruling in which the high court attempted to reconcile sedition law and the First Amendment came in 1951 in the case of *Dennis* v. *U.S.*[46] (see page 56). Eleven Communist party members had been convicted of advocating the violent overthrow of the government, a violation of the Smith Act. The defendants raised the clear and present danger test as a barrier to their convictions; the actions of a small band of Communists surely did not constitute a clear and present danger to the nation, they argued. Chief Justice Vinson, who wrote the opinion for the court, used a variation of the clear and present danger test enunciated by Holmes in the *Schenck* case. He called it a clear and probable danger test. Surely the Congress has a right to prevent the overthrow of the government, Vinson said. How likely is it that the words spoken or written by the defendants would lead even to an attempted overthrow? "In each case [courts] must ask whether the gravity of the 'evil' discounted by its improbability, justifies such invasion of free speech as is necessary to avoid the danger," Vinson wrote, quoting a lower-court opinion written by Judge Learned Hand.

The test went only slightly beyond the original Holmes test, and the court ruled that the defendants' First Amendment rights had not been violated. If the Brandeis test from *Whitney* had been applied, however, it is likely the convictions would have gone out the window.

It has been more than 35 years since the Supreme Court heard the case of *Brandenburg* v. *Ohio* (see page 57) and made its last and probably best attempt to resolve the apparent contradiction between sedition law and freedom of expression. A leader of the Ku Klux Klan was prosecuted and convicted of violating an Ohio sedition law for stating: "We're not a revengent [revengeful] organization, but if our President, our Congress, our Supreme Court, continues to suppress the white Caucasian race, it's possible there might have to be some revengeance [revenge] taken." In reversing the conviction, the high court said the law must distinguish between the advocacy of ideas and the incitement to unlawful conduct. "The constitutional guarantees of free speech and free press do not permit a state to forbid or proscribe advocacy of the use of force or of law violation except *where such advocacy is directed to inciting or producing imminent lawless action and is likely to incite or produce such actions.*"[47]

This test, which represents the current and modern version of Justice Holmes' old clear-and-present-danger standard, can be broken down into four components. First, the word "directed" represents an intent requirement on the part of the speaker: Did the speaker actually intend for his or her words to incite lawless action? Second, the word "imminent" indicates that the time between the speech in question and the lawless action must be very close or proximate. Third, the conduct itself must be "lawless action," requiring that there be a criminal statute forbidding or punishing the underlying action that is allegedly advocated. Finally, the word "likely" represents a probability requirement—that the lawless action must be substantially likely to occur and not merely a speculative result of the speech. All four of these elements must be proven before the speech can be considered outside the scope of First Amendment protection.

"The constitutional guarantees of free speech and free press do not permit a state to forbid or proscribe advocacy of the use of force or of law violation except where such advocacy is directed to inciting or producing imminent lawless action and is likely to incite or produce such actions."

46. 341 U.S. 494 (1951).
47. 395 U.S. 444 (1969).

The legal theory behind the law of sedition was outlined previously; if someone publishes something that incites another person to do something illegal, the publisher of the incitement can be punished. While charges of sedition are rarely filed today, it is not uncommon for private persons to sue the mass media on the grounds that something that was published or recorded or exhibited incited a third person to commit an illegal act. These cases are similar to sedition prosecutions in many ways, and the constitutional shield developed by the courts that protects the mass media against convictions for sedition is applied in these cases as well.

The Book Made Me Do It

In the late 1870s Boston police arrested what some believe to be America's first serial killer, a teenage boy who began torturing children when he was 11 and began killing kids three years later. After the arrest of Jesse Pomeroy many persons blamed his killings on the dime novels that were published at the time, graphically violent stories with titles like "Desperate Dan" and "The Pirates of Pecos," even though the young killer testified that he never read such books.[48] This may have been the first time, but surely not the last, that books or movies or magazines or recordings were said to be responsible for someone's death or injury.

Courts are frequently asked to rule in wrongful death, negligence, and product liability lawsuits whether a media artifact like a film or recording played some part in inciting the actual perpetrator of the crime to commit illegal acts. To determine the liability in such cases the courts often use the *Brandenburg* test for incitement to violence outlined earlier in this chapter. For example, in 2002 the 6th U.S. Court of Appeals ruled that the producers of the film "The Basketball Diaries," the makers of several video games and some Internet content providers were not liable in a lawsuit brought by the parents of students who were killed and wounded when teenager Michael Carneal went on a shooting rampage in the lobby of Heath High School in Paducah, Ky. The plaintiffs argued, among other things, that Carneal had watched the film, which depicts a student daydreaming about killing a teacher and several classmates. "We find it is simply too far a leap from shooting characters on a video screen (an activity undertaken by millions) to shooting people in a classroom (an activity undertaken by a handful, at most) for Carneal's activities to have been reasonably foreseeable to the manufacturers of the media Carneal played and viewed," the court ruled. The material in this case falls far short of the standard required by *Brandenburg,* the judges added.[49] Why did they reach this conclusion? First and foremost, the movie was not "directed" to cause violence. As the appellate court wrote in *James* v. *Meow Media,* "while the defendants in this case may not have exercised exquisite care regarding the persuasive power of the violent material that they disseminated, they certainly did not 'intend' to produce violent actions by the consumers, as is required by the *Brandenburg* test."[50] In addition, the appellate court reasoned that "it is a long leap from the proposition that Carneal's actions were foreseeable to the *Brandenburg* requirement that the violent content was 'likely' to cause Carneal to behave this way."[51]

48. Schechter, "A Movie."
49. *James* v. *Meow Media Inc., 300 F. 3d 683 (2002).*
50. Ibid. at 698.
51. Ibid. at 699.

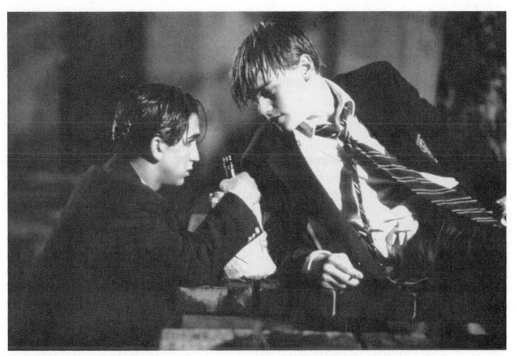

Source: © The Everett Collection

Leonardo Dicaprio, right, and James Madio, in a scene from "The Basketball Diaries," which was the focus of a lawsuit in 2002.

In 2001 a Louisiana trial court dismissed a lawsuit against Warner Brothers and other defendants brought by plaintiffs who claimed that a robbery and shooting at a convenience store was the result of the thieves' attempting to mimic characters in the film "Natural Born Killers."[52] Cases like those just outlined are typical of the way the courts have handled claims that the mass media have incited a criminal act by a reader or a viewer. It is very difficult for a plaintiff ever to prove the intent ("directed") prong of the *Brandenburg* test against the media. The media simply don't intend for violence to occur as a result of viewing, playing or reading their products. Rather, the typical intent is to entertain and to make a profit! But of course, there are exceptions to the rule.

In 1996 the families of Mildred and Trevor Horn and Janice Saunders filed a wrongful death suit against Paladin Enterprises and its president, Peter Lund. The company published a book titled "Hit Man: A Technical Manual for Independent Contractors." Lawrence Horn hired James Perry to kill his ex-wife, their 8-year-old quadriplegic son, and the son's nurse to gain access to the proceeds of a medical malpractice settlement. Both Perry and Horn were arrested and convicted of the murders; Perry was sentenced to death, Horn to life in prison. The plaintiffs contended that Perry used the Paladin publication as an instruction manual for

---

52. *Delgado* v. *American Multi-Cinema Inc.*, 85 Cal. Rptr. 2d 838 (1999) and *Byers* v. *Edmondson*, 29 M.L.R. 1991 (2001). See also *Pahler* v. *Slayer*, 29 M.L.R. 2627 (2001).

the killings. A U.S. District Court in Maryland ruled in August 1996 that the book was protected by the First Amendment. "However loathsome one characterizes the publication, 'Hit Man' simply does not fall within the parameters of any recognized exceptions to the First Amendment principles of freedom of speech." The book failed to cross the line between permissible advocacy and impermissible incitation to crime or violence, Judge Williams wrote.[53]

Fifteen months later the 4th U.S. Circuit Court of Appeals reversed the lower-court ruling. The defendant had agreed to a stipulation in the case that stated Paladin provided its assistance to Perry with both the knowledge and the intent that the book would immediately be used by criminals and would-be criminals in the solicitation, planning and commission of murder and murder for hire. The court said the book was not an example of abstract advocacy but a form of aiding and abetting a crime. The book "methodically and comprehensively prepares and steels its audience to specific criminal conduct through exhaustively detailed instructions on planning, commission, and concealment of criminal conduct," the panel ruled. There is no First Amendment protection for such a publication. The court noted that this case was unique and should not be read as expanding the potential liability of publishers and broadcasters when third parties copy or mimic a crime or other act contained in a news report or a film or a television program.[54] An appeal to the U.S. Supreme Court was denied and the case was returned to the U.S. District Court for trial. In May 1999 Paladin Press settled the case out of court. In spite of this case, the stringent requirements of the *Brandenburg* test make it difficult, bordering on impossible, for a plaintiff to win a lawsuit that alleges a play or book or song or movie was responsible for causing someone's illegal acts. The case law is highly one-sided in this regard.[55]

One media product—the video game—is under increasing legislative attacks from governmental entities across the United States. Both Indianapolis, Indiana, and St. Louis County, Missouri, as well as the state of Washington, enacted legislation in recent years that was designed to limit and restrict minors' access to video games that depict graphic images of violence. The rationale for restricting access to the games is that they allegedly cause the children who play them to aggress against others. But video games tell stories and have plots, however graphic they might be, and thus are subject to First Amendment protection as speech. All three laws were declared unconstitutional by federal courts.

In July 2004, a federal court issued an order[56] striking down, on First Amendment grounds, a Washington state law that restricted minors' access to video games containing "realistic or photographic-like depictions of aggressive conflict in which the player kills, injures, or otherwise causes physical harm to a human form in the game who is depicted, by dress or other recognizable symbols, as a public law enforcement officer."[57] The decision was anything but surprising. It followed in the footsteps of opinions issued by two federal

---

53. *Rice* v. *Paladin Enterprises Inc.,* 940 F. Supp. 836 (1996).
54. *Rice* v. *Paladin Enterprises Inc.,* 128 F. 3d 233 (1997).
55. See *Yakubowicz* v. *Paramount Pictures Corp.,* 404 Mass. 624 (1989) and *Herceg* v. *Hustler,* 814 F. 2d 1017 (1987).
56. Order Granting Plaintiffs' Motion for Summary Judgment and Granting in Part Defendants' Cross-Motion, *Video Software Dealers Ass'n* v. *Maleng* (W. D. Wash. 2004) (No. C03-1245L).
57. Wash. Rev. Code § 9.91.180 (2004).

appellate courts that held unconstitutional similar legislation regulating minors' access to fictional images of violence in video games.[58]

In striking down Washington's video game law, U.S. District Court Judge Robert S. Lasnik articulated a veritable laundry list of flaws that fatally plagued the statute.

- The current state of social science research was seriously lacking and failed to provide substantial evidence to support "the Legislature's belief that video games cause violence." In particular, the judge wrote that "neither causation nor an increase in real-life aggression is proven by these studies."

- The Washington law was "both over-inclusive and under-inclusive" in its attempt to single out "just one type of violence" for regulation, namely game-related aggression toward law enforcement officers. As Judge Lasnik reasoned, the law "sweeps too broadly in that it would restrict access to games that reflect heroic struggles against corrupt regimes" or "involve accidental injuries to officers," while it simultaneously "is too narrow in that it will have no effect on the many other channels through which violent representations are presented to children."

- The law's limitations on game-related violence "impact more constitutionally protected speech than is necessary to achieve the identified ends and are not the least restrictive alternative available." The judge observed that regulation was "not limited to the ultra-violent or the patently offensive and is far broader than what would be necessary to keep filth like Grand Theft Auto III and Postal II out of the hands of children."

- The law was "unconstitutionally vague." Judge Lasnik pointed out that attorneys for Washington state were unable, during oral argument, to answer the seemingly simple question of whether a firefighter would be a "public law enforcement officer" as that term is used in the statute.

It seems unlikely that anti-access video game legislation will ever survive judicial scrutiny. Nonetheless, attacking video games is a politically popular move—what politician doesn't want to stop violence?—so more unconstitutional legislation is likely to be produced throughout the rest of the decade.

It seems unlikely that anti-access video game legislation will ever survive judicial scrutiny.

For instance, in July 2005 Illinois Gov. Rod Blagojevich (D.) signed into law the "Safe Games Illinois Act" that bans the rental and sale to minors—defined as those under the age of 18 years—of video games depicting "violent" and "sexually explicit" content. The law also requires the labeling of packages for such games with a solid white "18" outlined in black that must be at least two inches tall and two inches wide. A federal lawsuit was immediately filed against the new law by the leading trade associations for the video game industry, including the Entertainment Software Association. In December 2005 a federal judge held that the Illinois law violated the First Amendment protection of free speech.

58. See *Interactive Digital Software Ass'n v. St. Louis County,* 329 F. 3d 954 (8th Cir. 2003), petition for reh'g en banc denied, 2003 U.S. App. LEXIS 13782 (2003) (striking down, on First Amendment grounds, a St. Louis County, Mo., ordinance that regulated minors' access to graphically violent video games); *American Amusement Machine Ass'n v. Kendrick,* 244 F. 3d 572 (7th Cir. 2001), petition for reh'g en banc denied, 2001 U.S. App. LEXIS 11010 (2001), cert. den. 534 U.S. 994 (2001) (declaring unconstitutional an Indianapolis, Ind., ordinance limiting minors' access to games deemed to be "harmful to minors" because of their "graphic violence").

Michigan Gov. Jennifer Granholm (D.) signed a similar law in 2005 barring access to "ultra-violent explicit video games," as did California Gov. Arnold Schwarzenegger (R.). Lawsuits were quickly filed by the video game industry against the laws in both Michigan and California, claiming the measures violated the First Amendment speech rights of both game creators and game players. In November 2005, a federal judge ruled in favor of the video game industry and issued a preliminary injunction against the Michigan law in the case of *Entertainment Software Association* v. *Granholm,* reasoning in part that the law would have a chilling effect on speech and that the social science evidence used to support it was too weak to show any harms allegedly caused by playing the games. And in December 2005 a federal judge issued an injunction against the enforcement of the California law. Every politician in 2005, it seemed, was jumping on the bandwagon of parent-pandering, video game legislation. Ultimately, best-selling games like "Grand Theft Auto: San Andreas," which was found in July 2005 to have secret sex scenes that can be accessed by savvy gamers through a "hot coffee" modification, will continue to draw the wrath of politicians and spawn legislation.

One of the most widely publicized recent cases involving the application of the *Brandenburg* test involved Web postings by anti-abortion activists that branded doctors who performed abortions as "baby butchers." The Web postings were prepared by a group called the American Coalition of Life Activists. They included dossiers—so-called Nuremberg files (a reference to the war crimes trials held after the Second World War)—on abortion rights supporters, including doctors, clinic employees, politicians and judges. The group said the files could be used to conduct Nuremberg-like war crime trials in "perfectly legal courts once the tide of this nation's opinion turns against the wanton slaughter of God's children." On the site the names of abortion supporters who had been murdered were struck through and the names of those wounded were grayed out. A Planned Parenthood affiliate in Oregon sued, claiming that the material constituted threats against the persons named. A jury agreed and awarded more than $100 million in actual and punitive damages. A three-judge panel of the 9th U.S. Court of Appeals overturned this verdict in 2001. The court said the postings may have made it more likely that third parties would commit violent acts against the physicians, but they did not constitute a direct threat from the anti-abortion activists against the doctors.[59] The plaintiffs petitioned for a rehearing by the court and 14 months later, in a 6-5 vote, the court changed its ruling, declaring that there was no First Amendment protection for the Web postings. "While advocating violence is protected," wrote Judge Pamela Ann Rymer, "threatening a person with violence is not." She noted that three abortion providers had been murdered after similar "wanted posters" had been circulated regarding them. By the time the posters at issue were published, the poster format itself had acquired currency as a death threat for abortion providers, she added. The postings connote something they do not literally say, Judge Rymer wrote, yet both the actor and the recipient get the message.[60] The Supreme Court denied a petition to review the case in June 2003.[61]

59. *Planned Parenthood at Columbia/Willamette, Inc.* v. *American Coalition of Life Activists,* 244 F. 3d 1007 (2001).

60. *Planned Parenthood of the Columbia/Willamette, Inc.* v. *American Coalition of Life Activists,* 290 F. 3d 1058 (2002).

61. 539 U.S. 958 (2003).

Source: Bettman/CORBIS

The Gitlow *Ruling and the Incorporation Doctrine*

Before leaving the discussion of sedition, one additional case must be noted, not for its impact on the law of sedition but for its impact on the civil liberties enjoyed by all Americans. In 1925 Benjamin Gitlow, a small-time, left-wing agitator, asked the U.S. Supreme Court to reverse his conviction for violating the New York criminal anarchy statute. Gitlow was a member of a radical left-wing splinter group within the Socialist party. The group adopted a "Left Wing Manifesto" that condemned the dominant "moderate socialism" and advocated a far more militant posture that called for mass political strikes for the destruction of the existing government. Gitlow arranged for the printing and distribution of 16,000 copies of the "Manifesto." While the description of the publication sounds somewhat threatening, legal scholar Zechariah Chafee, one of Gitlow's contemporaries, said that any agitator who read the pamphlet to a mob would "not stir them to violence, except possibly against himself. This manifesto would disperse them faster than the Riot Act."[62] Gitlow was nevertheless convicted by the state.

In his appeal to the high court, he argued that the statute violated his freedom of expression guaranteed by the U.S. Constitution. In making this plea, Gitlow was asking the court to overturn a 92-year-old precedent.

Benjamin Gitlow, the leader of a dissident faction of the Socialist party, was prosecuted by New York state for publishing thousands of copies of a "Left Wing Manifesto." While the Supreme Court of the United States upheld his conviction, the high court ruling nevertheless declared that the First Amendment protected individuals from prosecutions by the states as well as the federal government.

62. Chafee, *Free Speech.*

In 1833 the Supreme Court of the United States ruled in *Barron* v. *Baltimore* that the Bill of Rights, the first 10 amendments to the U.S. Constitution, were applicable only in protecting citizens from actions of the federal government. Chief Justice John Marshall ruled that the people of the United States established the U.S. Constitution for their government, not for the government of the individual states. The limitations of power placed on government by the Constitution applied only to the government of the United States. Applying this rule to the First Amendment meant that neither Congress nor the federal government could abridge freedom of the press, but that the government of New York or the government of Detroit could interfere with freedom of expression without violating the guarantees of the U.S. Constitution. The citizens of the individual states or cities could erect their own constitutional guarantees in state constitutions or city charters. Indeed, such provisions existed in many places.

As applied to the case of Benjamin Gitlow, then, it seemed unlikely that the First Amendment (which prohibited interference by the federal government with freedom of speech and press) could be erected as a barrier to protect the radical from prosecution by the state of New York. Yet this is exactly what the young Socialist argued.

Gitlow's attorneys, especially Walter Heilprin Pollak, did not attack Chief Justice Marshall's ruling in *Barron* v. *Baltimore* directly; instead they went around it. Pollak based his argument on the 14th Amendment to the Constitution, which was adopted in 1868, 35 years after the decision in *Barron* v. *Baltimore*. The attorney argued that there was general agreement that the First Amendment protected a citizen's right to liberty of expression. The 14th Amendment says, in part, "No state shall . . . deprive any person of life, liberty, or property, without due process of law." Pollak asserted that included among the liberties guaranteed by the 14th Amendment is liberty of the press as guaranteed by the First Amendment. Therefore, a state cannot deprive a citizen of the freedom of the press that is guaranteed by the First Amendment without violating the 14th Amendment. By jailing Benjamin Gitlow for exercising his right of freedom of speech granted by the First Amendment, New York state denied him the liberty assured him by the 14th Amendment. Simply, then, the First Amendment, as applied through the 14th Amendment, prohibits states and cities and counties from denying an individual freedom of speech and press.

The First Amendment, as applied through the 14th Amendment, prohibits states and cities and counties from denying an individual freedom of speech and press.

The high court had heard this argument before, but apparently not as persuasively as Mr. Pollak presented it. In rather casual terms, Justice Edward Sanford made a startlingly new constitutional pronouncement: "For present purposes we may and do assume that freedom of speech and of the press—which are protected by the First Amendment from abridgment by Congress—are among the fundamental personal rights and 'liberties' protected by the due process clause of the Fourteenth Amendment from impairment by the states."[63]

The importance of the ruling in *Gitlow* v. *New York* is that the high court acknowledged that the Bill of Rights places limitations on the actions of states and local governments as well as on the federal government. The *Gitlow* case states that freedom of speech is protected by the 14th Amendment. This is known as the incorporation doctrine: The free speech and free press clauses of the First Amendment have been "incorporated" through the 14th Amendment due process clause as fundamental liberties to apply to state and local government entities and officials, not just to "Congress." In later cases the court placed freedom of religion, freedom

---

63. *Gitlow* v. *New York,* 268 U.S. 652 (1925).

from self-incrimination and freedom from illegal search and seizure under the same protection. Today, most of the rights outlined in the Bill of Rights are protected via the 14th Amendment from interference by states and cities as well as by the federal government. The importance of the *Gitlow* case cannot be underestimated. It truly marked the beginning of attainment of a full measure of civil liberties for the citizens of the nation. It was the key that unlocked an important door.

In the end Gitlow lost his case anyway. He had won a major constitutional victory but was unable to persuade the high court that his political agitation was harmless. Justice Sanford ruled that New York state had not violated Gitlow's First Amendment rights when it prosecuted him for publishing his "Left Wing Manifesto," which the state contended advocated the violent overthrow of the government.

SUMMARY

Within eight years of the passage of the First Amendment, the nation adopted its first (and most wide-ranging) sedition laws, the Alien and Sedition Acts of 1798. Many leading political editors and politicians were prosecuted under the laws, which made it a crime to criticize both the president and the national government. While the Supreme Court never did hear arguments regarding the constitutionality of the laws, several justices of the Supreme Court presided at sedition act trials and refused to sustain a constitutional objection to the laws. The public hated the measures. John Adams was voted out of office in 1800 and was replaced by his political opponent and target of the sedition laws, Thomas Jefferson. The laws left such a bad taste that the federal government did not pass another sedition law until World War I, 117 years later.

Sedition prosecutions in the period from 1915 to 1925 were the most vicious in the nation's history as war protesters, socialists, anarchists and other political dissidents became the target of government repression. It was during this era that the Supreme Court began to interpret the meaning of the First Amendment. In a series of rulings stemming from the World War I cases, the high court fashioned what is known as the clear and present danger test to measure state and federal laws and protests and other expressions against the First Amendment. The test was rigid and was never used to overturn a lower-court conviction, although in 1927 Justice Louis D. Brandeis did fashion a broad and liberal interpretation of the clear and present danger test in his dissent in the case of *Whitney* v. *California*. In 1925 the court ruled that the guarantees of freedom of speech apply to actions taken by all governments, that freedom of speech under the First Amendment protects individuals from censorship by all levels of government, not just from actions by the federal government. This pronouncement in *Gitlow* v. *New York* opened the door to a much broader protection of freedom of expression in the nation.

The nation's most recent sedition law was adopted in 1940. The Smith Act, as it is known, prohibits the advocacy of the violent overthrow of the government. Following a series of trials and two Supreme Court rulings in the 1950s, the law has become a relatively benign prohibition. The Supreme Court made its last important attempt to reconcile the First Amendment and the law of sedition in 1969 when it ruled in *Brandenburg* v. *Ohio* that advocacy of unlawful conduct is protected by the Constitution unless it is directed toward inciting or producing imminent lawless action and is likely to incite or produce such action.

TAXATION AND THE PRESS

The First Amendment guarantees that the press shall be free from unfair and discriminatory taxes that have an impact on circulation or distribution. In this area the classic case concerns a U.S. senator from a southern state and the daily press of that state.[64]

During the late 1920s and early 1930s, the political leader of Louisiana was Huey P. Long. Long was a demagogue by most accounts and in 1934 held his state in virtual dictatorship. He controlled the legislature and the statehouse and had a deep impact on the judicial branch as well. Long started his career by attacking big business—Standard Oil of California, to be exact. He became a folk hero among the rural people of Louisiana and was elected governor in 1928. In 1931 he was elected to the U.S. Senate, and many people believe that he would have attempted to win the presidency had he not been assassinated in 1935.[65]

In 1934 the Long political machine, which the majority of the big-city residents had never favored, became annoyed at the frequent attacks by the state's daily newspapers against the senator and his political machine. The legislature enacted a special 2 percent tax on the gross advertising income of newspapers with a circulation of more than 20,000. Of the 163 newspapers in the state, only 13 had more than 20,000 subscribers, and of the 13, 12 were outspoken in their opposition to Long. The newspapers went to court and argued that the tax violated the First Amendment as well as other constitutional guarantees. The press won at the circuit court level on other grounds, but the state appealed. Then in 1936 the Supreme Court ruled in favor of the newspapers squarely on First Amendment grounds.

Justice George Sutherland, who wrote the opinion in this unanimous Supreme Court decision, said, that such taxes on newspapers were the direct cause of much civil unrest in England and were one of the chief objections Americans had had to British policy—objections that ultimately forced independence.

The justice wrote:

> It is impossible to concede that by the words "freedom of the press" the framers of the amendment intended to adopt merely the narrow view then reflected by the law of England that such freedom consisted in immunity from previous censorship. . . . It is equally impossible to believe that it was not intended to bring within the reach of these words such modes of restraint as were embodied in . . . taxation.[66]

Sutherland asserted that the tax not only restricted the amount of revenue the paper earned but also restrained circulation. Newspapers with fewer than 20,000 readers would be reluctant to seek new subscribers for fear of increasing circulation to the point where they would have to pay the tax as well. The justice added that any action by the government that prevents free and general discussion of public matters is a kind of censorship. Sutherland said

---

64. *Grosjean* v. *American Press Co.,* 297 U.S. 233 (1936).
65. Gerald, *The Press and the Constitution.*
66. *Grosjean* v. *American Press Co.,* 297 U.S. 233 (1936).

that in this case even the form in which the tax was imposed—levied against a distinct group of newspapers—was suspicious. He then wrote:

> The tax here involved is bad not because it takes money from the pockets of the appellees [the newspapers]. If that were all, a wholly different question would be presented. It is bad because, in the light of its history and of its present setting, it is seen to be a deliberate and calculated device in the guise of a tax to limit the circulation of information to which the public is entitled in virtue of the constitutional guaranties. A free press stands as one of the great interpreters between the government and the people. To allow it to be fettered is to fetter ourselves.[67]

"A free press stands as one of the great interpreters between the government and the people. To allow it to be fettered is to fetter ourselves."

Therefore, in *Grosjean* v. *American Press Co.,* the Supreme Court struck down a discriminatory tax against the press.

Despite the fact that Justice Sutherland specifically noted in his opinion that the ruling in *Grosjean* did not mean that newspapers are immune from ordinary taxes, some newspaper publishers apparently did not read the opinion that way, but saw it instead as a means of escaping other kinds of taxes. After *Grosjean,* for example, unsuccessful attempts were made to have a sales tax in Arizona declared inapplicable to newspapers because it was a restriction on freedom of the press.[68] Since 1953, when the U.S. Supreme Court refused to hear an appeal from a California decision affirming the constitutionality of a general business tax on newspapers, the matter has been fairly well settled. The California case involved the Corona Daily Independent, which challenged a business tax imposed by the city of Corona. A license tax of $32 had been levied for many years against all businesses. In 1953 the newspaper refused to pay the levy on the grounds that the tax violated its First Amendment rights to freedom of expression. The *Grosjean* case prohibited such taxation, lawyers for the publication argued. The trial court ruled in favor of the newspaper, but the California Appellate Court disagreed and reversed the ruling. Justice Griffin wrote that there is ample authority to the effect that newspapers are not made exempt from ordinary forms of taxation. Justice Griffin said that the newspaper had not shown that the amount of the tax was harsh or arbitrary, that the tax was oppressive or confiscatory, or that the tax in any way curtailed or abridged the newspaper's right to disseminate news and comment:

> We conclude that a nondiscriminatory tax, levied upon the doing of business, for the sole purpose of maintaining the municipal government, without whose municipal services and protection the press could neither exist nor function, must be sustained as being within the purview and necessary implications of the Constitution and its amendments.[69]

The U.S. Supreme Court refused to review the ruling in *City of Corona* v. *Corona Daily Independent,* and most people believed the refusal signaled concurrence with the opinion of the California court.

---

67. Ibid.
68. *Arizona Publishing Co.* v. *O'Neil,* 22 F. Supp. 117; aff'd. 304 U.S. 543 (1938).
69. *City of Corona* v. *Corona Daily Independent,* 252 P. 2d 56 (1953).

But in 1983 the U.S. Supreme Court did review an unusual tax placed on a handful of Minnesota newspapers.[70] Since 1971 Minnesota had imposed a use tax on the cost of the paper and ink products consumed in the production of a publication. The law was amended in 1974 to exempt from the tax the first $100,000 worth of paper and ink used. After the exemption was adopted, only about 15 newspapers in the state were forced to pay the tax. And the Minneapolis Star and Tribune Company ended up paying about two-thirds of all the revenues collected under the tax. The Star and Tribune Company challenged the tax, and in March 1983 the high court ruled that the levy against the newspapers was invalid.

Justice Sandra Day O'Connor described the tax as a "special tax that applies only to certain publications protected by the First Amendment." She added: "A power to tax differentially, as opposed to a power to tax generally, gives a government a powerful weapon against the taxpayer selected." Such a tax could be used to censor the press, a clear violation of the First Amendment. The tax is also deficient because it ends up hitting only a few of the newspapers in the state. "Whatever the motive of the legislature in this case," Justice O'Connor wrote for the court's majority, "we think that recognizing a power in the State not only to single out the press but also to tailor the tax so it singles out a few members of the press presents such a potential for abuse that no interest suggested by Minnesota can justify the scheme."[71]

The Supreme Court voided another tax scheme in 1987 because, Justice Thurgood Marshall said, "the taxing scheme was based solely on the content of the publication."[72] Arkansas had a sales tax on tangible personal property. Several items were exempt from the tax, including newspapers and "religious, professional, trade and sports journals and/or publications printed and published in the state." The publisher of a general interest magazine sued to be exempt from the tax. The publisher argued that his magazine was published in the state and therefore should be exempt. The Arkansas Supreme Court ruled that the publisher had read the statute incorrectly. The law only exempted religious, professional, trade and sports publications that were printed in the state, not all magazines printed in the state. This tax was unconstitutional because it was discriminatory, because its applicability depended solely on the content of the publication, the high court said. This is a violation of the First Amendment. The high court heard arguments in the autumn of 1988 in a similar case, *Texas Monthly, Inc.* v. *Bullock,*[73] in which a Texas statute exempted religious periodicals from the general state sales tax. The publisher of the Texas Monthly argued that the law not only discriminated against certain publications based on their content, but also violated the separation of church and state clause in the First Amendment. In February 1989, by a 6-3 vote, the Supreme Court declared the Texas tax invalid. Justice William Brennan, writing the court's opinion, said the tax violated the establishment clause of the First Amendment. In 1999 a U.S. District Court in California struck down a tax on cable and satellite broadcasters. The state had levied a 5 percent tax on the gross receipts of pay-per-view telecasts of boxing, wrestling, kickboxing and similar contests. Telecasts of movies or concerts or other sporting events were not taxed. The

70. *Minneapolis Star* v. *Minnesota Commissioner of Revenue,* 460 U.S. 575 (1983).
71. *Minneapolis Star* v. *Minnesota Commissioner of Revenue,* 460 U.S. 575 (1983).
72. *Arkansas Writers' Project* v. *Ragland,* 481 U.S. 221 (1987).
73. 489 U.S. 1 (1989).

court ruled that the tax violated the First Amendment because it imposed a financial burden on speakers because of the content of their speech.[74]

The basic rule of First Amendment law regarding taxes on the press is this: Newspapers, broadcasting stations, and other mass media must pay the same taxes as any other business. Taxes that are levied only against the press and tend to inhibit circulation or impose other kinds of prior restraints (such as very high taxes that keep all but very wealthy people from publishing newspapers) are clearly suspect and probably unconstitutional. Also, decisions by the state to tax or not tax cannot be based solely on the content of the publication. In some circumstances, however, states can distinguish between different mass media when levying taxes. This was a ruling by the Supreme Court in 1991 in a case from Arkansas. The state levied a 4 percent sales tax on cable television receipts; magazines and newspapers were exempt from paying this tax.

Justice Sandra Day O'Connor, writing for a 7-2 majority, restated the high court's doctrine that the First Amendment prevents government from singling out the press as a whole for special tax burdens. "The press plays a unique role as a check on government abuse and a tax limited to the press raises concerns about censorship of critical information and opinion," she wrote.[75] Nor may states discriminate among categories of mass media when taxing, if that discrimination is based on content or for purposes of censorship, she added. But "differential taxation of speakers, even members of the press, does not implicate the First Amendment unless the tax is directed at, or presents the danger of suppressing particular ideas," O'Connor wrote. Almost 20 other states have taxes on cable television but do not tax the print media, according to The New York Times. In 1995 the Pennsylvania Supreme Court upheld the constitutionality of a state sales tax on magazines but not on newspapers. The court ruled that the tax was based not on content but on format and frequency of publication, a reasonable basis for distinguishing between the two media.[76]

Today some politicians occasionally attempt to punish or to retaliate against the press for unfavorable news coverage by trying to change rules related to taxation. For instance, Missouri law provides a sales tax exemption for newspapers on their purchase of newsprint, ink and other supplies. In 2004, however, Republicans in the Missouri House of Representatives passed a bill that eliminated that tax break, but only for the state's two largest newspapers—the St. Louis Post-Dispatch and the Kansas City Star—based on their operating revenue and daily circulation.[77] Democrats contended the bill was in "retaliation for a Post-Dispatch editorial calling the [Republican] legislators hypocrites for cutting Medicaid when they use a state-subsidized health plan."[78] The editorial was accompanied by the names and photographs of 66 Missouri House Republicans. After the House voted to eliminate the tax exemption, Post-Dispatch columnist Bill McClellan wryly wrote that "it seems that some of these House Republicans will not tolerate criticism. They'll shout you down. They'll use the tax code to get you. Whatever it takes."[79] Fortunately for the Post-Dispatch and the Star, a Missouri Senate committee later voted to remove the House-passed section.

74. *United States Satellite Broadcasting Co.* v. *Lynch,* 41 F. Supp. 2d 1113 (1999).
75. *Leathers* v. *Medlock,* 499 U.S. 439 (1991).
76. *Magazine Publishers of America* v. *Pennsylvania,* 654 A. 2d 519 (1995).
77. Young, "Newspapers Would Retain Tax Benefit."
78. Ibid.
79. McClellan, "Criticizing the State's GOP."

SUMMARY   Governments have traditionally used taxation as a means of controlling the press. Since the 1930s and the U.S. Supreme Court ruling in *Grosjean* v. *American Press Co.,* the First Amendment has posed a substantial barrier to such efforts by governments in the United States. Newspapers, broadcasting stations and other mass media must surely pay the same taxes imposed on other businesses. But taxes that are levied only against the press and tend to inhibit circulation or impose other kinds of restraints are unconstitutional. Also, taxes levied against mass media that are based solely on the content of the particular medium are generally regarded as unconstitutional.

PRIOR RESTRAINT

The great compiler of the British law, William Blackstone, defined freedom of the press in the 1760s as freedom from "previous restraint," or prior restraint. Regardless of the difference of opinion on whether the First Amendment is intended to protect political criticism or to protect the press from unfair taxation, most agree that the guarantees of freedom of speech and press were intended to bar the government from exercising prior restraint. Despite the weight of such authority, the media in the United States in the 2000s still face instances of prepublication censorship.

Prior restraint comes in many different forms. The most obvious are those instances in which the government actually insists on giving prior approval before something may be published or broadcast, or simply bans the publication or broadcast of specific kinds of material. There are examples of these varieties in this chapter and the next. Similar kinds of prior restraint occur when the courts forbid the publication of certain kinds material before a trial (see Chapters 11 and 12) or when a court issues an order forbidding the publication of material that might constitute an invasion of privacy (Chapters 7 and 8). But there are subtler forms of prior restraint as well. For example, many states have laws aimed at discouraging convicted criminals from profiting from their crimes by making money from books or films that detail their exploits (see pages 138–139). These are called Son of Sam laws because the first state statute enacted was aimed at stopping a notorious New York serial murderer, David Berkowitz, nicknamed the Son of Sam, from earning money by selling an account of his rampage. Such laws are permissible, but broadly worded statutes have been ruled to be a prior restraint because they may stop the convicted felon from expressing his or her views on a variety of subjects. And some courts have considered laws that limit how or how much a political candidate can spend during an election campaign to be prior censorship as well (see pages 147–150). The discussion in this chapter focuses on the most blatant kind of prior restraint, direct government restrictions on publication.

NEAR v. *MINNESOTA*

The Supreme Court did not directly consider the constitutionality of prior restraint until more than a decade after it had decided its first major sedition case. In 1931, in *Near* v. *Minnesota,*[80] the high court struck an important blow for freedom of expression.

80. 283 U.S. 697 (1931).

City and county officials in Minneapolis, Minn., brought a legal action against Jay M. Near and Howard Guilford, publishers of the Saturday Press, a small weekly newspaper. Near and Guilford were self-proclaimed reformers whose ostensible purpose was to clean up city and county government in Minneapolis. In their attacks on corruption in city government, they used language that was far from temperate and defamed some of the town's leading government officials. Near and Guilford charged that Jewish gangsters were in control of gambling, bootlegging and racketeering in the city and that city government and its law enforcement agencies did not perform their duties energetically. They repeated these charges over and over in a highly inflammatory manner.[81]

Minnesota had a statute that empowered a court to declare any obscene, lewd, lascivious, malicious, scandalous or defamatory publication a public nuisance. When such a publication was deemed a public nuisance, the court issued an injunction against future publication or distribution. Violation of the injunction resulted in punishment for contempt of court.

In 1927 county attorney Floyd Olson initiated an action against the Saturday Press. A district court declared the newspaper a public nuisance and "perpetually enjoined" publication of the Saturday Press. The only way either Near or Guilford would be able to publish the newspaper again was to convince the court that their newspaper would remain free of objectionable material. In 1928 the Minnesota Supreme Court upheld the constitutionality of the law, declaring that under its broad police power the state can regulate public nuisances, including defamatory and scandalous newspapers.

The case then went to the U.S. Supreme Court, which reversed the ruling by the state Supreme Court. The nuisance statute was declared unconstitutional. Chief Justice Charles Evans Hughes wrote the opinion for the court in the 5-4 ruling, saying that the statute in question was not designed to redress wrongs to individuals attacked by the newspaper.[82] Instead, the statute was directed at suppressing the Saturday Press once and for all. The object of the law, Hughes wrote, was not punishment but censorship—not only of a single issue, but also of all future issues—which is not consistent with the traditional concept of freedom of the press. That is, the statute constituted prior restraint, and prior restraint is clearly a violation of the First Amendment.

One maxim in the law holds that when a judge writes an opinion for a court, he or she should stick to the problem at hand and not wander off and talk about matters that do not really concern the specific issue before the court. Such remarks are considered **dicta,** or words that do not really apply to the case. These words, these dicta, are never really considered an important part of the ruling in the case. Chief Justice Hughes' opinion in *Near* v. *Minnesota* contains a good deal of dicta.

In this case Hughes wrote that the prior restraint of the Saturday Press was unconstitutional, but in some circumstances, he added, prior restraint might be permissible. In what kinds of circumstances? The government can constitutionally stop publication of obscenity, material that incites people to acts of violence, and certain kinds of materials during wartime. (It is entirely probable that the chief justice was forced to make these qualifying statements in order to hold his slim five-person majority in the ruling.) Hughes admitted, on the other hand,

The object of the law, Hughes wrote, was not punishment but censorship—not only of a single issue, but also of all future issues—which is not consistent with the traditional concept of freedom of the press.

81. Friendly, *Minnesota Rag.*
82. *Near* v. *Minnesota,* 283 U.S. 697 (1931).

that defining freedom of the press as only the freedom from prior restraint is equally wrong, for in many cases punishment after publication (i.e., subsequent punishment) imposes effective censorship upon the freedom of expression.

Near v. *Minnesota* stands for the proposition that under American law prior censorship is permitted only in very unusual circumstances; it is the exception, not the rule. Courts have reinforced this interpretation many times since 1931. Despite this considerable litigation, there remains an incomplete understanding of the kinds of circumstances in which prior restraint might be acceptable under the First Amendment, as the following cases illustrate.

AUSTIN v. *KEEFE*

A case that to some extent reinforced the *Near* ruling involved the attempt of a real estate broker to stop a neighborhood community action group from distributing pamphlets about him. The Organization for a Better Austin was a community organization in the Austin neighborhood of Chicago. Its goal was to stabilize the population in the integrated community. Members were opposed to the tactics of certain real estate brokers who came into white neighborhoods, spread the word that blacks were moving in, bought up the white-owned homes cheaply in the ensuing panic, and then resold them at a good profit to blacks or other whites. The organization received pledges from most real estate firms in the area to stop these blockbusting tactics. But Jerome Keefe refused to make such an agreement. The community group then printed leaflets and flyers describing his activities and handed them out in Westchester, the community in which Keefe lived. Group members proclaimed that Keefe was a "panic peddler" and said they would stop distributing the leaflets in Westchester as soon as Keefe agreed to stop his blockbusting real estate tactics. Keefe went to court and obtained an injunction that prohibited further distribution by the activists of pamphlets, leaflets and literature of any kind in Westchester on the grounds that the material constituted an invasion of Keefe's privacy and caused him irreparable harm. The Organization for a Better Austin appealed the ruling to the U.S. Supreme Court. In May 1971, the high court dissolved the injunction. Chief Justice Warren Burger wrote, "The injunction, so far as it imposes prior restraint on speech and publication, constitutes an impermissible restraint on First Amendment rights." The injunction, as in the *Near* case, did not seek to redress individual wrongs, but instead sought to suppress on the basis of one or two handbills the distribution of any kind of literature in a city of 18,000 inhabitants. Keefe argued that the purpose of the handbills was not to inform the community but to force him to sign an agreement. The chief justice said this argument was not sufficient cause to remove the leaflets and flyers from the protection of the First Amendment. Justice Burger added:

> Petitioners [the community group] were engaged openly and vigorously in making the public aware of respondent's [Keefe's] real estate practices. Those practices were offensive to them, as the views and practices of the petitioners are no doubt offensive to others. But so long as the means are peaceful, the communication need not meet standards of acceptability.[83]

The *Keefe* case did a good job of reinforcing the high court's decision in *Near* v. *Minnesota*.

---

83. *Organization for a Better Austin* v. *Keefe,* 402 U.S. 415 (1971).

PENTAGON PAPERS CASE

While it is more famous, another 1971 decision is not as strong a statement in behalf of freedom of expression as either *Near* or *Keefe.* This is the famous Pentagon Papers decision.[84] The case began in the summer of 1971, when The New York Times, followed by the Washington Post and a handful of other newspapers, began publishing a series of articles based on pilfered copies of a top secret 47-volume government study officially entitled "History of the United States Decision-Making Process on Vietnam Policy." The day after the initial article on the so-called Pentagon Papers appeared, Attorney General John Mitchell asked The New York Times to stop publication of the material. When The Times' publisher refused, the government went to court to get an injunction to force the newspaper to stop the series. A temporary restraining order was granted as the case wound its way to the Supreme Court. The government also sought to impose a similar injunction on the Washington Post after it began to publish reports based on the same material.

At first the government argued that the publication of this material violated federal espionage statutes. When that assertion did not satisfy the lower federal courts, the government argued that the president had inherent power under his constitutional mandate to conduct foreign affairs to protect the national security, which includes the right to classify documents secret and top secret. Publication of this material by the newspapers was unauthorized disclosure of such material and should be stopped. This argument did not satisfy the courts either, and by the time the case came before the Supreme Court, the government argument was that publication of these papers might result in irreparable harm to the nation and its ability to conduct foreign affairs. The Times and the Post consistently made two arguments. First, they said that the classification system is a sham, that people in the government declassify documents almost at will when they want to sway public opinion or influence a reporter's story. Second, the press also argued that an injunction against the continued publication of this material violated the First Amendment. Interestingly, the newspapers did not argue that under all circumstances prior restraint is in conflict with the First Amendment. Defense attorney Professor Alexander Bickel argued that under some circumstances prior restraint is acceptable—for example, when the publication of a document has a direct link with a grave event that is immediate and visible. Apparently, both newspapers decided that a victory in that immediate case was far more important than to establish a definitive and long-lasting constitutional principle. They therefore concentrated on winning the case, acknowledging that in future cases prior restraint might be permissible.[85]

On June 30 the high court ruled 6-3 in favor of The New York Times and the Washington Post and refused to block the publication of the Pentagon Papers. But the ruling was hardly the kind that strengthened the First Amendment. In a very short per curiam opinion, the majority said that in a case involving the prior restraint of a publication, the government bears a heavy burden to justify such a restraint. In this case the government failed to show the court why such a restraint should be imposed on the two newspapers.[86] In other words, the government failed to justify its request for the permanent restraining order.

84. *New York Times* v. *U.S.; U.S.* v. *Washington Post,* 403 U.S. 713 (1971).
85. Pember, "The Pentagon Papers," 403.
86. *New York Times* v. *U.S.; U.S.* v. *Washington Post,* 403 U.S. 713 (1971).

Vietnam Archive: Pentagon Study Traces 3 Decades of Growing U. S. Involvement

By NEIL SHEEHAN

A massive study of how the United States went to war in Indochina, conducted by the Pentagon three years ago, demonstrates that four administrations progressively developed a sense of commitment to a non-Communist Vietnam, a readiness to fight the North to protect the South, and an ultimate frustration with this effort—to a much greater extent than their public statements acknowledged at the time.

The 3,000-page analysis, to which 4,000 pages of official documents are appended, was commissioned by Secretary of Defense Robert S. McNamara and covers the American involvement in Southeast Asia from World War II to mid-1968—the start of the peace talks in Paris after President Lyndon B. Johnson had set a limit on further military commitments and revealed his intention to retire. Most of the study and many of the appended documents have been obtained by The New York Times and will be described and presented in a series of articles beginning today.

Source: © The New York Times

> Three pages of documentary material from the Pentagon study begin on Page 35.

Though far from a complete history, even at 2.5 million words, the study forms a great archive of government decision-making on Indochina over three decades. The study led its 30 to 40 authors and researchers to many broad conclusions and specific findings, including the following:

¶That the Truman Administration's decision to give military aid to France in her colonial war against the Communist-led Vietminh "directly involved" the United States in Vietnam and "set" the course of American policy.

¶That the Eisenhower Administration's decision to rescue a fledgling South Vietnam from a Communist takeover and attempt to undermine the new Communist regime of North Vietnam gave the Administration a "direct role in the ultimate breakdown of the Geneva settlement" for Indochina in 1954.

¶That the Kennedy Administration, though ultimately spared from major escalation decisions by the death of its leader, transformed a policy of "limited-risk gamble," which it inherited, into a "broad commitment" that left President Johnson with a choice between more war and withdrawal.

¶That the Johnson Administration, though the President was reluctant and hesitant to take the final decisions, intensified the covert warfare against North Vietnam and began planning in the spring of 1964 to wage overt war, a full year before it publicly revealed the depth of its involvement and its fear of defeat.

¶That this campaign of growing clandestine military pressure through 1964 and the expanding program of bombing North Vietnam in 1965 were begun despite the judgment of the Government's intelligence community that the measures would not cause Hanoi to cease its support of the Vietcong insurgency in the South, and that the bombing was

Continued on Page 38, Col. 1

Front page from The New York Times, June 12, 1971. The so-called Pentagon Papers.

The decision in the case rested on the preferred position First Amendment theory or doctrine (see pages 46–47). The ban on publication was *presumed* to be an unconstitutional infringement on the First Amendment. The government had to prove that the ban was needed to protect the nation in some manner. If such evidence could be adduced, the court would strike the balance in favor of the government and uphold the ban on the publication of the articles. But in this case the government simply failed to show why its request for an injunction was vital to the national interest. Consequently, the high court denied the government's request for a ban on the publication of the Pentagon Papers on the grounds that such a prohibition was a violation of the First Amendment. Note: The court did not say that in all similar cases an injunction would violate the First Amendment. It did not even say that in this case an injunction was a violation of the First Amendment. It merely said that the government had not shown why the injunction was needed, why it was not a violation of the freedom of the press. Such a decision is not what one would call a ringing defense of the right of free expression.

What many people initially called the case of the century ended in a First Amendment fizzle. The press won the day; the Pentagon Papers were published. But thoughtful observers expressed concern over the ruling. A majority of the court had not ruled that such prior restraint was unconstitutional—only that the government had failed to meet the heavy burden of showing such restraint was necessary in this case.

PROGRESSIVE MAGAZINE CASE

What many people initially called the case of the century ended in a First Amendment fizzle.

The fragile nature of the court's holding became clear in 1979 when the government went to court to block the publication of material it claimed could endanger the national security.[87] Free-lance writer Howard Morland had prepared an article entitled "The H-Bomb Secret: How We Got It, Why We're Telling It." The piece was scheduled to be published in the April edition of the Progressive magazine, a 70-year-old political digest founded by Robert M. LaFollette as a voice of the progressive movement.

Morland had gathered the material for the article from unclassified sources. After completing an early draft of the piece, he sought technical criticism from various scholars. Somehow a copy found its way to officials in the federal government. With the cat out of the bag, Progressive editor Erwin Knoll sent a final draft to the government for prepublication comments on technical accuracy. The government said the piece was too accurate and moved into federal court to stop the magazine from publishing the story.

The defendants in the case argued that all the information in the article was from public sources, that any citizen could have gotten the same material by going to the Department of Energy, federal libraries and the like. Other nations already had this information or could easily get it. Experts testifying in behalf of the magazine argued that the article was a harmless exposition of some exotic nuclear technology.

The government disagreed. It said that while some of the material was from public sources, much of the data was not publicly available. Prosecutors and the government's battery of technical experts argued that the article contained a core of information that had never before been published. The United States also argued that it was immaterial where Morland had gotten his information and whether it had come from classified or public documents. Prosecutors argued that the nation's national security interest permitted the classification and censorship of even information originating in public if, when such information is drawn together, synthesized and collated, it acquires the character "of presenting immediate, direct and irreparable harm to the interests of the United States." The United States was arguing, then, that some material is automatically classified as soon as it is created if it has the potential to cause harm to the nation. The information in Morland's article met this description, prosecutors argued.

It fell to U.S. District Judge Robert Warren to evaluate the conflicting claims and reach a decision on the government's request to enjoin the publication of the piece. In a thoughtful opinion in which Warren attempted to sort out the issues in the case, the judge said he agreed with the government that there were concepts in the article not found in the public realm—concepts vital to the operation of a thermonuclear bomb. Was the piece a do-it-yourself guide for a hydrogen bomb? No, Warren said, it was not. "A number of affidavits make quite clear that a sine qua non to thermonuclear capability is a large, sophisticated industrial capability coupled with a coterie of imaginative, resourceful scientists and technicians."[88] But the article could provide some nations with a ticket to bypass blind alleys and help a medium-sized nation to move faster in developing a hydrogen bomb.

87. *U.S.* v. *Progressive,* 467 F. Supp. 990 (1979).
88. Ibid.

To the Progressive's argument that the publication of the article would provide people with the information needed to make an informed decision on nuclear issues, Warren wrote, "This Court can find no plausible reason why the public needs to know the technical details about hydrogen bomb construction to carry on an informed debate on this issue."

Looking to the legal issues in the case, Warren said he saw three differences between this case and the Pentagon Papers ruling of 1971.

- The Pentagon Papers were a historical study; the Morland article focuses on contemporary matters.
- The government failed to advance cogent national security interests in the Pentagon Papers case; the national security interest was considerably more apparent in the Progressive case.
- The government lacked substantial legal authority to stop the publication of the Pentagon Papers; in other words, there were no statutes or orders that specifically forbid such publication. There are several laws that specifically limit the disclosure of restricted data related to the design, manufacture or utilization of atomic weapons.

Warren concluded that the government had met the heavy burden of showing justification for prior restraint. The judge added that he was not convinced that suppression of the objected-to technical portions of the article would impede the Progressive in its crusade to stimulate public debate on the issue of nuclear armament. "What is involved here," Warren concluded, "is information dealing with the most destructive weapon in the history of mankind, information of sufficient destructive potential to nullify the right to free speech and to endanger the right to life itself."[89]

When the injunction was issued, the editors of the Progressive and their supporters inside and outside the press vowed to appeal the ruling. In September 1979, as the *Progressive* case began its slow ascent up the appellate ladder, a small newspaper in Madison, Wis., published a story containing much of the same information as was in the Morland article. When this occurred, the Department of Justice unhappily withdrew its suit against the Progressive. But the victory in the *Progressive* case was bittersweet at best. The publication of the article had been enjoined. A considerable body of legal opinion had supported the notion that the injunction would have been sustained by the Supreme Court, rightly or wrongly. It must be remembered that as a legal precedent the decision in the *Progressive* case has limited value. It was, after all, only a U.S. District Court ruling and doesn't carry the weight of the *Near* decision, for example. From a political standpoint, however, the case had important implications. Prior restraint, which had seemed quite distant in the years succeeding *Near* v. *Minnesota* and in the afterglow of the press victory in the Pentagon Papers case, took on realistic and frightening new proportions.

KOBE BRYANT CASE

The unfortunate media circus that was the criminal sexual assault case against basketball superstar Kobe Bryant in 2004 also involved a very different form of a prior restraint on the media. The prior restraint controversy began in June 2004 when a court reporter accidentally and

---

89. Ibid.

Source: © AP/Wide World Photos

mistakenly sent sealed transcripts of private, *in camera* (meaning "in private") proceedings by electronic transmission to seven media entities via an electronic mailing list. The transcripts, which went to media outlets such as the Associated Press and CBS News, related to and contained information about the alleged victim's sexual conduct before and after her encounter with Kobe Bryant in a hotel in Colorado.

Such evidence of prior and subsequent sexual conduct is presumed to be irrelevant and thus typically is inadmissible in court in sexual assault cases under what are known as rape shield laws. The primary policy behind rape shield laws such as the one in Colorado is to protect the privacy interests of the alleged victim, who technically is called a "complaining witness" in sexual assault cases. In addition, rape is a severely underreported crime, and some

Los Angeles Laker Kobe Bryant, shown here leaving a Colorado court house, became inadvertently involved in a prior restaint case when private documents about the sexual history of the woman who accused him of rape were mistakenly sent to reporters via e-mail.

81

women might be deterred from reporting sexual assaults upon them if they thought that their entire sexual history would be exposed in court and, in turn, in the mass media. Rape shield laws thus keep evidence of sexual conduct that is irrelevant and not material for the case at hand from being publicly reported.

An *in camera* proceeding, however, allows a judge to consider, in his or her private chambers and out of public view, whether there is any possibility that the prior or subsequent sexual conduct of the alleged victim is, in fact, relevant to the case at hand and thus should be admitted into evidence despite the presence of the shield law. Such a hearing took place in the Kobe Bryant case, and it was the record of that private hearing that was accidentally sent to the news media.

The seven media outlets that received the private and confidential transcripts wanted, of course, to publish their contents. There already had been much gossip and speculation about the alleged victim's sexual conduct before and after her encounter with Bryant, and the official records would either prove or disprove the rumors. Furthermore, the media had lawfully obtained the documents; the news outlets had neither stolen the documents nor taken them without permission. In brief, the seven news organizations that received the sealed transcripts had lawfully obtained truthful information about a matter of public significance, namely the rape case against one of the most high-profile basketball players in the United States. Under the U.S. Supreme Court's 1989 decision in *Florida Star* v. *B.J.F.*[90] (see page 321), if the media lawfully obtain truthful information about a matter of public significance, then they may publish it unless there is a government interest of the highest order that trumps the right to publish.

The trial court judge, however, wanted to protect the privacy of the alleged victim, and he immediately issued an order before the media published the contents of the document that read:

> It has come to the Court's attention that the *in camera* portions of the hearings in this matter . . . were erroneously distributed. These transcripts are not for public dissemination. Anyone who has received these transcripts is ordered to delete and destroy any copies and not reveal any contents thereof, or be subject to contempt of Court.

Such an order, however, constitutes a prior restraint on the media because it stops them from publishing information that they already possess. The order thus was presumptively an unconstitutional abridgment of the First Amendment right of a free press, and the news organizations that received the private transcripts of the *in camera* proceedings went to court to have the judge's order reversed. On July 19, 2004, the Supreme Court of Colorado, in a 4–3 split decision, upheld that part of the trial court's order preventing the media from revealing the contents of the documents.[91] The four-judge majority initially acknowledged that it was dealing with a prior restraint on speech, which it defined as a court order "forbidding certain communications when issued in advance of the time that such communications are to occur." The majority also recognized that such orders are presumptively unconstitutional, and it

---

90. 491 U.S. 524 (1989).
91. *Colorado* v. *Bryant,* 94 P. 3d 624 (2004).

identified a three-part test that such an order must pass or clear in order to be constitutional. In particular, the majority of the Supreme Court of Colorado wrote that a prior restraint is constitutional only if it

- serves a government interest of the "highest order" ;
- is the narrowest possible order available to protect that interest; and
- is "necessary to protect against an evil that is great and certain" to result from the reportage and that cannot be mitigated by less intrusive measures.

In applying this three-part test to the facts of the *Bryant* case, the majority began by emphasizing that it was forced to balance the "conflict between truthful reporting and state-protected privacy interests." The majority found that the privacy interests of sexual assault victims that are protected by rape shield laws constitute interests of the highest order. It wrote that if the trial court judge were "to allow publication of the mistakenly transmitted transcripts, it would abrogate all of its duties under the rape shield statute." The majority stated:

> The state's interests of the highest order in this case not only involve the victim's privacy interest, but also the reporting and prosecution of this and other sexual assault cases. Revealing the *in camera* rape shield evidence will not only destroy the utility of this very important legal mechanism in this case, but will demonstrate to other sexual assault victims that they cannot rely on the rape shield statute to prevent public airing of sexual conduct testimony the law deems inadmissible. This would directly undercut the reporting and prosecution of sexual assault cases, in contravention of the [Colorado] General Assembly's legislative purposes.

Turning to the second part of the test, the majority of the Supreme Court of Colorado found that the portion of the trial judge's order preventing the news media from revealing the contents of the transcripts was the narrowest possible method for protecting the privacy interests at stake. To its credit, however, the majority struck down that part of the trial judge's order that required the news media outlets "to delete and destroy any copies" of the transcripts. In other words, the news media organizations got to keep the transcripts, but they just couldn't publish or reveal their contents—a frustrating position for the news media. Finally, the court found that great and certain harm was sure to occur to the victim if the documents' contents were published, writing that "the harms in making these *in camera* judicial proceedings public would be great, certain, and devastating to the victim and to the state. These harms justify the remedy we fashion in this case."

The Supreme Court of Colorado thus upheld a prior restraint on the news media forbidding them from publishing information that they lawfully received and that concerned a matter of intense public interest. There was, however, a vigorous three-judge dissent that would have declared the prior restraint unconstitutional. In particular, the dissent wrote that

> two striking facts about this case make it obvious that the prior restraint issued by the district court is an unconstitutional violation of the freedom of the press guaranteed by the First Amendment. First, most of the private details of the alleged victim's sexual conduct around the time of the alleged rape, which is also the subject matter of the confidential hearings in this case, are already available through public court documents and other

sources and have been widely reported by the media. Second, the media did nothing wrong in obtaining the transcripts. Under well-established prior restraint doctrine, these two factors alone require this Court to direct the district court to vacate its order immediately.

Despite the dissent's passionate argument, it failed to carry the day in court and the majority allowed the prior restraint to remain in place. The media quickly asked the U.S. Supreme Court to step in and to prevent the enforcement of the prior restraint, but the nation's high court refused to do so.[92] Justice Breyer wrote that "the trial court's determination as to the relevancy of the rape shield material will significantly change the circumstances that have led to this application [for a stay of the prior restraint]. As a result of that determination, the trial court may decide to release the transcripts at issue here in their entirety, or to release some portions while redacting others. Their release . . . is imminent." In essence, the U.S. Supreme Court passed on the issue.

Ultimately, the trial court judge later did release most of the transcripts, with the exception of 68 lines relating to the alleged victim's name and sexual history. Yet the harm to the media was done; the Supreme Court of Colorado had upheld a prior restraint on the press despite the fact that the press had lawfully obtained truthful information of public interest. It is a terrible precedent from the perspective of anyone in the news media.

In the wake of the attacks on the World Trade Center and the Pentagon in 2001, and the subsequent wars in Afghanistan and Iraq, the question of prior restraint was again brought to the fore. Concerns about national security—the protection of the nation from further terrorist attacks—and war itself open the door to a reading of the First Amendment that will permit the kinds of prior restraints that would not be tolerated in more peaceful and secure periods. Legal historians would recall the words of the great liberal Justice Oliver Wendell Holmes written more than 85 years earlier: "When a nation is at war many things that might be said in time of peace are such a hindrance to its effort that their utterance will not be endured so long as men fight and that no court could regard them as protected by any constitutional right."[93] Or the fact that another liberal member of the high court, Chief Justice Charles Evans Hughes, declared in 1931 that information that threatened national security fell outside the general prohibition against prior restraint.[94] (The matter of military censorship is addressed in Chapter 3.) Shortly after the 9/11 terrorist attacks, many journalists were critical of a request by the U.S. government to television broadcasters that they resist telecasting the videotaped statements that Al Qaeda leader Osama bin Laden was providing to Arab broadcasting stations. The government noted that these were requests, not orders. But could the government restrain such broadcasts if the requests were ignored? That proposition was never tested; the statements were either heavily edited by the broadcasters or eliminated altogether. At this time, however, the very fragile nature of the ruling in the Pentagon Papers case once again became apparent.

92. *Associated Press* v. *District Court,* 125 S. Ct. 1 (2004).
93. *Schenck* v. *U.S.,* 249 U.S. 47 (1919).
94. *Near* v. *Minnesota,* 283 U.S. 697 (1931).

SUMMARY

While virtually all American legal scholars agree that the adoption of the First Amendment in 1791 was designed to abolish prior restraint in this nation, prior restraint still exists. A reason it still exists is the 1931 Supreme Court ruling in *Near* v. *Minnesota* in which Chief Justice Charles Evans Hughes ruled that while prior restraint is unacceptable in most instances, there are times when it must be tolerated if the republic is to survive. Protecting the security of the nation is one of those instances cited by Hughes and in the past quarter century in two important cases, the press has been stopped from publishing material the courts believed to be too sensitive. While the Supreme Court finally permitted The New York Times and the Washington Post to publish the so-called Pentagon Papers, the newspapers were blocked for two weeks from printing this material. And in the end the high court merely ruled that the government had failed to make its case, not that the newspapers had a First Amendment right under any circumstance to publish this history of the Vietnam War. Eight years later the Progressive magazine was enjoined from publishing an article about thermonuclear weapons. Only the publication of the same material by a small newspaper in Wisconsin thwarted the government's efforts to permanently stop publication of this article in the Progressive.

BIBLIOGRAPHY

Alexander, James. *A Brief Narrative on the Case and Trial of John Peter Zenger.* Edited by Stanley N. Katz. Cambridge: Harvard University Press, 1963.

Baker, C. Edwin. *Human Liberty and Freedom of Speech.* New York: Oxford University Press, 1989.

Barron, Jerome. "Access to the Press—A New First Amendment Right." *Harvard Law Review* 80 (1967): 1641.

Brooke, James. "Lawsuit Tests Legal Power of Words." *The New York Times,* 14 February 1996, A12.

Bunker, Matthew D. *Critiquing Free Speech.* Mahwah, N. J.: Erlbaum, 2001.

Carelli, Richard. "High Court Allows 'Killers' Lawsuit." *Seattle Post-Intelligencer,* 9 September 1998, A3.

Chafee, Zechariah. *Free Speech in the United States.* Cambridge: Harvard University Press, 1941.

Chemerinsky, Erwin. *Constitutional Law: Principles and Policies.* 2nd ed. New York: Aspen, 2002.

Farber, Daniel A. *The First Amendment.* 2nd ed. New York: Foundation Press, 2003.

Fick, Bob. "Jury Acquits Saudi Graduate Student." *Associated Press,* 11 June 2004, State & Local Wire.

Friendly, Fred. *Minnesota Rag.* New York: Random House, 1981.

Gerald, J. Edward. *The Press and the Constitution.* Minneapolis: University of Minnesota Press, 1948.

Helle, Steven. "Whither the Public's Right (Not) to Know? Milton, Malls and Multicultural Speech." *University of Illinois Law Review* 1991, no. 6 (1991): 1077.

Herman, Ken. "Suit Alleges Protesters Are Muzzled at Bush Events." *Atlanta Journal-Constitution,* 21 October 2004, 10A.

Levy, Leonard. *Emergence of a Free Press.* New York: Oxford University Press, 1985.

Marklein, Mary Beth. "It's Not Easy Being a Speaker." *USA Today,* 13 May 2004, 1D.

McClellan, Bill. "Criticizing the State's GOP is a Good Way to Get Shouted Down." *St. Louis Post-Dispatch,* 19 April 2004, B1.

Meiklejohn, Alexander. *Free Speech and Its Relation to Self-Government.* New York: Harper & Brothers, 1948.

O'Connor, Lesley. "Packed Crowd Gets First Look at Gallagher's Film." *Daily Collegian,* 25 October 2004, 3.

Parks, Louis B. "Chicks Face 'Landslide' of Anger after Remark." *Houston Chronicle,* 15 March 2003, A1.

Pember, Don R. "The Pentagon Papers: More Questions Than Answers." *Journalism Quarterly* 48 (1971): 403.

———. "The Smith Act as a Restraint on the Press." *Journalism Monographs* 10 (1969): 1.

Peterson, H. C., and Gilbert Fite. *Opponents of War, 1917–1918.* Seattle: University of Washington Press, 1957.

Rabban, David M. *Free Speech in Its Forgotten Years.* Cambridge, United Kingdom: Cambridge University Press, 1997.

Redish, Martin H., and Kirk J. Kaludis. "The Right of Expressive Access in First Amendment Theory." *Northwestern University Law Review* 93 (1999): 1083.

Richards, Robert D., and Clay Calvert. "Nadine Strossen and Freedom of Expression." *George Mason University Civil Rights Law Journal* 13 (2003): 185.

Roche, John P. *Shadow and Substance.* New York: Macmillan, 1964.

Rutland, Robert. *The Birth of the Bill of Rights.* Chapel Hill: University of North Carolina Press, 1955.

Schechter, Harold. "A Movie Made Me Do It." *The New York Times,* 3 December 1995, A17.

Schmitt, Richard B. "Acquittal in Internet Terrorism Case Is a Defeat for Patriot Act." *Los Angeles Times,* 11 June 2004, A20.

Siebert, Fredrick. *Freedom of the Press in England, 1476–1776.* Urbana: University of Illinois Press, 1952.

Smith, James M. *Freedom's Fetters.* Ithaca, N.Y.: Cornell University Press, 1956.

Smith, Jeffrey A. "Prior Restraint: Original Intentions and Modern Interpretations." *William and Mary Law Review* 28 (1987): 439.

Smolla, Rodney. *Free Speech in an Open Society.* New York: Knopf, 1992.

Vaigo, Joe. "Speaking Tonight; Moore Uproar Rouses Campus." *Press Enterprise,* 12 October 2004, A1.

Weiser, Benjamin. "Appellate Court Backs Convictions in '93 Terror Plot." *The New York Times,* 17 August 1999, A1.

Young, Cathy. "The Tyrrany of Hecklers." *Boston Globe,* 2 June 2003, A13.

Young, Virginia. "Newspapers Would Retain Tax Benefit." *St. Louis Post-Dispatch,* 29 April 2004, B1.

THE FIRST AMENDMENT
Contemporary Problems

While First Amendment battles over sedition and taxation have been fought and won, other important issues related to freedom of expression continue to be debated. Most prior restraints are unconstitutional. The use of prior restraint to protect the national security, however, continues to be regarded differently. Similarly, school authorities may censor school newspapers, magazines, and yearbooks without always running afoul of the First Amendment. In addition, prior restraint is an essential part of an entire class of government regulations called time, place and manner rules that frequently win judicial approval. Governments at all levels face the dilemma of what to do about so-called hate speech, given the constitutional guarantees of freedom of expression. These are some of the issues we explore in this second chapter on the First Amendment.

PRIOR RESTRAINT DURING WARTIME

Censorship of the press during wartime is not uncommon. There was censorship in every war in which the United States was involved, beginning with the Civil War. Censorship in both World War I and World War II was extensive. For example, the American people did not know the full extent of damage to the U.S. Pacific Fleet in the wake of the bombing of Pearl Harbor on December 7, 1941, until after the war was ended. During World War II reporters had few limits on where they could go or with whom they could talk, but all news reports were screened by military censors before they were allowed to be published or broadcast. The press accepted some kind of censorship as a given—something normal in time of war. Such a belief in the normalcy of wartime censorship was reasonable in light of the U.S. Supreme Court's statement in *Schenck v. United States* in 1919 that "when a nation is at war many things that might be said in time of peace are such a hindrance to its effort that their utterance will not be endured so long as men fight and that no Court could regard them as protected by any constitutional right."[1]

The war in Vietnam was different from earlier wars in a number of important ways. There was never the massive, unquestioning kind of public support for the war that had existed in World War II, for example. And this was reflected in the kinds of stories journalists filed from the war zone. Unlike previous wars, which began with an important event (e.g., the firing on Fort Sumter in 1861, the bombing of Pearl Harbor in 1941, or the North Korean attack on South Korea in 1950), the fighting in Vietnam seemed to sneak up on this nation. Small groups of U.S. advisors went to Southeast Asia to try to help the South Vietnamese pick up the pieces following the defeat of the French. A handful of reporters went along to cover this story. Slowly the American military presence increased. By 1968 when the United States had committed more than half a million personnel to the fighting, American reporters had gotten used to very loose controls. They could pretty much go where they wanted to go, talk

---

1. 249 U.S. 47, 52 (1919).

to whomever they met, and report on most military matters. Security guidelines existed, and according to the government officials who administered them, reporters generally abided by the guidelines. Still, reporters enjoyed a freedom to report that their colleagues in earlier wars had not experienced. Since U.S. officials doubted they could get the genie back in the bottle and institute stricter controls, they chose instead to use propaganda to counter what journalists reported. Government efforts at propaganda included attempts to undermine the journalists who reported the bad news from Vietnam by denying the truth of these reports and complaining to editors and publishers about their correspondents in the field.

The freedom journalists had to report the Vietnam War was not the result of a fundamental change in government policy. The administration did not suddenly reverse the course that had been followed in every other war the nation had fought and decide that the press needed more freedom to tell the public what was happening on the battlefield. The government simply never got sufficiently organized to initiate the kind of censorship that had been imposed in earlier conflicts. In pointing to reasons why the United States failed to win the Southeast Asia conflict, many military leaders cited press reports from Vietnam for fueling the anti-war sentiment, which in turn limited the government's ability to fully engage the enemy. This would not happen again, they vowed.

Beginning in 1983 the United States was involved in a series of military actions or wars. Censorship of the press was imposed with a heavy hand until the 2003 war with Iraq. Here is a brief and selective overview of what happened during those 20 years.

GRENADA

When the United States invaded the Caribbean island of Grenada in 1983 to stop a Cuban military buildup and protect U.S. citizens, reporters were not permitted in the war zone. Criticism of this policy led to the creation of the Department of Defense National Media Pool, a group of reporters who would be assigned to accompany the military when future secret invasions took place. The pool reporters would act as the eyes and ears of the remainder of the press corps, sharing what they learned with others in the mass media. The pool was used successfully during two small military operations in the late 1980s.

One of the legal highlights from the brief battle in Grenada was a lawsuit filed by Larry Flynt. The publisher of sexually explicit magazines such as Hustler and Barely Legal sued then-Secretary of Defense Casper Weinberger and the United States. Flynt challenged their decision to prohibit press coverage of the initial stages of the military intervention in Grenada when the only information available to the public about the events occurring on the island came from official U.S. government sources. A federal district court, however, ruled that Flynt's request for relief was moot, given the brevity of both the press ban and the military battle.[2] An appellate court upheld the mootness determination.[3]

It is important to note that none of the mainstream news media companies or networks dared to file a lawsuit against the federal government, possibly for fear of burning their important government sources. Sadly, only Flynt was willing to fund a fight for First Amendment access principles. Although people object to the content of most of his publications, Flynt

2. *Flynt* v. *Weinberger,* 588 F. Supp. 57 (1984).
3. *Flynt* v. *Weinberger,* 762 F. 2d 134 (1985).

Source: © AP/Wide World Photos

must be lauded for his efforts to secure press access both in Grenada and, as discussed later in this chapter, in Afghanistan and Iraq (see page 94).

PANAMA

In 1989, when the United States invaded Panama to capture its president, Manuel Noriega, who had been indicted in the United States on drug charges, the media pool that was supposed to accompany the troops was effectively shut out. By the time the reporters got onto the streets of Panama City, the fighting was over. "We missed the war," said NBC reporter and pool member Fred Francis.[4] News coverage of this invasion was limited largely to video and other material provided by the government.

4. Schmeisser, "Shooting Pool," 21.

PERSIAN GULF WAR

The United States went to war again in 1990 after Iraq invaded Kuwait. During the six-month military buildup and the short air war, control of the press by the government was almost complete. Once the ground fighting started, the huge numbers of reporters overwhelmed the efforts by the military to control them. Reports from the front improved substantially. At the peak of the military buildup as many as 800 journalists were in Saudi Arabia, the staging area for the war. They were kept on a short leash by their military handlers. Reporters who sought to leave the rear area and talk to ground troops or air force personnel had to travel in a pool of other reporters. The journalists were always accompanied by military public affairs officers, who stayed with the reporters even as they interviewed the troops. Reporters who ventured off by themselves, outside of the pools, could lose their press credentials if they were caught. Or they could get lost in the desert and even be captured by the enemy, the fate suffered by a CBS news team. Before any news reports' video or audio footage could be released it had to be reviewed by military public affairs officers.[5] Most journalists said the guidelines issued by the military, which outlined what could and could not be reported, were fair but were interpreted in a very conservative manner. The reviews also took time, especially if a journalist sought to challenge a decision made by a censor.

Before the actual ground fighting started, and to a lesser extent during the fighting, a majority of information about what was happening came not from the firsthand reports of journalists in the field but from military briefers and officials in the Pentagon. And this news was heavily colored to paint the best possible picture for the American people.[6] Most analyses undertaken after the war revealed two important themes. Americans got a fuzzy and incomplete picture of what actually happened during the war. And while the government surely bore the brunt of the blame for this censorship and deception, the members of the press were far too willing to go along with the stringent censorship rules, and complained far too little.[7]

Two lawsuits challenged the censorship during the Persian Gulf War, but neither succeeded. A handful of journalists and news organizations who had been routinely excluded from the press pools in deference to larger media organizations sued the government, claiming the censorship policies violated the First Amendment. But by the time the court heard the case, the fighting was over, the restrictions had ended, and the issue was, in the words of the law, moot. The issue still could have been decided under an exception to the rule of mootness that permits a court to rule on a case if the subject matter "is capable of repetition yet evading review," that is, if the issue is likely to arise over and over again and continue to become moot each time before it can be resolved. The federal district court chose not to do this, however, saying that the issues were too abstract to be decided in the absence of an actual case.[8]

In April 1993, a federal court ruled that the government did not violate the First Amendment when it barred journalists from Dover Air Force Base during the conflict. Since 1972 the air base had been open to the press and public to witness the arrival of the bodies of U.S. military personnel who died overseas in the defense of their country. But the first Bush administration

---

5. See, in general, Fialka, *Hotel Warriors.*
6. See, for example, Miller, "Operation Desert Sham," 17.
7. See Dennis et al. *The Media War,* and MacArthur, *Second Front.*
8. *Nation Magazine* v. *U.S. Department of Defense,* 762 F. Supp. 1558 (1991).

did not want Americans to see video or still pictures of dead American service personnel coming home in body bags. The federal court supported the government. Citing several earlier rulings by the Supreme Court of the United States, the judge dismissed the complaint and ruled that the First Amendment does not "mandate a right of access to government information or sources of information within government's control."[9] The District of Columbia U.S. Circuit Court of Appeals affirmed the dismissal of the claim by the lower court.[10] The court ruled that the closure of the site did not violate the First Amendment because military bases have traditionally been closed to the public and the press. The court also stated that the burden placed on news gathering was modest at worst because the policy did not impede public and press acquisition of basic facts. These rulings were not unexpected, because for a variety of reasons, judges are quite unwilling to overturn Pentagon policies, policies that might affect the national security. The issue over access to Dover Air Force Base and images of returning flag-draped coffins of U.S. military personnel would arise again in 2004 and 2005 when bodies came home from fighting in Iraq and Afghanistan (see pages 98–99).

THE BALKANS

The United States played the dominant role in the NATO military actions in Yugoslavia in the 1990s. Much of the campaign was carried out by air, and the world press—not just U.S. reporters—remained on the outside, trying to look in. The government gave out so little information in the early days of the campaign that the usually compliant American media publicly complained to the U.S. secretary of defense. As a result more information began to flow. But still, most doors remained shut.[11] British military historian Alistair Horne wrote in the Spectator in July 2003 that this was the most secret campaign in living memory. Historian Phillip Knightley quoted Sky news correspondent Jake Lynch as saying, "We were given lots of material, but no information."[12] Reporters, without military sources to answer their questions, began interviewing each other. To fill the vacuum of virtually no real information, NATO spokespersons provided largely news-free briefings. In his book, "The First Casualty," Knightley described the NATO public relations efforts in this manner:

> In the comparatively short history of media management in wartime there can have been no system so skillfully designed to win the propaganda war. Nothing was left to chance. The reporting of every correspondent writing about Kosovo was monitored and if necessary, instantly rebutted. NATO's line on every likely aspect of the war was developed, polished and rehearsed.[13]

When the bombing finally ended and troops entered Kosovo, 2,700 journalists accompanied them.

---

9. *JB Pictures, Inc.* v. *Defense Department,* 21 M.L.R. 1564 (1993).
10. *JB Pictures, Inc.* v. *Defense Department,* 86 F. 3d 236 (1996).
11. Sloyan, "The Fog of War."
12. Knightley, *The First Casualty,* 504.
13. Ibid., 513.

A highly sensitive issue during the war was the massive number of civilian casualties caused by the NATO bombing. While the United States did admit to such deaths, it didn't like the idea of its military actions becoming the target of criticism each day on the nightly news. U.S. officials were especially critical of Serbian television reports that graphically displayed the death and destruction in civilian areas, calling the reports phony. The U.S. media picked up these video reports from satellite transmissions made by the Serbian TV stations. The American military solved the problem by bombing the Serbian stations off the air. The action was justified, they said, because the stations were feeding propaganda and lies to the Serb viewers.[14]

AFGHANISTAN AND THE WAR ON TERRORISM

In September 2001, the violence that was prevalent throughout other parts of the world exploded in the United States. And from September 11 forward the nation and the world changed. Within weeks the American military was on the move again, this time into Afghanistan, a nation wracked by war since a Soviet invasion in 1979. U.S. officials said the Afghan Taliban government provided a safe haven and a staging area for the Al Qaeda terrorists responsible for the attacks in the United States.

During the early weeks of the war in Afghanistan, the fighting was similar to what took place in Yugoslavia two years before. It was an air war, with American planes bombing the central Asian nation from nearby bases and ships at sea. At this point, access for journalists was limited to areas where U.S. forces were carrying out the war: U.S. Navy ships at sea, distant air bases, and military posts outside Afghanistan. Small numbers of U.S. ground troops were inserted into Afghanistan, but no reporters were permitted to accompany these troops. The Pentagon cited its long-standing policy against coverage of what it called "special ops" missions, a policy it justified by saying it wanted to keep secret the tactics used by these elite troops. Briefings by the military were far less common than they had been during the Persian Gulf War or the bombing in Yugoslavia. Information about what was happening was in short supply. The U.S. government bought all access to high-level commercial satellite imagery to supplement its own satellite coverage of central Asia, but also to keep these images away from what it called "prying eyes," which undoubtedly included both the enemy and the press. As the Afghan Taliban government began to disintegrate in November 2001, many more Western reporters found their way into Afghanistan and stories on the ground fighting in that country became commonplace. Still, by most accounts, the reports on the fighting were far from complete as the military kept journalists away from areas regarded as dangerous or sensitive. And there were dangers. During 10 days in mid-November, for example, seven journalists were killed by the roving bands of bandits or tribal warlords that are endemic to the region. It turned out that even parts of neighboring Pakistan were not safe; Daniel Pearl from the Wall Street Journal was kidnapped and killed by members of a militant faction.

In an article published in early 2002 in the Columbia Journalism Review, the magazine's editor-at-large, Neil Hickey, said that journalists were being denied access to American troops in the field in Afghanistan to a greater degree than in any previous war involving U.S. forces.[15] Reporters also complained, Hickey said, about Pentagon press briefings, which were often devoid of meaningful information because they were conducted by upper-echelon defense

---

14. Sloyan, "The Fog of War."
15. Hickey, "Access Denied."

department officials and military officers who really didn't know specifics of what was happening in the war zone. Hustler publisher Larry Flynt went to federal court in early 2002 to try to bar the government from interfering with reporters' right of access to U.S. ground troops in Afghanistan. He argued that the media have a First Amendment right to gather and report on military operations abroad. A U.S. district court said it was sympathetic to Flynt's argument but refused to block the censorship by the government. In early 2004, a U.S. appellate court rejected Flynt's claim and ruled that the Pentagon has no constitutional obligation to provide the media with access to American troops while they are in combat.[16] In rejecting Flynt's claim, the unanimous three-judge panel from the District of Columbia Circuit Court of Appeals wrote that "there is no constitutionally based right for the media to embed with U.S. military forces in combat."[17] The court turned back Flynt's argument that precedent for such a right could be found in the U.S. Supreme Court's 1980 decision in *Richmond Newspapers, Inc.* v. *Virginia,* which recognized a constitutional right of public and press access to attend criminal trials (see Chapter 12). In October 2004, the U.S. Supreme Court denied Flynt's petition for a writ of certiorari, thus bringing the case to a disappointing close for American journalists.[18]

The government attempted to limit news coverage of military operations in other ways as well. Officials in the Department of Defense announced that government employees who leak classified information to the press might be prosecuted. Leaks from people in government to the press have been a standard practice for decades. Leaders in government often foster such leaks to see if the public likes an idea before officially proposing it. There is an elaborate classification system in place that restricts access to all manner of information held by the government. (See pages 376–377 for a complete discussion of this system.) So it is possible to keep such information secret. But there is no provision within this classification system that makes it a crime for someone to publish such information. The United States found that out when it attempted to stop the publication of the Pentagon Papers in 1971. (See pages 77–79 for a discussion of this case.) In 2000 Congress passed a law making it a crime to leak any kind of classified material, but President Bill Clinton vetoed this measure. In October 2001, Secretary of Defense Donald Rumsfeld said that government employees who give classified information to the press might be prosecuted under a federal law forbidding espionage, which makes it a crime to communicate information that might injure the United States. Rumsfeld said he was concerned that some Defense Department officials had leaked information to the press regarding the presence of U.S. special forces in Afghanistan. First Amendment lawyers debated whether this law might also be applicable to members of the press who report this information. Regardless, the prosecution of a federal employee for such a crime would undoubtedly involve reporters who would be required to testify in such a case. (See Chapter 10 for a discussion of how the law affects a reporter's relationship with a news source.)

THE WAR IN IRAQ

Approximately a year after the terrorist attacks in New York and Washington the U.S. government began to prepare the nation for an assault on Iraq. Administration officials, from the president on down, claimed there was evidence that linked the government of Saddam Hussein to

16. *Flynt* v. *Rumsfeld,* 355 F. 3d 697 (2004).
17. *Flynt* v. *Rumsfeld,* 355 F. 3d 697, 706 (2004).
18. 125 S. Ct. 313 (2004).

Source: © Mario Tama/Getty Images

the Al Qaeda terrorists, that the Iraqis probably had developed nuclear, biological and chemical weapons, arms that came to be called weapons of mass destruction, and that the Iraqi dictator was a destabilizing influence in the Middle East. Early in 2003 American and British forces (referred to as coalition forces) launched an attack against the Persian Gulf nation.

The Pentagon did an about-face when it came to managing the press coverage of the war. In the autumn of 2002 the Department of Defense announced that when the fighting began, reporters would be allowed to accompany military units into battle and report on what they saw, with only limited restrictions. The new policy was dubbed "embedding"; reporters would be embedded with the troops as they covered the war.[19] The government went so far as to arrange so-called weeklong boot camps for journalists, to prepare them for the rigors of accompanying the military units to which they were assigned.

At the height of the fighting there were about 700 foreign and U.S. reporters embedded with coalition forces. The journalists carried their own transmission equipment, often 140-pound video phones that were small enough to fit into two suitcases. They generally provided their own transportation as well, sometimes elaborate vehicles. The CBS Humvees, for example, carried five cameras, fuel, a portable generator, had polarized windows to reduce

In Iraq, reporters who were embedded were usually close to the coalition troops they covered. This journalist was attached to the Irish Guard's 7th Armored Brigade in fighting around Basra.

19. Bushnell and Cunningham, "Being There."

glare and were air-conditioned.[20] Some reporters chose not to be embedded and went off on their own. But being what the government called a "unilateral" had distinct drawbacks. Sixteen journalists died during the initial fighting in Iraq, though not all of them were unilaterals, many from either enemy or friendly fire. The number of journalistic casualties would later rise significantly; the Committee to Protect Journalists (http://www.cpj.org) reported that a total of 24 journalists from across the globe and 16 media workers—people working with journalists in supporting roles such as drivers, interpreters, fixers and guards—were killed in 2004 alone while working in Iraq.[21] By January 2006, the Committee to Protect Journalists claimed that at least 60 journalists and 22 media support staff had been killed in Iraq since March 2003.

The embedded reporters were free to report most of what they saw or heard. There were 19 categories of nonreleasable information. In general, these were the kinds of commonsense rules that didn't trouble most journalists. Reports about ongoing combat missions had to be cleared by the unit commanders. The time, date and place of military action, as well as the outcome of the action, could be reported only in general terms. There were limits on reporting on future or canceled missions. Some stories had to be held or "embargoed" until unit commanders said it was safe to report the actions. Stories about the specific number of troops, aircraft or ships in a particular area would not be reported, except in terms of very large numbers (e.g., there are 45,000 troops in northern Iraqi). Reports on battlefield casualties were permitted as long as the identities of the dead or injured were protected for 72 hours, or until their kin had been notified. Finally, reporters could not leave the units in which they were embedded.[22] The military had the right to terminate the embedded assignment at any time, for any reasons. At least two reporters had their assignment terminated. The most widely publicized was Geraldo Rivera, who was reporting the war for Fox News.[23] He was ousted after he, while on camera, drew a map in the sand, revealing the location of the 101st Airborne Division, the unit with which he was embedded. He also talked about an impending attack. Both lapses were violations of the rules, but Rivera was permitted to return to the 101st a few days later. A notable change in policy was that the reporters were not saddled with military public affairs officers, or handlers, everywhere they went.

The embedding process got mixed reviews in the immediate months after Saddam Hussein was toppled from power.[24] The censorship problems that were so common and troublesome from 1983 on were not evident in Iraq. Mark Sussman, a CBS reporter, said on PBS' "NewsHour with Jim Lehrer" in late April 2003 that there were no problems with censorship. But the record wasn't completely clean. When journalists working for the Washington Times revealed that two U.S. Marines had died when they were ordered to swim across a canal in full battle gear without a safety line, they were blackballed by the unit with which they were embedded, cut off from all information. They eventually joined another unit.[25] No one knows how many other negative stories were never reported for fear of such retaliation.

20. Harmon, "Improved Tools."
21. This information can be found at the Committee to Protect Journalists' Web site at http://www.cpj.org/Briefings/Iraq/Iraq_danger.html
22. See Bushnell and Cunningham, "Being There" and Blumenthal and Rutenberg, "Journalists Are Assigned."
23. Bauder, "NBC Fires Reporter."
24. See Smith, "Hard Lessons" for an excellent summary of this issue.
25. Donvan, "For the Unilaterals."

The Pentagon both applauded and criticized the new system. The positive, usually laudatory reports, transmitted from the battlefield to the American public, were music to the ears of Department of Defense officials. But when the fighting bogged down after two weeks of rapid advances, and reporters in the field told this story, the government complained that the American people were getting an incomplete and even incorrect picture of how the war was going. The TV reports of increasing Iraqi resistance, of slowed shipments of supplies and other problems, overwhelmed the assurances from the Pentagon that the advance was going very well. Department of Defense officials were particularly unhappy with press reports that quoted ground commanders complaining that the stiffened resistance had caught them off guard.[26] That much of the news was reported in real time—when it was happening—also troubled persons in the Pentagon. "American television often has images of downed United States aircraft before Central Command could confirm that any was missing, let alone whether it fell to Iraqi fire or mechanical malfunction," New York Times reporters Jim Rutenberg and Bill Carter said.[27]

Daily Pentagon and Central Command briefings were used to provide information, but also to put a spin on the news, as in the past. And for the most part the American press—as in the past—bought into the spin.[28] Pentagon officials called the Republican Guard a "formidable force"; so did the American press. It turned out to be less than formidable. Defense Department officials said Baghdad would be fiercely defended; much of the press reported this as fact, not as speculation. The defense around the city collapsed rather quickly. In the months after the Iraqi government was ousted, many in the American press said they probably should have asked many more questions before the war about whether or not the Iraqis really had weapons of mass destruction and what would happen in Iraq after Saddam Hussein was ousted.

Most reporters said they liked the new system, adding that they believed the public got a better picture of this war, compared with coverage of U.S. military involvements during the preceding 20 years. NBC correspondent Bob Arnet said, "The embedding process is the best single move the American military has ever made in its relations with the press."[29] But the praise was not universal. Reporter Chris Hedges wrote in The Nation, "The embedding process induces reporters to perpetuate the myth of war as an ennobling exercise."[30] And National Public Radio correspondent George Burnett called it a "flawed experiment that served the purposes of the military more than it served the cause of balanced journalism."[31] Even reporters who supported the system admitted that it provided viewers and readers with only a tiny slice of what was happening in the war. New York Post reporter Vincent Morris said, "This war is whatever piece of dirt you are sitting on."[32] He was attached to a helicopter unit, so the war is about helicopters, he said. Reporters were not permitted to leave their units to look outside, at what was happening elsewhere.

The embedded reporters depended on the men and women in the units they were attached to for food, water, companionship and indeed for their very survival at times. Gordon

26. Rutenberg and Carter, "Spectacular Success."
27. Ibid.
28. Smith, "Hard Lessons."
29. Arnet, "Embedded/Unembedded I."
30. Smith, "Hard Lessons."
31. Burnett, "Embedded/Unembedded II."
32. Carr, "Reporters' New Battlefield Access."

Dillow, a reporter for the Orange County Register, wrote in the Columbia Journalism Review that he found himself falling in love with his subjects. "I fell in love with 'my' Marines." In some stories, he said, "I wasn't reporting the truth; the point was I was reporting the Marine grunt truth—which had also become my truth."[33] There was no misrepresenting of facts, just an empathetic tone, reports that often lacked a skeptical edge.

In December 2004 a RAND Corp. study called "Reporters on the Battlefield: The Embedded Press System in Historical Context" was released.[34] It found that about 600 journalists engaged in the U.S. military's embedding program, out of the approximately 2,200 reporters and camera crews from the United States and other nations in Iraq. The report concluded that worries about embedded reporters becoming biased in favor of their assigned troops were unfounded, as surveys conducted by journalism groups found that embedded reporters' coverage of the war was "of reasonably high quality." The report noted, however, that tensions could arise between journalists and the military in the future if U.S. military forces suffer serious setbacks or heavy casualties. It also concluded that while embedding may foster so-called straw-hole journalism—each embedded reporter has only a very narrow perspective of the war, as if viewed through a straw—news organizations were able to put together the reporters' work to show the bigger picture.

In late 2003 and early 2004, as the coalition forces became frustrated as they attempted to reestablish civilian control in Iraq amid daily attacks from former Saddam Hussein supporters and other terrorists, U.S. soldiers became much more aggressive in their treatment of journalists who were covering the guerrilla war, especially Arab journalists working for non-U.S. or British media organizations. The Associated Press reported that media people were detained, news equipment was confiscated, and some journalists suffered both verbal and physical abuse while trying to report the aftermath of the attacks.

In April 2004, the Department of Defense called for a tightening of its policy preventing the release of photographs of coffins or funerals of American soldiers killed in Iraq and returning back to the United States (see pages 91–92). That occurred after the U.S. Air Force granted—much to the government's chagrin—the Freedom of Information Act[35] (see Chapter 9) request by a man named Russ Kick for "all photographs taken after February 2003 of caskets containing the remains of U.S. military personnel at Dover Air Force Base in Delaware."[36] Kick, who had made more than 200 previous FOIA requests, received from the Air Force "a CD-ROM of 361 photos not just of flag-draped coffins, but also of uniformed pallbearers or fellow soldiers in camouflage bowing their heads, caring for the remains of fallen comrades."[37] Kick displayed the photographs, 73 of which turned out to be of the deceased Columbia space shuttle astronauts, for the world to see on his Web site, The Memory Hole.[38] When the Washington Post, The New York Times, and the New York Daily News placed some of the photographs on their front pages, it sparked a public debate on privacy, access and freedom of information. The fact is, however, that "since 1991, the Pentagon has banned the media from taking pictures of

---

33. Dillow, "Grunts and Pogues."
34. The report can be found on the Web site of the RAND Corp. at http://www.rand.org.
35. 5 U.S.C. § 552 (2002).
36. Smith, "Coffins and Now Chaos."
37. Ibid.
38. The images can been seen at http://www.thememoryhole.org/war/coffin_photos/dover.

caskets being returned to the United States."[39] The administration of President George W. Bush had "issued a stern reminder of that policy in March 2003, shortly before the war in Iraq began."[40] In June 2004, the U.S. Senate rejected legislation proposed by Senator Frank Lautenberg (D.–N.J.) that would have instructed the Department of Defense to develop new rules permitting photographers on military bases to cover the arrival and departure of caskets containing the remains of soldiers killed overseas.

Then, in October 2004, a University of Delaware journalism professor and former CNN correspondent named Ralph J. Begleiter filed a lawsuit in federal court in Washington, D.C., seeking to force the Pentagon under the Freedom of Information Act to make available photographs and videos of the coffins of military members killed overseas and brought back to the United States.[41] Begleiter told the press at that time, "I think the public has a right—and maybe even a responsibility—to be aware of them."[42] His legal battle ultimately proved surprisingly successful when in April 2005 the Pentagon released hundreds of photographs taken by military photographers from 2001 (when the United States attacked Afghanistan) through 2004.[43] In some instances, the faces of U.S. honor-guard soldiers saluting caskets in tribute ceremonies were redacted or blacked out to protect their privacy. The release of the photographs in response to Begleiter's FOIA request, however, did not affect and failed to change the 1991 government ban on on-scene press coverage of returning casualties from the wars.

And if the efforts to thwart access to photographs of closed coffins weren't bad enough, Pentagon officials fought hard in 2004 to continue to suppress and withhold from the American public additional, undisclosed photographs and videotapes (beyond those previously released) of the torture in an Iraqi prison of detainees at the hands of U.S. soldiers. The Pentagon called for this censorship, "pointing to the ongoing criminal investigations, and the possibility of lawsuits based on privacy issues."[44] For the Pentagon, the public's need to know about the actions of its taxpayer-supported fighting forces takes a backseat to the government covering itself from legal liability based on privacy concerns. But in May 2005 in response to a Freedom of Information Act request filed by the American Civil Liberties Union, a federal district court judge ordered the Defense Department to release "dozens of photographs taken by an American soldier of Iraqi detainees in the Abu Ghraib prison in Iraq."[45]

Another issue that arose in 2004 was not government censorship of wartime information but private self-censorship. A vivid example of such self-censorship came in April 2004 when the Sinclair Broadcast Group "ordered its ABC affiliates to preempt Ted Koppel's 'Nightline: The Fallen' Roll Call Tribute to U.S. Military Killed in Iraq."[46] Sinclair is "known for including conservative commentary in its news and for its almost exclusively Republican political contributions."[47] Vietnam War veteran and U.S. Senator John McCain (R.–Ariz.) blasted Sinclair's self-censorship, stating "Your decision to deny your viewers an opportunity

39. Bernton, "Woman Loses Job."
40. Rivera, "Images of War Dead."
41. Edmonson, "Military Coffin Photos."
42. Ibid.
43. Garofoli, "Flag-Draped Coffin Photos."
44. Allen and Graham, "Bush Lauds Rumsfeld."
45. Preston, "U.S. Must Release Prison Photos."
46. Jensen, "Sinclair Broadcast Group."
47. Ibid.

to be reminded of war's terrible costs, in all their heartbreaking detail, is a gross disservice to the public, and to the men and women of the United States Armed Forces."[48]

A new dilemma for journalists in Iraq popped up in November 2004 when the Iraqi government's Media High Commission—an agency set up by the former U.S. governor there—directed the media to "set aside space in your news coverage to make the position of the Iraqi government, which expresses the aspirations of most Iraqis, clear."[49] The media were also told to distinguish between insurgents and ordinary residents of the Sunni Muslim city of Falluja where U.S. forces had just launched a major offensive. The directive, which carried the letterhead of the Iraqi prime minister's office, ominously concluded with the statement: "We hope you comply . . . otherwise we regret we will be forced to take all the legal measures to guarantee higher national interests."[50]

Reporting while a nation is at war has always presented the most difficult challenge for a free press in a democratic society. Some government secrecy is imperative to the protection of the nation and for successful prosecution of the war. Some censorship is not only justifiable, but needed. But how much? And for what reasons? Governments have traditionally asserted three reasons to justify such censorship: to deny to the enemy information that might be helpful in prosecuting the war; to try to protect the security of nation's fighting forces; and to sustain the morale of the people. Unfortunately, censorship is sometimes invoked to shield serious military blunders or questionable policies as well. How to establish a proper balance has always been the toughest question. The American people have demonstrated that they will support the government when they believe the nation is on the proper course (World War II is a prime example), but will withdraw that support when they believe the policies are flawed or foolish (the war in Vietnam). The challenge for the press is to provide the American people with the information they need to make these decisions but to not compromise the safety of the nation at the same time.

SUMMARY

Censorship of war news was common in the United States until the fighting began in Vietnam in the 1960s. Reporters were required to follow general security guidelines in their coverage of the war in Southeast Asia, but nevertheless went nearly everywhere, talked with nearly everyone, and presented the American people with a frank account of both the good and bad in that conflict. Many in the military said they believed the lack of restraints on the correspondents who reported the war in Vietnam was responsible for creating public sentiment against the war. Between 1983 and 2003 reporters who sought to cover the multitude of U.S. military actions faced a broad and varied array of censorship policies. When the United States invaded Iraq in 2003, government policies changed. Reporters were embedded with frontline troops and on naval vessels and permitted to report the war—with some restrictions—as they saw it. The system had mixed results but was surely better than the heavy censorship exercised in the previous two decades. As usual, the government exercised a heavy-handed public relations operation to try to put the best possible face on all the news that came from the war zone.

48. Carter, "Debate Over 'Nightline' Tribute."
49. Calvert, "Allawi's Warning to Journalists."
50. Ibid.

THE FIRST AMENDMENT IN THE SCHOOLS

Censorship of school newspapers and magazines is a serious First Amendment issue in America today. Consider the following instances that took place in just one month—May 2005—in three very different places across the United States:

- In Cobb County, Ga., the principal at Pebblebrook High School killed the final edition of the student newspaper, the BrookSpeak, because it previously had highlighted "negative stories at the expense of articles more favorable to the school's image" and because it allegedly displayed "a lack of thoroughness in its reporting of stories on teen pregnancy and vandalism in the school parking lot."[51]
- In Idaho Falls, Idaho, the principal at Bonneville High School asked the student newspaper editor to kill an opinion piece written by a sophomore that criticized school administrators for not paying enough attention to all of the students and stated that "it seems as if they just don't care."[52] The student editor obeyed the principal's request.
- In Collinsville, Ill., near St. Louis, Mo., the principal at Collinsville High School refused to release the April 2005 issue of the student newspaper, the Kahoki, until the final day of school in May 2005 in apparent retribution for an earlier issue that included a column by the student editor in chief, Sarah Lawrence, that "took some shots at the math department and guidance office."[53]

Not only does such censorship deprive students and others of information they should rightfully see, but when practiced in the schools, censorship can take on the aura of being good policy, the right thing for the government to do. School, after all, is where students are taught the difference between right and wrong, where students learn about the freedoms Americans enjoy under their Constitution.

CENSORSHIP OF THE HIGH SCHOOL PRESS

For centuries, students were presumed to have few constitutional rights of any kind. They were regarded as junior or second-class people and were told it was better to be seen and not heard. Parents were, and still are, given wide latitude in controlling the behavior of their offspring, and when these young people moved into schools or other public institutions, the government had the right to exercise a kind of parental control over them: in loco parentis, in the place of a parent. During the social upheaval of the 1960s and 1970s, students began to assert their constitutional rights, and in several important decisions the federal courts acknowledged these claims. In 1969, in the case of *Tinker* v. *Des Moines*, for example, the Supreme Court ruled that students in the public schools do not shed at the schoolhouse gate their constitutional rights to freedom of speech or expression.

On December 16, 1966, Christopher Eckhardt, 16, and Mary Beth Tinker, 13, went to school wearing homemade black armbands, complete with peace signs, to protest the war in Vietnam. Mary Beth's brother John, 15, wore a similar armband the following day. All three

During the social upheaval of the 1960s and 1970s, students began to assert their constitutional rights, and in several important decisions the federal courts acknowledged these claims.

51. Markiewicz, "Cobb School."
52. Stricker, "Student Paper."
53. Aguilar, "Newspaper Adviser."

Source: © Reuters/CORBIS

were suspended from school after they refused requests by school officials to remove the armbands. School administrators said they feared that wearing the armbands might provoke violence among the students, most of whom supported the war in Vietnam. The students appealed to the courts to overturn their suspensions. Three years later Justice Abe Fortas, writing for the Supreme Court, said that students have a First Amendment right to express their opinions on even controversial subjects like the war in Vietnam if they do so "without materially and substantially interfering with the requirements of appropriate discipline in the operation of the school and without colliding with the rights of others."[54]

The *Tinker* standard played a very important role in the 2003 federal district court opinion in *Barber* v. *Dearborn Public Schools*.[55] The case arose from a dispute in Dearborn, Mich. That city boasts, the court noted, "the largest concentration of Arabs anywhere in the world

54. *Tinker* v. *Des Moines School District,* 393 U.S. 503 (1969).
55. 286 F. Supp. 2d 847 (E.D. Mich. 2003).

outside of the Middle East" and "approximately 31.4% of Dearborn High's students are Arab." Many of these residents reportedly fled Iraq to escape the regime of the now-captured former dictator, Saddam Hussein. It was in this environment on February 17, 2003—just before the launch of the U.S. military offensive in Iraq—that Bretton Barber, then a high school junior, wore a T-shirt labeling President George W. Bush an "International Terrorist" in order "to express his feelings about President Bush's foreign policies and the imminent war in Iraq." Barber went through the first three class periods of the day without having anyone mention the shirt. It was during the lunch period, however, that one student (and one student only) complained to an assistant principal about Barber's political fashion statement. That student was upset because he had a relative in the military being sent to Iraq and at least one of his family members served in each of the country's prior wars. Barber soon was asked to remove the T-shirt—he was wearing a different shirt underneath it—or turn it inside out. Refusing to take either option, Barber called his father and went home from school that day. Shortly thereafter, he filed a federal lawsuit against the school district.

Judge Patrick J. Duggan faced the issue of whether the school violated Barber's First Amendment right to free speech and political expression when it prohibited him from wearing the anti-Bush T-shirt. He first held that Barber's case was controlled by the U.S. Supreme Court's 1969 opinion in *Tinker* v. *Des Moines Independent Community School District* that upheld the right of students to wear black armbands to school to protest the Vietnam War. Duggan thus decided that Barber's case was not guided by the high court's more recent decisions in either the sexually offensive, captive-audience expression case of *Bethel School District* v. *Fraser*[56] (see page 113) or the school-sponsored newspaper case of *Hazelwood School District* v. *Kuhlmeier*[57] (see pages 104–106). Barber's situation, in brief, was much more factually similar to *Tinker* than it was to either *Bethel* or *Hazelwood,* thus allowing the judge to distinguish the latter two cases.

Applying the *Tinker* precedent, Judge Duggan reasoned that the school officials' "decision to ban Barber's shirt only can withstand constitutional scrutiny if they show that the T-shirt caused a substantial disruption of or material interference with school activities or created more than an unsubstantiated fear or apprehension of such a disruption or interference." The judge found that only one student and one teacher had expressed negative opinions about the shirt and that there was "no evidence that the T-shirt created any disturbance or disruption in Barber's morning classes, in the hallway between classes or between Barber's third hour class and his lunch period, or during the first twenty-five minutes of the lunch period."

As for the school officials' arguments that the continued wearing of the shirt might cause trouble in the future, given the ethnic composition of the student body and the imminence of war, Judge Duggan found that "even if the majority or a large number of Dearborn High's Arab students are Iraqi, nothing in the present record suggests that these students were or would be offended by Barber's shirt which conveys a view about President Bush. More importantly, there is nothing in the record before this Court to indicate that those students, or any students at Dearborn High, might respond to the T-shirt in a way that would disrupt or interfere with the school environment." He added that "it is improper and most likely

---

56. 478 U.S. 675 (1986).
57. 484 U.S. 260 (1988).

detrimental to our society for government officials, particularly school officials, to assume that members of a particular ethnic group will have monolithic views on a subject and will be unable to control those views."

Comparing the fact situation in Bretton Barber's case with the Vietnam War protest scenario at issue in the seminal and controlling *Tinker* case, Judge Duggan wrote: "[C]learly the tension between students who support and those who oppose President Bush's decision to invade Iraq is no greater than the tension that existed during the United States' involvement in Vietnam between supporters of the war and war-protestors." The judge added that "students benefit when school officials provide an environment where they can openly express their diverging viewpoints and when they learn to tolerate the opinions of others." Judge Duggan thus ruled in favor of Bretton Barber in a decision that captured national attention in newspapers such as the Los Angeles Times and the Washington Post. And in April 2004 the Thomas Jefferson Center for the Protection of Free Expression named Dearborn High School one of the 13 most notorious censors in the nation and awarded it a "Jefferson Muzzle" for its actions against Barber.[58]

Unfortunately, decisions like Judge Duggan's opinion in *Barber* that are favorable to students' speech rights are few and far between today. The legal legacy of *Tinker* has largely failed to live up to Justice Fortas' bold language in the case. Although *Tinker's* material-and-substantial interference or disruption standard remains good law and has never been overruled, many lower federal and state courts attempt to factually distinguish *Tinker* in student-speech cases so as to avoid applying its precedent. It is a major problem for students' speech rights that has only grown worse after the tragedy at Columbine High School in Littleton, Colo., in April 1999. Judges today are extremely sensitive to the legacy of Columbine and other school shootings and, in turn, give great deference to school administrators and principals and are loathe to question their judgment about when speech might reasonably lead to a substantial and material disruption of the educational process or interference with the rights of other students.

By 1988, when the U.S. Supreme Court decided the case of *Hazelwood School District v. Kuhlmeier*, it became apparent that the promise of *Tinker* would not be fulfilled. Today, then, the place to begin to seek an understanding of students' First Amendment rights begins with *Hazelwood*.

The Hazelwood *Case*

In 1983 the principal at Hazelwood East High School near St. Louis censored the school newspaper by completely removing two pages from the publication. The pages contained articles about teenage pregnancy and the impact of parents' divorce on children. The articles on pregnancy included personal interviews with three Hazelwood students (whose names were not used) about how they were affected by their unwanted pregnancies. There was also information about birth control in the story. The story on divorce quoted students—again not identified—about the problems they had suffered when their mothers and fathers had split up. The censorship of the articles was defended on the grounds of privacy and editorial balance.

---

58. Associated Press, "Group Names Dearborn."

Source: AP/World Wide Photos

School officials said they were concerned that the identity of the three girls who agreed to anonymously discuss their pregnancies might nevertheless become known. School officials said they acted to protect the privacy of the students and the parents in the story on divorce as well. In addition, the principal said the latter story was unbalanced, giving the views of only the students. In January of 1988 the Supreme Court ruled that the censorship was permissible under the First Amendment.[59]

At the outset it is important to note that this ruling involved the censorship of a high school newspaper that was published as a part of the school curriculum. The court strongly suggested that the full force of the ruling would not necessarily apply to a high school paper published as an extracurricular activity where any student might contribute stories. Justice Byron White, author of the court's opinion, noted specifically in a footnote that the court did

In 1988 the Supreme Court ruled that school administrators had broad powers to censor high school newspapers. Pictured above is Tammy Hawkins, one of the editors of the Hazelwood East High School newspaper, Spectrum, holding a copy of the newspaper that generated the high court ruling.

59. *Hazelwood School District v. Kuhlmeier,* 484 U.S. 260 (1988).

not at that time have to decide whether its ruling might also be applied to school-sponsored college and university newspapers.

The Supreme Court refused to apply the *Tinker* standard by distinguishing the *Hazelwood* case from the earlier ruling. The *Tinker* ruling, Justice White said in the 5-3 decision, deals with the right of educators to silence a student's personal expression that happens to occur on school property. *Hazelwood* concerns the authority of educators over school-sponsored publications. "Educators are entitled to exercise greater control over this second form of student expression to assure that participants learn whatever lessons the activity is designed to teach, that readers or listeners are not exposed to material that may be inappropriate for their level of maturity, and that the views of individual speakers are not erroneously attributed to the school," he wrote. Educators do not offend the First Amendment by exercising editorial control over the style and content of student speech in school-sponsored publications as long as their actions are reasonably related to "legitimate pedagogical concerns." This means school officials could censor out material they found "ungrammatical, poorly written, inadequately researched, biased or prejudiced, vulgar or profane, or unsuitable for immature audiences." Justice White stressed at one point in the ruling that the education of the nation's youth is primarily the responsibility of parents, teachers, and state and local school officials, not federal judges. Only when the decision to censor has "no valid educational purpose" is the First Amendment directly and sharply involved.

In the years since the *Hazelwood* ruling censorship of the student press has escalated. Each year the Student Press Law Center, a clearinghouse and legal advocate for student First Amendment fights, reports hundreds of calls from student journalists seeking help with censorship problems. Most school administrators react aggressively against any hints of school violence, and the courts seem willing to support such actions. In July 2001, for example, the U.S. Court of Appeals upheld the expulsion of a student at a Washington state high school who had written a poem that detailed the methodical mass killing of 28 people at a school.

But some courts are willing to protect student expression that references violent conduct. In one of the most important decisions involving free speech and alleged threats of violence since the shootings at Columbine High School in 1999, the Supreme Court of California held in *In re George T.*[60] in 2004 that a student-authored poem that was labeled at the top of the page as "Dark Poetry" and that promised "I can be the next kid to bring guns to kill students at school. So parents watch your children cuz I'm BACK!!" was of such an "ambiguous nature" as to *not* constitute a criminal threat of violence under California statutory law.[61] The poem, entitled "Faces" and passed by its male student author to a female student during an

Educators do not offend the First Amendment by exercising editorial control over the style and content of student speech in school-sponsored publications as long as their actions are reasonably related to "legitimate pedagogical concerns."

---

60. 33 Cal. 4th 620 (2004).

61. The relevant provision of the California Penal Code provides: "Any person who willfully threatens to commit a crime which will result in death or great bodily injury to another person, with the specific intent that the statement, made verbally, in writing, or by means of an electronic communication device, is to be taken as a threat, even if there is no intent of actually carrying it out, which, on its face and under the circumstances in which it is made, is so unequivocal, unconditional, immediate, and specific as to convey to the person threatened, a gravity of purpose and an immediate prospect of execution of the threat, and thereby causes that person reasonably to be in sustained fear for his or her own safety or for his or her immediate family's safety, shall be punished by imprisonment in the county jail not to exceed one year, or by imprisonment in the state prison." California Penal Code § 422 (2004).

honors English class at Santa Teresa High School in Santa Clara County (the author later passed it to a second female student), read in its entirety:

Who are these faces around me?
Where did they come from?
They would probably become the
next doctors or loirs [sic] or something. All
really intelligent and ahead in their
game. I wish I had a choice on
what I want to be like they do.
All so happy and vagrant. Each
origonal [sic] in their own way. They
make me want to puke. For I am
Dark, Destructive, & Dangerous. I
slap on my face of happiness but
inside I am evil!! For I can be
the next kid to bring guns to
kill students at school. So parents
watch your children cuz I'm BACK!!

In holding that the poem did not constitute a criminal threat of violence in the case of *In re George T.,* the California high court observed that the text "is ambiguous and plainly equivocal. It does not describe or threaten future conduct since it does not state that the protagonist plans to kill students." The court added that "exactly what the poem means is open to varying interpretations because a poem may mean different things to different readers. As a medium of expression, a poem is inherently ambiguous." For the justices on the Supreme Court of California, "only the final two lines of the poem could arguably be construed to be a criminal threat."

The court also made it clear that the circumstances surrounding the communication and distribution of the poem did not indicate that it reasonably would have been interpreted as an actual threat. In particular, the court observed that "there was no history of animosity or conflict between" the author of the poem and the students to whom it was given. Furthermore, "no threatening gestures or mannerisms accompanied the poem." The court thus concluded that the poem "and the circumstances surrounding its dissemination fail[ed] to establish that it was a criminal threat because the text of the poem, understood in light of the surrounding circumstances, was not 'so unequivocal, unconditional, immediate, and specific as to convey to [the two students] a gravity of purpose and an immediate prospect of execution of the threat.'" While the decision marks an important victory for students' right to free expression, the issue now becomes how broadly other courts will interpret the decision in *In re George T.* In particular, will it be limited to the narrow context of student poetry cases or does it signal a broader change of heart by courts, now that more than a half-decade has passed since Columbine, not to treat student speech as a threat of violence? The answer to this question remains to be seen. In addition, it is important to note that the case of *In re George T.* did not involve the application of the *Tinker* material-and-substantial interference standard but rather applied a criminal code section on true threats. Thus it has no impact on how courts might apply *Tinker* to similar cases.

But it is not only stories about sexual behavior or violence that can provoke school administrators to censor student publications. School officials frequently seek to block the publication of stories that will make school administrators or teachers appear to be foolish or incompetent or lacking judgment. For example, the principal at a high school near Chicago censored an article about four school administrators who had spent $5,600 on trips to meetings when the district faced a serious budget crisis. The article included material about potential impropriety in the way the funds were spent. The principal ordered the names of the administrators taken out of the article.[62] Other reports of censorship are reported almost weekly in newspapers and magazines. In Snohomish, Wash., school administrators blocked the student newspaper from publishing a story about a vice principal who was suspended and later resigned in the face of charges of sexual harassment. A principal in New Jersey cut a story about the school's sex education program. In Ft. Wayne, Ind., a principal censored an article that outlined financial improprieties by a school coach, even though the principal acknowledged the story was accurate. Unfortunately, the *Hazelwood* ruling has acted as a kind of imprimatur for high school officials to wield the censor's blue pencil.

There are only a few rare instances on record in which courts have held that school administrators have gone too far and violated the rights of student journalists under *Hazelwood*'s expansive "legitimate pedagogical concerns" standard. One such case of a First Amendment violation involved the censorship of an article in the Utica High School Arrow in Utica, Mich. The student-authored article in question reported on a lawsuit filed against the Utica Community Schools (UCS) by two local residents, Joanne and Rey Frances, who lived next door to the UCS bus depot. The Frances' lawsuit claimed injuries and illnesses allegedly caused by breathing in the diesel fumes emitted by the UCS's idling buses each school day. A local newspaper had already covered the story about the lawsuit before student Katherine "Katy" Dean researched and wrote an article about the situation for her school newspaper, the Arrow. The Arrow is an officially sponsored publication of the UCS and, as part of the high school's curriculum for which students receive credit and grades, operates under the direction of a faculty advisor. The faculty advisor, however, does not regulate the subjects covered by students, but instead merely provides advice on which stories to run. She also reviews, criticizes, and checks the grammar contained in articles. The Arrow's staff of student journalists controls the content of the monthly paper, is responsible for major editorial decisions without significant administrative intervention, and typically does not submit its content to school administrators for prepublication review.

The article written by Dean was balanced and accurate, and it correctly reported that school district officials declined to comment on the lawsuit. One day before the article was scheduled to go to press, however, UCS administrators ordered that it be removed from the Arrow, citing so-called journalistic defects and "inaccuracies" (for instance, the UCS administration did not like the fact that Dean's article accurately attributed scientific data to a story in USA Today—apparently it was not a credible source in the minds of the school officials— and the fact that a draft of the story used pseudonyms for the Frances' real names). The American Civil Liberties Union filed a lawsuit on behalf of Dean, claiming the censorship violated Dean's First Amendment rights under *Hazelwood*.[63]

In November 2004 U.S. District Court Judge Arthur Tarnow applied the *Hazelwood* legitimate-pedagogical-concerns standard and ruled in favor of Dean and against the school.

---

62. "Suspension of Student" and "Students Censored."
63. *Dean* v. *Utica Community Schools,* 345 F. Supp. 2d 799 (E.D. Mich. 2004).

The judge called the school's censorship and suppression of the article "unconstitutional," adding that the school's "explanation that the article was deleted for legitimate educational purposes such as bias and factual inaccuracy is wholly lacking in credibility in light of the evidence in the record."[64] Judge Tarnow distinguished the Arrow's article about the lawsuit from the censored content in the *Hazelwood* case that dealt with teen pregnancy and divorce. He observed that Katy Dean's article about the bus-fumes lawsuit did not raise any privacy concerns since a local paper had already addressed the lawsuit, and it did not contain any sexual "frank talk" and thus could not reasonably be perceived as being unsuitable for immature audiences. Beyond such critical distinctions, Judge Tarnow found the article to be fair and balanced, noting that Dean's story "sets forth the conflicting viewpoints on the health effects of diesel fumes, and concludes that the link between diesel fumes and cancer is not fully established." Finally Tarnow noted that the story contained no serious grammatical errors and that "Dean's article properly and accurately attributes its quotations to their sources. The article qualifies any statement made by its sources. The article does not present the author's own conclusions on unknown facts." Judge Tarnow thus concluded that "Katy Dean had a right to publish an article concerning the Frances' side of the lawsuit so long as it accurately reported the Frances' side of the lawsuit."

In addition to holding that the school's actions against Dean violated the *Hazelwood* standard, Judge Tarnow ruled that the censorship of her article violated the more general but important First Amendment rule against **viewpoint-based discrimination.** In support of this holding, Judge Tarnow noted that the UCS attorney "conceded that Dean's article would not have been removed from the Arrow if it had explicitly taken the district's side with respect to the Frances' lawsuit against UCS." This is the essence of viewpoint-based discrimination: The government (in this case, the school district) restricts and restrains one side of a debate but not the other. For instance, it would violate the rule against viewpoint-based discrimination if a public school only allowed pro-choice views on the topic of abortion to be printed in the school newspaper while it simultaneously prohibited and censored pro-life views. More simply put, the government should remain neutral in the marketplace of ideas (see pages 48–49) and not favor one side of a debate over the other. By acknowledging that the school would have allowed Katy Dean to print an article that favored the UCS's position in the lawsuit filed against it by the Frances, the UCS attorney essentially admitted the viewpoint-based discrimination that drove it to censor Dean's story.

Dean's ACLU attorney, Andrew Nickelhoff, remarked after the victory that Dean's article "was an excellent piece of high school journalism, and I think they were trying to find problems with the article to have an excuse for censoring it."[65] The case of *Dean* v. *Utica Community Schools* thus should stand as a stark reminder to overzealous and censorious high school administrators that there are limits, even under the *Hazelwood* legitimate-pedagogical-concern standard, to censorship of the student press. As the Student Press Law Center observed, "the judge's ruling gives a clear mandate that content cannot be censored merely because officials dislike it."

High school journalism remains vigorous in many schools. And the legislatures in a handful of states, including Colorado, Arkansas, Iowa, Massachusetts and Kansas, have passed

64. Associated Press, "Utica Schools."
65. Ibid.

statutes granting student journalists in those states a fuller measure of freedom of expression than was granted by the Supreme Court in *Hazelwood*. Similar "anti-*Hazelwood*" statutes were proposed in 2005 in Vermont and Michigan. Some community newspapers are now actively supporting the fight for freedom of expression in the schools. For example, when school officials forbade a student newspaper at a Dallas high school to publish a picture of a student smoking off campus to illustrate an article on health and school regulations, the Dallas Morning News said it would run the photo and an article about censoring the school newspaper unless the school superintendent relented.[66] The student newspaper ran the photo as planned. And when officials at Venice High School in southern California in June 2003 killed a story about a relationship that a health teacher at the school had had when she was 29 with a 16-year-old child actor, the Los Angeles Times gave the student-journalists full space on its commentary pages to explain what happened.[67] The true victory for the student-journalists here was the Times' decision to cover this instance of censorship and thereby bring to even more light the story the students had sought to bring out in the first place. The students' decision to fight their battle in the pages of a major daily newspaper rather than in a court of law thus paid off.

Censorship Guidelines

While the decision in *Hazelwood* surely gave school administrators a strong hand in censoring high school newspapers, all the questions regarding the scope of such censorship have not been answered. But some general guidelines have emerged.

The question, In what ways can a high school newspaper be censored? cannot be answered until two other questions are. First, is the newspaper published at a public or private high school? Constitutional protections have substantially less meaning at private schools. The First Amendment is not considered an impediment at private high schools or private colleges and universities. A newspaper at a private school can be censored in just about any way imaginable. There is, however, one minor exception to this general rule. In particular, California has a statute known as the "Leonard Law" that applies First Amendment standards to private, secular high schools and to secondary schools; these private schools, in other words, are forbidden from violating students' First Amendment rights.[68] Although California is the only state to have such a law extending First Amendment rights to private school students, there is nothing to prevent legislative bodies in other states from drafting and approving similar legislation in the future.

The next question to ask when focusing on public schools is, What kind of newspaper is it? Three kinds of publications are possible:

▪ A school-sponsored newspaper, generally defined as a paper that uses the school's name and resources, has a faculty advisor, and serves as a tool to teach knowledge or skills. Typically this kind of newspaper is produced as part of a journalism class.

---

66. See Bonner and Hines, *Death by Cheeseburger*.

67. Estrada and Robles, "All the News."

68. California Education Code § 48950 (providing in relevant part that "school districts operating one or more high schools and private secondary schools shall not make or enforce any rule subjecting any high school pupil to disciplinary sanctions solely on the basis of conduct that is speech or other communication that, when engaged in outside of the campus, is protected from governmental restriction by the First Amendment to the United States Constitution").

- An unsupervised or student-controlled newspaper produced on the school's campus as an extracurricular activity.
- A student newspaper produced and distributed off campus.

The *Hazelwood* ruling spoke only to the first kind of newspaper. This type of paper can be most heavily censored. Most authorities agree that school officials have less power to censor the second kind of publication, and no power to censor the third kind of newspaper, unless students attempt to distribute it on campus. School administrators can ban the on-campus distribution of material produced elsewhere, and this authority provides them with a kind of informal censorship power if students seek to circulate the material on school property.

When a student standing on the steps of the school's main entrance passes out a newspaper he or she has fashioned off campus, it is pretty obvious the publication is being distributed on school property. But what about a student who creates a Web site on a home computer, a site that is accessible to anyone using the Internet—including students and teachers using school computers? Does this constitute distribution on school property? Can the student be punished for the content of the Web site? These are questions the courts are having a difficult time answering. Judges usually answer these questions with a no; what the student creates at home is protected by the First Amendment, even if the site is accessible via school computers. But contrary decisions have also been rendered as well. Here are a few examples of recent rulings.

- A student in Missouri was suspended from school for posting material on his home Web site that was critical of both the school and school administrators. A federal court blocked the school from enforcing the suspension, ruling that the student's First Amendment challenge was likely to succeed at a trial.[69]
- A federal court in Pennsylvania ruled that a student could not be punished for his postings on a message board that he made from his home computer unless the content caused "substantial disruption or interference with the work of the school." There was no evidence of such disruption, the court said.[70]
- In Washington state a student won $10,000 in damages (and $52,000 in attorney's fees) from a school district after he was suspended for creating a Web site that parodied an assistant principal at his school.[71]
- A U.S. District judge in Ohio ruled that a student who created a personal Web site on his own time, with his own equipment, could not be expelled because of the content of the site. He did access the site on a school computer to show his fellow students, but the court said the 80-day suspension was based on the content of the site, not on his use of the school computer. The suspension violated his First Amendment rights, the court said.[72]
- The Pennsylvania Supreme Court upheld the 10-day suspension of a student who generated a Web site that displayed derogatory comments about a teacher, including a photo of the teacher that morphed into a likeness of Adolph Hitler. A message on the site also solicited donations to hire a hit man and included

69. *Beussink* v. *Woodland R-IV School District,* 30 F. Supp. 2d 1175 (E.D. Mo. 1998).
70. *Flaherty* v. *Keystone Oaks School District,* 247 F. Supp. 2d 698 (W.D. Pa. 2003).
71. Stifler, "Ex-Student Awarded Damages."
72. *Coy* v. *Board of Education of the North Canton City Schools,* 205 F. Supp. 2d 791 (N.D. Ohio 2002).

offensive comments about the school principal. The court said that even though the Web site was generated off campus, the statements and images nevertheless constituted "on campus" speech because the message was aimed at the school community and was accessed by students using school computers. The school's need to maintain order and fulfill its educational mission outweighed the student's First Amendment rights, the court said.[73]

ACCEPTABLE CRITERIA APPLIED TO CENSOR HIGH SCHOOL NEWSPAPERS PRODUCED AS PART OF JOURNALISM CLASS

1. Stories or photos that materially and substantially interfere with the requirements of appropriate school discipline
2. Material that interferes with the rights of students
3. Material that fails to meet standards of academic propriety
4. Material that generates health and welfare concerns
5. Matters that are obscene, indecent or vulgar

What kinds of content can be censored? Five general categories of material emerge from studying the case law.

1. Publications or stories that materially and substantially interfere with the requirements of appropriate discipline. This is the old *Tinker* standard; its viability remains solid.
2. Material that interferes with the rights of students. This too was a part of the *Tinker* standard. The school can protect students from damage to their reputation or invasion of their privacy. The school can also protect itself from liability in such instances.
3. School-sponsored newspapers can be censored for reasons of academic propriety, what the court in *Hazelwood* called "legitimate pedagogical concerns." This rationale is potentially boundless and includes everything from censoring stories that are ungrammatical or poorly written, to blue-penciling stories about topics that school administrators believe are inappropriate for students of high school age, to cutting stories that might interfere with the school's basic educational mission.
4. Material that generates health and welfare concerns. School officials may censor stories and especially advertising that deals with tobacco and alcohol products, sexual behavior and so on. This category is another seemingly open-ended one that can probably be applied to school-sponsored and nonsponsored publications with equal vigor.
5. Matters that are obscene, vulgar or indecent. Obscenity is a narrowly, if not precisely, defined category of speech (see *Miller* v. *California* in Chapter 13). It is doubtful a high school publication would attempt to print such matter. Vulgarity and

---

73. *J.S.* v. *Bethlehem Area School District,* 807 A. 2d 847 (Pa. 2002).

indecency, however, are open-ended concepts. The Supreme Court dealt with this issue in a 1986 ruling, *Bethel School District* v. *Fraser*,[74] a case involving a student speech. The ruling applies equally to newspapers, however.

A student named Matthew Fraser spoke before a student assembly on behalf of his friend who was running for a student government post. Fraser's speech, which he cleared beforehand with three teachers, contained the following remarks about his friend: "He is a man who is firm, he's firm in his pants, firm in his shirt, his character is firm—but most of all his belief in you, the students of Bethel, is firm." The speech contained another, similar double entendre. Fraser was suspended from school for two days by school officials who claimed the speech was obscene and vulgar.

Chief Justice Warren Burger wrote the high court's opinion that upheld Fraser's suspension. "The undoubted freedom to advocate unpopular and controversial views in schools must be balanced against the society's countervailing interest in teaching students the boundaries of socially appropriate behavior," the chief justice wrote. The schools could reasonably conclude, he said, that the essential lessons of civil, mature conduct cannot be conveyed in a school that tolerates "lewd or offensive speech." Burger added that the "pervasive sexual innuendo" in Fraser's speech was plainly offensive to both teachers and students.[75] Dissenter John Paul Stevens questioned whether "a group of judges who are at least two generations and three thousand miles away from the scene of the crime" were as well qualified as Fraser to determine whether the speech would offend his contemporaries, who went on to elect the candidate for whom he spoke.

Although censorship of any kind is a problem, what deeply troubles most observers is the elasticity of many of the concepts used to justify the censorship of school newspapers, concepts like academic propriety, health and welfare, vulgarity. An additional problem is that the advisor to the newspaper, the adult supervisor, is an employee of the censoring agency, the school district. This person, who is in the best position to fight for the rights of the student journalists, may literally be putting a teaching career on the line if petty school administrators choose to use the annual teacher evaluation to punish an outspoken advisor.

"The undoubted freedom to advocate unpopular and controversial views in schools must be balanced against the society's countervailing interest in teaching students the boundaries of socially appropriate behavior."

CENSORSHIP OF COLLEGE NEWSPAPERS

The 1988 *Hazelwood* ruling by the Supreme Court left unresolved whether administrators at public colleges and universities enjoyed the same powers of censorship the court gave to high school administrators. (Remember, the Constitution is not a bar to the censorship of publications at private colleges and universities.)

One U.S. Court of Appeals ruling strongly suggests that the federal courts are reluctant to expand the censorial powers of college administrators via *Hazelwood*. In 2001 the 6th U.S. Court of Appeals sitting en banc ruled that when administrators at Kentucky State University refused to permit the distribution of the school's yearbook because they didn't approve of its content and the color of its cover, they violated the First Amendment rights of the students at the school. But the 10-3 ruling was based largely on the fact that the creation of the yearbook was

---

74. 478 U.S. 675 (1986).
75. *Bethel School District* v. *Fraser*, 478 U.S. 675 (1986); see also *Boroff* v. *Van Wert City Board of Education*, 220 F. 3d 465 (2000).

not a classroom activity in which students are assigned a grade. The yearbook was a designated public forum (see pp. 129–130) created by the university to exist in an atmosphere of free and responsible discussion and intellectual exploration, the court said. What the school officials did was clearly censorship. "There is little if any difference between hiding from public view the words and pictures students use to portray their college experience, and forcing students to publish a state-sponsored script. In either case, the government alters student expression by obliterating it," Judge R. Guy Cole wrote.[76] But in reality, the court had merely distinguished the production of the yearbook from the classroom-generated newspaper in *Hazelwood.*

A much more disturbing, disappointing and important federal appellate court decision affecting the college press was handed down in June 2005 in a case called *Hosty* v. *Carter,* 412 F. 3d 731 (7th Cir. 2005). The *Hosty* case centered on demands by university administrators in 2000 for prior review and approval—a classic prior restraint on speech, in other words—of the Innovator, the student-run newspaper at Governors State University, located slightly south of Chicago, Ill. The Innovator had previously published articles under the by-line of student Margaret Hosty that were critical of a school official, thus sparking the confrontation.

A major issue in the resulting lawsuit was whether the legitimate-pedagogical-concerns standard articulated by the U.S. Supreme Court in the *Hazelwood* case for controlling the censorship of school-sponsored, high school newspapers that are part of the curriculum is also applicable to college newspapers. The Supreme Court in *Hazelwood* had dropped a footnote in its opinion, leaving open this specific issue, that stated "we need not now decide whether the same degree of deference is appropriate with respect to school-sponsored expressive activities at the college and university level."

In *Hosty,* the student-journalist plaintiffs argued that *Hazelwood's* legitimate-pedagogical concerns standard was never made applicable to the college press, and they contended that university administrators cannot ever insist that student newspapers be submitted for review and approval. But by a 7-4 vote, the U.S. 7th Circuit Court of Appeals rejected these contentions and rebuffed the idea that there is a bright-line difference between high school and college newspapers. The 7th Circuit wrote that the Supreme Court's footnote in *Hazelwood* "does not even hint at the possibility of an on/off switch: high school papers reviewable, college papers not reviewable." It added that "whether *some* review is possible depends on the answer to the public-forum question, which does not (automatically) vary with the speakers' age." The key in *Hosty,* then, was whether the student newspaper constituted a public forum. Whether a particular physical venue or location constitutes a public forum for purposes of First Amendment speech protection is discussed later in this chapter (see pages 129–135). Writing for the seven-judge majority in *Hosty,* Judge Frank Easterbrook articulated a rule that "speech at a non-public forum, and underwritten at public expense, may be open to reasonable regulation even at the college level."

Thus, for Judge Easterbrook and the majority of the 7th Circuit, "*Hazelwood's* first question therefore remains our principal question as well: was the reporter a speaker in a public forum (no censorship allowed?) or did the University either create a non-public forum or publish the paper itself (a closed forum where content may be supervised)?" This meant that the appellate court had to examine the status of the particular student newspaper at issue in *Hosty,* namely the Innovator, to determine whether or not it was a public forum. The court noted that if the Innovator "operated in a public forum, the University could not vet its contents." The appellate court,

---

76. *Kincaid* v. *Gibson,* 236 F. 3d 342 (2001).

unfortunately, held that it was not possible on the record in front of it to determine what kind of forum the Governors State University had established with the Innovator. The court did, however, provide some guidance on this for the future, noting among other things that:

- while "being part of the curriculum may be a *sufficient* condition of a non-public forum, it is not a *necessary* condition. Extracurricular activities may be outside any public forum . . . without also falling outside all university governance." In other words, just because a college newspaper is an extracurricular activity and not part of the curriculum does not mean that it necessarily escapes all university control or regulation;
- "a school may declare the pages of the student newspaper open for expression and thus disable itself from engaging in viewpoint or content discrimination while the terms on which the forum operates remain unaltered."

Another important factor in the public forum determination of a university newspaper is whether the university underwrote and subsidized the newspaper without any strings attached or, conversely, whether it "hedge[d] the funding with controls that left the University itself as the newspaper's publisher."

What does all of this mean for college newspapers? First, it's important to remember that the decision is binding in only the three states that comprise the 7th Circuit Court of Appeals—Illinois, Indiana and Wisconsin (see page 25 for a map of the federal appellate court circuits). Second, many college newspapers, such as the Daily Collegian at Penn State University, are independent of the universities that their student-journalists attend and are not directly funded by the university. In an official press release on the *Hosty* decision, Mark Goodman, executive director of the Student Press Law Center that had filed a friend-of-the-court brief in the case, stated:

> As a practical matter, most college student newspapers are going to be considered designated public forums and entitled to the strongest First Amendment protection because that's the way they've been operating for decades. But this decision gives college administrators ammunition to argue that many traditionally independent student activities are subject to school censorship. I fear it's just a matter of time before a university prohibits a student group from bringing an unpopular speaker to campus or showing a controversial film based on the *Hosty* decision. Such actions invite havoc on college campuses.

It remains to be seen whether other federal courts will follow the lead of the 7th Circuit in *Hosty* or, instead, whether they will be more willing to focus on the age-level of the students involved and draw clear lines between high school and college newspapers that would relegate the reach of *Hazelwood* to high schools. Three student journalists at Governors State University did not give up, however, and they petitioned the U.S. Supreme Court in September 2005 for a writ of certiorari, asking the high court to reconsider the 7th Circuit's opinion. Among the three specific questions that Margaret Hosty and her high-powered First Amendment attorney Lee Levine asked the nation's high court to consider was the following key issue:

- "Does this Court's decision in *Hazelwood School District* v. *Kuhlmeier*, 484 U.S. 260 (1988), either authorize an official of a public university to impose a viewpoint-based system of prior restraint on a newspaper produced by adult students outside the university's educational curriculum, or limit the otherwise clearly established right of adult university students to be free from such a system of prior restraint in the publication of such a newspaper?"

A friend-of-the-court brief in support of the students was filed in October 2005 by a number of journalism schools, communication colleges and organizations such as the Pennsylvania Center for the First Amendment. Unfortunately the Supreme Court decided not to hear the *Hosty* case in February 2006, meaning that the 7th Circuit's 2005 opinion still stands in that circuit. The Student Press Law Center issued a press release lamenting the decision not to hear *Hosty* and "encouraging students in Illinois, Indiana and Wisconsin to call upon their schools to pledge their commitment to free speech by explicitly designating their student media as 'public forums' where student editors have the right to make editorial decisions free from administrative interference."

Problems for College Journalists

University administrators cite three reasons more than any others to support their arguments that at times, censorship is needed. The first is disruption of the school. This goes beyond physical disruption to include the publication or broadcast of material that may interfere with the purpose of the university, or even more broadly, that may interfere with the message the university is attempting to communicate to both its students and the larger community. As an example of the latter, school administrators have at times attempted to block the publication of stories about crimes committed on campus for fear of suggesting to students and their parents that the campus might be a dangerous place—in other words, a part of the real world, not the peaceful and idyllic setting pictured in promotional brochures.[77]

School officials also argue it is their responsibility to protect their students from offensive speech. Attempts to censor material regarded as racist or insensitive to ethnic minorities have been undertaken at times. Finally, college administrators argue they have a right to block the publication of material to ensure that the ideas or views contained in the material are not attributed to the school itself. Most college newspapers are not published like high school newspapers, as a part of a journalism class. They are extracurricular activities, usually independent of both the journalism program and the university. A board of student publications, made up of students, faculty, administrators and even outside professional journalists, is appointed to set the policy for the publication and select the editors. An advisor—who lacks the power to do anything but give advice—frequently works with student journalists on a day-to-day basis. Unfortunately, most people off campus, and even some on campus, fail to recognize the independence of the publication and are often quick to blame the college or university for offensive content.

What kinds of specific censorship problems affect the college press? Getting access to information is one problem. Student journalists often have difficulty gaining access to reports on faculty performance, student government meetings and school disciplinary hearings. It is not uncommon for a college to reject the criminal prosecution of a student apprehended for a minor crime, and instead punish the student through a disciplinary proceeding. The criminal trial would be open to the public and the press; disciplinary hearings are routinely closed. Hence, no bad publicity for the school. Campus administrators have even attempted to bar all reporters from access to university police reports, citing the Family Educational Rights and Privacy Act (see pages 403–404), which limits the public access to most student records.

77. Paulk, "Campus Crime."

School officials have argued—unsuccessfully—that crime reports that name students as victims, perpetrators or even witnesses are educational records and hence inaccessible under this law. If the press can't see the official police reports, stories about the incident generally won't be written. The courts have rejected this interpretation of the law.[78]

Some newspapers that have published advertising for alcohol, tobacco or other products regarded as harmful by some members of society, or that have published ads supporting controversial ideas or promoting certain speakers or books, have been the focus of censorship attempts. News stories, editorials, letters to the editor and columns that focus on racial, ethnic, gender and even political issues are often the target of protests and sometimes attempts at censorship. These matters especially provoke campus actions, not only by administrators but by students as well. The theft of all the issues of a single edition of a newspaper by those who disagree with the material published in the paper is a problem on some campuses.* About 30 to 40 such thefts occur each year, according to Mark Goodman, the executive director of the Student Press Law Center. For instance, the SPLC reported that more than 8,500 copies of a single edition of the student newspaper at the University of Utah, the Daily Utah Chronicle, were stolen from campus bins in November 2005. That same month more than 1,000 copies of a progressive student newspaper at Illinois State University were stolen. Campus police usually claim they are powerless to pursue the thieves, since, because the student newspapers are free, no law has been broken.

And therein lies the problem of quite literally stealing "free" speech: How can one steal something if it is free? In fact, only two states—Colorado[79] and Maryland[80]—have statutes making it a crime to steal free newspapers. Colorado enacted its law in 2004 after the apparent pilfering of 8,000 copies of three free newspapers, in and around Aspen in August 2003, by a man and woman who apparently didn't like a story printed about them. The Colorado law, which applies to publications distributed on a complimentary basis and to any student periodical distributed at any institution of higher education, provides in relevant part:

> A person commits the offense of newspaper theft when that person obtains
> or exerts unauthorized control over more than five copies of an edition of
> a newspaper from a newspaper distribution container owned or leased by
> the newspaper publisher with the intent to prevent other individuals from
> reading that edition of the newspaper. Control is unauthorized if there is a
> notice on the newspaper or on the newspaper distribution container that
> possession of more than five copies with intent to prevent other individuals
> from reading that edition of the newspaper is illegal.[81]

*Such problems are not confined to college campuses. In the midst of a heated election in a community in southern Maryland, several sheriff's deputies bought out, with the encouragement and support of the sheriff, all the copies of a weekly newspaper that published material critical of the sheriff, who was a candidate for re-election. The deputies paid for the papers, and conducted the buyout off duty. But the 4th U.S. Court of Appeals nevertheless ruled the action was a civil rights violation, calling the activity a classic example of the kind of suppression of political criticism that the First Amendment was intended to prohibit. *Rossignol* v. *Voorhaar,* 315 F. 3d 516 (2003).

78. See *Student Press Law Center* v. *Alexander,* 778 F. Supp. 1227 (1991) and *Ohio ex rel The Miami Student* v. *Miami University,* 79 Ohio St. 3d 168 (1997).
79. Colorado Revised Statute § 18-4-419.
80. Maryland Code Annotated, Criminal § 7-106.
81. Colorado Revised Statute § 18-4-419.

The Maryland statute, which was enacted in 1994 and is much more brief than its Colorado counterpart, provides: "[A] person may not knowingly or willfully obtain or exert control that is unauthorized over newspapers with the intent to prevent another from reading the newspapers."[82] The term "newspaper," as used within the statute, is defined as "a periodical that is distributed on a complimentary or compensatory basis."[83]

Because only two states have statutes targeting the theft of free newspapers, incidents of newspaper theft on college campuses are rampant today. The Student Press Law Center (SPLC) tracks and describes the incidents from a link on its Web site at http://www.splc.org/newspapertheft.asp and provides a helpful "Newspaper Theft Checklist" of strategies and advice for college newspaper journalists at http://www.splc.org/theftchecklist.asp. In 2004 the SPLC reported numerous instances of the pilfering of student newspapers across the country, including, among others, the theft of about

- 2,500 copies of the Poly Post at California Polytechnic Institute at Pomona by unidentified students;
- 1,500 copies of the Wichitan, the weekly newspaper at Midwestern State University in Wichita Falls, Texas, after a front-page story that featured a fight at a fraternity party that led to the fraternity being placed on alcohol probation;
- 2,500 copies of the West Georgian at West Georgia University after it ran a front-page story about a student softball player charged with homicide by vehicle, felony hit and run, and driving under the influence of alcohol;
- 1,600 copies of the Trailblazer at Vincennes University in Indiana on the same day the newspaper ran an article exposing a fraternity's suspension for alcohol use at rush events and implicating the fraternity in an alleged rape; and
- 5,000 copies of the Medium, an alternative weekly student publication at Rutgers University, by an anonymous group that claimed the paper disseminates hate speech and hate-charged commentary.

Newspaper thefts continued at a rapid pace in 2005. For instance, more than 5,000 copies of a single edition of the student newspaper at North Carolina State University were stolen in March 2005, and 7,000 copies of the newspaper at Morehead State University in Kentucky were pilfered on a single day in September 2005.

The entire press run of The Daily Californian at the University of California, Berkeley, was stolen in 1996 to protest an editorial that supported a state referendum aimed at ending affirmative action programs. The Daily Californian was victimized again on November 4, 2002—one day prior to local elections in Berkeley—when mayoral candidate Tom Bates allegedly stole approximately 1,000 copies of the student newspaper "from their kiosk on Sproul Plaza, birthplace of the Free Speech Movement."[84] The Daily Californian, which is distributed free of charge, had endorsed Bates' opponent in the race. Although Bates would win the election by slightly more than 5,000 votes, he was roundly criticized and chastised by other local press outlets for the paper-pilfering incident; as the neighboring Oakland Tribune

82. Maryland Code Annotated, Criminal § 7-106 (b).
83. Maryland Code Annotated, Criminal § 7-106 (a).
84. Burress, "Berkeley Mayor."

opined, "That the mayor of a city proud to call itself the home of the free-speech movement would trample on those First Amendment rights is not only ironic but also embarrassing."[85]

Shortly after the Bates incident, Berkeley became only the second city in the country's most populous state to adopt a statute against the theft of free newspapers. It passed, in October 2003, an ordinance targeting "the unauthorized removal of newspapers."[86] The other California city to possess such an ordinance is San Francisco,[87] which adopted its law after it dealt with a high-profile incident of newspaper theft back in 1992 when then-Police Chief Richard Hongisto allegedly ordered several police officers to remove more than 2,000 copies of an issue of the Bay Times, a gay-themed newspaper, that mocked Hongisto with a sexually suggestive illustration on its cover.[88]

Finally, attempts to censor college newspapers indirectly, by reducing or even ending their funding, have generally failed. In 1983 the 8th U.S. Court of Appeals handed down an important ruling that still represents the state of the law,[89] more than 20 years later. The case began in the late 1970s when the University of Minnesota Daily published a year-end edition containing content that, according to one university faculty member, offended Third World students, blacks, Jews, feminists, gays, lesbians and Christians.[90] In the wake of complaints from students and off-campus readers, the university regents embarked on a plan to cut the funding for the newspaper. The plan was to allow students to decide whether or not to contribute $2 each semester to fund the newspaper. The $2 fee had automatically gone to the newspaper in the past. Two university review committees advised the regents the plan was a bad idea, but it was adopted nevertheless. Before the vote many of the regents publicly stated they favored the plan because students should not be forced to support a newspaper that was "sacrilegious and vulgar."

A lawsuit followed the decision, and the appellate court ruled the move by the regents violated the First Amendment. A reduction in or even the elimination of fees is certainly permissible, the court said, so long as it is not done for the wrong reasons. But there was ample evidence in this case, the court said, that the reduction was enacted to punish the newspaper. As such it was an attempt at censorship. The court cited the negative comments about the newspaper by the regents during consideration of the plan, as well as the fact that the change was not made at other University of Minnesota campuses (which are governed by the same board of regents), only the Twin Cities campus, home of the offending newspaper, as evidence of the punitive nature of the new policy. "Reducing the revenues available to the newspaper is therefore forbidden by the First Amendment," the court concluded.[91]

More recently, in July 2004 the editors of the Mirror, the student newspaper at the University of Northern Colorado, filed a lawsuit in federal court alleging that funding cuts for the newspaper made by the Student Representative Council and later approved by the university's board of trustees violated the First Amendment rights of free speech and free press.[92] In particular, the newspaper's editors contended that the cuts were instituted by student leaders

85. Editorial, "Mayor Tom Bates."
86. Berkeley, Cal., Municipal Code § 13.54 (2003).
87. San Francisco, Cal., Municipal Police Code Art. 9, § 630 (2004).
88. Hoover, "Hongisto Fired."
89. *Stanley* v. *McGrath,* 719 F. 2d 279 (1983).
90. Gillmor, "The Fragile First."
91. *Stanley* v. *McGrath,* 719 F. 2d 279 (1983).
92. Associated Press, "UNC Students."

in retaliation for stories about a council member's arrest for drunk driving and the council's alleged violations of open-meeting laws. The lawsuit alleged that when the Student Representative Council discussed the newspaper's funding, one council member objected to the newspaper's content and urged others to vote to cut the Mirror's funding. The council later cut funding for the newspaper by 40 percent.

The State Press Magazine, a student-run publication at Arizona State University (ASU), faced a funding cut as well as the threat of heightened editorial control in 2004 after it ran a cover photo showing a woman's bare breast with a nipple piercing. The photograph was used to illustrate a story on "the popularity of body piercings among students and how they enhance college students' sex lives."[93] The State Press is editorially independent of ASU, but it receives a rent-free office on campus and about 10 percent of its operating budget comes from the university. ASU also threatened to remove the State Press from its campus offices. The situation reached a boiling point in 2005 when a member of the Arizona House of Representatives named Russell Pearce (R.–Mesa) added a line to the state's proposed 2006 budget that specified "no state funding for university student publications" due, in part, to the State Press's nipple-piercing cover. Fortunately for advocates of the college press, Governor Janet Napolitano (D.) in 2005 vetoed the proposed 2006 budget for Arizona that included the measure prohibiting funding to university publications. But the Arizona legislature did not give up, and Gov. Napolitano ultimately signed a budget in May 2005 for fiscal year 2006–2007 that included the following footnote inserted by Rep. Pearce: "The appropriated monies shall not be used to support any student newspaper." The effect of that single sentence might not even touch the State Press, however. Why? Because as the Student Press Law Center reported on its Web site, "the student newspapers the footnote is meant to affect—those at Arizona State University, the University of Arizona and Northern Arizona University—say they do not currently receive state money. The footnote only applies to money the universities receive through the legislature."

Alcohol Advertisements and the College Press

In 1996, the Commonwealth of Pennsylvania adopted a law known simply as Act 199. The law prohibited the paid dissemination of alcoholic beverage advertising in college newspapers.[94] In particular, it provided that no advertising of alcoholic beverages "shall be permitted, either directly or indirectly, in any booklet, program book, yearbook, magazine, newspaper, periodical, brochure, circular or other similar publication published by, for or in behalf of any educational institution." After Act 199 became law, the Pennsylvania Liquor Control Board issued an advisory notice clarifying how the law applied to universities and the collegiate press. The notice stated:

> Advertisements which indicate the availability and/or price of alcoholic beverages may not be contained in publications published by, for and in behalf of any educational institutions. Universities are considered educational institutions under this section. Thus, an advertisement in a college newspaper or a college football program announcing beverages would not be permissible.

93. DeFalco, "Body Piercing Photo."
94. 47 Pennsylvania Statutes Annotated § 4-498 (2004).

What does this statement mean? Under this law, an advertisement paid for by a local bar in State College, Pa., and placed in the student newspaper at the Pennsylvania State University, the Daily Collegian, that described the availability and/or price of beer at the bar during happy hours would not be permissible. The student newspaper at the University of Pittsburgh, the Pitt News, decided to challenge the law on First Amendment grounds because the Pitt News, like the Daily Collegian, had received a substantial portion of its advertising revenue from alcoholic beverage ads prior to the enactment of Act 199. But in 1998 alone, the Pitt News lost $17,000 in advertising revenue because of the law.

Pennsylvania, in contrast, argued that the law was necessary to curb both underage drinking (although many college students and all faculty are of at least the legal drinking age of 21) and binge drinking/alcohol abuse. The theory on the latter interest apparently was that if students didn't know where the cheap beer was being served because they couldn't find advertisements for it in college newspapers, then they wouldn't drink as much.

In July 2004, however, the U.S. Court of Appeals for the 3rd Circuit held in a case called *Pitt News* v. *Pappert* that Act 199 violated the First Amendment rights of the Pitt News and, by implication, other college newspapers in Pennsylvania.[95] The appellate court ruled that the law was "an impermissible restriction on commercial speech" (see Chapter 15) and that it was presumptively unconstitutional because it targeted a too narrow segment of the media—newspapers affiliated with colleges and universities—and thus conflicted with U.S. Supreme Court precedent on taxation of the press (see pages 70–74). The appellate court observed that Pennsylvania "has not pointed to any evidence that eliminating ads in this narrow sector [of the media] will do any good. Even if Pitt students do not see alcoholic beverage ads in the Pitt News, they will still be exposed to a torrent of beer ads on television and the radio, and they will still see alcoholic beverage ads in other publications, including the other free weekly Pittsburgh papers that are displayed on campus together with the Pitt News." The appellate court added that "in contending that underage and abusive drinking will fall if alcoholic beverage ads are eliminated from just those media affiliated with educational institutions, the Commonwealth relies on nothing more than 'speculation' and 'conjecture.'" The court suggested that rather than restricting the First Amendment speech and press rights of college newspapers, the "most direct way to combat underage and abusive drinking by college students is the enforcement of the alcoholic beverage control laws on college campuses." On an interesting side note, the appellate decision in favor of the Pitt News was authored by Judge Samuel A. Alito. Alito was nominated in late 2005 to the U.S. Supreme Court by President George W. Bush.

Mark Goodman, the executive director of the Student Press Law Center, which had filed a friend-of-the-court brief on behalf of the Pitt News, remarked: "Eight years after this law was enacted, a court has finally recognized how irrational and unconstitutional it was. The staff of The Pitt News deserves much credit for its willingness to fight this over the course of many years. College student newspapers around the state will be the beneficiaries of its courage." Pennsylvania attorney general spokesman Scott Connelly announced in September 2004 that his office would not appeal the appellate court's decision. The Student Press Law Center reported on its Web site in October 2004 that both the Pitt News and the Daily Collegian reported an increase in advertising sales following the end of the successful five-year legal battle.

---

95. *Pitt News* v. *Pappert*, 379 F. 3d 96 (2004).

BOOK BANNING

Jon Stewart, the quick-witted and acerbic host of Comedy Central's popular fake-news program, The Daily Show, earned a dubious accolade in 2005 when his best-selling book, "America (The Book): A Citizen's Guide to Democracy Inaction," was briefly banned from the Jackson-George Regional Library System in Mississippi. What provoked the ban? A digitally altered image of Supreme Court justices' faces superimposed on naked bodies. The director of the library system told a reporter for the Associated Press, "I've been a librarian for 40 years and this is the only book I've objected to so strongly that I wouldn't allow it to circulate. We're not an adult bookstore." The library board eventually rescinded its ban and put the book, which Wal-Mart stores refused to stock because of the satirical image, back on the shelves of its eight libraries. While the brief-lived ban suggests a humor-challenged library system in southern Mississippi that couldn't handle the naked truth, book banning is no laughing matter. In fact, it is all too common.

In the summer of 2003, Scholastic Press published "Harry Potter and the Order of the Phoenix." Like previous volumes in the series, the book immediately moved to the top of the best-seller lists. But the books in the series also top another list, according to the American Library Association.[96] They typically rank number one on lists of books that parents and censorship groups seek to have banned or restricted at school and public libraries. More serious books face similar challenges as well. David Guterson's "Snow Falling on Cedars," named book of the year in 1995 by the American Booksellers Association, was the frequent target of book banners in the late 1990s. The novel tells the story of a Japanese-American man charged with murder in Washington state after World War II. When the book, which sold more than three million copies, was put on reading lists at some high schools, parents objected, claiming it contained too much profanity, graphic violence, racial bigotry and sex. The most challenged book of 2004, according to the American Library Association, was "The Chocolate War" by Robert Cormier. It was the first time in five years that a Harry Potter book did not top the ALA's list.

Books are challenged for any number of reasons. Here is a list compiled by the American Library Association's Office for Intellectual Freedom of the most common reasons for challenging books between 1990 and 2000.[97] The reasons are listed in descending order:

- Sexual content
- Offensive language
- Unsuited to age group
- Occult/satanism
- Violence
- Homosexuality
- Promoting religion
- Nudity
- Racism
- Sex education
- Anti-family

---

96. Zeller, "Unfit: Harry Potter" and Wilgoren, "Don't Give Us Little Wizards."
97. Ibid.

While book-banning incidents usually pop up in widely separated local school districts, there is substantial evidence that most of these seemingly spontaneous eruptions have their genesis in well-orchestrated campaigns by national organizations with names like National Citizens for Excellence in Education, Association of Christian Educators, Eagle Forum, Concerned Women for America, and Focus on the Family. Entire school curricula for certain grade levels or subjects have also been attacked. In the accompanying box is a list of a few of the books commonly attacked. A complete list would take several pages.

LIST OF COMMONLY BANNED BOOKS

Several books by Judy Blume, a best-selling children's author

"Daddy's Roommate" by Michael Wilhoite

"Heather Has Two Mommies" by Leslea Newman

The Harry Potter series by J. K. Rowling

"Catching Alice" and the other Alice books by Clare Naylor

"Taming the Star Runner" by S. E. Hinton

The Captain Underpants series by Dav Pilkey

"Roll of Thunder, Hear My Cry" by Mildred Taylor

"Julie of the Wolves" by Jean Craighead George

"Scary Stories to Tell in the Dark" by Alvin Schwartz

"The Bridge to Terabithia" by Katherine Paterson

"The Chocolate War" by Robert Cormier

"The Diary of Anne Frank"

"The Martian Chronicles" by Ray Bradbury

"Catch-22" by Joseph Heller

If book banning is truly a constitutional issue, then the federal courts should be involved. And they have been, but only in a limited way. The one Supreme Court ruling on the matter is ambiguous and, in a sense, raised as many questions as it answered.

Members of the Board of Education of the Island Trees School District in eastern New York removed nine books from the high school library. Included among the banished books were "The Fixer" by Bernard Malamud, "Slaughterhouse Five" by Kurt Vonnegut, "The Naked Ape" by Desmond Morris, "Soul on Ice" by Eldridge Cleaver, and the "Best Short Stories by Negro Writers." Student council president Steven Pico and four other students challenged this action in the U.S. District Court. They argued that their First Amendment rights to read these books had been violated. But U.S. District Judge George Pratt rejected these arguments and ruled that a school board has the right to remove books that are irrelevant, vulgar, immoral, and in bad taste. The First Amendment was not violated by such action, Pratt ruled, citing a seven-year-old U.S. Court of Appeals decision, *President's Council District 25* v. *Community School Board.*[98] The judge's ruling came on the board of

---

98. 457 F. 2d 566 (1972).

education's motion for summary judgment. No trial was ever held to establish the facts, including the school board's motives for removing these volumes.[99]

The U.S. Court of Appeals for the 2nd Circuit reversed Judge Pratt's order and ordered the District Court to hold a trial. The appellate court stood by its earlier decision that permitted school authorities to remove vulgar or immoral books from the school library. But the court ruled that Steven Pico and the other students should have been given a chance at trial to persuade the court that the school board's ostensible justification for removing the books (that they were in bad taste, vulgar, etc.) was merely a pretext for the suppression of freedom of speech. The board could not ban the books if their decision to remove them was based on their political or moral disagreement with the content of the works.[100] In March 1982 the Supreme Court heard arguments in the case and three months later affirmed the Court of Appeals decision and returned the case to District Court for trial. However, the high court was fractured into several groups, and seven different opinions were written.

A school board cannot, under the First Amendment, remove books from a school library simply because it disapproves of the political ideas or philosophies expressed in the books.

The court's opinion was written by Justice William Brennan. A school board cannot, under the First Amendment, remove books from a school library simply because it disapproves of the political ideas or philosophies expressed in the books, wrote Justice Brennan. Books may be removed if they are persuasively vulgar or if they are educationally unsuitable. But the First Amendment guarantees to students a right to receive ideas, and the board of education cannot interfere with that right simply because it disagrees with those ideas. Brennan mustered the support of justices Thurgood Marshall and John Stevens behind his opinion.

Justice Harry Blackmun concurred with all of Brennan's opinion except his reference to a "right to receive ideas," a controversial notion Brennan promulgated. Blackmun said he based his opinion on a principle narrower and far more basic than the right to receive ideas. The state may not suppress exposure to ideas for the sole purpose of suppressing exposure to those ideas, he wrote. The fifth vote in the 5-4 decision came from Justice Byron White, who seemed dismayed at Brennan's exploration of constitutional issues. A trial was needed, he said, to find out what motivated the removal of the books. When the facts are established, he wrote, the court can develop constitutional law on the matter.

Chief Justice Warren Burger and Justices Lewis Powell, William Rehnquist, and Sandra O'Connor all dissented. All the dissenting opinions reflected the position that it was the responsibility of the school board, not of a federal court, to run the school. "The plurality [Brennan, Marshall, Blackmun, and Stevens] concludes that the Constitution requires school boards to justify to its teenage pupils the decision to remove a particular book from a school library,"[101] Burger wrote. Other dissenters echoed Burger's complaint.

The ruling was particularly unsatisfactory because the court failed to provide any clear guidance on an issue that is plaguing scores of school libraries across the nation. The splits within the court left even a careful reader of the decision with little certainty about how the court would act in a subsequent case. Four justices said school boards cannot remove books from a library for political or moral reasons; four justices said school boards can remove books for any reason; and Justice White refused to say where he stood on the issue. "We should not decide constitutional questions until it is necessary to do so," he wrote. Even the

99. *Pico* v. *Island Trees,* 474 F. Supp. 387 (1979).
100. *Pico* v. *Island Trees,* 638 F. 2d 404 (1980).
101. *Island Trees* v. *Pico,* 457 U.S. 853 (1982).

language in the court's opinion lacks clarity. Brennan said that a book can be removed from the shelves if it is "persuasively vulgar" or "educationally unsuitable." What do these terms mean?

No Supreme Court decision since 1982 has helped to clarify the meaning of the ruling in *Pico.* But school administrators have taken the strong mandate given to them in *Hazelwood School District* v. *Kuhlmeier*[102] to censor student publications and used it to justify the removal of books and other curricular material about which parents and other groups have complained. Courts have ruled such actions are permissible since they relate to the legitimate pedagogical concerns noted by the Supreme Court in *Hazelwood.*[103]

SUMMARY

In the 1960s courts ruled that both high school and college students enjoyed the rights of freedom of expression guaranteed by the First Amendment. But despite a seemingly broad First Amendment ruling by the Supreme Court in the case of *Tinker* v. *Des Moines,* lower courts refused to apply the high court's mandate and the censorship of high school publications and presentations continued. In 1988 even the Supreme Court turned its back on *Tinker* and gave high school authorities broad rights of censorship over newspapers produced as a part of the journalism curriculum. Today school authorities may censor school-sponsored publications or presentations for legitimate pedagogical reasons. They may also censor stories that materially and substantially interfere with the requirements of discipline in the school, that interfere with the rights of students, that generate health and welfare concerns, and that are obscene or vulgar. Censorship in the high school press is common at many schools; at other institutions, however, journalism seems to be robust. The college press suffers less censorship, but recently attempts have been made to censor college and university publications that present material deemed by authorities to be "politically incorrect," that present the college or administrators in a bad light, or that report on crime on the campus.

At least one federal court ruled that the kind of broad censorship high school administrators are permitted to impose under the *Hazelwood* ruling is not applicable at public colleges and universities. But another federal court in *Hosty* v. *Carter* suggested otherwise in 2005.

Book banning continues to be a problem at both school and public libraries. The courts have failed to articulate specific standards to guide librarians and school administrators and, at the same time, protect the rights of students and other library patrons.

TIME, PLACE AND MANNER RESTRICTIONS

Most attempts by the government to use prior censorship are based on the content of the material it seeks to censor. National security interests may be at stake, or a school official might fear that a news story in a student newspaper deals with a subject too mature for high school students. But the government can also base its attempts at prior censorship on other

102. 484 U.S. 260 (1988).
103. Kaplan, "Removal of Books."

Chapter 3

But the government can also base its attempts at prior censorship on other factors—specifically, the time, the place or the manner of the communication.

factors—specifically, the time, the place or the manner of the communication. There would certainly be few content-based objections to an individual presenting a speech on how to grow mushrooms. But the government (as well as citizens) would surely object if the speaker wanted to give the speech while standing in the middle of Main Street, or on a sidewalk at 2 a.m. in a residential neighborhood. These are called **time, place and manner restrictions.**

Such rules generate no serious First Amendment problems so long as they meet a set of criteria the courts have developed during the past 50 years. Let's look at the criteria first, and then see how they have been applied.

1. **The rule must be neutral as to content, or what the courts call content neutral, both on its face and in the manner in which it is applied.** A rule that is content neutral is applied the same way to all communications, regardless of what is said or printed. In other words, a law cannot permit the distribution of flyers promoting the construction of a new stadium, but restrict persons from handing out material in favor of tearing down a viaduct. A viable time, place and manner rule must be content neutral. In 2000 the Supreme Court ruled that a Colorado law that made it unlawful for any person within 100 feet of the entrance to a health care facility to approach within 8 feet of another person to pass out a handbill or a leaflet, display a sign, or engage in "oral protest, education or counseling" was content neutral. The statute prohibited unwanted approaches to all medical facilities in the state, *regardless* of the message the speaker was attempting to communicate, the court said.[104]

   A Gladstone, Mo., ordinance that prohibited property owners from placing political signs on their property more than 30 days before an election was ruled to be content based, not content neutral. The law singled out political speech for special regulation, but did not regulate for-sale signs or other such displays, the court said.[105] And the 9th U.S. Court of Appeals ruled that a Las Vegas ordinance that banned the distribution of commercial leaflets along Las Vegas Boulevard, commonly known as Las Vegas Strip, was not content neutral because it didn't apply to persons handing out other kinds of leaflets as well.[106]

   Sometimes a law will appear to be content neutral but is not because it gives far too much discretion to the officials who are assigned to administer it. Publishers in Calistoga, Calif., had to make an application to the city before they could install a news rack on a public sidewalk or parking way. Once they made the application, the city could, *in the city's discretion,* issue a permit for the news racks. The court said this standard was far too broad, that it placed no limits on the discretion of city officials who issued the permits. As such, it could be applied in a manner that was not content neutral.[107]

   In 1992 the Supreme Court struck down a county ordinance in Georgia that forced persons or groups seeking to have a rally or march to pay up to $1,000 to

104. *Hill* v. *Colorado,* 530 U.S. 703 (2000).
105. *Whitton* v. *Gladstone,* 354 F. 3d 1400 (1995).
106. *S.O.C.* v. *Clark County, Nevada,* 152 F. 3d 1136 (1998).
107. *Napa Valley Publishing Co.* v. *Calistoga,* 225 F. Supp. 2d 1176 (2002).

help defray county expenses in providing extra police protection and other services. The fee was variable and was supposed to reflect the county's costs, but whether it included all costs or just some, or whether the fee was required at all, was left to the discretion of the county administrator. "The decision [of] how much to charge for police protection or administration time—or even whether to charge at all—is left to the whim of the administrator," wrote Justice Harry Blackmun. "There are no articulated standards either in the ordinance or in the county's established practice," he added in the 5-4 ruling.[108]

2. **The law must not constitute a complete ban on a kind of communication.** There must be some alternative means of accomplishing this communication. In the 1980s several states sought to ban the polling of voters outside voting booths. The polling was conducted by the news media for several reasons, including an attempt to find out what kinds of people (age, political affiliation, occupation, etc.) voted for which candidates. Many of these statutes were struck down at least in part, the courts ruled, because the press could not ask these questions at any other place or in any other manner and expect to get the same data. There is no assurance, for example, that persons responding to such questions in a telephone survey had voted for anyone.[109] The ban on exit polling, then, constituted a complete ban on the kinds of questions reporters sought to ask.

3. **The state must articulate a substantial interest to justify this restraint on speech.** A ban against using loudspeakers to communicate a political message after 10 p.m. could surely be justified on the grounds that most people are trying to sleep at that time. A ban against passing out literature and soliciting money in the passageways between an airport terminal and the boarding ramps could also be justified by the state, which wants to keep these busy areas clear for passengers hurrying to board airplanes.[110] But attempts by the government to ban distribution of handbills on city streets because many people throw them away and cause a litter problem are typically rejected.[111] The state interest in keeping the streets clean can be accomplished by an anti-litter law. At times communities have attempted to raise aesthetic reasons to justify limiting or banning newspaper boxes. Some courts refuse to allow these concerns alone to justify limits on First Amendment freedoms, usually noting that many other common objects on the streets (telephone poles, trash cans, fire hydrants, street signs) are also eyesores.[112] Other courts have ruled that aesthetic considerations can be included in a community's justification for limits.[113] If the community can demonstrate a strong rationale for its aesthetic concerns, even a total ban on the placement of racks in a specific area might be acceptable. In 1996

108. *Forsyth County* v. *The Nationalist Movement,* 505 U.S. 123 (1992).
109. See, for example, *Daily Herald* v. *Munro,* 838 F. 2d 380 (1988).
110. See, for example, *International Society for Krishna Consciousness* v. *Wolke,* 453 F. Supp. 869 (1978).
111. *Schneider* v. *New Jersey,* 308 U.S. 147 (1939) and *Miller* v. *Laramie,* 880 P. 2d 594 (1994).
112. See *Providence Journal* v. *Newport,* 665 F. Supp. 107 (1987) and *Multimedia Publishing Co. of South Carolina, Inc.* v. *Greenville-Spartanburg Airport District,* 991 F. 2d 154 (1993).
113. See *Gold Coast Publications, Inc.* v. *Corrigan,* 42 F. 3d 1336 (1995) and *Honolulu Weekly Inc.* v. *Harris,* 298 F. 3d 1037 (2002).

the 1st U.S. Court of Appeals permitted the city of Boston to completely ban news racks from the public streets of a historic district of the city, where the architectural commission was trying to restore the area to what it looked like hundreds of years earlier.[114]

GUIDELINES FOR TIME, PLACE AND MANNER RESTRICTIONS

1. Rules must be content neutral.
2. Rules must not constitute a complete ban on communication.
3. Rules must be justified by a substantial state interest.
4. Rules must be narrowly tailored.

In addition to asserting a substantial interest, the state is required to bring evidence to court to prove its case. Southwest Texas State University in San Marcos attempted to restrict the distribution of a small community newspaper on its campus. It told the 5th U.S. Circuit Court of Appeals that it sought such restrictions in order to preserve the academic environment and the security of the campus, protect privacy on campus, control traffic, preserve the appearance of the campus, prevent fraud and deception, and eliminate unnecessary expenses. These were all laudable goals, but the court said the university presented no evidence to support the notion that restricting the sale of these newspapers to a few vending machines or direct delivery to subscribers on campus would accomplish these goals. "[T]he burden is on the defendants [university] to show affirmatively that their restriction is narrowly tailored to protect the identified interests. Defendants failed to carry this burden," the court ruled.[115] And in 2002 a U.S. District Court ruled that the city of Calistoga, Calif., would have to produce evidence to show how its new limits on the number of news racks in the city was arrived at, and how they would advance the goal of enhancing pedestrian safety and the flow of traffic on the streets and sidewalks.[116]

4. **The law must be narrowly tailored so that it furthers the state interest that justifies it, but does not restrain more expression than is actually required to further this interest.** "A regulation is narrowly tailored when it does not burden substantially more speech than is necessary to further the government's legitimate interests."[117] Officials in the city of Sylvania, Ga., believed they had a litter problem. The Penny-Saver, a weekly free newspaper, was thrown on the lawn or driveway of each residence in the city. Oftentimes residents just left the paper where it fell. These unclaimed papers were unsightly and sometimes wound up on the street or in the gutter. The city adopted an ordinance that made it illegal to distribute free,

---

114. *Globe Newspaper Company* v. *Beacon Hill Architectural Commission,* 100 F. 3d 175 (1996).
115. *Hays County Guardian* v. *Supple,* 969 F. 2d 111 (1992).
116. *Napa Valley Publishing Co.* v. *Calistoga,* 225 F. Supp. 1176 (2002).
117. *Ward* v. *Rock Against Racism,* 491 U.S. 781 (1989).

printed material in yards, on driveways or on porches. The publisher of the Penny-Saver sued, claiming the new law was a violation of the First Amendment. The Georgia Supreme Court agreed, rejecting the city's argument that this was a proper time, place and manner rule. The ordinance was certainly content neutral, but it was not narrowly tailored. The law blocked the distribution of the Penny-Saver but also barred political candidates from leaving literature on doorsteps, stopped many religious solicitors who hand out material, and blocked scores of others from passing out pamphlets door-to-door. In addition, the court ruled, the problem could be solved in other ways that do not offend the First Amendment. The city could require either the Penny-Saver publisher or the city residents to retrieve the unclaimed papers or could punish the publisher for papers that end up in the ditch or on the street.[118]

The City of Los Angeles adopted an ordinance banning the sale of goods or the solicitation of donations along the Venice Beach Boardwalk. The only exceptions were the sale of newspapers or other periodicals and solicitation or selling by nonprofit groups. City officials said the ordinance was needed to protect local merchants from unfair competition and to ensure the free flow of traffic on the boardwalk. The 9th U.S. Circuit Court of Appeals ruled that the ordinance was not narrowly tailored. If the city was truly concerned about unfair competition and traffic flow, there was no justification for allowing some vendors—those who sold newspapers or solicited for nonprofit groups—to use the boardwalk while barring all others. "There is no evidence," the court ruled, "that those without nonprofit status are any more cumbersome upon fair competition or free traffic flow than those with nonprofit status."[119]

A law or rule can be declared invalid for failing to pass any of the four tests just listed. The manner in which the rules are applied by the court (for example, how much justification must the state have?) is usually dependent on the kind of place to which the rule applies. The place is called a "forum" in the law, and what is called forum analysis has become quite popular with contemporary judges.

FORUM ANALYSIS

Courts have identified four kinds of forums:

Traditional Public Forum: Traditional public forums are public places that have by long tradition been devoted to assembly and speeches, places like street corners, public parks, the steps in front of a student union building or a plaza in front of city hall. The highest level of First Amendment protection is given to expression occurring in traditional public forums.

Designated Public Forum: Designated public forums are places created by the government to be used for expressive activities, among other things. A city-owned auditorium, a fairgrounds, a community meeting hall and even a student newspaper intended to be open for

---

118. *Statesboro Publishing Company* v. *City of Sylvania,* 516 S.E. 2d 296 (1999); see also *Houston Chronicle* v. *Houston,* 630 S.W. 2d 444 (1982) and *Denver Publishing Co.* v. *Aurora,* 896 P. 2d 306 (1995).
119. *Perry* v. *Los Angeles Police Department,* 121 F. 3d 1365 (1997).

use by all students are examples of designated public forums. First Amendment protections surely apply in such places, but the government has greater power to use time, place and manner rules to regulate speech and press in these areas than in traditional public forums.

Public Property That Is Not a Public Forum: Some kinds of public property not considered to be public forums are obvious—prisons and military bases, for example. But other kinds of public property are also regarded as off-limits for expressive activity. Concourses leading to boarding areas in airports are not considered public forums, although the public areas in the airport terminal (where the restaurants, shops and other facilities are located) are likely to be counted as designated public forums.[120] Courts in New York have ruled that subway stations are not public forums;[121] a court in South Dakota said that an interstate highway rest stop is not a public forum;[122] and a U.S. District Court in Oklahoma ruled in 1997 that the Oklahoma University computer network used by faculty and students is not a public forum.[123] At least three U.S. Courts of Appeals have had to decide whether the advertising space on the sides and backs of public transit buses constitute public forums. And the answer seems to focus less on where the space is located than on the transit systems' policies regarding the use of the space for advertising. Ad spaces on buses in both Chicago and New York were ruled to be designated public forums because the transit authorities permitted advertising for a wide variety of commercial, noncommercial and political advertising.[124] The 9th U.S. Circuit Court of Appeals in 1998 ruled that the buses in Phoenix were not public forums because the city sold space only to commercial advertisers. "The city has not designated the advertising space on the exterior of its buses as a place for general discourse," the court said.[125]

Private Property: Owners of private property, which includes everything from a backyard patio to a giant shopping mall, are free to regulate who uses their property for expres- sive activity. There are no First Amendment guarantees of freedom of expression on private property.

Let's examine briefly how the courts have treated First Amendment rights in a variety of public and private forums.

PUBLIC FORUMS

Public streets historically are regarded as places where people can speak and distribute handbills, pamphlets and other materials. But history isn't law, and before 1938 whether public streets were legally open to such activity was not a settled matter. But in the landmark case of *Lovell* v. *Griffin,*[126] the Supreme Court established that the First Amendment protects the distribution as well as the publication of ideas, opinions and news.

120. *International Society for Krishna Consciousness* v. *Lee,* 505 U.S. 672 (1992) and *Lee* v. *International Society for Krishna Consciousness,* 505 U.S. 830 (1992).
121. *Rogers* v. *New York City Transit Authority,* 89 N.Y. 2d 692 (1997).
122. *Jacobsen* v. *Howard,* 904 F. Supp. 565 (1995).
123. *Loving* v. *Boren,* DC WOkla. No. CIV. 96-657-A, 1/28/97.
124. *Planned Parenthood Association/Chicago Area* v. *Chicago Transit Authority,* 767 F. 2d 122 (1985) and *New York Magazine* v. *Metropolitan Transit Authority,* 136 F. 3d 123 (1998).
125. *Children of the Rosary* v. *City of Phoenix,* 154 F. 3d 972 (1998).
126. 303 U.S. 444 (1938).

The city of Griffin, Ga., had an ordinance that prohibited distribution of circulars, handbooks, advertising and literature of any kind without first obtaining written permission from the city manager. Under the law, the city manager had considerable discretion as to whether to give permission. Alma Lovell was a member of the Jehovah's Witnesses religious sect, an intense and ruggedly evangelical order that suffered severe persecution in the first half of this century. But the Witnesses doggedly continued to spread their word, passing out millions of leaflets and pamphlets and attempting to proselytize anyone who would listen.

Alma Lovell didn't even attempt to get a license before she circulated pamphlets, and she was arrested, convicted and fined $50 for violating the city ordinance. When she refused to pay the fine, she was sentenced to 50 days in jail. At the trial the Jehovah's Witnesses freely admitted the illegal distribution, but argued that the statute was invalid on its face because it violated the First Amendment guarantees of freedom of the press and freedom of religion.

On appeal the Supreme Court agreed that the law did indeed violate freedom of the press. Chief Justice Charles Evans Hughes wrote, "We think that the ordinance is invalid on its face" because it strikes at the very foundation of freedom of the press by subjecting it to license and censorship. The city argued that the First Amendment applies only to newspapers and regularly published materials like magazines. The high court disagreed, ruling that the amendment applies to pamphlets and leaflets as well: "These indeed have been historic weapons in the defense of liberty, as the pamphlets of Thomas Paine and others in our own history abundantly attest. The press in its historic connotation comprehends every sort of publication which affords a vehicle of information and opinion."[127]

"The press in its historic connotation comprehends every sort of publication which affords a vehicle of information and opinion."

Lawyers for Griffin also argued that the First Amendment was not applicable because the licensing law said nothing about publishing, but only concerned distribution. Again the court disagreed, noting that liberty of circulation is as essential to freedom of expression as liberty of publication. Chief Justice Hughes wrote, "Without the circulation, the publication would be of little value."

Public Streets

Nineteen months after the Lovell decision the Supreme Court handed down a second distribution decision, a ruling involving laws in four different cities. The four cases were decided as one. A Los Angeles ordinance prohibited the distribution of handbills on public streets on the grounds that distribution contributed to the litter problem. Ordinances in Milwaukee, Wis., and Worcester, Mass., were justified on the same basis—keeping the city streets clean.

An Irvington, N.J., law was far broader, prohibiting street distribution or house-to-house calls unless permission was first obtained from the local police chief. The police department asked distributors for considerable personal information and could reject applicants the law officers deemed not of good character. This action was ostensibly to protect the public against criminals.

The Supreme Court struck down all four city ordinances.[128] Justice Owen Roberts wrote for the court that cities can certainly enact regulations in the interest of public safety, health and welfare. Pedestrians, for example, could be prohibited from blocking a street or sidewalk in order to distribute pamphlets. And a city can certainly punish persons who litter the streets

127. *Lovell* v. *Griffin*, 303 U.S. 444 (1938).
128. *Schneider* v. *New Jersey*, 308 U.S. 147 (1939).

with paper. But a community cannot justify an ordinance that prohibits the distribution of handbills—conduct that is protected under the First Amendment—by asserting an interest in keeping the streets clean. The fourth ordinance, the one in Irvington, was declared unconstitutional because it was not content neutral. It gave police the discretion to determine who could express their ideas and who could not, Roberts said.

The following year the Supreme Court voided another anti-solicitation law, one enacted in New Haven, Conn. Solicitation of money for religious causes was prohibited unless the solicitors first gained the approval of local officials, whose job it was to determine what was and was not a "bona fide object of charity." Justice Roberts, writing for a unanimous court, ruled that a community could, in order to protect its citizens from fraudulent solicitations, require strangers in the community to establish identity and authority to act for the cause they purport to represent. A community could also adopt reasonable rules limiting the time such door-to-door solicitation might be made.

> But to condition the solicitation of aid for the perpetuation of religious views or systems upon a license, the grant of which rests in the exercise of a determination by state authority as to what is a religious cause, is to lay a forbidden burden upon the exercise of a liberty protected by the Constitution.[129]

Other Public Forums

Courts have ruled that a wide variety of public places are public forums for the purpose of communication. Government attempts to regulate speech and press activity in an airport, for example, have frequently been challenged on First Amendment grounds. (See, for example, *International Society for Krishna Consciousness* v. *Wolke*[130] and *International Society for Krishna Consciousness* v. *Lee.*[131]) Airports are created to facilitate air travel, and are often filled with hurried passengers who stream down concourses from one boarding area to another. Courts have generally ruled that the government has the right to limit the distribution of materials in the busy and crowded zones of an airport. Airport terminals, that area often containing shops, restaurants, rental car agencies and other businesses, are another matter. Generally, First Amendment concerns are more pronounced in these areas and a greater amount of speech activity is permitted. In 1992, however, the Supreme Court issued a pair of rulings that suggested the high court was having difficulty deciding how much solicitation should be permitted in air terminals. In the first case, *International Society for Krishna Consciousness* v. *Lee,*[132] a majority of the court ruled that airport terminals were not traditional public forums and that the government could forbid individuals to use the terminals to solicit money for any cause. But in the companion ruling, the high court declared that a government ban on the distribution of literature in these same terminals was a violation of the First Amendment, even though the terminal was not regarded as a traditional public forum.[133]

129. *Cantwell* v. *Connecticut,* 310 U.S. 296 (1940).
130. 453 F. Supp. 869 (1978).
131. 925 F. 2d 576 (1991).
132. 505 U.S. 672 (1992).
133. *Lee* v. *International Society for Krishna Consciousness,* 505 U.S. 830 (1992).

The first decision was explained in a lengthy opinion written by Chief Justice Rehnquist. The second ruling, however, was contained in a one-paragraph, unsigned opinion. Justices Kennedy and O'Connor shifted their votes in the two cases.

In 1981 the Supreme Court ruled that the state of Minnesota could regulate communication activities by a religious group, the Hare Krishnas, at the Minnesota State Fair. The crowds on the fairgrounds were too thick to permit the Krishnas to perform their ritualistic face-to-face solicitations. But the high court added that the group members could mingle with the crowds, talk with people, and propagate their views. The court added that the religious group members should also have the opportunity to have a booth at the fair like scores of other solicitors.[134]

Attempts by communities to regulate the street-corner vending machines that dispense newspapers and other publications is a common issue to confront the courts. Such regulations are permissible so long as the rules meet the normal tests for time, place and manner rules. In 1988 the Supreme Court voided a Lakewood, Ohio, ordinance because the city tied the placement of the machines to permit fees, insurance requirements, design standards and any other "such terms and conditions" the mayor deems reasonable and necessary. The high court ruled that the ordinance was invalid because it gave the mayor unbridled authority to reject a permit request. "It is apparent that the face of the ordinance itself contains no explicit limits on the mayor's discretion," wrote Justice William Brennan.[135] A similar regulation, struck down in New York, required vending machine owners to obtain permission from the city attorney to place their boxes on the streets, but the city council failed to give the city attorney any criteria to apply in the placement of these machines.[136]

What kinds of regulations are permissible? The government can charge a fee to those who seek to place the racks on public street corners or in other public places. The fee must be reasonable, that is, bear some resemblance to the costs incurred by the city or county to process and issue the permits. A fee for news rack space at the Atlanta airport was challenged because the charge exceeded the cost of processing the application and maintaining the racks. But the 11th U.S. Court of Appeals, sitting en banc, ruled that when a city or government acts as a proprietor, reasonable regulations may include a profit margin in the fee, similar to the kind of profit a private party would expect to earn for allowing someone to use a similar space.[137] In this case the airport used the fees it collected to help operate the terminal. Regulations regarding the location of the stands are also permissible, so long as they are reasonable. Rules that prohibit the placing of stands too close to fire hydrants or crosswalks are clearly acceptable.

Finally, rules on clustering or limits on the number of stands on a single corner are possible. California courts approved a Glendale ordinance that permits only eight newsstands in any one location and 16 on each side of a block. The ordinance also employed a preference system for newspapers wishing to place stands on the streets, giving priority to newspapers that are published most frequently and circulated most widely in Los Angeles County. The court said that space was limited and the city had an obligation to allocate it. The preference

134. *Heffron* v. *International Society,* 452 U.S. 640 (1981).
135. *Lakewood* v. *Plain Dealer Publishing Co.,* 486 U.S. 750 (1988).
136. *New York City* v. *American School Publications,* 509 N.E. 2d 311 (1987).
137. *Atlanta Journal and Constitution* v. *Atlanta Department of Aviation,* 322 F. 3d 129 (2003).

for one kind of newspaper over another was "simply a means of balancing the problem of public demand and supply."[138] Communities can also use a lottery to determine how to allocate the public space.[139]

Several states and cities have attempted to regulate the placement of billboards, with mixed results. The problem in such regulation is coping with the rights of store owners to advertise their businesses. The dilemma is best illustrated by a 1981 U.S. Supreme Court ruling on a San Diego billboard ordinance. The ordinance prohibited all outdoor advertising except on-site commercial signs that promoted goods or services offered by businesses on the premises. That is, owners of hardware stores could erect on their property signs that advertised materials sold in the hardware store. Acknowledging that the ban was prompted by substantial state interests in the aesthetic quality of the city and in traffic safety, the Supreme Court nevertheless struck down the city law. The flaw in the ordinance was the broad exemption granted for on-site commercial speech. "Insofar as the city tolerates billboards at all," Justice White wrote in the plurality court opinion, "it cannot choose to limit their content to commercial messages." The law is not content neutral; it reaches into the realm of protected speech, he wrote. To be constitutional, then, the ordinance must allow noncommercial (Save the Whales, Abortion Is a Crime, etc.) on-site billboards as well. A total ban on billboards, if properly justified, might also be acceptable.[140]

> *"Insofar as the city tolerates billboards at all, it cannot choose to limit their content to commercial messages."*

Are public television stations public forums? Does the public have a right to participate in determining what programming should be aired on a government-funded station or to appear on programs relating to public issues? In 1982 the 5th U.S. Circuit Court of Appeals ruled that the managers of public television stations enjoyed the same rights as managers of privately owned televisions to select programming to be broadcast.[141] While citizens may have a voice in setting broad policies regarding programming, they don't have the right to influence day-to-day programming choices. In 1998 the Supreme Court reinforced this earlier decision when it ruled that public television station managers can determine which political candidates will appear on political debates aired by the station. Ralph Forbes, a perennial independent candidate for Congress, was excluded from a debate sponsored by and aired on a public television station between the Democrat and Republican candidates for Arkansas' 3rd Congressional District seat. The Court of Appeals ruled that Forbes should have been included,[142] but the Supreme Court reversed. The high court ruled that public broadcasting stations do have the discretion to exclude candidates from political debates so long as the exclusion is not based on the candidate's views. The candidate debate was not a public forum, like a park or a street corner, but a "nonpublic" forum subject to reasonable restrictions, the court said. Justice Anthony Kennedy, writing for the six-person majority, noted that Nebraska public television stations had canceled their candidate debates in 1996 as a result of the earlier

---

138. *Socialist Labor Party* v. *Glendale,* 82 Cal. App. 3d 722 (1978).
139. *Honolulu Weekly Inc.* v. *Harris,* 298 F. 3d 1037 (2002).
140. *Metromedia* v. *San Diego,* 453 U.S. 490 (1981); see also *Donnelly* v. *Campbell,* 639 F. 2d 6 (1980); *Metromedia* v. *Baltimore,* 583 F. Supp. 1183 (1982); and *Norton* v. *Arlington Heights,* 433 N.E. 2d 198 (1982).
141. *Muir* v. *Alabama Educational Commission,* 656 F. 2d 1012 (1981), 688 F. 2d 1033 (1982); see also *Chandler* v. *Georgia Public Telecommunications Commission,* 917 F. 2d 486 (1990).
142. *Forbes* v. *Arkansas Educational Television Communications Network Foundation,* 22 F. 3d 1423 (1994); *Forbes* v. *The Arkansas Educational Television Commission,* 93 F. 3d 497 (1996).

Court of Appeals ruling. "A First Amendment jurisprudence yielding these results does not promote speech but represses it," Kennedy said. Even the dissenters agreed that the lower court was mistaken in ruling that every candidate on the ballot had a presumptive right to appear on the televised debate. The dissenters, however, argued that any decision to include or exclude a particular candidate must be based on "pre-established, objective criteria."[143]

Finally, in 1997 a U.S. District Court ruled that a public university's computer network was not a public forum. The University of Oklahoma, fearful of violating a state law that barred the distribution of obscene or indecent material over a computer-generated communication system, installed a two-tier access system to sites on the network. Anyone could gain access to a set of university-approved sites in the first tier. But users who sought access to a full-service server that carried a wider variety of sites had to click a button acknowledging that their use of the server was for legitimate research and teaching activities and that they were at least 18 years old. The limited access was challenged by a faculty member at the university, but the lawsuit failed when the professor was unable to introduce any evidence that his First Amendment rights had been violated. Nevertheless the court took the occasion to note that the university computer and Internet services did not constitute a public forum because there was no evidence that the facilities had ever been open to the general public or used for public communication. "The state, no less than a private owner of property, has the right to preserve the property under its control for the use to which it is lawfully dedicated. In this case the OU [Oklahoma University] computer and Internet services are lawfully dedicated to academic and research uses."[144] Although the issue was imperfectly argued at trial, the ruling was still the first judicial effort to define what kind of a forum is represented by a computer-generated communication system.

NONPUBLIC OR PRIVATE FORUMS

The cases just noted concern public forums. Courts have generally tolerated much more restriction on expression exercised in private forums—shopping centers and private residences, for example. Residential distribution and solicitation have consistently been a vexing problem as the rights of freedom of expression are measured against the rights of privacy and private property.

In 1943 the Supreme Court faced an unusual ordinance adopted by the city of Struthers, Ohio, which totally prohibited door-to-door distribution of handbills, circulars and other advertising materials. The law also barred anyone from ringing doorbells to summon householders for the purpose of distributing literature or pamphlets.

Justice Hugo Black wrote the opinion for the majority in the divided court. He said the arrest of Thelma Martin, another Jehovah's Witness, for ringing doorbells in behalf of her religious cause was a violation of her First Amendment rights. Door-to-door distributors can be a nuisance and can even be a front for criminal activities, Justice Black acknowledged. Further, door-to-door distribution can surely be regulated, but it cannot be altogether banned. It is a valuable and useful means of the dissemination of ideas and is especially important to those

143. *Arkansas Educational Television Commission* v. *Forbes,* 523 U.S. 666 (1998); see also *Alabama Libertarian Party* v. *Alabama Public Television,* 227 F. Supp. 2d 1213 (2002).
144. *Loving* v. *Boren,* DC WOkla. No. CIV-96-657-A, 1/28/97.

groups that are too poorly financed to use other, expensive means of communication with the people. Black said a law that makes it an offense for a person to ring the doorbell of house-holders who have appropriately indicated that they are unwilling to be disturbed would be lawful and constitutional. However, the city of Struthers cannot by ordinance regulate this decision on behalf of all its citizens—especially when such a rule clearly interferes with the freedom of speech and of the press. "The right of freedom of speech and press has broad scope. The authors of the First Amendment knew that novel and unconventional ideas might disturb the complacent, but they chose to encourage a freedom which they believed essential if vigorous enlightenment was ever to triumph over slothful ignorance."[145] The high court reinforced this ruling in 2002 when it ruled 8-1 that an ordinance in Stratton, Ohio, which prohibited any canvasser or solicitor to visit any home for the purpose of promoting or explaining any cause without first providing identification and obtaining permission from the mayor, was unconstitutional. Stratton is a village with less than 300 residents, about 50 miles south of Struthers, the community involved in the 1943 decision. Village officials interpreted "canvassers" to include Jehovah's Witnesses. Justice John Paul Stevens said in the majority opinion that the ordinance was so broad it appeared to include neighbors ringing one another's doorbells to solicit support for a political candidate or other political cause. "It is offensive, not only to the values protected by the First Amendment, but to the very notion of a free soci-ety," Stevens wrote. It was unthinkable in the United States that a citizen would have to get government permission before he or she could talk to a neighbor, he said. The decision, the high court said, did not limit communities from placing similar restrictions on persons con-ducting commercial activities or soliciting funds.[146] The Appellate Division of the New York Supreme Court ruled in 1996 that if a property owner tells the distributor of a free newspaper that he or she does not want the newspaper delivered, the distributor does not have a First Amendment right to continue to deliver the newspaper.[147]

The problem of dealing with distribution of materials at privately owned shopping cen-ters has also been a troubling one. In 1968, in *Amalgamated Food Employees Local 590* v. *Logan Valley Plaza,*[148] the Supreme Court ruled that the shopping center was the functional equivalent of a town's business district and permitted informational picketing by persons who had a grievance against one of the stores in the shopping center. Four years later in *Lloyd Corp.* v. *Tanner,*[149] the court ruled that a shopping center can prohibit the distribution of hand-bills on its property when the action is unrelated to the shopping center operation. Protesters against nuclear power, for example, could not use the shopping center as a forum. Persons protesting against the policies of one of the stores in the center, however, could use the center to distribute materials.

In 1976 the Supreme Court recognized the distinctions it had drawn between the rules in the *Logan Valley* case and the rules in the *Lloyd Corp.* case for what they were—restrictions based on content. The distribution of messages of one kind was permitted, while the distribution

---

145. *Martin* v. *City of Struthers,* 319 U.S. 141 (1943).
146. *Watchtower Bible & Tract Society of New York* v. *Village of Stratton, Ohio,* 536 U.S. 150 (2002); see also Greenhouse, "Court Strikes Down Curb."
147. *Tillman* v. *Distribution Systems of America, Inc.,* 648 N.Y.S 2d 630 (1996).
148. 391 U.S. 308 (1968).
149. 407 U.S. 551 (1972).

of messages about something else was banned. In *Hudgens* v. *NLRB*,[150] the high court ruled that if, in fact, the shopping center is the functional equivalent of a municipal street, then restrictions based on content cannot stand. But rather than open the shopping center to the distribution of all kinds of material, *Logan Valley* was overruled, and the court announced that "only when . . . property has taken all the attributes of a town" can property be treated as public. Distribution of materials at private shopping centers can be prohibited.

Just because the First Amendment does not include within its protection of freedom of expression the right to circulate material at a privately owned shopping center does not mean that such distribution might not be protected by legislation or by a state constitution. That is exactly what happened in California. In 1974 in the city of Campbell, Calif., a group of high school students took a card table, some leaflets and unsigned petition forms to the popular Pruneyard Shopping Center. The students were angered by a recent anti-Israel U.N. resolution and sought to hand out literature and collect signatures for a petition to send to the president and Congress. The shopping center did not allow anyone to hand out literature, speak or gather petition signatures, and the students were quickly chased off the property by a security guard. The students filed suit in court, and in 1979 the California Supreme Court ruled that the rights of freedom of speech and petitioning are protected under the California Constitution, even in private shopping centers, as long as they are "reasonably exercised."[151] The shopping center owners appealed the ruling to the U.S. Supreme Court, arguing that the high court's ruling in *Lloyd Corp.* v. *Tanner* prohibited the states from going further in the protection of personal liberties than the federal government. But six of the nine justices disagreed, ruling that a state is free to adopt in its own constitution individual liberties more expansive than those conferred by the federal Constitution.[152]

A state is free to adopt in its own constitution individual liberties more expansive than those conferred by the federal Constitution.

Courts in many states (Washington, Colorado, New Jersey, Oregon, New York and others) have interpreted their state constitutions as providing broader free speech and press rights than those provided by the First Amendment to the U.S. Constitution. This trend becomes particularly noticeable when the federal courts narrow the meaning of the First Amendment.

SUMMARY

The prior restraint of expression is permissible under what are known as time, place and manner regulations. That is, the government can impose reasonable regulations about when, where and how individuals or groups may communicate with other persons. Time, place and manner rules apply to both public forums (settings owned or controlled by a government, such as a public street or an airport) and private forums (privately owned settings, such as residences and shopping centers). In order to be constitutional, time, place and manner restraints must meet certain criteria:

1. The regulation must be content neutral; that is, application of the rule should not depend on the content of the communication.

150. 424 U.S. 507 (1976).
151. *Robins* v. *Pruneyard Shopping Center*, 592 P. 2d 341 (1979).
152. *Pruneyard Shopping Center* v. *Robins*, 447 U.S. 74 (1980).

2. The regulation must serve a substantial governmental interest, and the government must justify the rule by explicitly demonstrating this interest.

3. There cannot be total prohibition of the communication. The speakers or publishers must have reasonable alternative means of presenting their ideas or information to the public.

4. The rules cannot be broader than they need to be to serve the governmental interest. For example, the government cannot stop the distribution of literature on all public streets if it only seeks to stop the problem of congestion on public streets that carry heavy traffic.

OTHER PRIOR RESTRAINTS

Major issues regarding prior restraint have been outlined in the previous pages. Yet each year other instances of prior restraint are challenged in the courts, and frequently the Supreme Court is called on to resolve the issue. Here is a brief outline of some of these issues.

SON OF SAM LAWS

Americans have always been interested in crime and criminals. But in the past three decades our desire to know more about this sordid side of contemporary life has spawned a seemingly endless host of books and television programs about killers, rapists, robbers, hijackers and their victims. Indeed, it is often jokingly said of those accused of high-profile crimes that when they are captured they are more eager to contact an agent than a defense attorney. Efforts have been made by government to stop felons from receiving money that might be earned by selling stories about their crimes. Many civil libertarians say this is a prior censorship. The laws in question, which have been adopted in one form or another by 42 states and the federal government, are colloquially called "Son of Sam" laws after a serial killer in New York who was dubbed that name by the press. Before the Son of Sam (David Berkowitz) was caught, reports circulated that the press was offering to pay for the rights to his story. The New York legislature responded to those reports by passing a law that permits the state to seize and hold for five years all the money earned by an individual from the sale of his or her story of crime. The money is supposed to be used to compensate the victims of the crimes caused by the felon. The criminal/author collects what is left in the fund after five years.

Two separate challenges to the New York law were mounted in the late 1980s and early 1990s. Simon & Schuster contested the law when it was applied against the best-selling book "Wiseguys" (the basis for the film "GoodFellas"). Career mobster Henry Hill was paid for cooperating with the book's author, Nicholas Pileggi. Macmillan Publishing Co. also challenged the validity of the law when New York sought to seize the proceeds of Jean Harris' autobiography, "Stranger in Two Worlds," because some of the material in the work was based on her trial for the murder of her lover, diet doctor Herman Tarnower.

The statute was upheld in both federal and state courts. The 2nd U.S. Circuit Court of Appeals ruled in *Simon & Schuster* v. *Fischetti*[153] that the purpose of the law was not to suppress speech but to ensure that a criminal did not profit from the exploitation of his or her crime, and that the victims of the crime are compensated for their suffering. A compelling state interest is served, and the fact that this imposes an incidental burden on the press is not sufficient to rule the law a violation of freedom of expression.

But in late 1991 the U.S. Supreme Court disagreed and in an 8-0 decision ruled that the Son of Sam law was a content-based regulation that violated the First Amendment.[154] "The statute plainly imposes a financial disincentive only on a particular form of content," wrote Justice Sandra Day O'Connor. In order for such a law to pass constitutional muster, the state must show that it is necessary to serve a compelling state interest and that the law is narrowly constructed to achieve that end. The members of the high court agreed with the ruling of the lower court that the state has a compelling interest in ensuring that criminals do not profit from their crimes, but this law goes far beyond that goal; it is not narrowly drawn. The statute applies to works on any subject provided they express the author's thoughts or recollections about his or her crime, however tangentially or incidentally, Justice O'Connor noted. The statute could just as easily be applied to "The Autobiography of Malcolm X" or Thoreau's "Civil Disobedience" or the "Confessions of St. Augustine," she added. While Justice O'Connor specifically noted that this ruling was not necessarily aimed at similar laws in other states because they might be different, the decision has forced substantial changes in most of the existing laws. In Massachusetts, however, the Supreme Judicial Court of that commonwealth approved a probationary scheme that had clear earmarks of a Son of Sam law. Katherine Power, a 1970s radical who participated in a bank robbery in which a police officer was killed, surrendered to authorities in 1993 after spending 23 years as a fugitive. She pleaded guilty to her crimes and a trial court ordered the defendant to serve 20 years probation as part of her sentence. Attached to the probation sentence was a provision that Power could not in any way profit from the sale of her story to the news media during those 20 years. Power appealed the provision, citing the First Amendment and the Supreme Court ruling in *Simon & Schuster.* The Massachusetts high court rejected this appeal, arguing that a specific condition of probation (which frequently restricts a probationer's fundamental rights) is not the same as a Son of Sam law, which is a statute of general applicability.[155] So, are Son of Sam laws constitutional? They certainly can be, but most of the current laws are not narrowly tailored in such a way as to pass muster. Because the laws are content-based statutes, the state has to first demonstrate that a compelling state interest is at stake and then prove that the law does not bar more speech than is necessary to further that interest. The state has to convince the court that its law stops a criminal from profiting from his or her crime while the victim remains uncompensated. In addition the law must be aimed at only significant commercial exploitation, not at all expressive activity in which the author reflects his or her thoughts or recollections about the crime, however incidental they might be.

---

153. 916 F. 2d 777 (1990).
154. *Simon & Schuster, Inc.* v. *New York Crime Victims Board,* 502 U.S. 105 (1991); see also *Bouchard* v. *Price,* 694 A. 2d 670 (1998) and *Keenan* v. *Superior Court,* 40 P. 3d 718 (2002) in which courts in Rhode Island and California struck down similar laws.
155. *Massachusetts* v. *Power,* 420 Mass. 410 (1995).

PRIOR RESTRAINT AND PROTESTS

Two 1994 decisions by the Supreme Court focus on the prior restraint of those seeking to demonstrate or protest. In June the Supreme Court unanimously ruled that cities may not bar residents from posting signs on their own property. Margaret Gilleo had challenged the Ladue, Mo., ordinance by posting an 8-by-11-inch sign in a window of her house protesting the Persian Gulf War. The lower courts ruled that the ban on residential signs was flawed because the city did not ban signs on commercial property; the law favored one kind of speech over another. But the Supreme Court struck down the ordinance in a broader fashion, ruling that the posting of signs on residential property is "a venerable means of communication that is both unique and important. A special respect for individual liberty in the home has long been part of our culture and law," wrote Justice John Paul Stevens. "Most Americans would be understandably dismayed, given that tradition, to learn that it was illegal to display from their window an 8-by-11-inch sign expressing their political views," he added.[156]

In another ruling involving the right to protest, the high court upheld a Florida state court injunction that established a 36-foot buffer zone between an abortion clinic in Melbourne, Fla., and anti-abortion protesters.[157] The buffer zone, or ban on picketing, was designed to keep protesters away from the entrance to the clinic, the parking lot, and the public right-of-way. Chief Justice Rehnquist, who wrote the 6-3 ruling, said the ban "burdens no more speech than is necessary to accomplish the governmental interest at stake." The court did strike down, however, a 300-foot buffer zone within which protesters could not make uninvited approaches to patients and employees, as well as a buffer zone the same size around the houses of clinic doctors and staff members. The chief justice said a smaller zone or restriction on the size and duration of demonstrations would be constitutional.[*]

In 1995 the Supreme Court struck down an Ohio law (and for all intents and purposes laws in almost every other state in the nation) that prohibited the distribution of anonymous election campaign literature. Margaret McIntyre had circulated leaflets opposing an upcoming school levy, but failed to include her name and address on the campaign literature as required by law. She was fined $100. The state argued the statute was needed to identify those responsible for fraud, false advertising and libel, but seven members of the high court said the law was an unconstitutional limitation on political expression. "Under our constitution, anonymous pamphleteering is not a pernicious, fraudulent practice, but an honorable tradition of advocacy and of dissent," wrote Justice John Paul Stevens for the majority. "Anonymity is a shield from the tyranny of the majority." Stevens said anonymity might in fact shield fraudulent conduct, but our society "accords greater weight to the value of free speech than to the dangers of its misuse."[158]

---

[*]In 2003 the Supreme Court refused to permit two abortion clinics and the National Organization for Women to use the federal Racketeer Influenced and Corrupt Organizations Act (RICO; see p. 543 for a discussion of this law) when they sued anti-abortion activists who disrupted and blockaded abortion clinics in Chicago in the 1990s. The high court said the protests did not constitute extortion, a crime that might make the RICO law applicable. *Scheidler* v. *National Organization for Women,* 537 U.S. 393 (2003). The court implied that it was inappropriate to use the federal racketeering law as a weapon against political protests.

156. *City of Ladue* v. *Gilleo,* 512 U.S. 43 (1994).

157. *Madsen* v. *Women's Health Center,* 512 U.S. 753 (1994).

158. *McIntyre* v. *Ohio Elections Commission,* 514 U.S. 334 (1995).

The issue of home-posted political signs addressed by the Supreme Court in the case of Margaret Gilleo back in 1994 would rise again a decade later, but in a slightly different context—yard signs for candidates running for office. Across the country in the presidential election year of 2004, citizens challenged their local municipal ordinances that prohibited the posting of yard signs for political candidates.[159] As Dan Lewerenz reported that year for the Associated Press, "hundreds, probably thousands, of municipalities across the country have laws limiting when residents may plant campaign yard signs, how big those signs can be, even how many signs can sit in a single yard—restrictions that have almost universally been deemed unconstitutional."[160] Despite the fact that political speech is at the core of both the First Amendment and Meiklejohnian theory (pages 47–48), and despite the fact that judges in 2004 struck down the laws en masse, municipalities continue to enact these ordinances, which amount to unconstitutional prior restraints on expression.

In 2005, the U.S. Supreme Court considered a somewhat unusual case involving a prior restraint issued by a lower court against a lone individual who, like Margaret McIntryre and Margaret Gilleo, was engaged in protest-based expression. But unlike in those cases, this new dispute involved a very high-profile individual who actually had sought the court-ordered prior restraint—namely, attorney Johnnie L. Cochran Jr., who gained national fame for his successful defense in the 1990s murder case against former NFL and USC football star O.J. Simpson. The case of *Tory* v. *Cochran* centered on the speech activities of Ulysses Tory, who exercised his First Amendment right to express his opinion about Cochran in a very public forum by carrying signs on a public sidewalk. Tory, it seems, believed he had been treated badly by Cochran on a legal matter on which the attorney had represented Tory. Tory thus picketed in front of Cochran's offices on Wilshire Boulevard in Los Angeles, carrying signs with messages such as "Johnnie is a crook, a liar and a thief," "Can a lawyer go to HEAVEN? Luke 11:46" and "You've been a BAD BOY, Johnnie L. Cochran." Cochran claimed the statements constituted defamation and he sued Tory.

A trial court judge in 2002 granted Cochran's motion for a court order against such allegedly defamatory protests, and it issued a very broad and expansive permanent injunction as a remedy that forever prohibited Tory from all future speech in any public forum—regardless of content or context—about Cochran, an admitted public figure. Specifically, Ulysses Tory was permanently prohibited from

- standing, assembling or approaching within 300 yards of either Cochran or Cochran's place of business;
- carrying "in any public forum" signs or placards that mentioned Cochran; and
- "orally uttering statements about Cochran and/or Cochran's law firm" in any public forum.

It is important to note that the second and third bullet points apply in any public forum; they are not limited to the 300-yard boundary that applies to the first bullet point. A California appellate court upheld the order in 2003 in an "unpublished" opinion (while the opinion can be found online on LexisNexis, it is officially "unpublished" under California court rules,

159. Boas, "Front Yard Politics."
160. Lewerenz, "Local Governments."

meaning that it cannot be cited or used in any other case),[161] and the state Supreme Court refused to hear the case.[162] This forced Tory to take his dispute to the U.S. Supreme Court. The nation's high court faced the issue of whether a permanent injunction in a defamation action stopping all future speech anywhere about a well-known public figure violated the First Amendment free speech rights of Tory. Tory was represented at the Supreme Court by Duke University Law School's Erwin Chemerinsky. Chemerinsky, a leading First Amendment scholar, argued in a brief filed with the court:

> The stakes here are enormous. The California Court of Appeal's approach would allow every court in the country, in every defamation action, to issue a broad injunction as a remedy. Any act of defamation would mean that the speaker could be barred forever from saying anything—fact or opinion, true or false—about the defendant in any public forum. A newspaper that was found to have defamed a person could be perpetually enjoined from ever publishing anything about that individual. Such a permanent forfeiture of speech rights, especially about public figures and matters of public concern—which is exactly what occurred in this case—has no place in a country governed under the First Amendment.

Citing Chief Justice Charles Evan Hughes' 1931 majority opinion in *Near* v. *Minnesota* (see pages 74–76), Chemerinsky contended that a prior restraint is never a valid remedy for alleged defamation. Chemerinsky wrote in a court brief that "*Near* emphatically rejected the notion that injunctive relief is ever a permissible remedy in defamation cases, calling it the 'essence of censorship,' even though the injunction in that case followed a finding of defamation and involved false and anti-Semitic epithets—speech of minimal, if any, public value."

In an unusual bit of levity during oral argument in *Tory* v. *Cochran* in March 2005, Justice David Souter seemingly mocked the expansiveness of the injunction by noting that it would apparently sweep up even speech made by Chemerinsky on behalf of Ulysses Tory against Cochran in court. Looking at Chemerinsky, Souter queried, "How about you? You're in trouble too, aren't you?" And when Cochran's attorney, Jonathan Cole, acknowledged that all nine of the justices seemed to feel during questioning that the injunction was overbroad, Justice Antonin Scalia quipped back "very perceptive." It appeared, based on the justices' reactions during oral argument, that there would be a unanimous opinion in favor of Tory and striking down the injunction as fatally overbroad.

Just one week after the court heard oral argument, however, Cochran passed away at age 67 of an inoperable brain tumor. This seemingly rendered the injunction protecting him from Tory's picket signs meaningless and moot, but in April 2005 the Supreme Court accepted briefs from the parties on the issue of whether it should nonetheless issue a ruling on the merits. On May 31, 2005, the court ruled in the case of *Tory* v. *Cochran*,[163] initially noting that it "is not moot. Despite Johnnie Cochran's death, the injunction remains in effect. Nothing in its language says to the contrary." Yet the seven-justice majority opinion authored by Justice

---

161. *Cochran* v. *Tory*, 2003 Cal. App. Unpub. LEXIS 10227 (Cal. Ct. App. 2003).
162. *Cochran* v. *Tory*, 2004 Cal. LEXIS 2004 (Cal. 2004).
163. 125 S.Ct. 2108 (2005).

Stephen Breyer still avoided the critical issues in the case while holding the injunction was, as now applicable to Tory in light of the death of Cochran, overbroad. Breyer wrote:

> Johnnie Cochran's death makes it unnecessary, indeed unwarranted, for us to explore petitioners' basic claims, namely (1) that the First Amendment forbids the issuance of a permanent injunction in a defamation case, at least when the plaintiff is a public figure, and (2) that the injunction (considered prior to Cochran's death) was not properly tailored and consequently violated the First Amendment. . . . Rather, we need only point out that the injunction, as written, has now lost its underlying rationale. Since picketing Cochran and his law offices while engaging in injunction-forbidden speech could no longer achieve the objectives that the trial court had in mind (i.e., coercing Cochran to pay a "tribute" for desisting in this activity), the grounds for the injunction are much diminished, if they have not disappeared altogether. Consequently the injunction, as written, now amounts to an overly broad prior restraint upon speech, lacking plausible justification.

In reaching this conclusion, the nation's high court vacated the California appellate court's injunction and remanded the case back to state court. It was an odd and rather anticlimactic ending to a very interesting case that spanned issues of defamation, political protest and prior restraint.

SUMMARY

A wide variety of legal issues relate to prior restraint. In recent years the Supreme Court of the United States has voided a statute aimed at denying criminals the right to earn profits from books or films about their crimes and voided a city ordinance that barred residents from putting signs on their front lawns or in their windows. At the same time, the high court has permitted limited restrictions aimed at those seeking to protest abortion at a clinic in Florida.

HATE SPEECH/FIGHTING WORDS

Hate speech, words written or spoken that attack individuals or groups because of their race, ethnic background, religion, gender or sexual orientation, is a controversial but not altogether uncommon aspect of contemporary American life. Few people openly acknowledge a value in such speech, but there is a considerable debate over what to do about it. Most people agree that such invective can cause injury to the persons at which it is aimed, sometimes deep, lasting psychological injury. And it is argued that such speech should not be tolerated in an increasingly diverse society like that in the United States. If untempered enough, even words can provoke a violent response, something the state surely has an interest in preventing. But words are generally protected by the First Amendment, even words that can cause harm, like libelous accusations. How do you balance the need to protect the sensibilities of members of the community with the right to speak and publish freely, a right guaranteed by the First Amendment?

The Supreme Court endeavored to balance these issues more than 60 years ago when it ruled that those who print such invective in newspapers or broadcast them on the radio or paint them on walls or fences are generally protected by the Constitution, but those who utter the same words in a face-to-face confrontation do not enjoy similar protection. The case involved a man named Chaplinsky, who was a member of the Jehovah's Witness religious sect. Face-to-face proselytization or confrontation is a part of the religious practice of the members of this sect. Chaplinsky attracted a hostile crowd as he attempted to distribute religious pamphlets in Rochester, N.H. When a city marshal intervened, Chaplinsky called the officer a "God-damned racketeer" and a "damned fascist." The Jehovah's Witness was tried and convicted of violating a state law that forbids offensive or derisive speech or name-calling in public. The Supreme Court affirmed the conviction by a 9-0 vote. In his opinion for the court Justice Frank Murphy outlined what has become known as the **fighting words doctrine:**

"There are certain well-defined and narrowly limited classes of speech, the prevention and punishment of which have never been thought to raise any constitutional problems."

> There are certain well-defined and narrowly limited classes of speech, the prevention and punishment of which have never been thought to raise any constitutional problems. These include . . . fighting words—those which by their very utterance inflict injury or tend to incite an immediate breach of the peace. It has been well observed that such utterances are no essential part of any exposition of ideas, and are of such slight social value as a step to the truth that any benefit that may be derived from them is clearly outweighed by the social interest in order and morality.[164]

Fighting words may be prohibited, then, so long as the statutes are carefully drawn and do not permit the application of the law to protected speech. Also, the fighting words must be used in a personal, face-to-face encounter—a true verbal assault. The Supreme Court emphasized this latter point in 1972 when it ruled that laws prohibiting fighting words be limited to words "that have a direct tendency to cause acts of violence by the person to whom, individually, the remark is addressed."[165] It is important to note that the high court has given the state permission to restrict so-called fighting words because their utterance could result in a breach of the peace, a fight, a riot; not because they insult or offend or harm the person at whom they are aimed.

This test seems to work well in some kinds of cases. During the 1970s neo-Nazis sought to stage marches and hold rallies in communities that were particularly sensitive to such hate mongering, towns like Skokie, Ill., which has a large Jewish population. These communities tried a wide variety of means to block such demonstrations, but with little success. Courts consistently invalidated the laws, ruling that they were discriminatory or abridged constitutionally protected rights of free speech.[166] The Illinois Supreme Court, in a decision typical of several such rulings, declared that "Peaceful demonstrations cannot be totally precluded solely because the display [of the swastika] may provoke a violent reaction by those who view it. . . . A speaker who gives prior notice of his message has not compelled a confrontation with those who voluntarily listen."[167]

Hate speech is one thing, but what about symbolic acts that attempt to communicate the same kinds of messages, burning a cross on someone's lawn, for example? The Supreme Court faced this question in 1992 when it struck down a St. Paul, Minn., ordinance that forbade the display of a burning cross or a Nazi swastika or any writing or picture that "arouses

---

164. *Chaplinsky* v. *New Hampshire,* 315 U.S. 568 (1942).
165. *Gooding* v. *Wilson,* 405 U.S. 518 (1972).
166. *Collin* v. *Smith,* 578 F. 2d 1197 (1978); *Village of Skokie* v. *National Socialist Party,* 373 N.E. 2d 21 (1978).
167. *Village of Skokie* v. *National Socialist Party,* 373 N.E. 2d 21 (1978).

the anger, alarm or resentment in others on the basis of race, color, creed, religion or gender." Minnesota courts had approved the law, saying the phrase "arouses anger, alarm or resentment in others" was another way of saying "fighting words." But the statute violated the First Amendment, the high court said, because it was content based—that is, it only applied to fighting words that insult or provoke violence on the basis of race, color, creed or gender. What about fighting words used to express hostility toward someone because of their political affiliation, or their membership in a union or the place where they were born? Justice Antonin Scalia asked. The city has chosen to punish the use of certain kinds of fighting words, but not others, he said. The majority of the court agreed that cross burning was a reprehensible act, but contended there were other laws that could be used to stop such terroristic threats that did not implicate the First Amendment, such as trespass or criminal damage to property. Eleven years later the high court revisited the issue in a case involving Virginia's law against cross burning and ruled that a state could proscribe cross burning without infringing on First Amendment freedoms, so long as the state made it a crime to burn a cross *with the purpose to intimidate the victim.* The intimidation factor is the key, Justice Sandra Day O'Connor wrote. The state would have to prove that the cross burner intended to intimidate the victim; the threat could not be inferred simply because a cross was burned on the victim's lawn.[168]

The efforts to control hate speech in the past two decades have focused particularly on public schools and universities. More than 300 colleges promulgated speech codes in the 1980s and early 1990s, but after several court rulings against such policies, the school policies were either abandoned or simply unenforced.[169] The courts tended to follow the principles from *Chaplinsky* and *Gooding* that limit prosecution of such hate speech to face-to-face encounters that could result in physical injury or provoke violent acts. Public schools seem to be the focus of attempts to control uncivil rhetoric in the new century, as local school boards try to reduce instances of sexual harassment and bullying, which have been cited as the possible cause of shootings at some schools. But even in such circumstances the schools must abide by the limits imposed by the First Amendment. As one federal appellate court observed in 2002, "there is no constitutional right to be a bully. On the other hand, confining prohibited speech to that which constitutes 'harassment' is not alone sufficient to ensure constitutionality."[170] The appellate court in that case, *Sypniewski* v. *Warren Hills Regional Board of Education,* declared unconstitutional, on First Amendment grounds, that part of a New Jersey public school's racial harassment policy that was directed at speech that "creates ill will." The court also issued an injunction prohibiting the enforcement of the same policy as it was used by the school to prevent a student from wearing a T-shirt emblazoned with the word "Redneck." The shirt, based upon the work of "Blue Collar Comedy Tour" comedian Jeff Foxworthy, listed the "Top 10 Reasons You Might Be a Redneck Sports Fan," none of which involved racist, sexist or homophobic messages. The school, however, argued that the term "redneck" connoted racial intolerance and was akin to a "gang signifier" at the school, which had recently experienced racial tension. But the appellate court found "little or no evidence that the word 'redneck' had been used to harass or intimidate, or otherwise to offend," and it

168. *Virginia* v. *Black,* 538 U.S. 343 (2003); see also Greenhouse, "Justices Allow Bans."
169. See, for example, *John Doe* v. *University of Michigan,* 721 F. Supp. 852 (1989) and *UWM Post* v. *Board of Regents of the University of Wisconsin,* 774 F. Supp. 1163 (1991).
170. *Sypniewski* v. *Warren Hills Regional Board of Education,* 307 F. 3d 243, 264 (2002), cert. den. 538 U.S. 1033 (2003).

concluded that the policy could not be used to stop students from wearing the Foxworthy T-shirt in question.

Just one year earlier, a policy drafted by the school board in State College, Pa., was declared unconstitutional by a federal appeals court because it was vague and overbroad and would punish students for "simple acts of teasing and name calling." A lawsuit against the policy was filed in behalf of two students who said they feared they would be punished if they expressed their religious belief that homosexuality is a sin. The district defined harassment as verbal or physical conduct based on race, sex, national origin, sexual orientation or other personal characteristics that has the effect of creating an intimidating or hostile environment. Examples of such harassment included jokes, name-calling, graffiti and innuendo as well as making fun of a student's clothing, social skills or surname. The appeals court agreed that preventing actual discrimination in school was a legitimate, even compelling, government interest. But the school district's policy was simply overbroad, prohibiting a substantial amount of speech that would not constitute actionable harassment under either federal or state law.[171] The government cannot prohibit invective or epithets that simply injure someone's feelings or are merely rude or discourteous. The Pennsylvania ruling mirrors other similar decisions throughout the nation that pose a real dilemma for school administrators and legislators who are seeking to reduce the verbal aggressiveness common on many school yards.

At the college level, the difference between unprotected harassment and protected expression that merely offends was clarified by the Office of Civil Rights (OCR) of the U.S. Department of Education in a July 28, 2003, memorandum. That memorandum, authored by Gerald Reynolds, assistant secretary for the OCR at the time, provides that harassment

> must include something beyond the mere expression of views, words, symbols or thoughts that some person finds offensive. Under OCR's standard, the conduct must also be considered sufficiently serious to deny or limit a student's ability to participate in or benefit from the educational program. Thus, OCR's standards require the conduct be evaluated from the perspective of a reasonable person in the alleged victim's position, considering all the circumstances, including the alleged victim's age.

This statement is important because many public universities today have policies that, although they are no longer called or referred to as speech codes, nonetheless restrict students' expressive rights. A Philadelphia-based organization called the Foundation for Individual Rights in Education (FIRE) aggressively challenges such policies while it simultaneously defends college students' rights of free speech. FIRE keeps tabs on these policies online at http://www.speechcodes.org and encourages students to come forward with instances of campus censorship. In 2003, for instance, FIRE was successful in having a federal court issue an injunction prohibiting Shippensburg University in Pennsylvania from enforcing provisions of its speech code (the university called its policy a "code of conduct" rather than a speech code in a failed attempt to avoid First Amendment issues).[172] The court wrote that Shippensburg University's speech code "could certainly be used to truncate debate and free expression by students." In 2004, the university settled the lawsuit brought by FIRE and agreed to change its

171. *Saxe* v. *State College Area School District*, 240 F. 3d 200 (2001).
172. *Bair* v. *Shippensburg University*, 280 F. Supp. 2d 357 (2003).

speech code. The code had been applied by Shippensburg University to order students to take down posters denouncing Osama bin Laden, according to the deposition testimony of a resident advisor at the university.[173] FIRE, along with the Liberty Legal Institute and the Alliance Defense Fund, scored another victory in 2004 when a federal judge declared the speech code at Texas Tech University unconstitutionally overbroad as applied to speech in the public forums at the Lubbock-based public university.[174] U.S. District Court Judge Sam Cummings observed that "the students' interests in having a true public forum open to their free-expression interests must predominate" in these settings on campus. FIRE continued its "Speech Code Litigation Project" in 2005, filing a federal lawsuit in October of that year called *Dews* v. *Troy University* contending that the speech policies at Troy University, an Alabama public state university, are overbroad and vague (see page 12). The case was not resolved when this book went to press.

Hate speech is not a new problem in America, but for the first time in many years the courts have been called in to determine just how far the state may go in limiting what people say and write about other people when their language is abusive or includes racial, ethnic or religious invective. In the early 1940s the Supreme Court ruled that so-called fighting words could be prohibited, but these words have come to mean face-to-face invective or insults that are likely to result in a violent response on the part of the victim. The high court voided a St. Paul, Minn., ordinance that punished such abusive speech because, the court said, the law did not ban all fighting words, merely some kinds of fighting words (i.e., racial or religious invective) that the community believed were improper. The decision in this case has sharply limited attempts by state universities and colleges and public schools to use speech codes to discourage hate speech or other politically incorrect comments or publications.

SUMMARY

THE FIRST AMENDMENT AND ELECTION CAMPAIGNS

The First Amendment is clearly implicated in any election campaign. Candidates give speeches, publish advertising, hand out leaflets, and undertake a variety of other activities that clearly fall within the ambit of constitutional protection. But since the mid-1970s the First Amendment and political campaigns have intersected in another way as well. Attempts by Congress and other legislative bodies to regulate the flow of money in political campaigns have been consistently challenged as infringing on the right of freedom of expression.

Campaign reform laws tend to fall into one of two categories: those that limit how much candidates and their supporters can spend on the election, and those that limit how much money people can contribute to candidates and political parties. The courts have tended to find more serious First Amendment problems with the laws that limit spending than the laws that limit contributions, although this is not always the case. Any attempt to explain the law in this area

173. Associated Press, "Shippensburg Agrees."
174. *Roberts* v. *Haragan*, 346 F. Supp. 2d 853 (N.D. Tex. 2004).

begins with the 1976 Supreme Court ruling in *Buckley* v. *Valeo*.[175] In that case the high court said that 1974 amendments to the 1971 Federal Election Campaign Act that limited how much money candidates for federal office could spend on their campaigns were unconstitutional because they reduced "the quantity of expression by restricting the number of issues discussed, the depth of their exploration, and the size of the audience reached." The justices apparently recognized that the nation had moved from the town-hall democracy of the late 18th century to the media-dominated politics of modern times. Limits on spending implicated the First Amendment because "virtually every means of communicating ideas in today's mass society requires the expenditure of money," the court ruled. The limit on campaign spending "heavily burdens core First Amendment expression."

But the court looked at the amendments limiting campaign contributions differently. In *Buckley* the high court upheld limits on how much money an individual or an organization can contribute to a candidate for federal office. These laws were justified by Congress as a means of preventing both corruption and the appearance of corruption in the electoral process that could occur when candidates receive large political contributions. Remember, the court decision was rendered in the wake of the corruption revealed in the Nixon administration by the Watergate scandals. Since 1976 the high court has frequently expressed its willingness to accept limits on campaign contributions.

In 2001 the high court in a 5-4 vote upheld another portion of the 1974 amendments, which limited how much political parties can contribute to a candidate's campaign for federal office. Justice David Souter echoed the rationale of the earlier ruling when he wrote that unlimited contributions might give the appearance of corruption, something Congress has a right to prevent. "Parties function for the benefit of donors whose object is to place candidates under obligation, a fact that parties cannot escape."[176] The law places limits on how much can be spent, up to $33,780 in coordination with a candidate for the House of Representatives and up to $1.6 million to assist a Senate candidate. The amount varies based on the size of the district or the state. This money is usually spent for advertising for the candidate by the party.

The high court reiterated this position in 2000 when it upheld a Missouri statute that restricted contributions to candidates for state office to a maximum of $1,075. Justice David Souter said in his opinion for the court that the ruling in *Buckley* applied not only to federal regulation of campaign finance, but to state regulation as well.[177] In 2003 the high court upheld another section of the 1971 Federal Election Campaign Act that banned direct corporate contributions to candidates for federal office. A lower court had held the law was unconstitutional when applied to a nonprofit anti-abortion group, North Carolina Right to Life Inc., which, while organized as a corporation, had no shareholders. Justice David Souter, writing for the seven-person majority, said: "Restrictions on political contributions have been treated merely as 'marginal' speech restrictions subject to relatively complaisant [agreeable, obliging] review under the First Amendment, because contributions lie closer to the edges than to the core of political expression." Corporate contributions, he said, are the furthest from the core of political expression, since corporations' First Amendment speech and association

---

175. 424 U.S. 1 (1976).
176. *Federal Election Commission* v. *Colorado Republican Federal Campaign Committee,* 533 U.S. 431 (2001).
177. *Nixon* v. *Shrink Missouri Government PAC,* 528 U.S. 377 (2000).

interests are derived largely from those of their members.[178] So generally speaking, laws regulating contributions have passed muster under the First Amendment.

BIPARTISAN CAMPAIGN FINANCE REFORM ACT

In 2002 Congress passed the most comprehensive campaign reform legislation since the mid-1970s, the Bipartisan Campaign Finance Reform Act. The new law contains 15,000 words, but at its core are three major provisions.

- National political parties and their committees are prohibited from accepting or spending "soft money," the large unlimited contributions by corporations, unions and individuals. State and local political parties can accept up to $10,000 from individuals to fund voter-registration drives or get-out-the-vote efforts in federal elections. But these efforts can't refer to any identified candidate for federal office, and the money must be raised locally.
- Corporations, unions or other interest groups cannot use soft money to pay for "electioneering communications," television advertising that refers to specific candidates for federal office and that is broadcast within 30 days of a primary election or 60 days of a general election. These groups can only use money from their political action committees to pay for such ads, and these committees are subject to contribution limitations.
- Limits on "hard money" contributions, that is, contributions to candidates from individuals, have been increased. A person may now give a total of $95,000 in each two-year election cycle (up from $50,000) to all federal candidates, political parties and political action committees combined. A person may contribute $2,000 per election directly to a federal candidate (up from $1,000), and $25,000 to a political party, up from $20,000.

In December 2003 the Supreme Court rejected a constitutional challenge to the main provisions of the law.[179] Several opinions were written on the various parts of the complicated law, but in simple terms, the court upheld most aspects of the law by a 5-4 vote. The dissenters invoked the First Amendment, rejecting the notion that the huge soft-money contributions that generated the law presented the problems of electoral corruption that the high court had used to support its ruling in *Buckley* 27 years earlier. "Apparently, winning in the marketplace of ideas is no longer a sign that the ultimate good has been reached by free trade in ideas," Justice Clarence Thomas wrote. "It is now evidence of corruption."

But the majority, led by Justices Sandra Day O'Connor and John Paul Stevens, rejected that argument. "This crabbed view of corruption, and particularly the appearance of corruption, ignores precedent, common sense, and the realities of political fund-raising exposed by the record in this litigation," they wrote. The record demonstrates the manner in which political parties have sold the access to federal candidates and officeholders, the pair added. "It was not unwarranted for Congress to conclude that the selling of access gives rise to the appearance of corruption." The limits on so-called electioneering communication by unions

178. *Federal Election Commission* v. *Beaumont,* 539 U.S. 146 (2003).
179. *McConnell* v. *Federal Election Commission,* 540 U.S. 93 (2003). See also, Greenhouse, "Justices, in a 5-to-4 Decision, Back Campaign Finance Law."

and corporations, what many saw as a vulnerable port of the law, were also upheld and were discussed in only six pages of 119 pages of the majority opinion.

The new federal law applies only to federal candidates. But some states have been busy as well attempting to resolve their own campaign finance and election problems. A voter initiative in Washington state was approved in 1992 that limited the use of donations made to political parties to what are called "party-building activities," actions such as voter registration drives or political polling. Parties could not use such funds to support candidates with political advertising or direct mail promotions. The Washington Supreme Court ruled that the law was unconstitutional. Justice Barbara Madsen said that rulings by federal courts, including the U.S. Supreme Court, place sharp limits on the power of the state to regulate political advertising. "The right to speak out at election time is one of the most zealously guarded under the First Amendment," she said.[180]

But in 2002 the 2nd U.S. Court of Appeals ruled that Vermont lawmakers could constitutionally impose spending limits of $300,000 on candidates for governor, and $100,000 on candidates for lieutenant governor. The state argued the limits were needed to prevent the "corrupting influence of excessive fund-raising and campaign spending." The two judges who supported the limits said the state had the right to adopt rules it believed were "necessary to safeguard the democratic process and the public's faith in its representatives." A third judge on the panel said the rules violated candidates' First Amendment rights.[181] In September 2005, the U.S. Supreme Court granted a petition for a writ of certiorari in the Vermont case of *Randall* v. *Sorrell,* deciding to consider and review the 2nd Circuit's opinion.[182]

SUMMARY   Efforts to reform the expensive American electoral process seem to be gaining momentum in the early part of the 21st century, but under the Constitution there is only so much that the law can do. The Supreme Court has ruled that while it is permissible to place a limit on how much money one person or business can donate to a campaign, it may be a violation of the First Amendment to place a limit on how much a candidate may spend. Because the presentation of campaign messages via the mass media is so much a part of the current electoral process and because sending such messages costs money, campaign spending is tied closely to freedom of speech and press and is protected by the First Amendment, the court has ruled. In 2003 the high court ruled that a massive campaign-return law adopted by Congress that included some limits on campaign spending was constitutional.

THE FIRST AMENDMENT AND THE INFORMATION SUPERHIGHWAY

The First Amendment was drafted and approved in the late 18th century, a time when newspapers, magazines, books and handbills comprised the press that was intended to be protected by the constitutional provision. As each new mass medium has emerged—radio,

180. Galloway, "Political Spending Unchecked."
181. Stout, "Federal Appeals Panel."
182. *Randall* v. *Sorrell,* 126 S. Ct. 35 (2005).

motion pictures, over-the-air television, cable television and so forth—the courts have had to define the scope of First Amendment protection appropriate to that medium. And so it is with the Internet, computer-mediated communication. The next 13 chapters of this text contain references to laws regarding libel, invasion of privacy, access to information, obscenity, copyright and advertising, and they contain references to how these laws are being applied to computer-mediated communication. These emerging rules have in no small part been dictated by decisions by the federal courts that speak to the general question of the application of the First Amendment to the Internet. The next few pages focus on this general question.

How the government regulates a message communicated by any medium is generally determined by the content of that particular message. A plea to burn down city hall and kill the mayor is sedition; a call to vote the mayor out of office is not. Calling Mary Smith a thief is libelous; calling Mary Smith a good student is not. The law is applied, then, based on what the message says. But in some instances the regulation of a message is based on more than the content of the message; it is also influenced by the kind of medium through which the message is transmitted. As some have stated, there is a medium-specific First Amendment jurisprudence in the United States, meaning that the scope and amount of protection that speech receives will be influenced by the nature of the medium on which it is conveyed.

At least four categories of traditional communications media were in common use when the Internet first burst onto the scene, and even today each is regulated somewhat differently by the law. The printed press—newspapers, magazines, books and pamphlets—enjoys the greatest freedom of all mass media from government regulation. The over-the-air broadcast media—television and radio—enjoy the least amount of freedom from government censorship. Cable television is somewhere between these two, enjoying more freedom than broadcasting but somewhat less than the printed press. Few limits are placed on the messages transmitted via the telephone, and those that are must be very narrowly drawn.[183] There are some ifs, ands, or buts in this simple outline, but it is an accurate summary of the hierarchy of mass media when measured by First Amendment freedom. It should be noted, however, that many experts predict growing convergence in the mass media that will blur the lines among these four distinct media. The 1996 Telecommunications Act, for example, gave telephone companies the power to transmit television signals via phone lines to compete with cable television. At the same time cable companies were given the right to provide telephone service by buying phone systems or using the wires currently devoted to cable to carry telephone calls.[184]

Courts have distinguished among these four media by applying four basic criteria:

- **The capacity of the medium to carry messages.** Are there an unlimited number of channels, or is capacity limited in some way?
- **The traditional relationship between the government and the medium.** Has the medium traditionally been free, or has regulation been imposed from the inception of the medium?

183. *Sable Communications* v. *FCC*, 492 U.S. 115 (1989).
184. See Lively, "Information Superhighway"; see also "Message Is the Medium."

- **The pervasiveness or invasiveness of the medium.** What role does the receiver play in receiving the message? Does the receiver have to actively seek the message, or can he or she be a largely passive recipient?
- **The accessibility of the medium.** How easy is it for children to gain access to the messages communicated by the medium?

Why is the printed press allotted the most protection by the First Amendment? Using these criteria it is obvious. There are no physical limits on the number of newspapers and magazines or handbills that can be published. (Economic limits are another matter, but one not considered by the courts in this context.) Since the founding of the Republic in 1789, the printed press has traditionally been free. The receiver must generally take an active role in purchasing a book or a magazine or newspaper. Young people must have the economic where-withal to buy a newspaper or magazine, and then have the literacy skills to read it.

It is just as obvious, applying these criteria, why broadcast media have fared the poorest in First Amendment protection. There is an actual physical limit on the number of radio and television channels that exist. All but a very few are in use. Since not everyone who wants such a channel can have one, it is up to the government to select who gets these scarce broadcast frequencies and to make certain those who use the frequencies serve the interests of all listeners and viewers. Because of this and other reasons, broadcasting has been regulated nearly since its inception. It has no tradition of freedom. All the receiver must do to listen to the radio or watch television is to flick a switch. Even children who don't know how to read can do this; radio and television are easily accessible to kids.

Cable television and telephones fit somewhere in between. There is potentially an unlimited capacity for messages to be transmitted by each medium. Both have been historically regulated, but not to the extent that broadcasting has been regulated. Although a receiver can watch a cable television channel as easily as he or she can watch an over-the-air channel, the receiver must take a far more active role by subscribing to a cable system. While this action may seem like a trivial distinction, the courts have made much of it. Judges have presumed that the persons who subscribe to cable television should know what they will receive. Federal law mandates that cable television companies provide safeguards (called cable locks) for parents who want to shield their children from violent or erotic programming.* Such screening technology is only now coming into use for over-the-air television. The use of a telephone also requires a more active role by the receiver than simply switching on a radio or television set.

The application of these criteria over the past 60 years by judges in a wide variety of cases has resulted in the establishment of a hierarchy of mass media in relation to the First Amendment—the hierarchy just outlined. Where do computer-mediated communication systems fit into this hierarchy? In June 1997 the Supreme Court ruled in a 7–2 decision that communication via the Internet deserves the highest level of First Amendment protection, protection comparable to that given to newspapers, magazines and books.[185] (The dissenters on the court agreed with this portion of the ruling.) The high court made this decision as it ruled that the central provisions of the 1996 Communications Decency Act that restricted the transmission of indecent material over the Internet violated the U.S. Constitution. Recognizing that each medium

---

*But in *U.S.* v. *Playboy Entertainment Group Inc.,* 529 U.S. 803 (2000), the Supreme Court suggested that cable television enjoys the full protection of the First Amendment. This notion has yet to be fleshed out by the court.

185. *Reno* v. *American Civil Liberties Union,* 521 U.S. 844 (1997).

of communication may present its own constitutional problems, Justice John Paul Stevens wrote that the members of the high court could find no basis in past decisions for "qualifying the level of First Amendment scrutiny that should be applied to this medium [the Internet]."

The court rejected the notion prevalent among those in Congress who voted for the Communications Decency Act that communication via the Internet should be treated in the same manner as communication via over-the-air radio and television. The court said that the scarcity of frequencies that had long justified the regulation of broadcasting did not apply in the case of the Internet, which, it said, can hardly be considered a "scarce" expressive commodity. "The Government estimates that as many as 40 million people use the Internet today, and that figure is expected to grow to 200 million by 1999," Justice Stevens wrote. "This dynamic, multifaceted category of communication includes not only traditional print and news services, but also audio, video, and still images, as well as interactive, real time dialogue. Through the use of chat rooms, any person with a phone line can become a town crier with a voice that resonates farther than it could from any soapbox," Stevens added.

Neither before nor after the enactment of the Communications Decency Act have the "vast democratic fora of the Internet been subject to the type of government supervision and regulation that has attended the broadcast industry," Justice Stevens wrote. There is no tradition of censorship in cyberspace. The court added that computer-mediated communication is not invasive as are radio and television. Communications over the Internet do not "invade" an individual's home or appear on one's computer screen "unbidden." Almost all sexually explicit images are preceded by warnings as to content, and odds are slim that a user would come across a sexually explicit site by accident.

Finally, the Supreme Court rejected the government's assertion that the shielding of children from indecent communication was critical if the Internet was to grow as an important communications medium, that adults would not embrace the Internet because of the risk of exposing their children to offensive and harmful content. "We find this argument singularly unpersuasive," wrote Justice Stevens. The dramatic expansion of this new marketplace of ideas contradicts the factual basis of this contention, he said. "As a matter of constitutional tradition, in the absence of evidence to the contrary, we presume that governmental regulation of the content of speech is more likely to interfere with the free exchange of ideas than to encourage it," Stevens wrote. "The interest in encouraging freedom of expression in a democratic society outweighs any theoretical but unproven benefit of censorship," he added.

The importance of this ruling cannot be overestimated. Not only did the court strike down a restrictive federal law that was certain to retard the growth of computer-mediated communication, it ruled that any other governmental agency that seeks to regulate communication via the information superhighway must treat this medium in the same manner it would treat a newspaper or a book.

BIBLIOGRAPHY

Aguilar, Alexa. "Flap Leads Newspaper Adviser to Resign." *St. Louis Post-Dispatch,* 4 May 2005, B1.

Allen, Mike, and Bradley Graham. "Bush Lauds Rumsfeld for Doing 'Superb Job.'" *Washington Post,* 11 May 2004, A15.

Arnet, Bob. "Embedded/Unembedded I." *Columbia Journalism Review,* May/June 2003, 42.

Associated Press. "Group Names Dearborn a Notorious Free Speech Censor." 13 April 2004.

Associated Press. "Shippensburg Agrees to Drop Speech Code Rules." 25 February 2004.

Associated Press. "UNC Students Sue Over Newspaper Funding Cuts." 15 July 2004.

Associated Press. "U.S. Judge Says Utica Schools Illegally Censored Prep Paper." 13 October 2004.

Bauder, David. "NBC Fires Reporter Over Remark." *Seattle Post-Intelligencer,* 1 April 2003, A8.

Bernton, Hal. "Woman Loses Job Over Coffins Photo." *The Seattle Times,* 22 April 2004, A1.

Blumenthal, Ralph, and Jim Rutenberg. "Journalists Are Assigned to Accompany U.S. Troops." *The New York Times,* 18 February 2003, A12.

Boas, Katherine. "Front Yard Politics, or the Right to Bear Signs." *The New York Times,* 22 August 2004, 14CN 1.

Bonner, Alice, and Judith Hines. *Death by Cheeseburger: High School Journalism in the 1990s and Beyond.* Arlington, Va.: The Freedom Forum, 1994.

Boot, William. "Covering the Gulf War: The Press Stands Alone." *Columbia Journalism Review,* March/April 1991.

Bruni, Frank. "Dueling Perspectives: Two Views of Reality Vying on the Airwaves." *The New York Times,* 18 April 1999, A11.

Burnett, John. "Embedded/Unembedded II." *Columbia Journalism Review,* May/June 2003, 43.

Burress, Charles. "Berkeley Mayor Will Plead Guilty." *San Francisco Chronicle,* 12 December 2002, A25

Bushnell, Andrew, and Brent Cunningham. "Being There." *Columbia Journalism Review,* March/April 2003, 18.

Calvert, Clay. "Allawi's Warning to Journalists Is Wrong Turn for Democracy." *Sacramento Bee,* 20 November 2004, B7.

Carr, David. "Reporters' New Battlefield Access Has Its Risks as Well as Its Rewards." *The New York Times,* 3 March 2003, B2.

Carter, Bill. "Debate Over 'Nightline' Tribute to War Dead Grows, as McCain Weighs In." *The New York Times,* 1 May 2004, A5.

Cranberg, Gilbert. "The Gulf of Credibility." *Columbia Journalism Review,* March/April 1988, 19.

DeFalco, Beth. "Body Piercing Photo Causes Friction Between Administration, Student Press." *Associated Press,* 20 November 2004.

Delgado, Richard. "Words That Wound: A Tort Action for Racial Insults, Epithets, and Name Calling." *Harvard Civil Rights–Civil Liberties Law Review* 17 (1982): 133.

Dennis, Everette, et al. *The Media at War: The Press and the Persian Conflict.* New York: Gannett Foundation Media Center, 1991.

Denniston, Lyle. "Son of Sam Law vs. First Amendment." *Washington Journalism Review,* May 1991, 56.

Dillow, George. "Grunts and Pogues." *Columbia Journalism Review,* May/June 2003, 32.

Donvan, John. "For the Unilaterals, No Neutral Ground." *Columbia Journalism Review,* May/June 2003, 35.

Editorial. "Mayor Tom Bates Owes More Than Apology." *Oakland Tribune,* 12 December 2002, Opinions/Editorials.

Edmonson, George. "Suit Seeks Military Coffin Photos." *Atlanta Journal-Constitution,* 5 October 2004, 7A.

Estrada, Naldy, and Julio, Robles. "All the News That's Fit to Print and Won't Upset the Faculty." *Los Angeles Times,* 7 July 2003, California Metro 11.

Fialka, John J. *Hotel Warriors.* Washington, D.C.: Woodrow Wilson Press Center, 1992.

Galloway, Angela. "Political Spending Unchecked" *Seattle Post-Intelligencer,* 28 July 2000, A1.

Garofoli, Joe. "Flag-Draped Coffin Photos Released." *San Francisco Chronicle,* 29 April 2005, A10.

Greenhouse, Linda. "Court Strikes Down Curb on Visits by Jehovah's Witnesses." *The New York Times,* 18 June 2003, A12.

———. "Justices Allow Bans on Cross Burnings Intended as Threats." *The New York Times,* 8 April 2003, A1.

———. "Justices, in a 5-to-4 Decision, Back Campaign Finance Law That Curbs Contributions." *The New York Times,* 11 December 2003, A1.

Harmon, Amy. "Facts Are In, Spin Is Out." *The New York Times,* 25 March 2003, B14.

———. "Improved Tools Turn Journalists into a Quick Strike Force." *The New York Times,* 24 March 2003, B14.

———. "The Self-Appointed Cops of the Information Age." *The New York Times,* 7 December 1997, section 4, 1.

Hentoff, Nat. *Free Speech for Me–But Not for Thee: How the American Left and Right Relentlessly Censor Each Other.* New York: HarperCollins, 1992.

Hickey, Neil. "Access Denied." *Columbia Journalism Review,* January/February 2002, 26.

Hoover, Ken. "Hongisto Fired." *San Francisco Chronicle,* 15 May 1992, A1.

Jacobs, Matthew J. "Assessing the Constitutionality of Press Restrictions in the Persian Gulf War." *Stanford Law Review* 44 (1992): 674.

Jensen, Elizabeth. "Sinclair Broadcast Group Thrusts Itself into the News." *Los Angeles Times,* 8 May 2004, E14.

Kaplan, Julie B. "The First Amendment Standard for Removal of Books from Public School Curricula." *Dickinson Law Review* 95 (1991): 259.

Knightley, Phillip. *The First Casualty,* rev. ed. Baltimore: Johns Hopkins University Press, 2000.

Lewerenz, Dan. "Local Governments Back Off Laws That Limit Campaign Signs." *Associated Press*, 18 September 2004.

Lewis, Neil A., and Richard A. Oppel Jr. "U.S. Court Issues Discordant Ruling on Campaign Law." *The New York Times,* 3 May 2003, A1.

Lewis, Richard. "College Newspapers Stolen Over Reparations Ad." *The Seattle Times,* 18 March 2001, A5.

Lively, Donald. "The Information Superhighway: A First Amendment Roadmap." *Boston College Law Review* 35 (1994): 1066.

MacArthur, John R. *Second Front: Censorship and Propaganda in the Gulf War.* New York: Hill and Wang, 1992.

MacCormack, Zeke. "No Snow: Texas School Bans Book." *Seattle Post-Intelligencer,* 10 September 1999, A1.

Markiewicz, David. "Cobb School Loses Its 'Voice.'" *Atlanta Journal-Constitution,* 19 May 2005, 4C.

"The Message Is the Medium: The First Amendment on the Information Superhighway." *Harvard Law Review* 107 (1994): 1062.

Miller, Mark C. "Operation Desert Sham." *The New York Times,* 24 June 1992, A17.

Paulk, Crystal. "Campus Crime Real Despite What You Read." *Quill,* September 1997, 48.

Preston, Julia. "Judge Says U.S. Must Release Prison Photos." *The New York Times,* 27 May 2005, A10.

Riskin, Cynthia. "Communications Students Support Some Speech, Press Censorship." *The Washington Newspaper,* January/February 1994.

Rivera, Ray. "Images of War Dead a Sensitive Subject." *The Seattle Times,* 22 April 2004, A22.

Rutenberg, Jim, and Bill Carter. "Spectacular Success or Incomplete Picture? Views of TV's Coverage Are Split." *The New York Times,* 20 April 2003, B15.

Salamon, Julie. "New Tools for Reporters Make Images Instant, but Coverage No Simpler." *The New York Times,* 6 April 2003, B13.

Schmeisser, Peter. "Shooting Pool." *New Republic,* 18 March 1991, 21.

"School Censorship on Rise, Civil Liberties Group Says." *Seattle Post-Intelligencer,* 29 August 1991.

Sharkey, Jacqueline. "The Shallow End of the Pool." *American Journalism Review,* December 1994, 43.

Sloyan, Patrick J. "The Fog of War." *American Journalism Review,* June 1999, 32.

Smith, Lynn. "Coffins and Now Chaos." *Los Angeles Times,* 26 April 2004, E1.

Smith, Terrence. "Hard Lessons." *Columbia Journalism Review,* May/June 2003, 26.

Sterngold, James. "For Artistic Freedom, It's Not the Worst of Times." *The New York Times,* 20 September 1998, section 2, p. 1.

Stifler, Lisa. "Ex-Student Awarded Damages in His Free-Speech Lawsuit." *Seattle Post-Intelligencer,* 21 February 2001, B1.

Stout, David. "Federal Appeals Panel Upholds Vermont Limits on Campaign Spending." *The New York Times,* 8 August 2002, A16.

———. "Court Upholds Alaska Limits on Soft Money in State Races." *The New York Times,* 14 August 2003, A14.

Stricker, Nicole. "Student Paper Pulls Opinion Piece." *Idaho Falls Post Register,* 7 May 2005, A07.

"Students Censored, but Issue Lives On." *The New York Times,* 7 September 1997, A9.

"Suspension of Student for Poem of Violence Upheld." *Seattle Post-Intelligencer,* 21 July 2001, B2.

Tenhoff, Greg C. "Censoring the Public University Student Press." *Southern California Law Review* 64 (1991): 511.

Thompson, Mark. "The Brief Ineffective Life of the Pentagon's Media Pool." *Columbia Journalism Review,* March/April 2002, 66.

Wilgoren, Jodi. "Don't Give Us Little Wizards, The Anti-Potter Parents Cry." *The New York Times,* 1 November 1999, A1.

Zeller, Tom. "Unfit: Harry Potter and Potty Humor." *The New York Times,* 15 June 2003, B2.

Zernike, Kate. "Free-Speech Ruling Voids School District's Harassment Policy." *The New York Times,* 16 February 2001, A11.

LIBEL
Establishing a Case

The law of libel is centuries old. Its roots in this country spring directly from the British common law. Throughout most of this nation's history the states were left to fashion their own libel laws. But since the mid-1960s the U.S. Supreme Court has "federalized" basic elements of defamation law, obligating the states to keep their rules and regulations within boundaries defined by the First Amendment. This development has transformed what was a fairly simple aspect of American law into a legal thicket akin to a blackberry patch. In this first of three chapters about defamation some basic dimensions of this common tort action are characterized and the requirements that have been placed on the plaintiff to establish a cause of action for libel are outlined.

157

THE LIBEL LANDSCAPE

Defamation, or libel, is what lawyers call a **tort,** or a civil wrong. It is undoubtedly the most common legal problem faced by persons who work in the mass media, and often the most troublesome. Allegations of libel are included in about three-fourths of all the lawsuits filed against the mass media, according to a recent study by the Media Law Resource Center (MLRC). In simple terms, **libel** is the publication or broadcast of any statement that

■ injures someone's reputation or
■ lowers that person's esteem in the community.

Anyone who speaks or publishes (including material on the Internet) or broadcasts anything can become the target of a defamation action. Libel can lurk in a news story or editorial, press release, company newsletter, advertising copy, letters to the editor, comments made in an Internet chatroom or in a Web log, or even statements made orally at a public gathering.[1] The mainstream mass media face the vast majority of libel suits, and that is why most of the cases cited in the three subsequent chapters tend to involve lawsuits against newspapers, radio and television stations, magazines and books, and the growing number of information-oriented sites on the Internet. But the editors of company magazines and corporate public information specialists need to be cautious as well. The law, as it is applied to companies like CBS or the New York Times, applies just as well to other mediated forms of communication. However, the public press, such as newspapers and broadcast stations, enjoy some First Amendment protections in libel suits that may not accrue to defamation published in a company newsletter or a press release.

Libel suits are as troublesome for the press as they are common. While any lawsuit against any person or business creates problems, there are some special aspects to libel law that seem to make these problems even worse.

■ The protracted nature of many libel cases, plus the high cost of defending against such suits, can result in a heavy financial burden for the defendant.
■ Plaintiffs often make outrageous damage claims and at times even win enormous damage awards.
■ Libel law is especially complicated and often confusing, to the point that sometimes jurors and even judges don't understand the law and make erroneous decisions.
■ Some plaintiffs file frivolous libel lawsuits to try to silence their critics in the press and the public.

Let's examine each one of these factors briefly.

TIME AND MONEY

All lawsuits take time to resolve. Some libel suits take a very long time. The Knight-Ridder Company settled a libel suit in 1996 brought by a former Philadelphia prosecuting attorney.

---

1. See, for example, *Troy Group, Inc.* v. *Tilson,* 364 F. Supp. 2d 1149 (2005) for a suit based on an e-mail, and *600 West 115th Street Corp.* v. *von Gotfeld,* 80 N.Y. 2d 130 (1992) for a case based on a comment made at a public meeting.

The case began 23 years earlier. Consumers Union, the publisher of Consumer Reports, settled a libel suit in 2004 that had been brought by the Suzuki Motor Corporation. The case began in 1996.[2] Although these cases aren't necessarily typical, protracted litigation is always a threat in a defamation action because of the complex nature of libel law. And while the case goes on, the defense lawyers remain on the job, racking up billable hours.

Successfully defending a newspaper or broadcasting network in a libel suit requires the work of talented attorneys. It is far more complicated than writing a will or seeking damages for an automobile accident. Hourly fees of hundreds of dollars are not unusual. Book publisher Simon & Schuster and author James B. Stewart were sued in the 1990s by an attorney who claimed he was defamed in Stewart's book "Den of Thieves," an account of Wall Street figures who participated in the corporate takeover madness of the late 1980s. The plaintiff was mentioned only briefly in the book. By the time the lawsuit was dismissed in 1999, the defendants had spent more than $1 million defending the book.[3] The Washington Post spent $1.3 million in the mid-1980s defending itself in a libel suit brought by the then-president of the Mobil Oil Company for a story it had published about the executive's son. The Post won the case after a trial and appeal.[4] Author Stewart told a reporter that after he was sued for "Den of Thieves" he felt as if someone was trying to punish or harass him. "It is unpleasant, time-consuming and distracting. Its [the lawsuit] existence has clouded my credit rating and made it difficult for me to get a mortgage. I am sure it has intimidated other journalists and publishers," he said.

DAMAGES SOUGHT AND WON

Plaintiffs sometimes claim exaggerated damage and seek extraordinary sums. In 1994 Phillip Morris Co. sought $10 billion (that's right, billion) in damages in a libel action against ABC. The Church of Scientology, which has a reputation of being highly litigious, once sued Time Warner for $416 million because it described the church as a global racket.[5] Damage claims this high are never awarded. Phillip Morris settled for a televised apology and $3 million. But the lawsuits have to be defended. And damage awards are often very high. The Media Law Resource Center reported in the spring of 2005 that on average juries awarded $3.4 million to the plaintiff in libel actions during the first five years of the new millennium, up from $1.5 million during the 1980s and $2.9 million during the 1990s. Jury awards are typically lowered by the trial judge, or by an appellate court. Still, in February 2005 the Massachusetts Supreme Judicial Court affirmed a $2.1 million award against the Boston Globe in a lawsuit brought by a physician. Nine days earlier a Boston jury ordered the Boston Herald to pay the same amount to a superior court judge who had sued the newspaper for libel.[6]

2. Hakim, "Suzuki Resolves a Dispute."

3. Carvajal, "Libel Wrangle Over Miliken Book." The Appellate Division of the New York Supreme Court granted Simon & Schuster's motion for a summary judgment on September 27, 1999, and dismissed the lawsuit. See *Armstrong* v. *Simon & Schuster,* 27 M.L.R. 2289 (1999).

4. *Tavoulareas* v. *The Washington Post Co.,* 817 F.2d 726 (1987). See also Brill "1982: Behind the Verdict," 31.

5. *Church of Scientology International* v. *Time Warner Inc.,* 903 F. Supp. 637 (1995). The case brought by the church was ultimately dismissed in July 1996. Time Warner settled a parallel libel suit based on the same 1991 article brought by church member Michael Bayback in November 1996.

6. See MLRC 2005 Report on Trials and Damages. 2005 Issue 1, February 2005. See also *Ayash* v. *Dana-Farber Cancer Institute,* 443 Mass. 367 (2005), and Belluck, "Boston Herald Ordered to Pay."

THE LIBEL PUZZLE

Much of the law is complicated. Maybe it's not rocket science, but most laws and legal procedures are beyond the immediate grasp of even the educated average person. Libel law is more difficult to understand than most other areas of the law. (That is why we devote three chapters to the topic in this text.) The law of defamation is filled with amorphous concepts like actual malice, public figures, rhetorical hyperbole and truth. It is based on traditional common law, but has many statutory elements and is infused with a considerable number of constitutional elements. A trial judge can sit on the bench for a lifetime and never try a libel case. If one appears on his or her calendar it is usually a brand-new experience. As likely as not, the jurist hasn't even considered the topic since the two or three days it was discussed in a torts class at law school.

And if the topic is new to the judge, jurors who must decide the case, who often must apply the kinds of amorphous concepts outlined above, are frequently even more in the dark. Mistakes are made at the trial; wrong decisions are handed down. In the aforementioned case involving the Washington Post and the oil company executive, the foreman of the jury totally misunderstood the judge's instructions and the panel rendered a completely wrong decision in the case, a decision that was ultimately reversed on appeal.

This case reveals an important fact about libel suits. While most libel suits against the press are dismissed before they even go to trial—almost 75 percent according to a 2004 study by the Media Law Resource Center—if a case does go to trial, the mass medium will likely lose. Why? Well, sometimes the press is guilty of damaging a reputation and there is no viable defense. Or, as noted above, because the law is often hard to understand, the trial judge and jury will make an error that must be corrected on appeal. Just as important, however, is another factor. A lot of average people who sit on juries, for whatever reason, don't really like the press. "Reporters are arrogant. The press is too liberal. All that is reported is bad news. What about the good things that are happening in the country? The media are always criticizing our leaders or our celebrities or our sports heroes." Ad infinitum. A libel trial can provide an opportunity for a juror to express these frustrations with a damage award.

And then there is the First Amendment. Why should the First Amendment protect a newspaper when it has injured an individual's reputation? A Gallup poll taken in the 1990s revealed that most people interviewed strongly supported libel actions against the press. Other surveys indicate that while people say they theoretically believe freedom of the press is an important human right, they are far less likely to favor it as a right in a specific instance—such as a defense in a libel case.

Most good lawyers do everything they can to keep their media clients out of the courtroom. They work to get the case dismissed before trial. Even a settlement is not out of the question. Plaintiff's attorney Thomas D. Yannucci, who has brought numerous successful actions against the press, called the jury box the media's Achilles' heel. "If you take it to the jury, the ordinary citizen begins [the trial] thinking the media is unfair."[7]

Going to trial, then, is bad news. The good news is that most trial judgments are overturned on appeal. Between 1980 and 2000, only a little more than 25 percent of all the decisions that were appealed by the press were affirmed with no modification whatsoever,

---

7. Moscov, "Truth, Justice and the American Tort," 22.

according to a study by the Media Legal Resource Center. But appeals take more time, and more time costs more money.

THE LAWSUIT AS A WEAPON

No one likes to be criticized in public or in the press. A reputation can be a fragile element in the human psyche or a corporate image. Most individuals, companies and other organizations take the criticism in stride or respond in kind and go on about their business. But a few targets of such criticism seek to quiet their critics by filing or threatening to file a libel suit. Some of these suits are perfectly legitimate. But in the past quarter century, a growing number of these actions were illegitimate attempts by the targets of the criticism to silence the critics and warn other potential critics that they might suffer the same fate if they spoke out or published negative information or opinion.

These kinds of libel suits have been given a name: SLAPP suits, or Strategic Lawsuits Against Public Participation. SLAPP suits first emerged in an effort to block citizens or citizens' groups from speaking out against corporations or other businesses. For example, Victor Monia and several citizens' groups were sued for more than $40 million in a libel action brought by a land developer after they successfully led a fight to impose a one-year moratorium on real estate development in Saratoga, Calif. A school bus company sued parents who complained to the state that the school buses were unsafe. A coal company sued a blueberry farmer for telling the Environmental Protection Agency about the company's pollution of a river. And the Police Benevolent Association of Nassau County, N.Y., filed 50 lawsuits against citizens who complained of police misconduct.

At first the SLAPP suits seemed to accomplish their goal to stifle the voices of the critics. More were filed and even the mass media became a target. "Run that story and we will take you to court." But plaintiffs rarely win these lawsuits; of the few cases that actually go to trial, the defendants win more than 90 percent of the time. But winning is not the point for the plaintiffs; they don't expect to win. If they can force their critics to go to court, force them to pay the legal fees required to mount a defense, they have sent a powerful message. "It will cost you money, a lot of money, to criticize us." Usually if the speaker or publisher stops the criticism, the lawsuit is dropped. The actions are brought, some authorities have noted, to obtain a legal advantage over the defendant, not to vindicate a legally recognized right of the plaintiff.

As SLAPP suits became more common, legislatures and courts sought to fashion means to block them. There are laws in at least 20 states that bar or severely limit such lawsuits.* In many states the anti-SLAPP statutes even protect the mass media.[8]

California has what is probably the broadest statute. In 1992 the state legislature adopted a law that protects a speaker or publisher if he or she can demonstrate that the lawsuit

*California, Delaware, Florida, Georgia, Indiana, Louisiana, Maine, Massachusetts, Minnesota, Nebraska, Nevada, New Mexico, New York, Oklahoma, Oregon, Pennsylvania, Rhode Island, Tennessee, Utah, and Washington. The Colorado Supreme Court has ruled that protections similar to those in SLAPP statutes are contained in the state's common law. *Protect Our Mountain Environment* v. *District Court,* 677 P. 2d 136 (1984).

8. See, for example, *Lee* v. *Pennington,* 830 So. 2d 1037 (2002).

arises from comments on a public issue by the defendant in furtherance of his or her rights of petition or free speech guaranteed under the U.S. Constitution or the state constitution. The lawsuit must be dismissed by the court unless the plaintiff can demonstrate a probability of prevailing on the legal claim. That is, if the anti-SLAPP statute is invoked by the defendant, the court must presume that the legal action was brought to chill the defendant's exercise of his or her First Amendment rights. The plaintiff must convince the court there is substantial merit in the allegations even before the trial begins. If the lawsuit is dismissed, the plaintiff must pay the defendant's legal expenses. After several state court decisions seemed to dilute this statute, the legislature amended the law in 1997, informing judges they should construe the statute broadly; that is, give the defendant any benefit of the doubt. In 2002 the California Supreme Court handed down three rulings reinforcing the notion that courts are to be aggressive in controlling these harassment actions.[9]

But even the broadest laws are not without boundaries. When the office manager of a San Diego law firm sued a Vietnamese-language magazine for publishing stories suggesting he was taking sexual liberties with female employees, the magazine publisher tried to block the suit with the anti-SLAPP law. He claimed that it was a public issue whether a lawyer serving the Vietnamese community is representing the best interest of his clients and the community, and whether there is misconduct in the manner in which he operates. The California Court of Appeals, in an unpublished opinion, rejected this argument, noting that while statements concerning the quality of lawyers in the community may have substantial public interest, the allegedly libelous comments concerned the sexual activities of the office manager of the firm. The fact that he is employed by the law firm doesn't translate this into a public issue, the court said.[10]

Not all state laws are as broad as the California statute. In New York, for example, the law only applies to citizens who speak out on land-use issues at meetings of government planning commissions or zoning boards. But overall, the laws have proved to be effective, especially in protecting activists who seek to challenge government policies or the impact of private interest groups that try to influence government policy.

For the reasons outlined above, libel suits are a common and troublesome problem for the mass media in America. Many thoughtful people have asked, "Isn't there some way to resolve this problem that both protects the reputation of individuals and businesses, but at the same time lowers the costs and risks for the press?" That is the final matter to consider in this section.

RESOLVING THE PROBLEM

Going to court in a libel action is rarely a happy experience for any of the participants.

Going to court in a libel action is rarely a happy experience for any of the participants. Plaintiffs are rarely gratified. Lawyers' fees can take as much as 50 percent of their winnings. The typical case takes four years to litigate, four years during which their lives are disrupted. Two-thirds of

9. See for example, *Equilon Enterprise, LCC v. Consumer Cause, Inc.,* 29 Cal 4th 53 (2002). But the California statute was slightly modified in 2003 to give business and financial institutions a broader right to sue for label by limiting the scope of the anti-SLAPP statute. See California Code of Civil Procedure, §425.17(c). See also Pring, "SLAPPs; Pring and Canan, "Strategic Lawsuits;" and Dill, "Libel Law Doesn't Work."

10. *Quang v. Tran,* 32 M.L.R. 2198 (2004).

the plaintiffs questioned by researchers in the massive Iowa Libel Research Project said they were dissatisfied with their litigation experience.[11]

The press isn't happy either. Defense costs and damage awards cut into revenues. Reporters and editors are immobilized for long periods of time. Publicity about the lawsuit only reinforces the negative attitudes many people have about the news media. Even the public suffers in the end. Tax dollars subsidize the cost of litigation. Lawsuits often result in a more cautious press that may, to avoid the threat of lawsuits, deny readers and viewers important information.

Does every dispute between a mass medium and an injured party have to result in a lawsuit? Are there other means to solve these problems? Relatively simple solutions have been proposed, but ultimately rejected. Three-fourths of all plaintiffs interviewed in the Iowa Libel Research Project said they would never have filed a lawsuit if the news medium would have published or broadcast a correction, retraction or apology. That solution sounds simple enough. But some editors and broadcasters are reluctant to adopt a policy of routinely publishing corrections or retractions. Sometimes journalists disagree with a plaintiff that there is an error in the story. Sometimes the reluctance to admit mistakes is founded on the proposition that the publication or broadcast of corrections or retractions will damage the already fragile credibility that the news media enjoy. And without credibility, what can the press offer the public? But many observers question the validity of this argument. Only a fool, they say, believes that the press never makes an error. Admitting a mistake when one is made will only enhance the press's credibility. In any case, while many publications do in fact routinely publish corrections, many do not.

Other schemes have been suggested as well. Many proposals to take the issue out of the judicial system have emerged. Arbitration of some sort as opposed to court action would ameliorate the problem. But no large-scale arbitration program has been successfully initiated, despite the success of some small or experimental programs. Schemes that push plaintiffs to be more aggressive in seeking corrections and retractions and that reward the press for publishing such corrections or retractions have also been proposed. In fact, about 30 states in the nation already have what are called retraction statutes, which are designed to keep libel disputes out of the courthouse and make it easier and cheaper for both sides to resolve the issues. (See pp. 269–271 for a fuller description of these laws.) But the existing statutes have problems, and the new proposals seem to go too far, or not far enough, and rarely satisfy attorneys for both plaintiffs and defendants.[12] The press has tried to reduce frivolous lawsuits by suing plaintiffs who bring these legal actions for abuse of process or malicious prosecution or other causes of action.[13] But courts tend to resist such efforts, expressing worry that by routinely permitting such counterlawsuits they might deter a deserving plaintiff who has been truly damaged and is entitled to a day in court to seek a remedy. For the time being, at least, libel actions will continue to find their way into the judicial arena. And the process that ensues is the focus of the remainder of this chapter and Chapters 5 and 6 as well.

11. Bezanson, Cranberg, and Soloski, *Libel Law and the Press.*

12. See Dill, "Libel Law Doesn't Work."

13. See, for example, *Ward* v. *Roy H. Park Broadcasting Co.,* 400 S.E. 2d 758 (1991) and *Mitchell* v. *The Herald Co.,* 137 A. 2d 213 (1988).

SUMMARY   Libel is the most common and often the most troublesome problem faced by people who work in the mass media. It usually takes a great deal of money to successfully defend a libel suit. Damage claims are sometimes outrageous, and occasionally damage awards are extremely high and have little to do with the harm caused by the defamation. The law is very complicated, and mistakes made by judges and juries have to be rectified by lengthy and costly appeals. Some plaintiffs attempt to use the law to harass or punish defendants rather than simply repair a damaged reputation, but many states have attempted to block these so-called SLAPP suits with legislation. Researchers have demonstrated that most libel plaintiffs are unhappy about their experiences in litigation and would not sue if the mass medium simply corrected or retracted the libelous statement. The press, however, seems reluctant to follow this strategy. More ambitious schemes to resolve the libel problem have generally met with opposition or indifference from the press and from organizations of trial lawyers.

LAW OF DEFAMATION

The law of defamation is ancient; its roots can be traced back several centuries. Initially, the law was an attempt by government to establish a forum for persons involved in a dispute brought about by an insult or by what we today call a defamatory remark. One man called another a robber and a villain. The injured party sought to avenge his damaged reputation. A fight or duel of some kind was the only means of gaining vengeance before the development of libel law. It was obvious that fights and duels were not satisfactory ways to settle such disputes, so government offered to help solve these problems. Slowly the law of defamation evolved. Today the process of going to court to avenge one's honor is highly institutionalized.

In other parts of the world, different schemes are used to accomplish similar ends. In continental Europe libel suits are less common. When a newspaper defames a person, that person has the right—under law—to strike back, using the columns of the same newspaper to tell his or her side of the story. This right is called the right of reply, and it exists in the United States in a far less advanced form, as is noted near the end of Chapter 6. Many people favor this notion of letting the parties fight it out in print or by broadcast. They say it is far better to set out after the truth in this fashion than to rattle the chains on the courthouse door every time an insult is flung in the public press.

Parts of the law of libel do not concern those who work in mass communications. For example, elements of libel deal with allegations contained in private communications, a letter from one person to another, a job recommendation from a former employer to a prospective employer. The material in this chapter focuses on public communications—material that is published or broadcast via the mass media, using that term in its broadest sense to include advertising, company magazines, trade association newsletters, press releases, the Internet and so on. Similarly, because newspapers, broadcasting stations, magazines and the like tend to focus on material considered to be of public concern, courts often treat them differently from nonmedia defendants.[14] Unless otherwise stated, it can be presumed the discussion in this text focuses on the rights and responsibilities of media defendants.

Additionally, it must be remembered that libel law is essentially state law. It is possible to describe the dimensions of the law in broad terms that transcend state boundaries, and that is what this text attempts to do. But important variations exist in the law from state to state, as will be demonstrated in the next chapter in the discussion of fault requirements. It is important for students to focus on the specific elements of the law in their states after gaining an understanding of the general boundaries of the law.

Another problem in the law has to do with whether a communication is a libel (written defamation) or a **slander** (an oral defamation). The law in some states distinguishes between the two. The problem was simple 150 years ago. Because of the state of technology, a public communication, that is, one meant for a wide audience, was a printed communication—a newspaper, magazine or handbill. Therefore a law that dealt with libel more harshly than with slander made sense; libel caused more severe damage. A libel lasted longer than a slander since a libel was printed, more people saw it, and it was generally considered to be planned defamation, not words accidentally spoken in the heat of argument. Film, radio, television and the Internet have made these distinctions meaningless. If a performer defames someone on a television program, the defamation still has immense impact and is heard by millions despite the fact that the defamation is not printed. Although the law varies slightly from state to state, today published defamation, whether it is in a newspaper, on the Internet, on radio or television, in the movies, or whatever, is regarded as libel. And libel rules apply.

The purpose of this chapter is to give people in mass communications guidance and rules to apply in the process of gathering, writing, publishing, and broadcasting news, information or advertising. People who want to learn to litigate a lawsuit should go to law school. The goal in these chapters is to keep media practitioners out of libel suits or at least to keep them from losing libel suits.

ELEMENTS OF LIBEL

There are many definitions of defamation, and they are all about the same. In their book "Libel," Phelps and Hamilton include this definition:

> Defamation is a communication which exposes a person to hatred, ridicule, or contempt, lowers him in the esteem of his fellows, causes him to be shunned, or injures him in his business or calling.[15]

The "Restatement of Torts," a compilation by the American Law Institute of what it thinks the common law says, defines libel this way:

> a communication which has the tendency to so harm the reputation of another as to lower him in the estimation of the community or to deter third persons from associating with him.[16]

14. See, for example, *Philadelphia Newspapers, Inc.* v. *Hepps,* 475 U.S. 767 (1986).
15. Phelps and Hamilton, *Libel.*
16. American Law Institute, *Restatement of Torts.*

Defamation is any communication that holds a person up to contempt, hatred, ridicule or scorn.

Here is another definition: Defamation is any communication that holds a person up to contempt, hatred, ridicule or scorn.

Each of the preceding definitions reveals common and important elements of defamation:

1. **Defamation is a communication that damages the reputation of a person, but not necessarily the individual's character.** Your character is what you are; your reputation is what people think you are. Reputation is what the law protects.

2. **To be actionable defamation, the words must actually damage a reputation. There must be proof offered that the individual's reputation was harmed.** A U.S. District Court in Oklahoma granted a summary judgment to the defendant in a libel suit because the plaintiff, a man who was wrongly named as a seller of T-shirts and other memorabilia "celebrating" the death and destruction caused by the bombing of the federal building in Oklahoma City, failed to provide sufficient evidence that his reputation had been harmed.[17] Without proof of this harm, a party who claims injury will not be able to recover damages for the injury. But proof of harm is an elusive element, and evidence of damage to reputation is often speculative at best. Also, juries frequently are willing to assume damage to reputation upon the presentation of only the barest of evidence. Is it possible for a plaintiff to have such a poor reputation that a court will rule that there can be no further harm to that individual's reputation, that the defamatory words were incapable of causing additional damage to the plaintiff's reputation? Yes. Such a person is regarded as being "libel proof."

   For example, in the 1990s Dr. Jack Kevorkian, a controversial physician who assisted patients who sought to end their lives because they were terminally ill, was the frequent subject of both positive and negative media coverage. Dr. Kevorkian sued the American Medical Association and a handful of physicians in 1996, claiming he had been defamed in a letter that accused him of being "a reckless instrument of death," and a doctor who "engages in criminal practice" and who "poses a great threat to the public." The Michigan Court of Appeals declared Dr. Kevorkian to be libel proof when it ruled that the statements could not defame him. "In short, plaintiff's reputation in the community, if not the nation, is such that the effect of more people calling him either a murderer or a saint is de minimis [of very little significance]."[18] In those instances where an allegedly libelous statement "cannot realistically cause impairment of reputation because the person's reputation is already so low . . . the claim should be dismissed," the court said, quoting a 1991 federal court ruling *(Brooks* v. *American Broadcasting Co.).*[19] In 2003 a U.S. District Court in Kansas came to the same conclusion about Thomas Lamb, a man who was sentenced to three consecutive life terms for murder and rape he committed in 1969. Lamb contended that because 31 years had elapsed and he had not committed a subsequent crime, his reputation had been rehabilitated. The court disagreed.[20]

---

17. *Zeran* v. *Diamond Broadcasting Inc.,* 26 M.L.R. 1855 (1998).
18. *Kevorkian* v. *American Medical Association,* 602 N.W. 2d 233 (1999).
19. 932 F. 2d 495 (1991).
20. *Lamb* v. *Rizzo,* 31 M.L.R. 2513 (2003); affirmed on the U.S. Court of Appeals, 381 F. 3d 1133 (2004).

Source: © AP/Wide World Photos

3. **At least a significant minority of the community must believe that the plaintiff's reputation has been damaged, but the minority must not be an unrepresentative minority.** A Delaware superior court ruled that it was not defamatory for a television newscaster to refer to a convict as "an alleged FBI informant." The plaintiff complained that the statement hurt his reputation among his fellow prisoners at the state penitentiary. Conceding that the "informant" label might harm his prison reputation, the court ruled that "it is not one's reputation in a limited community in which attitudes and social values may depart substantially from those prevailing generally which an action for defamation is designed to protect." The public in general would not think any less of the plaintiff for being an informant for the FBI.[21] To summarize this point: The defamation must lower a person's reputation in the eyes of a significant number of people, and unless unusual circumstances exist, these people must fairly reflect representative views.

Dr. Jack Kevorkian, shown here giving his closing arguments in his murder trial in Pontiac, Mich., in March 1999, was ruled to be libel proof in his defamation action against his critics.

Persons can be injured through a libel in numerous ways. The statement may simply hurt their reputation, or it may be that lowering their reputation deprives them of their right to enjoy social contacts, which is a fancy way of saying that their friends don't like them anymore or their friends want to avoid them. A man's or woman's ability to work or hold a job or

---

21. *Saunders* v. *WHYY-TV,* 382 A. 2d 257 (1978). See also *Clawson* v. *St. Louis Post-Dispatch LLC,* 32 M.L.R. 2608 (2004), where a District of Columbia superior court rejected a plaintiff's argument that being identified as an "informer" was defamatory; he said he considered himself as a "whistle blower." It was not in the public interest, the court said, to allow comments that characterize a person as helping law enforcement or the government to be defamatory.

make a living may be injured. A person need only be injured in *one* of these three ways to have a cause of action for libel. If plaintiffs can show actual harm in any one of these areas, chances are good they will recover some damages. That is one of the reasons libel law exists—to compensate the plaintiff for injury. There are other reasons. A libel suit can help vindicate the plaintiff, help restore the damaged reputation. A victorious plaintiff can point a finger at the newspaper or television station and say, "See, they were wrong, they lied, they made an error." A damage judgment is also considered punishment for the defendant. Editors and broadcasters who have to pay a large damage award may be more cautious in the future. It can stand also as an example to other journalists to avoid such behavior.

Any living person can bring a civil action for libel. A dead person can't sue; that's obvious. The common law bars suits by the relatives of someone who has died in behalf of the deceased. Note, however, that if a living person is defamed, brings suit, and then dies before the matter is settled by the court, it is possible in some states that have what are called **survival statutes** for relatives to continue to pursue the lawsuit.[22] A business corporation can sue for libel. So can a nonprofit corporation, if it can show that it has lost public support and contributions because of the defamation. There is a division in judicial opinion about whether unincorporated associations like labor unions and political action groups can sue for libel. Some court rulings say no; others say yes. Find out what the law is in your state. Cities, counties, agencies of government and governments in general cannot bring a civil libel suit. This question was decided years ago and is settled law.[23]

One important key to understanding any lawsuit is to understand the concept of the burden of proof. Which party must prove what? While this point sounds like a trivial matter to many laypeople, it is a very significant element in a lawsuit. Remember, under our adversarial legal system, the court does nothing but evaluate and analyze the material that is brought before it by the adversaries. Judges and juries don't go out and look for evidence themselves. So the matter of who must bring the evidence before the court is a critical one. If a plaintiff, for example, is required to prove a specific element in a case and fails to bring sufficient evidence before the court to convince the judge or jury, the plaintiff loses the case. Theoretically, the defendant can just sit on his or her hands and do nothing until the plaintiff has brought forth the needed evidence to prove the point. But this is not likely to happen; the defendant is more likely to fight the plaintiff every step of the way, arguing that the evidence is not acceptable or is insufficient to prove the point.

TO WIN A LIBEL SUIT A PLAINTIFF MUST PROVE:
1. The libel was published.
2. Words were of and concerning plaintiff.
3. Material is defamatory.
4. Material is false.
5. Defendant was at fault.

---

22. See *MacDonald* v. *Time,* 554 F. Supp. 1053 (1983) and *Canino* v. *New York News,* 475 A. 2d 528 (1984).
23. *City of Chicago* v. *Tribune Publishing Co.,* 139 N.E. 2d 86 (1923).

In a libel case the plaintiff bears the initial burden of proof. He or she must establish five separate elements of the case in order to have any chance of winning (see boxed text on page 168).

Each of the five elements in this box is outlined in detail shortly. Items 4 and 5 are probably only required if the plaintiff is suing a mass media defendant. These elements are fairly recent additions to the law of libel, and the courts have not yet fully resolved the question of how far they should be extended.[24] Since this book is about mass media law, it is written with the assumption that plaintiffs will generally have to prove the falsity of the matter. The fifth element, proof of fault, is also presumed to be a requirement to be met by the plaintiff for purposes of this discussion. Fault will be discussed in Chapter 5.

PUBLICATION

Before the law recognizes a statement or comment as a civil libel, the statement must be published. Under the law, **publication** means that one person, in addition to the source of the libel and the person who is defamed, sees or hears the defamatory material. Just one person is all it takes. But isn't this a contradiction to what was written on page 166 that a significant number of persons must believe that the plaintiff's reputation has been harmed before he or she can collect damages? Here it is stated that only a single person must see or hear the libel for publication to take place. Two different concepts are being discussed. The first is publication. The plaintiff has to show that at least one other person saw the libelous material or the court will not allow the lawsuit to proceed. No publication, no lawsuit. Assume the plaintiff can show all five elements needed—publication, identification, defamation, falsity and fault—and the publisher of the libel fails to raise a workable defense. The plaintiff wins the case. Then comes the assessment of damages. At this point the plaintiff must show that the false statement that was published lowered his or her reputation among a significant number of the right-thinking people in the community. If the plaintiff cannot show this, the victory is a moral one at best. No damages will be awarded. It is even possible that the court might rule that the words are not defamatory if they don't lower the plaintiff's reputation in the eyes of a significant number of persons.

The question of publication is largely academic when the mass media is sued. If something is in a newspaper or on television or transmitted over the Internet, the court will presume that a third party has seen or heard the matter.[25]

Republication of a libel can also result in a successful lawsuit. Author and courtroom observer Dominick Dunne was sued when, during an appearance on a radio program, he repeated allegations he said he had heard from a third party that implicated a U.S. congressman in the disappearance of a legislative intern named Chandra Levy. When Congressman Gary Condit sued, Dunne said that he was only repeating what others had told him—he did not initiate the charge, but said he thought the charges might be true—and argued that he was protected by the First Amendment. A federal district court disagreed and rejected the motion

---

24. See *Columbia Sussex* v. *Hay,* 627 S.W. 2d 270 (1981); *Mutafis* v. *Erie Insurance Exchange,* 775 F. 2d 593 (1985); and *Philadelphia Newspapers* v. *Hepps,* 475 U.S. 767 (1986).
25. *Hornby* v. *Hunter,* 385 S.W. 2d 473 (1964).

for a summary judgment, noting that republication of false facts threatens the target's reputation as much as does the original publication. "The First Amendment does not absolutely protect a speaker who republishes false assertions of fact, then disclaims any awareness of the actual truth of the republication, then 'theorizes' that the defamatory implication of the republication is true."[26] After his motion was denied Dunne settled the lawsuit.

Some people mistakenly believe that attributing a libel to a third party will shield them from a lawsuit, but this is one of the great myths of American journalism.

Some people mistakenly believe that attributing a libel to a third party will shield them from a lawsuit, but this is one of the great myths of American journalism. For example, most good reporters know that it is libelous to label someone a murderer. But a remarkably high percentage of professionals erroneously believe you can label someone a murderer, as long as you attribute the statement to a third party. "Jones killed his wife" is obviously defamatory. So is "Jones killed his wife, according to neighbor Ned Block." The newspaper or broadcasting station has simply republished Block's original libel of Jones. (Because the reporter apparently quoted a source for the allegation of murder, the plaintiff might find it more difficult to prove the required fault element. And that could doom Mr. Jones' libel suit. But it doesn't change the fact that the allegation—attributed or not—is the republication of a libel.) Because of the republication rule, nearly everyone in the chain of production of a news story is technically liable in a lawsuit.

Publishers and Vendors

A long-standing exception to the republication rule is the notion that news vendors, bookstores, libraries and others who actually distribute the finished printed product cannot be held responsible for republishing the defamation unless the defendant can show that these people or institutions knew the printed matter contained a defamation, or should have had reason to know. This concept is called **scienter,** or guilty knowledge, and is fundamental in many areas of the law. For example, in 2003 the Tennessee Court of Appeals ruled that a shop owner was not liable when he allowed a publisher to place a free newspaper that contained allegedly defamatory content on a counter next to other free newspapers that anyone could pick up and take home.[27] The shop owner was a vendor, not a publisher. Similarly, network-affiliated television stations are not responsible for defamatory content in the programming they transmit for the networks. They too are regarded as vendors.

Libel on the Internet

The great bulk of the law of libel that is outlined in this chapter and the next two applies to defamation that is transmitted via the Internet. Courts regard communication on the World Wide Web the same way they regard material published in newspapers, magazines or books. Two issues have arisen, however, that have forced the courts and Congress to consider the relationship between libel and the Internet. The first has to do with the status of online service providers (OSPs) in the transmission of a libel; the second has to do with jurisdiction, a subject that will be discussed in Chapter 6.

---

26. *Condit.* v. *Dunne,* 317 F Supp 2d 344 (2004).
27. *Piper* v. *Mize,* 31 M.L.R. 1833 (2003).

There are many contexts in which a libel might be published on the Internet. A defamatory message might be sent to every person who logs on to an OSP's computers. Libelous material might be contained in a database that is viewed or downloaded by a user. Defamation might be posted on a bulletin board generally accessible to some or all of the OSP's customers. A libelous remark might be made during an online real-time discussion among users connected to an OSP. Or defamation might be contained in a message sent to an e-mail addressee.

If the online service provider is the author or originator of the libelous message, it will be regarded as a publisher of the material in a libel suit and be treated as a newspaper publisher is treated. It is liable for the defamatory publication and can be sued for libel.

More commonly, however, the OSP merely transmits what another party has posted on the system as an e-mail or a message on a bulletin board or on a Web site. In this case the system operator will be regarded as a vendor or distributor rather than a publisher. This was an issue that courts debated in a series of rulings in the early 1990s. Then Congress settled the matter in 1996 when it adopted the Communications Decency Act. That federal law states: "No provider . . . of an interactive computer service shall be treated as the publisher or speaker of any information provided by another information content provider."[28] Since the passage of that measure numerous online service providers have been exonerated in libel actions because of the federal law. In April 1998 a federal court, citing the federal law, dismissed a libel action against America Online by an aide to President Clinton who claimed he had been defamed by comments made by a political gossip columnist named Matthew Drudge, whose "Drudge Report" was transmitted online by the Internet service provider. But the court permitted Sidney Blumenthal to proceed with his lawsuit against Drudge.[29] The matter was settled out of court in May 2001. A court in New York ruled that an online service provider was not liable for defamation it had transmitted, but not originated, under New York common law. The court said the OSP was like a telephone company, "which one neither wants nor expects to superintend the content of its subscribers' conversations."[30] In 2001 in Washington state, an appellate court ruled that the federal law immunized Internet book vendor Amazon.com from tort liability when it was sued by an author for including readers' comments on its Web site that were critical of the author's work. A U.S. District Court in South Dakota ruled that a shop that rents the use of Internet-accessible computers to customers is also protected by the federal statute.[31] In 2003 the 3rd U.S. Court of Appeals ruled that holding America Online liable for failing to block transmission of allegedly defamatory online messages in a chat room would treat the OSP as "publisher or speaker of that content," and violate the immunity provided under the federal law. And the 9th U.S. Court of Appeals ruled during the same year that when an Internet dating service formulated open-ended profile questions and then posted third party's false answers on the Web, it did not become a publisher under the law.[32] Because the dating service

---

28. 47 U.S.C. § 230 (C) (1).
29. *Blumenthal* v. *Drudge,* 992 F. Supp. 44 (1998).
30. *Lunney* v. *Prodigy Services Co.,* 723 N.E. 2d 539 (1999).
31. *Schneider* v. *Amazon.com Inc.,* 31 P. 3d 37 (2001) and *Patent Wizard Inc.* v. *Kinkos, Inc.,* 29 M.L.R. 2530 (2001).
32. *Green* v. *America Online,* 3rd Cir. 01-1120, 1/16/03, and *Caratano* v. *Metrosplash.com Inc.,* 9th Cir., No. 02-55658, 8/31/03.

did not play a significant role in creating, developing or transforming the relevant information, it remained immune from a lawsuit.* Interestingly, the protection provided to OSPs under the federal law goes beyond libel to include other kinds of liability as well. For example, a U.S. District Court in Virginia ruled that America Online was not liable in a negligence action brought against the OSP by a man who claimed he was harmed when someone posted a notice on a bulletin board advertising T-shirts and other items glorifying the Oklahoma City bombing. Affixed to the ad were the plaintiff's name and telephone number. The court said the imposition of common law liability in the case would directly contradict the congressional mandate.[33]

While U.S. law appears to be effective in protecting the OSPs from libel suits initiated in the United States, it is unlikely to protect the OSPs from lawsuits filed in other countries. British law, for example, does not protect online service providers who simply act as distributors of a defamatory message that has been posted on the Web by a third party. An OSP in Great Britain, Demon Internet, agreed to pay $25,000 in damages plus several hundred thousand dollars in court costs to British physicist Laurence Godfrey in March 2000 for transmitting alleged defamatory comments that had been part of a discussion in a news group carried by Demon's new servers. If Demon had been a U.S. OSP and the suit brought in a U.S. court, Godfrey would have had no chance of winning. But British libel law is more heavily weighted toward plaintiffs than is the law in the United States, and the British government has not given OSPs immunity from libel actions when they merely act as distributors of the material.[34] Authorities disagree on whether a U.S. OSP could be successfully sued in a British court if it distributed defamatory matter about a British subject to Internet users in Great Britain. Courts will have to sort this out. The basic points to remember are these: At this time only U.S. law provides protection for OSPs regarding the content they simply distribute as opposed to originate. And the Internet, as a global medium, reaches nations with laws fundamentally different from those in the United States.

IDENTIFICATION

The second element in a libel suit is **identification:** the injured party must show the court that the allegedly defamatory statement is "of and concerning him, her, or it." Failing to do this, the plaintiff will lose the suit. Author William Peter Blatty, who wrote "The Exorcist" and other popular thrillers, once sued The New York Times for libel because the newspaper did not include one of the author's books on its best-selling book list. By not including the work,

---

*A 2004 decision by a California appellate court has muddied the waters somewhat in this area. The case involved eBay, the popular auction Web site. A seller on eBay posted allegedly defamatory comments on the site in response to complaints from a buyer. The buyer sued and eBay raised the federal law in its defense. But the court said eBay was not a "provider . . . of an interactive computer service" that was immunized from suit by the statute; it was a distributor or transmitter of the defamatory material. Distributors could be subject to liability. But the court excused eBay from liability because it had contractual agreements with buyers and sellers that protected it from suit. (*Grace* v. *eBay Inc.,* 16 Cal. Rptr. 3d 192 (2004). The California Supreme Court agreed to hear an appeal of this ruling.

33. *Zeran* v. *America Online Inc.,* 958 F. Supp. 1124 (1997), aff'd. 129 F. 3d 327 (1997). But see *Barnett* v. *Rosenthal,* Cal. Ct. App. A096461 10/15/03 for a different interpretation of the law.

34. Kaplan, "Suit Against," and Lyall, "British Internet Provider."

Blatty argued, this defamed him; it lowered his reputation. But the California Supreme Court dismissed the case. How could Blatty complain of libel for not being identified? the court asked. The plaintiff must establish that the defamatory remarks are "of and concerning" him, and if Blatty wasn't included on the list, there were no remarks at all of and concerning him.[35] This suit was surely an odd one, but it makes the point: The plaintiff must be identified. Not every reader or viewer needs to know to whom the libel refers. But certainly more than one or two people must be able to recognize the plaintiff as the subject of the derogatory remark. Libel authorities disagree on how many people must be able to identify the subject of the remark. But remember, to win damages the plaintiff must prove that his or her reputation has been lowered in the eyes of a significant minority of the members of the community. If only a handful of people can recognize the plaintiff, it is doubtful that he or she can prove sufficient harm to win damages.

Identification can occur in several ways. A plaintiff may be explicitly named. Or the defendant can use a similar name that suggests the plaintiff's actual name. The producers of the television show "Hard Copy" were sued for using the name Sweepstakes Clearing House when they aired a story on sweepstakes scams. Sweepstakes Clearing House is a made-up name, but there is a company called Sweepstakes Clearinghouse and its owners sued. The Texas Court of Appeals reversed the summary judgment granted the defendant and ruled that a publication is "of and concerning" the plaintiff if persons who knew or were acquainted with the plaintiff believed that the libelous material referred to the plaintiff.[36] A person can be identified in a number of ways. He or she may be explicitly named. The individual can be described, for example, as the host of the quiz show "Jeopardy" or the city's superintendent of public works. A picture or a drawing, even without a caption, can be sufficient if the likeness is recognizable. Even descriptive circumstances can sometimes point the finger at someone. In 1991 a young woman, after attending a party, was abducted as she was standing outside a house near the University of Pennsylvania campus. She said she was raped by her abductor. A local television station reported the attack, including comments by a police officer who cast some doubts on the victim's story. The young woman claimed these comments defamed her. The station did not use the victim's name, but described her as a female Bryn Mawr student (Bryn Mawr is a small college near the University of Pennsylvania that enrolls less than 1,500 undergraduates) who had been raped on a certain day, that she lived in a dorm at Bryn Mawr, that she drove a Nissan, and that she had attended a party at the University of Pennsylvania shortly before her abduction. The station claimed that broadcasting these facts did not constitute identification. But a U.S. District Court disagreed, noting the small school environment at Bryn Mawr. "In this type of environment, it would not be surprising if some people could identify the plaintiff from the information supplied in the broadcast."[37] In fact, the plaintiff presented affidavits from students attesting to the fact that the story of her rape had spread rapidly across campus after the broadcast. The Illinois Supreme Court held the publishers of Seventeen magazine liable for publishing a short story labeled fiction that described as a slut a girl identified only as Bryson. The author of the story, Lucy Logsdon, a native of southern

---

35. *Blatty* v. *The New York Times,* 728 P. 2d 1177 (1986).
36. *Allied Marketing Group Inc.* v. *Paramount Pictures Corp.,* 111 SW 3d 168 (2003).
37. *Weinstein* v. *Bullock,* 827 F. Supp. 1193 (1994).

Illinois, wrote a first-person narrative that recounts a conflict she said she had with a high school classmate. The classmate in the short story bore a slight physical resemblance to the plaintiff, Kimberly Bryson, who had attended high school with Logsdon. The court said that third persons familiar with both the plaintiff and the defendant would understand that the story was referring to the plaintiff despite the fiction label.[38]

It is possible for the plaintiff to put two or more stories together to establish identification. Police arrested eight people in Brookline, Mass., in connection with drug smuggling. One of the persons arrested was identified as a former employee of Haim's Deli in Brookline. Police said gang members at times met at the deli. An area radio station mistakenly reported: "The owner of a Brookline deli and seven other people are arrested in connection with an international cocaine ring." Haim Eyal, the owner of Haim's Deli, sued for libel. The radio station attempted to defeat the suit by arguing that its report did not include the name of the delicatessen and that there were scores of delis in Brookline. Therefore, it had not identified Mr. Eyal. But the Massachusetts Supreme Judicial Court ruled that because nearly all other news stories about the incident had mentioned Haim's Deli, listeners to the erroneous radio report would know which deli was involved and would think Haim Eyal was arrested as a gang member.[39]

If a libelous statement does not make an explicit identification, then the plaintiff must somehow prove that the defamatory words refer to him or her. There have been a handful of cases in which plaintiffs have sued for libel, arguing that they have been fictionally portrayed in a novel. This is not as difficult to prove as it sounds, as some publishers have discovered. The U.S. Court of Appeals for the 2nd Circuit ruled in 1980 that an identification might be established if "a reasonable reader rationally suspects that the protagonist is in fact the plaintiff, notwithstanding the author's and publisher's assurances that the work is fiction." To do this, the court said, the plaintiff must show that the fictional work "designates the plaintiff in such a way as to let those who knew her understand that she was the person meant. It is not necessary that all the world should understand the libel; it is sufficient if those who knew the plaintiff can make out that she is the person meant."[40] What courts tend to do in such cases is first look at the similarities between the character and the plaintiff, and then look at the dissimilarities. In the early 1980s Lisa Springer sued Viking Press, alleging that she had been depicted as a character in Robert Tine's novel "State of Grace." The heroine of the fictional work was Lisa Blake, the mistress of a ruthless Italian industrialist, a woman who had an unusual sexual appetite. Springer had had a personal relationship with the author just before the book was published, and both she and the fictional Lisa Blake had similar physical characteristics, attended college, and even lived on the same street in New York. But the court found that the dissimilarities between the two were more striking, noting that Springer lived a fairly modest, quiet life, while the fictional Blake inhabited a far more luxurious world. "The dissimilarities both in manner of living and in outlook are so profound that it is virtually impossible to see how one who had read the book and who knew Lisa Springer could attribute to Springer the lifestyle of Blake."[41]

---

38. *Bryson* v. *News America Publications Inc.,* 672 N.E. 2d 1207 (1996).
39. *Eyal* v. *Helen Broadcasting Corp.,* 583 N.E. 2d 228 (1991).
40. *Geisler* v. *Petrocelli,* 616 F. 2d 636 (1980).
41. *Springer* v. *Viking Press,* 457 N.Y.S. 2d 246 (1982).

Journalists face somewhat of a conundrum today regarding identification. Traditionally, reporters have been taught to include full identification when writing or talking about someone: John Smith, 36, of 1234 Boone Street, a carpenter. This information will separate this John Smith from any other person with the same name. But the issue of privacy is of great concern today, and many people don't want their ages or addresses in the newspaper or broadcast on television. Some news organizations now permit less than complete identification in sensitive situations. The reporter should always get complete identification for the subject of a news story, if only to confirm that he or she is writing about the correct person. Newspaper or broadcast station policy will determine how much of this information is used.

The reporter should always get complete identification for the subject of a news story, if only to confirm that he or she is writing about the correct person.

GROUP IDENTIFICATION

A troublesome question regarding identification is group identification. Can a member of a group sue when the group as a whole is libeled? Remember, the plaintiff must show the court that the injurious remarks are "of and concerning him or her." If the group is very small, the plaintiff usually has little difficulty convincing a court that identification has occurred. If the editor of a company's employee newsletter asserts that the three-person employee benefit board is incompetent, each member could claim identification. On the other hand, if the group is very big it is improbable that a suit will stand. In a 2002 "60 Minutes" broadcast the CBS network included a report on multimillion dollar verdicts against corporations rendered by juries in rural Mississippi, including Jefferson County. There were comments made by persons interviewed that jurors were "paying back these Yankee corporations or businesses for them being disenfranchised." The jurors were mad and held resentment, the interviewees said. One even suggested that the jurors benefited by receiving money under the table after their verdicts. Several former Jefferson County jurors sued, claiming that the defamatory statements were clearly "directed toward" and "of and concerning" them. The U.S. District Court judge disagreed, noting that none of the plaintiffs were named. The court said the segment referred to juries in rural, impoverished places like Jefferson County. But "no connection can be shown between the plaintiffs and the allegedly defamatory statement other than the fact that the plaintiffs served as jurors in Jefferson County." There were far too many people who had been jurors one time or another in that county.[42]

But what about the groups in between very small and very big? The "Restatement of Torts" says this:

> One who publishes defamatory matter concerning a group or class of persons is subject to liability to an individual member of it, but only if (A) the group or class is so small that the matter can reasonably be understood to refer to the individual, or (B) the circumstances of publication reasonably give rise to the conclusion that there is particular reference to him.[43]

There is really no magic number; it is not possible to say, for example, that a group with more than 40 is safe, or that groups with less than 25 pose problems. Courts will look at the

---

42. *Berry* v. *Safer*, 32 M.L.R. 2057 (2004). See also *Gales* v. *CBS*, 32 M.L.R. 2067 (2004), aff.d. 124 Fed Appx 275 (2005).

43. American Law Institute, *Restatement of Torts*.

circumstances as well as the number in the group. A police undercover agent reported to the owner of a paper mill in Maine that employee Harry Hudson had been drinking on the job. The agent was assigned to the mill to look for illegal drug use. A dozen workers at the mill were ultimately fired, 11 for illegal drug use, and Hudson for drinking on the job. A local television station subsequently reported that 12 workers had been terminated at the mill for involvement with illegal drugs. No names were given, but the mill was identified. Hudson sued and argued that it was common knowledge in the small community who the 12 workers were—and as such he had been erroneously identified as an illegal drug user. The station sought to have the suit dismissed, but the Maine Supreme Court refused, ruling that it was a jury question whether or not the broadcast had identified Hudson.[44] Courts have ruled that groups of 29 teachers,[45] 30 firefighters,[46] and 21 police officers[47] were all too large to permit identification.

The Virginia Supreme Court in 2002 blocked the attempt of a police officer to sue for libel after the mayor of the town accused the police department of corruption, dishonesty and felonious conduct. One member of the police department, Donald Dean Jr., sued and said because the department was small (from five to eight members when the mayor's comments were made), a statement like the mayor's was surely of and concerning individual members of the group. The court rejected the small group notion, ruling that a statement imputing misconduct to a government group—even a small group—constitutes a libel of government, for which there is no cause of action in American law. Dean would have to show the statement specifically implicated him or each member of the group. "Such an implication can be shown by extrinsic evidence, but evidence that others 'understood' the implication, based solely upon the plaintiff's membership in the referenced group will not satisfy the 'of and concerning' requirement," the court ruled.[48]

But caution is urged on reporters who describe even a very large group in a defamatory manner. Care is especially appropriate if only a small number of the defamed group live in the community. If the charge is made that all astrologers are frauds and there is only one astrologer in the community, the remark can be dangerous. The plaintiff could convince a sympathetic jury that the comment was aimed at him, and that he has been severely harmed by the remark.

DEFAMATION

The third element in the plaintiff's case focuses on the words themselves. There are two kinds of defamatory words. The first kind consists of words that are libelous on their face, words that obviously can damage the reputation of any person. Words like "thief," "cheat," and "traitor" are libelous per se—there is no question that they are defamatory.

The second kind of words are innocent on their face and become defamatory only if the reader or viewer knows other facts. To say that Duane Arnold married Jennifer Carter appears

44. *Hudson* v. *Guy Gannett Broadcasting,* 521 A. 2d 714 (1987).
45. *O'Brien* v. *Williamson Daily News,* 735 F. Supp. 218 (1990).
46. *Olive* v. *New York Post,* 16 M.L.R. 2397 (1989).
47. *Arcand* v. *Evening Call,* 567 F. 2d 1163 (1987).
48. *Dean* v. *Dearing,* 561 SE 2d 686 (2002); see also *Friends of Falun Gong* v. *Pacific Culture,* 109 Fed Appx 442 (2004).

safe enough. But if the reader knows that Arnold is already married to another woman, the statement accuses Arnold of bigamy. And that is a libelous accusation.

The distinction between these two kinds of words was once more important than it is now. At one time plaintiffs had to prove they were specifically harmed by the words in the second category, usually called "libel per quod." Damage was presumed from the words in the first category, usually called "libel per se." All plaintiffs today must prove they were damaged by the publication of the libel. Still, in many jurisdictions, courts have erected significant barriers that make it more difficult for persons who sue for libel per quod to win their case than persons who sue for words that are clearly defamatory on their face.

The law does not contain a list of words that are defamatory. In each case a court must examine the particular words or phrase or paragraph and decide whether these words lower the individual's reputation among a significant number of so-called right-thinking people in the community. Sometimes a precedent or many precedents will exist. Numerous cases, for example, establish that stating a woman is unchaste is libelous. But sometimes precedents aren't always that useful. Times change; the meanings of words change. Describing someone as a slacker today might be unkind, but hardly libelous. But during World War I the term "slacker" was used to identify a draft dodger and was certainly defamatory. Author Oscar Hijuelos used these phrases in his novel "The Mambo Kings Play Songs of Love": "Gloria huddled at a table drinking daiquiris." She touched the "skin and gnarly hair" of the Mambo King before saying to him, "Come on, ya big lug, why don't you kiss me?" Eighty years ago such a description of a woman's behavior might in fact harm her reputation. But in 1991, a U.S. District Court ruled that "reporting that a person has requested a kiss or [was] sipping a daiquiri, true or not, simply does not subject [a person] to the scorn of the average reader."[49]

At a libel trial a judge and jury are supposed to consider the words in light of their ordinary meaning unless the evidence is persuasive that the defendant meant something else when the statement was published. As a general rule, the judge will decide as a matter of law whether particular words are capable of conveying a defamatory meaning. Sometimes even negative descriptions of a person won't qualify as libel. Comedienne Martha Raye sued late-night television host David Letterman for a parody of her ads for denture cleaner. The ads always began, "Here is Martha Raye, actress, denture wearer." Letterman told his audience that he had seen "the most terrifying commercial on television last night, featuring Martha Raye, condom user." The court said that the words were not defamatory. "No one could reasonably understand this passage as expressing that the plaintiff actually uses condoms, that she is promiscuous, that she actually had made a condom commercial, or any other statement of fact," the California Superior Court judge ruled, dismissing the case.[50] The Rhode Island Supreme Court ruled in 2002 that a cartoon in the Sunday comics section of the Providence Journal was not capable of a defamatory meaning. Two workmen, one wearing a shirt that said Budget Pest Control, were shown standing in front of a blazing house. The one wearing the shirt was holding a gas can and grinning maniacally. The other worker was telling a distraught woman, "Easy now, ma'am. This is Billy Bob's first day on the job and them carpenter ants can be real stubborn." The court asked the question, would ordinary readers have reasonably

---

49. Cohen, "Use of Real Name."
50. *Raye* v. *Letterman,* 14 M.L.R. 2047 (1987).

understood the cartoon to be making a defamatory comment about the plaintiff, Budget Termite & Pest Control? The court said no. The comment carried an exaggerated comic tone and was published on the comics page. These factors would suggest a humorous idea, not a statement of fact. The court also noted that the name Budget Pest Control was almost a generic label and the plaintiff really couldn't connect its business with the cartoon.[51]

If the judge rules that the words *are capable* of a defamatory meaning, the fact finder—the jury, if there is one, or the judge—then must determine whether the words *in fact convey* a defamatory meaning. For example, a U.S. Court of Appeals ruled that it was up to a jury to decide whether the allegation that a scientist charged as much as $5,000 per day to testify as an expert in court cases carried with it the implication that the scientist was selling his testimony to the highest bidder, a clearly defamatory assertion.[52]

Innuendo as opposed to a flat assertion can be defamatory.

Innuendo as opposed to a flat assertion can be defamatory. Read the following actual news item from the Boston Record:

> The Veterans Hospital here suspected that 39-year-old George M. Perry of North Truro, whose death is being probed by federal and state authorities, was suffering from chronic arsenic poisoning.
>
> State police said the body of Perry, and of his brother, Arthur, who is buried near him, would probably be exhumed from St. Peter's Cemetery in Provincetown.
>
> George Perry died in the VA hospital last June 9, forty-eight hours after his tenth admission there. . . . His brother, who lived in Connecticut and spent two days here during George's funeral, died approximately a month later. About two months later, in September, George's mother-in-law, seventy-four-year-old Mrs. Mary F. Mott, who had come to live with her daughter, died too. Her remains were cremated.

While the story lacked a good deal in journalistic clarity, it didn't take a terribly insightful reader to understand what the reporter was trying to suggest. Mrs. Perry murdered her husband, her brother-in-law, and her mother. The insinuations are that Arthur died after visiting the plaintiff's home and that the mother had "died too." Isn't it too bad that her remains were cremated? This story cost the Hearst Corporation, publishers of the Boston Record, $25,000.[53]

A libel suit cannot be based on an isolated phrase wrenched out of context. The article as a whole must be considered. A story about baseball's legendary base stealer, Ricky Henderson, might contain the sentence "Henderson might be the best thief of all time," referring to his base-stealing ability. Henderson cannot sue on the basis of that single sentence. The story itself makes it clear the kind of thievery the writer is discussing. Nevertheless, a libelous remark in a headline—even though it is cleared up in the story that follows—may be the basis for a libel suit.

One week after O.J. Simpson was acquitted of the criminal charge of murdering his wife and her companion the National Examiner carried a headline on its cover, "COPS THINK KATO DID IT—He fears they will want him for perjury, pals say." The story appeared on page 17 and

---

51. *Budget Termite & Pest Control* v. *Bousquet,* 811 A 2d 1169 (2002).
52. *McBride* v. *Merrell Dow,* 717 F. 2d 1460 (1984).
53. *Perry* v. *Hearst Corp.,* 334 F. 2d 800 (1964).

carried the headline, "KATO KAELIN . . . COPS THINK HE DID IT." The story said the police were trying to prove that Kaelin lied under oath, that he committed perjury. The headlines suggest, Kaelin argued, that he was a suspect in the murders. Attorneys for the National Examiner said no, that was not what was intended. The word "it" meant perjury. Judges on the 9th U.S. Circuit Court of Appeals ruled that under California law the meaning of the publication must be measured by the effect it would have on the mind of the average reader, and in this case it was highly likely that an average, reasonable reader might conclude that the word "it" referred to murder.[54] Kaelin and the Examiner settled this suit in October 1999.

The Indiana Supreme Court was confronted with a situation in which a restaurant owner argued that a newspaper headline defamed his establishment. The court adopted the rule that if a headline fairly indicates the substance of an otherwise accurate article, the headline is not defamatory. In this case a county health inspector reported that there was evidence of roaches and rodents in the restaurant. The headline in the Ft. Wayne Journal Gazette stated: "Health board shuts doors of Bandido's. Inspectors find rats, roaches at local eatery." The state high court ruled that the headline was not an accurate indication of the article, because it contained the word "rats," and the story only referred to "rodents." Every rat is a rodent, the court ruled, but not every rodent is a rat.[55]

Sometimes a court will even allow reader habits to be taken into account. A story of about 50 paragraphs published in the Seattle Post-Intelligencer was a generally accurate account of the redemption of a home mortgage by a local attorney. But the headline and the first few paragraphs strongly hinted that the attorney had done something wrong. The jury agreed with the plaintiff that it was unlikely that most readers would follow the lengthy story as it was jumped onto the inside pages of the newspaper and would absorb only the defamatory connotations in the first few paragraphs. The lawyer won a $100,000 judgment.[56]

Factual assertions can obviously be the basis of a libel suit. Can a statement of opinion be defamatory? Well, that depends. If the question is, Can an opinion lower someone's reputation? which is the definition of defamation, the answer is yes, an opinion can be defamatory. But if the question is, Can a defamatory opinion be the basis for a libel suit? the answer is probably no. American courts have ruled on numerous occasions that pure opinion is protected by the First Amendment.[57] A plaintiff cannot successfully sue for libel based on a statement that is pure opinion. Why? Because pure opinion cannot be proved to be true or false—it is simply an opinion. For example, "I think Brenda Baylor is a stupid jerk." Even though this comment might lower Brenda's reputation in the eyes of the community, how can you prove or disprove that someone is a stupid jerk? Without proof of falsity, the libel suit fails. So pure opinion is not a problem. But unfortunately, courts frequently have a devil of a time determining what is and what is not pure opinion. Clearly, an opinion statement that contains a false fact can be libelous because of the false fact. "I think Brenda Baylor is a stupid jerk. You know, she only scored 150 on her SAT test." The second sentence is a factual assertion and if it is false, it could surely support a claim of libel. But other kinds of statements are not so clear. "Emissions from the Acme Smelter are harming the environment." Is that a statement of

54. *Kaelin v. Globe Communications Corp.,* 162 F. 3d 1036 (1998).
55. *Journal-Gazette Company v. Bandido's Inc.,* 712 N.E. 2d 446 (1999).
56. *McNair v. Hearst Corp.,* 494 F. 2d 1309 (1974).
57. See, for example, *Milkovich v. Lorain Journal Co.,* 110 S. Ct. 2695 (1991).

fact or an opinion? Some people might believe that any emission from a smokestack harms the environment. But Acme might be in full compliance with Environmental Protection Agency rules and will argue its emissions are safe. So it depends. This topic is explored far more fully on pages 258–264. Suffice to say for this discussion, opinion statements can harm a person's reputation and are therefore defamatory. But if such statements are free of false and libelous facts, they cannot sustain a defamation lawsuit.

Although there is no space in this book for a catalog of defamatory words, an outline of the most common categories of problem words, words to which writers and editors need to pay special attention, is feasible.

Crime

Imputations of criminal behavior are responsible for a great many libel suits. Saying someone has done something illegal—from jaywalking to murder—is libelous. The use of the word "alleged" in these cases is often of little help. The meaning of the word "alleged" is "to be declared or asserted to be as described." An alleged murderer is someone who has been declared or asserted to be a murderer. But by whom? If the state has charged Jones with murder, the state has alleged that he is a murderer. If that is the case, a reporter should say so: "Jones, who has been charged with murder" rather than simply, "the alleged murderer Jones." But if Jones is merely being questioned in connection with the murder, he is not an alleged murderer, he is an alleged suspect. To call him an alleged murderer is inaccurate and libelous. The best guide for the reporter is this: Report what you know to be true. If Jones is being questioned as a suspect, say that. If police consider him a suspect, say that. Take the word "alleged" and put it in the circular file next to your desk.

Sexual References

Sexual references and implications are also responsible for a great many libel suits. A statement that a woman is unchaste or is sleeping with a man to whom she is not married is defamatory. An allegation that a woman has been raped is equally libelous. The law traditionally has been less protective of men in this regard, but times may be changing. A young male model sued the publishers of gay and lesbian publications for including his photo in advertising for "Lust," a collection of photographs of naked, sexually aroused men engaged in explicit sex acts. The defendant was alone in the photo and was clothed from the waist down, but he argued that the use of the photo in advertising for such a publication suggests that he is sexually promiscuous. The defendants tried to argue that even if the use of the photo did imply sexual promiscuity, this was not a defamatory statement when made about a man rather than a woman. The Appellate Division of the New York Supreme Court disagreed, stating that "the notion that while the imputation of sexual immorality to a woman is defamatory per se, but is not so with respect to a man, has no place in modern jurisprudence. Such a distinction, having its basis in gender-based classification—would violate constitutional precepts."[58]

Comments about other kinds of sexual behavior are also sensitive, but as Americans seem to be developing a more open mind regarding sexual behavior, the law is changing. Twenty-five

58. *Rejent* v. *Liberation Publications, Inc.*, 197 A.D. 2d 240 (1994).

years ago any allegation that a man was gay or a woman was a lesbian was defamatory per se.[59] There are surely courts that would still abide by that rule today. But many courts have taken a different position. A federal court in Massachusetts ruled in mid-2004 that an accusation that an individual is gay no longer imputes criminal conduct and, therefore, cannot be the basis for a claim of libel per se. The plaintiff in the case argued that some people in the community believe that homosexuals are less reputable than heterosexuals and cited laws against gay marriage to support his case. The court rejected this argument, noting that in the past, statements misidentifying whites as blacks were also considered defamatory, but not so today.[60]

Personal Habits

Material about the personal habits of an individual need to be carefully screened. To raise questions about an individual's honesty, integrity or financial responsibility can be dangerous. Comments about consumption of alcohol or drugs can also cause problems. Libel law has traditionally protected persons from false assertions that they have a contagious disease. Such an allegation can cause friends and acquaintances to shun the supposed victim because they don't want to be infected by the disease themselves. This is not a common libel problem today. But it is a problem to suggest that someone suffers from a medical condition that implies, for example, sexual promiscuity or unsavory behavior on the part of the victim. The Nebraska Supreme Court in 1990 sustained a jury award of $23,350 to a Springfield, Neb., man who was falsely accused of having AIDS. This was a slander suit; it resulted when a prominent woman in a small town began spreading rumors about the plaintiff.[61] Finally, comments about an individual's personal religious faith ("She doesn't live up to the teachings of her church"), patriotism, or political activities have also generated libel actions.

Ridicule

A person can be libeled by ridicule. Not all humorous stories about someone are necessarily defamatory; only those in which the subject of the story is made to appear "uncommonly foolish" tend to be dangerous. Newspapers are commonly victimized by false obituaries. At times the "deceased" has brought a libel suit in response to such a publication, but the courts have consistently ruled that to say someone has died is not defamatory; it does not lower that person's reputation. But once a New England newspaper ridiculed a man by saying he was so thrifty that he built his own casket and dug his own grave. This story made the man appear to be foolish or unnatural.[62]

Business Reputation

Libel law probably goes furthest in protecting persons in their business and occupations. Any comment that injures people's ability to conduct a business, harms them in their job, or makes

59. *Gray* v. *Press Communications LLC,* 775 A 2d 678 (2001).
60. *Albright* v. *Morton,* 321 F. Supp. 2d 130 (2004). See also *Donovan* v. *Fiumara,* 114 N.C. App. 524 (1994); and *Miles* v. *National Enquirer,* 38 F. Supp. 2d 1226 (1999).
61. Robbins, "A Rumor of AIDS."
62. *Powers* v. *Durgin-Snow Publishing Co.,* 144 A. 2d 294 (1958).

Source: © AP/Wide World Photos

NBA player Latrell Sprewell sued the New York Post for defamation for publishing a story that, he said, hurt him in his business as a basketball player.

it more difficult for them to pursue their occupation is generally defamatory. And business-people are generally more likely to sue. They tend to be more acquainted with law and more comfortable initiating a legal suit. National Basketball Association star Latrell Sprewell sued the New York Post after it published a story that claimed Sprewell took a swing at someone, missed, hit a wall, and broke a bone in his hand. Then, the newspaper said, he delayed in reporting the injury to his team, the New York Knicks. Sprewell denied the story and said it harmed his business relationship with the Knicks, his employer. A New York Supreme Court agreed that the story could have had such an impact and denied the Post's motion to dismiss.[63]

There are some interesting quirks in libel law as it relates to comments about the way an individual does business. To report that a businessperson or professional person has made an error is not always defamatory. Business and professional people are not expected to be perfect. Everyone makes a mistake now and then. A story, for example, that suggests a physician has misdiagnosed a case or that a real estate developer has botched a deal may not be considered defamatory under what is called the **single mistake rule.** The community would not think less of a doctor or businessperson who made a single error, the reasoning goes. Hence, the statement is not defamatory. Stories that suggest a pattern of incompetence,

63. *Sprewell* v. *NYP Holdings Inc.,* 32 M.L.R. 2338 (2004).

that go beyond asserting a single error, are defamatory, however.[64] The single mistake rule should not be used as an excuse for sloppy reporting, but it can come in handy if an error is inadvertently made.

Corporations that believe their credit has been damaged or their reputation has been harmed can do exactly what an individual plaintiff can do and sue for this injury. The list of kinds of defamatory accusations is long. Assertions that a company is involved in illegal business or that it fails to pay its bills on time or that it deliberately manufactures unsafe products or that it is trying to break a union are all libelous. The law, however, does not hold a public business responsible for the bad behavior of its customers. The owner of a Biloxi lounge sued for a story that said a man had been killed in a fight in the bar. Actually the fight took place outside, about one-half block down the street. The Mississippi Supreme Court refused to hold the newspaper responsible, ruling that there was nothing in the story that harmed the lounge or its owner.[65] A suggestion that the proprietor of a public business encourages rowdy behavior, or tolerates fighting, or permits drug deals to be made is a different matter. In these cases the story does reflect on the behavior of the owner and would be libelous.

Criticism of a Product

Criticism of a product falls into a different legal category, called "disparagement of property." Such criticism is often called **trade libel,** but it is not really libel at all. What is the difference between libeling a business and disparaging a product?

Criticism of a product falls into a different legal category, called "disparagement of property."

- Trade libel, or product disparagement, focuses on the product itself. "Viking Runabout automobiles continually stall during a rainstorm." That is an attack on the product.
- A libel of a business tends to focus on the alleged failings of the people who operate the business. "Viking Runabout automobiles continually stall during a rainstorm. The manufacturer, in order to save a few dollars, did not shield the electrical system properly and water leaks in at alarming levels, causing a short circuit." This is an attack on the company as well as the product.

To win a trade libel suit the plaintiff must prove three things.

1. The plaintiff must show that the statements made about the products are false. This can be difficult. Organizations that test products and then publish their results tend to be very careful in the way they present their findings. Rather than report that the Viking Runabouts stall in a rainstorm, the story will usually say the Viking Runabout that was tested stalled. Viking may be able to prove that most of its Runabouts run properly; it is difficult to dispute that one car, the one tested, failed to run correctly.
2. The plaintiff must show specific monetary loss because of the false comments about the product. Courts insist on fairly precise dollars-and-cents losses from canceled orders, for example, or a drop in sales.

64. *Bowes* v. *Magna Concepts, Inc.,* 561 N.Y.S. 2d 16 (1990); see also *Sermidi* v. *Battistotti,* 27 M.L.R. 2523 (1999).
65. *Chatham* v. *Gulf Publishing,* 502 So. 2d 647 (1987).

3. The plaintiff must show that the false comments about the product were motivated by ill will and bad feelings, or by what the law calls actual malice. Actual malice, which is defined more completely on pages 222–233, means that the defendant knew that the statements about the product were false, or exhibited reckless disregard for the truth in making the comments.

This is a difficult challenge for the plaintiff. Even proving the that the statements were false is not always easy. For example, in 1989 the television program "60 Minutes" suggested that apples grown in Washington state were unsafe because they had been treated with a chemical called Alar, which some scientists contend causes an increased risk of cancer, especially to children. Farmers in the state sued CBS and others for $100 million, alleging among other things product disparagement, or trade libel. But the case came to an abrupt ending four years later when a U.S. District Court granted the network's motion for a summary judgment, ruling that the plaintiffs in the case could not possibly prove that the statements were false.

The apple growers contended that three statements made in the broadcast were false.

1. Daminozide (the active ingredient in Alar) is the most potent cancer-causing agent in our food supply.
2. Daminozide poses an imminent hazard and unacceptable cancer risk.
3. Daminozide is most harmful to children.

Judge Nielsen said that there was substantial debate within the scientific community about the potential harm caused by daminozide. CBS presented evidence that the Environmental Protection Agency considers daminozide to be among the most carcinogenic synthetic pesticides and that ingesting a carcinogen at any time could create the hazard of suffering a cancer in the future. But, the judge said, researchers have sharp differences of opinion regarding the potential harm that daminozide might cause to children. If science is seemingly in disagreement about the danger posed by this chemical, Judge Nielsen said, how did the plaintiffs think they were going to prove that these allegations were false?[66] The 9th U.S. Circuit Court of Appeals upheld this decision in 1995.[67]

Banks, Insurance Companies and Vegetables

Many states have adopted statutes aimed at protecting the reputations of specific kinds of businesses. Banks and insurance companies in many jurisdictions are shielded by special statutes designed to protect them from attacks on their fiscal integrity. If successful, such an attack could turn customers against these businesses and destroy them quite easily. In recent years many states have adopted statutes that outlaw publication of intentional lies about the fruits and vegetables grown in the state. These so-called veggie hate laws are aimed at preventing the kind of damage suffered by Washington apple growers because of the Alar controversy noted earlier. These laws generally give farmers and growers a cause of action to sue anyone who makes a statement about the health risks of a particular food product that is not based on "verifiable fact or scientific or other reliable evidence." Some of these laws also shift

66. *Auvil* v. *CBS "60 Minutes,"* 836 F. Supp. 740 (1993).
67. *Auvil* v. *CBS "60 Minutes,"* 67 F. 3d 816 (1995).

the burden of proving truth or falsity from the plaintiff to the defendant. Although such laws as these seem odd, they nevertheless exist and could result in legal woes for the careless journalist.

Talk show producer and host Oprah Winfrey was sued in 1998 by Texas cattle ranchers under that state's False Disparagement of Perishable Food Products Act. A guest on Winfrey's talk show had alleged that thousands of head of U.S. cattle were infected with bovine spongiform encephalopathy, the so-called mad cow disease, prompting the talk show host to declare that she was giving up eating hamburgers. Cattle prices dropped precipitously after the broadcast, and the ranchers sought millions of dollars in damages. Experts who viewed the case as the first important test of the constitutionality of the veggie hate laws were disappointed when U.S. District Judge Mary Lou Robinson ruled that the case could not proceed under the Texas law because the plaintiffs had not proved that cattle are "perishable food" as defined by the statute, or that "knowingly false" statements had been made, a requirement under the Texas law.[68] The 5th U.S. Circuit Court of Appeals affirmed the lower-court decision, but solely on the grounds that no knowingly false statements had been made about the cattle.[69]

FALSITY

While nearly all libel plaintiffs who sue the mass media must prove that the defamatory statements are false, not every plaintiff must meet this requirement. This is because of one of the quirks in libel law, something that will be discussed at far greater length beginning on page 193.

The world of libel plaintiffs is divided into two groups, public persons and private persons. A public person is a government official, an elected officer, someone who is leading a public crusade, a prominent entertainer, a visible religious or business leader. A private person is someone who is not a public person. As you will soon see, the law makes it far more difficult for a public person, as opposed to a private person, to win a libel suit.

In every instance a public-person plaintiff must prove that the libelous remarks are not truthful. But the Supreme Court has ruled that a private-person plaintiff must prove the falsity of the libelous statements only when the subject of the statement is a matter of public concern.[70] What is a matter of public concern? The Supreme Court has not given a definition but, in another case, noted that whether a statement dealt with a matter of public concern must be determined on the basis of the statement's "content, form and context."[71] Not a very clear definition.

Over time, courts will flesh out the definition of a "matter of public concern." This issue has simply not arisen often enough in the past 20 years for the courts to provide much meaningful insight on it. Most authorities will argue that when a solid definition emerges, it will be one that is broadly based and include most of what is published in mainstream newspapers and magazines, and what is aired on television or radio. It could be argued that when the editor at a publication or broadcasting station, which is aiming to attract and please a large, diverse audience, selects an item to report, that in itself is evidence that the content of the item is a matter of public concern. But no court has yet gone this far.

68. *Texas Beef Group* v. *Winfrey*, 11 F. Supp. 2d 858 (1998).
69. *Texas Beef Group* v. *Winfrey*, 201 F. 3d 680 (2000).
70. *Philadelphia Newspapers, Inc.* v. *Hepps*, 475 U.S. 767 (1986).
71. *Dun & Bradstreet* v. *Greenmoss*, 472 U.S. 749 (1985).

The first rule of proving truth or falsity is that the evidence presented in court must go to the heart of the libelous charge.

Most plaintiffs, then, must prove that the defamatory material is false. In those few instances when a private person sues for a story that is not a matter of public concern, the defendant must prove that the material is truthful. How does one prove falsity or truth?

The first rule of proving truth or falsity is that the evidence presented in court must go to the heart of the libelous charge. The proof must be direct and explicit. If there is conflicting evidence, the fact finder—the judge or the jury—will decide who is telling the truth. Every word of a defamatory charge need not be truthful, only the part that carries the gist or the sting of the libel.

What the court is looking for is substantial truth. For example, an article in American Medical News alleged that a physician was being sued for stock fraud. The doctor sued for libel, claiming that this statement was false. In fact, he said, he was being sued for making deceptive statements relating to stock transactions. The allegation of being sued for stock fraud suggests that he was being deceitful for personal gain, he argued. The 10th U.S. Circuit Court of Appeals agreed that the statement in the publication was not exactly accurate, but called the problem a layperson's inaccuracy. The gist of the statement was substantially true.[72]

A federal court in Pennsylvania ruled that a newspaper report that the plaintiff was convicted of embezzlement when the actual charges were tax evasion and mail fraud was substantially true and not actionable.[73] The National Geographic Society was sued in 2003 for reporting in a story on 21st century slavery that a Maryland couple had lured a 14-year-old schoolgirl from Cameroon to the United States with promises of schooling, then isolated her in their home, forced her to work as their servant, and "raped her." The magazine got the information for the article from Department of Justice documents that said the girl was "sexually assaulted" and "sexually abused." While the couple was charged with making the girl a slave, and there was substantial evidence they sexually abused her, they were not convicted of rape. They sued for libel, contending the rape allegation was false. But a federal court ruled against the plaintiffs, holding that there was ample precedent in the law that "technical errors in legal nomenclature in reports on matters involving violation of the law are of no legal consequence." The article was substantially true.[74]

In 2001 the Michigan Court of Appeals overturned a lower-court ruling in favor of former Congresswoman Barbara Collins who claimed she had been misquoted in a story in the Detroit Free Press. In a taped interview Collins said she didn't believe all white people were intolerant. "That's why I love the individuals, but I don't like the race," she said. In the quote carried by the Free Press, the last phrase was changed to this: "That's why I say I love the individuals, but I hate the race." The trial court agreed with the plaintiff that the words "don't like" and "hate" mean different things, and this made the statement in the newspaper false. But the appellate court disagreed and said the words have about the same meaning—the gist or the sting of the quoted matter was true.[75]

But don't be misled. It is not the size of the error that counts. The court will ask whether the inaccurate statement is defamatory. And a detail can be just as libelous as a major assertion.

72. *Schwartz* v. *American College of Emergency Physicians,* 215 F. 3d 1140 (2000).
73. *Reilly* v. *North Hills News Record,* 27 M.L.R. 1569 (1998).
74. *Nanji* v. *National Geographic Society,* 33 M.L.R. 2074 (2005).
75. *Collins* v. *Detroit Free Press,* 627 N.W. 2d 5 (2001).

Take the case of Anthony S. Jones, for example. Jones was hired as a firefighter in 1984 under a federal court order that required the employment of more minorities in the Des Moines (Iowa) Fire Department. Eighteen months later he was fired. Authorities said he had failed to pass a written emergency medical technician examination, a requirement to hold the job. Fire Chief Robert Armstrong told reporters that Jones had a reading problem. He had been tutored in reading at taxpayers' expense, Armstrong said, but the test revealed he still read at the third-grade level. Jones sued when the story was broadcast. The television station and other defendants asked the trial court to dismiss the case because the story was substantially true. The trial court denied the motion, and the Iowa Supreme Court sustained the denial. The state high court said there were two errors in the story. Jones personally had paid for a substantial part of the tutoring. Also, Jones was tested as reading at a level comparable with the lower one-third of community college students, not the third-grade level. These were details, but they were an important part of the substance of the story. The story was not substantially true, the court ruled, and sent the case back for trial.[76]

An Illinois appellate court in 2002 rejected a newspaper's argument that it was not libelous to report that a man pleaded guilty to felony possession of marijuana when in fact he had pleaded guilty to misdemeanor unlawful possession of marijuana. The publication's attorneys argued that either plea resulted in a criminal conviction for the plaintiff. There is a difference between a felony and a misdemeanor, the court ruled. A misdemeanor is a minor offense while a felony is a serious crime. The public will view a felon far differently than someone who has been convicted of a minor crime, the court added.[77]

Reporters must also remember that a jury in a libel suit will determine the truth or falsity of a story based on what the story said, not what the reporter meant. ABC was sued by the maker of a garbage recycling machine. Lundell Manufacturing sold the $3 million machine to a county in Georgia. After using the machine for a year or so, some people in the county said that the new machine had not solved the garbage problem. An ABC "World News Tonight" story included these comments:

> In this south Georgia county of tobacco farms and pecan groves taxpayers are angry that they are stuck with a three million dollar debt for this garbage recycling machine that they never approved and does not work.

Network attorneys argued that the reporter meant that the machine does not work in the larger sense, that it doesn't solve the county's garbage problem. But a jury agreed with the plaintiff instead and said that they interpreted the comment to mean that the garbage recycling machine did not work, that it was defective. In 1996 the 8th U.S. Circuit Court of Appeals upheld the more than $1 million jury award and ruled that a jury could conclude that the network's statement about the machine was false.[78]

How does the court evaluate the truth of the charge? The jury does this with guidance from the judge. The jurors are presented with both the libelous untruthful statement about the plaintiff and the truth about the plaintiff. The untruthful statement will leave a certain impression about the plaintiff in the jurors' minds. Does learning the truthful statement change that

---

76. *Jones* v. *Palmer Communications, Inc.,* 440 N.W. 2d 884 (1989).
77. *Myers* v. *Telegraph,* 30 M.L.R. 2463 (2002).
78. *Lundell Manufacturing Co.* v. *ABC Inc.,* 98 F. 3d 351 (1996).

impression? For example, a television station refers to Hal Jones as a wife beater. Jurors gain an impression of Jones based on that statement. In truth, Jones struck his wife only once, during an argument, after she threw a coffee pot at him. Does the truth leave a different impression of Jones in the jurors' minds? One court said that "a workable test of truth is whether the libel as published would have a different effect on the mind of the reader from that which the pleaded truth would have produced."[79]

The case of *Haynes* v. *Alfred A. Knopf, Inc.* provides a good example of this test. Author Nicholas Lemann wrote a best-selling book called "The Promised Land: The Great Black Migration and How It Changed America." In this work he recounted the migration of more than 5 million African-Americans from impoverished rural areas in the South to the North between 1940 and 1970. In some parts of the book he focused on the experiences of individuals to tell his story. What happened to Ruby Lee Daniels when she moved north from Mississippi was an important segment in the book. Seven years after she arrived in Chicago, Ruby Lee met Luther Haynes. Haynes had a good job at the time, and he and Ruby lived together and had children. But then, according to Lemann, Luther began to drink too much and problems began. The author recounted a whole series of incidents that reflected very badly on Haynes and certainly hurt his reputation. Included were allegations that Haynes was fired from a job for drinking, that he was arrested for assaulting a police officer, that he refused to support his family, and that he walked out on Ruby and the children. In a libel suit that followed, Haynes did not dispute the accuracy of most of these statements, but said that three of them were false. The court ruled that even if three of the many statements were false, most of the material written about Haynes was true. The reputation was damaged by the truthful statements. The harm caused by the three false statements really didn't hurt Haynes that much more. "Falsehoods that do not harm the plaintiff's reputation more than a full recital of the true facts about him would do are thus not actionable," the court said.[80]

Even if a story contains nothing but truthful statements it still might be regarded as false if important facts are left out and the story leaves a false impression. Some courts have called this defamation by implication. A South Carolina driver accidentally struck and injured the police chief of Eastover, S.C. She pleaded guilty to driving too fast for road conditions. A year later the police chief died and in two stories the newspaper repeated the account of the traffic accident, adding that the woman would not face additional charges despite the chief's death. Everything in both stories was true; but the newspaper did not report that the police chief died from cancer. Readers could easily conclude that he had died from injuries sustained in the accident, and this would be false, the South Carolina Court of Appeals concluded.[81] In Washington state the owner of a kitchen design and appliance store sued a Spokane television station for reporting that he had ejected and then had police arrest a mentally handicapped man who refused to leave the store. In the filmed report the handicapped man described how he had been forcefully escorted from the store by the owner. He told the reporter he simply wanted a job washing windows. The man, who suffered from Down's syndrome, had no prior criminal record, the reporter said. Nothing in the story was false. But the store owner argued

"Falsehoods that do not harm the plaintiff's reputation more than a full recital of the true facts about him would do are thus not actionable."

79. *Fleckstein* v. *Friedman,* 195 N.E. 537 (1934).
80. *Haynes* v. *Alfred A. Knopf, Inc.,* 8 F. 3d 1222 (1993); see also *Schmalenberg* v. *Tacoma News Inc.,* 943 P. 2d 350 (1997).
81. *Richardson* v. *State-Record Co.,* 499 S.E. 2d 822 (1998).

he had been defamed because the reporter failed to tell viewers that the man was the subject of numerous complaints because of his aggressive behavior, that he had made threats against the store owner, saying he would shoot the man and his wife, that the police had threatened to arrest him if he continued to trespass in the store, and that the only reason he had no criminal record was because courts had ruled him mentally incompetent to stand trial. The store owner, Eliot Mohr, argued that inclusion of these facts, would have made his actions appear to be reasonable and would have made him appear more sympathetic to the plight of the intruder. This, he said, amounted to defamation by implication. The Washington Court of Appeals agreed, but the state Supreme Court disagreed and overturned the grant of a summary judgment in Mohr's behalf. The court ruled defamation by implication was certainly possible in some cases, but that Mohr had not made a clear showing that the impression left in viewers' minds by the televised report would have been any different if the omitted facts had been included. The case was sent back for a trial.[82]

One more point should be stressed about truth and falsity. Correctly quoting someone or accurately reporting what someone else has said does not necessarily constitute publishing a truthful statement. Imagine that John Smith tells a reporter that the police chief changes arrest records of certain prisoners to simplify their getting bail and winning acquittal. This charge, attributed to John Smith, is contained in the reporter's story, which is subsequently published. The police chief sues for libel. It is not sufficient for the reporter to prove merely that the statement in the story was an accurate account of what Smith said. Even if the reporter's story contained an exact duplicate of Smith's charge, truth can be sustained only by proving the substance of the charge, that the police chief has altered arrest records. It is the truth of the libelous charge that is at issue, not merely the accuracy of the quote in the story. Accuracy, then, is not always the same thing as truth.

The initial burden in the libel suit rests with the plaintiff, who must prove five important elements: that the defamation was published, that it was of and concerning the plaintiff, that the words were defamatory, that the allegations were false, and that the defendant was at fault in causing this legal harm. The first four elements have been discussed in this chapter. Proving fault, the most complicated of the five elements, is the subject of Chapter 5.

SUMMARY

A plaintiff in a libel suit must first prove that the defamatory material was published; that is, that one additional person besides the plaintiff and the defendant has seen the material. The plaintiff must next show that the libel is of and concerning him or her. An individual can be identified for purposes of a libel suit by a name, nickname, photograph or even through a report of circumstances. Statements made about a very large group of people cannot be used as the basis for a libel suit for a single member of that group. However, if the group is smaller, individual members of the group may be able to sue for comments made about the entire group. The plaintiff must also prove that the words in the offensive statement are defamatory, that they lower his or her reputation. The most common kinds of defamatory statements contain allegations about criminal acts or sexual impropriety, include comments about personal

82. *Mohr* v. *Grant*, 68 P. 3d 1159 (2003); 108 P. 3d 768 (2005).

habits or characteristics, or reflect on the plaintiff's patriotism, political beliefs, or competence and qualifications in a business or occupation. Corporations or other businesses can be defamed, and the manufacturer of a product can sue, with great difficulty, for product disparagement. In lawsuits against the mass media the plaintiff normally must prove that the damaging statements are false. The evidence presented in court must go to the heart of the libelous charge; the gist or sting of the libel must be false. Minor errors, unless they relate directly to the gist of the libel, will not usually result in a finding of falsity. The test of falsity is whether the proven truth leaves a different impression of the plaintiff in the minds of the jury than the impression created by the defamatory falsehood.

BIBLIOGRAPHY

American Law Institute. *Restatement of Torts,* 2nd ed. Philadelphia: American Law Institute, 1975.

Ashley, Paul. *Say It Safely,* 5th ed. Seattle: University of Washington Press, 1976.

Bellock, Pam. "Boston Herald Is Ordered to Pay Judge $2 Million for Libel." *The New York Times,* 19 February 2005, A-8.

Bezanson, Randall P., Gilbert Cranberg, and John Soloski. *Libel Law and the Press.* New York: The Free Press, 1987.

Brill, Steven. "1982: Behind the Verdict in the Washington Post Libel Trial." *The American Lawyer,* May 1994, 31.

Carvajal, Doreen. "Libel Wrangle Over Miliken Book Drags On." *The New York Times,* 28 June 1999, C1.

Cohen, Roger. "Suit Over Novel's Use of Real Name Is Dismissed." *The New York Times,* 19 July 1991.

Dill, Barbara. "Libel Law Doesn't Work, But Can It Be Fixed?" In *At What Price? Libel Law and Freedom of the Press,* essays by Martin London and Barbara Dill. New York: Twentieth Century Fund Press, 1993.

Grossman, Lawrence K. "CBS, 60 Minutes, and the Unseen Interview." *Columbia Journalism Review,* January/February 1996, 39.

Hakim, Danny. "Suzuki Resolves a Dispute with a Consumer Magazine." *The New York Times,* 9 June 2004, C6.

Libel Law: A Report of the Libel Reform Project. Washington, D.C.: The Annenberg Washington Program, 1988.

Media Law Resource Center. MLRC 2005 Report on Trials and Damages. Bulletin 2005 No. 1 (February 2005).

Moscov, Jim. "Truth, Justice and the American Tort." *Editor & Publisher,* 27 November 2000, p. 16.

Phelps, Robert, and Douglas Hamilton. *Libel.* New York: Macmillan, 1966.

Pring, George. "SLAPPs: Strategic Lawsuits Against Public Participation." *Pace Environmental Law Review,* Fall 1989, 8.

————, and Penelope Canan. "Strategic Lawsuits Against Public Participation." *Social Problems* 35 (1988): 506.

Prosser, William L. *Handbook of the Law of Torts.* St. Paul: West Publishing, 1963.

Robbins, William. "A Rumor of AIDS, a Slander Suit." *The New York Times,* 23 July 1990.

Shepard, Alicia C. "Fighting Back." *American Journalism Review,* January/February 1996, 34.

Smolla, Rodney A. "Dun & Bradstreet, Hepps, and Liberty Lobby: A New Analytic Primer on the Future Course of Defamation." *Georgetown Law Journal* 75 (1987): 1519.

———, and Michael J. Garetner. "The Annenberg Libel Reform Proposal: The Case for Enactment." *William and Mary Law Review* 31 (1989): 25.

Yankwich, Leon R. *It's Libel or Contempt If You Print It.* Los Angeles: Parker & Sons Publications, 1950.

Chapter 5

LIBEL
Proof of Fault

In 1964, for the first time, the U.S. Supreme Court ruled that a libel plaintiff was required to show that a defendant had been at fault when the defamatory material was published. Until that time, civil libel law had been governed by what is known as the doctrine of strict liability. Under this doctrine a libel defendant was responsible for harming a plaintiff regardless of how cautious and careful he or she had been in preparing and publishing or broadcasting the story. This ruling changed the face of libel law. What had been a relatively simple tort became a complex legal morass when it was infused with First Amendment considerations. This chapter outlines the two basic considerations relevant to fault:

Who is the plaintiff?

How was the story or material processed or prepared?

NEW YORK TIMES v. SULLIVAN

A difficult and often violent struggle for civil rights was taking place in much of the Deep South in the late 1950s and early 1960s. Blacks, often accompanied by white civil rights workers, used various acts of nonviolent civil disobedience to challenge a wide range of voting, accommodation and education laws that had left them as second-class citizens. Network television news was still in its early adolescence in this era; NBC and CBS carried only 15 minutes of news each night. The story of the civil rights movement was carried throughout the nation via a handful of prestigious and frequently liberal newspapers, especially The New York Times. Segregationist leaders in the South hated these newspapers, which each day carried stories and pictures of another peaceful civil rights protest that had been met with violence or some other illegal act by city, county or state officials or by angry southern citizens.

On March 29, 1960, The Times carried a full-page editorial-advertisement entitled "Heed Their Rising Voices." The ad was placed by an ad hoc coalition of civil rights leaders called the "Committee to Defend Martin Luther King and the Struggle for Freedom in the South." The text of the ad leveled charges against public officials in the South who, the committee contended, had used violence and illegal tactics to try to quell the peaceful civil rights struggle. The basic thrust of the charges contained in the advertisement was true; but the ad was filled with small, factual errors. Several public officials in Alabama brought suit against the newspaper. The first case to go to trial was one brought by Montgomery, Ala., police commissioner L.B. Sullivan, who sought $500,000 in damages for false and defamatory statements about the conduct of the Montgomery police department.* Sullivan was never named in the ad but contended that comments about the behavior of the police reflected on him. A trial court ruled on behalf of Sullivan, and his $500,000 damage award was upheld by the Alabama Supreme Court. This was despite the fact that only 35 copies of the offending issue of The New York Times were circulated in Montgomery County.

The U.S. Supreme Court unanimously reversed the decision, ruling that Sullivan could not recover damages in this case unless he proved that The New York Times published the false and defamatory advertisement knowing it was false, or that the paper exhibited reckless disregard for the truth when it printed the material.[1] That is, the Montgomery police commissioner had to show that the newspaper had actually lied when it printed the ad (knowledge of falsity), or that the persons who published the ad (both the members of the committee and the members of the newspaper's staff) had been extraordinarily careless by not examining the charges made in the statement much more carefully (reckless disregard for the truth). Justice William Brennan labeled these two elements "actual malice"; proof of knowledge of falsity or proof of reckless disregard for the truth was proof of actual malice. The language in the court's opinion extended the ruling in this case to all persons whom the court called **public officials.** All public officials who sought to win a libel suit based on defamatory allegations about how they did their jobs or whether they were fit to hold those jobs henceforth would have to prove actual malice. Before examining the various elements in this new libel standard, let's look briefly at the rationale Brennan and his colleagues used to support this fundamental change in the law.

---

*Compared with the multimillion dollar damage awards sought today, $500,000 doesn't sound like much. But it was a staggering amount half a century age.
1. *New York Times Co. v. Sullivan,* 376 U.S. 254 (1964).

Source: © AP/Wide World Photos

The following are excerpts from the advertisement, "Heed Their Rising Voices," that was published in The New York Times on March 29, 1960, by the Committee to Defend Martin Luther King and the Struggle for Freedom in the South. The sections of the ad published below provoked a libel suit by L.B. Sullivan, police commissioner of Montgomery, Ala., against The New York Times, which resulted in the Supreme Court's application of the First Amendment as a shield against libel actions brought by public officials against the mass media.

"Heed Their Rising Voices"

"As the whole world knows by now, thousands of Southern Negro students are engaged in widespread non-violent demonstrations in positive affirmation of the right to live in human dignity as guaranteed by the U.S. Constitution and the Bill of Rights. In their efforts to uphold these guarantees, they are being met by an unprecedented wave of terror by those who would deny and negate that document which the whole world looks upon as setting the pattern for modern freedom. . . .

"In Montgomery, Alabama, after students sang 'My Country, Tis of Thee' on the State Capitol steps, their leaders were expelled from school, and truckloads of police

Associate Justice William Brennan, the author of the Supreme Court decision in New York Times v. Sullivan in 1964 and many other notable First Amendment rulings.

armed with shotguns and tear-gas ringed the Alabama State College Campus. When the entire student body protested to state authorities by refusing to re-register, their dining hall was padlocked in an attempt to starve them into submission. . . .

"Small wonder that the Southern violators of the Constitution fear this new, non-violent brand of freedom fighter . . . even as they fear the upswelling right-to-vote movement. Small wonder that they are determined to destroy the one man who, more than any other, symbolizes the new spirit now sweeping the South—the Rev. Dr. Martin Luther King, Jr., world-famous leader of the Montgomery Bus Protest. . . .

"Again and again the Southern violators have answered Dr. King's peaceful protests with intimidation and violence. They have bombed his home almost killing his wife and child. They have assaulted his person. They have arrested him seven times—for 'speeding,' 'loitering,' and similar 'offenses.' And now they have charged him with 'perjury'—a felony under which they could imprison him for ten years. . . .

"We urge you to join hands with our fellow Americans in the South by supporting, with your dollars, this Combined Appeal for all three needs—the defense of Martin Luther King—the support of the embattled students—and the struggle for the right-to-vote."

THE RATIONALE FOR THE RULING

▪ **Stripped of its cover, this case was clearly one of seditious libel.** A government official was criticized for the way he handled his public office. The newspaper was punished for publishing this criticism. The issues that generated the court ruling and the penalty for the newspaper were really not much different from what occurred in prosecutions under the Alien and Sedition Acts of 1798 and the Espionage and Sedition Acts of 1917 and 1918. Rulings by the Supreme Court had sharply limited the government's power to use seditious libel to punish those who criticize it (see pages 51–62). What Sullivan and his co-plaintiffs were attempting to do was to resurrect sedition law via a civil libel action.

▪ **The nation has a profound and long-standing national commitment to the principle that debate on public issues should be uninhibited, robust and wide open.** Debate on public issues is a fundamental part of the democratic process. All citizens are encouraged to take part in this debate. In the heat of any discussion it is inevitable that erroneous statements will be made by the participants. Many people will be fearful of taking part in the debate if they think they might be sued for libel if they make a misstatement that harms someone's reputation. Whatever is added to the field of libel, wrote Justice Brennan, is taken away from the field of free debate. Freedom of expression, Brennan noted, needs breathing space to survive.[2]

Freedom of expression, Brennan noted, needs breathing space to survive.

▪ **When public officials like Sullivan take a government post, they must expect that their work will be closely scrutinized and even criticized by the people they serve.** Officers of government have ample means to rebut this criticism. They

2. *New York Times Co.* v. *Sullivan,* 376 U.S. 254 (1964).

usually have easy access to the press to deny allegations made against them, to give their side of the story, and to even verbally attack their critics. This kind of speech is also a part of the important debate within a democracy. Police commissioner Sullivan could have easily talked to reporters in Montgomery if he sought to publish the truth. Instead he chose to punish The New York Times.

The actual malice rule imposed on the law of libel by the Supreme Court was already a part of the law in a handful of states prior to the 1964 ruling in *New York Times* v. *Sullivan*. In the wake of the Sullivan decision, all state and federal courts had to follow this rule. By the end of the decade, the Supreme Court had extended the actual malice rule to persons called **public figures.** Persons outside of government frequently try to lead public debate on important issues. These people should not be any more immune to criticism and complaints than government officials, the court rationalized.[3] Public figures would also have to prove actual malice in order to sustain a successful libel suit. Finally, in 1974, the high court added the final element to the libel fault rule when it declared that even private persons, persons who are not part of government or who have not tried to influence public opinion, must prove that the mass medium was at fault when the libel was published or broadcast.[4] The state courts were given some freedom in this ruling to determine just what kind of fault the private party suing a mass medium must prove. Under the First Amendment the private-person plaintiff at least must prove that the mass media defendant failed to exercise reasonable care in preparing and transmitting the story, or was negligent, the high court said. But a state could ask that these plaintiffs prove even more to sustain their libel suits, the court added. The issue of the level of fault that the plaintiff must prove will be discussed in the second half of this chapter (see pages 219–233).

Several words have been used in the past few pages that beg for fuller explanation. Who is a public official? Who is a public figure? How do you define negligence? How do you define actual malice? The next section of this chapter attempts to add flesh to these bones, to make these legal concepts come a bit more alive. Before moving to that, let's briefly summarize the fault rules to this point.

1. Private persons who sue the media for defamation must at least prove that the material was published through negligence. Negligence is defined in the law as the failure to exercise reasonable care.
2. Individuals who have been deemed to be public persons for purposes of a libel suit against a mass medium have to prove that the defendant exhibited actual malice when the material was published. Actual malice is defined in the law as publishing with the knowledge that the libelous assertion is false, or with reckless disregard for whether it is true or false.

PUBLIC PERSONS VERSUS PRIVATE PERSONS

All libel plaintiffs who sue the mass media must prove that the defendant in the case was at fault, that the publication or broadcast of the libelous material was not simply the result of an innocent error. Public officials and public figures have to prove a higher level of fault than do

3. *Curtis Publishing Co.* v. *Butts, A.P.* v. *Walker,* 388 U.S. 130 (1967).
4. *Gertz* v. *Robert Welch, Inc.,* 418 U.S. 323 (1974).

private individuals. But who are public officials and public figures in the eyes of the law? Before exploring this issue a brief caution is warranted. One of the problems in the law of libel is that courts have taken perfectly good words that most of us use daily and have attached a slightly different meaning to these words. Students need to exercise caution because of this. Most of us could probably agree on a general definition of a public figure, for example. But in libel law these words mean something different. What we need to remember is the legal definition of these words, not the common, ordinary, everyday definition.

WHO IS A PUBLIC OFFICIAL?

Two questions must be asked to determine whether a libel plaintiff should be considered a public official:

1. Who is this plaintiff; that is, what kind of government job does this person have?
2. What was the allegedly libelous story about?

Let us consider these questions separately.

Job Description

The kind of government job a person holds is one key to determining who is and who is not a public official for purposes of libel law. Let's start with three general rules:

1. Any person who is elected to public office, to even the most lowly public office, qualifies as a public official.
2. Persons who are appointed to or hired for government jobs *may qualify* as public persons in a libel action. It depends on the nature of the job.
3. But not everyone who works for the government will be regarded as a public official.

Determining if a non-elected government employee should be considered a public official in a libel action is often troublesome for the courts. What lawyers like to call a bright-line rule doesn't exist. (When courts consistently rule the same way on a legal question lawyers often say a bright-line rule has been established. If, for example, in every instance the courts rule that a school teacher or a public works supervisor is a public official, this would be considered a bright-line rule.) Nevertheless, the Supreme Court has provided some useful guidance for the lower courts.

The Supreme Court has said:

> It is clear that the "public official" designation applies at the very least to those among the hierarchy of government employees **who have or appear to have to the public a substantial responsibility for or control over the conduct of governmental affairs.**[5]

Justice Brennan added that when a position in government has such apparent importance that the public has an independent interest in the qualifications and performance of the person who holds it, beyond the general public interest in the qualifications and performance of all

---

5. *Rosenblatt* v. *Baer,* 383 U.S. 75 (1966).

government employees, the person in that position qualifies as a public official. While Brennan's remarks are fairly clear, let's try to translate a bit. Citizens are concerned that everyone who works for the government—from the clerk at the welfare office to the crossing guard outside the school to the person who reads the water meter—does his or her job efficiently and correctly. But some government employees have jobs that have responsibilities that go far beyond the responsibilities of the average government employee—persons like the head of the city's welfare department, the individual in charge of school safety programs, and the supervisor of the city water department. We have a special interest in their qualifications and how well they do their jobs. These people are likely to be counted as public officials.

The Supreme Court added that the person must hold a position that invites public scrutiny of the person holding it, entirely apart from the scrutiny and discussion occasioned by the particular charges in the controversy. In the late 1980s in Minneapolis, Minn., one of two Beluga whales kept by the city zoological park was injured and the wound refused to heal. News coverage of these problems continued for nearly three years until the whale and its female partner were sent to Sea World in San Diego. When zoo officials shortly thereafter announced they were contemplating buying two new whales, animal rights groups threatened to sue. The dispute prompted a study of what had caused the previous problem with the Beluga whale. A committee concluded that the curator of marine mammals at the zoo, Austin McDevitt, had been negligent because he maintained a level of chlorine in the whale tanks that was too high and that that was why the wound would not heal. McDevitt disputed the finding and when the report was made public, he sued for libel. The defendants in the lawsuit claimed McDevitt was a public official. Was he? McDevitt clearly worked for the government as curator of marine mammals at the zoo. But did he have substantial responsibility for the conduct of government affairs? Should the people in Minneapolis have an interest in the way he conducted his office beyond their general interest in how all government employees do their jobs? The defendants pointed to the controversy over the care of the whales, but the court rejected that argument. The critical aspect in determining who is and who is not a public official is the public interest in the person's job *before the controversy began,* not the public interest once a controversy has arisen. In this case the court ruled that the record did not manifest an independent interest in McDevitt's performance over and above an interest in how all government employees do their jobs.[6] In 1998 the 4th U.S. Circuit Court of Appeals ruled that Rex Baumback, timber management officer and contracting officer for timber sales in the Eldorado National Forest, was a public official. ABC News called the plaintiff "a bureaucrat who got away with a $25 million mistake" after he was accused of making serious errors in awarding 16 contracts for the sale of timber on federal lands. The Forest Service ultimately had to cancel the contracts and was being sued by timber companies. The appellate court said that Baumback's role in management of the sale of U.S. resources clearly marked him as one who had substantial responsibility for the administration of government matters.[7] Finally, the Ohio Court of Appeals ruled that even though he had not been elected to office, the chief of the criminal section of the city law department was a public official because of his responsibilities and the importance of his position in the eyes of the public.[8]

The critical aspect in determining who is and who is not a public official is the public interest in the person's job before the controversy began.

6. *McDevitt* v. *Tilson,* 453 N.W. 2d 53 (1990).
7. *Baumback* v. *American Broadcasting Cos.,* 26 M.L.R. 2138 (1998).
8. *Scaccia* v. *Dayton Newspapers Inc.,* 30 M.L.R. 1172 (2001).

Some state courts have developed criteria that are a little different from those used by the U.S. Supreme Court. The Tennessee Supreme Court ruled that a junior state social worker was a public official because her job carried with it "duties and responsibilities affecting the lives, liberty, money or property of a citizen that may enhance or disrupt his enjoyment of life."[9] The Washington Supreme Court in 1979 said that the administrator of a small county motor pool, who worked without direct supervision, had two assistants, and could independently spend up to $500 of county money on open charge accounts at several local parts dealers, was a public official. "The public quite naturally has a legitimate and continuing interest in how local tax revenues are spent by those county employees vested with the power to utilize the public purse," wrote Chief Justice Robert Utter for the court.[10] The defamation in this case was an allegation that the plaintiff had used small amounts of county funds to repair private vehicles. Similarly, police officers, who are relatively low-level government employees, have usually been held to be public officials because they hold the power of life and death over the citizens in a community.[11] A U.S. District Court in Washington state ruled in 2004 that the secretary and chief examiner of the City of Seattle's Public Safety Civil Service Commission was a public official for purposes of her lawsuit against KING television and the city. The court noted that in her job she supervised other city employees and managed the application process for persons seeking employment with the Seattle Police Department and the Seattle Fire Department. She also supervised the testing process for all the applicants. On this basis, the court said, she has, or certainly appears to have, substantial responsibility.[12]

What about a consulting firm that advises a government on a controversial but important government policy question? The Iroquois Research Institute was hired by Fairfax County, Va., to evaluate the historical and archeological value of an island in the Potomac River on which the county hoped to construct water-intake facilities. Lowes Island was the subject of a great zoning controversy in the community, and when Iroquois reported that the work could be done without harming the island, the research institute became the focus of sharp criticism. The Loudoun (Va.) Times Mirror published a story that challenged the competence of Iroquois researchers, and a libel suit followed. The U.S. Court of Appeals for the 4th Circuit ruled that the consulting firm could not be considered a public official in terms of the libel suit.[13] The court said that the institute made no recommendations to the county, participated in no policy determinations, and exercised no discretion. In short, it had no control over the conduct of governmental affairs. "Its position was not of such apparent importance that the public has an independent interest in its qualifications," the court ruled. The court conceded that in some instances a consultant employed by the government entity can be classified a public official, but not this time.[14]

The context in which the defamation occurs is often important. A planner with a state geological survey office might not normally hold a position that invites public scrutiny. But if

9. *Press* v. *Verran,* 589 S.W. 2d 435 (1978).

10. *Clawson* v. *Longview Publishing Co.,* 589 P. 2d 1223 (1979).

11. See, for example, *Soke* v. *The Plain Dealer,* 69 Ohio St. 3d 395 (1994) and *Clark* v. *Clark,* 21 M.L.R. 1650 (1993).

12. *Harris* v. *City of Seattle,* 315 F. Supp. 2d 1105 (2004).

13. *Artic* v. *Loudoun Times Mirror,* 624 F. 2d 518 (1980). But see also *Adey* v. *Action for Animals, Inc.,* 361 F. Supp. 457 (1973), where another federal court came to a contrary conclusion.

14. *Artic* v. *Loudoun Times Mirror,* 624 F. 2d 518 (1980).

this person is appointed by the governor to conduct a study of the feasibility of constructing a hazardous waste dump site near the state capital, this special assignment brings with it closer public scrutiny. In such a case a person who was not a public official might suddenly become one in terms of libel law.

To summarize, it is impossible to provide a nice, neat list of the kinds of jobs that elevate nonelected government employees to the status of public official. But some of the criteria to look for include the following:

- The level of responsibility the individual has. In other words, how important is the job?
- The kind of responsibility the person has. Police officers, teachers and social workers may be lower-level employees, but the way they do their jobs can have an important and immediate impact on people's lives.
- Does the individual have the authority to spend public money independently, without supervision?
- What is the nature of the person's job? The head of a task force to reorganize city employee health benefits and the head of the city's anti-terrorism task force might supervise the same number of workers, earn the same salary, and be at the same city management level. But it is likely that the public will take a far greater interest in the qualifications of the anti-terrorism task force supervisor and the way she does her job than in the qualifications and competency of the person heading the employee benefits task force.

The Nature of the Story

As noted previously, there are two parts to the test to determine whether a libel plaintiff is a public official. If the plaintiff is not an elected official, or if the job he or she holds simply doesn't include the kind of substantial responsibility outlined by the Supreme Court, a court will not consider this litigant a public official. That plaintiff will be asked to prove only some kind of negligence to establish fault.

But if the plaintiff is an elected officer, or is someone who meets the criteria outlined above, he or she may have to prove actual malice to sustain the fault requirement. Whether proof of actual malice will be required depends upon the focus of the libelous statement. If the statement concerns (1) the manner in which the plaintiff conducts himself or herself in office—in other words, the way he or she does the job—or (2) the plaintiff's general fitness to hold that job, then the plaintiff carries the burden of proving actual malice.

The first criterion relates to the plaintiff's official duties and focuses on matters directly related to public responsibilities. For example, in the Harris case noted above, the allegations against the chief examiner focused on a trip she took to Las Vegas to attend a black public administrators conference. The television station said she spent little time in seminars and workshops during the trip, but considerable time at the gaming tables. The court ruled that the strong nexus between her position and the alleged false statements meant that the story directly related to the way she conducted herself on the job.

But it must be remembered that public officials have private lives and not everything a government employee does in public necessarily relates to his or her official conduct. Dr. Lazelle Michaelis was the coroner of Otter Tail County, Minn., a position of substantial responsibility. She was also a private physician employed by a medical association. Because of her expertise in pathology she occasionally, as a favor, performed autopsies for the coroner in neighboring Becker County. A controversy developed when Michaelis concluded that the death of a young woman in Becker County was a suicide. Claiming her reputation was damaged by the publicity, she sued CBS broadcasting station WCCO for libel. The station argued that because Michaelis was the coroner in Otter Tail County she was a public official, obligated to prove actual malice. The court disagreed, saying that when Michaelis performed the autopsy in Becker County she was acting as a private doctor; she was paid by the medical association for which she worked. Her position in Otter Tail County had no relevance in this case.[15]

The second criterion is much broader and can relate to a public official's private life, personal habits or traits that may make someone unfit to hold a responsible job. For example, the fact that the fire chief's personal financial affairs are in considerable disarray probably doesn't have much to do with how well she performs her job as fire chief. But a city treasurer who has problems with personal finances could be a different story. This might suggest the treasurer is not fit to manage the city's financial affairs. The decision whether a particular allegation reflects on a public official's fitness to hold the job will necessarily be a subjective one. And it is complicated by the fact that courts, in making this determination, seem to use an elastic standard that relates to the importance of the plaintiff's job. It seems that almost anything about the personal life of the president of the United States is considered a measure of his or her fitness to hold that office. But the courts are unwilling to say the same thing about lower government officials. And the lower you go on the totem pole of public officeholders, the more the courts seem willing to rule that stories about private life have little to do with being a public official for purposes of a libel suit. It is incumbent on any journalist preparing a story on a public official's private life to demonstrate within the story just how these revelations affect the government officer's official responsibilities. This, in itself, could thwart a lawsuit.

ALL-PURPOSE PUBLIC FIGURES

Persons deemed to be public figures must also prove actual malice when suing for libel. The Supreme Court has said that there are two kinds of public figures: all-purpose public figures and limited-purpose public figures. It was Justice Lewis Powell who established these twin categories in his opinion in *Gertz* v. *Welch*.[16] He identified all-purpose public figures as those persons who "occupy positions of such pervasive power and influence that they are deemed public figures for all purposes."

While Justice Powell's description of an all-purpose public figure sounds simple enough, this is a category of libel plaintiffs that most courts have had difficulty identifying. Do the criteria relate to power or fame? Sometimes the powerful have little public recognition. Name the presidents of the 10 largest U.S. corporations—powerful individuals, but hardly widely known. For example, in the late 1980s, federal judges refused to classify William Tavoulareas, the president of Mobil Oil, one of the nation's largest companies, as a public figure, saying that such a person must be so well known that his or her name is a household word. (See page 159.) On the other hand, the famous often have little real power. People like Paris Hilton or Adam Sandler come to mind. So who is an all-purpose public figure?

15. *Michaelis* v. *CBS, Inc.,* 119 F. 3d 697 (1997).
16. 418 U.S. 323 (1974).

Entertainers Johnny Carson[17] and Wayne Newton[18] were both declared to be all-purpose public figures, largely because they were so famous. But so was conservative writer and editor William Buckley,[19] who was certainly well known among his readers and followers, but was hardly a household name. But these are old cases. Surprisingly, perhaps, there haven't been a lot of other similar cases since. In the past decade or so, it is typically the plaintiff himself or herself who agrees to the designation as an all-purpose public figure.[20] Why would a plaintiff agree to such a designation since it certainly makes it more difficult to win a libel action? Mostly likely they want to exaggerate their prominence in the public eye to support a higher damage claim. Then again, a lot of celebrities, sports stars and others have very large egos which need constant care and feeding.

But there is more than one way to look at the all-purpose public figure question. Some people might have the pervasive power and influence Justice Powell talked about on a national level; everyone, everywhere knows about them. But others may enjoy such power and influence strictly on a local level. Everyone in a specific town or region or state knows about them. And these people can be deemed all-purpose public figures as well. Consider the woman who lives in a community of 6,500 people. She was formerly the mayor, has served on the school board in the past, and has been a perennial choice for president of the parent-teacher association. She is the president of the largest real estate company in town, is a director on the board of the local bank, and owns the local pharmacy and dry cleaners. She is active in numerous service clubs, is a leader in various civic projects, and is instantly recognizable on the street by the town's residents. Her family founded the town 150 years earlier. If she is libeled in a community newspaper whose circulation remains almost exclusively in the community, it could be argued persuasively that this woman is an all-purpose public figure in the community. (See *Steere* v. *Cupp*,[21] in which the Kansas Supreme Court ruled such an individual was a total, or all-purpose, public figure.) In 1982, the Montana Supreme Court ruled that investment and commodity advisor Larry Williams was an all-purpose public figure for his libel suit based on a state Democratic Party press release that erroneously charged that he had been under federal indictment for political dirty tricks. The court listed the following activities by Williams, which convinced the court that he was an all-purpose public figure for the purposes of a libel suit based on the circulation of defamatory allegations in Montana: He published an investment advisory service; he wrote three books on stocks; he was the subject of an article in Forbes magazine and another article in the Wall Street Journal; he frequently gave speeches and ran unsuccessfully for the U.S. Senate; he was chairman of the Republican Party in Montana; and he was an active member of the National Taxpayers Union.[22]

But some courts have rejected the notion that because someone is well known in a community this automatically makes him or her an all-purpose public figure. A television reporter in Utah sued the station where she had worked for making false statements about why she was fired. The station argued she was an all-purpose public figure. She had reported stories for the station for three years, done promotional spots, and appeared at special events for the station.

17. *Carson* v. *Allied News,* 529 F. 2d 206 (1976).
18. *Newton* v. *NBC,* 677 F. Supp. 1066 (1985).
19. *Buckley* v. *Litell,* 539 F. 2d 882 (1976).
20. See *Masson* v. *New Yorker Magazine, Inc.,* 881 F. 2d 1452 (1989), for example.
21. 602 P. 2d 1267 (1979).
22. *Williams* v. *Pasma,* 565 P. 2d 212 (1982).

One could speculate that a large percentage of people in the community could recognize the plaintiff, Holly Wayment. At least that is what the trial court surmised. But the Utah Supreme Court rejected the ruling that she was an all-purpose public figure. There was no evidence presented that she wielded any particular social or political influence or even proof that the news show on which she appeared was widely watched. "If we accept these facts as sufficient evidence of general fame in the local community, any reporter would qualify as an all-purpose public figure," the court said.[23]

What if the defamatory material circulates outside the local community, as well, to persons who may not be familiar with the plaintiff? This question arose in 1985 in a libel suit by businessman George Martin against the Chariho Times in Rhode Island. Martin was clearly well known in the village of Shannock, where he owned and had developed a considerable amount of property over a period of 15 years. The Times was widely read by the 300 residents of the village, and a trial court ruled that Martin was a local all-purpose public figure. On appeal Martin argued that the newspaper had 3,000 subscribers, a far larger readership than just among the village residents by whom he was so well known. The Rhode Island Supreme Court, noting that Martin's fame had spread beyond the Shannock village limits, added that "very few individuals will be known to all subscribers or purchasers of any publication."[24] Wally Butts and Major General Edwin Walker were not known to all subscribers of the Saturday Evening Post, yet were declared to be public figures by the Supreme Court,[25] the Rhode Island justice noted, recalling that famous 1967 decision (see pages 226–228). "It is sufficient to attain a public figure status that the plaintiff should have been known to a substantial portion of the publication's readership," the court ruled.[26] And Martin met this test.

LIMITED-PURPOSE PUBLIC FIGURES

"More commonly, those classed as public figures have thrust themselves to the forefront of particular public controversies in order to influence the resolution of the issues involved."

Persons in the second category of public figures outlined by Justice Powell in the *Gertz* decision are called limited-purpose public figures. "More commonly," he said, "those classed as public figures have thrust themselves to the forefront of particular public controversies in order to influence the resolution of the issues involved."[27] This kind of libel plaintiff is regarded as a public person for a discrete part of his or her life, usually because of steps the person has taken to influence public opinion on a public issue. In a series of four rulings in the mid-1970s the Supreme Court developed three criteria to determine whether someone is a limited-purpose public figure:

- **A public controversy must exist before the publication or broadcast of the libelous matter.**
- **The plaintiff must have in some way participated voluntarily in this controversy.**
- **The plaintiff's participation must be such that he or she is actively seeking to influence public opinion regarding the controversial issues.**

23. *Wayment* v. *Clear Channel Broadcasting,* 116 P3d 271 (2005).
24. *Martin* v. *Wilson Publishing,* 497 A. 2d 322 (1985).
25. *Curtis Publishing Co.* v. *Butts, AP* v. *Walker,* 388 U.S. 130 (1967).
26. *Martin* v. *Wilson Publishing,* 497 A. 2d 322 (1985).
27. *Gertz* v. *Robert Welch, Inc.,* 418 U.S. 323 (1974).

While there have only been a handful of cases that focused on whether a plaintiff was or was not an all-purpose public figure, there have been hundreds of rulings regarding limited-purpose public figures. The three criteria highlighted here stem from four decisions handed down by the Supreme Court of the United States. State courts and lower federal tribunals have often offered their own sets of guidelines that differ in small ways from the criteria outlined by the Supreme Court. The limited-purpose public figure test offered by the nation's high court is generally regarded as a somewhat conservative test. That is, there are undoubtedly plaintiffs who would not be regarded as public figures under the Supreme Court's criteria, but who might qualify as such under the criteria used by a state court, or even a U.S. Court of Appeals. Overall, though, the various tests are much more alike than they are different. The central concern in all the tests is the plaintiff's role in a particular controversy. The differences tend to focus on the nature of the controversy and the role played by the plaintiff in that controversy. Anyone seeking to determine whether a particular person is or is not a limited-purpose public figure can be assured that if that person qualifies under the test outlined by the Supreme Court, there is a high probability that individual will qualify under the test used by any other court.

The Supreme Court test, and the cases that spawned it, are the focus of the next few pages. A brief outline of how other court tests differ from the high court's definition of a limited-purpose public figure follows.

In *Gertz* v. *Welch* the plaintiff was Elmer Gertz, a well-known and widely respected Chicago attorney who had gained prominence in civil rights disputes in that city. He had written several books and articles, and on many occasions had served on commissions and committees in Chicago and Cook County. When a young man was slain by a Chicago police officer, Gertz agreed to represent the family in a civil action against the officer. The policeman had been tried and convicted of murder in the shooting, but Gertz played no role in that criminal action. His only role in the entire matter was as an attorney representing the family in the action for civil damages. He became the subject of a vicious attack by American Opinion, a magazine published by the John Birch Society, which accused him of being a communist fronter, a Leninist, and the architect of a frame-up against the police officer. It also charged that Gertz had a long police record.

In the libel suit that followed, the Supreme Court ruled that despite his prominence in the civil rights area, Elmer Gertz was not a public figure for the purposes of this lawsuit. The words of Justice Powell stand as an important guideline:

> It is preferable to reduce the public figure question to a more meaningful
> context by looking to the nature and extent of an individual's participation
> in the particular controversy giving rise to the defamation.[28]

The key phrase is "extent of an individual's participation in the particular controversy giving rise to the defamation." To be a limited-purpose public figure, the plaintiff must be shown to have played a prominent role in the particular controversy giving rise to the defamation, the controversy prompting publication of the defamatory statement or comment. Gertz would have been considered a limited-purpose public figure if the dispute in the case had involved civil rights in Chicago. But the particular controversy that gave rise to the article in

28. *Gertz* v. *Robert Welch, Inc.,* 418 U.S. 323 (1974).

American Opinion was the murder of the young man and the subsequent trial of the police officer. Gertz was not an important participant in that issue. He was simply acting as an attorney—which was his profession—in representing the family of the youth in a civil action. He was acting as a private individual.*

Two years later the court ruled that a socially prominent Palm Beach woman was not a public figure with regard to the divorce action in which she was involved. The case, *Time, Inc.* v. *Firestone,*[29] resulted from a short notice published in Time magazine that Russell Firestone was granted a divorce from his wife on grounds of extreme cruelty and adultery. Firestone was in fact granted a divorce from his wife, but on grounds that neither member of the couple was "domesticated." Mary Alice Firestone sued Time for libel, claiming she had been called an adulteress. Time argued that her prominence in the Palm Beach community made her a public figure. On the record she clearly appeared to be a public figure: a leading member of the "Four Hundred of Palm Beach Society," an "active member of the sporting set," a person whose activities attracted considerable public attention. She even maintained a clipping service to keep track of her publicity. The divorce case became a cause célèbre in the community, prompting 43 articles in a Miami newspaper and 45 stories in the Palm Beach newspapers. She held several press conferences during the course of the 17-month legal dispute. Nevertheless, the Supreme Court refused to acknowledge that Mary Alice Firestone was a public figure in the context of the divorce case, the subject of the Time article that was defamatory. Justice William Rehnquist wrote:

> Respondent did not assume any role of especial prominence in the affairs of society, other than perhaps Palm Beach society, and she did not thrust herself to the forefront of any particular public controversy in order to influence the resolution of the issues involved in it.[30]

Time argued that because the trial was well publicized, it must be considered a public controversy and Mary Alice Firestone a public person. "But in doing so," Justice Rehnquist wrote, "petitioner seeks to equate 'public controversy' with all controversies of interest to the public." The justice said that a divorce proceeding is not the kind of public controversy referred to in *Gertz.* While there was public interest in the proceedings, the case was not an important public question.

Rehnquist also pointed out that Mrs. Firestone was not a voluntary participant in the divorce proceeding. She was forced to go into public court to dissolve her marriage. The subtle difference, then, that Rehnquist points to is the difference between voluntarily becoming involved in a public controversy and voluntarily becoming involved in something that results in a controversy. Firestone did the latter—she voluntarily went to court to get a divorce, and the divorce trial resulted in the controversy. Justice Powell did note in *Gertz* that "it may be possible for someone to become a public figure through no purposeful action of his own, but the instances of truly involuntary public figures are exceedingly rare."[31]

---

*This libel case, which began in 1969, finally ended in the summer of 1982 when a $400,000 judgment against American Opinion was upheld by the 7th U.S. Circuit Court of Appeals. Elmer Gertz died in 2000 at age 93.

29. 424 U.S. 448 (1976).

30. *Time, Inc.* v. *Firestone,* 424 U.S. 448 (1976).

31. *Time, Inc.* v. *Firestone,* 424 U.S. 448 (1976).

The meaning of *Gertz* and *Firestone* was re-emphasized in 1979 in two rulings by the Supreme Court that clearly indicated that the high court intended the limited-purpose public-figure category to be narrow. In both cases, *Hutchinson* v. *Proxmire*[32] and *Wolston* v. *Reader's Digest*,[33] the Supreme Court reversed rulings by lower federal courts, rulings that had declared that the plaintiffs were in fact limited-purpose public figures.

The plaintiff in the *Hutchinson* case was the research director at a public mental hospital in Michigan. He was also the recipient of about $500,000 in federal grants to support his research on animal aggression. Believing that such research was unimportant, Senator William Proxmire bestowed his monthly Golden Fleece Award on several federal agencies that had funded Hutchinson's research for nearly seven years. In the process the Wisconsin lawmaker accused Hutchinson of putting the "bite" on the American taxpayer and making "a monkey" out of the American people. Hutchinson sued.

Chief Justice Burger refused to consider the plaintiff a public figure. He said there was no controversy about the research until Proxmire's defamatory comments about Dr. Hutchinson. The scientist did not thrust himself or his views into a public dispute or issue. In fact, Burger said, the defendants "have not identified such a particular controversy; at most they point to concern about general public expenditures." Hutchinson, the chief justice noted, at no time assumed any role of public prominence in the broad question of concern about expenditures. The researcher, then, had no part in the controversy that gave rise to the defamation, according to Burger. Simply taking public money to do research is not enough to make a person like Hutchinson into a public figure, the court ruled. "If it were, everyone who received or benefited from the myriad public grants for research could be classified as a public figure."[34]

Finally, the chief justice drew on a basic rationale for the distinction between private and public persons and said that "we cannot agree that Hutchinson had such access to the media that he should be classified as a public figure." His access, Burger noted, was limited to responding to Proxmire's announcement of the Golden Fleece Award. The decision of the court was 8-1 in favor of Hutchinson's status as a private figure. The single dissenting vote by Justice Brennan was based solely on how the court had responded to another question, not to the public-figure issue.

The facts in the *Wolston* case are somewhat more complicated. Ilya Wolston was identified in a 1974 book, "KGB: The Secret Works of Soviet Secret Agents," as a Soviet agent. His description as such stemmed from events that had taken place nearly 20 years earlier when a federal grand jury in New York state was investigating the activities of Soviet agents in the United States. Wolston's aunt and uncle, Myra and Jack Soble, were well-publicized American Communists who were arrested in January 1957 and charged with spying. Wolston himself was interviewed by the Federal Bureau of Investigation and testified several times before a New York grand jury. In July 1958 he failed to respond to a grand jury subpoena. His failure to appear was reported in the press. He said he had not testified because he was in a state of mental depression. Later he changed his mind and offered to give testimony. He subsequently pleaded guilty to a charge of contempt and was sentenced to three years' probation. During the six weeks between the time he refused to testify and his sentencing, 15 news

---

32. 443 U.S. 111 (1979).
33. 443 U.S. 157 (1979).
34. *Hutchinson* v. *Proxmire,* 443 U.S. 111 (1979).

stories were published about Ilya Wolston in New York and Washington newspapers. He was never indicted for espionage.

Wolston's libel suit was based on his misidentification in the "KGB" book published by Reader's Digest. The publication argued that because of his contempt conviction in 1958, Wolston was a limited-purpose public figure for purposes of a discussion of Soviet agents and espionage. Eight members of the Supreme Court disagreed. Justice William Rehnquist, writing for the majority, stated that Wolston did not "inject" himself into any controversy, that he was dragged into the controversy when the government pursued him during the investigation of Soviet agents. "The mere fact that petitioner voluntarily chose not to appear before the grand jury, knowing that his action might be attended by publicity, is not decisive on the status of public figure," Rehnquist said.[35] The justice noted that Wolston played a minor role in whatever controversy there might have been over Soviet espionage, that he had never talked about this matter with the press. "We decline to hold that his mere citation for contempt rendered him a public figure for purposes of comment on the investigation of Soviet espionage."

Rehnquist stressed that Wolston had made no effort to influence the public on the resolution of any issue. The plaintiff did not in any way seek to arouse public sentiment in his favor or against the investigation. Quoting his own opinion in the *Firestone* case, Rehnquist wrote:

> While participants in some litigation may be legitimate "public figures," either generally or for the limited purpose of that litigation, the majority will more likely resemble respondent [Mary Firestone or Ilya Wolston], drawn into a public forum largely against their will in order to attempt to obtain the only redress available to them or to defend themselves against actions brought by the state or by others.[36]

"The mere fact that petitioner voluntarily chose not to appear before the grand jury, knowing that his action might be attended by publicity, is not decisive on the status of public figure."

WHO IS A LIMITED-PURPOSE PUBLIC FIGURE?

1. Limited-purpose public figures normally must voluntarily step into the public spotlight.
2. A limited-purpose public figure is someone who plays a role in the resolution of an important public or social issue.
3. There must have been some attempt by the individual to influence public opinion in the resolution of this issue. Usually this action implies access to the mass media.

The question now is, What can we learn from the language in these Supreme Court rulings? Three basic points seem to emerge:

1. Limited-purpose public figures normally must voluntarily step into the public spotlight. The court said it would be exceedingly rare for someone to be an involuntary public figure. Such instances as rising to deny charges made against you and going to court to end a marriage or to defend yourself from government charges

---

35. *Wolston* v. *Reader's Digest*, 443 U.S. 157 (1979).
36. Ibid.

do not represent voluntary behavior. They represent a response to the behavior of someone or something else.

2. A limited-purpose public figure is someone who plays a role in the resolution of an important public or social issue. A messy divorce, an investigation of aggression in animals, a charge of contempt for failure to testify before a grand jury are not the kinds of "affairs of society" that the court considers to be important. One gets the impression that the justices are looking to the discussion of social issues (abortion, discrimination), economic issues (taxpayers' revolt, city budget), educational problems (busing, minimum competency requirements), governmental policy (censorship, declaration of war), and the like to find the kinds of persons they would consider limited-purpose public figures. A public controversy might be defined as a controversy in which the resolution of the issues will affect the general public or at least a wider group of persons than those individuals directly involved in the controversy.

3. There must have been some attempt by the plaintiff to influence public opinion in the resolution of these issues. This speaks to the basic point made by Justice Powell in the *Gertz* case—the nature and extent of the individual's participation in the particular controversy giving rise to the defamation. In *Hutchinson* the issue was wasteful expenditures, but Dr. Hutchinson had said little, if anything, about that before being libeled by Senator Proxmire. Similarly, Ilya Wolston had said nothing about the issue of Soviet agents in this country—which is what the defendant contended was the issue in *Wolston* v. *Reader's Digest.*

Inherent in an attempt to influence the outcome of a public issue is the ability of the plaintiff to get access to the mass media. The plaintiff generally must have some means of speaking out on the issue or of responding to criticism. Also, the media cannot create a controversy through a news story, defame a person in reporting that story, and then argue that the individual is a public figure because of the controversy. Imagine that a television station reports without any foundation that a local private citizen has been abusing foster children in his care, something that would surely generate a controversy in a community. Imagine the story is completely false and the station is sued for libel. The broadcasting station cannot defend itself by arguing that the citizen is a public figure because of the controversy generated by the false story. This maneuver is called bootstrapping and has been generally rejected by the courts. These are the key points, then, in determining whether an individual is a limited-purpose public figure:

1. **There must be an important public controversy.**
2. **The plaintiff must inject himself or herself voluntarily into the controversy.**
3. **The plaintiff must attempt to influence public opinion about the resolution of the issue and have some access to the press to accomplish this feat.**

LOWER-COURT RULINGS

The four Supreme Court rulings discussed here provide important guideposts that can assist anyone seeking to determine whether a particular plaintiff is a limited-purpose public figure. But the set of cases is not a talisman that answers all questions in all circumstances. For one thing the four cases did not reveal who was a public figure, only who was *not* a public figure. For the past three decades the lower courts have been somewhat at sea, struggling with lawsuits involving different kinds of circumstances and different kinds of plaintiffs. It is not surprising, then, that in 1993 legal scholars Harry Stonecipher and Don Sneed concluded, after examining numerous lower-court rulings in which the limited-purpose public figure question was an issue, that state courts and lower federal courts are coming to some of their own conclusions regarding this question.[37] The tests emerging from the lower courts surely reflect the language of the high court rulings, but often four or five rather than three criteria are applied. In Washington state, for example, the test requires the judge to answer five questions:

- Did the plaintiff have access to the media?
- What was the nature of the plaintiff's role in the controversy?
- Were the defamatory comments germane to the controversy?
- Did the controversy exist before the defamation was published?
- Was the plaintiff still a public figure at the time of defamation?

The 4th U.S. Circuit Court of Appeals uses this test:

- Did a controversy exist prior to the publication of the defamatory matter?
- Did the plaintiff voluntarily assume a role of special prominence in the controversy?
- Did the plaintiff seek to influence resolution of the controversy?
- Does the plaintiff have access to effective channels of communication?
- Did the plaintiff retain the public-figure status at the time of the alleged defamation?[38]

While these two tests and tests used by other courts vary slightly from the test forged by the U.S. Supreme Court, they nevertheless retain the basic elements: A limited-purpose public figure voluntarily becomes involved in a pre-existing public controversy with both the hope and the means (media access) to help resolve that controversy. A few lower courts have viewed the "voluntary participation" element of the criteria in a more liberal fashion. These courts have ruled that if an individual behaves in a manner that is likely to generate a public controversy, even though he or she doesn't intend to generate a controversy, this person can be deemed to be a limited-purpose public figure. A criminal rarely seeks to attract attention; yet some courts have said that by committing a criminal act an individual can legitimately expect to draw the kind of public attention that fosters a definition of a public figure. But there is disagreement among the courts as well. In March 1998 a U.S. District Court in Connecticut ruled that the wife of a physician who had continuing legal problems was a public figure. The doctor, on probation for five years because of charges of incompetence, was arrested and charged with 20 counts of fraud. "Despite the fact that plaintiff has not sought a public role, she has been thrust into the role of a public figure by virtue of her marriage to Dr. Zupnik—who clearly is a public figure."[39] Three months later the Appellate Division of the New York Supreme Court ruled that the ex-husband of prominent television celebrity Joan Lunden was

---

37. Stonecipher and Sneed, "Survey," 328.
38. See *Clardy* v. *The Cowles Pub. Co.,* 912 P. 2d 1078 (1996) and *Carr* v. *Forbes,* 259 F. 3d 273 (2001).
39. *Zupnik* v. *Associated Press Inc.,* 26 M.L.R. 2084 (1998).

not a public figure simply because he was married for many years to the co-host of ABC's "Good Morning America." The Globe tabloid had suggested that prior to the divorce, while the couple was separated, Lunden's husband had an affair with a prostitute. "Plaintiff is not famous in his own right and his marriage to Ms. Lunden certainly did not bestow upon him the sort of fame that is necessary to be considered a general public figure."[40] The two cases present almost identical circumstances, yet the courts reached contrary decisions. What follows is a sampling of lower-court rulings that demonstrate both the consistencies and inconsistencies in the law.

The Nature of the Controversy

The kind of controversy that generated the libel is an obviously important factor in determining whether a plaintiff is a limited-purpose public figure. In 1994 in a decision that echoed earlier Supreme Court rulings, the 4th U.S. Circuit Court of Appeals declared that "a public controversy is a dispute that in fact has received public attention because its ramifications will be felt by persons who are not direct participants."[41] This is the same standard applied by the Georgia Supreme Court when it ruled that a group of plastic surgeons who were involved in a fight with other physicians over what kinds of medical specialists were qualified to perform plastic surgery were not public figures. This was a dispute that affected only members of the medical community, not the general public.[42] An interesting ruling from Colorado demonstrates the difference between varieties of controversies. Linda Lewis was arrested and convicted for shoplifting at a J.C. Penney store in Aurora, Colo. Linda and her husband then filed suit against the store, claiming that Mrs. Lewis, an African-American, had been beaten when she was detained by store security personnel. After the lawsuit was filed, local and national civil rights organizations became involved in the dispute. Public meetings were held at which the Lewis' charges against J.C. Penney were aired. The possibility of a boycott of the Penney stores was raised. Mrs. Lewis appeared and spoke at these meetings. Videotape of her arrest in the store was shown at the meetings.

A television station aired a report based on erroneous information that Mrs. Lewis had a prior criminal record. She sued for libel. The TV station contended that she was a public figure; Mrs. Lewis said she was a private citizen forced to go to court to protect her rights. What the Colorado Court of Appeals saw in this case were two controversies. The first was Linda Lewis' $15 million lawsuit against the J.C. Penney store. In this controversy Lewis was just a private person, trying to use the court system to correct what she believed was a legal wrong. Its outcome would affect only Lewis and her husband, and the retailer. There was, however, a second controversy created when public protests and calls for store boycotts erupted. If Lewis had stayed away from this controversy, she would have remained a private person. But when she spoke at public meetings to rally support for her cause, when she aired the videotape of her arrest, she became a leading player in a much broader controversy, a truly public controversy. Because of these actions, she became a public figure.[43]

The kind of controversy that generated the libel is an obviously important factor in determining whether a plaintiff is a limited-purpose public figure.

40. *Krauss* v. *Globe International Inc.,* 674 N.Y.S. 2d 662 (1998).
41. *Foretich* v. *Capital Cities/ABC, Inc.,* 37 F. 3d 1541 (1994).
42. *Georgia Society of Plastic Surgeons* v. *Anderson,* 363 S.E. 2d 710 (1987).
43. *Lewis* v. *McGraw-Hill Broadcasting Co., Inc.,* 832 P. 2d 1118 (1992).

In several instances courts have ruled that the mass media cannot generate a controversy and then label those persons ensnared in that controversy as limited-purpose public figures. In 1989, The Globe tabloid newspaper claimed that an agent of the CIA had named Khalid Khawar as the real assassin of Sen. Robert Kennedy; Sirhan Sirhan was innocent. The killing had been arranged by the Shah of Iran's secret police and the Mafia, the newspaper reported. The newspaper carried a photo of Khawar standing with a group of people who were talking with Kennedy shortly before he was killed. At the time of the killing Khawar was a free-lance photographer. The camera that hung around the plaintiff's neck in the photo was really a gun, The Globe reported. The newspaper got its story from a book that made the same allegations. The book was highly controversial and focused considerable attention on Khawar, who sued the author and the publisher, as well as The Globe. Book author Robert Morrow defaulted (did not defend himself) and the publisher settled the suit and retracted the allegations. The Globe fought the lawsuit and argued that Khawar was a public figure because of all the publicity that was focused upon him when the book was published. The California Supreme Court disagreed, saying that Khawar had done nothing to bring about the publicity; it was generated by the press during the controversy.[44] This is a classic case of bootstrapping, which is not permitted. A jury found the allegations false and defamatory.

The Plaintiff's Role

Once a court has ruled that a legitimate controversy existed it must then determine what role the plaintiff played in the controversy. This is a more difficult question. Was the plaintiff actually involved in the controversy that gave rise to the defamation? Or was he or she simply on the periphery? Was the participation voluntary or was the plaintiff drawn into the controversy by the mass media? Because no two cases are exactly alike, and because the answers to the questions raised above often involve subjective judgments, it is not surprising to find contradictory rulings among the courts in cases in which the facts seem somewhat similar. But this should stand as a warning to those who think the law is made up of a set of specific rules that are applied in exactly the same fashion in every case. This rarely happens, and perhaps never will, unless the human judges and jurors are replaced by computers. Let's look at a few cases to explore how various courts have dealt with the matter of the role of the plaintiff in the controversy.

A real controversy has simmered in the United States for the past 20 years as more and more women have joined the American armed forces. A sharp difference of opinion still exists on the role women should play in combat. One of the last bastions of male exclusivity was the job of combat pilot for the U.S. Navy. Carey D. Lohrenz was one of the first two women who became Navy combat pilots. She was at the top of her class during basic flight training, won the right to train in jet aircraft, and, after Congress changed the law barring women from flying combat jets, was assigned as an F-14 pilot on a Navy aircraft carrier. This controversy heated up after the change in U.S. policy, and then it escalated even more when the other female combat pilot died when her aircraft malfunctioned as she attempted a carrier landing. At this point some people began attacking both the idea of allowing women to fly high-performance combat aircraft and Lohrenz herself, saying she was incompetent and unqualified. She sued for libel.

44. *Khawar* v. *Globe International Inc.,* 965 P. 2d 696 (1998).

Was she a public figure? The defense argued that because of the controversy over whether women should be allowed to fly fighter aircraft, Lohrenz, a female combat pilot, surely was a public figure for purposes of this issue. But Lohrenz's attorney argued that she had not taken any part in this controversy—she simply trained as a Naval aviator, chose to fly jets, and accepted her assignment as a combat pilot when the opportunity presented itself. She certainly did not publicly participate in the debate over the wisdom of this change in policy.

The U.S. Court of Appeals sided with the defense. The court ruled that when Lohrenz *chose* to become a Navy aviator and when she *chose* to accept the assignment as an F-14 pilot, she should have realized she was becoming embroiled in the controversy over the role to be played by women in combat. She attained a special prominence in the dispute when she suited up to fly a Navy warplane. "A central role in the controversy came with the territory," the court said.[45]

In 1999 a Georgia court ruled that Richard Jewell was a public figure for purposes of his libel suit against Cox Enterprises Inc., publisher of the Atlanta Constitution and the Atlanta Journal. Jewell, a former deputy sheriff, is the man who discovered a bomb in a knapsack in a park during the 1996 Summer Olympic Games in Atlanta and then herded spectators out of the area before the device exploded. One person was killed, 11 others were injured. Jewell was regarded as a hero at first, and then law enforcement officers focused their attention on him as a suspect in the bombing. After the incident Jewell gave about a dozen interviews to local and national media about his role in clearing people out of the area after he discovered the bomb and about park security in general. He sued the Atlanta newspapers for comments published while he was regarded as a prime suspect in the bombing. He was later cleared. The court ruled that Jewell was a public person because he voluntarily stepped into the controversy by giving the interviews to the press. He was not at the time defending himself from accusations. "It is beyond argument," the court ruled, "that plaintiff did not reject any role in the debate, was a prominent figure in the coverage of the controversy, and, whatever his reticence regarding his media appearances, encountered them voluntarily."[46]

Courts in some states have ruled that an individual need not voluntarily inject himself or herself into a controversy to qualify as a limited-purpose public figure. In Wisconsin, for example, a state court ruled that a man who was falsely accused of a crime was a public figure for purposes of a libel suit because of his past behavior and the nature of the controversy. A teenager told police the plaintiff, Todd Erdmann, had come to his house looking for his sister. The boy told police that when he couldn't find the girl, Erdmann shot him. The plaintiff, who had earlier been warned about stalking the woman, was arrested five hours later. Police described the suspect as a survivalist who had access to several weapons. The following day the teenage boy admitted that he had made up the story, that he had in fact shot himself. Erdmann sued a local television station for libel for statements broadcast while he was a suspect. In the lawsuit the TV station contended that the plaintiff was a public figure. The Wisconsin Court of Appeals agreed. The court ruled that it was unfortunate that Erdmann had been thrust into the controversy primarily because of the boy's false report to the police and because of conclusions by the police that Erdmann was violent and dangerous and had access

---

45. *Lohrenz* v. *Donnelly,* 350 F. 3d 1272 (2003). The Supreme Court refused in 2004 to review this decision.

46. *Jewell* v. *Cox Enterprises Inc.,* 27 M.L.R. 2370 (1999), aff'd. *Atlanta Journal-Constitution* v. *Jewell,* Ga. Ct. App., 29 M.L.R. 2537 (2001).

to automatic weapons. "Although the police formulated these conclusions without any conduct or action by Erdmann, it is clear that it may be possible for someone to become a public figure through no purposeful action of his own," the court ruled.[47]

But other courts have demanded more active participation by the plaintiff before applying the public-figure designation. For example, Edward Mazur, a Polish immigrant, was a successful businessman, worked for various international companies, and owned parts of a number of businesses in the United States, Canada and Poland. He was also heavily involved in a variety of Polish-American social, community and athletic organizations. At the time the defamation was published, he was the director of the American Center of Polish Culture in Washington, D.C. In 2002 many stories appeared in the Polish press, and some were reprinted in this country, about crime and corruption that involved leaders of the Polish government. This was a controversy, a federal court noted, that affected Polish citizens, the Polish community in the United States, and others interested in Polish affairs. Statements were posted on the Internet in an online newsletter that said Mazur was linked to the murder of a police chief in Warsaw, Poland, and that there were rumors he had ties to organized crime and government corruption in Poland. When he sued for libel the defense asserted that there was surely a controversy about the allegations against current and former Polish government officials. And the court agreed. So as a leader in the Polish-American community, as Mazur was, he would surely have a central role in this controversy, the defense argued. The U.S. District Court disagreed on this point, noting that Mazur had taken no affirmative action to influence the outcome of the controversy. He was not a limited-purpose public figure.[48]

Contradictory decisions like these are often confusing, even to lawyers who specialize in libel law. They are evidence of two things. First, that the law of libel is still evolving, as it has during the past several centuries. And second, as noted in Chapter 4, libel is still basically state law. While the constitutionalization of the tort has added some consistency to the development of the libel law, state judges still have considerable room to shape their own law.

BUSINESSES AS PUBLIC FIGURES

Businesses and corporations can sue for libel; they can also be classified as public figures for purposes of a libel suit.

Businesses and corporations can sue for libel; they can also be classified as public figures for purposes of a libel suit. Surely if a business attempts to lead public opinion during a controversy over an important public issue, it could be categorized as a limited-purpose public figure. For example, General Motors could be classified as a limited-purpose public figure if it was libeled as it attempted to lead public opinion against government-imposed automobile emission standards. But businesses have been regarded as public figures based on other criteria as well, criteria hammered out over the past two decades. Some of the standards used to determine whether a business is a public figure include the following:

- **Whether a business has used a highly unusual advertising or promotional campaign to draw attention to itself.**
- **Whether a business is regulated by the government.**
- **Whether the libelous comment about the business focuses on a matter of great public concern.**

47. *Erdmann* v. *SF Broadcasting of Green Bay Inc.,* 599 N.W. 2d 1 (1999).
48. *Mazur* v. *Szporer,* 32 M.L.R. 1833 (2004).

Not all courts agree that these criteria are applicable. Here are some cases that offer guidelines in the application of these standards.

A company called Steaks Unlimited was deemed a public figure because it used a highly unusual method to advertise its low-priced, inspected, ungraded, frozen, tenderized, boxed beef. The advertising campaign featured unusually heavy radio and newspaper advertising, large signs erected at the sales location, and distribution of handbills to persons walking near the store. The sale attracted wide public attention, beyond the attention from consumers who sought to buy the meat.[49] And a U.S. District Court ruled in 1981 that the Bose Corporation, which was suing Consumer Reports, was a limited-purpose public figure because the audio equipment manufacturer had advertised its new 901 speakers in a highly unconventional manner that precipitated a public discussion on the merits of the product. The company intentionally emphasized the unconventional design of the product in its advertising and publicity.[50]

But normal advertising will not generally establish the level of notoriety required to turn a business into a public figure. A spirited, but typical, comparative advertising campaign between U.S. Healthcare Inc. and Blue Cross in Pennsylvania did not propel either company into the public-figure status, according to the 3rd U.S. Circuit Court of Appeals.[51] Similarly, extensive advertising and promotion by entrepreneur Thomas Jadwin of a double tax-exempt, no-load bond mutual fund he had developed did not make him a public figure. Soliciting media attention for such an offering is normal, the Minnesota Supreme Court ruled.[52] But the Nevada Supreme Court recently ruled that because a restaurant actively seeks out public patronage, it should usually be considered a public figure, at least for purposes of comments on the food.[53]

A nursing home in Rhode Island was declared to be a public figure by the state's high court because it was regulated by the government and because there was considerable public concern about the conditions at such facilities.[54] The Ohio Court of Appeals ruled in 1997 that despite the novelty at that time of interactive computer systems, advertising on the Internet is not unusual enough to turn a software company into a public figure in a libel suit.[55] In 1984 a U.S. District Court in Kansas ruled that the Beech Aircraft Company was a public figure for the purposes of a libel suit against Aviation Consumer magazine, which had published a story about Beech aircraft involved in accidents. The court said that "the defamatory statements relate to part of Beech's business that is federally regulated and arose in the context of a federal investigation." By entering into a regulated activity like the manufacture of aircraft, the company, in essence, invited public scrutiny, the court said.[56] And in 1988 the U.S. Court of Appeals for the 11th Circuit ruled that two businessmen who owned jai alai frontons in

49. *Steaks Unlimited* v. *Deaner,* 623 F. 2d 624 (1980).
50. *Bose Corp.* v. *Consumers Union of the United States, Inc.,* 508 F. Supp. 1249 (1981), rev'd 629 F. 2d 189 (1982), aff'd. 446 U.S. 485 (1984).
51. *U.S. Healthcare, Inc.* v. *Blue Cross of Greater Philadelphia,* 898 F. 2d 914 (1990).
52. *Jadwin* v. *Minneapolis Star,* 367 N.W. 2d 476 (1985).
53. *Pegasus* v. *Reno Newspapers Inc.,* 57 P. 3d 82 (2002).
54. *Harris Nursing Home Inc.* v. *Narragansett Television Inc.,* 24 M.L.R 1671 (1995).
55. *Worldnet Software Co.* v. *Gannett Satellite Information Network, Inc.,* 25 M.L.R. 2331 (1997).
56. *Beech Aircraft* v. *National Aviation Underwriters,* 11 M.L.R. 1401 (1984).

Florida were public figures in their libel suit brought against ABC. The court ruled the pair had put themselves in the public eye by becoming involved in a heavily regulated industry.[57] In 1995 the New Jersey Supreme Court said it would not consider an ordinary business to be a public figure unless the business was concerned with matters of public health and safety or was subject to substantial government regulation. The court added, however, that it would also regard as a public figure a business accused of consumer fraud when the allegations, if true, would constitute a violation of New Jersey's Consumer Fraud Act. In this case a lawn mower repair business was accused of cheating its customers. The state Supreme Court affirmed a lower-court ruling that the plaintiff business would have to prove actual malice to win its libel suit.[58] Other courts have rejected the government-regulation criteria, however. The Supreme Court of Oregon did not even consider the rationale that a regulated business is a public figure when it ruled that the Bank of Oregon was not a public figure for purposes of a lawsuit against the Willamette Week newspaper. "There simply is no public controversy into which plaintiffs arguably thrust themselves. Merely opening one's doors to the public, offering stock for public sale, advertising, etc., even if considered a thrusting of one's self into matters of public interest, is not sufficient to establish a public figure," the court ruled.[59]

Two court rulings in the 1990s, including one by the 5th U.S. Circuit Court of Appeals, have provided additional criteria that might be applied when determining whether a business is a public figure for purposes of a libel suit. In *Snead* v. *Redland Aggregates, Ltd.,* the Court of Appeals ruled that the notoriety of a business to the average person in the relevant geographical area (the area in which the libel is circulated), the public prominence of the business because it manufactures widely known consumer goods, and the frequency and intensity of media scrutiny of the business are all factors that need to be considered when a court makes a determination about the public-figure status of a business.[60] Also to be considered, the court said, is whether the libelous speech involves a matter of public or private concern. In this case the court ruled that a British firm that quarried sand, gravel and crushed stone was not a public figure. And a U.S. District Court in Pennsylvania ruled that a business's relative access to the media and the manner in which the risk of defamation came upon the business (i.e., the context of the dispute that generated the libel) must be considered when deciding whether a business was a public figure or not.[61] While the criteria in both these decisions lack precision, these rulings indicate that some courts seem willing to consider the public-figure status of businesses in a broader light.

As noted by the 5th U.S. Circuit Court of Appeals in the *Snead* decision, generalizations that have some value when determining the public or private status of an individual don't work well when applied to a business. Most courts seem more comfortable approaching the problem on a case-by-case basis. The lack of clear standards is an important reason journalists should be cautious when communicating about businesses, even those that have a high visibility in the community.

57. *Silvester* v. *ABC,* 839 F. 2d 1491 (1988).
58. *Turf Lawnmower Repair, Inc.* v. *Bergen Record,* 655 A. 2d 417 (1995).
59. *Bank of Oregon* v. *Independent News,* 963 P. 2d 35 (1985).
60. 998 F. 2d 1325 (1993).
61. *Rust Evader Corp.* v. *Plain Dealer Publishing Co.,* 21 M.L.R. 2189 (1993).

PUBLIC PERSONS OVER TIME

If someone is a public person (public official or public figure) today, will he or she still be regarded as a public figure 20 years from now? Yes, but only in regard to the issues or matters that generated the public-person status today. If Foster Pierson is a public figure today because he is at the forefront of a fight against a gun control initiative on the ballot in Indiana, he will still be regarded as a public figure in any story published or broadcast 20 years from now regarding this initiative battle. Similarly, a woman who retires to private life after being mayor of Houston will still be regarded as a public person if she sues for libel for a story published 25 years from now that focuses on her conduct while she was mayor.

The 10th U.S. Court of Appeals ruled in 2002 that the former associate deputy director of the Federal Bureau of Investigation was a public person for the purposes of a libel suit based on a book about the Oklahoma City bombing in 1995. Oliver Revell was retired from the FBI when the book was published, but the court ruled that this was immaterial. That

> the person defamed no longer holds the same position does not by itself strip him of this status as a public official for constitutional purposes. If the defamatory remarks relate to his conduct while he was a public official and the manner in which he performed his responsibilities is still a matter of public interest, he remains a public official within the meaning of *New York Times*.[62]

A U.S. District Court ruled that a U.S. Secret Service agent who saved the life of President Gerald Ford in 1975 must still be regarded as a public person for purposes of a libel suit based on a story broadcast in 1992 about the attempted assassination.[63] Two attempts were made on Ford's life in September 1975. Agent Larry Buendorf deflected the arm of assailant Lynette "Squeaky" Fromme on Sept. 5, 1975, and saved the life of President Ford while he was visiting Sacramento, Calif. Two weeks later a private citizen, Oliver Sipple, pushed away the arm of assailant Sara Jane Moore as she attempted to shoot the president when he was in San Francisco. This second incident became a major issue in the Bay Area when newspaper columnist Herb Caen speculated in print that the White House had not thanked Sipple for his heroic act because he was a homosexual. Sipple was gay, but sued the newspaper for invasion of privacy.[64] (See page 318 for more on this case.) Researchers at National Public Radio got the two incidents mixed up and commentator Daniel Schorr, in a report on how the press tramples on the privacy of public people, said it was revealed after he saved the president's life that agent Buendorf was a homosexual. The court ruled that Buendorf would have to prove actual malice to win his libel suit, something he was unable to do.[65] But in 1997 the Arkansas Supreme Court ruled that J. Michael Fitzhugh, a former federal prosecutor, was not a public person for purposes of a libel action he brought against the Arkansas Democrat-Gazette. The newspaper published a story that federal prosecutor Robert Fiske Jr. was about to initiate the first prosecution in the Whitewater investigation. Two men, Charles Matthews and Eugene

62. *Revell v. Hoffman*, 309 F. 3d 1228 (2002). See also *Newsom v. Henry*, 443 So. 2d 817 (1984) and *Contemporary Mission v. New York Times*, 665 F. Supp. 248 (1987), 842 F. 2d 612 (1988).
63. *Buendorf v. National Public Radio, Inc.*, 822 F. Supp. 6 (1993).
64. *Sipple v. Chronicle Publishing Co.*, 154 Cal. App. 3d 1040 (1984).
65. *Buendorf v. National Public Radio, Inc.*, 822 F. Supp. 6 (1993).

Fitzhugh, were the defendants in the case. The newspaper ran what it thought were pictures of the pair. The Matthews photo was correct, but the Democrat-Gazette mistakenly published a photo of J. Michael Fitzhugh instead of a picture of Eugene Fitzhugh. The newspaper argued that because the plaintiff had been a federal prosecutor for eight years—clearly a public official during those years—he surely should be considered a public person for the purposes of this lawsuit. The court disagreed, ruling that while J. Michael Fitzhugh was and still is a public person for any story relating to his work as a federal prosecutor, he was not a public person for stories about matters outside that realm, including the Whitewater investigation. The simple error cost the newspaper $50,000 in damages.[66]

PRIVATE PERSONS

In a libel action, if the plaintiff does not meet the definition of a public official, an all-purpose public figure, or a limited-purpose public figure, the court will regard the individual as a private person. This designation means the plaintiff will not be required to prove that the defendant lied or exhibited reckless disregard for the truth in publishing the libel. The plaintiff in most jurisdictions will only have to demonstrate that the defendant failed to exercise reasonable care in preparing and publishing the defamatory material. There are, however, a few exceptions to this rule. A few states, including California,[67] Colorado,[68] Indiana,[69] Alaska,[70] and New York,[71] have decided that plaintiffs who are considered private persons must prove a higher degree of fault than simple negligence when they sue a mass medium for libel based on a story about a matter of public interest. In some states these plaintiffs must prove gross negligence or gross irresponsibility; in others these private-person plaintiffs must prove actual malice. Gross negligence is a higher degree of fault than simple negligence, but a lesser degree of fault than actual malice. To find out the rule in your state, locate the most recent state supreme court ruling on libel. Within the text of this decision there is very likely to be a reference to the level of fault required by private-person plaintiffs.

SUMMARY Under the fault requirement all persons who sue a mass medium for libel must prove that the defendant was somehow at fault in publishing the defamatory material, that the publication (or broadcast) did not result from an innocent error.

What the courts call a "public person" must normally prove that the defendant acted with actual malice in publishing the libel; that is, the defendant knew the material was false but still published it or exhibited reckless disregard for the truth. What the courts define as "private persons" must prove at least that the defendant acted negligently, that is, in such a

66. *Little Rock Newspapers* v. *Fitzhugh,* 954 S.W. 2d 187 (1997).
67. *Rollenhagen* v. *City of Orange,* 172 Cal. Rptr. 49 (1981).
68. *Walker* v. *Colorado Springs Sun, Inc.,* 538 P. 2d 450 (1975).
69. *AAFCO Heating and Air Conditioning Co.* v. *Northwest Publications, Inc.,* 321 N.E. 2d 580 (1974).
70. *Gay* v. *Williams,* 486 F. Supp. 12 (1979).
71. *Chapadeau* v. *Utica Observer-Dispatch, Inc.,* 341 N.E. 2d 569 (1975).

way as to create an unreasonable risk of harm. The courts have ruled that there are three kinds of "public persons":

   I. *Public officials:* Persons who work for a government in a position of authority, who have substantial control over the conduct of governmental affairs, and whose position in government invites independent public scrutiny beyond the general public interest in the qualifications and performance of all government employees. Libelous comments must focus on the plaintiff's official conduct (the manner in which the plaintiff conducts his or her job) or on the plaintiff's general fitness to hold public office.

  II. *All-purpose public figures:* Persons who occupy persuasive power and influence in the nation or in a community, persons who are usually exposed to constant media attention.

 III. *Limited-purpose public figures:* Persons who voluntarily inject themselves into an important public controversy in order to influence public opinion regarding the resolution of that controversy. The key elements are these:

    a. Public controversy, the resolution of which must affect more persons than simply the participants. The outcome must have an impact on people in a community.

    b. Plaintiffs who voluntarily thrust themselves into this controversy. An individual who has been drawn involuntarily into a controversy created by someone else (such as the press) is not a limited-purpose public figure.

    c. Plaintiffs who attempt to influence the outcome of the controversy, to shape public opinion on the subject. This implies that a plaintiff has some access to the mass media to participate in the public discussion surrounding the controversy.

Using a variety of criteria, courts have ruled that businesses can be deemed public figures in a libel suit. Persons who become public persons remain public persons throughout their lives with regard to stories published or broadcast that relate to incidents or events that occurred while they were public persons.

THE MEANING OF FAULT

> Negligence = Failure to Exercise Reasonable Care
> Actual Malice = Knowledge of Falsity or Reckless Disregard for the Truth

NEGLIGENCE

"Negligence" is a term that has been commonly used in tort law for centuries, but has only been applied to libel law since 1974. In simple terms, **negligence** implies the failure to exercise ordinary care. In deciding whether to adopt the negligence or the stricter actual malice fault requirements, state courts are providing their own definitions of the standard. Washington state adopted a "reasonable care" standard. Defendants are considered negligent if they do not exercise reasonable care in determining whether a statement is false or will create a false impression.[72] The Tennessee Supreme Court has adopted a "reasonably prudent person test": What would a reasonably prudent person have done or not have done in the same circumstance? Would a reasonably prudent reporter have checked the truth of a story more fully? Would such a reporter have waited a day or so to get more information? Would a reasonably prudent reporter have worked harder in trying to reach the plaintiff before publishing the charges?[73] In Arizona negligence has been defined as conduct that creates unreasonable risk of harm. "It is the failure to use that amount of care which a reasonably prudent person would use under like circumstances," the Arizona Supreme Court ruled.[74]

Some of the more common reasons a defendant might be found negligent are these:

- **Reliance on an untrustworthy source**
- **Not reading or misreading pertinent documents**
- **Failure to check with an obvious source, perhaps the subject of the story**
- **Carelessness in editing and news handling**

Did the reporter make a good faith effort to determine the truth or falsity of the matter?

The question the court will always ask is, **Did the reporter make a good faith effort to determine the truth or falsity of the matter?** Here are some cases that illuminate these criteria.

Courts will often scrutinize the source of the reporter's story when deciding whether or not there was negligence. After a reporter relied on a source whom police described as being an unreliable informant, and even the reporter admitted in court that he had found some of his source's information to be incorrect, the Massachusetts Supreme Judicial Court ruled that a jury might find negligence in such a case.[75] But a superior court in New Jersey ruled in 2003 that when a criminal suspect was misidentified in a news story there was no negligence, because the reporter had gotten the wrong name from both the police and an assistant prosecutor.[76] And the courts have consistently ruled that a newspaper or broadcast station is not negligent when it relies on reports received from the Associated Press, Reuters or other news services.[77]

Reportorial techniques are often scrutinized when a plaintiff asserts that a news medium has been negligent. But courts do not expect superhuman efforts from journalists, only general competence. The San Antonio Express-News was sued for libel when it inadvertently ran the wrong picture with a story it published on a woman convicted of prostitution, selling a child into prostitution and drug-related offenses. The plaintiff, who had the same name as the woman described in the Express-News story, had also been convicted of selling a child into

---

72. *Taskett* v. *King Broadcasting Co.,* 546 P. 2d 81 (1976).
73. *Memphis Publishing Co.* v. *Nichols,* 569 S.W. 2d 412 (1978).
74. *Peagler* v. *Phoenix Newspapers,* 547 P. 2d 1074 (1976).
75. *Jones* v. *Taibbi,* 512 N.E. 2d 260 (1987).
76. *Yeager* v. *Daily Record,* 32 M.L.R. 1667 (2003).
77. *Appleby* v. *Daily Hampshire,* 395 Mass. 2 (1985); *McKinney* v. *Avery Journal, Inc.,* 393 S.E. 2d 295 (1990); and *Cole* v. *Star Tribune,* 26 M.L.R. 2415 (1998).

prostitution, but was clearly not the woman described in the newspaper. Was there negligence in this case? The reporter had seven years of experience covering the courthouse and had spent six months researching the series of articles on the Texas Department of Correction's parole system. She had submitted a request to the county sheriff's office for a mug shot of the woman who was the subject of the story. The request included the woman's name, date of birth, and Department of Corrections identification number. The sheriff's office gave her the wrong photo. The plaintiff insisted that the reporter failed to verify that she had the correct photo, that the reporter should have checked with the woman's mother to make certain the correct photo was being used. The court disagreed. "The issue was not what Fox [the reporter] could have done to avoid the mistake. It is whether she acted reasonably; that is, as a reasonable reporter under similar circumstances would have acted." The court said there was no negligence in this case.[78]

The South Carolina Supreme Court ruled that the failure of a reporter to examine a public judicial record when writing about a criminal case could be negligence. The plaintiff in the case had been arrested with four other men and charged with pirating stereo audiotapes. Two months later four of the men arrested pleaded guilty to the charges, but the charges were dismissed against the plaintiff. The newspaper published a story saying that the plaintiff had also pleaded guilty to the charges. The reporter had gotten his information about the case in a telephone conversation with the prosecuting attorney. The attorney testified that he had given the reporter the correct information. Six days elapsed between the dismissal of charges and the erroneous story. The South Carolina high court concluded that the correct information was available to the reporter in the court records and that he could have looked at this material before publishing the story. He instead chose to rely on a telephone conversation and in doing so got the story fouled up. The jury could readily conclude that the reporter was negligent, the court ruled.[79]

Finally, the Virginia Supreme Court ruled that when a newspaper published a very negative story about a local teacher, based largely on complaints from parents who called the newspaper, it exhibited negligence. Parents were quoted in the article as saying the teacher was erratic, disorganized, forgetful, unfair and demeaning to students. The reporter who wrote the story talked to a couple of students, the principal, and two of the teacher's colleagues, but got very little information. As such, the story was very one-sided. The court said that the reporter could have contacted many more students to try to verify the accusations since there was no deadline pressure. It was obvious, the court ruled, that the parents who contacted the reporter bore the teacher ill will. This should have pushed the reporter to do a more thorough job.[80]

The editorial process itself may be examined when a plaintiff seeks to prove negligence. And carelessness in the way that editors handle news copy can result in a finding of fault. In 1985 the editors at USA Today planned to run a special feature commemorating the 10th anniversary of the capture of Saigon by the North Vietnamese, the end of the Vietnam War. In typical USA Today fashion, the editors wanted a short story from each state. An editor in

78. *Garza* v. *The Hearst Corporation,* 23 M.L.R. 1733 (1995).
79. *Jones* v. *Sun Publishing,* 292 S.E. 2d 23 (1982).
80. *Richmond Newspapers* v. *Lipscomb,* 362 S.E. 2d 32 (1987).

Virginia called the paper's stringer in Vermont and asked him for a contribution. The stringer, Ron Wyman, talked with an acquaintance, Jeffrey Kassel, a clinical psychologist at a Veterans Administration hospital, and asked if he had any ideas for a short story. The thrust of Kassel's remarks was the notion that many American soldiers who fought in Vietnam felt as if they were victims, forced to fight in a war they didn't want. As Wyman was leaving, Kassel noted that he had recently seen an article in another newspaper that said that former Vietnamese soldiers were amused by the idea that their painful experiences in the war might leave them with "post-traumatic stress disorder," the scourge of many U.S. veterans. Wyman put his notes together and read them over the telephone to his editor in Virginia. She in turn routed the notes to another editor who wrote the final story, which quoted Kassel as saying, "We've become a nation of handwringers. . . . It's amusing that vets feel they are the victims when the Vietnamese had the napalm and bombs dropped on them."[81] This, of course, was not what Kassel had said. USA Today had attributed to the psychologist the observations in the newspaper article he noted to reporter Wyman. Testimony at the trial revealed that no one ever called Kassel before publication to check the quote, no editor checked with Wyman after the story was written, and the individual who wrote that short story never even checked with the editor who had transcribed Wyman's notes over the telephone. The 1st U.S. Circuit Court of Appeals ruled that a jury might certainly construe this behavior as negligent.[82]

The definition of the term "negligence" will undoubtedly vary from state to state and possibly from judge to judge within a state. It is going to be some time before any kind of broad, consistently applied guidelines emerge. It is unlikely the Supreme Court will be of any help in this matter as it appears to be the intention of the court to leave the matter to the states.

ACTUAL MALICE

Defining actual malice is somewhat easier than defining who is and who is not a public figure or public official. In *New York Times Co.* v. *Sullivan*,[83] Justice Brennan defined **actual malice** as "knowledge of falsity or reckless disregard of whether the material was false or not." The two parts of this definition should be considered separately.

Knowledge of Falsity

"Knowledge of falsity" is a fancy way of saying "lie."

"Knowledge of falsity" is a fancy way of saying "lie." If the defendant lied and the plaintiff can prove it, actual malice has then been shown. In 1969 Barry Goldwater was able to convince a federal court that Ralph Ginzburg published known falsehoods about him during the 1964 presidential campaign in a "psychobiography" carried in Ginzburg's Fact magazine. Ginzburg sent questionnaires to hundreds of psychiatrists, asking them to analyze Goldwater's mental condition. Ginzburg published only those responses that agreed with the magazine's predisposition that Goldwater was mentally ill and changed the responses on other questionnaires to reflect this point of view. Proof of this conduct, plus other evidence, led the

81. *Kassel* v. *Gannett Co., Inc.,* 875 F. 2d 935 (1989).
82. Ibid.
83. 376 U.S. 254 (1964).

court to conclude that Ginzburg had published the defamatory material with knowledge of its falsity.[84]

Quoting a subject exactly can present a real challenge to a reporter. Most people talk a lot faster than most reporters can write. There are two kinds of quotes in news stories. Statements that are enclosed within quotation marks are called direct quotes and are supposed to represent an exact (or as close as possible) copy of what the subject said. But reporters also use indirect quotes. These represent the substance of what the subject said, but are not an exact replica. Indirect quotes are never enclosed in quotation marks.

For example, Cathy Miller tells a reporter, "The mayor is going to have to cut spending on public safety to balance the budget."

- **Direct quote:** "The mayor is going to have to cut spending on public safety to balance the budget," Cathy Miller said.
- **Indirect quote:** Cathy Miller said she believed that the mayor will have to reduce spending for police and fire services to get a balanced budget.

Most people believe that a direct quote contains the exact words of the speaker and an indirect quote contains at least an accurate reflection of what the speaker said. What happens if a reporter changes these words, and in doing so changes the meaning of the statement in such a way that it defames the speaker? Is this knowledge of falsity?

This was the question faced by the Supreme Court of the United States in 1991 when it heard an appeal by psychoanalyst Jeffrey Masson of an adverse lower-court ruling in his lawsuit against the New Yorker magazine and writer Janet Malcolm. For many years Masson was projects director of the prestigious Sigmund Freud Archives. As time went on, he became disillusioned with some of Freud's ideas and began to advance his own theories. His superiors disapproved of this and fired the noted psychoanalyst. Writer Malcolm talked with Masson for more than 40 hours about Freud, his own ideas about psychoanalysis, and his relationship with others who worked at the archives. The New Yorker published a long article that resulted from the interviews, and the piece was expanded and ultimately published as a book. Malcolm's article presented an unflattering picture of Jeffrey Masson. Some of the most damning prose came from long direct quotations that the writer attributed to the psychoanalyst. Malcolm said she had taken these quotes from 18 hours of taped interviews, as well as notes she had kept during the interviews. But Masson contended that he had never said many of the things attributed to him, that Janet Malcolm had fabricated these quotes. And these quotes made him look egotistical, irresponsible, sexually promiscuous and dishonest. Malcolm said she had made only minor changes in the quotations.

In the lawsuit that followed, Masson stipulated he was a public figure. But he argued that when Malcolm changed or fabricated his remarks for the article, she was guilty of actual malice. The trial court granted the defendant's motion for a summary judgment, and the case went into appeal. The key question was whether evidence of changing the words in a direct quote is, in and of itself, proof of knowledge of falsity.

In a 7-2 ruling, the high court reversed the lower-court ruling. It said that readers presume that the words contained within quotation marks are a verbatim reproduction of what the

---

84. *Goldwater* v. *Ginzburg*, 414 F. 2d 324 (1969).

Courtesy, Knopf Publishing © Jerry Bauer

▼

Janet Malcolm, author of "The Journalist and The Murderer," and defendant in a libel suit brought by Jeffrey Masson. A jury found in her behalf in 1994. Published by Knopf.

speaker said. But, Justice Kennedy wrote, to demand that the press meet such a high standard is unrealistic. "If every alteration [of a quote] constituted the falsity required to prove actual malice, the practice of journalism, which the First Amendment is designed to protect, would require a radical change, one inconsistent with our precedents and First Amendment principles," he added. "We conclude that a deliberate alteration of the words uttered by a plaintiff does not equate with knowledge of falsity . . . unless the alteration results in a *material change* [author's emphasis] in the meaning conveyed by the statement."[85]

85. *Masson* v. *The New Yorker, Inc.,* 111 S. Ct. 2419 (1991).

The case was sent back to lower court for a jury trial on critical fact issues in the case. The appeal to the Supreme Court, after all, was based on the unproven premise that Malcolm had in fact altered the quotes. The Supreme Court insisted that before convicting Malcolm of libel the jury answer three questions affirmatively:

1. Were the statements attributed to Masson false (i.e., the meaning of the quotes had been materially changed)?
2. Did these false statements defame Masson?
3. Did Malcolm act with actual malice; did she know the quotes were false but publish them anyway, or exhibit reckless disregard for the truth?

In 1993 a jury in San Francisco found that five quotations attributed to Masson were false, that two were libelous, and that there was sufficient evidence of actual malice to sustain a conviction for libel. But the jury members could not agree on a damage award to the plaintiff.[86] A new trial on both damages and liability was scheduled. In late 1994 another San Francisco jury ruled that two quotes were false, and one of those defamed Masson, but that Janet Malcolm had not acted with actual malice in publishing these quotes. In other words, the jury believed the reporter when she said she believed that what she wrote was what Jeffrey Masson had told her. Trial observers attributed the reversal in the verdict to two factors. The defense spent much more time in the second trial on the actual malice standard, trying to educate jurors in how irresponsible or careless a journalist must be for a libel claim to prevail. Also, most observers said that Janet Malcolm was far more persuasive in her testimony in the second trial, that jurors seemed more inclined to believe her.[87] Masson appealed the adverse verdict on the grounds that the trial judge erred in instructing the jury on actual malice. In June 1996 the U.S. Court of Appeals affirmed the lower-court verdict and barred Masson from trying to bring another libel action against The New Yorker based on the same libel claims.[88]

In a similar vein the Texas Supreme Court in 2005 ruled that it is not evidence of knowledge of falsity simply to show that a headline on a news story paraphrases the remarks of a speaker and is not a verbatim recitation of what the speaker said. The court said two questions must be answered. Would a reasonable reader believe these were the actual words of the speaker? And did the paraphrased comment alter the meaning of what the speaker actually said? If a reasonable reader would understand that this was a paraphrase or interpretation of what the speaker said, and not a recitation of the exact remark attributed to him or her, there can be no finding of actual malice.

Reckless Disregard for the Truth

Reckless disregard for the truth is a bit more difficult to define. In 1964 the Supreme Court said that reckless disregard could be shown by proving that the defendant had "a high degree of awareness of [the] probable falsity" of the defamatory material when it was published.[89] Four years later the Supreme Court said that in order to show reckless disregard for the truth,

---

86. Gross, "Impasse Over Damages," A1.
87. Margolick, "Psychoanalyst Loses Libel Suit," A1.
88. *Masson* v. *The New Yorker, Inc.,* 85 F. 3d 1394 (1996).
89. *Garrison* v. *Louisiana,* 379 U.S. 64 (1964).

Proof that the defendant failed to investigate a charge that later turns out to be false is not in and of itself sufficient evidence to prove actual malice.

the plaintiff must bring forth "sufficient evidence to permit the conclusion that the defendant in fact entertained serious doubts as to the truth of his publication."[90] Proof that the defendant failed to investigate a charge that later turns out to be false is not in and of itself sufficient evidence to prove actual malice.

KNOWLEDGE OF FALSITY

A high degree of awareness of the probable falsity of the defamatory
material when it was published

or

Sufficient evidence to permit the conclusion that the defendant in fact entertained
serious doubts as to the truth of the publication

These definitions of reckless disregard are certainly useful in a theoretical sense. It is surely possible to envision a reporter or editor entertaining serious doubts about the truth of an allegation and publishing it anyway. However, neither of these definitions is terribly helpful in a practical sense. As Judge Kozinski of the 9th U.S. Circuit Court of Appeals wrote in his decision in a case involving the National Enquirer and Clint Eastwood, "As we have yet to see a defendant who admits to entertaining serious subjective doubt about the authenticity of an article it published, we must be guided by circumstantial evidence."[91] There is language in a 1967 Supreme Court ruling that has been extremely helpful to both jurists and journalists in charting a course by using such evidence. The ruling involved two cases, *Curtis Publishing Co.* v. *Butts* and *AP* v. *Walker.*[92] Justice John Harlan outlined a test in his opinion to evaluate the conduct of both defendants in these libel cases. It is important to note that Justice Harlan never called the criteria he outlined a test for reckless disregard for the truth. He said he was attempting to establish a test to see whether the defendants in the two cases had seriously departed from the standards of responsible reporting. A few courts have rejected the Harlan criteria as a test for actual malice.[93] But even some members of the Supreme Court have referred to this test as a measure of reckless disregard. And it has become a commonly used test in the lower courts.

The two cases that generated these criteria came before the Supreme Court at about the same time and were joined and decided as one case. In the first case, Wally Butts, the athletic director at the University of Georgia, brought suit against the Saturday Evening Post for an article it published alleging that Butts and University of Alabama football coach Paul "Bear" Bryant had conspired prior to the annual Georgia-Alabama football game to "fix" the contest. The Post obtained its information from a man who said that while making a telephone call, he had been accidentally plugged into a phone conversation between Butts and Bryant. George Burnett, who had a criminal record, told the Post editors that he had taken careful notes. The story was based on Burnett's recollection of what was said.

---

90. *St. Amant* v. *Thompson,* 390 U.S. 727 (1968).
91. *Eastwood* v. *National Enquirer Inc.,* 123 F. 3d 1249 (1997).
92. 388 U.S. 130 (1967).
93. See, for example, *Clyburn* v. *News World Communications,* 903 F. 2d 29 (1990).

Source: Used with permission from The Saturday Evening Post © 1963. Article originally appeared in the March 23, 1963 issue of The Saturday Evening Post. Photo © Atlanta Journal Constitution

The Saturday Evening Post alleged that Wally Butts and Paul "Bear" Bryant conspired to fix the Georgia-Alabama football game during the 1962 college football season. Publication of this article ultimately resulted in the famous Curtis Publishing Co. v. Butts *ruling in 1967.*

In the other case, Major General (retired) Edwin Walker, a political conservative and segregationist from Texas, brought suit against The Associated Press and a score of publications and broadcasting stations for publishing the charge that he led a mob of white citizens against federal marshals who were attempting to preserve order at the University of Mississippi in September of 1962, during the crisis over the enrollment of James Meredith. Walker was on campus during the disturbances, but did not lead a mob. The AP report was filed by a young AP correspondent on the scene.

The court ruled that in the *Butts* case the Post had exhibited highly unreasonable conduct in publishing the story but that in the *Walker* case no such evidence was present. Again, it is important to note that although Justice John Marshall Harlan did not call the conduct reckless disregard at the time, most authorities accept these cases as good indicators of what the court means by reckless disregard. Look at the details of each case.

In the *Butts* case, the story was not what would be called a hot news item. It was published months after the game occurred. The magazine had ample time to check the report. The source of the story was not a trained reporter, but a layman who happened to be on probation on a bad-check charge. The Post made no attempt to investigate the story further, to screen the game films to see if either team had made changes in accord with what Bryant and Butts supposedly discussed. Many persons were supposedly with Burnett when he magically overheard this conversation and none were questioned by the Post. The magazine did little, then, to check the story, despite evidence presented at the trial that one or two of the editors acknowledged that Burnett's story needed careful examination. Finally, both Butts and Bryant had strong reputations for integrity. There had never even been hints of this kind of behavior in the past.

In the *Walker* case, different circumstances were present. For the AP editor back in the office who was responsible for getting the story on the wires, it was hot news, a story that should be sent out immediately. The information was provided in the "heat of battle" by a young, but trained, reporter who in the past had given every indication of being trustworthy. All but one of the dispatches from the correspondent said the same thing: Walker led the mob. So there was internal consistency. Finally, when General Walker's previous actions and statements are considered, the story that he led a mob at Ole Miss was not terribly out of line with his prior behavior. There was nothing in the story to cause AP editors to suspect that it might be in error. The journalist did not report, for example, that the mob was being led by the Roman Catholic Archbishop of New Orleans. A red light should signal those instances that suggest further checking because the story doesn't sound very likely.[94]

When all these are sorted out, three key factors emerge:

1. Was the publication of the story urgent? Was it a hot news item? Or was there sufficient time to check the facts in the story fully?
2. How reliable was the source of the story? Should the reporter have trusted the news source? Was the source a trained journalist? Should the editor have trusted the reporter?
3. Was the story probable? Or was the story so unlikely that it cried out for further examination?

It is very difficult for a plaintiff to prove actual malice. Proving that a defendant did in fact entertain serious doubts about the truth or falsity of the matter that was subsequently published or broadcast is an imposing task. But the Supreme Court has placed additional burdens on the plaintiff as well.

■ **The plaintiff must prove actual malice with "clear and convincing" evidence.**[95] Normally in a civil lawsuit the plaintiff must prove his or her allegations with a "preponderance of the evidence," which means that the plaintiff has more evidence than the defendant. "Clear and convincing" means that there can be little or no dispute about the evidence.

---

94. *Curtis Publishing Co.* v. *Butts, AP* v. *Walker,* 388 U.S. 130 (1967).
95. *Gertz* v. *Robert Welch, Inc.,* 418 U.S. 323 (1974).

■ **The Supreme Court has instructed appellate courts to re-examine the evidence in the case to determine that the record "establishes actual malice with convincing clarity."**[96] Typically an appellate court is bound to accept the evidentiary findings of the trial court (see page 17). But in a libel case the appellate court is mandated to take a close look and make certain the evidence supports the finding of malice. Allotting the appellate court such evidentiary power not only gives the defendant a second chance to win the case on the basis of the facts, but it also forces trial court judges to take extra pains when examining the facts, knowing that their work will likely be closely scrutinized in the future. The following overview of court rulings on actual malice will help illuminate both the criteria for such a finding and these two defense advantages.

In many instances the subject of a defamatory story will deny its truth before the story is published. When the story is published anyway, the plaintiff will argue that its publication in the face of the denial is evidence of reckless disregard for the truth. The vast majority of courts have rejected this argument.[97]

In sorting out claims of actual malice, courts often are forced to delve deeply into the reporting process. Sports Illustrated published an article on fixed boxing matches. The article cited a match between Randall "Tex" Cobb and Paul "Sonny" Barch, which was promoted by Rick Parker, as an example of a fixed fight. A senior editor at the magazine had gotten a call from Barch in which he alleged the fix. He told the editor that he had given sworn testimony to the Florida State Athletic Commission (FSAC) regarding the fight. Barch said that he and Cobb had agreed that Barch would take a dive in the first round. He also said that he and Cobb and Parker had all used cocaine before the match. The editor assigned an experienced reporter to check out the story. She had worked for both the magazine and the Wall Street Journal, but she was not a boxing expert. The magazine took the following steps to check out the story:

■ The reporter talked at length with an official at the FSAC who confirmed Barch's story.
■ She talked with promoter Parker's ex-business partner who confirmed the allegations.
■ Barch was a last-minute substitute in the fight, so the reporter interviewed the original opponent, who said he was replaced on the fight card at the last minute under phony circumstances.
■ The reporter also talked with Barch and with Parker.
■ Cobb was a reluctant interview subject, but the reporter finally talked with him on the telephone. He denied the whole story.
■ Several reporters, including some who regularly covered boxing, watched a tape of the fight.

But the magazine did not do the following:

■ No one at Sports Illustrated talked with the referee for the fight or the ringside judges.

96. *Bose Corporation* v. *Consumers Union of the United States, Inc.*, 446 U.S. 485 (1984).
97. See, for example, *Worrell-Payne* v. *Gannett Co.*, 30 M.L.R. 2893 (2002).

▪ No one reviewed the sworn testimony that Barch said he gave to the FSAC.

▪ No outside boxing experts were consulted.

▪ No one other than Barch was ever consulted about whether Cobb had been a knowing participant in the scheme.

A trial court awarded Cobb almost $10 million in damages, but the 6th U.S. Court of Appeals reversed the judgment, ruling that there was not clear and convincing proof that the magazine's editors or reporters entertained serious doubts about the truth or falsity of the story. The court agreed that the investigation could have been more comprehensive, noting that someone should have interviewed the referee and the judges. But the court ruled that while failure to take additional steps might not have been prudent, and could be considered negligence, this did not amount to actual malice.[98]

In another case a financial advisor by the name of Brian Freeman sued for libel, saying he was misquoted in a book by reporter Moira Johnson called "Takeover: The New Wall Street Warriors—The Men, The Money, The Impact." Freeman is a lawyer and was representing a machinists' union during the closed-door negotiations about the future of Trans World Airlines. Two financiers, Carl Ichan and Frank Lorenzo, were fighting over control of the airline. Johnson wrote: "Brian Freeman, the lawyer to represent the machinists, compounded the threats of a strike, warning that being sold into bondage to Lorenzo would provoke nighttime trashing of airplanes and other sabotage." Reporter Johnson did not attend the meeting, but two people who did talked with her about what Freeman had said during the negotiations. The first person Johnson talked to said the quoted statement accurately reflected what Freeman had said. The other person, who testified in the lawsuit for Freeman, said he didn't exactly remember what Freeman said, but that Freeman was cautious as a lawyer. "It was no big deal," the witness said. Freeman contended that the two witnesses to the conversation obviously disagreed and that Johnson should have done more checking on the quote because of this disagreement. Failure to do so amounted to actual malice. The New York Court of Appeals disagreed, noting that nothing the second witness said actually contradicted what the first witness told Johnson. "Given these different possible interpretations, no rational fact finder could, in this case, find actual malice by clear and convincing evidence."[99]

Disputes over the validity of evidence, often scientific evidence, frequently figure in libel disputes. That a reporter accepts one set of findings rather than another is not regarded as evidence of actual malice. Documentary filmmaker Michael Moore produced a segment of his "TV Nation" program on a company that disposed of New York City sewer sludge by shipping it to Texas and spreading it over a large plot of land. The company, Merco Joint Venture, said the application of the sludge increases vegetation on arid grassland, adds nutrients to the soil, and conditions the soil to make better use of limited water. Moore's "Sludge Train" broadcast made fun of this process and questioned the safety of such an application of waste matter. Merco sued for libel, claiming that there was scientific evidence that the matter was safe. The 5th U.S. Circuit Court of Appeals ruled that there was no consensus from experts on whether land application of the sludge was safe. And even if there were, it would not be proof that the defendants knew the broadcast was false or should have known it was false. "Because an

---

98. *Cobb* v. *Time Inc.,* 278 F. 3d 629 (2002).
99. *Freeman* v. *Johnson,* 614 N.Y.S. 2d 377 (1994).

'expert' endorses a certain practice does not mean that all reasonable debate on the merits or safety of that practice is foreclosed," the court said as it reversed the $5 million judgment against the defendants.[100]

The U.S. Supreme Court spoke to the question of actual malice in 1984 when it ruled that a sound engineer employed by Consumer Reports had not acted with actual malice when he knowingly changed the wording of the results of a test panel that had evaluated an audio speaker system, even though his testimony that he didn't think he had changed the meaning of the statement was unbelievable.[101] In its review of the Bose 901 speakers, Consumer Reports magazine said the sound from the speakers "tended to wander about the room." This statement was written by engineer Arnold Seligson, who supervised the test. But the listener panel had actually said that the sound tended to move along the wall, in front of and between the two speakers. At the trial Seligson testified that he believed the two statements meant the same thing. The district court found this testimony incredible and said that Seligson obviously knew he had changed the meaning of the statement.[102] This was evidence of actual malice. The Supreme Court disagreed, saying Seligson's testimony, in and of itself, was not evidence of actual malice. "He had made a mistake," Justice John Paul Stevens wrote, "and when confronted with it he refused to admit it and steadfastly attempted to maintain that no mistake had been made—that the inaccurate was accurate. The attempt failed, but the fact that he made the attempt does not establish that he realized the inaccuracy at the time of publication."[103]

The lower courts have been somewhat more consistent in applying the criteria developed by the Supreme Court regarding actual malice than they have in applying criteria used to determine who is and who is not a public figure. Many courts have used elements of the three-part *Butts-Walker* test to measure actual malice. For example, Was the journalist on a deadline? A reporter for the St. Louis Globe-Democrat, preparing a story on deadline, told a rewrite person on the city desk that a city alderwoman admitted at a public meeting to having had two abortions. The copydesk botched the story and attributed the statement to another alderwoman, an outspoken foe of abortion. The Missouri Supreme Court said the journalists' behavior was negligent but not reckless disregard for the truth. The deadline pressure made rechecking the information impossible.[104]

The law does not require the complete verification of a story, especially a breaking story. (Most editors, however, will demand the most thorough verification possible.) The District of Columbia U.S. Circuit Court of Appeals ruled that evidence that a book publisher failed to completely verify defamatory allegations written by an author whose credibility had been frequently questioned was not sufficient to demonstrate that the publisher had in fact entertained serious doubts about the truth of these allegations. The book in question is "Profits of War" by Ari Ben-Menashe, a man, the publisher acknowledged, whose credibility was often suspect. But Ben-Menashe was relied on as a credible source by many writers and television producers. The book contained allegations that Robert C. McFarlane, a former national security advisor, was really an Israeli agent who facilitated spying by the Israelis on the

The law does not require the complete verification of a story, especially a breaking story.

100. *Peter Scalamandre & Sons, Inc.* v. *Kaufman,* 113 F. 3d 556 (1997).
101. *Bose Corporation* v. *Consumers Union of the United States, Inc.,* 446 U.S. 485 (1984).
102. *Bose Corporation* v. *Consumers Union of the United States, Inc.,* 508 F. Supp. 1249 (1981).
103. *Bose Corporation* v. *Consumers Union of the United States, Inc.,* 446 U.S. 485 (1984).
104. *Glover* v. *Herald Co.,* 549 S.W. 2d 858 (1977).

United States. Many of Ben-Menashe's allegations about McFarlane were proved to be false four months after the book was published when a congressional task force released a report on many topics related to relations between the United States and Middle Eastern nations. At the time the book was published, however, much of the evidence contained in the task force report had not yet been made public.

McFarlane argued that because Ben-Menashe's credibility was dubious at best, the book publisher had a duty to verify every one of his defamatory assertions. The court disagreed with that argument. "When the source of potentially libelous material is questionable . . . the investigatory efforts of the publisher are important only to the extent that they serve as evidence that it did not publish the material in reckless disregard for the truth," the judges said. The publisher does not have to corroborate every allegation, the court said. In this case the publisher did attempt to verify all the defamatory statements but was unable to find evidence to substantiate many of the charges. At the same time no contradictory evidence was uncovered either. "To hold that a publisher who relies upon a questionable source must not only investigate the allegations but actually corroborate them . . . would be to turn the inquiry away from the publisher's state of mind and to inquire instead whether the publisher satisfied an objective standard of care," the court ruled. The plaintiff had failed to demonstrate actual malice.[105]

The 11th U.S. Circuit Court of Appeals handed down a similar ruling in 1999 in a libel suit brought by a financial corporation against ABC television for a "20/20" broadcast. The plaintiff, BFC Financial Corporation, said it had been libeled when the network portrayed it as knowlingly misleading investors about the benefits and risks of limited real estate partnerships. ABC countered with the argument that it interviewed many sources and not one of them regarded what BFC had done as being fair to investors. The plaintiff argued that the network reporters had not interviewed the real estate expert it had recommended and this was proof of actual malice. The court disagreed. "ABC was not required to continue its investigation until it found somebody who would stand up for Levan [a plaintiff]," the court said. The law only required that the network reporters not proceed to broadcast while entertaining serious doubts as to the truth of the allegations.[106]

One evolving issue related to actual malice is the matter of the defendant's motivation for publishing the defamatory material. Before the ruling in *New York Times* v. *Sullivan* the term "malice" was related to the question, Why did the defendant make these defamatory charges? Was it simply to inform the public of a problem or a concern, or were the charges published because the defendant didn't like the plaintiff or was angry with the plaintiff? In other words, was the publication fostered by ill will, spite or malice? The actual malice standard outlined by the Supreme Court in 1964 doesn't address why something was published or broadcast, but focuses instead on the defendant's behavior or belief that the matter is truthful. The high court called this actual malice, to distinguish it from traditional or common-law malice.

The Supreme Court has ruled on at least two occasions that a showing of ill will or spite by a plaintiff is not sufficient to prove actual malice.[107] But more and more lower courts are

---

105. *McFarlane* v. *Sheridan Square Press Inc.,* 91 F. 3d 1501 (1996).

106. *Levan* v. *Capital Cities/ABC Inc.,* 27 M.L.R. 2555 (1999).

107. See *Harte-Hanks Communications Inc.* v. *Connaughton,* 109 S. Ct. 2678 (1989) and *Beckley Newspapers* v. *Hanks,* 389 U.S. 81 (1967). See also *Johnson* v. *E.W. Scripps Co.,* 31 M.L.R. 1503 (2003).

being asked to consider this question. State supreme courts in Kentucky[108] and Washington[109] have ruled that evidence of ill will and spite can be used as evidence of actual malice in some circumstances. The 2nd U.S. Circuit Court of Appeals ruled in 2001 a reporter's bias against an organization could be relevant to show a purposeful avoidance of the truth (actual malice) if it were coupled with evidence of an extreme departure from standard investigative techniques.[110] But even those courts willing to hear such evidence have set a fairly high standard for the plaintiff to meet. A recent case from South Carolina demonstrates this point.

A newspaper in a small South Carolina town ran a column in which it simply printed questions and comments from readers who submitted them by letter or telephone. One comment included in the column was a telephone message that questioned why the police chief had not stopped drug dealers in the community from selling their wares and questioned whether the chief was being paid by the dealers to allow their business to continue. The chief sued for libel and won at trial. The state's high court had to evaluate the evidence that the material was published with actual malice; the police chief is a public official and the comments related to his official duties. The plaintiff argued that the editor of the paper had failed to investigate or verify the information left on the telephone message. The phone message that was the supposed basis for the item was erased by someone at the newspaper. Four years earlier the paper's editor had been arrested for manufacturing marijuana. He pleaded guilty. And the chief said the editor had been rude to his wife on a recent occasion. Mere failure to investigate a charge is not evidence of actual malice, the plaintiff acknowledged. But the last three elements, the chief said, surely showed that the item in the newspaper was published with ill will and spite. The court ruled that while the defendant's motivation may bear some relation to the inquiry into actual malice, the courts must be careful not to place too much reliance on it. It is irrelevant in this case, the court said. Even if the editor's conviction on a drug charge and his rudeness do show some ill will toward the chief, these factors fall far short of the clear and convincing evidence required to prove that he had a high degree of awareness of the falsity of the charges.[111] The question of what motivates a broadcaster or editor to carry a story is a developing issue, and journalists need to remember that it is best to keep personal feelings out of the stories they prepare.

SUMMARY

In a lawsuit against a mass medium, a private person must prove that the defendant was at least negligent in publishing the defamatory matter. Negligence has been defined as the failure to exercise reasonable care or as acting in such a way as to create a substantial risk of harm. In some states, in certain cases private persons will be required to prove more than simple negligence. They may be required to prove gross negligence, which is a standard that implies a greater degree of carelessness on the part of the defendant. An individual who has been declared to be a public person for the purposes of a libel suit must prove actual malice. Actual malice is defined as knowledge of falsity or reckless disregard of the truth. Transmitting a story with the knowledge of its falsity means that the publishers of the story knew it was

108. *Ball* v. *E.W. Scripps Co.,* 801 S.W. 2d 684 (1990).
109. *Herron* v. *King Broadcasting Co.,* 746 P. 2d 295 (1987).
110. *Church of Scientology International* v. *Behar,* 238 F. 3d 168 (2001).
111. *Elder* v. *Gaffney Ledger,* 533 S.E. 2d 899 (2000).

not true but still communicated it to the public. To prove reckless disregard for the truth, the plaintiff must show that the publisher of the defamation had a "high degree of awareness of the probable falsity of the material" when it was published or that the publisher in fact "entertained serious doubts about the truth of the material" before it was published. The courts have established a set of three criteria to help determine whether material was published with reckless disregard for the truth. The jurists tend to look at these factors:

1. Whether there was time to investigate the story or whether the material had to be published quickly
2. Whether the source of the information appeared to be reliable and trustworthy
3. Whether the story itself sounded probable or farfetched

If the item was hot news, if the source was a trained journalist, and if the information in the story sounded probable, there can be no finding of reckless disregard. However, if there was plenty of time to investigate, if the source of the material was questionable, or if the information in the story sounded completely improbable, courts are more likely to permit a finding of reckless disregard for the truth.

INTENTIONAL INFLICTION OF EMOTIONAL DISTRESS

As more and more plaintiffs lost their libel suits because they were unable to prove actual malice, attorneys began to look to a means to avoid the heavy burden of proof placed on their clients by the *New York Times* ruling. They turned to an alternative tort called the intentional infliction of emotional distress as a means to cirucumvent the actual malice rule. Lawsuits alleging this tort injury first appeared in the late 19th century, according to Susan Kirkpatrick in an article in the Northwestern University Law Review.[112] But it wasn't recognized by the "Restatement of Torts," the synthesis of tort law published by the American Law Institute, until 1948. In 1965 the "Restatement" provided for the first time a definition of the tort, which has four parts.

- **The defendant's conduct was intentional or reckless.**
- **The defendant's conduct was extreme and outrageous.**
- **The defendant's conduct caused the plaintiff emotional distress.**
- **The emotional distress was severe.**[113]

In practice, Kirkpatrick said, courts really focus on a single criterion—whether the defendant acted outrageously. Or as one court put it, the defendant's conduct went beyond all possible bounds of decency and was regarded as atrocious and utterly intolerable in a civilized community. An Illinois appellate court ruled in late 1998 that ethnic slurs like "stupid Polack," the portrayal of a buffoonish Polish Pope, and Polish jokes on three separate NBC programs

---

112. Kirkpatrick, "Intentional Infliction of Emotional Distress," 993.
113. American Law Institute, *Restatement of Torts.*

were not sufficiently outrageous to maintain an action for intentional infliction of emotional distress.[114]

An unusual case from Florida demonstrates the kind of communication that might support such a finding. A 6-year-old girl was abducted in June 1985. Two years later police found a child's clothing and parts of a skeleton, but it took authorities another year to make the connection between the grisly remains and the missing child. In August 1988 a television reporter and camera operator went to the chief of police and asked to see the child's skull. The officer was videotaped as he lifted the skull out of the box containing the remains, and the video was shown on the evening news. Family members unexpectedly saw the video and were shocked. They sued for invasion of privacy and outrage, the Florida version of the emotional distress tort. The Florida Court of Appeals ruled against the invasion of privacy claim, but said that the video had clearly exceeded the bounds of decency. "Indeed," the court said, "if the facts as alleged herein do not constitute the tort of outrage, then there is no such tort."[115]

In the 1980s a case emerged in which a public-person plaintiff tried to use the emotional distress tort as a way to avoid having to meet the strict requirements of proof mandated by the actual malice standard in a libel suit. The lawsuit was prompted when Hustler magazine published a parody of a series of widely circulated ads for Campari liquor. The real Campari ads featured interviews with celebrities who discussed the first time they tasted the liquor. The printed advertisements had fairly strong sexual overtones as the subjects talked about their "first time." The Hustler parody was a fictitious interview with the Rev. Jerry Falwell, an evangelical preacher who in the 1980s led a conservative political action group called The Moral Majority. Falwell described his first sexual experience as an incestuous encounter with his mother. Falwell was also characterized by the parody as a drunkard. There was a small disclaimer at the bottom of the parody, and it was listed in the table of contents as fiction.

Falwell sued the magazine for libel, invasion of privacy and intentional infliction of emotional distress. The trial judge dismissed the invasion of privacy claim, but sent the other two to the jury. Jurors rejected the libel claim on the grounds that the parody was so farfetched, no person could possibly believe that it described actual facts about Falwell. The jury did award the Baptist preacher $200,000 in damages for emotional distress.

Hustler appealed the ruling, but a unanimous three-judge panel of the U.S. Court of Appeals for the 4th Circuit upheld the damage award, noting that all the proof that was needed in such a case was that the item was sufficiently outrageous as to cause emotional harm and that it was published intentionally.[116] While most journalists did not condone the Hustler style of parody, they nevertheless viewed the decision as a serious threat to freedom of expression. The sturdy First Amendment barrier built up to protect the mass media from libel suits brought by persons in the public eye was neatly circumvented by Falwell in this case. Because of his presence as a spokesman for the conservative religious right in this nation, Falwell would likely be considered a public figure in a libel action and be forced to prove actual malice before he could collect damages. In this suit he did not even have to show negligence. Nor did the broad First Amendment protection that is granted to statements of opinion apply outside the law of libel. In the future, persons suing for satire or parody could avoid having to

114. *Polish-American Guardian Society* v. *General Electric Co., 27* M.L.R. 1443 (1998).
115. *Armstrong* v. *H & C Communications, Inc.,* 575 So. 2d 280 (1991).
116. *Falwell* v. *Flynt,* 797 F. 2d 1270 (1986).

surmount the constitutional barriers in libel law by instead filing an action for intentional infliction of emotional distress.

Hustler appealed to the Supreme Court and in 1988, in a unanimous ruling, the high court reversed the appellate court ruling. Chief Justice Rehnquist, noting that most people would see the Hustler parody as gross and repugnant, nevertheless rejected Falwell's argument that because he was seeking damages for severe emotional distress rather than reputational harm, a standard different from that applied in libel should apply. "Were we to hold otherwise," the chief justice wrote, "there can be little doubt that political cartoonists and satirists would be subjected to damages awarded without any showing that their work falsely defamed its subject." Rehnquist added:

> The appeal of the political cartoon or caricature is often based on exploration of unfortunate physical traits or politically embarrassing events—an exploration often calculated to injure the feelings of the subject of the portrayal. The art of the cartoonist is often not reasoned or evenhanded, but slashing and one-sided.[117]

Falwell contended it was making a mockery of serious political cartoons to compare them to the Hustler parody, which was truly outrageous. The law should protect even public figures from such outrageous caricatures. Rehnquist disagreed, noting the outrageousness standard of liability would not work.

> "Outrageousness" in the area of political and social discourse has an inherent subjectiveness about it which would allow a jury to impose liability on the basis of jurors' tastes and views or perhaps on the basis of their dislike of a particular expression.[118]

The court ruled that in order for a public figure or public official to win an emotional distress claim, it would be necessary to prove three things:

1. That the parody or satire amounted to statement of fact, not an opinion.
2. That it was a false statement of fact.
3. That the person who drew the cartoon or wrote the article knew it was false, or exhibited reckless disregard for the truth or falsity of the material. In other words, proof of actual malice is necessary.

The ruling in the Hustler case that added a First Amendment element to the defense against emotional distress cases has proved to be a valuable protection for the press. For example, in 2005 the Arizona Supreme Court said the guarantees of freedom of speech and press protected the Tucson Citizen newspaper after it was sued for intentional infliction of emotional distress for publishing an inflammatory letter to the editor. The letter writer suggested that the best way to stop the murders of American soldiers in Iraq was for Americans to murder Muslims living in this country as a kind of retribution. "After all," the writer said, "this is a 'Holy War' and although such a procedure is not fair or just, it might end the horror."

---

117. *Hustler Magazine* v. *Falwell*, 108 S. Ct. 876 (1988).
118. Ibid.

In dismissing the case the court said it assumed the statement would cause emotional distress, but because the comment concerned a matter of public concern, it was protected by the constitutional guarantees of freedom of expression. "In the world of debate about public affairs, many things done with motives that are less admirable are protected by the First Amendment," the court said.[119] The court also ruled that the letter was not an incitement to violence because there was no call for imminent action, nor did it qualify as fighting words.

SUMMARY

The intentional infliction of emotional distress is a new tort and punishes a wide range of conduct, including the publication or broadcast of material that is outrageous and causes severe emotional distress. Courts have made it extremely difficult for plaintiffs to win such suits by placing a substantial burden of proof on the injured party. The Supreme Court added to this burden in 1988 when it ruled that public-person plaintiffs would have to show actual malice as well to win their lawsuits.

BIBLIOGRAPHY

American Law Institute. *Restatement of the Law of Torts,* 2nd ed. Philadelphia: American Law Institute, 1975.

Ashley, Paul. *Say It Safely,* 5th ed. Seattle: University of Washington Press, 1976.

Barron, Jerome, and C. Thomas Dienes. *Handbook of Free Speech and Free Press.* Boston: Little, Brown, 1979.

Gross, Jane. "Impasse Over Damages in *New Yorker* Libel Case." *The New York Times,* 4 June 1993, A1.

Kirkpatrick, Susan. "*Falwell* v. *Flynt:* Intentional Infliction of Emotional Distress as a Threat to Free Speech." *Northwestern University Law Review* 81 (1987): 993.

Lee, Douglas E. "Public Interest, Public Figures, and the Corporate Defamation Plaintiff: Jadwin v. Minneapolis Star and Tribune." *Northwestern University Law Review* 81 (1987): 318.

Lewis, Anthony. *Make No Law.* New York: Random House, 1991.

Margolick, David. "Psychoanalyst Loses Libel Suit Against a *New Yorker* Reporter." *The New York Times,* 3 November 1994, A1.

O'Connor, Clint. "Setting the Paper of Record Straight." *Washington Journalism Review,* September 1987, 10.

Prosser, William L. *Handbook of the Law of Torts.* St Paul: West Publishing, 1963.

Smolla, Rodney A. *Suing the Press.* New York: Oxford University Press, 1986.

———. "Dun & Bradstreet, Hepps, and Liberty Lobby: A New Analytic Primer on the Future Course of Defamation." *Georgetown Law Journal* 75 (1987): 1519.

Stonecipher, Harry, and Don Sneed. "A Survey of the Professional Person as Libel Plaintiff." *Arkansas Law Review* 46 (1993): 303.

119. *Citizen Publishing Co.* v. *Miller,* 115 P3d 107 (2005).

LIBEL
Defenses and Damages

Libel defenses are hundreds of years old. Most of them grew out of the common law, but today many defenses are contained in state statutes as well. Before the mid-1960s when the Supreme Court began to add substantial new burdens upon libel plaintiffs, defenses were the primary means of warding off a defamation lawsuit. Most plaintiffs today lose because they can't meet the required burden of proof; but defenses remain a viable and important part of the law. A libel defense can not only protect a defendant from a successful suit, it can stop a plaintiff's case quickly, saving the publication or broadcasting outlet both time and money. Citing an appropriate defense, a defendant can ask a judge to dismiss a case even before a hearing is held. Such a dismissal is called a summary judgment. The judge may issue such a ruling if he or she does not think the plaintiff can prove what is required, as outlined in Chapters 4 and 5, or believes the defendant had a legal right (a defense) to publish or broadcast the defamatory material. Libel defenses are the primary subject of this chapter. Following this material is a brief outline of both civil libel damages and criminal libel.

SUMMARY JUDGMENT/STATUTE OF LIMITATIONS

The **summary judgment** is undoubtedly one of the best friends the mass media libel defendant has. About three-fourths of media requests for a summary judgment are granted by the courts. If the defendant's request for such a judgment is granted by the court, the case ends without a trial. Trials cost a lot of money and the press has not established a good track record for winning cases sent to a jury. Here is a brief outline of what happens in the summary judgment procedure.

After the plaintiffs have made their initial written allegations to the court, but before the trial begins, the defendants can argue that the lawsuit should be dismissed either because the plaintiff has failed to prove what is necessary to sustain the libel suit (publication, identification, defamation, falsity, and the requisite level of fault) or because there is a legal defense that blocks a successful lawsuit. As it considers this motion by the defense, the court is obligated to look at the plaintiff's allegation in the most favorable possible way. And if there is any dispute regarding facts (which would be settled at a subsequent trial), it must be for now resolved in favor of the plaintiff. If, having considered these factors, the court determines that a reasonable juror, acting reasonably, could not find for the plaintiff, then the motion for summary judgment will be granted.[1] (Please note that the plaintiff can also ask for a summary judgment, arguing there is no possible way a juror could find for the defendant.)

Here's a hypothetical example of how the summary judgment works. Imagine that Laura Parker, the editor of a small newsletter, the Iowa Consumer News, publishes a story that accuses Argot Farms, a giant corporate grain producer, of selling corn to cereal makers that has been labeled as adulterated and unfit for human consumption by the U.S. Department of Agriculture. For many years Argot has portrayed itself in television advertising as an environmentally friendly and responsible corporation. "Healthy food for healthy families" is the corporate slogan. Argot sues for libel, claiming that the story is false. Parker asks the court for a summary judgment and makes two arguments to support her request:

1. The story is true and therefore the case should be dismissed.
2. Argot Farms, because of its heavy television advertising, is a public figure. Therefore it must have proof of actual malice to win its case. It has made no allegations regarding actual malice, only charges of simple negligence on Parker's part.

1. See, for example, *Nader* v. *DeToledano,* 408 A. 2d 31 (1979).

Argot Farms asks the court to deny the motion for a summary judgment and makes the following three arguments:

1. It is not a public figure, simply a business trying to win customers through normal advertising. Therefore it must only show negligence.
2. The story is false.
3. Parker got the information for her story from an unreliable source.

In ruling on Parker's motion for a summary judgment the court must assume that the facts, as stated by Argot Farms, are true; that is, that the story is false, and that Parker got the information from an unreliable source. If the case later goes to trial, both these "facts" will be examined through the presentation of evidence.

Based on the record as presented by the plaintiff, the judge can

1. agree with Parker that Argot Farms is a public figure and, since there is not even an allegation of actual malice, grant the summary judgment; or
2. agree with Argot Farms that it is not a public figure and, based on the assumptions that the story is false and there is evidence of negligence, refuse to grant the motion for a summary judgment.

The loser in either case can appeal the ruling. The appellate court will reconsider the matter. Is Argot a public figure? Do the company's allegations present sufficient evidence of negligence or actual malice? If the appellate court agrees with the trial court, it will sustain the summary judgment. The case will end unless Argot appeals to an even higher court. But the appellate court may reverse the lower court ruling, finding that the company is not a public figure and must prove only negligence or that it is a public figure but there is sufficient suggestion of actual malice in its allegations to go to trial. The case will then return to the lower court for a trial, unless Parker takes a subsequent appeal. When the case goes to trial, Argot and Parker must present evidence to support their allegations. The assumption that the plaintiff's allegations are true is no longer valid.*

The Supreme Court has given both trial and appellate courts wide latitude in granting summary judgments in libel cases, especially in suits brought by public persons. In 1986 the justices said that federal courts must grant a summary judgment in favor of the media defendants in cases involving actual malice unless the plaintiffs can demonstrate that they will be able to offer a jury clear and convincing evidence of actual malice.[2] Some trial judges had been hesitant about granting summary judgments because they believed that proof of actual malice calls the defendant's state of mind into question, which is a matter better considered at trial. But judges who force a trial even in the face of a weak libel claim are playing into the hands of those litigants who like to use the law to harass the press. Federal Judge Stanley Sarokin explained the importance of a summary judgment to the press in a 1985 ruling:

> Possibly the giants of the industry have both the finances and the stamina
> to run the risk in such situations [the threat of a libel suit]. But the
> independent will of smaller magazines, newspapers, television and radio

The Supreme Court has given both trial and appellate courts wide latitude in granting summary judgments in libel cases.

*Please note: This is a simplistic outline of how a motion for summary judgment may be treated by the courts and not a detailed explanation of how a libel suit may proceed.
2. *Anderson* v. *Liberty Lobby,* 477 U.S. 242 (1986).

stations undoubtedly bends with the spectre of a libel action looming. Even if convinced of their ultimate success on the merits, the costs of vindication may soon be too great for such media defendants to print or publish that which may entail any risk of a court action. If that is the result, it is a sorry state of affairs for the media, and, more important, for the country. Therefore, probably more than any other type of case, summary judgments in libel actions should be readily available and granted where appropriate.[3]

STATUTE OF LIMITATIONS

For nearly all crimes and most civil actions, there is a **statute of limitations.** Courts do not like stale legal claims. They have plenty of fresh ones to keep them busy. Prosecution for most crimes except homicide and kidnapping must be started within a specified period of time. For example, in many states if prosecution is not started within seven years after an armed robbery is committed, the robber cannot be brought to trial. He or she is home free. (However, the robber can still be prosecuted for failing to pay income tax on money taken from a bank, but that is another story.)

The duration of the statute of limitations for libel actions differs from state to state, varying from one to three years (Figure 6.1). In most states the duration is one or two years. What this means is that a libel suit must be started within one or two years following publication of the offending material. The date of publication on a newspaper determines when the duration of the statute begins. In television and radio the statute of limitations begins on the day the program is telecast or broadcast. Magazines pose a somewhat different problem. The publication date on the magazine rarely coincides with the date the publication is actually distributed. Magazines dated November are usually distributed in October, sometimes even in late September. Courts have ruled that the statute of limitations begins on the date that a magazine is distributed to a substantial portion of the public. For example, Business Week magazine was sued for libel for an article published in its issue dated Sept. 12, 1994. The lawsuit was filed on Sept. 11, 1997, the day before the three-year statute of limitations expired. Attorneys for the magazine demonstrated to the court that the Sept. 12, 1994, edition of Business Week was on the newsstands and on its way to subscribers on Sept. 6, 1994. The U.S. District Court in New Mexico ruled that the statute of limitations begins on the earliest date that the publication is available to a substantial portion of the public rather than the cover date on the magazine.[4] Case dismissed.

The libel republication rule can be a factor in considering the statute of limitations. In some states buying a back issue of a publication is considered new publication, and the statute of limitations starts over. More and more jurisdictions have rejected this rule and substituted the single publication rule. This rule states that the entire edition of a newspaper or magazine is a single publication and that isolated sales in the months or years to come do not constitute republication. Therefore the statute of limitations starts on the day the edition hit the

---

3. *Schiavone Construction* v. *Time,* 619 F. Supp. 684 (1985).

4. *Printon Inc.* v. *McGraw-Hill Inc.,* 35 F. Supp. 2d 1325 (1998). See also *MacDonald* v. *Time,* 554 F. Supp. 1053 (1983); *Wildmon* v. *Hustler,* 508 F. Supp. 87 (1980); *Bradford* v. *American Media Operations, Inc.,* 882 F. Supp. 1508 (1995); and *Williamson* v. *New Times Inc.,* 980 S.W. 2d 706 (1998).

MAP SHOWING DURATION OF STATUTE OF LIMITATIONS IN LIBEL ACTIONS

☐ = One year

▨ = Two years

▓ = Three years

▼ FIGURE 6.1

Plaintiffs must file libel suits before the statute of limitations expires. This chart indicates the duration of this filing period in the 50 states.

newsstands and ends one or two or three years later. The statute cannot be reactivated by a later sale. Courts have also ruled that the single publication rule applies to material published on the Internet. The clock begins to run when the material is posted on the Web. But a subsequent alteration of the material will likely restart the one-, two- or three-year statutory clock.[5] The rebroadcast of defamatory material on radio or television is generally considered a new publication, since it is intended to reach a new audience, and therefore creates a new opportunity for injury.[6]

Jurisdiction

Is it possible for a plaintiff who has not filed a libel suit within the statute of limitations in his or her home state to file an action in another state that has a longer statute of limitations? The answer is yes, so long as the libel has been circulated in this other state. The Supreme Court clarified this question in two 1984 rulings, *Keeton* v. *Hustler*[7] and *Calder* v. *Jones*.[8] Kathy Keeton, a resident of New York, sued Hustler magazine, an Ohio corporation, for libel in the

5. *Firth* v. *New York,* 747 N.Y.S. 2d 69 (2002); *Van Buskirk* v. *New York Times,* 325 F 3d 87 (2003); *Mitan* v. *Davis,* W. D. Ky., Civil Action No. 3:00 CV-841-5, 2/3/03; *McCandliss* v. *Cox Enterprises Inc.,* 593 SE2d 856 (2004); and *Traditional Cat Ass'n.* v. *Gilbreath,* Cal. Ct. App. No. D041421, 5/6/04.
6. *Lehman,* v. *Discovery Communications Inc.,* 32 M.L.R. 2377 (2004).
7. 465 U.S. 770 (1984).
8. 465 U.S. 783 (1984).

state of New Hampshire. Hustler challenged the action, arguing that the suit should be brought in New York or Ohio but not New Hampshire, which had a six-year statute of limitations. (The statute of limitations is now three years in New Hampshire.) Only about 15,000 copies of the 1-million-plus circulation of the magazine were sold in New Hampshire, the defendant argued. A court of appeals ruled that the plaintiff had too tenuous a contact with New Hampshire to permit the assertion of personal jurisdiction in that state, but the Supreme Court unanimously reversed the ruling. Hustler's regular circulation of magazines in New Hampshire is sufficient to support an assertion of jurisdiction in a libel action, Justice William Rehnquist wrote. "False statements of fact harm both the subject of the falsehood and the readers of the statement: New Hampshire may rightly employ its libel laws to discourage the deception of its citizens," the justice continued. The state may extend its concern to the injury that in-state libel causes to a nonresident as well, he added.[9]

The same day, the high court ruled that California courts could assume jurisdiction in a case brought by a California resident against the authors of a story that was written and published in a newspaper in Florida but circulated in California. Shirley Jones sued two journalists for an article they wrote and edited in Florida and that was then published in the National Enquirer. At that time the Enquirer had a national circulation of about 5 million and distributed about 600,000 copies each week in California. A trial court ruled that Jones could certainly sue the publishers of the Enquirer in California, but not the reporters. Requiring journalists to appear in remote jurisdictions to answer for the contents of articles on which they worked could have a chilling impact on the First Amendment rights of reporters and editors, the court said. But again a unanimous Supreme Court disagreed, with Justice Rehnquist noting that the article was about a California resident who works in California. Material for the article was drawn from California sources and the brunt of the harm to both the career and the personal reputation of the plaintiff will be suffered in California where the Enquirer has a huge circulation. In other words, the primary negative effect of the libel will be in California, he added. "An individual injured in California need not go to Florida to seek redress from persons who, though remaining in Florida, knowingly cause the injury in California," Rehnquist wrote. The justice said that the potential chill on protected First Amendment activity stemming from libel actions is already taken into account in the constitutional limitations on the substantive law governing such suits. "To reinforce those concerns at the jurisdictional level would be a form of double counting," he said.[10]

Jurisdiction and the Internet

 These two Supreme Court rulings stand for the proposition that publishers may be sued in any jurisdiction in which they distribute even a relatively small portion of their publication—even if the plaintiff does not reside in that jurisdiction. How does this principle apply to communication on the Internet? Any message contained on any Web site is conceivably accessible in any state in the nation. Can the Web site operator or publisher of the allegedly defamatory material be sued in any or every jurisdiction? Is evidence that the message was received and downloaded by residents of the jurisdiction sufficient to begin a lawsuit in that jurisdiction? Or must there be stronger ties to the jurisdiction? These are questions that have yet to be

---

9. *Keeton* v. *Hustler,* 465 U.S. 770 (1984).
10. *Calder* v. *Jones,* 465 U.S. 783 (1984).

completely answered. The Supreme Court of the United States has passed on reviewing at least three cases that involve this jurisdiction question.[11] The lower courts seem to be more or less following one of two strategies: one that fairly broadly applies the so-called "effects" test from the *Calder* case, or one that applies the *Calder* test much more narrowly. Remember in *Calder* the Supreme Court ruled that California courts could exercise jurisdiction over journalists who resided in Florida because the article concerned California activities of a California resident and was published in a national publication that had a large circulation in California.[12] The lower courts that read this test broadly are ruling that a court in Montana, for example, can exercise jurisdiction only if there is evidence that the out-of-state Internet publisher was aware that the material could cause harm in Montana, that the material was aimed at the residents of Montana, and that the out-of-state publisher had some contact with someone or something in Montana. In one recent case articles were posted on the Web site of a Connecticut newspaper that allegedly defamed a Virginia resident. The 4th U.S. Court of Appeals ruled that the Virginia courts could not exercise jurisdiction in the matter because there was no evidence that the newspaper aimed the content of the site at Virginia residents. The article had to do with a Virginia prison warden and allegations that he had permitted guards to abuse inmates in the Virginia prison who had been relocated there from Connecticut. The court said the article was directed toward Connecticut residents, and the lawsuit should be filed in that state.[13] The 5th U.S. Court of Appeals made a similar ruling in 2002 when it held a Massachusetts resident and the operator of a New York Web site could not be sued in a Texas court simply because the plaintiff lived in Texas, and would suffer damage to his reputation in that state. The key is the geographic focus of the article, not the location of the harm inflicted, the court said. The article contained no references to Texas, no references to any of the plaintiff's activities in Texas, and was not directed at Texas readers. The story was about an FBI official who was accused of covering up a possible advance warning of the 1988 bombing of Pan Am flight 103. This activity occurred when the plaintiff lived outside of Texas. He moved to Texas when he left the Bureau.[14]

But a federal court in Louisiana ruled that a court in a distant state or forum could exercise jurisdiction if the brunt of the harm felt by the plaintiff was in that forum. Questions about whether the material was about activities in that state or whether it was directed to readers in that state were not material, the court said.[15] Check to see how the courts in your state have ruled on this question.

One final point: Courts in Australia and Great Britain, among others, have asserted jurisdiction in cases involving allegedly defamatory Internet messages that originated in the United States. The High Court of Australia ruled that because the plaintiff lived in Australia, and because the harm from the allegedly defamatory message did not occur until it was downloaded in Australia, the courts there could exercise jurisdiction.[16] The British case involved a

---

11. *Als Scan Inc.* v. *Digital Services Consultants Inc.,* U.S. No. 02-483, cert den. 1/13/03; *Griffs* v. *Luban,* U.S. No. 02-754, cert. den. 3/10/03, and *Young* v. *New Haven Advocate,* 315 F. 3d 256 (2002).
12. 465 U.S. 783 (1984).
13. *Young* v. *New Haven Advocate,* 315 F. 3d 256 (2002). In May 2003 the Supreme Court declined to review this decision.
14. *Revell* v. *Lidov,* 317 F. 3d 467 (2002). See also *Novak* v. *Benn,* 32 M.C.R. 2259 (2004).
15. *Planet Beach Franchising Corp.* v. *C3ubit Inc., d/b/a Tantoday,* E.D. La. No. Civ. A. 02-1859, 8/12/02.
16. *King* v. *Lewis,* High Court of Justice, Queen's Bench Division, No. [2004] EWHC, 168 (QB), 2/6/04.

U.S. resident, boxing promoter Don King, who the court said, had many friends and acquaintances in England. The court ruled that the publication of an Internet posting takes place when it is downloaded. Please note that when a court in a foreign nation asserts jurisdiction in a libel case, the many important First Amendment protections that apply in a case tried in the United States rarely protect a defendant tried outside this country.

SUMMARY   A libel suit must be started before the statute of limitations expires. Each state determines how long this period will be. In all states it is one, two, or three years. A libel suit started after the expiration of the statute of limitations will be dismissed. Jurisdiction questions in Internet-based libel suits are still being sorted out by the courts, but usually are based upon where the content of the message was aimed, where the harm was caused, and where the message was downloaded.

TRUTH

The First Amendment provides defendants in libel suits considerable protection. The defendant in a lawsuit filed against a newspaper or other mass medium is in fact well defended by the constitutional fault requirements placed on the plaintiff. But there were defenses for libel even before the ruling in *New York Times* v. *Sullivan.*[17] These emerged through the common law and via statutes in many states. Truth, privileged communication, fair comment, consent and right of reply all work to protect the libel defendant—no matter who he or she might be. The applicability of each of these defenses in a particular case is determined by the facts in the case—what the story is about, how the information was gained, and the manner in which it was published.

Traditionally, truth has been regarded as an important libel defense that completely protected defendants in lawsuits for defamation. To use this defense, the defendant was required to prove the truth of the libelous allegations he or she published. Truth is still a defense in a libel action, but it has lost much of its importance in light of recent rulings that require most libel plaintiffs to carry the burden of proving a defamatory allegation to be false when the story focuses on a matter of public concern. In those few instances when a private-person plaintiff sues for a libelous statement that does not focus on something of public concern and therefore does not have to show the falsity of the matter as a part of proving negligence, the libel defendant can escape liability in the case by showing that the defamatory matter is true. But the defendant carries the burden of proof; truth becomes a defense. The same rules apply to proving truth that apply to proving falsity, only they are reversed. The defendant must show that the allegations are substantially true. Extraneous errors will not destroy the defense. See pages 185–189 to refresh your memory on these matters.

17. 376 U.S. 254 (1964).

PRIVILEGED COMMUNICATIONS

The people of the United States have traditionally valued robust debate as one means of discovering the truths essential to building consensus. The law takes pains to protect this debate, making sure that speakers are not unduly punished for speaking their minds. Article 1, Section 6, of the federal Constitution provides that members of Congress are immune from suits based on their remarks on the floor of either house. This protection is called a privilege. The statement in question is referred to as a privileged communication.

ABSOLUTE PRIVILEGE

Today this privilege, sometimes called the privilege of the participant, attaches to a wide variety of communications and speakers. Anyone speaking in a legislative forum—members of Congress, senators, state representatives, city council members and so forth–enjoys this privilege. Even the statements of witnesses at legislative hearings are privileged. But the comments must be made in the legislative forum. The Supreme Court ruled in 1979 that while a speech by a senator on the floor of the Senate would be wholly immune from a libel action, newsletters and press releases about the speech issued by the senator's office would not be protected by the privilege. Only speech that is "essential to the deliberations of the Senate" is protected, and neither newsletters to constituents nor press releases are parts of the deliberative process.[18]

Today, privilege attaches to a wide variety of communications and speakers.

Similarly, the privilege attaches to communications and documents made in judicial forums—courtrooms, grand jury rooms, and so forth. Judges, lawyers, witnesses, defendants, plaintiffs and all other persons are protected so long as the remark is uttered during the official portions of the hearing or trial and the statement or document is in some way relevant to the proceeding. An attorney in Pennsylvania filed a complaint in a lawsuit and then faxed a copy of this complaint to a reporter. He was sued for libel by the person named in the complaint, who argued that when he sent the complaint to the journalist, he was publishing its defamatory allegations. The attorney argued that since the complaint was a privileged judicial document, which it is, his act of sending the complaint was also privileged. The Supreme Court of Pennsylvania disagreed, ruling that sending the document to a reporter was an extrajudicial act and was not relevant in any way to the legal proceedings.[19] A question that arises after this ruling is this: What if the attorney had merely told the reporter about the lawsuit that had been filed, and suggested he or she look at the complaint? Would that act be protected? Most likely.

Finally, persons who work in the administrative and executive branches of government enjoy the privilege as well. Official communications including reports, policy statements, even press conferences, presented by presidents, governors, mayors, department heads, and others are protected. The Supreme Court of the United States ruled in 1959 that the privilege applies to any publication by government officials that is in line with the discharge of their official duties.[20] This case involved a press release issued by an official explaining why two federal workers were fired. The New York Court of Appeals echoed this ruling 20 years later

---

18. *Hutchinson* v. *Proxmire,* 443 U.S. 111 (1979). Proxmire was sued when he attacked a Michigan man in a press release critical of wasteful government spending.

19. *Bochetto* v. *Gibson,* 32 M.L.R. 2474 (2004).

20. *Barr* v. *Mateo,* 353 U.S. 171 (1959).

when it said that a press release issued by an assistant attorney general concerning the investigation of a possible fund-raising scam was protected by the privilege.[21] The difference in the manner in which the courts treated the press releases by Senator William Proxmire in a case noted previously (see page 207) and the two cases cited just above stems from the different roots of the privilege. The congressional privilege stems directly from the U.S. Constitution and is limited by constitutional language that focuses on the deliberative process and lawmaking. Proxmire's remarks fell outside these boundaries. The common law and/or state statutes are the sources of all other parts of the privilege, and courts have construed this protection quite liberally.

The privilege just discussed is an **absolute privilege.** The speaker cannot be sued for defamation on the basis of such a remark. A similar kind of privilege applies also to certain kinds of private communications. Discussions between an employer and an employee are privileged; the report of a credit rating is privileged; a personnel recommendation by an employer about an employee is privileged. These kinds of private communications remain privileged so long as they are not disseminated beyond the sphere of those who need to know.

QUALIFIED PRIVILEGE

What is called **qualified privilege** goes far beyond the absolute immunity granted to speakers at public and official meetings and the conditional immunity granted to certain types of private communications. Under the qualified privilege, sometimes called the privilege of the reporter, an individual may report what happens at an official governmental proceeding or transmit the substance of an official government report or statement and remain immune from libel even if the publication of the material defames someone. This is how the privilege is outlined in the "Restatement of Torts":

> The publication of defamatory matter concerning another in a report of any official proceeding or any meeting open to the public which deals with matters of public concern is conditionally privileged if the report is accurate and complete, or a fair abridgment of what has occurred.[22]

Actually, this definition of the privilege in the "Restatement" is a bit conservative, as courts continually extend the protection of qualified privilege to reports of more diverse kinds of government activity. This qualified privilege is sometimes called the privilege of the reporter, as opposed to the absolute immunity noted previously, which is often referred to as the privilege of the participant. The use of the term "reporter" signifies someone who reports on what has happened, as opposed to the journalistic meaning of the term, a newspaper or television reporter.

CRITERIA FOR APPLICATION OF QUALIFIED PRIVILEGE

▪ Report of a privileged proceeding or document

▪ A fair and accurate summary published or broadcast as a report

---

21. *Gautsche* v. *New York,* 415 N.Y.S. 2d 280 (1979).
22. American Law Institute, *Restatement of Torts.*

At the start it is important to note that qualified privilege is a conditional privilege; that is, the privilege only works as a libel defense if certain conditions are met. First, the privilege only applies to reports of certain kinds of meetings, hearings, proceedings, reports and statements. Second, the law requires that these reports be a fair and accurate or truthful summary of what took place at the meeting or what was said in the report. In the past there was a third condition—that the report containing the defamatory charges was published or broadcast in order to inform the people, not simply to hurt the plaintiff. It is generally considered today that this third condition no longer applies; the defendant's motivation for publishing or broadcasting the material is irrelevant.[23]

The defendant bears the burden of proving that the privilege applies to the libelous material. The court will determine whether the particular occasion (meeting, proceeding, report) is privileged. The jury will determine whether the defendant's report of the occasion is a fair and accurate report.

Before going into the details relating to the application of this defense, let's look at a brief hypothetical example. During a meeting of the Mayberry City Council, Councilman Floyd Lawson, while discussing an increase in the garbage rates for city residents, says this: "Allied Garbage Co., which supposedly gives us a good rate to pick up the trash, is run by a bunch of crooks who are intent on cheating this city and all its citizens. I mean, I read it in the newspaper. These guys are a part of organized crime." Because of the protection of the absolute privilege, the owners of Allied Garbage cannot sue Lawson. When the reporter who attended the meeting includes this comment in her story, the newspaper also is shielded from a lawsuit so long as the story is a fair and accurate summary of what Lawson said: "Councilman Floyd Lawson charged last night during a city council meeting that the owners of Allied Garbage Co. are a part of organized crime and are cheating the city."

Let's first examine the kinds of occasions that courts have found to be covered by the privilege.

Legislative Proceedings

The privilege applies to what occurs during meetings of legislative bodies, from the U.S. Congress down to the lowly village council meeting. But courts have ruled that only what is said during the official portion of the meeting is included within the protective ambit of the defense. A Pennsylvania superior court recently ruled that the privilege did not apply to a newspaper report of comments made by citizens while a township board of supervisors meeting was in recess.[24] The privilege also applies to the reports of committee meetings of such organizations as well as to stories about petitions, complaints and other communications received by these bodies. The only requirement that must be met with regard to this aspect of the privilege is that the official body, such as a city council, must officially receive the complaint or petition before the privilege applies. If the Citizens for Cleaner Streets bring to a city council meeting a petition charging the street superintendent with incompetence and various and sundry blunders in his or her job, publication of these charges is privileged as soon as the city council officially accepts the petition. Nothing has to be done with the document. It must

---

23. See *Schiavone Construction* v. *Time,* 569 F. Supp. 614 (1983).
24. *DeMary* v. *Latrobe Printing and Publishing Co.,* 28 M.L.R. 1337 (2000).

merely be accepted. But if copies of the petition are merely circulated to citizens attending the meeting and never officially presented to the city council, the privilege may or may not apply, depending on how willing a judge is to apply a broad reading of the protection. The privilege usually applies to stories about the news conferences of members of a legislative body following a session, to stories about what was said during a closed meeting by the body, and to stories about what was said during an informal gathering of legislators before or after the regular session, especially if what is said or what occurs during these kinds of events is of great public interest.

Judicial Proceedings

The privilege of the reporter also applies to actions that take place in judicial forums: testimony and depositions of witnesses, arguments of attorneys, pronouncements of judges and so forth. Stories about trials, decisions, jury verdicts, court opinions, judicial orders and decrees, and grand jury indictments are all protected by the privilege. A New York trial court ruled in 2002 that reports of attorney disciplinary hearings were protected by the privilege, because the hearings are quasi-judicial.[25] A woman's charge of marital rape made in open court against her husband was regarded as privileged when it was published in a local newspaper.[26] Probably the most difficult problem a reporter on the court beat has to face is what to do when a lawsuit is initially filed. Under our legal system a lawsuit is started when a person files a complaint with a court clerk and serves a summons on the defendant. The complaint is filled with charges, most of which are libelous. Can a reporter use that complaint as the basis for a story?

Traditionally states have followed one of two rules on this question. In some states a complaint that has been filed is not considered privileged until some kind of judicial action has been taken.[27] The scheduling of an appearance by the litigants may be sufficient. This rule, which requires a judge to become involved in the matter before the complaint is privileged, is designed to protect an innocent party from being smeared in a news report written about a lawsuit that has been filed but then quickly withdrawn. Advocates of this system argue that it is much more difficult to withdraw such a lawsuit after a judge has gotten involved in the proceeding. Those who oppose this rule say the idea is a good one but it is out-of-date. Libel expert Bruce Sanford contends that "courts now recognize that the old rule can be easily circumvented by anyone determined to defame; judicial action may be obtained simply by filing a procedural motion."[28] Consequently, more and more states today follow the rule that the complaint becomes privileged as soon as it has been filed with the court and a docket number has been assigned or the defendant has been issued a summons. Two cautionary notes are important. A reporter should never take a lawyer's word that the lawsuit has been filed. The announcement may be a hoax to get publicity favorable to a client. A call to the courthouse is always in order. Also, ignore what the lawyer says about the case when he or she proclaims that the legal action has been filed. Normally, only comments or material contained in the

25. *Wong* v. *World Journal,* 31 M.L.R. 1214 (2002).
26. *Tonnessen* v. *Denver Publishing Co.,* 3 P. 3d 959 (2000).
27. See *Amway Corp.* v. *Procter and Gamble Co.,* 31 M.L.R. 2441 (2003), for example.
28. Sanford, *Libel and Privacy.*

formal judicial proceedings or court documents are protected by privilege. The Iowa Supreme Court ruled that comments made to a reporter by an attorney after the lawyer had filed the complaint initiating the lawsuit were not protected by privilege.[29]

Stories about those parts of the judicial process that are closed to the public may or may not be protected by the privilege. For example, court sessions for juveniles and divorce proceedings are frequently closed to protect the privacy of the individuals involved.[30] Some states regard these closures as important public policy and attempt to discourage publicity about such proceedings by denying the mass media the opportunity to apply the privilege if a lawsuit should result from press coverage. But this rule is changing. The 9th U.S. Circuit Court of Appeals has ruled that under California law, the press enjoyed the privilege to publish reports of proceedings in a family court that excluded the general public during its hearings.[31] And a broad reading of U.S. Supreme Court rulings in certain privacy lawsuits that were generated because of press reports of court hearings suggests that the First Amendment may place substantial limits on libel plaintiffs as well who are suing because of a report of a closed legal proceeding.[32]

Executive Actions

Reports of the statements and proceedings conducted by mayors, department heads and other persons in the administrative and executive branches of government are generally privileged. The best guideline is that the privilege is confined to stories about actions or statements that are official in nature, the kinds of things that are substantially "acts of state." By law, administrators are required to prepare certain reports and to hold certain hearings, and the privilege certainly covers stories on these activities. Although not required by law, other actions are unmistakably part of the job. Reports on these activities are protected as well. For example, the district attorney of Delaware County in Oklahoma held a news conference to discuss a drug investigation previously conducted by his office. At the news conference he distributed the transcript of a conversation between two undercover narcotics agents who had worked on the investigation. A local newspaper published a verbatim report of the conversation and was sued by a man named Ace Wright, who said it defamed him. The Oklahoma Supreme Court ruled that the publication was privileged. "District attorneys in Oklahoma have historically used press conferences to distribute information about the activities of their office to the citizens they represent," the court said.[33] The news conference was an activity conducted as a part of the official duties of the district attorney's office. But the Massachusetts Supreme Judicial Court refused to extend the privilege to remarks made by a police chief about an internal investigation into whether one of his officers was working part-time at a second job while he was supposed to be on duty. "The conditional privilege to publish defamatory material is

"The conditional privilege to publish defamatory material is designed to allow public officials to speak freely on matters of public importance in the exercise of their official duties,"

29. *Kennedy* v. *Zimmerman,* 601 N.W. 2d 61 (1999).
30. See *Riemers* v. *Grand Forks Herald,* 32 M.L.R. 2381 (2004) for a ruling by the North Dakota Supreme Court that reports of divorce proceedings are protected by the privilege.
31. *Dorsey* v. *National Enquirer, Inc.,* 973 F. 2d 1431 (1992).
32. See *Cox Broadcasting Co.* v. *Cohn,* 420 U.S. 469 (1975) and *Florida Star* v. *B.J.F.,* 109 S. Ct. 2603 (1989).
33. *Wright* v. *Grove Sun Newspaper Co., Inc.,* 873 P. 2d 983 (1994).

designed to allow public officials to speak freely on matters of public importance in the exercise of their official duties," the court said.[34] But it was not an official duty of the chief to report to the press on an internal departmental investigation. The New York Supreme Court ruled that reports of investigations by an environmental agency are privileged.[35] Even stories based on confidential government documents that focused on possible government misconduct were declared to be privileged under Massachusetts law.[36] Finally, a Nevada court ruled that defamatory remarks contained in an official press release issued by the Bureau of Land Management, a federal agency, were privileged.[37]

Reports of police activities also fall under the heading of executive actions. It is fairly well settled that a report that a person has been arrested and charged with a crime is privileged. Official statements made by police about an investigation are privileged in many instances. The U.S. Court of Appeals for the 2nd Circuit ruled that public statements made by the head of the New York City office of the FBI about an FBI search of law offices in Brooklyn were privileged. CNN had quoted the FBI agent as describing the offices as the headquarters for a dangerous left-wing group that sought to topple the U.S. government.[38] The U.S. Court of Appeals for the 3rd Circuit ruled that information obtained legally by Time magazine from FBI investigatory documents is also protected by a qualified privilege.[39] Caution needs to be exercised here, however. The privilege surely does not apply to every statement made by every police officer on every topic. The Idaho Supreme Court refused to apply the privilege to statements that were made privately to a reporter by a police officer. The court said these statements went beyond the official police reports, which are clearly privileged documents.[40] A note of caution. Some American courts have refused to allow the privilege defense when the document that contained the defamatory statement was not generated in the United States. In 2001 the Nevada Supreme Court refused to extend the privilege to portions of a book based on a confidential report from British police. This kind of report is generally not available to the public, the court said, and does not qualify as an official act or proceeding. Four years later a U.S. District Court refused to allow the privilege defense to protect allegations that two Russians were involved in corrupt and criminal conduct. The court said, "the privilege is unavailable to defendants in this case because it does not extend to official reports of the actions of a foreign government."[41]

The privilege is not confined to those instances of reporting official government proceedings. The Washington Supreme Court ruled that the reporting of the charges on recall petitions is privileged.[42] A federal court in Idaho ruled that the privilege applied to a story about a meeting called by citizens to protest the actions of a judge. It clearly was not an official meeting but concerned important public business, the conduct of a public official.

34. *Draghetti* v. *Chimielewski,* 416 Mass. 808 (1994).

35. *Quarcini* v. *Niagara Falls Gazette,* 13 M.L.R. 2340 (1987).

36. *Ingerere* v. *ABC,* 11 M.L.R. 1227 (1984).

37. *Mortensen* v. *Gannett Co.,* 24 M.L.R. 1190 (1995).

38. *Foster* v. *Turner Broadcasting,* 844 F. 2d 955 (1988).

39. *Medico* v. *Time,* 634 F. 2d 134 (1981).

40. *Wiemer* v. *Rankin,* 790 P. 2d 347 (1990).

41. *Wynn* v. *Smith,* 16 P. 3d 424 (2001); *OAO Alfa Bank* v. *Center for Public Integrity,* D.D.C., No. 00-2208 (JDB). 9/27/05.

42. *Herron* v. *Tribune Publishing Co.,* 736 P. 2d 249 (1987).

The court said, "There is a general doctrine that what is said at a public meeting, at which any person of the community or communities involved might have attended and heard and seen for himself, is conditionally privileged for publication."[43]

The "Restatement of Torts" says that reports of what occurs at meetings open to the public at which matters of public concern are discussed are privileged.[44] Paul Ashley, libel authority and author of "Say It Safely," wrote that the privilege probably applies to a public meeting even though admission is charged, so long as everyone is free to pay the price. "By supplying them with information about public events," Ashley wrote, "the publisher is acting as the 'eyes and ears' of people who did not attend."[45] In such a circumstance, the report of a public meeting, the key element undoubtedly is the subject of debate. Was it of public concern? Was it of limited public concern? Was it a purely private matter?

NEUTRAL REPORTAGE

In 1977 the 2nd U.S. Court of Appeals created a new variety of qualified privilege called **neutral reportage.**[46] In a nutshell this privilege says that when the press reports newsworthy but defamatory allegations made by a responsible and prominent source, these reports are privileged, even if the reporter believed the allegations were false when he or she included them in the story. Very few other courts have joined the 2nd Circuit in accepting this privilege.[47] Most other courts that have been confronted with the defense have rejected it, most recently the Pennsylvania Supreme Court.[48] These courts have argued that neutral reportage is incompatible with previous Supreme Court rulings such as *Gertz* v. *Robert Welch Inc.,* that it is unnecessary because of other high court rulings, or that there is simply no basis in the law to support the defense. Neutral reportage is simply not a viable defense in most jurisdictions. The courts that have accepted this defense seem to agree that it has four distinct elements.

- **The defamatory allegations must be newsworthy charges that create or are associated with a public controversy.**
- **The charges must be made by a responsible and prominent source.**
- **The charges must be reported accurately and neutrally.**
- **The charges must be about a public official or public figure.**[49]

ABUSE OF PRIVILEGE

Whether qualified privilege applies to a particular story is the first part of the test. Next, a court will ask whether the story is a fair and accurate or true report of what took place or what is contained in the record.

A court will ask whether the story is a fair and accurate or true report of what took place or what is contained in the record.

43. *Borg* v. *Borg,* 231 F. 2d 788 (1956).
44. American Law Institute, *Restatement of Torts.*
45. Ashley, *Say It Safely.*
46. *Edwards* v. *National Audubon Society, Inc.,* 556 F. 2d 113 (1977), cert. den. 434 U.S. 1002 (1977).
47. See *Price* v. *Viking Penguin, Inc.,* 881 F. 2d 1426 (1989); and *Schwartz* v. *Salt Lake City Tribune* (2005).
48. See, for example, *Dickey* v. *Columbia Broadcasting System, Inc.,* 583 F. 2d 1221 (1978); *Young* v. *The Morning Journal,* 76 Ohio St. 3d 627 (1996); and *Norton* v. *Glenn,* 797 A. 2d 294 (2002); aff'd. Nos. 18 & 19 MAP 2003, 10/20/04.
49. See *Khawar* v. *Globe International Inc.,* 46 Cal. App. 4th 22 (1996); aff'd. 79 Cal. Rptr. 2d 178 (1998).

■ Fair means balanced. The story should be complete and include all sides of a contentious dispute. If at a public meeting speakers both attack and defend Conrad Nagel, the story should reflect both the attack and the defense. If a court record contains both positive and negative references about the subject, the news account should contain both kinds of references as well. If a reporter writes a story about a lawsuit that has been filed against a local doctor, the story should also contain the doctor's response to the charges. There has to be balance; that is the key.

■ An accurate or true report means that the story should honestly reflect what is in the record, or what was said. The story doesn't have to be a verbatim account of what was said. The Connecticut Court of Appeals recently ruled, "It is not necessary that it be exact in every immaterial detail or that it conform to the precision demanded in technical or scientific reporting."[50] And the California Court of Appeals noted, "The privilege applies unless the differences between the facts and the manner in which they are described are of such a substantial character that they produce a different effect on the readers."[51] The story must be an accurate summary of the statement or document. If the original statement or document contains erroneous material, it will not affect the privilege. The 1st U.S. Court of Appeals ruled in 2003 that a story which accurately summarized what a police chief told a reporter about a possible criminal suspect was privileged, even though what the chief said turned out to be inaccurate.[52]

But stories that contain even seemingly small errors can lose the privilege, if the errors are such that they change the impact of the report in the minds of the average reader. In 1988 Glamour magazine printed a story about a widely publicized child custody case. The writer used a variety of sources for the story, including some depositions filed during the custody battle. These are privileged documents. A deposition from a clinical psychologist who had talked with the father in this case, Eric Foretich, discussed the death of his infant sister. The psychologist said that Foretich "was making funeral arrangements, selecting burial plots, you know, seeing the dead infant, things of that sort. . . . He spoke about his dead infant sister and being given this child to hold as his mother is running screaming through the house." The story in Glamour, however, contained these phrases: "When he [Foretich] was in his teens, a sister died shortly after birth. Eric's mother handed him the dead infant, and he arranged for the funeral."

A U.S. District Court in the District of Columbia said the magazine's statement was not a fair and accurate summary of the material in the deposition. The description of Eric's mother in the deposition suggests a woman who was distraught, distressed by grief. The description of her in the magazine shows a cold, uncaring woman.[53]

Other kinds of errors are not as important. A New Jersey newspaper was sued when it reported that a police officer was having sex with a woman at police headquarters. The source of the story was a letter read at a township council meeting by a county prosecutor. The

---

50. *Burton* v. *American Lawyer Media Inc.,* 847 A. 2d 1115 (2004).
51. *Colt* v. *Freedom Communications Inc.,* 109 Cal. App. 4th 1551 (2003).
52. *Yohe* v. *Nugent,* 321 F. 3d 35 (2003).
53. *Foretich* v. *Advance Magazine Publishers, Inc.,* 18 M.L.R. 2280 (1991).

occasion was privileged, the plaintiff agreed, but the story was in error. The official record said the sexual encounter took place in the Municipal Building, not the police station. The police station is in the Municipal Building, the court noted, and the slight error was not material.[54] A Spokane, Wash., newspaper was sued after it reported that a businessman had lost a $250,000 judgment in a suit brought against him by Microsoft. The software maker accused T. James Le of selling counterfeit copies of Microsoft software. There were a couple of minor inaccuracies in the story, which was based on a privileged court file. One statement was false. The story said that Le had sold counterfeit copies of Office Pro and Windows 95 in December of 1998. Actually, he sold only copies of Windows 95 in December of 1998. But the Washington Court of Appeals ruled that the error was insubstantial. "Viewed in context with the entire story, the challenged passage is substantially accurate and fair as a matter of law," the court said.[55]

The story should also be in the form of a report. If defendants fail to make it clear that they are reporting something that was said at a public meeting or repeating something that is contained in the public record, the privilege may be lost. The law says the reader should be aware that the story is a report of what happened at a public meeting or at an official hearing or is taken from the official record. These facts should be noted in the lead and in the headline if possible, as noted in the following boxed example. The U.S. Court of Appeals for the District of Columbia Circuit ruled that qualified privilege did not apply to a magazine summary of statements contained in an official report from the National Transportation Safety Board. The report is an official record; it is clearly covered by the reporter's privilege. But the summary in the magazine gave readers no clue that the statements constituted a summary of an official document. "The challenged [defamatory] assertion is simply offered as historical fact without any particular indication of its source," the court said. The reader was left with the impression that the author of the article reached the conclusion contained in the defamatory allegations based on his own research.[56]

**AT CITY COUNCIL SESSION: MAYOR BLASTS
CONTRACTOR WITH CHARGES OF FRAUD**

Mayor John Smith during a city council meeting today charged the Acme Construction Company with fraudulent dealings.

The privilege protects only that part of a story based on an official proceeding or a public record or report. Anything added to the story from outside these sources will not be protected by the qualified privilege.

One last point needs to be made. Traditionally, under the common law, if even a fair and true report was published not to inform the public but because the publisher wanted to hurt the target of the defamation, the privilege could be lost. Courts called this intent to harm the plaintiff common-law malice because the publisher had a malicious intent. In most states today,

---

54. *Rabbitt* v. *Gannett Satellite Information Network Inc.,* 32 M.L.R. 1410 (2003).
55. *Alpine Industries Computers Inc.* v. *Cowles Publishing Co.,* 57 P. 3d 1178 (2002).
56. *Dameron* v. *Washingtonian,* 779 F. 2d 736 (1985).

even if the plaintiff is able to prove common-law malice, the privilege will still protect the publisher. But this protection is not the law everywhere. The Minnesota Court of Appeals decided in June 1999 that proof of common-law malice can defeat the privilege in that state.[57] Be forewarned.

SUMMARY   The publication of defamatory material in a report of a public meeting, legislative proceeding, or legal proceeding or in a story that reflects the content of an official government report is conditionally privileged. The privilege extends to the meetings of all public bodies, to all aspects of the legal process, to reports and statements issued by members of the executive branch of government, and even to nonofficial meetings of the public in which matters of public concern are discussed. Such reports cannot be the basis for a successful libel suit as long as the report presents a fair (balanced) and accurate (truthful) account of what took place at the meeting or what is contained in the record.

PROTECTION OF OPINION

The law has traditionally shielded statements of opinion from suits for defamation. Opinion is a basic part of mass media in the 21st century, with art, music, film, and television reviews; political commentary; news analysis; and editorials. Opinion-filled exchanges, often heated and exaggerated, are part of the basic political and social discourse in the United States. For several centuries a common-law defense, called fair comment and criticism, was the shield used to protect opinion statements from libel suits. In the past 30 years, however, two other defenses have been added, and there is some question whether the common-law protection afforded to opinion statements by the fair comment defense is needed or viable. In the following pages we examine all three of these potential defenses.

RHETORICAL HYPERBOLE

In the late 1960s, a real estate developer had engaged in negotiations with a local city council for a zoning variance on some land he owned. At the same time the developer was also negotiating with the same city council regarding another parcel of land that the city wanted him to buy. The local newspaper published articles on the bargaining and said that some people had characterized the developer's negotiating positions as "blackmail." The libel suit that followed ultimately found its way to the U.S. Supreme Court. The high court rejected the plaintiff's notion that readers would believe the developer had committed the actual crime of blackmail. The court said the stories gave readers all the background needed to understand the negotiations. "Even the most careless reader must have perceived that the word was no more than rhetorical hyperbole, a vigorous epithet used by those who considered the [developer's] negotiating position extremely unreasonable."[58]

---

57. *Moreno* v. *Crookston Times Printing Co.,* 594 N.W. 2d 555 (1999).
58. *Greenbelt Publishing Assn., Inc.* v. *Bresler,* 398 U.S. 6 (1970).

Four years later the high court rendered a similar ruling in a case involving a dispute among postal workers. The National Association of Letter Carriers was trying to organize workers at a post office in Virginia. The monthly union newsletter included the names of those who had not yet joined the union under the heading, "List of Scabs." To emphasize their point, the editors of the newsletter published a definition of a scab written years ago by American author Jack London. London said, among other things, that a scab carries a tumor of rotten principles where others have a heart, and is a traitor to his god, his country, his family and his class. A postal worker sued, claiming he was not a traitor. The high court cited the earlier decision in *Greenbelt* and said it was impossible to believe that any readers would have understood the newsletter to be charging the plaintiff with the criminal offense of treason. It was rhetorical hyperbole—lusty, imaginative expression.[59]

Opinion statements, then, may be defended as being unbelievable rhetoric. Here are some examples of the kinds of statements courts have ruled are rhetorical hyperbole:

> *Opinion statements, then, may be defended as being unbelievable rhetoric.*

- A talk-show host in Alabama said this about a host on a competing program: "These two guys really slobbered over each other. I mean, I really thought they were going to start performing oral sex on one another."[60]
- A caption under a photo of motorcycle stuntman Evel Knievel and two women (one of whom was his wife) posted on the ESPN extreme sports Web site EXPN.com said, "Evel Knievel proves that you're never too old to be a pimp."[61]
- A talk show host stated that a woman, who ran an unlicensed and understaffed day-care center in her home, was no better than a murderer. Authorities found a three-month-old baby dead in a crib at the woman's home and she had been convicted of endangering the welfare of a child and making false statements to police.[62]
- Television personality Geraldo Rivera called a man who maintained anti-abortion Web sites that listed the names, addresses, and Social Security numbers of doctors who performed abortions an accomplice to murder, someone who was aiding and abetting homicide.[63]

Rhetorical hyperbole is protected, then, because the language is so expansive that the reader or listener knows it is only an opinion, that it is not an assertion of fact. The tone of the language is normally the key. But in cases of satire or parody, the writer or broadcaster must be certain that a reasonable reader will in fact realize that the assertions are not meant to be taken as statements of fact. And this can be a close call sometimes. In 2002 a Texas appellate court was faced with a difficult case after a Dallas alternative weekly newspaper published what was purported to be a news story but was actually a fictional satirical piece. A seventh grader in the small town of Ponder, Texas, had been held in juvenile detention for five days after he read a Halloween story to his classmates that was laced with references to

---

59. *Old Dominion Branch No. 496, National Association of Letter Carriers* v. *Austin*, 94 S. Ct. 2770 (1974); see also *Delaney* v. *International Union UAW Local 94*, 32 M.L.R. 1454 (2004).
60. *Finebaum* v. *Coulter*, 31 M.L.R. 1560 (2003).
61. *Knievel* v. *ESPN*, 393 F. 3d 1068 (2005).
62. *Anslow* v. *Gach*, 32 M.L.R. 2438 (2003).
63. *Horsley* v. *Rivera*, 292 F. 3d 695 (2002).

drugs and violence. Local authorities said the story amounted to a threat of violence and punished the boy. A reporter for the Dallas Observer apparently thought the punishment was nonsense and wrote a satirical fictional story about the same Ponder judge and prosecutor. The satire said authorities locked up a first-grade girl for preparing a book report on Maurice Sendak's "Where the Wild Things Are," a popular children's book. The story described the 6-year-old as being shackled in court and quoted the prosecutor as saying he had not yet decided whether to try the child as an adult. The story mentioned the earlier case, but everything else was pure fiction. It was published under a "News" heading in the newspaper. Some readers apparently thought the story was factual and many complaints were filed against the two public officials. The judge and prosecutor sued for libel. The newspaper sought a summary judgment, arguing that the column was rhetorical hyperbole. The trial court rejected the motion and an appellate court affirmed the refusal. The court said the story had to be viewed in the light of several years of media attention to violence in the schools, and the earlier real incident that occurred in Ponder, which involved two of the public officials quoted in the satirical column.[64] The Texas Supreme Court reversed and granted the summary judgment, ruling that reasonable readers would not understand the story as stating actual facts. There were clues within the column that the column was fiction, the court said, noting that the judge was quoted as calling for "panic and overreaction." The story also quoted former Texas governor George Bush as stating that Maurice Sendak's book "clearly has deviant sexual overtones," and that "zero tolerance means just that. We won't tolerate anything." The court said the article did have a superficial degree of plausibility, but that is the hallmark of satire.[65] The paper won in the end, but it took about five years and undoubtedly cost a considerable sum. Satirists need to be careful.

THE FIRST AMENDMENT

The Supreme Court ruled in 1991 that a statement of "pure opinion" on a matter of public concern is protected by the First Amendment.[66] A libel action based on such a statement cannot succeed. Courts across America have adopted this principle as a fundamental rule of libel law. There has been substantially less agreement, however, on how to identify a statement of "pure opinion." Chief Justice Rehnquist, the author of the 1991 ruling, said a statement of pure opinion is a statement that is incapable of being proved true or false. Pure opinion, Rehnquist said, does not assert or even imply a provably false fact.

The Supreme Court decision flowed from a case in which an Ohio sports columnist wrote that a high school wrestling coach and a school superintendent "lied" during a hearing in which they argued for the reinstatement of the wrestling team, which had been disqualified from participating in the state wrestling tournament. It's hard to know what writer Ted Diadiun really meant when he wrote his column, but after a libel suit was filed against the newspaper, the sportswriter argued that he was simply stating his opinion that the coach and the school superintendent had not been honest when they testified at the hearing.

---

64. *New Times Inc.* v. *Isaacks,* 91 SW 3d 844 (2002).
65. *New Times Inc.* v. *Isaacks,* 32 M.L.R. 2480 (2004).
66. *Milkovich* v. *Lorain Journal Co.,* 110 S. Ct. 2695 (1991).

The case meandered through state and federal courts for nearly 15 years before the Supreme Court ultimately ruled in 1991 that Diadiun's statement was an assertion of a fact, not simply an opinion. Rehnquist said the columnist would not have helped his case had he written "In my opinion, Milkovich [the coach] lied" or "I think Milkovich lied." He is still asserting a fact. He is telling readers, the chief justice said, that "I know something that leads me to believe that this man lied under oath." And this is the assertion of a fact, nothing more, nothing less. The newspaper ultimately paid $116,000 in damages to the plaintiffs. More important, perhaps, the publication spent close to a half million dollars defending itself.

It is unusual for lower courts to reject outright a principle of law enunciated by the Supreme Court, but that is what has happened in this case. The majority of lower courts in the United States that since 1991 have decided cases involving statements of opinion have indicated a dissatisfaction with the *Milkovich* standard. The consensus seems to be that defining an opinion statement using the single criterion of proving a statement true or false is far too conservative, that it would deny First Amendment protection to statements that an author intended to be opinion and that a reader or viewer would assume was opinion.

Many courts have gravitated to a different test for determining whether a remark is intended as an assertion of fact or a statement of opinion. This test includes the criterion outlined by the high court—can the statement be proved true or false—but requires the court to look at other dimensions of the published comment as well.

The Ollman *Test*

In 1984 the U.S. Court of Appeals for the District of Columbia Circuit outlined a four-part test to determine whether a statement should be regarded as the assertion of a fact or as simply the speaker's or writer's opinion. The test, which emerged from the case of *Ollman* v. *Evans,*[67] is known as the *Ollman* test for obvious reasons. Here are the four elements:

- **Can the statement be proved true or false?** This is the basic test from *Milkovich.*
- **What is the common or ordinary meaning of the words?** Some words that appear to be factual assertions are more often used as statements of opinion. If you call someone a turkey, you don't really mean to suggest that the person has feathers and says gobble-gobble. Calling someone a moron doesn't normally mean that his or her IQ score is way below average.
- **What is the journalistic context of the remark?** Newspaper readers expect to find factual assertions in news stories on the front page. They don't expect to find facts in editorial columns, they expect to find opinions. NBC news anchor Brian Williams gives us the news; Rush Limbaugh gives us his opinions, no matter how he happens to word the statements.
- **What is the social context of the remark?** Certain kinds of speech are common to certain kinds of political or social settings. The audience attending a lecture by an eminent scientist on the need to vaccinate young children is expecting to hear facts. In a debate between two candidates for the legislature, the audience is

67. 750 F. 2d 970 (1984).

prepared to hear opinion. Labor disputes, political meetings, protest rallies and other such settings usually generate high-spirited and free-wheeling commentary. People don't usually expect to hear factual assertions.

OLLMAN TEST

1. Can the statement be proved true or false?
2. What is the common or ordinary meaning of the words?
3. What is the journalistic context of the remark?
4. What is the social context of the remark?

Free Speech and Chimpanzees

The first important court to reject the single-criterion *Milkovich* test was the New York Court of Appeals, the high court in that state. The case, *Immuno, A.G.* v. *Moor-Jankowski,*[68] involved a scholarly scientific journal. The journal published a letter from a researcher who asserted that a plan by an Austrian pharmaceutical company to establish a laboratory in Sierra Leone that would use chimpanzees for research on hepatitis was simply a ploy to avoid the restrictions in place in Western Europe and North America that prohibit the importation of the primates, which are regarded as an endangered species. The researcher, Dr. Shirley McGreal, further asserted that the plan could cause serious harm to the chimpanzee population in the region. The comments were published in a letter to the editor and were prefaced by an editorial note that identified McGreal as an animal rights advocate and stated that the company regarded the charges as inaccurate and reckless. The state high court said the letter was protected opinion. Under the single-criterion *Milkovich* standard some of the statements would likely be regarded as factual assertions. But Chief Judge Judith Kaye rejected the single-criterion test, calling it a "hypertechnical" test that paid no attention to contextual matters. The defamatory matter was published in a letter to the editor, a forum where readers expect to find opinion statements. The page carried a warning that the views expressed in the letters were those of the letter writers. Judge Kaye noted that the readers of this journal were highly specialized researchers who were aware of the ongoing debate over the use of primates in medical research. The statements were protected, the court ruled, under the free press provisions of the New York state constitution.[69]

Since this ruling, numerous courts have followed the lead of the New York high court and applied the broader *Immuno* test to determine whether a statement is pure opinion or an assertion of fact. A New York trial court recently rejected a libel suit against the New York Post by a woman who was a toll collector for the Port Authority. Because of complaints from commuters about her rude behavior, the newspaper ran a story about her, describing her as "nasty," "an ogre," and "the toll collector from hell." The court said the story was supported

---

68. 77 N.Y. 2d 235 (1991).
69. *Immuno, A.G.* v. *Moor-Jankowski,* 77 N.Y. 2d 235 (1991).

by truthful facts, and that the context provided by the remainder of the story clearly revealed that the derogatory comments were statements of opinion.[70] Both a U.S. District Court and the 9th U.S. Circuit Court of Appeals have ruled that a statement published in a New York Post column about Johnnie Cochran, one of O.J. Simpson's attorneys, was protected by the First Amendment. The columnist called Cochran a "legal scoundrel" who "will say or do just about anything to win, typically at the expense of the truth." The trial court ruled that the tenor of the column and the context of the statements dictated the readers would view the remarks as opinion, not allegations of fact. The appellate court agreed.[71] And the 1st U.S. Circuit Court of Appeals ruled that statements in a biography of Robert K. Gray that said the former Republican politician and public relations practitioner had faked his closeness to Ronald Reagan and other senior administration officials were protected opinions. "This is just the kind of subjective judgment that is only minimally about 'what happened,' but expresses instead a vague and subjective characterization of what happened," the court said.[72] Again, context was a key.

But the lines can be finely drawn. The 2nd U.S. Circuit Court of Appeals ruled that an unflattering description of an attorney could imply factual assertions to readers. The key, the court said, is the overall context in which the defamatory statements were made. This context was a national directory compiled and distributed by a reputable professional organization. It listed the names, addresses and areas of expertise of attorneys who were willing to work with women who were contemplating gender discrimination suits against employers and others. The directory reported that one woman described the plaintiff-attorney as an ambulance chaser who was only interested in slam dunk cases. "In such a fact-laden context," the court said, "the reasonable reader would be less skeptical and more willing to conclude that [the directory] stated or implied facts," the court said.[73]

And the Nevada Supreme Court ruled in 2002 that just because a factual statement is contained in a restaurant review, a typical vehicle for opinion, doesn't mean it can't be considered a statement of fact. The reviewer suggested in her article that she thought a Mexican-American restaurant was using packaged or canned ingredients in its dishes. The reviewer wrote that after tasting her meal, "I was beginning to realize all of this [food] came out of some sort of package." She later noted that she saw a can of pinto beans sitting on a counter in the kitchen. The newspaper argued that every statement in the review should be regarded as protected opinion. But the court disagreed. The statement "this food came out of some sort of package" should be considered opinion, given the context—a restaurant review—and the opinion-laden tenor of the article. But the statement about the canned beans was an assertion of fact and, if untrue, could be regarded as defamatory. The restaurant owner denied using packaged products in the food but admitted he kept a can of pinto beans on the premises in

70. *Wilkins* v. *New York Post*, 195 Misc. 2d 119 (2003).
71. *Cochran* v. *NYP Holdings Inc.*, 27 M.L.R. 1108 (1998); aff'd. 210 F. 3d 1036 (2000).
72. *Gray* v. *St. Martin's Press, Inc.*, 221 F. 3d 243 (2000). See also *Moldea* v. *New York Times Co.*, 22 F. 3d 310 (1994); *Dworkin* v. *L.F.P., Inc.*, 839 P. 2d 903 (1992); *Maynard* v. *The Daily Gazette Co.*, 447 S.E. 2d 293 (1994); *Keohane* v. *Stewart*, 882 P. 2d 1285 (1994); *Stolz* v. *KSFM* 102 FM, 30 Cal. App. 4th 195 (1995); *Vail* v. *The Plain Dealer Publishing Co.*, 72 Ohio St. 3d 279 (1995); *Portington* v. *Bugliosi*, 56 F. 3d 1147 (1995); and *Biospherics, Inc.* v. *Forbes, Inc.*, 26 M.L.R. 2164 (1998).
73. *Flamm* v. *American Association of University Women*, 201 F. 3d 144 (2000).

case he ran out of fresh beans. So the appellate court affirmed the newspaper's motion for a summary judgment.[74]

Leaving out facts in a story can also be a problem when the defendant attempts to assert the opinion defense. It could give readers an impression of the plaintiff that was unintended by the opinion writer. A case in point was decided several years ago in Rhode Island.

A man picketing and protesting the dismissal of an employee at a YMCA branch collapsed. The president of the branch was a physician who was conducting a board meeting while protesters marched outside. When he was informed that a picketer had collapsed, he offered his assistance. He was told his help was not needed because an aid unit was expected momentarily. When the protester died the story received widespread publicity. The press reports included criticism of the doctor for not aiding the stricken man. All the stories left out the fact that the physician had offered to help the victim. The doctor sued and argued that the stories made him appear to be indifferent, uncaring and even callous. The defendants argued that the defamatory criticisms were opinions. A jury agreed with the plaintiff, noting that by leaving out the essential fact that the doctor had offered to help, the stories implied something that was untruthful.[75] The absence of this information turned protected opinion statements into defamatory factual allegations.

FAIR COMMENT AND CRITICISM

Fair comment is a common-law defense that protects the publication of statements of opinion. It has worked satisfactorily for several centuries. But like many other elements in the law of libel, fair comment has been seriously affected by the application of First Amendment protections to libel law. With the emergence of the First Amendment privilege for statements of opinion that has been outlined in the previous section, most lawyers say it makes more sense to rely on the power of the Constitution to protect their clients as opposed to using a workable, but less powerful, common-law defense. Hence, the status of the fair comment defense is in a kind of legal limbo right now.[76] The hundreds of fair comment precedents remain on the books as good law, but no one seems to cite them anymore.

The use of a fair comment defense requires the court to apply a three-part test:

1. **Is the comment an opinion statement?** Courts have traditionally used a single-criterion test to answer this question: Can the statement be proved true or false?

2. **Does the defamatory comment focus on a subject of legitimate public interest?** The courts have defined legitimate public interest very broadly to include everything from cultural artifacts to religion to medicine to advertising. If the defamatory comment is aimed at an individual it must focus on that person's public life, not his or her private life. What Britney Spears does on stage is one thing; what she does in her bedroom is something else.

---

74. *Pegasus* v. *Reno Newspapers Inc.,* 57 P. 3d 82 (2002).
75. *Healy* v. *New England Newspapers,* 520 A. 2d 147 (1987).
76. But see *Magnusson* v. *New York Times Co.,* 32 M.L.R. 2496 (2004) where the Oklahoma Supreme Court ruled the fair comment defense was applicable in a lawsuit brought against a TV station by a physician.

3. **Is there a factual basis for the comment?** The third requirement of the three-part test is critical, for it is grounded in the legal rationale for the defense: the notion that both our democratic system of government and our culture are enhanced by the free exchange of ideas and opinions. Almost 200 years ago, Great Britain's Lord Ellenborough wrote that "Liberty of criticism must be allowed, or we should have neither purity of taste nor of morals. Fair discussion is essentially necessary to the truth of history and the advancement of science."[77] Those who read the opinions of others certainly have the right to express opinions of their own on the same topic. But it is impossible for a person to challenge another individual's opinion without knowing the basis for that opinion. The facts supporting the opinion must accompany the opinion.

Under fair comment the facts may be outlined in the article or broadcast that contains the opinion. For example:

> In 2002 Mayor Robert Allen bought six road graders for the city, none of which were needed or used. Two years later he spent $60 million of the people's money to build an auditorium that stands vacant 350 nights a year. Last year he sent four of his staff to Europe to study how mass transit is operated there, and three of the cities his staff visited have no mass transit system. Mayor Allen has been squandering taxpayers' money for too long; he is wasteful and pays little heed to need for fiscal caution.

The opinion—that Allen has been squandering taxpayers' money—was supported by the factual statements in the first part of the story.

But if the facts regarding a situation are already widely known, it is not necessary for the commentator to spell them out afresh for readers or viewers. For example, the comment that "No American president has damaged the position of the United States as a world leader in diplomacy more than George W. Bush" need not be accompanied by an outline of how most foreign governments opposed the nation's invasion of Iraq in 2003. On the other hand there is a well-regarded school of thought in libel law that suggests it is a good idea in any commentary or analysis to present the facts that support the opinion. This inclusion can enhance even the First Amendment defense for opinion statements. A presentation of the facts gives the defamatory remarks important context. It can help explain what is meant. And it is more equitable to readers and listeners and to the individual who is the focus of the criticism. In any lawsuit, judges and jurors are always impressed by fairness.

It is a good idea in any commentary or analysis to present the facts that support the opinion.

The defendant who is sued for defamatory opinion, then, may attempt to defeat the lawsuit using any or all of the three strategies just outlined. The defendant can argue that the defamatory statements are so broad, so exaggerated, that no one would regard them as factual assertions; that they are rhetorical hyperbole. The defendant may also argue that the statement is a pure opinion and protected by the Constitution. Finally, the defendant can argue that the common-law defense of fair comment provides a shield against a lawsuit.

---

77. *Tabart* v. *Tipper,* 1 Camp. 350 (1808).

**TIPS ON AVOIDING A LIBEL SUIT BASED
ON STATEMENTS OF OPINION**

Journalists can take steps to avoid such a lawsuit in the first place. Mass media attorney David Utevsky suggests the following:

- When stating an opinion, try to make certain it is understood as such. But remember the words "in my opinion" don't change a statement of fact into protected opinion.

- Don't rely on journalistic context to protect you. Just because the libel appears in a review or a column or a commentary does not mean a court will regard it as opinion.

- Clearly state and summarize the facts on which your opinion is based. Ask yourself whether you believe a court could find that these facts support your opinion about the matter.

- Make certain the facts are true. If there is a dispute about the fact, refer to both sides of the dispute when stating your opinion.

SUMMARY

Statements of opinion are often immune to a successful libel action. The courts have said that rhetorical hyperbole—broad, exaggerated comments about someone or something—are obviously not assertions of fact and cannot stand as the basis for a successful libel suit. The Constitution also protects statements of opinion, but only pure opinion, according to the Supreme Court. Opinion statements that imply the assertion of falsehoods are not protected. The Supreme Court has ruled that the test to determine whether a statement is opinion or not is whether the statement may be proved false. Other courts have applied somewhat broader tests for opinion that focus on the ordinary meaning of the words and the journalistic and social context of the statement in addition to whether the statement can be proved to be false. Finally, opinion is protected by the common-law defense of fair comment. A plaintiff cannot recover damages for an opinion statement about a subject of legitimate public interest that is based on true facts that are clearly stated or well known.

DEFENSES AND DAMAGES

The privilege of the reporter and the defenses for opinion are not the only means at hand to thwart a libel suit. At least two other common-law defenses exist: **consent** and **right of reply.** Like fair comment, these defenses are old. Both have been used on occasion in the past with substantial success. Yet they are not universally accepted, and only rarely have they been applied in a libel suit in the last 30 years. Let's briefly examine each.

CONSENT

Many legal authorities agree that an individual cannot sue for libel if he or she consented to the publication of the defamatory material.[78] Imagine that Mary Jones, a reporter for the River City Sentinel, hears rumors that John Smith is a leader of organized crime. Jones visits Smith and tells him that she has heard these rumors. Then Jones asks Smith if he cares if the rumors are published in the newspaper. Smith says it is OK with him, and Jones writes and publishes the story. In this instance Smith consented to publication of the defamation. Now this event is not too likely to happen, is it? Cases of this kind of express consent are extremely rare. Courts insist that the plaintiff either knew or had a good reason to know the full extent of the defamatory statement in advance of its publication before consent can be said to exist.

But there is another kind of consent that some courts have recognized. It is called indirect or implied consent. A plaintiff can give this kind of consent in at least a couple ways. Courts have ruled that when an individual comments on a defamatory charge and this response is published with the charge, the injured party has given indirect consent to publish the libel.[79] The logic to this argument is simple: If the response is printed, the charge must be printed as well or the story won't make any sense. Courts have also ruled that if the plaintiff has told others of the defamatory charges against him or her, this amounts to implied consent to publication elsewhere.[80] Implied consent is constructed on sound legal theory, but only a handful of courts have accepted this theory. Nevertheless, getting a comment from an individual you are about to libel is a very good idea. Giving the subject of the story a chance to reply might reveal mistakes in the story, mistakes that can be corrected before publication or broadcast. It is the fair and equitable thing to do as well. Judges and jurors appreciate fairness. The goal, after all, is to publish a complete story. There is no reason to believe that the subject of the story might not have information that would help the reporter attain that goal.

Implied consent is constructed on sound legal theory, but only a handful of courts have accepted this theory.

RIGHT OF REPLY

Right of reply is another secondary defense. Like consent, it has not been commonly applied in recent years. Right of reply is sometimes called "the self-defense." If an individual has been defamed, he or she may answer the defamation with a libelous communication and not be subject to a successful libel suit. It might be termed "giving as good as you got." The only limitation here is that the reply must approximate the original defamation in magnitude. Self-defense has this same limitation. The response cannot greatly exceed the provocation. The court will not accept a claim of self-defense if you shoot and kill someone who threw a spit-wad at you.

In a famous lawsuit two American journalists assailed one another in print. Newsman Quentin Reynolds suggested that columnist Westbrook Pegler had once called a third journalist, Heywood Broun, a liar. This bothered Broun, Reynolds wrote, to the extent that he could not sleep. Broun became ill and finally died. Pegler was incensed by this comment, claiming it

---

78. Phelps and Hamilton, *Libel,* and Sanford, *Libel and Privacy.*
79. See *Pulverman* v. *A.S. Abell Co.,* 228 F. 2d 797 (1956), for example.
80. *Pressley* v. *Continental Can Co.,* 250 S.E. 2d 676 (1978).

charged him with moral homicide. So he attacked Reynolds, calling him sloppy, a sycophant, a coward, a slob and a four-flusher. Pegler accused Reynolds of public nudism, of being a war profiteer, and of being an absentee war correspondent. Pegler also attacked the deceased Broun, calling him a liar and someone who made his living by controversy.

In the libel suit that followed, Pegler raised the defense of right of reply. The court agreed that Pegler's comments about Broun bore a resemblance to a reply but determined that the columnist had gone too far in his attack on Quentin Reynolds. This portion of the article had no conceivable relationship to a reply. Reynolds was awarded $175,000 from Pegler, the New York Journal-American, and the Hearst Corporation.[81]

The case just described is not a typical lawsuit. Journalists still fight with one another, but they rarely settle the matter in court. As such, what good is the right-of-reply defense for those who work in the mass media? Some authorities have argued that the mass media have the right to publish a reply to a defamatory attack and remain immune from a libel suit.[82] In several cases it was held that where the plaintiff's charge was made in a newspaper, the newspaper was privileged to carry the defendant's reply.[83] Otherwise the right of reply is of no avail to the defendant; no one would be able to see or read the reply if the defendant were denied use of the press. Similarly, it was held that the reply can even be carried in a newspaper or a medium different from the medium used for the attack.

In "Cases and Materials on Torts," law professors Charles Gregory and Harry Kalven wrote:

> The boundaries of this privilege are not clearly established and it gives rise to questions amusingly reminiscent of those raised in connection with self-defense: How vigorous must the plaintiff's original aggression have been? Must the original attack itself have been defamatory? What if it [the original attack] is true or privileged? How much verbal force can the defendant use in reply? Can he defend third parties?[84]

Questions like these continue to reduce the true effectiveness of the defense of right of reply.

DAMAGES

If the court gets to the point in a libel suit of assessing damages, it is obvious that the plaintiff has met all requirements, including proving fault, and that none of the defenses just outlined have worked. How damages are assessed is not an essential piece of information for a journalist to carry, yet some feeling for the subject is useful. Libel law operates with four kinds of damages today. In each instance, before any damages can be awarded, the plaintiff must prove one thing or another to the court.

---

81. *Reynolds* v. *Pegler,* 223 F. 2d 449 (1955).
82. See Phelps and Hamilton, *Libel.*
83. See *Fowler* v. *New York Herald,* 172 N.Y.S. 423 (1918).
84. Gregory and Kalven, *Cases and Materials on Torts.*

Actual Damages

The most common libel damages are called **actual damages,** or damages for actual injury. Plaintiffs must bring evidence to the court to show that because of the publication of the defamation they have suffered actual harm, which might include impairment of reputation or standing in the community, monetary loss, personal humiliation, or mental suffering and anguish.[85] Some of these concepts are pretty nebulous. How can mental suffering or anguish be proved in court and then measured in dollar amounts? As such, the awarding of even so-called actual damages is rarely a precise process. The plaintiff will ask for an amount that may or may not bear any relationship to the actual harm inflicted, and the court—usually the jury—will award what it thinks the plaintiff deserves, often regardless of the amount of damage inflicted. If the amount is too high the trial judge or an appellate court will frequently modify the amount of money awarded. The gross imprecision in awarding damages puts considerable pressure on both parties, but especially the defendant, to settle the case without going to trial.

The most common libel damages are called actual damages, or damages for actual injury.

Special Damages

Special damages are specific items of pecuniary loss caused by published defamatory statements. Special damages must be established in precise terms, much more precise terms than those for the actual damages just outlined. If a plaintiff can prove that he or she lost $23,567.19 because of the libel, that amount is then what the plaintiff can ask for and what will likely be awarded if he or she can convince the jury of the validity of the case. Special damages represent a specific monetary, and only monetary, loss as the result of the libel. Most plaintiffs do not seek special damages. However, in some cases special damages are all that can be sought. In trade libel, for example, the only award a plaintiff can get is special damages.

Presumed Damages

Presumed damages are damages that a plaintiff can get without proof of injury or harm. A public-person plaintiff or a private-person plaintiff suing for a libelous statement that focuses on a matter of public concern can only be awarded presumed damages (sometimes called general or compensatory) damages on a showing of actual malice, knowledge of falsity or reckless disregard of the truth. However, a private person suing on the basis of a libelous statement that focuses on a private matter and not a public concern need only show negligence to collect presumed damages.[86]

Punitive Damages

Lawyers frequently call **punitive damages,** or exemplary damages, the "smart money." Punitive damage awards are usually very large. The other kinds of damages just discussed are

---

85. See Justice Lewis Powell's opinion in *Gertz* v. *Robert Welch, Inc.,* 4118 U.S. 323 (1974).
86. *Dun* & *Bradstreet* v. *Greenmoss Builders,* 472 U.S. 479 (1985).

designed to compensate the plaintiff for injury. Punitive damages are designed to punish defendants for misconduct and to warn other persons not to act in a similar manner.

A public-person plaintiff or a private-person plaintiff suing for a libelous statement that focuses on a matter of public concern can only win punitive damages on a showing of actual malice, knowledge of falsity or reckless disregard for the truth. A private person suing for libel based on remarks made about a private matter, and not a public concern, can win punitive damages on a showing of negligence.

Punitive damages are the most onerous aspect of any libel suit, and many persons think they are grossly unfair. Punitive damages have been barred in Louisiana, Massachusetts, Nebraska, New Hampshire, Oregon, and Washington and have been limited in Colorado, Florida, Georgia, Kansas, Montana, Mississippi, North Dakota and Virginia.[87] Legislatures in other states, such as Alabama, Illinois and Indiana, have considered placing some kind of limits on punitive damages. Few, if any, legal authorities will argue that punitive damages ought to be completely abolished. They do in some instances serve a purpose. A business that consciously and aggressively sells harmful or dangerous products must be punished, most legal experts will argue. A publisher who consistently prints gross lies that shred the reputations of innocent people should suffer serious consequences. But the gargantuan size of some punitive damage awards, amounts that bear no resemblance whatsoever to the harm inflicted, has led many attorneys to argue that such awards violate the Eighth Amendment to the U.S. Constitution, which forbids the levying of excessive fines. The Supreme Court has never fully agreed with this argument but in recent years has attempted, albeit subtly, to put the brakes on the imposition of excessive punitive awards. In 1991, the high court ruled that the methods used by the courts to assess punitive damages are not "so inherently unfair as to be per se unconstitutional." But, Justice Harry Blackmun wrote for the court, "the general concerns of reasonableness and adequate guidance from the court when the case is tried to a jury properly enter into the constitutional calculus."[88] Five years later the high court overturned as "grossly excessive" an award of $2 million to an Alabama man who sued BMW for selling him, as a new car, an automobile that had been repainted to correct minor paint damage incurred in shipping. Again, the court declined to provide a specific test that should be applied at trial to guide the assessment of punitive damage awards, but offered three guideposts that could be used: the degree of reprehensibility of the defendant's conduct, the ratio between punitive and actual damages, and a comparison between the punitive damage award and any criminal or civil fines that could be levied by the state for similar conduct.[89] In 2001 the high court again spoke to the problem, warning lower appellate courts that they must give "searching scrutiny" to whether a jury's punitive damage award is excessive.[90] In 2003 the high court made its sharpest attack on punitive damages when it overturned an award of $145 million that a Utah jury had given a couple who had sued State Farm insurance company. The lawsuit focused on the insurer's refusal to settle a claim and other related matters. Justice Anthony Kennedy, writing for the six-person majority, said that the wealth of a defendant cannot justify an otherwise unconstitutional punitive damage award. The couple had been awarded $1 million in

87. Dill, "Libel Law Doesn't Work."
88. *Pacific Mutual Life Insurance Co. v. Haslip,* 111 S. Ct. 1032 (1991).
89. Greenhouse, "Justices Reject Punitive Award," A1.
90. Greenhouse, "Punitive Damages."

compensatory damages, the remaining $144 million as punitive damages. Kennedy said the ratio of 145 to 1 resulted in a damage award that was "neither reasonable nor proportionate to the wrong committed." He called the award irrational and arbitrary and suggested it was based less on the harm caused by the defendants and more on the fact that State Farm was a wealthy defendant. He said the state courts had used the case as a platform to expose and punish the insurer for its perceived deficiencies throughout the country.[91] Whether rulings like these that talk in rather abstract terms about "reasonable" ratios between compensatory damage and punitive awards will reduce egregious awards handed out in state courts remains to be seen.

RETRACTION STATUTES

The phrase "I demand a retraction" is common in the folklore of libel. What is a **retraction?** A retraction is both an apology and an effort to set the record straight. Let us say you blow one as an editor. You report that Jane Adams was arrested for shoplifting, and you are wrong. In your retraction you first tell readers or viewers that Jane Adams was not arrested for shoplifting, that you made a mistake. Then you might also apologize for the embarrassment caused Ms. Adams. You might even say some nice things about her. At common law a prompt and honest retraction is usually relevant to the question of whether the plaintiff's reputation was actually harmed. After all, you are attempting to reconstruct that part of her reputation that you tore down just the day before. She might have difficulty proving actual harm.

The phrase "I demand a retraction" is common in the folklore of libel.

RETRACTION STATUTE FROM STATE OF OREGON

A typical retraction statute looks much like this one from the state of Oregon. Publishers and broadcasters who meet the letter of such laws can substantially reduce the amount of damages a plaintiff can win in a libel suit.

30.165 Publication of correction or retraction upon demand.

1. The demand for correction or retraction shall be in writing, signed by the defamed person or the attorney of the person and be delivered to the publisher of the defamatory statement, either personally or by registered mail at the publisher's place of business or residence within 20 days after the defamed person receives actual knowledge of the defamatory statement. The demand shall specify which statements are false and defamatory and request that they be corrected or retracted. The demand may also refer to the sources from which the true facts may be ascertained with accuracy.

2. The publisher of the defamatory statement shall have not more than two weeks after receipt of the demand for correction or retraction in which to investigate the demand; and, after making such

---

91. *State Farm* v. *Campbell,* No. 01-1289; Greenhouse, "Justices Limit."

investigation, the publisher shall publish the correction or retraction in:

(a) The first issue thereafter published, in the case of newspapers, magazines or other printed periodicals.

(b) The first broadcast or telecast thereafter made, in the case of radio or television stations.

(c) The first public exhibition thereafter made, in the case of motion picture theatres.

3. The correction or retraction shall consist of a statement by the publisher substantially to the effect that the defamatory statements previously made are not factually supported and that the publisher regrets the original publication thereof.

4. The correction or retraction shall be published in substantially as conspicuous a manner as the defamatory statement. [1955 c.365 §3]

Thirty-three states have some kind of retraction law, according to libel authority Bruce Sanford.[92] Some of these laws are very comprehensive; others provide extremely limited protection. The Washington state law, for example, only relates to the liability of editors and others who process the news, and most persons who work in the media in Washington don't even regard the law as a retraction statute.[93] Under a typical retraction statute, a plaintiff must give the publisher an opportunity to retract the libel before a suit may be started. If the publisher promptly honors the request for a retraction and retracts the libelous material in a place in the newspaper as prominent as the place in which the libel originally appeared, the retraction will reduce, and in some instances cancel, any damage judgment the plaintiff might later seek in a lawsuit. Failure to ask for a retraction or failure to ask for a retraction in the way prescribed by the statute can result in a dismissal of the libel complaint.[94]

In at least two states, retraction statutes adopted by the legislature have been ruled unconstitutional. In both Arizona[95] and Montana,[96] the state high courts have ruled that the state constitution gives citizens the right to sue for injury to person, property or character. The retraction statute diminishes that right and is hence unconstitutional, the courts ruled.

A court in at least one state applied a retraction statute to libel published on the Internet. The Georgia Supreme Court ruled in 2002 that the state's law, which applies only to punitive damages, not the right to sue, is applicable to publications occurring on the Internet. Both the trial court and the state court of appeals had ruled it did not apply to Internet publications, that it applied only to publications in the traditional media. In this case the plaintiff had failed to ask for a retraction and therefore was denied the opportunity to seek punitive damages.[97]

92. Sanford, *Libel and Privacy.*
93. Washington Rev. Code Ann. § 9: 58. 040 (1977).
94. *Milsap* v. *Stanford,* 139 F. 3d 902 (1998).
95. *Boswell* v. *Phoenix Newspapers,* 730 P. 2d 186 (1986).
96. *Madison* v. *Yunker,* 589 P. 2d 126 (1978).
97. *Mathis* v. *Cannon,* 573 SE 2d 376 (2002).

SUMMARY

Secondary defenses, consent and right of reply, exist and may in rare instances aid a libel defendant. To collect damages in a libel suit, plaintiffs must demonstrate to the court that there was actual harm to their reputations. These are called *actual damages*. If plaintiffs can demonstrate specific items of monetary loss, *special damages* may be awarded. Plaintiffs may also seek to win *punitive damages*. In many states, a timely retraction of the libel can reduce damages significantly and even lessen the likelihood of a libel suit. These rules are governed by state laws called *retraction statutes.*

CRIMINAL LIBEL

Criminal libel has been a part of the law of defamation for as long as the law has existed. It is a close cousin to seditious libel and civil libel. Chapters 4, 5, and the better part of this chapter have dealt with civil libel, one person suing another for defamation. Criminal libel is founded on the theory that sometimes it is appropriate for the state to act on behalf of the party injured by the libel and bring criminal charges against the defendant. Criminal libel has been justified traditionally with the argument that if the state fails to act, the injured party or parties may take violent action against the libeler to compensate for the damage they have suffered. The state has a substantial interest in preventing this violence from occurring. In fact, however, most criminal libel prosecutions are generated for political reasons, according to a recent study by the Media Law Resource Center (MLRC). There were 77 criminal libel cases filed or threatened in the 40 years following the Supreme Court ruling in *New York Times* v. *Sullivan,* and more than 65 percent of these cases involve speech about public officials, public figures or matters of public interest, the MLRC reported. Law enforcement officers and elected public officials are the most frequent complainants in these prosecutions. For example, in August of 2005 a 32-year-old Farmington, N.M., man was found guilty of criminal libel because he circulated a petition asking the local police department to investigate one of its officers, and picketed the police station with signs calling the officer "dirty" and "liar." The city attorney who prosecuted the case told the local newspaper that he was extremely thankful that "we live in a country with free speech, but certain kinds of speech are not free." The man, Juan Mata, had previously filed a civil rights lawsuit against the city and five police officers alleging police brutality. The state's criminal libel statute had been declared unconstitutional 13 years earlier by a state appellate court.[98] In another recent case officials in Kansas City, Kan., filed criminal libel charges against an irregularly published periodical called The New Observer. During an election campaign the newspaper reported that one of the candidates for mayor lived in an affluent county to the south of the district in which she sought election, and thus was ineligible for the mayor's job. This wasn't true, and the county prosecutor, who was a frequent target of attacks by the irreverent newspaper's publisher and editor, arrested both men five days after the candidate who was attacked won the mayor's job. The pair were convicted of criminal defamation the following year and could have been sentenced to a year-long jail

98. Mayeux, "Jury Finds Mata."

term. The Kansas Court of Appeals affirmed the conviction in 2004 and a fine, instead of jail time, was levied against the elderly journalists. Attempts in the legislature to repeal the Kansas law failed as well.[99]

Only 17 states* and two U.S. possessions (Puerto and the U.S. Virgin Islands) had criminal libel statutes in 2005. Authorities in most states are unwilling to take on someone else's troubles and prosecute for criminal libel so long as a civil remedy is available. A prosecutor will generally gain very little public support by taking such an action. In an age when people are murdered, robbed, raped and assaulted with alarming frequency, most voters would rather see government officers arrest and prosecute real criminals. Years ago in New York, a judge stated this proposition very well.

> The theory, in simplest terms, is that when an individual is libeled, he has an adequate remedy in a civil suit for damages. The public suffers no injury. Vindication for the individual and adequate compensation for the injury done him may be obtained as well in the civil courts. Thus the rule has always been that the remedy of criminal prosecution should only be sought where the wrong is of so flagrant a character as to make a criminal prosecution necessary on public grounds.[100]

Criminal libel differs from civil libel in several important respects. First of all, it is possible to criminally libel the dead. The state can use a criminal libel statute to prosecute an individual for damaging the reputation of someone who is deceased. In some states criminal libel is tied to causing or potentially causing a breach of the peace. This charge used to be quite common. If a publication, speech or handbill so provoked the readers or listeners that violence became possible or did in fact occur, criminal libel charges might result. In 1966 the U.S. Supreme Court undermined most of the "breach of the peace" statutes as well as the actions of those states that brought criminal libel actions under the common law. The case was *Ashton* v. *Kentucky*[101] and involved a mining dispute in Hazard, Ky. An agitator was arrested for circulating a pamphlet that contained articles attacking the chief of police, the sheriff and a newspaper editor, among others. At the criminal libel trial, the judge defined the offense as "any writing calculated to create a disturbance of the peace, corrupt public morals or lead to any act, which when done, is indictable."

The Supreme Court reversed the conviction. Writing for a unanimous court, Justice William O. Douglas said the crime, as defined by the trial court, was too general and indefinite. It left the standard of responsibility—whether something is illegal or not—wide open to the discretion of the judge. Also, Douglas noted, the crime is determined not by the character of the person's words, not by what that person says or writes, but rather by the boiling point of those who listen to or read those words. The law makes someone a criminal simply because his or her neighbors have no self-control and cannot refrain from violence. This decision was

---

*Colorado, Florida, Idaho, Kansas, Louisiana, Michigan, Minnesota, Montana, New Hampshire, New Mexico, North Carolina, North Dakota, Oklahoma, Utah, Virginia, Washington and Wisconsin.

99. *Kansas* v. *Carson,* No. 01-CR-301 (Kansas Dist. Ct.); affirmed No. 90-690 (Kansas Ct. App., Aug. 20, 2004). See also "Criminalizing Speech About Reputation"; "Developments in Criminal Defamation Law"; and Barriner, "A Criminal Defamation Verdict."

100. *People* v. *Quill,* 177 N.Y. 2d 380 (1958).

101. 384 U.S. 195 (1966).

an important factor, but only one factor, in the passing of "breach of the peace" as an aspect of criminal libel. It is extremely rare for such a case to occur today.

The Supreme Court has heard one criminal libel case since the *New York Times* v. *Sullivan*[102] ruling. The court ruled in *Garrison* v. *Louisiana*[103] that when the defamation of a public official is the basis for a criminal libel suit, the state has to prove actual malice on the part of the defendant—that is, knowledge of falsity, reckless disregard for the truth or falsity of the matter. Justice Brennan wrote that the reasons that persuaded the court to rule that the First Amendment protected criticism of public officials in a civil libel suit apply with equal force in a criminal libel suit. "The constitutional guarantees of freedom of expression compel application of the same standard to the criminal remedy," he added. The Supreme Court has never answered the question of whether the actual malice rule applies to cases involving the criminal libel of private persons. Nevertheless, this ruling was a potent blow against criminal libel. The laws in 33 states have either been repealed or struck down since the *Garrison* decision.[104] Most of the state laws that still exist fail to meet even the minimum constitutional requirements sent out by the high court in 1966.*

This ruling was a potent blow against criminal libel.

BIBLIOGRAPHY

American Law Institute. *Restatement of Torts.* 2nd ed. Philadelphia: American Law Institute, 1975.

Ashley, Paul. *Say It Safely.* 5th ed. Seattle: University of Washington Press, 1976.

Barringer, Felicity. "A Criminal Defamation Verdict Roils Politics in Kansas City, Kan." *The New York Times,* 29 July 2002, A14.

"Criminalizing Speech About Reputation: The Legacy of Criminal Libel in the U.S. After *Sullivan* and *Garrison.*" *Media Law Resource Center Bulletin 2003:* 1.

"Developments in Criminal Defamation Law Since 2002." *Media Law Resource Bulletin,* 2004, No. 4, Pt. 2.

Dill, Barbara. "Libel Law Doesn't Work, But Can It Be Fixed?" In *At What Price? Libel Law and Freedom of the Press,* by Martin London and Barbara Dill. New York: The Twentieth Century Fund Press, 1993.

Gleason, Timothy W. "The Fact/Opinion Distinction in Libel." *Hastings Journal of Communications and Entertainment Law* 10 (1988): 763.

Greenhouse, Linda. "For First Time Justices Reject Punitive Award." *The New York Times,* 21 May 1996, A1.

*In 2004 a U.S. District Court in California struck down on First Amendment grounds a state law that made it a crime to make a false accusation against a police officer. This wasn't technically a criminal libel law, but it had many elements common to such laws. *Hamilton* v. *City of San Bernardino,* 32 M.L.R. 2594 (2004). The 9th U.S. Court of Appeals made a similar ruling on this law in 2005. See *Chaker* v. *Crogan,* 33 M.L.R. 2569 (2005). The California Supreme Court had two years earlier upheld the same statute. *People* v. *Stanistreet,* 58 P. 3d 465 (2002).

102. 376 U.S. 254 (1964); see also *Ivey* v. *State,* 29 M.L.R. 2089 (2001).

103. 379 U.S. 64 (1964).

104. See, for example, *Mangual* v. *Rotger-Sabat,* 317 F. 3d 45 (2003), where the 1st U.S. Court of Appeals ruled that the Puerto Rican criminal libel statute was unconstitutional as it applied to public figures.

———. "Justices Limit Punitive Damages—Victory for Tort Reform." *The New York Times,* 8 April 2003, A16.

———. "Punitive Damages Must Get a Searching Review on Appeal, Justices Rule." *The New York Times,* 15 May 2001, A18.

Gregory, Charles O., and Harry Kalven. *Cases and Materials on Torts.* 2nd ed. Boston: Little, Brown, 1969.

Mayeux, Debra. "Jury Finds Mata Guilty of Criminal Libel." *The Daily Times,* 9 August 2005.

McGraw, David. "The Right to Republish Libel: Neutral Reportage and the Reasonable Reader." *Akron Law Review* 25 (1991): 335.

Phelps, Robert, and Douglas Hamilton. *Libel.* New York: Macmillan, 1966.

Pogrebin, Robin. "Publication Date Open to Dispute in Internet Age." *The New York Times,* 3 November 1997, C1.

Prosser, William L. *Handbook of the Law of Torts.* St. Paul: West Publishing, 1963.

Sanford, Bruce W. *Libel and Privacy.* 2nd ed. Englewood Cliffs, N.J.: Prentice-Hall Law & Business, 1993.

INVASION OF PRIVACY
Appropriation and Intrusion

Invasion of privacy is a multifaceted tort that is designed to redress a variety of grievances. These include the commercial exploitation of an individual's name or likeness, the intrusion on what might be called our private domains, the revelation of intimate information about someone, and the libel-like publication of embarrassing false information about a person. After an initial exploration of the broader dimensions of the right to privacy, we will explore these four discrete legal areas in Chapters 7 and 8.

INVASION OF PRIVACY

The right to privacy in the United States has been diminishing bit by bit for over 100 years. The growth of the government, the growth of the mass media, numerous technological innovations, all of these developments and others too numerous to name, have contributed to the shrinking of that sphere of privacy which supposedly surrounds each of us and protects us from the prying eyes of the outside world. The terrorist attacks on September 11, 2001, made the problems of protecting our privacy even worse, much worse. The federal government adopted the Patriot Act (the Uniting and Strengthening America by Providing Appropriate Tools Required to Intercept and Obstruct Terrorism Act), a wide-ranging federal law that made it easier for the government to gather information about terrorists, and those they only think are terrorists. In late 2005 it was revealed that the President had ordered the National Security Agency to eavesdrop on telephone conversations originating here and abroad without seeking warrants, as required by law. The President defended his actions on national security grounds. But federal agencies are restricted by the Privacy Act of 1974 from building databases of dossiers on citizens unless these files are directly related to an agency's mission. Also, the 1974 law requires that these files be accurate, and citizens are given the right to access their own files and force the government to correct mistaken information in the files. In order to avoid the limits placed upon it by the Privacy Act, the government has been outsourcing to private companies the job of data gathering, creating what some have called a "security-industrial complex," a 21st-century version of the "military-industrial complex" President Dwight D. Eisenhower warned the nation against half a century ago. These companies, like LexisNexis, ChoicePoint and others, do not face the restrictions the Privacy Act places on the government. And they tend to be vulnerable to security breaches, as nearly 150,000 people discovered in February 2005 when ChoicePoint sent them notification that con artists had gained access to their Social Security numbers, addresses and other personal data the company had gathered about them.

No one doubts the need for the government to gather data to help thwart future terrorist operations. The problem is that individuals rarely wear signs proclaiming to be terrorists, so attempts to gather data have had an impact upon a wide range of people beyond those who pose a threat to the nation. And many Americans are now beginning to bridle at the extent to which the government has moved to "peer into the lives of ordinary people," as author Robert O'Harrow Jr. wrote in "No Place to Hide." Of course, not everyone shares these feelings. In fact, many Americans seem more than willing to trade a measure of privacy for increased security, or for the ability to participate more fully in the credit-card society, or simply for the convenience of being able to do things like conduct their business via the Internet.

But government snooping is not the only problem faced by Americans who value their privacy. In recent years many mass media organizations and the people who work for them have given new meaning to the concept of the intrusive or prying reporter. The "anything goes" attitude of not most, but too many in the journalism business, has angered not only the objects of this aggressive reporting but thoughtful members of the audience as well. And this is where this text intersects with the right to privacy, for over the past century state legislatures and courts have fashioned legal rights that permit persons who believe they have been injured to sue the mass media for infringing on their rights of privacy. The law is ragged in many ways because it is young and still developing, unlike libel law, which has existed for several centuries. And today, while concerns over the right to privacy range far beyond the behavior of the mass media, it is interesting to note that it was the intrusive newspaper reporting of the late 19th century that is the likely genesis of the law that exists today.

THE GROWTH OF PRIVACY LAWS

Most rights that Americans believe to be basic are guaranteed by the U.S. Constitution and contained in the Bill of Rights. But a guarantee of a right to privacy is not to be found in this document. In fact, the word "privacy" is not even contained in the Constitution. Privacy, or at least the concept of privacy as we know it today, was not on the minds of many Americans in the largely rural America of the 17th and 18th centuries. The U.S. Supreme Court has ruled in the past century that the protection of the right to privacy is at the core of several amendments contained in the Bill of Rights, but this notion has been generated by 20th-century legal thinking and cannot necessarily be attributed to the nation's founders.*

It wasn't until the end of the 19th century that the need for a right to privacy became a public issue. Of course the nation had changed dramatically. America was rapidly becoming an urban nation. The streets of many cities were clogged with poor immigrants or first-generation Americans. Big city daily newspapers used a variety of sensational schemes to attract these potential readers. Editors often played out the lives of the "rich and famous" on the pages of their newspapers, permitting their readers to vicariously enjoy wealth, status and celebrity.

It was this kind of journalism that apparently pushed two Boston lawyers, Samuel D. Warren and Louis D. Brandeis, to use the pages of the Harvard Law Review to propose a legally recognized right to privacy. Warren, the scion of a prominent Boston family, urged his friend (and future Supreme Court justice) Brandeis to help him write the piece, "The Right to Privacy."[1] The article appeared in 1890 and can be legitimately regarded as the fountain from which the modern law of privacy has flowed.

The pair argued, "Instantaneous photographs and newspaper enterprise have invaded the sacred precincts of private and domestic life; and numerous mechanical devices threaten to make good the prediction that 'what is whispered in the closet shall be proclaimed from the house-tops.'" Warren and Brandeis said they were offended by the gossip in the press, which they said had overstepped in every direction the obvious bounds of propriety and decency:

> To satisfy a prurient taste the details of sexual relations are spread broad-
> cast in the columns of the daily papers. To occupy the indolent, column
> upon column is filled with idle gossip, which can only be procured by
> intrusion upon the domestic circle. . . .

*In 1965 the Supreme Court ruled in *Griswold* v. *Connecticut,* 381 U.S. 479, that something like a right to privacy was implicit in the Bill of Rights. In that case and others the high court has decided that the First Amendment's guarantee of freedom of association, the Third Amendment's limits on the government's power to quarter soldiers in private homes during peacetime, the protection from unreasonable search and seizure in the Fourth Amendment, and the protection against self-incrimination in the Fifth Amendment all speak indirectly, at least, to protection of the right of privacy. This constitutional right to privacy has been cited several times by the high court since 1965, including the *Roe* v. *Wade* abortion ruling in 1973 and the decision in *Lawrence* v. *Texas* in 2003 that declared the Texas anti-sodomy law to be unconstitutional.
1. Warren and Brandeis, "The Right to Privacy," 220.

> The common law has always recognized a man's house as his castle, impregnable, often, even to its own officers engaged in the execution of its commands. Shall the courts thus close the front entrance to constituted authority, and open wide the back door to idle or prurient curiosity?[2]

To stop this illicit behavior, the two young lawyers proposed that the courts recognize the legal right of privacy; that is, citizens should be able to go to court to stop such unwarranted intrusions and also secure money damages for the hardship they suffered from such prying and from publication of private material about them.

It was 13 years from the time the Warren and Brandeis article was first published until the first state recognized the law of privacy. The state of New York adopted a law that prohibited the commercial exploitation of an individual and called it a right to privacy. Interestingly, the right this new statute sought to safeguard was not even mentioned in the famous Harvard Law Review article.

The law of privacy grew slowly and sporadically over the next 90 years.

The law of privacy grew slowly and sporadically over the next 90 years. All but three states today recognize some kind of legal right to privacy. North Dakota has thus far refused to recognize the tort, and there have been no reported privacy cases in either Vermont or Wyoming.[3] Other states have rejected one or more of the four torts that constitute the modern right to privacy.* And until the European Convention on Human Rights became a part of the law in Western Europe, nations like England and France didn't recognize the invasion-of-privacy tort.

Privacy law is far more idiosyncratic from state to state than is libel law. In other words, it is somewhat easier to make generalizations about libel law that reflect the law in every state or in most states than it is to make these generalizations about the law of privacy. Part of the problem is that some states have protected the right to privacy through statutes, and these often are very particular. The New York statute, for example, is quite explicit about how the right to privacy is protected in that state, and some aspects of the law common in most states are not a part of the New York law.

Today the law of privacy encompasses protection for at least four separate legal wrongs. Three of these have absolutely nothing to do with the law as outlined in 1890 by Warren and Brandeis.

FOUR AREAS OF PRIVACY LAW

1. Appropriation of name or likeness for trade purposes
2. Intrusion upon an individual's solitude
3. Publication of private information about an individual
4. Publishing material that puts an individual in a false light

---

*Several states have rejected the false-light invasion-of-privacy tort, for example, because it is too much like libel. See *Denver Publishing* v. *Bueno,* 54 P. 3d 893 (2002), for example.
2. Warren and Brandeis, "The Right to Privacy," 220.
3. Sanford, *Libel and Privacy.*

The first kind of invasion of privacy is called **appropriation** and is defined as taking a person's name, picture, photograph or likeness and using it for commercial gain without permission. Appropriation is technically the only right of privacy guaranteed in some of the states that have privacy statutes. The laws are limited to outlawing this one kind of behavior. But as a matter of fact, judicial construction of these laws has allowed them to encompass some of the other aspects of invasion of privacy as well.

Intrusion is the second type of invasion of privacy, an area of the law growing rapidly today, and is what most people think of when invasion of privacy is mentioned. Intrusion upon the solitude and into the private life of a person is prohibited.

The third arm of the law prohibits **publication of private information**—truthful private information—about a person. What is truthful private information? Gossip, substance of private conversations, and details of a private tragedy or illness have all been used as the basis of a suit.

Finally, the publication of material that places a person in a **false light** is the fourth category of the law of privacy. This category is an outgrowth of the first area of the law, appropriation, and doesn't at first glance seem like an invasion of privacy at all, but it is regarded as such by the law.

The tremendous growth of communication via interactive computer systems (i.e., the Internet) has generated substantial challenges in the application of the law of privacy. The relative ease of access and use of these systems has resulted in numerous privacy problems. While research indicates many Internet users remain skittish about the safety and security of this communication channel, many users plow on ahead, oblivious to serious privacy problems. In many ways the Internet is just like any other mass communication system. And all four elements of the law of privacy are applicable in the lawsuits that result from claims of invasion of privacy via interactive computer systems. Practically, however, most problems fall under two of the privacy subtorts—intrusion and publication of private information. It is not difficult for outsiders to collect data from Internet users, with and without their knowledge. This can be categorized as intrusion. Similarly, these data can then be published in a variety of ways and for a variety of purposes. This can be regarded as the publication of private information. We will explore these Internet-related problems in the sections of Chapters 7 and 8 that focus on those topics.

A few caveats or warnings are appropriate before each of the four aspects of privacy law is detailed. First, only people enjoy protection for their right to privacy. Corporations, labor unions, associations and so forth can protect their reputations through libel law, but they do not have a right to privacy.* (Other laws protect businesses against unfair commercial exploitation.)

The right to privacy is most easily understood if each of the four areas of the law is considered as a discrete unit. Don't try to apply the defenses that may be applicable in appropriation to publication of private information. They don't work.

There is much about the law of privacy that defies logic. Why is putting someone in a false light considered an invasion of privacy, for example? Challenging the logic of the law serves little purpose and usually makes learning the law more difficult.

---

*See *Felsher* v. *University of Evansville*, 755 N.E. 2d 589 (2001), for example.

The law of privacy is young—just over 115 years old if you start with the Warren and Brandeis proposal. There are a lot of legal questions that haven't been answered, or at least answered satisfactorily. Bad court decisions are abundant. Trial judges rarely see invasion-of-privacy cases; most lawyers are equally distant from the law. If you mix those two elements together, it is not uncommon for courts to render wrong-headed decisions. A trial court in Louisiana once ruled that a house had a right to privacy, for example.

Finally, it is worthwhile to raise the issues of ethics and morality. The following pages provide for journalists, photographers, and advertising and public relations practitioners a kind of road map of how to stay within the law. But these roads aren't necessarily the ones that should be followed at all times. Today, more than ever, many readers and viewers are asking the mass media to exercise restraint in certain areas, restraint that often falls well within the boundaries of what is legal. Journalists would do well to ponder these requests. Publish and be damned is still an appropriate response in some situations. But more often a thoughtful journalist will take a different tack.

APPROPRIATION

It is illegal to appropriate an individual's name or likeness for commercial or trade purposes without consent.

Appropriation is the oldest of the four privacy torts. Until recently it was the most comprehensible. Appropriation protects an individual's name or likeness from commercial exploitation. Two of the earliest privacy cases on record are good examples of how the appropriation tort is supposed to protect an individual from commercial exploitation. In 1902 young Abigail Roberson of Albany, N.Y., awoke one morning to find her picture all over town on posters advertising Franklin Mills Flour. Twenty-five thousand copies of the advertisement had been placed in stores, warehouses, saloons and other public places. Abigail said she felt embarrassed and humiliated, that she suffered greatly from this commercial exploitation, and she therefore sued for invasion of privacy. But she lost her case, and the state's high court ruled that

> an examination of the authorities leads us to the conclusion that the so-called "right of privacy" has not yet found an abiding place in our jurisprudence, and, as we view it, the doctrine cannot now be incorporated without doing violence to settled principles of law by which the profession and the public have long been guided.[4]

Following this decision a great controversy arose in New York, led by newspapers and magazines, many of whom expressed outrage at the way the court had treated Abigail. The controversy settled on the state legislature, which during the following year, 1903, adopted the nation's first privacy law. The statute was very narrow; that is, it prohibited a very specific kind of conduct. Use of an individual's name or likeness without the individual's consent for advertising or trade purposes was made a minor crime. In addition to the criminal penalty, the statute allowed the injured party to seek both an injunction to stop the use of the name or picture and money damages.

4. *Roberson v. Rochester Folding Box Co.,* 171 N.Y. 538 (1902).

Two years later Georgia became the first state to recognize the right of privacy through the common law. Paolo Pavesich, an Atlanta artist, discovered that a life insurance company had used his photograph in newspaper advertisements. Pavesich's photograph was used in a before-and-after advertisement to illustrate a contented, successful man who had bought sufficient life insurance. A testimonial statement was also ascribed to the artist. He sued for $25,000 and won his case before the Georgia Supreme Court, which ruled that

> the form and features of the plaintiff are his own. The defendant insurance company and its agents had no more authority to display them in public for the purpose of advertising the business . . . than they would have had to compel the plaintiff to place himself upon exhibition for this purpose.[5]

RIGHT OF PUBLICITY

The appropriation tort actually encompasses two slightly different legal causes of action. One is the right to privacy, the other is called the **right of publicity.** The differences between these two sound legalistic, but they are actually quite important.

- Traditionally, the right-to-privacy dimension of appropriation was designed to protect an individual from the *emotional damage* that can occur when a name or likeness is used for a commercial or trade purpose. Imagine how embarrassed Abigail Roberson felt the morning she awoke to find her picture on all those advertising posters. The right to publicity, on the other hand, is an attempt to remunerate individuals for the *economic harm* suffered when their name or picture is used for advertising or trade purposes, and they are not compensated for it. The proposition is a simple one: An individual's name or likeness has monetary value, and using it without permission is akin to theft. But the difference between emotional harm and economic harm is sometimes easier to state than to apply.[6]

- The second distinction between the right of privacy and the right of publicity often helps resolve this question. Because the right of publicity protects a property right—the economic value in a name or likeness—only someone whose name or likeness has a commercial value can successfully allege a violation of his or her right of publicity. An average person—Jane Doe, example—would likely be embarrassed to find her picture on a box of Wheaties. But it would be extremely difficult for Jane to argue in court that General Mills was actually promoting its cereal this way because kids all over America want to eat what Jane Doe eats. But kids may want to eat the same cereal that Derek Jeter or Sue Bird eats. The names and pictures of these professional athletes have commercial value and would enhance the value of the cereal (or the cereal box) in the eyes of consumers. Simply put, only well-known persons have a legally recognized economic value in their names or likeness, and except in unusual cases, they are the only ones who can sue for damage to their right to publicity. The average person can only assert emotional damage in a right of privacy suit.

5. *Pavesich* v. *New England Mutual Life Insurance Co.,* 122 Ga. 190 (1905).
6. See *Villalovos* v. *Sundance Associates Inc.,* 31 M.L.R. 1274 (2003), for example.

■ Finally, something that has an economic value, like a house or a painting or a ring, can usually be passed on to an heir when the owner dies. Something of emotional value, like a reputation or mental health, is gone when its owner passes on. Consequently, it is possible in some states for a celebrity or sports star or some other well-known person who has died to pass on the property right in his or her name to his or her heirs. The heirs can sue for violation of the deceased's right to publicity. Lawyers say that the right of publicity is descendible. For the rest of the people, their right to privacy dies when they do.

As noted, the right to privacy is over 100 years old. But the right to publicity is only half that old, and it has been only in recent years as more and more states pass laws to protect this aspect of appropriation that substantial case law has been generated.[7] Today there are probably as many right-to-publicity cases being litigated as right-to-privacy lawsuits. In the following discussion of the appropriation tort, the two—right of publicity and right of privacy—will be intermingled. The law is basically the same; only the damage asserted by the plaintiff in the lawsuit is different.

USE OF NAME OR LIKENESS

Everybody knows what a name is, and it is therefore unnecessary to dwell on that term. It should be noted, however, that stage names, pen names, pseudonyms and so forth count the same as real names in the eyes of the law. If the name of actor-musician Snoop Dogg is used in an advertisement for pizza without his permission, the suit cannot be defended on the basis that because Snoop Dogg's real name is Calvin Broadus, his "name" was not appropriated illegally. Only the names of people are protected under appropriation. The names of businesses, corporations, schools and other "things" are not protected under the law. However, the use of a trade name like Kodak or Crest can create other serious legal problems (see Chapter 14).

What is a likeness? Obviously a photograph, a painting and a sketch—anything that suggests to readers and viewers that the plaintiff is pictured—is a likeness. Federal courts in New York state ruled that a sketch of a black man sitting in the corner of a boxing ring was, for purposes of an invasion-of-privacy suit, the "likeness" of former heavyweight champion Muhammad Ali. The boxer looked a little like Ali, and the sketch was accompanied by a verse that referred to the boxer as "the Greatest."[8] Even something like a statue could be a likeness.

Whether a likeness or representation of a plaintiff has been appropriated is often a jury question. Susan Cohen sued a cosmetics maker in 1984 after the firm published an ad containing what Cohen said was a photo of herself and her daughter bathing in a stream while nude. But only the backs and the sides of the bathers can be seen, and the company argued no appropriation had taken place because the plaintiffs were not identifiable. Cohen's husband said he recognized his wife and daughter, as did friends of the family. A lower court dismissed the suit, ruling that the plaintiff's identities cannot be determined from the picture. But the appellate division of the New York Supreme Court overturned the dismissal. The requirement that a portrait or picture of a plaintiff be appropriated "does not require that there be an identifiable facial representation as a prerequisite to relief," the court said. A jury should decide

7. *Haelan Laboratories, Inc.* v. *Topps Chewing Gum,* 202 F. 2d 866 (1953).
8. *Ali* v. *Playgirl,* 447 F. Supp. 723 (1978).

whether the advertisement contains a recognizable likeness.[9] In January 1997 a U.S. District Court ruled that a baby, photographed as she was carried by a firefighter away from the bombed Alfred P. Murrah Federal Building in Oklahoma City on April 19, 1995, was not identifiable. The judge rejected the plea from the child's mother to bar the use of the photograph for commercial purposes without her consent. The photographer had sold the rights to use the picture to several publications as well as to a T-shirt manufacturer and a commemorative statuette maker.[10]

In recent years celebrities have sought to expand the range of protection under appropriation in a variety of ways. As the people of the nation tend to dwell more on the lives of the rich and famous, the value in the names and likenesses of these media icons has dramatically increased. Some performers have argued that their likeness can include the identity of a film or television character whom they have played for several years. In other words, their real persona has become entwined with the identity of a fictional person, and the commercial use of the fictional persona violates their right to publicity. Some courts have agreed.

For example, the 3rd U.S. Circuit Court of Appeals ruled in 1994 that when a role played by an actor becomes so associated with that actor that it becomes inseparable from the actor's own public image, the actor obtains an interest in this fictional identity. The case involved George McFarland, an actor who as a child played a character called Spanky in a series of short films produced during the Great Depression known as the "Our Gang" comedies. (The series was later shown on television under the title "The Little Rascals.") This role was pretty much McFarland's film career and he became indelibly remembered by movie fans as Spanky. When a restaurant called Spanky McFarland's opened in New Jersey in 1989, the former child actor sued. The eating establishment was filled with Our Gang memorabilia, and the menu featured items named after the characters in the films, for example, Spanky's Steak Sandwich. A lower court ruled that McFarland had no proprietary right in the identity of the Spanky character since it was, after all, a fictional person. But the appellate court reversed and said there was clearly a triable issue of fact as to whether the actor had become so identified with the character that the use of that name in a commercial venture would invoke McFarland's own image.[11]

The 9th U.S. Circuit Court of Appeals reached the same conclusion three years later when it reversed a summary judgment granted to Host International, which had installed animatronic robots that resembled "Cheers" patrons Norm Peterson and Cliff Clavin in airport bars designed to look like the set of the long-running television comedy. Host named the figures Bob and Hank. The company said that since Paramount owned the copyright to the characters as well as the set design, actors George Wendt (Norm) and John Ratzenberger (Cliff) could not claim that their identities had been appropriated. The appellate court sent the case back for trial, stating that an actor or actress does not lose the right to control the commercial exploitation of his or her likeness merely by portraying a fictional character owned by someone else.[12]

Other celebrities have argued, some successfully, that their right to publicity is violated when businesses use in their advertisements people who look or sound like the real celebrities.

9. *Cohen* v. *Herbal Concepts,* 473 N.Y.S. 2d 426 (1989).
10. Queary, "Mother Denied Say," A8.
11. *McFarland* v. *Miller,* 14 F. 3d 912 (1994).
12. *Wendt* v. *Host International,* 125 F. 3d 800 (1997).

The growing public fascination with celebrities has generated a small growth industry in the use of so-called look-alikes and soundalikes. All that some talent agencies do is provide actors and actresses of this ilk for everything from appearances in television and magazine ads to cocktail parties. The legal aspect of this development first reached the courts in the 1980s when an actress named Barbara Reynolds, a woman who bears a striking resemblance to the late Jackie Kennedy Onassis, was featured in a Christian Dior ad, along with three real celebrities. Reynolds was made up and dressed to look like Onassis, who sued, arguing that her likeness had been appropriated for the advertisement. The New York State trial court agreed, noting that the law prohibits the use of a representation "which conveys the essence and likeness of an individual." Reynolds, as Reynolds, could pose for ads or make public appearances, but she could not attempt to convey the appearance of someone else, someone much better known.[13] Phil Boroff, who might easily be mistaken for Woody Allen, appeared in several ads for firms like National Video and Men's World. In April 1986 he appeared in a Men's World ad in Newsday holding a clarinet, very reminiscent of the character played by Allen in the film "Annie Hall." Beneath the photo, in small, lightfaced type, were these words:"This is a Ron Smith celebrity look-alike." Allen sued. A U.S. District Court ruled that despite the disclaimer and despite the fact that it was Phil Boroff, not Woody Allen, in the photo, "the use of Boroff's photograph in their [Men's World] advertisement creates a likelihood of consumer confusion over plaintiff's endorsement or involvement."[14] A bigger, bolder disclaimer might have solved the legal problem, the judge ruled.

Contemporary advertising strategies include the notion of attempting to build an emotional bond between the product and the consumer, to suggest a sharing of values. Advertisers have found that the use within television and radio ads of songs that were popular at the time members of the target audience came of age will invoke favorable memories among the viewers and the listeners; a great summer trip, a special prom, a wedding day. But many performers are reluctant to re-perform the song in a commercial. So the advertiser sometimes does the next best thing and hires another artist to imitate the singer's original performance. The ad may or may not include a disclaimer, "celebrity voice impersonator."

Singer Bette Midler was the first to go to court because of such an impersonation. She sued the Ford Motor Company and its ad agency, Young & Rubicam, for using a "soundalike" to imitate a song—"Do You Want to Dance?"—that she made popular in the 1970s. (The Beach Boys originally made the song popular in the 1960s.) The agency first asked Midler to do the commercial, but she refused. The agency then hired a performer who had worked as a backup singer for Midler for 10 years to imitate Midler's performance.

The U.S. Court of Appeals for the 9th Circuit ruled in favor of Midler and sustained a jury verdict of $400,000 against Young & Rubicam. "The singer manifests herself in the song. To impersonate her voice is to pirate her identity," the court ruled. Not every voice imitation to advertise goods is necessarily actionable, the court noted; however, "we hold that when a distinctive voice of a professional singer is widely known and is deliberately imitated in order to sell a product, the sellers have appropriated what is not theirs and committed a tort in California."[15]

In the wake of the Midler ruling, other performers sought to block similar voice impersonations in commercials. Singer Tom Waits successfully sued Frito-Lay for using an

---

13. *Onassis* v. *Christian Dior,* 472 N.Y.S. 2d 254 (1984).
14. *Allen* v. *Men's World Outlet,* 679 F. Supp. 360 (1988).
15. *Midler* v. *Ford Motor Co.,* 849 F. 2d 460 (1988).

impersonator to imitate him on a commercial jingle for Salso Rio Dorito corn chips. The jingle was a copy of Waits' hit song "Step Right Up." A jury awarded the singer $2.5 million. Performers Chris Isaak, Mitch Ryder and Carlos Santana also sought to stop similar voice impersonations. A variety of legal strategies were used by the plaintiffs in these cases. Midler won her case using a California statute that specifically prohibits the misappropriation of an individual's "voice" or "likeness" for advertising or selling without the individual's consent. Waits used the federal Lanham Act (see pages 632–633), a statute that prohibits unfair competition. To win, Waits had to prove that he had a distinctive voice that was recognizable by the public and that the advertiser attempted to pass off the commercial as being performed by the singer. Jurors had to find that they recognized Waits' voice in the commercial, not merely that they thought it was Waits' voice because he had popularized the song used in the jingle.*

The power of the right of publicity to protect identity as well as name and likeness was demonstrated in 1992 when a federal court ruled in favor of game show hostess Vanna White in her "look-alike" suit against Korean electronics manufacturer Samsung. White, of course, is the very recognizable woman whose claim to fame is lighting up letters on the game board of one of America's most popular syndicated television quiz shows, "Wheel of Fortune." Samsung Electronics America and its advertising agency developed a campaign in the early 1990s that tried to suggest that while lots of things in our society might change or become dated, Samsung products would remain state-of-the-art despite the passage of time. The ads featured two illustrations purporting to display items from the 21st century. One would contain a picture of a Samsung product like a VCR, the other a humorous message. One ad, for example, had a picture of a raw beefsteak with the caption, "Revealed to be health food, 2010 A.D."

White sued Samsung for publishing an ad that included a photo-parody of the celebrated letter turner. Near the center of the color photo was a robot, reminiscent of C3PO of "Star Wars" fame, decked out in a blond wig, evening dress and jewelry, standing next to a video board with large letters on it. Beneath the illustration was the caption, "Longest running game show, 2012 A.D." The joke in the parody ad was that Samsung products would still be around after Vanna White had been replaced by a robot on "Wheel of Fortune." A lower court dismissed the lawsuit, but the 9th U.S. Circuit Court of Appeals reinstated the action, ruling that the use of the image of the formally dressed robot in the advertisement surely could effectively "eviscerate" White's right to publicity. "The identities of the most popular celebrities are not only the most attractive for advertisers, but the easiest to evoke without resorting to obvious means such as a name or likeness or voice," the court ruled.[16] Performers need to be protected from such exploitation.

Is an advertiser who seeks to create the illusion of a celebrity with a look-alike or a voice impersonator protected from an appropriation suit if the ad contains a disclaimer? Yes, if the disclaimer is prominent in the ad. Small type at the bottom of a full-page newspaper ad will not do the trick, nor will an audio disclaimer camouflaged by music or noise in a radio spot.

A phrase that hasn't been used yet in this discussion is "the First Amendment." Do the limits placed on the use of celebrity likenesses in any way have an impact on freedom of

---

*Waits continues to fight for the right to his voice. In January 2006 he won a lawsuit against the Audi division of Volkswagen, and still had a suit pending against the Opel division of General Motors.

16. *White* v. *Samsung Electronics America, Inc.,* 971 F. 2d 1395 (1992); rehearing den. 989 F. 2d 1512 (1992).

expression? If this question was even raised, until recently it really hasn't seemed to trouble the courts. But in two rulings judges have wondered aloud for the first time whether in some instances increasing the protection of the images of performers and athletes isn't at the same time prohibiting those who appropriate these images from using their constitutional rights to comment on these performers and athletes. In 1996 the 10th U.S. Circuit Court of Appeals was faced with a lawsuit based on what was arguably a commercial parody. A company called Cardtoons had published since 1992 a series of baseball cards that feature caricatures of well-known major league baseball players. The back of the cards contained humorous commentary. The card depicting Barry Bonds of the San Francisco Giants, for example, carried a recognizable likeness of Bonds on the front, with the name Treasury Bonds of the Gents. The commentary on the back of the card described Treasury Bonds and focused on his high salary and his interest in money. Ricky Henderson of the Oakland Athletics was referred to as Egotisticky Henderson of the Pathetics.

The court ruled that the cards were parodies, social commentary on popular American celebrities, and protected by the First Amendment.

The Major League Baseball Players Association sued to block distribution of the cards. The suit alleged, among other things, that the cards violated the ballplayers' right to publicity. Their likenesses were used for commercial purposes without their consent. The lower court ruled in favor of Cardtoons and the Court of Appeals affirmed. The court ruled that the cards were parodies, social commentary on popular American celebrities, and protected by the First Amendment. "While not core political speech . . . this type of commentary on an important social institution constitutes protected expression," Judge Tacha wrote.[17] The players association argued that this case was identical to *White* v. *Samsung* and that the same outcome was warranted. Judge Tacha disagreed, noting that the White case involved an advertisement for a product and this case did not. But that didn't matter, the judge wrote, because he and his colleagues disagreed with the result of the earlier case. The court stressed the importance of parody and said that the Major League Baseball Players Association would never consent to a parody of its members. "Because celebrities are an important part of our public vocabulary, a parody of a celebrity does not merely lampoon the celebrity, but exposes weakness of the idea or value that the celebrity symbolizes in society," Judge Tacha added.

In 2001 the California Supreme Court was faced with a more blatant example of the piracy of a performer's image, but still raised the First Amendment issue in deciding the matter. Because it is the home of the so-called American Dream Factory, California has a comprehensive statute that protects images and names of celebrities. An artist named Gary Saderup created a charcoal drawing of the Three Stooges comedy team. Making a single drawing is not a problem since the law exempts single and original works of fine art from the purview of the statute. But Saderup went on to create lithographic prints and T-shirts that also contained the drawing and was sued by Comedy III Inc., a company that owns the rights to the Stooges. Justices on the California high court noted immediately the First Amendment implications in the issue. "Because celebrities take on public meaning, the appropriation of their likenesses may have important uses in uninhibited debate on public issues, particularly debates about culture and values," the court noted. The creative appropriation of celebrity images can be an important avenue of individual expression, the justices added. The importance of celebrities in society means that the right to publicity has the potential of censoring significant expression by suppressing alternative versions of celebrity images that are "iconoclastic, irrelevant,

17. *Cardtoons* v. *Major League Baseball Players Association,* 95 F. 3d 959 (1996).

Source: © Columbia/The Kobal Collection

The comedy team of the Three Stooges was the focus of a California lawsuit based on the right to publicity.

or otherwise attempt to redefine the celebrity's image." There must be a test, then, that takes these values into account, the justices went on. The court focused on what is called the transformative elements in the reproduction. If the reproduction is simply a literal translation of the celebrity's image, then the First Amendment concerns are surely minimal. But it is a different matter if the user has added other elements to the image, has transformed the image into a parody, used the name in a song, lampooned the prominent person, or in some way used the celebrity's likeness as a vehicle for the expression of opinion or ideas. Then the rights of free expression take precedence over the right of the celebrity to protect his or her right to publicity. In this case, the court said, Saderup used a literal depiction of the Stooges for commercial gain without adding significant expression beyond his trespass on the right to publicity. He was guilty of violating the law.[18]

The 6th U.S. Court of Appeals, citing both the Cardtoons and Saderup decisions, ruled in 2003 that artist Rick Rush did not violate Tiger Woods' right to publicity when he painted a picture of the golfer commemorating his 1997 Master's golf tournament victory. The picture featured Woods in the foreground and six other golfing greats in the background. Rush produced 250 limited edition serigraphs, which he sold for $700 each, and 5,000 smaller lithographs, which were priced at $15 each. He was sued by ETW Corporation, which holds

---

18. *Comedy III Inc.* v. *Gary Saderup Inc.,* 21 P. 3d 797 (2001). The Supreme Court of the United States refused to hear an appeal of this ruling.

the exclusive marketing rights to Woods, for trademark infringement and violation of the golfer's right to publicity. (The court held a person's image or likeness cannot function as a trademark. See Chapter 14 for more on trademark law.) As for the right to publicity, the court said Rush's work was creative and transformative, and this made it worthy of First Amendment protection. The substantial creative content in the work outweighed any adverse effect on ETW's market.[19]

ADVERTISING AND TRADE PURPOSES

What are advertising and trade purposes? While minor differences exist among the states—especially among the states with statutes—a general guideline can be set down: Advertising or trade purposes are commercial uses; that is, someone makes money from the use. Here are examples of the kinds of actions that may be regarded as a commercial use:

1. **Use of a person's name or photograph in an *advertisement* on television, on radio, in newspapers, in magazines, on the Internet, on posters, on billboards and so forth. Rapper 50 Cent sued a Philadelphia car dealer for $1 million in 2005 for using his name in an ad for a Dodge Magnum. The ads used the Slogan, "Just Like 50 Says."**

2. **Display of a person's photograph in the window of a photographer's shop to show potential customers the quality of work done by the studio.**

3. **A testimonial falsely suggesting that an individual eats the cereal or drives the automobile in question.**

4. **Use of an individual's name or likeness in a banner ad or some other commercial message on a Web site.**

5. **The use of someone's likeness or identity in a commercial entertainment vehicle like a feature film, a television situation comedy or a novel.**

Numerous court cases document liability outlined in these uses. For example, in 1992 the former wife of National Football League Hall of Fame running back John Riggins decided to sell the house the two had lived in, a home she had won as a part of the divorce settlement. As a real estate agent she created a brochure that used John Riggins' name in several spots to advertise the house. The Virginia Supreme Court ruled that this was a commercial purpose and sustained the award of more than $50,000 to the former NFL star.[20] Sometimes the use is more oblique. After Third Coast Entertainment Inc. obtained an option on the film rights of an unauthorized biography of Priscilla Presley, the wife of Elvis Presley and a celebrity in her own right, the company attempted to generate interest in the possible video production by suggesting that Presley would work with them on preparing a film. Press releases included headlines that said Presley had been offered a consultant role on the film, something that wasn't true. The suggestion of her willingness to participate in the production certainly enhanced the potential value of the project, since the film would have been difficult if not impossible to produce without her cooperation. The California Court of Appeals said this was a commercial use

19. *ETW Corp.* v. *Jireh Publishing Inc.,* 6th Cir. No. 00-3584, 6/20/03. See also Chambers, "Case of Art, Icons and Law."
20. *Town & Country Properties, Inc.* v. *Riggins,* 457 S.E. 2d 356 (1995).

Source: Photofest

of her name without her consent. Truthful use of a celebrity's name in advertising that is merely an adjunct to a legitimate film or book, and only promotes the work itself, is protected, the court ruled. In this case, the use was merely an attempt to generate publicity for Third Coast Entertainment and its efforts to promote the project.[21]

The kinds of uses outlined in Example 5 pose the most complicated legal problems because of the varied circumstances involved. And courts often have difficulty sorting through these circumstances to arrive at consistent decisions. What if a producer just happens to pick the name of a real person for use in a television program? Michael Costanza sued Jerry Seinfeld and others for use of the name Costanza in the successful situation comedy. But the fictional character was named George and the plaintiff's full name or photo was never associated with the show. The similarity of the plaintiff's last name and the fictional character did not amount to an illegal appropriation, the New York court ruled.[22] A Michigan case presented a far more complicated problem. NBC aired a docudrama depicting the story of the popular singing group, the Temptations. The estate of David Ruffin, the lead singer in the group from 1964 to 1968, sued, claiming that by depicting Ruffin in the film the producers had appropriated his identity and violated the right to publicity. The U.S. District Court ruled against

Popular television programs like "Seinfeld" are often sued by individuals who claim their identity is reflected in a character on the program. Jason Alexander, second from the left, played George Costanza, the target of just such a lawsuit.

21. *Presley* v. *Grant,* 31 M.L.R. 1385 (2002).
22. *Costanza* v. *Seinfeld,* 719 N.Y.S. 2d 29 (2001).

Ruffin's heir, ruling that the depiction of a person's life even in an entertainment film is not a violation of the right to publicity. The term "likeness" does not include general incidents from a person's life, the court said. The narrative of an individual's life standing alone lacks the value of a name or likeness that the appropriation tort protects.[23] And in 2005 the Florida Supreme Court ruled that the state's commercial misappropriation statute did not apply to a motion picture or any other use that does not "directly" promote a product or service. The children of two of the crew members of the Andrea Gail, the fishing boat that was lost during "The Perfect Storm" sued Time Warner for using the names of the men in the feature film of the same name without permission. The fact that the motion picture was created for profit did not warrant defining the term "commercial purpose" in the statute to include a motion picture, the court said.[24] But caution should be exercised in such cases as a cause of action for false light privacy might be generated because the events included in the film have been fictionalized in some manner. (See pages 335–337.)

NEWS AND INFORMATION EXCEPTION

What about this argument? A newspaper runs a photograph of John Smith on the front page after his car rolled over several times during a high-speed police pursuit. Smith sues for invasion of privacy, arguing that his picture on the front page of the newspaper attracted readers to the paper, resulted in the sale of newspapers, and therefore was used for commercial or trade purposes. Despite the arguments of many persons—even today—courts have consistently rejected this claim.

This plea was first made in 1907 by a New Yorker who objected to having his picture appear on the front page of the New York World. The state Supreme Court rejected the argument, noting that surely the intent of the state legislature was not to prohibit a newspaper or magazine from publishing people's names or pictures in a single issue without their consent. Two years later another New York court reiterated this stand, ruling that advertising and trade purposes referred to commercial use, not to the dissemination of information.[25] The U.S. Supreme Court has ruled that the fact that newspapers and books and magazines are sold for profit does not deny them the protection of liberty of expression.[26]

Asking 15 different judges what is news or what is information could very likely result in getting 15 different answers. This is especially true today when much of what passes for news is really provided as entertainment. A New Jersey appellate judge recently noted this problem when he wrote, "It is neither feasible nor desirable to make a distinction between news for information and news for entertainment in determining the extent to which the publication is privileged." This was a case where several individuals who had been admitted to an emergency room at a hospital were videotaped for a television program, "Trauma: Life in the ER," which was telecast on The Learning Channel. (The fact that all had signed consent forms

---

23. *Ruffin-Steinbeck* v. *de Passe*, 82 F. Supp. 2d 723 (2000), aff'd. 267 F. 3d 457 (2001).
24. *Tyne* v. *Time Warner Entertainment Co.*, 901 S.2d 802 (2005); 33 M.L.R. 2318 (2005).
25. *Moser* v. *Press Publishing Co.*, 109 N.Y.S. 963 (1908); *Jeffries* v. *New York Evening Journal*, 124 N.Y.S. 780 (1910).
26. *Time, Inc.* v. *Hill*, 385 U.S. 374 (1967). See *Small* v. *WTMJ Television Station*, 542 N.W. 2d 239 (1995) for a recent statement of this rule.

before the taping seriously undercut their cases, which they lost.) Nevertheless, the court ruled the production was privileged: It was not a commercial use.[27] It is fair to say that most judges have a fairly broad view of the news and information exception and don't insist that only stories about politics, economics, the environment or international affairs qualify.

A California Court of Appeals recently dismissed a lawsuit by a man who complained about the broadcast of an episode of the television show "Cops" in which he was filmed talking to Los Angeles County Sheriff's deputies after he was assaulted by someone from whom he was trying to buy drugs. Police didn't detain him, but the conversation was aired many times in the program. (His face was obscured, but his voice was not altered.) The court ruled that the law exempts news broadcasts, and other public affairs programming, and this use fell under that exemption.[28] In another case a 14-year-old Florida girl posed for a series of pictures that she believed would appear in Young and Modern, a magazine aimed at teenage girls. The photos appeared in a 1995 edition of the publication, but not exactly in the context the young model expected. They illustrated a regularly published column called Love Crisis. In this edition a 14-year-old letter writer told the columnist she had gotten drunk at a party and had sex with three different boys. What should I do? she asked. Don't do it again, the advice columnist replied, and be sure to get tested for both sexually transmitted diseases and pregnancy. The column was headlined, "I got trashed and had sex with three guys," and three photos of the plaintiff were used to illustrate the letter. She alleged the photos were published for commercial purposes, but the New York Court of Appeals disagreed. The article was newsworthy, the court said. It was not an advertisement in disguise. The fact that a publication may have used the photos primarily to enhance the value of the magazine by increasing its circulation did not mean that the photos were used for purposes of trade.[29]

The "Cops" show and the teen magazine are just two examples of the merger in contemporary mass media of news and entertainment. An even greater problem in privacy law is the convergence of information and marketing. The close association between advertising and the content of publications or television programs raises real questions about whether a particular use should be considered an exemption to the general prohibition against a commercial use. Two recent cases make the point.

Actor Dustin Hoffman sued a Los Angeles magazine in 1999 for using his photo in a fashion feature called Grand Illusions. Using computer imaging technology, the magazine combined still photos of actresses and actors (both living and dead) with photos of contemporary models wearing the latest fashions by many designers who were advertisers in the magazine. But the photo feature was not an advertisement; it was editorial copy. Hoffman's picture was taken from a publicity still used to publicize the film "Tootsie," in which the actor is made up like a woman. Hoffman's face and head was attached to the body of a female model and the new photo appeared over this caption: "Dustin Hoffman isn't a drag in a butter-colored silk gown by Richard Tyler and Ralph Lauren heels." A trial court ruled that the use of the photo was for commercial purposes, but the 9th U.S. Circuit Court of Appeals disagreed. "Viewed in context the article as a whole is a combination of fashion photography, humor, and visual and verbal editorial content on classic films and famous actors. Any commercial aspects

27. *Castro* v. *NYT Television,* 32 M.L.R. 2555 (2004).
28. *Ingerson* v. *Twentieth Century Fox Film Corp.,* 31 M.L.R. 1289 (2003).
29. *Messenger* v. *Gruner + Jahr Printing and Publishing,* 94 N.Y. 2d 436 (2000).

are 'inextricably entwined' with expressive elements and so they cannot be separated out 'from the fully protected whole,'" the court ruled.[30]

About the same time the Hoffman case was decided, the same U.S. Court of Appeals was faced with a somewhat similar fact situation. In this case the plaintiff's likeness was used in a 250-page Abercrombie & Fitch quarterly clothing catalog. Each issue of the retailer's catalog has a theme and contains information as well as product descriptions. The issue in question focused on the sport of surfing and included stories about famous California surfing venues and other similar material. The plaintiff's photo had been taken in 1965 and was printed adjacent to a page offering T-shirts for sale, shirts similar to the ones worn by surfers in the 1960s. In this case the court said the catalog at issue was a sales catalog and was published to sell Abercrombie & Fitch merchandise. This was unlike the feature article that was the genesis of the Hoffman lawsuit. The court didn't categorize the use of the photo as "commercial speech," but said it was far more commercial than the use of Hoffman's photo in Los Angeles Magazine. The publishers of the magazine had done nothing to try to connect the photo to the information articles in the catalog. The court called the use "window dressing" that would not justify the application of the information exemption under the law.[31]

OTHER EXCEPTIONS

The doctrine of incidental use, for example, is recognized in many jurisdictions and permits a fleeting or brief use of an individual's name or likeness in some kinds of commercial creations.

The right to publish or broadcast an individual's name or likeness for news and information purposes is a broad exception to the appropriation rule. Other courts have found other exceptions as well, but this is where the law of privacy gets a little dicey. Not all courts view the same actions as exceptions to the appropriation rule. The doctrine of incidental use, for example, is recognized in many jurisdictions and permits a fleeting or brief use of an individual's name or likeness in some kinds of commercial creations. A U.S. District Court in California said that the use of a retired actress's name and likeness in advertising for videos of two feature films in which she had appeared 30 years earlier was incidental to the release of the videos themselves. The use of her image and name in the video was protected by a release she had signed when she made the original movies.[32] A brief filmed scene of a pedestrian walking on the street that ends up in a feature motion picture may not support an action for appropriation either. A U.S. District Court in New York rejected Pamela Preston's claim that her likeness had been appropriated when she appeared for a total of nine seconds walking on a New York street in a scene that ran behind the opening credits of the film "Sea of Love." "The doctrine of incidental use was developed to address concerns that penalizing every unauthorized use, no matter how insignificant or fleeting, of a person's name or likeness would impose undue burdens on expressive activity," the court ruled.[33] In 1994 a federal court in New York ruled that it was an incidental use when publisher Random House used, without permission, the names and photographs of five other authors in advertising for its book on the Kennedy assassination, "Case Closed" by Gerald Posner. In his book Posner argued that the conspiracy theories proposed by

---

30. *Hoffman* v. *Capital Cities/ABC Inc.,* 33 F. Supp. 2d 867 (1999), rev'd. 255 F. 3d 1180 (2001).
31. *Downing* v. *Abercrombie & Fitch,* 265 F. 3d 994 (2001).
32. *Page* v. *Something Weird Video,* 25 M.L.R. 1489 (1996).
33. *Preston* v. *Martin Bregman Productions, Inc.,* 765 F. Supp. 116 (1991). See also *University of Notre Dame* v. *20th Century Fox,* 22 App. Div. 2d 452, 15 N.Y.S. 2d 907 (1962).

the five pictured authors were bogus. The headline "Guilty of Misleading the American Public" was above the pictures. The court acknowledged that this case was somewhat unusual, in that earlier applications of the incidental use doctrine in this regard had generally related to the media's reuse of previously published material for the purposes of self-promotion. (This is called the *Booth* rule; see the following section.) "Nonetheless," Judge Martin said, "it is clear that what drives the exception is a First Amendment interest in protecting the ability of the media to publicize its own communications."[34] But remember, courts in different states may take a decidedly different view of the arguments that seem so persuasive here.

Booth *Rule*

The *Booth* rule is closely related to the incidental use doctrine; in fact, some courts refer to it as part of that doctrine. The rule has developed slowly over the past 40 years and today provides fairly broad protection to the mass media in most states if an individual's name or likeness is used in advertising for a particular information medium. In other words, the use of a person's name or likeness in an advertisement *for* a magazine or a newspaper or a television program is usually not regarded as an appropriation if the photograph or name has been or will be a part of the medium's news or information content.

The controversy that sparked this rule involved Academy Award–winning actress Shirley Booth.* She was photographed in Jamaica, and the picture was published in a feature story in Holiday magazine. Holiday then used the same picture to advertise the magazine itself. The full-page advertisement told readers that the picture was typical of the material appearing in Holiday magazine and urged people to advertise in the periodical or subscribe to Holiday. Ms. Booth did not object to her photograph in the feature story, only to its use in the subsequent advertisement. The courts, however, refused to call the use an invasion of privacy. The New York Supreme Court ruled that the maintenance of freedom of expression depends in no small part on the economic support of the press by advertisers and subscribers. And to win such support a publication or broadcasting station must be able to promote itself. Since the picture in this case was first used in an information story, its subsequent use in a promotion for the magazine was really only incidental to its original use and was merely to show the quality and content of the magazine. The picture was not used to sell spaghetti or used cars. Hence the use did not constitute an invasion of privacy.[35]

Originally it was believed that the *Booth* rule protected only the *republication* or *rebroadcast* of material previously used in the medium. And some courts still follow this rule. But other courts have enunciated a broader protection. For example, a U.S. District Court ruled that it is permissible for a newspaper or magazine to use previously published material in a television advertisement for the publication.[36] That is, a name or likeness that appeared in a newspaper story can be *republished* in a television advertisement for that newspaper. In New Jersey a woman was photographed as a part of a television news story on the dangers of smoking in the presence of infants. Her photo was used in station promotions for the news story, but

---

*Ms. Booth won an Oscar as Best Actress in 1952 for her role in the film "Come Back Little Sheba."
34. *Groden* v. *Random House Inc.*, 22 M.L.R. 2257 (1994), aff'd. 61 F. 3d 1045 (1995).
35. *Booth* v. *Curtis Publishing Co.*, 11 N.Y.S. 2d 907 (1962).
36. *Friedan* v. *Friedan*, 414 F. Supp. 77 (1976).

her comments and picture were cut from the story when it was broadcast. The court ruled that this use still was an incidental and protected use.[37] In 1995 the New York Supreme Court ruled that the use of radio personality Howard Stern's photo without his permission in advertisements for an online service was not an invasion of privacy under this incidental republication rule. After Stern announced he was a candidate for the job of governor of New York, the Delphi online service set up a bulletin board for debates on his political candidacy. It used an outlandish photo of Stern (which he had earlier posed for) showing him with bare buttocks. The picture appeared in ads in New York Magazine and the New York Post with the caption, "Should this man be the next governor of New York?" Readers were invited to debate the issue on the bulletin board. Stern argued that Delphi wasn't a news or information medium like a newspaper or magazine and shouldn't be allowed to raise the incidental republication exception. The court disagreed, stating that the online service is analogous to news vendors, bookstores, letters to the editor and other news disseminators.[38] No one yet knows just how far the courts will go in extending the *Booth* rule. The tendency, however, seems to be to expand the protection rather than restrict it.

Clearly the use of a name or photo to promote a medium cannot be an explicit or even implied endorsement of the medium. Cher won a lawsuit against Forum magazine after it used her photo to promote an edition of the publication. The advertisements clearly implied that the actress-singer endorsed Forum, which was not true. That issue of the magazine did contain an interview with Cher, but the court ruled that the advertisements went far beyond establishing the news content and quality of the publication for potential readers.[39]

Finally, the use of an individual's name or likeness in a political advertisement is not regarded as an appropriation. A campaign advertisement that says "Vote for Jones, not Smith," would not give Smith a legal right to sue for appropriation. The use of an individual's name or likeness in an issue-oriented advertisement such as "Save the Whales" or "Stop Racism" likewise would not sustain an appropriation lawsuit. What about the use of a name or likeness in an advertisement or promotion for a nonprofit organization like the YMCA or the Red Cross? Many such groups put out brochures or pamphlets to stimulate donations to further their community work. Would the unauthorized use of the picture of a child swimming in the pool at the YMCA sustain a lawsuit? That is unlikely, but the 6th U.S. Circuit Court of Appeals did uphold a small damage award to a child whose picture was used without permission in a direct mail solicitation by a Kentucky religious order. The Little Sisters of the Assumption Order included the photo with a letter that was sent to 125,000 homes asking for donations for the poor. The appellate court affirmed the lower court award of $100 in damages for appropriation.[40] And the New York Supreme Court came to a similar conclusion in 1995 when it found that the use of an individual's photo on a solicitation by a nonprofit corporation, the Community Service Society of New York, was an advertisement under the terms of the New York privacy statute. The defendant had used the plaintiff's picture in its newsletter aimed at soliciting funds for needy New Yorkers.[41] These two cases stand alone at present, but suggest that caution should

37. *Linder* v. *Capital Cities ABC Inc.,* 27 M.L.R. 2375 (1999).
38. *Stern* v. *Delphi Internet Services Corp.,* 626 N.Y.S. 2d 694 (1995).
39. *Cher* v. *Forum International,* 692 F. 2d 634 (1982).
40. *Bowling* v. *The Missionary Servants of the Most Holy Trinity,* 972 F. 2d 346 (1992).
41. *Vinales* v. *Community Service Society of New York, Inc.,* 23 M.L.R. 1638 (1995).

be exercised by any organization, commercial or otherwise, that seeks to use the names and faces of real people in fund-raising efforts. The simplest solution to the problem is to get consent from these persons.

CONSENT AS A DEFENSE

The law prohibits only the unauthorized use of a name or likeness for commercial or trade purposes. States with privacy statutes usually require that written authorization or consent be given before the use. The rule in the states that follow the common law is less specific with regard to the need for written consent. But in any legal action the defendant is going to have to prove that he or she had consent to use the name or photograph. Written consent is usually uncontestable and will stand as a solid defense against an appropriation claim, even if the plaintiff argues that he or she didn't really understand what he or she was signing. When a photographer took pictures of professional tennis player Anastasia Myskina, the athlete signed a consent form, or release, permitting Conde Nast publishers to include the photos in the 2002 sports issue of GQ magazine. But she sued the magazine for invasion of privacy, claiming that the magazine appropriated her likeness when it used the photos in ways she did not approve of or anticipate. In their defense the magazine raised the matter of the consent form she had signed. She said she misunderstood the document she signed; English was not her first language. A federal court said her assertion—even if true—was irrelevant. When a party signs a contract, which a release is, she is bound by the terms of the contract, whether or not she understood it, whether or not she read it.[42] Attempts to convince a court that oral consent was given can be met by the plaintiff's denial, and then the fact finder will have to decide who is telling the truth. Also, oral consent can be withdrawn up to the moment of publication or broadcast.

The consent issue is most easily resolved if the subject has signed a model release similar to the one printed on page 296. But such legal documents are not always required to establish consent. Two rulings make this point. Sam and Joseph Schifano sued the Greene County Greyhound Park, a dog racing track, for including their photo in an advertising brochure for the facility. The plaintiffs, who visited the park often, were photographed while they sat with several other persons in what is called The Winner's Circle, a section of the park that can be reserved by interested groups of spectators. There was no written consent for the use of their picture, but there was ample evidence that park officials had told the plaintiffs why they were taking the photos and gave them a chance to leave if they did not want to be in the picture. "Plaintiffs, neither by objecting nor moving, when those options were made available by park employees, consented to having their photograph taken at the Park," the Alabama Supreme Court ruled in 1993.[43]

A year later the 9th U.S. Circuit Court of Appeals handed down a similar ruling in a lawsuit involving a popular television situation comedy called "Evening Shade." Country music songwriter and performer Wood Newton sued the producers of the program because the lead character in the show, played by Burt Reynolds, was also named Wood Newton. The creator of the program, Linda Bloodworth-Thomason, grew up in the same town as the real Wood Newton, and there are some similarities between the real and fictional characters. Newton

The law prohibits only the unauthorized use of a name or likeness for commercial or trade purposes.

42. *Myskina* v. *Conde Nast Publications Inc.,* 33 M.L.R. 2199 (2005).
43. *Schifano* v. *Greene County Greyhound Park, Inc.,* 624 So. 178 (1993).

never signed a release for the use of his name, but when the program was first telecast he sent a letter to the producers that said, "I want you to know that I'm flattered that you are using my name, everyone who I've talked to thinks it's exciting and so do I." The lawsuit was filed many months later, after the producers of the program had rejected music that Newton had written and submitted for use on the program. "Although Newton never uttered the words 'I consent,' it is obvious that he did consent," the court ruled.[44]

MODEL RELEASE OR CONSENT FORM USED BY A PHOTOGRAPHER

For and in consideration of my engagement as a model/subject by (insert photographer's name), hereafter referred to as the photographer, on terms or fee hereinafter stated, I hereby give the photographer, his/her legal representatives, and assigns, those for whom the photographer is acting, and those acting with his/her permission, or his/her employees, the right and permission to copyright and/or use, reuse, and/or publish, and republish photographic pictures or portraits of me, or in which I may be distorted in character, or form, in conjunction with my own or a fictitious name, on reproductions thereof in color, or black and white made through any media by the photographer at his/her studio or elsewhere, for any purpose whatsoever; including the use of any printed matter in conjunction therewith.

I hereby waive any right to inspect or approve the finished photograph or advertising copy of printed matter that may be used in conjunction therewith or to the eventual use that it might be applied.

I hereby release, discharge and agree to save harmless the photographer, his/her representatives, assigns, employees or any person or persons, corporation or corporations, acting under his/her permission or authority, or any person, persons, corporation or corporations, for whom he/she might be acting, including any firm publishing and/or distributing the finished product, in whole or in part, from and against any liability as a result of any distortion, blurring, or alteration, optical illusion, or use in composite form, either intentionally or otherwise, that may occur or be produced in the taking, or processing or reproduction of the finished product, its publication or distribution of the same, even should the same subject me to ridicule, scandal, reproach, scorn, or indignity.

When Consent Won't Work

There are times when even written consent does not work as a defense, and the media must be aware of such situations:

1. **Consent given today may not be valid in the distant future, especially if it is gratuitous oral consent.** In Louisiana a man named Cole McAndrews gave permission to the owner of a health spa to use his before-and-after pictures in

---

44. *Newton* v. *Thomason,* 22 F. 3d 1455 (1994). But express oral or written consent is required under some state right-of-publicity statutes. See, for example, *Bosley* v. *Wildwet T. Com,* 310 F. Supp. 2d 914 (2004), rev'd. on other grounds, 32 M.L.R. 1641 (2004).

advertisements for the gym. But the owner, Alvin Roy, waited 10 years to use the photographs, and in the interim McAndrews' life had changed considerably. He sued Roy, who argued that it was McAndrews' responsibility to revoke the consent if he no longer wanted the pictures used. But a Louisiana court of appeals agreed instead with the plaintiff. Judge Robert D. Jones wrote:

> We are of the opinion that it would be placing an unreasonable burden on the plaintiff to hold he was under duty to revoke a gratuitous authorization given many years before. As the defendant was the only person to profit from the use of the pictures then, under all the circumstances, it seems reasonable that he should have sought renewal of the permission to use the old pictures.[45]

Reauthorization may be required when a name or photograph is used many years after consent was first given. A professional actor in New York gave the manufacturer of artificial Christmas trees permission to use his picture in a commercial for one year. When the commercial was used after one year, he sued for appropriation, and the New York high court sustained his privacy suit against the challenge by the defendant that only an action for breach of contract should be permitted.[46]

2. **Some persons cannot give consent.** A teenage girl is perfect to appear in a Luster-Glo Shampoo advertising campaign. She agrees to pose and signs a release authorizing use of her picture in the advertisements. The pictures are great, the advertisements are great, everything is great—until notice arrives that the model is suing for invasion of privacy! But she signed the permission form. Right. But she is only 16 years old, and under the law minors cannot give consent. Parental consent is required in such instances. What if the girl said she was 18 years old? The court will determine how believable such a statement was and will frequently ask whether the defendant sought any proof of this claim. If parents or guardians do give consent for the use of a minor's name or picture, under the common law in many states it is possible for the minors to revoke that consent when they reach the legal age.

Other people are unable to give consent as well. CBS was sued on behalf of David Delan by his guardian for including the young man in its film "Any Place But Here," a documentary about mental illness. Delan had been hospitalized for more than five years as a psychotic at the Creedmor State Hospital in New York. Because of his illness, he could not legally sign a consent form, and the network failed to gain a signed release from a physician. A psychologist gave CBS permission to film David, but the New York state law specifically requires the signature of a medical doctor on the release agreement before patients in the state's mental hospitals can be photographed or interviewed.[47] CBS ultimately prevailed in the case when the appellate division of the New York Supreme Court ruled that the broadcast was not made for advertising or trade purposes, and therefore consent from David Delan was

45. *McAndrews* v. *Roy,* 131 So. 2d 256 (1961).
46. *Welch* v. *Mr. Christmas Tree,* 57 N.Y. 2d 143 (1982).
47. *Delan* v. *CBS,* 445 N.Y.S. 2d 898 (1981).

It is important to know that the person from whom consent is obtained is legally able to give consent.

not required.[48] But the point made by the trial court is well taken. Persons who are unable to give consent because, for one reason or another, they are wards of the state, are risky subjects for publications or broadcasts that are made for advertising or trade purposes. It is important to know that the person from whom consent is obtained is legally able to give consent.

3. **Consent to use a photograph of a person in an advertisement or on a poster cannot be used as a defense if the photograph is materially altered or changed.**
Many years ago a well-known and well-paid New York fashion model posed for pictures to be used in an advertising campaign for a bookstore. After the photography session, model Mary Jane Russell signed this standard release form:

> The undersigned hereby irrevocably consents to the unrestricted use by Richard Avedon [the photographer], advertisers, customers, successors, and assigns, of my name, portrait, or picture for advertising purposes or purposes of trade, and I waive the right to inspect or approve such completed portraits, pictures, or advertising matter used in connection therewith.

It sounds as though she signed her life away, and with regard to the pictures Avedon took, she did. However, the bookstore sold one of the photographs to a maker of bedsheets. The bedding manufacturer had a reputation for running sleazy advertising campaigns and consequently had trouble getting first-class models to pose for advertising pictures. The textile manufacturer had the Avedon photo substantially retouched, changing the context. Mary Jane Russell sued for invasion of privacy, but the manufacturer answered by telling the court that the model had given irrevocable consent for anyone to use those pictures, that she had waived her right to inspect the completed pictures and the advertising, and so forth.

The court agreed that Russell had given up her right of privacy with regard to the pictures Avedon took. But the picture used by the sheet maker in its advertising was not the same picture taken by Avedon. It had been altered. And Russell won her case. Justice Matthew Levy of the New York Supreme Court wrote:

> If the picture were altered sufficiently in situation, emphasis, background, or context, I should think that it would no longer be the same portrait, but a different one. And as to the changed picture, I would hold that the original written consent would not apply and that liability would arrive when the content of the picture has been so changed that it is substantially unlike the original.[49]

What is substantial alteration? Because only a couple of court decisions have been rendered on this topic there is no line of precedents to answer this question. For the time being every judge who is asked this question is free to fashion his or her own answer. Substantially retouching a photo, as was done in the *Russell* case, was, until recently, a complicated undertaking. But today computers and software make such alterations close to child's play. Just because it is easy, however, doesn't make it legal. Magazine editors and the providers of content for the Web must take special

---

48. *Delan* v. *CBS,* 458 N.Y.S. 2d 698 (1983).
49. *Russell* v. *Marboro Books,* 183 N.Y.S. 2d 8 (1959).

Source: © Warner Brothers/Kobal Collection

care. A signed consent will only protect the use of the original photo with slight retouching, not wholesale modification of the particular subject in the picture or the setting in which the subject has been photographed.[50]

LIFE AFTER DEATH

The right to privacy is a personal right that dies with the individual. But the right to publicity may live on after death. The word "may" is essential to the sentence because there is inconsistency in the law in the states that have faced this question. And the question remains unanswered in many jurisdictions. State courts have handed down a mixed bag of rulings.[51] The legislatures in several states have passed statutes guaranteeing to heirs the right to protect the commercial exploitation of dead public figures for as long as 50 years.* And in at least one state, New York, the notion that an heir should be able to control such publicity has been flatly rejected. So where a particular lawsuit is tried is usually critical to the outcome.

The use of dead celebrities to sell products is a growing phenomenon. Viewers of the Super Bowl telecast in 1997 saw Fred Astaire, who died in 1987, dancing with a Dirt Devil vacuum cleaner. James Dean sells Levi's jeans and Converse shoes; Steve McQueen promotes

The 1968 film "Bullitt" featured one of the great motion picture car chases as Lt. Frank Bullitt, played by Steve McQueen, driving a Ford Mustang, chased two killers through the streets of San Francisco. Ford recently began using McQueen's images from the film to market the sporty automobile.

*California, Florida, Indiana, Kentucky, Nebraska, Oklahoma, Tennessee, Utah and Virginia are among the states that have statutes that speak to this matter in some way.

50. See, for example, *Dittner* v. *Troma,* 6 M.L.R. 1991 (1980).

51. See, for example, *Reeves* v. *United Artists,* 572 F. Supp. 1231 (1983); *Lugosi* v. *Universal,* 160 Cal. App. 3d 323 (1979); *Acme* v. *Kuperstock,* 711 F. 2d 1538 (1983); and *The Martin Luther King Center* v. *American Heritage Products,* 296 S.E. 2d 697 (1982).

Ford Mustangs. There are major American companies that do nothing but license the likenesses of dead celebrities. Advertisers who seek to associate their products with images of dead celebrities must be wary of the law in this area, which is generally unsettled in most states. It is usually worth the money and the effort to pay for the licensing rights rather than risk a lawsuit, which can be costly even if it is successfully defended.

New challenges in this area of privacy law will continue to emerge in the coming years as computer technology makes it possible to bring the images of creatures, aliens, starships and even dead celebrities to the motion picture and television screen. Using technologies pioneered by individuals like George Lucas and others, it is possible to create entire commercials and even feature films that contain the images of celebrities long since departed from this earth, images that look as real as photographs of living, breathing people. There is no doubt that the individuals who are charged with crafting the law in this realm will have to be as creative as the men and women who have generated this remarkable technology.

SUMMARY

Appropriation of a person's name or likeness for commercial or trade purposes without permission is an invasion of privacy and may be a violation of a person's right to publicity. Use of an individual's photograph, a sketch of the person, a nickname or a stage name are all considered use of a name or likeness. However, the publication of news and information in magazines, books, newspapers and news broadcasts is not considered a trade purpose, even though the mass medium may make a profit from such publication. Consequently, persons who are named or pictured in news stories or other such material cannot sue for appropriation. Also, a news medium may republish or rebroadcast news items or photographs already carried as news stories in advertising for the mass medium to establish the quality or kind of material carried by the medium.

Anyone who seeks to use the name or likeness of an individual for commercial or trade purposes should gain written consent from that person. Even written consent may be invalid as a defense in an invasion-of-privacy suit if the consent was given many years before publication, if the person from whom the consent was gained cannot legally give consent, or if the photograph or other material that is used is substantially altered.

Courts have also recognized what is known as the right to publicity. Right-to-publicity actions are most often instituted by well-known persons who believe the unauthorized use of their name or likeness has deprived them of an opportunity to reap financial gain by selling this right to the user. In some states the right to publicity can be passed on to heirs like any other piece of property, which means that an individual's estate can control the use of his or her name and likeness after the person's death.

INTRUSION

It is illegal to intrude, physically or otherwise, upon the seclusion or solitude of an individual.

When people hear the phrase invasion of privacy, the intrusion tort is what frequently comes to mind. Cameras with telephoto lenses, hidden microphones, snooping through records—all of these are associated with intrusion. Intrusion has a lot in common with both civil and criminal trespass. It is not unusual for a plaintiff to sue for both trespass and intrusion in the same lawsuit. But the causes of action are different. Not every intrusion is a trespass, and vice versa. Trespass is usually defined as the intentional and unauthorized entry onto land or property occupied or possessed by another. An illegal intrusion may be accomplished without physical entry onto private property. It could be done by taking a photo of someone who is in a private and secluded location, for example. And the law governing the two legal actions is different as well. Intrusion is the focus of this section; trespass and other laws that regulate the use of hidden microphones or video cameras will be outlined in the section on news gathering in Chapter 9.

The intrusion tort differs from the other three invasion-of-privacy torts in a very important way. Intrusion cases focus exclusively on how information is assembled. The act of gathering the material constitutes the intrusion. In appropriation, publication of private facts and false-light invasion of privacy, publication of the material generates the legal wrong. How the information was gathered is much less important, if not totally immaterial.

The most important legal element in an intrusion case is what the courts call "a reasonable expectation of privacy." This is a subjective determination in many cases. But if a court rules that a plaintiff did not enjoy a reasonable expectation of privacy when the defendant gathered or attempted to gather the information at issue, the intrusion suit will fail.

INTRUSION AND THE PRESS

An illegal intrusion can occur in myriad ways. Eavesdropping to overhear a conversation could be an intrusion. Gathering personal information from an individual's private records could also be an intrusion. The use of a telephoto lens on a camera to photograph a subject might violate the law as well. The court will ask in every case in which an intrusion is alleged whether the subject of the intrusion "enjoyed a reasonable amount of privacy" when the information was collected. This issue is the key to determining whether an invasion of privacy took place. A reporter who sits at a table in a restaurant and eavesdrops on the conversation at the next table is not committing an intrusion. If other diners can hear the conversation, the speakers did not enjoy a reasonable expectation of privacy.[52] If, however, the reporter hides in a closet in the subject's office and listens to a conversation, this would be an intrusion. Two people talking in a private office have a reasonable expectation of privacy. Courts are just beginning to sort out when an Internet user can expect to enjoy a reasonable expectation of privacy, and the decisions have not been favorable to those who think the Web should be a secure haven. At least two lower courts have ruled that the user of an online service who participated in a chat room conversation and sent e-mail messages to other chat room participants did not have a reasonable expectation of privacy with regard to the content of these messages.[53] A federal court in Massachusetts ruled in 2002 that two employees of an insurance company did not enjoy a reasonable expectation of privacy in the content of the sexually explicit e-mail messages they sent and received at work.[54] A U.S. District Court in Maine

---

52. See *Simtel Communications* v. *National Broadcasting Company Inc.,* 84 Cal. Rptr. 2d 329 (1999).

53. See *U.S.* v. *Charbonneau,* DC, S. Ohio, CR-2-97-83, 9/30/97, and *Pennsylvania* v. *Proetto,* Pa. Super. Ct. No. 1076 EDA 2000, 3/28/01.

54. *Garrity* v. *John Hancock Mutual Life Insurance Co.,* D. Mass., No. 00-12143-RWZ-5/7/02.

ruled that a student lacked a reasonable expectation of privacy in files that he accessed on a shared-usage university computer.[55] And in the summer of 2004 the 1st U.S. Court of Appeals ruled that if e-mail messages were stored for even a millisecond on the computers of an Internet service provider that transmitted them, federal wiretap laws were not violated if employees of the provider read the messages. A company called Interloc Inc., a literary clearinghouse, made copies of the messages its subscribers sent to competitor Amazon.com. Interloc's customers were dealers in rare and out-of-print books, and while Amazon did not offer its customers out-of-print and rare books, it did help customers track down such books. The court ruled that while the wiretap law prohibits eavesdropping on messages that are not stored, it does not protect stored messages.[56] The courts have yet to rule on whether an Internet user who is sending or receiving signals through a wireless connection—so-called wi-fi—enjoys a reasonable expectation of privacy.

NO PRIVACY IN PUBLIC

What occurs in public is generally not regarded as being private. If what takes place is visible or what is said is audible by any person who happens to be in the vicinity, it is difficult if not impossible for a plaintiff to argue that there should be a reasonable expectation of privacy in such a situation. American Airlines flight attendant Beverly Deteresa sued ABC for secretly recording a conversation she had with ABC producer Anthony Radziwill. The plaintiff worked the flight that O.J. Simpson took to Chicago the night that Nicole Brown Simpson and Ronald Goldman were killed. Radziwill asked Deteresa to appear on television as the two talked at her front door. She declined, but Radziwill secretly taped the conversation and instructed a camera crew across the street to videotape the discussion between the producer and the flight attendant. A brief segment was later shown on ABC news. The 9th U.S. Circuit Court of Appeals affirmed a lower-court decision granting a summary judgment to the television network. The court ruled that there was no reasonable expectation of privacy when the plaintiff was talking with a journalist in plain sight of anyone who passed by on the public street.[57]

It is just as unreasonable for individuals to expect privacy in other settings where people gather. A woman sitting in a restaurant complained of intrusion after a television news crew videotaped patrons sitting in the room. The Iowa Supreme Court ruled that someone sitting in a restaurant could not have a legitimate expectation of privacy. If the patron was in a private dining room in the restaurant such an expectation may exist, but what happens in a public dining room happens in public.[58] But the courts have recognized gradations in an expectation of privacy as well. ABC sent a reporter to work as a telephone psychic at a telemarketing company in California. While there the reporter secretly photographed and tape-recorded conversations with several co-workers. The network was sued for intrusion, among other things. ABC argued that there was no legitimate expectation of privacy in the office setting because workers shared small, three-walled cubicles. Conversations could

---

55. *U. S.* v. *Bunnell,* D. Me., Crim. No. 0213-B-S, 5/10/02.

56. *Jewell,* "Setback Seen for E-mail Privacy."

57. *Deteresa* v. *American Broadcasting Co. Inc.,* 121 F. 3d 460 (1997).

58. *Stressman* v. *American Blackhawk Broadcasting Co.,* 416 N.W. 2d 685 (1987).

be heard by other employees. The California Supreme Court disagreed with the network, ruling that

> in an office or other workplace to which the general public does not have unfettered access employees may enjoy a limited, but legitimate expectation that their conversations and other interactions will not be secretly videotaped by undercover television reporters, even though their conversations may not have been completely private.[59]

ABC suffered another setback in 2004 when its motion for a summary judgment was denied in an intrusion case in which one of its reporter/producers had secretly taped conversations at a workshop given for aspiring actors and actresses by casting directors. By paying a fee to attend the workshops the performers got to meet and talk with casting directors, the persons who play an important role in employing actors and actresses who appear in movies and on television. This was a controversial practice in California and the network did a segment on it for a "20/20" broadcast. The reporter taped not only the actual presentations during the workshop but also private conversations among the performers during breaks. Some of the performers sued. In California all parties must agree to the recording of a conversation unless it takes place at a public gathering. ABC asked that the case be dismissed, claiming the conversations took place in public spaces.

The U.S. District Court ruled that even though some of their conversations could have been overheard by other students, the plaintiffs still had a reasonable expectation of privacy. They could not have expected as they talked among themselves in the corners or against the walls of the classroom, much less in the restrooms, that a reporter was covertly recording their conversations. This was not a public place.[60]

But the 9th U.S. Court of Appeals ruled three years later in a similar situation that medical laboratory operators who invited reporters and photographers who were posing as someone else to tour the lab could not enjoy a reasonable expectation of privacy. The journalists secretly recorded and photographed what they heard and saw and broadcast this material on a segment of ABC's "Primetime Live" that focused on problems in medical laboratories that tested Pap smears for cancer. The appellate court said the situation was not quite the same as that in the *Sanders* case noted above, because the laboratory was semipublic. Nonemployees could enter the facilities for blood tests and other lab work. Also, because the lab was in Arizona, the federal court applied that state's law, which, according to the ruling, was far less protective of privacy rights than the law in California. No personal or private information was recorded by the journalists, the court noted, and what was revealed was not terribly offensive. So there was no intrusion.[61]

Finally, another California ruling demonstrates how carefully judges will sometimes look at a situation to judge the extent of a potential intrusion. A car containing four members of the Shulman family accidentally left Interstate 10, tumbled down an embankment, and came to rest upside down in a drainage ditch. Rescue apparatus arrived at the scene, including

59. *Sanders* v. *American Broadcasting Companies,* 978 P. 2d 67 (1999). Sanders received a settlement of more than $900,000 from ABC.
60. *Turnbell* v. *American Broadcasting Companies,* 32 M.L.R. 2442 (2004). However, the plaintiff lost the case at trial.
61. *Medical Laboratory Management Consultants* v. *American Broadcasting Co.,* 306 F. 3d 806 (2002).

a Mercy Air helicopter with a medic and a flight nurse. Also on board was a camera operator who worked for a television production company. The photographer was accumulating footage for a television program called "On Scene: Emergency Response." Nurse Laura Carnahan was wearing a microphone that supplied the audio stream for the video. As rescue workers cut Ruth Shulman out of the car, she was comforted by Carnahan. The conversation was recorded as the photographer videotaped the rescue. Shulman was placed in the rescue helicopter, and during the flight to the hospital more video and audio material was gathered. Shulman, who ended up a paraplegic because of her injuries, sued for invasion of privacy, both intrusion and publication of private facts. The California courts dismissed the private facts claim, noting that there was tremendous public interest in what happened in this case. But the California Supreme Court said a jury could certainly find a valid intrusion claim with regard to the video and audio recordings of Mrs. Shulman while she was in the rescue helicopter on the way to the hospital, and the audio recording of conversations between the flight nurse and the victim as firefighters removed Mrs. Shulman from the wrecked car.[62]

Caution is warranted. The maxim that there can be no expectation of privacy in public is not invulnerable, especially as an increasing number of American courts demonstrate a growing sensitivity to the way in which information is gathered by some news organizations in the 21st century. (See pages 353–364.) A U.S. Court of Appeals recently upheld the claim made by a criminal defendant that a so-called perp walk, the traditional parading of a prisoner in front of the press so pictures can be taken, violated the defendant's constitutional right to privacy guaranteed under the Fourth Amendment. The walk in this case was clearly staged; the prisoner was taken out of the police precinct, paraded in front of the press, and then returned to the precinct. And the court made clear that permitting the press to take photos of a criminal defendant during the legitimate transporting of a prisoner from one site to another was not at issue in the case.[63] Nevertheless, the ruling represents an important departure from the normal outcome of such cases. Almost 30 years ago a federal court barred a photographer from coming within 10 yards of Jacqueline Kennedy Onassis and her children because he previously had been harassing the family with his incessant photography.[64] A court in Pennsylvania fashioned a similar order to protect a family in that state from the intense scrutiny of reporters from the television program "Inside Story."[65] (See pages 358–359 for more on this case.) Paparazzi—the aggressive photographers who dog celebrities in hopes of getting a picture they can sell to the multitude of tabloid newspapers and magazines that focus on the entertainment business—have become a growing, and some say, serious problem, especially in California and New York. The celebrity-obsessed American culture has provided a fertile field for these journalistic gadflys. Pictures of some entertainers have become so valuable that some paparazzi are actually using cars and vans to ram the vehicles of the

62. *Shulman* v. *Group W. Productions Inc.,* 955 P. 2d 469 (1998). The case was subsequently settled out of court.
63. *Lauro* v. *Charles,* 219 F. 3d 202 (2000). See also *Cardarola* v. *County of Westchester,* 142 F. Supp. 2d 431 (2001), where a court ruled that permitting a suspect to be photographed during the course of legitimate transportation of the individual was not an invasion of privacy.
64. *Gallela* v. *Onassis,* 487 F. 2d 986 (1973), 533 F. Supp. 1076 (1982).
65. *Wolfson* v. *Lewis,* 924 F. Supp. 1413 (1996).

publicity-shy celebrities in order to force them to leave their cars to deal with the accident. This presents the so-called photo opportunity. California has passed laws to try to limit some of these excesses. A state statute creates tort liability for physical and "constructive" invasions of privacy through photographing, videotaping or recording a person engaged in "personal or familial activity." In October 2005 another law that triples the damages celebrities can win from paparazzi if they are assaulted during a photographic shoot, and denies the photographer any profits from the sale of a picture taken during an altercation, went on the books. Critics of the new laws say they could interfere with legitimate newsgathering in some circumstances, and that they are unfair in that they treat paparazzi differently than other California citizens.[66] The simple theme of these rulings and laws is that the growing sensitivity expressed by many persons about intrusive journalistic behavior is getting a friendlier hearing in many venues. The rule that there can be no expectation of privacy regarding what happens in public is still viable, but perhaps not impregnable.

THE USE OF HIDDEN RECORDING DEVICES

The miniaturization of video and audio equipment has made it possible for anyone, including reporters, to secretly record conversations, confrontations, meetings and other happenings. Can such recording constitute an intrusion, an invasion of privacy? It is not easy to answer this question definitively.

In 1971 a U.S. Court of Appeals in California ruled that such surreptitious recording could constitute an illegal intrusion. The case was an odd one. Two reporters for Life magazine agreed to cooperate with Los Angeles police who sought to arrest a man who was practicing medicine without a license. Posing as man and wife, the pair went to the "doctor's" home where he conducted his practice. While A.A. Dietemann examined the woman, the man secretly photographed the procedure. At the same time the conversation was secretly recorded. Police arrested Dietemann several weeks later, and following his apprehension the magazine published a story with a transcript of the recorded conversation and some of the photos taken in his home. The appellate court sustained his suit for intrusion, ruling that a homeowner should not "be required to take the risk that what is heard or seen [in his or her home] will be transmitted by photography or recording . . . to the public at large."[67] Other courts have not followed this precedent, although none of the subsequent cases involved recording or photography in a private home.

For example, in 1975 Arlyn Cassidy and several other Chicago police officers were acting as undercover agents, investigating massage parlors in the city. The owner of one massage parlor where police previously had made arrests believed he was being harassed by the officers and invited a television news camera crew to come in and secretly film an encounter between an undercover agent and a model at the parlor. The camera was set up behind a two-way mirror and was filming when officer Cassidy came in, paid $30 for deluxe lingerie modeling, and subsequently arrested the girl for solicitation. Three other agents came into the room at about the same time the television news crew burst through another door, filming as

---

66. California Civil Code, Section 1708.8.; "Schwarzenegger Signs Law."
67. *Dietemann* v. *Time, Inc.,* 499 F. 2d 245 (1971).

they left the building. The officers sued the station for intrusion, using the *Dietemann* case as precedent.

But an Illinois appellate court ruled in favor of the journalists, distinguishing the *Dietemann* case in some important ways. First, Cassidy and the other plaintiffs were public officers acting in the line of duty as the filming took place. Second, the film crew was not in a private home but in a public business. And third, the crew was on hand at the invitation of the operator of the premises. "In our opinion," the court ruled, "no right of privacy against intrusion can be said to exist with reference to the gathering and dissemination of news concerning discharge of public duties."[68]

A Kentucky circuit court ruled that it was not an intrusion when a young woman, at the instigation of a newspaper, secretly recorded a conversation she had with an attorney in the attorney's office. After the newspaper published a transcript of the conversation, during which attorney John T. McCall proposed an unethical fee arrangement with the woman, the lawyer sued for intrusion. Again, the court distinguished *Dietemann,* noting that the woman was in McCall's office at his invitation. "A lawyer, an officer of the court, discussing a public court with a potential client, is not in seclusion within the meaning of the law," the court ruled.[69] A Kentucky appellate court subsequently upheld this ruling.[70]

"A lawyer, an officer of the court, discussing a public court with a potential client, is not in seclusion within the meaning of the law."

Finally, a U.S. District Court in Illinois in 1994 rejected an intrusion claim made against ABC News after it had secretly photographed and recorded eye examinations at an ophthalmology clinic. The owners of the clinic sued. The court ruled that the plaintiffs in the case had alleged no damage from the recording, other than that it had been broadcast. The court also rejected the claim that the recording violated the doctor-patient privilege. That privilege, the court said, belongs to the patient, not the doctor. If the doctor had filmed the examination, it would have been a violation of this privilege and likely an intrusion. But when the patients authorized the recording (they were working for the network), no legal wrong occurred.

The 5th U.S. Circuit Court of Appeals upheld this ruling in early 1995. The appellate court specifically rejected the plaintiff's arguments that the 1971 *Dietemann* ruling should control in this situation. The court said Dietemann was operating out of his home, not a public place of business like the ophthalmology clinic. And Dietemann did no advertising whereas the eye clinic actively solicited the public to visit the facility.[71] Cases like those cited here have chipped away at the substance of the *Dietemann* ruling.

The use of hidden cameras or concealed microphones generates controversy among journalists as well as among the public. In some states (see page 363), laws regulate the use of these reporting tactics. But whether such reporting techniques are illegal or not, they are regarded by many people as sneaky, intrusive and unethical. A journalist who uses such means without careful consideration of the alternatives risks undermining the public trust in his or her work and in the craft in general. In 1992 the Society of Professional Journalists and the Poynter Institute for Media Studies drafted guidelines for the use of hidden cameras. These

68. *Cassidy* v. *ABC,* 377 N.E. 2d 126 (1978).
69. *McCall* v. *Courier-Journal,* 4 M.L.R. 2337 (1979).
70. *McCall* v. *Courier-Journal,* 6 M.L.R. 1112 (1980).
71. *Desnick* v. *Capital Cities/ABC, Inc.,* 851 F. Supp. 303 (1994), aff'd. *Desnick* v. *American Broadcasting Companies, Inc.,* 44 F. 3d 1345 (1995).

guidelines, outlined in the *American Journalism Review,*[72] state that hidden cameras should be used only

- when the information is of profound importance.
- when all other alternatives for obtaining the same information have been exhausted.*
- when the individuals involved and their news organizations apply—through outstanding quality of work as well as the commitment of time and funding—the excellence needed to pursue the story fully.
- when the harm prevented by the information revealed through deception outweighs any harm caused by the act of deception.
- when the journalists involved have conducted a meaningful, collaborative and deliberative decision to justify deception.

The guidelines say that winning a prize, beating the competition, getting a story cheaply, doing it because others have done it, or doing it because the subjects of the story are unethical are not sufficient reasons to justify the use of hidden cameras.

INTRUSION AND THE PUBLICATION OF INFORMATION OBTAINED ILLEGALLY

Gathering information through illegal intrusions is not the way journalists typically behave. But using information gathered illegally by others is another matter altogether, and while not a common practice, it does occur. Can a newspaper or broadcasting station or Web-site operator be successfully sued for publishing or broadcasting material obtained via an illegal intrusion by a third party? The Supreme Court, echoing some older lower-court decisions, recently said no when asked this question.[73] But it was a qualified no at best. The case involved the broadcast of an audiotape recording of a cell phone conversation between two officials of a teachers' union. Not-so-veiled threats were made during the conversation against local school board members. The conversation was illegally intercepted and taped by unknown persons and then distributed to the local press. The two union officials brought suit under the federal wiretap statute, which makes it a violation for anyone to disclose the contents of an illegally intercepted communication. In the 6-3 ruling, the high court acknowledged that the case presented a tough choice between protecting the free flow of information in society and the individual's right to privacy and the protection of private speech. Justice John Paul Stevens noted that the framers of the Constitution "surely did not foresee the advances in science that produced the conversation, the interception or the conflict" that generated the case. But while the majority of the court ruled that there was no liability in this case for broadcasting the tape, the justices said they did so only because the broadcasters in the case had played no part in intercepting or obtaining the taped conversation, and because of the public significance—not simply the newsworthiness—of the content of the conversation. Concurring justices Stephen

---

*In the *Turnbell* case noted on page 303, ABC admitted in court it could have done the story without the secret recording.

72. Lissit, "Gotcha," 17.

73. *Bartnicki* v. *Vopper,* 121 S. Ct. 1753 (2001).

Breyer and Sandra Day O'Connor made clear that had the facts been even slightly different, their decision could have gone the other way. Longtime New York Times Supreme Court reporter Linda Greenhouse accurately characterized the ruling as "a cautionary tale for the nation's newsrooms."[74]

Previous rulings had focused on cases in which a right-to-privacy intrusion claim was made. In three separate rulings, two by U.S. Courts of Appeals[75] and a third by a Maryland state court,[76] the judge found that no liability for intrusion could be assessed against the publisher of that material so long as it had been obtained innocently. In the Maryland case several former and current members of the University of Maryland basketball team sued the Washington Evening Star for publishing an article that revealed portions of their academic records. Somebody gave the newspaper the information. There was no evidence presented that the reporters had either personally inspected the records or asked someone else to do it. Consequently, no suit could be maintained by the athletes on the intrusion theory.

Remember, none of the rulings just cited protects a journalist who actually makes the illegal intrusion by pilfering documents or intercepting telephone conversations. And in some instances, as noted by the high court in the *Bartnicki* case, even the obvious newsworthiness of a story might be insufficient to shield a news medium that publishes the contents of illegally obtained material in direct violation of statutes such as the federal wiretap laws. And beyond just the law, ethical considerations abound as well and must be factored into the equation. Journalists whose decision to publish or broadcast is based on their often self-serving declaration of "serving the public good" will not always prevail in the 21st century.

SUMMARY   Intruding on an individual's solitude, or intrusion, can be an invasion of privacy. The legal wrong occurs as soon as the information about the individual is illegally collected. Subsequent publication of the material is not needed to establish a cause of action, and defending an intrusion by arguing that in publishing the information the defendant was serving the public interest rarely succeeds. The plaintiff carries the burden of convincing the court that when the intrusion occurred, he or she enjoyed a reasonable expectation of privacy. The general rule is that there can be no such expectation if the plaintiff was in a public place. Public streets, restaurants, even areas in private businesses normally accessible to the public are not places were an individual can reasonably expect to find privacy. The use of hidden cameras and microphones frequently prompts intrusion suits and the courts have viewed such intrusions in various ways, depending on where the information was gathered. But in some jurisdictions the use of such devices is barred by other laws. The subsequent publication or broadcast of material obtained through an intrusion by a third party (i.e., not the publisher or broadcaster) has not been regarded as a violation of privacy law.

74. Linda Greenhouse, "Court Says Press Isn't Liable."
75. *Liberty Lobby* v. *Pearson,* 390 F. 2d 489 (1968) and *Pearson* v. *Dodd,* 410 F. 2d 701 (1969).
76. *Bilney* v. *Evening Star,* 406 A. 2d (1979).

INTRUSION AND THE INTERNET

The explosive growth of interactive computer systems has generated a revolution in communication worldwide. For most Americans today, using e-mail and the Internet is as common as communicating by telephone or U.S. mail. Users pull mounds of data out of the systems; users pour mounds of data into the systems. With all these data floating through these electronic canals, it is no wonder that privacy problems have arisen almost as rapidly as the Internet has grown. And intrusion problems are among the most stubborn difficulties. Computers are not liked locked files, or secure telephone lines, or even desk drawers. In too many situations they present an open door to those who seek to uncover whatever it is the user has stored in the machine or is attempting to communicate via the system. While 10 years ago this was probably news to most Internet users, today it must be regarded as common knowledge.[77] Careful computer users try to increase the odds in their favor by adopting security measures. Many users, however, simply push ahead with fingers crossed, hoping they won't have problems.

Since the mid-19th century most Americans have been of two minds about their privacy. On the one hand they aggressively demand protection for their personal information. But on the other, they willingly give away personal information simply to enjoy the benefits of modern society. The law even recognized this in a perverse kind of way. A legal doctrine has developed, applicable in most jurisdictions, called the assumption of risk analysis. Under this doctrine an individual loses a privacy interest in personal information that is voluntarily made accessible to another person or is otherwise placed in the flow of commerce. The courts have said there can be no expectation of privacy when a customer fills out an application for a bank loan or applies for a credit card, dials a telephone number* or even puts out the trash on the edge of the driveway.[78] For some reason, a lot of people think sharing information via the Internet is somehow more secure. But it isn't.

At least people are aware that they are giving up their personal information when they apply for a credit card or fill out a government form and are admitted to a hospital. But Web users often aren't even aware they are giving up personal information when they communicate via the Internet. It is almost commonplace to see news stories about one business or another finally admitting they have been secretly mining data off the Internet, data about their subscribers or people who access their Web sites. Even the federal government has admitted undertaking this practice.[79] A whole new language has developed filled with exotic words like cookies and mouse droppings and sniffers, terms that identify programming devices that permit the user to gather personal information in a clandestine manner. E-mail is another problem. Messages sent via e-mail pass through several exchange points on their way to recipients, and it is possible to copy, reroute or tamper with the message at any one of these points. In many cases reading someone else's e-mail is a violation of federal law, but not always. It often depends on whose computer server the message sender is using. Employers, for example, are

---

*It is illegal to intercept a telephone conversation. But the numbers dialed by phone users are much more legally accessible.

77. See Fixmer, "New Ways to Travel" and Stellin, "Consumers' Views Split."
78. Stuckey, *Internet and Online Law.*
79. "Senator Raises Privacy."

not prohibited by law from exploring an employee's e-mail messages if the employee is sending them via the company server.[80] Students who use university computer servers to send their messages lack substantial protection as well. And as noted earlier, a federal court ruled (see page 302) that federal wiretap laws are not violated when an Internet service provider reads its subscriber's e-mails.

The movement of government records from manila files to computers has also created privacy problems. Many government records and court documents were always accessible to the public (see Chapter 9), but it was not easy to gain access to them. It required a trip, often to the state capitol or a courthouse, and a search through sometimes dusty archives. With this material online, someone can sit at home and scan these files. When Hamilton County, Ohio (Cincinnati is the county seat), put its court records on the Web, many citizens were outraged to discover that their neighbors were using the Internet to gain access to information about them: state tax liens, arrest warrants, bond postings, documents posted in divorce cases and other official records.[81] But other jurisdictions are also making public records electronically accessible. In California many years ago a man used data he obtained online to locate the victim he later killed. The California law permitting access to the records the killer used was changed. Make no mistake about it; governments are not making records that were previously closed open to public inspections. These records were always accessible. It simply took a lot of effort for the average citizen to see them. The trend toward making such documents Internet-accessible is either good news or bad news, depending on where an individual stands in the debate between those who favor open government and those who seek greater privacy.

LEGISLATIVE ACTION

Even a casual observer could only conclude that the government—especially Congress—has done little to solve the problem of data theft from Internet users. This is true despite two compelling facts:

The personal information of more than 50 million consumers has been lost, stolen or even sold to thieves, according to one credible report.

Most Americans—71 percent according to a poll taken in 2005—say they believe Congress should pass laws to keep the Internet safe, as well as insist that the few laws that do exist are enforced more rigorously.[82]

Surprisingly perhaps, the theft, misuse and sale of personal information is primarily an American problem. Every other Western country has a comprehensive set of national privacy laws and an office of data protection, led by a privacy commissioner. Most European nations begin with the idea that data protection is a human right, regulated by comprehensive principles that apply to both business and government. "Where American businesses are given

---

80. "AMA Survey Charts Extent of Workplace Monitoring," 2 E.P.L.R. 560 (1997). A federal court in Nebraska ruled in 2003 that an employee has no objectively reasonable expectation of privacy that his online activities are private. See *United States* v. *Bailey,* D. Neb., 4: OZCR3040, 7/23/03.
81. Lee, "Dirty Laundry."
82. Bridis, "Citizens fret."

relatively free rein to collect and sell information, European companies are severely restricted from those activities without individual consent," wrote Eric Dash in a 2005 article in The New York Times headlined "Europe Zips Lips; U.S. Sells ZIPs."[83]

Why this disparity between nations which have so many other laws in common? American business has diligently fought any attempts by Congress to adopt laws that would restrict its ability both to gather and to disperse (e.g., sell) personal information. During the past decade through lobbying and other techniques businesses have stalled most congressional efforts at regulation by successfully arguing (with the support of both the Clinton and Bush administrations) that self-regulation is the best way to deal with the problem. The Federal Trade Commission fought diligently for new legislation for several years, but ultimately gave up the fight in late 2001 when it became clear that Congress was not about to adopt any meaningful new laws.

Some laws already exist that focus directly on protecting privacy on the Internet and other contemporary communication devices like mobile telephones. But most of these are not rigorously enforced. Twenty years ago Congress amended existing statutes that regulated wiretapping so it applied to many more kinds of electronic communication, including communication via the Internet. The Electronic Communications Privacy Act, or ECPA, has many provisions.[84] The law makes it illegal, for example, to intentionally intercept a cellular telephone conversation or disclose or air the communication with knowledge or reason to believe that the call was intercepted illegally. The law forbids the manufacturers and importers of radio scanners from making or selling scanners that can intercept communications on frequencies used for cellular telephones. Scanners that are sold should not be easily modified to enable them to intercept such communications, but most authorities agree that it is fairly easy for someone with a rudimentary training in radio electronics to make such modifications. The 1986 statute also prohibits the intentional interception of online communication and outlaws such practices as keystroke monitoring, tapping a data line, and rerouting electronic communication to provide contemporaneous acquisition. It is also illegal under the ECPA to use or disclose the contents of any electronic communication if the user or discloser knew or had reason to know that the information was obtained through an illegal interception. This means it is illegal to use any device to read other users' private messages and to divulge the contents of another person's electronic mail. The online system provider cannot read the contents of users' e-mail, but the law does not apply to employers. The statute also prohibits "hacking," or gaining unauthorized access to other users' files or documents.

Two other important laws have been adopted during the past decade. In 1994 Congress adopted the Drivers' License Protection Act, which barred state departments of motor vehicles from disclosing personal information about individuals that is contained in driver's license records, information including photos, names, addresses, telephone numbers and the like. This data is used by many nongovernment entities, like the press, and many state governments do a lucrative business in selling this information to all sorts of businesses that market goods and services to drivers and automobile owners. Several states challenged the law, claiming that it violated the 10th Amendment to the U.S. Constitution because it forced state officials to perform a federal task—the protection of personal privacy. State officials said this federal

---

83. Dash, "Europe Zips Lips."
84. See Stuckey, *Internet and Online Law.*

mandate exceeded Congress' authority under the commerce clause and encroached on state authority. In January 2000 the Supreme Court ruled unanimously that the law did not violate the 10th Amendment. The court said the statute regulated states as owners of databases containing information that is an article of interstate commerce; it did not compel states to enact any laws or commandeer their officials to assist in administering federal programs.[85]

A frequent target for surreptitious data-gathering on the Internet in the 1990s were Web sites aimed at younger children. Using contests, games, chat rooms, message boards and other diversions, site operators (often food makers and toy manufacturers) would attempt to collect personal information from children, including names, addresses, e-mail addresses, telephone numbers and even Social Security numbers. Under pressure Congress responded to this problem by adopting the Children's Online Privacy Protection Act in 1998. This law authorized the FTC to regulate Internet sites that collect personal information from users under the age of 13. The law was implemented by the federal regulators and requires site operators to inform users that information is being collected, limits the kind of information that can be collected, and provides a means for parents to review or even delete personal information that is being collected. Adopting the law is one thing; making it work is another. In the wake of its adoption a study done at the University of Pennsylvania revealed that only about 50 percent of the children's Web sites that collect information were following the rules. (See Chapter 15 for more on this law.)

The collection of data via the Internet about people who use the system could in many instances qualify as an illegal intrusion. The problem, however, is that the user usually doesn't know the data has been collected. Also, because of the international nature of the Internet, while such data collection may be illegal in the United States, it might not be in another part of the world. Where did the intrusion take place? when the information was snatched from the user's computer, which is located in Detroit? or when it was downloaded by the site operator, who lives in Brussels, Belgium?

What happens to the data that is gathered by cookies and intercepted e-mail and other means? It is often sold or released to the public for other purposes. These problems will be explored when publication of private facts is discussed in Chapter 8.

SUMMARY   The surreptitious collection of data from Internet users is a serious problem. Personal data flows freely through these electronic channels, and gathering this information is a common task performed by both honest and not-so-honest entrepreneurs and even the government. Laws dating back as far as the 1980s regulate some of this behavior, but Congress has resisted adopting stringent rules because businesses have argued self-regulation is a better solution. Congress has, however, adopted the Drivers' License Protection Act and the Children's Online Privacy Protection Act in an attempt to control some of the more egregious problems.

85. *Reno* v. *Condon,* 120 S. Ct. 666 (2000).

BIBLIOGRAPHY ⟶

"Abdul Serves Lawsuit to Diet Promoter." *Seattle Post-Intelligencer,* 16 June 1999, A3.

Bernstein, Nina. "Proposals to Protect Privacy Seem to Face Stalemate on Contradictory Goals." *The New York Times,* 20 October 1997, A12.

Bridis, Ted. "Citizens Fret over Internet Security." *Seattle Post-Intelligencer,* 15 June 2005, C-2.

Brooks, Brian. *Journalism in the Information Age.* Boston: Allyn and Bacon, 1997.

Chambers, Marcia. "Case of Art, Icons and Law, with Woods in the Middle." *The New York Times,* 3 July 2002, C13.

——— "New Privacy Rules for Children's Web Sites." *The New York Times,* 21 October 1999, D11.

"College Report Finds That Most Kids' Web Sites Fall Short of COPPA Requirements." *Electronic Commerce & Law Report,* 11 April 2001, 375.

Corr, O. Casey. "Cybersnoops on the Loose." *The Seattle Times,* 10 August 1997, B5.

Dash, Eric. "Europe Zips Lips; U.S. Sells ZIPs." *The New York Times,* 7 August 2005, Sec 4, p9.1.

Fixmer, Rob. "New Way to Travel the Web While Leaving Fewer Footprints." *The New York Times,* 16 August 1999, C5.

Greenhouse, Linda. "Court Says Press Isn't Liable for Use of Ill-Gotten Tapes." *The New York Times,* 22 May 2001, A14.

Jewell, Mark. "Setback Seen for E-mail Privacy." *Seattle Post-Intelligencer,* 2 July 2004, C2.

Kuczynski, Alex. "Dustin Hoffman Wins Suit on Photo Alteration." *The New York Times,* 23 January 1999, A30.

Labaton, Stephen. "White House and Agency Split on Internet Privacy." *The New York Times,* 23 May 2000, C1.

Lee, Jennifer S. "Dirty Laundry, Online for All to See." *The New York Times,* 5 September 2002, E1.

Lewis, Peter. "Web Cookies: Trail of Crumbs." *The Seattle Times,* 9 August 1998, C1.

———. "What's on Your Hard Drive." *The New York Times,* 8 October 1998, D1.

Lissit, Robert. "Gotcha." *American Journalism Review,* March 1995, 17.

Lohr, Steve. "Industry Group to Offer Standards for Privacy on Internet." *The New York Times,* 26 May 1997, C3.

Markoff, John. "At the New Frontier of Eavesdropping." *The New York Times,* 19 January 1997, B5.

Pember, Don R. "The Burgeoning Scope of Access Privacy and the Portent for a Free Press." *Iowa Law Review* 64 (1979): 1155.

———. *Privacy and the Press.* Seattle: University of Washington Press, 1972.

Prosser, William L. "Privacy." *California Law Review* 48 (1960): 383.

Queary, Paul. "Mother Denied Say Over Baby's Photo." *The Seattle Times,* 19 January 1997, A8.

Sanford, Bruce W. *Libel and Privacy.* 2nd ed. Englewood Cliffs, N.J.: Prentice-Hall Law and Business, 1993.

"Schwarzenegger Signs Law Aimed at Paparrazi Wallet." *The New York Times,* 2 October 2005, 17.

"Senator Raises Privacy as Federal Web Site Issue." *The New York Times,* 17 April 2001, C3.

Stellin, Susan. "Consumers' Views Split on Internet Privacy." *The New York Times,* 21 August 2000, C3.

Stuckey, Kent. *Internet and Online Law.* New York: Law Journal Seminars-Press, 1996.

Warren, Samuel D., and Louis D. Brandeis. "The Right to Privacy." *Harvard Law Review* 4 (1890): 220.

Weber, Bruce. "High-Tech Film Casting: Death Is No Drawback." *The New York Times,* 11 March 1994, B15.

Weinraub, Bernard. "2 Paparazzi Convicted of Stalking Celebrities." *The New York Times,* 4 February 1998, A36.

INVASION OF PRIVACY
Publication of Private Information and False Light

Giving publicity to private facts about someone's life is what provoked legal scholars Samuel D. Warren and Louis D. Brandeis to propose in 1890 that the law should protect an individual's right to privacy. Some label this gossip-mongering, others describe it as legitimate journalism. Whatever it is called, it has become the stock-in-trade of a growing number of American periodicals and television programs. And the law, as you will see in the next section of this text, has been largely ineffective in stopping it. We also explore in this chapter the strangest of the privacy torts, false light invasion of privacy.

PUBLICITY ABOUT PRIVATE FACTS

It is illegal to publicize private information about a person if the matter that is publicized

a. would be highly offensive to a reasonable person, and

b. is not of legitimate public concern or interest.

"Keyhole journalism" is what press critics in the late 19th century called it. The snooping, prying, gossipy, scandal-driven reporting that many of us today have come to take for granted in both the print and electronic media was just emerging at the end of the 19th century.

A lot of people believed it was offensive and should be stopped. Attorneys Samuel Warren and Louis Brandeis even proposed a legal solution, a right of privacy, enforceable in a court of law.[1] But American courts have been less than enthusiastic in their support for such ideas. Of all the four tort actions encompassed by the right to privacy, this one, a cause of action based on giving publicity to private facts, has gained the least acceptance from the judiciary. The courts in many states have not yet recognized or have refused to recognize this tort. The North Carolina Supreme Court, in refusing to recognize the tort action, called it "constitutionally suspect."[2] What makes this tort "constitutionally suspect" in the eyes of many judges and legal scholars is that it punishes the press, or whomever, for publishing truthful information that has been legally obtained. Making the press liable in such instances seems to run against basic American First Amendment tenets and a substantial body of case law. So although the courts in about 80 percent of U.S. jurisdictions are willing to hear arguments in such a case, plaintiffs rarely win these arguments. More than one legal scholar has argued that few would suffer if this entire tort area of privacy simply disappeared. University of Chicago law professor Harry Kalven wrote 40 years ago that the size and strength of the defenses in a private facts lawsuit raise the question of whether it is a viable tort remedy. "The mountain, I suggest, has brought forth a pretty small mouse," he said.[3]

But the courts and legal scholars may be out of step with public opinion on this question.

But the courts and legal scholars may be out of step with public opinion on this question. There seems to be a growing sensitivity among many Americans regarding the protection of personal privacy. Many persons in the United States expressed a belief that press revelations about President Bill Clinton's private life were simply out of place on the front pages of American newspapers. A majority of persons surveyed by researchers at Middle Tennessee State University in the early 1990s told the researchers that they believed the press deserves less than the full protection of the First Amendment when journalists delve into the past lives of public figures or report the sexual activities of persons in the public eye. Congress took action in 1996 to protect the privacy of health care records when it adopted the Health Insurance Portability and Accountability Act. Provisions in the law make it much harder for the press to get even routine information from health care providers about patients in their care. For example, when a nightclub burned down in West Warwick, R.I., in 2003, killing 100 persons, reporters who contacted hospitals about the status of the injured patrons were usually rebuffed by hospital officials, even though the law had not yet gone into effect. Some observers regard it as ironic that at the same time Americans seem to be growing concerned about protecting their own and others' private lives, the television programs, magazines and newspapers that focus on such material seem to be thriving as never before.

The law clearly favors the press when the mass media is sued for publishing private facts. But reporters need to be careful. This area may be one of those in which journalists need to ask some tough questions of themselves before pushing the law to its outer limits. What is legal may not always be what is right, either on an ethical/moral scale or in the eyes of readers and viewers. There are times when it is absolutely essential for the journalist to have the protection to publish what many would regard as offensive and embarrassing private information. But the routine publication of this kind of information may someday seriously dilute this valuable protection. (See pages 324–330 for a discussion of legitimate public concern.)

1. Warren and Brandeis, "The Right to Privacy," 220.
2. *Hall* v. *Post,* 15 M.L.R. 2329 (1988).
3. Kalven, "Privacy in Tort Law," 326.

It is easiest to understand this aspect of the law by taking the tort apart and looking at each element separately (see boxed text). The plaintiff in a private facts case carries the burden of proving each element. Failure to convince the court of any one of these three parts of the law means the lawsuit is doomed.

PUBLICITY TO PRIVATE FACTS

1. There must be publicity to private facts about an individual.
2. The revelation of this material must be offensive to a reasonable person.
3. The material is not of legitimate public concern.

PUBLICITY

The words "publicity" and "publication" mean different things in privacy law than they do in libel law. In defamation, "publication" means to communicate the material to a single third party. The word "publicity" in privacy law implies far more. It means that the material is communicated to the public at large or to a great number of people, making it certain that the facts will shortly become public knowledge. This kind of publicity can usually be presumed when a story is published in a newspaper or broadcast over radio and television, or contained on a Web site, a chat room or an electronic bulletin board.

PRIVATE FACTS

Before an invasion-of-privacy suit can be successful, the plaintiff must demonstrate that the material publicized was indeed private. What happens in public is considered public information. When the Associated Press reported the identity of the victim of a sexual assault who testified at the sentencing hearing of the molester, the young man sued for invasion of privacy. The name was not in the court records and had not been made public before the hearing. But the testimony was given in open court. The 4th U.S. Court of Appeals ruled in favor of the news-gathering agency, saying "we cannot understand how the voluntary disclosure of information in an unrestricted, open courtroom setting could be anything but a matter of public interest."[4] One of two young women who were photographed while attending a rock concert at the Big Cypress Indian Reservation in Florida sued when her picture—showing her exposed breasts adorned with tattoos or body paint—was published in Stuff magazine with the caption "Their Parents Must Be Proud." She argued that because the picture was taken on privately owned land at a concert open only to ticket holders it was a private affair. The Florida Circuit Court disagreed, noting that as a matter of law and common sense, a rock concert is a public event.[5]

---

4. *Doe 2* v. *Associated Press*, 331 F. 3d 417 (2003).
5. *Mayhall* v. *Dennis Stuff Inc.*, 31 M.L.R. 1567 (2002).

The California Supreme Court ruled in 2004 that it was not an invasion of privacy when the Discovery cable channel broadcast a documentary on a criminal trial that had taken place some 10 years earlier. One of the defendants had pled guilty to being an accessory after the fact to a murder for hire, served three years in prison, and since being released lived an obscure, lawful life. He argued that dredging up the past revealed a part of his life that was unknown to many of his contemporary friends and business associates. The court ruled that the First Amendment precludes holding the news media liable for the publication of truthful information contained in public court records, regardless of how much time had passed or what the plaintiff had subsequently done with his life.[6] A U.S. District Court ruled that the publication in Penthouse magazine of pictures of celebrities Tommy Lee and Pamela Anderson Lee, showing them on their honeymoon in various states of undress, "sexually touching," would not support a private facts case since the photos had been previously published in other magazines. The scenes were no longer private when Penthouse published the pictures.[7]

If a large segment of the public is already aware of supposedly intimate or personal information, it is not private. Oliver Sipple, who deflected a gun held by a woman who tried to assassinate President Gerald Ford, sued the San Francisco Chronicle after a columnist noted that the fact that Sipple was a homosexual was probably the reason Ford had never thanked his benefactor for his heroic act. But Sipple's suit failed, in part at least, because his sexual orientation was hardly a secret in San Francisco. A California Court of Appeals noted that Sipple routinely frequented gay bars, marched in parades with other homosexuals, and openly worked for the election of homosexual political candidates, and that many gay publications had reported stories about his activities in the homosexual community. That he was a homosexual was not a private fact, the court ruled.[8] A court in Massachusetts ruled that because the plaintiff in a privacy action had told three other persons about some embarrassing personal information, the information was not a private fact for purpose of an invasion-of-privacy lawsuit.[9]

Information contained in documents and files that are considered public records—that is, open to public inspection—is generally not regarded as private. What if no person has ever inspected the file, but then its contents are published? It is still not regarded as private. The Idaho Statesman in Boise was sued when it published a photo of a handwritten statement that was given to the police in 1955 during the investigation of a sex scandal. The individual who gave the statement was charged and convicted, but the statement implicated other people who were never charged in the case. The document was never part of a criminal proceeding and never made it into a public court record, but was kept for 40 years in a public criminal case file that was stored in the court clerk's office. It was discovered and published in 1995 in an article about the earlier scandal during a debate on a public initiative to limit the rights of gays in Idaho. An individual who was linked to a homosexual relationship (but never charged with a crime) in the original 40-year-old document sued for invasion of privacy. The Idaho Court of Appeals said the publication was protected because it was a part of

6. *Gates* v. *Discovery Communications Inc.,* 101 P. 3d 552 (2004).
7. *Lee* v. *Penthouse International Ltd.,* 25 M.L.R. 1651 (1997).
8. *Sipple* v. *Chronicle Publishing Co.,* 154 Cal. App. 3d 1040 (1984).
9. *Peckham* v. *Levy,* 26 M.L.R. 1222 (1997).

an official criminal court file. Quoting an opinion by Justice Warren Burger from 1975, the Idaho court noted, "A responsible press is an undoubtedly desirable goal, but press responsibility is not mandated by the Constitution and like many other virtues it cannot be legislated." After two hearings the Idaho Supreme Court affirmed the lower court rulings, saying the newspaper could not be held liable for accurately reporting what was contained in a court record open to the public.[10]

Journalists must be careful when dealing with health records. What seems to be a public record may not be. New York City was sued by an individual who complained to the City Commission on Human Rights that he had been discriminated against by his employer because he was infected with the AIDS virus. The commission arranged an agreement between the employer and the man, and then distributed a press release outlining the settlement. The plaintiff was not identified, but he alleged that there were sufficient details in the release that made him readily identifiable to persons who knew him or worked with him. The city maintained that when the man filed a complaint, he put his name on a public record. But Human Rights Commission staffers failed to realize that part of the arranged settlement included an agreement that the complainant would not be identified. The city code regarding such a conciliation agreement specifically states that the information shall be made public, *unless the complainant and the commission determine that disclosure is not required.* The 2nd U.S. Circuit Court of Appeals ruled that the plaintiff's medical status did not automatically become a public record when he filed his complaint.[11]

Naming Rape Victims

Some of the most difficult decisions journalists must make today relate to the naming of the victims of crimes, especially sexual crimes. The name is usually a part of a public record (a public police file, a public information or indictment, or a court record) and thus not private. But the individual has already been a victim of an assailant. Some people say that the way some publications and television stations operate today, putting the name in the public press is akin to assaulting the victim again. Rape victims have been the most common litigants in privacy suits aimed at newspapers or television stations that publicize the names of sexual assault victims. Not many newspapers and broadcasting outlets routinely publicize the name of a rape victim today, but some do, and lawsuits have occurred.[12]

Not many newspapers and broadcasting outlets routinely publicize the name of a rape victim today, but some do, and lawsuits have occurred.

Critics of the practice of naming rape victims in news articles raise three arguments:

■ Someone who is sexually assaulted is victimized three times: the first during the assault, the second during interrogation by often unsympathetic police and during public trial testimony and cross-examination, and the third by knowing that friends, neighbors, co-workers and others are aware of the rape because of the publicity.

■ Society often judges the rape victim to be as guilty as the rapist. This attitude can stigmatize the victim for many years.

---

10. *Uranga* v. *Federated Publications Inc.,* 28 M.L.R. 2265 (2000), aff'd. 67 P. 3d 29 (2003).
11. *Doe* v. *New York,* 15 F. 3d 275 (1994).
12. Marcus and McMahon, "Limiting Disclosure," 1019.

■ Because of the first two factors, victims who realize that their identities will be revealed frequently fail to report the crime, especially if the rape has been committed by an acquaintance. The rapist is not punished and may go on to attack another victim.

The validity of the arguments is difficult to dispute. But some journalists will publish or broadcast the victim's name regardless of the consequences. They argue that it is important for society to know the names of all crime victims. Publishing the name of a victim adds credibility to a news story, makes the story more meaningful to readers or viewers. Others argue that when the press fails to publish the name of a rape victim it is treating this victim differently from the victim of a simple assault or a robbery. This reinforces the notion that rape victims are at least partly responsible for their fate, or that they are "damaged goods." "Now is the time for us to understand that keeping the hunted under wraps merely establishes her as an outcast and implies that her chances for normal social relations are doomed forevermore," said Karen DeCrow, former president of the National Organization for Women. "Pull off the veil of shame. Print the name," she added. Geneva Overholser, former editor of the Des Moines Register, argues that by not printing the name, the press is reinforcing the idea that rape is a different kind of attack, not a crime of brutal violence. She said that this "sour blight of prejudice is best subjected to strong sunlight."[13] Some newspapers are trying to reach a compromise on this matter by not printing the victim's name unless she or he consents to the use. Victims who fear the publicity are protected; using the names of those who don't mind undermines the myth noted by Karen DeCrow.

Four states, Florida, Georgia, South Carolina and Wisconsin, adopted statutes early in the century that prohibited the press from identifying the victim of a rape. Among other provisions, these laws gave victims a right to sue for invasion of privacy if their name was revealed. The statutes in both Wisconsin[14] and South Carolina[15] were tested and courts ruled that the laws did not infringe on freedom of the press. The Supreme Court of the United States first became involved in the issue in the mid-1970s. A reporter for an Atlanta, Ga., television station, in violation of station policy, broadcast the name of a 17-year-old woman who had been raped and murdered. He had obtained the name from public court documents. The parents sued, using the Georgia rape victim identification law as the basis for the legal action. Georgia courts supported the privacy claim, but in 1975, in the case of *Cox Broadcasting Co.* v. *Cohn,* the U.S. Supreme Court overturned the decision. The high court ruled that the press cannot be held liable for invasion of privacy for reporting information that was already part of a public record. Justice Byron White noted that most people depend on the mass media for information about the operation of government. The press gathers this information at public meetings and from the public record. Judicial proceedings are an important part of our governmental system and are something in which the public has always expressed a great interest. By making judicial records and proceedings public, the state of Georgia must have concluded that the public interest was being served:

> We are reluctant to embark on a course that would make public records generally available to the media but forbid their publication if offensive to the sensibilities of the supposed reasonable man. Such a rule would make it very

13. Marcus and McMahon, "Limiting Disclosure," 1019.
14. *State* v. *Evjue,* 253 Wis. 146 (1948).
15. *Nappier* v. *Jefferson Standard Life Insurance Co.,* 322 F. 2d 502 (1963).

difficult for the press to inform their readers about the public business and yet stay within the law. The rule would invite timidity and self-censorship and very likely lead to the suppression of many items that would otherwise be put into print and that should be made available to the public.[16]

Quoting the "Restatement of Torts," which attempts to summarize the law of torts, the court said, "There is no liability when the defendant merely gives further publicity to information about the plaintiff which is already public. Thus there is no liability for giving publicity to facts about the plaintiff's life which are matters of public record."

But the 1975 ruling did not completely resolve the issue. The high court was confronted with a somewhat different case 14 years later. The Florida Star, a weekly newspaper in Jacksonville, mistakenly published the name of the victim of a sexual assault. Such publication was against the newspaper's own policy and in violation of a state policy that deemed that such records were not to be made public. Law enforcement officers inadvertently gave the record to a new reporter, and it was included in the weekly outline of police activity published by the newspaper. The privacy suit was based on a Florida law that made it illegal to "print, publish, or broadcast . . . in any instrument of mass communication" the name of the victim of a rape. Justice Thurgood Marshall, writing for the six-person majority, said the newspaper could not be held liable in this case. It had published accurate information that it had lawfully obtained, information contained in public records. The plaintiff argued that the police reports that were mistakenly given to the reporter were not public records. Marshall said that this fact was immaterial. "The fact that state officials are not required to disclose such reports does not make it unlawful for a newspaper to receive them when furnished by the government," Marshall wrote.* But the jurist stressed that the court's ruling was not without limits.

> Our holding today is limited. We do not hold that truthful publication is automatically constitutionally protected, or that there is no zone of personal privacy within which the state may protect the individual from intrusion by the press, or even that a State may never punish publication of the name of a victim of a sexual offense. . . . We hold only that where a newspaper publishes truthful information which it has lawfully obtained, punishment may be imposed, if at all, only when narrowly tailored to a state interest of the highest order.[17]

The issue in Florida continued to play itself out two years later when the national tabloid newspaper The Globe and other print and broadcast media revealed the name of the young woman who claimed she was raped by William Kennedy Smith at the Kennedy estate in Palm Beach. Smith was acquitted of the charges, but Florida prosecuted The Globe under

---

*In 2005 the U.S. 3rd Court of Appeals ruled that it was not an invasion of privacy when a Pennsylvania newspaper published a report that a young male had been charged with raping a seven-year-old girl, even though state law barred the disclosure of juvenile law enforcement records. The court said the information had been lawfully gathered from a police officer, who, in giving the story to the press, violated a state law. "His unlawful release of the information does not make the receipt of that information by the Herald Standard unlawful," the court said. *Bowley* v. *City of Uniontown Police Department,* 404 F. 3d 783 (2005).
16. *Cox Broadcasting Co.* v. *Cohn,* 420 U.S. 469 (1975).
17. *Florida Star* v. *B.J.F.,* 109 S. Ct. 2603 (1989).

the statute just cited. In August 1993, a Florida District Court of Appeals ruled that the state statute was unconstitutional. In an attempt to respond to Justice Marshall's instruction in the earlier Florida Star decision, the state of Florida argued that the statute was justified because the state had a high interest in protecting the identity of rape victims. State attorneys cited many of the same arguments previously noted on pages 319–320 to support their contention that the victim's name should not be revealed. The Court of Appeals was apparently unimpressed. "The fact that forty-six states are able to conduct sexual assault investigations and trials without punishing the press criminally for disclosure of the victim's identity is, in itself, a circumstance which leads this court to conclude that the state's expressed concerns about a victim's safety and privacy are somewhat exaggerated and overblown," the court said.[18]

The debate on whether publishing the name of a victim of a sexual assault is good policy goes on. But court rulings seem to be generally consistent in protecting the press. In 1993 the Georgia Supreme Court reversed a lower-court judgment against a newspaper that had published the name of a woman who shot and killed an intruder in her home, an individual whom she believed was about to sexually assault her. The police regarded the shooting as self-defense and treated the attack as a sexual assault, so the victim sued the press when stories about the incident were published. The state high court ruled that the newspaper had merely published information about a matter of public importance that it had obtained legally. The shooting story was a subject of legitimate public interest, and the newspaper had a right to accurately report facts about the incident, including the woman's name, the court said.[19] Two years later the Texas Supreme Court ruled that it was not an invasion of privacy when a newspaper revealed extensive personal details about the unnamed victim of a rape. The court acknowledged that the details made it likely the victim of the crime could be identified, but said it would not hold the newspaper to the task of sifting through all the details in a story to decide which ones were safe to publish and which ones were not. The court called this an impossible task, one that could cause critical information of legitimate public interest to be withheld until it becomes untimely and worthless to an informed public.[20]

OFFENSIVE MATERIAL

If the determination has been made that private facts about a person's life have been published, a court must then ask two subsequent questions:

1. Would the publication of the material offend a reasonable person?
2. Was the published material of legitimate public concern?

Judges and juries are often faced with the dilemma of deciding whether the revelation of important, but offensive or embarrassing, information is an invasion of privacy. The law on this question is pretty clear; if the material is of legitimate public concern, it doesn't matter how offensive or embarrassing the revelation is. There was no invasion of privacy. For the past

18. *Florida* v. *Globe Communications Corp.,* 622 So. 2d 1066 (1993), aff'd. Florida Supreme Court, 648 So. 2d 110 (1994).
19. *Macon Telegraph Publishing Co.* v. *Tatum,* 436 S.E. 2d 655 (1993). In October 2001, the Georgia statute was declared unconstitutional by the state Supreme Court. *Dye* v. *Wallace,* 553 S.E. 2d 561 (2001).
20. *Star-Telegram Inc.* v. *Doe,* 23 M.L.R. 2492 (1995).

100 years courts have been extremely reluctant to fashion narrow limits on the kinds of information people need to receive. Time and time again judges have ruled that it is not only the responsibility of the press to bring important public information to the public, but also that it is the job of editors and reporters, not the courts, to decide what is and what isn't important. If there is any legitimate public interest at all in the material, the press will usually win the case, regardless of how embarrassing revelation of the material might be. This notion is more fully discussed on pages 324–330.

It is the job of editors and reporters, not the courts, to decide what is and what isn't important.

Remember the revelation of the material must be offensive to a reasonable person, not someone who is overly sensitive. Peggy Jo Fry sued the Ionia (Mich.) Sentinel-Standard for invasion of privacy when it reported that her husband and another woman had died in a fire that destroyed a cottage near Lake Michigan. The story mentioned that Ted Fry had been seen with Rita Hill at a tavern prior to the fire and related details about Fry's wife and children. The court ruled that these details were simply not highly offensive to a reasonable person.[21] Another Michigan woman sued Knight-Ridder Newspapers after the Miami Herald published a story about the murder of her daughter. The plaintiff in the case was mentioned incidentally in the story. It was noted that four of her six children were deaf and that she was a hardworking woman who had great faith in her daughter's ability to succeed in life. The court said such information is not offensive.[22]

But judges are human beings with feelings and sensitivities, and though they will most often bend over backward to support the right of the press to publish truthful information, once in a while a case comes along that presents what the court believes are outrageous circumstances that cry out for some punishment of the newspaper or broadcasting station. Three out-of-the-ordinary cases are cited here as a warning that there are exceptions to what even the experts regard as the hard-and-fast rules in the law of privacy.

Many years ago a woman with a rather unusual disorder—she ate constantly, but still lost weight—was admitted to a hospital. Journalists were tipped off and descended on her room, pushed past the closed door, and took pictures against the patient's will. Time magazine ran a story about the patient, Dorothy Barber, and in it referred to her, in inimitable Time style, as "the starving glutton." Mrs. Barber sued and won her case. The judge said the hospital is one place people should be able to go for privacy.[23] More than the patient's expectation of privacy in a hospital room influenced the ruling, because there are several decisions in which persons in hospitals have been considered to be the subject of legitimate concern and did not therefore enjoy the right to privacy. The story about the unusual disorder was surely offensive, almost mocking. The disorder was not contagious, and the implications for the general public were minimal. The Time story seemed to focus on Mrs. Barber almost as if she were a freak, and in doing so the revelation of this information was highly offensive to any reasonable person, the court ruled.

An Alabama housewife took her two sons to the county fair and finally succumbed to their pressure to be taken through the fun house. As she left the building, an air jet blew Mrs. Flora Bell Graham's dress up over her head, and she was exposed from the waist down except for her underclothing. As fate would have it, a photographer was nearby and captured

---

21. *Fry* v. *Ionia Sentinel-Standard,* 300 N.W. 2d 687 (1980).
22. *Andren* v. *Knight-Ridder Newspapers,* 10 M.L.R. 2109 (1984).
23. *Barber* v. *Time,* 159 S.W. 2d 291 (1942).

the moment on film. The picture was featured in the Sunday edition of the local newspaper as a publicity piece for the fair. Mrs. Graham sued. By logical legal analysis one could suggest that she should not have won. Many people saw her. It was a public occurrence. She could not be readily identified in the picture because her dress was over her head. However, persons who knew the children, who were also in the picture, could make the connection between mother and children. Mrs. Graham did win.[24] She had suffered an immense amount of embarrassment from the most intimate kind of revelation, and the public value of the photograph was extremely low.

Finally, the South Carolina Supreme Court affirmed a jury verdict against a newspaper that, in publishing a story about teenage pregnancies, had identified a young man—a minor—as the father of an illegitimate child. The teenage mother of the baby had given the reporter the father's name. The reporter talked to the young man, who understood that the newspaper was doing a survey on teenage pregnancy. He said he was never told that his name might be used in the story. The newspaper argued that the information—including the boy's name—was of great public interest. The state Supreme Court said that was a jury question, and a jury ruled that it was not of great public interest[25] and that its publication was highly offensive.

LEGITIMATE PUBLIC CONCERN

The rulings just noted are not typical decisions by courts in cases involving the publication of private facts. Normally, a legitimate public interest in the subject matter or the people involved will outweigh any embarrassment to the plaintiff. As noted previously, public interest trumps offensiveness. And public interest has been broadly defined. Courts are more interested in what people find interesting, not what people *should* be interested in reading about. The relatively narrow definition of public concern fashioned to apply in defining a limited-purpose public figure in a libel case (see pages 202–217) is simply not used in these privacy cases.

Subjects as diverse as a 12-year-old girl giving birth to a child,[26] the investigation of a death in a boating accident,[27] the sterilization of an 18-year-old girl,[28] a young man getting substance abuse treatment at a hospital,[29] the activities of a bodysurfer,[30] the photograph of a murder victim,[31] and others have all been ruled to be of legitimate concern and interest to the public. Even the seemingly frivolous subject of romance was declared to be newsworthy by a New York court that found no liability in the broadcast of a television film of a man and a woman walking hand in hand along Madison Avenue. The couple objected to being photographed; he was married to another woman, she was engaged to be married to another man. The court said that the film, used to show people behaving in a romantic fashion in order to explore the prevailing attitudes on this topic, is newsworthy.[32]

24. *Daily Times-Democrat* v. *Graham,* 162 So. 2d 474 (1962).
25. *Hawkins* v. *Multimedia,* 344 S.E. 2d 145 (1986).
26. *Meetze* v. *AP,* 95 S.E. 2d 606 (1956).
27. *Partin* v. *Fox Televisiion Stations of Birmingham, Inc.,* 28 M.L.R. 1630 (1999).
28. *Howard* v. *Des Moines Register,* 283 N.W. 2d 789 (1979).
29. *Carter* v. *Superior Court of San Diego County,* 30 M.L.R. 1193 (2002).
30. *Virgil* v. *Time, Inc.,* 527 F. 2d 1122 (1975).
31. *Barger* v. *Courier-Journal and Louisville Times,* 20 M.L.R. 1189 (1992).
32. *DeGregario* v. *CBS,* 43 N.Y.S. 2d 922 (1984).

The courts have been most generous to the press in their understanding of American reading and viewing habits. In a 1975 ruling in California, the U.S. Court of Appeals for the 9th Circuit noted that "in determining what is a matter of legitimate public interest, account must be taken of the customs and conventions of the community; and in the last analysis what is proper becomes a matter of community mores."[33] Thirty-five years earlier, another federal judge noted that the public enjoyed reading about the problems, misfortunes and troubles of their neighbors and other members of the community. The case involved an article in The New Yorker about the failure of a child prodigy to fulfill the promise many had predicted for him (see boxed excerpt). "When such are the mores of the community, it would be unwise for a court to bar their expression in the newspapers, books, and magazines of the day," Judge Charles Clark wrote.[34]

The following are excerpts from an article written by Jared L. Manley (a pen name for noted writer James Thurber) about William James Sidis. The piece was published in The New Yorker on August 14, 1937, and provoked one of the nation's most celebrated invasion-of-privacy lawsuits (*Sidis* v. *F-R Publishing Co.*).

"Where Are They Now?" "April Fool!"
"One snowy January evening in 1910 about a hundred professors and advanced students of mathematics from Harvard University gathered in a lecture hall in Cambridge, Massachusetts, to listen to a speaker by the name of William James Sidis. He had never addressed an audience before, and he was abashed and a little awkward at the start. His listeners had to attend closely, for he spoke in a small voice that did not carry well, and he punctuated his talk with nervous, shrill laughter. . . . The speaker wore black velvet knickers. He was eleven years old. . . . When it was all over, the distinguished Professor Daniel F. Comstock of Massachusetts Institute of Technology was moved to predict to reporters, who had listened in profound bewilderment, that young Sidis would grow up to be a great mathematician, a famous leader in the world of science."

(The next section of the article explains how Sidis, as a small child, had become a kind of guinea pig for his psychologist father who used experimental techniques to educate his son when he was little more than a baby. Manley goes on to describe Sidis's education, his extreme efforts to hide from the spotlight of publicity, his series of mundane jobs, and his rejection of a career in science or mathematics.)

"William James Sidis lives today, at the age of thirty-nine, in a hall bedroom of Boston's shabby south end. . . . He seems to get a great and ironic enjoyment out of leading a life of wandering irresponsibility after a childhood of scrupulous regimentation. . . . Sidis is employed now, as usual, as a clerk in a business house. He said that he never stays in one office long because his employers or fellow-workers soon find out that he is the famous boy wonder, and he can't tolerate a position after that. 'The very sight of a mathematical formula makes me physically ill,' he said."

---

33. *Virgil* v. *Time, Inc.*, 527 F. 2d 1122 (1975).
34. *Sidis* v. *F-R Publishing Co.*, 113 F. 2d 806 (1940).

(Manley relates that Sidis has become a passionate collector of streetcar transfers, that he enjoys the study of certain aspects of the history of Native Americans, and that he is writing a treatise on floods.)

"His visitor [Manley] was emboldened, at last, to bring up the prediction, made by Professor Comstock . . . back in 1910, that the little boy who lectured that year on the fourth dimension to a gathering of learned men would grow up to be a great mathematician, a famous leader in the world of science. 'It's strange,' said William James Sidis, with a grin, 'but you know, I was born on April Fool's Day.'"

Even the way a story is presented is normally not a factor: Sensationalism and sensational treatment generally do not remove the protection of newsworthiness. The parents of two young children who had suffocated in an abandoned refrigerator said the sensational way the story was presented was as objectionable as the story itself. However, the court ruled that the manner in which the article was written was not relevant to whether the article was protected by the constitutional guarantees of free speech and free press—which, by the way, it was.[35] In another case a Boston newspaper published a horrible picture of an automobile accident in which the bloodied and battered body of one of the victims was clearly visible and identifiable, and the court rejected the plaintiff's claim. The Massachusetts Supreme Court noted, "Many things which are distressing or may be lacking in propriety or good taste are not actionable."[36] And in 1994 the 5th U.S. Circuit Court of Appeals ruled that sensational television stories about the discovery of child pornography, including homemade sex films, among the belongings of a Roman Catholic priest did not turn newsworthy reports into invasion of privacy. The judge agreed the information was embarrassing and the news stories demonstrated a distinct lack of sensitivity on the part of the broadcasters, but ruled that the material was clearly of public interest. "We are not prepared to make editorial decisions for the media regarding information directly related to matters of public concern," the court declared.[37]

Persons who are famous or become well known because of something that has happened to them lose a considerable amount of their privacy. Revelations about them, which might be actionable if made about a typical individual, usually do not generate liability. Such is the nature of celebrity in the 21st century. But people whose lives intersect with famous or well-known individuals also lose some of their privacy. A story published in a Utah newspaper in 1997 said hikers had found the body of a man near a dirt trail whose death, officers said, "looks like one of those autoerotic things." Murder charges were subsequently filed in the case. Later the body was identified, as were the victim's wife and children. The family members sued for invasion of privacy, saying the story contained information that reflected upon the intimate details of the marital relationship. The U.S. District Court dismissed the complaint and the 10th U.S. Court of Appeals affirmed this ruling. The court said it was almost impossible to define the limits of the right to privacy if it encompassed information about a spouse's behavior that reflected on the marital relationship. But the court said it would draw the line around the individual directly implicated by the personal material revealed, in this

35. *Costlow* v. *Cuismano,* 311 N.Y.S. 2d 92 (1970).
36. *Kelley* v. *Post Publishing Co.,* 327 Mass. 275 (1951).
37. *Cinel* v. *Connick,* 15 F. 3d 1338 (1994).

case the dead husband. "Any other conclusion would stretch the right to privacy beyond any reasonable limits," the judges added.[38] Another similar ruling involved a woman named Pamela J. Howell, who was secretly committed to a private psychiatric facility by her family. Few of her friends or relatives knew of the hospitalization. Another patient at the facility, Hedda Nussbaum, had been in the national news for many months as the adoptive mother of a 6-year-old girl who had died from child abuse. A photographer, using a telephoto lens, snapped a photo of Nussbaum as she stood next to Howell at the hospital, and the photo was published in The New York Post. Howell's name was not mentioned in the newspaper, but she was clearly recognizable in the photo. She sued for invasion of privacy, but lost. The New York Court of Appeals ruled that if Howell's picture accompanied a newspaper article on a matter of public interest, and the Nussbaum story still had substantial public interest, she would have to demonstrate that her photo bore no real relationship to the article. The court said she could not carry that burden of proof in this case. Unfortunately, she just happened to be in the wrong place at the wrong time.[39]

But even the most widely known public person retains at least a small portion of his or her life that the courts seem willing to shield. How far can the press delve into the private affairs of a public person? While not officially enunciated, courts have nevertheless recognized that a kind of sliding scale is applicable. The more famous the person, the smaller the zone of privacy. Just as important in many instances, however, is the reason for the publication of private information. The press is not required to justify its publication of private information, but a court will frequently try to determine why the material was published. Did it help readers understand something? Did it illuminate a problem? Did it give viewers important insights? Or was it merely an attempt to titillate readers or viewers, to satisfy a craving for the odd or unusual? A good example of this analysis is a case from California.

How far can the press delve into the private affairs of a public person?

The story focused on Mike Virgil, widely regarded in southern California at the time as one of the best bodysurfers along the Pacific Coast. Sports Illustrated wanted to publish a story on bodysurfing, and writer Curry Kirkpatrick chose to emphasize the prowess of Virgil. Virgil was known for his almost total disregard for personal safety and talked freely with the writer about his private life as well as about his surfing. He told Kirkpatrick that he was reckless in private as well and described several incidents to demonstrate this attitude. These incidents include putting out a burning cigarette with his mouth, burning a hole in his wrist with a cigarette, diving headfirst down a flight of stairs, and eating live insects. After the interview, Virgil had second thoughts about the story and asked Sports Illustrated not to include the material about his private life. The magazine published the story as Kirkpatrick had written it, and Virgil sued. The U.S. Court of Appeals for the 9th Circuit ruled that the line between private and public information "is to be drawn when the publicity ceases to be the giving of information to which the public is entitled, and becomes a morbid and sensational prying into private live *for its own sake* [emphasis added]." In applying this standard to the Virgil case, a U.S. District Court ruled that "any reasonable person reading the article would conclude that the personal facts concerning the individual were revealed in a legitimate journalistic attempt to explain his extremely daring and dangerous style of bodysurfing."[40] Judge Thompson ruled

38. *Livsey* v. *Salt Lake County,* 275 F. 3d 952 (2002).
39. *Howell* v. *New York Post Co., Inc.,* 612 N.E. 2d 699 (1993).
40. *Virgil* v. *Time, Inc.,* 527 F. 2d 1122 (1975).

that no one could reasonably conclude that these personal facts were included for any inherent morbid, sensational or curiosity appeal they might have. If Sports Illustrated had published these personal details about Virgil without any information about his performance as a talented bodysurfer, it might have been an invasion of privacy. But in the context of the story about his public life as a surfer, the publication was not an invasion of privacy.

This standard was applied by the Iowa Supreme Court when it ruled that a story about a girl who had been sterilized when she was 18 years old was not an invasion of privacy. The story focused on the activities at a county juvenile home that had come under investigation by the state. As an example of what occurred there, the Des Moines Register recounted the story of a girl who was sterilized against her will because a psychiatrist reported to officials that she was "impulsive" and "hair-triggered" and would probably have psychological problems in the future. The girl's name was used but was not prominent in the story. The court ruled that the paper had not pried into the girl's life simply to shock or outrage the community. The facts were presented to demonstrate to the community the kind of unethical, even illegal, activities taking place at the home. As such, the material was of legitimate public concern. But was it necessary to use the victim's name in this story? Was it not possible for the newspaper to present this story to readers without identifying an unfortunate victim of this county home? The Iowa high court ruled it was legitimate to conclude that the name was an essential ingredient in the story:

> In the sense of serving an appropriate news function, the disclosure [of the name] contributed constructively to the impact of the article. It offered a personalized frame of reference to which the reader could relate, fostering perception and understanding. Moreover, it lent specificity and credibility to the report. In this way the disclosure served as an effective means of accomplishing the intended news function. . . . Moreover, at a time when it was important to separate fact from rumor, the specificity of the report would strengthen the accuracy of the public perception of the merits of the controversy.[41]

What courts often look for in these kinds of cases, then, is a nexus between the admittedly private and embarrassing information and the newsworthy subject of the story. How far the press can go in reporting the private life of public persons often depends not only on what was said—how private the information is—but also on why the material was used. When an individual's public life is explained, many parts of that person's private life are of legitimate public concern.

FACTORS SOME COURTS TAKE INTO ACCOUNT IN DETERMINING LEGITIMATE PUBLIC CONCERN

▮ How much public interest or importance there is in the material.

▮ How deeply does publication of these facts intrude into an individual's privacy?

▮ How public or private is the individual who is the focus of the story?

---

41. *Howard* v. *Des Moines Register,* 283 N.W. 2d 789 (1979).

It is important at this point in the discussion of public persons and public figures to note that these terms are not being used as they are used in the law of libel. Recall, when discussing defamation, the label "public figure" had a distinct and quite narrow meaning. That is not the definition of public person used in privacy law. Also, many courts have rejected the concept of the "involuntary public figure" in libel cases, a private individual who just happens to get caught in a big story. Since 1929 American courts have recognized that involuntary public figures do exist in privacy law. The Kentucky Supreme Court first noted such a person and gave this definition of the status:

> The right of privacy is the right to live one's life in seclusion, without being subjected to unwarranted and undesired publicity. In short, it is the right to be let alone . . . . There are times, however, when one, whether willing or not, becomes an actor in an occurrence of public or general interest. When this takes place he emerges from his seclusion, and it is not an invasion of his right of privacy to publish his photograph with an account of such occurrence.[42]

The court later noted that private citizens can become "innocent actors in great tragedies in which the public has a deep concern." The scope, therefore, of the rubric involuntary public figure is wide. In Kansas City a young man was arrested by police outside the local courthouse on suspicion of burglary. A local television news crew filmed the arrest, and it was broadcast on television that night. The young man, however, had been released by police, who admitted they had arrested the wrong man. An invasion-of-privacy suit followed, but the courts rejected it, stating that the plaintiff must show a serious, unreasonable, unwarranted and offensive invasion of private affairs before recovery can be allowed:

> In the case at bar, plaintiff was involved in a noteworthy event about which the public had a right to be informed and which the defendant [television station KCMO] had a right to publicize. This is true even though his involvement therein was purely involuntary and against his will.[43]

An Illinois appeals court ruled in 1978 that a story that reported the death of a boy from an apparent drug overdose and then went on to outline details of the youth's life was not an invasion of privacy. The subject was of legitimate concern; in addition, the youth became an involuntary public figure by his actions within the drug culture in the community. "It is not necessary for an individual to actively seek publicity in order to be found in the public eye," the court ruled.[44]

Some legal scholars have speculated that because the Supreme Court has ruled in libel cases that a public figure must be a voluntary participant in a controversy or public event, a similar rule might be applied in the law of privacy. But there seems to be nothing on record to suggest that will happen. Indeed, two factors strongly mitigate against such a development. First, to abandon the involuntary public figure rule in privacy law would be to radically reshape a part of the law that is more than 75 years old. That seems unlikely. Second, in private facts cases the law is focusing on the publication of truthful, albeit private information,

42. *Jones* v. *Herald Post Co.,* 18 S.W. 2d 972 (1929).
43. *Williams* v. *KCMO Broadcasting Co.,* 472 S.W. 2d (1971).
44. *Beresky* v. *Teschner,* 381 N.E. 2d 979 (1978).

not defamatory falsehoods. American judges have been extremely reluctant to find liability where the charge is based on truthful or factual material. A narrowing of the definition of public figure to meet the criteria established in libel law would significantly enlarge the scope of liability. The records suggest most American jurists oppose such a move.

ETHICS AND PRIVACY

Journalists have to remember that liability in a private facts case is usually determined by a judge or jury asking questions about some fairly elastic concepts. Was the material offensive to a reasonable person? Was the material of legitimate public concern? The law in this area is not carved in stone and could change as public sentiments change. If nothing else, in the long term, decisions by judges and juries usually reflect public opinion. And this is why people who work in the mass media need to begin to ask more questions as well—especially, what are the ethical implications of revealing this personal information?

Journalism is in many ways a tough business. Many reporters and editors spend a lot of time, too much time it sometimes seems, reporting the sordid or tragic side of life. It is easy to become desensitized, to become immune to the anguish such reporting can cause. There are often hard choices to be made. Many years ago distinguished editor John Sigenthaler related to a television audience what takes place each day when the editors at a newspaper decide what stories and photos should go on the front page. He said he recalled one such meeting where the staff had to decide what picture to put on page one: a photo of a tragic automobile accident or a photo of a field full of spring flowers. He said they chose the picture of the flowers, but then reminded his audience that life is not just a field of flowers. There are many darker matters that must be reported.

When it comes to privacy, good editors agree that the feelings and sensibilities of the subject of the story should always be considered. But, at the same time, these feelings and sensibilities should never be used as a reason to deny to the public information that has legitimate public concern. The last three words are the key. Legitimate public concern. The decision on whether to publish or broadcast a story will always be a judgment call that must be made carefully and thoughtfully. Too many journalists are reluctant to make this call. Instead, they declare that their job is to simply report the news, to pass along whatever they discover. Journalists are not supposed to make judgments, they argue. Some people call this the sewer pipe school of journalism. What goes in one end of a sewer pipe comes out the other end with little change. But today people in the mass media, and even members of their audience, know that journalists make judgments every day of the week. What stories should be covered? Who should be quoted? How should the story be played? Journalism is not now nor ever has been a purely objective activity.

It is worth noting that the ethics code of the Society of Professional Journalists (SPJ), an organization of reporters and editors, reminds reporters to "recognize that gathering and reporting information may cause harm and discomfort. Pursuit of the news is not a license for arrogance." The SPJ's ethics code also instructs journalists to "show good taste. Avoid pandering to lurid curiosity." Such ethical considerations are clearly relevant when considering whether to publish private facts.[45]

45. http://www.spj.org/ethics.asp

The courts and the public will continue to support the endeavors of the press in privacy actions so long as there is some assurance that journalists are willing to ask the question, Is there legitimate public concern in this story? At present, this is primarily an ethical issue. But if journalism is pursued with the kind of reckless abandon that is common today at a few media outlets, it could one day become a defining legal question as well. We must constantly remember the words of the great U.S. jurist Learned Hand. Liberty rests in the hearts and minds of the people, Hand wrote. When it dies there, no court or constitution can revive it.

RECOUNTING THE PAST

If an individual is in the public eye, revelations about his or her private life are normally fair game for the press. As noted above, courts have erected an almost impenetrable defense that blocks such lawsuits. But lawsuits by persons who were once in the public eye, but have retreated to a quiet life of solitude out of the public spotlight, are fairly common. These litigants usually argue that the passing of time dims the public spotlight and that a person stripped of a right to privacy because of his or her notoriety regains at least some of that protection after an indeterminate period of time.

There are at least two kinds of cases that usually occur. The first is the simplest to describe: a news story or book or TV documentary that simply recounts the past. In other words, history. "On this day in 1990 Mary Beth Ellroy was convicted of killing her two-week-old baby and sentenced to 15 years in prison." These kinds of lawsuits are never successful. Typical is a decision by the New Jersey Supreme Court in a case involving a book that recounted a crime spree that occurred eight years earlier. Joseph Kallinger and his son were apprehended by police in 1975 after their criminal rampage that included killing, robbing and raping. In 1983 a professor of criminal justice at City University of New York published a book about Kallinger's life and crimes. One of Kallinger's victims sued, arguing that replaying this tragedy in public print was traumatic and disturbing and would be highly offensive. The court agreed with that assessment but ruled that the case failed because the facts revealed were not private but public, and "even if they were private, they are of legitimate concern to the public."[46] The lapse of time did nothing to insulate the plaintiff from such publicity. The facts were taken from the public trial record in the case, and the court noted that the Supreme Court ruling in *Cox* v. *Cohn*[47] was not limited to contemporaneous events.

The second kind of story is a bit more problematic. A report that film star Sid Feldman was accused in 1995 by his former wife of possessing child pornography is again retelling history. But the added sentence, "Today, Feldman is selling real estate in Dade County, Florida," pushes the report beyond history. Some courts have ruled that such "Where are they now" kinds of stories are permissible, so long as the report was not designed to purposely embarrass or humiliate the plaintiff.[48] But other judges are less tolerant of such publicity and will sometimes ask the question, What is the relevance of tying Feldman's current job with these

---

46. *Romaine* v. *Kallinger,* 537 A. 2d 284 (1988).

47. 420 U.S. 469 (1975).

48. See *Kent* v. *Pittsburgh Press,* 349 F. Supp. 622 (1972); *Sidis* v. *F-R Publishing Co.,* 113 F. 2d 806 (1940); and *Bernstein* v. *NBC,* 232 F. 2d 369 (1955).

accusations from the past?[49] And to defend such a suit, the press needs a good answer. If Feldman were running for public office, if he ran a popular photographic studio that specialized in taking pictures of youngsters, if he were arrested today for possessing child pornography—all of these would supply the rationale for tying the past to the present. But simply reporting that he is selling real estate might not convince the court that such a story should be immune from suit.

Perhaps the most important question any journalist can ask when preparing to publish a story is Why? Why is this information being published? If there is a good reason, most judges will bend over backward to protect the press. But without a good reason, the legal terrain can get a lot more complicated.

PRIVATE FACTS ON THE INTERNET

In Chapter 7 the problem of gathering personal information via the Internet was explored as an intrusion. Disclosing personal information gathered through such an intrusion, or simply publishing private facts on the Internet, falls under the publication-of-private-facts area of privacy law. The law will apply in exactly the same way as it would if the information were published in a newspaper. Were private facts publicized, facts that would be offensive to a reasonable person, that are not of legitimate concern or public interest? But it is worth briefly mentioning other kinds of publication-of-private-facts issues that have arisen.

 The collection of personal data is an important task for both government and business, and was going on for decades, long before the Internet was even a glint in someone's eye. But in the past, data about individuals was usually stored in folders or files and was not easy or inexpensive to share with others. "Today, with commercial databases, networks, and CD-ROMS, you can match data sets with a few keystrokes and literally surf through people's lives," noted Leslie L. Byrnes, a White House consumer affairs adviser.[50] Not many years ago, LexisNexis P-Trak databases promised purchasers access to the names and addresses of 300 million people. Some personal entries included a good deal more, such as birth dates, telephone numbers, prior addresses and even Social Security numbers, which are the primary registration numbers that key Americans to their bank accounts, insurance policies, medical records, and scores of credit card companies. For a short time even the federal government made citizens' Social Security numbers available when it put the Social Security system online.

There is no shortage of people in government and private business who regard the disclosure of such data as a threat to personal privacy. There is a distinct shortage, however, of people within these same venues who think government should do something about the problem. Most civic and business leaders regard the free flow of personal data as something that can be controlled through self-regulation and stricter internal business and government practices. The Federal Trade Commission has been an exception to this general rule, and in

---

49. See, for example, *Hall* v. *Post,* 355 S.E. 2d 816 (1987).
50. "White House Consumer Advisor Sees Role for Encryption in Privacy Protection," 2 E.L.P.R. 156 (1997).

the past has moved against some of the more egregious offenders. (See pages 640–644 in Chapter 15 for examples.)

Each session of Congress seems to generate new attempts to adopt laws to protect personal privacy. There were promises made by members of the House of Representatives that a comprehensive Internet privacy law that would pre-empt all state laws would be adopted in 2002. But it never happened. Debate continues in each legislative session, but proponents of such a law face considerable opposition from powerful interests in the business community as well as officials in the executive branch of government, who proclaim they are sensitive to the needs of business. There was pressure on the government to adopt some kind of law at the end of the 1990s in order to facilitate U.S. compliance with the broad privacy protections contained in the European Data Protection Directive that was adopted by member nations of the European Union in 1995. Failure to comply with the provisions of this directive would have limited American businesses and industries from operating in nations belonging to the European Union, which includes almost all the nations of Europe. But agreements were ultimately reached that permitted American commercial enterprises to continue to operate in Europe without the adoption of privacy legislation in the United States. All the American businesses had to do was to promise they would abide by certain privacy guidelines that were a part of the European Data Privacy Directive. Even then, many businesses failed to follow the guidelines but continued to operate abroad. The complicated issues have not yet been fully resolved.

SUMMARY

It is an invasion of privacy to publicize private information about another person's life if the publication of this information would be embarrassing to a reasonable person and the information is not of legitimate public interest or concern. To publicize means to communicate the information to a large number of people. There is no liability for giving further publicity to information that is already considered public. The press is free, for example, to report even embarrassing and sensitive matters contained in public records. The information that is publicized must be considered offensive to a reasonable person; the law does not protect hypersensitive individuals.

Courts use many strategies to determine whether information has legitimate public concern. Stories that are of great interest have legitimate public concern. Stories about both voluntary and involuntary public figures are normally considered of legitimate public concern. When private information is published or broadcast, it is important that a connection exists between the revelation of the embarrassing private information and the newsworthy aspects of the story. Embarrassing details about a person's private life cannot be publicized simply to amuse or titillate audiences. News stories that recount past events—including embarrassing details of an individual's life—are normally protected from successful privacy suits. However, courts will usually insist on a good reason for relating these embarrassing past events to an individual's current life or work. There is no complete resolution of issues relating to the use of personal data gathered via the Internet.

FALSE-LIGHT INVASION OF PRIVACY

It is illegal to publicize material that places an individual in a false light if

a. **the false light in which the individual was placed would be offensive to a reasonable person, and**

b. **the publisher of the material was at fault when the publication was made.**

This fourth tort in the invasion-of-privacy quartet has engendered the most disputes within the law. What in the world does this have to do with invasion of privacy? Many state courts have refused to recognize this variety of invasion of privacy. In 1998 the Minnesota Supreme Court recognized a cause of action for appropriation, private facts and intrusion, but rejected the false-light tort. Four years later the Colorado Supreme Court also refused to recognize false-light invasion of privacy. Both courts said the cause of action was largely coextensive with libel and didn't see the need to embrace both torts.

The courts' logic is sound to a point—libel and false-light privacy are similar in some ways. At the base both involve the publication of something derogatory about the plaintiff. The practical difference between the two is that the nasty words published about the plaintiff don't have to actually be strong enough to harm a reputation to qualify for a false-light action. In other words, the plaintiff doesn't have to show the court that his reputation was harmed, only that something false was published and that this caused him to suffer embarrassment or humiliation. Also, defendants in false-light cases are unable to take advantage of some of the procedural safeguards and defenses that exist in libel law.[51] The origins of the false-light tort are murky. It was created by judges more than half a century ago as an amalgam of the appropriation and private facts torts. There are three important elements in the tort. The plaintiff must first prove that the specific allegations are false. The same rules that apply in a libel action when truth or falsity is at issue apply. (See pages 185–189.) The key is whether or not the words that carry the sting, that cause humiliation or embarrassment, are substantially true. Errors in details don't matter much. For example, Deangelo Bailey sued rapper Marshall Bruce Mathers III (better known as Eminem) for false-light invasion of privacy because of the lyrics in the 1999 song "Brain Damage." The supposedly autobiographical song described how Mathers was bullied when he was in school, how Bailey banged his head against a urinal, broke his nose, soaked his clothes in blood, etc. Bailey argued that there was no proof of these specific allegations, but the court said the sting in the song lyrics was that Bailey was a bully—and he had admitted that he picked on Mathers when they were younger. This amounted to substantial truth. Case dismissed.[52]

The plaintiff must also prove that the false statements are offensive to a reasonable person, and that the defendant was at fault in publishing this material. The definition of fault in privacy law is the same one that is applied in libel law. (See pages 219–233.) A false-light case can develop from a simple error made by the publisher, but there are other ways such cases arise as well. Here is a summary of the more common kinds of cases.

---

51. *Lake* v. *Wal-Mart Stores Inc.,* 582 N.W. 2d 231 (1998) and *Denver Publishing* v. *Bueno,* 54 P. 3d 893 (2002).

52. *Bailey* v. *Mathers,* 33 M.L.R. 2053 (2005).

> **FALSE-LIGHT PRIVACY**
> 1. Publication of material must put an individual in a false light.
> 2. The false light would be offensive to a reasonable person.
> 3. The publisher of the material was at fault.

FICTIONALIZATION

Fictionalization is really the purposeful distortion of the truth, usually for dramatic purposes. Some of the earliest false-light cases involved radio and television dramatizations of actual news events. Because they did not know exactly what happened, and because real life is generally boring, script writers often changed these events to increase the drama. False-light suits were often a consequence of this creativity.[53] Television programming and motion pictures are filled these days with stories that supposedly represent events that really happened. Television producers even have a name for these kinds of programs—docudramas. These kinds of productions pose risks for their creators because of libel and false-light invasion-of-privacy suits. The simple way to avoid these problems is for a television or motion picture company to buy the rights to the story from the real people they plan to portray. By signing a standard contract (and accepting a few dollars in payment), the real-life characters in the story forfeit their right to sue if they are unhappy with how they are portrayed. Individuals who refuse to sign such an agreement are simply written out of the story; they don't exist as far as the video story is concerned. (And you always thought these presentations were accurate and truthful.) More and more, production companies try to avoid involving the real characters in the story and simply advertise their productions as being "based on a true story." This is shorthand for a more honest statement—"most of this story is fiction."

It was not uncommon years ago for reporters and editors at many magazines and some newspapers to try to dramatize their stories a bit by adding what they suggested was real-life dialogue or maybe some additional "facts" to their news reports.[54] Today, most of this kind of journalism is confined to supermarket tabloid newspapers, or what most would call sleazy magazines. This kind of journalism has prompted more than its share of libel and false-light privacy claims. And some of the antics that prompt these lawsuits are hard to believe. A 96-year-old Arkansas resident sued the Sun tabloid newspaper for using her photo to illustrate a totally fabricated story about a 101-year-old female newspaper carrier who had to give up her route because she was pregnant. Plaintiff Nellie Mitchell's photo had been published 10 years earlier in another tabloid owned by the same company in a true story about the Mountain Home, Ark., woman. But the editors at the Sun needed a picture to illustrate their phony story and simply used Mitchell's, undoubtedly thinking she was dead. A U.S. District Court jury awarded the elderly woman $1.5 million in damages.[55] The simple rule for writers who want

---

53. See, for example, *Strickler* v. *NBC,* 167 F. Supp. 68 (1958).
54. See *Acquino* v. *Bulletin Co.,* 190 Pa. Super. 528 (1959), for example.
55. *Peoples Bank & Trust Co. of Mountain Home* v. *Globe International, Inc.,* 786 F. Supp. 791 (1992). See also *Varnish* v. *Best Medium,* 405 F. 2d 608 (1968).

to be dramatists is this: If you change the facts, change the names and don't use photos of real people.

Real names often appear in novels, feature films, TV shows or even advertisements. Oftentimes individuals will sue (normally unsuccessfully) under appropriation when this occurs. (See pages 289–290.) But false-light cases can result as well. In such actions the decision usually rests on whether just the name was taken, or whether the identity was taken as well. The New York Times, an advertising agency and the United Negro College Fund were recently sued for false-light invasion of privacy by Lawrence Botts Jr., a well-educated white man who complained that he and his family had been put in a false light by an ad carried in the newspaper for the educational charity. The ad depicts a fictional black man who has turned to alcohol and "wasted" his mind because he could not afford a college education. The man's name in the ad was Larry Botts. The 3rd U.S. Court of Appeals rejected the suit, saying the name in the ad was simply a John Doe, "a generic place holder for the prototypical underprivileged black youth."[56]

The differences between taking just a name and taking an identity can be subtle, but they are easy to grasp. Look at these hypothetical situations. Let's say that author Nora Roberts writes a novel about a popular actress who has AIDS. In the book, the actress's best friend is a short, chubby nurse named Julia Roberts. The writer has taken actress Julia Roberts' name, but not her identity. But if, in the novel, an actress who has AIDS is named Julia Roberts, if she is rather tall and thin, if she won an Academy Award, if she had been married to a country/pop singer named Lyle Lovett, and so on, then the writer has taken the identity as well as the name. How many characteristics must be the same before plaintiffs can claim their identity was taken and they were placed in a false light? Courts decide this question on a case-by-case basis.

For example, the author and publisher of a book entitled "Match Set" was sued by a woman who had the same name as the central character in the novel. Both women were named Melanie Geisler. The character in the novel was a female transsexual tennis player who was induced to participate in tennis fraud. The plaintiff in the case worked for a small publishing company for six months and was acquainted with the defendant author who also worked at the same company for a short time. The plaintiff and the fictional Melanie Geisler shared many physical characteristics. Geisler argued that the similarity of names and physical descriptions, coupled with the fact that she and the author were acquainted for a short time, led many persons to believe the book was about her. The U.S. Court of Appeals for the 2nd Circuit ruled that a reasonable person could come to such a conclusion, rejected the defendant's motion for dismissal, and sent the case back for trial.[57] Some authors can face a problem even if the plaintiff does not have the same name as a character in the novel. In an old Florida case a novelist knowingly used a real person with whom she was acquainted as the basis for a character in a novel, but changed the name in the book. She was sued for invasion of privacy and lost the case. The court ruled that because the character described in the novel was so unusual, many persons in the community recognized her even though the name had been changed.[58]

56. *Botts* v. *New York Times Co.,* 106 Fed. Appx. 109 (2004).
57. *Geisler* v. *Petrocelli,* 616 F. 2d 636 (1980).
58. *Cason* v. *Baskin,* 159 Fla. 131 (1947).

Novels and feature films often carry a disclaimer: "This is a work of fiction. All the characters and events portrayed are fictitious. Any resemblance to real people and events is purely coincidental." Will this ward off a false-light suit? No. Although the statement has minimal value in showing the intent of the author or publisher or producer, the rule is simple: You cannot escape liability for committing a legal wrong by announcing that you are not liable. If you put a large sign on the top of your car that said, "Stay out of my way. I am a very bad driver and if I hit someone, it is not my fault," this would not relieve you from any liability if you caused an accident. Similarly, the disclaimer that a book is a work of fiction and the characters are fictitious will not prevent a successful privacy suit if the author has obviously appropriated someone's identity and put him or her in a false light.

OTHER FALSEHOODS

False-light privacy suits based on fictionalization are not too common today. False-light lawsuits more typically involve simple editing or writing errors, or errors in judgment. Misuse of photographs, both still and video, is a common problem. The Saturday Evening Post was plagued by such lawsuits in the 1940s and 1950s. For example, the magazine once published a picture of a little girl who was brushed by a speeding car in an intersection and lay crying in the street. The girl was the victim of a motorist who ignored a red traffic light, but in the magazine the editors implied that she had caused the accident herself by darting into the street between parked cars. The editors simply needed a picture to illustrate a story on pedestrian carelessness and plucked this one out of the files. The picture was totally unrelated to the story, except that both were about people being hit by cars. Eleanor Sue Leverton sued the Post and won. Judge Herbert F. Goodrich ruled that the picture was clearly newsworthy in connection with Eleanor's original accident.

Misuse of photographs, both still and video, is a common problem.

> But the sum total of all this is that this particular plaintiff, the legitimate subject for publicity for one particular accident, now becomes a pictorial, frightful example of pedestrian carelessness. This, we think, exceeds the bounds of privilege.[59]

WJLA-TV in the nation's capital was sued in a case that graphically demonstrates how a broadcasting station or publication can and cannot use unrelated pictures to illustrate a story. The station broadcast a story on a new medical treatment for genital herpes. The report appeared on both the 6 p.m. and 11 p.m. newscasts. Both reports carried the same opening videotape of scores of pedestrians walking on a busy city street. Then the camera zoomed in on one woman, Linda Duncan, as she stood on a corner. Duncan turned and looked at the camera. She was clearly recognizable. On the 6 p.m. news there was no narration during the opening footage. The camera focused on the plaintiff Duncan and then the tape cut to a picture of the reporter, who was standing on the street, and said, "For the twenty million Americans who have herpes, it's not a cure." The remainder of the story followed. But for the 11 p.m. news, the reporter's opening statement was read by the news anchor as viewers watched the opening videotape, including the close-up of Linda Duncan. A defense motion to dismiss the privacy and defamation actions was granted as it related to the 6 p.m. newscast. The court said there was not a sufficient connection between pictures of the plaintiff and the reporter's statement.

59. *Leverton v. Curtis Publishing Co.,* 192 F. 2d 974 (1951).

But the court denied a summary judgment relating to the 11 p.m. broadcast. "The coalescing of the camera action, plaintiff's action (turning toward the camera), and the position of the passerby caused plaintiff to be the focal point on the screen. The juxtaposition of this film and commentary concerning twenty million Americans with herpes is sufficient to support an inference that indeed the plaintiff was a victim," the court ruled. A jury should decide whether the connection was strong enough.[60]

Sometimes an error simply occurs, and there is little anyone can do about it. A newspaper in Oklahoma published an article concerning the death of a former local schoolteacher who had been convicted of murder and who was reportedly mentally ill. But the photo used to accompany the story was that of Frenche Colbert, who lived in Phoenix, Ariz. Colbert's picture had been sent to the newspaper years earlier when he graduated from law school. Somehow, his photo got mixed up with that of the schoolteacher. There is no question that this publication put Colbert in a false light.[61] In such cases the fault requirement is a strong defense.

A simple precaution will protect publishers and broadcasters against many false-light suits. Refrain from using unrelated photos to illustrate stories and articles. When a story is published in the employee magazine about worker carelessness as a prime cause of industrial accidents, control the impulse to pull from the files a random picture of one of the employees working on the assembly line. That employee could contend that the story and photo suggest she is careless. Similarly, don't use old photos of kids hanging around the parking lot at a local park to illustrate a news story on neighborhood complaints about drug dealing in the park. Juxtaposing the wrong pictures with the wrong words could give viewers the impression that one of these kids is selling or using drugs.

HIGHLY OFFENSIVE MATERIAL

Before a plaintiff can win a false-light case, the court must be convinced that the material that is false is highly offensive to a reasonable person. Although the records contain a handful of cases where nonoffensive material was the basis for a successful false-light suit,[62] these cases are old and should not be regarded as authoritative today. Typical of modern decisions is the case of *Cibenko* v. *Worth Publishers*. The plaintiff was a New York–New Jersey Port Authority police officer whose photograph appeared in a college sociology text. In a section of the book entitled "Selecting the Criminals," the picture depicted a white police officer (Cibenko) in a public place apparently prodding a sleeping African-American man with his nightstick. The caption for the picture stated:

> The social status of the offender seems to be the most significant determinant of whether a person will be arrested and convicted for an offense and of the kind of penalty that will be applied. In this picture a police officer is preventing a black male from falling asleep in a public place. Would the officer be likely to do the same if the "offender" were a well-dressed, middle-aged white person?

60. *Duncan* v. *WJLA-TV,* 10 M.L.R. 1395 (1984).
61. *Colbert* v. *World Publishing,* 747 P. 2d 286 (1987).
62. See *Molony* v. *Boy Comics Publishers,* 65 N.Y.S. 173 (1948) and *Spahn* v. *Julian Messner, Inc.,* 18 N.Y. 2d 324 (1966).

Officer Cibenko claimed the photograph and caption made him appear to be a racist, and this portrayal was false. A U.S. District Court in New Jersey disagreed and ruled that there was no offensive meaning attached to the photograph and caption, especially not a highly offensive meaning.[63] A U.S. District Court in Maine dismissed a suit by a man who had fallen out of the hatch of a small airplane, but managed to cling to the door rails until the pilot made an emergency landing. An article in National Enquirer embellished the story somewhat, adding material on what the plaintiff had thought about as he clung to the airplane. The reporter had never communicated with the accident victim and therefore could not have known what went through his mind. The court ruled that the description of physical sensations and predictable fears, though possibly exaggerated or maybe even fanciful, was not offensive to a reasonable person.[64]

THE FAULT REQUIREMENT

Since 1967, plaintiffs in false-light suits have been required to carry a fault requirement much like the one applied in libel cases. The case in which this fault requirement was applied to invasion of privacy was the first mass media invasion-of-privacy suit ever heard by the U.S. Supreme Court.[65] In the early 1950s the James Hill family was held captive in their home for nearly 24 hours by three escaped convicts. The fugitives were captured by police shortly after leaving the Hill home. The incident became a widely publicized story. At about the same time there were other similar hostage-takings in other parts of the United States. Author Joseph Hayes wrote a novel about such an occurrence called "The Desperate Hours," which focused on a fictional four-member Hilliard family that was held hostage by three escaped convicts. The book was made into a movie and a play. Before the play "The Desperate Hours" opened on Broadway, Life magazine published a feature story about the drama, stating that the play was a reenactment of the ordeal suffered by the James Hill family (see Figure 8.1). The actors were even taken to the home in which the Hills had lived (now vacant) and were photographed at the scene of the original captivity.

James Hill sued for invasion of privacy. He complained that the magazine had used his family's name for trade purposes and that the story put the family in a false light. "The Desperate Hours" did follow the basic outline of the Hill family ordeal, but it contained many differences. The fictional Hilliard family, for example, suffered far more physical and verbal indignities at the hands of the convicts than did the Hill family.

The family won money damages in the New York state courts,[66] but the Supreme Court of the United States vacated the lower-court rulings and sent the case back for yet another trial. The Hill family gave up at this point, and no subsequent trial was held.

Justice William Brennan, in a 5-4 ruling, declared that the family's name and photographs had not been used for trade purposes. Brennan reminded all concerned that

---

63. *Cibenko* v. *Worth Publishers,* 510 F. Supp. 761 (1981).
64. *Dempsey* v. *National Enquirer Inc.,* 687 F. Supp. 692 (1988).
65. *Time, Inc.* v. *Hill,* 385 U.S. 374 (1967).
66. *Hill* v. *Hayes,* 207 N.Y.S. 2d 901 (1960), 18 App. Div. 2d 485 (1963).

THEATER

ACTUAL EVENT, as reported in newspaper, took place in isolated house about 10 miles from Philadelphia. There three convicts from

Lewisburg penitentiary held family of James Hill as prisoners while they hid from manhunt. All three convicts were later captured.

TRUE CRIME INSPIRES TENSE PLAY

The ordeal of a family trapped by convicts gives Broadway a new thriller, 'The Desperate Hours'

Source: LIFE Magazine © 1955 Time Inc. Reprinted with permission. Photo © Cornell Capa/Magnum Photos.

FIGURE 8.1 ▼

Life magazine published this article about the James Hill family, which led the family to sue for invasion of privacy.

informative material published in newspapers and magazines is not published for purposes of trade (see pages 290–292), even though these publications generally are considered profit-making businesses.

Turning to the false-light action, Brennan applied the same First Amendment standards he had developed in the *New York Times* v. *Sullivan* libel suit to this category of invasion-of-privacy litigation (see pages 194–197). "We hold that the constitutional protections for speech and press preclude the application of the New York [privacy] statute to redress false reports of matters of public interest in the absence of proof that the defendant published the report with knowledge of its falsity or in reckless disregard of the truth."[67]

The *Time* v. *Hill* case was decided in 1967, three years after the *Sullivan* ruling. But since 1967 the high court has substantially modified the fault requirement in libel cases. In 1974 in *Gertz* v. *Welch* the court reiterated that so-called public persons must prove actual malice to maintain a successful libel action, but added that private persons must also prove fault—at least negligence.[68] Did the high court intend that this two-part fault standard be applied to false-light invasion-of-privacy cases as well? The Supreme Court had an occasion to answer this question shortly after its ruling in *Gertz* but declined to do so. In *Cantrell* v. *Forest City Publishing Co.,*[69] a false light invasion-of-privacy case, the high court concluded that there was sufficient evidence to show that the defendant newspaper had acted with

67. *Time, Inc.* v. *Hill,* 385 U.S. 374 (1967).
68. 418 U.S. 323 (1974).
69. 419 U.S. 245 (1974).

reckless disregard for the truth. Because the defendant could prove actual malice in this case, the court said it did not have to consider whether a private-person plaintiff would have to prove only negligence to sustain the fault requirement in a false-light privacy action. "This case presents no occasion to consider whether a state may constitutionally apply a more relaxed standard of liability for a publisher or broadcaster of false statements injurious to a private individual under a false light theory of invasion of privacy or whether the constitutional standard announced in *Time, Inc.* v. *Hill* applies to all false light cases," wrote Justice Stewart for the court.

Whether the *Gertz* variable-fault standard is applicable to false-light cases remains an open question. Most authorities tend to think that the rule of *Time, Inc.* v. *Hill*—that all plaintiffs are required to show actual malice, knowledge of falsity, or reckless disregard of the truth—will stand as the law in most jurisdictions. Several factors prompt this conclusion. The Supreme Court could have changed the rules in the *Cantrell* case, but did not. The high court could have modified the *Time, Inc.* v. *Hill* rule in *Gertz,* but did not. Finally, a statement that is not defamatory is likely to be far less damaging to a plaintiff. Less harm, higher fault requirement. Some courts have taken a different point of view and ruled that private-person false-light plaintiffs must prove only negligence.[70] But more courts have stayed the course, requiring all plaintiffs to show actual malice.[71]

Whether the Gertz *variable-fault standard is applicable to false-light cases remains an open question.*

Before the discussion of the right of privacy comes to an end, a few points should be reiterated. First, remember that only people have the right of privacy. Corporations, businesses and governments do not enjoy the legal right of privacy as such. Second, unlike libel, the law of privacy does provide that the plaintiff may seek an injunction to stop an invasion of privacy. Courts are very hesitant to enjoin tortious conduct, however, unless the plaintiff can show that the action will cause irreparable injury and that the tortious conduct will likely be continued. Such was the case in the *Galella* v. *Onassis*[72] suit. A plaintiff is far more likely to get an injunction in either an intrusion or an appropriation case than in a private facts or false-light suit. Normally, courts refuse to grant injunctions because they believe an adequate legal remedy is available or because they believe that the injunction could constitute prior censorship in violation of the First Amendment. The plaintiff bears an immense burden in convincing a court that prior restraint is called for. While it is possible to get an injunction, it is difficult. Third, it is impossible to civilly libel a dead person, but a few state privacy statutes make it possible for an heir to maintain an action for invasion of privacy.

Although privacy law is not as well charted as libel law, and although there are fewer privacy cases, suits for invasion of privacy are a growing menace to journalists. If journalists stick to the job of responsibly reporting the news, they may rest assured that the chance for a successful privacy suit is slim.

---

70. See *Wood* v. *Hustler,* 736 F. 2d 1084 (1984) and *Crump* v. *Beckley Newspapers,* 370 S.E. 2d 70 (1984).
71. See *Dodrill* v. *Arkansas Democrat Co.,* 5 M.L.R. 1090 (1979); *McCall* v. *Courier-Journal and Louisville Times Co.,* 4 M.L.R. 2337 (1979), aff'd. 6 M.L.R. 1112 (1980); *Goodrich* v. *Waterbury Republican-American Inc.,* 448 A. 2d 1317 (1987); and *Colbert* v. *World Publishing Co.,* 747 P. 2d 286 (1987).
72. 487 F. 2d 986 (1973); 533 F. Supp. 1076 (1982).

SUMMARY

It is an invasion of privacy to publish false information that places an individual into what is called a false light. However, this false information must be considered offensive to a reasonable person. Also, the plaintiff must prove that the information was published negligently, with knowledge of its falsity, or with reckless disregard for the truth.

One common source of false-light privacy suits is any drama that adds fictional material to an otherwise true story. The use of fictional rather than real names in such a drama will normally preclude a successful invasion-of-privacy suit. The coincidental use of a real name in a novel or stage play will not stand as a cause of action for invasion of privacy. Most false-light cases, however, result from the publication of false information about a person in a news or feature story. Pictures of persons who are not involved in the stories that the pictures are used to illustrate frequently provide false-light privacy suits.

BIBLIOGRAPHY

Andrews, Edmund. "European Law Aims to Protect Privacy of Data." *The New York Times,* 26 October 1998, A1.

Brinkley, Joel. "Web Site Agrees to Safeguards in First On-Line Privacy Deal." *The New York Times,* 14 August 1998, A13.

Kalven, Harry, Jr. "Privacy in Tort Law—Were Warren and Brandeis Wrong?" *Law and Contemporary Problems* 31 (1966): 326.

Marcus, Paul, and Tara L. McMahon. "Limiting Disclosure of Rape Victims' Identities." *Southern California Law Review* 64 (1991): 1019.

Pember, Don R. "The Burgeoning Scope of Access Privacy and the Portent for a Free Press." *Iowa Law Review* 64 (1979): 1155.

———. *Privacy and the Press.* Seattle: University of Washington Press, 1972.

Pember, Don R., and Dwight L. Teeter. "Privacy and the Press Since *Time* v. *Hill*." *Washington Law Review* 50 (1974): 57.

Pilgrim, Tim A. "Docudramas and False Light Invasion of Privacy." *Communications and the Law,* June 1988, 3.

Prosser, William L. "Privacy." *California Law Review* 48 (1960): 383.

Warren, Samuel D., and Louis D. Brandeis. "The Right to Privacy." *Harvard Law Review* 4 (1890): 220.

Wyatt, Robert O. *Free Expression and the American Public.* Murfreesboro, Tenn.: Middle Tennessee State University, 1991.

GATHERING INFORMATION
Records and Meetings

This chapter is about how the law affects the efforts of reporters and ordinary citizens to gather information about what is going on in the nation and their communities. And until about 15 years ago the text focused almost exclusively on federal and state statutes that either permit or limit the gathering of information from government records or from meetings of government agencies. But times have changed, and today the law regarding news gathering is also focused on efforts by the government and others to stop the press from collecting data about a wide range of people and activities. Both topics are covered in this chapter. Additional material on gaining access to the judicial process and judicial records is covered in Chapter 12.

Information is the lifeblood of American journalism and American politics. Because the government is the biggest and most important institution in our lives, information about the government and information gathered by the government is a central focus of the news media. Until the mid-20th century there were few significant rules that defined the rights of citizens, including journalists, to gain access to the information generated and kept by the government. Reporters developed sophisticated but informal schemes with news sources in government to get the material they needed. The average citizen was shut out.

Since the 1950s state and federal governments have passed laws defining public access to records and meetings. If there was a "Golden Age of Access" to information it was likely in the 1970s and early 1980s. Since then there has been a growing government resistance to public (especially press) access to such materials—a resistance exacerbated by the events of September 11, 2001. As Lucy A. Dalglish, executive director of the Reporters Committee for Freedom of the Press, wrote in that organization's comprehensive September 2005 sixth edition of its report called *Homefront Confidential,* "led by secrecy-loving officials in the executive branch, secrecy in the United States government is now the norm."[1]

For instance, in 2004 a group called the Coalition of Journalists for Open Government (http://www.cjog.net) asserted that a new set of federal rules[2] that took effect that year relating to the Transportation Security Administration's (TSA) ability to withhold records and data that it deemed sensitive security information (SSI) would have "a seriously adverse impact on traditional citizen and media oversight of the governance of our seaports, airports and transit systems."[3] The coalition, which includes more than 30 journalism organizations such as the American Society of Newspaper Editors and the Society of Professional Journalists, contended in comments filed with the TSA that the new regulations "will result in vast amounts of information being designated sensitive security information and withheld from the public for unknown lengths of time. There appears to be no limits to the type of information that

---

1. *Homefront Confidential,* 1.
2. 49 C.F.R. § 1520 et seq. (2004).
3. *In the Matter of Protection of Sensitive Security Information,* "Comments of the Coalition of Journalists for Open Government," available online at http://www.cjog.net/protest_sensitive_security_inform.html.

might be gathered or generated as SSI and then sealed." Of particular concern was the definition of SSI, which is described in the new federal rules simply as "information obtained or developed in the conduct of security activities, including research and development, the disclosure of which TSA has determined would . . . be detrimental to the security of transportation."[4] The new rules also provide a laundry list of specific categories of items such as "critical aviation or maritime infrastructure asset information" that may constitute SSI. The Coalition of Journalists for Open Government contends, however, that "there are no criteria to guide those who must decide which items of information within any one of the categories are appropriate for safeguarding."

In August 2004, an organization called OpenTheGovernment.org issued its inaugural "Secrecy Report Card: Quantitative Indicators of Secrecy in the Federal Government." It found that "the federal government spent $6.5 billion last year [2003] creating 14 million new classified documents and securing accumulated secrets—more than it has for at least the past decade."[5] The report noted that secrecy "increased dramatically" under the policies of the administration of President George W. Bush. One of the more astonishing findings of the report was that "for every $1 the federal government spent in 2003 releasing old secrets, it spent an extraordinary $120 maintaining the secrets already on the books." But the censorial and secrecy hits didn't stop there. In an April 2005 update to its first secrecy report card, the group reported:

> In 2004, the federal government set a new record for keeping secrets. Last year, federal employees chose to classify information a record 15.6 million times, according to new government figures released this week. The figure is 10 percent higher than the total in the previous year. And when given a choice, government employees last year chose to keep their secrets longer than in years past: Two-thirds (66 percent) of the time government employees chose to keep those new secrets for more than a decade.[6]

In addition, the Columbia Journalism Review reported in late 2004 that the federal government and its contractors spent $7.5 billion—one billion more than the initial "Secrecy Report Card" figure from OpenTheGovernment.org—in 2003 to make information classified.[7] The bottom line, to put it bluntly, is that secrecy comes at a very high cost, both financially and, perhaps more important, to the processes and practices of democracy.

In November 2005, the Coalition of Journalists for Open Government released another report. This one showed that the use of FOIA exemptions by government agencies to screen and withhold information increased by 22 percent between 2000 and 2004. This result is somewhat shocking because it comes in spite of the fact that federal agencies actually responded to 13 percent *fewer* requests for information in 2004 when compared with 2000, according to the Coalition.

To the extent the tragic events of September 11, 2001, have been used as a rationale (cynics might say excuse) for foreclosing access to information and limiting, more generally,

---

4. 49 C.F.R. § 1520.5 (2004).
5. A copy of the report can be found on the organization's Web site at http://www.openthegovernment.org.
6. OpenTheGovernment.org, "Secrecy Report Card: An Update April 5, 2005"; available online at http://www.openthegovernment.org/article/articleview/130/1/68/?TopicID.
7. "Hard Numbers."

constitutional rights and liberties, it is important to keep in mind the words in October 2004 of the 11th U.S. Circuit of Appeals: "We cannot simply suspend or restrict civil liberties until the War on Terror is over, because the War on Terror is unlikely ever to be truly over. September 11, 2001, already a day of immeasurable tragedy, cannot be the day liberty perished in this country."[8]

But rights and liberties are grounded in the law.

Journalists and citizen activists are often forced to go to court to try to assert rights they believe have been abridged by government restrictions on access to information. But rights and liberties are grounded in the law. We don't enjoy rights in the United States just because they feel good, or because they are inherent to human nature. When someone goes to court and asks for something, the first thing the judge will say is "Show me the law." So if journalists hope to use the law for assistance, they must find support in one of those sources of the law discussed in Chapter 1.

NEWS GATHERING AND THE LAW

In order for journalists to gather news, they must have access to information. While information to courts, trials and judicial proceedings is discussed in Chapter 12, there are three primary sources of law to which journalists might look or turn in order to find a legal right of access to information such as documents, records, meetings, and venues. Those three sources of law are

- Common Law
- Constitutional Law (the First Amendment to the U.S. Constitution)
- Statutory Law (both state and federal statutes)

Despite the tradition of open government both in this country and in Great Britain, the common law provides only bare access to government documents and to meetings of public agencies. In Great Britain, where the common law developed, complete and total access to Parliament, for example, was not guaranteed until 1874, and even then the House of Commons could exclude the public by a majority vote. Initially the public was excluded because members of Parliament feared reprisal from the Crown for statements made during floor debate. Later this fear subsided, but secret meetings continued in order to prevent voters from finding out that many members of the legislative body were not faithful in keeping promises to constituents.

Secrecy in England had a direct impact on how colonial legislatures conducted their business. The Constitutional Convention of 1787 in Philadelphia was conducted in secret. The public and the press had almost immediate access to sessions in the U.S. House of Representatives, but it was not until 1794 that spectators and reporters were allowed into the Senate chamber. Although today access is guaranteed to nearly all sessions of Congress, much (maybe even most) congressional business is conducted by committees that frequently meet in secret.

Common-law precedents exist that open certain public records to inspection by members of the public, but distinct limitations have been placed on this common-law right. For

---

8. *Bourgeois* v. *Peters,* 387 F. 3d 1303 (2004).

example, under the common law a person seeking access to a record normally must have an "interest" in that record. And most often this interest must relate to some kind of litigation in which the person who seeks the record is a participant. Also, only those records "required to be kept" by state law are subject to even such limited disclosure under the common law. Many important records kept by the government are not "required to be kept" by law. Hence, the common law must be found wanting as an aid in the process of news gathering.

THE CONSTITUTION AND NEWS GATHERING

Does the U.S. Constitution provide any assistance to citizens who seek to scrutinize government records or attend meetings of government bodies? Surprisingly the First Amendment plays a rather insignificant role in defining the rights of citizens and journalists in the news-gathering process. The amendment was drafted in an age when news gathering was not a primary function of the press. The congressional records of the drafting and adoption of the First Amendment fail to support the notion that the protection of the news-gathering process was to be included within the scope of freedom of the press. On August 15, 1789, during the House debate on the adoption of the First Amendment, James Madison, its principal author in the Congress, stated that if freedom of expression means nothing more than that "the people have a right to express and communicate their sentiments and wishes, we have provided for it already" (in what was to become the First Amendment). "The right of freedom of speech is secured; the liberty of free press is expressly declared to be beyond the reach of this government; the people may therefore publicly address their representatives, may privately address them, or declare sentiments by petition to the whole body," Madison added. One is hard-pressed to find within this description of the First Amendment guarantee of freedom of expression expansive notions about the right to gather news and information. The First Amendment was seen as a means by which the public could confront its government, not necessarily report on its activities.[9]

The Supreme Court has on at least two occasions explored the nexus between freedom of expression and news gathering. In a non-press-related case in 1964, the members of the high court ruled that the constitutional right to speak and publish does not carry with it the unrestrained right to gather information.[10] Eight years later Justice Byron White, speaking as well for three other members of the high court, said: "Nor is it suggested that news gathering does not qualify for First Amendment protection; without some protection for seeking out the news, freedom of the press could be eviscerated."[11] Many First Amendment lawyers regard this statement as a fountain from which a constitutionally based right to gather news springs, but others disagree. White's statement was dictum in a case that involved the right of journalists to refuse to reveal the names of confidential news sources (see Chapter 10). And White said he didn't see any connection at all between news gathering and a reporter's right to protect the name of a news source. The sentence was hardly a ringing endorsement of a First Amendment right of access to information. These comments are as far as the high court has gone in dealing with this issue in an abstract or theoretical way.

9. See Rourke, *Secrecy and Publicity,* and Padover, *The Complete Madison.*
10. *Zemel* v. *Rusk,* 381 U.S. 1 (1964).
11. *Branzburg* v. *Hayes,* 408 U.S. 665 (1972).

The high court has been asked on three separate occasions whether the First Amendment guarantees a journalist the unobstructed right to gather news in a prison. In each case the court said no. In *Pell* v. *Procunier*,[12] reporters in California attempted to interview specific inmates at California prisons. In *Saxbe* v. *Washington Post*,[13] reporters from that newspaper sought to interview specific inmates at federal prisons at Lewisburg, Pa., and Danbury, Conn. In both instances the press was barred from conducting the interviews. The U.S. Bureau of Prisons rule, which is similar to the California regulation, states:

> Press representatives will not be permitted to interview individual inmates.
> This rule shall apply even where the inmate requests or seeks an interview.

At issue was not access to the prison system. The press could tour and photograph prison facilities, conduct brief conversations with randomly encountered inmates, and correspond with inmates through the mails. Outgoing correspondence from inmates was neither censored nor inspected, and incoming mail was inspected only for contraband and statements that might incite illegal action. In addition, the federal rules had been interpreted to permit journalists to conduct lengthy interviews with randomly selected groups of inmates. In fact, a reporter in the Washington Post case did go to Lewisburg and interview a group of prisoners.

The argument of the press in both cases was that to ban interviews with specific inmates abridged the First Amendment protection afforded the news-gathering activity of a free press. The Supreme Court disagreed in a 5-4 decision in both cases. Justice Stewart wrote in the majority opinion that the press already had substantial access to the prisons and that there was no evidence that prison officials were hiding things from reporters. Stewart rejected the notion that the First Amendment gave newspeople a special right of access to the prisons. "Newsmen have no constitutional right of access to prisons or their inmates beyond that afforded the general public," the justice wrote.[14] Since members of the general public have no right to interview specific prisoners, the denial of this right to the press does not infringe on the First Amendment.

The high court did not disagree with the findings of the district court in the *Saxbe* case that face-to-face interviews with specific inmates are essential to accurate and effective reporting about prisoners and prisons. What the court seemed to say was that while the First Amendment guarantees freedom of expression, it does not guarantee effective and accurate reporting. In fact, about five months after the *Saxbe* and *Pell* decisions, in a speech at the Yale Law School Sesquicentennial Convocation, Justice Stewart made this exact point:

"There is no constitutional right to have access to particular governmental information, or to require openness from the bureaucracy."

> The press is free to do battle against secrecy and deception in government. But the press cannot expect from the Constitution any guarantee that it will succeed. There is no constitutional right to have access to particular governmental information, or to require openness from the bureaucracy. The public's interest in knowing about its government is protected by the guarantee of a free press, but the protection is indirect. The Constitution itself is neither a Freedom of Information Act nor an Official Secrets Act. The Constitution, in other words, establishes the contest, not its resolution.[15]

12. 417 U.S. 817 (1974).
13. 417 U.S. 843 (1974).
14. *Pell* v. *Procunier*, 417 U.S. 817 (1974).
15. Stewart, "Or of the Press," 631.

In 1978 the high court split along similar lines on a case involving press access rights to a county jail.[16] An inmate at the Santa Rita County, Calif., jail committed suicide in 1975. Following the death and a report by a psychiatrist that jail conditions were bad, KQED television in San Francisco sought permission to inspect and take pictures in the jail. Sheriff Houchins announced that the media could certainly participate in one of the six tours of the jail facility that were given to the public each year. However, the tours did not visit the disciplinary cells nor the portion of the jail in which the suicide had taken place. No cameras or tape recorders were allowed, but photographs of some parts of the jail were supplied by the sheriff's office.

Reporters at KQED took a jail tour, but were not happy at the limits placed on them. Sheriff Houchins contended that unregulated visits through the jail by the press would infringe on the inmates' right of privacy, could create jail celebrities out of inmates that would in turn cause problems for jailers, and would disrupt jail operations. Houchins noted that reporters did have access to inmates—they could visit individual prisoners, could visit with inmates awaiting trial, could talk by telephone with inmates, could write letters to prisoners, and so forth. But KQED argued that it had a constitutionally protected right to gather news and challenged the limits.

Chief Justice Warren Burger wrote the opinion for the court in the 4-3 decision in which neither Justice Blackmun nor Justice Marshall took part. "Neither the First Amendment nor the Fourteenth Amendment mandates a right of access to government information or sources of information within the government's control," Burger asserted. The chief justice seemed troubled by the argument of KQED that only through access to the jail could the press perform its public responsibility.

> Unarticulated but implicit in the assertion that the media access to jail is essential for an informed public debate on jail conditions is the assumption that the media personnel are the best qualified persons for the task of discovering malfeasance in public institutions. . . . The media are not a substitute for or an adjunct of government. . . . We must not confuse the role of the media with that of government.[17]

In 1980 in a case that many commentators hailed as the beginning of a general constitutionally guaranteed "right to know," the Supreme Court ruled that the First Amendment does establish for all citizens the right to attend criminal trials.[18] (See Chapter 12 for a full discussion of this case.) But while Chief Justice Burger's opinion was quite explicit regarding the First Amendment and attendance at criminal trials, it was obscure regarding the larger constitutional right to gather news in other contexts. And the high court has done little in the past two decades to clarify its position on this question. Although it has decided a number of right-of-access cases since *Richmond Newspapers,*[19] the Supreme Court has never explicitly recognized this right outside of judicial proceedings.

16. *Houchins* v. *KQED,* 438 U.S. 1 (1978).
17. *Houchins* v. *KQED,* 438 U.S. 1 (1978).
18. *Richmond Newspapers* v. *Virginia,* 448 U.S. 555 (1980).
19. See, for example, *Press-Enterprise Co.* v. *Riverside Superior Court,* 464 U.S. 501 (1984).

The lower federal courts and state courts tend to mirror the rulings by the Supreme Court that reject the notion of a First Amendment right of access to information and meetings. There are, however, significant exceptions:

- The 5th U.S. Circuit Court of Appeals ruled in 1977 that news gathering was protected by the First Amendment but still denied a reporter's request to film the execution of a condemned man.[20]
- When the White House staff tried to exclude camera crews with CNN from the pool of network television photographers who cover the president, a U.S. District Court forbade the discriminatory action, noting that the First Amendment includes a "right of access to news and information concerning the operations and activities of government."[21]
- In 1985 a federal court in Utah ruled that the public and the press had a First Amendment right to attend a formal administrative fact-finding hearing by the Mine Safety and Health Administration to investigate the causes of a mine fire that killed 27 people. The 10th U.S. Circuit Court of Appeals later overturned this ruling, noting that the hearings had ended and the issue was moot.[22]
- A U.S. District Court in Ohio ruled in 1988 that the press and the public have a qualified First Amendment right of access to the legislative process—in this case a city council meeting. The court said there was always a First Amendment presumption in favor of open government meetings, a presumption that can only be overcome by a formal showing of a need for privacy and confidentiality.[23]
- Finally, in 2002 the 9th U.S. Circuit Court of Appeals held that the public enjoys "a First Amendment right of access to view executions from the moment the condemned is escorted into the execution chamber."[24] This right of access, the appellate court wrote, includes the right to watch so-called initial procedures, including the forcible restraint of the condemned and the fitting of that person "with the apparatus of death." The court reasoned, in part, that "informed public debate is the main purpose for granting a right of access to governmental proceedings."

Unfortunately decisions like these stand in stark contrast to a larger body of case law that denies this proposition. For instance, in 2004 the 8th U.S. Circuit Court of Appeals held in *Rice* v. *Kempker* that "the First Amendment does not protect the use of video cameras or any other cameras or, for that matter, audio recorders in the execution chamber."[25] In this case, a religious-based group in Missouri called New Life Evangelistic Center wanted to videotape the execution of a convicted murderer, Daniel Basile, in a Missouri correctional facility, and it asserted a First Amendment right of public access. The organization contended that allowing

20. *Garrett* v. *Estelle,* 556 F. 2d 1274 (1977).
21. *CNN* v. *ABC et al.,* 518 F. Supp. 1238 (1981).
22. *Society of Professional Journalists* v. *Secretary of Labor,* 11 M.L.R. 2474 (1985), rev'd. 832 F. 2d 1180 (1987).
23. *WJW* v. *Cleveland,* 686 F. Supp. 177 (1988).
24. *California First Amendment Coalition* v. *Woodford,* 299 F. 3d 868 (2002).
25. *Rice* v. *Kempker,* 374 F. 3d 675 (2004).

viewers to see the horror of a man put to death would convince people that capital punishment is wrong and thus would help to end capital punishment in Missouri and in the United States. The appellate court, however, reasoned that "neither the public nor the media has a First Amendment right to videotape, photograph, or make audio recordings of government proceedings that are by law open to the public." Most courts have refused to recognize the First Amendment as a means to gain access to government records, government meetings or government facilities. A key point that must be remembered regarding these rulings: In virtually all the instances noted in which a court has ruled that the First Amendment does provide a means of gaining access to a meeting or a record, the court has emphasized that this right belongs to both the press and the public. Reporters are not given any special rights in this regard, only those rights that all citizens enjoy.

"Neither the public nor the media has a First Amendment right to videotape, photograph, or make audio recordings of government proceedings that are by law open to the public."

Access to Government Officials: A Right to Interview?

Each example described so far has involved a question of First Amendment access to either a place, such as a government-run prison, or to a proceeding like a government meeting or an execution. But what happens when a reporter simply wants access to speak with a person—namely, a government official such as a mayor or a governor—and that official has issued a "no-comment policy" and refuses to speak with specific members of the press? Is there, in other words, a First Amendment right of access possessed by the media to conduct one-on-one interviews with government officials such that the officials cannot refuse to speak with the news media?

These were the questions at the heart of *Youngstown Publishing Co.* v. *McKelvey* decided in May 2005 by a federal district court in Ohio.[26] George McKelvey, the mayor of Youngstown, Ohio, was upset at critical, negative coverage of him and his administration by a local newspaper called the Business Journal. In response to the criticism, Mayor McKelvey decided to strike back and to severely restrict the Business Journal's access to him and other government employees. He issued a statement providing that he had "instructed members of my administration not to make statements to the Business Journal except to fulfill the City's obligations regarding public records requests. . . . I have made the determination that City administrators and employees may not comment to the Business Journal on behalf of the City."

The Business Journal sued the mayor, claiming that he and the City of Youngstown unlawfully retaliated against it for exercising its rights under the First Amendment. The Business Journal argued that it "was engaged in the constitutionally protected activity of publishing news reports which questioned the actions of local government officials on a matter of great public concern" and that the mayor's no-comment policy "is an attempt to prevent the Business Journal from engaging in this activity and is motivated by Mayor McKelvey's displeasure with the Business Journal's reporting."

To establish such a claim for unlawful retaliation in violation of the First Amendment, U.S. District Court Judge Peter Economus wrote that "the Business Journal must first demonstrate that this 'give-and-take of information' in the form of one-on-one interviews with and comments from city employees, is a constitutionally protected activity." In other words, the newspaper would need to prove that there is a First Amendment right of access to conduct

26. 2005 U.S. Dist. LEXIS 9476 (N.D. Ohio 2005).

one-on-one interviews with and receive comments from government employees. Economus ruled against the Business Journal. He held that the mayor's freeze-out of the newspaper's reporters from one-on-one interviews did not violate a constitutional right. The judge initially drew a critical "distinction between access to events and facilities opened to the press and access to one-on-one interviews and off-the-record comments." The latter constitute "information not otherwise available to the public." Economus reasoned that "enforcing media access to 'information not otherwise available to the public' would be affording the media a special privilege of access over and above that of the general public." No such special privilege for the press, as distinct from the public, exists. He concluded:

> The right of access sought by the Business Journal is to information not otherwise available to the public, and, therefore, is a privileged right of access above that of the general public to which no constitutional right of access applies. . . . The no-comment policy does not impede the Business Journal from engaging in a constitutionally protected activity, and plaintiffs cannot establish this element of their First Amendment retaliation claim.

What does this mean? In a nutshell, members of the press have no special right of access to government officials to conduct one-on-one private interviews. A government official like Mayor McKelvey may freely discriminate against particular members of the media in choosing to grant or deny such interviews. As Judge Economus wrote, "the fact that one newspaper or reporter may gain access to an interview or comment by a city employee does not require that all reporters be given access to the same information."

Sadly the situation in *Youngstown Publishing Co.* v. *McKelvey* is not isolated. A similar case also was decided in 2005 in *Baltimore Sun Co.* v. *Ehrlich* [27] in which Maryland governor Robert Ehrlich issued a very precise order in November 2004 stating:

> No one in the Executive Department or Agencies is to speak with David Nitkin or Michael Olesker until further notice. Do not return calls or comply with any requests. The Governor's Press Office feels that currently both are failing to objectively report on any issue dealing with the Ehrlich-Steele Administration. Please relay this information to your respective department heads. Any questions or concerns can be directed to the following contact information.

Both Nitkin and Olesker are reporters for the Baltimore Sun. The Sun sued the governor, claiming the governor's order violated a First Amendment right of access of its two reporters to speak with government officials. In ruling against the newspaper, however, U.S. District Court Judge William D. Quarles Jr. wrote that "a government may lawfully make content-based distinctions in the way it provides press access to information not available to the public generally" and that the 4th U.S. Circuit Court of Appeals in which Maryland sits has "declined to recognize a journalist's right to have equal access to public information sources and to be treated the same as other journalists."

Taken together, the results in *Youngstown Publishing Co.* v. *McKelvey* and *Baltimore Sun Co.* v. *Ehrlich* indicate that there is no special press right of First Amendment access to

---

27. 356 F. Supp. 2d 577 (D. Md. 2005), affirmed, 2006 U.S. App. LEXIS 3581 (4th Cir. 2006).

interview or to speak with politicians in one-on-one situations. Government officials may pick and discriminate in choosing the reporters with whom they speak and grant access.

So the First Amendment is not a terribly effective sword, a weapon or tool to gain access to information or records. In recent years journalists have been accused of invasion of privacy trespass, disorderly conduct and unlawful news gathering when they have attempted to get a news story. Has the First Amendment been an effective shield in warding off these prosecutions? The answer is no; the First Amendment has been of little use at all. Let's examine some of these issues.

The First Amendment Protection of News Gathering

Since the 1960s the legal landscape in which American journalists operate has become far friendlier to the kind of aggressive reporting that many people regard as a hallmark of the press in the United States. Rulings by the Supreme Court and lower tribunals have made it harder and harder for plaintiffs alleging libel and invasion of privacy to win in court. The likelihood of winning any lawsuit against the press for what has been published or broadcast has become substantially lower. Therefore many plaintiffs' attorneys have taken a different tack in their attacks on the mass media, basing their legal claims not on what was published or broadcast, but on how the material for the story was gathered.

American journalists and their allies have attempted to defend themselves against charges of illegal news gathering by arguing that the press has a responsibility to bring the news to the people if the democratic system is expected to function. And to bring the news to the people, journalists sometimes have to bend the rules a little bit, use information-gathering techniques that would result in civil or even criminal liability if used by nonjournalists. These news-gathering tactics must be protected by the First Amendment, they argue. But American courts have been largely unswayed by this argument. In 1998, for example, a U.S. District Court in Maryland refused to dismiss charges of transporting and receiving child pornography against a free-lance journalist who attempted to block the prosecution by arguing that he was gathering news, not child pornography. Lawrence Matthews said that law enforcement officials were too zealous in their prosecution of Internet users and that the news stories resulting from his investigation would reveal this overly aggressive official action. His work was in the public interest, he said. But the court was not moved. "It is well settled that the First Amendment does not grant the press automatic relief from laws of general application," Judge Williams said. "If law enforcement officials are doing something improper in their investigations the court does not understand how the defendant would uncover malfeasance by receiving and disseminating the materials himself."[28] In 2000, the 4th U.S. Circuit Court of Appeals affirmed Judge Williams' decision and rejected Matthews' assertion that the First Amendment entitled him to assert a legitimate-journalistic-purpose defense to conviction under federal child pornography laws.[29] It also rejected the friend-of-the-court argument of the Reporters Committee for Freedom of the Press that there should be a more general journalistic news-gathering exemption from those laws. The appellate court cited with approval the Supreme

28. *U.S.* v. *Matthews,* 11 F. Supp. 2d 656 (1998). Matthews was sentenced to 18 months in prison.
29. *U.S.* v. *Matthews,* 209 F. 3d 338 (2000), cert. den., 531 U.S. 910 (2000).

Court's opinion in *Branzburg* v. *Hayes* for the proposition that the First Amendment does not provide "a license on either the reporter or his news sources to violate valid criminal laws."[30]

Most reporters don't violate criminal statutes, as Matthews said he was charged with doing, to investigate how the police enforce those statutes. But reporters do break other laws. An overview of some of these kinds of situations will demonstrate that the courts are no more tolerant of these actions.

Trespass **Trespass** typically is defined as an intentional, unauthorized (i.e., without consent) entry onto land that is occupied or possessed by another. While consent is a defense to a claim of trespass, journalists who exceed the scope of consent by taking actions in abuse of the authorized entry or by going into places beyond where they have permission may be held liable for trespass.

Reporters may face both civil liability and criminal prosecution when they trespass. It is important for journalists to remember, as one federal appellate court wrote in 1995, that "there is no journalists' privilege to trespass."[31] What's more, reporters don't have the right to trespass on private property or even government-owned property. The latter point was emphasized recently when a U.S. District Court in Puerto Rico ruled that reporters who illegally entered the Camp Garcia Naval Installation at Vieques, Puerto Rico, were not immune from trespass charges because of the constitutional guarantees of freedom of the press. The journalists were reporting on protests by Puerto Ricans and others who objected to the use of the area as a bombing range. The court said the First Amendment neither immunizes trespassers nor creates any special status for reporters who violate criminal or civil laws.[32]

A recent case illustrates the dangers of criminal trespass. Reporter Bryon Wells of the East Valley Tribune near Phoenix, Ariz., sought to interview a recently fired local police officer named Daniel Lovelace. Lovelace had been involved in a fatal shooting and was charged, at the time, with second-degree murder. Wells went through a closed but unlocked gate, posted with a "no trespassing" sign, and entered Lovelace's fenced property. The reporter walked to the front door, rang the bell and was told by the woman who answered, Lovelace's wife, to leave. Wells apparently left peacefully, but in July 2004 a judge upheld Wells' conviction for misdemeanor criminal trespass—he was fined $300 and sentenced to a year of probation—based on the incident.[33] In upholding a ruling by a lower-court judge, Judge Michael D. Jones wrote that "reporters who are in violation of a criminal trespass statute are not exempt from prosecution simply because they are exercising a First Amendment right." The Arizona criminal trespass law at issue provides: "A person commits criminal trespass in the first degree by knowingly . . . entering or remaining unlawfully in a fenced residential yard."[34]

Not all reporters who enter private property uninvited are necessarily trespassing. Whether or not the owner or occupant of the property asks the reporter to leave is a critical factor. A woman who permitted a CBS television crew to accompany a crisis intervention team that entered her home was later unable to maintain that the visit had been a trespass, a

30. 408 U.S. 665, 691 (1972).
31. *Desnick* v. *American Broadcasting Companies, Inc.,* 44 F. 3d 1345, 1351 (1995).
32. *United States* v. *Maldonado-Norat,* 122 F. Supp. 2d 264 (2000); see also *Stahl* v. *Oklahoma,* 665 P. 2d 839 (1983).
33. "Judge Upholds Reporter's Trespassing Conviction." *Arizona* v. *Wells,* 2004 WL 1925617 (Ariz. Super. 2004).
34. Arizona Revised Statute § 13-1504 (2004).

court ruled.[35] Also, the public is invited to visit some kinds of private property, and the press is a part of the public. ABC sent a camera crew to secretly film eye examinations being given to patients at an optical business. The exams were being administered in the portion of the business that was open to customers who wandered in seeking information, medication or other services. The 7th U.S. Circuit Court of Appeals rejected a trespass action brought by the owners of the property, saying that there was no invasion in this case of any of the interests that the tort of trespass is designed to protect, namely the use and enjoyment of one's property without interference. The offices were open to anyone who sought ophthalmologic services offered by the business. The activity in the office was not disrupted; there was no invasion of anyone's private space.[36] And in Michigan the state Court of Appeals similarly rejected a trespass action against a television station who sent a reporter carrying a hidden camera into a transmission repair shop. Even though she was posing as a customer, which she was not, the court said she had only entered those areas of the business open to the public.[37]

Even when the media are found civilly liable for trespass, they may not always be responsible under trespass law for so-called publication damages—monetary losses that flow from the actual publication or broadcast of footage. In a case discussed earlier (see page 303) in the context of a different cause of action—intrusion into seclusion—the operators of a medical laboratory filed a trespass complaint against ABC for the broadcast of a report that included footage obtained by ABC employees when they trespassed into certain areas of the laboratory.[38] The report, however, contained only 52 seconds of relatively innocuous videotape obtained during the trespass itself. The 9th U.S. Circuit Court of Appeals held that the plaintiff "fails to identify any damages flowing specifically from this 52-second videotape clip" and concluded that "the alleged trespass was not the legal cause of the publication damages that Medical Lab seeks." The real damage, the appellate court reasoned, was caused by other information broadcast by ABC that was obtained without trespassing. It thus refused to award the plaintiff damages under trespass law for the broadcast.

This ruling reinforces the 4th U.S. Circuit Court of Appeals' 1999 decision in *Food Lion, Inc.* v. *Capital Cities/ABC, Inc.* in which the appellate court refused to award publication damages based on a trespass cause of action.[39] In particular, ABC employees trespassed at Food Lion stores to obtain hidden-camera footage that was later aired on "Primetime Live" regarding alleged food mishandling practices at the then-growing supermarket chain. Food Lion's business was markedly hurt by the "Primetime Live" report, which clearly damaged the store's reputation. Rather than sue for defamation or how the story was reported, however, Food Lion sued for how the news was gathered, using causes of action for trespass and fraud (see page 359). The appellate court concluded that Food Lion, by suing for trespass in order to collect damages for the actual broadcast of the report (publication damages), was trying to make what it called "an end-run around First Amendment strictures" such as actual malice that apply in libel law (see pages 222–234). The court wrote that "Food Lion attempted to

---

35. *Baugh* v. *CBS, Inc.,* 828 F. Supp. 745 (1993).
36. *Desnick* v. *American Broadcasting Companies, Inc.,* 44 F. 3d 1345 (1995).
37. *American Transmission Inc.* v. *Channel 7 of Detroit Inc.,* 609 N.W. 2d 607 (2000).
38. *Medical Laboratory Management Consultants* v. *American Broadcasting Companies, Inc.,* 306 F. 3d 808 (2002).
39. 194 F. 3d 505 (1999).

avoid the First Amendment limitations on defamation claims by seeking publication damages under non-reputational tort claims [i.e., trespass], while holding to the normal standard for these torts." Food Lion would need to prove actual malice, as required in libel law, in order to recover damages caused by the broadcast; trespass would not work, even if some of the material obtained for the broadcast had come from trespassory conduct. As a result, the appellate court awarded Food Lion nominal damages of only $1 on its cause of action for trespass—an amount designed to show that while trespass had occurred when the ABC employees used hidden cameras in nonpublic areas of the Food Lion stores, Food Lion was not harmed in its actual use or possession of the property by this trespass.

Is it a trespass to photograph or film a person from above his or her home or other private property using a helicopter to get the desired images?

Is it a trespass to photograph or film a person from above his or her private property using a helicopter to get the desired images? It all depends on how high the chopper passes. Television newsmagazines often try to capture images of celebrity weddings using aerial shots taken from hovering helicopters. In a slightly different twist, a news helicopter hovered for 10 minutes above the home of Gail Bevers to obtain footage for a story about the poor condition of rental properties. Bevers, who was "scared to death" by the helicopter, sued for trespass. In 2002, a Texas appellate court hearing her case observed that "one of the key facts in ascertaining whether a flight through airspace constitutes a trespass is the altitude of the aircraft."[40] The court noted that while "landowners have no right to exclude overflights above their property because airspace is part of the public domain," flights that are within the "immediate reaches of the airspace next to the land" and that also interfere substantially with the use and enjoyment of that land may constitute a trespass. In Bevers' case, the court concluded "a single ten-minute hover over her property at 300 to 400 feet does not, as a matter of law, rise to the level of 'substantial interference' with the use and enjoyment of the underlying land." The appellate court thus affirmed summary judgment for the media defendants.

What if the reporter accompanies government officials, police or firefighters onto the property? Can these government agents give permission for the press to illegally enter private property? The simple answer is no. And the courts have ruled that not only are reporters potentially liable for damages in such a case, but the law officers themselves may be at risk for bringing reporters along. These kinds of cases have developed in recent years because of a growing number of instances in which the press and government agents are cooperating with each other, behavior that was largely unthinkable only a quarter-century ago. But the so-called reality television programs have a seemingly insatiable appetite for video footage of police or firefighters or paramedics in action, and deals are routinely made in which reporters get to accompany the government agents in exchange for positive press coverage of the police or rescue agency. So it is not uncommon to find reporters and photographers routinely accompanying federal, state and local police officers as they execute search warrants, arrest fugitives, and investigate crimes.

In 1999 the Supreme Court of the United States unanimously ruled that when law enforcement officers permit reporters to accompany them when they enter private homes to conduct searches or witness arrests, the officers violate "the right of residential privacy at the core of the Fourth Amendment." Two cases had found their way to the high court. The first, *Wilson* v. *Layne,* resulted when members of a joint federal and local law enforcement task

---

40. *Bevers* v. *Gaylord Broadcasting Co.,* 30 M.L.R. 2586, 2590 (2002).

force invited a Washington Post reporter and photographer to accompany them when they arrested fugitives in Rockville, Md., just outside the nation's capital. The other case, *Hanlon v. Berger,* involved agents of the U.S. Fish and Wildlife Service who invited reporters and photographers from CNN to accompany them as they searched the property of a Montana rancher for evidence that the property owner was illegally poisoning wildlife. The issue the Supreme Court focused upon was whether the government agents who brought the journalists onto the private property could be held responsible for civil rights violations; in other words, could the property owners sue the government agents for violating their Fourth Amendment rights against an illegal search? The government agents attempted to justify the invitations by arguing that such close-up coverage of their action will assist the public in understanding law enforcement problems and help the police in getting more public cooperation. "Surely the possibility of good public relations for the police is simply not enough, standing alone, to justify the ride-along intrusion into a private home," Chief Justice William Rehnquist wrote for the court. The chief justice quoted an almost 400-year-old British court ruling in supporting the high court's decision: "The house of everyone is to him as his castle and fortress, as well for his defence [*sic*] against injury and violence, for his repose." But because the law concerning media ride-alongs had not been developed when these arrests took place, the high court ruled that it would be unfair to subject the police officers in this case to money damages for their behavior. The officers could not have clearly foreseen that what they did would be a violation of the Constitution.[41]

"Surely the possibility of good public relations for the police is simply not enough, standing alone, to justify the ride-along intrusion into a private home."

The court did not in this instance rule on the matter of the liability of reporters and photographers who enter private premises with the permission of police. The *Berger* case was remanded to the 9th U.S. Circuit Court of Appeals for disposition in light of the high court ruling regarding the liability of the police.[42] In an earlier decision, the Court of Appeals had ruled that, because of the extremely close cooperation between the journalists and the government agents who searched the Montana ranch, the television reporters and producers were actually "state actors" or "joint actors" with the wildlife agents and could be subject to the same kind of Fourth Amendment action brought against the federal officers.[43] After the Supreme Court decision, the appellate court ruled that the journalists did not enjoy the kind of qualified immunity that had shielded the government agents in the *Wilson* case, reinstated Berger's Fourth Amendment claim against the reporters, and also reversed a lower court's dismissal of claims for trespass and the intentional infliction of emotional distress against the media defendants.[44] In 2001, Paul Berger finally reached a confidential settlement agreement with CNN, bringing the case to a close for an undisclosed amount of cash.[45] Berger died in April 2003 and the terms of the agreement were never made public.[46]

The 9th U.S. Circuit Court of Appeals revisited in 2002 the question of when the media can be successfully sued for violating the Fourth Amendment right against unreasonable

---

41. *Wilson* v. *Layne,* 526 U.S. 603 (1999).
42. *Hanlon* v. *Berger,* 526 U.S. 808 (1999).
43. *Berger* v. *Hanlon,* 129 F. 3d 505 (1997).
44. *Berger* v. *Hanlon,* 188 F. 3d 1155 (1999). The rancher and his wife were absolved of all felony charges, but the search was nevertheless broadcast 10 different times by CNN.
45. "CNN, Federal Government Settle Suit with Montana Rancher."
46. "Rancher at Center of Lawsuit Over Televised Raid Dies."

searches and seizures. In *Brunette* v. *Humane Society of Ventura County,* the plaintiff complained that a journalist who accompanied members of the Humane Society—a government-created agency and thus a state actor—on a search of the plaintiff's ranch to investigate alleged instances of animal cruelty acted "in cahoots with the Humane Society" and thereby also became a state actor.[47] The appellate court, however, rejected her Fourth Amendment claim against the journalist and his newspaper, writing that "Brunette's allegations do not establish any substantial cooperation or inextricably intertwined activity between the media and the Humane Society." Comparing the case to *Berger,* the appellate court wrote:

> Unlike CNN in *Berger,* the Media neither planned the raid nor participated in any pre-raid briefings. Nor did the Humane Society in this case disclose to the Media any confidential information like the USFWS disclosed to CNN in *Berger.* Moreover, [the journalist] arrived at Brunette's ranch independently in his own vehicle, *after* the Humane Society had cut the gate lock and begun to search.

The court thus concluded that although the Humane Society and the journalist were both present at Brunette's ranch, they "acted independently" and the journalist's "news gathering mission was entirely distinct from the Humane Society's investigation of animal cruelty charges." The media could not be held liable as a state actor under such circumstances.

These rulings should send a clear message to the press that reporters who want to enter private property need the permission of the occupant or the owner of the property. Police and firefighters are unable to give the press this permission. Reporters who are sent to cover demonstrations or protests that may stray onto nonpublic areas are advised to meet with the police beforehand and explain what they will be doing. They should carry full press credentials and obey all legitimate police orders. For instance, a photographer for The New York Times, Edward Keating, was arrested and charged with criminal trespass in 2002 at "ground zero" in Manhattan when he was caught carrying someone else's press pass and his own credentials had expired.[48] Reporters need to be careful not to interfere with police or have a verbal confrontation with officers who are attempting crowd control. Tensions run high, and the police often fear losing control of the situation. There are a myriad of catchall laws in most cities and states, laws like interfering with an officer in the execution of his or her duty, that might be the basis for an arrest even if a trespass is not involved (see pages 361–363). When applied to the press, these laws might be unconstitutional,[49] but such a ruling will not be made until weeks or months after the journalist has been arrested.

Harassment In 1996 a federal judge in Pennsylvania took the extraordinary action of enjoining the news-gathering activities of two reporters who worked for the television infotainment program "Inside Edition." Reporters Paul Lewis and Stephen Wilson were preparing a story on the high salaries paid to corporate executives at U.S. HealthCare while the company was imposing severe cost cutting on patients. The story focused on Leonard Abramson, chairman of the board, and Abramson's daughter and son-in-law, Nancy and Richard Wolfson, who also worked at U.S. HealthCare. The Wolfsons argued that the reporters used ambush

---

47. 294 F. 3d 1205 (2002), cert. den., 537 U.S. 1112 (2003).
48. "Photographer Is Arrested."
49. *City of Houston* v. *Hill,* 482 U.S. 451 (1987).

interviews, shotgun microphones, and other electronic equipment to harass them and invade their privacy after they rejected requests for on-camera interviews. The reporters went so far, the couple said, as to follow their daughter to school and to follow the entire family when they took a vacation in Florida. The Wolfsons sued the reporters for tortious stalking, harassment, trespass, and invasion of privacy–intrusion upon seclusion, and asked the judge to stop the reporters from using the intrusive news-gathering techniques until a jury trial was held. The judge ruled that he thought the Wolfsons would prevail in their lawsuit against the reporters. He said that through their unreasonable surveilling, hounding and following, the two news-gatherers had effectively rendered the family captive in their own home. The judge entered a preliminary injunction that barred Lewis and Wilson from any conduct, with or without the use of cameras, that invades the Wolfsons' privacy, actions including but not limited to harassing, hounding, following, intruding, frightening, terrorizing or ambushing the family.[50] In January 1997, the parties reached a settlement and the judge dissolved the preliminary injunction he had issued against "Inside Edition." The case thus never went to trial, as the plaintiffs agreed to withdraw their amended complaint against the television show and the journalists for "Inside Edition" agreed not to follow or go to the homes of the Wolfsons or certain family members.

Fraud Fraud can be defined as a knowingly false statement of a material or significant fact that is communicated with the intent to induce the plaintiff to rely on that statement and that does, in fact, induce the plaintiff to reasonably rely upon it to the plaintiff's harm or injury. Typically we think of sellers of goods as engaging in fraud when they lie to buyers about the quality of those goods. But can journalists be held liable for fraud when they try to obtain information by telling a lie? Imagine this scenario. A newspaper editor hears well-founded rumors that a local retail business is cheating its customers. To check out this story, two newspaper reporters apply for jobs at the business to take a look at what goes on inside. The pair use false names, fake work histories, and tell the business owners they are looking for work. They do not reveal they are newspaper reporters and will be spying on the other workers at the business. Are the reporters' activities legal? In 1996 a jury in North Carolina decided that ABC television journalists had committed fraud and an assortment of other legal wrongs when they lied about their backgrounds and intentions in order to get jobs at a supermarket chain the network was investigating for potential health code violations. A damage award of $5 million was later reduced to all but nothing ($2) when a U.S. Court of Appeals ruled that the behavior of the two journalists did not meet the strict legal standard for fraud required by North Carolina statutes.[51] But this high-profile case, which generated considerably more news coverage than the original ABC broadcast about the supermarket chain, brought into sharp focus the issue of reporters pretending to be persons they are not in order to secretly gather news. In a different state with a different statute the fraud conviction might have been sustained. Indeed, in Minnesota just a year later, WCCO television and one of its reporters were found guilty of both fraud and trespass in a situation that mirrored the ABC case. In this instance the reporter lied about her background and her reportorial intentions when she

---

50. *Wolfson* v. *Lewis,* 924 F. Supp. 1413 (1996).
51. *Food Lion Inc.* v. *Capital Cities/ABC,* 194 F. 3d 505 (1999); see also Barringer, "Appeals Court Rejects Damages."

applied for a position as a volunteer at a care facility for mentally retarded persons. She secretly videotaped activities at the facility and portions of the tape were later telecast.[52]

An issue closely related to fraud is impersonation by journalists of government officials in order to obtain information. Such impersonation is prohibited by both federal and state law and the First Amendment provides no defense. For instance, journalist Avi Lidgi was sentenced in April 2002 to one-year probation and 60 hours of community service by a federal court for posing as both a federal prosecutor and a federal judge's aide in order to obtain secret legal documents in an espionage case in Cleveland, Ohio.[53] The 27-year-old journalist agreed to plead guilty to one count of impersonating a federal official after a grand jury had indicted him on three counts and he faced up to nine years in prison.

Misrepresentation   In the autumn of 1994 NBC approached Raymond Veilleux, owner of a trucking company in Maine, and sought permission to send a reporting team with a long-haul truck driver as he drove a California-to-Maine run. Veilleux and driver Peter Kennedy said they were suspicious of the offer because of the growing pressures for stricter regulation of truckers in the wake of a fatal accident in 1993. Four young people had been killed when the car in which they were riding was struck by a long-haul driver who had exceeded the number of hours he was legally allowed to drive. Veilleux and Kennedy agreed to work with the network only after NBC promised to present a positive view of trucking. The network producers said that they would not ask Kennedy to violate any trucking regulations or deviate from his normal driving routine during the trip and that the report would not include any comments from an organization called Parents Against Tired Truckers, an advocacy group fighting for tougher trucking regulations. The 1995 "Dateline" segment did not portray the industry in a positive way. The opening line was, "American highways are a trucker's killing field." The report included interviews with members of Parents Against Tired Truckers, alleged that driver Kennedy repeatedly violated hours-of-service regulations, falsified his driver's log book, and lied to federal inspectors. NBC also revealed that Kennedy had previously tested positive for marijuana and amphetamine use in a random drug test. Kennedy was shown admitting to some of these allegations during the program. Veilleux and Kennedy sued. A U.S. District Court rejected NBC's motion for a summary judgment and permitted a jury to hear allegations of misrepresentation, false-light privacy and negligent infliction of emotional distress.[54] In July 1998 the jury awarded the plaintiffs $525,000 in damages. Twenty months later, the 1st U.S. Circuit Court of Appeals dismissed many of the charges against NBC on the grounds that most of the statements in the broadcast were not materially false and could not sustain a claim of intentional infliction of emotional distress or false-light privacy. The court also said the claim of misrepresentation against the network for promises it made to portray the trucking company in a positive way could not be sustained because in the course of the investigation, NBC uncovered negative information about the trucking company that it was free to report. But the network remained liable for misrepresentation for failing to fulfill its promise not to involve the Parents Against Tired Truckers in the broadcast.[55]

52. *Special Force Ministries* v. *WCCO Television,* 584 N.W. 2d 789 (1998).
53. "Journalist Gets Probation."
54. *Veilleux* v. *National Broadcasting Co.,* 8 F. Supp. 2d 23 (1998).
55. Schiesel, "Jury Finds NBC Negligent," and *Veilleux* v. *National Broadcasting Co.,* 206 F. 3d 92 (2000).

Failure to Obey Lawful Orders   Police and fire officials at the scene of disasters, accidents and fires frequently restrict the access of the press and public to the site. Reporters are bound to respect these rules or face charges of disorderly conduct or worse. For instance, a reporter for the Fayetteville Observer named Robert Boyer was convicted in 2005 of failing to leave a crime scene and sentenced to 60 hours of community service.[56] The case arose in March 2004 after Boyer went to the scene of a homicide in a neighborhood of Fayetteville, N.C. After reportedly refusing to cooperate after being asked and ordered by police six different times to move back from the crime scene, Boyer was arrested and charged with the misdemeanor offense of resisting, delaying or obstructing an officer. Boyer unsuccessfully argued to the district court judge that the local police broke department policy by failing to use crime-scene tape to block public access to the dead-end street where the crime occurred. The police, instead, stationed an officer, along with his car, on the street to tell others it was a crime scene. According to a local newspaper account, "the officers chose not to use crime-scene tape to block the entrance because police vehicles would be coming in and out, and it would have been more work to repeatedly raise and lower the flimsy tape." The lesson here is this: Journalists must be careful not only to notice and obey the location of crime-scene tape but also to obey the lawful commands and orders of the police when no tape is present.

The New Jersey Supreme Court upheld the disorderly person conviction of a press photographer who was charged with impeding a police officer in the performance of his duty at the scene of a serious traffic accident. The photographer was standing near the wreckage when the state trooper, who feared a fire might begin and who also wanted to preserve the accident scene for investigation, ordered the area cleared of spectators. The news photographer moved back five feet, but when he refused to move any farther, he was arrested. The journalist, Harvey J. Lashinsky, argued that the state's disorderly person statute was inapplicable to him because he was a member of the press. The state's high court disagreed, noting that "the constitutional prerogatives of the press must yield under appropriate circumstances to other important and legitimate interests." Acknowledging that the press does play a special role in society, the court nevertheless said that the photographer clearly impeded the officer by refusing his request to leave the area. While the officer was arguing with the journalist, he could have been giving assistance to the accident victims and beginning the investigation of the crash.[57]

When a commuter aircraft crashed near Billy Mitchell Field outside Milwaukee in September 1985 police cordoned off the crash site so rescue workers and federal safety officials could do their work. WTMJ news photographer Peter Ah King and three other journalists who had run through a police roadblock to reach the crash site were told by authorities to leave the area. But Ah King jumped a fence and ran to the top of a small hill 30 yards away. When a police officer caught up with him he was told to leave, but he refused and continued to take video pictures of the crash site. He told authorities he would only leave if he was arrested, so police arrested him. Shortly thereafter the crash site was opened to the press. Ah King was convicted of disorderly conduct. He appealed his conviction to the Wisconsin Supreme Court, which affirmed the lower-court ruling. The court said that the refusal to obey a police command does not normally constitute disorderly conduct. But in this case the

---

56. Woolverton, "Ex-Reporter for Observer Found Guilty."
57. *State* v. *Lashinsky,* 404 A. 2d 1121 (1979).

photographer's repeated refusal to obey the order to leave the area in a situation in which crowd control was a major concern, coupled with "his continued penetration into a nonpublic restricted area," must be regarded as disorderly conduct because the conduct had the tendency to disrupt good order. The court acknowledged that reporters have a right to gather the news by any means within the law, but they do not have a First Amendment right to access, solely because they are news-gatherers, to the scene of an airplane crash from which the general public has been excluded.[58] (Note: At least one state, California, has a statute that gives the news media the right to enter disaster areas closed to the general public. But reporters must sign a waiver of liability of the government before access is allowed.)

Grand juries work behind closed doors, and courts are very sensitive when anyone attempts to elicit information from the jurors about what has taken place. Two reporters in Indiana were held in contempt of court when they attempted to induce former grand jury members to reveal secret testimony. But the Indiana Supreme Court dismissed the contempt charges in this case. The court bluntly affirmed that unlawful news-gathering activities are not protected by the First Amendment and that any attempt to induce grand jurors to reveal secret testimony can surely be punished by the courts. But in this case, the reporters attempted to gain information from former grand jurors more than two years after the closure of the particular grand jury proceeding. The attempts to obtain information in this case could hardly impede the administration of justice, the state court declared.[59]

Note the point made in these cases that a journalist has an obligation to obey "lawful" orders by police and other officials. Photographer David Connell obeyed the orders of police officers, but he believed they were unlawful. A U.S. District Court in New Hampshire agreed and ruled that Connell's civil rights had been violated when he was barred from taking pictures at an automobile accident. One person was killed, another seriously injured in the collision. Connell began taking pictures from a spot about 25 feet away from the accident. When the police asked him to move, he retreated to a spot about 30 yards away, and then 40 yards away. Police still weren't satisfied, so Connell went into a home and began taking pictures from a second-floor window. Other people were viewing the wreck from a similar vantage point. Police and emergency medical technicians still weren't happy, and Connell was ordered to stop taking pictures or face arrest for disturbing the peace. He complied but brought the civil rights action against the town of Hudson. "It is hard to imagine how Connell could have interfered with police or emergency activities by taking pictures from the second floor of a house that others were using to view the accident," the court said. The real reason for the restriction on the photographer seemed to be that emergency personnel did not want Connell to take pictures of the dead and injured as they were removed from the automobiles. The court said this was an insufficient justification. The court awarded Connell only nominal damages, one dollar. But the ruling nevertheless makes the strong point that police and fire officials must respect the rights of journalists, who also have a job to do.[60]

58. *City of Oak Creek* v. *Ah King,* 436 N.W. 2d 285 (1989).
59. *Indiana* v. *Helzel,* 522 N.E. 2d 31 (1990).
60. *Connell* v. *Town of Hudson,* 733 F. Supp. 465 (1990).

Other Laws   Many other laws may directly affect news-gathering. And the First Amendment does not offer a shield to reporters who violate these, either. For example, in most states and the District of Columbia, a reporter can secretly record a conversation or interview with a news source. But in about a dozen states, including California, Pennsylvania and Washington, a reporter must have the permission of all parties involved in a conversation before it can be recorded. These laws prohibit anyone from secretly recording a conversation face-to-face, on the telephone, or almost anywhere. For instance, California Penal Code Section 632 provides that a crime is committed by anyone (including, of course, a journalist) who

> intentionally and *without the consent of all parties* to a confidential communication, by means of any electronic amplifying or recording device, eavesdrops upon or records the confidential communication, whether the communication is carried on among the parties in the presence of one another or by means of a telegraph, telephone, or other device, except a radio.

California courts have held that a "confidential communication" is one in which a party to the conversation has an objectively reasonable expectation that it is not being overheard or recorded.[61] A violation occurs at the moment the recording is made, *regardless* of whether the material recorded is later published or aired. The California law also provides for a civil remedy for individuals who are recorded in violation of the statute. In 2003, a California appellate court held that a physician had successfully stated a prima facie case demonstrating a violation of California Penal Code Section 632 based upon the undercover and secretive recording by broadcast journalists of conversations in the physician's private office between the physician and journalists posing as patients.[62] In an important blow to the journalists involved, the appellate court refused to create or adopt an affirmative defense for the journalists based upon what they claimed was a legitimate news-gathering motive.

What about recording or storing e-mail messages or conversations conducted through a private chat room? Courts are just now being asked this question. And in Washington, one of the states in which the consent of all parties is required before a conversation can be recorded, a superior court ruled that storing computer messages was not governed by the all-party consent law because computer messages were not specifically mentioned in the statute.[63] Nearly half the states and the federal government have laws prohibiting eavesdropping. And in a growing number of states it is even against the law to secretly take a video or still photograph of someone. These laws target video voyeurs, but they impact journalists and legitimate photographers. Anyone who hopes to practice journalism without violating the law needs to know the laws in his or her particular state that relate to news gathering. There are subtle differences among the state laws, and the statutes change from time to time. Awareness of the law is the best protection a reporter can have. A good resource on taping can be found online at the Reporters Committee for Freedom of the Press Web site at http://www.rcfp.org/taping.

---

61. *Flanagan* v. *Flanagan*, 41P. 3d 575 (2002).
62. *Lieberman* v. *KCOP Television, Inc.,* 110 Cal. App. 4th 156 (2003).
63. Kaplan, "Recording of Electronic Chats."

SUMMARY   Gaining access to government-held information is an important problem for journalists and citizens alike. Since the early 1980s government has become more reticent about providing easy access by reporters to the vast amounts of information held by agencies within the government. Public opinion tends to support the government in this regard, and journalists have been forced to exercise legal means to accomplish some reporting tasks. But the law is not always helpful. The common law offers little assistance to persons attempting to inspect government records. The U.S. Constitution was drafted at a time when news gathering was not the central role of the press. There is little evidence to suggest that the right to gather news was intended to be guaranteed by the First Amendment. Federal courts have in recent years suggested that news and information gathering is entitled to some protection under the U.S. Constitution, but they have been stingy in granting such protection. The U.S. Supreme Court has limited the rights of reporters to gather information at prisons and jails to the same rights enjoyed by other citizens. Lower courts have found broader, albeit qualified, constitutional rights of access. Courts have not permitted, however, the use of the First Amendment to immunize reporters from legal consequences that result when the law is broken while news is being gathered. Many plaintiffs are finding that it is easier to sue the press for how the news has been gathered than for libel or invasion of privacy. Suits for trespass, fraud, misrepresentation, failure to obey lawful orders and other causes of action are becoming more common today.

THE FREEDOM OF INFORMATION ACT

Neither the common law nor the Constitution has provided the clear and well-defined right of access to government information that most citizens believe is needed. Beginning in the early 1950s, there were concerted efforts by press and citizen lobbying groups to pass statutes that guarantee to public and press alike the right to inspect records and other information held by the government and to attend meetings held by public agencies. These laws now exist in almost every state. In addition, there are federal open-records and open-meetings laws. Let us look at the federal legislation first.

In 1966, after many years of hearings and testimony and work, Congress adopted the **Freedom of Information Act,** which was ostensibly designed to open up records and files long closed to public inspection. The documentary evidence left by Congress relating to the passage of this measure leaves little doubt that the purpose of this bill was to establish a general philosophy of the fullest possible disclosure of government-held records. The Senate Report's Purpose of the Bill section quotes James Madison:

> Knowledge will forever govern ignorance, and a people who mean to be their own governors, must arm themselves with the power knowledge gives. A popular government without popular information or the means of acquiring it, is but a prologue to a farce or a tragedy or perhaps both.[64]

Both the public and the press have accepted this philosophy.

---

64. U.S. Senate, *Clarifying and Protecting,* 2–3.

The Freedom of Information Act (FOIA) has been an important tool for journalists seeking answers to important questions. In the past four decades reporters have used the law to expose serious safety defects in the gas tank on the Ford Pinto, to find out why the Hubble Space Telescope mirror failed to work, and to alert citizens in several states about environmental crises at Department of Energy nuclear weapons plants. During the presidential campaign of 2004, the Washington Post successfully used a FOIA request to obtain portions of the military records of Larry Thurlow.[65] Thurlow, a critic of Democratic candidate John Kerry's military record and a member of a group called "Swift Boat Veterans for Truth," claimed that the Navy Swift boat that Kerry commanded in Vietnam alongside one skippered by Thurlow never came under fire during a particular mission up the Bay Hap River. The military records of Thurlow produced under the FOIA request, however, stated that "all units began receiving enemy small arms and automatic weapons fire from the river banks." The phrase "all units" indicates that Kerry's boat did come under attack, as the then-presidential candidate had claimed. As the Post wrote, this statement in the records "contradicts his [Thurlow's] own version of events." Another FOIA request in 2004 uncovered and exposed the fact that about 99 percent of the complaints filed that year with the Federal Communications Commission over allegedly indecent programming (see Chapter 16), aside from complaints about the infamous Janet Jackson breast-baring Super Bowl halftime show, came from just one organization—the Parents Television Council. That organization has a link on its Web site devoted solely to the filing of e-mail complaints about indecent broadcasts with the FCC. The FOIA request to the FCC thus exposed a major force behind the massive censorship campaign of one organization.

In 2005 a FOIA request by the Associated Press for Pentagon records relating to evidence against more than 550 terror suspects and alleged enemy combatants detained by the United States at Guantanamo Bay, Cuba, produced a "summary of evidence" document that included a startling factual assertion: One of the Guantanamo detainees "associated with" Al-Qaeda had "assisted in the escape of Osama bin Laden from Tora Bora" in Afghanistan.[66] The Associated Press called it "the first definitive statement from the Pentagon that bin Laden was at Tora Bora and evaded U.S. pursuers."[67] The document and statement seemed to contradict the claims of some in the military and the Bush administration that they did not know whether bin Laden was in Tora Bora, which was bombed and attacked by U.S. forces in December 2001. Cave-to-cave searches there at the time by American ground forces did not find bin Laden, and Senator John Kerry had asserted during his campaign for president in 2004 that Bush had missed an excellent opportunity to capture or kill bin Laden in Tora Bora. In 2005 the Pentagon also produced hundreds of photographs taken by official military photographers of flag-draped coffins containing U.S. armed forces members killed in Iraq and Afghanistan. The production of the pictures, which vividly brought home the realities of war yet simultaneously showed the dignity and respect of military ceremonies, occurred in response to a FOIA request by a journalism professor named Ralph Begleiter (see pages 98–99).

Too often FOIA fights for documents, although perhaps ultimately successful, are both lengthy and expensive. The San Francisco Chronicle published a two-part series in June 2002

---

65. Dobbs, "Records Counter a Critic of Kerry."
66. Burns, "Document: Bin Laden Evaded U.S. Forces."
67. Ibid.

called "The Campus Files" that demonstrated how the FBI used a covert campaign to conduct unlawful intelligence activities and disrupt the Free Speech Movement at the University of California-Berkeley in the 1950s and 1960s.[68] The report was based on FBI records obtained after a 17-year legal battle over an FOIA request made by then-journalism student Seth Rosenfeld back in 1981. The series prompted U.S. senator Dianne Feinstein (D.-Calif.) to ask FBI director Robert Mueller in 2002 whether the FBI is currently engaged in such activities and to call for it to take specific steps from misusing its powers for political purposes. The protracted FOIA battle, which demonstrates the obstacles sometimes faced by those making FOIA requests, cost the FBI more than $1 million in trying to suppress the documents.

Unfortunately, lengthy battles like that involving the Free Speech Movement are not unusual. For instance, a University of California-Irvine professor named Jonathan Wiener gained access in late 2004 to the last 10 pages of an approximately 300-page file the FBI kept on the late Beatles member John Lennon.[69] The FBI maintained files on what it considered to be anti-government activists of the era, and from 1971 to 1972 it gathered data on Lennon, such as memos describing his donations to a group that planned to demonstrate at the 1972 Republican National Convention. Wiener filed his original FOIA request with the FBI back in 1983, and he received 248 pages from the file on Lennon 14 years later in 1997. But it was not until September 2004 that U.S. District Court Judge Robert Takasugi ordered the release of the last 10 pages–pages that the FBI claimed would pose a national security risk because an unidentified foreign government had secretly provided the agency with the information—and the two-decade-long battle finally ended. An exhausted Wiener told a reporter for the Los Angeles Times, "I never wanted to spend—what has it been?—21 years on this. I just wanted to write something about Lennon."[70] Weiner has now posted the documents from Lennon's file at http://www.lennonfbifiles.com/fbi.html on his own Web site. In another FOIA battle that concluded in 2004—this one on a quite different matter—U.S. District Court Judge Shira A. Scheindlin ordered the Occupational Safety and Health Administration (OSHA) to turn over to The New York Times the company names and worker injury and illness rates of the workplaces in the United States with the worst safety records.[71] The Times had sought the information back in 2002 under the Freedom of Information Act because OSHA had previously only given the names of workplace locations where work injuries were above the national average and had failed to give rankings that would identify the worst locations. OSHA's prior practice thus made it "difficult for reporters or the public to know where it was riskiest to work and whether the agency was effective in bringing about improvements."[72]

In August 2002, the Center for National Security Studies and more than 20 other public-interest organizations successfully used FOIA to sue the Department of Justice to release the identities of all individuals detained in connection with the investigation of the September 11, 2001, terrorist attacks, as well as the identities of their attorneys.[73] The government had

---

68. Rosenfeld, "The Campus Files: Reagan, Hoover and the UC Red Scare." The complete series, including a description of the FOIA battles, is available online at http://sfgate.com/campus/.
69. Yi, "Professor Wins Release of Last FBI Data on Beatle."
70. Ibid.
71. Preston, "Judge Orders Agency to Disclose Safety Records."
72. Ibid.
73. *Center for National Security Studies et al.* v. *U.S. Dept. of Justice,* 215 F. Supp. 2d 94 (2002).

asserted several sections under Exemption 7 of FOIA relating to information compiled for "law enforcement purposes" (see pages 384–390). Judge Gladys Kessler, however, stayed her order later that same month so that the issue could be heard by the appellate court. That court, the U.S. Circuit Court of Appeals for the District of Columbia, handed the Bush administration a victory in June 2003 when it ruled in a split 2-1 decision that the Justice Department can keep secret the names of foreign detainees.[74] The appellate court majority reasoned that "America faces an enemy just as real as its former Cold War foes, with capabilities beyond the capacity of the judiciary to explore." It concluded that Exemption 7(A) (see pages 384–390) regarding interference with law enforcement proceedings justified the withholding of this information, writing that

> the government's expectation that disclosure of the detainees' names would enable al Qaeda or other terrorist groups to map the course of the investigation and thus develop the means to impede it is reasonable. A complete list of names informing terrorists of every suspect detained by the government at any point during the September 11 investigation would give terrorist organizations a composite picture of the government investigation, and since these organizations would generally know the activities and locations of its members on or about September 11, disclosure would inform terrorists of both the substantive and geographic focus of the investigation.

Hundreds of thousands of ordinary citizens have also used the law to gain access to more mundane records held by a myriad of government agencies. But using the law has not always been easy, for the government often has been genuinely hostile to Freedom of Information Act requests made by reporters. "From Lyndon Johnson's reluctant signing of the FOIA in 1966, every administration since has viewed it with some degree of distaste," said Professor Lotte Feinberg, an FOIA expert at John Jay College of Criminal Justice. An illustration of the Bush administration's hostility to FOIA requests was the battle fought in 2004 over information related to the government's so-called no-fly lists for suspected terrorists. The lists identify individuals who are not allowed to board airplanes, as well as "selectees" who are subjected to extra searches. For instance, the singer formerly known as Cat Stevens ("Peace Train" and "Morning Has Broken" were among his hits), who converted to Islam and now goes by Yusuf Islam, was removed in September 2004 from a plane headed from London to the United States because he was on a no-fly list for giving money to a group suspected to be terrorist-related.[75] In a case called *Gordon* v. *FBI*[76] filed in federal court in San Francisco, the American Civil Liberties Union and several individuals in 2004 sought information from the Transportation Security Administration (TSA) and the FBI about how the no-fly lists are compiled and how innocent people can have their names removed from the lists. The TSA, citing FOIA exemptions for privacy and national security, refused to turn over the information. A federal judge in 2004, however, criticized the TSA in *Gordon* v. *FBI,* stating that it was making "frivolous claims of exemption" and that "the government has not come close to

---

74. *Center for National Security Studies et al.* v. *U.S. Dept. of Justice,* 331 F. 3d 918 (2003). In January 2004, the Supreme Court declined to hear the case. 540 U.S. 1104 (2004).
75. Boule, "No-Fly List Clips Singer."
76. 32 M.L.R. 2288 (N.D. Cal. 2004).

meeting its burden." The TSA, upon a court order, eventually produced 301 pages of redacted documents in October 2004, but those documents failed to reveal how many people currently are barred from flying or are subject to extra screening because they are on watch lists.[77]

APPLYING THE LAW

The usefulness of any freedom of information act depends in no small part on the way the government chooses to interpret and apply it. Some observers said that George W. Bush had a greater penchant for secrecy than any recent president—even before the terrorist attacks of 9/11. This contention seemed to be borne out by resistance in the Bush administration to provide Congress and the public with even the barest of details on the government's energy policies and the Enron scandal. "This administration has a knee-jerk response—reflexive secrecy," said Thomas S. Blanton, director of the National Security Archive, a research center at George Washington University.[78]

The terrorists attacks in New York and Washington, D.C., and the subsequent move to tighten homeland security had an immediate impact on the application of the federal freedom of information law. In October 2001 then-Attorney General John Ashcroft ordered all agencies covered by the law to review more closely which documents they release under the law. The attorney general's policy permits agencies to withhold information on any "sound legal basis" and to carefully consider threats to national security and law enforcement effectiveness. Under President Clinton a looser criteria was applied: Agencies could hold back information only to prevent "foreseeable harm." Lucy Dalglish, head of the Reporters Committee for Freedom of the Press, said that the change "sends a message throughout the entire federal government to stonewall or deny requests whenever possible." In addition, government agencies began after September 11, 2001, to remove information from their official Web sites, sites that are accessible to any Internet user. The kinds of data expunged included the location and operating status of nuclear power plants, maps of the nation's transportation infrastructure, and information about chemicals used at industrial sites. This action stirred debate even among advocates of greater access to government-held data. The Federation of American Scientists—whose Project on Government Secrecy was created in the early 1990s to force the government to move more information into the open by posting such data on its own Web site—decided to remove information on intelligence sites, nuclear weapons facilities and similar matters from its Internet postings. The Bush administration also sought to limit public access to information about critical infrastructure systems like energy, telecommunications and banking that it had been asking private businesses to provide to the government. This plan was aimed at denying terrorists access to such data, but it also encouraged private companies to cooperate by reducing the fear that important business-related secrets might be made accessible to competitors.[79] And in 2006 The New York Times revealed that the CIA and other agencies were removing from public use at the National Archives tens of thousands of pages of previously declassified material and then secretly restoring them to classified status.

---

77. Kravets, "No Fly List."
78. Weinberg, "Trashing the FOIA," and Rosenbaum, "When Government Doesn't Tell."
79. Helm, "Policy Tightens Access to Federal Records"; Toner, "Reconsidering Security"; and Mitchell, "Limits Sought on Access."

A recent blow to access advocates came in November 2002 when President George W. Bush signed into law the Homeland Security Act of 2002.[80] One of the most controversial provisions of this law is known as the Critical Information Infrastructure Act. It makes exempt from FOIA, as well as state and local disclosure laws, so-called critical infrastructure information that is voluntarily submitted to the federal government—specifically, to the Homeland Security Department—by private persons and, more notably, business entities. What is the problem with this? As the San Francisco Chronicle opined in an editorial, the law "allows private parties to hide information about 'critical infrastructure'—including concerns about health and safety— simply by submitting the data voluntarily to the new department. The information could apply to privately operated power plants, bridges, dams, ports or chemical plants."[81] The new law also keeps private the name of the person or entity submitting the information.

The result, as Senator Patrick Leahy (D.-Vt.) observed, is "most severe weakening of the Freedom of Information Act in its 36-year history" and "a big-business wish-list gussied up in security garb." In particular, the act encourages businesses to submit information concerning critical infrastructure information—defined broadly to include "information not customarily in the public domain and related to the security of critical infrastructure or protected systems"—not only by making that information exempt from FOIA and state disclosure laws but also by granting those companies immunity from "any civil action arising under Federal or State law if such information is submitted in good faith." It creates criminal penalties for anyone who discloses the submitted information. The potential for abuse is clear—companies may file information with the government to keep it out of the hands of the press and to shield themselves from lawsuits arising from wrongdoing that information otherwise exposes.

In March 2003, Senator Leahy introduced a bill, called the "Restoration of Freedom of Information Act," designed to narrow the reach of the Homeland Security Act. The bill, however, failed to gain support in the Senate. But Leahy did not give up. In 2005 the Vermont Democrat was back, re-introducing along with co-sponsors Carl Levin (D.-Mich.) and Joe Lieberman (D.-Conn.) the "Restoration of Freedom of Information Act."[82] Once again, the measure addressed the "critical infrastructure information" exemption from FOIA created by the Homeland Security Act (HSA) of 2002. By February 2005, the Department of Homeland Security (DHS) had received a total of 29 submissions under the critical infrastructure exemption and rejected only seven of those. As Leahy stated in announcing his new bill in March 2005, the problem was clear:

> We know nothing of the substance of the accepted submissions, what vulnerabilities they may describe, or what is being done to address them. Most businesses are good citizens and take seriously their obligations to the government and the public, but this "disclose-and-immunize" provision [of the HSA of 2002] is subject to abuse. . . . The HSA lays out the perfect blueprint to avoid legal liability: funnel damaging information into this voluntary disclosure system and preempt the government or others harmed by the company's actions from being able to use it against the company. This is not the kind of two-way public-private cooperation that serves the public interest.

80. Public Law No. 107–296.
81. Editorial, "Reinforce Anti-Secrecy Law," A24.
82. S. 622, 109th Cong. (2005). The short title of the 2005 measure was "Restore FOIA Act."

To rectify some of these alleged problems, the 2005 bill proposed by Leahy and his co-sponsors would have

- ended civil immunity from lawsuits for companies that voluntarily submit critical infrastructure information to the DHS;
- ended criminal liability for legitimate whistle-blowers at the DHS who disclose such submitted information; and
- limited the HSA exemption to cover only "records" from the private sector, not any and all "information" labeled by the private entities as critical infrastructure.

This third change—replacing the word "information" with "records"—is more than just a matter of semantics or verbal gymnastics. In particular, the term "records" is limited in definition to well-defined communications such as paper and electronic documents, reports and e-mails, whereas "information" is much broader, untested in court, and could sweep up verbal conversations and the content of telephone calls. As with Leahy's earlier bill, however, the 2005 version of the Restoration of Freedom of Information Act failed to become law.

High-level policy decisions are not the only reason freedom of information laws often fail to work as they were intended. For whatever reason, most government bureaucrats at all levels find it extremely difficult to share the records they hold with the nation's citizens. Consequently, bizarre stories emerge as agencies try to block access to records that by all accounts should be made public. When former Associated Press correspondent Terry Anderson asked the FBI for access to material in his personal files that related to Arab terrorists who had held him hostage in Lebanon for six years, the agency refused, claiming that releasing the records would violate the terrorists' right of privacy. Public ridicule forced Attorney General Janet Reno to reverse the FBI on this point, but she still denied Anderson's request, citing national security reasons. The fact of the matter is that no administration since the Freedom of Information Act was adopted nearly 40 years ago has truly invested sufficient time and energy to make it work the way it was envisioned. Only the dogged efforts of private citizens, scholars and journalists have occasionally broken down the walls between the bureaucracy and the citizenry it is supposed to serve.

How many FOIA requests do government agencies receive each year? At a May 2005 hearing called "Privacy, Security and Information: A Look at FOIA in the Post-9/11 Era," a U.S. House of Representatives subcommittee on government management, finance and accountability was told by various panelists that, for 25 major agencies:

- FOIA requests increased by a remarkable 71 percent from 2002 to 2004;[83]
- the number of pending backlog requests—requests carried over from year to year—rose by 14 percent since 2002;
- despite the increasing backlog, government agencies in 2004 provided responsive records in full to requesters 92 percent of the time;
- government agencies now receive a total of four million requests annually;
- it costs the government $300 million a year to process those requests; and

83. This figure and many others presented at the hearing are found in a May 2005 report prepared by the U.S. Government Accountability Office entitled "Information Management: Implementation of the Freedom of Information Act." It can be located by visiting the GAO's Web site at http://www.gao.gov.

■ while most requests are processed within the current 20-day deadline (see page 390), some government agencies—most notably, the State Department, the Central Intelligence Agency and the National Science Foundation—are considerably slower in responding.

In an effort to both expedite the processing of requests for information and better keep tabs on such requests, two FOIA-centered bills were introduced in 2005. In particular, the "OPEN Government Act of 2005" was proposed in both the U.S. Senate[84] and the House of Representatives.[85] A tortured acronym for "Openness Promotes Effectiveness in our National Government Act," this measure would have required each government agency to establish a FOIA request tracking system that would

■ provide a person making a FOIA request with an individualized tracking number within 10 days of the receipt of the request;
■ establish a telephone line or Internet service allowing a requester to find out both the date on which the agency originally received the request and an estimated date on which it would complete its processing of the request; and
■ create an Office of Government Information Services that would both audit agencies' compliance with FOIA policies and offer mediation services, as an alternative to litigation in an ombudsman-like role, between people making FOIA requests and the agencies that deny them.

By the end of 2005, however, the OPEN Government Act had failed to become law. It had gained fewer than 30 co-sponsors in the U.S. Senate. One can expect, however, to see similar bills proposed in the near future.

There was some good news on the FOIA front in 2005. In particular, in December that year President Bush issued an executive order calling for each government agency to appoint a chief FOIA officer with agency-wide responsibility for efficient and appropriate compliance with the FOIA.[86] In addition, the executive order mandated that each agency establish at least one FOIA requester service center to be the first place that a FOIA requester can contact to seek information concerning the status of a FOIA request and appropriate information about the agency's FOIA response. Finally, the order called for each agency to appoint at least one FOIA public liaison to serve as a supervisory official to whom FOIA requesters can raise concerns about service. Whether such measures will be effective in expediting FOIA requests remains to be seen.

FOIA AND ELECTRONIC COMMUNICATION

By the year 2000 the vast majority of government records were created, transported and stored electronically. As computer technology replaced paper records, agencies within the federal government balked at allowing access to these electronic records. Most bureaucrats seemed to hold the opinion that the electronic records were a special class of data, outside the range of FOIA and off limits to the public.[87] Officials argued that if they had to perform even simple

84. S. 394, 109th Cong. (2005).
85. H.R. 867, 109th Cong. (2005).
86. The official White House press release describing the Dec. 14, 2005, order is available online at http://www.whitehouse.gov/news/releases/2005/12/20051214-4.html.
87. Morrissey, "FOIA Foiled?" 29.

computer programming to retrieve the information sought by the requester, the information fell outside the broad mandate of disclosure of the Freedom of Information Act. This mind-set was not confined to the lower echelons of the administration. High officials in both the first Bush and the Clinton administrations fought efforts by the National Security Archives to force the government to save electronic messages (e-mail) sent by computer. Officials in the Bush administration sought to erase from computer files all records of communications among officials during the eight years of the Reagan presidency. The case was still in the courts when Clinton was inaugurated in 1993 and his administration continued to argue the position taken by the Bush administration that the government had a right to dispose of this information as it saw fit. The U.S. Court of Appeals for the District of Columbia Circuit rejected this argument in August 1993, ruling that the government must preserve electronic messages and memos under the same standards that have always been applied to paper communications.[88]

In 1996, after a couple of previous tries, Congress finally adopted an amendment to the Freedom of Information Act that requires government agencies to apply the same standards of disclosure to electronic records that they have always applied to paper documents. This includes all e-mail correspondence as well as letters or notes. The Electronic Freedom of Information Act, as codified at 5 U.S.C. § 552 and known as e-FOIA, also establishes priorities that the agencies must apply when faced with multiple requests for computer searches for records. Top priority goes to FOIA requests in which a delay would threaten the life or safety of an individual. Next in line comes the news media and others in the business of disseminating information to the public. The new law also requires agencies to publish an online index of the documents they have and to make a reasonable attempt to provide documents in the requested format, that is, on tapes, diskettes, paper and so on. The law does not, however, define electronic information, instead leaving this important question to federal agencies and the courts.

Initial compliance with the act was slow. The U.S. General Accounting Office reported in 2001 that most agencies had opened electronic reading rooms but had not yet provided all the required electronic material. It said the quality of the agencies' annual reports needed improvement. Most agencies had implemented e-FOIA requirements but had not made all required documents available. While nearly all the agencies had Web pages, only about half could accept electronic requests for documents. The introduction of electronically stored and transmitted documents and messages has caused problems for reporters who cover all levels of government. The growing use of e-mail has made it possible for members of governmental boards or commissions to hold a "virtual" meeting via the computer.

Freedom of information laws are only as helpful as the administration that must administer them. Multitudes of means exist for thwarting the law. Despite the problems, the federal FOIA continues to operate.

AGENCY RECORDS

The broad outlines of the federal Freedom of Information Act, the nine areas of exempted information, and suggested ways in which a journalist or citizen can use the law are sketched out in the next few pages. One can write an open-records law in two basic ways. The first way

88. Lewis, "Government Told to Save Messages," A1.

is to declare that the following kinds of records are to be accessible for public inspection and then list the kinds of records that are open. The second way is to proclaim that all government records are open for public inspection except the following kinds of records and then list the exceptions. Congress approved the second kind of law in 1966, and it went into effect in 1967. The law has been amended several times, with substantial changes being enacted in 1974, 1976, 1986 and 1996, as well as in 2002 with the adoption of the Homeland Security Act (pages 369–370), which directly affects FOIA.

What Is an Agency?

The U.S. Freedom of Information Act gives any person access to all the records kept by all federal agencies, unless the information falls into one of nine categories of exempted material. An agency has been defined under the law as

> any executive department, military department, government corporation, government-controlled corporation or other establishment in the executive branch of government (including the executive office of the president), or any independent regulatory agency.

The law governs records held by agencies in the executive branch of government and all the independent regulatory agencies like the **Federal Trade Commission,** the Federal Aviation Agency, the Nuclear Regulatory Commission, the Social Security Administration, and the Securities and Exchange Commission. The law does not cover records held by Congress or the federal courts. Some agencies associated with the executive branch of government also fall outside the purview of the law. In 1985 the U.S. Court of Appeals for the District of Columbia Circuit ruled that the Council of Economic Advisors, which works closely with the president on economic matters, is not covered by the law because it exists solely to advise and assist the president and makes no policy on its own. The agency has no regulatory power; it cannot issue rules or regulations. Although the FOIA does govern some operations in the executive office of the president, the law does not reach "the president's immediate personal staff or units in the executive office whose *sole function* is to advise and assist the president," the court ruled.[89]

A U.S. District Court ruled in 1995 that the National Security Council, which is also a part of the executive office of the president, is an agency under the FOIA because it operates independently of the president in many instances.[90] The U.S. Court of Appeals reversed this decision a year later. The court said that three factors have to be considered when determining whether a unit in the executive office of the president exercises enough substantial independent authority to be regarded as an agency. The court must look at how closely from an operational standpoint the group is to the president, at whether it has a self-contained structure, and at the nature of its delegated authority. The NSC certainly has a self-contained structure with its own staff and budget, the court acknowledged. But the "intimate organizational and operating relationship between the President and the NSC is . . . entitled to significantly greater weight in evaluating the NSC's arguable status as an agency than is the

---

89. *Rushforth* v. *Council of Economic Advisors,* 762 F. 2d 1038 (1985).
90. *Armstrong* v. *Executive Office of the President,* 877 F. Supp. 690 (1995).

self-contained structure of the entity,"[91] the court ruled. Also, in this case, the plaintiff failed to show that the NSC exercised any meaningful nonadvisory authority. Because the NSC operates in close proximity to the president and because it does not exercise substantial independent authority, the NSC is not an agency within the meaning of the law, the court concluded.

What Is a Record?

Congress did not specify the physical characteristics of a record in the Freedom of Information Act. Certainly records are paper documents, e-mail and other computer-generated material.[92] But the term "record" also includes films, tapes and even three-dimensional objects such as evidence in a criminal prosecution.

What Is an Agency Record?

"Agency" has been defined under the law; so has "record." What is an agency record? It is not, unfortunately, simply a combination of the definition of these two terms. In this case the whole, the term "agency record," involves a good deal more than the sum of its parts. Courts have established the following definition of an agency record:

> **If the agency has created the document and is in possession of that document, it is very likely an agency record.**
>
> **If the agency has created the document but does not possess or control it, it is not an agency record.**
>
> **If the agency merely possesses the document but has not created it, it might be an agency record, or it might not. If the agency came into possession of the document as a part of its official duties, it is probably an agency record. If it just happens to have the document, it is probably not an agency record.**

A great volume of case law supports this definition. The high court rejected in 1980 the requests of the Reporters Committee to gain access to notes created by Henry Kissinger when he was secretary of state. Kissinger gave these notes to the Library of Congress when he left office. The high court refused to accede to the FOIA request, noting that the material had certainly been created by Kissinger, but that he was no longer in possession of the documents.[93]

The U.S. Court of Appeals refused to permit the inspection of telephone slips and desk calendars possessed by two different agencies because neither kind of document was related to agency business.[94] The same court also refused to provide access to a report prepared by

---

91. "National Security Council Not Subject to FOIA," 1 E.P.L.R. 438 (1996).

92. *Long* v. *IRS,* 596 F. 2d 362 (1979).

93. *Kissinger* v. *Reporters Committee,* 445 U.S. 136 (1980).

94. *BNA* v. *Baxter; Environmental Defense Fund* v. *Office of Management and Budget,* 742 F. 2d 1848 (1984).

members of Ronald Reagan's transition staff prior to his inauguration as president. The document was kept by the Department of Health and Human Services, an agency covered by FOIA. "In this case," the court said, "although copies of the report are physically located in HHS, the report was not generated by HHS, is not within the control of HHS, and indeed never entered the department's files or was ever used by the department for any purpose."[95]

In *Justice Department* v. *Tax Analysts,*[96] the Supreme Court ruled that the Justice Department was required to make available copies of district court decisions it receives in the course of litigating tax cases. The opinions were sought by a company called Tax Analysts, which publishes a weekly magazine called Tax Notes, a report on federal tax matters. Because the Justice Department is routinely sent these opinions, editors at Tax Analysts decided it would save the company a great deal of time to get copies of the opinions from the Department of Justice, rather than soliciting them from courts around the nation. But the Justice Department refused, arguing that these were not agency records. These decisions, the Justice Department lawyers argued, originated with the courts, agencies not covered by the Freedom of Information Act. But Justice Thurgood Marshall disagreed and wrote for the 8-1 majority that the relevant question is whether an agency covered by the Freedom of Information Act has "created or obtained the materials sought . . . not whether the organization from which the documents originated is itself covered by the FOIA." The Justice Department controls these records, even though it did not generate them. (This statement distinguishes the ruling from the case of *Wolfe* v. *Department of Health and Human Services,* in which the records were stored at the agency but were not under agency control.) If the Justice Department wanted to continue to refuse to provide these materials to the Tax Analysts, it would have to cite an appropriate exemption.

FOIA EXEMPTIONS

A document or tape or file that has been determined to be an agency record accessible via the Freedom of Information Act may still be withheld from public inspection if it properly falls into one of the nine categories of exempted material. Please note, federal agencies *are not required* to withhold documents from disclosure simply because they are included in an exempted category.[97] The law simply says they may withhold such material. The nine exemptions outlined in the following pages are fairly specific, yet not specific enough to be free from substantial judicial interpretation. How a judge defines a word or phrase in these exemptions can result in a significant change in the meaning of the law and can lead to either expanded public access or, more likely in recent years, substantially reduced public access. We will examine each exemption separately, try to outline its meaning, and briefly explore case law that illuminates how the exemption is applied. It is important to remember that in light of the war on terrorism it is likely that many of these exemptions will be viewed even more broadly by government agencies and even the courts.

Federal agencies are not required to withhold documents from disclosure simply because they are included in an exempted category.

95. *Wolfe* v. *Department of Health and Human Services,* 539 F. Supp. 276 (1987); 711 F. 2d 1077 (1983).
96. 492 U.S. 136 (1989).
97. See *Chrysler Corp.* v. *Brown,* 441 U.S. 281 (1979).

EXEMPTIONS TO DISCLOSURE UNDER THE FREEDOM OF INFORMATION ACT

1. National security matters
2. Housekeeping materials
3. Material exempted by statute
4. Trade secrets
5. Working papers/Lawyer-client privileged materials
6. Personal privacy files
7. Law enforcement records
8. Financial institution materials
9. Geological data

National Security

Exemption 1: Matters specifically authorized under criteria established by an executive order to be kept secret in the interest of national defense or foreign policy and in fact properly classified pursuant to such an executive order. This exemption deals with a wide range of materials, but primarily with information related to national security and national defense, intelligence gathering and foreign relations. The system has a three-tier classification. Material, the release of which could reasonably be expected to damage national security, is classified as "confidential," the lowest level of classification. The "secret" classification is used to shield material that if disclosed could be expected to cause serious damage to national security. "Top secret," the highest level of classification, is reserved for material that if revealed could be expected to cause exceptionally grave damage to national security.[98]

As originally adopted in 1966, this exemption excluded from disclosure any document or record that the president, through executive order, chose to classify in the name of national security. Courts, including the Supreme Court, ruled that there could be no challenge to the classification of the document or record, no judicial examination of whether the material was sensitive or even related to national security.[99] The exemption was abused by administrations, especially during the Nixon presidency, and was amended by Congress in 1974. The change in the law has given the courts the power to inspect classified documents to determine whether they have been properly classified.

The law only states that a court *may* determine whether the material was properly classified, not that it *must* do so. Most courts refuse to even examine the documents. Although occasionally a judge will take the initiative to apply the exemption as Congress intended,[100]

---

98. Exec. Order No. 12958, 3 C.F.R. 333 (1996).
99. *Epstein* v. *Resor,* 296 F. Supp. 214 (1969), aff'd. 421 F. 2d 930 (1970) and *EPA* v. *Mink,* 401 U.S. 73 (1973).
100. *Browde* v. *Navy,* 713 F. 2d 864 (1983).

more commonly judges refuse to evaluate the classification of the material, claiming they lack the expertise to make such a judgment.[101]

Housekeeping Practices

Exemption 2: Matters related solely to the internal personnel rules and practices of an agency. This exemption covers what are known as "housekeeping" materials: vacation schedules, coffee break rules, parking lot assignments and so forth. Little harm would result if these materials were made public; the exemption is offered simply to relieve the agencies of the burden of having to maintain such material in public files.

Whether this exemption applies to agency training and procedure manuals has been regularly litigated. For example, a citizen sought access to a Bureau of Alcohol, Tobacco and Firearms staff manual entitled "Surveillance of Premises, Vehicles, and Persons." The bureau released all but 20 pages of the manual, which it said described internal personnel rules and practices of the agency. The U.S. Court of Appeals for the District of Columbia Circuit ruled in favor of the agency in the lawsuit that followed. The court noted that during the debate on the FOIA in Congress, members spoke without contradiction that Exemption 2 was designed to shield material in law enforcement manuals on investigation procedures.[102] But in 1997 the 10th U.S. Circuit Court of Appeals ruled that maps depicting the location of the Mexican spotted owl that were used by the U.S. Forest Service to protect the owl habitat pursuant to the Endangered Species Act did not relate to the agency's personnel practices and were not exempt from disclosure.[103]

The exemption cannot be used to hide all agency procedures and policies, especially if they involve questionable agency practices. The Boston Globe sought information from the FBI and the Drug Enforcement Administration regarding the amount of money these agencies paid to Charles Matta, a former confidential informant. During the 12 years Matta was a paid FBI/DEA informant he was continually in trouble with local law enforcement authorities. In 1990 he was convicted in state courts for gambling and alcohol- and drug-related offenses. The newspaper wanted to find out if the federal agencies had been inadvertently subsidizing Matta's local criminal activities. The federal law enforcement agencies rejected the Freedom of Information Act requests made by The Globe, citing various exemptions, including Exemption 2. Officials said that the amount of money paid to Matta related to internal agency practices. The U.S. District Court rejected government efforts to block the disclosure of these records. The court said two questions must be asked regarding the applicability of Exemption 2:

1. Is the matter about which information is sought predominantly internal, such that there can be no legitimate public interest in the information?

If there is public interest, then the court must determine

2. Would disclosure significantly risk circumventing any of the agencies' regulations or statutes?

---

101. *Knopf* v. *Colby,* 502 F. 2d 136 (1975).
102. *Crooker* v. *Bureau,* 670 F. 2d 1051 (1981); see also *Hardy* v. *Bureau of Alcohol, Tobacco and Firearms,* 631 F. 2d 653 (1980).
103. *Audubon Society* v. *United States Forest Service,* 104 F. 3d 1201 (1997).

This is not a balancing test, the court said. If there is no public interest in having this information released, then Exemption 2 applies. Similarly, if release of this material might seriously compromise the operation of the agency, then the material must remain secret. In this case, the court said, "The public has a right to know whether in a combined effort to enforce criminal laws the agencies instead bankrolled Matta's ongoing criminal activities." In addition, the agencies failed to cite any regulations or statutes that might be circumvented by the release of this information. "Where the plaintiffs have demonstrated a strong public interest and where the identity of the informant has been publicly acknowledged; the total amount paid to the informant is not exempt [from disclosure]," the court concluded.[104]

Statutory Exemption

Exemption 3: Matters specifically exempted from disclosure by statute (other than section 552b of this title) provided that such statute (a) requires that the matters be withheld from the public in such a manner as to leave no discretion on the issue, or (b) establishes particular criteria for withholding or refers to particular types of matters to be withheld. This exemption is designed to protect from disclosure information required or permitted to be kept secret by scores of other federal laws. A wide range of records fall under this exemption, including Census Bureau records, public utility information, trade secrets, patent applications, tax returns, bank records, veterans benefits and documents held by both the CIA and the National Security Agency.

Courts generally ask three questions when determining whether Exemption 3 applies to a specific record or document:

1. Is there a specific statute that authorizes or requires the withholding of information?
2. Does the statute designate specific kinds of information or outline specific criteria for information that may be withheld?
3. Does the record or information that is sought fall within the categories of information that may be withheld?

If all three questions are answered yes, disclosure can be legally denied.

The CIA has managed to use this exemption to almost completely shield its operations from public scrutiny.

Via congressional action and numerous court rulings the CIA has managed to use this exemption to almost completely shield its operations from public scrutiny. In 1984 Congress voted to exempt all CIA operational files from release under the Freedom of Information Act. In 1985 the Supreme Court ruled that records relating to CIA-funded research from 1952 to 1966 at 80 universities to study the effects of mind-altering substances on humans were off-limits to public inspection. A lawyer named John Sims wanted to see the names of the schools and the individuals who had participated in the research projects. The agency argued that the names were exempt from disclosure because, under a 1947 law, the names of intelligence sources cannot be disclosed by the CIA. The Supreme Court agreed and ruled that the director of the spy agency had broad authority under the 1947 National Security Act to protect all sources of information, confidential or not.[105] In 1996 a U.S. District Court ruled that the CIA

104. *Globe Newspaper Co.* v. *FBI*, 21 M.L.R. 1013 (1992).
105. *Sims* v. *CIA,* 471 U.S. 159 (1985). Sims today is a constitutional law professor at the University of the Pacific McGeorge School of Law in Sacramento, Calif.

didn't even have to respond to a formal FOIA request, since its response might reveal whether it even had a record sought by the requester. The court said the agency had to maintain its strict policy of not revealing sources.[106]

In recent years, federal agencies have cited nearly 100 different statutes to try to justify withholding documents. In some instances courts have rejected these attempts, but frequently the denial goes unchallenged, according to researchers at the Reporters Committee on Freedom of the Press. Courts have upheld denial of access to records based on laws governing the Census Bureau, Consumer Products Safety Commission, Internal Revenue Service, the Patent and Trademark Office, the Postal Service, National Security Agency and a few others.

Trade Secrets

Exemption 4: Trade secrets and financial information obtained from any person and privileged or confidential. Two kinds of information are exempt from disclosure under this exemption—trade secrets and financial or commercial information. The trade secret exemption has not been heavily litigated. In 1983 the U.S. Court of Appeals for the District of Columbia Circuit fashioned a definition of a trade secret that considerably narrowed the exemption. In litigation initiated by Ralph Nader's Public Citizen Health Research Group, the court said a trade secret is "an unpatented, commercially valuable plan, appliance, formula, or process which is used for the making, preparing, compounding, treating, or processing of articles or materials which are trade commodities, and that can be said to be the end product of either innovation or substantial effort." The court rejected a broader definition of a trade secret proposed by the Food and Drug Administration: "any . . . compilation of information which is used in one's business and which gives him an opportunity to obtain an advantage over competitors who do not know or use it."[107]

The "financial information" exemption applies only to information supplied to the government by individuals or private business firms. It is this second section of the exemption that has undergone the most thorough judicial interpretation. When the Miami Herald sought records from the Small Business Administration regarding loans made to small contractors that had become delinquent, the agency said these records were financial or commercial information that it did not have to disclose under Exemption 4. But courts had previously ruled that Exemption 4 only applies if the disclosure of the information would either impair the government's ability to obtain similar information in the future or would cause competitive harm to the individual or business that submitted the information. The SBA was unable to produce evidence that either of these conditions existed, and the court ordered the material disclosed.[108] Federal courts have followed this doctrine consistently. In 1998 the Federal Aviation Administration attempted to use "financial information" arguments to support its decision not to reveal specific data to the Chicago Tribune when the newspaper sought documents relating to in-flight medical emergencies. While the agency gave some material to the newspaper, it deleted all references to the names of airlines, flight numbers, aircraft tail numbers, routes, and remarks regarding individual medical emergencies. Because the "events occurred while

106. *Earth Pledge Foundation* v. *Central Intelligence Agency,* DC SNY 96 CIV. 0257 (1996).
107. *Public Citizen Health Research Group* v. *Food and Drug Administration,* 704 F. 2d 1280 (1983).
108. *Miami Herald* v. *Small Business Administration,* 670 F. 2d 65 (1987).

the aircraft were in revenue producing operations," the FAA said, the data were commercial or financial information. Noting at the outset that the fundamental premise of the FOIA is disclosure, not secrecy, the U.S. District Court said that only material that bears a direct relationship to the operations of a commercial venture is exempt from disclosure. The information must be commercial in nature. The flight information did not meet that standard.[109]

Working Papers/Discovery

Exemption 5: Interagency and intra-agency memorandums and letters which would not be available by law to a party other than an agency in litigation with the agency. This exemption shields two kinds of materials from disclosure. The first are best described as working papers: studies, reports, memoranda and other sorts of documents that are prepared and circulated to assist government personnel to make a final report, an agency policy or a decision of some kind. This section of the law also exempts from disclosure communications between an agency and its attorney, material that is traditionally protected by the attorney-client privilege. (In any lawsuit, communications between an attorney and a client are private.)

The rationale for protecting working papers from public disclosure was well outlined in 1982 when the U.S. Court of Appeals refused to require the Air Force to give up materials that were used in preparing a final report on the use of herbicides in Vietnam. The court explained in *Russell* v. *Air Force:*[110]

> There are essentially three policy bases for this privilege. First, it protects creative debate and candid consideration of alternatives, within an agency, and thereby improves the quality of the agency policy decisions. Second, it protects the public from the confusion that would result from premature exposure to discussions occurring before the policies affecting it had actually been settled upon. And third, it protects the integrity of the decision-making process itself by confirming that "officials should be judged by what they decided, not for matters they considered before making up their minds."

The portions of the first draft of the report sought by the plaintiff in the case were considerations, not decisions, and part of the decision-making process designed to be protected by this exemption. Factual portions of predecisional documents are not normally exempt. For example, imagine there is a long policy memorandum containing advisory recommendations on a proposed jet fighter and the cost of the construction of the warplane. While the advisory recommendations are exempt, the factual cost data is not and must be segregated out of the memo and released on request.

Sometimes documents generated to help formulate a policy become the basis for that policy and are noted or discussed in the final decision or policy statement. The Supreme Court ruled in 1975 that Exemption 5 cannot be used to shield such documents. Once the decision has been made, the court said, public disclosure of these materials cannot damage the decision-making process.[111]

---

109. *Chicago Tribune* v. *Federal Aviation Administration,* 27 M.L.R. 1059 (1998).
110. 682 F. 2d 1045 (1982).
111. *NLRB* v. *Sears, Roebuck and Company,* 421 U.S. 132 (1973).

The courts have interpreted Exemption 5 very broadly. For example, the U.S. Court of Appeals for the District of Columbia Circuit ruled that Exemption 5 goes so far as to shield draft book manuscripts from disclosure. A historian working for the Office of Air Force History prepared a draft history of the role of the U.S. Air Force in South Vietnam in the early 1960s. Senior OAFH officers rejected the manuscript—the second time such a manuscript was turned down. A reporter sought a copy of the manuscript, believing it might contain information about unreported war crimes. The Air Force turned down the request, arguing that disclosure of the manuscript might reveal the deliberative editorial process used by the Air Force. The court agreed. "The simple comparison of the draft with the final manuscript would expose an editorial judgment made by Air Force personnel," the court ruled. This exposure of the editorial judgment would inhibit creative debate and candid considerations in the future, the court added.[112]

The second part of the exemption protects from public disclosure material that would not normally be open to inspection in a civil legal proceeding. There is something called the discovery process that is a part of all litigation. Through discovery one party is able to gain access to evidence, testimony and other kinds of material possessed by the other party. But some kinds of material are not accessible through this discovery process. When a private person consults an attorney and discusses matters relevant to a lawsuit, what is said during those conversations is confidential. The attorney cannot be forced to reveal the substance of the conversation. Similarly, most documents that pass between the client and the attorney are considered confidential or privileged. This part of Exemption 5 shields the same kinds of conversations and materials that are generated between a federal agency and its attorneys. For example, in 1984 the U.S. Supreme Court ruled that confidential statements obtained by U.S. Air Force officials during the investigation of an air crash were protected from FOIA disclosure under Exemption 5. The public is entitled to see all such memos or letters that a private party could discover in litigation with the agency, Justice John Paul Stevens wrote. But the material being sought in this case under the FOIA would not normally be open through discovery in a civil lawsuit. The high court ruled that the exemption clearly incorporates the civil discovery privilege; Congress did not intend to permit litigants to use the Freedom of Information Act to circumvent this privilege.[113]

In 2001 the Supreme Court limited the scope of Exemption 5 when it said communication between a group of Native-American tribes and the Bureau of Indian Affairs, a government agency that represents the United States in the nation's relationships with the tribes, was not covered by Exemption 5. The issue focused on a dispute about the allocation of water from the Klamath River Basin in Oregon and northern California. A group of irrigators filed a series of FOIA requests to see copies of correspondence between the tribes and the BIA regarding water issues. The government rejected the request, claiming that because of the special relationship between the tribes and the BIA, the records should be protected under Exemption 5 in much the same way that correspondence between lawyers and clients is protected. The Supreme Court, in a unanimous ruling, rejected this argument. Justice David Souter wrote for the court that although there are surely exceptions to the general rule of public disclosure mandated by the Freedom of Information Act, these exceptions are to be applied narrowly. "All of this boils down to requesting that we read an 'Indian trust' exemption into

112. *Dudman Communications Corp.* v. *Air Force,* 815 F. 2d 1565 (1987).
113. *U.S.* v. *Weber Aircraft Corp.,* 465 U.S. 792 (1984).

Exemption 5 also incorporates the common-law concept called executive privilege.

the statute, a reading that is out of the question," Souter wrote. The court also rejected the notion that the communication between the tribes and the BIA was comparable to communication between an agency and an outside consultant, material that is sometimes regarded as interagency or intra-agency memoranda.[114]

Exemption 5 also incorporates the common-law concept called **executive privilege.** Beginning with President George Washington in 1794, American chief executives have asserted that the president enjoys a common-law privilege to keep secret all presidential papers, records and other documents. Washington asserted the privilege when Congress called for all papers and records in the possession of the president that would facilitate its investigation of the negotiation of the Jay Treaty, a controversial agreement with Great Britain. Washington refused to comply with the congressional demand, citing executive privilege. Andrew Jackson refused to give Congress information relating to a boundary dispute in Maine. Millard Fillmore refused a request from the Senate that he provide that body with information regarding negotiations with the Sandwich (Hawaiian) Islands.

Modern-day presidents have asserted executive privilege as well, but usually with less success. President Richard Nixon tried to argue that access to the infamous White House tapes that played a critical role in the Watergate scandal should be protected by an absolute executive privilege. The Supreme Court ruled that the absolute privilege was developed to protect military and diplomatic secrets. A qualified privilege might be applicable in other situations, but in those cases the need for confidentiality must be balanced against other values. In this case, the need for the tapes in a criminal investigation outweighed the need for secrecy, the court said.[115] President Clinton asserted executive privilege numerous times during his eight years in office. Citing the privilege the president rejected congressional attempts in 1996 to obtain documents related to White House travel office firings, a joint FBI–Drug Enforcement Agency memo to the president on drug enforcement, and foreign-policy documents on the administration's Haiti policy. In 1999 Clinton invoked the privilege again when Congress sought documents relating to his decision to offer clemency to jailed members of a Puerto Rican separatist group.[116] Clinton tried but failed to use executive privilege to protect his senior aides from questioning by prosecutors in the office of the independent counsel during the Monica Lewinsky investigation.

Personal Privacy

Exemption 6: Personnel and medical files and similar files the disclosure of which would constitute a clearly unwarranted invasion of privacy. This exemption shields "personnel and medical files and similar files." Personnel files and medical files are fairly easy to identify. The courts have had more of a problem determining the nature of a "similar file." At one time courts declared that similar files were files *like* personnel and medical files.[117] But the Supreme Court rejected that interpretation. The key consideration, the high court said, is not the kind of file that is at issue, but the kind of information in the file that is the object of the

114. *Department of the Interior* v. *Klamath Water Users,* 532 U.S.I. (2001).
115. *U.S.* v. *Nixon,* 418 U.S. 683 (1974).
116. Galvin, "Clinton Invokes Executive Privilege."
117. *Washington Post* v. *State Department,* 647 F. 2d 197 (1981).

FOIA request. An individual's medical and personnel files contain highly personal information about an individual. A file is a "similar file" if it contains this same kind of personal information.[118] Not every file that contains personal information will be considered a similar file. "The test is not merely whether the information is in some sense personal," a U.S. Court of Appeals ruled, "but whether it is of the same magnitude—as highly personal in nature—as contained in personnel or medical records."[119]

In December 2005, the U.S. Court of Appeals for the 2nd Circuit held that administrative investigative records may constitute files similar to personnel or medical files. In this case, *Wood v. FBI,* 2005 U.S. App. LEXIS 26556 (2005), a reporter for the Journal Inquirer of Manchester, Connecticut, used FOIA to seek documents relating to the investigation of Connecticut Federal Bureau of Investigation agents accused of lying in affidavits supporting arrest warrant applications. The appellate court ruled against the reporter, however, concluding that disclosure of the names and identifying information of the government investigators located in administrative investigation files of the FBI would constitute a clearly unwarranted invasion of privacy and thus could be withheld under Exemption 6. In reaching this conclusion, the court reasoned that "the records at issue are highly detailed and contain personal information about the subjects of the investigation—the Connecticut FBI agents accused of misrepresenting search warrant information" and "also contain private information about other individuals, particularly witnesses."

In the late 1980s The New York Times sought access to the voice communications tape recorded aboard the space shuttle Challenger just before it exploded in January 1987. The National Aeronautics and Space Administration argued that the tape was shielded from disclosure because it contained personal information similar to that contained in personnel and medical files. Both the U.S. District Court[120] and a panel of judges on the U.S. Court of Appeals[121] ruled that the tape contained nothing as personal as material in personnel or medical files. But the government petitioned for a rehearing of the case by the full membership of the appellate court, and in a 6-5 ruling the appellate court overturned the earlier decisions. "While the taped words do not contain information about the personal lives of the astronauts, disclosure of the file would reveal the sound and inflection of the crew's voices during the last seconds of their lives," the court said. The information recorded through the capture of a person's voice is distinct and is in addition to the information contained in the words themselves, the six judges noted.[122]

A ruling that a file is a medical or personnel or similar file does not automatically bar the release of data in the file. Establishing that the information or material sought is the kind of information protected by Exemption 6 is just the first step. The court must then determine that

1. the release of this information will constitute an invasion of personal privacy, *and*
2. this invasion of personal privacy is clearly unwarranted.

The Supreme Court made it clear in 1976 that exemption is not intended to preclude every incidental invasion of privacy, but rather "only such disclosures as constitute clearly

118. *State Department* v. *Washington Post,* 456 U.S. 595 (1982).
119. *Kurzon* v. *Health and Human Services,* 649 F. 2d 65 (1981).
120. *New York Times* v. *NASA,* 679 F. Supp. 33 (1987).
121. *New York Times* v. *NASA,* 852 F. 2d 602 (1988).
122. *New York Times* v. *NASA,* 970 F. 2d 1002 (1990).

unwarranted invasions of personal privacy."[123] The government normally carries the burden of proof that the release of the information will amount to an unwarranted invasion of privacy. But this burden is not a terribly heavy one. For example, a U.S. District Court accepted government arguments that the release of the voice communications tape-recorded aboard the space shuttle Challenger would be an unwarranted invasion of privacy.[124] The ruling was made despite the fact that a printed transcript of the tape had been previously released.

In 1991 the Supreme Court ruled that the revelation of personal information contained in U.S. State Department interviews with Haitian nationals who had been returned to their homeland after coming to the United States would constitute an invasion of privacy.[125] The U.S. Supreme Court sided with the State Department, ruling that release of the names, addresses, marital status, employment status, living conditions and other material would be an invasion of privacy of the interview subjects. Justice John Paul Stevens said linking such data to the names of the former refugees would be a "significant" invasion of their personal privacy. The high court ruling was unanimous.

In 1994 the Supreme Court ruled that in some circumstances it is an unwarranted invasion of privacy to make public the home addresses of government employees. The issue arose as two labor unions sought the names and home addresses of employees of the Department of Defense and other federal agencies. The U.S. Supreme Court in a unanimous decision said the names and addresses could be withheld from disclosure by virtue of Exemption 6.[126] Justice Clarence Thomas wrote that he couldn't imagine how this information would further citizens' rights to be informed about what their government was up to. In addition the privacy interests are substantial, he said. The union seeks the addresses of those employees who have chosen not to join the union. These employees may want to avoid an influx of union-related mail or telephone calls or visits. "Many people simply do not want to be disturbed at home by work-related matters," Thomas wrote. When the privacy interest outweighs the public interest in the information, the disclosure would constitute a clearly unwarranted invasion of privacy, the associate justice concluded.

Law Enforcement

Exemption 7: Records or information compiled for law enforcement purposes, but only to the extent that the production of such law enforcement records or information (a) could reasonably be expected to interfere with enforcement proceedings, (b) would deprive a person of a right to a fair trial or an impartial adjudication, (c) could reasonably be expected to constitute an unwarranted invasion of personal privacy, (d) could reasonably be expected to disclose the identity of a confidential source, including a state, local or foreign agency or authority or any private institution which furnished information on a confidential basis, and, in the case of a record or information compiled by criminal law enforcement authority in the course of a criminal investigation or by an agency conducting a lawful national security intelligence investigation, information furnished by confidential source, (e) would disclose techniques and procedures for law

---

123. *Department of the Air Force* v. *Rose,* 425 U.S. 352 (1976).
124. *New York Times* v. *National Aeronautics and Space Administration,* 782 F. Supp. 628 (1991).
125. *State Department* v. *Ray,* 502 U.S. 164 (1991).
126. *Department of Defense* v. *Federal Labor Relations Authority,* 114 S. Ct. 1006 (1994).

enforcement investigations or prosecutions, or would disclose guidelines for law enforcement investigations or prosecutions if such disclosure could reasonably be expected to risk circumvention of the law, or (f) could reasonably be expected to endanger the life or physical safety of any individual.

Exemption 7 provides an agency a broad exception to the general rule of access. Like Exemption 6, Exemption 7 requires a two-tiered test in its application. The first tier or question (what lawyers and judges often call the threshold question) is this: Was the information or record sought compiled for law enforcement purposes?

If the government is unable to show that the records were compiled for law enforcement purposes, the exemption does not apply. But the courts are generally willing to grant the government wide latitude in applying this test. For example, the Supreme Court ruled in 1982 that summaries of investigatory records qualified as law enforcement records. In 1969 President Nixon's staff members requested that the FBI summarize and transmit to the president information in its files concerning particular individuals who had criticized the administration, a so-called enemies list. When Howard Abramson sought to see these summaries in 1976, he was told they were investigatory records shielded by Exemption 7. Abramson argued that while the original records may have been compiled for law enforcement purposes, the summaries of these records sent to the president did not meet this criterion. The summaries were prepared, if for any reason, for political and not law enforcement purposes. But the high court disagreed in a 5-4 ruling. "We hold that information initially contained in a record made for law enforcement purposes continues to meet the threshold requirements of Exemption Seven where that recorded information is reproduced or summarized in a new document prepared for a non-law enforcement purpose," Justice Byron White wrote for the court.[127]

In another decision in 1989, the high court ruled that the reason the material is originally compiled is not relevant in determining whether Exemption 7 is applicable. The key question, the high court ruled, is whether the information is being used for law enforcement purposes when the response to the FOIA inquiry is sent to the person seeking the data.

The key question, the high court ruled, is whether the information is being used for law enforcement purposes when the response to the FOIA inquiry is sent to the person seeking the data.

Grumman Aircraft provided routine information for a government audit in 1978. The information compiled at this time by the Defense Contract Audit Agency was not compiled for law enforcement purposes. Seven years later a federal investigation into possible fraudulent practices by the company began and Grumman sought to gain copies of the information it had provided the auditors in 1978. The agency refused, citing Exemption 7, and transferred the records to the FBI. Grumman then sought the records from the FBI. This agency said no, arguing that the records had been compiled for law enforcement purposes and their release could reasonably be expected to interfere with an ongoing proceeding. Grumman argued that the records were not originally compiled for law enforcement purposes, but the Supreme Court said this was immaterial. "The plain words [of the statute] contain no requirement that compilation be effected at a specific time. The objects sought merely must have been compiled [for law enforcement purposes] when the government invokes the exemption," Justice Harry Blackmun wrote for the court in the 6-3 ruling.[128]

Law enforcement agencies, however, are not given carte blanche discretion to designate any record they choose as one gathered for law enforcement purposes. Seth Rosenfeld sued the Department of Justice and the FBI to gain access to records of FBI investigations of faculty,

---

127. *FBI* v. *Abramson,* 456 U.S. 615 (1982).
128. *John Doe Agency* v. *John Doe Corporation,* 110 S. Ct. 471 (1989).

students and journalists at the University of California in the early 1960s when the so-called Free Speech Movement challenged the university administration's regulations barring political activities on campus. The federal agencies argued that the material had been gathered for the purpose of examining whether the student movement had been captured from within by communists. The U.S. Court of Appeals for the 9th Circuit agreed that while some of the material sought by Rosenfeld had indeed been gathered for legitimate law enforcement purposes, other records were gathered long after the need for such an investigation ceased to exist. The law enforcement purpose argument was only a pretext, the court said, invoked to pursue routine monitoring of many individuals and to shield the harassment of the political opponents of the FBI.[129]

Information compiled for law enforcement purposes may still be accessible under the Freedom of Information Act. The court next must determine whether the release of the material would result in one of the six consequences outlined in *a* through *f* in the exemption; for example, would the release of the information be expected to interfere with law enforcement proceedings or deprive a person of a right to a fair trial?

Congress amended Exemption 7 in 1986 and gave federal law enforcement agencies far broader authority to refuse FOIA requests. Courts have read the exemption in an expansive manner, giving the FBI, the Secret Service, the Drug Enforcement Administration and other federal police agencies even more legal excuses to deny access to information they possess. For example, in 1989 the Supreme Court agreed that the release of computerized arrest records (often called "rap sheets") held by the FBI could reasonably be expected to constitute an unwarranted invasion of personal privacy. The rap sheets contain information indicating arrests, indictments, acquittals, convictions and sentences on about 24 million people in the nation. Some of this material is highly sensitive, but much of it has been publicized previously when individuals were being processed by the criminal justice system. In addition, all of this data is available from state and local law enforcement agencies across the nation. The FBI has simply put together all the bits and pieces of data about an individual held by various police agencies into a single, computerized file.

CBS reporter Robert Schnake sought such information from the FBI on Charles Medico. The agency denied the request, citing the personal privacy factor in Exemption 7. A U.S. District Court supported the agency, saying the material sought by Schnake would be personal to Medico. But the U.S. Court of Appeals for the District of Columbia Circuit reversed this decision, noting that the government cannot assert a privacy interest in records it holds when the records are already available from state and local authorities.[130] The Supreme Court reversed this ruling in a 9-0 decision. The privacy interest in a rap sheet is substantial, wrote Justice John Paul Stevens for the court. "The substantial character of that interest is affected by the fact that in today's society the computer can accumulate and store information that would have otherwise surely been forgotten long before a person attains the age of 80, when the F.B.I.'s rap sheets are discarded," Stevens added. Stevens rejected the argument that because arrests and convictions are almost always public knowledge when they happen, an individual has only a minimal privacy interest in a federal compilation of such information. Federal computers, he said, make easily available information that would be difficult to obtain

---

129. *Rosenfeld* v. *U.S. Dept. of Justice,* 57 F. 3d 803 (1995).
130. *Reporters Committee for Freedom of the Press* v. *Justice Department,* 816 F. 2d 730 (1987).

by other means. "Plainly there is a vast difference between the public records that might be found after a diligent search of courthouse files, county archives, and local police stations throughout the county and a computerized summary located in a single clearinghouse of information," Stevens noted.[131]

Federal courts also supported the FBI when it cited the privacy exemption to block access to information it held about the possible disciplinary proceedings against an FBI agent for misconduct,[132] and the U.S. Postal Service when it refused to make public nearly one-half of a 4,700-page record amassed by the agency when it investigated the shooting deaths of 14 postal service workers at the Edmond, Okla., post office in 1986.[133] It is not overstating the case to say that the judges in the federal courts, many of whom have worked in law enforcement as prosecutors and U.S. attorneys, seem more than willing to support the attempts by law enforcement agencies to block access to a wide range of documents and records.[134]

In May 2003, the U.S. Supreme Court agreed to hear oral argument later that year in a case involving a request of 10 Polaroid death-scene photographs of Vincent W. Foster, former deputy counsel to President Bill Clinton.[135] Foster was found dead in 1993 of a gunshot wound in a Fort Marcy Park in northern Virginia and all official federal investigations concluded that it was a suicide. A California attorney named Allan J. Favish, however, was skeptical of these investigations and sought under FOIA certain autopsy photographs to see if it really was a suicide. Clinton-critic Favish, in fact, documents his search for the photographs online from his own Web site at http://www.allanfavish.com/foster.htm and gives his perspective on the case.

At issue in the case was whether Exemption 7(c), which protects from disclosure law enforcement records that "could reasonably be expected to constitute an unwarranted invasion of personal privacy," applies to deny Favish's request. The argument was that disclosure would intrude upon the privacy of the Foster family. The U.S. Court of Appeals for the 9th Circuit ruled in June 2002 that some autopsy photographs could be released per a January 2001 district court order but that others were to be withheld.[136]

In 2004 Justice Anthony Kennedy delivered a unanimous opinion for the U.S. Supreme Court in *National Archives and Records Administration v. Favish*.[137] It was a resounding victory for privacy—in particular, for relational/familial privacy rights and, especially, those of Vincent Foster's family—and a defeat for Allan Favish. Justice Kennedy initially framed the opinion as pivoting on two related questions:

> The initial question is whether the exemption [7(c)] extends to the decedent's family when the family objects to the release of photographs showing the condition of the body at the scene of death. If we find the decedent's family does have a personal privacy interest recognized by the statute, we must then consider whether that privacy claim is outweighed by the public interest in disclosure.

131. *Justice Department v. Reporters Committee,* 109 S. Ct. 1486 (1989).
132. *Dunkelberger v. Justice Department,* 906 F. 2d 779 (1990).
133. *KTVY-TV v. U.S. Postal Service,* 919 F. 2d 1465 (1990).
134. See, for example, *Schmerler v. FBI,* 900 F. 2d 333 (1990).
135. *Office of Independent Counsel v. Favish,* 538 U.S. 1012 (2003).
136. *Favish v. Office of Independent Counsel,* 37 Fed. Appx. 863 (2002).
137. 541 U.S. 157 (2004).

Source: © AP/Wide World Photos

Allan Favish took his fight to obtain death-scene photographs of Vincent Foster all the way to the U.S. Supreme Court in 2004. The high court ruled against Favish.

In answering the first question, Justice Kennedy reasoned, "We have little difficulty . . . in finding in our case law and traditions the right of family members to direct and control disposition of the body of the deceased and to limit attempts to exploit pictures of the deceased family member's remains for public purposes." Citing an eclectic mix of nontraditional sources such as the Encyclopedia Britannica and Sophocles' story in Antigone, Kennedy wrote that "family members have a personal stake in honoring and mourning their dead and objecting to unwarranted public exploitation that, by intruding upon their own grief, tends to degrade the rites and respect they seek to accord the deceased person who was once their own." The court thus concluded that FOIA recognizes surviving family members' right to personal privacy with respect to their close relative's death-scene images. Kennedy wrote, "Our holding ensures that the privacy interests of surviving family members would allow the Government to deny . . . gruesome requests in appropriate cases. We find it inconceivable that Congress could have intended a definition of 'personal privacy' so narrow that it would allow convicted felons to obtain these materials without limitations at the expense of surviving family members' personal privacy."

As to the second issue—whether the Foster family's privacy claim was outweighed by the public interest in disclosure of the photographs—the court reasoned that the 7(c) exemption for law enforcement records that could reasonably be expected to constitute an unwarranted invasion of personal privacy

> requires the person requesting the information to establish a sufficient reason for the disclosure. First, the citizen must show that the public interest sought to be advanced is a significant one, an interest more specific than having the information for its own sake. Second, the citizen must show the information is likely to advance that interest. Otherwise, the invasion of privacy is unwarranted.

Kennedy added that "the justification most likely to satisfy Exemption 7(c)'s public interest requirement is that the information is necessary to show the investigative agency or other responsible officials acted negligently or otherwise improperly in the performance of their duties" and that "the requester must establish more than a bare suspicion in order to obtain disclosure. Rather, the requester must produce evidence that would warrant a belief by a reasonable person that the alleged Government impropriety might have occurred."

Applying this standard to the facts of the Vincent Foster death-scene photographs case, the court concluded that the requester, Allan Favish, "has not produced any evidence that would warrant a belief by a reasonable person that the alleged Government impropriety might have occurred to put the balance into play." Favish thus lost his case. He wrote a lengthy response to the Supreme Court's opinion, however, that can be found on his Web site at http://www.allanfavish.com/ajf_response_to_decision.htm.

The *Favish* opinion ranks as an important victory for privacy rights advocates and a blow to access supporters, including journalists. A statutory right to privacy now has been extended to protect the privacy interests of surviving family members of a deceased individual. It will be recalled from Chapter 7 that "only people enjoy protection for their right to privacy" (page 279). After the *Favish* opinion, and in the very limited but important context of FOIA actions, this now means that the relatives of dead people enjoy protection for their right to privacy in some circumstances. It is important here to note the limitations of the decision in *Favish*. In particular, the Supreme Court did not create a general "survivor right of privacy" for purposes of other contexts or tort-based privacy lawsuits (see Chapters 7 and 8). Rather, the court engaged in the very precise and limited practice of **statutory construction** when it interpreted the meaning of a single statutory FOIA exemption, namely 7(c). As attorneys might put it, the holding in the *Favish* opinion was "narrow."

Records and documents held by federal law enforcement agencies enjoy additional shielding from public disclosure beyond the broad language of Exemption 7. The 1986 amendment to the FOIA permits such agencies to refuse to confirm or deny the existence of

1. records concerning a criminal investigation, if disclosure could reasonably be expected to interfere with enforcement proceedings;
2. informant records requested by third parties, if the informant's status as an informant has not been officially confirmed; and
3. classified records of the FBI pertaining to foreign intelligence, counterintelligence and international terrorism investigations.

The purpose of these additional limits on access to information is to try to stop the bad guys, crooks, spies, terrorists and so on from using the Freedom of Information Act as a means of finding out how much the government knows about their activities. And if the limits are applied in this fashion, few will object. But remember, the government does not always work from such noble principles. Recall the case earlier where White House operatives wanted FBI files on persons who criticized the president. The broad law enforcement exemptions to the FOIA make it very difficult for the press or others to discover and publicize this kind of misuse of government power.

Financial Records

Exemption 8: Matters contained in or related to examination, operating, or condition reports prepared by, on behalf of, or for the use of any agency responsible for the regulation and supervision of financial institutions. This is a little-used exemption that is designed to prevent the disclosure of sensitive financial reports or audits that, if made public, might undermine the public confidence in banks, trust companies, investment banking firms and other financial institutions.

Geological Data

Exemption 9: Geological and geophysical information and data, including maps concerning wells. People who drill oil and gas wells provide considerable information about these wells to the government. This exemption prevents speculators and other drillers from gaining access to this valuable information.

HANDLING FOIA REQUESTS

Filing a FOIA request these days is a relatively simple matter. For instance, the Reporters Committee for Freedom of the Press actually has an online request letter generator on its Web site at http://www.rcfp.org/foi_letter/generate.php. Government agencies also provide extensive online information about filing FOIA requests. For example, the U.S. Department of Justice maintains a link on its Web site at http://www.usdoj.gov/04foia devoted to the Freedom of Information Act.

Government departments must answer requests for records and documents within 20 business days.

Government departments must answer requests for records and documents within 20 business days. A journalist can, however, ask for an "expedited review" if there is an urgent need for the information. A requester is entitled to an expedited review if he or she is a person primarily engaged in disseminating information and there is an urgency to inform the public about an actual or alleged governmental activity. If an appeal is filed after a denial, the agency has only 20 days to rule on the appeal. Each agency must publish quarterly, or more frequently, an index of the documents and records it keeps.

Agencies are required to report to Congress each year and must include in the report a list of the materials to which access was granted and to which access was denied and the costs incurred. If a citizen or a reporter has to go to court to get the agency to release materials and the agency loses the case, the agency may be assessed the cost of the complainant's legal fees and court costs. Finally, agency personnel are now personally responsible for granting or denying access, a requirement federal agencies object to strenuously. An employee of an agency who denies a request for information must be identified to the person who seeks the material, and if the access is denied in an arbitrary or capricious manner, the employee can be disciplined by the Civil Service Commission.

Agencies may charge fees to cover the actual cost of searching for and copying the records that are sought. These fees can be very high if a large amount of material is requested. In 1986 Congress passed legislation that set out specific fee provisions for four kinds of requesters:

1. Commercial-use requesters must pay fees for document search, duplication and review.

2. Noncommercial requesters from educational or scientific institutions pay no search fees and receive one hundred pages of free duplication.

3. Representatives of the news media pay no search fees and receive copies of one hundred pages free.

4. All other requesters receive two hours of search time and one hundred pages at no charge.

Anyone who seeks a fee waiver under the FOIA must show that the disclosure of the information is "in the public interest because it is likely to contribute significantly to public understanding of the operations or activities of the government and is not primarily in the commercial interest of the requester."

News media representatives are defined as persons actively working for an organization that publishes or broadcasts the news to the public. Free-lance writers working on magazine articles or books may qualify as a representative of the news media if they can demonstrate a solid basis for expecting publication of their work. This evidence could be a contract, a response to a query letter, or some other document or device that indicates probable publication. News has been defined as "information about current events or of current interest to the public."

The Freedom of Information Act is not difficult to use. There is a sample request letter on page 393. In addition, both the Student Press Law Center and the Reporters Committee for Freedom of the Press offer free automated open-records request letters. The fill-in-the-blank format is easy to complete before printing it out on a computer. The online services of the Student Press Law Center can be accessed through http://www.splc.org. The online address for the Reporters Committee is http://www.rcfp.org/foi.html. For only $5 (plus $1.50 for shipping and handling) it is possible to get a highly informative booklet, "How to Use the Federal FOI Act," 9th edition, published by the Reporters Committee for Freedom of the Press, 1101 Wilson Blvd., Suite 1100, Arlington, VA 22209. Longtime right-of-access proponent Sam Archibald offers these suggestions to journalists on making the law work:[138]

1. Find out which agency or agencies have the material that you are interested in. The U.S. Government Manual lists all federal agencies, explains what they are supposed to do and usually lists local street and Web addresses and telephone numbers.

138. Archibald, "The Revised F.O.I. Law," 54.

2. Call, write or e-mail the agency to get background information about the material and information that is being sought.

3. When you determine what specific records you seek and which agency has them, prepare a specific Freedom of Information Act request (see sample letter on page 393).

4. If the request is denied, file an appeal. Send along a copy of the rejection letter and make a strong argument why the material should be released.

5. If the appeal is rejected—and you really want to get the material—go to court. This final point, more than any other, needs to be emphasized. As long as government agencies are confident that the press and public will not bother with lawsuits, the tendency to withhold information will be reinforced. But strong sanctions can be applied against government officials who are found to have deliberately withheld material illegally. Sanctions can only be applied, however, after judicial determination of the matter. The application of this kind of pressure on a regular basis by the press and the public can have a generally positive impact in the battle for open government.

TIPS ON HOW TO GET RECORDS

Many old journalistic hands argue that formal FOIA requests should be a last resort. Jack Briggs, former editor of the Tri-City (Wash.) Herald, advises reporters to do the following:

- Ask informally for documents—a formal FOIA request often takes much longer.
- Look to public court records for information that takes longer to get through an FOIA request.
- Cultivate trusted sources within federal agencies.
- Follow up FOIA requests with telephone calls.
- Don't kick and scream, unless kicking and screaming is justified. And don't forget to occasionally praise the FOIA officer who helps you.

FEDERAL OPEN-MEETINGS LAW

In 1976 Congress passed and the president signed into law the **Government in Sunshine Act, the federal open-meetings law.** The statute affects approximately 50 federal boards, commissions and agencies "headed by a collegial body composed of two or more individual members, a majority of whom are appointed to such position by the president with the advice and consent of the Senate." These public bodies are required to conduct their business meetings in public. Notice of public meetings must be given one week in advance, and the agencies are required to keep careful records of what occurs at closed meetings. The law also prohibits informal communication between officials of an agency and representatives of companies and other interested persons with whom the agency does business unless this communication is recorded and made part of the public record.

SAMPLE FOI ACT REQUEST LETTER

Your address
Daytime phone number
Date

Freedom of Information Office
Agency
Address

FOIA Request

Dear FOI Officer:

Pursuant to the federal Freedom of Information Act, 5 U.S.C. § 552, I request access to and copies of *(here, clearly describe what you want. Include identifying material, such as names, places, and the period of time about which you are inquiring. If you think they will help to explain what you are looking for, attach news clips, reports and other documents describing the subject of your research).* Please include any e-mail correspondence that relates to this matter.

(Optional:) I would like to receive the information in electronic *(or microfiche)* format.

I agree to pay reasonable duplication fees for the processing of this request in an amount not to exceed $ _____. However, please notify me prior to your incurring any expenses in excess of that amount.[1]

(Suggested request for fee benefit as a representative of the news media:) As a representative of the news media I am only required to pay for the direct cost of duplication after the first 100 pages. Through this request, I am gathering information on *(subject)* that is of current interest to the public because *(give reason).* This information is being sought on behalf of *(give the name of your news organization)* for dissemination to the general public. *(If a free-lancer, provide information such as experience, publication contract, etc., that demonstrates that you expect publication.)*

(Optional fee-waiver request:) Please waive any applicable fees. Release of the information is in the public interest because it will contribute significantly to public understanding of government operations and activities.[2]

If my request is denied in whole or part, I ask that you justify all deletions by reference to specific exemptions of the act. I will also expect you to release all segregable portions of otherwise exempt material. I, of course, reserve the right to appeal your decision to withhold any information or to deny a waiver of fees.

Because I am making this request as a journalist *(or author or scholar)* and this information is of timely value, I would appreciate your communicating with me by telephone, rather than by mail, if you have questions regarding this request.[3] *(If you are a reporter or a person who is "primarily engaged in disseminating information," and your request concerns a matter of "compelling need," a request for expedited review may be honored. If so, include the next three paragraphs:)*

Please provide an expedited review of this request, which concerns a matter of urgency. As a journalist, I am primarily engaged in disseminating information.

The public has an urgent need for information about *(describe the government activity involved)* because *(establish the need for bringing information on this subject to the public's attention now).*

I certify that my statements concerning the need for expedited review are true and correct to the best of my knowledge and belief. I look forward to your reply within 20 business days, as the statute requires.

Thank you for your assistance.

Very truly yours,

Your Signature

Footnotes

1. Most agencies will not consider your request properly filed unless you state something about the fees—either your willingness to pay or your request for a fee waiver. By setting an amount up front, the agency will begin to process your request, and you can retain some control over the ultimate amount you will have to pay.

2. You may wish to address each criterion for waiver, except that, as a representative of the news media, you need not show how you will use the information to contribute to public understanding or that its use is noncommercial. An author or scholar may show how the information will ultimately be available to the public. A library may identify researchers who will use it.

3. It is always a good idea to call the agency's FOI office several days after your request is mailed, to be sure of its arrival and to talk directly with the officer processing your request. Quite often you can resolve any minor problems concerning your request at that time and avoid delays.

Sample FOIA request letter, based on *How to Use the Federal FOI Act,* 8th ed., FOI Service Center Publication.

Chapter 9

Courts have strictly interpreted the requirement that the law only applies to bodies whose members are appointed by the president.

Courts have strictly interpreted the requirement that the law only applies to bodies whose members are appointed by the president. In 1981 the U.S. Court of Appeals for the District of Columbia Circuit ruled that the Government in Sunshine Act did not govern meetings of the Chrysler Loan Guarantee Board, a body created by Congress to oversee federal loan guarantees for the financially troubled automaker. Persons who served on the board were not actually named by the president, but served because they held other federal offices (i.e., secretary of the treasury, comptroller general, chairman of the Federal Reserve). "If Congress had wanted to subject the board to the provisions of the Sunshine Act, it could have so provided when the board was established," the court noted.[139] A board or agency must also have some independent authority to act or take action before the law applies. A U.S. Court of Appeals ruled that the law does not apply to the president's Council of Economic Advisors. The sole function of the CEA is to advise and assist the president, the court said. It has no regulatory power. It cannot fund projects, even though it may appraise them. It has no function, save advising and assisting the president. Hence, it is not subject to either the FOIA or the Government in Sunshine Act.[140] Even agencies or commissions that fall under the aegis of the law may meet behind closed doors. The 1976 law lists 10 conditions or exemptions under which closed meetings might be held. The first nine of these exemptions mirror the exemptions in the Freedom of Information Act. The 10th exemption focuses on situations in which the agency is participating in arbitration or is in the process of adjudicating or otherwise disposing of a case.

This exemption was used to block access to a meeting of the Nuclear Regulatory Commission. The NRC was discussing the reopening of the nuclear power plant at Three Mile Island in Pennsylvania. The federal district court ruled that this meeting would likely focus on the final adjudication of the federal action involving the nuclear reactor and hence could be closed to press and public.[141]

There has been relatively little litigation under the Government in Sunshine Act, and reporters who work in Washington, D.C., report that compliance with the law is not good. The same problems existed in the early years of operation of the Freedom of Information Act. Constant pressure and frequent litigation against agencies that refused to comply with the FOIA finally made the law more effective. The same pressure is needed to make the Government in Sunshine Act live up to its promise.

SUMMARY

Statutes provide public access to both federal records and meetings held by federal agencies. The federal records law, the Freedom of Information Act, makes public all records including electronic records and e-mail held by agencies within the executive branch of government and the independent regulatory commissions. Courts have given a broad meaning to the term "record" but have ruled that an agency must normally create and possess such a record before it becomes subject to the Freedom of Information Act. Nine categories of information are excluded from the provisions of the law. These include exemptions for national security, agency working papers, highly personal information, and law enforcement files. Agencies

139. *Symons* v. *Chrysler Corporation Loan Guarantee Board,* 670 F. 2d 238 (1981).
140. *Rushforth* v. *Council of Economic Advisors,* 762 F. 2d 1038 (1985).
141. *Philadelphia Newspapers* v. *Nuclear Regulatory Commission,* 9 M.L.R. 1843 (1983).

must publish indexes of the records they hold and must permit copying of these materials. It is important to follow specific procedures when making a Freedom of Information Act request to see certain records or documents.

The Government in Sunshine Act is the federal open-meetings law. This law reaches about 50 agencies in the executive branch and the regulatory commissions. Members of these organizations are not permitted to hold secret meetings unless they will discuss material that falls into one of 10 categories. These categories mirror the Freedom of Information Act exemptions but also include a provision that permits closed-door meetings to discuss attempts to arbitrate or adjudicate certain cases or problems.

STATE LAWS ON MEETINGS AND RECORDS

It is not as easy to talk about access at the state level as it is at the federal level, because the discussion involves hundreds of different statutes. (Most states have multiple laws dealing with access to meetings, access to records, and other access situations.) The following pages provide at best a few generalizations. Harold Cross made some of the most astute generalizations in 1953 in his pioneering book "The People's Right to Know."[142] Cross was really the first scholar to present a comprehensive report on access problems. In his book he listed four issues, or questions, common to every case of access:

1. Is the particular record or proceeding public? Many records and meetings kept or conducted by public officers in public offices are not really public at all. Much of the work of the police, though they are public officers and work in public buildings, is not open to public scrutiny.

2. Is public material public in the sense that records are open to public inspection and sessions are open to public attendance? Hearings in juvenile courts are considered public hearings for purposes of the law, but they are often not open to the public.

3. Who can view the records and who can attend the meetings open to the public? Many records, for example, might be open to specific segments of the public, but not to all segments. Automobile accident reports by police departments are open to insurance company adjusters and lawyers, but such records are not usually open to the general public.

4. When records and meetings are open to the general public and the press, will the courts provide legal remedy for citizens and reporters if access is denied?

The last question is probably not as important today as it was when Cross wrote his book in 1953, for at that time access to many public records and meetings in the states was based on the common law. Today this fact is no longer true. Access to meetings and records is nearly always governed by statute, and these statutes usually, but not always, provide a remedy for citizens who are denied access. This provision is more widespread in open-meetings

142. Cross, *The People's Right to Know.*

laws, which tend to be more efficient in providing access, than in open-records laws, which are still weak and vague in many jurisdictions.

STATE OPEN-MEETINGS LAWS

All 50 states have specific statutes that mandate open meetings, and these laws range from good to awful. The need for **open-meetings laws** is obvious. There never was a solid common-law right to attend the meetings of public bodies, and as noted earlier, the constitutional provisions regarding freedom of expression have proved inadequate with regard to access.

It is difficult to make generalizations about these 50 different state laws. The Reporters Committee on Freedom of the Press in 2001 published its fourth edition of "Tapping Officials' Secrets," a comprehensive examination of both the open-meetings laws and the open-records laws in all 50 states. A quick perusal of this volume demonstrates the variety in the laws among the states. One of the most important aspects of any open-meetings law is the strong sanctions that may be imposed on government officials who fail to follow the mandate of the law. Laws that provide for substantial personal fines against these individuals are generally more desirable than laws that impose only small fines or no personal penalties at all. Another important part of an open-meetings law is the legislative declaration at the beginning of the law. A clear, strong statement in favor of open access to meetings of government bodies can persuade a judge who is trying to interpret the law to side with the advocates of access rather than with the government. For example, in the state of Washington the open-meetings law begins as follows:

> The legislature finds and declares that all . . . public agencies of this state and subdivisions thereof exist to aid in the conduct of the people's business. It is the intent of this chapter that their actions be taken openly and that their deliberations be conducted openly.

State open-meetings laws are normally written in one of two ways. Some laws declare that all meetings are open, except the following. Meetings that are closed are then listed. Other state laws simply list the agencies that must hold open meetings. The Congress of the United States is clearly excluded from the provisions of the federal open-meetings law. State legislatures are generally excluded from the provisions of their state open-meetings laws as well. But the issue is not quite as clear-cut as the situation at the federal level. Some state open-meetings laws do in fact cover some kinds of legislative proceedings. State open-meetings laws routinely do not include meetings of parole and pardon boards, of law enforcement agencies, of military agencies like the National Guard, of medical agencies like hospital boards, and so forth.

A good open-meetings law will specifically define a meeting by giving the number of members of the board or commission who must be present to constitute a public meeting (a quorum? at least two? etc.), by stating that all deliberative stages of the decision-making process are considered meetings and must be open to the public, and by stating that social gatherings and chance encounters are not considered meetings and are therefore excluded from the provisions of the law. Some laws are not this specific and merely refer to all meetings, all regular or special meetings, all formal meetings, or whatever. As noted earlier, courts are still struggling to determine whether so-called e-meetings, communication by group members via the computer, constitute a meeting under the law.

Most open-meetings laws provide for closed meetings, or **executive sessions,** in certain kinds of cases. Meetings at which personnel problems are discussed are an obvious example. A public airing of a teacher's personal problems could be an unwarranted invasion of privacy. The discussion of real estate transactions is another obvious example. Meetings involving public safety are sometimes best conducted in private rather than in public. Usually laws will permit an official body to meet with its attorney behind closed doors if potential or actual litigation is on the agenda. This exception is merely an extension of the traditional lawyer-client privilege. Labor negotiations may also be held in private in about half the states. All but 13 state open-meetings laws contain a provision that no final action can be taken at an executive session, that the board or commission must reconvene in public before a final determination can be made on any issue.

When a presiding officer of a governmental body announces at a meeting that the body is going into executive session, a reporter at the meeting should make certain of the following items:

1. The presiding officer has specified what topics will be discussed during the closed session, or why the executive session has been called.

2. A reporter who believes that a meeting is being closed improperly should formally object. He or she should ask members of the body specifically which provision in the law they are using to go into closed session. It is not inappropriate to ask for a vote of the body to make certain the required simple majority (or two-thirds majority in some states) approves of the closed session.

3. The reporter should also ask what time the closed session will end, so he or she can attend a reconvened public session.

Most open-meetings statutes require not only that meetings be open to the public, but also that the public be notified of both regular and special meetings far enough in advance that they can attend if they wish. Time requirements vary, but normally a special meeting cannot be held without an announcement a day or two in advance.

Virtually all laws provide some kind of injunctive or other civil remedy if the law is violated; almost half the statutes provide for criminal penalties if the statute is knowingly violated. In many states any action taken at a meeting that was not public, but should have been public, is null and void. The action must be taken again at a proper meeting. Most laws provide fines and short jail terms for public officers who knowingly violate the law, but prosecution is rare.

What should a reporter do when asked to leave a meeting that he or she believes should be open to the press and public? First, find out who has denied you access to the meeting and ask for the legal basis of this denial. Never leave a meeting voluntarily; but if ordered to leave, do so and contact your editor immediately. Resistance is not advised, for criminal charges may be filed against you. While open-meetings laws provide a good means of access to proceedings, the reporter possesses what is probably a more powerful weapon—the power of publicity. Public officials don't like stories about secret meetings. If an agency abuses its right to meet in executive session, describe these meetings as they really are—secret sessions. A photo essay showing a meeting room door open, closing, and closed, accompanied by a caption citing appropriate parts of the open-meetings law, will often get a reporter back into a proceeding faster than a court action.

While open-meetings laws provide a good means of access to proceedings, the reporter possesses what is probably a more powerful weapon—the power of publicity.

OPEN-MEETINGS TIPS FOR REPORTERS

▮ Ask for legal basis for closure.

▮ Find out who is asking that meeting be closed and why.

▮ Never leave a meeting voluntarily, but don't resist being escorted out the door.

▮ Call your editor immediately.

▮ Use publicity as well as the law to gain access.

STATE OPEN-RECORDS LAWS

Every state in the union also has some kind of **open-records law.** The access laws either follow the federal formula—all records are open except the following—or list the kinds of records that the public does have a right to inspect. A good online resource for these state laws is the Citizen Access Project at http://www.citizenaccess.org.

State freedom of information laws can be very important tools for journalists. For instance, in 2004 The New York Times used New York's Freedom of Information Law (FOIL)[143] to obtain portions of the transcripts of oral histories conducted by the New York City Fire Department with firefighters concerning their activities at the World Trade Center on September 11, 2001.[144] New York's FOIL statute requires state and municipal agencies to "make available for public inspection and copying all records," unless one of 10 exceptions applies. One of those exceptions is a privacy exception that guards against the release of a record if its disclosure "would constitute an unwarranted invasion of personal privacy." The appellate division of the New York court in 2004 directed the disclosure under FOIL of the "personal expressions of feelings contained in the oral histories." The Times also was able to obtain the words of 911 operators contained in the transcripts of the 911 emergency telephone calls made on September 11, 2001. The court, however, ruled that the personal privacy exception applied to the words of the callers/victims and prevented their disclosure. The court wrote that "disclosure of the highly personal expressions of persons who were facing imminent death, expressing fear and panic, would be hurtful to a reasonable person of ordinary sensibilities who is a survivor of someone who made a radio dispatch call before dying." In other words, The Times could get one side of the telephone conversations—the words of 911 operators—but not the other half spoken by the callers and victims.

In 2005, the case of *New York Times Co.* v. *City of New York Fire Dept.* finally reached the highest appellate court in New York state, known as the Court of Appeals (in a rather odd quirk in New York, state trial courts are called supreme courts while the top court is known simply as the Court of Appeals). The question again hinged on whether the fire department and the administration of Mayor Michael Bloomberg were required under New York's FOIL

---

143. N.Y. Public Officers Law § 84 et seq. (2004).

144. *New York Times Co.* v. *City of New York Fire Dep't.,* 770 N.Y.S. 2d 324 (N.Y. App. Div. 1st Dept. 2004).

statute to disclose the tapes and transcripts of the 911 calls and the transcripts of the oral interviews with firefighters.[145] New York's high court largely affirmed the earlier appellate division ruling, but modified it slightly to direct that "the entire oral histories [of the interviews with firefighters] be disclosed, except for specifically-identified portions that can be shown likely to cause serious pain or embarrassment to an interviewee." This marked a clear victory for The Times on its quest for the oral histories of the firefighters.

When it came to the 911 emergency tapes between callers and operators, however, the Court of Appeals balanced competing interests. On the one hand, there were concerns for privacy of the victims of the terrorist attacks and, more specifically and importantly, the privacy interests of the victims' surviving relatives in keeping private the affairs of their dead loved ones. Balanced against the privacy concerns of the relatives was the public interest in the disclosure of the information, which might show how well and effectively emergency workers in New York City responded to the terrorist attacks of September 11, 2001. Specifically, The New York Times argued that "the public has a legitimate interest in knowing how well or poorly the 911 system performed on that day." In affirming the earlier ruling blocking disclosure of the words of the victims but allowing release of the words of the 911 operators, the court held that it was "not persuaded" that complete disclosure of all of the 911 calls was required to serve the public interest. It wrote that "the public interest in the words of the 911 callers is outweighed by the interest in privacy of those family members and callers who prefer that those words remain private." In ruling in favor of the privacy interests of the victims' surviving relatives, the New York high court reasoned that "it is highly likely in this case—more than in almost any other imaginable—that, if the tapes and transcripts are made public, they will be replayed and republished endlessly, and that in some cases they will be exploited by media seeking to deliver sensational fare to their audience. This is the sort of invasion that the privacy exception exists to prevent."

The court did, however, allow the disclosure of the words of eight specific callers/victims. Why? Because their surviving relatives had sought the disclosure, specifically intervened in the case on the side of The New York Times to obtain the disclosure and had no privacy objections regarding the taped, dying words of their own relatives. The case finally came to a close in August 2005 with the release by New York City officials of what the New York Times called "a digital avalanche of oral histories, dispatchers' tapes and phone logs so vast that they took up 23 compact discs" and that included "about 200 accounts of emergency medical technicians, paramedics and their supervisors." *

FOIL, incidentally, was strengthened later in 2005 when Governor George Pataki signed into law a bill that required state government agencies to grant or deny FOIL requests within 20 days of their filing, with violations of the rule creating a right to a civil cause of action for the requesting party. The mandating of such a swift turnaround time (year-long delays in answering requests were previously not uncommon in the Gotham State) was designed to eliminate the accuracy in New York of what had become a sad but often-quoted maxim—access delayed is access denied.

New York is not the only place where state laws affecting access are important. Across the country, voters in California overwhelmingly approved a ballot initiative called Proposition 59 in November 2004 that expanded access to government records in the Golden State.

---

*Dwyer, "Vast Archive Yields New View of 9/11."
145. *New York Times Co.* v. *City of New York Fire Dept.*, 2005 N.Y. LEXIS 452 (N.Y. Mar. 24 2005).

The measure, which was supported by the California Newspaper Publishers Association, provides in relevant part that "the people have the right of access to information concerning the conduct of the people's business, and, therefore, the meetings of public bodies and the writings of public officials and agencies shall be open to public scrutiny." It was immediately seized upon successfully by the California First Amendment Coalition—a group of journalists and civic activists—to request the official appointment calendars, daily schedules and meeting logs for Governor Arnold Schwarzenegger (R.-Calif.).[146] After Schwarzenegger agreed to make his daily calendar public, other high-ranking California officials soon followed suit. And in April 2005, Schwarzenegger announced that he would require state agencies to obtain approval directly from his office before withholding access to public records. Of particular importance here is that Proposition 59 actually placed a right of public access to government "writings" into the state constitution, not simply the California statutory provisions known as the California Public Records Act, which has been in place since 1968. The California Supreme Court had held back in 1991 that the state's Public Records Act did *not* provide access to the same documents requested by the First Amendment Coalition under the Proposition 59 amendment to the state Constitution.[147]

The California Public Records Act was used successfully in 2004, however, by the Sacramento Bee to obtain the disciplinary termination letters for five local firemen, each of whom was a government employee.[148] The letters revealed multiple abuses of public resources. For instance, one firefighter took an ambulance to a local adult bookstore to get a porn star's autograph, and another drove a fire engine, carrying women that he had picked up in bars, to emergency response calls. While the firefighters' union claimed that privacy interests should have prevented disclosure of the disciplinary letters, a judge disagreed. As the Bee's attorney stated, "firefighters don't have privacy protection that trumps the Public Records Act."

Most state laws permit inspection of records by any person, but a few limit access to public records to citizens of the state. The reason persons want to see a record is normally considered immaterial when determining whether they can gain access to the record. The freedom of information laws provide access to records held by public agencies in the state, and normally these statutes provide a broad definition of these agencies. Normally included are state offices, departments, divisions, bureaus, boards and commissions. Records kept by local government agencies (cities, counties, villages) are also included, as are those kept by school districts, public utilities and municipal corporations. In some states these laws also apply to records held by the governor.[149] These state laws do not normally govern records kept by courts or the legislature. Frequently these branches of government have established their own policies regarding access to records. State laws follow either a liberal or conservative definition of a public record. *All records possessed by an agency* are deemed to be public records in those states with liberal definitions of a public record. But some state laws are more conservative and provide access only to those *records that are required to be kept by law.*

146. Berthelsen, "Governor Asked to Open Records."
147. *Times Mirror Co. v. Superior Court of Sacramento County,* 53 Cal. 3d 1325 (1991).
148. Hume and Coronado, "Letters Detail Probe Results."
149. Bush, "Access to Governors' Records," 135.

The continuing validity of state open records laws with "citizens-only" provisions that facially discriminate against out-of-state citizens was thrown into serious doubt in May 2005 when a federal district court in a case called *Lee v. Minner,* 369 F. Supp. 2d 527 (2005), struck down such a measure in Delaware's freedom of information law for violating the privileges and immunities clause of the U.S. Constitution. That clause is designed to prevent the discriminatory treatment of citizens from other states and it is intended, as the U.S. Supreme Court wrote long ago an 1868 opinion called *Paul v. Virginia,* "to place the citizens of each state upon the same footing with citizens of other states, so far as the advantages resulting from citizenship in those states are concerned." The district court in *Lee v. Minner* held that Delaware had failed to justify its distinction between citizens and non-citizens of that state when it came to accessing state-government documents. In reaching this conclusion, the court reasoned that "access to public records is the hallmark of effective participation in a democracy. As the 'corporate home' for thousands of corporations in the United States, Delaware's regulations have nation-wide political and economic impact, and therefore, it seems reasonable that non-citizens should have the same access to public records as Delaware citizens."

All state freedom of information laws provide exemptions to disclosure. Agencies *may* withhold material that falls under an exemption in some states; agencies *must* withhold this information in other states. Six common exemptions to the state open-records laws are the following:

1. Information classified as confidential by state or federal law
2. Law enforcement and investigatory information
3. Trade secrets and commercial information
4. Preliminary departmental memorandums (working papers)
5. Personal privacy information
6. Information relating to litigation against a public body

The federal Freedom of Information Act requires agencies to maintain an index of documents and records; not many state laws have the same requirement. But in every state, the right to inspect records includes the right to copy records. Procedures to gain access to state agency records follow the federal FOIA model. Two-thirds of the state statutes have provisions for judicial review of agency rulings in which the state bears the burden to show that the record should remain undisclosed.

Obtaining copies of state records can sometimes be an expensive proposition. For instance, in 2005 the sheriff in Tuscaloosa, Alabama—home of the University of Alabama— began a policy of charging $1 per page for copying plus an additional $38-per-hour fee for processing state open-records requests if it takes more than 15 minutes to find and copy reports. Records, in other words, might be available under state open-records laws, but journalists should bring either a credit card or a thick wad of cash with them to the local courthouse or police station. Sometimes the local fees charged are so high that they are ruled excessive under the applicable open-records act. That was the case in April 2005 when the attorney general of Kentucky issued an order declaring that a 50-cent-per-page fee charged for copying by the City of Hartford, Ky., violated that state's open-records act. Attorney General Gregory Stumbo wrote that Hartford "must recalculate its copying fee" unless it "can substantiate that its actual costs exceed ten cents per page." Stumbo added that the 50-cent-per-page fee "constitutes a subversion of the intent" of Kentucky's open-records act.

This brief summary of the state laws provides the barest of outlines and guidelines. Reporters, government information officers and even just interested citizens should be well-acquainted with state rules and regulations on public access to meetings and records. Such information is easily developed with a little research. Many state press associations or organizations of journalists publish handbooks or guides to the laws in their states. A simple phone call is often all that is needed to get one of these guides. Many of these same organizations periodically sponsor seminars on access, open to all for the price of the registration fee. Knowledge about state access laws is truly power. Without such knowledge reporters and citizens alike can be easily misled by misguided public officials.

THE PRIVATIZATION OF PUBLIC GOVERNMENT

One of the real challenges facing the press in the 21st century results from the growing trend of private companies taking over what has been traditionally regarded as government business. For-profit and nonprofit organizations today are replacing the government in operating public schools, jails and prisons, state and local welfare agencies, and many other state services. These private agencies are not generally regarded to have the same responsibilities as public agencies to maintain open records or hold meetings in public. The Tennessee Court of Appeals in 2001 ruled that a nonprofit corporation that contracted with the state to help administer a state-subsidized day-care program was not a state agency for purposes of the state's public records act. This ruling came even though the corporation signed a contract stipulating that all its records were to be considered state property, that all its employees performed work for the state, that 99 percent of its income came from the state, and that many of its employees worked in state offices.[150] Fortunately for journalists and all access advocates, the Supreme Court of Tennessee reversed the Court of Appeals decision in September 2002. The state's high court concluded in a unanimous opinion that the agency in question—Cherokee Children & Family Services, Inc.—operates as the functional equivalent of a government agency and therefore "all of its records are subject to the Tennessee Public Records Act and therefore are accessible by the public."[151]

Some government agencies, frustrated with the time it takes to deal with record management and access problems, have turned over government records to private companies who sell access to these records for a profit. In DuPage County, Illinois, the administrators of the judicial system gave exclusive control of the court's records to a private firm that sold access to the records. Other counties considered using the same system before an editorial campaign by the state's newspapers stopped the practice from spreading.[152] In Indiana, Illinois, Michigan, Ohio and Wisconsin, a company called CivicLink, owned by Ameritech, a telephone company, provides computer access to court proceedings, meetings, property and tax records, and other types of public information—for a price. Journalists seeking information about such "private" government systems are sure to face denials based on corporate privacy,

---

150. *Memphis Publishing Co. et al.* v. *Cherokee Children & Family Service, Inc.,* 29 M.L.R. 1545 (2001).
151. *Memphis Publishing Co. et al.* v. *Cherokee Children & Family Services, Inc.,* 87 S.W. 3d 67 (2002).
152. Fought, "Privatization Threatens Access."

confidentiality of private financial records, and other arguments that businesses have used for decades to shield their operations from public scrutiny. New laws will be needed to break down these walls.

SUMMARY

All states have laws that govern access to public meetings and public records. Good state open-meetings laws have strong legislative declarations in support of public meetings, specifically define a public meeting by listing the number of members who must gather to constitute a meeting, and declare void all actions taken during a meeting that was improperly closed to the public. Most laws provide for closed sessions to discuss such matters as personnel actions, real estate transactions and litigation.

State open-records laws tend to mirror the federal law. Both state and local agencies are governed by the laws, which apply to most governmental bodies except the legislature and the courts. Most state laws govern all records kept by these agencies, but a few are applicable only to records that are required to be kept by law. Exemptions to state open-records laws include material specifically excluded by other statutes, law-enforcement investigatory information, working papers and highly personal information. Most laws provide for access to the judicial system in case a request for data is rejected, but both New York and Connecticut have established commissions to act as arbiters in these matters, and Florida has adopted a constitutional amendment that governs access throughout state government. A major concern facing both journalists and the public today is the growing use of private businesses to carry out governmental functions.

LAWS THAT RESTRICT ACCESS TO INFORMATION

Just as there are laws that provide for public access to government-held documents, there are laws that specifically preclude access to government-held information. There are provisions in scores of federal laws alone that limit the right of access. Tax statutes, espionage laws, legislation on atomic energy and dozens of other kinds of laws are filled with limitations on the dissemination of information (e.g., personal information on taxes, national security questions, and matters relating to nuclear weapons). But in addition to these kinds of laws, the federal government has adopted in the past four decades at least three rather broad sets of regulations regarding information held by the government. All three were adopted in the name of protecting the right to privacy. While these regulations cannot be considered here in a comprehensive sense, persons who gather information for a living need to be aware of their implications.

All three were adopted in the name of protecting the right to privacy.

SCHOOL RECORDS

An amendment, the Family Educational Rights and Privacy Act (sometimes called the Buckley Amendment), to the General Education Provisions Act (1974) is aimed at increasing both the parental access to, and the confidentiality of, educational records. On the one hand, the law forces all federally funded schools and educational agencies to permit parents to inspect and review their children's educational records. On the other hand, the statute prohibits the distribution of personally identifiable information, excluding what is called directory data, to unauthorized persons without consent of the parents. The result is that student records or files must be kept confidential. This goal is hardly a hardship on the press in most instances. However, because of the stiff penalty in the law—possible loss to the school of federal funds—educators have occasionally overreacted and declared data that are actually unprotected by the statute to be confidential. Some university officials, for example, have tried to use this provision to deny reporters access to campus police records in an effort to squelch stories about crime on campus (see page 116). In one absurd case, a reporter-photographer said that school officials chased him off school property when he attempted to photograph children playing outside at recess. The officials cited the 1974 law as a reason that picture taking was no longer permitted on school property. Of course, instances like that are rare, and the significance of the law is its indication of the extreme interest in privacy today rather than its threat to the legitimate news-gathering tasks of the press.

In 2002 the U.S. Supreme Court issued a 7-2 opinion interpreting the Family Educational Rights and Privacy Act that could help the media obtain campus crime reports and records by reducing universities' worries about being sued for violating the law. In particular, the court held that the Buckley Amendment does not give students the personal right to sue their schools for releasing personal material covered by that statute.[153] The remedy for violation, the court held, is not an individual lawsuit but, as noted above, solely the loss to schools of federal funds.

HEALTH AND MEDICAL RECORDS

In April 2003, a new set of privacy rules and regulations went into effect that limit the ability of journalists to obtain information about patients in hospitals and in the custody of other health care providers. The rules, officially known as the Federal Standards for Privacy of Individually Identifiable Health Information, were enacted pursuant to the Health Insurance Portability and Accountability Act of 1996, which is commonly known by the acronym HIPAA (see page 316). The Seattle Times wrote that "for the news media, HIPAA rules will mean that in the event of a shooting, car crash or other newsworthy event, hospitals will disclose no information unless a reporter knows the patient's name. In the past, reporters could ascertain a patient's condition in those situations without a name."[154] In a special white paper called "The Lost Stories," Jennifer LaFleur of the Reporters Committee for Freedom of the Press (RCFP) observed that "under HIPAA, hospitals may release only the name and one-word status of the patient—but only if the patient has agreed to have his or her name released and then only if the reporter has the individual's full name."[155] LaFleur added that many "journalists around the country report that police and fire departments have cited HIPAA for not disclosing accident information."

In September 2004, the RCFP reported on its Web site that HIPAA has been cited by police and other emergency officials in denying important information to journalists, according to the National Newspaper Association. For example, the Beaver County Times and

---

153. *Gonzaga University* v. *Doe,* 536 U.S. 273 (2002).
154. Ostrom, "Privacy Rules to Limit Word on Patients."
155. LaFleur, "The Lost Stories."

Allegheny Times in Pennsylvania reported that a local hospital cited HIPAA in not reporting a hepatitis outbreak to the public. In Oklahoma, the law has been used to justify withholding information about inmates who died in prison and failing to inform nursing home residents that registered sex offenders lived in the homes, the Tulsa World reported.

It is important to note that police and fire departments, along with other law enforcement agencies, are *not* entities covered by HIPAA. Thus HIPAA does not give the police the power or the right to keep secret information in their reports and logs about accident or shooting victims. The entities covered by HIPAA, in contrast, are health plans, health care clearinghouses and health care providers.

The Department of Health and Human Services maintains a Web site devoted to HIPAA and its privacy provisions. It is located at http://www.hhs.gov/ocr/hipaa and journalists seeking information from health care providers should be familiar with its myriad relevant terms and provisions. One very important statement for journalists on that Web site relates to the relationship between HIPAA and state open-records laws. It can be found on a link for frequently asked questions about state public records laws. In particular, the Web site provides that "if a state agency is not a 'covered entity' . . . it is not required to comply with the HIPAA Privacy Rule and, thus, any disclosure of information by the state agency pursuant to its state public records law would not be subject to the Privacy Rule." This makes it clear that police and fire departments, which are not covered entities, cannot hide behind HIPAA to keep information secret that is otherwise open under a state law.

In an important decision related to this last matter, the attorney general for the state of Kentucky, Greg Stumbo, handed journalists a victory when he issued an opinion in August 2004 declaring that HIPAA does not apply in that state to the names of injured people mentioned in police reports.[156] Parsed differently, police in Kentucky cannot use HIPAA to withhold their incident reports mentioning injured people who were taken to health care providers. That opinion came on the heels of a February 2004 opinion by Greg Abbott, the attorney general of Texas, holding that, regardless of HIPAA, governmental agencies such as police and fire departments in Texas still must release medical information required to be disclosed under the state's open-records laws.[157] Rulings such as those in Kentucky and Texas are vital for journalists performing their jobs, and it can be hoped that attorneys general in other states will issue similar opinions in the future.*

In another early development of the law related to HIPAA as it affects the news media, a federal judge in Colorado ruled in 2004 that HIPAA does not create a private cause of action for hospitals and medical care providers to sue news entities that publish medical records.[158] In that case, the Rocky Mountain News had obtained and published material contained in a hospital's secret peer review report, and the hospital sued the newspaper alleging that its use of the report violated HIPAA. Judge Walker D. Miller dismissed the lawsuit, however. He

---

*In addition to attorneys general in Kentucky and Texas, the assistant attorney general of Mississippi, Heather P. Wagner, wrote a letter in late 2004 to the city attorney in Hattiesburg advising that state open-records laws, including the Mississippi Public Records Act, trump HIPAA's privacy guarantees and therefore require police and fire departments to release information about those injured in crimes and fires.

156. "Medical Privacy Law Does Not Apply."

157. Pasztor, "Abbott: In Battle of Laws, State Comes First."

158. *Univ. of Colo. Hospital Authority v. Denver Publishing Co.,* 32 M.L.R. 2251 (D. Colo. 2004).

reasoned that "federal courts have consistently refused to find a private right of action under HIPAA" and observed that both the language and structure of HIPAA do not provide for a private cause of action. Rather than a private lawsuit, Judge Miller wrote, HIPAA "provides a method for enforcing its prohibition upon use or disclosure of [an] individual's health information—the punitive imposition of fines and imprisonment for violations." Indeed, under HIPAA, one can be fined up to $250,000 and imprisoned for 10 years.

THE FEDERAL PRIVACY LAW

The **Privacy Act** of 1974 has two basic thrusts. First, it attempts to check the misuse of personal data obtained by the federal government, the quantity of which has, of course, reached staggering proportions. Second, the law is intended to provide access for individuals to records about themselves that are held by federal agencies. The first objective of the law could be the more troublesome to the press.

The act requires that each federal agency limit the collection of information to that which is relevant and necessary, to collect information directly from the subject concerned when possible, and to allow individuals to review and amend their personal records and information. Also, under the act agencies are forbidden from disclosing what is called "a personally identifiable record" without the written consent of the individual to whom the record pertains. Since this section of the law is seemingly contradictory to the spirit of the federal FOIA, Congress was forced to clarify the responsibilities of federal agencies with regard to the law. A provision was added to the Privacy Act that declares that records required to be disclosed under the FOIA are not subject to the provisions of the Privacy Act and consequently cannot be withheld from inspection. To the government official with control of information, however, neither the Privacy Act nor the FOIA is unambiguous.

The difficulty in resolving aspects of the Privacy Act and the Freedom of Information Act is graphically illustrated by a case decided by the U.S. Court of Appeals for the District of Columbia Circuit. Frank Greentree was indicted and convicted in federal court on drug charges. He filed a civil suit to block state prosecution based on the same events. Greentree sought information from both the Drug Enforcement Administration and the U.S. Bureau of Customs to assist him in his civil action. When the agencies refused to give him the material he sought, he filed both a Freedom of Information Act request and a Privacy Act request to get the information. The documents sought by Greentree were contained in something called the Investigations Record System, and this system of records has been declared to be exempt from the access provisions of the Privacy Act. Hence it was unavailable to Greentree through the federal privacy law. Because the information could not be released under the Privacy Act, the government argued that it was also unavailable under FOIA Exemption 3. Remember Exemption 3: It provides that the Freedom of Information Act does not apply to matters "specifically exempt from disclosure by statute." The material Greentree sought was exempt from disclosure under the federal privacy statute; therefore, the government argued, it was also exempt from disclosure under Exemption 3 of the Freedom of Information Act. In two previous appellate court rulings, this government argument was sustained.[159] But in *Greentree,* the

159. See *Terkel* v. *Kelly,* 599 F. 2d 214 (1979) and *Painter* v. *Federal Bureau of Investigation,* 615 F. 2d 689 (1980).

U.S. Court of Appeals for the District of Columbia Circuit denied the validity of this argument and ruled against the government. Judge Wald said that throughout its consideration of the Privacy Act, Congress struggled to hold separate the Privacy Act and the FOIA. That effect was ultimately successful, he said. Judge Wald noted that section (b) (2) of the Privacy Act clearly states that "no agency shall disclose any record which is contained in a system of records . . . *unless disclosure of the record would be required under section 552 (The Freedom of Information Act) of this title* [author emphasis]." "We must conclude," Wald wrote, "that this section of the Privacy Act represents a congressional mandate that the Privacy Act not be used as a barrier to FOIA access." Congress could not have intended that a section of the Privacy Act could serve as a withholding statute under FOIA Exemption 3, the judge said. It is possible, he noted, that the government might still be able to block access to this information because of Exemption 7 (the law enforcement exemption of the FOIA), but the government would have to prove that the material sought by Greentree was exempt from disclosure.[160]

Other conflicts exist in the administration of the two laws. Before passage of the Privacy Act, materials that were not required to be disclosed under the FOIA were nevertheless permitted to be disclosed at the discretion of a government agency. Now, information falling under an FOIA exemption, and thus not required to be disclosed, will routinely be withheld out of fear of violating the Privacy Act.

CRIMINAL HISTORY PRIVACY LAWS

In accordance with the broad scope of the Omnibus Crime Control and Safe Streets Act of 1968, the federal Law Enforcement Assistance Administration, an agency created by the Nixon administration to help local police forces fight crime, sought to develop a national computerized record-keeping system. The system that was established permits any police department in the nation to have access to the records of virtually all other police departments.

Congressional concern about the misuse of this record system led to limitations on access to the data. Police records have always contained a considerable amount of information that is erroneous, out-of-date or private. The centralized record-keeping system presents a problem referred to by some writers as the "dossier effect." The contrast between these computerized and centrally maintained records immediately accessible across the country and those police records of the past was sharp and immediately evident: Fragmented, original-source records kept by a single police agency for a limited geographical area were not readily accessible because of their bulk and associated indexing problems. Hence, federal policy mandated that states, if they wish to participate in the national record-keeping system, adopt rules that, among other things, limit the dissemination of some criminal history nonconviction data.

The "Code of Federal Regulations" ("Criminal Justice Information Systems") defines nonconviction data as follows:

> arrest information without disposition if an interval of one year has elapsed from the date of arrest and no active prosecution of the charge is pending, or information disclosing that the police have elected not to refer a matter to a prosecutor, or that a prosecutor has elected not to commence criminal proceedings, or that proceedings have been indefinitely postponed, as well as all acquittals and all dismissals.

160. *Greentree* v. *Customs Service,* 674 F. 2d 74 (1982).

As a result of the state laws, press access to criminal history records kept by the police has been virtually eliminated unless data sought are pertinent to an incident for which a person is currently being processed by the criminal justice system, are conviction records, or are original records of entry, such as arrest records, that are maintained chronologically and are accessible only on that basis. Reporters can also obtain information about arrests not resulting in conviction, however, if they are aware of the specific dates of the arrests. It is hard to determine whether these laws have substantially affected the press's ability to report on the criminal justice system. A good police reporter usually can gain access to information he or she wants to see. Nevertheless, potential problems are apparent. One commentator noted:

> On the one hand, the uncontrolled dissemination and publication of certain criminal history records can adversely affect the individual himself. On the other hand, the public and the press must have access to basic records of official action if they are to effectively scrutinize and evaluate the operations of the police, the prosecuting agencies, and the courts.[161]

The ability to achieve that scrutiny is important. For example, it is possible to envision a situation in which a prosecutor is accused of favoring friends or certain ethnic or racial groups when deciding whether to prosecute arrested persons. Without access to arrest records that can be compared with prosecution records, such a charge would be difficult to investigate. Persons within the criminal justice system could gain access to the needed records, but history indicates that these people must be prodded before they take action. And, of course, prodding is the function of the press.

STATE STATUTES THAT LIMIT ACCESS TO INFORMATION

All states have statutes that limit access to information that would otherwise be available under a freedom of information law.

All states have statutes that limit access to information that would otherwise be available under a freedom of information law. The state of Washington, for example, has more than 100 different laws that govern the access to particular information. Arizona has 39 laws that block access to specific records. Some of these state statutes are aimed at blocking access to trade secrets; others limit access to information submitted to the state in compliance with environmental laws. In 2001, in direct response to the racetrack death of driver Dale Earnhardt at the Daytona 500 and the subsequent request for autopsy photographs by the Orlando Sentinel and other newspapers, the Florida legislature passed a bill that was signed into law by Governor Jeb Bush that makes confidential and exempt from that state's public records act photographs and videotapes of autopsies.[162] The newspapers had sought access to the photographs to determine the reasons for Earnhardt's death and, in particular, whether a particular safety device might have saved his life. In 2002, a Florida appellate court upheld the constitutionality of that statute and its retroactive application, and the Supreme Court of Florida declined to hear the case in July 2003, letting the appellate court decision stand.[163] Finally, in December 2003, the

---

161. Higgins, "Press and Criminal Record Privacy," 509.
162. Florida Statute § 406.135 (2001).
163. *Campus Communications, Inc.* v. *Earnhardt,* 821 So. 2d 388 (2002). The Supreme Court of Florida's decision not to hear the case came in a close 4-3 vote.

U.S. Supreme Court declined to hear the case.[164] There now is a danger that other states will follow Florida's lead and adopt similar legislation.

Divorce is another area where some states adopt statutes limiting public access to certain records. For instance, a new law took effect in California in 2004 after being signed by Governor Schwarzenegger (R.) that allowed parties in divorce proceedings, upon their request, to require judges to seal any and all documents that mention financial information such as their assets and liabilities.[165] Judges had no option under the law to deny such a request, and the placement of financial data in a solitary footnote of an otherwise lengthy document was enough to require the sealing of the document in its entirety. While court-filed pleadings and documents like those in divorce cases, of course, are presumptively and traditionally open to the public, there are many rich people going through divorces who simply don't want their financial data to suddenly appear in a public file. Such was the case in *Burkle* v. *Burkle*[166] when a Los Angeles billionaire investor named Ronald W. Burkle with an estimated wealth of $2.3 billion became the first person to use the new divorce-secrecy California law. He requested that a judge seal what the Sacramento Bee described as a stack of financial documents "about 2 feet tall"[167] in his divorce case from Janet Burkle. Mrs. Burkle, on the other hand, wanted the documents open to the public because she thought her soon-to-be former husband was hiding assets. The Los Angeles Times and the Associated Press also objected to the law, and those media entities intervened in the Burkle divorce case to have the documents unsealed. In March 2005, Superior Court Judge Roy L. Paul ruled in the media's favor and held that the new California law violated the First Amendment. Judge Paul weighed the right of privacy in financial data against what he called "the competing right of public access." He determined that judges must have "some discretion on a case-by-case basis before entire pleadings are sealed on behalf of some small portion within them." Paul added that "there is no compelling state interest in streamlining the process to the point that the court is totally divested of discretion in all instances." Rather than requiring that an entire document be sealed as the new California law did, the better answer is for the judge to edit out and redact (to black out with a marker or colored tape) only those portions of documents that, in his or her discretion, are particularly privacy sensitive, such as social security and bank account numbers. The judge thus concluded that "the statute is overbroad because it mandates sealing entire pleadings to protect a limited class of specified material." In 2006 a California appellate court upheld Paul's ruling in *Burkle*, reasoning that "the First Amendment provides a right of access to court records in divorce proceedings" and concluding "while the interest in protecting divorcing parties from identity theft and other financial crimes may override the First Amendment right of access in a proper case, [the statute] is not narrowly tailored to serve that interest" and thus is unconstitutional.[168]

---

164. *Campus Communications, Inc.* v. *Earnhardt,* 124 S.Ct. 821 (2003).

165. *See* California Family Code § 2024.6 (2005) (providing that "upon request by a party to a petition for dissolution of marriage, nullity of marriage or legal separation, the court shall order a pleading that lists the parties' financial assets and liabilities and provides the location or identifying information about those assets and liabilities sealed").

166. Superior Court, Los Angeles County, Cal. 2005.

167. Lundstrom, "The Privacy Boogeyman Runs Amok."

168. 135 Cal. App. 4th 1045 (2006). In addition to the dispute in California over access to documents in divorce proceedings, the Supreme Court of New Hampshire in December 2005 declared unconstitutional parts of a law in that state that limited the ability of the media to obtain financial affidavits in divorce cases. *Associated Press* v. *New Hampshire,* 888 A.2d 1236 (Dec. 30, 2005).

SUMMARY All the states and the federal government have laws that specifically exclude certain kinds of information from the public scrutiny. Some of these exclusions were noted in the discussion of Exemption 3 of the Freedom of Information Act. Today, the right to privacy has been erected as a substantial barrier to access to information held by government agencies. The federal government has adopted a law protecting the privacy of student records. Congress passed a federal privacy law, which often conflicts with the provisions of the Freedom of Information Act. The federal government has also insisted that states pass statutes that control access to criminal history records. Much privacy legislation has been passed by the states themselves, and today the right to privacy is being used frequently to block access to public records.

BIBLIOGRAPHY ⟶

Archibald, Sam. "The Revised F.O.I. Law and How to Use It." *Columbia Journalism Review,* July/August 1977, 54.

Barringer, Felicity. "Appeals Court Rejects Damages Against ABC in Food Lion Case." *The New York Times,* 21 October 1999, A1.

Beesley, Susan L., and Theresa Glover. "Developments Under the Freedom of Information Act, 1986." *Duke Law Journal* (1987): 521.

Berthelsen, Christian. "Governor Asked to Open Records." *San Francisco Chronicle,* 6 November 2004, B3.

Boule, Margie. "No-Fly List Clips Singer, But Parent Who Abducts Kids Glides," *Oregonian,* 30 September 2004, E01.

Burns, Robert. "Document: Bin Laden Evaded U.S. Forces." *Associated Press,* 22 March 2005.

The Bush Administration and the News Media. Washington, D.C.: Reporters Committee for Freedom of the Press, 1992.

Bush, Ellen M. "Access to Governors' Records: State Statutes and the Use of Executive Privilege." *Journalism Quarterly* 71 (1994): 135.

The Clinton Administration and the News Media. Washington, D.C.: Reporters Committee for Freedom of the Press, 1996.

Clymer, Adam. "Government Openness at Issue as Bush Holds on to Records." *The New York Times,* 3 January 2003, A1.

"CNN, Federal Government Settle Suit with Montana Rancher." *Associated Press,* 5 June 2001.

Cross, Harold. *The People's Right to Know.* New York: Columbia University Press, 1953.

Denniston, Lyle. "Reagan Legacy: Law Against Leaks." *Washington Journalism Review,* December 1988, 10.

Dobbs, Michael. "Records Counter a Critic of Kerry." *Washington Post,* 19 April 2004.

Dwyer, Jim. "Vast Archive Yields New View of 9/11." *The New York Times,* 13 August 2005, A1.

Editorial. "Reinforce Anti-Secrecy Law." *San Francisco Chronicle,* 4 April 2003, A24.

Fought, Barbara C. "Privatization Threatens Access." *Quill,* September 1997, 8.

Galvin, Kevin. "Clinton Invokes Executive Privilege on Clemency Deal." *Seattle Post-Intelligencer,* 17 September 1999, A3.

Greenhouse, Linda. "Police Violate Privacy in Home Raids with Journalists." *The New York Times,* 25 May 1999, A25.

Halstuk, Martin. "In Review: The Threat to Freedom of Information." *Columbia Journalism Review,* January-February 2002, 8.

"Hard Numbers." *Columbia Journalism Review,* September/October 2004, 19.

Hayes, Michael J. "Whatever Happened to 'The Right to Know'? Access to Government-Controlled Information Since *Richmond Newspapers.*" *Virginia Law Review* 73 (1987): 111.

Helm, Mark. "Policy Tightens Access to Federal Records." *Seattle Post-Intelligencer,* 17 November 2001, A3.

Higgins, Steven. "Press and Criminal Record Privacy." *St. Louis University Law Journal* 20 (1977): 509.

Homefront Confidential: How the War on Terrorism Affects Access to Information and the Public's Right to Know. Arlington, VA: Reporters Committee for Freedom of the Press, 6th ed. 2005.

How to Use the Federal FOI Act, 8th ed. Arlington, Va.: FOI Service Center, 1998.

Hume, Elizabeth, and Coronado, Ramon. "Letters Detail Probe Results," *Sacramento Bee,* 29 December 2004, A1.

"Journalist Gets Probation for Posing as Federal Official." *Plain Dealer,* 13 April 2002, B2.

"Judge Upholds Reporter's Trespassing Conviction." *Associated Press,* 6 July 2004.

Kaplan, Carl S. "Judge Says Recording of Electronic Chats Is Legal." *Cyber Law Journal,* 14 January 2000.

Kirtley, Jane E., ed. *The First Amendment Handbook.* Washington, D.C.: Reporters Committee for Freedom of the Press, 1986.

LaFleur, Jennifer. *The Lost Stories: How a Steady Stream of Laws, Regulations and Judicial Decisions Have Eroded Reporting on Important Issues.* Arlington, VA: Reporters Committee for Freedom of the Press, 2003.

Lewis, Neil. "White House Holds Up Release of Regan-Era Documents." *The Oregonian,* 9 June 2001, A10.

Lundstrom, Margie, "The Privacy Boogeyman Runs Amok as Public Records Are Sealed." *Sacramento Bee,* 5 March 2005, A3.

Marwick, Christine M., ed. *Litigation Under the Amended Freedom of Information Act.* 2nd ed. Washington, D.C.: American Civil Liberties Union and Freedom of Information Clearing House, 1976.

"Medical Privacy Law Does Not Apply." *Associated Press,* 28 August 2004.

Meier, Barry. "Jury Says ABC Owes Damages of $5.5 Million." *The New York Times,* 23 January 1997, A1.

Middleton, Kent. "Journalists, Trespass, and Officials: Closing the Door on *Florida Publishing Co.* v. *Fletcher.*" *Pepperdine Law Review* 16 (1989): 259.

Mifflin, Laurie. "Judge Slashes $5.5 Million Award to Grocery Chain for ABC Report." *The New York Times,* 30 August 1997, A1.

Mitchell, Alison. "Limits Sought on Access to Company Data." *The New York Times,* 29 November 2001, B9.

Morrissey, David H. "FOIA Foiled?" *presstime,* March 1995, 29.

Ostrom, Carol M. "Privacy Rules to Limit Word on Patients." *The Seattle Times,* 13 April 2003, B1.

Padover, Saul, ed. *The Complete Madison.* New York: Harper & Row, 1953.

Pasztor, David. "Abbott: In Battle of Laws, State Comes First." *Austin American-Statesman,* 14 February 2004, B1.

Pember, Don R. "The Burgeoning Scope of 'Access Privacy' and the Portent for a Free Press." *Iowa Law Review* 64 (1979): 1155.

"Photographer Is Arrested." *The New York Times,* 12 January 2002, B3.

Preston, Julia. "Judge Orders Agency to Disclose Safety Records." *The New York Times,* 3 August 2004, A14.

"Rancher at Center of Lawsuit Over Televised Raid Dies." *Associated Press,* 17 April 2003.

Riechmann, Deb. "Congress Fears Nuclear Secrets May Slip Out in Old Documents." *The Seattle Post-Intelligencer,* 25 August 1999, A5.

Ritter, Bob. *New Technology and the First Amendment.* Greencastle, Ind.: SPJ Reports, 1993.

Rosenbaum, David E. "When Government Doesn't Tell." *The New York Times,* 3 February 2002, D1.

Rourke, Francis. *Secrecy and Publicity.* Baltimore: Johns Hopkins University Press, 1961.

Schiesel, Seth. "Jury Finds NBC Negligent in 'Dateline' Report." *The New York Times,* 9 July 1998, A19.

Schulz, David A. "Troubling Ruling Restricts News Gathering." *Editor & Publisher,* 29 June 1996, 5.

Sherer, Michael D. "Free-Lance Photojournalists and the Law." *Communications and the Law* 10 (1988): 39.

Stewart, Potter. "Or of the Press." *Hastings Law Journal* 26 (1975): 631.

Toner, Robin. "Reconsidering Security, U.S. Clamps Down on Agency Web Sites." *The New York Times,* 28 October 2001, B4.

U.S. Senate. *Clarifying and Protecting Right of Public to Information.* 89th Cong., 1st sess., 1965, S. Rept. 813.

Weinberg, Steve. "Trashing the FOIA." *Columbia Journalism Review,* January/February 1985, 21.

Weiner, Tim. "Lawmaker Tells of High Cost of Data Secrecy." *The New York Times,* 28 June 1996, A9.

———. "U.S. Plans Secrecy Overhaul to Open Millions of Records." *The New York Times,* 18 March 1994, A1.

Wicklein, John. "FOIA Foiled." *American Journalism Review,* April 1996, 36.

Yi, Daniel. "Professor Wins Release of Last FBI Date on Beatle." *Los Angeles Times,* 1 October 2004.

PROTECTION OF NEWS SOURCES/CONTEMPT POWER

The lifeblood of journalism is information. Each day reporters gather information that is then published or broadcast. It is not uncommon today for people outside the news-gathering business to want access to the information gathered by journalists. Sometimes they merely seek copies of what has already appeared in print or been carried over the airwaves. Sometimes they want more: information that has not been published; photos or video that have not been broadcast; the names of persons who provided the information to

413

the journalists. Judges, grand juries and even legislative committees all have the power to issue subpoenas to try to force reporters to reveal this information. In the first part of this chapter we explore exactly how much protection the law provides to reporters who refuse to cooperate when they are presented with subpoenas and how the actions of the journalist ultimately affect what we all read in our newspapers and magazines and see and hear on television and radio.

Anyone who refuses to submit to a court order can be punished with a citation for contempt of court, a swift judicial ruling in which the target can find himself or herself in jail in a matter of hours. That was the case in 2005 when New York Times reporter Judith Miller spent nearly three months in jail for refusing to reveal a confidential source to a special prosecutor and grand jury.

JOURNALISTS, JAIL AND CONFIDENTIAL SOURCES

On July 6, 2005, New York Times reporter Judith Miller was jailed at a detention facility in Alexandria, Va. She would spend the rest of the summer there, and then remain confined for 85 days until Sept. 29, 2005. Why was the then-57-year-old Miller locked up? What had she done wrong? A federal judge had found her in civil contempt for refusing to reveal to a special prosecutor and federal grand jury the identity of a confidential source for a potential story about which Miller ultimately never wrote a single article. Miller was jailed, in other words, for keeping a promise and for protecting a source. And sources, of course, are the lifeblood of journalism—something that Miller herself would later say in testimony before a federal committee studying the need for a federal shield law to protect confidential sources (see pages 448–449). Miller was only released from jail after her source—I. Lewis "Scooter" Libby, then chief of staff to Vice President Dick Cheney—waived and released her from the confidentiality promise and Miller's attorneys reached an agreement with the government to provide limited testimony before the grand jury. As Judith Miller, who later resigned from The New York Times after her release, stated in October 2005 during an award ceremony hosted by the California First Amendment Coalition, "I am free today only because of a federal prosecutor's agreement to limit his questions to me and because my once confidential source wrote me a letter and called me in jail to say he really, really wanted me to testify."

The jailing of a reporter like Miller who refuses to cooperate with government authorities who want him or her to divulge confidential information is not a common occurrence in the United States today. But it does happen. In 1996 a judge in Florida sentenced Miami Herald reporter David Kidwell to 70 days in jail because he refused to answer a prosecutor's questions about an interview he had with a man accused of killing his stepdaughter. Kidwell spent two weeks in jail before a federal judge freed him and directed the state appeals court to reconsider the case in light of numerous federal court rulings that recognize a First Amendment privilege for reporters.[1] In February 2000 reporter Tim Crews of the Sacramento Valley Mirror was jailed for five days for refusing to reveal the names of the sources for his story that a former California Highway Patrol officer had stolen a gun from a county police drug task force. And in 2001 a free-lance writer named Vanessa Leggett was jailed for more than five

1. *Kidwell* v. *Florida*, 696 So. 2d 399 (1997); rev'd. 26 M.L.R. 2466 (1998).

Source: © AP/Wide World Photos

months in Texas because she refused to give her notes from an interview to a grand jury investigating a murder. Leggett appealed to the U.S. Supreme Court, urging it to clarify the law surrounding a journalist's First Amendment privilege to protect confidential sources and contending that federal courts apply the law unequally in different parts of the country. The Supreme Court, however, declined in 2002 to hear her case, denying Leggett's petition for a writ of certiorari.[2] Although she lost in court, Leggett won the support and admiration of journalists across the country, as well as the PEN/Newman's Own First Amendment Award (including a $25,000 prize) in recognition of the 168 days she spent in jail in Houston for refusing to reveal her confidential sources.

The years 2004 and 2005 proved particularly dangerous for journalists who refused to reveal their confidential sources' identities. The Boston Globe reported in 2004 that "at least 10 journalists [were] facing possible jail terms or major fines for declining to disclose confidential sources in federal court battles."[3] Examples of some of those cases are described later in the section on contempt (see page 457), but it is important here to understand the significance of this disturbing turn of events.

One high-profile dispute involved Time magazine White House correspondent Matthew Cooper and, as noted earlier, New York Times reporter Judith Miller. Cooper was found in civil contempt in 2004 by a federal judge and "ordered confined at a suitable place until such time as he is willing to comply with [a] grand jury subpoena" regarding who leaked and disclosed the name of then-covert CIA operative Valerie Plame in July 2003 to several members of the news media, including columnist and TV pundit Robert Novak.[4] Novak then blew

Journalists Judith Miller and Matthew Cooper were at the center of a major battle in 2005 over the ability of reporters to keep secret the identity of confidential sources. Miller ultimately served time in a detention facility that year for protecting her source's identity.

2. *Leggett* v. *United States,* 535 U.S. 1011 (2002).
3. Jurkowitz, "Reporters Found in Contempt."
4. *In re Special Counsel Investigation,* 332 F. Supp. 2d 33 (D.D.C. Aug. 9, 2004).

Plame's cover by printing her name in his syndicated column later that month. The conservative columnist cited the sources for the scoop on Plame's employment as "two senior administration officials," neither of whom he identified by name.

It is a violation of federal law to reveal the name of covert CIA agents, and the Justice Department named a special prosecutor, U.S. Attorney Patrick J. Fitzgerald, to conduct a grand jury investigation into who leaked Plame's name to Novak. With Novak refusing to tell anyone whether he had even spoken with the special prosecutor or was cooperating with the government investigation, Fitzgerald soon began "aggressively taking on other journalists who reported on the story."[5] Among those journalists was Time's Matthew Cooper.

In addition to meting out possible jail time for Cooper, U.S. District Court Judge Thomas Hogan "ordered [Time] to pay a fine of $1,000 per day until such time as it is willing to comply with the grand jury subpoena."[6] The judge, however, stayed both orders pending appeal. Initially Cooper had submitted to questioning in a two-hour deposition by special prosecutor Fitzgerald after one of Cooper's sources waived his confidentiality agreement with Cooper.[7] However, the Time reporter was later called before a grand jury for a second time and, once again, Cooper refused to testify. Thus in October 2004, Judge Hogan held Cooper in contempt of court for a second time and ordered him jailed for as long as 18 months.[8] As he did the first time, the judge imposed a $1,000-a-day fine on Time magazine but stayed both Cooper's jail term and the magazine's fine pending appeal. As Cooper remarked about the similarity between his two contempt citations, "as Yogi Berra says, 'It's deja vu all over again.'"[9]

In the same matter, Hogan ordered Judith Miller to testify before a grand jury as part of the investigation conducted by Fitzgerald into the leak and disclosure of Plame's name.[10] Although the Pulitzer Prize–winning Miller had worked on the Plame case, she had never written about it. In issuing his September 2004 order, the judge rejected Miller's assertion that, as a journalist, she could not be compelled to testify about confidential sources. And in October 2004, Hogan held Miller in contempt of court for her refusal to testify before the grand jury.[11] Hogan ordered Miller to be jailed for up to 18 months, but as he did with Matthew Cooper, Hogan allowed her to remain free pending an appeal.

Miller told a reporter for USA Today after she was held in contempt that "it's frankly frightening that, just for doing my job and talking to government employees about public issues, I may be deprived of my freedom. Confidential sources, especially in Washington, are vital for balanced reporting if the public is to hear from government critics."[12] As The New York Times later opined, special prosecutor Fitzgerald's "investigation . . . has veered terribly off course. It threatens grievous harm to freedom of the press and the vital protection it provides against government misconduct."[13] Citing the cases of both Matthew Cooper and Judith Miller, The Times' editorial observed that "the specter of reporters being imprisoned merely

---

5. Schmitt, "Prosecutor's Lips Still Sealed."

6. *In re Special Counsel Investigation,* 332 F. Supp. 2d 33 (D.D.C. Aug. 9, 2004).

7. Steinberg, "Threat of Jailing Is Lifted."

8. Schmidt, "Reporter Held in Contempt of Court."

9. Ibid.

10. *In re Special Counsel Investigation,* 338 F. Supp. 2d 16 (D.D.C. Sept. 9, 2004).

11. Leonnig, "Journalist Cited for Contempt."

12. Johnson, "Times' Reporter Held in Contempt."

13. Editorial, "Press Freedom on the Precipice."

for doing their jobs is something that should worry everyone who cherishes the First Amendment and the essential role of a free press in a democracy."

But there would be no relief for the reporters at the appellate court level. In February 2005, a three-judge panel of the U.S. Circuit Court of Appeals for the District of Columbia upheld the district court's findings against both Miller and Cooper. The appellate court, citing the U.S. Supreme Court precedent in *Branzburg* v. *Hayes*[14] (see later in this chapter) ruled that "there is no First Amendment privilege protecting the evidence sought" and that "if any such common law privilege exists, it is not absolute, and in this case has been overcome by the filings of the Special Counsel [Fitzgerald] with the District Court."[15] Put more bluntly, the court in the case of *In re Grand Jury Subpoena* held that there is no privilege to protect journalists from being compelled to reveal their confidential sources when called to testify before grand juries.

In April 2005, the same appellate court denied a petition for rehearing the matter, thus leaving the two reporters to face 18 months in jail or take their case to the nation's highest court. Finally, in May 2005, both Cooper and Miller filed petitions with the U.S. Supreme Court asking it to hear their cases and throw out the contempt orders against them. The attorneys general of 34 states filed a friend-of-the-court brief in the matter urging the justices to take up the case and calling for the recognition of a privilege.

Unfortunately for Cooper and Miller, the U.S. Supreme Court in June of 2005 denied the journalists' petition for a writ of certiorari and refused to hear their case. That meant that Cooper and Miller had exhausted their legal appeals and now faced a difficult choice—either go to jail for civil contempt or break a promise to a confidential source. Time magazine agreed to cooperate with the investigation of special prosecutor Patrick Fitzgerald and turned over Cooper's notes and e-mails about the matter, and Cooper decided to obey the order of U.S. District Court Judge Thomas Hogan and to testify after his source gave him permission to testify. Cooper thus escaped jail, and it became apparent that the secret source and leaker may have been Karl Rove, deputy chief of staff for President George W. Bush, although Rove denied this (I. Lewis "Scooter" Libby, Vice President Dick Cheney's chief of staff, ultimately was indicted on five charges by Fitzgerald's federal grand jury in October 2005).

Cooper and Miller had exhausted their legal appeals and now faced a difficult choice— either go to jail for civil contempt or break a promise to a confidential source.

Although Cooper and Time Magazine caved in, Judith Miller and The New York Times refused to back down. On July 6, 2005 Miller was taken into custody and jailed in Alexandria (Va.) Detention Center for refusing to name her source. The Reporters Committee for Freedom of the Press deplored the jailing of Miller, and the organization soon began keeping a running tab on its Web site on the number of days she spent in jail until, eventually, she was released on Sept. 29, 2005. The jailing of Miller also reinvigorated calls for a federal shield law; 31 states had such statutes in 2005, but there was no federal shield statute. In October of 2005, the Senate Judiciary Committee heard testimony from a number of individuals, including Judith Miller and ABC News President David Westin, regarding Senate Bill 1419, known as the Free Flow of Information Act of 2005. That measure was designed to create a shield law in the federal courts. By early 2006, however, the measure had yet to become law, and there was strong disagreement among some people about whether such a law was necessary in that it could be misused by reporters for their own benefit or exploited by confidential sources who use and manipulate journalists by getting to hide behind the cloak of confidentiality. Some

14. 408 U.S. 665 (1972).
15. *In re Grand Jury Subpoena,* 397 F. 3d 964 (D.C. Cir. 2005).

people, for instance, believed that Miller acted as she did only to gain martyrdom status; others believe she was used by the Bush administration to protect I. Lewis "Scooter" Libby's identity. Libby was indicted by a federal grand jury on five felony charges including, among others, obstruction of justice and perjury in regard to the leak of CIA agent Valerie Plame's name. The Justice Department also opposed the federal shield law measure on the grounds that it might harm national security interests by preventing the government from obtaining important information from journalists.

Veteran media defense attorney Floyd Abrams, who represented both Cooper and Miller at the lower-court levels and who filed the May 2005 petition to the Supreme Court on behalf of Miller (at the Supreme Court level, Cooper was represented by Theodore Olson, former solicitor general), remarked that in 2004 it was "becoming a perilous time for journalists who rely on information provided under terms of confidentiality."[16] That trouble extended beyond the realm of politics and cases such as the Valerie Plame dispute to the arena of sports. For instance, the U.S. Attorney's Office in San Jose, Calif., in 2004 targeted three San Francisco Chronicle reporters, as well as journalists from the San Jose Mercury News, in a search for confidential sources in the steroid controversy involving BALCO.[17] The controversy made national headlines because of rumors that baseball home-run king Barry Bonds and other prominent athletes such as track star Marion Jones may have used steroids supplied by BALCO. The two Bay Area newspapers were supplied by anonymous sources with investigative reports and transcripts of confidential grand jury proceedings in the BALCO investigation. After Major League Baseball eventually adopted a new steroid-use policy in early 2005, the editor of the San Francisco Chronicle, Phil Bronstein, said he had absolutely no intention of giving up his newspaper's sources for the confidential grand jury testimony and that the league's new policy, in fact, vindicated the reporting efforts of his staff.[18] Bronstein stated, "The press has certain responsibilities in society, but one of them is not to enforce the provisions of the federal grand jury system. Obviously, there are people who disagree with that, including the Justice Department. But that's not the view from here."

New calls for a federal shield law arose in 2004 and 2005.

The situation was so bad that in November 2004, U.S. Senator Christopher Dodd (D.-Conn.) introduced a bill called the "Free Speech Protection Act of 2004"[19] that was designed to create a federal shield law to protect individuals and organizations involved in gathering and disseminating news from being hauled into federal court and forced to disclose their sources or other unpublished information. There was good reason to think that the public would support the measure; a national survey of more than 650 adults conducted in October 2004 on behalf of the First Amendment Center in Nashville, Tenn., found that 72 percent of respondents agreed with the statement that "journalists should be allowed to keep a news source confidential." Although Senator Dodd's bill died when Congress adjourned in December 2004, he reintroduced the measure in 2005 as "The Free Speech Protection Act of 2005."[20] In addition, a different bill called the "Free Flow of Information Act of 2005,"[21] which would take similar measures but would more narrowly define the class of journalists that it would protect, was introduced in the

16. Tucker, "Wen Ho Lee Reporters Held in Contempt."
17. Strupp, "Now Feds Target 'Merc' Reporters."
18. Broder, "From Grand Jury Leaks Comes a Clash of Rights."
19. S. 3020, 108th Cong. (2004).
20. S. 369, 109th Cong. (2005).
21. H.R. 581, 109th Cong. (2005).

U.S. House of Representatives in 2005 by Mike Pence (R.-Ind.) and Rick Boucher (D.-Va.), along with an identical companion Senate bill from Richard Lugar (R.-Ind.).[22] The Pence-Boucher and Lugar bills, as originally proposed, would provide for an absolute privilege to protect the identity of confidential sources, which means that a journalist's right to keep the source's name secret cannot be overcome in any situations by a subpoena. In introducing the Senate version of the bill, Lugar stated in a press release that "it is important that we ensure reporters certain rights and abilities to seek sources and report appropriate information without fear of intimidation or imprisonment. Without such protection, many whistleblowers will refuse to step forward and reporters will be disinclined to provide our constituents with the information that they have a right to know." The measures were still under debate in early 2006.

The Reporters Committee for Freedom of the Press maintains a very helpful link on its Website that is designed "to keep journalists up to date on the federal shield law effort and the other legal controversies involving reporters' subpoenas." It can be found at http://www.rcfp .org/shields_and_subpoenas.html. The RCFP also has an excellent page about shield laws and the reporter's privilege not to testify that is found at http://www.rcfp.org/privilege/index.html.

So why are journalists subject to subpoenas, requests for information and court orders? There are several answers to that question.

So why are journalists subject to subpoenas, requests for information and court orders? There are several answers to that question.

Most journalists are highly efficient information gatherers. Some information that journalists gather is not included in the newspaper stories or television reports they prepare. Sometimes the source of a story doesn't want to be named and asks the reporter to promise not to reveal his or her identity. The obvious example here is the Watergate source known only as Deep Throat until he finally came forward in 2005 to reveal his identity as W. Mark Felt. But reporters are not only efficient gatherers, they are excellent record keepers as well. Unreported material is often retained in notebooks and computer memories, or on videotape and audiotape. For some persons this undisclosed information is important, even vital. Law enforcement officials frequently want to know what a criminal suspect told a journalist during an interview— only parts of which have been published or broadcast. Libel plaintiffs often need to know the identity of the sources used by reporters in preparation of a story in order to try to prove the story was untrue or fabricated or published with malice. Video recordings of a violent demonstration are often useful to police who seek to identify those who incited the violence or committed criminal acts. Hence, reporters are often asked to reveal information they have gathered but chosen not to publish or broadcast. Most of the time journalists comply with such requests. At times, however, they refuse. When this happens, the persons interested in obtaining this information often get a court order or **subpoena** to force the journalist to reveal the name of the news source or to disclose the confidential information. Or government agents may get a **warrant** to search a newsroom or a reporter's home to find the information they want.

In our society the press is supposed to represent a neutral entity as it gathers and publishes news and information. When the government or anyone else intrudes into the newsroom or the reporter's notebook, it compromises this neutrality. A news source who normally trusts journalists may choose not to cooperate with a reporter if government agents can learn the source's name by threatening the reporter with a court order. Television news crews will hardly be welcome at protest rallies if the demonstrators know that the government will use the film to identify and prosecute the protesters. The effectiveness of the reporter as an information

In our society the press is supposed to represent a neutral entity as it gathers and publishes news and information.

22. S. 3440, 109th Cong. (2005).

gatherer may be seriously compromised if government agents or civil and criminal litigants can force journalists to reveal information they choose not to disclose. Society also may ultimately suffer because the flow of information to the public may be reduced.

This chapter is about the problems a reporter can face when government agents or other persons use the power of the judicial system to gain access to the news-gathering processes. We study the problems of source confidentiality and newsroom searches. We also look at recent judicial and legislative attempts to resolve these issues. Finally, we examine the powerful weapon the government may employ to get its way in these disputes: the contempt power.

NEWS AND NEWS SOURCES

If news and information are the lifeblood of the press, then news sources are one of the important wells from which that lifeblood springs. Many journalists are often no better than the sources they can cultivate. News sources come in all shapes and sizes. Occasionally their willingness to cooperate with a reporter is dependent on assurances from the journalist that their identity will not be revealed. Why would a news source wish to remain anonymous? There are many reasons. Often the source of a story about criminal activities has participated in criminal activities and has no desire to publicize this fact. Frequently the source of a story about government mismanagement or dishonesty is an employee of that government agency, and revelation of his or her identity as a whistleblower could result in loss of the job for informing the press of the errors made by the employee's superiors. Some persons simply do not want to get involved in all the hassle that frequently results when an explosive story is published; by remaining anonymous they can remain out of the limelight.

So just how often do journalists use and rely on confidential sources today? A study released in 2005 by the Project for Excellence in Journalism that examined hundreds of news stories published in 16 papers across the United States, including major ones such as The New York Times and the Washington Post, found a significant drop in the use of anonymous sources between 2003 and 2004.[23] Only 7 percent of the stories published in 2004 that were examined as part of the massive content analysis used anonymous sources, compared with 29 percent—more than four times as many—just a year before in 2003. It is unclear why there was such a precipitous drop, but it could be that increased pressure by the government in 2004 to force journalists to reveal their sources in cases such as those described earlier involving Matthew Cooper and Judith Miller are already having a chilling effect on the gathering of news from anonymous sources.

Journalists have always used confidential sources and obtained information that government officials sought to uncover. The earliest reported case of a journalist's refusal to disclose his sources of information took place in 1848 when a reporter for the New York Herald refused to reveal to the U.S. Senate the name of the person who had given him a secret copy of the treaty the United States was negotiating to end the Mexican-American War. He was held in contempt of the Senate and jailed. A U.S. Court of Appeals denied the journalist's petition for release.[24] But the issue of journalists protecting the identity of a confidential source surfaced infrequently

---

23. Seelye, "Fewer Sources Go Nameless in the Press."
24. *Ex parte Nugent,* 16 Fed. Cas. 471 (1848).

in the next 120 years. In fact, from 1911 to 1968 only 17 cases involving a reporter's confidential sources were reported, according to an article in the California Law Review.[25]

There is little mystery as to why the requests to journalists to reveal the names of sources or share confidential information with authorities escalated at the end of the 1960s and into the 1970s. The nation went through a period of great social upheaval, and the press played a significant role in documenting the confrontations between blacks and whites, between war protesters and police, between the mainstream culture and the nascent counterculture. The press was often privy to information that government officials wanted and thought they needed. In 1999 Dan Rather and CBS News producers were told they would have to provide the videotape of an interview the CBS anchorman had with one of the men on trial in Texas for murdering a black man by dragging him behind a pickup truck. Portions of the interview were telecast on "60 Minutes II." Texas authorities wanted to see the entire interview.* The confidential relationship between a journalist and a news source often sparks the interest of authorities who are seeking to discover who leaked confidential information to the press. Leaks, apparently from the office of independent counsel Kenneth Starr, facilitated much of the early reporting about the Clinton-Lewinsky affair. Stopping such "leaks" is given a high priority by others in government. Members of the U.S. Senate grilled reporters Nina Totenberg of National Public Radio and Timothy Phelps of Newsday in early 1992 to try to get them to reveal the names of confidential informants who leaked to them a statement made by law professor Anita Hill during the Senate confirmation hearings for Judge Clarence Thomas. Thomas was being considered for an appointment to the U.S. Supreme Court at the time, and Hill charged the jurist with sexual harassment. The pair of reporters were threatened with subpoenas and possible contempt charges for failing to cooperate. But leadership in the Senate finally abandoned the quest for the information, letting Totenberg and Phelps off the hook.

GROUNDS CITED BY NEWS ORGANIZATIONS FOR SUCCESSFUL CHALLENGE OF SUBPOENA

Shield law	54%
Constitutional privilege	18%
Information not needed	31%
Other sources for same information	31%
Lack of relevance	18%
Order too broad	33%
Other	1%

Note: Figures total more than 100 percent because more than one reason was cited in several cases.

Source: Agents of Discovery, 2003.

---

*When Texas judicial authorities threatened to put a news producer in jail and the appellate courts rejected the television network's requests for help, CBS agreed to provide the material sought by the court.
25. "The Newsman's Privilege," 1198.

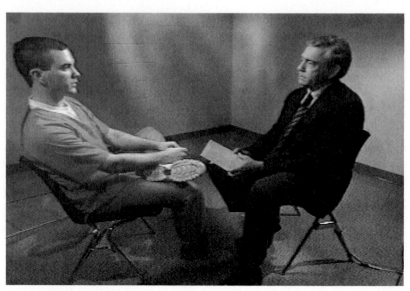

Courtesy CBS News/60 Minutes II.

Law enforcement officials frequently try to gain access to information generated by journalists, as Texas authorities did when CBS News reporter Dan Rather interviewed this murder suspect.

A 2003 study conducted by the Reporters Committee on Freedom of the Press examined reporter-source problems during 2001.[26] The data revealed that television stations received more subpoenas than newspapers. Criminal litigation generated 56 percent of all subpoenas; civil cases spawned about 36 percent (see Figure 10.1). The great bulk of subpoenas issued to the news media were generated by state court proceedings. Only 9 percent were issued in connection with proceedings in federal court. The press fully complied with about 68 percent of all subpoenas issued; that is, they gave the authorities the information that was sought. The remaining subpoenas were either voluntarily withdrawn by the party seeking the information or were challenged in court. About 67 subpoenas were challenged by the press in 2001, and journalists succeeded in getting about 75 percent of these quashed, or set aside (see box). Finally, the vast majority of the subpoenas were issued for nonconfidential information. Typically in this era reporters and photographers are more commonly called on to reveal what they saw as eyewitnesses or to share videotapes or photographs that were generated without any promise of confidentiality to anyone.

A journalist served with a subpoena has few options. The reporter or news organization can cooperate with those who seek the information and reveal what it is they want to know. This cooperation could damage the reporter/source relationship or threaten the image of independence fostered by most news media. The journalist can seek to have the subpoena withdrawn or attack the order in court and hope to have it quashed. Going to court can be expensive and is time-consuming. The statistic cited earlier, that 75 percent of the subpoenas challenged by the press are quashed, is deceptive. The press usually only challenges a court order when it thinks it can win. Of the 823 subpoenas reported in the 2003 study, only about 6 percent were actually quashed. Another 19 percent were ultimately withdrawn. If in the end

26. *Agents of Discovery,* 2003.

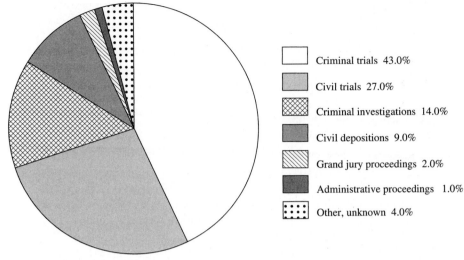

Criminal trials 43.0%

Civil trials 27.0%

Criminal investigations 14.0%

Civil depositions 9.0%

Grand jury proceedings 2.0%

Administrative proceedings 1.0%

Other, unknown 4.0%

Source: Agents of Discovery, 2003.

▼FIGURE 10.1

Kind of proceeding or process that generates subpoenas to reporters.

the journalist refuses to cooperate, he or she will likely be held in contempt of court. A fine and a jail sentence usually follow. So the choice for the journalist is not an easy one.

But the choice for society is difficult as well. The interests that are involved in this dilemma are basic to our system of government and political values. On the one hand, it is clearly the obligation of every citizen to cooperate with the government and testify before the proper authorities. This concept was so well-established by the early 18th century that it had become a maxim. John Henry Wigmore, in his classic treatise on evidence, cites the concept thus: "The public has a right to everyman's evidence."[27] The Sixth Amendment to the U.S. Constitution guarantees the right to have witnesses and to compel them to testify in our behalf. And surely this right is a valuable one, both to society and to the individual seeking to prove his or her innocence of charges of wrongdoing. The Supreme Court in 1919 wrote on the duties and rights of witnesses:

> [I]t is clearly recognized that the giving of testimony and the attendance upon court or grand jury in order to testify are public duties which every-one within the jurisdiction of the government is bound to perform upon being properly summoned, . . . the personal sacrifice involved is a part of the necessary contribution to the public welfare.[28]

But society surely benefits from the information provided by the news media. Many believe that when a reporter is forced to break a promise of confidentiality or is used as an arm of law enforcement investigators, it harms this flow of information. People who know things, often important things, simply won't give this information to journalists for fear of being exposed if the reporter is squeezed for the information. The fragile reporter/source relationship may be damaged.

27. Wigmore, *Anglo-American System of Evidence.*
28. *Blair* v. *U.S.,* 250 U.S. 273 (1919).

> ### TIPS FOR REPORTERS ON PROMISING CONFIDENTIALITY
>
> Here are some suggestions that were given by newspaper attorney David Utevsky to reporters and writers at a seminar in Seattle.
>
> - Do not routinely promise confidentiality as a standard interview technique.
> - Avoid giving an absolute promise of confidentiality. Try to persuade the source to agree that you may reveal his or her name if you are subpoenaed.
> - Do not rely exclusively on information from a confidential source. Get corroboration from a nonconfidential source or documents.
> - Consider whether others (police, attorneys, etc.) will want to know the identity of the source before publishing or broadcasting the material. Will you be the only source of this information, or can they get it elsewhere?
> - Consider whether you can use the information without disclosing that it was obtained from a confidential source.
>
> Reporters should always consult with a supervisor or editor before promising anonymity to a source; if a legal action results the journalist will have to rely on the news outlet to assist in defending the action.

The reporter's privilege that emerged during the past three decades is hardly a nice, neat, legal proposition.

As more and more reporters were called on to cooperate with legal authorities during the last 40 years, the courts and state legislatures were asked to fashion protection for both the legal system and the press. What was needed were rules that required the reporter to share valuable information with the parties that needed it, but only in those rare circumstances when severe harm might result without this cooperation. These rules are called the reporter's privilege. Such a privilege is not a novelty in the law. A variation of this privilege is given to doctors, lawyers, members of the clergy and even accountants in some instances. The reporter's privilege that emerged in the past three decades is hardly a nice, neat, legal proposition. The source of the privilege varies from jurisdiction to jurisdiction. In some places its genesis is in the U.S. or state constitution; in other places it flows from the common law or state statute. The scope of the privilege also varies from jurisdiction to jurisdiction. A reporter in Michigan may be legally immune from a certain kind of subpoena, whereas her counterpart in Ohio may not enjoy the same immunity. What follows is a general outline of the broad provisions of the privilege, focusing especially on the rights that spring from the First Amendment. To be safe a journalist should know the specific law in his or her own state. An excellent online resource for the rules of each state that is prepared by the Reporters Committee for Freedom of the Press is called "The Reporter's Privilege." It can be found on the Web site of the Reporters Committee for Freedom of the Press at http://www.rcfp.org/privilege/index.html and is billed by that organization as "a complete compendium of information on the reporter's privilege—the right not to be compelled to testify or disclose sources and information in court—in each state and federal circuit."

THE FAILURE TO KEEP A PROMISE

Many journalists are reluctant to reveal the names of their sources because they think it would be unethical or would diminish their ability to use the source at some point in the future. About 15 years ago reporters discovered another reason to protect the identity of a source. They could be sued it they broke their promise of confidentiality.

This story begins in Minnesota more than 20 years ago, in the last days of a political campaign. In 1982 Dan Cohen, who was closely associated with the Republican campaign for the governorship of Minnesota, approached reporters for both the Minneapolis Star and Tribune and the St. Paul Pioneer Press Dispatch and said he would give them previously unpublicized information about Marlene Johnson, the Democratic-Farmer-Labor candidate for lieutenant governor. All the reporters had to do was to promise never to reveal Cohen's name when asked where they got the information. The reporters agreed and Cohen supplied them with 12- and 13-year-old court records showing that Johnson had been arrested for unlawful assembly (she was at a protest rally) and that she had been convicted of petty theft for leaving a store without paying for $6 worth of sewing goods (the conviction was later vacated).

Editors at both newspapers decided to publish the information about the candidate, but because the election was just days away, they felt it was necessary to include Cohen's name as the source of the information to give readers the opportunity to evaluate the charges against Johnson. When Cohen's name was published, he lost his job. He angrily sued for breach of contract, claiming he and the reporters had entered into a contractual agreement when he provided the information for a promise of confidentiality. A Minnesota trial court agreed and awarded the public relations man $200,000 in compensatory damages and $500,000 in punitive damages. The Minnesota Court of Appeals affirmed the conviction but threw out the punitive damages, saying Cohen had failed to prove fraud in this case, the only claim that would permit a punitive damage award.[29] The Minnesota Supreme Court reversed the conviction. The state high court said the agreement between Cohen and the reporters was not an enforceable contract. The plaintiffs had raised an alternative theory of law at the oral argument, the doctrine of promissory estoppel. The high court said it was unnecessary to consider whether the agreement between Cohen and the reporters was governed by this doctrine, because enforcement of the doctrine would violate the First Amendment.[30]

Cohen appealed to the Supreme Court of the United States, which in June 1991 reversed the Minnesota Supreme Court ruling and told the state court to reconsider whether the doctrine of promissory estoppel did in fact apply in this case. Enforcement of this doctrine, wrote Justice Byron White, would not violate the First Amendment. "Generally applicable laws [that is, laws that can be applied to all citizens equally] do not offend the First Amendment simply because their enforcement against the press has incidental effects on its ability to gather and report the news." Here, White added, "Minnesota law simply requires those making promises to keep them."[31] A year later the Minnesota Supreme Court awarded Cohen $200,000 in damages in his suit against the newspapers.[32]

---

29. *Cohen* v. *Cowles Media Co.,* 445 N.W. 2d 248 (1989).
30. *Cohen* v. *Cowles Media Co.,* 457 N.W. 2d 199 (1990).
31. *Cohen* v. *Cowles Media Co.,* 111 S. Ct. 2513 (1991).
32. *Cohen* v. *Cowles Media Co.,* 479 N.W. 2d 387 (1992).

Promissory estoppel is an old Anglo-American legal rule that was promulgated to prevent injustice when someone fails to keep a promise that he or she has made, a promise that by itself does not add up to an enforceable contract, but a promise someone else has relied on. It is typically codified in the common law in words like these: "A promise that the promisor reasonably expects to induce reliance and that does induce reliance is binding if injustice can be avoided only by enforcement of the promise." To prevail in an action for promissory estoppel the plaintiff is usually required to show

1. *that the defendant made a clear and definite promise to the plaintiff;*
2. *that the defendant intended to induce the plaintiff's reliance on that promise;*
3. *that the plaintiff, in fact, reasonably relied on that promise to his or her detriment and harm; and*
4. *that the promise must be enforced by the court in the interests of justice to the plaintiff.*

Imagine a journalist tries to convince a lab technician at a chemical company to reveal specific information that proves that her employer is polluting a nearby stream. She is reluctant; she fears she will be fired if her cooperation with the reporter is discovered. But the reporter presses her and clearly promises that he will never, under any circumstance, reveal her name if she gives him the information. The story is published. The employee is subsequently fired after the reporter provides her name to a state legislative committee investigating the pollution. She then could bring an action for promissory estoppel.

In the immediate wake of the *Cohen* ruling another lawsuit began in Minnesota in which a woman named Jill Ruzicka sued Glamour magazine. The periodical published an article on therapist-patient sexual abuse that included an interview with Ruzicka, who had previously sued both her therapist and the state agency whose job it was to regulate such practitioners. Ruzicka agreed to be interviewed on the condition that she not be identified. She wasn't named in the article, but she argued that the reporter's description of her story made her identity obvious to most readers. The case made several stops in federal courts[33] before the 8th U.S. Circuit Court of Appeals ordered a lower court to hold a trial. The appellate judges said that the promise to shield Ruzicka's identity was definite enough under state law to support an action for promissory estoppel. The court said that because the magazine editors had added identifying details to the description of Ruzicka after she had approved the original draft of the article, a jury could find that the magazine had failed to keep its promise not to disclose the plaintiff's identity.[34]

Although other promissory estoppel lawsuits have been reported in the past decade,[35] the firestorm of litigation that some observers predicted has never materialized. It is exceedingly difficult for a plaintiff to win such a lawsuit; indeed, some jurisdictions don't even recognize the cause of action. In 2000 a woman named Julie Steele brought a lawsuit for promissory estoppel (and a variety of other legal claims) against Newsweek reporter Michael Isikoff and the Washington Post (which owns Newsweek) based on what she claimed was the

33. *Ruzicka* v. *Conde Nast Publications, Inc.,* 939 F. 2d 578 (1991), 774 F. Supp. 303 (1992).
34. *Ruzicka* v. *Conde Nast Publications, Inc.,* 999 F. 2d 1319 (1993).
35. See *Anderson* v. *Strong Memorial Hospital,* 573 N.Y.S. 2d 828 (1991) and *Morgan* v. *Calender,* 780 F. Supp. 307 (1992).

reporter's failure to honor a promise not to reveal her name as the source of information about Kathleen Willey, a woman who reportedly figured in the Clinton administration sex scandal. A U.S. District Court in Virginia dismissed the promissory estoppel action, noting that the state did not recognize the cause of action.[36]

Perhaps the most significant recent opinion in this area was handed down in 2005 by the 6th U.S. Circuit Court of Appeals in a case called *Ventura* v. *Cincinnati Enquirer*.[37] Plaintiff George G. Ventura sued the newspaper and its publisher, the massive conglomerate Gannett Co., for causes of action including breach of contract and promissory estoppel. Ventura claimed that Enquirer reporters disclosed his identity as a confidential news source to a grand jury investigating the illegal news-gathering actions of one of the paper's reporters, Michael Gallagher. Specifically, Ventura had entered into an agreement in 1997 with Gallagher, who was then working on an exposé of Chiquita Brands International, Inc. Ventura, an attorney, had worked as legal counsel for the massive firm best known for its bananas, but he had left under what the appellate court described as "less than amicable circumstances." Ventura thus agreed to give Gallagher, under a promise of confidentiality, private passwords and secret access codes to Chiquita's internal voice-mail systems. Gallagher then used the passwords and codes to illegally invade the Chiquita voice-mail system—conduct for which Gallagher was both fired by the Enquirer and subpoenaed to testify before a grand jury. It was during this testimony that Gallagher provided to the grand jury tape recordings of telephone conversations he had with Ventura regarding Chiquita's voice-mail system. The tape recordings supplied by Gallagher ultimately led, in part, to the indictment of Ventura on multiple counts of attempted unauthorized access to a computer system. Ventura, however, sought civil redress from Gallagher, the Enquirer and Gannett, claiming the disclosure of the tapes to the grand jury violated his confidentiality agreement with Gallagher. Ventura, however, would lose his civil lawsuit.

In sustaining the trial court's grant of summary judgment in favor of the Enquirer and against Ventura on causes of action breach of contract and promissory estoppel, the 6th Circuit found that "Ohio public policy precludes enforcement of agreements to conceal a crime where, as here, the plaintiff [Ventura] is effectively urging the court to enforce an agreement he reached with a co-conspirator [Gallagher] to withhold evidence of plaintiff's crimes." The appellate court determined that "that public policy precludes the plaintiff from enforcing any promise by Gallagher to conceal the plaintiff's criminal activity." Put differently, the 6th Circuit recognized an absolute privilege or immunity for Gallagher to give up Ventura's name without facing civil liability because such a privilege "will encourage the reporting of criminal activity by removing any threat of reprisal in the form of civil liability. This, in turn, will aid in the proper investigation of criminal activity and the prosecution of those responsible for the crime."

What does all of this mean? If—and that's a very big if—other courts adopt the logic of the 6th U.S. Circuit Court of Appeals, the outcome in *Ventura* v. *Cincinnati Enquirer* suggests that reporters may be free to breach agreements of confidentiality to sources, without fear of civil liability, but only if they are revealing the names of the confidential sources to a prosecutor in a grand jury setting. The 6th Circuit's decision only examined the public policy of one state—Ohio—and reporters should not assume that the holding will be stretched to other jurisdictions.

---

36. *Steele* v. *Isikoff*, 28 M.L.R. 2630 (2000).
37. 396 F. 3d 784 (6th Cir. 2005).

**TIPS FOR REPORTERS WHEN CONFRONTED WITH
A SOURCE WHO DEMANDS CONFIDENTIALITY**

1. Assume the interview is on the record unless the subject seeks anonymity.

2. There is no obligation to grant anonymity for information that has already been provided.

3. Before making any promise to a source, try to find something out about the information and where it comes from.

4. Talk with an editor or news director before making any promises to a source.

5. Keep any promise made to a source simple and easy to fulfill, and be certain both you and the source completely understand the conditions to which you have agreed.

6. Record any promise you make to a source.

7. Avoid adding material to a story that a source has already approved, or try to avoid promising the source that he or she has story approval.

CONSTITUTIONAL PROTECTION OF NEWS SOURCES

In 1972 the Supreme Court of the United States ruled, in a 5-4 decision, that there was no privilege under the First Amendment for journalists to refuse to reveal the names of confidential sources or other information when called to testify before a grand jury.[38] This ruling is the last word the nation's high court has spoken on the subject. It was recently upheld by the United States Court of Appeals for the District of Columbia Circuit in the high-profile case of *In Re: Grand Jury Subpoena, Judith Miller,* 397 F. 3d 964 (2005), when the appellate court wrote that "the Supreme Court decided in *Branzburg* that there is no First Amendment privilege protecting journalists from appearing before a grand jury or from testifying before a grand jury or otherwise providing evidence to a grand jury regardless of any confidence promised by the reporter to any source. The Highest Court has spoken and never revisited the question. Without doubt, that is the end of the matter." Yet today, a limited constitutional protection as well as common law protection, has been applied by federal appeals courts and federal district courts in many parts of the nation. The story of how judges in many of the lower and intermediate federal courts rewrote the *Branzburg* ruling is an example of the pragmatic genius of American law.

The Supreme Court consolidated three similar cases when it first faced the question of whether journalists could find a privilege in the First Amendment to permit them to refuse to testify when called before a grand jury. One case involved Paul Branzburg, a reporter for the Louisville Courier-Journal. Branzburg was called to testify in 1971 about drug use in Kentucky after he wrote two stories about drugs and drug dealers in the area. In the second case, Paul Pappas, a television reporter for a Massachusetts television station, was called before a grand

---

38. *Branzburg* v. *Hayes,* 408 U.S. 665 (1972).

jury to relate what he had seen and heard when he spent three hours at a Black Panther head-quarters in July 1970. Finally, New York Times reporter Earl Caldwell was subpoenaed to appear before a grand jury investigating the activities of the Black Panthers in Oakland, Calif. Caldwell, an African-American, had gained the confidence of the leaders of the militant group and had consistently written illuminating stories about the Panthers that demonstrated an astute awareness of their activities. The decisions in the three cases are referred to collectively as the *Branzburg* ruling.

In two instances—*Branzburg* and *Pappas*—lower courts had rejected arguments that the First Amendment provided a privilege for the reporters, a privilege that would permit them to refuse to testify. In *Caldwell,* however, the U.S. Court of Appeals for the 9th Circuit ruled that forcing the journalist to even appear before a grand jury could damage the public's First Amendment right to be informed. The court therefore found that journalists enjoyed a qualified privilege that protected them when called to testify about confidential information. The government must show a compelling need for the witness's presence in order to overcome this privilege, the court ruled.[39]

The Supreme Court fractured into three groups in deciding this case. Four justices, led by Byron White, who wrote the court's opinion, ruled that there was no First Amendment privilege for reporters called to testify before a grand jury. White said that although the court was sensitive to First Amendment considerations, the case did not present any such considerations. There were no prior restraints, no limitations on what the press might publish, and no order for the press to publish information it did not wish to. No penalty for publishing certain content was imposed. White wrote:

> The use of confidential sources by the press is not forbidden or restricted. . . .
>
> The sole issue before us is the obligation of reporters to respond to grand jury subpoenas as other citizens do and answer questions relevant to an investigation into the commission of crime. Citizens generally are not constitutionally immune from grand jury subpoenas; and neither the First Amendment nor other constitutional provisions protect the average citizen from the disclosing to a grand jury information that he has received in confidence.[40]

Reporters are no better than average citizens, White concluded.

The four dissenters differed sharply with the other justices. Justice William O. Douglas took the view that the First Amendment protection provides the press with an absolute and unqualified privilege. In any circumstance, under any condition, the reporter should be able to shield the identity of a confidential source. Justices Potter Stewart, William Brennan, and Thurgood Marshall were unwilling to go as far as Justice Douglas and instead proposed that reporters should be protected by a privilege that is qualified, not absolute. These three dissenters argued that the reporter should be able to protect the identity of the confidential source unless the government can show the following:

1. That there is a probable cause to believe that the reporter has information that is clearly relevant to a specific violation of the law

---

39. *Caldwell* v. *United States,* 434 F. 2d 1081 (1970).
40. *Branzburg* v. *Hayes,* 408 U.S. 665 (1972).

2. That the information sought cannot be obtained by alternative means less destructive of First Amendment rights

3. That the state has a compelling and overriding interest in the information

When the government cannot fulfill all three requirements, Justice Stewart wrote for the dissenters, the journalist should not be forced to testify.

Justice Lewis Powell provided the fifth vote needed for the court to reject the notion of a constitutional privilege for reporters. But while Powell voted with those who could find no privilege in the First Amendment, his brief concurring opinion seemed to support the opposite proposition. "The Court does not hold that newsmen, subpoenaed to testify before a grand jury, are without constitutional rights with respect to the gathering of news or in safeguarding their sources," he wrote. No harassment of reporters will be allowed, and a balance must be struck between freedom of the press and the obligation of all citizens to give relevant testimony. "In short, the courts will be available to newsmen under circumstances where legitimate First Amendment interests require protection," Powell wrote. Two years later, in a footnote in another case, *Saxbe* v. *Washington Post,*[41] Powell emphasized that the high court's ruling in *Branzburg* was an extremely narrow one and that reporters were not without First Amendment rights to protect the identity of their sources.

LOWER-COURT RULINGS

Most lower federal courts have treated the high court's decision in Branzburg *as the very narrow ruling that Justice Powell said it was in 1974.*

Most lower federal courts have treated the high court's decision in *Branzburg* as the very narrow ruling that Justice Powell said it was in 1974. The *Branzburg* ruling focused on a reporter's responsibility to testify before a grand jury. And that is generally how the lower courts have applied the precedent, granting reporters a qualified right to refuse testimony in other kinds of circumstances. Note the language from the 3rd U.S. Circuit Court of Appeals in a 1979 ruling, which characterized *Branzburg* in this fashion:

> There (in *Branzburg*), the Supreme Court decided that a journalist does not have an absolute privilege under the First Amendment to refuse to appear and testify before a grand jury to answer questions relevant to an investigation of the commission of a crime. No Supreme Court case since that decision has extended the holding beyond that which was necessary to vindicate the public interest in law enforcement and ensuing effective grand jury proceedings.[42]

Not all the U.S. Courts of Appeals have looked at *Branzburg* in such an expansive manner. In 1998 a panel of judges in the 5th Circuit wrote:

> Although some courts have taken from Justice Powell's concurrence a mandate to construct a broad, qualified news reporters' privilege in criminal cases, we decline to do so. Justice Powell's separate writing only emphasizes that at a certain point, the First Amendment must protect the press from government intrusion.[43]

41. 417 U.S. 843 (1974).
42. *Riley* v. *Chester,* 612 F. 2d 708 (1979).
43. *U.S.* v. *Smith,* 135 F. 2d 363 (1998); see also *WTHR-TV* v. *Cline,* 693 N.E. 2d 1 (1998).

The court went on to require a television station to surrender the unaired portions of a video-tape interview with a man accused of arson.

Ten of 12 of the U.S. appeals courts have ruled that the First Amendment provides at least limited protection for reporters who are asked to testify or produce photos or other materials at hearings other than grand jury proceedings.* The 6th U.S. Circuit Court of Appeals (Kentucky, Michigan, Ohio and Tennessee) rejected this notion in 1987. "Because we conclude that acceptance of the position . . . would be tantamount to our substituting, as a holding in *Branzburg,* the dissent written by Justice Stewart, we must reject that position. . . . That portion of Justice Powell's opinion certainly does not warrant rewriting the majority opinion to grant a First Amendment testimonial privilege to news reporters," the court ruled.[44] And the 7th Circuit Court of Appeals (Illinois, Indiana and Wisconsin), in an August 2003 opinion called *McKevitt* v. *Pallasch,* 339 F. 3d 530 (2003), that was authored by the prominent Judge Richard Posner, skeptically questioned the existence of a federal reporter's privilege in the context of a case involving nonconfidential sources. Judge Posner wrote that when the information in a reporter's possession does not come from a confidential source, it is difficult to see what possible bearing the First Amendment could have on the question of compelled disclosure. He articulated a test for this situation that simply requires an analysis of whether the service of a subpoena is reasonable in the circumstances. While the ultimate impact of this decision is yet unclear, one thing definitely is certain: It represents a substantial rethinking of the *Branzburg* decision by an extremely well-respected jurist. In the year following Judge Posner's opinion suggesting that the First Amendment does not provide journalists with any form of special protection against having to answer subpoenas, there were only two district court opinions that applied the reasonable-in-the-circumstances standard adopted in *McKevitt*—too few opinions from which to draw any conclusions. Thirty-one of the United States have enacted a statutory protection called a **shield law** that offers reporters some protection against being forced to reveal the identities of confidential sources. (See page 449 for a list of those states.) Appellate courts in nearly all of the remaining 19 states have recognized various kinds of constitutional or common-law testimonial privileges for reporters.

The constitutional privilege has considerable elasticity. Its successful application depends on several factors. What kind of proceeding is involved? The privilege is more readily granted to a journalist involved in a civil suit than to one called to testify before a grand jury. What kind of material is sought? A journalist is more likely to be protected by the privilege when the name of a confidential source is sought than when courts are seeking testimony about information that is not confidential or about events actually witnessed by the reporter. Finally, testimonial privilege derived by both federal and state courts through the Constitution or the common law is qualified by the various tests that courts have developed, tests that usually mirror the one outlined by Justice Stewart in *Branzburg.* Is the information important? Is it clearly relevant to the proceedings? Is there somewhere else to get the information? It is important to remember that without a binding Supreme Court ruling, the lower federal and state courts have been permitted

---

*The 5th U.S. Circuit Court of Appeals is included among the 10 because, despite the 1998 ruling in *U.S.* v. *Smith,* judges in the circuit have ruled that a privilege exists at least for civil suits. (See, for example, *Miller* v. *Transamerican Press, Inc.,* 621 F. 2nd 721 [1980]). The 1998 decision did not reject these earlier rulings, but argued that because a criminal case was at issue, a different standard should apply.
44. *Storer Communications* v. *Giovan,* 810 F. 2d 580 (1987).

to fashion their own rules; and there is distinct variance from state to state, federal circuit to federal circuit. Look to the court precedents in your region as the final authority in this matter.

Civil Cases

A reporter could be called to testify in three different kinds of court proceedings: a civil lawsuit, a criminal case or a grand jury. Courts are most likely to recognize the right of a journalist to refuse to testify in a civil action, and least likely to recognize this right if the reporter is called before a grand jury. Recognition of the privilege in civil cases came only a year after the *Branzburg* ruling, when a U.S. District Court in Washington, D.C., quashed a subpoena issued to reporters from a variety of newspapers and magazines who were thought to have materials obtained during their coverage of the Watergate break-in. The materials were sought by members of the Democratic National Committee who were suing to win damages from some of the Watergate burglars.[45] The court said that reporters had at least a qualified privilege under the First Amendment to refuse to answer such questions or provide such material. Four years later the 10th U.S. Circuit Court of Appeals ruled that filmmaker Arthur Hirsch could not be forced to reveal confidential information he had obtained in connection with a civil suit by the estate of Karen Silkwood against the Kerr-McGee Corporation.[46] Silkwood died mysteriously in an auto accident after she threatened to expose improper safety conditions at the nuclear facility at which she worked. Hirsch was preparing a documentary film on Karen Silkwood's life and death.

In a typical civil suit, the court will ask three questions when deciding whether to force the reporter to testify:

1. Has the person seeking the information from the reporter—normally the plaintiff—shown that this information is of *certain relevance* in the case? It must be related to the matter before the court.
2. Does this information go to the heart of the issue before the court? That is, is it critical to the outcome of the case?
3. Can the person who wants the information show the court that there is no other source for this information?

If all three questions are answered yes, the chances are good that the court will require the reporter to reveal the confidential information. How rigorously the judge applies this test often depends on the reporter's relationship to the lawsuit. If the reporter is not a party to the lawsuit but merely has information that may be of value to one or both parties, a judge typically applies the test very rigorously and normally the journalist will not be required to testify. But that is not always the case. In 1996 a federal judge in Connecticut ruled that a reporter had to testify in a securities case as to whether one of the defendants had actually made the statements that were attributed to him in a newspaper article written by the reporter.[47] The judge ruled that the testimony sought was directly relevant to the case and was unavailable from another source. The court also noted that it was not seeking information about a confidential

---

45. *Democratic National Committee* v. *McCord,* 356 F. Supp. 1394 (1973).
46. *Silkwood* v. *Kerr-McGee,* 563 F. 2d 433 (1977).
47. *SEC* v. *Seahawk Deep Ocean Technology, Inc.,* 166 F.R.D. 268 (1996).

source. If the reporter is a party in the lawsuit, either as a plaintiff or a defendant, courts are less willing to let the journalist off the hook. In these instances it is more likely, but still not common, for the court to require the reporter to cooperate.

There is but a single recorded case in which a reporter who was a plaintiff in the case was asked to testify and refused. Columnist Jack Anderson sued former President Richard Nixon and other former administration officials in 1978 for trying to deprive him of his civil rights. His lawsuit was founded on reports he said he received from confidential informants, but when asked by the defendants to reveal the names of these informants, Anderson refused. The court ruled that the columnist could not have things both ways. "He cannot ask for justice and deny it to those he accuses."[48] Anderson was forced to withdraw his lawsuit when he refused to testify.

Reporters far more commonly find themselves as defendants in lawsuits, typically a libel suit. Oftentimes the plaintiff seeks to know about sources the reporter used to prepare the libelous story, or where and how the reporter got information for the libelous story. Whether the court will force the reporter to testify in such instances usually depends on several factors, all of which are related to the three-part test outlined earlier. A plaintiff will often be required to show that the information held by the reporter goes to the very heart of the lawsuit. For example, the plaintiff may have to show that he or she cannot possibly prove negligence or actual malice (see pages 219–234 to refresh your memory on these matters) without information from the reporter.[49] Or, the court will require that the plaintiff show that the libel claim actually has merit, that it is not simply an attempt to harass the defendant.[50] Finally, the court will usually require the plaintiff to show that there is no other source for this information, that the plaintiff has exhausted all other potential means of gaining this information. In 1979 the U.S. Supreme Court ruled that it was not an infringement of the reporters' First Amendment rights for the defendant to ask reporters what they were thinking about as they prepared the libelous story.[51] Such questions may or may not involve confidential sources.

The reporter who refuses to obey a court order and give the plaintiff critical information in a libel suit surely faces a **contempt of court** charge and potentially a fine and a jail sentence. But that is not all. In a few cases when a reporter has refused to reveal his or her source for a libelous story, the court has ruled as a matter of law that no source for the story exists.[52] This declaration effectively strips away the libel defense for a newspaper or broadcasting station. In effect, the judge is saying that the reporter made up the story. This is not a common occurrence, but it certainly is a frightening one.

For instance, in the case of *Ayash* v. *Dana-Farber Cancer Institute*[53] the Supreme Judicial Court of Massachusetts in 2005 affirmed a default judgment against The Boston Globe in a libel suit because the newspaper failed to disclose confidential sources. In this lawsuit Dr. Lois J. Ayash of the Dana-Farber Cancer Institute alleged that The Globe published a series of scathing and inaccurate articles in 1995 written by reporter Richard A. Knox about

48. *Anderson* v. *Nixon et al.,* 444 F. Supp. 1195 (1978).
49. *Cervantes* v. *Time,* 446 F. 2d 986 (1972).
50. *Senear* v. *Daily Journal-American,* 641 P. 2d 1180 (1982).
51. *Herbert* v. *Lando,* 441 U.S. 153 (1979).
52. See *Downing* v. *Monitor Publishing,* 415 A. 2d 683 (1980) and *Sierra Life* v. *Magic Valley Newspapers,* 623 P. 2d 103 (1980).
53. 822 N.E. 2d 667; 33 M.L.R. 1513 (Mass. 2005).

Ayash's treatment of several patients who allegedly were given overdoses of a highly toxic chemotherapy drug, thereby destroying the doctor's reputation. One article even ran under the blunt (and, if false, defamatory) headline "Doctor's Orders Killed Cancer Patient" (remember from Chapter 4 and the description from the case involving Kato Kaelin that, if false, headlines can form the basis for a libel suit). During the discovery stage of the litigation, Ayash sought the identities of sources consulted by Knox before writing articles that were subsequently published in The Globe and that formed, at least in part, the basis of the doctor's lawsuit. At the trial court level, The Globe had refused to provide information that would lead to the identities of Knox's confidential sources, despite a court order to disclose their identities. Massachusetts is one of 19 states that does not have a shield law giving some protection to reporters against disclosure of confidential information (see pages 449–452). A judgment of civil contempt was entered by the trial court judge against The Globe and Knox and, in turn, the judge awarded a pretrial judgment against them. A jury was allowed to determine damages and it meted out a whopping $2.1 million award to Ayash. In particular, the jury gave the doctor $1.68 million against The Globe ($240,000 in economic damages and $1.44 million in emotional distress damages) and $420,000 against Knox ($60,000 in economic damages and $360,000 in emotional distress damages).

In affirming both the default judgment and the damage award, the Massachusetts high court noted that "the Globe defendants had no special constitutional or statutory testimonial privilege, based on their status as a newspaper publisher or reporter, that would justify their refusal to obey the orders." It agreed with the trial court judge's determination that "the plaintiff's need for the requested information outweighed the public interest in the protection of the free flow of information to the press." The Massachusetts high court's decision affirming the award sparked renewed discussion in that state's legislature in 2005 about the need to join the majority of states and adopt a shield law to protect reporters such as Richard Knox from making the uncomfortable choice between either breaching promises of confidentiality to their sources or facing entry of default judgments with potentially devastating jury awards.

Finally, the 9th U.S. Circuit Court of Appeals handed down an important ruling in mid-1993 when it extended the reporter's privilege in a civil suit to the authors of books as well. Typically the privilege has been granted to so-called working journalists, salaried employees of newspapers, magazines and broadcasting stations. Free-lance writers like book authors were often denied the protection. The case involved a defamation action between Leonard Shoen, the founder of the U-Haul Corporation, and his sons, Mark and Edward. The libel case was an offshoot of a long-running and highly acrimonious fight among these family members over control of the company. Ronald Watkins, an author of books on topical and controversial subjects, was working on a manuscript about the family feud. He was subpoenaed to testify regarding his interviews with Leonard Shoen, but he refused, citing the First Amendment privilege among other reasons. The lower court rejected his argument and, when Watkins still refused to testify, held the author in contempt of court.

The Court of Appeals reversed the lower-court order. The court ruled that a book author clearly had a right to invoke the First Amendment privilege.[54] "The journalist's privilege is designed to protect investigative reporting regardless of the medium used to report the news to the public," Judge Norris wrote. And there was no question that when Watkins was

54. *Shoen* v. *Shoen,* 5 F. 3d 1289 (1993).

gathering information as he interviewed Leonard Shoen, he intended to disseminate it to the public. The plaintiff raised the issue that Watkins had not given a promise of confidentiality when he interviewed the elder Shoen. Judge Norris said that fact was not controlling. The privilege could apply even in the absence of a promise of confidentiality. It is simply one factor to be considered when all the interests are balanced. In this case the plaintiffs failed to show that they exhausted other potential sources for the same information. Why didn't they talk directly with Leonard Shoen, the court asked. This factor alone meant that the plaintiffs had failed to demonstrate sufficient cause to overcome the First Amendment protection afforded Watkins, Judge Norris said.

Criminal Cases

Courts have granted the First Amendment privilege to reporters quite freely in civil actions in part, at least, because there is no competing constitutional right involved. In a criminal case, however, the privilege for the reporter must be balanced against the Sixth Amendment right of the defendant to compel testimony on his or her behalf. Consequently, it is somewhat less likely that a court will permit a reporter to refuse to answer questions about the identity of a confidential source or other confidential information. Courts most often apply slight variations of the Stewart test from the *Branzburg* case (see pages 428–430) to determine whether the journalist will be compelled to testify.

In a criminal case, the privilege for the reporter must be balanced against the Sixth Amendment right of the defendant to compel testimony on his or her behalf.

In *U.S.* v. *Burke,* for example, the defendant was indicted for conspiracy in connection with a basketball point-shaving scheme at Boston College and attempted to impeach the testimony of the prosecution's chief witness, a reputed underworld figure. The defendant asked the court to subpoena the unpublished notes and drafts of Sports Illustrated reporter Douglas Looney, who had interviewed the witness. The U.S. Court of Appeals for the 2nd Circuit quashed the subpoena, noting that a court may order reporters to reveal confidential sources only when the information is (1) highly material and relevant, (2) necessary or critical to the defense, and (3) unobtainable from other sources.[55]

This same test was applied in a New York case relating to the trial of mob boss John Gotti. Bruce Cutler had served as Gotti's attorney until he was disqualified by the court. Prior to Cutler's disqualification, the court had warned all lawyers in the case to refrain from making out-of-court statements about the highly publicized trial. During the course of the trial, and after his disqualification, Cutler made comments about the case that were published in newspapers and broadcast on television. Cutler was charged with criminal contempt of court for violating the court order. Before his jury trial Cutler subpoenaed several reporters, seeking their notes, video outtakes and other materials. The journalists sought to quash the subpoena, but the 2nd U.S. Circuit Court of Appeals said that Cutler could have limited access to some of these materials because it constituted the only significant evidence he had to defend the charge of contempt that had been levied against him. In other words, the material he sought was relevant, unobtainable from other sources, and critical to his defense.[56]

In 1984 the Washington state Supreme Court ruled that an Everett (Wash.) Herald reporter did not have to reveal the names of several confidential sources he had used to prepare an article

55. *U.S.* v. *Burke,* 700 F. 2d 70 (1983).
56. *U.S.* v. *Cutler,* 6 F. 3d 67 (1993).

about alleged cult activities at an 80-acre farm near rural Snohomish, Wash. The owner of the farm, Theodore Rinaldo, had been convicted of statutory rape, assault, coercion and intimidating a witness. A year after his conviction, several persons who had testified on Rinaldo's behalf at his trial stepped forward and admitted they had committed perjury. It was during his second trial for tampering with witnesses and other offenses that Rinaldo tried to force reporter Gary Larson to reveal the names of persons who gave the reporter information for six articles that had brought the activities at the farm to the attention of local authorities. Justice James Dolliver, speaking for the court, ruled that Rinaldo would have to show that the information was necessary or critical to his defense and that he had made a reasonable effort to get the material by other means. He could not make such a showing, and the subpoena was quashed.[57]

More recently, the First Amendment privilege came into play in a high-profile criminal case involving John Phillip Walker Lindh, the so-called American Taliban who was indicted in February 2002 after he allegedly joined certain terrorist organizations in Afghanistan to fight against American forces. Robert Young Pelton, a free-lance journalist who was covering the military conflict in Afghanistan on behalf of CNN, had interviewed Lindh after Lindh was captured by U.S. troops in November 2001. Attorneys for Lindh subpoenaed Pelton to testify about the interview at a hearing on various motions they had filed to suppress evidence in the case against their client. Pelton moved to quash the subpoena on the ground that he had a First Amendment privilege against disclosure of information obtained during the news-gathering process in Afghanistan. In July 2002, however, Pelton's motion to quash was denied by a federal district court judge in Alexandria, Virginia.[58] The judge held that the First Amendment privilege grounded in Justice Powell's concurrence in *Branzburg* applies only "where the journalist produces some evidence of confidentiality or governmental harassment." Pelton conceded that there was no confidentiality of sources involved—Lindh was the source—and thus the judge held that "he cannot invoke any First Amendment privilege on the basis of confidentiality of sources or government harassment." Pelton, however, raised another argument that was also rejected by the court—"that the special circumstance of his role as a war correspondent in Afghanistan is a sufficient factor to trigger application of the privilege." The judge called this a "novel claim," found absolutely no case law precedent to support it, and thus denied Pelton's motion to quash the subpoena. Ultimately, Lindh pleaded guilty just three days after the judge's decision to two charges of aiding the Taliban and carrying explosives and therefore Pelton never was forced to testify.

Grand Jury Proceedings

While the qualified privilege for reporters to refuse to reveal the identities of confidential sources in civil and criminal actions has been recognized by most lower federal courts and state supreme courts that have considered the question, these same courts have routinely refused to extend the First Amendment privilege to grand jury proceedings. This was the case in 2005 when a federal appellate court refused to extend a privilege to either Judith Miller or Matthew Cooper in the Valerie Plame leak controversy described earlier in this chapter. This refusal is true even though the grand jury's power to force disclosure is not constitutionally

57. *State* v. *Rinaldo,* 684 P. 2d 608 (1984).
58. *United States* v. *Lindh,* 210 F. Supp. 2d 780 (E.D. Va. 2002).

guaranteed, as is the criminal defendant's right to compel a witness to testify. The obvious explanation for this reluctance on the part of judges is that the single U.S. Supreme Court precedent on the question focused on grand jury testimony and in that case, *Branzburg* v. *Hayes*,[59] the high court ruled that no privilege existed.

For example, in August 2001, the 5th U.S. Circuit Court of Appeals rejected an appeal from a free-lance writer named Vanessa Leggett who refused to turn over research materials to a federal grand jury in Houston. Leggett was trying to write a book about a 1997 murder that was being investigated by the Justice Department. Texas has no shield law to protect reporters (see pages 449–452), but there was considerable doubt Leggett would have qualified for protection under the law in any case since she was a free-lancer, not a staff reporter for a publication. The appellate court rejected her effort to invoke the constitutional privilege. The court said while the privilege under the First Amendment may protect a journalist's confidential sources in civil cases, its applicability is diminished in criminal cases and it reaches its nadir or lowest point in grand jury proceedings. "The public's interest in law enforcement proceedings always outweighs the media interests," the court ruled.[60] The Supreme Court declined in 2002 to hear Leggett's case (see pages 414–415).

This case is typical. There are, however, a few decisions that have recognized the journalist's privilege even in the face of a grand jury subpoena. One of these rare and huge victories came in 2005 when a federal judge in New York held that both a qualified First Amendment privilege and a federal common law privilege protected against the seizure by a federal grand jury sitting in Illinois of the telephone records of two New York Times reporters. In this case, *New York Times Co.* v. *Gonzales*,[61] the government was investigating an alleged breach and leak of a government secret by one or more unknown government employees. The telephone records at issue, which were held by an unidentified third-party telephone company, were those of New York Times reporters Judith Miller (yes, the same Judith Miller who was involved in the Valerie Plame leak dispute described earlier in the chapter) and Philip Shenon. The federal government wanted to learn the identity of its employees who allegedly leaked to either Miller or Shenon or both information relating to the government's plans to block the assets and search the offices of two Islamic charity organizations in the fall of 2001, in and around the time of the terrorist attacks on New York City and Washington, D.C. Collectively, Miller and Shenon had written multiple articles for The New York Times during that time period and in the past on the subject of terrorism and the possible involvement of Islamic charities with terrorism (Miller, in fact, had written on that topic since 1993). The federal government thus believed that if it could obtain the telephone records of Miller and Shenon, then it could determine who might have leaked information to them. The New York Times, however, countered that "the disclosure of the telephone records at issue would not only constitute an unacceptable violation of the privacy of both Miller and Shenon but would also likely reveal the identities of dozens of confidential sources who are of no relevance to the government's investigation."

U.S. District Court Judge Robert W. Sweet ruled in favor of The New York Times, Miller and Shenon. He found that a qualified First Amendment privilege and a federal common-law privilege protecting journalists' confidential sources applied in the context of grand jury

A federal judge in New York held that both a qualified First Amendment privilege and a federal common law privilege protected against the seizure by a federal grand jury sitting in Illinois of the telephone records of two New York Times reporters.

59. 408 U.S. 665 (1972).
60. *In re Grand Jury Subpoenas,* 29 M.L.R. 2301 (2001).
61. 382 F. Supp. 2d 457 (2005).

proceedings. In reaching his conclusion, Sweet initially acknowledged that the "issue is the proper relationship between two vitally important aspects of our democracy: the free press on the one hand and the fair and full administration of justice on the other," and that the case centered on "the conflicting interests of the press and the federal criminal justice system." Sweet then interpreted the U.S. Supreme Court's holding in *Branzburg* v. *Hayes* to recognize, at least within the U.S. Court of Appeals for the 2nd Circuit in which New York is located, "a qualified First Amendment privilege, applicable in civil actions and in all phases of a criminal prosecution, that protects reporters from compelled disclosure of confidential sources." More important, he found that "the government has not offered a principled basis for concluding that the qualified First Amendment reporter's privilege applies in the context of a criminal trial but not in the context of a grand jury investigation." Sweet thus determined that "whether there is a qualified privilege rooted in the First Amendment is *not* dependent on the nature of the case." In other words, the qualified privilege applies regardless of whether it is a civil or criminal case or a grand jury investigation. Sweet also found that the federal common law embraced such a privilege, reasoning that "this recognition of a qualified privilege with respect to confidential sources is consonant with the conclusions reached by the courts or legislatures [citing legislative-created shield laws in 31 states] of forty-eight states as well as the District of Columbia on the issue of reporter's privilege against compelled disclosure."

To overcome such a qualified First Amendment and federal common law privilege, Sweet wrote that the government would need to prove that the subpoenaed documents—in this case, the reporters' telephone records—were

1. *highly material and relevant to the government's case;*
2. *necessary or critical to the maintenance of the claim; and*
3. *not obtainable from other available sources.*

Applying this three-part test to the facts of the case, Sweet concluded that the government had failed to show the materiality, relevance and necessity of the telephone records to its investigation, and that it had similarly not shown that the information about who leaked the information to The Times' reporters was not available from other sources. Sweet finished his opinion by writing:

> To deny the relief sought by the Times under these circumstances, i.e., without any showing on the part of the government that the sought records are necessary, relevant, material and unavailable from other sources, has the potential to significantly affect the reporting of news based upon information provided by confidential sources. The record before this court has demonstrated that the reporters at issue [Miller and Shenon] relied upon promises of confidentiality to gather information concerning issues of paramount national importance—e.g., the nation's preparedness for the attacks of September 11, the government's efforts to combat Al Qaeda post-September 11, and the risk posed to the American people by biological weapons. The government has failed to demonstrate that the balance of the competing interests weighs in its favor.

But again, these rulings are really atypical; more often than not, reporters have found themselves forced to testify when subpoenaed to appear before a grand jury. It is thus not wise to rely on First Amendment protection if called before a grand jury.

Source: © AP/Wide World Photos

What happens when the individual requesting the information is a special prosecutor rather than a grand jury? The 1st U.S. Circuit Court of Appeals squarely addressed this question in 2004 when it handed down its decision in *In re Special Proceedings.*[62] The appellate court, in a blow to journalists, held that "*Branzburg* governs in this case even though we are dealing with a special prosecutor rather than a grand jury," adding that "the considerations bearing on privilege are the same in both cases." The court thus refused to extend a reporter's privilege when confidential information is requested by a special prosecutor.

The case transpired in the context of an FBI investigation, called "Operation Plunder Dome," into governmental corruption at City Hall in Providence, R.I. The investigation was important and successful, as it sent several city officials, including former Mayor Vincent "Buddy" Cianci, to federal prison. The First Amendment dispute involved efforts to obtain the name of a source that leaked to James Taricani, a veteran investigative television reporter covering "Operation Plunder Dome," a copy of a secret surveillance videotape of an FBI informant handing an envelope that allegedly contained a $1,000 cash bribe to a Providence city official named Frank E. Corrente. Corrente was later convicted of bribery.

Taricani's station, the Providence NBC-affiliate, WJAR-TV, aired a portion of the secret tape, and a federal judge appointed a special prosecutor to determine who leaked it to Taricani. When Taricani refused to give up his confidential source, he was hit by the judge with civil contempt and a $1,000-a-day fine. In holding that the opinion in *Branzburg,* which rejected a testimonial privilege in grand jury proceedings (see page 428), also controlled cases involving special prosecutors, the 1st U.S. Circuit Court of Appeals affirmed the district court judge's civil contempt finding against Taricani. It wrote that "there is no doubt that the request to Taricani was for information highly relevant to a good faith criminal investigation" and that

Investigative broadcast journalist Jim Taricani was sentenced to six months of home confinement in late 2004 for refusing to divulge the identity of a confidential source.

62. 373 F. 3d 37 (1st Cir. 2004).

"reasonable efforts were made to obtain the information elsewhere." Importantly, the appellate court cited somewhat favorably Judge Posner's 2003 opinion in the *McKevitt* case (see page 431) that was skeptical of the *Branzburg* opinion offering any protection to journalists beyond what ordinary relevance and reasonableness requirements would demand.

With the appellate court decision going against Taricani, the district court began assessing the $1,000-a-day fine against the reporter in August 2004. Clare Eckert, the vice president for marketing at WJAR-TV, would not reveal at the time who was covering the bill, but she noted that arrangements between NBC Universal, WJAR-TV and Taricani were private. By early November of 2004, Taricani still had not revealed his source and, in the process, he had racked up (and paid) fines of about $85,000. Recognizing the civil fine was not forcing Taricani to give up his confidential source, U.S. District Court Judge Ernest Torres then ordered that Taricani be tried for criminal contempt unless the reporter gave up his source. In taking this step, the judge suspended the $1,000 fine because the case was now about *criminal* contempt, not a *civil* penalty. Judge Torres soon found Taricani guilty of criminal contempt, prompting the Emmy Award–winning journalist to proclaim, "When I became a reporter 30 years ago, I never imagined that I would be put on trial and face the prospect of going to jail simply for doing my job."[63] NBC issued a prepared statement supporting Taricani, writing that "Jim did exactly what an investigative reporter should do: he informed the public about corrupt political officials who were tried, convicted and incarcerated for their crimes."

In December 2004, shortly before Taricani was to be sentenced for his criminal contempt conviction, an attorney named Joseph Bevilacqua Jr. came forward and admitted under oath that he was Taricani's source for the videotape. Bevilacqua had represented one of the city officials, Joseph Pannone, convicted in the corruption scandal in Providence that Taricani was investigating. Bevilacqua's admission, however, did not negate the criminal contempt conviction of journalist Taricani. On December 9, 2004, the 55-year-old Taricani was sentenced to six months of home confinement. Judge Torres chose home confinement rather than prison because of health concerns about Taricani, who is a heart-transplant recipient. The judge stated from the bench, "Except for his health and history of a good record, all of the factors call for a meaningful prison sentence."[64] During his confinement, Taricani was denied access to the Internet and prohibited from doing media interviews; he could leave his home only for medical treatments. NBC officials, in a prepared statement, called the sentence "a sad day for journalism. The facts here do not justify punishing a journalist who did nothing illegal in receiving and airing a videotape." Taricani chose not to appeal the sentence, but NBC Universal issued a final statement on the matter in December 2004:

> We believe Jim's criminal contempt conviction and sentence should be reviewed by the court of appeals because the severe punishment imposed on him is not warranted. In NBC Universal's view, the key factors weighing against severe punishment were: the corrupt government officials involved in the original case were convicted; no claim was ever made by those convicted that the airing of the videotape compromised the trial; by the time of the contempt sentencing, the source had come forward and a civil contempt fine had already been paid. However, we respect Jim's health concerns and accept his decision not to seek an appeal.

63. Belluck, "Reporter Is Found Guilty."
64. Belluck, "Reporter Who Shielded Source."

Taricani ultimately was released from home confinement in April 2005 upon recommendation from his probation officer, about two months earlier than originally scheduled, after he was found by Judge Torres to have fully complied to that point with all of the conditions of his home detention. Despite the early release, the case of Jim Taricani, in the opinion of the authors of this textbook, represents a very low mark in recent years in terms of the legal protection that journalists have—or don't have—in protecting their sources. It must be remembered that had it not been for his fragile health, Taricani would have landed in jail for protecting his source rather than getting home confinement.

ANONYMITY AND THE INTERNET

An interesting problem that has developed recently and is related to the matter of reporters' protecting the identity of their sources is whether or not the parties in a lawsuit can force Internet service providers to reveal the names of persons who post anonymous messages on the Web. There have been a handful of cases that clearly reveal the courts are struggling to accommodate various competing interests. A New Jersey appellate court ruled that a subpoena to ascertain the identity of anonymous Internet posters in a libel case should not be issued unless the plaintiff could first make a prima facie case for libel.[65] The court outlined a four-part test it said lower courts should follow that is known as the *Dendrite* test:

> The plaintiff must first make an effort to notify the anonymous poster that he or she is the subject of an application for disclosure.
>
> The plaintiff must identify and set forth the allegedly defamatory statements.
>
> The plaintiff must provide sufficient evidence to support each element of the cause of action, including the harm that has allegedly been incurred.
>
> The court must then balance the defendant's right to anonymous speech under the First Amendment (see page 140) against the strength of the plaintiff's case and the necessity of disclosure to allow the plaintiff to proceed properly.

In the New Jersey case the unidentified posters were named as defendants in the lawsuit. A federal court in Washington state fashioned a somewhat similar rule in a suit in which the anonymous posters were not a party in the lawsuit. It said the subpoena would not be issued unless the information sought went to a core claim made by the plaintiff or the defense, the information was directly or materially relevant to the case, and the party seeking the identities had demonstrated that the information was unavailable from other sources.[66]

More recently, the Supreme Court of Virginia concluded in 2002 that America Online must reveal the name of one its subscribers who allegedly libeled and engaged in unfair business practices against Nam Tai Electronics.[67] A person using the login name of "scovey2" had obtained Internet access through America Online. He had posted a statement on a message board about Nam Tai Electronics stating, "Sinking is not a province in China but an observation about this company's stock market performance. This low tech crap they produce is in an extremely competitive and low profitability industry. I see see-sawing of the stock with no real direction." The high court of Virginia affirmed the trial court's denial of America Online's

---

65. *Dendrite International Inc.* v. *Doe,* 775 A. 2d 756 (N.J. Super. Ct. 2001).

66. *Doe* v. *2TheMart.com Inc.,* 140 F. Supp. 2d 1088 (W.D. Wash. 2001). See also *Columbia Insurance Co.* v. *Seescandy.com,* 185 F.R.D. 573 (1999).

67. *America Online, Inc.* v. *Nam Tai Electronics, Inc.,* 571 S.E. 2d 128 (2002).

motion to quash the subpoena served on it by Nam Tai Electronics. Nam Tai had subpoenaed the identity of "scovey2" as part of a complaint against more than 50 unknown individuals, alleging libel, trade libel and violations of California's unfair-business-practice statutes.

Finally, in a 2005 libel opinion called *Doe* v. *Cahill* that was based on statements posted on a Web log (a "blog"), the Supreme Court of Delaware held that "the summary judgment standard is the appropriate test by which to strike the balance between a defamation plaintiff's right to protect his reputation and a defendant's right to exercise free speech anonymously."[68] What does this mean? The court called it a "modified" two-part version of the four-part *Dendrite* test mentioned earlier. In particular, the plaintiff must: 1) make reasonable efforts to notify the defendant (the anonymous poster) that he is the subject of a subpoena or application for an order of disclosure; and 2) provide sufficient evidence to support and sustain each and every element of the plaintiff's cause action versus the defendant (in this case, defamation) against a motion for **summary judgment** (see glossary).

NONCONFIDENTIAL INFORMATION AND WAIVER OF THE PRIVILEGE

While U.S. courts have been willing to permit journalists to protect confidential sources and confidential information, most of the same courts have been far more reluctant to protect reporters when nonconfidential information is at issue. And most subpoenas issued today to journalists are to gain access to nonconfidential information.

In 1999 the 2nd U.S. Circuit Court of Appeals, vacating an earlier decision it had announced, ruled that the federal law does recognize a qualified privilege for journalists with regard to nonconfidential information. In order to get unedited videotape possessed by NBC, the plaintiff, who had filed a civil rights action against a Louisiana police officer, would have to show that the information contained on the tape was highly material and relevant, necessary, or critical to the maintenance of his civil rights claim and was not obtainable from other sources.[69] This ruling is an unusual one because most other courts have rejected this notion. More typical is a ruling by the 5th U.S. Circuit Court of Appeals a year earlier that said that reporters do not enjoy any privilege, qualified or otherwise, not to disclose nonconfidential information in a criminal case.[70] This ruling seems to be more in line with previous court rulings. A U.S. District Court ruled in 1990 that a journalist who witnessed a beating of a criminal suspect by police had to testify on behalf of the injured party. "This court knows of no authority to support the proposition that such personal observations are privileged simply because the eyewitness is a journalist," the judge ruled.[71]

Photographers have been forced to surrender photos they have taken of building fires,[72] industrial accidents,[73] fatal auto accidents,[74] or even of an individual who has filed a personal injury lawsuit against an insurance company.[75] The press has generally been unable to convince

68. *Doe* v. *Cahill,* 884 A.2d 451 (Del. 2005).
69. *Gonzales* v. *National Broadcasting Co., Inc.,* 155 F. 3d 618 (1999).
70. *U.S.* v. *Smith,* 135 F. 3d 963 (1998).
71. *Dillon* v. *San Francisco,* 748 F. Supp. 722 (1990).
72. *Marketos* v. *American Employers Insurance Co.,* 460 N.W. 2d 272 (1990).
73. *Stickels* v. *General Rental Co., Inc.,* 750 F. Supp. 729 (1990).
74. *Idaho* v. *Salsbury,* 924 P. 2d 208 (1996).
75. *Weathers* v. *American Family Mutual Insurance Co.,* 17 M.L.R. 1534 (1990).

judges that it has an important interest at stake when it refuses to cooperate with those who seek nonconfidential information. The arguments that have been made so well about the importance of protecting confidential sources aren't nearly as persuasive when nonconfidential material is at stake.

Reporters must worry about another aspect of the privilege, the problem that through some action they may actually waive their right to refuse to testify. A case in Washington, D.C., focuses on this dilemma. Six police officers brought a $9 million lawsuit against the city and top police officials. They were disciplined by the police department after a botched 1986 drug operation that failed to net the hundreds of arrests expected. In the wake of the failed raid, Washington Post reporter Linda Wheeler revealed in a newspaper story that the Post had obtained secret plans for the raid. The six officers who were disciplined argued that leaks from high-level police officials, not from them, caused the raid to fail. And they subpoenaed Wheeler to find out where she got the plans for the operation.

Reporters must worry about another aspect of the privilege, the problem that through some action they may actually waive their right to refuse to testify.

The reporter refused to identify her source and was found in contempt of court. The court said that any privilege a reporter might enjoy in such an instance was waived when, in 1986, she told her husband and another man, both officers in the U.S. Park Police, the name of her confidential source. "A reporter cannot choose in 1986 to disclose her source to others . . . and then choose in 1991—as a witness in a judicial proceeding—not to make this same disclosure," wrote Judge Richard A. Levie. The District of Columbia Court of Appeals upheld this ruling.[76]

Wheeler was excused from testifying in the summer of 1991 when a mistrial was declared in the lawsuit. But a retrial was scheduled. The reporter's husband, to whom she had revealed the identity of her source, was forced to testify before the hearing was adjourned. "This could become a very effective harassment technique," said Jane Kirtley, who was then executive director of the Reporters Committee for Freedom of the Press. She suggested that a judge or attorney might say, "Well, journalists, I recognize you're covered by a shield law or a reporter's privilege, but I'm just going to bring in your spouse, your kid, your parents, your dog, anybody who's around, and see what they know."

There is really no bright line marking when and how a reporter may in fact waive the privilege. The law is too diffuse for such a generalization. But reporters who have promised confidentiality should keep the information completely confidential. In fact, if Wheeler did reveal the name of her source to her husband, and she denied doing so, she broke a Washington Post rule that forbids a reporter from telling anyone outside the newspaper the name of a confidential source.

WHO IS A JOURNALIST?

An emerging problem relating to the constitutionally based journalist's privilege is, Who is a journalist?[77] When the privilege was developed in the 1970s and 1980s the definition of a journalist was relatively clear: A journalist was someone who gathered news for a news medium. In the 21st century, with the growth of interactive computer communication and 900 number information services, virtually anyone can report the news, or what he or she might refer to as

76. *Wheeler* v. *Goulart,* 18 M.L.R. 2296 (1990) and *Goulart* v. *Barry,* 18 M.L.R. 2056 (1991).
77. Calvert, "And You Call Yourself a Journalist?"

the news. Should anyone who uses the Internet or a 900 telephone number to spread information be regarded as a journalist for purposes of the law? This issue has not been resolved, but at least one court has attempted to solve the dilemma.

Mark Madden is an irrepressible professional-wrestling commentator who "broadcast" his commentary via 900-number telephone calls. His commentaries were usually sarcastic, sometimes fanciful, and always provocative. To listen to these messages callers paid $1.69 per minute. World Championship Wrestling (WCW) owns the line and paid Madden $350 per week to operate it.[78] During a commentary Madden reported that the World Wrestling Federation (WWF), the archrival of the WCW, was in serious financial difficulty. WCW and WWF were suing each other, claiming unfair competition. Madden was subpoenaed to testify about the sources for his report on WWF's financial difficulties. Madden raised the First Amendment privilege, claiming he was a journalist entitled to constitutional protection. A U.S. District Court agreed in 1997,[79] but the U.S. Court of Appeals overturned the lower-court decision in July 1998. The appellate judges said that Madden was an entertainer disseminating hype, not news.

In ruling that Madden was not a journalist, the three-judge panel from the 3rd U.S. Circuit Court of Appeals defined a journalist (for purposes of application of the privilege) in this fashion: a journalist is one

- who is engaged in investigative reporting;
- who is gathering news; and
- who possesses the intent at the beginning of the news-gathering process to disseminate this news to the public.[80]

Since this ruling other cases have been reported. A U.S. District Court in the District of Columbia has ruled that cyberjournalist/rumor-monger Matt Drudge was protected by the constitutional journalistic privilege in the libel suit brought against him by Sydney Blumenthal.[81] (See page 171.) But a federal court ruled in 1999 that a cyberscribe in Colorado who maintained a Web site offering information about the University of Colorado athletic programs did not have a constitutional right to be given the same privileges that school officials accord to other "accredited members of the news media." Theodore Smith was not a journalist.[82] These cases are just the opening chapters of what is surely to be a long saga regarding who is and who is not a journalist.

Indeed, in 2003 the 2nd U.S. Circuit Court of Appeals jumped into the fray and denied journalistic status to a financial ratings agency called Fitch, Inc., which had sought to quash a subpoena under New York's shield law.[83] Although not addressing the constitutional journalistic privilege, the federal appellate court nonetheless considered whether the New York shield law, which protects journalists from contempt for refusing to comply with a nonparty subpoena when the subpoena seeks to discover information conveyed to a journalist in confidence, included protection for a financial ratings company. New York's law defines a professional journalist as "one who, for gain or livelihood, is engaged in gathering, preparing, collecting,

78. Glaberson, "Wrestling Insults."
79. *Titan Sports Inc.* v. *Turner Broadcasting Systems Inc.,* 967 F. Supp. 142 (1997).
80. *In re Madden,* 151 F. 3d 125 (1998).
81. *Blumenthal* v. *Drudge,* 186 F.R.D. 236 (1999).
82. *Smith* v. *Plati,* D. Colo., No. 99-K-491, 7/22/99.
83. *In re Fitch, Inc., & American Savings Bank, FSB,* v. *UBS Painewebber, Inc.,* 330 F. 3d 104 (2003).

writing, editing, filming, taping or photographing of news intended for a newspaper, magazine, news agency, . . . or other professional medium or agency which has as one of its regular functions the processing and researching of news intended for dissemination to the public." Fitch contended that it fits this definition because "it conducts research, fact-gathering, and analytical activity that is directed towards matters of general public concern, just like any journalist, and notes that it makes its information available on its web site to the general public." The appellate court rejected this argument, reasoning in part that "Fitch only 'reports on' specific transactions for which it has been hired. Unlike a business newspaper or magazine, which would cover any transactions deemed newsworthy, Fitch only 'covers' its own clients. We believe this practice weighs against treating Fitch like a journalist." The appellate court did, however, leave open some breathing room for future cases and debate when it wrote, "we conclude that the district court did not abuse its discretion in finding that Fitch was not entitled to assert the journalist's privilege for the information at issue. For the sake of clarity, we note that we are not deciding the general status of a credit rating agency like Fitch under New York's Shield Law: Whether Fitch, or one of its rivals, could ever be entitled to assert the newsgathering privilege is a question we leave for another day."

One of the newest and most intriguing issues involving the question of who is a journalist, for purposes of both state shield laws (see pages 449–452) and the First Amendment journalistic privilege protection, centers on the status of so-called "bloggers"—individuals who keep and maintain Web logs ("blogs"). The question first came to public attention in late 2004 and early 2005 when Apple Computer, Inc., filed two separate, high-profile lawsuits in state court in California related to the alleged leak of some of its trade secrets, apparently by unknown current or former Apple employees, to several bloggers, who then posted the secret information on their Web sites for all to see.

In one case, *Apple Computer, Inc.* v. *Does,*[84] the giant computer and iPod manufacturer sued 25 unnamed individuals or entities (identified in the complaint as "Does" given their unknown identities), alleging the "Does" had leaked specific, trade secret information about new Apple products to the operators of several online Web sites, including AppleInsider (http://www.appleinsider.com) and PowerPage (http://www.powerpage.org). In an effort to obtain the identity of the unknown "Doe" defendants, Apple subpoenaed a company called Nfox. Nfox is the e-mail service provider for the PowerPage Web site and blog. Specifically, Apple subpoenaed Nfox for e-mail messages that may identify the confidential sources who supplied the various blogs with trade secret information. Although Nfox did not object to the subpoena as it was merely the service provider, the operators of blogs like PowerPage that use Nfox's e-mail service strenuously objected, and they intervened in the lawsuit seeking a protective order blocking the subpoena. Specifically, the bloggers asserted that they are "journalists" and thus are entitled to claim a privilege from disclosing their confidential sources under California's shield law.

California is one of 31 states with a shield law. Its shield law generally protects journalists from being held in contempt of court for refusing to disclose the identity of confidential sources. The problem is how the California shield law, which is codified as California Evidence Code Section 1070, defines the individuals who are protected by it. In particular,

84. Complaint, *Apple Computer, Inc.* v. *Does,* Case No. 1-04-CV-032178 (Superior Ct., Santa Clara County, Calif., filed Dec. 13, 2004).

that section protects "[a] publisher, editor, reporter or other person connected with or employed upon a newspaper, magazine or other periodical publication, or by a press association or wire service, or any person who has been so connected or employed." The law is silent about the status of those who run blogs.

In March 2005, Superior Court Judge James P. Kleinberg denied the bloggers' motion for a protective order and refused to quash the subpoena that Apple served on Nfox. More important, the judge sidestepped and dodged the direct question of whether bloggers are journalists for purposes of protecting their sources under either the California shield law or the First Amendment.[85] Judge Kleinberg wrote that even if the bloggers are journalists, "this is not the equivalent of a free pass. The journalist's privilege is not absolute." He added, "The right to keep and maintain proprietary information [trade secrets] . . . is a right which the California legislature and courts have long affirmed and which is essential to the future of technology and innovation generally. The Court sees no reason to abandon that right even if it were to assume, *arguendo,* movants [the bloggers] are 'journalists' as they claim to be." Finding the trade secrets of Apple to be the equivalent of stolen property under California's Uniform Trade Secrets Act and the state's penal code, Kleinberg wrote that regardless of whether the operator of the PowerPage Web site "fits the definition of a journalist, reporter, blogger or anything else need not be decided at this juncture for a fundamental reason: There is no license conferred on anyone to violate criminal laws." This language should sound familiar for students who closely read Chapter 9, which emphasized in the section "The First Amendment Protection of News Gathering" that the First Amendment does not grant the press automatic relief from laws of general application.

The bloggers, who are supported by the Electronic Frontier Foundation (http://www.eff.org) in the case, vowed to appeal the matter and, indeed, filed an appeal within a month of the adverse decision. Among other things, the appeal contends that the judge's ruling violates the First Amendment and Apple must first subpoena its own employees or use computer forensics to determine who leaked the information.[86] Adding to the magnitude of the case, the Reporters Committee for Freedom of the Press (RCFP) and 11 other media entities, including the publishers of all major newspapers in California as well as the Associated Press, filed a lengthy friend-of-court brief in April 2005. The amicus brief urged protection of the bloggers' confidential sources and objected to the subpoenaing by Apple Computer of the third-party, e-mail service provider (Nfox) as the means for indirectly obtaining those confidential sources. On appeal, the case is called *O'Grady* v. *Superior Court,* because it was filed on behalf of Jason O'Grady (the blogger and owner of the PowerPage Web site) appealing the order of a superior court judge. The case was still ongoing in 2006.

In the other case, called *Apple Computer, Inc.* v. *Nick dePlume,*[87] Apple directly sued in January 2005 the operator of a blog called Think Secret.[88] The individual at the center of this case is Nicholas Ciarelli, a Harvard University student who goes by the alias "Nick dePlume"

---

85. Order After Hearing, *Apple Computer, Inc.* v. *Does,* Case No. 1-04-CV-032178 (Superior Ct., Santa Clara County, Calif., Mar. 11, 2005).

86. The Electronic Fronteir Foundation maintains a link on its Website at http://www.eff.org/Censorship/Apple_v_Does with current information on the case.

87. Complaint, *Apple Computer, Inc.* v. *Nick dePlume,* Case No. 1-05-CV-033341 (Superior Ct., Santa Clara County, Calif., filed Jan. 4, 2005).

88. Fost, "Bay Judge Weighs Rights of Bloggers."

and runs a blog called "Think Secret" (www.thinksecret.com). The blog publishes articles primarily on the topic of Apple computers and, in early 2005, published an average of 13 articles a month. In March 2005 Ciarelli and Think Secret filed, under California's anti-SLAPP statute (see pages 161–162 regarding SLAPP suits), a motion to dismiss Apple's lawsuit, contending that Think Secret is a journalistic Web site engaged in journalism and that its information is both newsworthy and lawfully obtained. The case was in progress in early 2006.

TELEPHONE RECORDS

The names of confidential news sources, reporters' notes, news film and photographs are not the only records that have been sought by government agents and attorneys through the use of a subpoena. In a 1994 libel action initiated by the Philip Morris Companies against ABC, the cigarette maker sought access to a reporter's credit card bills and to airline and rental car bills as well as to private telephone records. The goal of this effort was to try to discover the identity of a former R. J. Reynolds Tobacco Co. executive who told the network reporter that tobacco companies regularly added nicotine to cigarettes. Telephone records present a special problem.

The telephone company maintains subscriber records for toll telephone calls for about six months. For long-distance calls billed to the subscriber's telephone number, these records indicate the telephone number called as well as the date, time and duration of the call. The fact that the phone company keeps these records is hardly a secret; a copy of the monthly toll-call record is provided to each subscriber with each month's bill.

In 1974 AT&T announced that in the future it would not release these records to the government without a subpoena and, as a general policy, would seek to notify subscribers immediately when their individual records had been subpoenaed by a government agency. However, when records were subpoenaed pursuant to a felony investigation, the telephone company said it would not notify the subscriber of the subpoena as long as the government certified that an official investigation was being conducted and that notification to the subscriber could impede the investigation.

The Reporters Committee for Freedom of the Press challenged the telephone company's policy of releasing *any* records to the government, arguing that the government could use such records to determine reporters' sources. Journalists raised both the Fourth Amendment and the First Amendment as bars to this cooperation between AT&T and the government.

A U.S. Court of Appeals seemed unpersuaded that this cooperation created a real problem and ruled against the Reporters Committee. The Fourth Amendment claim lacked merit, the court said, because the constitutional prohibition against illegal search and seizure "does not insulate all personal activity from official scrutiny." The First Amendment claim was similarly rejected. The court asserted that the First Amendment offers no additional protections against good faith criminal investigations beyond that afforded by the Fourth and Fifth amendments.

> The principle is clear. To the extent individuals desire to exercise their First Amendment rights in private, free from possible good faith law enforcement investigation, they must operate within the zone of privacy secured by the Fourth Amendment. When individuals expose their activities to third parties, they similarly expose these activities to possible government scrutiny.[89]

89. *Reporters Committee* v. *AT&T,* 593 F. 2d 1030 (1978).

SUMMARY

In recent years more and more reporters have been called to testify in legal proceedings. Often they are asked to reveal confidential information to aid police in criminal investigations, to assist in the defense of a criminal defendant, or to help a libel plaintiff establish negligence or actual malice. Failure to comply with a court order can result in a citation for contempt of court. The Supreme Court of the United States ruled in 1972 that reporters were like all other citizens; they did not enjoy a First Amendment privilege that permitted them to refuse to testify before a grand jury. Despite this high court ruling, the lower federal courts and state courts have fashioned a constitutional, common-law privilege that often protects a journalist who has been subpoenaed to testify at a legal hearing. The privilege is qualified. In many instances a court will not require a journalist to testify unless the person seeking the information held by the journalist can demonstrate that the reporter has information that is relevant to the hearing, that there is a compelling need for the disclosure of this information, and that there are no alternative sources for this information.

Courts tend to apply this three-part test differently in different types of legal proceedings. Journalists are most likely to escape being forced to testify in a civil suit, especially if the reporter is not a party to the suit in some way. Reporters are more likely to be forced to testify in a criminal case, but there are numerous examples of reporters being granted a qualified privilege to escape such testimony as well. Reporters called to testify before a grand jury, however, usually are required to honor the subpoena. More and more courts are seeking journalists' testimony regarding nonconfidential information, and the law is of substantially less protective value in these cases. A U.S. Court of Appeals has ruled that the records of toll telephone calls made by journalists may also be subpoenaed to further legitimate law enforcement proceedings.

LEGISLATIVE AND EXECUTIVE PROTECTION OF NEWS SOURCES

Virtually every state offers some protection for reporters. Oftentimes it has been generated by the courts through the state and federal constitutions, or through the common law. But the state legislatures and the U.S. Department of Justice have attempted to protect reporters as well. Thirty-one states have statutes that shield reporters in one way or another from subpoenas that might force them to reveal confidential information. There is no federal shield law, but the Department of Justice has developed an extensive set of guidelines that sharply limit when and how federal agents may use subpoenas against journalists. Although there currently is no federal shield law, U.S. Senator Christopher Dodd (D.-Conn.) introduced a bill in November 2004 that would have created such a statute. Dodd's bill, dubbed the "Free Speech Protection Act of 2004,"[90] would have provided an absolute privilege from disclosing sources in federal court regardless of whether the sources are promised confidentiality or not. The bill also would have given a limited or qualified privilege to withhold other information except

90. S. 3020, 108th Cong. (2004).

under certain circumstances. Dodd's bill failed to become law when the congressional session closed at the end of 2004, but he reintroduced the measure in early 2005. In addition, a new bill called the "Free Flow of Information Act"[91] that would take similar steps quickly was introduced in the U.S. House of Representatives in 2005 by Mike Pence (R.-Ind.) and Rick Boucher (D.-Va.), along with an identical companion measure in the U.S. Senate sponsored by Richard Lugar (R.-Ind.).[92] The 2005 congressional bills originally called for an absolute privilege for protecting the identities of confidential sources, with a qualified privilege covering other materials. Neither bill, however, had become law by early 2006.

SHIELD LAWS

In 1896 Maryland became the first state to grant journalists a limited privilege to refuse to testify in legal proceedings. Since that time 30 additional states and the District of Columbia have adopted similar rules, either by state statute, the state constitution or even rules of court. The states that have such laws are Alabama, Alaska, Arizona, Arkansas, California, Colorado, Delaware, Florida, Georgia, Illinois, Indiana, Kentucky, Louisiana, Maryland, Michigan, Minnesota, Montana, Nebraska, Nevada, New Jersey, New Mexico, New York, North Carolina, North Dakota, Ohio, Oklahoma, Oregon, Pennsylvania, Rhode Island, South Carolina and Tennessee.

In 1896 Maryland became the first state to grant journalists a limited privilege to refuse to testify in legal proceedings.

These laws, in more or less limited terms, outline the reporter's privilege that has been established by the state. The statutes generally establish who can use the privilege (i.e., who is a reporter?), the kinds of information the privilege protects (i.e., confidential and nonconfidential; sources only or sources and information), and any qualifications that might accrue (i.e., the privilege is waived through voluntary disclosure of other parts of the material; instances when disclosure is mandated).

For example, the Alabama shield law provides:

> No person engaged in, connected with, or employed on any newspaper, radio broadcasting station or television station, while engaged in a news gathering capacity shall be compelled to disclose, in any legal proceeding or trial, before any court or before a grand jury of any court, before the presiding officers of any tribunal or his agent or agents, or before any committee of the legislature, or elsewhere, the sources of any information procured or obtained by him and published in the newspaper, broadcast by any broadcasting station, or televised by any television station on which he is engaged, connected with or employed.[93]

The precise language of state shield laws is very important in determining what they will and will not cover or protect. This was illustrated in 2005 in the case of *Price* v. *Time, Inc.* in which the 11th U.S. Circuit Court of Appeals held that Alabama's shield law, quoted immediately above in this section, did not apply to the magazine Sports Illustrated. Engaging in the process of **statutory construction** (see page 10), the appellate court held that the Alabama statute's phrase "newspaper, radio broadcasting station or television station" did not cover

---

91. H.R. 581, 109th Cong. (2005).
92. S. 3440, 109th Cong. (2005).
93. Ala. Code, 12-21-142 (2003).

magazines like Sports Illustrated. In reaching this conclusion, the appellate court followed the plain meaning rule—it gave the statutory words their ordinary meaning and did not impart its own views on the legislative language. The 11th Circuit wrote that "it seems to us plain and apparent that in common usage 'newspaper' does not mean 'newspaper and magazine.'"

Some legal authorities have speculated that the mere existence of a shield law is valuable because it will deter the issuance of subpoenas to journalists. But the study by the Reporters Committee for Freedom of the Press doesn't support that notion. In fact, in 2001 news media outlets in states with shield laws received significantly more subpoenas per outlet than did such organizations in non-shield-law states. That said, however, the report also notes that "the responses from media organizations suggest that shield laws did make a difference in 2001 in whether a subpoena was quashed. The quash rate from shield-law states was 22 percent, compared to 5 percent in non-shield-law states."[94] For example, the Michigan shield law protected several newspapers and television stations that were ordered to turn over videotapes and photographs that had been taken of rioters who roamed the streets of East Lansing after Michigan State University's loss to Duke University in the NCAA Division I basketball tournament in 1999. Police and prosecutors wanted to use the material to try to identify lawbreakers. The media voluntarily provided copies of the tapes and photos that were broadcast and published, but refused to provide copies of material that had not been published or aired. The state Supreme Court threw out the subpoenas, ruling that journalists were subject only to court orders that sought to gain information already disseminated to the public or court orders in which the journalist was the subject of the criminal inquiry.[95] And in 1997 the Minnesota Court of Appeals ruled that before a reporter could be compelled to testify in a libel suit, the trial court must, because of the state's shield law, find that the information was unavailable from other sources, that it was clearly relevant to the case, and that the defamatory statements were false.[96]

Many other cases could be cited to show how shield laws have protected journalists. But these laws have problems as well. Not the least of these problems is that many judges don't like shield laws. They believe the laws unfairly impinge on judicial discretion, denying judges the authority to compel testimony when it is needed in a lawsuit. Hence, in many instances the laws are interpreted very narrowly. Judges follow the letter of the law, but not the spirit of the legislation. For example, the California Supreme Court ruled that while a reporter could not be held in contempt for refusing to produce unpublished photos he had taken of an automobile accident, he might still be subject to other sanctions, such as money damages, for failing to comply with the order. The state shield law only protects a reporter from a contempt citation.[97] The New York shield law failed to protect NBC when it was ordered to provide video outtakes of a protest demonstration staged in early 1998 by thousands of construction workers. The trial judge ruled that the government—which wanted to use the videotape to identify workers so they could be prosecuted—had demonstrated that the material was highly relevant and unavailable from other sources.[98] This showing defeated the protection of the shield law.

94. *Agents of Discovery,* 2003.
95. *People* v. *Pastor,* 613 N.W. 2d 310 (2000).
96. *Bauer* v. *Gannett Co.,* 557 N.W. 2d 608 (1997).
97. *The New York Times* v. *Santa Barbara Superior Court,* 796 P. 2d 811 (1990).
98. *In re Grand Jury Subpoenas,* 27 M.L.R. 1723 (1998).

SHADED STATES HAVE SHIELD LAWS

Source: Agents of Discovery, 2003.

Shield laws suffer from other deficiencies as well. Here are some of the problems:

- Few of the laws give a protection that exceeds, or is even equal to, that given by the constitutional privilege.
- The laws in most of the states are significantly qualified. For example, the laws in Alaska, Louisiana, New Mexico and North Dakota can be overcome by a mere judicial determination that justice or public policy requires the privilege to yield to some other interest.[99]
- In some states the reporter waives the privilege upon disclosure of any portion of the confidential matter.[100]
- In other states the shield law will not apply unless there was an understanding of confidentiality between the reporter and the source.[101]
- State shield laws often exclude free-lance writers, book authors and cable television operators. Courts have not yet considered whether such laws apply to people who use a computer as a mass medium.[102]
- Shield laws rarely cover what a reporter witnesses, only what a reporter has been told or given.[103] For instance, an appellate court in Maryland held in May 2003 that

99. *Confidential Sources and Information,* 1993.
100. *In re Schuman,* 537 A. 2d 297 (1988).
101. *Outlet Communications, Inc.* v. *Rhode Island,* 588 A. 2d 1050 (1991).
102. Alexander and Cooper, "Words That Shield."
103. *Delaney* v. *Superior Court,* 249 Cal. Rept. 60 (1988) and *Minnesota* v. *Knutson,* 523 N.W. 2d 909 (1994).

state's shield law did not protect reporters from complying with administrative subpoenas seeking their testimony at police department administrative hearings when those reporters personally observed and witnessed the relevant event about which their testimony was sought.[104]

The perfect shield law would likely be preferable to the First Amendment privilege; but the perfect shield law does not exist. Hence, even in those states that have a shield law, reporters frequently end up relying on the constitutional privilege.

FEDERAL GUIDELINES

As a kind of corollary to a shield law, the Department of Justice has adopted rules that define when and how a federal prosecuting attorney can obtain a subpoena against a working reporter.[105] Here is a summary of the guidelines:

I. **The Department of Justice must attempt to strike a balance between the public's interest in the free dissemination of ideas and information and the public interest in effective law enforcement when determining whether to seek a subpoena for a journalist's confidential information.**

II. **All reasonable attempts should be made to obtain the information from alternative sources before considering issuing a subpoena to a member of the news media.**

III. **Negotiations with the news media to gain the information sought shall be pursued in all cases in which a subpoena to a member of the news media is contemplated.**

IV. **If the negotiations fail (if the reporter won't provide the material voluntarily), the attorney general must approve the subpoena based on the following guidelines:**

   a. There must be sufficient evidence of a crime from a nonpress source. The department does not approve of using reporters as springboards for investigation.

   b. The information the reporter has must be essential to a successful investigation—not peripheral or speculative.

   c. The government must have unsuccessfully attempted to get the information from an alternative, nonpress source.

   d. Great caution must be exercised with respect to subpoenas for unpublished information or where confidentiality is alleged.

   e. Even subpoenas for published information must be treated with care, because reporters have encountered harassment on the grounds that information collected will be available to the government.

   f. The subpoena must be directed to specific information.

104. *Prince George's County, Maryland v. Hartley,* 31 M.L.R. 1679 (2003).
105. See 28 C.F.R. §50.10.

TELEPHONE RECORDS

Rules 1 through 3 in the guidelines just listed apply as well when federal agents seek to subpoena the toll telephone records of members of the media. If the negotiations to get the records fail, the agents must seek permission from the attorney general to issue the subpoena. In such a case the following guidelines apply:

1. There should be reasonable grounds to believe that a crime has been committed and that the information sought is essential to the successful investigation of that crime.
2. The subpoena should be directed at only relevant information regarding a limited subject matter and should cover a limited period of time.
3. The government should have pursued all reasonable alternative means before seeking the subpoena.
4. Reporters must be given timely notice that the government intends to issue a subpoena.
5. Information obtained through the subpoena must be closely guarded so that unauthorized persons cannot gain access to it.

These federal guidelines have worked well. Remember, the Reporters Committee on Freedom of the Press reported that less than 10 percent of the subpoenas issued in 2001 were generated in federal proceedings. In some federal cases judges have insisted that the government must demonstrate that it has followed these guidelines before it will force a reporter to testify. But they are not an absolute shield, as Associated Press reporter John Solomon discovered in August 2001, when he was notified that the Justice Department had subpoenaed his telephone records from the previous May in order to help them trace a possible source for a story the journalist had written concerning a federal investigation of U.S. Senator Robert G. Torricelli. Justice Department officials were apparently worried that the information had been leaked to Solomon by someone in the agency. But this was a rare occurrence, most government officials and journalists agree.[106] Some state and local law enforcement agencies have adopted rules similar to these federal rules. The federal guidelines apply to criminal cases, civil matters and subpoena of telephone records.

NEWSROOM SEARCHES

Is a newsroom or a journalist's home protected by the First Amendment from a search by the police or federal agents? The Supreme Court of the United States refused to extend the First Amendment in such a manner in 1978.[107] Since then, however, Congress and many state legislatures have provided qualified legislative protection for premises where news and scholarship are produced. This legislation apparently has been successful in reducing searches of newsrooms. For instance, the 2003 survey by the Reporters Committee for Freedom of the Press reported zero newsroom searches in 2001 for the 823 respondents.[108] The lawsuit that

Is a newsroom or a journalist's home protected by the First Amendment from a search by the police or federal agents?

106. Barringer, "Justice Department."
107. *Zurcher v. Stanford Daily,* 436 U.S. 547 (1978).
108. *Agents of Discovery,* 2003.

resulted in the Supreme Court ruling stemmed from the political turmoil of the early 1970s, a period that generated many of the previously discussed cases regarding reporters' sources.

In April 1971 police were asked to remove student demonstrators who were occupying the administrative offices of Stanford University Hospital. When police entered the west end of the building, demonstrators poured out of the east end, and during the ensuing melee outside the building, several police officers were hurt, two seriously. The battle between the police and the students was photographed by a student, and the following day pictures of the incident were published in the Stanford Daily student newspaper. In an effort to discover which students had attacked the injured police officers, law enforcement officials from Santa Clara County secured a warrant for a search of the Daily's newsroom, hoping to find more pictures taken by the student photographer. There was no allegation that any member of the Daily staff was involved in the attack or other unlawful acts. No evidence was discovered during the thorough search.

This type of search is known as an innocent third-party search, or simply a third-party search. Police search the premises or a room for evidence relating to a crime even though there is no reason to suspect that the owner of the premises or the occupant of the room is involved in the crime that is being investigated. Such searches are not uncommon, but in the lawsuit that followed, the student newspaper argued that this kind of search threatened the freedom of the press and should not be permitted unless police officials first obtain a subpoena—which is more difficult for police to get than a simple search warrant is. The subpoena process would also provide the press with notice prior to the search and allow editors and reporters to challenge the issuance of the subpoena.

The newspaper argued that the unannounced third-party search of a newsroom seriously threatened the ability of the press to gather, analyze and disseminate news. The searches could be physically disruptive for a craft in which meeting deadlines is essential. Confidential sources—fearful that some evidence that would reveal their identity might surface in such a search—would refuse to cooperate with reporters. Reporters would be deterred from keeping notes and tapes if such material could be seized in a search. All of this, and more, could have a chilling effect on the press, lawyers for the newspaper argued.

The Supreme Court, in a 5-3 ruling, disagreed with the newspaper. Justice Byron White ruled that the problem was essentially a Fourth Amendment question (i.e., was the search permissible under the Fourth Amendment?), not a First Amendment question, and that under existing law a warrant may be issued to search any property if there is reason to believe that evidence of a crime will be found. "The Fourth Amendment has itself struck the balance between privacy and public need and there is no occasion or justification for a court to revise the Amendment and strike a new balance," White wrote. The associate justice conceded that "where the materials sought to be seized may be protected by the First Amendment, the requirements of the Fourth Amendment must be applied with 'scrupulous exactitude.'" He added, "Where presumptively protected materials are sought to be seized, the warrant requirement should be administered to leave as little as possible to the discretion of the officer in the field." But Justice White rejected the notion that such unannounced searches are a threat to the freedom of the press, arguing that the framers of the Constitution were certainly aware of the struggle between the press and the Crown in the 17th and 18th centuries, when the general search warrant was a serious problem for the press. Yet the framers did not forbid the use of search warrants where the press was involved,

White asserted. They obviously believed the protections of the Fourth Amendment would sufficiently protect the press.[109]

Newsroom searches by the police, a rarity in the decades before the *Zurcher* case, suddenly became a common occurrence. Journalists sought legislative relief from this onslaught and Congress responded by adopting the Privacy Protection Act of 1980.[110] The law limits the way law officers and government agents can search for or seize materials that are in the hands of persons working for the mass media or persons who expect to publicly disseminate the material in some other manner (e.g., public speech). The statute designates two categories of material that are protected: work products and documentary materials. The law says a work product "encompasses the material whose very creation arises out of a purpose to convey information to the public." In layperson's language, work products are reporters' notes, undeveloped film, outtakes and so forth. Documentary materials are described as "materials upon which information is formally recorded," such as government reports, manuscripts and the like. Congress based the statute on the commerce clause in the U.S. Constitution in order to extend the reach of the law to include state and local agencies as well as federal law enforcement personnel. To obtain either work products or documentary materials, law enforcement agencies must obtain a subpoena; a search warrant will not do. There are, however, exceptions to the rule. A law enforcement agency may conduct a warranted search of a newsroom to find work products in either of the following two situations:

1. When there is a probable cause to believe that the person possessing such materials has committed or is committing a criminal offense to which the materials will relate.
2. Where there is reason to believe that the immediate seizure of such materials is necessary to prevent the death of or serious harm to a person.

A search warrant may be used instead of a subpoena to obtain documentary materials if either of the two conditions just listed is met or in either of these two situations:

1. There is reason to believe that the giving of notice pursuant to gaining a subpoena would result in the destruction, alteration, or concealment of such materials.
2. That such materials have not been provided in response to a court order directing compliance with a subpoena, all other legal remedies have been exhausted, and there is reason to believe that further delay in gaining the material would threaten the interests of justice.

In most instances, then, law enforcement personnel will be forced to seek a subpoena to gain access to information kept in a newsroom or a reporter's home.

HOW TO RESPOND TO A SUBPOENA

What should a reporter do if he or she is subpoenaed? First, try to avoid the problem altogether. Don't give a promise of confidentiality to a source without first carefully considering whether such a promise is actually needed to get the story. Discuss the matter with an editor or the news director before agreeing to keep the name of a source confidential. Also, don't

What should a reporter do if he or she is subpoenaed?

109. *Zurcher v. Stanford Daily,* 436 U.S. 547 (1978).
110. See 42 U.S.C §§ 2000aa–2000aa-12.

talk, even informally, with persons outside the newspaper about stories in which confidential information or sources are involved. Such discussions may be ruled to constitute a waiver of the privilege you seek to assert at a later date.

But if a subpoena should arrive, the first thing to remember is that the police are not coming to your door to arrest you. The subpoena is simply an order that you have been called to appear at some type of proceeding or supply certain documents. So don't panic. Tell your editor or news director immediately. Ask to talk with your news organization's legal counsel. Don't attempt to avoid being served with the subpoena. While a reporter is under no obligation to make the job easier for the person serving the subpoena, resistance to this service may result in the subpoena being abandoned and a search warrant issued in its place. Don't ever accept a subpoena for someone else.

If the subpoena requests only published material, or video that has previously been broadcast, the newspaper or broadcasting station may simply provide this material without dispute. Journalists should be familiar with their news organization's policy on retaining notes, tapes, first drafts and so on. If there is no policy, it is worthwhile to ask management to consider adopting one. Once the subpoena has been served, the material sought is considered official evidence, and if it is destroyed to avoid having to produce it, the reporter very likely will be held in contempt of court. So once you have been served, begin gathering the material together in case you have to surrender it at some later time.

If you believe that the material or names of sources should be withheld, and your news organization disagrees, it is in your interest to hire your own attorney to represent you. The company attorney is working for the company, not you. Finally, remember that the odds of being forced to give up the material or names are low. The law is, for the most part, on your side these days.

SUMMARY   State legislatures and the federal government have adopted statutes and rules that offer some protection to journalists who hold confidential information sought by government agents and other individuals. Thirty-one states have adopted so-called shield laws, which provide a qualified privilege for reporters to refuse to testify in legal proceedings. Although sometimes these statutes can be helpful, they are not without problems. There is a lack of consistency among the state shield laws. These laws have definitional problems that permit courts to construe them very narrowly if they choose to. The laws usually protect only what someone tells a reporter, not what a reporter personally sees or hears. Often courts see the statutes as legislative interference with judicial prerogatives and go out of their way to interpret the laws in the least useful manner.

The Department of Justice has adopted rules that govern when and how federal agents may subpoena journalists, records possessed by journalists, and journalists' telephone toll records. The rules require federal agents to strike a balance between the public's interest in the free flow of information and effective law enforcement.

Congress passed the Privacy Protection Act of 1980 in response to a ruling by the U.S. Supreme Court that the First Amendment does not ban searches of newsrooms or reporters' homes. This act requires federal, state and local police agencies who seek a journalist's work products or other documentary materials to get a subpoena for these materials rather than seize them under the authority of a search warrant. The statute does provide exceptions to these rules. For example, premises may be searched and materials seized under a search warrant if police believe the reporter has committed a crime, if there is reason to believe someone will be harmed if the materials are not seized, or if police fear the materials might be destroyed if a subpoena is sought.

THE CONTEMPT POWER

Those who work in the mass media and run afoul of judicial orders or the commands of legislative committees can quickly feel the sharp sting of a contempt citation. Reporters who refuse to respond to a subpoena, editors who criticize a judge, newspapers that refuse to pay a libel or invasion-of-privacy judgment, all of these and more can be held in contempt. This was the case with both Matthew Cooper and Judith Miller in 2004 and 2005. In August 2004, Cooper was held in contempt of court by a federal judge for refusing to reveal to a grand jury the name of the government official or officials who leaked and revealed the identity of undercover CIA officer Valerie Plame to several journalists.[111] The judge ordered Cooper to be jailed and he fined the magazine $1,000 a day until Cooper revealed the name of the source who leaked Plame's name to members of the media. Cooper was allowed to remain free while the order was appealed, and he later submitted to a two-hour deposition in the matter, initially relieving Time and himself of legal repercussions. However, when Cooper was called before a grand jury for a second time later in 2004, he refused to testify and was held in contempt and ordered to jail for a second time (see page 416). His appeal to an appellate court was denied in 2005, and the Supreme Court refused to hear his case that same year.

In another high-profile case in 2004, U.S. District Judge Thomas Penfield Jackson held five different reporters in contempt of court.[112] Why? Because they refused to comply with an earlier order he had issued requiring them to reveal the identity of the confidential sources they used in reporting on the espionage investigation of Dr. Wen Ho Lee, a former Los Alamos nuclear scientist who was later cleared of all but one of the 59 charges against him.[113] In August 2004, Judge Jackson ordered each reporter, including journalists from such prestigious papers as the Los Angeles Times and The New York Times, to pay a fine of $500 a day until the reporter complied with the earlier order seeking the identity of the sources. Lee sought the names as part of a lawsuit he filed against the federal government. In June 2005, a unanimous three-judge panel of the U.S. Court of Appeals for the District of Columbia in *Lee* v. *Department of Justice* upheld the contempt charges and the $500-a-day fines issued by Judge Jackson against four of five reporters Lee had subpoenaed and deposed. In November 2005, a fifth reporter—Walter Pincus of the Washington Post—was held in civil contempt in the *Lee* case for refusing to reveal a confidential source.

111. *In re Special Counsel Investigation,* 332 F. Supp. 2d 33 (D.D.C. Aug. 9, 2004). Liptak, "Reporter from Time Is Held in Contempt."
112. *Lee* v. *U.S. Dept. of Justice,* 327 F. Supp. 2d 26 (D.D.C. Aug. 18, 2004).
113. Jurkowitz, "Reporters Found in Contempt."

HISTORY OF CONTEMPT

In 1631 in England, a British subject was convicted of a felony, a common enough event. This particular subject was angered at being found guilty, and after the sentence was read he threw a brickbat (a piece of broken brick) at the judge. The brickbat missed the judge, but the man was quickly seized, his right hand was cut off and nailed to the gallows, and he was immediately hanged in the presence of the court.[114]

While such judicial retribution is an uncommon exercise of the contempt power, it nevertheless is a representative example of the power of judges to control what goes on in their courtrooms. Even today, at the beginning of the 21st century, disobedience of or disrespect for the court is normally put down swiftly by exercise of the power of contempt. Any act that interferes with the orderly processes of justice is usually promptly stopped and the offender is quickly punished. While other governmental bodies (legislative bodies, for example) can use the contempt power, its use by judges, which is the subject of this section, is far more common today.

Courts today rarely justify the exercise of the contempt power on the grounds that it protects the integrity of the judge. Instead, protection of the authority, order and decorum of the court is the usual reason given for the use of the contempt power. Alternatively, the court will use contempt to protect the rights of the litigants using the court to settle a dispute.

KINDS OF CONTEMPT

Varieties of contempt are recognized through the common law, and efforts have been made to label these varieties. But these efforts have been unsatisfactory; there is frequently disagreement among courts about what kinds of behavior constitute what kinds of contempt. No attempt will be made to resolve these discrepancies in this book. It is sufficient to note that judges use the contempt power for two purposes:

A court can use the contempt power to protect the rights of a litigant in a legal dispute. A reporter who refuses to reveal the name of a source critical to the defense of a person charged with larceny could endanger the person's right to a fair trial. The contempt power can be used to force the reporter to testify. Similarly, a broadcasting station that refuses to pay the plaintiff a judgment after losing a libel case endangers the right of the injured party to repair his or her reputation. Again, the contempt power can be used to force the broadcaster to pay the judgment.

The contempt power can be used to vindicate the law, the authority of the court, or the power of the judge. A defendant who refuses to stop talking during a trial or an attorney who continually ignores judicial warnings against talking to reporters about the merits of the case can be punished with a contempt citation. So can a writer who carelessly and aggressively criticizes a court ruling in a newspaper editorial.

Judges who use the contempt power to protect the rights of litigants usually impose an indeterminate sentence against the target of the contempt. That is, a judge can jail a reporter until he or she is willing to reveal the name of the critical source. Or the court can fine the broadcaster a specific amount each day until the civil judgment is paid. The punishment is used to coerce the target of the citation to take some action.

Judges who use the contempt power to vindicate the law, the authority of the court, or the power of the judge will generally impose a determinate sentence. That is, a specific fine

114. Goldfarb, *The Contempt Power.*

($25,000) or jail sentence (30 days in jail). Here the sentence is strictly punishment; no coercion is implied.

The most onerous application of the contempt power occurs when it is summarily applied. When a judge uses summary contempt power, the jurist acts as a prosecutor ("I accuse you of . . ."), jury ("Guilty as charged") and judge (I sentence you to . . ."). This power is normally reserved for those occasions when the judge has actual firsthand knowledge of the contemptuous act—for example, if the defendant misbehaves in the courtroom or if the reporter refuses to answer questions relating to the identity of a source. When the summary power is applied, the accused has few of the rights normally associated with due process of law. There is no jury trial, no right to call witnesses. The accuser and the judge are one and the same.

Any contempt conviction can be appealed. As in any other case, the appeal is taken to the next higher court in the state or in the federal system. Normally the punishment is suspended pending the outcome of the appeal.

Contempt and the Press

The contempt power is broad and touches all manner of persons who run afoul of a judge. Journalists are among persons at jeopardy. What kinds of situations are most likely to result in contempt problems for the press? To list a few:

1. Failure to pay a judgment in a libel or invasion-of-privacy case.
2. Failure to obey a court order. The judge rules that no photos may be taken in the courtroom, or orders reporters not to publish stories about certain aspects of a case. If these orders are disobeyed, a contempt citation may result.
3. Refusal of a journalist to disclose the identity of a source or to testify in court or before a grand jury.
4. Critical commentary about the court. This might be an editorial critical of the court or a cartoon mocking the judge. Contempt citations have been issued to punish the press in such cases.
5. Tampering with a jury. A reporter tries to talk with jurors during a trial, asking questions about their views on the defendant's innocence or guilt.

These situations are some of the more common ways that members of the press might become involved in a contempt problem, although the list is by no means exhaustive.

LIMITATIONS ON CONTEMPT POWER

The early years of the 20th century must be regarded as a high-water mark for the contempt power, because since that time the opponents of this power have succeeded in placing rather severe limitations on its use. Make no mistake; it is not a sterile power. Judges can and still do use their contempt power. Great Falls (Mont.) Tribune reporter Melody Perkins found that out when she asked Judge John M. Marvel why the proceeding she had just been ushered out of was closed to the public. The judge declared that her question disrupted the courtroom, held her in contempt, and fined her $300. The Montana Supreme Court upheld the citation.[115] But

---

115. *Great Falls Tribune Co. v. Montana Eighth District Court*, 777 P. 2d 345 (1989).

today judges throughout the United States have far less freedom in how they use this power than they had in the first quarter of the 20th century.

Legislative Limits

One important limitation on the power of the court to use contempt comes from legislatures. For nearly 90 years, Congress has passed laws that limit use of the summary power by federal judges to dispose of contempt citations. The 1914 Clayton Antitrust Act, for example, requires that judges provide a jury trial in a contempt case when the contemptuous action is also a crime under federal or state law. In 1932, as a part of the Norris-LaGuardia Act, Congress mandated jury trials for all contempts arising out of labor disputes. The 1957 civil rights law provided for a jury trial for contempt when the sentence imposed exceeded 45 days in jail. The 1964 civil rights law contains the same provision.

Court-Imposed Limits

The bench itself imposes limitations on the use of the summary power. The Federal Rules of Criminal Procedure requires that in many instances notice be given the contemnor and a hearing be allowed. In addition, there is the right to counsel, the right to cross-examine witnesses, the right to offer testimony, and in many instances the right to a jury trial. If the contempt citation is based on criticism or disrespect of a judge, that judge is disqualified from the proceeding. Bail is also allowed. The courts and legislatures in many states also deem that a jury trial is a requirement in an indirect contempt.

In the instances just noted, the legislature or the bench itself grants the right to a jury trial. Is there a constitutional right to a jury trial in such cases? The U.S. Supreme Court grappled with this question in the 1960s.

In 1964 the high court ruled that there is no constitutional right to a jury trial in a contempt case in upholding the contempt conviction of the governor of Mississippi, Ross Barnett, who willfully disobeyed an order of the U.S. Court of Appeals for the 5th Circuit. As one might expect at that time and in that place, the substantive question involved was civil rights. However, a footnote to the court's opinion states, "Some members of the Court are of the view that, without regard to the seriousness of the offense, punishment by summary trial without a jury would be constitutionally limited to that penalty provided for petty offenses."[116]

Petty offenses generally carry a sentence of six months or less. What the court seemed to be hinting at is that a jury trial is constitutionally required if the penalty exceeds more than six months in jail. In 1966 in *Cheff* v. *Schnackenberg,*[117] the high court specifically said what it had implied in the *Barnett* case—that sentences exceeding six months cannot be imposed in cases of criminal contempt without giving the accused a jury trial. Two years later, in *Bloom* v. *Illinois,*[118] the high court took the last step and ruled that criminal contempt is a crime in the ordinary sense and that since the U.S. Constitution guarantees the right to a jury trial in criminal cases, prosecutions by state courts for serious criminal contempts (those with more than a six-month penalty) must be heard by a jury.

116. *U.S.* v. *Barnett,* 376 U.S. 681 (1964).
117. 384 U.S. 373 (1966).
118. 391 U.S. 194 (1968).

In 1941 the U.S. Supreme Court placed a distinct limit on the power of federal judges to use their summary power in punishing contempts. An 1831 statute had limited the use of this power to contempts committed in the presence of the court or "so near thereto" as to obstruct the administration of justice. In 1918 the high court ruled that the words "so near thereto" had a causal meaning. Any act that was in close relationship to the administration of justice could be punished summarily.[119] Twenty-three years later the Supreme Court reversed itself on this matter in the case of *Nye* v. *U.S.*[120] Justice William O. Douglas cited research that had been done on the 1831 statute by legal scholars during the mid-1920s that showed Congress had intended the words to have a geographic, not a causal, meaning. Before the summary power can be used, Douglas wrote, the misbehavior must be in the courtroom or in the physical proximity of the courtroom. Most people today believe this interpretation permits a federal judge to exercise the summary power to punish acts that take place in the courtroom, in the hallway outside the court, and perhaps in the lobby of the courthouse, but not much farther. Conceivably, a noisy demonstration just outside the building might also be ruled to be "so near thereto" to affect the administration of justice.

Through various means, then, during this century the summary power of judges has been limited, and in turn the limitations have reduced the contempt power. Through statutes that explicitly limit the use of the summary power and through court rulings that limit the severity of punishment that may be applied in the absence of a jury, the absolute power of judges has been trimmed. Nevertheless, the summary power is still a threat. And even six months in jail is a long time!

First Amendment Limitations

The First Amendment was not raised as a barrier to contempt conviction until relatively modern times—in 1941 to be exact. In 1941, and again in 1946 and 1947, the U.S. Supreme Court ruled that freedom of the press to comment on the judiciary must be protected, except in those circumstances in which the commentary presents a serious threat to the proper functioning of the legal process. These three decisions—*Bridges* v. *California* and *Times Mirror Co.* v. *Superior Court*,[121] *Pennekamp* v. *Florida*,[122] and *Craig* v. *Harney*[123]—stand as the bedrock support for the argument that the First Amendment protects the press in writing about the judiciary.

The first case, *Bridges* v. *California* and *Times Mirror Co.* v. *Superior Court*,[124] consisted of two appeals from decisions by California courts, and the cases were decided together by the Supreme Court. In the first case, labor leader Harry Bridges was held in contempt of court when he publicly threatened to take the dockworkers out on strike if the courts attempted to enforce a judicial ruling against Bridges and his union. In the second case, the Los Angeles Times was ruled in contempt for publishing a series of anti-labor editorials. The trial court claimed that the editorials were aimed at influencing the disposition of cases concerning labor unionists that were before the court.

---

119. *Toledo Newspaper Co.* v. *U.S., 247 U.S. 402 (1918).
120. 313 U.S. 33 (1941).
121. 314 U.S. 252 (1941).
122. 328 U.S. 331 (1946).
123. 331 U.S. 367 (1947).
124. 314 U.S. 252 (1941).

In a 5-4 decision, the high court repudiated the idea that the contempt power is valid because it is deeply rooted in English common law. Justice Hugo Black wrote that even if this were the case, the idea ignores the generally accepted historical belief that "one of the objects of the Revolution was to get rid of the English law on liberty of speech and press." Black said that before a judge can use the contempt power to close off discussion of a case, there must be a "clear and present danger" that the discussion will produce interference with the proper administration of justice. In applying Holmes' famous World War I clear-and-present-danger sedition test to contempt, Black meant that only those threats to justice that are imminent or immediate can be punished. The substantive evil must be extremely serious and the degree of imminence extremely high before utterances can be punished, he wrote.

Black said that before a judge can use the contempt power to close off discussion of a case, there must be a "clear and present danger" that the discussion will produce interference with the proper administration of justice.

The government argued in these cases that commentary on a case is clearly proper, but only *after* the case is completed so that the course of justice will not be influenced. Black rejected this notion, saying that it is while a trial is under way that the public interest about a case is highest. He wrote:

> We cannot start with the assumption that publications actually do threaten to change the nature of legal trials and that to preserve judicial impartiality it is necessary for judges to have a contempt power by which they can close all channels of public expression to matters touching on the pending cases.[125]

It should be noted parenthetically that in using the clear-and-present-danger test to block contempt convictions, Justice Black made better use of those four words than did the high court in its application of the test in sedition trials. The clear-and-present-danger test indeed became an effective means of stopping contempt convictions against the press.

This concept was reinforced five years later when in the second case, *Pennekamp* v. *Florida,* the court reviewed an appeal from the Florida Supreme Court involving a contempt citation against the Miami Herald. The Herald had been highly critical of the trial courts in Dade County, Fla., for many months. In at least two editorials, it was argued that the courts worked harder to protect the criminals than they worked to protect the people. But the newspaper's evaluation of the courts' performance was founded on serious misstatement of facts. The court found both the editor, John D. Pennekamp, and the newspaper in contempt and levied fines against them both.

The Supreme Court overturned the convictions, noting, "We are not willing to say under the circumstances of this case that these editorials are a clear and present danger to the fair administration of justice in Florida." Justice Stanley Reed wrote that although he could not precisely define clear and present danger, certainly the criticism of a judge's actions in a non-jury trial would not affect the legal process. What about the factual errors in the editorials? Justice Reed said the errors were immaterial. Free discussion, Reed said, is a cardinal principle of Americanism. Discussion after a trial ends might be inadequate and can endanger the public welfare. Freedom of discussion should be given the widest range compatible with the essential requirement of the fair and orderly administration of justice. "We conclude," Reed wrote, "that the danger under this record to fair judicial administration has not the clearness and immediacy necessary to close the door of permissible public comment. When that door is closed, it closes all doors behind it."[126]

---

125. *Bridges* v. *California* and *Times Mirror Co.* v. *Superior Court,* 314 U.S. 252 (1941).
126. *Pennekamp* v. *Florida,* 328 U.S. 331 (1946).

The following year, the court once again reinforced the First Amendment barrier to the use of the contempt power in its decision in *Craig* v. *Harney,* the third case. In this case a Texas newspaper had been highly critical of a judge who directed a jury to return a verdict against a well-liked citizen in a civil suit. The Corpus Christi Caller-Times was found in contempt of court, and again the high court struck down the conviction. Justice William O. Douglas admitted that in the court's opinion the critical articles were unfair because they contained significant errors about what had actually occurred at the trial. "But inaccuracies in reporting," he wrote, "are commonplace. Certainly a reporter could not be laid by the heels for contempt because he missed the essential point in a trial or failed to summarize the issues to accord with the views of the judge who sat on the case."[127]

Douglas wrote that it took more imagination than the court possessed to find "in this sketchy and one-sided report of a case any imminent or serious threat to a judge of reasonable fortitude." Douglas added, "Where public matters are involved, the doubts should be resolved in favor of freedom of expression rather than against it."

The three cases just discussed—*Bridges, Pennekamp,* and *Craig*—represent three strong statements in favor of a broad discussion of judicial matters, of trials, and of the legal process. To some degree they also represent a limitation on the contempt power of the courts. The clear-and-present-danger test is a formidable hurdle for any judge to clear before punishing a newspaper or television station with a contempt citation. However, lest we get swept away by the court's rhetoric, it is important to look at what was involved in each of these cases, or rather what was not involved. In none of the cases did the judge first issue an order banning certain kinds of publicity about the case. In none of the cases could a jury have been influenced by the media publicity. In none of the cases did the press publish or broadcast evidence or statements prohibited at the trial. As a matter of fact, all three cases involved the same question— commentary or criticism directed toward a judge. From these cases it is clear that the Supreme Court expects the nation's judges to be strong, not to bend in the wind of public opinion, not to be influenced by journalistic commentary. But the court has never indicated that it has the same expectations with regard to juries. It has never said that a judge must allow the press free rein in its comments on a pending case with regard to material evidence or the credibility of witnesses. The caution, then, is not to read more into these decisions than is actually there.

COLLATERAL BAR RULE

When a journalist violates a court order, a contempt citation is probably forthcoming. But what if the court order appears to be illegal or unconstitutional on its face? Can a journalist still be held in contempt of court for violating such an order? The answer to that important question is maybe, for there is no clear resolution of this matter at present. The legal concept involved is called the **collateral bar rule,** a rule that requires that all court orders, even those that appear to be unconstitutional and are later deemed to be unconstitutional by an appellate court, must still be obeyed until they are overturned. The collateral bar rule states that a person who violates a court order cannot collaterally challenge the order's constitutionality as a defense to the contempt charge. Instead, that person must obey the order and hope to get it overturned on appeal. While this rule has been rarely invoked against the press, a U.S. Court of Appeals ruling from 1972 stands as a stark reminder of its meaning. In that case reporters

127. *Craig* v. *Harney,* 331 U.S. 367 (1947).

Gibbs Adams and Larry Dickinson of the Baton Rouge (La.) Morning Advocate and State Times ignored what they believed was an unconstitutional court order forbidding them from publishing information about what took place in an open federal court hearing. The pair, who were each fined $300, appealed the order and the 5th U.S. Circuit Court of Appeals ruled that the trial judge's actions were clearly unconstitutional. At the same time, the court upheld the contempt citations, ruling that a person may not, with impunity, violate a court order that later turns out to be invalid.[128]

While this rule, sometimes called the Dickinson rule, seems grossly unfair, there is a logic to it.

While this rule, sometimes called *the Dickinson rule,* seems grossly unfair, there is a logic to it. The court system would cease to operate as it does if people had a choice of whether or not to obey a court order. Without the power to coerce behavior, judges would be unable to discharge their duties and responsibilities, and courts would become mere boards of arbitration that issue advisory opinions. Temporarily obeying a court order that is later deemed unconstitutional certainly poses a hardship to anyone subjected to the order, but it is especially onerous to members of the press. A delay in publishing a news story can seriously diminish the value of the news. And even a speedy or expedited appeal to an appellate court might take two weeks to two months. But the judge who wrote the opinion in the *Dickinson* case probably spoke for many jurists when he wrote, "Newsmen are citizens too. They too may sometimes have to wait."[129]

Only one important collateral bar case involving the press has occurred since this 1972 ruling. In this case a federal judge in Rhode Island found the Providence Journal and its editor, Charles Hauser, in contempt of court for violating the judge's order forbidding the publication of any information that had been obtained by the government from an illegal FBI wiretap.[130] The 1st U.S. Circuit Court of Appeals ruled that the trial judge's order was transparently invalid and could not serve as a basis for a contempt citation. The appellate court added, however, that in the future publishers and broadcasters should first try to get an appellate review before violating a court order.[131] With the 5th Circuit and the 1st Circuit somewhat in disagreement about this matter, the Supreme Court agreed to hear an appeal. But after reading briefs and hearing arguments, the members of the high court dismissed the appeal because the special prosecutor who handled the appeal for the government had failed to obtain proper authorization from the Solicitor General of the United States to petition for a writ of certiorari.[132] At the federal level, then, the issue remains unresolved. But courts in Washington and Illinois have flatly rejected the rationale of the *Dickinson* case,[133] and courts in Arizona,[134] California,[135] Massachusetts[136] and Alabama[137] have considered the matter but have issued ambiguous rulings.

---

128. *U.S.* v. *Dickinson,* 465 F. 2d 496 (1972).
129. *U.S.* v. *Dickinson,* 465 F. 2d 496 (1972).
130. *In re Providence Journal,* 630 F. Supp. 993 (1986).
131. *In re Providence Journal,* 820 F. 2d 1354 (1987).
132. *U.S.* v. *Providence Journal,* 108 S. Ct. 1502 (1998).
133. *State ex rel Superior Court* v. *Sperry,* 483 P. 2d 609 (1971) and *Cooper* v. *Rockford Newspapers,* 365 N.E. 2d 746 (1977).
134. *Phoenix Newspapers* v. *Superior Court,* 418 P. 2d 594 (1966) and *State* v. *Chavez,* 601 P. 2d 301 (1979).
135. *In re Berry,* 493 P. 2d 273 (1968).
136. *Fitchburg* v. *707 Main Corp.,* 343 N.E. 2d 149 (1976).
137. *Ex parte Purvis,* 382 So. 2d 512 (1980).

SUMMARY

The power of a judge to punish for contempt of court is a remnant of the power of English royalty. Today, courts have broad powers to punish persons who offend the court, interfere with legal proceedings, or disobey court orders. Contempt is used both to protect the rights of private persons who are litigating matters in the courts and to punish a wrong committed against the court itself.

Some limits have been placed on the contempt power. Legislatures often restrict the kinds of sentences judges may impose for contempt or require a jury trial before a contempt conviction. The Supreme Court has ruled that before criticism of a court may be punished by contempt, it must be shown that the criticism created a clear and present danger of the likelihood of interference with the administration of justice. In some jurisdictions appellate courts have ruled that persons must obey even unconstitutional contempt orders (the *Dickinson* rule).

BIBLIOGRAPHY ⟶

Agents of Discovery. Washington, D.C.: Reporters Committee for Freedom of the Press, 2003.

Alexander, Laurence B., and Leah Cooper. "Words That Shield: A Textual Analysis of the Journalist's Privilege." *Newspaper Research Journal* 18 (1997): 51.

Barringer, Felicity. "Justice Department in Rare Move, Obtains a Reporter's Phone Records." *The New York Times,* 29 August 2001, A18.

Belluck, Pam. "Reporter Is Found Guilty for Refusal to Name Source." *The New York Times,* 19 November 2004, A24.

———. "Reporter Who Shielded Source Will Serve Sentence at Home." *The New York Times,* 10 December 2004, A28.

Berger, Robert G. "The 'No Source' Presumption: The Harshest Remedy." *American University Law Review* 36 (1987): 603.

Broder, John M. "From Grand Jury Leaks Comes a Clash of Rights." *The New York Times,* 15 January 2005, A8.

Calvert, Clay. "And You Call Yourself a Journalist? Wrestling With a Definition of 'Journalist' in the Law." *Dickinson Law Review* 103 (1999): 411.

Confidential Sources and Information. Washington, D.C.: Reporters Committee for Freedom of the Press, 1993.

Editorial. "Press Freedom on the Precipice." *The New York Times,* 16 October 2004, A16.

Fost, Dan. "Bay Judge Weighs Rights of Bloggers." *San Francisco Chronicle,* 8 March 2005, A1.

Frazer, Douglas H. "The Newsperson's Privilege in Grand Jury Proceedings: An Argument for Uniform Recognition and Application." *Journal of Criminal Law and Criminology* 75 (1984): 413.

Glaberson, William. "Wrestling Insults Fuel Free Speech Case." *The New York Times,* 24 October 1998, A10.

Goldfarb, Ronald. *The Contempt Power.* New York: Columbia University Press, 1963.

Johnson, Peter. "'Times' Reporter Held in Contempt in CIA Leak Inquiry." *USA Today,* 8 October 2004, 3A.

Jurkowitz, Mark. "Reporters Found in Contempt in Nuclear Case." *The Boston Globe,* 19 August 2004, A3.

Kase, Kathryn. "When a Promise Is Not a Promise: The Legal Consequences for Journalists Who Break Promises of Confidentiality to Sources." *Hastings Communications and Entertainment Law Journal* 12 (1990): 565.

Langley, Monica, and Lee Levine. "*Branzburg* Revisited: Confidential Sources and First Amendment Values." *George Washington Law Review* 57 (1988): 13.

Leonnig, Carol D. "Journalist Cited for Contempt in Leak Probe." *Washington Post,* 8 October 2004, A02.

Liptak, Adam. "Reporter from Time Is Held in Contempt in C.I.A. Leak Case." *The New York Times,* 10 August 2004, A1.

Malheiro, Sharon K. "The Journalist's Reportorial Privilege—What Does It Protect and What Are Its Limits?" *Drake Law Review* 38 (1988–89): 79.

Mullen, Lawrence J. "Developments in the News Media Privilege: The Qualified Constitutional Approach Becoming Common Law." *Maine Law Review* 33 (1981): 401.

"The Newsman's Privilege: Government Investigations, Criminal Prosecutions, and Private Litigation." *California Law Review* 58 (1970): 1198.

Parrell, Mark J. "Press/Confidential Source Relations: Protecting Sources and the First Amendment." *Communications and the Law* 47, March 1993.

Schmidt, Susan. "Reporter Held in Contempt of Court Again in Leaks Probe." *Washington Post,* 14 October 2004, A19.

Schmitt, Richard B. "Prosecutor's Lips Still Sealed in Probe of Leaked Information." *Los Angeles Times,* 23 October 2004, A10.

Seelye, Katharine Q. "Fewer Sources Go Nameless in the Press, Survey Shows." *The New York Times,* 14 March 2005, C6.

Steinberg, Jacques. "Threat of Jailing Is Lifted with Reporter's Testimony." *The New York Times,* 25 August 2004, A16.

Strupp, Joe. "Now Feds Target 'Merc' Reporters in BALCO Probe." *Editor & Publisher Online,* 13 September 2004, News.

Tucker, Neely. "Wen Ho Lee Reporters Held in Contempt." *Washington Post,* 19 August 2004, A02.

Utevsky, David. "Protection of Sources and Unpublished Information." Paper presented at the meeting of Washington Volunteer Lawyers for the Arts, Seattle, Wash., 27 January 1989.

Wigmore, John H. *A Treatise on the Anglo-American System of Evidence in Trials at Common Law.* 2nd ed. Boston: Little, Brown, 1934.

Chapter 11

FREE PRESS/FAIR TRIAL
Trial Level Remedies and Restrictive Orders

Legal problems frequently arise as the press and the criminal justice system intersect in our society. These problems are usually cast as the result of two seemingly conflicting constitutional rights: the right to a free press guaranteed by the First Amendment, and the right to a fair trial guaranteed by the Sixth Amendment. If the press publishes and broadcasts anything it chooses about a crime or a criminal suspect, isn't it possible readers and viewers will make up their minds about the guilt or innocence of the accused? And if they do, won't the members of the jury (who are also readers and viewers) approach the case with prejudice either for or against the defendant? What will happen to the guarantee of a fair trial? But if the court moves to restrict this publicity by the mass media to protect the integrity of the trial process, won't this interfere with the rights of the press? What about the First Amendment? We explore these issues in Chapters 11 and 12. Included is a discussion of the kinds of publicity that may damage the right to a fair trial, and the various schemes adopted by the courts to try to minimize the impact of this publicity or restrict the flow of this kind of information.

PREJUDICIAL CRIME REPORTING

Americans' fascination with news about crime is not a recent fetish. Indeed, the people of this nation have always found stories about crime and criminals alluring. In the 19th century, hangings were public spectacles with a carnival-like atmosphere and were usually well attended. Today so-called true crime and mystery novels are among the most popular print genres, and dramas about crime and criminals usually rank among the most popular TV shows. (See the various episodes of "Law and Order" and "CSI," and their multiple offspring, for example.)

The news media, especially television news, are also saturated with stories about crime and the administration of criminal justice. Many television news producers salivate at the prospect of yet another celebrity trial—be it Robert Blake, Kobe Bryant, Michael Jackson, Martha Stewart or whoever. It is hard to judge whether there are more stories about crime in a particular news medium today, say the Detroit News or WCCO-TV in Minneapolis, or whether it just seems that way because there are so many more mass media covering crime. Five hundred or so print and broadcast reporters were on hand for the first day of the Michael Jackson trial in California in early 2005. That is clearly more than cover most institutions of the federal government, major political events, or even more important trials like the prosecution of the executives of Enron, a case in which there were millions of victims of the company's fraudulent operations. And in vying for the short attention span of most Americans, many members of the press have few qualms about reporting stories that go beyond the facts of a case to include rumors, their own opinions about guilt or innocence, and speculations by the scores of so-called experts who dwell just beyond the boundaries of the actual courthouse proceedings.

This quasi–news reporting of crime and the criminal justice system is at the heart of the long-standing matter that journalists and lawyers alike call the free press–fair trial controversy. This controversy—like the news coverage of crime—also dates to the early years of the republic. Many lawyers and judges argue that it is extremely difficult or even impossible for a defendant to get a fair trial—a right guaranteed by the Sixth Amendment—when important segments of the press have already decided the individual is guilty. This kind of publicity, they say, will surely influence members of the community who will ultimately sit on the jury that decides the defendant's guilt or innocence. Reporters and editors argue that the influence of the press is seriously exaggerated in such arguments, and regardless, the First Amendment protects the press from government interference, even if it occasionally acts irresponsibly.

No one claims that all reporting about crime or criminals is a problem. While the heavy emphasis by the press on reporting crime is regarded as misplaced by most observers, even the severest critics agree that most stories are straightforward and fair. But potential problems arise in those instances when the press saturates a community with stories about a particular crime or criminal defendant—the killing of Matthew Shepard in Wyoming and JonBenet Ramsey in Colorado; the Washington, D.C., sniper shootings; the Laci Peterson murder; the sexual assault charges against Kobe Bryant; or the child molestation allegations against Michael Jackson. What kind of news creates the greatest danger of prejudice? Here is a list of some of the more common kinds of stories that critics say can endanger the defendant's rights:

1. **Confessions or stories about the confession that a defendant is said to have made, which include even alluding to the fact that there may be a confession.**

Source: © AP/Wide World Photos

The Fifth Amendment says that a person does not have to testify against him- or herself. Sometimes confessions that are made are later retracted. The Associated Press reported in June 2001 that a man who spent 22 years in prison in Florida after he confessed to six murders and a rape was released when DNA evidence indicated he didn't commit the crimes. The man, who had the mental capacity of an 8-year-old, confessed to the crimes to please the detectives, whom he regarded as his buddies, lawyers said.[1]

2. **Stories about the defendant's performance on a test, such as a polygraph, lie detector or similar device, and about the defendant's refusal to take such a test.** Many kinds of so-called scientific or forensic evidence, which may help police identify a suspect, are not admissible as evidence at a trial.

3. **Stories about the defendant's past criminal record or that describe the defendant as a former convict.** This information is not permitted at the trial. It may seem entirely logical to some people that when someone has committed 99 robberies and is again arrested for robbery, the accused probably did commit the crime. As a matter of fact, past behavior is immaterial in the current trial for robbery. The state must prove that the defendant committed *this* robbery.

The trial of Michael Jackson in 2005 on charges of child molestation was just one more in a seemingly endless parade of celebrity trials. Jackson was ultimately acquitted of the charges.

1. Farrington, "DNA Indicates Confessions."

4. **Stories that question the credibility of witnesses and that contain the personal feelings of witnesses about prosecutors, police, victims or even judges.**

5. **Stories about the defendant's character** (he or she hates children and dogs), **associates** (he or she hangs around with known syndicate mobsters), **and personality** (he or she attacks people on the slightest provocation).

6. **Stories that tend to inflame the public mood against the defendant.** Such stories include editorial campaigns that demand the arrest of a suspect before sufficient evidence has been collected; person-on-the-street interviews concerning the guilt of the defendant or the kind of punishment that should be meted out after the accused is convicted; televised debates about the evidence of the guilt or innocence of the defendant. All these kinds of stories put the jury in the hot seat as well as circulate vast quantities of misinformation.

7. **Stories that are published or broadcast before a trial that suggest, imply or flatly declare that the defendant is guilty.** Months before Scott Peterson went on trial in 2004 for the murder of his wife and unborn child, many people in the mass media, espcially television commentators, opined that he was guilty of the crime. That the jury ultimately agreed is immaterial. Even a person who is ultimately convicted is guaranteed a fair trial.

IMPACT ON JURORS

That intensive press coverage of a criminal case *might* jeopardize the rights of the defendant is generally assumed. But whether it *will* in fact harm the defendant's Sixth Amendment rights remains more of an open question. There are those who argue vigorously that any publicity can result in a jury biased for or against the defendant. And many of these true believers don't stop with criticism of the news media. In the spring of 2005 U.S. News and World Report magazine published a long story on how the popular drama "C.S.I." (and its various clones), a program about crime scene investigators, was influencing jury verdicts across the nation. Some prosecutors argued that many jurors who regularly watched the program were demanding scientific evidence, including positive DNA test results, before they were willing to convict. Some defense attorneys argued the opposite side, claiming that the television programs portrayed forensic or scientific evidence as being unambiguous and more certain than it really is. The problem with both sets of assertions is that there was, at that time, simply no evidence to support them. The advocates could only point to a handful of cases in which they said they believed the jury made the incorrect decision, and then blamed it on the television show.

In fact, there is a serious lack of evidence that even intensive press coverage of a particular case can have a negative impact on the defendant. For more than 50 years, social scientists have attempted to prove or disprove this assumption with less than great success. The law prohibits the use of real jurors in actual trials as subjects for this research. Consequently, researchers have tried to generate other means to gather the data that is needed. Some have attempted to replicate a trial in an experimental setting. Others have used survey research methods to poll members of a community about what they know and think about highly publicized criminal cases in the area. Neither technique has provided totally satisfactory results. Complicating the resolution of this problem is the fact that many social scientists are beginning to believe that people tend to remember far less about what they read or watch on television than has been traditionally assumed. Social scientists, then, have failed to establish the validity of the assumption that prejudicial publicity will seriously damage the defendant's fair trial rights.

Some persons familiar with the controversy have expressed reservations about this traditional assumption. After a substantial study, University of Wisconsin researcher Robert E. Drechsel concluded that "the evidence also indicates that the magnitude of the fair trial–free press issue may be overblown. Most trial judges and other judicial sources do not seem to perceive frequent major problems with prejudicial publicity."[2] And the judges on at least two U.S. appeals courts have expressed a similar sentiment. "Pretrial publicity does not, however, lead in every criminal case to an unfair trial," noted judges on the 9th U.S. Circuit Court of Appeals in 1988.[3] And judges on the 4th U.S. Circuit Court of Appeals said that "it verges upon insult to depict all potential jurors as nothing more than malleable and mindless creations of pre-trial publicity." They added, "There is somewhat of a tendency to frequently overestimate the extent of the public's awareness of news."[4]

The next issue to focus on is the jury itself. Just what is an impartial juror?

"Most trial judges and other judicial sources do not seem to perceive frequent major problems with prejudicial publicity."

THE LAW AND PREJUDICIAL NEWS

The definition of an impartial juror used by the courts in the United States is almost 200 years old and stems from a ruling in 1807 by Chief Justice John Marshall in the trial of the former U.S. vice president Aaron Burr for treason. Charges that the jurors were biased were made at the trial. Marshall proclaimed that an impartial juror was one free from the dominant influence of knowledge acquired outside the courtroom, free from strong and deep impressions that close the mind. "Light impressions," Marshall wrote, "which may fairly be supposed to yield to the testimony that may be offered, which leave the mind open to a fair consideration of that testimony, constitute no sufficient objection to a juror."[5]

In the last 55 years the U.S. Supreme Court has fashioned other tests to guide trial judges and appellate courts, tests constructed on Chief Justice Marshall's words. The high court has decided several cases relating to pretrial publicity, but three decisions stand out. The first stemmed from a series of brutal killings in Indiana. Leslie Irvin was arrested in connection with a series of six murders. Statements that Irvin had confessed to all six killings received widespread publicity. At the trial, of 430 persons called as potential jurors, 375 told the judge that they believed Irvin was guilty. Of the 12 jurors finally selected, eight told the court they thought he was guilty before the trial started. The Supreme Court overturned Irvin's murder conviction, noting that in this case, in which so many persons so many times admitted prejudice, statements of impartiality could be given little weight.[6]

Fourteen years later surfer Jack Murphy, nicknamed "Murph the Surf," appealed his conviction for robbery and assault, arguing he had been denied a fair trial because of pretrial

2. Drechsel, "Media-Judiciary Relations," 1.
3. *Seattle Times* v. *U.S. District Court,* 845 F. 2d 1243 (1988).
4. *The Washington Post Co.* v. *Hughes,* 923 F. 2d 324 (1991).
5. *U.S.* v. *Burr,* 24 Fed. Cas. 49 No. 14692 (1807).
6. *Irvin* v. *Dowd,* 366 U.S. 717 (1961).

publicity. Murphy was involved in theft of millions of dollars in jewels (including the fabled Star of India sapphire) from New York City's Museum of National History. He claimed the jury had been prejudiced by the massive publicity about the burglary as well as stories about his previous criminal record and other shady exploits. The Supreme Court disagreed. Only 20 of the 78 potential jurors who were questioned told the Florida trial judge they believed Murphy was guilty. The high court said that this ratio was not comparable to the evidence of hostility or overwhelming prejudice toward the defendant that was found in the *Irvin* case. The Constitution requires that the defendant have a "panel of impartial, indifferent jurors," ruled Justice Thurgood Marshall; "they need not, however, be totally ignorant of the facts and issues involved."[7] It is sufficient that a juror can lay aside his or her impressions and personal opinions and render a considered opinion based on the evidence presented in court. Many people see this 1975 ruling in *Murphy* v. *Florida* as rejecting the often-asserted principle that publicity about a criminal case automatically results in bias toward the defendant.

The high court re-emphasized this point nine years later in the case of *Patton* v. *Yount*.[8] In this ruling the court said that "the relevant question is not whether the community remembered the case, but whether the jurors at Yount's trial had such a fixed opinion that they could not judge impartially the guilt of the defendant."

WHAT IS AN IMPARTIAL JUROR?

An impartial juror is one whose mind is free from the dominant influence of knowledge acquired outside the courtroom, free from strong and deep impressions that close the mind. *U.S.* v. *Burr,* 1807.

"The constitution requires that the defendant have a panel of impartial, indifferent jurors. They need not, however, be totally ignorant of the facts and issues involved." *Murphy* v. *Florida,* 1975.

"The relevant question is not whether the people in the community remember the case, but whether the jurors had such a fixed opinion they could not judge impartially the guilt of the defendant." *Patton* v. *Yount,* 1984.

On the basis of these rulings and others, two important generalizations emerge. The high court is willing to permit jury service by a person who possesses knowledge or has opinions about a case, so long as

1. the knowledge or opinions are not so closely held that they cannot reasonably be put aside in the face of evidence; and
2. the publicity surrounding the case is not so widespread and prejudicial as to render a potential juror's assurances of impartiality as unbelievable.[9]

---

7. *Murphy* v. *Florida,* 421 U.S. 784 (1975).
8. 467 U.S. 1025 (1984).
9. See Minow and Cate, "Who Is an Impartial Juror?" 631.

SUMMARY

The First Amendment to the U.S. Constitution guarantees freedom of the press; the Sixth Amendment guarantees every criminal defendant a fair trial. Many people believe these two amendments are in conflict because, often, publicity about a criminal case can prejudice a community against a defendant and make it impossible to find a fair and impartial jury in the case. The kinds of publicity that can be most damaging to a defendant include material about confessions or alleged confessions, stories about a past criminal record, statements about the defendant's character, comments about the defendant's performance on scientific tests or refusal to take such tests, and statements made before a trial suggesting the defendant's guilt.

Social science has not yet proved that such publicity does in fact create prejudice or that persons cannot set aside their beliefs about a case and render a verdict based on the facts presented at the trial. An impartial juror is not required to be free of all knowledge or impressions about a case; the juror must be free of deep impressions and beliefs that will not yield to the evidence that is presented in court during the trial.

TRADITIONAL JUDICIAL REMEDIES

For more than 200 years American judges have had tools at their disposal to try to mitigate or lessen the impact that pretrial publicity might have on a trial. These tools range from carefully examining potential jurors about their knowledge of the case, to moving the trial, to delaying a hearing while publicity abates. As a last resort a criminal conviction can be reversed if there is evidence that the trial was tainted by publicity. But this last resort is costly because it usually involves a retrial, resulting in added expense and inconvenience for all parties involved. These traditional judicial tools, sometimes called trial level remedies, permit the court to reduce the impact of the publicity on the trial without inhibiting the press in any way.

As a last resort a criminal conviction can be reversed if there is evidence that the trial was tainted by publicity.

TRIAL LEVEL REMEDIES FOR PRETRIAL PUBLICITY

1. Voir dire
2. Change of venue
3. Change of veniremen
4. Continuance
5. Admonition
6. Sequestration

VOIR DIRE

Before prospective jurors finally make it to the jury box, they are questioned by the attorneys in the case and oftentimes the judge. These interviews are designed to protect the judicial process from jurors who have already made up their minds about the case or who have strong biases toward one party or the other. In a process called **voir dire,** each prospective juror is questioned prior to being impaneled in an effort to discover bias. Pretrial publicity is only one source of juror prejudice. If the prospective juror is the mother of a police officer, she is likely to be biased if the defendant is on trial for shooting a police officer. Perhaps the juror is a business associate of the defendant. Possibly the juror says she doesn't believe in psychology or psychiatry, and the defendant intends to use an insanity defense.

When a pool of potential jurors (called the venire) is assembled, a preliminary screening may take place through the use of a written questionnaire. After this initial screening both sides in the case then question the remaining members of the venire, and either side can ask the court to excuse a potential juror. This procedure is called challenging a juror. There are two kinds of challenges: **challenges for cause** and **peremptory challenges.** To challenge a juror for cause, an attorney must convince the court that there is a good reason for this person not to sit on the jury. Deep-seated prejudice is one good reason. Being an acquaintance of one of the parties in the case is also a good reason. Any reason can be used to challenge a potential juror. All the attorney must do is to convince the judge that the reason is proper. There is no limit on the number of challenges for cause that both prosecutor and defense attorney may exercise.

A peremptory challenge is somewhat different. This challenge can be exercised without cause, and the judge has no power to refuse such a challenge.* There is a limit, however, on the number of such challenges that may be exercised. Sometimes there are as few as two or three and sometimes as many as 10 or 20, depending on the case, the kind of crime involved, the state statute, and sometimes the judge. This kind of challenge is reserved for use against persons whom the defense or the prosecution does not want on the jury but whom the judge refuses to excuse for cause. An attorney may have an intuitive hunch about a potential juror and want that person eliminated from the final panel. Or the juror's social or ethnic background may suggest a problem to the attorney.

To select jury members for the typical criminal trial, attorneys rely on the answers to the questions they ask potential jurors and on their intuition. In the occasional high-profile trial it is not uncommon for attorneys on both sides to undertake a far deeper scrutiny of the panel of potential jurors. For example, for the trial in the spring of 2001 of a former Ku Klux Klansman accused of murdering four young black girls when he bombed a Birmingham, Ala., church in 1963, the prosecution organized focus groups and polled nearly 500 residents of the Birmingham area to help them understand racial attitudes in the community. Government attorneys used the information they got from this research to help them select a jury, a jury of eight whites and four blacks, which later deliberated for just over two hours before bringing in a conviction.[10] And before Martha Stewart went to trial in early 2004 for obstruction of justice and securities fraud, her lawyers and advisors used polling and focus groups to try to uncover the kind of person who might make a favorable juror in her case.

Is voir dire a good way to screen prejudiced jurors? In the early 1970s nearly 80 percent of a large number of judges surveyed said they thought the question-and-answer process was

---

*The Supreme Court has placed limits on the use of preemptory challenges by attorneys to exclude persons from a jury solely on the basis of their race or gender. For example, the high court in 2005 overturned the 20-year-old murder conviction of a Texas man because, the court said, the jury selection had been infected by racial bias. The prosecution had used its preemptory challenges to remove 10 of 11 black potential jurors. *Miller-El* v. *Dreke,* No. 03-9659.

10. Sack, "Research Guided Jury Selection."

either highly effective or moderately effective in screening out biased jurors.[11] But media coverage of especially high-profile trials has increased dramatically since that time, and the results of a similar survey today might be different. Most lawyers say they agree that voir dire can be effective, to a point. Still, it is difficult to argue with critics who say that voir dire uncovers only the prejudice that the prospective juror is aware of or is not too embarrassed to admit. Biased jurors can lie when questioned about their biases. They may not even know their mind is made up about the guilt or innocence of the defendant. And the prejudices may have nothing to do with pretrial news coverage of the crime. Potential jurors may be prejudiced against defendants because of their race, the kind of work they do, or the neighborhood in which they live.

Good lawyers walk a fine line in selecting jurors. A defense attorney certainly doesn't want a juror who knows all about the case and has already made up his or her mind regarding a defendant's guilt. On the other hand, a juror who doesn't know anything about a widely publicized case might be just as bad. Mark Twain once facetiously suggested that "ignoramuses alone could mete out unsullied justice."* Few attorneys want the jury box filled with ignoramuses. The feelings of most good attorneys are reflected in remarks made by U.S. Attorney Jay B. Stephens, who suggested that the best jurors are intelligent jurors who listen to the evidence, who evaluate the evidence, and who do not go off on extraneous kinds of issues. "That purpose is served, I think, by informed jurors, by jurors who are an integral part of the community, who participate in the community, who are aware of what is going on in the community and who stay informed."[12]

CHANGE OF VENUE

A serious crime that has been heavily publicized in one community might have received scant press coverage in another community in the state. The court can, in order to impanel a jury of citizens who know much less about the case, move the trial to the second community. This change of location of the trial is called a **change of venue.** If this relocation of the trial is ordered, all the participants in the trial—the prosecutor, defense attorney, judge, defendant, witnesses and others—will go to this new location for the trial. The jury will be selected from citizens in the new community. In 2003, for example, the trials of the snipers who terrorized the Washington, D.C., suburbs were moved a considerable distance from communites where the crimes were committed. And the trial of Scott Peterson was moved 50 miles from his hometown of Modesto, Calif., the following year.

A trial in a state court can be moved to any other venue in the same state. A federal case can be moved to any other federal court, although keeping the trial as close as possible to the site of the crime is considered desirable. The federal trial of the defendants charged in the Oklahoma City bombing was moved to Denver, a city in the adjacent state of Colorado. In that case the move out of state rather than to another city in Oklahoma was prompted by the need to find courtroom facilities that could accommodate a trial of that magnitude.

Change of venue is costly. Witnesses, attorneys and other persons must be transported and housed and fed while the trial takes place in a distant city. The defendant must surrender

---

*Mark Twain, *Roughing It* (New York: New American Library Edition, 1962).
11. Bush, *Free Press and Fair Trial.*
12. U.S. Senate Subcommittee, *Federal Jury Selection,* 581.

Often the effectiveness of the change of venue depends on how far the trial is moved from the city in which the crime was committed.

the constitutional right to a trial in the district in which the crime was committed. Publicity about the case could appear in the media located in the community in which the trial is scheduled to be held, defeating the purpose of the change of venue. Often the effectiveness of the change of venue depends on how far the trial is moved from the city in which the crime was committed. A trial judge in Washington state who was concerned about newspaper coverage of a local murder case granted a change of venue. But he moved the trial to an adjoining county, the only other county in the state in which the "offending" newspaper had significant circulation. The move accomplished very little, and the judge ultimately was forced to close portions of the proceedings to the press.[13] While a change of venue can reduce the risk of prejudicial publicity influencing a jury, other equally problematic factors may be introduced into the trial. The difference in the ethnic and racial composition of one community as opposed to another could possibly change the outcome of a trial. When the trial of four white police officers accused of beating Rodney King, a black man, was moved to the largely white distant suburbs of Los Angeles in a change of venue, three of the officers were acquitted of the charges and the jury failed to reach a verdict regarding the fourth officer. This despite the fact that the beating was captured on videotape by a bystander. The officers' federal trial for violation of King's civil rights was held in the city of Los Angeles with a racially mixed jury, and all the officers were convicted.

In some states it is possible for the defense to seek a **change of veniremen** rather than a change of venue. Instead of moving the trial to another city, the court imports a jury panel from a distant community. In the summer of 2004 a federal judge in Alabama agreed to a plan to try Eric Rudolph, who was accused of planting a bomb outside a clinic in Birmingham, in Birmingham, but ruled that the jurors in the trial would be picked from communities in the northern part of the state instead of the three-county area surrounding that city. Rudolph later pleaded guilty to the crime. When this procedure is employed it usually means that the judge and attorneys visit the distant communities and select a jury panel, then transport the jurors to the community in which the trial will be held. This procedure costs the state less money, since all it must do is pay the expenses of the jurors for the duration of the trial.

CONTINUANCE

When a trial is continued, or a **continuance** is granted, the trial is delayed. By postponing a trial for weeks or even months, a judge expects that the people in the community will forget at least some of what has been written or broadcast about the case, and that expectation is probably legitimate. However, before a trial may be postponed, the defendant must sacrifice his or her right to a speedy trial, something guaranteed under the Constitution. Because the courtrooms in America are clogged, there are few truly speedy trials today, but a continuance delays a trial even longer. The defendant may spend this additional time in jail if bail has not been posted. It is also possible, even likely, that when the trial is finally set to begin, publicity about the case will reappear in the mass media.

But a continuance is a perfect solution in some cases. One judge told of how, just as he was scheduled to begin hearing a malpractice suit on a Monday morning, the Sunday paper, quite innocently, carried a long feature story on the skyrocketing costs of physicians' malpractice

---

13. *Federated Publications* v. *Kurtz,* 94 Wash. 2d 51 (1980).

insurance because of the large judgments handed down in courts. The article pointed out that physicians passed the additional insurance charges along to patients. The story was widely read. Jurors, who also pay doctors' bills, might hesitate to award a judgment to an injured patient knowing that it would raise insurance rates and ultimately cost patients more. The judge therefore continued the case for two months to let the story fade from the public mind.

ADMONITION TO THE JURY

Once a jury is impaneled, its members are instructed by the judge to render their verdict in the case solely on the basis of the evidence presented in the courtroom. Judges say they believe that most jurors take this **admonition** quite seriously. Jurors are also warned not to read newspaper stories or watch television broadcasts about the case while the trial is being held. Often jurors are excused from the courtroom while the trial judge hears arguments from the attorneys or even testimony from witnesses. In such instances the court usually wants to determine whether certain evidence is admissible in the case before the evidence is presented to the jury. The press may publish or broadcast reports about this evidence, whether or not it is admitted in the case. It would accomplish very little to keep such evidence from the jury during the trial if jurors could watch news stories about it during the evening television newscasts.

The following admonition, which is one used by King County, Wash., superior court judges, is typical:

> Do not discuss this case or any criminal case or any criminal matter among yourselves or with anyone else. Do not permit anyone to discuss such subjects with you or in your presence. . . . Do not read, view, or listen to any report in a newspaper, radio, or television on the subject of this trial or any other criminal trial. Do not permit anyone to read about or comment on this trial or any criminal trial to you or in your presence.

Evidence shows that most jurors pay close attention to these instructions. In the single major study in which real jury deliberations were examined to determine the impact of mass media publicity on the trial process, researchers found that jurors listen carefully to the cautionary instructions given to them by judges. The coordinator of that research project, Harry Kalven, noted in a letter to the director of the American Law Institute:

> We do . . . have evidence that the jurors take with surprising seriousness the admonition not to read the paper or discuss the case with other people. . . . Our overall impression . . . is that the jury is a pretty stubborn, healthy institution not likely to be overwhelmed either by a remark of counsel or a remark in the press.[14]

SEQUESTRATION OF THE JURY

Once a jury is selected, or impaneled, the problem of pretrial publicity diminishes. But other problems emerge. It is not uncommon for jurors to be removed from the courtroom during a trial while attorneys make arguments about the admissibility of evidence or the possible testimony of

14. Bush, *Free Press and Fair Trial.*

a witness. Except in extraordinary cases the public and press remain in the courtroom during these episodes, and what is discussed can and likely will be reported in newspapers and on television. Or prejudicial information may be generated by persons outside the courtroom during the trial and, again, be reported by the news media. In some instances the aforementioned admonition to the jurors may be considered insufficient to shield them from this publicity, and so the members of the panel are isolated from outsiders during the trial. They are not allowed to go home each evening but are housed in a hotel. They eat their meals together, relax together, go to and from the courthouse together. Telephone calls and e-mail (if permitted) are screened by court personnel. Newspapers and television news broadcasts are also screened for stories about the trial. This process is called **sequestration of the jury** and is mandatory in some states for trials that last longer than a day, unless both the state and the defense agree to waive the procedure. In a few other states sequestration of the jury is required in all death penalty cases. In most jurisdictions, however, the jurors are isolated only if the judge specifically orders it.

Sequestration of the jury can have serious drawbacks for the state, the jurors and the criminal justice system. It costs the state a lot of money to house and feed the jurors. New York reportedly spent $2.5 million a year putting up jurors overnight until mandatory sequestration was abandoned in 2001.[15] It cost jurors both time and money. Staying in a hotel and eating in restaurants for two or three days may be considered a lark by some people, but the trials in which jurors are sequestered often last weeks or even months. Lives are seriously disrupted, and few jurors can afford a loss of income over such a prolonged period of time. In extremely long trials, some jury members suffering hardships will ask to be excused before the trial is completed. And many attorneys fear the criminal justice system may be compromised as well. Sequestration may keep jurors free from unwanted prejudicial publicity about the case, but could generate a prejudice in jurors of a different kind, a prejudice against one party or the other for keeping them away from family and friends for an extended period. Defense attorneys express this fear most often, saying they believe jurors will blame the defendant for their hardships. But it was reported after the 1995 O.J. Simpson criminal trial that some jurors, who were sequestered for almost as long as Simpson was jailed, said they empathized with the defendant because of this.[16] The jurors in the second O.J. trial, the civil suit in which he was found guilty, were not sequestered.

SUMMARY   Trial courts have many ways to compensate for the prejudicial pretrial publicity in a criminal case. Each citizen is questioned by the attorneys and the judge before being accepted as a juror. During this voir dire examination, questions can be asked of the potential jurors about the kinds of information they already know about the case. Persons who have already made up their minds about the defendant's guilt or innocence can be excluded from the jury.

Courts have the power to move a trial to a distant county to find a jury that has not been exposed to the publicity about the case that has been generated by local mass media. While such a change of venue can be costly, it can also be an effective means of compensating for sensational publicity about a case.

15. Sengupta, "New York State."
16. Labaton, "Lessons of Simpson Case."

A trial can be delayed until the publicity about the case dies down. The defendant must waive the right to a speedy trial, but, except in highly sensational cases, granting a continuance in a trial can thwart the impact of the massive publicity often generated in the wake of a serious crime.

Jurors are always admonished by the judge to base their decision on the facts presented in court and not to read or view any news stories about the case while they are on the jury. There is evidence that they take these warnings quite seriously.

In important cases it is always possible to seclude, or sequester, the jury after it is chosen to shield it from publicity about the trial.

RESTRICTIVE ORDERS TO CONTROL PUBLICITY

Judges have been trying for many, many years to compensate for prejudicial pretrial publicity using the remedies outlined in the previous section. Some jurists and lawyers feel that these schemes are badly out-of-date. It costs the state more money to try a defendant when there is a change of venue or when an extensive voir dire is needed. These remedies don't always work, it is contended. There is a better solution to the problem: The court should control the kind and amount of information that is published or broadcast about the case. If this is done, it won't be necessary later on to compensate for any prejudicial publicity.

In the late 1960s and early 1970s the tool of choice for trial judges who sought to control pretrial publicity in a criminal case was the **restrictive order.** These judicial orders are called **gag orders** by many journalists, and this is an apt description. They are designed to stop the parties, the attorneys, the witnesses and sometimes even the press from making comments about specific aspects of a case. The growth in the use and popularity (among judges) of the restrictive order was primarily the result of a serious misunderstanding in the judiciary about what the U.S. Supreme Court said, or meant to say, about one of this century's most widely publicized murder cases: the prosecution of Dr. Sam Sheppard for the murder of his pregnant wife, Marilyn. Mrs. Sheppard was killed early in the morning on July 4, 1954. Her husband, Sam, claimed she was bludgeoned to death by an intruder who attacked her in her bedroom as she slept. From the very beginning of the investigation local police thought Sheppard was the killer. The case, which had all the elements of a good murder mystery, caught the fancy of the nation's press and was front-page news in all parts of the country. After three weeks of intense publicity, Sheppard was arrested and charged with murder. Publicity increased during the preliminary examination and trial, and few were surprised when the wealthy osteopath was convicted. Twelve years later, after several appeals had been denied, the U.S. Supreme Court reversed Sam Sheppard's conviction, ruling that he had been denied a fair trial because of pretrial and trial publicity about the case.[17]

17. *Sheppard* v. *Maxwell*, 384 U.S. 333 (1966). Sheppard was retried by the state of Ohio after the Supreme Court ruling. He was acquitted in this second trial. But his life was in ruins, and he died several years later of a liver disease. And yes, this case was the inspiration for both the television series and the movie called "The Fugitive."

Quit Stalling and Bring Him In!

CELEBREZZE SAYS BAY MAYOR IS PROTECTING MURDER SUSPECT

Special thanks to Cleveland State University Library

Headlines like these in the Cleveland Press pressured police to move against Sam Sheppard in 1954.

Justice Tom Clark, who wrote the Supreme Court's opinion in the *Sheppard* case, came down hard on the press, noting that bedlam reigned during the trial and that "newsmen took over practically the entire courtroom, hounding most of the participants in the trial, especially Sheppard." Justice Clark saved his sharpest criticism for Judge Blythin, who conducted the trial, and the other officers of the court for allowing the publicity about the case and the coverage of the trial to get out of hand. Here are some excerpts from Clark's opinion:

> Bearing in mind the massive pretrial publicity, the judge should have adopted stricter rules governing the use of the courtroom by newsmen . . . the court should have insulated witnesses [from the media]. . . . The court should have made some effort to control the release of leads, information and gossip to the press by police officers, witnesses and the counsel for both sides. . . . And it is obvious that the judge should have further sought to alleviate this problem by imposing control over the statements made to the news media by counsel, witnesses, and especially the coroner and police officers. . . . The court might well have proscribed extrajudicial statements by any lawyer, party, witness or court official which divulged prejudicial matters . . . the court could also have requested the appropriate city and county officials to promulgate a regulation with respect to dissemination of information about the case by their employees. In addition, reporters who wrote or broadcast prejudicial stories could have been warned as to the impropriety of publishing material not introduced in the proceedings.[18]

The Supreme Court made it quite clear in the *Sheppard* decision that it holds the trial judge responsible for ensuring that the defendant's rights are not jeopardized by prejudicial press publicity. While the court was critical of the press's behavior, no suggestion was made

---

18. *Sheppard* v. *Maxwell,* 384 U.S. 333 (1966).

that the judicial system launch an attack on the press. Nevertheless, at a conference following the decision, a professor of law, in explaining the high court's opinion in *Sheppard,* suggested that the court had proposed that judges use restrictive orders and the contempt power to control the press. Justice Clark, who was at the same meeting, told the assembled trial lawyers that the professor misinterpreted the court's ruling:

> The Court never held up contempt and it may well be that it will never hold up contempt because the restraint is too stringent. . . . The Court's opinion never mentioned any guidelines for the press. . . . I am not proposing that you jerk a newspaper reporter into the courtroom and hold him in contempt. We do not have to jeopardize freedom of the press.[19]

"I am not proposing that you jerk a newspaper reporter into the courtroom and hold him in contempt."

As we will see shortly, the remarks by Justice Clark were soon forgotten.

Two years after the ruling in *Sheppard* v. *Maxwell,* the American Bar Association proposed that trial judges use court orders (restrictive orders) to control the public statements and activities of the many participants in a trial—the prosecutor, witnesses, defense attorneys, jurors and others. (The document containing this proposal is known as the Reardon Report.) The bar association also recommended that judges use the contempt power against any persons who knowingly violated a valid judicial order not to disseminate information about the case. No state court system ever officially adopted the ABA recommendations, but the suggestions were taken to heart by many individual judges. Restrictive court orders became a common tool for a judge who sought to control the publicity about a pending criminal trial. One observer estimated that in the 10 years between 1966 and 1976, trial courts issued almost 175 restrictive orders, 39 of which prohibited the press from reporting or commenting on some aspect of a pending criminal case. In addition, nearly all the federal courts adopted standing orders regarding publicity in criminal cases.

Court orders aimed at blocking the flow of information about a legal proceeding fall into one of two categories. First, there are orders aimed directly at the press, prohibiting newspapers, magazines, and radio and television stations from printing or broadcasting specific information about a case. The second kind of restrictive order is aimed at the participants in the trial. It endeavors to stop the attorneys or witnesses or police or whomever from making statements or releasing information regarding the case. If the information is not made public, the press will be unable to publish it. Or so the theory goes. The Supreme Court has sharply limited the application of the first type of restrictive order, those aimed at the press. Fewer limitations have been placed on restrictive orders directed at trial participants. Let's explore both kinds of orders.

RESTRICTIVE ORDERS AIMED AT THE PRESS

There is no such thing as a typical restrictive order; in fact, that is one of the virtues seen in them by judges. Each order can be fashioned to fit the case at hand. They are often quite comprehensive. Orders aimed at the press usually limit the press coverage of certain specific details about a case; a defendant's confession or prior criminal record, for example. Orders aimed at the participants in a trial are usually much broader, forbidding comments by attorneys,

19. Friendly and Goldfarb, *Crime and Publicity.*

witnesses and others about any aspect of the case. In 1975 another sensational murder case began, one that would ultimately bring the issue of pretrial publicity and gag orders before the Supreme Court.

Erwin Simants was arrested and charged in North Platte, Neb., with the murder of all six members of the Henry Kellie family. Like the *Sheppard* case, the arrest of Simants caught the eye of the national news media, and local judge Hugh Stuart had his hands full with scores of reporters from around the state and the nation. Stuart responded by issuing a restrictive order barring the publication or broadcast of a wide range of information that he said would be prejudicial to Simants. The order was later modified by the Nebraska Supreme Court to prohibit only the reporting of the existence and nature of any confessions or admissions Simants might have made to police or any third party and any other information "strongly implicative" of the accused. The order was to stand in effect until a jury was chosen.

The press in the state appealed the publication ban to the U.S. Supreme Court, and in June 1976 the high court ruled that Judge Stuart's order was an unconstitutional prior restraint on the press. All nine members of the court agreed that Judge Stuart's court order was a violation of the First Amendment. But is such a restrictive order aimed at the press a violation of the First Amendment in every case? This is where the high court split. Four justices—Potter Stewart, William Brennan, Thurgood Marshall and John Paul Stevens—said that this kind of restrictive order would never be permissible. Four other justices—Warren Burger, Harry Blackmun, William Rehnquist and Lewis Powell—said that such orders may be permissible in extraordinary circumstances. And the ninth justice—Byron White—said there was really no need in this case to decide whether this kind of restrictive order might be permissible in extreme cases, but concurred with Chief Justice Burger's opinion that became the court's opinion.

The chief justice wrote that a restrictive order levied against the press might be permissible where the "gravity of the evil, discounted by its improbability, justifies such an invasion of free speech as is necessary to avoid the danger."[20] Burger then outlined a three-part test to be used to evaluate whether a restrictive order that limited the press would pass First Amendment scrutiny. He said that such an order could be constitutionally justified only if these conditions are met:

1. Intense and pervasive publicity concerning the case is certain.
2. No other alternative measure might mitigate the effects of the pretrial publicity.
3. The restrictive order will in fact effectively prevent prejudicial material from reaching potential jurors.

Prior restraint is the exception, not the rule, Chief Justice Burger wrote. There must be a clear and present danger to the defendant's rights before such a restrictive order can be constitutionally permitted, he said. In Simants' case, Burger said, while there was heavy publicity about the matter, there was no evidence that Judge Stuart had considered the efficacy of other remedies to compensate for this publicity. Also, the small community was filled with rumors about Simants and what he had told the police. Burger expressed serious doubts whether the restrictive order would have in fact kept prejudicial information out of public hands.

20. *Nebraska Press Association* v. *Stuart,* 427 U.S. 539 (1976).

> ### *NEBRASKA PRESS ASSOCIATION* TEST FOR
> ### RESTRICTIVE ORDERS AIMED AT THE PRESS
> 1. There must be intense and pervasive publicity about the case.
> 2. No other alternative measure might mitigate the effects of the pretrial publicity.
> 3. The restrictive order will in fact effectively prevent prejudicial publicity from reaching potential jurors.

Please note, the Supreme Court did not declare restrictive orders aimed only at *trial participants* to be unconstitutional. This issue was not raised in the trial, but it was and still is assumed that courts have much broader power to limit what attorneys, police and other trial participants can say about a case out of court. "Guidelines on Fair Trial/Free Press," issued by the United States Judicial Conference, for example, specifically recommends that federal courts adopt rules that limit public discussion of criminal cases by attorneys and court personnel and suggests that courts issue special rules in sensational criminal cases to bar extrajudicial comments by all trial participants. But, in light of the ruling in *Nebraska Press Association* v. *Stuart,* the guidelines state:

> No rule of court or judicial order should be promulgated by a United States
> district court which would prohibit representatives of the news media from
> broadcasting or publishing any information in their possession relating to a
> criminal case.

In both 1978 and 1979 the Supreme Court issued opinions in cases that had the effect of reinforcing the rule from the *Nebraska Press Association* decision; that is, restrictions on what the press may publish are to be tolerated only in very rare circumstances. In 1978 the high court prohibited the state of Virginia from punishing the Virginian Pilot newspaper for publishing an accurate story regarding the confidential proceedings of a state judicial review commission.[21] A Virginia state statute authorized the commission to hear complaints of a judge's disability or misconduct, and because of the sensitive nature of such hearings, the Virginia law closed the proceedings to the public and the press. The state argued that confidentiality was necessary to encourage the filing of complaints and the testimony of witnesses, to protect the judge from the injury that might result from the publication of unwarranted or unexamined charges, and to maintain confidence in the judiciary that might be undermined by the publication of groundless charges. While acknowledging the desirability of confidentiality, the Supreme Court nevertheless ruled against the state. Chief Justice Burger, writing for a unanimous court, stated that the "publication Virginia seeks to punish under its statute lies near the core of the First Amendment, and the Commonwealth's interests advanced by the imposition of criminal sanctions are insufficient to justify the actual and potential encroachments on freedom of speech and of the press." The court did acknowledge that the state commission could certainly meet in secret and that its reports and materials could be kept

---

21. *Landmark Communications* v. *Virginia,* 435 U.S. 829 (1978).

confidential. But while the press has no right to gain access to such information, once it possesses the information, it cannot be punished for its publication. In this sense the court followed the *Nebraska Press Association* rule limiting restraints placed on the press's right to publish.

In 1979 the high court declared unconstitutional a West Virginia statute that made it a crime for a newspaper to publish, without the written approval of the juvenile court, the name of a youth charged as a juvenile offender.[22] Again Chief Justice Burger wrote the opinion for the court and stressed the fact that once the press has legally obtained truthful information, it may publish this information. In this case two Charleston, W.Va., newspapers published the name of a 14-year-old boy who was arrested for the shooting death of a 15-year-old student. Reporters for the newspapers got the name from persons who had witnessed the shooting. "If the information is lawfully obtained," the chief justice wrote, "the state may not punish its publication except when necessary to further an interest more substantial than is present here."

"If the information is lawfully obtained, the state may not punish its publication except when necessary to further an interest more substantial than is present here."

In the past 27 years, in light of these three rulings, the number of restrictive orders aimed at the news media has dwindled substantially. Most trial judges won't even bother to issue an order when it is requested. Typical is the reaction of a California superior court judge who was asked by a defendant in a trial for the embezzlement of public funds to bar the press from publishing any information concerning the case, pending the outcome of the trial. The judge ruled there was no evidence that publicity about the case was creating a deep and hostile prejudice in the community, and any prejudice that did result could be treated more than adequately with a good voir dire.[23]

When a trial court does issue such an order, it is typically overturned on appeal. For example, the Utah Supreme Court struck down a gag order aimed at the Salt Lake City media that prohibited the media from referring to a defendant in a 1981 rape trial as the "Sugarhouse rapist." Ronald D. Easthope, the man on trial, had been convicted in the early 1970s for a series of rapes in the Sugarhouse area of Salt Lake City. He was arrested again for rape after he was paroled. The state's high court first outlined the three standards raised in the *Nebraska Press Association* case:

1. Did the publicity threaten his right to a fair trial?
2. Would measures short of the judge's restrictive order ensure the defendant a fair trial?
3. Will the restraint on the press achieve the desired results?

The state high court said the order was unconstitutional because the court had failed to consider any of these elements. The order was also invalid procedurally because the court had issued the order without notice or hearing. In addition, the state Supreme Court said, it was hard to see how the term "Sugarhouse rapist" could harm Easthope, since he had previously admitted his crimes in open court.[24]

The Supreme Court of Mississippi in December 1998 threw out both a contempt citation and a gag order in a case involving the publication of material relating to a defendant's

---

22. *Smith* v. *Daily Mail Publishing Co.,* 443 U.S. 97 (1979).
23. *People* v. *McPeters,* 32 M.L.R. 2278 (2004).
24. *KUTV* v. *Conder,* 668 P. 2d 513 (1983).

juvenile record.[25] The juvenile record was discussed by the prosecutor at an open sentencing hearing in an effort to convince the judge to impose a maximum sentence on a defendant who had been convicted of manslaughter. The judge told the reporter, Cynthia Jeffries of the Delta Democrat Times, not to include any material about the juvenile record in her story. Three days after the hearing the newspaper carried a story containing this information. Jeffries was arrested and brought before the judge, who found her in contempt for violating the order and sentenced her to three days in jail. The state's high court said the judge's action was improper in two ways. First, the judge treated this situation as a direct contempt—a contempt committed in the presence of the court (see page 458)—when in fact the contempt was committed outside the courtroom as the article was published. Jeffries should have had the benefit of procedural safeguards that accompany charges of an indirect or constructive contempt, the court ruled. Second, the court order regarding the juvenile record was invalid. The judge did not even consider the *Nebraska Press Association* test, the court ruled. The order should not have been issued had that test been applied, since it would not have been effective in protecting the defendant's rights. The courtroom was full of other people during the hearing, all of whom heard the same information the newspaper published. Also, the court could have used other means to avoid the problem in the first place, such as having the discussion about the juvenile record in the judge's chambers, away from the open courtroom.

Although the law regarding gag orders issued against the press is generally unambiguous, some trial judges still believe that circumstances exist in a case they are trying that justify issuing a restrictive order. In 1995 U.S. District Judge John Feikens barred Business Week magazine from publishing an article it had prepared based on sealed court documents. The documents had been sealed by Feikens during litigation between Procter & Gamble Co. and Bankers Trust Co. Procter & Gamble was suing the bank for using improper sales tactics to sell the company derivative securities. The giant home products company said it suffered a $100 million loss on the securities.

A Business Week reporter, Linda Himelstein, was given copies of the sealed documents by one of the lawyers from the law firm representing Bankers Trust. The lawyer later said he did not realize the documents had been sealed. Upon discovering that the magazine was about to publish a story based on the documents, both litigants asked Judge Feikens to issue the restrictive order. He complied with this request and the order was issued three hours before the magazine was to go to press. Instead of asking Judge Feikens to reconsider the order or to hold a hearing on the matter, Business Week challenged the order at the U.S. Court of Appeals for the 6th Circuit. A three-judge panel dismissed the appeal.[26] Associate Justice John Paul Stevens of the U.S. Supreme Court also refused to grant relief in the case. The high court jurist said the magazine should have first asked Judge Feikens for a hearing so he could gather relevant facts in the case and consider the merits of the First Amendment arguments.

Three weeks after the order was issued, Judge Feikens unsealed the relevant documents and permitted Business Week and other news media to publish stories related to the contents of these materials. Judge Feikens refused, however, to throw out his original order. He affirmed in

---

25. *Jeffries* v. *Mississippi,* 724 So. 2d 897 (1998).
26. *McGraw-Hill Cos.* v. *Procter & Gamble Co.,* 116 S. Ct. 6 (1995).

court his right to issue the ban because of the confidential nature of the materials in question.[27] Six months later the U.S. Court of Appeals for the 6th Circuit ruled 2-1 that Judge Feikens had been wrong to bar the magazine from publishing the story. "At no time," the court ruled, "even to the point of entering a permanent injunction after two temporary restraining orders, did the District Court appear to realize that it was engaging in a practice that, under all but the most exceptional circumstances, violates the Constitution: preventing a news organization from publishing information in its possession on a matter of public concern." In the circumstances existing in this case, the appellate tribunal ruled, the court had no power to issue the restraining order.[28]

Finally, in 2005 the 2nd U.S. Court of Appeals ruled that a trial judge's fear of a mistrial was not a sufficient reason to issue an order barring the press from revealing the names of the jurors in a trial of a former bank executive for obstructing a federal stock investigation. The appellate court noted that the jurors' names had been announced in open court, and that the record simply did not show that reporting these names would impair the defendant's right to a fair trial. Also, the trial judge had not even considered whether a viable alternative to the gag order might prevent the harm the judge assumed would result if the names were published, the court said.[29]

Are gag orders against the press ever affirmed by appellate courts? If there is good reason, such an order may be sustained. During the pretrial proceedings in the Kobe Bryant rape trial an electronic transcript of an in-camera (nonpublic) hearing that would have revealed the rape victim's identity was accidentally disseminated to seven media outlets. The trial court issued an order barring the press from disseminating the information contained in this document. The Colorado Supreme Court upheld the trial court's order. While the court noted the U.S. Supreme Court rulings on permitting the publication of rape victims' identities (see pages 319–322), it also noted Justice Marshall's statement that the state courts were not completely without the power to shield the identity of the victim of a sexual assault if such shielding were needed to protect an interest of the highest order, in this case the mandate of the Colorado rape shield statute.[30] Of course the rape charges against the NBA star were subsequently dropped. (See pages 82–84 for more details on this case.)

RESTRICTIVE ORDERS AIMED AT TRIAL PARTICIPANTS

While the law regarding restrictive orders aimed at the press is generally clear and has evolved swiftly since 1976, the law regarding restrictive orders barring participants from speaking or publishing about a case is less distinct and is still developing. The theory behind gagging the participants in the trial is simple: If attorneys, police officers, witnesses and others are forbidden from speaking about the case, reporters will be denied access to a considerable amount of material that might very well be prejudicial. Stories will not be written or broadcast, and potential jurors will not see or hear such information.

---

27. *Procter & Gamble Co.* v. *Bankers Trust Co.,* 900 F. Supp. 186 (1995).
28. *Procter & Gamble Co.* v. *Bankers Trust Co.,* 78 F. 3d 219 (1996). See also Peterson, "Court Voids Restraint."
29. *United States* v. *Quattrone,* 402 F. 3d 304 (2005).
30. *Colorado* v. *Bryant,* 94 P. 3d 624 (2004).

Gag orders aimed at the trial participants are not common, nor are they unusual, especially in high-profile cases involving celebrities or other high-visibility defendants. The judge in the Michael Jackson trial barred attorneys from discussing the case outside the courtroom. Lawyers, witnesses and police officers were barred from discussing the case against Scott Peterson for the murder of his wife and unborn child. These orders are often quite comprehensive. When the federal government prosecuted Richard Scrushy, the former corporate chairman and CEO of HealthSouth, a giant HMO, the case generated substantial publicity. A federal judge in Alabama issued a broad-based restrictive order to block extrajudicial statements by parties and the attorneys.[31] The order said:

- No extrajudicial statements until the final verdict by any participant, including witnesses, concerning
    1. materials provided in discovery in preparation for the case;
    2. character, credibility, reputation or criminal record of a party or witness, or the expected testimony of a party or witness;
    3. matters that counsel should know would be inadmissible at the trial, and would create a substantial risk of prejudicing a trial jury; and
    4. with the exception of Scrushy personally, any opinions as to the defendant's guilt or innocence.
- Participants must remove from their existing Web pages extrajudicial comments, allegations of prosecutorial misconduct and information discovered in the course of criminal discovery.
- Counsel for parties must avoid commenting in court papers that are not filed under seal on evidence that is irrelevant to legal matters involved in the case.
- All court personnel must not disclose any information relating to the case that is not part of the public record.

In 2002 the California Supreme Court even refused to hear appeals from the Associated Press and two newspapers of an order barring lawyers and witnesses in two criminal cases from talking to journalists.[32] Eight years earlier the 4th U.S. Circuit Court of Appeals gave its approval to a restrictive order that stopped the witnesses in a highly publicized trial of members of the Ku Klux Klan and the Nazi party from discussing their testimony with reporters. The publication of the proposed testimony could endanger the fair trial rights of the defendants, the court ruled.[33]

But judges must be careful about the manner in which they shape these orders. During the 1993 World Trade Center bombing trial in New York, Judge Kevin Duffy barred the lawyers for all parties from discussing any aspect of the case. "There will be no more statements [in the press, on TV, on radio, or in any other electronic media] issued by either side or their agents," Judge Duffy said. "The next time I pick up a paper and see a quotation from any of you, you had best be prepared to have some money. The first fine will be $200. Thereafter, the fines will be squared," he said. The threat of a $40,000 fine could certainly have a chilling effect on freedom

---

31. *United States* v. *Scrushy,* 32 M.L.R. 1814 (2004).
32. "California: No-Talking Order Stands."
33. *In re Russell,* 726 F. 2d 1007 (1984).

of expression. The 2nd U.S. Circuit Court of Appeals, while sympathetic to Judge Duffy's problems, nevertheless ruled that the order was inappropriate. "The limitations on attorney speech should be no broader than necessary to protect the integrity of the judicial system and the defendant's right to a fair trial," the court ruled. This order was too broad. In addition, the judge made no finding that an alternative to this kind of blanket order would not work as well.[34]

A gag ordered issued by a Georgia trial court in a case against members of a church accused of child cruelty and aggravated assault was deemed too broad by an appellate panel. The order required all participants in the case to respond to all media inquiries about the case by saying "no comment" or "whatever we have to say will be or has been said in court." The court said the order certainly barred statements that could prejudice the trial, but also barred statements that are not likely to have such an impact.[35] Finally, in a highly unusual case from New York, a trial court rejected a request for a gag order against a witness in a racketeering case, a witness who just happened to be a member of the media. John A. Gotti Jr. was indicted for racketeering and other offenses that were related to the attempted murder in 1992 of Curtis Sliwa, the man who founded the Guardian Angels, a community-based anti-crime group. For years Sliwa insisted that Gotti ordered him killed, and he said so repeatedly on a talk radio program he aired on WABC-AM. The show has a large listenership. Gotti asked the court to bar Sliwa from making such extrajudicial statements, or talking in any way about the merits of the case since he would almost certainly be a witness at Gotti's trial. The court agreed that the comments could be prejudicial, but said a restrictive order would be less effective than a thorough voir dire and strong jury instructions. The court said it hoped that Sliwa would respect Gotti's right to a fair trial and refrain from making prejudicial comments on the radio, but that a gag order was a last resort it was not willing to impose at that time.[36]

Until recently it has been difficult for the press to intervene in cases in which gag orders are aimed at participants. Most courts ruled that because the order is aimed at lawyers or witnesses and not reporters, the press does not have a direct interest in the case. The order doesn't directly affect reporters. The news media lack what lawyers call standing. But press attorneys vigorously attacked that idea, arguing that the press enjoys a First Amendment right to publish, but if trial participants cannot give reporters information, there will be nothing to publish. And some courts have accepted that argument.[37] In these instances many judges have applied the standards from the *Nebraska Press Association* ruling to evaluate the constitutionality of the court order. Other courts have rejected this notion.[38] But even in some instances when the press is permitted to challenge the order, the order is still sustained. The South Dakota Supreme Court permitted the press to challenge a gag order imposed on the attorneys, witnesses and other parties in a heavily publicized manslaughter and child abuse case, but ruled that the order was constitutional. "The media's First Amendment right," the court ruled, "consists of the right to gather and report the news. However, it has no constitutional right to information about a trial beyond what is seen and heard in the courtroom."[39]

34. *U.S.* v. *Salameh,* 992 F. 2d 445 (1993).
35. *Atlanta Journal-Constitution* v. *State,* 596 S.E. 2d 694 (2004).
36. *United States* v. *Gotti,* 33 M.L.R. 1083 (2004).
37. See, for example, *Connecticut Magazine* v. *Moraghan,* 676 F. Supp. 38 (1987).
38. See, for example, *Radio & Television News Ass'n* v. *U.S. District Ct.,* 781 F. 2d 1443 (1986).
39. *Sioux Falls Argus Leader* v. *Miller,* 610 N.W. 2d 76 (2000).

Lawyers specifically may be barred under court rules or codes of conduct from making extrajudicial comments on a case, whether or not a restrictive order has been issued. The U.S. Supreme Court made that clear in a 1991 ruling that focused on an alleged violation of general court rules that applied to attorneys. A lawyer named Dominic Gentile, who represented a client charged with taking money and drugs from a safety deposit box rented by undercover police agents, held a press conference in which he claimed that police were using his client as a scapegoat. Gentile said his client was innocent, that a police officer was the likely thief who took the money and drugs, and described some of the witnesses for the prosecution in the case as drug dealers. Gentile's client was acquitted, but the Nevada Supreme Court ruled that the attorney's comments at the press conference violated a court rule that limits what an attorney can say about a pending case. The rule prohibited attorneys in a criminal case from making prejudicial statements about the character, credibility, reputation or criminal record of a party, suspect or witness. The rule did provide a so-called safe haven for lawyers who were permitted to "elaborate the general nature" of the defense.

The Supreme Court ruled by a 5-4 vote that states may prohibit out-of-court statements by attorneys if these statements have a substantial likelihood of materially prejudicing the proceeding.[40] But the court also ruled by the same 5-4 margin that the Nevada rule prohibiting extrajudicial comments by attorneys was a violation of Gentile's constitutional rights because it was too vague. The so-called safe-haven provisions contained terms that were so imprecise that they failed to give fair notice of what is permitted and what is forbidden, which could lead to discriminatory enforcement of the rule. What the court said, then, was that rules like these are permissible limits on free speech so long as they spell out specifically what can and cannot be said.

It is common following the completion of a lawsuit for attorneys to talk with jurors to discover what factors led to the verdict the jurors reached. Today in highly publicized trials, reporters also want to talk with the jurors. It is not uncommon today for tabloid television programs and tabloid newspapers to offer jurors large sums of money if they will talk on the record about their deliberations. Many people believe such juror interviews are detrimental to the legal system. "It is now assumed that jurors must deliberate in secret so that they may communicate freely with one another, secure in the knowledge that what they say will not be passed along to others," noted Yale law professor Abraham S. Goldstein.[41]

A judge can certainly bar a juror from speaking with reporters while the trial is in progress or before the jury deliberations are completed. But once a jury has completed its work and is dismissed by the judge, the law becomes considerably murkier. Judges raise several concerns relating to the jury. One is to protect the jurors from harassment by the press. The pushing and shoving to get an interview can sometimes get intense. Another is to protect the sanctity of the deliberations. There are as many as 12 people on a jury. If one member speaks with reporters, it often reveals the actions and comments of other members of the panel. Finally, there are cases where subsequent trials of other defendants may involve the same crime, and juror comments about their deliberations could have an impact on these forthcoming hearings. And there is always the potential of a retrial following an appeal by the defendant who was

It is not uncommon today for tabloid television programs and tabloid newspapers to offer jurors large sums of money if they will talk on the record about their deliberations.

---

40. *Gentile* v. *Nevada State Bar,* 111 S. Ct. 2770 (1991).
41. Goldstein, "Jury Secrecy and the Media," 295.

found guilty by the jurors. In New Jersey in 2002 a jury was unable to reach a verdict in the trial of a former rabbi who was charged with killing his wife. The trial was extensively covered by the press and was televised by Court TV. Following the first trial the court forbade the press from contacting or attempting to interview the jurors. The New Jersey Supreme Court affirmed this order, ruling that interviews with jurors might reveal insights into the juror deliberative process, including the reaction to evidence presented in the trial. This would give the prosecution an advantage at the retrial, the court said.[42]

Courts have tried a variety of schemes to limit press communications with jurors following trials. Some judges have tried to solve this problem by denying the press and the public access to the names and addresses of the jurors (see page 510). Courts have gone so far as to shield all identifying information about the jurors, such as names, addresses, professions, ages and so on. The members of such an anonymous jury are referred to only by number. For example, before the so-called Unabomber, Ted Kaczynski, pleaded guilty, all identifying information about the 12 jurors and six alternates selected to hear his case was confidential. Anonymous juries were also used in both Oklahoma City bombing prosecutions and in the trials of the Branch Davidian survivors, Oliver North, and the World Trade Center bombers. First Amendment advocates note that the anonymous jury, once a rarity, seems to be becoming far more commonplace today.[43] But others note that this kind of jury was typically used in the past with very high-profile trials, and the nation has simply experienced a great many more such trials in recent years.

Other judges have issued restrictive orders barring the news media from questioning jurors about their deliberations. These efforts have had mixed results. As a general rule, orders prohibiting media access to jurors for an unlimited duration are unconstitutional. But general rules are hard to fashion because of the significant differences that often exist among trials. In November 1997 the 5th U.S. Circuit Court of Appeals upheld such an order in a high-profile racketeering trial. Trial judge Sarah Vance told jurors they could not be interviewed "by anyone concerning the deliberations of the jury" unless she issued an order permitting it. The appellate court said the order was justified, considering the intense media scrutiny of the trial. The U.S. Supreme Court refused to review the decision.[44]

Judges have only limited discretion in this matter. For example, "The Handbook for Jurors," published by the Judicial Conference of the United States, specifically says that it should be up to each juror to decide whether he or she talks with the press following a trial. Some appellate courts have not permitted trial judges to ban such interviews. The 9th U.S. Circuit Court of Appeals struck down a lower-court order that prohibited anyone from interviewing jurors after a trial. The order was issued by the trial court to minimize harassment of jurors, according to the trial judge, but the Court of Appeals ruled that not all jurors might regard media interviews as harassing.[45] The Kentucky Supreme Court in 2000 overturned a trial court's order forbidding anyone to initiate contact with a juror even after the trial was completed. The order was needed, the trial judge said, to ensure jurors' personal safety and privacy. The state high court said the order was too broad. If a former juror doesn't

---

42. *State* v. *Neulander,* 30 M.L.R. 2281 (2002).
43. Kirtley, *The Privacy Paradox.*
44. *U.S.* v. *Cleveland,* 128 F. 3d 267 (1997).
45. *United States* v. *Sherman,* 581 F. 2d 1358 (1978).

want to talk with a reporter, he or she should refuse the interview. If the reporter persists, the former juror can complain to authorities about harassment or intimidation. He or she can even institute a civil suit against the reporter. But the court order barring anyone from contacting the former jurors after the trial went far beyond the court's jurisdiction, which ended when the trial ended.[46] And the 5th U.S. Circuit Court of Appeals ruled that an order by a lower court in a highly publicized federal fraud trial went too far when it barred the press from independently trying to reach the members of a jury after the trial ended. The jurors were impaneled anonymously, and the press sought their names and addresses after the trial ended. The trial court refused to give reporters this information and barred them from trying to uncover this information themselves. The appellate court upheld the lower-court decision to refuse to reveal the jurors' identities, but said the journalists could certainly seek this information from sources other than confidential court records, court personnel or trial participants.[47]

Finally, the U.S. Supreme Court ruled in 1990 that a Florida statute prohibiting witnesses who testified before a grand jury from revealing what they had said, even after the grand jury's term had expired, was unconstitutional.[48] Proceedings before grand juries are ultrasecret. Nothing but the true bill, or indictment, issued by a grand jury is a part of the public record. A reporter was working on a story when he uncovered information the prosecutor believed the grand jury should hear. The reporter was subpoenaed and testified before the grand jury. After he had given his testimony, he sought to write a news story about his investigation as well as his experiences before the grand jury. But the statute blocked his effort. So he sued in U.S. District Court to have the law declared to be unconstitutional. Ultimately, the Supreme Court did just that.

Chief Justice William Rehnquist wrote that traditionally courts have taken very seriously the need for secrecy in grand jury proceedings. But, he said, "we have recognized that the invocation of grand jury interests is not some talisman that dissolves all constitutional protections." In this case, the chief justice said, the situation involved a reporter's right to divulge information of which he was in possession before he testified before the grand jury, not information he had gained as a result of his participation in the grand jury proceeding. Citing the ruling in *Smith* v. *Daily*[49] (see page 484), Rehnquist said the state could not punish a journalist for publishing information that he or she had legally obtained. While important interests were at stake in maintaining a veil around the activities of a grand jury, these interests in this case were insufficient to outweigh the First Amendment interests.

Restrictive orders that bar the press from publishing information about a criminal case have ceased to be a serious problem for journalists. Orders that limit what trial participants can say remain a nuisance, however, and probably do not serve the judicial system as well as many observers might imagine. Rumors tend to thrive in an atmosphere in which the release of accurate information is stifled. It would be better perhaps to provide journalists determined to publish something about a case with accurate and truthful statements rather than push them to report what is ground out by a rumor mill.

46. *Cape Publications Inc.* v. *Braden,* 39 S.W. 3d 823 (2001).
47. *United States* v. *Brown,* 250 F. 3d 907 (2001).
48. *Butterworth* v. *Smith,* 110 S. Ct. 1376 (1990).
49. *Smith* v. *Daily Mail Publishing Co.,* 443 U.S. 97 (1979).

SUMMARY   In some instances trial courts have attempted to limit the publication of prejudicial information about a case by issuing court orders restricting what the press may publish or what the trial participants may publicly say about a case. These restrictive orders grew out of a famous U.S. Supreme Court decision in the mid-1960s that ruled a trial judge is responsible for controlling the publicity about a case.

In 1976 the Supreme Court ruled that the press may not be prohibited from publishing information it has legally obtained about a criminal case unless these conditions are met:

1. Intense and pervasive publicity about the case is certain.
2. No other reasonable alternative is likely to mitigate the effects of the pretrial publicity.
3. The restrictive order will prevent prejudicial material from reaching the jurors.

In two subsequent rulings the high court reaffirmed its 1976 decision that confidential information legally obtained by the press may be published. These cases involved the name of a juvenile suspect in a murder case and the names of judges whose conduct had been reviewed by a confidential state judicial commission.

Although judges may still limit what trial participants say publicly about a case, even these restrictive orders have come under constitutional scrutiny in recent years.

BIBLIOGRAPHY ⟶

Bush, Chilton R., ed. *Free Press and Fair Trial: Some Dimensions of the Problem.* Athens: University of Georgia Press, 1971.

"California, No-Talking Order Stands." *The New York Times,* 23 August 2002, A12.

Carmody, Deirdre. "Business Week Files Appeal to Supreme Court." *The New York Times,* 20 September 1995, A10.

Drechsel, Robert E. "An Alternative View of Media-Judiciary Relations: What the Non-Legal Evidence Suggests about the Fair Trial–Free Press Issue." *Hofstra Law Review* 18 (1989): 1.

Farrington, Brendan. "DNA Indicates Confessions Were False." *Seattle Post-Intelligencer,* 16 June 2001, A3.

Friendly, Alfred, and Ronald Goldfarb. *Crime and Publicity.* New York: Random House, Vintage Books, 1968.

Goldstein, Abraham S. "Jury Secrecy and the Media: The Problem of the Postverdict Interview." *University of Illinois Law Review* 1993 (1993): 295.

Kirtley, Jane, ed. *The Privacy Paradox.* Arlington, Va.: Reporters Committee for Freedom of the Press, 1998.

Labaton, Stephen. "Lessons of Simpson Case Are Reshaping the Law." *The New York Times,* 6 October 1995, A1.

Minow, Newton, and Fred Cate. "Who Is an Impartial Juror in an Age of Mass Media?" *The American University Law Review* 40 (1991): 631.

Pember, Don R. "Does Pretrial Publicity Really Hurt?" *Columbia Journalism Review,* September/October 1984, 16.

Peterson, Iver. "Court Voids Restraint on Business Week." *The New York Times,* 6 March 1996, C12.

Rutenberg, Jim. "Presumed Innocence? Not on Cable TV News." *The New York Times,* 26 April 2003, A15.

Sack, Kevin. "Research Guided Jury Selection in Bombing Trial." *The New York Times,* 3 May 2001, A12.

Sengupta, Somini. "New York State Ends the Mandatory Sequestration of Jurors." *The New York Times,* 31 May 2001, A20.

U.S. Senate Subcommittee on Improvement in Judicial Machinery of the Senate Judiciary Committee. *Hearings on Federal Jury Selection.* 90th Cong., 1st sess., 1967, 581.

Faced with Supreme Court rulings that blocked the use of restrictive orders to stop press coverage of the criminal justice system, judges in the 1980s began to close judicial proceedings to deny to reporters information that may be prejudicial to the defendant's fair trial rights. The press challenged these closures, and as with the restrictive orders, appellate courts found that such closures usually violated the First Amendment. This issue, as well as a discussion of voluntary press guidelines and the right to take photographic and electronic recording equipment into the courtroom, is the focus of this chapter.

CLOSED PROCEEDINGS AND SEALED DOCUMENTS

Press coverage of crime and the criminal justice system has always been a staple of the American press. And, as noted in the previous chapter, judges and lawyers have worried about the impact of this press coverage on the fair trial rights of defendants throughout the history of this republic. Many people think the problem has gotten worse since the middle of the last century because of the ability of the mass media to literally saturate the nation with the news of a particular case. It was in the 1960s that restrictive orders became popular weapons to blunt the impact of such publicity, but the Supreme Court sharply curbed the power of judges to issue such orders a decade later. (See pages 481–486.)

Unable to restrict what the press printed or broadcast, some judges began to limit the access of the press and public to portions of the criminal justice process. It is a simple idea; if journalists can't attend a hearing or see a document, they will have little to report. But the Supreme Court curbed the power of judges to deny such access in a series of rulings. Unfortunately this matter has not been resolved quite as neatly as the restrictive-order issue. The closure of hearings and the sealing of judicial documents continues today, and some observers think such closures are occurring more frequently than in the recent past.

A panel of First Amendment attorneys speaking at the 2004 Practising Law Institute's Communications Law conference described the previous 12 months as a troublesome year for access. Hearings involving suspected terrorists and an unusual number of so-called celebrity trials have exacerbated the situation, putting pressure on judges to find ways to mitigate the intense media coverage. But it probably goes beyond that. The press today just seems to find certain cases that are irresistible and then literally saturates the entire nation with news and features about the case. And it often makes little sense. About 16,000 people were murdered in the United States in 2002. Why, then, did the killing of Laci Peterson, a pregnant housewife, dominate national news coverage for almost a year? The man charged with the crime, her husband, wasn't a rock star or a television personality or even a sports celebrity. He was a fertilizer salesman. When the nation's press grabs onto a story like this the news coverage can be like a blanket, smothering the efforts of the court to give the defendant the fair trial rights guaranteed by the constitution.

This chapter will explore the issue of access to the justice system. The Supreme Court first attempted to resolve the growing tendency to close hearings and seal documents in 1980. Two other decisions followed in the middle of the decade. Today a judge who is asked to close a judicial hearing or seal court documents faces a considerable hurdle if he or she agrees to bar the press and the public from the proceeding or deny access to documents. An outline of the judicial test that establishes this hurdle follows. Following this outline there will be an examination of how this test has been applied in a variety of situations.

OPEN COURTS AND THE CONSTITUTION

In 1980 the U.S. Supreme Court ruled in a 7-1 ruling (Justice Lewis Powell took no part in this case) that there was a right under both the common law and the First Amendment to the U.S. Constitution for the public and the press to attend a criminal trial.[1] Six years later the high court extended this right of access to other judicial proceedings and records. In its ruling in this case, *Press-Enterprise* v. *Riverside Superior Court*,[2] the justices fashioned a rather complicated test that a judge must apply before he or she can constitutionally close off access to the judicial process.

The first thing a judge must determine if the closure issue arises is whether the proceeding or document is what the law regards as presumptively open or closed. A hearing that is presumptively open, for example, is one that is normally open to the public and the press. To determine whether the proceeding or document is presumptively open or not, the judge

1. *Richmond Newspapers* v. *Virginia,* 448 U.S. 555 (1980).
2. 478 U.S. 1 (1986).

must ask a couple of questions:

1. **whether this kind of hearing (or document, if access to a court record is involved) has traditionally and historically been open to the press and public, or**
2. **whether public and press access to this hearing will play a positive role in the functioning of the judicial process.**

If the court determines that this kind of hearing has traditionally been open, *or* that allowing the press and the public to attend the hearing will have a positive impact on the judicial process, then he or she must declare the hearing to be presumptively open. Then it is up to the persons seeking to close the hearing, the defendant or the state, to convince the court that there is a good reason to close it. In doing this, the advocates of closure must

1. **advance an overriding interest that is likely to be harmed if the proceeding remains open or the court permits access to the court document.** Examples of such interests include the right to a fair trial for the defendant, or protection of a witness's privacy. Then the advocate of closure must
2. **prove to the court that if the hearing or document is open to the press and public, there is a *substantial probability* that this interest will be harmed,** that the jury will be prejudiced or the privacy of the witness will be invaded, for example.

If the advocate of closure proves that there is a substantial probability that such harm may occur, then the judge must

3. **consider whether there are reasonable alternatives to closure that might solve the problem.** Perhaps a thorough voir dire or change of venue would reduce the probability of prejudice. Closure of the hearing or the sealing of the document should be the last option, not the first option, considered by the court.

If there are no viable alternatives, then it is the responsibility of the judge to

4. **narrowly tailor the closure so there is an absolute minimum of interference with the rights of the press and public to attend the hearing or see the document.** A pretrial hearing on evidence might include many issues beyond the single issue that could harm the defendant. The court must close only that portion of the hearing dealing with the single issue. Or the court must exclude the press and public from only that portion of a witness's testimony that might cause embarrassment or humiliation, not the entire testimony.

Finally, the trial judge must

5. **make evidentiary findings to support this decision and prepare a thorough factual record relating to the closure order, a record that can be evaluated by an appellate court.** This final element is important. Appellate courts want to be certain that the trial judge thoughtfully and carefully considered options other than closure as a solution to the problem. The Georgia Supreme Court voided an order closing the pretrial phase of a sensational murder trial because the judge had stated simply that alternatives to closure were considered and found to be insufficient. "A closure order must fully articulate the alternatives to closure and the reasons why the alternatives would not protect the movant's [the party seeking closure] rights," the court ruled.

And in 2005 the Illinois Court of Appeals rejected a trial court's order blocking public and media access to certain pretrial hearings and records. The court issued the order because, it said, media access to the material, which included inadmissible evidence, would "tend" to create "more than a potential problem." The appellate court said the judge failed to cite any facts to support his fears of potential problems, and he did not even consider alternatives to sealing the evidence.[3]

This *Press-Enterprise* test applies to documents as well as to hearings, and a decision by the 10th U.S. Circuit Court of Appeals is instructive in how the test is applied. Journalists covering the trials of Timothy McVeigh and Terry L. Nichols, who were charged with bombing the federal building in Oklahoma City, sought access to documents relating to the proceedings. They sought redacted (censored) portions of Nichol's motion to suppress certain evidence and exhibits, notes made by an FBI agent who initially interviewed Nichols, and redacted portions of McVeigh's and Nichol's motions for separate trials. The court said that while suppression motions are traditionally open, access has not been historically extended to evidence ruled inadmissable, and in this case only the inadmissable material has been sealed. Access to raw notes, such as those written by the FBI agent, is not supported by either tradition or logic, because it would provide exposure to hearsay and other unsupported and inadmissable matter. Finally, the court said it would assume, because of traditional practice, that there is a right of access to some portions of the documents relating to separate trials. With regard to the latter set of documents, the court said release of the material could endanger both defendants' right to a fair trial since these papers contained candid material needed by the court to assess whether separate trials were necessary. The appellate court said it would not second-guess this decision, since the trial judge had made adequate findings to support the closure order.[4]

PRESS-ENTERPRISE TEST FOR THE CLOSURE OF PRESUMPTIVELY OPEN JUDICIAL PROCEEDINGS AND DOCUMENTS

1. The party seeking closure, the defendant or the government or sometimes both, must advance an overriding interest that is likely to be harmed if the proceeding or document is open.

2. Whoever seeks the closure must demonstrate that there is a "substantial probability" that this interest will be harmed if the proceeding or document remains open.

3. The trial court must consider reasonable alternatives to closure.

4. If the judge decides that closure is the only reasonable solution, the closure must be narrowly tailored to restrict no more access than is absolutely necessary.

5. The trial court must make adequate findings to support the closure decision.

---

3. *Rockdale Citizen Publishing Co.* v. *Georgia,* 463 S.E. 2d 864 (1995); *People* v. *LaGrone,* Ill. App. Ct. No. 4-05-0509, 10/24/05.
4. *U.S.* v. *McVeigh,* 119 F. 3d 806 (1997).

OPEN AND CLOSED TRIALS

With guidance from the Supreme Court, courts have applied the *Press-Enterprise* test to a wide variety of hearings and documents. The widest access is granted to trials, and that is where this section will start.

Judges have an exceedingly difficult time closing off access to traditional criminal trials. The Supreme Court spoke unambiguously about such hearings in the 1980 ruling, *Richmond Newspapers* v. *Virginia.*[5] The case stemmed from a state court ruling in a Virginia trial.

In March 1976 John Stevenson was indicted for murder. He was tried and convicted of second-degree murder, but his conviction was reversed. A second trial ended in a mistrial when a juror asked to be excused in the midst of the hearing. A third trial also resulted in a mistrial because a prospective juror told other prospective jurors about Stevenson's earlier conviction on the same charges. This exchange was not revealed until after the trial had started. As proceedings were about to begin for the fourth time in late 1978, the defense asked that the trial be closed. The prosecution did not object and the court closed the trial. Richmond newspapers protested the closure to no avail. An appeal came before the U.S. Supreme Court in February 1980.

Chief Justice Burger wrote the court's opinion, noting that "through its evolution the trial has been open to all who cared to observe." A presumption of open hearings is the very nature of a criminal trial under our system of justice, the chief justice added. Although there is no specific provision in the Bill of Rights or the Constitution to support the open trial, the expressly guaranteed freedoms in the First Amendment "share a common core purpose of assuring freedom of communication on matters relating to the functioning of government," Burger wrote. "In guaranteeing freedoms such as those of speech and press the First Amendment can be read as protecting the right of everyone to attend trials so as to give meaning to those explicit guarantees," he added. The First Amendment, then, the chief justice noted, prohibits the government from summarily closing courtroom doors, which had been open to the public at the time that amendment was adopted.

The First Amendment, then, the chief justice noted, prohibits the government from summarily closing courtroom doors, which had been open to the public at the time that amendment was adopted.

But the chief justice refused to see the First Amendment as an absolute bar to closed trials. He noted that in some circumstances, which he explicitly declined to define at that time, a trial judge could bar the public and the press from a trial in the interest of the fair administration of justice. But, while the court did not outline such circumstances, it was clear from both the tone and the language of the chief justice's opinion that in his mind such circumstances would indeed be unusual. Justices White, Stevens, Brennan, Marshall, Stewart, and Blackmun all concurred with the chief justice in five separate opinions. All but Stewart went further in guaranteeing access to trials than did Chief Justice Burger. Justice Rehnquist dissented.

The Supreme Court has not yet ruled that civil trials are open to the press and public, but lower federal and state courts have made such rulings. In 1984 the U.S. Court of Appeals for the 3rd Circuit ruled that civil proceedings are also presumptively open to the public and the press. In *Publicker Industries* v. *Cohen,*[6] a lawsuit involving a corporate proxy fight, the court noted that a "survey of authorities identifies as features of the civil justice system many of those attributes of the criminal justice system on which the Supreme Court relied in holding

5. 448 U.S. 555 (1980).
6. 733 F. 2d 1059 (1984).

that the First Amendment guarantees to the public and to the press the right of access to criminal trials." The right is not absolute, the court said, but absent a clear showing that closing the trial serves an important governmental interest and that closing the trial is the only way to serve this interest, the civil proceeding should be open. In 1999 the California Supreme Court became the first state high court to make the same ruling, that the press and the public have a constitutional right of access to a civil proceeding.[7]

There are, of course, exceptions to the rule that trials are open to the press and the public. Here are a few examples.

Juvenile hearings: For decades the government manifested a strong interest in protecting the identities of juveniles who find themselves enmeshed in the judicial system, either as victims or defendants. It was not uncommon for all hearings involving juveniles to be closed to the press and the public. And courts generally supported this position.

The New Mexico Supreme Court ruled in 2001 that the press did not have an unqualified right of access to child abuse and neglect proceedings, especially when extensive prehearing media coverage made it impossible for reporters to cover the proceeding without divulging the identity of the parties involved.[8] The Vermont Supreme Court supported a trial judge's decision to bar public access to a proceeding in which the judge was to consider the legal status (adult or juvenile) of a 15-year-old boy accused of murdering one girl and assaulting another. Publicity is often seen as a reward for hard-core juvenile offenders, the court noted.[9] The Ohio Supreme Court supported the closure of a juvenile custody hearing, saying there was no qualified right of access to juvenile court proceedings to determine if a child is abused, neglected, or dependent, or to determine custody of a minor child.[10] The 8th U.S. Circuit Court of Appeals ruled that it was proper for a trial court to close a hearing set to determine whether a disabled student who threatened classmates with a pistol could be expelled from school. The appellate court cited the privacy rights of the student and his classmates guaranteed under federal law as justification for closing the hearing and sealing the transcript.[11] Finally, the District of Columbia U.S. Circuit Court of Appeals ruled that reporters should be barred from the trial of a 14-year-old charged with killing another juvenile. Reporters covering the case agreed not to divulge the juvenile's name or other identifying information in exchange for the right to cover the trial. When one newspaper broke the agreement, the court banned all reporters from covering the proceeding.[12]

But the traditional concern to shield the identities of juveniles involved in the judicial process is eroding in many states. Most states now classify juvenile hearings into two groups: those in which the juvenile was charged with a criminal offense, and those in which the juvenile was the subject of a hearing relating to parental neglect, abuse or some other similar concern. In most states that have done this, hearings in the first category are presumptively open, and in at

---

7. *NBC Subsidiary (KNBC-TV Inc.)* v. *Superior Court,* 980 P. 2d 337 (1999). See also *Brown & Williamson Tobacco Corp.* v. *FTC,* 710 F. 2d 1165 (1983); *Grove Fresh Distribs., Inc.* v. *Everfresh Juice Co.,* 24 F. 3d 893 (1994); and *Doe* v. *Santa Fe Independent School Dist.,* 933 F. Supp. 647 (1996).

8. *Albuquerque Journal* v. *Jewell,* 18 P. 3d 334 (2001).

9. *In re J. S.,* 438 A. 2d 1125 (1981).

10. *In re T. R.,* 52 Ohio St. 3d 6 (1990).

11. *Webster Groves School District* v. *Pulitzer Publishing Co.,* 898 F. 2d 1371 (1990).

12. *In re J.D.C.,* 594 A. 2d 70 (1991).

least a dozen states the abuse and neglect hearings are also open to the press and public.[13] In some instances judges who allow the press to attend such hearings will insist that reporters not reveal the juvenile's identity, and the press routinely agrees. The 3rd U.S. Court of Appeals ruled in 1994 that the federal Juvenile Delinquency Act, a statute that governs the treatment of persons under the age of 18 who violate federal law, does not require that the federal juvenile proceedings and records be closed. Rather, federal courts must make rulings regarding the closure of such hearings and records on a case-by-case basis, balancing the interests of all parties involved.[14]

Victim and witness protection: The Supreme Court has ruled that it is permissible for a state to attempt to protect the victim of a sexual assault by permitting the closing of a trial during the victim's testimony. Laws exist in many states that provide for such closure. But these laws can only permit the court to close the proceeding during the testimony; they cannot require that such a closure take place. A Massachusetts statute required closure of a trial during the testimony of a juvenile sex offense victim. The U.S. Supreme Court ruled that the law was unconstitutional. Justice William Brennan agreed that the state has a strong interest to protect the victim in this kind of a case. The law was nevertheless flawed, he said, because it *required* closure of the proceeding. "As compelling as that interest is, it does not justify a mandatory closure rule, for it is clear that the circumstances of the particular case may affect the significance of the [state] interest," Brennan wrote. Under the statute, the trial judge is not permitted to allow testimony in open court, even if the victim desires it, the jurist noted.[15] A 1992 Washington state law that required courts to ensure that the identities of juvenile victims of sexual assault were not disclosed was ruled unconstitutional as well, since it would have required trial judges to close the courtroom during such hearings.[16] Finally, the 10th U.S. Circuit Court of Appeals ruled that before the press and public can be excluded from the courtroom during the testimony of a juvenile rape victim, the trial court must ascertain whether the victim's emotional and psychological condition warrants such an exclusion, as the prosecution asserted in arguments.[17]

Appellate courts usually permit the closure of those portions of a trial during which an undercover police officer testifies. The Appellate Division of the New York Supreme Court ruled in 1997 that a trial court acted properly when it closed the courtroom during the testimony of undercover officers because these police officers continued to work ongoing investigations in the specific area in which the defendant was arrested and they said they feared for their safety if the courtroom remained open during their testimony.[18] But such closure is not automatic. In a 1993 case the state's high court ruled that it was improper for a trial judge to close the court during an undercover officer's testimony based only on the showing that this officer continued to operate undercover in "the Bronx area." The Bronx encompasses 41 square miles and includes 2.1 million people, the court said. Closing a trial based on this interest would in effect require automatic closure every time any undercover officer testified.[19]

13. Stack, "Opening Juvenile Courts."
14. *U.S. v. A.D.,* 28 F. 3d 1353 (1994); see also *U.S. v. Three Juveniles,* 61 F. 3d 86 (1995).
15. *Globe Newspapers* v. *Superior Court,* 457 U.S. 596 (1982).
16. *Allied Daily Newspapers* v. *Eikenberry,* 848 P. 2d 1258 (1993).
17. *Davis* v. *Reynolds,* 890 F. 2d 1105 (1989).
18. *New York* v. *Rivera,* 656 N.Y.S. 2d 884 (1997); see also *Ayala* v. *Speckard,* 131 F. 3d 62 (1997).
19. *New York* v. *Martinez,* 82 N.Y. 2d 436 (1993).

Military tribunals: Press and public access to military courts is generally open under both military law (Rules for Courts Martial 806(b)) and the First Amendment,[20] according to media attorneys Richard L. Cys and Andrew M. Mar.[21] But there are exceptions. When classified information is introduced at trial, closure will be permitted if the order is narrowly tailored—that is, no more of the hearing is closed than is necessary to protect the government's interest in protecting the security of the classified information. But in the wake of the terrorist attacks of September 2001, President Bush signed a military order allowing special military tribunals or commissions to try persons suspected of terrorist activities. Such commissions were to be used to determine the fate of the hundreds of persons who had been detained in the wake of the attacks and were imprisoned at a military facility at Guantanamo Bay in Cuba. These are people who may or may not be terrorists, may or may not have aided terrorists, or may or may not be illegal aliens. These commissions are supposed to determine the combatant status of the so-called detainees, or whether or not these people are a threat to the United States.

Many important questions about these commissions remained unresolved in early 2006. Foremost, are they even legal? A federal district court ruled that the administration exceeded its constitutional authority in establishing such tribunals, but in July of 2005 the U.S. Court of Appeals for the District of Columbia reversed this decision and said that the Bush plan did not violate the constitution, international law or military law. In November of 2005 the Supreme Court agreed to hear an appeal of this ruling.

If the high court agrees that the special military panels are legal, will they be open to the press and public? The government has pressed diligently to keep any hearings or legal documents related to the detainees and others it suspects of terrorist activities out of the public eye. Government lawyers have advanced what some attorneys call the "mosaic theory" to support their arguments for secrecy. This theory holds that any information, even seemingly innocuous bits of data, when disclosed in newspapers, on television, over the Internet or wherever, can be assimilated by other terrorists and help them understand the direction of government investigations, thereby compromising national security. Many courts have accepted this argument, but not all. For example, when the federal government sought to prosecute Zacarias Moussaoui, who was charged with conspiracy in connection with the September 11, 2001, terror attacks, it sought to close a hearing in which it would argue against certain testimony Moussaoui wanted to introduce at this trial, testimony the defendant said would exonerate him. The government said this testimony was improper and told the court it would make that argument in a closed hearing, because national security secrets would be presented to bolster its case. But the U.S. Court of Appeals rejected this argument, saying that the government sought too broad of a closure order. "The value of openness in judicial proceedings can hardly be overstated," the court wrote.[22] "This value, of providing the community at large a sense that justice has been done, is particularly relevant in the prosecution of Moussaoui." The court said there should be two hearings, one open to the public involving nonclassified information, and a later hearing in which classified evidence could be discussed. But the details

---

20. *ABC, Inc.* v. *Powell,* 47 M.J. 363 (1997).
21. Cys and Mar, "Media Access to the New Special Tribunals."
22. *United States* v. *Moussaoui,* 65 FedAppx 881 (2003); see also Shenon, "In Shift, Appeals Court Opens."

of this second hearing would also be made public after the arguments have been made. A transcript of the hearing—with classified information deleted—would be released to the public within several days after the hearing, the court said.

One issue after another arose in the Moussaoui case, and at times the proceedings appeared to take on the qualities of a never-ending story. But in March 2005 the Supreme Court, without comment, denied an appeal by the defendant of an appellate court ruling that restored his liability for the death penalty and held that he was not entitled to have access to captured members of Al Qaeda who, he said, would provide helpful testimony at his trial. Abruptly Moussaoui pleaded guilty to participating in a broad conspiracy to fly planes into American buildings. And at least this aspect of the case ended—as did the questions about press access to hearings and documents.

Another case involved an Algerian who was in the United States on a student visa when he was detained due to his alleged contact with three of the September 11 hijackers. He was later released on bond. All the proceedings involving the South Florida resident, Mohamed Kamel Bellahouel, were conducted in secret. The court proceedings were conducted in total secret, a violation, he argued, of both the common law and the First Amendment guarantees governing public access to judicial proceedings. Not only were the court proceedings and records closed in this case, but there was no public record that the case even existed until a clerk made a docketing error. This was a straightforward habeas corpus hearing (a hearing in which the government must justify its reason for the detention of any person), the kind of hearing that has traditionally been open. Bellahouel's appeal to the 11th U.S. Court of Appeals was publicly docketed, but entire pages in the public record are blank. He lost and was eventually deported. The Supreme Court denied certiorari.

The issue of access to proceedings related to alleged terrorist activities involves a variety of hearings, including trials, military commissions, habeas corpus hearings and even deportation hearings. (See page 508.) These are difficult issues, and thus far the Supreme Court has offered little guidance. While the court has made rulings involving the legality of some of the proceedings themselves, it has not yet dealt with the issue of access.[23]

SUMMARY

American courtrooms have been traditionally open to the press and the public, but in the wake of the rejection of restrictive orders as a means to control publicity, some judges attempted to resolve this problem by closing off access to judicial proceedings and records. In the 1980s the Supreme Court fashioned a legal test, the *Press-Enterprise* test, for judges to use to determine if access to hearings and documents could be limited without violating the First Amendment. Since that time courts have ruled that both criminal and civil trials must generally remain open. Exceptions have been granted for closure during the testimony of crime victims and some witnesses, and some juvenile proceedings. Also, military tribunals, a tool that the government can use to try persons accused of terrorism, may also be closed.

23. See *Hamdi* v. *Rumsfeld*, 124 S. Ct. 2633 (2004), for example.

CLOSURE OF OTHER HEARINGS

To laypersons, the judicial process generally means trials. But a surprisingly large percentage of the process takes place in hearings that are not trials, hearings that often resolve many of the issues formerly decided at trials. The growth of the wide array of especially pretrial hearings is the result of court decisions in the 1960s that substantially expanded defendants' rights in criminal cases, major changes in the way in which the criminal justice system works, and attempts by members of the judiciary to work more closely with people who staff the penal institutions and social service agencies.

There are evidentiary or suppression hearings, pretrial detention hearings, plea hearings, presentence and postsentence hearings, and so on. Many of these hearings take place long before the trial begins, weeks before the jury is even selected. Many of these hearings focus on information that may be highly prejudicial to the defendant. At an evidentiary hearing, for example, the court may rule that a key piece of evidence, such as a weapon, is inadmissible at the trial because it was improperly seized by the police. The fact that the defendant had a weapon is certainly prejudicial. If this fact is publicized, some argue, it won't matter that the evidence is barred from trial because the members of the community, the jurors, will already know it exists. Or the state may believe that the publicity about certain kinds of evidence may adversely affect the future prosecution of other defendants.

Since 1986 American courts have ruled that a wide range of judicial proceedings are presumptively open to the press and public.

Since 1986 American courts have ruled that a wide range of judicial proceedings are presumptively open to the press and public. Remember, if a hearing is presumptively open, the party seeking to close the proceeding bears the burden of convincing the court—as outlined in the *Press-Enterprise* test (see pages 496–497) that the hearing should be closed. And this is a big hurdle to cross.

The Supreme Court has specifically ruled that both pretrial evidentiary hearings[24] and voir dire proceedings[25] are presumptively open. These rulings apply to all courts, everywhere. Other rulings on open hearings have come from U.S. Courts of Appeals and state appellate courts. Consequently, these rulings don't apply as broadly; they may, in fact, be confined to a single federal jurisdiction or a state. It is fair to say, however, that in most situations the following kinds of proceedings are regarded as open and can only be closed by a strong showing of the substantial probability of harm to some other compelling interest:

- Pretrial detention hearings
- Bail hearings
- Plea hearings
- Voir dire proceedings
- Sentencing hearings
- Attorney disciplinary hearings

But because a kind of hearing is presumptively open doesn't mean it will always be open. Voir dire hearings offer a good example. Most of the time they are open. Lawyers for Martha Stewart sought closure of the examination of prospective jurors because of the intense media interest in the case and fears that potential jurors would be reluctant to tell the truth

---

24. *Press-Enterprise* v. *Riverside Superior Court,* 478 U.S. 1 (1986).
25. *Press-Enterprise* v. *Riverside Superior Court,* 464 U.S. 501 (1984).

Source: © AP/Wide World Photos

when questioned in front of the press. The trial court agreed, but the ruling was reversed by the 2nd U.S. Court of Appeals. The appellate judges noted that the media interest in the case had not resulted in disruption of the proceedings or disclosure of information the court had barred the press from revealing. Also, the judges refused to buy the notion that jurors would be less likely to be candid if they testified in front of the press. "It is difficult to conceive of a potential juror who would be willing to reveal a bias against the defendants in their presence, but not in the presence of reporters," the court said.[26] In 2004 the Washington state Supreme Court overturned a first-degree murder conviction because the trial court violated the defendant's right to a public trial when it barred the public—including the defendant's family—from the voir dire proceeding because the courtroom was too small. The judge also failed to apply the *Press-Enterprise* test, the court noted.[27]

Lawyers for Martha Stewart attempted to close the voir dire proceedings in her obstruction of justice trial. The trial court agreed, but the U.S. Court of Appeals didn't, and the examination was open.

26. *ABC Inc.* v. *Stewart,* 360 F. 3d 90 (2004).
27. *In re Personal Restraint Petition of Orange,* 32 M.L.R. 2569 (2004).

In other cases, the appellate courts have permitted closure of the jury selection process in order to protect the identity of the jurors,[28] or to ensure getting frank and candid responses from potential jurors.[29] For example, lawyers for controversial boxing promoter Don King asked the court to close the voir dire during his trial for wire fraud. The lawyers said they were concerned that, because of the long stream of negative publicity about King, jurors who had a neutral or positive view of the fight promoter would not answer questions honestly during the voir dire. The trial judge agreed.[30] "Prospective jurors, if made aware that their views will be publicly disseminated in the next day's newspapers or on radio or television broadcasts, will be under pressure not to express unpopular opinions relevant to their choice as trial jurors." And in Detroit in 2003 the trial judge closed several phases of the voir dire during the trial of four men charged with conspiracy in relation to the September 11, 2001, terrorist attacks. The judge said he issued the order to protect the privacy rights of the jurors, to shield them from undue harassment by the press and others. He said he was also concerned that press coverage of the voir dire could influence the responses given by the potential jury members.[31]

Some courts use other strategies to deal with potential or real juror problems. The U.S. Court of Appeals for the 5th Circuit ruled that it was permissible for a trial judge to question two jurors privately in his chambers about possible misconduct. This ruling came during the second trial of Edwin Edwards, who was then between his terms as governor of Louisiana. The first trial ended in a mistrial. During the second trial a juror reported to the marshal that another juror had remarked, "Did you know the last jury got paid for voting acquittal?" The judge questioned both jurors in chambers about the matter. He said he did so to keep the matter away from other jurors. The same thing happened a few days later and the judge responded in the same fashion. After the trial ended, the press sought a transcript and received an edited version with the jurors' names and other details stricken from the record. The court of appeals supported the judge. It noted that historically such questioning of jurors has been conducted in private. In addition, opening up such a hearing could be extremely harmful in this case, turning what the court called a "tempest in a teapot" into a mistrial. The court also supported the judge's decision to edit the transcript in order to protect the jurors from embarrassment.[32]

The 3rd U.S. Circuit Court of Appeals responded somewhat differently when it had to review an unusual situation that developed in a racketeering and extortion trial in Philadelphia. After the trial ended, one of the jurors claimed that other members of the jury had watched television reports about the case, read newspaper accounts of the trial, and discussed the case with their spouses, all contrary to the instructions from the court. These allegations received considerable press coverage and the defendant, who had been convicted, requested that the jurors be examined by the judge regarding these charges. The judge proceeded to question the jurors in private, despite press requests that the examination be conducted in

28. Liptak, "Nameless Juries on the Rise."
29. *In re South Carolina Press Association,* 946 F. 2d 1037 (1991).
30. *U.S.* v. *King,* 26 M.L.R. 1464 (1998), aff. *U.S.* v. *King,* 140 F. 3d 76 (1998).
31. *U.S.* v. *Koubriti,* 252 F. Supp 3d 424 (2003).
32. *U.S.* v. *Edwards,* 823 F. 2d 111 (1987).

public. The Court of Appeals issued an order stopping the proceeding until a hearing could be held, but by that time the judge said there was no further need to question the jurors. The trial judge denied the defendant's motion for a new trial and released the transcript of the examination, from which the jurors' names had been deleted. He said he had conducted the inquiry in private because he feared that the presence of the press in the courtroom during the examination would be coercive and interfere with the expressions of candor of the jurors. In addition, the judge said that jurors might inadvertently talk about matters discussed in the jury room, and that the public should not hear about such matters.[33]

But there are some kinds of proceedings that the courts have said are not presumptively open and generally remain closed to public scrutiny. The 6th U.S. Circuit Court of Appeals ruled that the press and public do not enjoy a presumptive right of access to what is called a summary jury trial, a rather unusual judicial proceeding sometimes used in civil cases. The **summary jury trial** is a device used by courts to attempt to get the parties in the case to settle their dispute before going to a full-blown jury trial. In such a case the attorneys present much-abbreviated arguments to jurors. There are no witnesses called, and objections to evidence or other matters are strongly discouraged. After hearing the arguments, the jurors issue an informal verdict that can then be used to settle the case. For example, if plaintiff Jones loses the verdict in the summary jury trial, she may be more willing to settle the case without a normal trial. The court said that there was no First Amendment right of access to such proceedings because such a right was not historically recognized and that permitting access might actually work against the purpose of the summary trial, that is, the settlement of the dispute.[34]

Grand jury proceedings are secret—and always have been. This is not an issue the press has disputed, but in two recent instances sensitive grand jury materials have been leaked by the press, much to the distress of defense lawyers, who argue that the release of this material violates the rights of defendants and can taint potential jurors. In December 2004, the San Francisco Chronicle published parts of federal grand jury testimony that suggested several major-league baseball players had used steroids. The following month both ABC News and a Web site called thesmokinggun.com carried substantial excerpts from grand jury proceedings in the Michael Jackson child molestation case. Under California law grand jury transcripts are usually made public before the start of a trial, but in this case the judge had barred the release of the material because of the intense media coverage of the case. No penalties were exacted against the press in these cases,[35] but the mass media walk on very thin legal ice when they publish secret material generated by a grand jury hearing. The First Amendment provides little protection in such a case. (See pages 436–440 to see how the First Amendment rarely protects journalists who refuse to reveal the names of sources of such grand jury materials.)

Rules that preserve the secrecy of grand jury proceedings apply equally to proceedings ancillary to grand jury proceedings. The press in 1998 sought access to proceedings that focused on whether "Monica Lewinsky or others suborned perjury, obstructed justice, intimidated witnesses, or otherwise violated federal law" in dealing with persons involved in Paula Jones'

33. *U.S.* v. *Simone,* 14 F. 3d 833 (1994).
34. *Cincinnati Gas and Electric Co.* v. *General Electric,* 854 F. 2d 900 (1988).
35. Broder, "From Grand Jury Leaks."

lawsuit against President Clinton. While these proceedings were related to Kenneth Starr's grand jury proceedings into Whitewater and the Clinton-Lewinsky affair, they were outside the scope of the primary focus of the proceedings. The District of Columbia Circuit of the U.S. Court of Appeals said there was no First Amendment right of access to such proceedings.[36]

Finally, there is a dispute among the courts today whether deportation hearings should be open or closed. The press generally ignored such hearings until the government began to deport Middle-Eastern aliens who they said were in some way connected to terrorist activities. These hearings then became news, and questions began to arise whether they should be open or closed. Two U.S. Courts of Appeal have split on whether press and public access should be permitted. In a case from Michigan, the 6th U.S. Court of Appeals ruled that because the proceedings exhibited substantial, quasi-judicial characteristics, they should be treated like criminal trials and were presumptively open.[37] The court said the hearings had been traditionally open to the public, and the openness plays a significant, positive role, ensuring fairness and preventing mistakes. Thus, any order to close a hearing is governed by the requirements of the *Press-Enterprise* test and must be narrowly tailored. But the 3rd U.S. Court of Appeals, in a case from New Jersey, ruled just the opposite, that deportation hearings are not presumptively open.[38] The court said the deportation hearing process had been codified by Congress and never explicitly contained a guarantee of access. Many hearings have been closed and must be closed, the court said, because they are often held in places that are inaccessible to the public, such as prisons. In addition, the court said, the harm that opening such hearings could do outweighs the potential positive impact of permitting public and press access. The court agreed with the government that an open hearing could reveal government sources and methods of investigation, could assist members of terrorist cells that are still operating, and could damage the privacy interests of the detainees. The ruling in this case was appealed by a group of New Jersey newspapers that challenged the blanket policy of closing the hearings, arguing the government should have to justify the closings on a case-by-case basis. The Supreme Court rejected the appeal in the late spring of 2003. So the law remains unsettled.

PRESUMPTIVELY OPEN DOCUMENTS

A wide range of documents has been ruled to be presumptively open. But remember, this presumption can be rebutted if the party seeking closure can convince the court that suppression of the material is essential to serve a substantial interest, and the order is narrowly tailored to serve that interest. Here are some common examples of the kind of material that courts have ruled to be open to inspection by the press and the public.

Court docket sheet: The 2nd U.S. Court of Appeals ruled in 2004 that there is a qualified First Amendment right to inspect these sheets that provide an index to judicial proceedings and documents.[39]

36. *In re Dow Jones & Co.,* 142 F. 3d 896 (1998).
37. *Detroit Free Press* v. *Ashcroft,* 30 M.L.R. 2313 (2002).
38. *North Jersey Media Group Inc.* v. *Ashcroft,* 308 F. 3d 198 (2002).
39. *Hartford Courant* v. *Pellegrino,* 371 F. 3d 49 (2004).

Documents filed in pretrial proceedings: The 9th U.S. Court of Appeals ruled that pretrial proceedings are open and "there is no reason to distinguish between pretrial proceedings and the documents filed in regard to them."[40]

Presentencing and postsentencing reports: The U.S. Court of Appeals for the 9th Circuit ruled that unless a judge could demonstrate a compelling need to keep such records sealed, they should be open for public inspection.[41] But this isn't always the rule. In 2001 a federal court in Pennsylvania sealed a presentencing report on a former state senator who had pleaded guilty to charges of corruption. The court cited the defendant's right to privacy and the court's need for confidentiality to support its ruling.[42]

Plea agreements: These are written agreements between a prosecutor and a defendant in which the accused agrees to plead guilty, usually to a lesser charge that originally filed.

Informations, indictments, search warrants and supporting affidavits, evidence and other materials related to sentencing: The first four items all relate to materials generated in charging a suspect with a crime, or gathering material needed for prosecution. Sentencing materials may go beyond these kinds of documents and include items that are not admissible as evidence in determining an individual's guilt or innocence.

But judges are often willing to draw a line if they feel that public interest will be harmed if some kinds of material are made public. Some recent cases make this point. A federal court in New York ruled in 2001 that while the press could have access to letters sent to the clerk of courts about a defendant who was about to be sentenced, similar letters that were sent to the court itself and used by the judge in the sentencing process were off-limits. The judge ruled that the people who sent those letters had an expectation of privacy about their comments, and there was a need for uninhibited commentary on the sentencing issue, something that might be deterred if citizens thought their ideas and opinions would be made public.[43] The Kentucky Supreme Court ruled in 2002 that a trial court could permanently seal some of the allegations of sexual abuse that were made against Roman Catholic priests in the diocese. The trial court said these particular allegations were a sham, immaterial, redundant and "scandalous." The state high court said it was difficult to see how access to such allegations would further the public's understanding of the judicial process and agreed that release of this material could cause irreparable harm to the diocese.[44]

Finally, the Virginia Supreme Court rejected a request by several newspapers that they be allowed to retest some of the evidence that was part of a criminal prosecution. A man had been convicted of rape and murder in 1982, before DNA testing was available. Eight years later the state did DNA testing of hair samples and blood types prior to his execution. The tests were inconclusive and the man was executed. Ten years later, experts said new DNA tests could prove once and for all the man's guilt or innocence, but the state refused to retest the material. The newspapers sought to conduct the tests themselves. But the court rejected their bid for access to this material. The press does have access to evidence introduced at a criminal trial, the court acknowledged, but "what the newspapers seek to do in this case is expand

40. *A.P.* v. *U.S. District Court,* 705 F. 2d 1143 (1983).
41. *U.S.* v. *Schlette,* 685 F. 2d 1574 (1988).
42. *United States* v. *Loeper,* 132 F. Supp. 2d 337 (2001).
43. *U.S.* v. *Lawrence,* 29 M.L.R. 2294 (2001).
44. *Roman Catholic Diocese of Lexington* v. *Noble,* 92 S.W. 3d 724 (2002).

the definition of 'access' to include the right to conduct independent testing of evidence in criminal proceedings." The newspapers in this case, the court ruled, sought access to something that really did not exist—new evidence in the form of new test results. No court in the land has accepted this novel argument, the court concluded.[45]

Juror records: Records related to jurors are also sometimes off-limits to public and press inspection. Some judges have refused to reveal the names and addresses of jurors, even after a trial has concluded. The appellate courts are of at least two minds on this question. The 4th U.S. Circuit Court of Appeals has explicitly said there is such a right. And in 1999 the Michigan Court of Appeals ruled that there was a qualified right of access when the press seeks postverdict names and addresses of jurors. The court said that trial courts have the discretion to impose appropriate restrictions on the manner and time of disclosure and, in some circumstances perhaps, to refuse disclosure when legitimate safety concerns of jurors are raised. Juror privacy concerns alone, the court said, are not sufficient to block disclosure.[46] But other courts, like the 5th U.S. Circuit Court of Appeals, have ruled that there is no such right of access.[47] As the activity in criminal courts increases, fewer Americans seem willing to serve as jurors. Judges have become increasingly protective of those citizens who are willing to perform this important public duty. For example, a U.S. District Court in Massachusetts ruled that a newspaper had the right of access to the names and addresses of jurors in a highly publicized civil trial, but not until 10 days after the verdict was returned. The judge wanted to give the jurors time to receive a court order he had prepared, which instructed the jurors that they could refuse any request to be interviewed and that once they had indicated they did not wish to be interviewed, no further requests need be tolerated.[48]

Publishing the names and addresses of jurors, whether permitted or not, is a decision that journalists have to study closely as an ethical issue. The knee-jerk reaction—"if we can get it, we'll publish it"—is inappropriate. In the wake of the first Rodney King trial in southern California in which the officers accused of the beating were exonerated, rioting broke out on the streets of Los Angeles by people protesting the verdict. One newspaper still published jurors' names, something that could have jeopardized the safety of each of these citizens. Key questions need to be asked: What is the purpose of publishing these names? Will publishing the names enlighten readers and viewers in an important way? Or will this action jeopardize the jurors' privacy or even safety? Responsible editors and broadcasters will take the high road.

At least one federal court has also ruled that the notes sent by members of the jury to the judge seeking instructions on matters of law or evidentiary questions are off-limits as well. The judge denied a request by a newspaper to see such records in a complicated case against five defendants that produced 90 separate verdicts. The sanctity of jury deliberations outweighed any First Amendment considerations, the court said. "Just as there is no right of access to the jury's deliberations while they are deliberating . . . there is no right of access to problems which the jurors perceived were preventing them from deliberating," the court ruled.[49]

Out-of-court settlements: There are some areas in which public and press access to court documents is routinely denied. Civil lawsuits often end with an out-of-court settlement;

---

45. *Globe Newspaper Co.* v. *Commonwealth,* 570 S.E. 2d 809 (2002).
46. *In re Baltimore Sun,* 14 M.L.R. 2379 (1988), and *People* v. *Mitchell,* 592 N.W. 2d 798 (1999).
47. *U.S.* v. *Edwards,* 823 F. 2d 111 (1987).
48. *Sullivan* v. *National Football League,* 839 F. Supp. 6 (1993).
49. *United States* v. *Kemp,* 366 F. Supp. 2d 255 (2005).

that is, both parties agree to a settlement without completing the trial. In the past, cases involving defective tires on Ford Explorers, the dangers of silicone breast implants, exploding cigarette lighters, and defective television receivers were all settled out of court, and the terms and nature of the settlements were shrouded under confidentiality orders. Oftentimes judges play an important role in generating such settlements. These settlement agreements have traditionally been considered a private matter between the parties in the lawsuit.[50] Today more and more of these agreements contain provisions that the terms of the settlement are to remain confidential. Defendants often seek confidentiality to avoid the disclosure of sensitive or potentially damaging information. Plaintiffs are willing to agree to confidentiality in order to obtain a higher amount of money in the settlement. Therefore, the sealing of out-of-court settlements has become somewhat commonplace. At first glance there seems little difficulty with such sealed agreements; after all, these are private agreements between private parties. But the public interest can be harmed in some instances. The confidential settlement of a malpractice suit against a doctor, for example, will provide compensation to the injured patient. But such a settlement denies other patients knowledge of the doctor's wrongdoing. If an auto manufacturer obtains a confidential settlement with a customer who was injured because of a faulty part in the car, other owners of the same vehicle may not be warned of the danger. Journalists are increasingly seeking access to such sealed agreements. Their quest for information is somewhat compromised by the fact that newspapers and broadcasting stations sometimes will seek the confidential settlement of a libel or invasion-of-privacy action. Most judges have not been receptive to the arguments that the press and public should have access to sealed agreements. Many jurists believe that the secrecy clause in these agreements encourages the settlement of lawsuits, and with courts in America as crowded as they are, judges favor anything that will reduce their caseload.* In 1986 the 3rd U.S. Circuit Court of Appeals ruled that there is a right of public access to sealed settlement agreements, the first important court to make such a ruling.[51] Since then a few other courts have ordered that such agreements be open for inspection.[52] As a rule, however, these agreements remain beyond the reach of even First Amendment arguments. Reporters who expose the terms of such secret settlements can face severe consequences. A court clerk mistakenly gave reporter Kirsten Mitchell a file containing the details of a secret settlement between Conoco Inc. and residents of a trailer park who alleged that Conoco had contaminated their water supply. When the Wilmington (N.C.) Morning Star published a story about the settlement, the court held both the reporter and the newspaper in contempt. They were jointly fined $500,000.[53]

Many jurists believe that the secrecy clause in these agreements encourages the settlement of lawsuits, and with courts in America as crowded as they are, judges favor anything that will reduce their caseload.

Protective court orders: Other documents normally closed to inspection are records provided by litigants to the opposing party in a lawsuit that are covered by a protective court order. During the discovery process, both sides in a legal dispute are permitted to explore the records and witnesses and other material held by the opposing party. The court assists in the

---

*In 1995 the Judicial Conference of the United States, a policy-making body for the federal courts, rejected a proposal that would have made the sealing of records almost automatic in civil cases.

50. See Bechamps, "Sealed Out-of-Court Settlements," 117.
51. *Bank of America v. Hotel Rittenhouse Assoc.,* 800 F. 2d 339 (1986).
52. See *EEOC v. The Erection Co.,* 900 F. 2d 168 (1990); *Pansy v. Stroudsburg,* 22 F. 3d 772 (1994); and *Des Moines School District v. Des Moines Register and Tribune Co.,* 487 N.W. 2d 667 (1992).
53. *Ashcraft v. Conoco Inc.,* 26 M.L.R. 1620 (1998).

process by compelling disclosure of this information when necessary. Sometimes a party will refuse to disclose some material unless the court will guarantee that material will not be made public. The court then enters a protective order, shielding the material from public disclosure.

For example, a black couple filed a civil rights complaint against persons who had twice firebombed their home. In preliminary proceedings it was discovered that one of the defendants was an officer in the Ku Klux Klan. The plaintiffs sought from him a list of local Klan members, and the court issued a subpoena ordering the production of the names. The Klansman resisted, but finally provided the list when it was put under a protective order, meaning that only the attorneys involved in the case could see the names. The court later sealed all access to the list in an effort to protect the privacy and associational rights of those named. The Court of Appeals upheld the ruling, noting that the list would never have been generated if it had not been for the protective order.[54] The court in this case relied on a 1984 U.S. Supreme Court ruling in a somewhat similar issue. In that case, *Seattle Times Co.* v. *Rhinehart*,[55] the high court said that an order prohibiting the dissemination of information generated during the discovery process is not the classic kind of prior restraint that requires "exacting First Amendment scrutiny. . . . Where a protective order is entered on a showing of good cause . . . and does not restrict the dissemination of the information if gained from other sources, it does not offend the First Amendment." In all likelihood, courts will continue to resist the disclosure of those documents that are generated during the discovery process and protected from public scrutiny by a court order.

National security: Finally, the nation's fight against terrorism and terrorist acts has resulted in the closure of court records. The case in point is the previously discussed trial of Zacarias Moussaoui (see pages 502–503). The government not only sought to deny access to certain portions of the proceedings, it also successfully convinced the judge to seal most of the court records. The questions focused on whether Moussaoui, a French citizen, could have access to captured Al Qaeda witnesses who he contended would help him prove his innocence. In August 2002 Judge Leonie Brinkema sealed many of the proceedings when the government contended that Moussaoui could use the material he placed in the record to secretly communicate with co-conspirators or sympathizers with coded messages. At the time, Moussaoui, who was ostensibly defending himself, was filing great numbers of highly inflammatory pleadings. Judge Brinkema modified her order a month later and said materials would be unsealed 10 days after they were filed, giving the government time to challenge the release of individual documents.[56] In April 2003 several news organization went to court to try to gain access to these materials.[57] The following day the judge announced that she had serious doubts whether the government could actually prosecute Moussaoui in a civilian court "under the shroud of secrecy under which it seeks to proceed."[58] The case, then, might have to be moved to a military tribunal, in which secrecy would be more readily tolerated. (See page 502.) As noted previously Moussaoui pleaded guilty in April 2005 and the access issues became moot.

The qualified First Amendment right of access to judicial proceedings and documents has gone a long way to block attempts by courts to keep the public and the press out of the

54. *Courier-Journal* v. *Marshall,* 282 F. 2d 361 (1987).
55. 104 S. Ct. 2199 (1984).
56. *United States* v. *Moussaoui,* 31 M.L.R. 1574 (2002).
57. Shenon, "News Groups Want Terror Case Files."
58. Shenon, "Judge Critical of Secrecy."

courtroom. Many trial judges, however, still see closure as a simple solution to the problem of publicity about a criminal case. And often the motion for closure is made totally unexpectedly. What should a reporter do when faced with such a problem? Here are some tips for journalists from "The First Amendment Handbook" prepared by the Reporters Committee for Freedom of the Press.

■ If you know your news organization will send an attorney to court to argue against closure, ask if you may speak with the judge for a moment.

■ Inform the judge that your news organization objects to the closure and would like an opportunity to argue against it. Ask for a brief recess so the attorney can come to court. If you know the name of the attorney, give his or her name to the judge. This information will bolster your credibility. Ask that your objection to the closure be made a part of the record.

■ If the judge won't let you speak and orders you to leave, leave. If you refuse, you could be arrested and cited for contempt of court.

■ When you leave the courtroom, write a short note to the judge explaining that your news organization wants to oppose the closure and that you will contact your editor or lawyer immediately. Give the note to a court officer and call your superiors.

TIPS FOR REPORTERS WHEN JUDICIAL HEARING IS CLOSED

■ Call the editor immediately to get a lawyer on the job.

■ Make a formal objection to closure.

■ Ask the judge to delay the closure until the lawyer arrives.

ACCESS AND THE BROADCAST JOURNALIST

It is far easier for the courts to serve the needs of the print media than the broadcast media when it comes to providing access to judicial proceedings and documents. In many instances it suffices for the broadcast journalist to attend the hearing or inspect the document like colleagues who work for newspapers or magazines. But other times the broadcast journalist wants to show viewers the actual document or allow listeners to hear the testimony or view the proceeding. Courts have been much slower to respond to these needs than the simpler needs of the working print reporter.

Two Supreme Court rulings initially loomed as major stumbling blocks for broadcast journalists: a 1965 ruling (*Estes* v. *Texas*[59]) that generally supported the ban on the telecast or broadcast of judicial proceedings, and a 1978 ruling (*Nixon* v. *Warner Communications*[60]) in which the high court refused to recognize the right of the journalists to make copies of audiotaped evidence for broadcast on the news. *Estes* will be discussed shortly. The second case involved tapes made by President Richard Nixon at the White House that were used as

It is far easier for the courts to serve the needs of the print media than the broadcast media when it comes to providing access to judicial proceedings and documents.

---

59. 381 U.S. 532 (1965).
60. 434 U.S. 591 (1978).

evidence in many of the Watergate trials of the 1970s. Broadcasters wanted to make copies of these tapes and play them for radio listeners and television viewers. The Supreme Court agreed that there is a generally recognized right of access to inspect evidentiary records in a case but said that this right was not an absolute right. "The decision as to access is one best left to the sound discretion of the trial court, a discretion to be exercised in light of the relevant facts and circumstances of the particular case," the court ruled. Courts have come a long way in granting press access to judicial evidence since 1978. But because the Nixon case focused specifically on the broadcast of taped evidence, those judges who wish to resist the broadcasters' efforts to use taped evidence in their newscasts have a fairly strong precedent on their side.[61] This section first focuses on gaining access to audio- or videotape evidence, then, the recording or televising of judicial proceedings.

Access to Evidence

The courts have considered a variety of factors in reaching a decision on whether to permit the broadcast or telecast of audio- or videotape evidence. Whether transcripts of the recordings have already been published is an important factor. Courts have also considered whether the broadcast or telecast of the material would enhance public understanding of an important historical or public occurrence. The rights of the defendant are also considered: Would the broadcast of this material prejudice the right to a fair trial? In Maryland a television station sought to broadcast a home videotape that was introduced as evidence during a murder trial. The victim's husband had shot the video of his wife as she got into her car to take their daughter to nursery school. Appearing in the background of the videotape are two men whom police charged with the subsequent murder of the woman. The defendants were being tried separately. A television station asked permission to broadcast the tape after it was shown in court during the first trial. The trial court said the station could broadcast the tape, but not until after the second trial. The Maryland Court of Special Appeals affirmed this ruling. The appellate court rejected the argument that there was a First Amendment right to copy trial evidence, but conceded a limited common-law right did exist. Nevertheless, the court said that the trial judge was correct in balancing this limited right against the fair trial rights of the second defendant.[62]

Most courts will insist on clear evidence that the broadcast or telecast of the material will harm the rights of the defendant or someone or something else before blocking access to the material. The U.S. Court of Appeals for the 3rd Circuit ruled that there is a strong presumption favoring access and that this presumption is not outweighed by mere speculations on the potential impact the telecast of the material may have on related proceedings.[63] The Washington state Supreme Court voided a contempt citation against a radio station that had broadcast, in violation of a court order, tape-recorded testimony that had been placed into evidence. The trial court had "accepted the most superficial showing of justification and then shifted to KHQ [the radio station] the burden of proving that the prior restraint was not necessary,"[64] the court said.

It is often important whether the tapes that are sought have been introduced into evidence. When John Hinckley was tried for the attempted assassination of Ronald Reagan, the

61. See, for example, *Group W Television Inc.* v. *Maryland,* 626 A. 2d 1032 (1993).
62. *Group W Television Inc.* v. *Maryland,* 626 A. 2d 1032 (1993).
63. *U.S.* v. *Martin,* 746 F. 2d 964 (1984).
64. *Washington* v. *Coe,* 101 N.W. 2d 364 (1984).

television networks sought to televise the videotaped deposition given by actress Jodie Foster in the case.* The court refused the request, noting that the testimony was never admitted into evidence. It was simply a statement from a witness; it just happened to be videotaped. No right existed to videotape and telecast the testimony of other witnesses. The videotaped deposition would not be an exception to that rule.[65] The New Mexico Supreme Court denied the press the right to copy and broadcast recordings of wiretaps that resulted in criminal indictments but were never played in open court or received into evidence.[66] Who has been videotaped is also an important consideration when a court examines a request to broadcast the material. Videotapes of defendants and police agents are more likely to be released than are recordings of innocent third parties. Jodie Foster was an "innocent witness" in the Hinckley case. She had been pulled into the case inadvertently. A U.S. District Court in Minnesota rejected requests from broadcasters to air videotapes of a hostage recorded by her kidnapper. The court ruled that it would create serious hardship for the victim of the crime and would serve no proper purpose.[67] A good way to outline the dimensions of this problem is to look at cases where access was granted and where it was denied.

The government presented a considerable amount of evidence on both videotape and audiotape on Congressman John Jenrette and John Stowe in a trial that stemmed from an FBI sting operation that started in 1978 and resulted in the conviction of one U.S. senator and five congressmen. The tapes were recordings of the defendants in the case making what the government alleged were illegal deals with undercover FBI agents. The networks sought to copy and broadcast these tapes. The U.S. District Court refused the request, fearing that if the tapes were televised it would be difficult to later impanel an impartial jury should a retrial be ordered by a higher court. The U.S. Court of Appeals for the District of Columbia Circuit disagreed and promulgated this test:

> Access may be denied only if the district court, after considering the relevant facts and circumstances of the particular case, and after weighing the interests advanced by the parties in light of the public interest and the duty of courts, concludes that justice so requires. . . . The court's discretion must clearly be informed by this country's strong tradition of access to judicial proceedings. In balancing the competing interests the court must also give appropriate weight and consideration *to the presumption—however gauged—in favor of public access to judicial records* [author emphasis].[68]

Several factors favored release of the tapes, the court concluded. They were admitted into evidence and played to a jury at a public trial. The tapes contained only admissible evidence. This was a trial in which the defendant was a high public official charged with betraying the public trust. The court admitted a retrial *might* be a problem, but there was no evidence that if there were a retrial, impartial jurors could not be found. What about protecting innocent third parties who were also pictured or heard in the tapes? There were only one or two instances of that, and the trial court can delete these sections, the court said. The tapes must be released.

---

*Hinckley was apparently infatuated with the actress, and this infatuation played some role in his attempt to kill Reagan.

65. *In re Application of ABC,* 537 F. Supp. 1168 (1982).
66. *New Mexico* v. *Brennan,* 645 P. 2d 982 (1982).
67. *In re Application of KSTP,* 504 F. Supp. 360 (1980).
68. *In re Application of NBC,* 653 F. 2d 609 (1981).

The 8th U.S. Circuit Court of Appeals ruled in December 1996 that neither the press nor the public had a First Amendment or common-law right of access to President Bill Clinton's videotaped deposition for a criminal trial in Arkansas. Transcripts of what was said in the deposition were made public and this satisfied the First Amendment requirements, the court ruled.[69] Finally, the U.S. 2nd Circuit Court of Appeals ruled in 2001 that a U.S. District Court did not err when it ordered copies of audio- and videotapes presented by the government at a pretrial detention hearing to be made available to the broadcast media. The court said that the tapes played at the hearing were part of the judicial record and subject to the common-law right of copying and inspection. Defendants objected and argued that broadcast of the tapes could be prejudicial to their fair trial rights, but the appellate court said that these concerns could be met by imposing other remedies such as a change of venue or a more thorough voir dire.[70]

RECORDING AND TELEVISING JUDICIAL PROCEEDINGS

In 1976, only about 30 years ago, cameras and other recording equipment were barred from courtrooms in all but two states, Texas and Colorado. Today, such equipment is permitted in at least some courtrooms in all 50 states. Mississippi and South Dakota became the final two states to join in this massive reversal of the older rules. The rules vary from state to state and are often complex. Here is a brief overview of some of the kinds of variations that exist:

- ▌ In most states cameras and/or recording equipment are permitted in both trial and appellate courts. In six states—Delaware, Illinois, Indiana, Louisiana, New York and South Dakota—cameras are permitted only in appellate chambers. Courts in Maine limit trial coverage to arraignments, sentencing and other nontestimonial proceedings, and the judiciary in Utah permits only still photography at trials.*
- ▌ In some states the right to use this equipment in a courtroom is presumed. In other states broadcasters and photographers must first get the permission of the judge or justices or even the parties. But in either case, a judge can bar electronic equipment if there is sufficient reason.
- ▌ In some instances parties involved in the legal proceeding must agree before they can be photographed. But their refusal to be photographed cannot totally block cameras from recording the rest of the participants or the proceedings in general.
- ▌ Jurors cannot be photographed in some states.

This swift reversal of the rules regarding the use of cameras in the courtroom climaxed a 40-year struggle by the press for relaxation of prohibitions that were instituted in the 1930s. At that time the press had conducted itself in an outrageous fashion in covering the trial of Bruno Hauptmann, who in 1934 was charged with kidnapping the baby of Charles and Anne Lindbergh. The trial judge, who had great difficulty in controlling the press, ordered that no pictures be taken during the court sessions. But photographers equipped with large, bulky, flash-equipped cameras moved freely about the courtroom and took pictures whenever there

At that time the press had conducted itself in an outrageous fashion in covering the trial of Bruno Hauptmann, who in 1934 was charged with kidnapping the baby of Charles and Anne Lindbergh.

*These rules change periodically. It is worth checking the Web site maintained by the Radio-Television News Directors Association for current information on your state: www.rtnda.org.
69. *U.S.* v. *McDougal,* 103 F. 3d 651 (1996).
70. *United States* v. *Graham,* 257 F. 3d 143 (2001).

was a recess, a delay or a pause in the trial. As a result of this episode, the American Bar Association adopted rules prohibiting the use of cameras and other electronic equipment in courtrooms. The rules, known as Canon 35, were adopted in most states and were followed in practice in those states that did not officially adopt the rules.[71]

After World War II, when the photographic equipment became smaller and less obtrusive and faster film permitted photography indoors without flash equipment, the press began to agitate for changes in the rules. The television industry especially chafed under the proscriptions (the ABA rules had been amended in 1952 to include television), as they put broadcast reporters, who depended on film to tell a story, at a distinct disadvantage in the competition with word-smiths of the printed press. In the mid-1960s the U.S. Supreme Court had a chance to consider the constitutionality of the ban on cameras in the courtroom in a case that began in Texas, one of a handful of states that occasionally allowed photography and recording in the courtroom.

The defendant was Billie Sol Estes, who was accused of a swindle involving fertilizer tanks. The story was important in the Lone Star State; television was therefore permitted at the initial pretrial hearing, and still photographers were permitted throughout the trial. But there was disruption at the pretrial hearing. Twelve camera operators crowded into the tiny courtroom, cables and wires snaked across the floor, microphones were everywhere, and the distraction caused by this media invasion was significant. The situation improved during the trial when television and recording equipment was housed in a booth at the back of the courtroom. Estes appealed his conviction to the U.S. Supreme Court on the grounds that he had been denied a fair trial because of the presence of the cameras and recorders. The court agreed with the defendant. "While maximum freedom must be allowed the press in carrying out this important function [informing the public] in a democratic society, its exercise must necessarily be subject to the maintenance of absolute fairness in the judicial process," wrote Justice Tom Clark for the majority.[72] The photography and broadcasting equipment simply created too many impediments to a fair trial.

However, experimentation with cameras in the courtroom continued. Telecasting equipment improved. Journalists demonstrated to judges that they could act responsibly if they were permitted access to courtrooms with their cameras and recorders. More and more states began to permit telecasts and broadcasts of criminal and civil trials as well as of the oral arguments at appellate hearings. In the early 1980s two former Miami police officers challenged the new rules in Florida that permitted cameras in the courtroom. They argued that television coverage of their trial in and of itself had deprived them of a fair trial. The Florida Supreme Court rejected their contention, and the U.S. Supreme Court agreed to hear the case. In a unanimous decision the high court ruled that the mere presence of cameras in the courtroom or simply televising or broadcasting portions of a trial does not in and of itself cause prejudice to the defendant or interfere with the right to a fair trial.[73] Chief Justice Burger wrote that at present "no one has been able to present empirical data sufficient to establish that the mere presence of the broadcast media inherently has an adverse effect on that [trial] process." It is true the presence of such equipment in the courtroom or the broadcast of a trial could endanger the defendant's right to a fair trial. But, Burger said, "an absolute constitutional ban on broadcast coverage of trials cannot

71. White, "Cameras in the Courtroom."
72. *Estes v. Texas,* 381 U.S. 532 (1965).
73. *Chandler v. Florida,* 449 U.S. 560 (1981).

be justified simply because there is a danger that, in some cases, prejudicial broadcast accounts of pretrial and trial events may impair the ability of jurors to decide the issue of guilt or innocence uninfluenced by extraneous matter." The chief justice said that in order to block the use of cameras and recorders at a trial, a defendant must demonstrate to the court how the trial will be adversely affected by the presence of this equipment. To overturn a conviction at a trial that has been televised, the defendant will need to show that the recording and photography equipment actually made a substantial difference in some material aspect of the trial. Proof that the jurors were aware of the cameras or that the presence of television cameras "told" jurors this was a big trial will not be sufficient to demonstrate prejudice, Burger wrote.

State courts have started to develop standards to assess complaints of prejudice from defendants who do not want their trials televised. In Florida, for example, the state Supreme Court has ruled that the trial court must hold an evidentiary hearing if a defendant or other participant in the trial protests the television coverage. Before cameras and recorders may be excluded, there must be a finding that electronic coverage of the trial would have an important "qualitatively different effect" on the trial than would other types of coverage.[74] Another Florida case demonstrates how such a difference might be shown. The defendant in the case had previously been found incompetent to stand trial. Treatment subsequently rendered her competent to proceed with the case. Her attorneys, armed with testimony from psychiatrists, asserted that television cameras in the courtroom would adversely affect the defendant's ability to communicate with her counsel and she might lapse into psychosis. The Florida Supreme Court ruled that this kind of evidence satisfied the standard for excluding television cameras.[75] Some states provide exemptions from coverage to certain classes of trial participants such as juvenile offenders, victims of sex crimes, or police informants.

State rules on the admission of cameras to the courtroom vary. In some states cameras will not be permitted unless various key trial participants agree. In more states the cameras are allowed on the discretion of the judge. If a participant objects to the admission of cameras to the courtroom, the press must honor this objection and refrain from photographing or recording this individual. And judges can and do require cameras to be turned off during the presentation of certain kinds of evidence, such as gory crime scene photos. Most states have adopted guidelines that establish the number of still and motion picture cameras permitted in the courtroom at any one time. Rules often specify where the cameras may be placed, require that all pictures be taken with available light, and even set standards of dress for photographers and technicians. The press must often be willing to share the fruits of the photography through pooling agreements, since most states have guidelines limiting movement and placement of cameras to when the court is in recess only.

Getting cameras and recording equipment into federal courtrooms is a far greater problem. Such equipment is barred in most instances. In January 2002, for example, mass media representatives petitioned U.S. District Judge Leonie Brinkema to permit the broadcast of the trial of suspected terrorist Zacarias Moussaoui. The judge rejected the request. The federal

74. *Florida* v. *Palm Beach Newspapers,* 395 So. 2d 544 (1981). The Mississippi Supreme Court ruled in 2005 that a trial court could not bar a television station from televising a sentencing hearing unless the court—in applying the *Press-Enterprise* test (see pages 496–498)—could justify closing the proceeding to all mass media—not just television. *In re WBLT Inc.,* 905 So. 2d 1196 (2005).
75. *Florida* v. *Green,* 395 So. 2d 532 (1981).

ban on cameras in the courtroom was not a violation of the First Amendment, Judge Brinkema said. In this particular case, televising the trial would likely intimidate witnesses and jurors, and could pose security problems as well.[76] The federal judiciary has considered changing its rules, and some modifications have been made in relation to appellate hearings. Experimentation with cameras in federal courtrooms in the early 1990s was regarded by most observers as successful, but despite the apparent success of that test, the members of the U.S. Judicial Conference voted in 1994 to continue the ban on cameras and recorders. Eighteen months later the federal judges who make up the conference voted to give the 13 appellate courts the power to permit the televising of arguments in civil cases.[77] At the end of 2005 judges in only the 2nd and 9th U.S. Courts of Appeal (San Francisco and New York) permitted cameras in their appellate courtrooms, and only in extremely limited circumstances. Legislation was introduced in the U.S. Senate in 1999, 2001 and again in 2003 that would give federal trial and appellate judges the discretion to permit cameras in their courtrooms on a three-year trial basis, but it failed to pass each time.

Why do the federal judges generally oppose permitting cameras in the courtroom? Chief Judge Edward Becker of the 3rd U.S. Court of Appeals probably spoke for many of his colleagues when he testified against the Senate proposal in 2000. Becker said that television coverage of court proceedings could have a positive impact on the judicial system, but it was unlikely that it would have such an impact. "Television news coverage appears to use the courtroom for a backdrop or a visual image for the news story," he said, "which like most stories on television are delivered in short sound bites and not in depth."[78] The Supreme Court released audiotapes in December 2000 of the oral argument presented during a hearing on the Florida presidential election recount. But despite this unprecedented move, there seems little likelihood of greater electronic coverage of the federal judiciary in the immediate future.

Courts have barred the televising of executions in the United States, most recently in the summer of 2004 when the 8th U.S. Court of Appeals ruled that there was no First Amendment right to videotape an execution. The decision upheld a Missouri corrections department policy barring all cameras and recording devices from execution chambers.[79] Similar decisions have been rendered for the past 15 years.[80]

Broadcasters have also failed in their attempts to get cameras and other recording equipment into the jury room. In November 2002 a trial judge in Houston said he would allow the PBS documentary series "Frontline" to film the jury deliberations in a death penalty case. The 17-year-old defendant and his mother agreed to the filming, as did the young man's attorney. "If the State of Texas wants to execute a 17-year-old, the whole world should be watching to make sure it is done right," attorney Ricardo Rodriquez said. But the state argued against the filming, claiming the process would turn the deliberations into a "Survivor"-style reality program. Scholars who study juries tended to agree, calling the comparison with the popular TV program correct. "Conscripting citizens for a reality television program strikes me as a bad

---

76. *United States* v. *Moussaoui,* 30 M.L.R. 1251 (2002).

77. Greenhouse, "Panel Allows TV."

78. Greenhouse, "Not Exactly Made for TV."

79. *Rice* v. *Kemker,* 374 F. 3d 675 (2004).

80. See *KQED, Inc.* v. *Vasquez,* 18 M.L.R. 2323 (1991). See also *Campbell* v. *Blodgett,* 982 F. 2d 1356 (1993); *California First Amendment Coalition* v. *Calderon,* 130 F. 3d 976 (1998); and *Entertainment Network Inc.* v. *Lappin,* 134 F. Supp. 2d 1002 (2001).

idea," Shari Diamond, a law professor at Northwest University told New York Times reporter Adam Liptak.[81] "It involves jurors in signing on for a national public performance. The potential for that having a distorting effect on their work is palpable," she added.

Three months later the Texas Criminal Court of Appeals, the state's highest criminal appeals court, rejected the judge's plan. The court cited a state statute that said, "No person shall be permitted to be with a jury while it is deliberating." This prohibits the taping, the court said, adding that it believed that the filming would introduce "outside influence and pressure" on the jury.[82]

Courts in Arizona and Wisconsin have on occasion permitted the filming of jury deliberations in criminal cases. And the taping of jury deliberations in civil cases for research or educational purposes has also taken place.[83] But as a general rule, cameras and audio recording equipment are barred from the jury room, and it is unlikely that this prohibition will change anytime soon.

SUMMARY

The right of access to pretrial proceedings and documents is qualified. The presumption that these hearings are open can only be overcome by a showing that there is an overriding interest that must be protected, that there is a "substantial probability" that an open hearing will damage this right, that the closure is narrowly tailored to deny access to no more of the hearing than is necessary to protect this interest, that the court has considered reasonable alternatives to closure, that closure of the hearing would in fact protect the interest that has been raised, and that the trial judge has articulated findings—which may be reviewed by an appellate court—that support these four points.

Broadcast journalists are given somewhat less access when they seek to obtain copies of audio- or videotaped evidence or seek to record or televise a judicial proceeding. Access to the taped evidence is developing through a case-by-case approach, and courts have granted journalists increasing rights to make copies of this material for later broadcast. Cameras and recording devices are now permitted in courts in all but two states and the District of Columbia. The Supreme Court has ruled that the mere presence of such devices does not in and of itself prejudice a defendant's right to a fair trial. The federal courts refuse to permit cameras in the courtroom. Cameras are barred from executions, and the filming of jury deliberations is generally prohibited.

BENCH-BAR-PRESS GUIDELINES

Both restrictive orders and the closure of court proceedings are admittedly effective ways of stopping publicity from reaching the hands of potential jurors, but they are equally dangerous in a representative democracy where information about how well government is operating is fundamental to the success of the political system. The bench, the bar and the press in many states

81. Liptak, "Inviting TV into Jury Room."
82. *State ex rel Rosenthal v. Poe,* Tex. Crim. App. No. 74, 515, 2/13/03.
83. Liptak, "Inviting TV into Jury Room."

have found that cooperation, restraint and mutual trust can be equally effective in protecting the rights of a defendant, while at the same time far less damaging to rights of the people.

In more than two dozen states the members of the bench, the bar and the press have tried to reach a common understanding of the problems of pretrial news coverage and have offered suggestions as to how most of these problems might be resolved. These suggestions are usually offered in the form of guidelines or recommendations to the press and to participants in the criminal justice system. **Bench-bar-press guidelines** normally suggest to law enforcement officers that certain kinds of information about a criminal suspect and a crime can be released and published with little danger of harm to the trial process. The guidelines also suggest to journalists that the publication of certain kinds of information about a case (see the list of damaging kinds of statements on pages 468–470) can be harmful to the defendant's chances for a fair trial without providing the public with useful or important information. The guidelines are often presented in a very brief form; at other times they encompass several pages of text.

Bench-bar-press guidelines have existed in some states for more than 50 years. In some communities these guidelines work very well in managing the problems surrounding the free press–fair trial dilemma. A spirit of cooperation exists between press, courts, attorneys and law enforcement personnel. In such communities it is rare to find a restrictive order or a closed courtroom. But most communities and states have found it takes considerable effort to make the guidelines work. Drafting the guidelines is only the first step. If, after agreement is reached on the recommendations, the bench, the bar and the press go their separate ways, the guidelines usually fail as a means of resolving the free press–fair trial problems.

Most communities and states have found it takes considerable effort to make the guidelines work.

A good deal of space has been devoted to the free press–fair trial problem because it is an important issue and because it continues to be a problem. Within both the press and the law, sharp divisions regarding solution of the problem remain. Many years ago, during a battle over a free press–fair trial issue in one southern state, the national office of the American Civil Liberties Union filed an amicus curiae (friend of the court) brief supporting a free and unfettered press, while the state chapter of the same civil liberties group filed a brief in favor of the court's position supporting a fair trial.

Crime, especially violent crime, has become the focus of many segments of the American press. Television news is especially afflicted by this trend. But serious reporting on the criminal justice system remains in short supply, despite the importance to society of the tasks undertaken by the police, the prosecutors and the courts. In "Crime and Publicity" Alfred Friendly and Ronald Goldfarb wrote:

> To shackle the press is to curtail the public watch over the administration of criminal justice. . . . The press serv es at the gatehouse of justice. Additionally, it serves in the manorhouse itself, and all along the complicated route to it from the police station and the streets, to the purlieus of the prosecutor's office, to the courtroom corridors where the pressures mount and the deals are made.[84]

The two authors also point out that we do not want a press that is more or less free, just as we should not tolerate trials that are almost fair. "And to complicate the issue," they note,

84. Friendly and Goldfarb, *Crime and Publicity*.

"it is evident that a free press is one of society's principal guarantors of fair trials, while fair trials provide a major assurance of the press's freedom."

Reporters dealing with the courts and the court system must be extremely sensitive to these issues. They should not be blinded to the sensitive mechanisms that operate in the courts to provide justice and fairness as they clamor for news. At the same time they should not let the authoritarian aspects of the judicial system block their efforts to provide the information essential to the functioning of democracy.

SUMMARY

In some states the press, attorneys and judges have agreed to try to solve the problems surrounding the free press–fair trial controversy through voluntary bench-bar-press agreements. Such agreements usually contain suggestions to all parties as to what information should and should not be publicized about criminal cases. When the guidelines work, there is usually a cooperative, rather than a combative, spirit among the members of the press, the judiciary and the bar. These guidelines often reduce or eliminate the need for restrictive orders or closed hearings.

BIBLIOGRAPHY ⟶

Bechamps, Anne T. "Sealed Out-of-Court Settlements: When Does the Public Have a Right to Know?" *Notre Dame Law Review* 66 (1990): 117.

Broder, John M. "From Grand Jury Leaks Comes a Clash of Rights." *The New York Times,* 15 January 2005, A8.

Bush, Chilton R., ed. *Free Press and Fair Trial: Some Dimensions of the Problem.* Athens: University of Georgia Press, 1971.

Cys, Richard L., and Andrew M. Mar. "Media Access to the New Special Tribunals: Lessons Learned from History and the Military Courts." *First Amendment Law Letter.* Winter 2002, p. 1.

Friendly, Alfred, and Ronald Goldfarb. *Crime and Publicity.* New York: Random House, Vintage Books, 1968.

Goldstein, Abraham S. "Jury Secrecy and the Media: The Problem of the Postverdict Interview." *University of Illinois Law Review* 1993 (1993): 295.

Greenhouse, Linda. "Not Exactly Made for TV, But Think of the Ratings." *The New York Times,* 26 November 2000, B4.

———. "Panel Allows TV in Appeals Courts." *The New York Times,* 13 March 1996, C6.

Judicial Records: A Guide to Access in State and Federal Courts. Washington, D.C.: Reporters Committee for Freedom of the Press, 1990.

Lindsey, Richard P. "An Assessment of the Use of Cameras in State and Federal Courts." *Georgia Law Review* 18 (1984): 389.

Liptak, Adam. "Inviting TV into Jury Room in Capital Case." *The New York Times,* 11 November 2002, A1.

———. "Nameless Juries on the Rise in Crime Cases." *The New York Times,* 26 November 2002, A1.

Minow, Newton, and Fred Cate. "Who Is an Impartial Juror in an Age of Mass Media?" *The American University Law Review* 40 (1991): 631.

Raskopf, Robert. "A First Amendment Right of Access to a Juror's Identity: Toward a Fuller Understanding of the Jury's Deliberative Process." *Pepperdine Law Review* 17 (1990): 357.

Shenon, Philip. "In Shift, Appeals Court Opens Hearing on a 9/11 Suspect." *The New York Times,* 14 May 2003, A15.

———. "Judge Critical of Secrecy in Terror Case Prosecution." *The New York Times,* 5 April 2003, B13.

———. "News Groups Want Terror Case Files." *The New York Times,* 4 April 2003, B13.

Stack, Barbara. "Opening Juvenile Courts." *Columbia Journalism Review,* March/April 2002, p. 62.

White, Frank W. "Cameras in the Courtroom: A U.S. Survey." *Journalism Monographs* 60 (1979).

REGULATION OF OBSCENE AND OTHER EROTIC MATERIAL

The attempts by the government to regulate obscenity and other so-called erotic material have little impact on most professional communicators who work in the mass media. Yet it is fair to argue that the legal battles fought over such materials are taking place on the front lines of the continual war to protect freedom of expression. In no other area of the law is the First Amendment under such intense siege. Emboldened by victories in the 2004 elections, a variety of political factions and advocacy groups have attacked a wide variety of books, movies, magazines, television and radio programs and the content of the Internet in an attempt to purge these channels of material they find obscene, indecent, offensive or merely distasteful. The court decisions that result from these battles define freedom of the press for all Americans, not just those who work on the fringes of our cultural landscape. This chapter briefly explores the history of regulation of obscenity, outlines current judicial definitions, and discusses a wide range of government efforts to control the content of mass communications.

THE LAW OF OBSCENITY

No First Amendment issue generates more emotion in Americans than does the regulation of the sale and distribution of obscene and other erotic materials. U.S. Judge H. Lee Sarokin noted more than 20 years ago that sexually explicit materials are supposed to arouse sexual passion.

> They also seem to arouse passions of an entirely different sort. If a merchant announced his intention to open a store dedicated to murder mysteries, no matter how violent or bloody, nary a picket or protestor would appear. But should one announce that sex is to be the main theme, then organized opposition is inevitable.[1]

IMPORTANT DATES IN OBSCENITY LAW

1791—Adoption of First Amendment

1815—First recorded obscenity prosecution

1842—First federal obscenity law

1873—Comstock Act adopted

1957—*Hicklin* rule abandoned

       Roth test emerges

1967—First presidential obscenity commission appointed

1973—*Miller* test enunciated

1985—Second presidential commission on obscenity appointed

1997—Communications Decency Act ruled unconstitutional

1998—Child Online Protection Act adopted

2001—Children's Internet Protection Act adopted

2004—Enforcement of Child Online Protection Act blocked by Supreme Court

---

The Supreme Court of the United States has defined what is legally obscene (see pages 531–536). This particularly narrow range of material is considered beyond the ambit of First Amendment protection. Today, however, war is being waged against a far wider range of erotic material, much of it material that is not considered legally obscene. Song lyrics and music videos have been attacked. Public libraries have come under siege for owning admittedly

---

1. *E-Bru, Inc.* v. *Graves,* 566 F. Supp. 1476 (1983).

frank but clinically sound sex education books. The Department of Justice with the support of various citizens groups successfully impaired the distribution of so-called men's magazines like Penthouse and Playboy during the 1980s. In a few states, efforts have been made to block the cablecasting of some R-rated movies. The mantra of many would-be censors today is the protection of young people from sexually explicit materials. Many state legislatures as well as the Congress of the United States have passed a wide variety of laws in an effort to accomplish this end.

Those who seek to limit the flow of erotic material in the marketplace often raise legitimate concerns. Many women believe sexually explicit material fuels violence against women. Parents express concern about what children may see and hear. Many individuals find such material antithetical to their religious beliefs. But there are compelling reasons to be concerned about the censorship of obscene and other erotic materials. The U.S. Supreme Court has declared with a bare minimum of justification that obscenity is outside the protection of the First Amendment. The high court has based this ruling largely on the dubious proposition that the Founding Fathers who drafted the First Amendment did not intend that it protect obscenity. It has been noted previously that there is little evidence to support any conclusions about the intent of the drafters of the First Amendment and the people who supported it. Colonial Americans often have been mistakenly described as a humorless, drab, sanctimonious people rooted in the strong Christian traditions that flowered in Puritan and other religious societies in the 17th century. In fact it was a lusty and often bawdy people who created this nation and who approved the constitutional guarantee of freedom of expression. What many today would call sexually explicit material was freely circulated in the late 18th century and people seemed unconcerned about it. The first civil prosecution for the distribution, sale or display of erotic material was not recorded until 1815, nearly 25 years after the adoption of the First Amendment.* Contemporary American attitudes about sex and erotic material were shaped far more by the Victorian values of the middle-to-late 19th century than by the values of the non-Native Americans who inhabited this continent and helped build this nation.

The Supreme Court has also attempted to justify the suppression of obscenity on the grounds that such books or magazines or movies are in some way detrimental to the community. But unassailable evidence to support this conclusion is also absent. Contemporary studies that suggest harmful consequences result from the circulation of obscenity are usually matched by equally persuasive studies that suggest the opposite conclusion. It is hardly a comforting proposition that the government can declare, with such limited justification, an entire category of speech and press to be outside the protection of the Bill of Rights. On this basis it may be obscenity that is banned today; it might be a religious dogma or political philosophy that is banned tomorrow. And that is an important reason to be concerned about the regulation of obscenity.

There is another reason as well, however. Although the descriptions we use today to define obscenity are surely better than the ones used a half-century ago, they still lack sufficient precision to adequately warn booksellers or video retailers or Web-site operators what it is they may or may not legally distribute. Consequently there is substantial self-censorship of nonobscene material. Record companies, magazine distributors, booksellers and Internet

It is hardly a comforting proposition that the government can declare, with such limited justification, an entire category of speech and press to be outside the protection of the Bill of Rights.

*Religious laws that governed some colonies in the 17th century forbade blasphemy, and blasphemous conduct could certainly involve sexually oriented books or pamphlets.

Source: Everett Collection

Steven Spielberg's Academy Award winning film, "Saving Private Ryan," also won the dubious honor of being censored by several U.S. television stations because of its graphic depiction of the violence that is a part of war.

service providers are often reluctant to take a chance and distribute material that might be illegal. In the wake of Janet Jackson's "wardrobe malfunction" at the 2004 Super Bowl halftime show, the government issued stern warnings to broadcasters about transmitting so-called indecent programming. These warnings resulted in a spate of self-censorship that included television stations refusing to broadcast Steven Spielberg's award-winning film "Saving Private Ryan" because of the violence that was depicted as American soldiers landed at Omaha Beach on D-Day in 1944, to some public television stations barring the telecast of a documentary on the war in Iraq because of the language used by American armed forces, to ABC barring a satirical skit by Robin Williams on the 2005 Academy Award telecast that made fun of such censorship. The government didn't order such censorship—the broadcasters did it themselves because they feared the consequences of offending the government. The convenience store operator who drops the sale of Playboy to avoid a boycott or prosecution limits public access to the monthly centerfold pictures and other material some people regard as salacious or offensive. But also limited is public access to the not-infrequent news article or informative essay also contained in that magazine. Even the strongest proponents of the free flow of erotic material do not suggest that this kind of material should be thrust in the faces of those who are legitimately offended by erotic magazines or books or videos. Harm to the individual psyche can be real even if undocumentable. All that advocates of freedom of expression seek is a society in which people can make up their own minds and have access to those materials that they want to read or watch.

COMMON TERMS

Obscenity—A narrow class of material defined by the Supreme Court in the *Miller* test (see pages 531–536). Material that is legally obscene is not protected by the First Amendment. Obscene material is sometimes referred to as hard-core pornography.
Indecent Material—Material that may be sexually graphic; often referred to as adult material or sexually explicit material. This material is protected under the First Amendment. However, such material may be barred in works available to children (see variable obscenity laws on pages 537–538) and in over-the-air (as opposed to cable or satellite-generated) radio and television broadcasts. (See pages 686–696 for a full discussion of broadcast indecency.)
Pornography—This term has no legal significance but is often used by laypersons and politicians to describe anything from real obscenity to material such as a passionate love scene that is simply offensive to the viewer. The overuse (and misuse) of this imprecise term tends to add more confusion to an already muddled legal landscape.

EARLY OBSCENITY LAW

The first recorded obscenity prosecution in the United States occurred in 1815, when a man named Jesse Sharpless was fined for exhibiting a painting of a man "in an imprudent posture with a woman." There are on record earlier convictions for offenses tied to obscenity; these were prosecutions under common law for crimes against God, not for merely displaying erotic pictures. In 1821 Peter Holmes was convicted for publishing an erotically enhanced version of John Cleland's *Memoirs of a Woman of Pleasure*.

As the 19th century progressed, obscenity laws and prosecutions became more common, ebbing and flowing with major reform movements in the 1820s and 1830s and in the wake of the Civil War. The first federal obscenity statute, a customs law regulating the importation of obscene articles, was adopted in 1842. The most comprehensive federal statute adopted during the century became law in 1873. Known as the Comstock Act because of the intense pressure applied on Congress by a young man named Anthony Comstock, the law declared that all obscene books, pamphlets, pictures and other materials were nonmailable. No definition of obscenity was provided by Congress, however. The Comstock law, as amended, remains the federal law today.

Federal agencies such as the Bureau of Customs and the Post Office Department were the nation's most vigilant obscenity fighters during the late 19th and first half of the 20th centuries. Sometimes straying beyond what the law actually permitted, these agencies banned, burned and confiscated huge amounts of erotic materials, including religious objects, pieces of art, books (including some of the best written during that era), magazines (including science and diving publications), and a wide array of material on birth control. When the motion picture industry began to grow in the early part of this century, local and state censors went after films that they believed to be obscene as well. The courts, especially the federal courts, became inundated with obscenity prosecutions and appeals. The U.S. Supreme Court seemed especially drawn to such litigation. Between 1957 and 1977, for example, the high court heard arguments in almost 90 obscenity cases and wrote opinions in nearly 40 of those cases. The remainder were decided by memoranda orders (see page 23 for a definition of this term).

DEFINING OBSCENITY

Outlawing obscenity is one thing. Defining it is something else. When American courts, in the wake of the adoption of the Comstock Act in 1873, first began considering what is and what is not obscenity they borrowed a British definition called the *Hicklin* rule.[2] Under this rule a work is obscene if **it has a tendency to deprave and corrupt those whose minds are open to such immoral influences and into whose hands it might fall.** If something might influence the mind of a child, it was regarded as obscene for everyone, under this definition. In addition, if any part of the work, regardless of how small, met this definition, the entire work was regarded as obscene. This very broad and loose definition made it possible for both federal and state authorities to wage an aggressive and highly successful war against erotic materials in the first half of the 20th century.

In 1957 the Supreme Court abandoned the *Hicklin* rule, declaring that because of this rule American adults were permitted to read or watch only what was fit for children. "Surely this is to burn the house, to roast the pig," Justice Felix Frankfurter noted.[3] In abandoning the *Hicklin* rule, the high court was forced to fashion a new definition of obscenity, beginning with the case of *Roth* v. *U.S.*[4] in 1957. Over the next nine years, in a variety of obscenity rulings, what was called the *Roth-Memoirs* test was developed by the Supreme Court.[5] The test had three parts.

First, the dominant theme of the material taken as a whole must appeal to prurient interest in sex.

Second, a court must find that the material is patently offensive because it affronts contemporary community standards relating to the description or representation of sexual matters.

Third, before something can be found to be obscene, it must be utterly without redeeming social value.

While this entire test was far narrower than the *Hicklin* rule, it was the third part of the test that continually bedeviled government prosecutors. If a work had even the slightest social value, it could not be deemed to be obscene.

---

2. *Regina* v. *Hicklin,* L.R. 3 Q.B. 360 (1868).
3. *Butler* v. *Michigan,* 352 U.S. 380 (1957).
4. 354 U.S. 476 (1957).
5. See *Manual Enterprises, Inc.* v. *J. Edward Day,* 370 U.S. 478 (1962); *Jacobellis* v. *Ohio,* 378 U.S. 184 (1964); and *Memoirs of a Woman of Pleasure* v. *Massachusetts,* 383 U.S. 413 (1966).

SUMMARY

Prosecutions for obscenity did not occur in this nation until the early 19th century. In the 1820s and 1830s, many states adopted their first obscenity laws. The first federal law was passed in 1842. The government actively prosecuted obscenity in the wake of the Civil War, and in 1873 Congress adopted a strict new obscenity law. Obscenity was defined as being anything that had a tendency to deprave and corrupt those whose minds might be open to such immoral influences and into whose hands it might happen to fall. This rule, called the *Hicklin* rule, meant that if any part of a book or other work had the tendency to deprave or corrupt any person (such as a child or overly sensitive individual) who might happen to see the work, the material was obscene and no person could buy it or see it. This definition facilitated government censorship of a wide range of materials.

In the 1950s and early 1960s, the Supreme Court adopted a new definition or test for obscenity, the *Roth-Memoirs* test. The test had three main parts:

1. The dominant theme of the material, taken as a whole, appeals to an average person's prurient interest in sex.
2. The material is patently offensive because it affronts contemporary community standards relating to sexual matters. It was assumed that there was a single, national standard that was applicable to all parts of the country.
3. The material is utterly without redeeming social value. It has no social value at all.

CONTEMPORARY OBSCENITY LAW

President Lyndon Johnson appointed a commission in 1967 to study the regulation of obscenity in the United States. Two years later a majority of the members of this blue-ribbon panel issued a report recommending the repeal of all laws that restricted the use of erotic materials by consenting adults.[6] But this was 1969 and Johnson was no longer president. Richard Nixon sat in the White House and flatly rejected the report. He vowed never to relax in the fight against obscenity, rejecting the commission's conclusion that the regular viewing or reading of obscenity produced no harmful effects in normal adults. The new president substantially changed the makeup of the Supreme Court as he made four appointments in three years.* By 1973, when the case of *Miller* v. *California*[7] was decided, a more conservative Supreme Court had its chance to redefine obscenity. This new test is the one courts must use today.

THE *MILLER* TEST

Marvin Miller was convicted of violating the California Penal Code for sending five unsolicited brochures to a restaurant in Newport Beach. The brochures, which advertised four erotic books and one film, contained pictures and drawings of men and women engaging in a

---

*President Nixon appointed Chief Justice Warren Burger and Associate Justices Harry Blackmun, Lewis Powell and William Rehnquist.
6. *Report of the Commission on Obscenity and Pornography.*
7. 413 U.S. 15 (1973).

In Miller, *for the first time since 1957, a majority of the Supreme Court reached agreement on a definition of obscenity.*

variety of sexual activities. The recipient of the mailing complained to police, and Miller was prosecuted by state authorities.

In *Miller,* for the first time since 1957, a majority of the Supreme Court reached agreement on a definition of obscenity. Chief Justice Warren Burger and four other members of the high court agreed that material is obscene if the following standards are met:

1. **An average person, applying contemporary local community standards, finds that the work, taken as a whole, appeals to prurient interest.**
2. **The work depicts in a patently offensive way sexual conduct specifically defined by applicable state law.**
3. **The work in question lacks serious literary, artistic, political or scientific value.**

The implications and ambiguities in these three elements create the need for fuller explanation. As a result of the *Miller* ruling and subsequent obscenity decisions handed down by the court since 1973, some guidelines have emerged.

An Average Person

The first element of the *Miller* test asks if an average person, applying contemporary community standards, would find that the work, taken as a whole, appeals to prurient interest. It is the trier of fact who will make this determination. This can be the trial judge, but more commonly it is the jury. The Supreme Court expects the trier of fact to rely on knowledge of the standards of the residents of the community to decide whether the work appeals to a prurient interest. The juror is not supposed to use his or her own standards in this decision. The Supreme Court noted in 1974:

> This Court has emphasized on more than one occasion that a principal concern in requiring that a judgment be made on the basis of contemporary community standards is to assure that the material is judged neither on the basis of each juror's personal opinion nor by its effect on a particular sensitive or insensitive person or group.[8]

Note the last phrase in this quote. The court expects the standards of an average person to be applied in making this critical determination. In California a trial judge told jurors to consider the effect of the material on all the members of the community, including children and highly sensitive persons. The Supreme Court ruled that these jury instructions were faulty.[9] "Children are not to be included for these purposes as part of the 'community,'" wrote Chief Justice Burger. However, instructing the jury to consider the impact of the material on sensitive or insensitive persons is permissible, so long as these persons are looked on as part of the entire community, Burger wrote. "The community includes all adults who comprise it, and a jury can consider them all in determining relevant community standards," Burger wrote. "The vice," he said, "is in focusing upon the most susceptible or sensitive members when judging the obscenity of the material."

Prurient interest has been defined by the courts to mean a shameful or morbid interest in nudity, sex or excretion. Judges must be careful when they instruct jurors on the specific legal

8. *Hamling* v. *United States,* 418 U.S. 87 (1974).
9. *Pinkus* v. *U.S.,* 98 S. Ct. 1808 (1978).

meaning of these terms. The Nebraska Supreme Court recently overturned the conviction of two men who were accused of distributing obscene material because the trial judge failed to define "prurient interest" completely. Prurient means, among other things, having the tendency to excite lustful thought. If this is the definition the jurors used, someone could be convicted of obscenity for simply distributing material that provokes a normal, healthy sexual desire. This would be wrong, the court ruled.[10]

Community Standards

The definition of community standards is a key to the first part of the *Miller* test. The Supreme Court had failed to define which community standards governed a determination of obscenity under the *Roth-Memoirs* test; were these local, regional or national standards? Two members of the court had declared in a plurality opinion that national standards were to be applied.[11] Chief Justice Burger made it clear in the *Miller* decision that local standards were to be applied. In most jurisdictions the term "local standards" has been translated to mean "state standards." All communities within the same state share the same standards. In fact, some state supreme courts have even ruled that local communities have no right to pass obscenity laws; the state has preempted this field.[12] The question of applicable community standards becomes an important factor in cases that involve the shipment of erotic material over long distances within the United States and in cases involving the importation of sexually explicit material from outside the United States.

In prosecutions initiated by the U.S. Postal Service, the government is free to choose the venue in which to try the case. This might be the city from which the material was sent; it might be the city in which it was received; or it might be any city through which the material passed during its transit. For example, a trial involving a magazine sent from Boston to Dallas might be held in Boston, Dallas, or anywhere in between. So Massachusetts standards might apply at the trial, or Texas standards, or even Pennsylvania or Kentucky standards if the publication passed through or over those states during its shipment. This government practice is called "venue shopping," or selecting a site where a conviction is most easily obtained. A postmaster in Oregon asked a postmaster in Wyoming to solicit (using a false name) erotic material distributed by an Oregon man. After the defendant sent material to Wyoming he was tried using Wyoming standards, not Oregon standards. The record shows that the defendant had never resided in, traveled through, or had any previous business contact in Wyoming. The 10th U.S. Circuit Court of Appeals upheld the conviction, noting that under the existing law "federal enforcement officers . . . are free to shop for venue from which juries with the most restrictive views are likely to be impanelled."[13] When imported erotic material is seized, the standards of the state in which the material is seized are applied at trial.

The growth of the Internet, which is a global communication system, has generated numerous difficulties in the application of the concept of local or even state standards. It is one thing to shut down a bookstore in Dallas or prosecute a distributor in Minneapolis. But a Web site operator in Seattle can reach users in all parts of the world in a matter of seconds. Whose

10. *State* v. *Halton*, 30 M.L.R. 2301 (2002).
11. *Jacobellis* v. *Ohio*, 378 U.S. 184 (1964).
12. *Spokane* v. *Portch*, 94 Wash. 2d 342 (1979).
13. *U.S.* v. *Blucher*, 581 F. 2d 244 (1978).

community standards should apply? The standard where the sender lives, or any of the various standards where the receivers live? In 2004 Judge James R. Spencer, in writing an opinion for the 4th U.S. Court of Appeals that struck down a Virginia law that made it a crime to disseminate online material that is harmful to juveniles, wrote poetically but accurately: "The content of the Internet is analogous to the content of the night sky. One state simply cannot block a constellation from the view of its own citizens without blocking or affecting the view of citizens of other states."[14]

But this decision is not typical. What is taking place, for the most part, is that courts are permitting the government to select the venue for prosecution, as they have done in the past with material shipped by the Postal Service. In the late 1980s, for example, Home Dish Satellite Corporation of New York City was beaming hard-core sex films to 30,000 subscribers across the nation and soft-core movies to 1.2 million other customers. Fifty persons in Montgomery County, Ala., subscribed to the service, and law enforcement officials there indicted the company on charges of violating the state obscenity statutes. Home Dish pleaded guilty to the charges and paid $150,000 in penalties. The grand jury also indicted GTE Corporation and its satellite subsidiaries. To escape the long arm of Alabama law, GTE dumped Home Dish off the satellite, which put the company out of business. Lawyers said that this case was the first time in the nation's history that local criminal laws were applied to programs carried nationwide by satellite technology. In 1994 a California couple was prosecuted for sending sexual images over a computer bulletin board carried on the Internet. The Amateur Action Computer Bulletin Board (AACBB) system featured e-mail, chat lines, public messages and explicit sexual files that only paying bulletin board members could access, transfer and download to their own computers. Robert and Carleen Thomas of Milpitas, Calif., were each convicted of 10 counts of transmitting obscenity through interstate telephone lines. Each count carried a penalty of up to five years in jail and a $250,000 fine. The Thomases had previously been investigated by the San Jose, Calif., police department, which ruled that the erotic material on the AACBB was not obscene under California standards. A postal inspector in Memphis joined the bulletin board under a false name and received the images through his computer in Tennessee. He initiated the complaint against the Thomases. Mike Godwin, a lawyer for the Electronic Frontier Foundation, said that the case had "one community attempting to dictate standards for the whole country." The trial court's verdict was upheld by the 6th U.S. Circuit Court of Appeals in January 1996, which noted that if the defendants didn't want to face a trial in Tennessee, they should not have enrolled a member from Tennessee.[15] The Supreme Court rejected an appeal by the California couple.

Patent Offensiveness

The second element of the *Miller* test says that a work is obscene if it depicts in a patently offensive way sexual conduct specifically defined by applicable state law. Patent offensiveness is also to be judged by the trier of fact, using contemporary community standards. But the Supreme Court has put limits on this judgment, ruling that only what it calls hard-core sexual

14. *PSINet Inc.* v. *Chapman,* 4th cir., No. 01-2352, 3/25/04.
15. "Couple Guilty of Pornography," 12; Wallace and Mangan, *Sex, Laws, and Cyberspace;* and *U.S.* v. *Thomas,* 74 F. 3d 701 (1996).

material meets the patently offensive standard. Georgia courts ruled that the motion picture "Carnal Knowledge," an R-rated film, was patently offensive. The Supreme Court reversed this ruling, saying that the Georgia courts misunderstood this second part of the *Miller* test.[16] Material that was patently offensive, Justice Rehnquist wrote, included "representations or descriptions of ultimate sexual acts, normal or perverted, actual or simulated" and "representations or descriptions of masturbation, excretory functions, and lewd exhibition of genitals." Rehnquist acknowledged that this catalog of descriptions was not exhaustive, but that only material like this qualifies as patently offensive material. The second part of the *Miller* test was "intended to fix substantive constitutional limitations . . . on the type of material . . . subject to a determination of obscenity," he added.

State laws are supposed to define the kinds of material or conduct that are prohibited as obscene. Many state obscenity statutes contain Rehnquist's descriptions as their definition of obscenity. Other state laws are less precise. The Supreme Court has even given its approval to state laws that contain no descriptive phrases so long as the state supreme court has construed (or interpreted) the law to prohibit only the narrowly defined kind of material outlined by Justice Rehnquist.[17]

State laws are supposed to define the kinds of material or conduct that are prohibited as obscene.

Serious Value

To be legally obscene a work must lack serious literary, artistic, political or scientific value. While not as broad as the "utterly without redeeming social value" element in the *Roth-Memoirs* test, this third criterion in the *Miller* test nevertheless acts as a brake on judges and juries eager to convict on the basis of the first two parts of the test. The judge is supposed to play a pronounced role in deciding whether a work has serious value. The serious value element is not judged by the tastes or standards of the average person. The test is not whether an ordinary person in the community would find serious literary, artistic, political or scientific value, but whether a reasonable person *could* find such value in the material.[18] Jurors are supposed to determine whether a reasonable person would see a serious value in the work. Both the state and the defense will frequently introduce expert testimony to try to "educate" the jury on the relative merit of the material in question.

The Supreme Court has not provided lower courts with specific guidelines regarding serious value, at least not as specific as the guidelines for patently offensive material. But the high court has continually warned lower courts "to remain sensitive to any infringement on genuinely serious literary, artistic, political, or scientific value."[19] The Supreme Court has also instructed lower appellate courts not to hesitate to scrutinize trial court judgments regarding serious value. The determination of whether a book or magazine or film lacks value "is particularly amenable to appellate review," wrote Justice Harry Blackmun.[20] So while a trial judge or an appellate court should be reluctant to second-guess a jury on a determination of contemporary community standards or patent offensiveness, the judge or court should not be hesitant in making an independent determination that a work has literary, artistic, political or scientific value.

16. *Jenkins* v. *Georgia,* 418 U.S. 153 (1974).
17. *Ward* v. *Illinois,* 431 U.S. 767 (1977).
18. *Pope* v. *Illinois,* 107 S. Ct. 1918 (1987).
19. *Miller* v. *California,* 413 U.S. 15 (1973).
20. *Smith* v. *U.S.,* 431 U.S. 291 (1977).

THE *MILLER* TEST

1. An average person, applying contemporary local community standards, finds that the work, taken as a whole, appeals to prurient interest.
2. The work depicts in a patently offensive way sexual conduct specifically defined by applicable state law.
3. The work in question lacks serious literary, artistic, political or scientific value.

Extreme Associates: *A Change in the Wind or a Fluke?*

In early 2005 a U.S. District Court Judge in Pittsburgh ruled that several long-standing federal obscenity laws were unconstitutional, a burden on an American's fundamental right "to possess, read, observe and think about what he chooses in the privacy of his own home by completely banning the distribution of obscene materials." The government prosecuted Extreme Associates Inc., a Southern California company that distributes sexually explicit material both through the mail and online, including "films of women being gang raped, defecated on and having their throats slit." Both sides in the case agreed that the material could be considered legally obscene, so there was no application of the *Miller* test by the judge to the films in question.

The decision by Judge Gary L. Lancaster was not based on a First Amendment rationale. Instead, he anchored his ruling on the Supreme Court's 2003 decision in *Lawrence* v. *Texas,*[21] which voided a Texas state anti-sodomy law. In that case the high court ruled that the liberty guaranteed by the due process clause in the Constitution "protects the person from unwarranted government intrusions into a dwelling or other private places." Lancaster said he interpreted that ruling to mean that "public morality is not a legitimate state interest sufficient to justify infringing on adult, private, consensual, sexual conduct even if that conduct is deemed offensive to the general public's sense of morality." The obscenity laws violate constitutional guarantees of personal liberty and sexual privacy of consenting adults who wish to view the films provided by Extreme Associates in the privacy of their own homes, Lancaster concluded.[22]

Eleven months later a three-judge panel of the 3rd U.S. Court of Appeals overturned this ruling, arguing the Judge Lancaster had ignored ample Supreme Court Precedent. This is the same appellate court, interestingly enough, which ruled that both the Communications Decency Act and the Child Online Protection Act were unconstitutional. The case could easily end up before the U.S. Supreme Court. But that could be years down the road. For now, it is a highly interesting legal artifact that may be the precursor of a change in the law, or merely a footnote in the long history of obscenity prosecutions.

---

21. 539 U.S. 558 (2003).
22. *U.S.* v. *Extreme Associates Inc.,* W.D. Pa., No. 03-0203, 1/21/05.

OTHER STANDARDS

The three-part test developed by the Supreme Court in *Miller* v. *California* is the legal test for obscenity in the United States today. But the Supreme Court, lower courts and other elements of the government have with varying degrees of success attempted to raise additional standards by which to judge erotic material. Here is a brief outline of some of these standards.

Variable Obscenity

The Supreme Court has ruled it is permissible for states to adopt what are known as **variable obscenity statutes.** Material that may be legally distributed and sold to adults may be banned as obscene for distribution or sale to juveniles, usually persons under the age of 18. This is not a return to the old *Hicklin* rule in which if something is obscene to a child, it is obscene for everyone and its distribution or sale can be completely banned. Variable obscenity means a state can have two standards for obscenity, one for adults and one for minors. This concept emerged from the high court ruling in *Ginsberg* v. *New York* in 1968.[23] In *Ginsberg* the Supreme Court ruled that the First Amendment did not bar New York state from prosecuting the owner of a Long Island luncheonette who sold four so-called girlie magazines to a 16-year-old boy. The magazines, which contained female nudity, could have been legally sold to an adult. Justice Brennan said the state could maintain one definition of obscenity for adults and another for juveniles because the Supreme Court recognized the important state interest in protecting the welfare of children. But even variable obscenity statutes are not without constitutional limits. In 1975 the Supreme Court struck down such a law in *Erznoznik* v. *City of Jacksonville*[24] because the definition of material that could not be distributed to juveniles was not specific enough. A city ordinance barred drive-in theaters from showing films in which either female breasts or buttocks were exposed if the theater screen was visible from the street. The ordinance was justified as a means of protecting young people from exposure to such material. "Only in relatively narrow and well-defined circumstances may government bar dissemination of protected material to children," Justice Lewis Powell wrote. Banning the exhibition of nudity is simply not narrow enough; only materials that have significant erotic appeal to juveniles may be suppressed under such a statute, he added. A simple ban on all nudity, regardless of context, justification or other factors, violates the First Amendment.

Although states and cities may adopt variable obscenity laws, these regulations cannot in any way interfere with the flow of constitutionally protected material to adults. Some communities have failed to meet this challenge. In 1992 the state of Washington adopted a statute that barred the sale of "erotic" recordings, tapes and CDs to young people. Under the statute a county prosecutor would obtain a recording from a music store and then ask a local judge to declare the recording to be erotic in terms of the law.* This was called the stage one ruling. If such a declaration was made, the store owner could either label the recording "Adults Only"

---

*The statute defined erotic material as material "the dominant theme of which taken as a whole, appeals to the prurient interest of minors in sex; which is patently offensive because it affronts contemporary community standards relating to the description or representation of sexual matters or sado-masochistic abuse; and is utterly without redeeming social value."

23. 390 U.S. 51 (1968).
24. 422 U.S. 205 (1975).

and not sell it to anyone under 18 years old, or stop selling it to any person. Then, if that store owner, *or any other store owner in the state,* either failed to label the record or sold it to a minor, he or she could be prosecuted for violating the statute. Washington courts ruled that the law was unconstitutional for a variety of reasons. There was no provision in the law that required a local court that had declared a recording to be obscene to notify all record stores in the state of this determination.[25] Therefore another retailer could be prosecuted for selling to a minor a record that he or she did not know had been declared fit only for adults. The law was also overbroad, the courts ruled, because it regulated speech that is not obscene for adults by creating a massive chilling effect that would inhibit the legally permissible sale of material to record buyers over the age of 18. Finally, a record store owner was entitled under law to a jury trial on the matter of whether a record was erotic. The ruling by the judge was insufficient.[26]

Laws regulating the sale of books and magazines to young people are perhaps the toughest for legislatures to craft. How can you require a bookseller to limit juvenile access to books acceptable to adults without limiting adult access to these same books? A Virginia statute prohibited the commercial display of books and magazines that contained nudity and sexual conduct or described "sexual excitement," if such works were accessible to persons under the age of 18. But everything from steamy novels to classical art catalogs contain such material. It is not possible to simply keep such material behind the counter. Does the bookseller have to maintain a separate adults-only section for every category of books? Or does the bookseller ban juveniles from the store? A federal court found the statute seriously deficient.[27] The only way the state was able to salvage this law was for the state Supreme Court to first narrowly define the kind of material prohibited by the statute, and then rule that in order for the state to win a conviction under the law, it would have to show that the bookseller knowingly afforded juveniles an opportunity to study the cover of the publication, or leaf through its pages, or that the bookseller took no reasonable steps to prevent such activity.[28] During the past decade the federal government, as well as many states, has attempted to restrict the flow of adult material on the Internet in order to shield young people from such matter. But the application of variable obscenity concepts has largely failed in this situation because by blocking the flow of such material to juveniles, the state also denied adults access to legally protected matter. (See pages 552–555 for a full discussion of this issue.)

Child Pornography

For more than 20 years both the states and the federal government have had laws restricting the distribution and even the possession of material called child pornography. The previous section of this chapter discussed variable obscenity, the court doctrine that permits the state to stop the distribution and sale of certain kinds of nonobscene material to children, material that may be freely sold and distributed to adults. As such, variable obscenity focuses on the receiver of the material: Is it a child or an adult? Child pornography laws focus on content of the suspect material. Originally these laws were aimed only at photographic depictions of

25. *Soundgarden* v. *Eikenberry,* 21 M.L.R. 1025 (1992).
26. *Soundgarden* v. *Eikenberry,* 871 P. 2d 1050 (1994).
27. *American Booksellers* v. *Strobel,* 617 F. Supp. 698 (1985).
28. *American Booksellers Association* v. *Virginia,* 12 M.L.R. 2271 (1986).

children involved in erotic acts or poses. The justification for the laws is circular, but logical. The state has a real interest in stopping the use of minors in the making of erotic material. Someone who uses children in this way can certainly be prosecuted, but the makers of such material are often hard to find. If the law makes the distribution and sale and possession of this kind of material a crime, then the market for the material will likely be reduced, and if the market is reduced, fewer children will be exploited. The first state law to be tested was the New York child pornography statute, which prohibits any person from knowingly promoting a sexual performance by a child under the age of 16 by distributing material that photographically depicts such a performance. It is important to note that the kind of material outlawed by this law, and other similar statutes, does not have to meet the test of obscenity outlined in the *Miller* ruling. That is, it isn't necessarily legally obscene. When the Supreme Court ruled that the New York law did not violate the First Amendment, Justice Byron White wrote that when evaluating child pornography the test for obscenity should be adjusted in the following respects: "A trier of fact need not find that the material appeals to the prurient interest of the average person; it is not required that the sexual conduct portrayed be done so in a patently offensive manner; and the material at issue need not be considered as a whole."[29]

The New York statute banned the sale and distribution of such matter. Subsequent state laws also banned the possession of this material, and the Supreme Court ruled in 1990 that these laws, when narrowly defined, are also constitutional. An Ohio statute banned the possession of any depiction of a minor in a state of nudity who is not the person's child or ward. This statute would have, for example, barred grandparents from possessing nude baby pictures of their grandchildren. The Ohio Supreme Court narrowed the meaning of the language of the statute, ruling it could only bar "depictions of nudity involving a lewd exhibition or graphic focus on a minor's genitals." The U.S. Supreme Court gave its approval to such an interpretation.[30]

In 1996 Congress adopted an amendment to the original federal child pornography law that barred the sale and distribution of any images that "appear" to depict minors performing sexually explicit acts. Under this statute child pornography is defined to include not only actual images (photos, videotapes, films) of children but also computer-generated images and other pictures that are generated by electronic, mechanical or other means in which "such visual depiction is, or appears to be, a minor engaging in sexually explicit conduct." Drawings, cartoons, sculptures and paintings are not included under the new law. Whereas the original child pornography laws were justified as a means to protect children from being exploited, the 1996 Child Pornography Prevention Act (CPPA) was justified as a means to protect children from pedophiles and child molesters, people whose criminal behavior may be stimulated by such images. The law specifically stated that no prosecution can be maintained if the material was produced by adults and was not advertised, promoted, described or presented in such a way as to suggest children were in fact depicted in the images. Four U.S. Courts of Appeals, the 1st,[31] 4th,[32] 5th,[33] and 11th[34] Circuits, upheld the constitutionality of

29. *New York* v. *Ferber,* 458 U.S. 747 (1982).
30. *Osborne* v. *Ohio,* 110 S. Ct. 169 (1990).
31. *U.S.* v. *Hilton,* 167 F. 3d 61 (1999).
32. *U.S.* v. *Mento,* 231 F. 3d 912 (2000).
33. *United States* v. *Fox,* 5th Cir., No. 00-40034, 4/13/01.
34. *United States* v. *Acheson,* 195 F. 3d 645 (1999).

the law. The 9th U.S. Circuit Court of Appeals ruled that the law violated the First Amendment.[35] In April 2002 the Supreme Court, in a 6-3 decision, ruled that important segments of the law violated the First Amendment. Justice Anthony Kennedy wrote that the CPPA "prohibits speech that records no crime and creates no victims by its production." Instead, he said, "the statute prohibits the visual depiction of an idea—that of teenagers engaging in sexual activity—that is a fact of modern society and has been a theme in art and literature throughout the ages." The court also ruled that the justification for the law was insufficient since Congress had failed to produce any evidence of more than a remote connection between speech that might encourage thoughts or impulses and any resulting child abuse. "The mere tendency of speech to encourage unlawful acts is not a sufficient reason for banning it," Kennedy added.[36]

Obscenity and Women

Some women have argued for many years that sexually explicit matter both discriminates against women and provokes violence against women.[37] Several communities considered adopting laws that revise the definition of obscenity to reflect this argument. Such a law was adopted in Indianapolis in 1984. The law declared that works that portrayed the graphic, sexually explicit subordination of women, whether in pictures or in words, were pornographic if they also included scenes or pictures in which women were presented as sexual objects who enjoy pain or humiliation; who experience sexual pleasure in being raped; who are tied up, cut up or mutilated; and who are presented as being dominated, violated, exploited or possessed through postures or positions of servility or submission. U.S. District Judge Sarah Evans Barker ruled that the law was unconstitutionally vague and that the kind of expression it sought to bar was protected by the First Amendment. The 7th U.S. Circuit Court of Appeals sustained this ruling, noting that under the law, sexually explicit speech or expression is obscene or is not, depending on the perspective of the author. Speech that subordinates women is obscene, no matter how great the literary or political value of the work. Speech that portrays women in positions of equality is lawful, no matter how graphic the sexual conduct.[38] This ruling ended the movement to adopt such laws in the United States. But one of the proponents of this view, law professor Catharine MacKinnon, was among a team of advocates who convinced the Canadian Supreme Court to rule that erotic material harmful to women can be legally banned in that country.

35. *Free Speech Coalition* v. *Reno,* 198 F. 3d 1083 (1999).
36. *Ashcroft* v. *Free Speech Coalition,* 122 S. Ct. 1389 (2002). State courts have followed the Supreme Court's lead in this regard. For example, in August 2003 the Appellate Division of the Superior Court of New Jersey ruled that the state's child pornography statute only applies to real images of children, not computer-drawn or virtual images of children. *New Jersey* v. *May,* N.J. Super. Ct. App. Div., A-3392-01TA, 8/18/03.
37. See "Pornography," 32; "First Amendment under Fire," 40; and Strossen, *Defending Pornography* for discussions of these issues.
38. *American Booksellers Association* v. *Hudnut,* 598 F. Supp. 1316 (1984), aff'd. 771 F. 2d 232 (1985).

The *Miller* test is used today by American courts to determine whether something is obscene. **SUMMARY**
It has three parts. Material is legally obscene under the following conditions:

1. An average person, applying contemporary local community standards, finds that the work, taken as a whole, appeals to prurient interest. This test requires the fact finder to apply local (usually state) standards rather than a national standard. The jury (or the judge if there is not a jury) determines the standard, based on its knowledge of what is acceptable in the community.

2. The work depicts in a patently offensive way sexual conduct specifically defined by applicable state law. Again, the fact finder in the case determines patent offensiveness, based on local community standards. But the Supreme Court has ruled that only so-called hard-core pornography can be found to be patently offensive. Also, either the legislature or the state supreme court must specifically define the kind of offensive material that may be declared to be obscene.

3. The material lacks serious literary, artistic, political or scientific value. This is a question of law, not of fact, to be decided in large part by the judge.

The three-part *Miller* test is the test that courts must use in defining obscenity in all cases except those involving juveniles. The Supreme Court has ruled that states may use a broader definition of obscenity when they attempt to block the sale or distribution of erotic material to children or when they attempt to stop the exploitation of children who are forced to engage in sexual conduct by filmmakers. But such laws must be careful so as not to unconstitutionally ban legal material as well. Laws aimed at stopping the use of children in preparing sexually explicit material have also been permitted by the high court. The federal courts blocked an attempt by the city of Indianapolis to outlaw written and visual material that might result in discrimination against women or provoke violence against women and children.

CONTROLLING OBSCENITY

For more than 100 years, the typical manner in which the state has attempted to control obscenity has been through a criminal prosecution. Such lawsuits are complicated, and to be successful in these cases, prosecutors must follow carefully prescribed paths in deciding whether material is obscene, in collecting and seizing evidence, and in making arrests. Often persons charged with exhibiting or selling obscene materials seek to plea-bargain with the state to reduce the charge. Booksellers, theater owners and other merchants who deal in sexually explicit materials often do not want to fight the government in an obscenity prosecution. They are not in the business to crusade for the First Amendment. Their goal is to stay out of jail and to return to selling books or showing movies. If the state can be convinced to reduce the obscenity charge in exchange for a guilty plea, the defendant can often get by with paying a fine instead of going to jail and be back in business within a few days of the arrest. Prosecutors seem amenable to such plea bargaining because, as one noted, "our business is to stop public distribution of certain obscene materials, not put people in jail."

If a case goes to trial, the judge and the jury are the ones who must determine whether the material sold or exhibited is obscene. The fact finder in the trial—the jury, or the judge if there is not a jury—determines Parts 1 and 2 of the *Miller* test, prurient appeal and patent offensiveness. A jury can also rule on the serious value of a work, but since this determination is normally regarded as a matter of law, a judge plays a far greater role in this determination.

In addition to determining whether the material is obscene, jurors are also called on to answer the question of whether the defendant was knowledgeable about the contents of what was being sold, distributed or published. This is called *scienter,* or guilty knowledge. In a 1959 case, *Smith* v. *California,*[39] the U.S. Supreme Court ruled that before a person can be convicted for selling obscene books or magazines or whatever, the state has to prove that the seller was aware of the contents of this material. "If the bookseller is criminally liable without knowledge of the contents . . . he will tend to restrict the books he sells to those he has inspected; and thus the state will have imposed a restriction upon the distribution of constitutionally protected as well as obscene literature," Justice Brennan wrote.

But what exactly must the state prove under the scienter requirement? Does the government have to produce evidence that the seller of the erotic material knew that it was legally obscene, but sold it anyway? No. The high court has ruled that it is sufficient that the government prove that the defendant had a general knowledge of the contents of the material, that a movie contains sadistic scenes, for example.[40] In the mid-1990s the prosecutor of Whatcom County, Wash., brought obscenity charges against two persons who operated a newsstand in the city of Bellingham for selling a publication called "Answer Me!" a magazine devoted to the discussion of rape. The newsstand operators insisted that the contents of the magazine, though sexually graphic, were nevertheless a satire. The prosecutor disagreed. But in the end that issue proved to be irrelevant. The jury acquitted the couple because, jurors said, the state had failed to prove that the newsstand operators were aware of the contents of the publication. There was insufficient evidence of scienter, or guilty knowledge.[41]

The criminal prosecution of obscenity in any community depends on whether the local prosecutor wants to be aggressive in this area of the law and on how the local courts have defined obscenity. Some prosecutors are militant foes of erotic material and continually prosecute purveyors of adult material. A great many more, however, find obscenity prosecutions far less important than the murder, rape, assault, robbery and burglary cases that deluge their offices. At the same time, the citizens of some communities are far more tolerant of adult material than their counterparts in other regions. Within certain parameters, the people in a community can generally read the books they want to read, watch the films they want to watch, and buy the magazines they want to buy. What appellate courts and the Supreme Court say about obscenity is relevant in only an indirect way.

In addition to simple criminal statutes banning the production, sale and distribution of obscene material, the government uses other means to stop the flow of such material. Some communities have tried to use what are called civil nuisance laws in this effort. These are laws that define the sale or distribution of obscenity as a public nuisance. Obscenity is defined by the three-part *Miller* test. Prosecutors can bring a nuisance suit against an adult bookstore or

---

39. 361 U.S. 147 (1959).
40. *Hamling* v. *United States,* 418 U.S. 87 (1974).
41. Sheehan and Buller, "Jury Acquits."

an adult theater, much as they can bring a nuisance action against a factory that is generating too much noise or a home owner who is running a commercial auto repair operation out of his garage. A judge will first rule on whether the material that is being sold or distributed is in fact obscene. If the court finds that it is, an injunction will be issued ordering the defendant to stop such sale or distribution—to abate the nuisance.

Statutes originally aimed at fighting organized crime are also being used by government to curb the manufacture and flow of obscenity. These statutes are called RICO laws, in reference to the 1970 federal Racketeering Influence and Corrupt Organizations Act. The purpose of this statute was to eradicate organized crime in the United States by establishing new penal provisions and enhanced remedies to deal with the unlawful activities of organized crime. About 30 states have joined the federal government in adopting RICO laws. These statutes provide significantly stiffer penalties—up to 20 years in jail and a large fine—for violating the provisions of the law, and they also permit the government to seek forfeiture of any profits and proceeds derived from the illegal activity.[42] To win convictions under the RICO laws the government must show that there has been a pattern of illegal activities, which is generally defined as two or more illegal acts. The Supreme Court has permitted the government to use these laws in prosecuting persons who generate and distribute pornography. And while their application seems fitting with regard to large-scale pornography purveyors, the laws have also been used against small chains of bookstores and even single-store adult businesses. Constitutional challenges have been raised to the seizure of assets of booksellers and distributors, confiscations that involve not only obscene material but nonobscene books and magazines and films as well. But the Supreme Court rejected the argument that such seizures constitute prior restraints or unconstitutional censorship, and called the forfeitures criminal punishments.[43]

POSTAL CENSORSHIP

No government agency is more diligent in policing obscenity in the United States than the U.S. Postal Service. The Post Office has been on the job for more than a century. In 1878 the U.S. Supreme Court ruled that the use of mail in the United States is a privilege, not a right.[44] This ruling has given the Postal Service substantial power to control the content of the mail. Although the government cannot legally tamper with first class mail, it is still illegal to send obscenity through the mail regardless of how it is delivered. Magazine sellers, book distributors and others who use other postal classifications (2nd class, 4th class) to ship their goods face even more serious problems. Postal inspectors also police the Internet.

The 1873 Comstock Act (see page 529) provides the basic authority for the U.S. Postal Service to regulate the flow of erotic material in the mail. But many other laws are also applicable. For example, postal patrons who have received unwanted solicitations for what they define as obscene material can request the Postal Service to inform the mailer that they no longer wish to receive such material. Once this notice is sent by the Postal Service to the mailer, any subsequent mailing to that particular patron is a violation of the law. Because the mail patron decides whether the material is obscene, this law can affect a broad range of

---

42. Bunker, Gates, and Splichal, "RICO and Obscenity Prosecutions," 692.
43. *Alexander* v. *U.S.,* 113 S. Ct. 2766 (1993).
44. *Ex parte Jackson,* 96 U.S. 727 (1878).

solicitations. The Supreme Court upheld the constitutionality of this law, Section 3008 of Title 39 of the U.S. Code, in a 1970 ruling.[45] Chief Justice Burger wrote: "It seems to us that a mailer's right to communicate must stop at the mailbox of an unreceptive addressee."

Section 3010 of Title 39 of the U.S. Code permits a mail patron to block the delivery of sexually oriented advertising, even if he or she has never received such a mailing. The mail patron simply informs the Postal Service that he or she does not wish to receive any advertising for sexually explicit material. The statute contains a definition of such material. The Postal Service periodically publishes a list of all mail patrons who have indicated they don't want to receive such advertisements, and it is up to the mailers to buy a copy of this list or face the possibility of criminal and civil penalties if convicted of sending such material to a person whose name is on the list. The federal courts have upheld the constitutionality of this law as well.[46]

FILM CENSORSHIP

Censorship of motion pictures by cities and states is an infrequent occurrence today.

Censorship of motion pictures by cities and states is an infrequent occurrence today. The operators of so-called adult or X-rated theaters in most communities generally have a good idea of what kinds of films can be shown and what kinds of films will invite prosecution from local authorities, and they tend to operate within the permissible limits. As recently as the mid-1960s, however, there were active censorship boards in nearly 50 American cities. The application of a voluntary film rating system by the Motion Picture Association of America (G, PG, PG-13, R and NC-17) has satisfied the concerns of most persons worried about the content of the movies.

Motion pictures were not granted First Amendment protection until 1952.[47] During the 1960s and 1970s courts scrutinized several local film censorship ordinances and established rigid guidelines to force local communities to conform to First Amendment principles.[48] Generally, censorship boards and the courts must make prompt rulings on whether a film may be exhibited, and the government bears the burden of proving that a film is not protected by the First Amendment.

Video dealers are not bound by the MPAA rating code, and often stock films that would only be exhibited in so-called X-rated movie houses. The constitutional rules that limit censoring movies in theaters apply in no small measure to video sales and rentals as well. Oklahoma City officials discovered this when they raided video stores and confiscated copies of the 20-year-old Academy Award–winning German film "The Tin Drum." The R-rated film was seized because authorities said it violated state child pornography laws. Police submitted a copy of the film to a judge, who later told them in his opinion the motion picture contained child pornography. No hearing was held, no written order was issued, and there was no evidence that the judge had watched any part of the film. Nevertheless, police confiscated all nine copies of the motion picture on the shelves of rental stores and in the home of at least one rental customer. A U.S. District Court intervened and enjoined city officials from withholding

---

45. *Rowan* v. *Post Office,* 397 U.S. 728 (1970).
46. *Pent-R-Books* v. *U.S. Postal Service,* 328 F. Supp. 297 (1971).
47. *Burstyn* v. *Wilson,* 343 U.S. 495 (1952).
48. See, for example, *Freedman* v. *Maryland,* 380 U.S. 51 (1965); *Interstate Circuit* v. *Dallas,* 390 U.S. 676 (1968); and *Star* v. *Preller,* 95 S. Ct. 217 (1974).

the film until a proper hearing was conducted. "The admitted goal to remove the film from public access without a prior adversarial hearing runs afoul of the First Amendment," the judge ruled.[49] Ten months later the same U.S. District Court ruled that distribution of the film did not violate the Oklahoma child pornography statute, which excludes from its purview material that does not have as its dominant theme an appeal to purient interests and that has literary, artistic, educational or scientific value. The court said the film does not have a dominant sexual theme and has undisputed artistic merit.[50]

SUMMARY

Postal censorship has historically been an important means used by the U.S. government to control the flow of obscene material in the United States, including material on the Internet. Today the postal service is less aggressive and permits postal patrons themselves to block the delivery of solicitations for adult materials and other obscene publications. Communities may also censor films before they are shown, or limit video and DVD rentals, so long as the community follows strict procedures laid down by the U.S. Supreme Court.

REGULATION OF NONOBSCENE EROTIC MATERIAL

Battles over obscenity have gone on for more than a century. But as the Supreme Court narrowed its definition of legal obscenity during the past 40 years, more and more pressure has been applied by advocacy groups and even some government agencies to stop the flow of nonobscene, adult matter, material that would probably have been considered legally obscene half a century ago, but is protected by the First Amendment today. In fact, in many respects, this has become the primary battleground in the fight over the distribution and exhibition of adult, sexually explicit material. Magazines like Penthouse and Playboy, rap music, homoerotic art exhibits, adult films and sexually oriented sites on the Internet are among a wide variety of mass media targeted for control and even censorship in various parts of the nation. Although this material is certainly offensive to some persons, it generally enjoys the full protection of the First Amendment because it does not qualify as obscenity under the *Miller* test. Here is an outline of some of these legal skirmishes.

ZONING LAWS

Many communities have attempted to use zoning ordinances to regulate businesses that sell or display sexually explicit but not legally obscene material. Seattle passed a law in 1977 that requires all adult theaters to be located within a small area downtown. City officials said that the character and quality of Seattle neighborhoods could be preserved and protected by isolating this adult activity to a small area downtown. Detroit took just the opposite approach. A city law passed in 1972 prohibits adult theaters from being located within 1,000 feet of other adult theaters, adult bookstores, cabarets, bars, taxi dance halls, hotels, pawnshops, pool halls,

49. *Video Software Dealers Assoc., Inc.* v. *Oklahoma City,* 6 F. Supp. 2d 1292 (1997).
50. *Oklahoma ex rel Macy* v. *Blockbuster Videos Inc.,* 27 M.L.R. 1248 (1998).

secondhand stores and shoeshine parlors, or within 500 feet of areas zoned residential. The city did not want such businesses clustered together or near other types of "problem" businesses in the community. Both these statutes were upheld by the courts.[51]

The owners of these adult establishments have found that zoning, while perhaps inconvenient, provides them with a kind of safe haven from police harassment. They are normally permitted to operate their businesses without trouble unless they attempt to sell or exhibit material that is legally obscene (i.e., meets the definition of obscenity in the *Miller* test) or unless other criminal laws are violated as a result of the traffic frequenting the adult establishments.

LEGAL TEST FOR ZONING REGULATIONS

1. A community cannot, under the guise of zoning, completely bar or even significantly reduce the number of adult bookstores, movie theaters or newsstands.

2. The ordinance must be justified by showing that it furthers a substantial state interest.

3. The ordinance must be narrowly drawn, so as not to restrict more speech than is necessary.

Because these zoning laws are aimed at regulating constitutionally protected material, the government must follow strict rules in instituting and maintaining these laws. Courts have applied a three-part test to evaluate these zoning ordinances.

1. **A community cannot, under the guise of zoning, completely bar or even significantly reduce the number of adult bookstores, movie theaters or newsstands.** The ordinance in Detroit that was approved by the Supreme Court in the *Young*[52] ruling did not substantially reduce the number of establishments selling adult material. And it left ample room for the introduction of new establishments. This point has been overlooked in some communities in which zoning regulations were used to try to close adult bookstores, theaters and other businesses. In 1981 the Supreme Court struck down a Mount Ephraim, N.J., zoning regulation that effectively barred all live entertainment from the parts of the city zoned commercial. The high court called the ordinance unreasonable and said that it excluded from the city a wide range of protected expression. The high court also rejected Mount Ephraim's argument that its citizens had access to such entertainment, despite the zoning rules, because adult entertainment was readily available outside the city in nearby areas.[53] The U.S. Court of Appeals for the 6th Circuit threw out a Keego Harbor, Mich., zoning law that prohibited adult theaters within 500 feet of a tavern or bar, a church or a school. There was no place in the

---

51. *Northend Cinema* v. *Seattle*, 585 P. 2d 1153 (1978) and *Young* v. *American Mini-Theaters, Inc.*, 427 U.S. 50 (1976).
52. *Young* v. *American Mini-Theaters, Inc.*, 427 U.S. 50 (1976).
53. *Schad* v. *Mount Ephraim*, 452 U.S. 61 (1981).

small community that was not within 500 feet of such an establishment.[54] But a U.S. District Court approved a zoning law in Brice, Ohio, that left only 27 percent of the town open for adult business.[55]

The federal courts have, however, shown a willingness to permit zoning laws that indirectly reduce the number of adult establishments in a community because of conditions in the real estate market. A Minneapolis ordinance was designed to force adult bookstores and theaters into the city's central business district. This was a small area in the city, and proprietors of some of the existing adult establishments said they simply could not afford to pay the very high cost of obtaining space in this area. One theater operator testified he could find only one suitable spot, and the owner wanted $3.5 million for the property. So although the zoning law did not physically or geographically reduce the number of adult businesses, the existing economic conditions and real estate market caused a substantial reduction in such establishments. A U.S. District Court said the law was unconstitutional,[56] but this decision was overturned by the 8th U.S. Circuit Court of Appeals.[57] "The inquiry for First Amendment purposes is not concerned with economic impact," the court said, quoting a portion of a concurrence by Justice Lewis Powell in the 1976 *Young* v. *American Mini-Theaters, Inc.* Supreme Court ruling. The appellate court said that the adult theater owner must fend for himself in the real estate market. "That Alexander could not secure property meeting his economic or commercial criteria does not render Section 540.410 [the zoning ordinance] invalid," the court ruled. All the city must do is provide a reasonable opportunity for him to open and operate his theater.

2. **The ordinance must be justified by showing that it furthers a substantial state interest.** The city or town cannot justify these ordinances by simply arguing that sexually explicit material is bad or offensive and therefore should be segregated into one part of town or should be spread out all over town. The community must demonstrate that the existence of these businesses causes undesirable *secondary effects* in the neighborhoods in which they exist. Government officials must demonstrate that these bookstores and movie theaters generate decay in the neighborhood where they are located, or, because of the kinds of persons attracted to such businesses, threaten harm to the schoolchildren who must pass them each day, or result in an increase in crime in that part of the community, or even cause unwarranted traffic or parking problems. The nature of the evidence presented by the community to justify the regulation is currently a matter of debate in the federal courts. In 1981 a U.S. Court of Appeals ruled that the data must be substantial and persuasive. "When a city effectively zones protected activities out of a political entity, the justification required is more substantial than when the First Amendment is merely incidental," the court ruled.[58] That was the position taken recently by the 9th U.S. Court of Appeals when it ruled that the closure in Los Angeles of two adult

---

54. *Keego Harbor Company* v. *Keego Harbor,* 657 F. 2d 94 (1981).
55. *Wolfe* v. *Village of Brice, Ohio,* 37 F. Supp. 2d 1021 (1999).
56. *Alexander* v. *Minneapolis,* 713 F. Supp. 1296 (1989).
57. *Alexander* v. *Minneapolis,* 928 F. 2d 278 (1991).
58. *Keego Harbor Company* v. *Keego Harbor,* 657 F. 2d 94 (1981).

businesses located in the same building was not justified by any studies that showed the negative secondary effects of such an operation. The city had an ordinance that outlawed the establishment of an adult business within 1,000 feet of another adult business or within 500 feet of a church, school, park, and so on. Studies had been generated by the city that found a positive correlation between the concentration of adult businesses in a single location and an increase in prostitution, robberies, assaults and theft. The city argued that having two businesses in the same building amounts to such a concentration; they were within 1,000 feet of each other. In the case in question the adult bookstore and the video arcade, with separate owners, were located in the same small building. There were no other adult businesses within 1,000 feet, and there were no schools, churches, parks or whatever nearby. The appellate court ruled that the city had no evidence that showed that having two businesses in the same building generated the same kind of negative secondary effects that occurred when adult businesses in separate buildings were concentrated together.[59] But the Supreme Court disagreed in a close decision by a badly split court. The court said that a city considering an *innovative* solution to secondary effects shouldn't have to have specific data that could demonstrate the efficacy of its proposed solution. The city can rely on any evidence that is "reasonably believed to be relevant" in demonstrating a connection between the speech in question and furthering a substantial government interest, wrote Justice Sandra Day O'Connor for four members of the court.[60] Justice Anthony Kennedy concurred in the judgment but rejected some of Justice O'Connor's rationale, saying the opinion focused too much on the secondary-effects problem and did not sufficiently consider the impact of the rule on protected speech.

Although a community must produce evidence to support its zoning regulation, it doesn't necessarily have to generate fresh evidence that relates directly to that community. It can rely on the experience of other communities in the region. The city of Renton, Wash., a suburb of Seattle, relied on the evidence generated by Seattle and other nearby communities to justify its zoning statute, and the Supreme Court ruled in 1986 that this was acceptable.[61] But when a community uses evidence from other cities to support its zoning regulations, the secondary effects evaluated must be comparable. In 1995 San Antonio adopted an ordinance that barred sexually oriented businesses from operating within 1,000 feet of a residential area. Encore Videos was within 1,000 feet of such an area but was separated from this area by a highway. The store owners argued that the ordinance was inapplicable because Encore Videos only provided sales for off-premise viewing. No in-store viewing was permitted. When the ordinance was adopted, the city relied on studies of secondary effects done in Seattle, Garden Grove, Calif., and Austin, Texas. But these studies either entirely excluded businesses that provided only take-home videos—like Encore Videos—or mixed this data with data on the effects of on-site adult establishments. The 5th U.S. Court of Appeals ruled that stores that sell

59. *Alameda Books Inc.* v. *City of Los Angeles,* 22 F. 3d 719 (2000).
60. *City of Los Angeles* v. *Alameda Books, Inc.,* 122 S. Ct. 1728 (2002).
61. *Renton* v. *Playtime Theatres,* 475 U.S. 41 (1986).

videos only for off-site use are different, and it is reasonable to assume that these businesses are less likely to produce harmful secondary effects. Consumers of this material are not likely to linger in the area and engage in public alcohol consumption and other undesirable activities. The court said the ordinance must be justified by some proof of the secondary effects of stores that sell for off-site consumption.[62]

Finally, it appears that the secondary effects must occur in reality, and not in what one court called "virtual space." An entrepreneur in Tampa, Fla., converted a house in a residential neighborhood into an adult entertainment feature by installing 30 Internet television cameras throughout the building and then hiring several attractive young women to live in the house and conduct their lives in front of the cameras. "The girls of Voyeur Dorm are fresh, naturally erotic and as young as 18," the ads said. "Catch them in their most intimate acts of youthful indiscretion." Subscribers to the Web site paid $35 per month to watch the girls and an additional $16 to chat with them. The city prosecuted, claiming this was in violation of its zoning ordinance which prohibited adult entertainment in such neighborhoods. But the zoning law was of course based on the secondary effects that result when patrons visit these businesses, for example, traffic and parking problems and an influx of undesirable customers. But none of this happened in this situation. The 11th U.S. Circuit Court of Appeals ruled that the adult entertainment offerings are dispersed over the Internet, not into the community. Patrons enjoy the activities in virtual space; zoning laws are indelibly anchored to particular geographic locations. The court ruled that the code was misapplied and reversed a lower-court ruling against Voyeur Dorm.[63] (The Supreme Court refused to review this ruling.)

3. **The ordinance must be narrowly drawn, so as not to restrict more speech than is necessary.** This criterion applies to a variety of problems. For example, if the ordinance regulates "adult bookstores and theaters," the statute must define these terms. What is an adult bookstore? What is an adult motion picture? An Ann Arbor, Mich., zoning ordinance declared that any business whose "principal activity" was the sale of "adult material" had to locate in a specific area of the city. The law adequately defined adult material. Principal activity, however, was defined as involving 20 percent or more of the merchant's business. That is, if one out of five books sold by the merchant was an adult book, the merchant ran an adult bookstore, according to the law. The law was too restrictive, the U.S. Court of Appeals ruled. "A limitation of adult materials up to twenty percent of a bookseller's wares conditions the constitutional right to speak in one way on the bookseller's willingness to speak in a different way eighty percent of the time," the court said.[64] In the *Mount Ephraim* case, the city had banned all forms of live entertainment, putting any sort of play or performance off-limits.[65] This restricted more speech than was needed to control adult entertainment. And the city of Galveston defined an adult theater as any

62. *Encore Videos Inc.* v. *San Antonio,* 330 F. 3d 288 (2003).
63. *Voyeur Dorm L.C.* v. *City of Tampa, Fla.,* 265 F. 3d 1232 (2001).
64. *Christy* v. *Ann Arbor,* 824 F. 2d 489 (1987).
65. *Schad* v. *Mount Ephraim,* 452 U.S. 61 (1981).

theater that regularly screened films that the state of Texas prohibited minors from seeing. Of course, this description includes all R-rated films. Again, the city went too far and banned too much expression.[66] The city of Keego Harbor, on the other hand, might have used other methods—short of banning adult theaters—to handle its traffic problems. The court suggested that the increased ticketing of violators was a less intrusive means of serving the governmental interest involved.[67]

Zoning laws can be used to control the sale and exhibition of adult materials in a community, but only if they meet the three requirements just outlined: There can be no complete ban on such establishments or substantial reduction of the availability of such material in the community; a government must strongly justify—with evidence—such rules; and the laws must be narrowly drawn.

ATTACKS ON THE ARTS

A nation's popular culture has always been a target for censors. In America the so-called dime novels of the late 19th century were generally condemned because they were thought to corrupt young men and women. Ragtime music, followed by jazz and rock 'n' roll, were all regarded as vulgar and corrupting influences. In the 1980s and 1990s a wide range of American popular culture was subject to attacks by both the government and organized pressure groups. Rap and heavy metal music, erotic and anti-religious art, violent movies and television programs, and other cultural artifacts were all the targets of censors. Explanations for this censorship are wide-ranging. Some artists always test the boundaries of conventional taste and mainstream standards, and their work offends the majority of people. Many Americans, trying to explain what seemed to be, at least according to television news, a growing epidemic of child molestation, spousal abuse, drive-by and school yard shootings, and serial killings, found the mass media a convenient scapegoat. "Protecting family values" became a popular shibboleth to many conservative Americans in the 1980s, and politicians of all stripes, anxious to take advantage of a trend in public opinion, echoed the same sentiments. The election of Ronald Reagan as president in 1980, in no small part due to the growing strength of the so-called Christian Right, seemed to embolden many conservatives who had always regarded much of American popular culture as being out of bounds. The election victory in 2004 by George W. Bush, wrought in no small measure by a large turnout of Christian conservatives who were angered and frightened because of efforts throughout the nation to legalize gay marriage, emboldened leaders of the religious right to push even harder for restrictions on adult-oriented cultural material. The most visible result of these efforts has been the crackdown on the content of over-the-air broadcasting. (See pages 686–696.) But the push for restrictions really began in the last decades of the 20th century. Here are a few examples.

■ For the first time in the nation's history a record album was declared by a court to be obscene. In 1990 a U.S. District Court in Florida ruled that the sale of the 2 Live Crew album "As Nasty As They Wanna Be" violated obscenity laws. After listening to the recording the trial judge ruled, among other things, that the music

66. *Basiardanes* v. *City of Galveston,* 682 F. 2d 1203 (1982).
67. *Keego Harbor Company* v. *Keego Harbor,* 657 F. 2d 94 (1981).

lacked serious artistic merit.[68] A U.S. Court of Appeals reversed, noting among other things that the trial judge was not qualified to determine whether the recording lacked serious artistic value.[69]

■ For the first time in the nation's history a legitimate, public art museum, the Cincinnati Contemporary Arts Center, faced criminal charges for violating obscenity laws. The museum and its director were prosecuted for exhibiting the homoerotic photographs created by Robert Mapplethorpe. A jury, only three of whose members said they had ever been in an art museum, took only two hours to find the defendants not guilty.

■ In 1996 Congress barred the sale of sexually explicit magazines like Penthouse, Hustler and Playgirl, as well as adult videos, on military bases. A U.S. Court of Appeals upheld the law, citing a judicial deference to military regulations, and because the act sought to uphold the military's image of professionalism and proper decorum.[70]

■ The recording industry succumbed to pressure from both Congress and vocal advocacy groups to place warning labels on CDs, tapes and vinyl albums. The argument that parents needed help in monitoring their youngsters' listening habits made sense to many people. After all, this wasn't censorship; it simply provided additional information to buyers about the product, supporters said.

Unfortunately, recordings with warning labels became an easy target for groups seeking to censor the music, and today the recording industry has difficulty placing all but the most heavily promoted recordings with warning labels in most record stores. Some giant retailers like Wal-Mart and K-Mart, which account for a substantial percentage of CD and tape sales, simply refuse to stock many recordings with lyrics or cover art they find objectionable, including those with a warning label. Some record labels have gone so far as to prepare alternate versions of the song lyrics, cover art, and CD and tape inserts, which omit material the retailers find objectionable, for these stores. Unfortunately, many buyers don't even realize they are getting an expurgated version of the product. Eroticism is not the only reason for such censorship. Wal-Mart refused to sell a recording by Sheryl Crow because one song on the album was critical of the retailer for selling firearms.

■ Finally, the federal government tried to censor artists who sought federal grants to help pay for their work. Members of Congress complained they were offended that some of the money provided by the National Endowment for the Arts was given to artists whose work they disapproved, work they found offensive or even obscene. Congress made an effort to put decency stipulations on the grants, but this was short-circuited by the federal courts.[71]

Battles like these continue to rage today. Advocacy groups are louder and more militant than ever, and legislators at all levels of government are easy targets for

---

68. *Skywalker Records, Inc.* v. *Navarro,* 739 F. Supp. 578 (1990).
69. *Luke Records, Inc.* v. *Navarro,* 960 F. 2d 134 (1992).
70. *PMG International Division L.L.C.* v. *Rumsfeld,* 30 M.L.R. 2523 (2002).
71. *Finley* v. *NEA,* 795 F. Supp. 1457 (1992), aff'd. 100 F. 3d 671 (1996) and *National Endowment for the Arts* v. *Finley,* 66 Law Week 4586 (1998).

such pressure groups. It is rare that a politician is voted from office for supporting laws regulating what advocacy groups call "public decency." At the same time, politicians who oppose such laws are frequently described as attacking family values and decency standards—difficult baggage to carry at election time. While the efforts often appear to be local and grassroots in nature, most are very well funded and orchestrated by a handful of national groups, like Focus on the Family.

EROTIC MATERIALS IN CYBERSPACE

The introduction of new technology into a society has always been met with suspicion by segments of that society. The introduction of new communications technology—from the printing press on—has certainly been viewed this way during the past five centuries. In recent times nothing has vexed segments of the American public more than the introduction and growth of the Internet. The advantages of this interactive communications system are obvious to even the most casual observer. But the power inherent in such a point-to-point system is also seen as a danger by many in the nation, especially those who find the free flow of information and other materials to be threatening. It is hard enough to control what magazine and book publishers, radio and television stations, film producers and others push into the media markets. The specter of 280 million individuals each flooding the new channels of communication with messages of hate, conspiratorial plans and even obscenity is a fearful prospect to many.

Since the mid-1990s the problem of keeping the Internet free of seamy, salacious, adult materials has consumed many Americans, including large numbers of the members of Congress. An article published in 1995 in the George Washington Law Review seems to have been the trigger for a series of legislative efforts.[72] The article was based on the dubious research findings of an undergraduate engineering student at a Pittsburgh university. The findings, which suggested that the Internet was flooded with sexual materials, were quickly dismissed by serious researchers. But the article nevertheless provided the impetus for many members of Congress and the leaders of a variety of anti–adult matter advocacy groups to push for legislation to clean up the Web. Beginning in 1996 Congress passed a series of three federal statutes designed to control what Americans could see on the Internet. It should be noted parenthetically, that the transmission of legally obscene (see the *Miller* standards, pages 531–536) material over the Internet is clearly banned by federal law. Statutes that make it a crime to transport obscene material in interstate commerce, whether in a truck or car, via the U.S. Postal Service or UPS, or by television transmission or satellite relay, also bar the movement of such material over the Internet, even through e-mail.[73] Transmission of child pornography via computers is also banned under federal law.

The statutes adopted by Congress focused on nonobscene, adult-oriented, sexually explicit material—material that is protected by the First Amendment. The laws were

- ▮ the 1996 Communications Decency Act;
- ▮ the 1998 Child Online Protection Act; and
- ▮ the 2001 Children's Internet Protection Act.

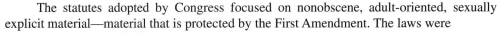

72. Rimm, "Marketing Pornography," 1849.
73. *Apollo Media* v. *Reno,* U.S. 98-933, 4/1/99.

What follows is a brief summary of these regulations, as well as the court rulings that focused on the laws.

The Communications Decency Act

The Communications Decency Act (CDA) was one part of a massive law that restructured telecommunication regulations. Among other things, the act made it a crime to transmit indecent material or allow indecent material to be transmitted over public computer networks to which minors have access. Fines of up to $250,000 and a jail sentence of up to five years were possible for persons convicted of violating this measure. The law defined indecency as "any comment, request, suggestion, proposal, image or other communication that, in context, depicts or describes in terms patently offensive as measured by contemporary community standards, sexual or excretory activities or organs." The law also resurrected language from the 1873 Comstock Act that barred the dissemination of information about birth control over the Internet. Under provisions contained in the statute, any challenge to law would be heard by a three-judge panel of federal judges. An appeal directly to the Supreme Court could follow.

Two separate three-judge panels declared the law unconstitutional in 1996.[74] A year later the Supreme Court agreed with this conclusion.[75] The court stressed that its ruling did not in any way limit the government in prosecuting those who disseminate obscenity or child pornography over the Internet. Its ruling was aimed exclusively at provisions in the law that barred the transmission of indecency. As noted earlier (see page 000), the court rejected the government's argument that the Internet should be regulated like a broadcasting station.

Justice John Paul Stevens, writing for the 7-2 majority, agreed with the lower court that the statute was plagued by vagueness. Without a definition of either "indecency" or "patent offensiveness," "could a speaker confidently assume that a serious discussion about birth control practices, homosexuality . . . or the consequences of prison rape would not violate the CDA?" he asked. "This uncertainty undermines the likelihood that the CDA has been carefully tailored to the congressional goal of protecting minors from potentially harmful materials." The high court said just because the term "patently offensive" was accepted by the court as a part of the definition of obscenity in the 1973 *Miller* ruling does not mean that the term standing alone is not vague. "We are persuaded," Stevens wrote, "that the CDA lacks the precision that the First Amendment requires when a statute regulates the content of speech." Justice Stevens added that by attempting to deny minors access to potentially harmful speech, the Communications Decency Act effectively suppresses a large amount of speech that adults have a constitutional right to receive and to address to one another. "It is true," Stevens wrote, "that we have repeatedly recognized the governmental interest in protecting children from harmful materials. But that interest does not justify an unnecessarily broad suppression of speech addressed to adults."

---

74. *American Civil Liberties Union* v. *Reno*, 929 F. Supp. 824 (1996) and *Shea* v. *Reno*, 930 F. Supp. 916 (1996); see also 1 E.P.L.R. 415 (1996).
75. *Reno* v. *American Civil Liberties Union*, 117 S. Ct. 2329 (1997).

The Child Online Protection Act

The following year Congress tried again when it adopted the Child Online Protection Act. The statute prohibits commercial Web sites from knowingly transmitting to minors (persons under 17 years of age) material that is harmful to minors. Harmful material was defined as material that, with respect to minors, is specifically created to appeal to prurient interests, that graphically depicts lewd or sexual behavior, and that lacks serious literary, artistic or scientific value. The law requires jurors to apply "contemporary community standards" when assessing material. A fine of $50,000 and a six-month jail sentence may be imposed for each violation. But the law includes provisions that bar any prosecution of a Web site operator who has restricted access to the site to persons with credit cards, debit accounts, adult access codes or adult personal ID numbers. The idea of this provision is that only adults would have access to one of these items, and therefore the site operator could honestly believe he or she is communicating with an adult, not a minor.

In 1999 a U.S. District Court declared the new law, referred to as COPA, unconstitutional.[76] Judge Lowell Reed Jr. said that while the new law differed in many respects from the Communications Decency Act, it nevertheless suffered the same defects. In attempting to protect minors from commercial sex sites, Congress once again passed a law that interferes with the receipt by adults of constitutionally protected material. The following year the 3rd U.S. Court of Appeals affirmed the lower-court ruling, but its decision focused only on a single aspect of the law—the contemporary community standards provision.[77] The Internet is a national—indeed an international—medium. If jurors are supposed to apply community standards—local standards under the *Miller* test—the material that is available in every community in the country will be judged by what is acceptable in the community with the narrowest of standards. What might be acceptable in 99 percent of the nation could be banned because it is offensive to people in Uptight, Utah. "The inability of Web publishers to restrict access to their Web sites based on the geographic locale of the site visitor, in and of itself, imposes impermissible burdens on constitutionally protected speech," the court ruled. In a nutshell, then, the law was overbroad.

In May 2002 the Supreme Court looked at the single criterion used by the lower appellate court to evaluate the law and reversed the decision.[78] The court ruled in an 8-1 decision that the law was not overbroad simply because of the community standards element in the test. But the high court was badly fractured, and four separate opinions were written. The only common ground among the four was that the analysis of the law by the Court of Appeals was incomplete. So the case was sent back to the Court of Appeals for another evaluation. In March 2003 the U.S. Court of Appeals again ruled the law was unconstitutional because, among other reasons, in its efforts to shield minors from certain Web sites, it restricted the access of adults to the material.[79] Again the case went to the Supreme Court, and in June 2004 the high court gave a second opinion on the Child Online Protection Act. In this 5-4 ruling, the court said that the law likely violates the First Amendment and continued the injunction against the enforcement of the act. Justice Anthony Kennedy and four colleagues said that the

---

76. *ACLU* v. *Reno,* 31 F. Supp. 2d 473 (1999).
77. *American Civil Liberties Union* v. *Reno,* 217 F. 3d 162 (2000).
78. *Ashcroft* v. *American Civil Liberties Union,* 122 S. Ct. 1700 (2002).
79. *American Civil Liberties Union* v. *Ashcroft,* 322 F. 3d 240 (2003).

government had failed to rebut the plaintiff's contention that there are plausible, less restrictive means—such as the use of software filters—that would block the objectionable material on the Internet and would be far less intrusive on First Amendment rights than the criminal statute. (Under First Amendment precedents, restrictions imposed by the government on expression must go no further than necessary to accomplish the government interest. In other words, the government must show it is using the least restrictive means to accomplish its goals.) Kennedy pointed out that about 40 percent of all Web content is posted outside the United States, and COPA—even if it were upheld—would do nothing to stop the flow of this material. In addition, U.S. Web site operators could move their operations out of the country to avoid prosecution. "It is not an answer to say that COPA reaches some amount of materials that are harmful to minors; the question is whether it would reach more of them than less restrictive alternatives." Kennedy said that the verification system built into COPA to protect the rights of adults was subject to evasion and circumvention, noting that even minors have their own credit cards these days. Kennedy admitted that filters are not perfect, but added: "Whatever the deficiencies of filters, however, the government failed to introduce specific evidence that existing technologies are less effective than the restrictions in COPA."[80] As of early 2006, nothing had happened either in the courts or in Congress that might lead to a resolution of the status of this legislation. But it is not being enforced.

The Children's Internet Protection Act

Congress made its third attempt at limiting access to the Internet in 2001 when it adopted the Children's Internet Protection Act. The law requires public libraries to install anti-pornography filters on all their computers that provide Internet access in order to continue to receive federal funding (so-called e-rate funds) that subsidizes their Internet access. About 14 million Americans access the Web via library computers. The federal government provides about $200 million each year to pay for this access.

Anti-pornography software filters are controversial for two reasons. Many people don't believe libraries should ever be in the business of censoring what their patrons seek to read or view. But many more people are critical of the filters because they don't work very well. They tend to screen out a lot of material that has no pornographic element at all. For example, a study conducted by the Henry J. Kaiser Family Foundation in 2002 revealed that the filters screen out important health sites that would be highly useful to all Web users, especially teenagers. Researchers found that filters set at the least restrictive level blocked about 1.4 percent of health sites, and those set at the most restrictive level blocked about 25 percent of the health sites. Many of the sites blocked focused on safe-sex topics. And even with the filters set at the highest restrictive level, about one in 10 pornography sites was still accessible.[81]

The trustees at libraries in a few states attempted to install filters on their computers before Congress acted. But in each case courts ruled that the laws violated the First Amendment.[82]

---

80. *Ashcroft* v. *American Civil Liberties Union*, 124 S. Ct. 2783 (2004).
81. Schwartz, "Internet Filters Block Many Useful Sites."
82. See *Mainstream Loudoun* v. *Board of Trustees of the Loudoun County Library*, 24 F. Supp. 2d 552 (1998), for example.

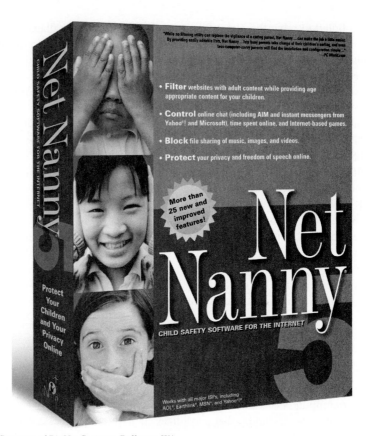

Courtesy of BioNet Systems, Bellevue, WA.

Net Nanny is one of several software filters available for parents, libraries and schools to use to attempt to limit children's access to adult material on the Internet.

Under the Children's Internet Protection Act the library must block access to any material that might be considered "harmful to minors." Adults have a right to ask library supervisors to override a filter for their use, but only if they are doing bona fide research or for any other "lawful purpose." Because of court challenges, the law was never enforced.

In May 2002 a three-judge federal panel ruled that the filtering statute was unconstitutional.[83] The law violated the First Amendment, the court said, because it required libraries to violate the First Amendment rights of their patrons as a condition of gaining federal funding. The spending power cannot be used to induce states to engage in unconstitutional conduct. The court called the filters a "blunt instrument" that typically blocks access to large quantities of material that librarians do not wish to exclude and that is constitutionally protected. Other, less restrictive means were available to protect minors, the court said. The computers minors used could be filtered and segregated from the unfiltered computers used by adults.

83. *American Library Association* v. *United States*, E.D. Pa., No. 01-1303, 5/31/02.

The unfiltered computers could be placed behind privacy screens or in separate areas, out of the line of sight of both children and adults who feel they would be offended by even glancing at such material.

Thirteen months later the Supreme Court, in a 6-3 ruling, reversed the lower-court decision.[84] There was no majority opinion. Chief Justice Rehnquist wrote the court's opinion, in which three other justices concurred. He said that limitations on access to the Internet were, for library users, of no greater significance than limitations on the access to books that librarians, for whatever reasons, chose not to acquire. All nine justices agreed that libraries could constitutionally restrict children's access to pornography. And all agreed that the available filters were blunt instruments. The resulting limits on access by adults to constitutionally protected materials were unacceptable to the three dissenters, Justices Ginsburg, Stevens and Souter. But this problem evidently did not trouble Chief Justice Rehnquist and his three colleagues, Justices Scalia, O'Connor and Thomas. The fact that the statute is not a direct requirement that all computers be filtered, but only a condition that must be met in order for libraries to receive federal funds, was noted by the chief justice. "Congress has wide latitude to attach conditions to the receipt of federal assistance in order to further its policy objectives," he said. But the two remaining members of the six-person majority seemed less convinced that the law's impact on adult access would be negligible. Both Justices Breyer and Kennedy said they assumed that libraries would be readily able to disable filters to ensure that adult users' access to online material was not substantially curtailed. If that were not true, Justice Kennedy wrote in his concurrence, critics can bring a new challenge based on that real-world experience.

The issue of controlling the access of young people to the adult-oriented sites on the Internet is surely not over. Many states have attempted to legislate in this area, without much success.[85] And it is unlikely that Congress will let the issue rest. But the difficulties with such legislation will continue to remain as well. Adopting a variable obscenity law—and that is what these are—is a simple prospect. Finding a way to apply the law in such a manner that does not interfere with the legitimate rights of adults is a far more difficult task.

In August 1997, The American Civil Liberties Union expressed concern over the push toward filtering in a policy paper it released on the topic entitled "Fahrenheit 451.2: Is Cyberspace Burning?" The title of the paper is a reference to the classic anti-censorship novel by author Ray Bradbury. The theme of the paper was that screening and filtering programs "limit the free marketplace of ideas." The authors of the paper continued:

> The administration's push for content ratings and blocking mechanisms is leading to a situation where the free market is not deciding what people want. The industry is moving in large part because it feels under the gun from the government. Moreover, by giving the government the tools with which to try to control speech on the Internet, labeling and blocking regimes will lead to the creation of an Internet infrastructure that will empower government censorship.[86]

84. *United States* v. *American Library Association,* 539 U.S. 194 (2003).
85. See *American Booksellers Foundation* v. *Dean,* 342 F. 3d 96 (2003).
86. Drolte, "Net Ratings Chill Speech."

SUMMARY   Significant efforts were made on many fronts during the 1980s to control the flow of non-obscene, sexually explicit material. Many communities attempted to use zoning ordinances to regulate such material. These laws are permissible so long as they are strongly justified, don't exclude or substantially reduce the number of such businesses, and are drawn in a narrow fashion to limit only the narrowest possible range of speech. Conservative groups applied considerable pressure to music and the arts in the past two decades. Rock groups like 2 Live Crew were tried (but acquitted) of obscenity. Pressure on the record industry resulted in a labeling scheme that troubles many civil libertarians. Controversies surrounding art erupted in Congress, and one gallery director was charged with obscenity for displaying a photographic exhibit. In the end there were few legal victories for the conservative critics. But some observers fear that intimidation and the threat of lawsuits will result in a growing conservatism in the arts community. Government efforts at censorship today are increasingly aimed at computer networks. In 1997 the Supreme Court ruled that the Communications Decency Act violated the First Amendment. Congress adopted the Child Online Protection Act in 1998 in an attempt to overcome the objections to the CDA voiced by the Supreme Court; its status has not yet finally been resolved, but it too is likely to be deemed an infringement on the First Amendment rights of adults. A law mandating the installation of software filters on computers at public libraries was given the green light by the Supreme Court, but the final status of the law will not be resolved until it is tested in everyday use.

BIBLIOGRAPHY ⟶

Above the Law: The Justice Department's War against the First Amendment. Medford, N.Y.: The American Civil Liberties Union, 1991.

Attorney General's Commission on Pornography. *Final Report.* Washington, D.C.: U.S. Department of Justice, 1986.

Blakely, C. "Is One Woman's Sexuality Another Woman's Pornography?" *Ms.,* April 1985, 37.

"Couple Guilty of Pornography Offered on Computer Network." *The New York Times,* 31 July 1994, 12.

"Court Upholds Conviction in Child Pornography Case." *The New York Times,* 12 June 1994, 16.

de Grazia, Edward. *Girls Lean Back Everywhere: The Law of Obscenity and the Assault on Genius.* New York: Random House, 1992.

Drolte, Angela. "ACLU Says Net Ratings Chill Speech." *Electronic Information Policy & Law Report* 2 (15 August 1997): 858.

"The First Amendment under Fire from the Left." *The New York Times,* 13 March 1994, 40.

Garber, Marjorie. "Maximum Exposure." *The New York Times,* 3 December 1993, 15.

Golden, Tim. "Court Bars Decency Standards in Awarding of U.S. Arts Grants." *The New York Times,* 6 November 1996, A10.

Greenhouse, Linda. "Decency Act Fails." *The New York Times,* 27 June 1997, A1.

———. "Justices Give Reprieve to an Internet Pornography Statute." *The New York Times,* 14 May 2002, A17.

———. "Justices Uphold Decency Test in Awarding Arts Grants, Backing Subjective Judgments." *The New York Times,* 26 June 1998, A17.

Mendels, Pamela. "Child Pornography Issue Raised in Budget." *The New York Times,* 3 October 1996, A11.

———. "Setback for a Law Shielding Minors From Smut Web Sites." *The New York Times,* 2 February 1999, A10.

"Pennsylvania: Child-Pornography Ruling." *The New York Times,* 8 March 2003, A15.

"Pornography." *Ms.,* January/February 1994, 32.

Report of the Commission on Obscenity and Pornography. New York: Bantam Books, 1978.

Rimm, Marty. "Marketing Pornography on the Information Superhighway." *Georgetown Law Journal* 83 (1995): 1849.

Schwartz, John. "Internet Filters Block Many Useful Sites, Study Finds." *The New York Times,* 12 November 2002, A27.

Sheehan, Kathy, and Helen Buller. "Jury Acquits Newsstand Operators." *The Bellingham Herald,* 2 February 1996, A1.

Stein, Ronald M. "Regulation of Adult Businesses through Zoning after *Renton.*" *Pacific Law Journal* 18 (1987): 351.

Stern, Ronald M. "Sex, Lies, and Prior Restraints: 'Sexually Oriented Business'—The New Obscenity." *University of Detroit Law Review* 68 (1991): 253.

Strossen, Nadine. *Defending Pornography, Free Speech, Sex, and the Fight for Women's Rights.* New York: Scribner, 1994.

Wallace, Jonathan, and Mark Mangan. *Sex, Laws, and Cyberspace.* New York: Henry Holt, 1996.

Chapter 14

COPYRIGHT

The law of copyright is almost 500 years old. British King Henry VIII issued the first royal grant of printing privilege, the forerunner of copyright law, in 1518. American copyright law springs from the U.S. Constitution and protects a wide variety of intellectual creations. While case law today still focuses on the rights of authors and artists who generate traditional creative compositions like books, photographs and poetry, the courtroom battles also involve the protection of videotapes, databases, e-books, and CDs. The rapid growth of the Internet has generated myriad new copyright problems. In this chapter we explore what the law of copyright protects, the important defense of fair use, infringement, and how creators can protect their work from thievery.

IMMATERIAL PROPERTY LAW

Copyright is an area of the law that deals with intangible property—property that a person cannot touch or hold or lock away for safekeeping. This concept is sometimes confusing to people; how can the law protect something you can't hold or touch? Consider that new paperback novel you just purchased at the bookstore. You own that book; you can do with it what you wish. After you read it you can sell it, donate it to Goodwill, give it to a friend to read, or tear out the pages and use them to start a campfire. But you don't own the arrangement of the words in that book; whoever holds the copyright, the book publisher or author, owns that part of the book. Hence, you can't reprint the book or copy long sections of it without permission. That book consists of two pieces of property, then: the physical or material book, and the words and artwork printed on the pages. An interesting legal dispute that erupted in late 2004 illustrates the heart of this matter. An unknown story and a handwritten letter attributed to Ernest Hemingway came to light when the owner sought to have them published.[1] But under the law, he can't do that. The story and the letter cannot be published without the permission of the Hemingway estate—which owns the rights to the author's unpublished work, and early indications were the estate did not want the material published. Hemingway gave the typed story and letter to a friend, who passed them on to his son. The owner of the physical artifacts can sell them; he owns that piece of property. But he cannot publish them.

Copyright is a close cousin to the law regulating patents and trademarks, which also affects intangible property. But all three of these areas protect something different.

PATENTS

Patent protection has served for many decades as an important element in the technological development of the nation. Without patent law it's doubtful that this society would have enjoyed the fruits of geniuses like Thomas Edison, Alexander Graham Bell and the Wright Brothers. The Constitution has given Congress the right to promote the sciences and the useful arts by protecting the rights of inventors. Hence, as author James Gleick wrote in The New York Times Magazine, the patent office is charged with the enforcement of a Faustian bargain: "Inventors give up their secrets, publishing them for all to see and absorb, and in exchange they get 20-year government-sanctioned monopolies on their technologies."[2]

---

1. Cowell, "Hemingway Bullfight Tale."
2. Gleick, "Patently Absurd."

There are at least three different kinds of patent protections. One variety protects inventions that have utility, such as a machine or a process. A typewriter can be patented; so can a specific way of reducing the hiss or noise on an audiotape. Patent law also protects designs—the appearance of an article of manufacture. The design of a piece of furniture or a tire tread or a belt buckle can be patented. A variety of patents protect plants, but only those kinds that can be reproduced asexually through means other than seeds, like cuttings or grafting. Patent rights do not exist until the patent is issued by the U.S. government. Hence, the famous abbreviation on many items, "pat. pending," which means the patent has been applied for and is pending.

TRADEMARKS

A trademark is any word, symbol or device—or combination of the three—that differentiates an individual's or company's goods and services from the products or services of competitors. The trademark on a particular item assures the buyer that he or she is getting the real item and protects the manufacturer or service provider from the unfair business practices of others. The function of trademark law is to stop confusion in the marketplace, to clearly identify the products and services created by specific businesses. Popsicles, Q-Tips, Jell-O, Super Glue, Velcro, Walkman, and thousands of other brand names are protected by trademark. Anyone can manufacture and sell a portable or pocket-size cassette tape player, but only Sony can call its player a Walkman. But it is possible to get trademark protection for more than simply a trade name. The hourglass shape of the classic Coca-Cola bottle is a registered mark. So is the art deco spire of the Chrysler Building in New York and the neoclassic facade of the New York Stock Exchange Building in the same city. In 1998 the stock exchange sued New York–New York Hotel and Casino in Las Vegas for constructing a one-third scale model of the building at its gambling and entertainment complex. A growing number of landlords are seeking to control the ways in which images and likenesses of their distinctive buildings are used by others, claiming that this protection is no different than a celebrity protecting the property value of his or her name or image. In 2005 a man named Leo Stoller claimed he had trademarked the word "stealth" and attempted to block Columbia Pictures from using the word as the title of a movie about elite U.S. Navy aviators. Legal experts pointed out that trademark law doesn't give someone exclusive rights in words, only the right to prevent consumer confusion. But Stoller continued to send out cease-and-desist letters anyway, according to an article in The New York Times.[3] Slogans such as "Don't Leave Home Without It" and "Just Do It" are registered trademarks. A generic term, one that is widely used by businesses and individuals, cannot be protected as a trademark, even if someone tries to register it. In 2004 the 4th U.S. Court of Appeals ruled that the publisher of Freebies Magazine could not claim trademark protection for the term "freebie" because it was a generic term that was in scores of dictionaries and used in hundreds of publications, advertisements and Web sites. The defendant in the case was using the term within its normal definition, a slang word for something that was given or received without charge.[4] Some telephone numbers can be

---

3. Dunlap, "What Next?"; Moynihan. "He Says He owns."
4. *Retail Services Inc.* v. *Freebies Publishing,* 4th Cir., No. 03-1272, 4/13/04.

protected as trademarks (e.g., 1-800-FLOWERS). In 1985 a federal court overruled a decision by the Patent and Trademark Office and granted trademark registration to a color for the first time. The Owens-Corning Fiberglas Corporation won protection for the color pink, the hue of its popular home insulation. The company showed the court it was the only manufacturer to use the color pink on insulation, it had been selling this pink product since 1956, the color pink was a basic part of its advertising and marketing strategy for the product, and that consumers, questioned in a sample survey, recognized the color pink as identifying a specific brand. In 1995 the Supreme Court reinforced this concept when it ruled unanimously that the Qualitex Company, which since the 1950s used a particular shade of green-gold on the pads it makes for use on dry-cleaning presses, can register that color as a trademark.

This area of the law also provides protection for what are called service marks for businesses such as Holiday Inn and McDonald's and certification marks for goods and services, such as Dolby for cassette decks and Real cheese for food products. Finally, what are called collective marks identify and protect members of organizations, such as the National Association of Realtors. There is also protection for something called trade dress, the way a product is packaged. Merriam-Webster, which published the Webster's Ninth New Collegiate Dictionary, collected more than $4 million in damages in 1991 when it successfully sued Random House for trademark infringement. When Random House published its Webster's College Dictionary it copied the look of the Merriam-Webster volume. The color, the design of the dust jacket, and the placement of the word "Webster's" on the spine of the book were all intended to fool potential customers, the plaintiffs argued. The jury agreed. Once registered, a trademark must be renewed after five years. Renewal is then required at 10-year intervals. But as long as it is properly renewed, a trademark can be maintained indefinitely. Some of the earliest American trademarks still in use date to the 18th and 19th centuries. Colgate dates to 1806; Gordon's (Gin) was first used in 1769. Chiquita bananas were first sold in 1876; Kodak cameras and film, 1886; and Tabasco pepper sauce, 1868.

THE FOUR MAIN FUNCTIONS OF TRADEMARKS AND SERVICE MARKS

- They identify one seller's goods and distinguish them from goods sold by others.
- They signify that all goods bearing the trademark or service mark come from a single source.
- They signify that all goods bearing the mark are of an equal level of quality.
- They serve as a prime instrument in advertising and selling goods.

While personal ownership of a trademark may exist perpetually, the ownership of a trademark or trade name can also be lost.

While personal ownership of a trademark may exist perpetually, the ownership of a trademark or trade name can also be lost. The Ford Motor Company in 2003 wanted to name one of its automobiles "Futura," a name it had used from 1959 to 1962 and in the late 1970s and early 1980s. But when it stopped using the name, Pep Boys, an auto parts retail chain, registered the name as a trademark. Pep Boys went to court to block Ford, and a federal court ruled in 2004 that the company had abandoned the trademark when it stopped using the name some 20 years earlier. Failure to use a name for as little as three years can constitute abandonment. It is also possible that trademark protection can be lost if the owner of the mark allows others to use the mark in a generic way. For example, if the makers of Super Glue (a trade name) adhesive failed to try to stop other adhesive makers from referring to their products as super glues, the trademark protection could be lost. These generic words—nylon, dry ice, escalator, toasted corn flakes, raisin bran, aspirin, lanolin, mimeograph, cellophane, linoleum, shredded wheat, zipper, yo-yo, and brassiere—were all at one time registered trademarks that slipped away from owners who failed to protect these names. Angry letters, threats of lawsuits, even legal action must be initiated to stop others from illegally using the name or phrase or mark. This responsibility falls on the owner of the mark; no government agency polices such misbehavior.

The United States Trademark Association, a trade group that works to protect the value of trademarks, frequently reminds journalists and others through advertisements in trade publications and by other means that trademarks are proper adjectives and should be capitalized; they are not nouns or verbs. Hence, you can use a Xerox photocopier to duplicate a letter, but you can't make a xerox, or xerox a letter. Printed or broadcast references of the latter variety will usually earn journalists a stern letter from the trademark holder reminding them of the law. Simple innocent infractions like these rarely cause serious problems for the offender. Calculated trademark infringement can be costly. A federal court in Chicago ordered the Quaker Oats Co., at the time the maker of the sport drink Gatorade, to pay a small company in Vermont nearly $43 million in damages for infringing on the trademark Thirst-Aid.

As previously noted, trademark law is designed to reduce the likelihood of confusion in the marketplace. For many years U.S. trademark law only forbade the use of a registered trademark or trade name on a product that was similar to the product produced by the owner of the trademark or trade name. A competitor to Sony could not call its portable cassette player a Walkman, but the manufacturer of exercise equipment could call its treadmill a Walkman. In January 1996 Congress, following the lead of the legislatures in 27 states, added more muscle to trademark protection when it adopted the Federal Dilution Trademark Act. This law gives the owners of trademarks and trade names legal recourse against anyone who uses the same or similar trademarks on even dissimilar products. In other words, in the past Maytag could only block the use of its trademark and name on home appliances made by its competitors. Under the new law Maytag could block the use of its name and registered trademark on an automobile or a camera as well. And Sony could stop the exercise equipment manufacturer from calling its treadmill a Walkman. Supporters of this new legislation argued that any use of another's name or mark weakened or diluted its value and distinctiveness, even in the absence of confusion as to the source of the goods. This law does not apply to the use of a registered name or mark in news reports or news commentary, or in parody, satire or other such forms of expression.

The new law was controversial when adopted because, opponents argued, "trademark dilution" was too elusive a concept. What is dilution of a trademark? Trademark infringement requires proof of consumer confusion and is not easy to prove. The new law is supposed to give trademark holders the ability to sue for behavior that falls short of actual infringement.

Recently the Supreme Court attempted, with limited success, to resolve some of this confusion in a case involving a national retailer and a small entrepreneur. In 1998 Victor Moseley of Elizabethtown, Ky., opened Victor's Little Secret, a small shop in a strip mall that sells sex toys, lingerie and novelty items. Subsequently the owners of Victoria's Secret, the catalog and retail seller of lingerie and women's clothing, sued under the new law, claiming the store's name was causing dilution of the distinctive quality of their famous brand. The Supreme Court ruled in the spring of 2003 that Victoria's Secret did not have to prove actual economic harm from the appropriation of its name in its lawsuit against Moseley, but the company must show some kind of current harm (as opposed to future harm), such as a loss of its distinctive identity or a blurring of its image. But the court did not specifically outline what factors might be considered in proving such a case. The court said it would not be enough to show a mental association between the two trademarks, that consumers think of one when they see the other. It would have to be shown that consumers had a different impression of the Victoria's Secret trademark because of the competitor's branding. Justice John Paul Stevens added that it would not be enough to show only that a trademark's image had been tarnished.[5] The case was sent back to the lower court for resolution of the matter.

To establish a trademark the applicant must submit a registration application to the Patent and Trademark Office in Washington, D.C. Before submitting the application a search should first be undertaken to determine whether someone else has already registered the trademark. This search can be done at the Patent and Trademark Office Library in Arlington, Va., or at about 60 regional sites (libraries) around the nation, or through the U.S. Trademark Electronic Search Systems via the Internet. A registration fee of $325 if you file online, or $375 if you file with paper, must accompany the application. Although it is not mandatory to precede the application with a search, it is advisable. If the examiner discovers in his or her search that the mark has been previously registered, the application fee is forfeited. Anyone who claims the right to a trademark can use the™ designation with the mark to alert the public to the claim. It is not necessary to have a registration or even a pending application to use this designation. And under the law, it is the person who first uses the mark, not the person who first registers the mark, who holds the rights to the symbol or word or phrase.*

It is not often that a case involving the content of a creative work falls into the trademark legal domain, but an unusual and interesting case developed in 2003 that demonstrates how the law can respond to unusual situations. Rosa Parks, a black tailor's assistant in Montgomery, Ala., boarded a city bus in 1955 and sat in a section normally reserved for white riders. When the bus driver asked her to "move to the back of the bus," she refused. She was arrested. News of her arrest spread quickly through the black community and generated a boycott of the city bus system by blacks in an effort to undermine the city's bus segregation law. The year-long boycott, which was ultimately successful, was a seminal event in the civil rights struggles of the mid-20th century, and Rosa Parks became a national icon of the civil rights movement.

---

*A booklet entitled *Basic Facts About Registering a Trademark* is available from the Patent and Trademark Office, Washington, D.C., 20231. The same information (and a lot more) is available via the Web site at www.USPTO.gov.

5. *Moseley* v. *V. Secret Catalogue, Inc.,* 537 U.S. 418 (2003). See also Greenhouse, "Ruling on Victor vs. Victoria."

Source: © AP/Wide World Photos

Recently the rap duo OutKast put out a record called "Rosa Parks." The song has nothing to do with Parks, but contains a frequently repeated refrain, "move to the back of the bus." Rapper Andre "Dre" Benjamin explained to the court that the song was a message to the duo's musical competitors who he did not believe were as good as OutKast, and the pair were telling them they had to take a back seat to the duo's talent, in other words, "move to the back of the bus." Parks sued under Section 43(a) of the federal Lanham Act (see page 632), a law that bans anti-competitive business behavior. But the case reflected trademark law, in that to prevail Parks would have to show that the use of her name is likely to cause confusion as to the "affiliation, connection or association" between herself and the defendant's goods or services. This element of the law is used by celebrities and businesses to vindicate the property rights in their identities against misleading commercial use by others. It is similar to elements of the right-to-publicity cause of action, outlined in Chapter 7. In fact, Parks sued for right to publicity as well. OutKast claimed that they had a First Amendment right to use the name, and that Parks did not have a trademark right in her name. A trial court had issued a summary judgment against Parks, but the 6th U.S. Court of Appeals reversed this ruling. The court said it was not necessary for OutKast to have made a "trademark" use of Parks' name for the civil rights warrior to use the Lanham Act to make a claim of false advertising. The court added that Parks' notoriety during the civil rights movement, plus her use of her

Rosa Parks, an icon of the civil rights movement, brought suit against the rap group OutKast for using a phrase in a song that she said violated her rights under trademark law.

status to promote various causes, as well as books and TV programs about her life, had made her a celebrity.

Parks claimed that the song misled consumers who might think the song is about her, or that she is affiliated with OutKast, or that she had sponsored or approved the song or the album. She said she was promoting her own album of songs, and this confusion could hurt the sales of that work. The court ruled that the First Amendment defense would hold up for OutKast only if they were able to show that the title has "artistic relevance" to the song. While the case was remanded to a lower court for disposition, Judge John D. Holschuh and his two colleagues on the appellate bench made it clear that they believed the relevance of the song title to the song's lyrics was highly questionable. "In lyrics that are laced with profanity, and in a 'hook' or chorus that is pure egomania, many reasonable people could find that this is a song that is clearly antithetical to the qualities identified with Rosa Parks," Holschuh wrote. The duo could clearly portray Parks in an unfavorable way in the song or do a parody or satire about Parks and be protected under the First Amendment. But in this case the name is used simply to attract attention to the song, the court said.[6] The Supreme Court refused to review the ruling.

After the denial of certiorari the case became badly muddled, with allegations that Parks, who was 91 and was diagnosed with dementia, had little to do with bringing the legal action. There were charges that associates and lawyers brought the lawsuit without Parks' knowledge or approval. The lawsuit was settled in April 2005. OutKast, Sony BMG Music Entertainment and the other defendants admitted no wrongdoing, but agreed to work on projects to "enlighten today's youth about the significant role Rosa Parks played in making America a better place for all races," Parks' court-appointed guardian, former Detroit mayor Dennis Archer, said.[7] Parks died in October 2005.

Happily, not all trademark infringement cases end in court. When a rock band called the Postal Service put out an album in 2003 called "Give Up" on a Seattle-based independent label called Sub Pop Records, they received a cease-and-desist letter from the real Postal Service informing them that Postal Service was a registered trademark of the United States Postal Service. But 15 months later the USPS sent the band members another letter, giving them permission to use the name if they would agree to promote the use of the mail. Subsequent copies of the album and any follow-up work would have to carry a notice about the trademark. The Postal Service agreed to sell the band's CD on its Web site, potentially earning some money. The band may be asked to do some commercials for the post office and also agreed to perform at a national postal service executive conference.[8] And just think, no judges got involved.

PLAGIARISM

Editors at The New York Times expressed embarrassment and shock in May 2003 when they revealed that one of their reporters, Jayson Blair, was guilty of fabrication and plagiarism in his reporting for the venerable newspaper. Plagiarism occurs when a writer takes the ideas,

6. *Parks* v. *LaFace Records,* 329 F. 3d 437 (2003).
7. Kinzer, "Legal Cloud Lingers," and "OutKast Settles."
8. Sisario, "Postal Service Tale."

thoughts, or words from another and passes them off as his or her own. The notion of taking credit for the work of another is a key element in plagiarism. While the mass media is certainly not rife with plagiarism, it is probably more common than many people suspect, especially editors. One of the most disturbing revelations about the Jayson Blair case was that so few of the subjects he wrote about complained to the newspaper about his stories. They said they just assumed reporters make things up. Most cases of plagiarism that are uncovered are usually resolved outside the legal system. The plagiarist is humiliated and often fired from his or her job. The publicity damages his or her reputation. A plagiarist may lose future book contracts or assignments. When instances of plagiarism reach the courts they are generally litigated as copyright cases. The television and film industries seem particularly vulnerable to problems of plagiarism. For example, writer-director Amy Heckerling and TriStar Pictures were sued in 1991 by other writers who claimed that the script from the 1989 hit film "Look Who's Talking" had been stolen from them. The case was settled out of court after the trial judge issued an opinion that he saw substantial similarity between the movie script and the plaintiffs' work. In 1997, one month before the release of the film "Amistad," Steven Spielberg's Dreamworks was sued for copyright infringement by author Barbara Chase-Riboud. The novelist claimed that the filmmaker had stolen important parts from her historical novel "Echo of Lions." Spielberg's lawyers denied the charges, saying the portions of the film Chase-Riboud cited in her complaint were based on history, which cannot be owned by any person, and on another novel, "Black Mutiny," a book published 36 years before "Echo of Lions." The producers of the film "Amistad" bought the rights to "Black Mutiny" in 1989. Lawyers for the film producers argued that extensive passages in Chase-Riboud's book had been in fact lifted from "Black Mutiny," and that she was the plagiarist. Judge Audrey Collins of U.S. District Court in Los Angeles rejected Chase-Riboud's request for an injunction to halt the release of the film. This was the second time in 10 years that Chase-Riboud had sued, complaining that someone had stolen her work for a play or a film[9] (see page 603).

But book authors and journalists also have been guilty of taking the work of others without giving proper credit. In 2001 historian Stephen E. Ambrose acknowledged he had improperly borrowed some material for his book "The Wild Blue." As critics condemned the practice, reports surfaced that another prominent historian, Doris Kearns Goodwin, admitted using borrowed passages in her 1987 work, "The Fitzgeralds and the Kennedys." Plagiarism occurs in journalism as well. A 1995 report published in the Columbia Journalism Review summarized 20 cases of such theft that occurred in some of the nation's leading newspapers and magazines.[10] And journalists are frequently disciplined—sometimes severely—when these practices are revealed. For example, in February 2005 the editors at the Worcester Telegram & Gazette in Massachusetts fired a sportswriter because, they said, he had used material from other publications at least six times. Most plagiarists aren't sinister or evil people. Few books or movies or plays or stories or songs are completely new or original; most creative people in one way or another borrow from their predecessors or colleagues. But there are ways to pay this debt, through acknowledgment or other means, that credit the author whose work is being

9. Weinraub, "'Amistad' Plagiarism Charge Rebutted."
10. Lieberman, "Plagiarize, Plagiarize, Plagiarize."

used. Use of such material with intent to deceive is clearly morally wrong, and the law makes passing off the work of another as one's own work illegal as well.

Copyright law protects "all works of authorship fixed in a tangible medium of expression." This description includes writings, photographs, paintings, music, drama and other similar works. Ideas are usually protected by the law relating to patents or contracts. Copyright does not protect ideas, but the specific expression of those ideas. Trademark protection is based on marketplace use; patents and copyright are statutory creations. Trademark protection can last forever; copyright and patent protection is limited by law. The remainder of this chapter focuses exclusively on copyright. Persons who work in the mass media do not need to become copyright attorneys to avoid lawsuits in the 21st century. But news writers, broadcasters, advertising copywriters and public relations specialists should know both how to protect their own work from theft and how to avoid illegally taking the work of someone else.

ROOTS OF THE LAW

Copyright protection was unneeded until the development of mechanical printing. The time and effort it took to hand-copy a manuscript made the theft of such work both tedious and unprofitable. But the printing press gave thieves the ability to reproduce multiple copies of a work relatively quickly and cheaply, and this capability changed things dramatically. Each subsequent technological development has put new stress and strain on copyright law. The development of motion pictures and the broadcast media, recorded music, audio- and then videotape, photocopying, and most recently interactive computer-mediated communication have all required modifications or new interpretations in the law as the government has sought to protect the right to literary property.

The British were the first to attempt such protection. Copyright law developed in England in the 16th century as the government sanctioned and supported the grant of printing privileges to certain master printers in exchange for their loyalty and assistance in ferreting out anti-government writers and publishers. But the rights of authors, as opposed to printers, were not protected until the early 18th century when the British Parliament passed the nation's first copyright law. The law gave the legal claim of ownership of a piece of literary property to the person who created the work or to a person who acquired the rights to the work from the author. The statute was a recognition by the Crown that in order to encourage the creation of books, plays and art, the creators of these works had to be assured that they would be rewarded for their labor. And that is the real logic behind copyright law, the fostering of the creative spirit. If a dramatist knew, for example, that as soon as her play was published she would lose control of the work because others could freely copy it, there would be little stimulation for the creation of plays.

And that is the real logic behind copyright law, the fostering of the creative spirit.

British copyright law was applied in the colonies until American independence. American copyright law derives directly from the U.S. Constitution. In Article I, Section 8, of that document lies the basic authority for modern United States copyright law:

> The Congress shall have Power . . . To promote the Progress of Science and useful Arts, by securing for limited Times to Authors and Inventors the exclusive Right to their respective Writings and Discoveries.

This provision gives Congress the power to legislate on both copyright and patent. The Congress did just that in 1790 by adopting a statute similar to British law. The law gave authors who were U.S. citizens the right to protect their books, maps and charts for a total of 28 years—a 14-year original grant plus a 14-year renewal. In 1802 the law was amended to include prints as well as books, maps and charts. In 1831 the period of protection was expanded by 14 years. The original grant became 28 years with a 14-year renewal. Also, musical compositions were granted protection. Protection for photography, works of fine art and translations were added later in the 19th century.

A major revision of the law was enacted in 1909, and our current law was adopted in 1976. The 1976 federal law pre-empted virtually all state laws regarding the protection of writing, music and works of art. Hence, copyright law is essentially federal law and is governed by the federal statute and by court decisions interpreting this statute. Parenthetically, it might be noted that in 1988 Congress finally approved U.S. participation in the 102-year-old Berne Convention, the world's pre-eminent international copyright treaty. The United States had been hesitant in the past to join the treaty because of significant differences between United States and international law, but after the 1976 revision of U.S. copyright law, the differences were minimal. American media companies, anxious to expand their international business, sought to improve trade relations and strengthen U.S. influence on matters relating to international copyright law and therefore put pressure on the government to join the convention.

WHAT MAY BE COPYRIGHTED

The law of copyright gives to the author, or the owner of the copyright, the sole and exclusive right to reproduce the copyrighted work in any form for any reason. There are actually six exclusive rights recognized under the law:

- **The right of reproduction of the work**
- **The right of preparation of derivative works**
- **The right of public distribution of the work**
- **The right of public performance of the work**
- **The right of public display of the work**
- **The right of public digital performance of a sound recording**

These rights are fairly clear with regard to traditional mass media. If Bogus Publishing prints 1,000 copies of a copyrighted Stephen King novel and distributes them to bookstores, this is a violation of King's exclusive distribution rights under the law. But the rights are less clear when it comes to computers and the Internet. Is storing a copyrighted document on a hard disk or a diskette or even in the computer's RAM a violation of the exclusive right to reproduce a copyrighted item? Probably, the courts seem to indicate. Does transmitting a copyrighted work via the Internet constitute a public performance of the work? Most likely. The courts are just now sorting out these questions. Several lower courts have ruled that it can be an infringement of copyright to download material off the Internet for unauthorized use or upload copyrighted material onto a Web site or bulletin board without the permission of the copyright holder.[11] A federal court in Texas ruled in December 1997 that an online service provider that provided subscribers unauthorized copies of copyrighted images infringed on the copyright holder's rights of reproduction, distribution, and display and was liable for direct copyright infringement. The provider argued that it was merely a conduit between the subscription service that scanned the photos into the system and the subscribers who downloaded them. The defendant said that all it sold was access to the subscription service, not images. The court disagreed, ruling that "Webbworld didn't sell access—it sold images."[12] However, under a federal statute adopted in 1998 an online service provider that acts as merely a *conduit* during the infringement of copyrighted works will not be held liable for the illegal act in most instances (see page 605). A U.S. District Court in Nevada ruled in 1999 that scanning a copyrighted photo into a computer for graphic manipulation and insertion into a new work constitutes a copyright infringement. The court said that digitizing any copyrighted material may support an infringement finding—even if it has only the briefest existence in a computer's memory.

Before a copyrighted work may be printed, broadcast, dramatized or translated, the consent of the copyright owner must first be obtained. The law grants this individual exclusive monopoly over the use of that material. To quote the statute specifically, copyright extends to "original works of authorship fixed in any tangible medium of expression." Congress has defined *fixed in a tangible medium* as that work that is "sufficiently permanent or stable to permit it to be perceived, reproduced, or otherwise communicated for a period of more than a transitory duration." Under these standards such items as newspaper stories or entire newspapers, magazine articles, advertisements, and almost anything else created for the mass media can be copyrighted. Material that is created in digital form and stored or transmitted electronically via computer diskettes or CD-ROM can also be protected by copyright. Extemporaneous performances and speeches, and improvised sketches are examples of materials that are not fixed in a tangible medium and are not protected by the federal copyright statute. But this lack of protection does not mean that someone can film or record a performer's act, for example, without the performer's permission. A federal law criminalizes the unauthorized recording of a live musical performance.[13] This action would also be forbidden by other laws, such as the right to publicity (see Chapter 7) and common-law copyright.*

*Under the 1909 law the United States had two kinds of copyright protection: common-law copyright and statutory copyright. Much as it did in 18th-century England, the common law protected any work that had not been published. Common-law protection was automatic; that is, the work was protected from the point of its creation. And it lasted forever—or until the work was published. In order to protect published works, the author, photographer or composer had to register the book or picture or song with the U.S. government and place a copyright notice on the work. The 1976 statute does away with common-law copyright for all practical purposes. The only kinds of works protected by the common law are works like extemporaneous speeches and sketches that have not been fixed in a tangible medium. They are still protected from the point of their creation by common-law copyright. Once they are written down, recorded, filmed or fixed in a tangible medium in any way, they come under the protection of the new law.

11. See, for example, *Playboy Enterprises Inc.* v. *Starware Publishers Corp.,* 900 F. Supp. 433 (1995).
12. *Playboy Enterprises Inc.* v. *Webbworld Inc.,* D.C.N. Texas Civil No. 3196-CV-3222-H, 12/11/97.
13. *United States* v. *Moghadam,* 11th Cir., No. 98-2180, 5/19/99.

The federal statute lists a wide variety of items that can be copyrighted, but this list is only illustrative. It includes the following:

1. Literary works (including computer software)
2. Musical works, including any accompanying words
3. Dramatic works, including any accompanying music
4. Pantomimes and choreographic works
5. Pictorial, graphic and sculptural works
6. Motion pictures and other audiovisual works
7. Sound recordings

Copyright law is equally specific about what cannot be copyrighted:

1. Trivial materials cannot be copyrighted. Such things as titles, slogans and minor variations on works in the public domain are not protected by the law of literary property. (But these items might be protected by other laws, such as unfair competition, for example.)

2. Ideas are not copyrightable. The law protects the literary or dramatic expression of an idea, such as a script, but does not protect the idea itself. "This long established principle is easier to state than to apply," notes law professor David E. Shipley. It is often difficult to separate expression from the ideas being expressed.

3. Facts cannot be copyrighted. "The world is round" is a fact. An author cannot claim that statement as his or her own and protect it through copyright.

4. Utilitarian goods—things that exist to produce other things—are not protected by copyright law, according to William Strong in "The Copyright Book." A lamp is a utilitarian object that exists to produce light. One cannot copyright the basic design of a lamp. But the design of any element that can be identified separately from the useful article can be copyrighted, according to Strong. The design of a Tiffany lamp can be copyrighted. The unique aspects of a Tiffany lamp have nothing to do with the utilitarian purpose of producing light; these aspects are purely decorative.

5. Methods, systems, and mathematical principles, formulas, and equations cannot be copyrighted. But a description, an explanation or an illustration of an idea or system can be copyrighted. In such an instance the law is protecting the particular literary or pictorial form in which an author chooses to express herself or himself, not the idea or plan or method itself. For example, an individual writes and publishes a book in which she outlines a new mathematical formula. Although the book itself may be protected by copyright, the formula cannot be, and others may use it freely. In other words, the copyright on an article or a book does not preclude the public from making use of what the book teaches.

Can all books and other creative works be copyrighted? No. The law specifically says that only "original" works can be copyrighted. What is an original work? In interpreting this term in the 1909 law, courts ruled that the word "original" means that the work must owe its origin to the author. In 1973 a court reporter (an employee of the court who transcribes the proceedings) attempted to claim copyright over a transcript he had made of some of the proceedings during the investigation of the death of Mary Jo Kopechne. This young woman drowned when a car driven by Senator Edward Kennedy went off a bridge and into a creek near Chappaquiddick, Mass. In *Lipman* v. *Commonwealth*,[14] a federal judge ruled that the transcript could not be copyrighted. "Since transcription is by very definition a verbatim recording of other persons' statements, there can be no originality in the reporter's product."

In 1985 an organization called Production Contractors Inc., or PCI, tried to block Chicago television station WGN from televising a Christmas parade on Thanksgiving Sunday. PCI, which put on the parade, sold the exclusive right to televise it to another station, WLS. The plaintiff claimed the parade was copyrighted, and WGN would be in violation of the law by televising it. A federal district court disagreed and ruled that a Christmas parade is not something that can be copyrighted; it is a common idea, not an event of original authorship.[15]

The work must be original. Must it be of high quality or be new or novel? The answer to both questions is no. Even common and mundane works are copyrightable. Courts have consistently ruled that it is not the function of the legal system to act as literary or art critic when applying copyright law. In 1903 Justice Oliver Wendell Holmes wrote in *Bleistein* v. *Donaldson Lithographing Co.,* "It would be a dangerous undertaking for persons trained only to the law to constitute themselves final judges of the worth of pictorial illustrations, outside of the narrowest and most obvious limits."[16] Even the least pretentious picture can be an original, Holmes noted in reference to the posters involved in this case.

The 9th U.S. Circuit Court of Appeals echoed this statement in 1992 when it ruled that raw, unedited video footage of news events was sufficiently original to be protected by copyright.[17] The case involved the Los Angeles News Service and Audio Video Reporting Service. LANS records live news events on video and then sells the unedited but copyrighted footage to television stations. The TV stations take the raw footage, edit it any way they want, and use it in newscasts. Audio Video Reporting Services videotapes newscasts and then sells clips of the newscasts to interested parties. A businesswoman who has been interviewed for a news story, for example, may want to buy a copy of the story from Audio Video. Or the parents of children featured in a news story on a school project might want to have a copy of that story.

LANS sued Audio Visual, claiming that in selling these video clips, which were taken from the copyrighted raw footage LANS had provided to local television stations, Audio Video was infringing on the copyright LANS held on the videotape. Audio Visual attempted to defend the suits on several bases, including the argument that raw, unedited videotape was not sufficiently original to be protected by copyright; all the photographer did was switch on the camera and point it at the news event. No creativity or intellectual input was required. The Court of Appeals disagreed, noting that there were several creative decisions involved in producing a photograph. The photographer must select the subject, the background, the

---

14. 475 F. 2d 565 (1973).
15. *Production Contractors* v. *WGN Continental Broadcasting,* 622 F. Supp. 1500 (1985).
16. 188 U.S. 239 (1903).
17. *Los Angeles News Service* v. *Tullo,* 973 F. 2d 791 (1992).

perspective, consider the lighting and the action, and so on. The "requisite level of creativity [to qualify as an original work] is extremely low; even a slight amount will suffice," the court said. Likewise, novelty is not important to copyright: The author does not have to be the first person to say something in order to copyright it. "All that is needed to satisfy both the Constitution and the statute is that the 'author' contributed something more than a merely trivial variation, something recognizably his own," one court ruled.[18]

COPYRIGHT AND FACTS

Facts cannot be copyrighted. That the film "Million Dollar Baby" won the Oscar in 2005, or that John Kennedy was killed in November 1963, or that George Washington was the nation's first president are all facts. No one can claim ownership of these facts; anyone can publish or broadcast them. But this simple concept can get a bit more complicated when someone works dilligently to collect a set of facts and then seeks to copyright his or her work. This section focuses on three such areas: databases, news events and research findings.

Telephone Books and Databases

Long before the birth of the computer, most homes contained relatively sophisticated databases. These are called telephone directories—a listing of phone company customers' names, addresses and telephone numbers. In 1991 the Supreme Court decided a seemingly innocuous case involving copyright protection for a white-pages telephone book—by any measure a collection of thousands of facts. But the ruling would have a profound impact on other kinds of databases and generate problems that have not yet been completely resolved.

The plaintiff in this case was Rural Telephone Service, a small, rural telephone company that issued a white-pages directory listing the names, addresses and phone numbers of its 1,309 subscribers. The defendant was Feist Publications, a business that specializes in publishing telephone directories. Feist published a single directory that included the names and telephone numbers contained in several small directories, creating a kind of regional phone book that included the subscribers of several small telephone companies. When Feist asked Rural for permission to take the 1,309 names from its telephone book for use in its regional directory, Rural refused to grant permission. Feist used the names anyway and Rural sued for copyright infringement. The plaintiff proved to the court that four of the 1,309 names in the directory were fictitious, planted there to snare a thief who reproduced the directory without permission.

Rural made two arguments to try to overcome the difficulty in establishing copyright protection for facts. First, the plaintiff argued that the directory was more than just facts, it was a compilation or collection of facts. The law has recognized limited protection for compilations of facts. Second, Rural raised what was known in copyright law as the "sweat of the brow" doctrine. This is a legal proposition recognized in the past by some courts that even though facts are not copyrightable, a man or woman who invests great energy and hard work in amassing these facts deserves some reward for this hard work. Hence, the law should protect a collection of facts like a directory or a road map not because it is necessarily original, but because it took a lot of work to create.

---

18. *Amsterdam* v. *Triangle Publishing Co.*, 189 F. 2d 104 (1951).

In a unanimous decision the Supreme Court rejected both arguments. With regard to the latter, Justice Sandra Day O'Connor said the "sweat of the brow" doctrine was a bogus argument. Quoting former justice William Brennan, she said, "The primary objective of copyright law is not to reward the labor of authors, but to promote the process of science and the arts." O'Connor agreed that some compilations of facts can be protected by copyright. The key to determining whether protection is merited is whether there is *some novelty or originality in the manner in which the facts are organized or selected or coordinated.* An alphabetical listing of names—the organization of the Rural directory and indeed all white pages—is not novel enough to generate copyright protection for the directory.[19]

The high court ruling was important, but seemingly narrow in its reach. How many cases involving copyright protection for white-pages directories emerge each year? Yet in recent years the importance of the *Feist* ruling has expanded exponentially. What can be said about the originality of an alphabetical list of names in a telephone book can be said as well about any alphabetically ordered list of facts. And the creation of alphabetically ordered lists of facts, which are also called databases, is among the fastest-growing and profitable uses for CD-ROM computer software and interactive Web sites on the Internet. Because of the *Feist* ruling, only those databases in which the factual items are organized or selected or coordinated in some novel or original manner will be protected by copyright law. Such organization or arrangement doesn't have to be unique or especially artful. But it surely must go beyond a simple alphabetical organization of the items it contains.[20] Otherwise, the compiler's investment of time, money and effort in gathering the data is not protected by copyright law. Many states have misappropriation laws (see pages 578–579) that may be used to bar database piracy. Congress, under pressure from the owners of large, commercial databases, has tried several times to pass legislation to protect these collections of facts, most recently in 2004. But in every case the legislators have run into roadblocks. Organizations outside the database industry, notably libraries and some technology companies, have opposed such legislation, claiming that such laws would allow some companies to monopolize facts, and this would hamper research projects. And there of course is the constitutional issue. The Supreme Court ruled that the so-called sweat-of-the-brow doctrine was constitutionally invalid in 1991, and this doctrine is at the heart of such legislation. There was no resolution of this issue by late 2005.

News Events

When the news is reported correctly it is basically an account of facts. Can a news account be copyrighted? Can one journalist claim the exclusive right to report on a story? Suppose a TV reporter gets an exclusive interview with a reclusive public figure and then broadcasts the

---

19. *Feist Publications, Inc.* v. *Rural Telephone Service Co., Inc.,* 111 S. Ct. 1282 (1991).

20. The same year the *Feist* case was decided the 2nd U.S. Circuit Court of Appeals ruled that the creator of a directory of businesses in New York City had demonstrated novelty by arranging and selecting the businesses to be included in the directory in a creative fashion. See *Key Publications, Inc.* v. *Chinatown Today,* 945 F. 2d 509 (1991). And in 1997 the 7th U.S. Circuit Court of Appeals ruled that a taxonomy (a way of describing items in a body of knowledge or practice) of dental procedures was a creative work, far different from a simple compilation. *American Dental Association* v. *Delta Dental Plan Association,* CA 7, 96-4140, 9/30/97. See also *Warren Publishing Co.* v. *Microdos Data Corp.,* CA 11 en banc, No. 93-8474, 6/10/97.

copyrighted interview on the evening news. Does the law of copyright prevent other journalists from relating the substance of what was revealed in that interview? The answer is no. Other stations cannot replay the same interview. Newspapers cannot publish a transcript of the interview. But both broadcast and print journalists can tell their viewers and readers what the public figure said in the interview. Copyright law doesn't even require the competitors to credit the TV journalist for the interview. Failing to give proper credit to the TV journalist who got the interview is grossly unethical but happens all too often. Charges of plagiarism might be made and a lawsuit might even be filed.

Copyright law protects the expression of the story—the way it is told, the style and manner in which the facts are presented—but not the facts in the story. For many writers this concept is a difficult one to understand and to accept. After all, if one reporter works hard to uncover a story, shouldn't he or she have the exclusive right to tell that story? This argument again reflects the sweat-of-the-brow doctrine that has been rejected by the Supreme Court. Shouldn't hard work be rewarded? In this case the law is clear. Hard work must be its own reward. Copyright only protects the way a story is told, not the facts in the story.

Research Findings and History

Gene Miller, a Pulitzer Prize–winning reporter for the Miami Herald, wrote a book entitled "83 Hours Till Dawn," an account of the widely publicized kidnapping of Barbara Mackle. Miller said he had spent more than 2,500 hours on the book, and many aspects of the kidnapping case were uncovered by the journalist and reported only in his book. Universal Studios wanted to film a dramatization of the 1971 incident but was unable to come to terms with Miller on payment for the rights. The studio produced the so-called docudrama anyway, and Miller sued for infringement of copyright. The similarities between Miller's book and the Universal script were striking—even some of the errors Miller had made in preparing the book were found in the film. But Universal argued that it was simply telling a story of a news event, and as such the research that Miller had done in digging out the facts regarding the story was not protected by copyright law. A U.S. District Court agreed with Miller's contention. "The court views the labor and expense of the research involved in the obtaining of those uncopyrightable facts to be intellectually distinct from those facts, and more similar to the expression of the facts than the facts themselves," the court said. The judge ruled that it was necessary to reward the effort and ingenuity involved in giving expression to a fact.[21] But the U.S. Court of Appeals for the 5th Circuit reversed the lower-court ruling. "The valuable distinction in copyright law between facts and the expression of facts cannot be maintained if research is held to be copyrightable. There is no rational basis for distinguishing between facts and the research involved in obtaining the facts," the court said. To hold research copyrightable, the court said, is no more or less than to hold that the facts discovered as a result of research are entitled to copyright protection.[22] The court added: "A fact does not originate with the author of a book describing the fact. Neither does it originate with the one who 'discovers' the fact. The discoverer merely finds and records. He may not claim that the facts

21. *Miller* v. *Universal City Studios,* 460 F. Supp. 984 (1978).
22. *Miller* v. *Universal City Studios,* 650 F. 2d 1365 (1981).

are 'original' with him, although there may be originality and hence authorship in the manner of reporting, i.e. the 'expression' of the facts."

The 7th U.S. Circuit Court of Appeals handed down a similar ruling in 1990 in a case involving the infamous John Dillinger, the subject of a widely publicized manhunt by local police and the FBI during the 1930s. Most historians believe that Dillinger was killed on July 22, 1934, when he was shot by government agents who ensnared him in an ambush as he left the Biograph movie theater in Chicago. Jay Robert Nash has written at least two books that dispute this conclusion. Nash argues that Dillinger learned about the ambush and sent a look-alike to the theater instead. The FBI, embarrassed that its setup failed, kept quiet. And Dillinger retired from a life of crime and lived the rest of his life on the West Coast.

A 1984 episode of the CBS television series "Simon and Simon" involved a story that suggested that Dillinger was still alive, living in California. Nash sued the network, claiming copyright infringement. The officials at the network admitted that they had seen Nash's books and said they had used some of his ideas. But, they argued, Nash claimed to be writing history, and history is a collection of facts. Such material cannot be copyrighted. The court agreed. The network might be liable if Nash portrayed his work as a novel, as fiction. But he didn't. "The inventor of Sherlock Holmes controls that character's fate while the copyright lasts; the first person to conclude that Dillinger survives does not get his dibs on the history," Judge Easterbrook wrote. Nash's rights lie in his expression, not in the naked truth.[23]

MISAPPROPRIATION

Although this chapter focuses on copyright, an ancillary area of the law needs to be briefly mentioned, as it too guards against the theft of intangible property. **Misappropriation,** or **unfair competition,** is sometimes invoked as an additional legal remedy in suits for copyright infringement. Unlike copyright, which springs largely from federal statute today, misappropriation remains largely a creature of the common law. One of the most important media-oriented misappropriation cases was decided by the Supreme Court more than 80 years ago and stemmed from a dispute between the Associated Press (AP) and the International News Service (INS), a rival press association owned by William Randolph Hearst. (INS merged with the United Press in 1958 and today is represented by the *I* in UPI.)

The Associated Press charged that the International News Service pirated its news, saying that INS officials bribed AP employees to gain access to news before it was sent to AP member newspapers. The press agency also charged that the Hearst wire service copied news from bulletin boards and early editions of newspapers that carried AP dispatches. Sometimes INS editors rewrote the news, and other times they sent the news out on the wire just as it had been written by AP reporters. Copyright was not the question, because AP did not copyright its material. The agency said it could not copyright all its dispatches because there were too many and they had to be transmitted too fast. The International News Service argued that because the material was not copyrighted, it was in the public domain and could be used by anyone.

---

23. *Nash* v. *CBS,* 899 F. 2d 1537 (1990). Also see *Burgess* v. *Chase-Riboud,* 765 F. Supp. 233 (1991) on pages 603–604.

Justice Mahlon Pitney wrote the opinion in the 7-1 decision. He said there can be no property right in the news itself, the events, the happenings, which are publici juris, the common property of all, the history of the day. However, the jurist went on to say:

> Although we may and do assume that neither party [AP or INS] has any remaining property interest as against the public in uncopyrighted matter after the moment of its first publication, it by no means follows that there is no remaining property interest in it as between themselves.[24]

Pitney said there was a distinct difference between taking the news collected by AP and publishing it for use by readers and taking the news and transmitting that news for commercial use, in competition with the plaintiff. This action is unfair competition, he said—interference with the business of the AP precisely at the point where profit is to be reaped.

In 1963 a Pennsylvania broadcasting station was found guilty of pirating the news from a local newspaper and reading it over the air as if it were the fruits of its own news-gathering efforts.[25] In 1994 the Reading (Pa.) Eagle Co., which publishes the morning Times and the afternoon Eagle, sued another Pennsylvania radio station, WIOV in Reading, charging copyright infringement, misappropriation and unfair competition. The publisher claimed the station was lifting its news stories and sought $50,000 in damages.[26]

The law of misappropriation is intended to stop

- **a person trying to pass his or her work off as the work of someone else, and**
- **a person trying to pass off the work of someone else as his or her own work.**

Imagine that a new magazine is published with the title News-Week. The cover design mirrors that of Newsweek. The design and title would be an attempt to confuse readers and pass off the new magazine as the well-established original, a publisher trying to pass his or her work off as the work of someone else. Or imagine a daily newspaper reporter picking up a story that was published in a small weekly paper, rewriting the story, and then passing it off as his or her original reporting. Such an action would be trying to pass off the work done by someone else as the daily reporter's own work.

The critical legal issue in an unfair competition or misappropriation suit is whether there is a *likelihood* that an appreciable number of ordinarily prudent purchasers are likely to be misled, or simply confused, as to the source of the goods in question.

DURATION OF COPYRIGHT PROTECTION

The length of time that a copyright will protect a given work depends on when the work was created. The major revision of the copyright law in 1976 included a significant extension of the duration of copyright protection. In 1998 Congress adopted the Sonny Bono Copyright Extension Act, adding 20 more years to the protection of a copyrighted work. Any work created after January 1, 1978, will be protected for the life of the creator, plus 70 years. This rule allows creators to enjoy the fruits of their labor until death and then allows the heirs to profit

---

24. *Associated Press* v. *International News Service,* 248 U.S. 215 (1919).
25. *Pottstown Daily News Publishing* v. *Pottstown Broadcasting,* 192 A. 2d 657 (1963).
26. Shepard, "Does Radio News Rip Off Newspapers?" 15.

from the work of their fathers, mothers, sisters or brothers for an additional length of time. After 70 years the work goes into what is called public domain. At that point it may be copied by any person for any reason without the payment of royalty to the original owner. The copyright on a work created by two or more authors extends through the life of the last author to die plus 70 years. What is called a "work for hire" is protected for 95 years after publication. Works for hire include books written by an author for a publisher, which then holds the copyright. Also included are most motion pictures, sound recordings, television programs and so on that are created through a collaborative effort.*

HOW LONG DOES COPYRIGHT PROTECTION LAST?

Works Created After January 1, 1978
The life of the creator plus 70 years.

Works Created by More Than One Person
The life of the last living creator plus 70 years.

Works for Hire
Ninety-five years after publication.

Works Created Before January 1, 1978
Ninety-five years.

What about works created before 1978? Prior to the revision of copyright law in 1976, works were protected for a term of 28 years. The owner could renew the copyright and add a second 28-year term for a total of 56 years. Under terms of the 1976 law, works created before 1978 are protected for a total of 95 years. If a work is in its initial 28-year term, it is protected for the remainder of that 28-year term plus 67 more years. Imagine that a book was copyrighted in 1970. It was protected until 1998 under its original 28-year term, plus 67 more years, until 2065. But to gain the additional 67 years, the copyright holder had to renew the copyright as was required under the previous statute.

If the copyrighted work is already in its renewal term—the second 28 years under the old law—it will be protected for a total of 95 years. Imagine, for example, that a song was originally copyrighted in 1940. The copyright was renewed in 1968, the end of the first 28-year term. It will be protected for an additional 67 years from 1968, or until 2035. No renewal request is needed in this case.

The federal statute that extended copyright protection for an additional 20 years was challenged by critics who saw the law as a means of protecting large corporate copyright holders, who lobbied Congress vigorously for the extension, not individual creators. Some critics derisively referred to the law as the Disney Copyright Extension, since without a

---

*The Copyright Office has available a myriad of booklets regarding all matters relating to copyright law, including duration of protection. Inquiries can be sent to the Copyright Office, Library of Congress, 101 Independence Ave. S.E., Washington, D.C. 20559-6000. The Copyright Office also has a Web site that provides similar information: lcweb.loc.gov/copyright/.

change in the law many of Walt Disney's cartoon characters would have fallen into the public domain. The legal challenge rested on the constitutional language that authorized Congress to protect the works of authors and inventors for a "limited time." Challengers said they did not object to the new duration of protection—the life of the creator plus 70 years; they instead said applying this extension retroactively to works already protected by copyright law violated the reasoning behind copyright law—which is to stimulate the creation of new works. Extending existing copyrights would not promote new creativity, they argued. In addition, a duration that is virtually perpetual, they said, violates the notion of "limited time." In 2003 the Supreme Court upheld the congressional action. Justice Ruth Bader Ginsburg said that the extension—the most recent of many extensions enacted by Congress since 1790—was within the power of Congress. She said that while it could be argued that the extension was bad public policy, it was within the power granted to the legislators by the Constitution.[27]

SUMMARY

American copyright law derives from rules and regulations established by the British government in the 16th and 17th centuries. The contemporary basis for the protection of intangible property is contained in the U.S. Constitution, and since 1789 the nation has had numerous federal copyright statutes. The current law, adopted in 1976, gives to the author or owner of a work the sole and exclusive right to reproduce the copyrighted work in any form for any reason. The statute protects all original works of authorship fixed in any tangible medium. Included are such creations as literary works, newspaper stories, magazine articles, television programs, films and even advertisements. Trivial items, utilitarian goods, ideas, and methods or systems cannot be copyrighted.

News events cannot be copyrighted, but stories or broadcasts that endeavor to describe or explain these events can be copyrighted. What is being protected is the author's style or manner of presentation of the news. Similarly, facts cannot be copyrighted, but works that relate these facts can be protected as expression. While news and facts cannot be copyrighted, anyone who attempts to present news or facts gathered by someone else as his or her own work may be guilty of breaking other laws, such as misappropriation, or unfair competition. In most cases copyrighted works are protected for the life of the author or creator plus 70 years. Different rules apply for works created before 1978 and for works made for hire.

FAIR USE

Owners of a copyright are granted almost exclusive monopoly over the use of their creations. The word "almost" must be used, for there are really four limitations on this monopoly. Three of the limitations have been discussed already. First, the work must be something that can be copyrighted. There can be no legal monopoly on the use of something that cannot be protected by the law. Second, the monopoly only protects original authorship or creation. If the creation

Owners of a copyright are granted almost exclusive monopoly over the use of their creations.

27. *Eldred* v. *Ashcroft,* 537 U.S. 186 (2003). See also, Greenhouse, "20-Year Extension."

is not original, it cannot be protected. Third, copyright protection does not last forever. At some point the protection ceases and the work falls into the public domain.

The fourth limitation on exclusive monopoly is broader than the other three, is certainly more controversial, and is concerned with limited copying of copyrighted material. This is the doctrine of **fair use,** which has been defined by one court as follows:

> A rule of reason . . . to balance the author's right to compensation for his work, on the one hand, against the public's interest in the widest possible dissemination of ideas and information on the other.[28]

This doctrine, then, permits limited copying of an original creation that has been properly copyrighted and has not yet fallen into the public domain.

One hundred and thirty years ago all copying of a copyrighted work was against the law. This absolute prohibition on copying constituted a hardship for scholars, critics and teachers seeking to use small parts of copyrighted materials in their work. A judicial remedy for this problem was sought. It was argued that since the purpose of the original copyright statute was to promote art and science, the copyright law should not be administered in such a way as to frustrate artists and scientists who publish scholarly materials. In 1879 the U.S. Supreme Court ruled in *Baker* v. *Selden:*

> The very object of publishing a book on science or the useful arts is to communicate to the world the useful knowledge which it contains. But this object would be frustrated if the useful knowledge could not be used without incurring the guilt of piracy of the book.[29]

The doctrine of fair use emerged from the courts, and under this judicial doctrine small amounts of copying were permitted so long as the publication of the material advanced science, the arts, criticism and so forth.

In 1976 Congress included the judicial doctrine of fair use in the revision of the copyright law. Section 107 of the measure declares, "The fair use of a copyrighted work . . . for purposes such as criticism, comment, news reporting, teaching (including multiple copies for classroom use), scholarship or research is not an infringement of copyright."

In determining whether the use of a particular work is a fair use, the statute says that courts should consider the following factors:

1. **The purpose and character of the use**
2. **The nature of the copyrighted work**
3. **The amount and substantiality of the portion used in relation to the copyrighted work as a whole**
4. **The effect of the use on the potential market for or value of the copyrighted work**

Each factor on this list will be considered separately as the doctrine of fair use is explored. Interestingly, the fair-use criteria included in the statute and just listed here (1 through 4) are very close to the criteria that courts used under the old common-law fair-use doctrine. This similarity is no accident. In a report issued by committees in the House and the

---

28. *Triangle Publications* v. *Knight-Ridder,* 626 F. 2d 1171 (1980).
29. *Baker* v. *Selden,* 101 U.S. 99 (1879).

Senate on Section 107, the legislators said that the new law "endorses the purpose and general scope of the judicial doctrine of fair use" but did not intend that the law be frozen as it existed in 1976. "The courts must be free to adapt the doctrine to particular situations on a case-by-case basis. Section 107 is intended to restate the present judicial doctrine of fair use, not to change, narrow, or enlarge it in any way."

PURPOSE AND CHARACTER OF USE

The purpose and character of the use of a work is the initial factor to be considered. A use is more likely to be considered a fair use if it is a noncommercial or nonprofit use. But simply because material is used in a commercial venture doesn't disqualify it as a fair use. The U.S. Court of Appeals for the 2nd Circuit noted that according to committee reports compiled when the new copyright law was adopted, Congress did not intend that only nonprofit educational uses of copyrighted works would qualify as fair use. The reports, said the court, are "an express recognition that . . . the commercial or nonprofit character of an activity, while not conclusive with respect to fair use, can and should be weighed along with other factors in fair-use decisions."[30]

The law lists several categories of use that may be protected by fair use. These include

- criticism and comment,
- teaching, and
- scholarship and research.

Just because a use falls into one of these categories doesn't mean a fair-use defense will automatically be successful. At the same time, uses that fall outside one of these categories may still qualify as a fair use. Here are some cases that illustrate these principles.

"The Daily Show" on Comedy Central used a video clip from a public access television show, "The Sandra Kane Blew Comedy Show," to introduce a segment called Public Excess. The segment features examples of public access television. Sandra Kane, a comedienne and former stripper, sings, dances and tells jokes on her show while wearing little or no clothing. She sued for copyright infringement, but the federal court said the use of the clip by Jon Stewart on "The Daily Show" was a fair use because it was used for critical purposes. "In presenting plaintiff's clip, defendant sought to critically examine the quality of plaintiff's public access television show," the court ruled.[31] And the 2nd U.S. Court of Appeals ruled that when an operator of two Web sites that are used to criticize cults and other groups accused of mind control quoted long segments of a manual used at executive training seminars it was a fair use because he used the segments to support his criticism of the company that conducted the seminars.[32]

But a federal court in California rejected a fair-use argument made by the operator of an Internet bulletin board who posted complete copyrighted articles from the Los Angeles Times and the Washington Post on the site so people could comment on the news and

---

30. *Maxtone-Graham* v. *Burtchaell*, 803 F. 2d 1253 (1986).
31. *Kane* v. *Comedy Partners*, 32 M.L.R. 1113 (2003).
32. *NXIVM Corp.* v. *Ross Inst.*, 2d Cir., 03-7952, 4/20/04.

criticize the manner in which the news stories were reported. The court noted that adding commentary to a verbatim copy of a copyrighted work does not automatically protect it as a fair use. The court issued an injunction barring future postings and assessed $1 million in damages against the defendant.[33] How do you explain the seemingly opposite rulings? Surely the concepts "comment" and "criticism" are elusive and subject to interpretation. But a more obvious explanation involves the amount of copyrighted material used in these three instances. In the California case, the defendants used a great many copyrighted articles from the two newspapers. Significantly smaller amounts of copyrighted material were used in the other two cases.

The comment and criticism element is more aptly applied to republishing small segments of a work. A book reviewer is clearly protected when quoting even long passages from a work being evaluated. A journalist could undoubtedly publish one or two stanzas from a poem by a poet who was named the winner of a Pulitzer Prize. Yet if a poster publisher took the same two stanzas of poetry, printed them in large type on 11-by-14-inch stock, and tried to sell them for $10 each, the publisher would be guilty of an infringement of copyright. The purpose of the use in the case of the journalist was to give readers an example of the poet's work, but the poster publisher simply wanted to make a few bucks.

Copyright law has traditionally regarded the limited use of copyrighted material for educational purposes as a fair use. The teacher who makes copies of a short article from Newsweek and distributes them to class members is normally considered an innocent infringer. But more substantial copying may not receive the same protection, especially when commercial interests are involved. In 1991 U.S. District Judge Constance B. Motley ruled that businesses that commercially copy collections of articles and excerpts from books without first gaining permission from copyright holders are violating the copyright laws, even if the copies are designed for classroom use.[34] This suit was launched by eight U.S. publishers against Kinko's, a national chain of copy shops based in California. Many college instructors collect magazine and journal articles, chapters from books, and other written material and create a kind of instant anthology for use in a class. Kinko's would copy this material, put it together into course packets or course resource books, and then sell it to the students enrolled in the course for $10 or $20, considerably less than the cost of a published anthology or a textbook. Teachers liked the scheme because they could fashion an individual collection of materials for each class. Students liked it as well because the resource books cost less than a published book. And, of course, Kinko's liked it because it was a very profitable endeavor. But the copyright holders did not appreciate the scheme and went to court to block it. Kinko's argued that the fair-use standard permits photocopying of material for educational use. Judge Motley agreed, but ruled that the nature and extent of the copying and Kinko's profit-making intent had clearly exceeded fair use. Citing the photocopier's "historic willful blindness to the copyright laws," Judge Motley ordered Kinko's to stop copying this material without first getting permission from the copyright holder. Most publishers will require Kinko's to pay a licensing fee or royalty to do such copying. In addition, the court ordered the copy shop to pay the publishers more than a half-million dollars in damages plus court costs and attorneys' fees.

33. *Los Angeles Times* v. *Free Republic,* 29 M.L.R. 1028 (2000).
34. *Basic Books Inc.* v. *Kinko's Graphics Corp.,* 758 F. Supp. 1552 (1991).

The decision in the Kinko's case was reinforced five years later when the 6th U.S. Circuit Court of Appeals, sitting en banc, also ruled that the creation of anthologies of copyrighted material for classroom use was a violation of the law. In this case the defendant argued that, because the professors who required the students to buy the anthologies had placed the same material on reserve in the library where students were free to copy it on their own, selling the same materials in a course pack was not a copyright infringement. The court said the copying of the material by the Michigan Document Service was a commercial use, regardless of how the copying would be regarded if a student did it on his or her own. The court noted that when the 1976 Copyright Act was approved, Congress had accepted guidelines for educational use copying that would be regarded as a fair use. The copying must

- **be brief—under 1,000 words;**
- **be spontaneous—there would be no time to get permission;**
- **not occur more than 9 times a term, with a limited number of copies from a single author;**
- **carry a copyright notice;**
- **not be a substitute for purchase of the original work and not cost the student more than the actual copying cost.**

These guidelines also make clear, the court said, that the kinds of anthologies created by the Michigan Document Service could not be regarded as a fair use.[35] The Supreme Court declined to review the Court of Appeals ruling.

At times defendants have argued that the use of copyrighted material serves a public interest and hence should be protected. In 1966 the 2nd U.S. Circuit Court of Appeals ruled that the use by Random House of copyrighted material in a biography of, at that time, America's best-known recluse, multimillionaire Howard Hughes, was a fair use. In an attempt to thwart the publication of the biography, a Hughes company called Rosemont had purchased the rights to a series of articles published in Look magazine that were heavily quoted in the book. The court ruled that the purpose of copyright law was not to stop the dissemination of information about publicity-shy public figures. It would be contrary to the public interest to permit individuals to buy up the rights to anything published about them to stop authors from using the material, the court ruled.[36] The public interest criteria came to the fore again two years later when a federal court permitted the author of a book to use copyrighted frames of 8mm motion picture film to illustrate his theory regarding the assassination of John F. Kennedy. The motion picture, taken by a spectator named Abraham Zapruder, was then owned by Time, Inc., which had bought the film shortly after the killing.[37]

Today, some judges talk about "transformative uses" when they consider claims of fair use. What does this mean? If an individual takes a portion of a copyrighted work and uses it for another purpose, in other words transforms it, it is much more likely to be regarded as a fair use. For example, when ABC broadcast a television news report about how the advocates of the legalization of marijuana have changed the image of the typical user from the long-haired

35. "Copying of Materials for Coursepack Does Not Constitute Fair Use, CA6 Rules," 1 E.P.L.R. 809 (1996).
36. *Rosemont* v. *Random House,* 366 F. 2d 303 (1966).
37. *Time, Inc.* v. *Bernard Geis Associates,* 239 F. Supp. 130 (1968).

pothead to a seriously ill medical patient, it used both the cover from a recent issue of Newsweek and a photo from a story in the issue to illustrate its video story. The magazine story had focused on the medical use of marijuana. The federal court said the use of the cover and the photo was a fair use because it was transformative use.[38] The network had taken the original copyrighted art and transformed it into a story about the news coverage of a current issue. Three years later in 2001 a federal court in New York ruled that when the Cable News Network used clips from the feature film "G.I. Joe" in its obituary on actor Robert Mitchum, the star of the film, it had transformed the clips into something different, a story about the death of a popular motion picture actor. This too was a fair use.[39]

NATURE OF THE COPYRIGHTED WORK

Courts look at several considerations when applying this criterion in a copyright infringement action.

- **Is the copyrighted work still available?** Using a part of a work that is out of print is far less serious than using a segment of a book that can be readily purchased at the local bookstore.
- **Is the copyrighted work what is called a consumable work?** A consumable work is something that is intended to be used just once: a workbook that accompanies a text, or a book of crossword puzzles. Consumables are usually cheaply priced and are intended to be used and then discarded. It would not be a fair use for a teacher to purchase a single copy of a biology workbook, make 30 photocopies of each page, and then pass out the photocopies for use by the students. But it would very likely be a fair use for the same teacher to make 30 copies of an article in Science magazine for class distribution.
- **Is the work an informational work or a creative work?** It is more likely to be a fair use if the copying involves a work like a newspaper or newsmagazine or encyclopedia rather than a novel or play or poem. This doesn't mean that copying an informational work is always a fair use; just that it is more likely to be.
- **Is the work published or unpublished?** The author's right of first publication—that is, the right to turn an unpublished work into a published one—is regarded as a valuable right by most courts and was the center of a spirited judicial and legislative battle in recent years.

This story begins in the backwash of the seminal mid-20th-century political event, the Watergate scandal, and involves the unpublished memoirs of Richard Nixon's successor, Gerald Ford. Weeks prior to the publication of the Ford book, The Nation magazine published a 2,250-word article containing paraphrases and quotes from the unpublished manuscript. An unnamed source had given a copy of the 200,000-word manuscript to the magazine, and although the article contained only about 300 words that were legitimately protected by copyright (the remainder of the article was uncopyrightable accounts of news and history), the

---

38. *Morgenstein* v. *ABC Inc.,* 27 M.L.R. 1350 (1998).
39. *Video-Cinema Films Inc.* v. *Cable News Network Inc.,* 29 M.L.R. 2551 (2001).

Nation piece contained the heart of Ford's work—his discussion of the pardon he gave to former President Nixon. A U.S. District Court said the publication amounted to copyright infringement, but a U.S. Court of Appeals disagreed, saying the publication of the material was a fair use.[40] The U.S. Supreme Court rejected the fair-use claim and reversed the lower appellate court ruling. "In using generous verbatim excerpts of Mr. Ford's unpublished manuscript to lend authenticity to its account of the forthcoming memoirs, The Nation effectively arrogated to itself the right of first publication, an important marketable subsidiary right," Justice Sandra Day O'Connor wrote. The 1976 Copyright Act clearly recognizes the right of first publication for an author, O'Connor said. The scope of fair use is narrowed where unpublished works are concerned. The Senate report that accompanied the 1976 law specifically states: "The applicability of the fair-use doctrine to unpublished works is narrowly limited since, although the work is unavailable, this is the result of a deliberate choice on the part of the copyright owner. Under ordinary circumstances the copyright owner's 'right of first publication' would outweigh any needs of reproduction." Justice O'Connor concluded that "the unpublished nature of a work is a key, though not necessarily determinative, factor, tending to negate a defense of fair use."[41]

Mark Twain once noted that it is possible to get more out of a lesson than the teacher intended. A cat that sits on a hot stove will likely never sit on another hot stove, he noted. It is just as likely, he added, the cat won't sit on a cold stove either. Such was the case when some lower courts interpreted Justice O'Connor's opinion in the Nation decision. When judges read the sentence, "We conclude that the unpublished nature of a work is a key, *though not necessarily determinative,* [author emphasis] factor, tending to negate a defense of fair use," they ignored the italicized phrase. In a series of increasingly restrictive rulings, judges on the 2nd U.S. Circuit Court of Appeals, a court with considerable national authority, ruled that the copying of an unpublished work *can never* be a fair use.[42] The impact of these rulings especially affected scholars who frequently use unpublished letters, diaries and other materials in preparing serious biographies of important public persons. Many in the publishing industry panicked. Editors at Harper & Row made author James Reston Jr. remove sections of a biography he had prepared of former Texas governor John Connally. Reston had quoted from unpublished letters Connally had sent to President Lyndon Johnson. And former New York City mayor Ed Koch substantially altered a book he was preparing that contained letters he had written to New Yorkers while he was mayor. He chose to not publish segments of the letters that had been written to him that prompted his written responses.

Congress came to the rescue in the autumn of 1992 when it amended the federal copyright statute. The law now states that "the fact that a work is unpublished shall not itself bar a finding of fair use," if such a finding is justified based on the application of all four fair-use

Justice O'Connor concluded that "the unpublished nature of a work is a key, though not necessarily determinative, factor, tending to negate a defense of fair use."

---

40. *Harper & Row Publishers* v. *Nation Enterprises,* 557 F. Supp. 1067 (1983), rev'd. 723 F. 2d 195 (1983).
41. *Harper & Row Publishers* v. *Nation Enterprises,* 471 U.S. 539 (1985). A newspaper or television broadcast or Web site can surely summarize what it has learned from a copy of an unpublished memoir or book, but it cannot quote sentences, paragraphs or pages from the manuscript. This may be a fine line to some, but it is an important dividing line to the courts.
42. See *Salinger* v. *Random House,* 811 F. 2d 90 (1987) and *New Era Publications* v. *Henry Holt & Co., Inc.,* 873 F. 2d 576 (1990).

*Excerpt from The Nation,
April 7, 1979, recounting
Ford's memoirs.*

THE FORD MEMOIRS

BEHIND THE NIXON PARDON

In his memoirs, *A Time to Heal*, which Harper & Row will publish in late May or early June, former President Gerald R. Ford says that the idea of giving a blanket pardon to Richard M. Nixon was raised before Nixon resigned from the Presidency by Gen. Alexander Haig, who was then the White House chief of staff.

Ford also writes that, but for a misunderstanding, he might have selected Ronald Reagan as his 1976 running mate, that Washington lawyer Edward Bennett Williams, a Democrat, was his choice for head of the Central Intelligence Agency, that Nixon was the one who first proposed Nelson Rockefeller for Vice President, and that he regretted his "cowardice" in allowing Rockefeller to remove himself from Vice Presidential contention. Ford also describes his often prickly relations with Henry Kissinger.

The Nation obtained the 655-page typescript before publication. Advance excerpts from the book will appear in *Time* in mid-April and in *The Reader's Digest* thereafter. Although the initial print order has not been decided, the figure is tentatively set at 50,000; it could change, depending upon the public reaction to the serialization.

Ford's account of the Nixon pardon contains significant new detail on the negotiations and considerations that surrounded it. According to Ford's version, the subject was first broached to him by General Haig on August 1, 1974, a week before Nixon resigned. General Haig revealed that the newly transcribed White House tapes were the equivalent of the "smoking gun" and that Ford should prepare himself to become President.

Ford was deeply hurt by Haig's revela-

(Continued on Page 363)

criteria. This change puts the law back to where it was immediately after the ruling in *Harper & Row Publishers* v. *Nation Enterprises,* before appellate courts began to misinterpret it. It remains exceedingly dangerous, though not necessarily fatal, to publish or broadcast material that has never before been published. Such a use will likely only be sustained provided the user can make a strong case under the other three fair-use criteria.

THE PORTION OR PERCENTAGE OF A WORK USED

The amount of a work used is not as important as the relative proportion of a work used. Word counts, for example, really don't mean as much as percentages. The use of 500 words from a 450-page book is far less damaging than the use of 20 words from a 40-word poem. How much of the work, in relation to the whole, was used? Courts will consider exact copying when looking at this question; but they will also often consider paraphrasing. Pirates will find little refuge in a dictionary of synonyms. For example, in the mid-1980s respected writer Ian Hamilton sought to publish a biography of reclusive novelist J.D. Salinger, the author of "Catcher in the Rye." Lacking Salinger's cooperation in the endeavor, Hamilton sought to prepare the biography by using portions of numerous unpublished letters the novelist had written to friends and acquaintances. Salinger sued for copyright infringement, claiming the contents of the letters were his literary property. To avoid the lawsuit Hamilton reworked the manuscript, deleting most phrases and sentences copied directly from the letters. But he extensively paraphrased the contents of the correspondence in place of using Salinger's actual words. The 2nd U.S. Circuit Court of Appeals ruled that this use was an infringement of copyright, not a fair use. Paraphrasing Salinger's words did not protect Hamilton. "What is protected is the manner of expression, the author's analysis or interpretation of events—the way he structures his material and marshalls facts, his choice of words and the emphasis he gives to particular developments," wrote Judge Jon O. Newman.[43] The paraphrasing was too close to Salinger's own choice of words, to his creativity. The biographer had taken the "heart of the material" from the letters. Hamilton abandoned his initial effort and instead wrote "In Search of J.D. Salinger," a book about Salinger's literary life (without the material from the letters) and his unsuccessful efforts to publish a biography of the reclusive author.

One of the toughest tasks facing a judge is measuring fair use when someone presents a parody of a copyrighted work. A parody is a critical and usually humorous effort to lampoon a creation. But in order to be a successful parody, the work must reflect the content of the original book or movie or song, not simply the style and presentation of the original creation. The question of parody was at the heart of one of the silliest legal actions in recent years when the Fox News Network tried to stop author Al Franken from calling his book, a critical evaluation of the conservative press in America, "Lies and the Lying Liars Who Tell Them: A Fair and Balanced Look at the Right." Fox claimed that it owned the rights to the phrase "fair and balanced," a slogan it uses to identify its newscasts. Franken said the book was a social commentary on the network and others, and that the use of the phrase was a parody. A federal court agreed, saying the lawsuit was wholly without merit, both factually and legally. "Parody is a form of artistic expression protected by the First Amendment. The keystone to parody is

---

43. *Salinger* v. *Random House,* 811 F. 2d 90 (1987).

imitation. Here, whether you agree with him or not in using the mark [fair and balanced], Mr. Franken is clearly mocking Fox," wrote judge Denny Chin.[44]

How much of the original work can be used? The U.S. Court of Appeals for the 9th Circuit ruled that it was a fair use for disc jockey Rick Dees to use the melody and some of the words from the first six bars of the song, "When Sunny Gets Blue," in his comic parody, "When Sonny Sniffs Glue." The lyrics in the original song are: "When Sunny gets blue, her eyes get gray and cloudy, then the rain begins to fall" in Dees' version: "When Sonny sniffs glue, her eyes get red and bulgy, then her hair begins to fall." The court noted that "like a speech, a song is difficult to parody effectively without exact or near-exact copying. If the would-be parodist varies the music or the meter of the original substantially, it simply will not be recognizable to the general audience." It is this special need for accuracy that gives the parodist some license in these cases, the court added.[45]

In 1992 the 6th U.S. Court of Appeals ruled that a commercial parody, whether a book or a movie or a song, could never be a fair use. Such a work was commercial and could not be regarded as artistic comment or criticism, something usually protected under the fair-use doctrine.[46] The ruling, if widely accepted, would have had a devastating impact on an entire range of creative work. But the Supreme Court rejected this notion two years later in one of the most colorful copyright cases ever decided. The case focused on a rap music parody of the song "Oh, Pretty Woman," a 1964 rock/country hit written by Roy Orbison (who performed the song) and William Dees. Rapper Luther Campbell, leader and founder of the group 2 Live Crew, was rebuffed when he sought permission from the publisher of the song, Acuff-Rose Music, to record his version of "Oh, Pretty Woman." Campbell was sued by Acuff-Rose when he made the recording anyway. A trial court called the 2 Live Crew version a parody and rejected the suit, but the Court of Appeals reversed, ruling that a commercial parody could never be a fair use. The Supreme Court sided with the trial court and sent the case back for trial, ruling that a jury trial was needed to determine whether the parody was a fair use. "The language of the statute," wrote Justice David Souter, "makes it clear that the commercial or nonprofit educational purpose of a work is only one element of the first factor enquiry into its purpose and character. . . . Accordingly, the mere fact that a use is educational and not for profit does not insulate it from a finding of infringement, any more than the commercial character of a use bars a finding of fairness. If indeed, commerciality carried presumptive force against a finding of fairness, the presumption would swallow nearly all of the illustrative uses listed [in the statute] . . . including news reporting, comment, criticism, teaching, scholarship and research since these activities are generally conducted for profit in this country."[47]

The Court of Appeals had also ruled that the fair-use defense was inapplicable because Campbell had taken too much of the song, the heart of the original work. Not only had the - rapper used the first line of the song, he had taken the melody and the signature bass riff that opens the original recording and is repeated as a kind of a musical signature throughout the recording. Souter acknowledged that it is important for the court to consider not only how much but the importance of the material taken in a use. But he said that a parody presents a

A parody presents a difficult problem.

44. *Fox News Network LLC* v. *Penguin Group (USA) Inc.* 31 M.L.R. 2254 (2003).
45. *Fisher* v. *Dees,* 794 F. 2d 432 (1986).
46. *Campbell* v. *Acuff-Rose Music, Inc.,* 92 F. 2d 1429 (1992).
47. *Campbell* v. *Acuff-Rose Music, Inc.,* 114 S. Ct. 1164 (1994).

difficult problem. Parody, he said, springs from its allusion to the original. "Its art lies in the tension between a known original and its parodic twin," he said. It is true the parody here took the opening lines and the musical signature. "But if quotation of the opening riff and the first line may be said to go to the 'heart' of the original, the heart is also what most readily conjures up the song for parody, and it is the heart at which parody takes aim. Copying does not become excessive in relation to parodic purpose merely because the portion taken was the original's heart." It was significant, Souter said, that after taking the first line, 2 Live Crew added its own lyrics. And while the bass riff was copied, other original sounds were added as well.

The ruling in the Luther Campbell case failed to provide precise guidelines for parodists regarding how much original material can be used in a parody that can be defined as a fair use. Maybe such precise guidelines are impossible to fashion. But without them the matter of fair use and parody continues to bedevil the judiciary. In 2001 the trust that owns the rights to Margaret Mitchell's best-selling novel from the 1930s, "Gone with the Wind," went to court to block Houghton Mifflin from publishing what reviewers described as a parody of the work. The plaintiffs argued that author Alice Randall had infringed on the copyright of the book in her novel, "The Wind Done Gone," a retelling of Mitchell's story from the point of view of a slave who lived on the plantation that was the setting for the Civil War–era novel. The narrator of the Randall book is a half-sister to Mitchell's heroine, Scarlett O'Hara, and the daughter of Mammy, a character in the original story. The plaintiffs also accused Randall of including 15 characters from the original work in her novel as well as several scenes from "Gone with the Wind," and of using verbatim dialogue from the original work. A trial court enjoined the publication of the new novel, ruling that Randall had taken far more from the original work than was necessary to mount a successful parody of the book.[48] A month later the 11th U.S. Circuit Court of Appeals overturned the injunction, calling it a drastic remedy and an unlawful prior restraint in violation of the First Amendment.[49] The book, suddenly the benefactor of millions of dollars in free publicity because of the notoriety of the lawsuit, was published as the parties continued to resolve the issue in the courts. In the spring of 2002 the parties settled their suit, but terms of the settlement were not disclosed.

EFFECT OF USE ON MARKET

The effect of the use on the potential market for, or value of, the copyrighted work is the fourth criterion. While a cautionary note should be sounded against assigning relative weight to the four criteria, this final one—harm to the plaintiff—is given greater weight by most courts than any of the other three. In a congressional committee report on the 1976 law, the legislators noted that "with certain special exceptions . . . a use that supplants any part of the normal market for a copyrighted work would ordinarily be considered an infringement." And in the action by Harper & Row against The Nation, Justice Sandra Day O'Connor noted that "this last factor is undoubtedly the single most important element of fair use."[50] "More important," Justice O'Connor

48. Kirkpatrick, "Court Halts Book."
49. *Suntrust Bank* v. *Houghton Mifflin Company,* 268 F. 3d 1257 (2001). See also Kirkpatrick, "'Wind' Book Wins Ruling."
50. *Harper & Row Publishers* v. *Nation Enterprises,* 471 U.S. 539 (1985).

wrote, "to negate fair use one need only show that if the challenged use should become wide-spread, it would adversely affect the potential market for the copyright work."

The inability of the plaintiff to demonstrate an adverse economic impact from the copying can frequently in and of itself sustain a fair-use ruling. In 1997 Warner Books published a book by Gerald Celente entitled "Trends 2000: How to Prepare for and Profit from the Changes of the 21st Century." In a chapter on power generation the author criticized the nuclear power industry and used a photo that was previously included in an advertisement published by the United States Council for Energy Awareness. The photo was a picture of a dairy farmer, Louise Ihlenfeldt, and a cow standing in a field of clover framed against a blue sky. A print message accompanying the photo in the ad described the harmonious relationship between the Ihlenfeldt family and a nuclear power plant located only a mile away. The book author belittled the message in the ad and criticized the industry. When a copyright action was brought against Warner Books for using the photo without permission, the publisher argued fair use. The use was for profit, and the entire picture was used, the court noted, but ruled that the black-and-white reprint of the color photo was unlikely to have a negative impact on the market for the original. "The idea that a thriving market for photographs of Louise Ihlenfeldt and the cow (however dramatically portrayed) actually exists is dubious to say the least," the court ruled.[51] In 1998 a federal judge in Washington state threw out a nearly $700,000 jury award to author Wade Cook after a trial where Cook asserted that motivational writer and speaker Tony Robbins had copied two phrases originated by Cook. The jury decided that Robbins had used the two phrases, "meter drop" and "rolling stocks," as many as 12 times in a workbook he (Robbins) distributed at financial seminars. But Judge Jack Tanner said there was not a scintilla of evidence that the use of these phrases caused any harm at all to plaintiff Cook.[52] In 2002 a federal court in New York ruled that when Web site operator Susan Pitt created a "Dungeon Doll" based on an altered head of a Barbie doll for a story about sexual slavery and torture, the use of Barbie was a fair use chiefly because the erotic dolls were unlikely to affect the market for the original Barbies.[53] And the 2nd U.S. Court of Appeals rejected the claim of negative economic impact made by a company that argued that when the defendant used some of the plaintiff's copyrighted materials to support his criticism of the company, which conducted executive training seminars, this would seriously reduce the demand for the company's service. "If criticisms on the defendants' web sites kill the demand for plaintiff's services, that is the price that, under the First Amendment, must be paid in the open marketplace of ideas," the court said.[54] Of course, if the defendant had used the plaintiff's materials to operate competing training seminars, the case would likely have ended differently.

In evaluating economic impact the court considers not only direct impact, but also the impact that using the copyrighted material might have on some derivative creation. Imagine the hypothetical situation in which a screenwriter, Virginia Miller, uses a Stephen King novel as the basis of a screenplay she prepares. The screenplay contains a great deal of material from the book. In a copyright action King would have difficulty maintaining that Miller's screenplay, in and of itself, had a direct impact on the sale of his novel. Not many screenplays are

---

51. *Baraban* v. *Time Warner Inc.,* 28 M.L.R. 2013 (2000).
52. "Jury Award for Wade Cook Overruled."
53. *Mattel Inc.* v. *P.H.,* 50 N.Y., No. 01 CIV. 1864 (LTS), 10/30/02.
54. *NXIVM Corp.* v. *Ross Inst.,* 2d Cir., 03-7952, 4/24/04.

sold on the retail market. But clearly, should Miller sell her screenplay to a motion picture producer, this action would probably deprive King of the likelihood that he could sell his own screenplay based on the novel. King would lose a derivative right, the right of an author to market a creation derived from the original work.

In the mid-1990s the Carol Publishing Group published "The Seinfeld Aptitude Test," a trivia book based on material contained in various episodes of the "Seinfeld" TV program. When sued by Castle Rock Entertainment for copyright infringement, Carol Publishing raised fair use as a defense, arguing first that the book just contained a collection of uncopyrightable facts from the TV program and second that the publication of the book had no impact on the market value of the television show. Judge Sonia Sotomayor rejected the first argument by noting that "Seinfeld is fiction. Both the 'facts' in various Seinfeld episodes and the expression of those facts, are the plaintiff's creation." The only unprotected facts in the show were the actors' real names, the names of the director and producer, and the number of seasons the show has run, she added. With regard to impact on the market value of the work, the judge reminded the defendants that the book was a derivative work and its publication deprived the plaintiffs of the opportunity to sell a similar work. The plaintiff controls these rights, she said.[55]

Another case involved professional photographer Art Rogers, who took a picture of a man, his wife and their eight German Shepherd puppies. He displayed the photo and ultimately had it published as a postcard that was sold in card shops. Artist Jeff Koons bought a copy of the postcard, tore off the copyright notice, and sent it to an Italian art studio with instructions to make four exact polychromed wood sculptures of the scene depicted in the photo. The lab complied and Koons sold three of the four sculptures for more than $350,000. Rogers sued, but Koons claimed his work was a parody of the original photo, an attempt to point out the banality of contemporary American society. The 2nd U.S. Circuit Court of Appeals rejected this argument as well as Koons' assertion that his sculpture would not have an impact on the market for Rogers' photograph. Although the two pieces of art are not in direct competition, Koons' unauthorized use of the photo deprived Rogers of the potential income he could earn by selling the right to reproduce the photo to another sculptor, the court ruled.[56] He lost the opportunity of the sale of a derivative right.

FACTORS TO BE CONSIDERED IN DETERMINING FAIR USE

1. The purpose and character of the use
2. The nature of the copyrighted work
3. The amount and substantiality of the portion used in relation to the copyrighted work as a whole
4. The effect of the use on the potential market for or value of the copyrighted work

55. *Castle Rock Entertainment* v. *Carol Publishing Group Inc.,* DC SNY 95 CIV. 0775 (SS), 2/27/97.
56. *Rogers* v. *Koons,* 960 F. 2d 301 (1992).

APPLICATION OF THE CRITERIA

When a court is faced with a defendant who claims fair use, it must apply the four criteria to the facts in the case. A decision by the 9th U.S. Court of Appeals provides a good example of how the criteria might be applied. When a Los Angeles jury in 1992 acquitted four police officers accused of beating a black man, Rodney King, the verdict sparked rioting in the California city. More than 50 people were killed, 2,000 injured and nearly 7,000 arrested. An indelible incident from that rioting was the beating of Reginald Denny by a mob of rioters. Pictures of a man named Damien Williams throwing a brick at Denny's head were broadcast continually. The Los Angeles News Service, an independent video news-gathering service, owned the rights to the nine minutes of video and licensed it for limited use. A subsidiary of CBS, Group W, used portions of the video without permission, as a short teaser before its broadcast of the trial of Damien Williams on Court TV. It also incorporated the brick-throwing footage in an introductory montage of video clips for its television program, "Prime Time Justice." In the copyright suit that followed, CBS argued that use of the video was a fair use. The trial court granted a summary judgment in favor of CBS.

What was the purpose and character of the use? The use was largely commercial—the promotion of Court TV coverage. But the use in the montage was a transformative use (see page 585), and the use before the trial was closely associated with news reporting. Despite the commercial nature of the cablecast, these uses have aspects about them that distinguish them from pure infringement, the court said, and this slightly favors the defendant. What was the nature of the material used? The video clips were informational, factual, and this favors Court TV as well. Only a small amount of the nine-minute video was used, but it was the heart of the film, the scene showing Williams throwing the brick at Denny. Weighing the brevity of the portion against its significance, the court said the third factor was neutral, not favoring either party. What was the effect on the market for continued licensing of this video by the Los Angles News Service? Small, if any, the court concluded. The parties worked in different markets; there was no competition between them to show riot coverage or any breaking news. Based on this assessment, three factors favor Court TV, especially the second factor. This makes the use a fair use.[57]

SUMMARY	While the copyright statute gives the author or owner of a copyrighted work an exclusive monopoly over the use of that work, the law recognizes that in some instances other persons ought to be able to copy portions of a protected work. No liability will attach to such copying if the use is what the law calls a "fair use."

A court will consider four factors when determining whether a specific use is fair use:

1. What is the purpose of the use? Why was the material copied? Was it a commercial use or for nonprofit educational purpose? Was the use intended to further the public interest in some way?

57. *Los Angeles News Service* v. *CBS Broadcasting Inc.,* 30 M.L.R. 2473 (2002).

2. What is the nature of the copyrighted work? Is it a consumable item such as a workbook, or is it a work more likely to be borrowed from, such as a newspaper or magazine article? Is the copyrighted work in print and available for sale? Has the work been previously published or is it unpublished?

3. How much of the copyrighted work was used in relation to the entire copyrighted work? Was it a small amount of a large work? Or was it a large portion of a small work?

4. What impact does the use have on the potential market or value of the copyrighted work? Has the use of the material diminished the chances for sale of the original work? Or is the use unrelated to the value or sale of the copyrighted material?

Although a court considers each of these items closely, most courts tend to give extra weight to item 4. In a close ruling the impact on the market or value of the copyrighted work often becomes the most crucial question.

COPYRIGHT PROTECTION AND INFRINGEMENT

Until 1989 when the provisions of the Berne Convention (see page 571) became applicable to American copyright law, a work would not be protected from infringement unless it contained a **copyright notice.** Failure to affix a notice meant the automatic loss of most copyright protection. Under international law, however, the affixing of a copyright notice is not required to protect a work. Once a work is created it is protected. American law now states that a copyright notice "may" be placed on works that are publicly distributed. The U.S. Copyright office, however, still strongly urges creators to include notice on all their works. Copyright law protects the "innocent infringer" from liability for infringement. Someone who copies a work that does not contain a notice could claim an innocent infringement, that is, could argue that she did not realize the work she copied was actually protected by copyright. Although the absence of notice doesn't guarantee a finding of innocent infringement, putting notice on a work eliminates the possibility of an innocent infringement defense. Placing a proper notice on the work is simply prudent behavior.

COPYRIGHT NOTICE

A copyright notice should contain the word "Copyright," the abbreviation "Copr." or the symbol © (the letter *C* within a circle; the symbol ℗ is used on phonorecords). The year of publication must also be included in the notice. For periodicals the date supplied is the date of publication. For books the date is the year in which the book is first offered for sale (e.g., a book printed in November or December 2005 to go on sale January 2006 should carry a 2006 copyright). The notice must also contain the name of the copyright holder or owner. Most authorities recommend that both the word "Copyright" and the symbol © be used, since the use of the symbol is required to meet the standards of the international copyright agreements. The symbol © protects the work from piracy in most foreign countries. A copyright notice should look something like this:

> Copyright © 2007 by Jane Adams

The copyright notice can be placed anywhere that it "can be visually perceived" on all publicly distributed copies.

The copyright notice can be placed anywhere that it "can be visually perceived" on all publicly distributed copies. (The rules are different for sound recordings, which by nature cannot be visually perceived.) The Copyright Office of the Library of Congress has issued rules that implement the statutory description that the notice be visually perceptible. For example, the rules list eight different places where a copyright notice might be put in a book, including the title page, the page immediately following the title page, either side of the front cover, and so forth. For photographs, a copyright notice label can be affixed to the back or front of a picture or on any mounting or framing to which the photographs are *permanently* attached.*

The law also provides that omission of the proper notice does not destroy copyright protection for the work if the notice is omitted from only a relatively small number of copies, if an effort is made within five years to correct the omission, or if the notice is omitted in violation of the copyright holder's express requirement that as a condition of publication the work carry a copyright notice.

At the same time, the law protects persons who copy a work on which the copyright notice was inadvertently omitted. Such an innocent infringer incurs no liability—cannot be sued—unless this infringement continues beyond the time notice is received that the work has been copyrighted.

REGISTRATION

Under the law, once a work is created and fixed in a tangible medium it is protected by copyright. Putting notice on the work is not required, but strongly advised. The work is then protected for the life of the author plus 70 years. However, before a copyright holder can sue for infringement under the law, the copyrighted work must be registered with the federal government. To register a work the author or owner must do three things:

1. Fill out the proper registration form. The type of form varies, depending on the kind of work being registered. The forms are available from the Information and Publications Section, Copyright Office, Library of Congress, Washington, D.C. 20559. Registration forms for some kinds of material are available through the Internet.

*The Copyright Office has available a myriad of booklets regarding all matters relating to copyright law, including how to affix a proper copyright notice. Inquiries can be sent to the Copyright Office, Library of Congress, 101 Independence Ave. S.E., Washington, D.C. 20559-6000. The Copyright Office also has a Web site that provides similar information: lcweb.loc.gov/copyright/.

2. Pay a $30 fee.
3. Deposit two complete copies of the work with the Copyright Office. (One complete copy is all that is required for unpublished works.)

The statute gives an author or owner 90 days to register a work. What happens if the work is still not registered after 90 days and an infringement takes place? The owner can still register the work and bring suit. But a successful plaintiff in such a suit cannot win statutory damages (see page 612) or win compensation for attorney fees. It is best to get into the habit of registering a work as soon as it is published or broadcast. Courts are of at least two minds regarding when a work is officially registered. Some courts have said a work is not registered—prohibiting a court from exercising jurisdiction in a case—until a certificate of registration is actually issued by the Copyright Office.[58] Other courts have ruled that official registration begins once the registration application has been mailed to the Copyright Office.[59]

INFRINGEMENT

Litigating intellectual property lawsuits has become a burgeoning cottage industry in the United States as the Muses of the creators of books, films, songs, articles and photos are seemingly unable to keep up with the insatiable appetite of the mass media for new products. A careful newspaper reader will routinely see references to new infringement actions. Most of these lawsuits don't amount to much, but they all play havoc with film producers, book publishers and others. In the spring of 2001 a woman named Nancy Stouffer sued author J.K. Rowling and the publishers of the celebrated Harry Potter books. Stouffer claimed that much earlier she had published a series of books about a bespectacled boy named Larry Potter, books that feature a set of characters called "muggles." For the uninitiated, muggles are also characters in the Harry Potter stories. Stouffer's attorneys claimed that Rowling had pirated the term, and because the Harry Potter books are so popular, the market for Stouffer's muggle merchandise dried up.[60] In September 2002 a federal judge rejected the infringement claim, saying he found only minimal similarities between the Harry Potter books and books written by Stouffer. In addition, the court found that the plaintiff had submitted fraudulent claims and lied in testimony.[61] But like the book series, the legal saga of Harry Potter continues. J.K. Rowling brought suit seven months later against a Dutch publisher, Byblos, claiming that books about an orphan named Tanya Grotter who has magical powers and a funny mark on her face are infringing on her copyright.

Persons who believe their exclusive right to control the use of a copyrighted work has been violated will sue for infringement. The federal copyright statute does not actually define infringement. The law simply states that anyone who violates any of the "exclusive rights" of the copyright holder is guilty of an infringement of copyright. Courts that litigate copyright cases seem to focus most often on three criteria to determine whether a particular use is an infringement (see following boxed text). A brief outline of each of these three points follows.

58. See *Goebel* v. *Manis,* 39 F. Supp. 2d 1318 (1999), for example.
59. *Denenberg* v. *Berman,* D. Neb. No. 4: 02CV7, 7/23/02; and *Well-Made Toy Mfg. Corp.* v. *Goffa Intern Corp.,* 210 F. Supp. 2d 147 (2002), for example.
60. Kirkpatrick, "Harry Potter."
61. "In a Plagiarism Case."

Source: Hulton Archive/Getty Images

NBC was sued by a man who claimed he had given the network the idea for "The Cosby Show" years before the series appeared on the network. But a federal court ruled that the plaintiff's idea for such a show was not original enough to be protected by copyright.

▮ Is the copyright on the plaintiff's work valid? While this inquiry will look at matters such as the proper registration of the work, the heart of this examination is to determine whether the copyrighted work is an original work that can be protected by copyright.

▮ Did the defendant have access to the plaintiff's work prior to the alleged infringement?

▮ Are the two works the same or substantially similar?

Originality of the Plaintiff's Work

The copyright on the plaintiff's work must be valid before a successful infringement suit can be maintained. As has been previously noted, a work that is not original cannot be protected by copyright. When a work is initially copyrighted there is no government assessment of whether it is original and can be legitimately copyrighted. The question of originality only arises if a lawsuit ensues. A central question, then, in many infringement suits is whether the plaintiff's work is original, or is the plaintiff attempting to bring suit on the basis of the theft of material that cannot be legally copyrighted because it lacks originality or novelty?

History, for example, exists for all to use in a book or a story. Margaret Alexander brought an infringement suit against Alex Haley, claiming that he had copied portions of her novel "Jubilee" and her pamphlet "How I Wrote Jubilee" when he wrote and published his successful novel "Roots" in 1976. But the court noted that most of what Alexander claimed Haley had stolen was history—the story of the slave culture in the United States—or material in the public domain, such as folktales about early American black culture. "Where common sources exist for the alleged similarities, or the material that is similar is not original with the plaintiff, there is no infringement," the court ruled.[62]

An NBC employee sued the network, arguing that he had originally proposed the concept for the highly successful "Bill Cosby Show" in 1980, some four years before the television program premiered. At that time NBC said it was not interested in the idea, the plaintiff said. But the court said that there was really nothing original in the concept proposed by plaintiff Hwesu Murray or in the Cosby show itself, for that matter. It merely combined two ideas that had been circulating for years: a family situation comedy, and the casting of blacks in nonstereotypical roles. The portrayal of a nonstereotypical black family in a half-hour show was a breakthrough in television broadcasting, the court noted, comparing the Cosby program with shows like "The Jeffersons," "Good Times," "Diff'rent Strokes," and "Sanford and Son," all of which featured blacks in fairly stereotypical roles. But the fact that such a show had never before been broadcast does not necessarily mean that the idea for the program itself was novel. "Whereas here, an idea consists in essence of nothing more than a variation on a basic theme—in this case the family situation comedy—novelty cannot be found."[63]

The author of a book entitled "Fort Apache" sued the producers of the film "Fort Apache—The Bronx" for copyright infringement. Both the book and the movie focused on the 41st Precinct of the New York City Police Department. Police officers had dubbed the South Bronx precinct Fort Apache because of the high incidence of violent crime in the area. Thomas Walker, a former police officer who was assigned to the 41st Precinct for 15 months, wrote and published his book in 1976. The book was a series of stories about his work in the precinct, a narrative moving from one anecdote to the next with no real plot. The film, on the other hand, was intensely plotted, with several interrelated story lines all taking place at once. Walker claimed the producers of the film had stolen his material, but a U.S. Court of Appeals disagreed. "To be sure, the book and the film share an identical setting, and police officers are central characters in both works," the court noted. "But the South Bronx and the 41st Precinct are real places known to the public through media coverage. Accordingly, the notion of telling a police story that takes place there cannot be copyrightable," the court ruled. The parts of the film that were similar to the book were not original with the book's author.[64]

Access

The second dimension of an infringement suit is access: The plaintiff must convince the court that the defendant had access to the copyrighted work. An opportunity to copy has to exist.

62. *Alexander* v. *Haley,* 460 F. Supp. 40 (1978).
63. *Murray* v. *NBC,* 844 F. 2d 988 (1988).
64. *Walker* v. *Time-Life Films,* 784 F. 2d 44 (1986).

If plaintiffs cannot prove that the so-called literary pirate had a chance to see and read the work, they are hard-pressed to prove piracy. As Judge Learned Hand once wrote:

> If by some magic a man who had never known it were to compose anew Keats's, "Ode on a Grecian Urn," he would be an 'author' and if he copyrighted it, others might not copy that poem, though they might of course copy Keats's.[65]

Translating Hand's reference to John Keats' early 19th-century poem into contemporary terms, consider this hypothetical situation. A young woman, who has lived all her life on a deserted island, with no exposure to outside influences, manages to write and then publish an exact duplicate of John Grisham's novel "The Last Juror." Grisham would be hard-pressed to win a copyright infringement case because he would be unable to show that the young writer had access to his work. Obviously, such a scenario is unlikely to occur. But it makes the point. The plaintiff must prove not simply that the two works are the same, but that the defendant stole his work. And to do that there must be proof that the defendant had access to the stolen work.

There must be proof that the defendant had access to the stolen work.

In 1998 Marion Leon Bea sued Home Box Office, claiming it had infringed on his script for a film called "N and Out" when it made the HBO motion picture "First Time Felon." The similarities between the two scripts were thin, the court noted. But what killed the suit was the plaintiff's inability to prove that HBO had access to his script before "First Time Felon" was produced.[66] Failure to prove that the defendant had access to a copyrighted book was also fatal to a lawsuit brought by Sonya Jason against the writers and producers of the 1978 film "Coming Home." Defendants Jane Fonda and others stated that their film was conceived in the late 1960s, that a first draft of the screenplay was completed by late 1973 and was revised in 1977. Jason's book, "Concomitant Soldier," was first printed in April 1974. Only 1,100 copies were printed. About 500 copies were sold in New Jersey, 100 were sold through the plaintiff's church, 200 copies were returned to the printer because they were defective, and the remaining copies were sold in southern California. Jason claimed that a copy of the book might have been given to Nancy Dowd, a screenwriter for the film, but there was no evidence that Dowd or anyone else connected with the film had seen the book. Jason was only able to prove that several hundred copies of "Concomitant Soldier" were sold in southern California where Fonda, Dowd and others associated with the film lived and worked. "That level of availability creates no more than a 'bare possibility' that defendants may have had access to plaintiff's book," the court said. "In and of itself, such a bare possibility is insufficient to create a genuine issue of whether defendants copied plaintiff's book."[67]

Copying and Substantial Similarity

The final factor the court will consider is whether the defendant copied the plaintiff's work. In some cases evidence of such copying is irrefutable. The defendant has dubbed copies of a videocassette or CD, or has reprinted a short story or a song lyric. In other instances it is a bit

---

65. *Sheldon v. Metro-Goldwyn-Mayer Pictures,* 81 F. 2d 49 (1939).
66. *Bea v. Home Box Office,* 26 M.L.R. 2373 (1998).
67. *Jason v. Fonda et al.,* 526 F. Supp. 774 (1981).

more complicated. A photo looks a lot like a copyrighted picture, for example. In these cases judges must often take on the role of art critic to flesh out the differences between two seemingly identical works. In 1993 Random House commissioned Jack Leigh to photograph the Bird Girl statue in the Bonaventure Cemetery in Savannah, Ga., to use on the cover of a novel it was publishing called "Midnight in the Garden of Good and Evil." The book was successful and the photo became famous. When Warner Brothers made the book into a film, it wanted to use a similar photo in its advertising for the motion picture. But the owner of the statue, which had become famous because of the Leigh photo, had removed the object from the cemetery. With the statue owner's permission, the film studio had a replica crafted, took it to the cemetery, and had it photographed for promotion of the movie. When the movie came out, Leigh sued for copyright infringement. Warner Brothers had not used Leigh's picture; but it had generated a photo that was remarkably similar to the original. Judges at the 11th U.S. Circuit Court of Appeals had to analyze the similarities and differences between the two. There was a difference in the contrast of the lighting; the statue was smaller and more distant in the Warner Brothers photo; the movie poster picture had a green/orange tint; and there was a Celtic cross on the new statue. But both photos were taken from the same low angle; hanging Spanish moss bordered both photos; the statue was in the center of both pictures; the light source is from above in both shots; and the remainder of the cemetery is obscured. In this case the court ruled that there were sufficient similarities to preclude a summary judgment for Warner Brothers and sent the case back for a jury trial.[68]

More often than not, however, direct or literal copying is not an issue. In these cases the defendant is not accused of taking a particular line or segment of a work, but of appropriating "the fundamental essence or structure of the work." There must be more than minor similarities between the two works; they must be *substantially similar.* But this is another instance in which it is easier to state a rule than to apply it. How can you determine whether two works are substantially similar? Courts use a variety of tests to determine substantial similarity, but virtually all the tests focus on two aspects of the work.[69] The courts will first ask whether the general idea or general theme of the works is the same. If the general idea of the two works is not similar, there is no infringement. But if the general idea is substantially similar, then the court looks at how the idea is expressed, how the theme is carried out. For example, the themes of the 1953 Alan Ladd film "Shane" and the 1985 Clint Eastwood movie "Pale Rider" are quite similar. Good people in a western town are being pushed around by bad men. Mysterious stranger comes to town and cleans out the villains. Good gunfighter rides off into the sunset. End of movie. But is this theme expressed in the same way in both films? Not really. The townspeople are different; the villains are different; the slight romantic subplot is different; even the leading characters are different. The expression of the common theme is not substantially similar. Let's examine how these criteria were applied in some actual copyright cases.

Warner Brothers, which owns the film rights to "Superman," sued ABC in the early 1980s for broadcast of the network series "The Greatest American Hero." The general idea of both the "Superman" films and the ABC series was similar—a character, who wears a red and

---

68. *Leigh* v. *Warner Brothers Inc.,* 212 F. 3d 1210 (2000).
69. See, for example, *Sid and Marty Krofft Television Productions* v. *McDonald's Corporation,* 562 F. 2d 1157 (1977) and *Apple Computer Inc.* v. *Microsoft Corp.,* 35 F. 3d 1435 (1994).

blue suit with a cape and is able to fly, battles the forces of evil. But the court ruled that Warner Brothers could not "claim a protected interest in the theme of a man dressed in a cape and tights who has the power to fly, resist bullets, crash through walls, break handcuffs, etc." The plaintiff must show that the concrete expression of the Superman idea has been appropriated. Warner Brothers could not do this. The characters in "Superman" and "The Greatest American Hero" were quite different. The hero of the ABC program was Ralph Hinckley, an ordinary man who reluctantly takes on abnormal abilities through a magic costume and is comically inept. Superman is naturally endowed with these powers, which he wields with grace and confidence. As a person Hinckley is the antithesis of the strong Superman character, the court said. In some ways the ABC show was a parody of Superman. "As a comedy that parodies American superheroes," Judge Motley wrote, "'The Greatest American Hero' has a very different appeal from Superman, a real superhero, and plaintiffs have not sufficiently proven that it will reduce demand for movies and programs about Superman, and products bearing the Superman image."[70]

The U.S. Court of Appeals for the 9th Circuit was asked to determine whether writer/director Michael Crichton had stolen a screen treatment for his 1978 film "Coma," which was based on a book by Robin Cook. Plaintiff Ted Berkik in 1968 wrote a 54-page screen treatment for a story he called "Reincarnation, Inc." Crichton apparently saw the screen treatment but did not use it 10 years later when he wrote the screenplay for "Coma." Berkik alleged that both the film and Robin Cook's book were taken from his screen treatment.

The stories have certain similarities, the court noted. Both deal with criminal organizations that murder healthy young people and then remove and sell their vital organs to wealthy people in need of organ transplants. And in both stories, courageous young medical professionals investigate and finally expose the criminal organization. But these similarities are at a high level of generality. When one looks at the manner in which these similar ideas are expressed in the two works, the similarity ends. The plots of the two stories develop differently; the settings are different. "Coma" is replete with medical terminology and is an old-fashioned detective story; "Reincarnation, Inc." is more of a romance. Yes, there are some similarities, but general ideas are not protected. Nor are situations and incidents that flow naturally from a basic plot premise, so-called *scènes à faire*. "These familiar scenes [depictions of the small miseries of domestic life or romantic frolics at the beach] and themes are among the very staples of modern American literature and film. The common use of such stock material cannot raise a trial issue of fact on the plaintiff's copyright claim," the appellate court ruled. "It merely reminds us that in Hollywood, as in the life of real men generally, there is only rarely anything new under the sun."[71]

A federal court in Pennsylvania ruled that a playwright had infringed on a copyrighted novel when he wrote a drama about Thomas Jefferson and his alleged romantic relationship with a slave he owned. Allegations that Jefferson was romantically involved with a woman named Sally Hemings were first aired by his political opponents in 1802. Biographers of the third U.S. president have variously rejected and accepted these charges. In 1974 author Fawn Brodie published a sensational biography of Jefferson, which she subtitled "An Intimate

---

70. *Warner Bros.* v. *ABC,* 523 F. Supp. 611 (1981).
71. *Berkik* v. *Crichton,* 761 F. 2d 1289 (1985).

History," and gave a full airing to the allegations, which she suggested she believed. Five years later Barbara Chase-Riboud wrote "Sally Hemings: A Novel," a work of fiction that explored in considerable detail the woman's supposed love affair with the man from Monticello. Three years later Granville Burgess wrote a play based on the same subject, "Dusky Sally." The play was about to be produced when Chase-Riboud sent letters to Burgess threatening a copyright suit. The playwright went to court seeking a declaratory judgment that "Dusky Sally" did not infringe upon the copyrighted novel.

Burgess argued that both works were based on history, and history cannot be copyrighted. But Chase-Riboud disagreed, noting that little historical data about the Jefferson-Hemings relationship existed and that the play was instead based largely on her work of fiction. Both works did use the few historical facts known about the supposed relationship, but Judge Robert Kelly said that beyond that there was a substantial similarity in the two works. "Chase-Riboud's assertion that other than the few facts which are known, practically everything about Sally Hemings, which appears in both works, was 'invented' by Chase-Riboud is not much of an overstatement," the jurist said. In both works, for example, Jefferson initiates the sexual relationship while in Europe on the night before he is to leave on a trip. In both works Sally Hemings seems somewhat resigned to his romantic advances. In the novel she says a prayer to herself in this scene. Stage directions for the play tell the character playing Sally Hemings to close her eyes, perhaps in prayer. It is known that Jefferson did injure his wrist while in Paris in 1787. But both works contain a scene where the slave is massaging the future president's wrist, a kind of prologue to the sexual relationship. Many other similarities existed as well, the court ruled.[72]

It is not easy to prove infringement of copyright; yet surprisingly, a large number of suits are settled each year in favor of plaintiffs. Most of these cases are settled out of court. In such instances the obvious theft of the material would generally appall an honest person. An individual who works to be creative in fashioning a story or a play or a piece of art usually has little to fear. The best and simplest way to avoid a suit for infringement is simply to do your own work, to be original.

COPYRIGHT INFRINGEMENT AND THE INTERNET

The law regulating mass media has had to adapt to changes in media technology many times in the past 215 years. When the nation's first copyright law was adopted, printed material comprised the mass media. But since then, the law has been forced to cope with photography, radio, motion pictures, sound recordings, television, audio- and videotaping, photocopying, computer programs, CD-ROM, and so on. But no technology has challenged the law to the extent the Internet has. By its very nature the new medium lends itself to the theft of the work of others. As one legal expert noted, digitized information can be copied quickly, easily and cheaply, and the copy is every bit as good as the original. Once the information is copied, it can be easily distributed via the Web to receivers who can make their own copies of the material and further distribute it: an almost endless chain.[73]

---

72. *Burgess* v. *Chase-Riboud,* 765 F. Supp. 233 (1991).
73. Johnson-Laird, "Exploring the Information Superhighway."

The ease of copying and distribution is only one problem. Many Internet users apparently don't believe that other peoples' works should enjoy copyright protection. When cartoonist Gary Larson pleaded with Web users to stop duplicating his "The Far Side" cartoons on the Internet, a substantial number of users replied that they would not cease the practice. "All this copyright infringement enforcing ticks me off," one user responded. "What is the Net for if we can't view a Far Side cartoon, or listen to a sound file from the Simpsons," the user asked rhetorically. There have always been people who disdained the notion that a writer or photographer should be able to protect his or her own work. But until the Internet, all that most of these people could do was steal it for themselves: illegally dub a CD or a movie, photocopy a series of short stories. Now it is possible for an individual not only to make the illegal copy, but to distribute it to 100,000 of his or her close friends in a matter of seconds.

The courts have been applying traditional copyright law to these new problems with some success. And some jurists say the application of existing law is all that is required to solve the problems. "New technologies—from television, to video cassette recorders, to digitized transmissions—have all been made to fit within the overall scheme of copyright law and to serve the ends to which copyright was intended to promote," wrote U.S. District Judge Leonie Brinkema. "The Internet is no exception."[74] Other observers say they believe that new laws are needed. An international group, the World Intellectual Property Organization, framed new copyright rules in two treaties in the mid-1990s that give copyright protection to the owners of digitized works. The treaties also provide for the fair-use defense in cyberspace.[75] The United States agreed to abide by these new rules in adopting the Digital Millennium Copyright Act (DMCA) in 1998. But this law went beyond the WIPO treaties and also prevents the circumvention of technological measures that control access to copyrighted works—so-called encryption codes—and outlaws the manufacture, importation or sale of devices used to circumvent such protections. In the summer of 2001, a 27-year-old Russian cryptographer named Dmitry Sklyarov was arrested in Las Vegas after giving a presentation to a convention of computer hackers on ways to decrypt the software used to protect electronic books. Six months later the government agreed to defer the prosecution of Sklyarov in return for his promise to testify against his employer, Elcomsoft, a Russian software company. A basic question in this case and others that spring from this section of the 1998 act is this: Can the government make it a crime to manufacture and sell a device that can be used to circumvent copyright protection if that device can be used for other, legal purposes as well? In 1984 the Supreme Court was asked that question about another technological invention, the video-cassette recorder. Hollywood television production companies sought to stop the sale of the new device in the United States because it could be used to make copies of the copyrighted programs broadcast on television. At that time the Supreme Court ruled that even though some people may use the device illegally, there were numerous legal purposes for the VCR as well. The manufacturer of the machine could not be held liable for those who used the device illegally.[76] But times have changed, people in the entertainment industry argue. Copying protected material has become too easy and can be done too rapidly for rights holders to catch up with the illegal users. It is time to ban the devices. This is a basic legal issue in any case to

---

74. *Religious Technology Center* v. *Lerma,* 24 M.L.R. 2473 (1996).
75. Schiesel, "Global Agreement Reached."
76. *Sony Corp.* v. *Universal City Studios, Inc.,* 464 U.S. 417 (1984).

determine whether software or hardware violates the DMCA. Does the machine or the program that permits illegal activity have functions that are clearly legal as well? Federal courts have upheld the constitutionality of the DMCA.[77] The 2nd U.S. Court of Appeals agreed that computer code is protected by the First Amendment but said a narrowly drawn statute—like the DMCA—would not violate the Constitution. But the issue is far from resolved, as more litigation enters the halls of justice. The law carries criminal penalties, a possible $500,000 fine and a five-year jail sentence. The 1998 law also exempts Internet service providers from copyright liability for simply transmitting information users have put on the Internet, and it imposes a compulsory licensing and royalty scheme for the transmission of music on the Internet similar to the scheme used to collect royalties for the broadcast of music on radio or television.

Prior to the development of interactive computer systems copyright problems were far simpler. Imagine this: John Doe reads a short story in a science fiction magazine, thinks a couple of his friends might enjoy the story, makes two photocopies and passes them along to his buddies. Technically a copyright infringement, but hardly a major problem. With interactive computer systems, however, things become a lot easier for John, and a lot more threatening to the magazine's publisher. John can upload the story into his computer, and then tell his friends that if they want to see it he will send it to them. And his friends can tell other friends, who tell other friends. And before long, the story is in the hands of several hundred people, people who never bought the magazine. Clearly a copyright infringement, and a much bigger problem. This is called file sharing, and it has generated considerable copyright litigation. It affects a wide range of mass media, most notably the motion picture industry, television producers, and the recording business. A brief review of the problems in the music industry will illustrate the issues.

File Sharing

The theft of recorded music via the Internet wasn't a serious problem until the late 1990s because it took too long to download a song. But the development of inexpensive data compression technology solved this problem, and the introduction of MP3 players, which brought this technology within reach of music lovers, resulted in the dramatic growth of illegal music file sharing. The music industry tried to block the manufacture and sale of the MP3 players, but the courts ruled they were simply space shifters, not audio recording devices. "The player merely makes copies in order to render portable . . . files that already reside in a user's hard drive," the court said, comparing the new device to a home video recorder, which the Supreme Court had ruled was legal.[78] (See page 604.)

When the new technology became popular, entrepreneurs provided computer users the means to swap the music files. The most prominent player was Napster, which was promptly sued by the recording industry. The company said it did nothing wrong; it did not collect or store recordings illegally. It simply provided the pathway via software for one Internet user to

---

77. *Universal City Studios Inc.* v. *Corley,* 2d Cir., No. 00-9185, 11/28/01. See also *Felten* v. *Recording Industry Association of America,* D.N.J., No. CV-01-2669 (GEB), 11/27/01.
78. *Recording Industry Association of America* v. *Diamond Multimedia Systems,* 9th Cir., No. 98-56727, 6/15/99.

gain access to music files stored by another user. This was simply like one person buying a CD and allowing a friend to dub a copy of the recording. Napster's attorneys said the company provided the transportation between the two music lovers.

In a short time the downloading of music began to reach massive proportions. Record sales plummeted—for many reasons, but illegal downloading was an important factor. The industry argued in court that what Internet music services were doing in facilitating this exchange—providing the transportation, so to speak—amounted to contributory copyright infringement. In 2001 the 9th U.S. Circuit Court of Appeals agreed with the recording industry and ordered Napster to stop facilitating the free transfer of recorded music.[79] The court ruled that the music service was abetting copyright infringement by its users, who were repeatedly exploiting the recording industry by making unauthorized copies of copyrighted works to avoid the expense of purchasing the authorized copies. The court rejected Napster's argument that the exchange of files between users was a fair use of the protected music. The court ruled that it was not Napster's obligation to prevent any exchange of the record company's copyrighted works. The industry carries the burden of communicating to Napster which works are being infringed on during the exchange. But for all intents and purposes the game was over for Napster, and the music service began signing licensing agreements with recording companies to avoid future litigation.

But the victory by the recording industry over Napster was not the end of the story; more likely it was only the end of the beginning. Other file-sharing services began to proliferate, and the industry began new lawsuits. In the spring of 2003 the industry lost a major case against two file-sharing software programs, StreamCast Networks and Grokster, because, the court said, they were different from Napster.[80] Napster provided a centralized database— the site and the facilities needed for users to find the digital materials, the music, they wanted. When Napster closed down, the file-sharing network disappeared. The two services involved in this suit simply provide the software that permits peer-to-peer file sharing. That is, it gives a pair of users the ability to share the music they already have. The services distribute the software free. They make their money by selling advertising that appears on the screen when the software is opened.

The court ruled that this was not contributory copyright infringement. "Liability for contributory infringement accrues where a defendant has actual—not merely constructive—knowledge of the infringement and a time during which the defendant materially contributes to that infringement," the court said. StreamCast Network and Grokster did not do this. Indeed, if both defendants went out of business today, copyright infringement by StreamCast and Grokster software users would continue unabated, the court noted. The software also permitted computer users to share lots of legally accessible material, such as music in the public domain, or other noncopyrighted work. Because there are numerous legal uses for the software, the product was more like the home video recorder that the Supreme Court had ruled was legal some 20 years earlier. It is the file-sharing users who were breaking the law, the court noted, not the companies that provide the software that permits them to do this.

---

79. 6 E.C.L.R. 144 (2001).
80. *Metro-Goldwyn-Mayer Studios Inc.* v. *Grokster Ltd.,* 259 F. Supp. 2d 1029 (2003).

In August of 2004 the 9th U.S. Court of Appeals affirmed the lower court decision, ruling that the distributors of the peer-to-peer software are not liable for aiding copyright infringement because they do not have the ability to monitor or control how users of their software exchange files.[81] Less than a year later the Supreme Court reversed this ruling. While accepting the notion that in some cases the makers and sellers of peer-to-peer sharing software or equipment (e.g., a videocassette recorder) would be immune from a suit for contributory copyright infringement, a company that is shown to *induce* copyright infringement can be liable even if the products also have lawful uses. Liability depends on showing that the distributor acted "with the object of promoting [the software's] use to infringe copyright." In this case, wrote Justice David Souter for a unanimous court, the record was "replete with evidence" that Grokster and StreamCast Networks "acted with a purpose to cause copyright violations by use of software suitable for illegal use." The high court sent the case back for trial, adding the observation that evidence against the two companies was so strong that the entertainment-industry plaintiffs might be entitled to a summary judgment.[82] In the wake of the ruling Grokster announced it was calling it quits on sharing music files, but StreamCast Networks vowed to fight on in court.

This ruling certainly did not end the problems faced by the recording industry related to file sharing of songs. So the recording industry attacked the actual file sharers as well. Students operating peer-to-peer file sharing services on university campuses and others were targeted. The International Federation of the Phonographic Industry filed more than 7,000 lawsuits in 2004 and reported that it had shut down more than 60,000 illegal music sharing sites.[83] The antipiracy push by the industry was accompanied by the introduction of Apple Computer's iPod digital players. Together these developments spurred the growth of legal file sharing services, which in 2004, accounted for more than 200 million downloads compared with only 20 million the year before. Music file-sharing services like Apple's popular iTunes, a new and legal Napster, Rhapsody, Yahoo and others began working with record companies instead of against them.[84] The recording companies give these services access to their music catalogs. And the file-sharing services pay the recording companies a royalty based on the number of the label's songs that have been downloaded by their customers, who pay for the music. The royalties are then distributed by the recording company to the artists and song publishers.

The growth of the legal file-sharing services has at least somewhat ameliorated the problem of illegal downloading. But exactly how much it has helped is clearly debatable. People in the record industry say the theft of copyrighted music continues unabated and it is still hurting the industry. Illegal downloaders often justify their actions by pointing out that most recorded music is put out by a small number of massive entertainment conglomerates that are highly profitable. Losing a few million dollars here or there really won't hurt. Industry representatives point out that it is not the companies that suffer the most damage, but the artists,

81. *Metro-Goldwyn-Mayer Studios Inc. v. Grokster Ltd.,* 380 F.3d 1154 (2004).
82. *Metro-Goldwyn-Mayer Studios Inc. v. Grokster Ltd.,* 125 S Ct. 2264 (2005).
83. Harmon, "Suit Settled for Students"; "Record Labels to Sue 261 Major Offenders," 34 E.C.L.R. 853 (2003); Holloway, "Recording Industry to Sue;" and Bridis, "Music Industry Gets Serious."
84. Whitley, "Legal Downloads Soar."

Source: © 20th Century Fox/ZUMA/CORBIS

"The Revenge of the Sith" was already illegally available online before the film was released in theaters.

who lose the royalties they should earn for their recordings and sometimes end up losing money on an album or a single after they have paid off all the expenses involved in making and promoting the record.

Both the television and film industries face similar albeit not as extensive problems. Following the model of the recording industry the film industry began cracking down on the Internet pirates who download copyrighted films. Government officials reported that Episode III of the Star Wars series, "The Revenge of the Sith," was downloaded illegally even before the film was commercially released in May 2005, and more than 10,000 times in the first 24 hours the film was in the theaters. In May 2005 federal investigators shut down one Web site—Elite Torrents—that they said was engaging in high-tech piracy by letting people download copies of movies and other copyright material free of charge.[85] President Bush signed a law in April 2005 that set penalties of up to 10 years in prison for anyone caught distributing a movie or song before its commercial release.

The TV industry is trying to solve its problems by embedding so-called digital flags in its programs. The industry has asked the government to require that all new consumer electronics equipment capable of receiving over-the-air digital signals—digital televisions, computers equipped with TV tuner cards and other devices—include technology that will recognize the broadcast flags and prevent the content from being distributed to other devices unless they too contain the same technology. The Federal Communications Commission (FCC) adopted such rules in 2004, but in May 2005 a U.S. Court of Appeals threw out the rules, saying the agency had exceeded its authority in requiring such technology in digital televisions and consumer devices.[86] Opponents of the rules argue that the FCC requirement would drive up the cost of the new digital TV sets, and also prevent consumers from recording and viewing programs in ways permitted by the copyright laws. Congress does have the authority to require such anti-copying technology on new products, but no action had yet been taken as this was chapter was prepared.

85. Sherman, "Revenge of the Government."
86. Bridis, "Rules Blocked on TV," American Library Ass'n. v. FCC, 33 M.L.R. 2459 (2005).

The file-sharing dilemma is a scenario that is still playing out. And the law of copyright is rife with other problems related to the Internet as well. The uploading, distribution and downloading of copyrighted photographs is a serious matter—especially from publications like Playboy where the photos (as well as the serious articles and essays) entice most people to buy the magazine.[87] The question of whether Internet service providers (ISPs) are liable for infringement when they act as a passive conduit for photos posted by their customers is an emerging issue, with at least one court ruling that the ISPs were not liable under the federal copyright law.[88]

SUMMARY

To protect the copyright of a work, the author or owner should give proper notice and register the work with the government. A proper copyright notice looks like this:

Copyright © 2007 by Jane Adams (use the symbol Ⓟ for phonorecords)

Notice must be placed where it can be visually perceived. To gain the full benefits of the law, a work must be registered with the Copyright Office in the Library of Congress as well. The proper registration form along with $30 and two complete copies of the work must be sent to the Register of Copyrights.

When a plaintiff sues for infringement of copyright, the court will consider three important criteria. First, is the plaintiff's work original? If the plaintiff has attempted to copyright material that legitimately belongs in the public domain, the plaintiff cannot sue for infringement of copyright. Second, did the defendant have access to the plaintiff's work? There must be some evidence that the defendant viewed or heard the copyrighted work before the alleged infringement took place. Finally, is there evidence that the defendant actually copied the plaintiff's work? If no such evidence exists, are the two works substantially similar? In examining this last issue, the court seeks to determine whether the ideas in the two works are similar. If the general idea of the two works is similar, is the expression of these ideas similar as well? Problems of copyright infringement via the Internet are just beginning to be litigated, with both traditional copyright law and new statutes being applied by the courts.

FREE-LANCING AND COPYRIGHT

What rights does a free-lance journalist, author or photographer hold with regard to stories or pictures that are sold to publishers? The writer or photographer is the creator of the work; he or she owns the story or the photograph. Consequently, as many rights as such free-lancers choose to relinquish can be sold or given to a publisher. Beginning writers and photographers

87. *Playboy Enterprises Inc.* v. *Starware Publishers Corp.,* 900 F. Supp. 433 (1995) and *Playboy Enterprises Inc.* v. *George Frena et al.,* 839 F. Supp. 1552 (1993).
88. *CoStar Group Inc.* v. *LoopNet Inc.,* 4th Cir., No. 03-1911, 6/21/04.

often do not have much choice but to follow the policy of the book or magazine publisher. Authors whose works are in demand, however, can retain most rights to the material for their future benefit. Most publishers have established policies on exactly what rights they purchase when they decide to buy a story or photograph or drawing. The annual edition of "The Writer's Market" is the best reference guide for the free-lancer. The boxed text lists some of the rights that publishers might buy.

1. All rights: The creator sells complete ownership of the story or photograph.
2. First serial rights: The buyer has the right to use the piece of writing or picture for the first time in a periodical published anywhere in the world. But the publisher can use it only once, and then the creator can sell it to someone else.
3. First North American serial rights: The rights are the same as those provided in number 2, except the publisher buys the right to publish the material first in North America, not anywhere in the world.
4. Simultaneous rights: The publisher buys the right to print the material at the same time other periodicals print the material. All the publishers, however, must be aware that simultaneous publication will occur.
5. One-time rights: The publisher purchases the right to use a piece just one time, and there is no guarantee that it has not been published elsewhere first.

It is a common practice for publishers to buy all rights to a story or photograph but to agree to reassign the rights to the creator after publication. In such cases the burden of initiating the reassignment rests with the writer or photographer, who must request reassignment immediately following publication. The publisher signs a transfer of rights to the creator, and the creator should record this transfer of rights with the Copyright Office within two or three weeks. When this transaction has taken place, the creator can then resell the material.

The sale of subsidiary or additional rights to publishers by free-lance writers has become far more complicated and more serious with the technological developments of the past decade. The growth of huge databases on CD-ROM and in computer memories accessible through the Internet has magnified the consequences for both the writers and photographers and the publishers. There is considerable money to be made on all sides. Six writers who sold work to The New York Times, Newsday, Sports Illustrated and other publications objected when these publications sold the contents of the newspapers and magazines to the Mead Corp., which operates the LexisNexis database, and to University Microfilms, which produces The New York Times on Disc. The writers argued they deserved at least a royalty payment. But a U.S. District Court ruled in favor of publishers in a lawsuit initiated by the free-lance writers. U.S. copyright law, the court said, gave the owners of a collective work (like a newspaper or magazine) the right to reproduce and distribute any "revision" of that collective work without the permission of the contributors to that work. So when a free-lance writer sold an article to a newspaper, the writer was also in effect giving the publisher of the paper the right to resell the article for inclusion on a CD-ROM or a database.[89] Two years later the 2nd U.S. Circuit Court of Appeals disagreed. The judges said that while a newspaper or magazine publisher did have the right to sell a revised edition of such a publication, the law was intended to apply to later editions of the newspaper or reissues of the magazine. Databases and CD-ROMs are not revised editions of the original publications. Databases contain many articles, the court noted, that may be retrieved according to criteria unrelated to the particular edition of the magazine or newspaper in which the articles first appear.[90] In June 2001 the Supreme Court sustained the appellate court ruling. Justice Ruth Bader Ginsburg, who wrote the opinion in the 7-2 ruling, said that publishers' "encompassing construction" of their republication rights was simply unacceptable. The massive databases, which include many published issues, "no more constitutes a revision of each constituent edition than a 400-page novel quoting a sonnet in passing would represent a revision of that poem," the justice wrote. Electronic databases are not simply modern versions of old-fashioned microfilm records, she added.[91]

But the *Tasini* ruling did not answer all questions regarding subsequent use of a free-lancer's material. After the U.S. Court of Appeals ruling in *Tasini,* but three months before the Supreme Court ruling, the 11th U.S. Court of Appeals ruled that the National Geographic Society (NGS) had infringed on a group of free-lance photographers' copyrights when it published their work in a 30-disc CD-ROM version ("The Complete National Geographic") of the magazine. This electronic version contained every page of every issue published since 1888, so it was essentially like a huge bound volume of all the magazines. The NGS argued that it was simply republishing the original issues, a revision that is permitted under the law. The court disagreed, noting that the electronic edition contained some material not included in the original issues, notably some animated sequences and special interactive software. This was a new work, and violated the copyright of the photographers.[92]

But more than two years later a U.S. District Court ruled in an opposite fashion in a case involving the same NSG CD-ROM disc set in a lawsuit brought by a different set of free-lance photographers. The court said the 11th Circuit had misread the law, which was clarified by the Supreme Court's *Tasini* decision. So long as an individual's work (the photographer's pictures) appears in its original context in the new version, it qualifies as a permissible reproduction or revision of a collective work. What distinguishes a revision from an entirely different work is the manner in which the free-lancers' work is presented to the user, the court said. In this case, the CD-ROM contains exactly the same pages as appeared in the original print editions of the magazine. The addition of the software, the animated opening sequence and music does not fundamentally change the manner in which the work is presented.[93] The 2nd U.S. Court of Appeals affirmed this decision in March 2005.[94]

89. *Tasini* v. *The New York Times,* 972 F. Supp. 804 (1997).
90. *Tasini* v. *The New York Times,* 192 F. 3d 356 (1999).
91. *New York Times Co.* v. *Tasini,* 121 S. Ct. 2381 (2001).
92. *Greenberg* v. *National Geographic Society,* 244 F. 3d 1267 (2001).
93. *Faulkner* v. *National Geographic Society,* 294 F. Supp. 2d 523 (2003).
94. *Faulkner* v. *Mindscape Inc.,* 402 F. 3d 304 (2005).

Finally, a federal court in New York ruled in 2001 that the basic rights granted by an author to a publisher that include the right to publish a work in book form do not include the right to publish the work as an interactive e-book. A separate agreement would be needed to permit the publication of the electronic version of the work. The case was decided under state contract law rather than federal copyright law, but the ruling is regarded as being generally applicable in other jurisdictions. The 2nd U.S. Court of Appeals affirmed this ruling in 2002.[95]

Now, more than ever, writers and photographers should be careful in spelling out the exact rights being offered to a publisher. This clarification should be done in the original query letter offering the material or in the cover letter that accompanies the final product. Contracts should be read carefully, and beginners should be wary of statements included on payment checks. It is not uncommon for a publisher to include a statement on a royalty check to the effect that "the endorsement of this check constitutes a grant of reprint rights to the publisher." In order to cash the check, the writer must agree to grant the reprint rights. In such cases writers should quickly notify the publisher that such an agreement is unacceptable and demand immediate payment for the single use of the story. Other pitfalls too numerous to mention await the inexperienced free-lancer. The best advice is to understand exactly what you are doing at all times during the negotiation of rights. Take nothing for granted; just because you are honest and ethical does not mean everyone else is. And if questions come up, consult a qualified attorney. Legal advice is costly, but it can save a writer or photographer money in the long run.

DAMAGES

Plaintiffs in a copyright suit can ask the court to assess the defendant for any damage they have suffered, plus the profits made by the infringer from pirating the protected work. Damages can be a little bit or a lot. In each case the plaintiff must prove to the court the amount of the loss or the amount of the defendant's profit. But, rather than prove actual damage, the plaintiff can ask the court to assess what are called statutory damages, or damage amounts prescribed by the statute. The smallest statutory award is $750, although in the case of an innocent infringement, the court may use its discretion and lower the damage amount. The highest statutory award is $30,000. However, if the plaintiff can prove that the infringement was committed willfully and repeatedly, the maximum damage award can be as much as $150,000.

In addition, the courts have other powers in a copyright suit. A judge can restrain a defendant from continued infringement, can impound the material that contains the infringement, and can order the destruction of these works. Impoundment and destruction are rare today. A defendant might also be charged with a criminal offense in a copyright infringement case. If the defendant infringed on a copyright "willfully and for purposes of commercial advantage or private financial gain," he or she could be fined and jailed for not more than one year.

The law of copyright is not difficult to understand and should not be a threat to most creative persons in the mass media. The law simply says to do your own work and not to steal

---

95. *Random House Inc.* v. *Rosetta Books LLC,* 150 F. Supp. 2d 613 (2001), aff.d. 2d Cir., No. 01-7912, 3/8/02.

from the work of other persons. Some authorities argue that copyright is an infringement on freedom of the press. In a small way it probably is. Nevertheless most writers, most authors, and most reporters—persons who most often take advantage of freedom of the press—support copyright laws that protect their rights to property that they create. Judge Jerome Frank once attempted to explain this apparent contradiction by arguing that we are adept at concealing from ourselves the fact that we maintain and support "side by side as it were, beliefs which are inherently incompatible." Frank suggested that we keep these separate antagonistic beliefs in separate "logic-tight compartments."

The courts have recognized the needs of society as well as the needs of authors and have hence allowed considerable latitude for copying material that serves some public function. Because of this attitude, copyright law has little, or should have little, impact on the information-oriented mass media.

BIBLIOGRAPHY

Ames, E. Kenly. "Beyond *Rogers* v. *Koons:* A Fair Use Standard for Appropriation." *Columbia Law Review* 93 (1993): 1473.

Bridis, Ted. "Music Industry Gets Serious About Suing Internet Users." *Seattle Post-Intelligencer,* 19 July 2003, C1.

———. "Rules Blocked on TV Anti-piracy Technology." *Seattle Post-Intelligencer,* 7 May 2005, E6.

Chervokas, Jason. "Internet CD Copying Tests Music Industry." *The New York Times,* 6 April 1998, C3.

Cowell, Alan. "Hemingway Bullfight Tale from 1924 Turns Up." *The New York Times,* 27 September 2004, A1.

Dunlap, David W. "What Next? A Fee for Looking?" *The New York Times,* 22 August 1998, B1.

Finn, Michael. "From Tarzan to Threepeat." *American Journalism Review,* April 1994, 41.

Ginsburg, Jane C. "No Sweat? Copyright and Other Protection of Works of Information After *Feist* v. *Rural Telephone." Columbia Law Review* 92 (1992): 339.

Gleick, James. "Patently Absurd." *The New York Times Magazine,* 12 March 2000, 44.

"Gone for a Song on the Internet." *Seattle Post-Intelligencer,* 9 June 2000, D2.

Greenhouse, Linda. "Ruling on *Victor* vs. *Victoria* Offers Split Victory of Sorts." *The New York Times,* 5 March 2003, A16.

———. "20-Year Extension of Existing Copyrights Is Upheld." *The New York Times,* 16 January 2003, A22.

Harmon, Amy. "Suit Settled for Students Downloading Music Online." *The New York Times,* 2 May 2003, A20.

Helfand, Michael T. "When Mickey Mouse Is as Strong as Superman: The Convergence of Intellectual Property Laws to Protect Fictional Literary and Pictorial Characters." *Stanford Law Review* 44 (1992): 623.

Holloway, Lynette. "Recording Industry to Sue Internet Music Swappers." *The New York Times,* 26 June 2003, C4.

Holusha, John. "A Clash over Course Work and Copyrights." *The New York Times,* 25 April 1996, C7.

"In a Plagiarism Case, Harry Potter Wins the Day." *The New York Times,* 19 September 2002, C5.

Johnson-Laird, Andy. "Exploring the Information Superhighway: The Good, the Bad, and the Ugly." Paper presented at the Electronic Information Law Institute meeting, San Francisco, March 2–3, 1995.

"Jury Award for Wade Cook Overruled." *Seattle Post-Intelligencer,* 18 December 1998, E4.

Kaplan, Benjamin, and Ralph S. Brown Jr. *Cases on Copyright.* 2nd ed. Mineola, N.Y.: Foundation Press, 1974.

Kaplan, Carl S. "In Court's View, MP3 Player Is Just a 'Space Shifter.'" *The New York Times on the Web,* 9 July 1999.

Kinzer, Stephen. "Legal Cloud Lingers for Civil Rights Hero." *The New York Times,* 18 October 2004, A12.

Kirkpatrick, David. "Court Halts Book Based on 'Gone With the Wind.'" *The New York Times,* 21 April 2001, A1.

———. "Harry Potter and the Court Battle over Creativity." *The New York Times,* 1 April 2001, A1.

———. "'Wind' Book Wins Ruling in U.S. Court." *The New York Times,* 26 May 2001, B1.

Kramer, David H. "Who Can Use Yesterday's News? Video Monitoring and the Fair Use Doctrine." *The Georgetown Law Journal* 81 (1993): 2345.

Lee, Jennifer. "U.S. Arrests Russian Cryptographer as Copyright Violator." *The New York Times,* 18 July 2001, C8.

Lewis, Peter. "A Posting on Internet Is Ruled Illegal." *The New York Times,* 26 January 1996.

Lieberman, Trudy. "Plagiarize, Plagiarize, Plagiarize." *Columbia Journalism Review,* July/August 1995, 21.

Moynihan, Colin. "He Says He Ows the Word 'Stealth.'" *The New York Times,* 4 July 2005, C5.

Muchnick, Irvin. "Protecting Writers' Rights Online." *Macworld,* July 1996, 236.

"A New Suit Against Online Music Sites." *The New York Times,* 4 October 2001, C4.

"OutKast Settles with Rosa Parks." *St. Petersburg Times,* 17 April 2005, 2B.

Richtel, Matt. "Web Sites and Recording Labels at Impasse on Fees." *The New York Times,* 29 November 1999, C19.

———. "With Napster Down, Its Audience Fans Out." *The New York Times,* 20 July 2001, A1.

———. "A New Suit Against Online Music Sites." *The New York Times,* 4 October 2001, C4.

———. "File Sharing Sites Found Not Liable for Infringement." *The New York Times,* 20 August 2004, C1.

Richtel, Matt, and Sara Robinson. "Ear Training: A Digital Music Primer." *The New York Times,* 19 July 1999, C6.

Riordan, Teresa. "Writing Copyright Law for an Information Age." *The New York Times,* 7 July 1994, C1.

Robinson, Sara. "3 Copyright Lawsuits Test Limits of New Digital Media." *The New York Times,* 24 January 2000, C8.

Sack, Kevin. "Appeals Panel Revives Suit on Use of Dr. King Speech." *The New York Times,* 7 November 1999, A18.

Schiesel, Seth. "Global Agreement Reached to Widen Law on Copyright." *The New York Times,* 21 December 1996, A1.

Shepard, Alicia. "Does Radio News Rip Off Newspapers?" *American Journalism Review,* September 1994, 15.

Sherman, Mark. "Revenge of the Government: Agents Close Pirate Web Site." *Seattle Post-Intelligencer,* 26 May 2005, C2.

Sisario, Ben. "Postal Service Tale: Indie Rock, Snail Mail and Trademark Law." *The New York Times,* 6 November 2004, A1.

Sorkin, Andrew Ross. "Software Bullet Is Sought to Kill Musical Piracy." *The New York Times,* 4 May 2003, A1.

Strauss, Neil, and Matt Richtel. "Pact Reached on Downloading of Digital Music." *The New York Times,* 29 June 1999, C1.

Strong, William. *The Copyright Book.* Cambridge, Mass.: The M.I.T. Press, 1981.

Tatum, Kevin. "Demonstration on Internet Piracy of Copyright Properties Reinforces the Need for Legislation." *Journal of Copyright Information,* May 1996, 6.

"Textbook Anthologies on Campuses Are Curbed by Rulings on Copyrights." *The New York Times,* 16 April 1991.

"Trademarks and the Press." *American Journalism Review,* October 1993, 43.

Weinraub, Bernard. "'Amistad' Plagiarism Charge Rebutted." *The New York Times,* 4 December 1997, B9.

Whitley, Angus. "Legal Downloads Soar in iPod World." *Seattle Post-Intelligencer,* 20 January 2005, C1.

Yen, Alfred C. "When Authors Won't Sell: Parody, Fair Use, and Efficiency in Copyright Law." *University of Colorado Law Review* 62 (1991): 79.

REGULATION OF ADVERTISING

Advertising, as a form of expression subject to legal regulation and potential First Amendment protection, is the dominant cultural icon of our time. It also is a huge business. Media critic Ken Auletta estimates that more than $500 billion was spent in 2004 in the United States alone on advertising and marketing. A 30-second television spot on the 2005 Super Bowl cost $2.4 million, while a similar spot on the 77th annual Academy Awards in 2005 averaged $1.6 million. Many

Americans are themselves walking advertisements, wearing T-shirts that sport and promote brand names like Hollister and Abercrombie & Fitch and carrying Von Dutch bags. Advertising dollars make possible most of the media content that we consume; were it not for ads, network television and daily newspapers would not exist. Advertising is, then, a very important form of speech.

Advertising messages are regulated by the government; in fact, advertising is probably the most heavily regulated form of modern speech and press. Laws at every level—federal, state and local—have been adopted to control what businesses and institutions may claim about their products and services. This chapter is an outline of the most common kinds of regulations that affect advertising. It is not comprehensive. There are thousands of laws that regulate advertising messages, far too many to cover in a single chapter. Persons in advertising, especially copywriters, need to have a comprehensive understanding of the law and should use this material only as a starting point.

ADVERTISING AND THE FIRST AMENDMENT

From 1791, when the Bill of Rights became law, until 1942, the Supreme Court of the United States never considered whether advertising was protected by the First Amendment. In 1942, in an unusual case involving a man named Chrestensen who sought to pass out handbills on the streets of New York City urging recipients to make a paid visit to a submarine he had moored at a nearby wharf, the high court ruled that "the Constitution imposes . . . no restraint on government as respects purely commercial advertising." What the Supreme Court called commercial speech, advertising, is not shielded by the constitutional guarantee of freedom of expression.[1]

In 1964 the Supreme Court implicitly rejected this precedent in the landmark case of *New York Times* v. *Sullivan*[2] (see pages 194–197). The cause of that libel suit against The Times was a paid advertisement, albeit an ad containing a political message, not a commercial one. Today we might call it an "advertorial." Therein lies the explanation, many said. Nine years later, however, the high court explicitly rejected the *Chrestensen* ruling. The case involved a small newspaper, the Virginia Weekly, which was published in Charlottesville and widely distributed on the University of Virginia campus. In February 1971, two years before the Supreme Court ruling in *Roe* v. *Wade*[3] that legalized abortion in the United States, the newspaper published a small ad for the Women's Pavilion of New York City. The ad announced that the Pavilion would help women with unwanted pregnancies to obtain "immediate placement in accredited hospitals and clinics at low cost," and would make all arrangements on a strictly confidential basis. When the advertisement was published, abortion was legal in New York but not in Virginia. Jeffrey Bigelow, a director and managing editor of the Weekly, was charged

---

1. *Valentine* v. *Chrestensen,* 316 U.S. 52 (1942).
2. 376 U.S. 254 (1964).
3. 410 U.S. 113 (1973).

with violating a Virginia state law that made it a misdemeanor for "any person by publication, lecture, advertisement, or by the sale or circulation of any publication, or in any other manner," to encourage or prompt the procuring of abortion or miscarriage. Four years later Bigelow's appeal ended up before the U.S. Supreme Court. Authorities in Virginia argued that because the offending material was a newspaper advertisement, there was no First Amendment prohibition against punishing Bigelow for this publication. The high court disagreed. "The existence of commercial activity in itself, is not justification for narrowing the protection merely because it appears as a commercial advertisement," wrote Justice Harry Blackmun for the seven-person majority on the court.[4]

Since 1975 the Supreme Court and lower federal courts have built upon the *Bigelow* ruling in a number of cases, fashioning what legal experts now call the **commercial speech doctrine.**

- In 1976 the Supreme Court ruled that a Virginia statute that forbade the advertising of the price of prescription drugs violated the First Amendment.[5]
- In 1977 the high court invalidated a township ordinance in New Jersey that banned the placement of "for sale" and "sold" signs on front lawns. Township authorities said the law was needed because such signs contributed to panic selling by white homeowners who feared that property values would decline because the township was becoming populated by black families. The Supreme Court rejected this argument and ruled that the placement of such signs was protected by the First Amendment.[6]
- In 1980 a New York Public Service Commission rule that forbade utilities from publishing or broadcasting advertising that promoted the use of electricity was ruled to be an infringement on the First Amendment rights of these businesses.[7]

Not all decisions involving advertising and freedom of expression resulted in First Amendment victories. The Supreme Court allowed the Commonwealth of Puerto Rico to prohibit the owners of legal gambling casinos to advertise these establishments to the local population, the people of Puerto Rico.[8] (Commonwealth officials said the gambling casinos were for the tourists who came to the island.) In addition, the high court has granted states fairly extensive authority to regulate advertising for professional services by individuals like doctors, lawyers, dentists and others. For example, while the Supreme Court would surely rule that advertising claims by plumbers or electricians or piano teachers that extol the quality of their services are completely permissible, the states may restrict these claims and many other kinds of advertising messages generated by doctors or lawyers.[9]

---

4. *Bigelow* v. *Virginia,* 421 U.S. 809 (1975).
5. *Virginia State Board of Pharmacy* v. *Virginia Citizens Consumer Council, Inc.,* 425 U.S. 748 (1976).
6. *Linmark Associates* v. *Township of Willingboro,* 431 U.S. 85 (1977).
7. *Central Hudson* v. *Public Service Commission,* 447 U.S. 557 (1980).
8. *Posadas de Puerto Rico Assoc.* v. *Tourism Co.,* 478 U.S. 328 (1986). However, the high court rejected the rationale of this ruling in 1996.
9. See, for example, *Bates and Van O'Steen* v. *Arizona,* 433 U.S. 350 (1977); *Zauderer* v. *Office of Disciplinary Council,* 471 U.S. 626 (1985); *Ohralik* v. *Ohio State Bar Association,* 436 U.S. 447 (1978); and *Florida Bar* v. *Went For It, Inc.,* 515 U.S. 618 (1995).

Why did the Supreme Court change its mind and decide that advertising enjoyed the protection of the First Amendment?

Why did the Supreme Court change its mind and decide that advertising enjoyed the protection of the First Amendment? Undoubtedly there are many reasons. But at the core of the rationale in most rulings by the high court is the assertion that advertising frequently transmits important information. Justice Harry Blackmun probably best stated this argument in the 1976 ruling that struck down a Virginia statute that forbade the advertising of prescription drug prices by pharmacies:

> Advertising, however tasteless and excessive it sometimes may seem, is nonetheless dissemination of information as to who is producing and selling what product, for what reason, and at what price. So long as we preserve a predominantly free enterprise economy, the allocation of our resources in large measure will be made through numerous private economic decisions. It is a matter of public interest that those decisions in the aggregate be intelligent and well informed. To this end, the free flow of commercial information is indispensable.[10]

COMMERCIAL SPEECH DOCTRINE

Government may regulate advertising that is false or misleading, and advertising for unlawful goods and services.

Government may regulate truthful advertising for legal goods and services if the following conditions are met:

    a. There is a substantial state interest to justify the regulation.

    b. There is evidence that the regulation directly advances this interest.

    c. There is a reasonable fit between the state interest and the government regulation.

COMMERCIAL SPEECH DOCTRINE

While advertising enjoys First Amendment protection, it does not enjoy the broad range of protection that shields political speech, for example. The constitutional protection for advertising is limited.

But distinguishing speech that is commercial from speech that is political is not always easy. The line can be blurry between the two, especially when a corporation engages in speech designed to defend its labor practices, as happened recently with Nike, the sporting goods and apparel manufacturer. In a case called *Nike* v. *Kasky,* the U.S. Supreme Court in 2003 faced the issue of whether Nike's public relations campaign to refute and rebut nagging allegations about unsafe working conditions and subpar wages at its plants in Southeast Asia constituted commercial speech (and thereby received reduced and limited First Amendment protection) or whether it was noncommercial speech subject to full First Amendment protection.

---

10. *Virginia State Board of Pharmacy* v. *Virginia Citizens Consumer Council, Inc.,* 425 U.S. 748 (1976).

The case arose in state court in California in 1998 when a man named Marc Kasky sued Nike, claiming the corporation made false and misleading statements—statements constituting unlawful and deceptive business practices, Kasky alleged—in defending itself against the much-covered allegations. Nike had refuted the claims in multiple press releases, letters to newspapers, letters to university presidents and athletic directors, and full-page advertisements in leading newspapers. Nike wasn't technically selling shoes or clothes with such speech, but obviously curing its ailing reputation could help sell more products. Thus the issue: Was this speech really advertising or not?

The U.S. Supreme Court had defined commercial expression 30 years earlier as "speech that does no more than propose a commercial transaction"[11] and as "expression related solely to the economic interests of the speaker and its audience."[12] These definitions, however, often are criticized by both attorneys and legal scholars as too vague or too limited.

Before reaching the U.S. Supreme Court, the Supreme Court of California weighed in on the case. In May 2002, it held that Nike's speech was commercial and thus entitled to only limited First Amendment protection. The California high court wrote that "when a corporation, to maintain and increase its sales and profits, makes public statements defending labor practices and working conditions at factories where its products are made, those public statements are commercial speech that may be regulated to prevent consumer deception."[13] Most startling to Nike and other corporations was the court's statement that "for purposes of categorizing Nike's speech as commercial or noncommercial, it does not matter that Nike was responding to charges publicly raised by others and was thereby participating in public debate."

Nike petitioned the U.S. Supreme Court for a writ of certiorari that was granted in 2003, and the court heard oral argument that same year. But in a very rare and disappointing decision, the court ruled in June 2003 that the writ had been "improvidently granted" on technical grounds (jurisdictional issues as well as premature adjudication) and dismissed the case.[14] The decision not to decide the case was a victory for Marc Kasky, who could continue his lawsuit in California with Nike's expression subjected to limited First Amendment protection as commercial speech. In September 2003, Nike agreed to settle the case for $1.5 million—an amount that would go to the Fair Labor Association for factory monitoring. The Supreme Court of California's opinion, of course, only has authority in that state, and the issue may someday again return to the nation's high court for final resolution. For now, we are left with the definitions of commercial speech provided above—"speech that does no more than propose a commercial transaction" and "expression related solely to the economic interests of the speaker and its audience."

The 9th U.S. Circuit Court of Appeals considered the question of how to define commercial speech in 2004 in a case called *United States* v. *Schiff*.[15] In this case the defendant, Irwin Schiff, was a longtime opponent of the federal income tax.* He argued that commercial speech was limited to only "advertising pure and simple," while the government contended

---

*In February 2006, Schiff was sentenced to 13 years in federal prison for his fraudulent tax advice.

11. *Pittsburgh Press Co.* v. *Pittsburgh Commission on Human Relations,* 413 U.S. 376, 385 (1973).

12. *Central Hudson* v. *Public Service Commission,* 447 U.S. 557, 561 (1980).

13. *Kasky* v. *Nike, Inc.,* 27 Cal. 4th 939, 969 (2002).

14. *Nike, Inc.* v. *Kasky,* 539 U.S. 654 (2003).

15. 379 F. 3d 621 (2004).

that commercial speech was more broadly defined in *Central Hudson* as "expression related solely to the economic interests of the speaker and its audience." At issue was a book, *The Federal Mafia: How the Government Illegally Imposes and Unlawfully Collects Income Taxes,* that Schiff had authored. It was sold individually by a company Schiff ran and also as a part of so-called tax-avoidance packages. The government claimed the book constituted fraudulent commercial speech (federal statutory law penalizes individuals who organize, market, or promote tax evasion schemes),[16] and it sought a court-ordered injunction preventing Schiff from selling it. Schiff, in contrast, argued that his book was really political speech (and not commercial speech, since Schiff claimed that commercial speech meant only "advertising pure and simple"), and he contended that granting such an injunction would be an unconstitutional prior restraint on speech (see pages 74–85). The difference is important, of course, because political speech receives heightened First Amendment protection while commercial speech that is false, misleading or deceptive falls outside the scope of the First Amendment's safeguards for expression. Fraudulent commercial speech, in other words, may be enjoined without violating the First Amendment.

To help resolve this question, the appellate court considered whether the commercial speech and expressive political components of the book were so "inextricably entwined" that the book had to be deemed political content. The court held the book constituted commercial speech, reasoning that "the protected and unprotected parts of the book are *not* inextricably intertwined" and that "Schiff cannot use the protected portions of *The Federal Mafia* to piggyback his fraudulent commercial speech into full First Amendment protection." The book, the appellate court observed, was "intended to help sell his [Schiff's] other products." It noted that "Schiff has created an entire line of tax avoidance products and services, of which *The Federal Mafia* is the linchpin. . . . The extravagant claims made in *The Federal Mafia* are designed to convince readers that they can lawfully avoid paying their income taxes so that the readers will buy other products in Schiff's line." The appellate court thus ruled in favor of the government and upheld a lower-court injunction preventing the sale of the book by Schiff.

In a case with remarkable factual similarities to *United States* v. *Schiff,* the 3rd U.S. Circuit Court of Appeals in July 2005 in *United States* v. *Bell,* 414 F. 3d 474 (2005), affirmed a district court's grant of a permanent injunction barring defendant Thurston Paul Bell from promoting and selling unlawful tax advice. The appellate court in *Bell* articulated a three-part test for determining whether speech is "commercial" for purposes of First Amendment protection and the commercial speech doctrine. It wrote that courts should consider whether

1. The speech is an advertisement;
2. The speech refers to a specific product or service; and
3. The speaker has an economic motivation for the speech.

In concluding that Bell's speech was commercial and, in particular, false commercial speech not entitled to any First Amendment protection, the appellate court observed that "[p]ackaging a commercial message with token political commentary does not insulate commercial speech from appropriate restrictions." Describing Thurston Paul Bell as "a professional tax protester who ran a business and a website selling bogus strategies to clients endeavoring to

---

16. 26 U.S.C. §§ 6700-6701.

avoid paying taxes," the appellate court concluded that his speech was both misleading and promoted an unlawful activity in that his Web site invited visitors to violate the tax code and sold them materials instructing them how to do so.

While commercial speech typically receives limited First Amendment protection, two types of commercial speech receive no protection whatsoever:

- **The government may regulate advertising that is false, misleading or deceptive.** Much of the rest of this chapter is devoted to defining and explaining such regulation.
- **The government may regulate advertising for unlawful goods and services.** This broad exception to the protection of the First Amendment was established primarily to permit the government to bar discriminatory employment advertising. It is illegal for an employer to discriminate on the basis of race or religion or ancestry or even gender when hiring employees. Help wanted ads that offer employment to "whites" or "men only" or whatever are also illegal.[17]

Even truthful advertising for legal goods and services can be regulated, provided that the government can satisfy the three requirements outlined here.

- **The government must assert a substantial state interest to justify the regulation.** States that seek to limit advertising by doctors and lawyers will argue that the public is not sophisticated enough to evaluate many claims that might be made by these professionals, and even perfectly truthful claims could be deceptive. Protecting the public from such deception is a substantial state interest.[18] The state of New York justified its ban on advertising by electrical utilities as part of the state effort to conserve energy.[19] But the interest must be a valid one in the eyes of the court. A statute in the state of Washington forbade the publication or broadcast of lies in political advertising for initiative and referenda issues. In 1998 the Washington Supreme Court said the state had failed to assert a substantial state interest in its defense of this 13-year-old statute. Justice Richard Sanders wrote that the state's interest, to shield the public from falsehoods during a political campaign, "is patronizing and paternalistic. It assumes the people of this state are too ignorant or disinterested to investigate, learn, and determine for themselves the truth or falsity in political debate."[20]
- **Next, the government must demonstrate that the ban on advertising it has instituted will directly advance the interest outlined in the previous paragraph.** Think of the interest as a kind of goal the state is seeking to reach. Will the ban on advertising help the state reach this goal? Will limiting advertising claims by doctors and lawyers protect the public from confusion and deception? Will a prohibition on advertising by electrical utilities result in the conservation of energy? A Baltimore ordinance that banned outdoor advertising for alcoholic

---

17. *Pittsburgh Press Co.* v. *Pittsburgh Commission on Human Relations,* 413 U.S. 376 (1973).
18. *Bates and Van O'Steen* v. *Arizona,* 433 U.S. 350 (1977).
19. *Central Hudson* v. *Public Service Commission,* 447 U.S. 557 (1980).
20. *Washington* v. *119 Vote No.! Committee,* 957 P. 2d 691 (Wash. 1998).

beverages in areas in which children walk to school or neighborhoods in which children play was ruled permissible because it directly and materially advanced the city's interest in promoting the welfare and temperance of minors.[21] There should be some evidence to support any conclusion that the court might reach, evidence beyond simple speculation that this ban may work.

■ **Finally, the state must show that there is a "reasonable fit" between the state interest being asserted and the government regulation.** All the parts of this test except this last requirement were generated in the *Central Hudson* case about advertising by electrical utilities, a 1980 ruling.[22] In the *Central Hudson* decision the court said the government regulation must be the "least restrictive means" of accomplishing the goal established by the state. That is, the regulation could prohibit no more communication than absolutely necessary to satisfy this state interest. But in a 1989 ruling, *Board of Trustees of the State University of New York* v. *Fox,* the high court abandoned this "least restrictive means" test and substituted the "reasonable fit" test. What does reasonable fit mean? Justice Scalia, in writing the decision, said: "What our decisions require is a 'fit' between the legislature's ends and the means chosen to accomplish those ends."[23] A reasonable fit means the regulation must be narrowly tailored to achieve the desired objective, but it doesn't have to be the least restrictive means available. The 10th U.S. Circuit Court of Appeals, for example, ruled that reasonable fit means that "the governmental goal must be substantial and the cost carefully calculated. The possibility of less extensive means or regulations does not require the conclusion that the chosen means are impermissible."[24]

A reasonable fit means the regulation must be narrowly tailored to achieve the desired objective, but it doesn't have to be the least restrictive means available.

Several recent commercial speech cases illustrate how the Supreme Court applies this test, often referred to as the *Central Hudson* test, that it has developed. None of these cases involved advertising that was deceptive or for unlawful goods and services.

A recent illustration of the application of the *Central Hudson* test and commercial speech doctrine is found in *El Dia, Inc.* v. *Puerto Rico Dept. of Consumer Affairs,* 413 F. 3d 110 (2005). In June 2005 the 1st U.S. Circuit Court of Appeals declared unconstitutional a Puerto Rico regulation that required nonresidents seeking to advertise on television in Puerto Rico to first deposit and post a bond of $25,000 to cover any expenses and damages should the advertisement be false or deceptive. No similar bond, however, was required from residents of Puerto Rico seeking to advertise on television. What was the justification for such a nonresident versus resident distinction? The Puerto Rico Department of Consumer Affairs claimed that the nonresident, bond-posting requirement in advance of commercial speech was necessary because of the alleged difficulty in enforcing Puerto Rico's consumer protection rules against nonresident advertisers. The bond, Puerto Rico argued, provided both a mechanism for securing jurisdiction over such nonresident advertisers who often lack assets in Puerto Rico and a fund for the payment of fines or damages charged to them.

21. *Anheuser-Busch Inc.* v. *Schmoke,* 101 F. 3d 325 (1996).
22. *Central Hudson* v. *Public Service Commission,* 447 U.S. 557 (1980).
23. *Board of Trustees of the State University of New York* v. *Fox,* 492 U.S. 469 (1989).
24. *Adolph Coors Co.* v. *Brady,* 944 F. 2d 1543 (1991).

In analyzing the constitutionality of this regulation, the federal appellate court applied the commercial speech doctrine and found that the regulation failed the *Central Hudson* test for several reasons. In applying this test, the court initially quoted U.S. Supreme Court precedent for the principle that "a governmental body seeking to sustain a restriction on commercial speech must demonstrate that the harms it recites are real and that its restrictions will in fact alleviate them to a material degree." Puerto Rico, the appellate court held, "has failed to provide any evidence, other than conclusory assertions, that nonresident advertisers pose a greater enforcement problem than resident advertisers, who are not subject to the bond requirement." The court noted that "there was no evidence of difficulty enforcing fines levied against nonresident advertisers" and that there was "no record of any resolution or adjudication requiring execution of a bond posted by a nonresident advertiser or a resident intermediary." In brief, there was no substantial state interest to justify the law; as the court put it, the government failed to demonstrate that the harms it sought were real. Even assuming the harms and interests Puerto Rico claimed were real, there still was no evidence to show that the law directly advanced them. Here the federal appellate court quoted from the *Central Hudson* opinion for the proposition that a "regulation may not be sustained if it provides only ineffective or remote support for the government's purpose." Again, the court found that no evidence of the effectiveness of the law had been introduced. Finally, on the last prong of the *Central Hudson* test—whether there is a "reasonable fit" between the government objectives and the terms of the statute—the 1st Circuit held that Puerto Rico made no effort to explain why less drastic methods of ensuring nonresident advertisers' compliance with the consumer regulations are not available. The appellate court wrote that Puerto Rico's "net is cast too broadly for such a small catch" of alleged nonresident violators of consumer protection regulations. The case thus demonstrates that the government carries the evidentiary burden of demonstrating that the interests asserted behind a law are real; that those interest will, in fact, be directly advanced by the law; and that the fit between the means and ends really is reasonable and does not sweep too far.

A regulation may not be sustained if it provides only ineffective or remote support for the government's purpose.

In 1995 the Supreme Court struck down a federal rule that forbade brewers from listing the alcohol content on labels attached to bottles and cans of beer and malt liquor. The government justified the rule by arguing that it sought to discourage young drinkers from buying a particular beer or malt liquor simply because it had the highest alcohol content. It is certainly legitimate for the government to try to dissuade young people from drinking too much and this rule assists the state in this role, U.S. attorneys argued. The government's interest in reducing the amount of alcohol consumed by young people is a laudable goal, a unanimous Supreme Court said, but added that there is really no evidence this rule advances that goal. There was no government ban on the disclosure of the alcohol content in advertising for these brews, Justice Clarence Thomas wrote. Nor were there limits on the words a brewer could use to describe these products. "To be sure," Thomas wrote, "the Government's interest in combating strength wars is a valid goal. But the irrationality of this unique and puzzling framework ensures that the labeling ban will fail to achieve that end."[25]

In 1996 the Supreme Court ruled that a Rhode Island statute that barred liquor stores from advertising the price of distilled spirits ran afoul of the First Amendment. The state attempted to justify the law by arguing that the ban on advertising reduced competition in the

25. *Rubin v. Coors Brewing Co.,* 514 U.S. 476 (1995).

sale of liquor, which resulted in higher liquor prices that in turn led to reduced consumption. But in his principal opinion for the badly splintered Supreme Court, Justice John Paul Stevens referred to the state's assertions that the ban would significantly reduce liquor consumption as speculation and conjecture. He said the court was not prepared to restrict truthful speech about a legal product on such flimsy justification and that the state had not even considered other means that did not restrict speech to accomplish its clearly valid goals. The justice added that raising liquor prices through taxation would have the same impact. Justice Stevens wrote, "The First Amendment directs us to be especially skeptical of regulations that seek to keep people in the dark for what the government perceives to be their own good."[26]

In the late 1990s the federal courts were asked to consider the constitutionality of a ban on broadcast advertising for casino gambling in states where such gambling was legal. Restrictions on the broadcast of advertising for lotteries and other gambling had been in place since the 1930s. But beginning in 1950 the government began to permit exceptions to what had always been an absolute ban. The government permitted broadcasting stations in states with state-run lotteries to advertise these contests. Exceptions were also granted to broadcast advertising for gambling casinos on Indian reservations, for fishing contests, for not-for-profit lotteries, and for lotteries conducted as promotional activities by commercial organizations.

The Supreme Court weighed into the fray and in 1999 unanimously ruled that the ban on broadcast advertising was a violation of the First Amendment because it "sacrifices an intolerable amount of truthful speech about lawful conduct." Justice John Paul Stevens wrote that the government failed to prove that the ban on such advertising will reduce either gambling or the social costs of gambling. While the government's interest in reducing the demand for gambling is valid, Stevens said, the law as it exists "is so pierced by exemptions and inconsistencies" that this valid state interest could not salvage the regulation or overcome the presumption "that the speaker and the audience, not the government, should be left to assess the value of accurate and nonmisleading information about lawful conduct."[27]

In 2001 the Supreme Court ruled that a Massachusetts law that banned both outdoor ads and point-of-sale ads for smokeless tobacco products and cigars within 1,000 feet of public playgrounds and schools was unconstitutional.[28] The high court conceded that the state had a substantial interest in reducing the use of such products by youngsters. And a majority also agreed that there was substantial evidence that tobacco sellers had boosted the sale of these products by targeting young males in their advertising. But the rule went too far; it was not a reasonable fit. Coupled with pre-existing zoning laws in the state, the rule constitutes a complete ban on the communication of truthful information about smokeless tobacco products and cigars to adult consumers, Justice Sandra Day O'Connor wrote. The law also fails to distinguish among the types of signs with respect to their appeal to children as opposed to adults, or even their size. The law is simply not tailored narrowly enough to advance the state's declared interest without impeding protected speech as well, the justices ruled. The Massachusetts statute was typical of laws in several other states as well, and these laws were also put in jeopardy.

26. *44 Liquormart, Inc.* v. *Rhode Island,* 517 U.S. 484 (1996).
27. *Greater New Orleans Broadcasting Association* v. *U.S.,* 527 U.S. 173 (1999).
28. *Lorillard Tobacco Co.* v. *Reilly,* 533 U.S. 525 (2001).

Finally, in 2002 the U.S. Supreme Court applied the commercial speech doctrine and the *Central Hudson* test to strike down as unconstitutional a federal law restricting the advertisement and promotion by pharmacies of so-called compounded drugs.[29] Drug compounding is a traditional component of pharmacy practice in which a pharmacist combines and mixes ingredients to create specially tailored medications in response to doctor prescriptions. Compounded drugs are exempted from the Food & Drug Administration's standard rigorous and lengthy drug approval process. The FDA became concerned that some pharmacists were abusing this exemption and were manufacturing and selling drugs, in some cases on a large-scale basis, under the guise of compounding and thus avoiding the standard drug approval procedures. Congress thus passed a law prohibiting pharmacies from advertising "the compounding of any particular drug, class of drug, or type of drug."[30] The government believed, as the U.S. Supreme Court wrote, "that without advertising it would not be possible to market a drug on a large enough scale to make safety and efficacy testing economically feasible."

The Supreme Court ruled that the government had a substantial interest in preserving the effectiveness and integrity of the drug approval process. The court also assumed as true the government's assertion that the advertising prohibition would directly advance this goal by preventing the large-scale manufacturing of compounded drugs. But the court concluded that the law failed the final part of the *Central Hudson* test—there were other ways, it observed, to serve the government's substantial interest that did not restrict so much speech. The fit, in brief, between the means and the ends was not reasonable. For instance, the FDA "could limit the amount of compounded drugs, either by volume or by numbers of prescriptions, that a given pharmacy or pharmacist sells out of state." Such a quantity, volume or revenue limitation would serve the government's interest but in no way impact the lawful and otherwise nonmisleading advertising of compounded drugs.

One other dimension of the relationship between the First Amendment and advertising needs to be briefly explored. Is it a violation of the First Amendment for a newspaper or magazine or broadcasting station to refuse to carry an advertisement? No. The long-standing legal doctrine is that the First Amendment is not even implicated; such a situation is one private entity, the mass medium, refusing to do business with another private entity.* In 1996 a U.S. District Court extended this doctrine to the Internet when it ruled that a private company called Cyber Promotions had no right under the First Amendment to e-mail unsolicited promotional advertisements to America Online subscribers. The court ruled that although the Internet provides the opportunity to disseminate vast amounts of information, the Internet does not have at the present time the means to police the dissemination of that information. "We therefore find that . . . the private online service has a right to prevent unsolicited e-mail solicitations from reaching its subscribers over the Internet," Judge Weiner wrote.[31]

---

*Broadcasters do have certain obligations related to carrying political advertising. See Chapter 16. In addition, if the publication is not privately owned but rather is published by a government entity, such as a state university's alumni magazine, there may be some situations in which advertisements cannot be rejected. See *Rutgers 1000 Alumni Council* v. *Rutgers*, 803 A. 2d 679 (2002).

29. *Thompson* v. *Western States Medical Center*, 535 U.S. 357 (2002).
30. Food and Drug Administration Modernization Act of 1997, 21 U.S.C. § 353a(c).
31. *Cyber Promotions, Inc.* v. *America Online, Inc.*, 1 E.P.L.R. 756 (1996), 24 M.L.R. 2505 (1996).

COMPELLED ADVERTISING SUBSIDIES AND GOVERNMENT SPEECH

Almost anyone with a discernable pulse who has watched network television advertisements during the past decade or so is familiar with trademarked slogans such as "Beef. It's What's for Dinner" and "Got Milk?" The former phrase actually played a pivotal role in a case decided by the U.S. Supreme Court in May 2005. The case did not involve the just-discussed commercial speech from *Central Hudson* but, instead, addressed the issue of "whether a federal program that finances generic advertising to promote an agricultural product violates the First Amendment."[32] In particular, *Johanns* v. *Livestock Marketing Association* centered on a federal statute and related federal order adopted in the 1980s under which the U.S. Secretary of Agriculture imposes a $1-per-head assessment, known in legal terms as a checkoff, on all sales of cattle in the United States. Although $1 taken alone may seem like a small amount for each sale, the program has collected more than $1 billion since 1988. A large portion of that money, under the federal law known as the Beef Promotion and Research Act, has gone to finance generic advertising for the beef industry, including the "Beef. It's What's for Dinner" campaign.

While that slogan at first may seem rather innocuous and to benefit the entire beef and cattle industry, a number of cattle producers objected to it because, as the Supreme Court put it, "the advertising promotes beef as a generic commodity, which, they contended, impedes their efforts to promote the superiority of, *inter alia,* American beef, grain-fed beef, or certified Angus or Hereford beef." In other words, the Livestock Marketing Association and the other plaintiff in the case objected to the fact that they were compelled to subsidize speech—the generic beef advertising campaign—to which they objected. They would, instead, rather spend their own money on distinctive advertising for a particular niche or premium variety of beef, such as organically fed. The plaintiffs thus alleged a violation of their First Amendment right not to be compelled to fund speech—an unenumerated right to remain silent, as it were—with which they disagreed.

A First Amendment right not to be compelled by the government to speak has been recognized by the Supreme Court in some situations. For instance, in the seminal 1943 opinion in *West Virginia Board of Education* v. *Barnette,* the court held that children in public schools could not be forced or compelled to recite the Pledge of Allegiance or salute the American flag.[33] The students had a right, in other words, to not speak. The majority of the court in *Livestock Marketing Association,* however, distinguished that case and others like it on the ground that the beef situation was a compelled-subsidy case—not a true compelled-speech case—and, more important, the advertising campaign itself represented "government speech," not speech by a private person against his or her wishes. Writing for a six-justice majority, Justice Antonin Scalia wrote that "the message set out in the beef promotions is from beginning to end the message established by the Federal Government" and that the Secretary of Agriculture "exercises final approval authority over every word used in every promotional campaign." The majority concluded that while "citizens may challenge compelled support of private speech" they "have no First Amendment right not to fund government

---

32. *Johanns* v. *Livestock Marketing Association,* 125 S. Ct. 2055 (2005).
33. 319 U.S. 624 (1943).

speech." To illustrate his point, Scalia noted that a person may not opt out of paying income taxes just because he or she doesn't agree with how the government is spending the money. In brief, the majority of the court concluded that the beef advertising is the government's own speech and, as such, does not raise First Amendment problems. The court thus ruled in favor of the federal beef promotion program and its compelled subsidization of advertising to which some cattlemen and farmers object. The Los Angeles Times observed that the decision was "likely to sweep aside legal challenges to dozens of similar promotional programs" run by federal and state government entities for products such as "cotton, potatoes, peanuts and eggs."[34]

SUMMARY

American advertising is regulated by scores of laws adopted by all levels of government. Persons in advertising must be aware of such rules as well as all other regulations (libel, invasion of privacy, obscenity, etc.) that restrict the content and flow of printed and broadcast material. Since the mid-1970s commercial advertising has been given the qualified protection of the First Amendment because much advertising contains information that is valuable to consumers. The government may prohibit advertising (1) that promotes an unlawful activity or (2) that is misleading or untruthful. The state may also regulate truthful advertising for lawful activities and goods if it can prove (1) that there is a substantial state interest to justify the regulation, (2) that such regulation directly advances this state interest, and (3) that there is a "reasonable fit" between the state interest being asserted and the governmental regulation. Advertising by professionals such as attorneys and physicians may be regulated in a somewhat more restrictive fashion.

THE REGULATION OF ADVERTISING

The regulation of deceptive or untruthful advertising is a large and difficult task policed by the advertising industry itself, the mass media, and various governmental agencies. During the 1980s, a time when advertising claims were increasing in intensity and in number, the federal government, a primary player in the regulation of advertising, pulled back from the aggressive stance it had taken during the 1970s. New means to control the content of commercial messages were explored. Let's briefly examine this process of regulation today.

SELF-REGULATION

Newspapers, magazines, broadcasting stations, online service providers and other mass media all have rules that more or less regulate the kind of advertising they will carry. These guidelines spring from a variety of concerns. Sometimes the owner of the medium thinks the product that is being advertised is offensive, like NC-17 or adult movies, or condoms. Other times

---

34. Savage, "Supreme Court Upholds Fees."

the ads themselves might be regarded as tasteless, like an advertisement for clothing in which the models are scantily dressed or posed erotically. It is not uncommon that an advertisement is rejected because of economic interests. A television station won't advertise a sporting event that will be telecast on a competing channel. Ads that promote illegal goods and services, that contain claims that appear to be deceptive or are not substantiated, or that unfairly trash a competitor's products might also be rejected. For instance, in late 2004 CBS, NBC and ABC stopped running certain television ads produced for the Miller Brewing Co. that poked fun at rival Anheuser-Busch's top-selling product, Budweiser, and that allegedly made unsubstanti-ated claims about taste tests comparing Miller Genuine Draft and Miller Lite with Budweiser and Bud Light.[35] CBS found the three Miller ads to be "unduly disparaging." These policies ebb and flow and are frequently enforced more rigorously in times when advertising is abun-dant than in times when advertising is scarce. Remember, a mass medium is permitted to reject any content it chooses, with or without a reason.

But the screening of advertising by the mass media does not present an unbreachable wall.

But the screening of advertising by the mass media does not present an unbreachable wall. Misleading, unfair, false and deceptive advertising is published and broadcast, and because of this the advertising industry has constructed a self-regulatory scheme to try to resolve as many problems as possible. The Better Business Bureau has two divisions available to advertisers who believe a competitor's claims are hurting the sale of their own products. The **National Advertising Division** and the **National Advertising Review Board** have been hearing advertiser complaints for several decades. While decisions by these components of the Better Business Bureau are not binding on advertisers, the mass media tend to take such findings of false or misleading claims quite seriously and usually bar such advertisements from newspapers, magazines or broadcast stations. And usually advertisers will pay heed as well. In 1993 Wal-Mart Stores changed its corporate slogan from "Always the low price, always," to "Always Low Prices, Always" after the Better Business Bureau found that the first slogan could mislead some shoppers. In rare instances an advertiser's complaint about a com-petitor's practices will be referred to the Federal Trade Commission.

Sometimes an advertiser will not believe that a complaint to the Better Business Bureau is sufficient and instead will take more formal action such as filing a lawsuit in federal court. This is another level of self-regulation.

Another vital layer of independent self-regulation relates to the National Advertising Review Council (NARC), which was established in 1971 by the Association of National Advertisers, the American Association of Advertising Agencies, and the American Advertis-ing Federation, along with the Council of Better Business Bureaus, to provide guidance and set standards of truth and accuracy for national advertisers. The NARC Web site can be found at http://www.narcpartners.org. NARC establishes polices for both the National Advertising Division, mentioned above, and the Children's Advertising Review Unit—the self-regulatory body for advertising to children under the age of 12 years, with its Web site located at http://www.caru.org—of the Council of Better Business Bureaus.

Although it was founded more than three decades ago, NARC remains a vital entity. For instance, in 2004 it published an 87-page white paper called "Guidance for Food Advertising Self-Regulation." Among other things, the white paper, which was designed to increase the

---

35. Daykin, "Networks Blow Whistle on Ads" and Cancelada, "CBS and NBC Will Stop Running Some Miller Ads."

understanding of the role of self-regulation of food advertising to children and adults, set forth the following guidelines:

- Copy, sound and visual presentations should not mislead children about product or performance characteristics.
- Advertising presentation should not mislead children about benefits from use of the product, including the acquisition of strength, status, popularity, growth, proficiency and intelligence.
- Fantasy, including animation, while appropriate for younger as well as older children, should neither create unattainable performance expectations nor exploit the younger child's difficulty in distinguishing between the real and the fanciful.
- The performance and use of a product should be demonstrated in a way that can be duplicated by the child for whom the product is intended.
- Products should be shown being used in safe ways, environments and situations.

LAWSUITS BY COMPETITORS AND CONSUMERS

Using mouthwash is just as effective as flossing when it comes to fighting tooth and gum decay. Pfizer Inc. made that claim in a massive multimedia advertising campaign launched in June 2004 called "The Big Bang" on behalf of its well-known Listerine brand mouthwash. One television commercial asserted, "Listerine's as effective as floss at fighting plaque and gingivitis. Clinical studies prove it." But a subsidiary of Johnson & Johnson that manufactures dental floss contended the assertion on behalf of Listerine was false and deceptive, and it sued Pfizer in federal court under the federal Lanham Act, saying the campaign constituted an unfair threat against sales of dental floss. In 2005, a federal court in New York ruled in favor of Johnson & Johnson, holding that "Pfizer's implicit message that Listerine can replace floss is false and misleading."[36] U.S. District Court Judge Denny Chin issued an injunction that ordered Pfizer to stop its campaign. Chin wrote, "I find that Pfizer's advertisements do send the message, implicitly, that Listerine is a replacement for floss—that the benefits of flossing may be obtained by rinsing with Listerine, and that, in particular, those consumers who do not have the time or desire to floss can switch to Listerine instead." Pfizer, in fact, had to spend $2 million dollars in 2005 to deploy about 4,000 workers across the United States to place stickers on Listerine bottles that were sitting on store shelves in order to cover up its claim and to remove tags carrying the claim that were hung around bottlenecks of the mouthwash.

In 1999 a federal judge did what virtually nobody else had been able to do in myriad television ads: He stopped the Energizer Bunny. A U.S. District Court ruled that Energizer's manufacturer, the Ralston Purina Company, must stop advertising that its batteries are superior to competing batteries, including Duracell's Ultra. Gillette, which makes Duracell batteries, initiated the lawsuit. The court said the Energizer claims were based on a study that was flawed and could not be used to substantiate a claim of superiority. Gillette won another lawsuit in 1999 when it convinced a jury that the Optiva Co., maker of the Sonicare electric toothbrush, made false and misleading claims about its product, claims that hurt the sales of a Gillette electric toothbrush, the Braun Oral-B. The jury awarded Gillette $2.5 million in damages.

36. *McNeil-PPC, Inc.* v. *Pfizer, Inc.,* 351 F. Supp. 2d 226 (S.D. N.Y. 2005).

Lawsuits for false advertising claims were relatively rare until the last quarter of the 20th century. With the rapid growth of comparative advertising (in which the advertised product is compared to a competitor's product), more and more advertisers have taken competitors to court over what they claim is deceptive and false advertising. In the fall of 1996 Gillette sued Norelco, charging that a Norelco campaign for electric shavers was false because it included exaggerated and distorted statements about wet shaving in an attempt to sell electric shavers. One of the longest-running legal battles was waged between American Home Products, the maker of Anacin and Advil, and Johnson & Johnson, the manufacturer of Tylenol, who were in court for more than a decade fighting over claims of the relative effectiveness of the two pain relievers.[37] Neither pharmaceutical manufacturer wanted to give the other any competitive edge while fighting for market share in the sale of over-the-counter pain relievers, a $3-billion-a-year business in the mid-1990s.

Another example of a competitor-versus-competitor lawsuit, based on alleged false advertising and filed under the federal Lanham Act, is the 2005 federal district court opinion of *Schick Manufacturing, Inc.* v. *Gillette Co.,* 372 F. Supp. 2d 273 (2005). The case pitted the two shaving-razor giants against each other. The plaintiff, Schick, contended that Gillette made false claims in 2004 about the prowess of the Gillette M3 Power razor system on television commercials and that, in turn, those misleading ads hurt the sales of Schick's own Quattro razor. The M3 includes a battery-powered feature that causes the razor to oscillate. One aspect of the Gillette M3 commercial to which Schick objected included an animated representation of the purported effect of the M3 Power razor on hair. In particular, as the court noted, "the animation, which lasts approximately 1.8 seconds, shows many hairs growing at a significant rate, many by as much as four times the original length." Schick believed this illustration showed a false amount of extension of the beard allegedly generated by the M3. The court ruled in favor of Schick, rejecting Gillette's creative yet unsuccessful argument that animated exaggeration does not constitute falsity. U.S. District Court Judge Janet C. Hall wrote that "a defendant cannot argue that a television advertisement is 'approximately' correct or, alternatively, simply a representation in order to excuse a television ad or segment thereof that is literally false." She concluded that while "a cartoon will not exactly depict a real-life situation, . . . a party may not distort an inherent quality of its product in either graphics or animation. Gillette acknowledges that the magnitude of beard hair extension in the animation is false. The court finds, therefore, that any claims with respect to changes in angle and the animated portion of Gillette's current advertisement are literally false." This is an important lesson for all undergraduates majoring in advertising to understand—be careful not to exaggerate claims, either in words or in images, such as commercial animation. Each can be deemed false in a court of law.

These lawsuits were filed under provisions of the federal Lanham Act, which was adopted more than 60 years ago by Congress to stop unfair competition in the marketplace. Section 43(a) creates a legal cause of action for false advertising. The statute, set forth at 15 U.S.C. § 1125, provides that a person who generates "any false designation of origin, false or misleading description of fact, or false or misleading representation of fact, which . . . in commercial advertising or promotion, misrepresents the nature, characteristics, qualities, or geographic origin of his or another person's goods, services, or commercial activities" is

---

37. See Mann and Plummer, "The Big Headache," 39.

liable for civil damages. As originally written, the law only prevented one advertiser from making false statements about his or her own goods ("The new Escalade will get 60 miles to the gallon in city driving"). But Congress amended the act in 1989, and now the law also prohibits an advertiser from making false claims about a competitor's product as well ("The new Escalade will get 26 miles per gallon in city driving, while the Dodge Neon only gets 5 miles to the gallon"). This provision of the Lanham Act was seldom used by advertisers until the 1970s. Between 1946 and 1968 the courts heard fewer than 30 false advertising cases.[38] Several developments propelled the growth of Lanham Act false advertising activity:

- ▪ Comparative advertising, in which an advertiser not only promotes his or her own goods but tends to disparage the product made by a competitor, became more common. Television networks had arbitrarily refused to air such commercials until urged to do so by the Federal Trade Commission, which suggested that such advertising would enhance the competitive nature of the marketplace.
- ▪ Advertising, as a part of the marketing mix for all products, took on more importance in the past 50 years. Sellers invested huge sums in building product images and establishing product claims. Attempts by competitors to undermine or dilute these images or claims were regarded more seriously than in the past.
- ▪ It became somewhat easier for plaintiffs to win Lanham Act false advertising suits.[39] The test of false advertising, for years a complex configuration of criteria, was reduced to basically three parts:

  1. What message, either explicitly or implicitly, does the ad convey?
  2. Is this message false or misleading?
  3. Does this message injure the plaintiff?

- ▪ The size of damage awards skyrocketed. Plaintiffs in Lanham Act cases had traditionally sought only to stop the competitor's advertising claims. For example, in 1976 American Brands won an injunction that forced R.J. Reynolds to stop using the slogan "The lowest tar of all cigarettes" in advertising for its Now brand cigarettes.[40] It was easier to block a competitor's claims than to win damages, because in order to gain a monetary award the plaintiff had to show specific monetary loss, something that is often difficult to do given the nebulous nature of advertising claims and the forces that motivate a consumer to buy a specific brand of a product. But courts began to ease this standard at about the same time that they began to increase the size of damage awards.[41] Not only is it now possible for plaintiffs to win actual damages and court costs from the defendant, but they can also tap into any profit made by the competitor through the use of a bogus advertising campaign. On top of this, the judge can double or triple the damage award in cases of especially flagrant falsity.

---

38. Pompeo, "To Tell the Truth," 565.
39. Singdahlsen, "The Risk of Chill," 339.
40. *American Brands, Inc.* v. *R.J. Reynolds Tobacco Co.,* 413 F. Supp. 1352 (1976).
41. See *PPX Enterprises* v. *Audiofidelity Enterprises,* 818 F. 2d 266 (1987) and *U-Haul International* v. *Jartran, Inc.,* 793 F. 2d 1034 (1986).

For example, in the mid-1980s U-Haul, which rents trucks and trailers, sued a competitor, Jartran, claiming false advertising. U-Haul had pretty much had its own way in this business, even in the face of new competition. But the Jartran advertising campaign (which won a prestigious marketing award) hurt U-Haul badly. The advertising featured price comparisons between the two companies that were computed in a manner unfair to U-Haul. The campaign also asserted that Jartran trucks were better. The size of the trucks pictured in the print advertising had been altered photographically to make the Jartran trucks appear larger. And nice, shiny new Jartran trucks were compared with less desirable-looking U-Haul models. U-Haul presented several consumer-perception surveys to the court that showed considerable consumer confusion regarding the advertising and charted a direct link between its lost sales and the Jartran campaign. During the year of the campaign, Jartran experienced a $92 million revenue increase; U-Haul, a $49 million revenue decline. The court computed the damages by adding Jartran's advertising expense for the misleading campaign, about $6 million, to the money spent by U-Haul to counteract the Jartran campaigning, close to $14 million. The judge then doubled this total and awarded U-Haul $40 million in damages, the largest award by far ever given in a Section 43(a) case.[42]

Consumers, as opposed to competitors, have a much more difficult time in maintaining an action for false advertising.

Consumers, as opposed to competitors, have a much more difficult time in maintaining an action for false advertising. Part of the reason for this is that the Lanham Act's rules against false advertising, which are designed to remedy unfair competition, generally allow only economic competitors to sue. It is very difficult for noncompetitors to gain standing to sue for false advertising under the Lanham Act. This was vividly illustrated in 2002 when a federal district court rejected tennis player Anna Kournikova's motion for a preliminary injunction based on a Lanham Act claim for false advertising against Penthouse magazine after it had published photos of a woman sunbathing topless whom it falsely represented on its cover and on its inside pages as Kournikova.[43] The June 2002 issue of Penthouse proclaimed on its cover in bold capital letters, "EXCLUSIVE ANNA KOURNIKOVA CAUGHT CLOSE UP ON NUDE BEACH." The photos inside, however, were not of the Russian-born tennis player, who is known more for her beauty than for her on-court prowess. Kournikova sued the company that publishes Penthouse magazine, General Media Communications, Inc., on several causes of action, one of which was false advertising under the Lanham Act. But the court, while calling the magazine's conduct "reprehensible," rejected the claim for a preliminary injunction, writing that "Kournikova cannot seriously argue that she is a competitor of Penthouse in any meaningful sense. Although Penthouse and Kournikova may be competing for the use of Kournikova's name and identity, this is not sufficient to constitute a 'competitive injury' for

---

42. *U-Haul International* v. *Jartran,* 793 F. 2d 1034 (1986).
43. *Kournikova* v. *General Media Communications, Inc.,* 2002 U.S. Dist. LEXIS 25810 (2002), aff'd. 51 Fed. Appx. 739 (9th Cir. 2002). In May 2003, the same judge reheard Kournikova's Lanham Act claim for false advertising, but this time on the defendant's motion for summary judgment. Judge Gary Allen Fees now found that while Kournikova may actually be a competitor with Penthouse in the "entertainment business" by selling sexually appealing products like her 2003 calendar, she once again had presented no evidence of competitive injury. The judge thus granted Penthouse's motion for summary judgment on the false advertising Lanham Act claim. Once again, Kournikova lost, something she is now accustomed to both on court and in court. *Kournikova* v. *General Media Communications, Inc.,* 278 F. Supp. 2d 111 (2003).

standing under a false advertising claim." There is no common-law tort for deceptive advertising. As George and Peter Rosden point out in their massive compendium "The Law of Advertising," historically, common-law courts have not been receptive to protecting consumers. "During the most formative period of common law," they write, "only a few goods in the marketplace were manufactured products so that the buyer was in an excellent position to judge for himself goods offered to him."[44] The basic slogan in those days was caveat emptor, or buyer beware.

While today consumers are far better protected—there is little consumers can do themselves to attack the dishonest advertiser, short of reporting the advertisement to the proper authorities. The Rosdens point out that it is possible for a consumer to sue under product liability laws, but in such cases the advertisement must contain a commitment about the product that is not fulfilled after purchase by the consumer.

STATE AND LOCAL LAWS

State regulation of advertising predates federal regulation by several years. This fact is not surprising when you consider that at the time the public became interested in advertising regulation—around the turn of the century—the federal government was a minuscule creature relative to its present size. Harry Nims, a New York lawyer, drafted a model law called the **Printers' Ink statute** (it was Printers' Ink magazine that urged passage of the law) in 1911. Most states today have such laws. In addition, many states have what are called unfair and deceptive acts and practices statutes, which give consumers the right to seek a judicial remedy in false advertising cases. These acts are often called "Little FTC Acts," and the guidelines developed by the FTC in applying federal advertising law (discussed shortly) are used by the state courts in administering these state regulations.[45] In addition, many local governments have consumer protection laws that apply broadly to false advertising.

Enforcement of state and local regulations is in the hands of attorneys general and local prosecutors. The intensity of such enforcement varies dramatically from one jurisdiction to another. Local prosecutors often find it difficult to devote staff time to consumer problems when faced with growing amounts of violent crimes, drug cases and other seemingly more serious threats to the public safety and welfare.

At times local enforcement of consumer protection laws is aggressive. During the late 1980s and early 1990s the federal government tended to relax its policing of false advertising claims. The Reagan administration mandate to "get government off the back of business" dictated a tempering of advertising regulation. At this time the states tried to pick up some of the slack. For example, Texas sued Volvo for false advertising for a television commercial that showed a giant pickup truck with huge tires drive over the tops of a line of cars, including a Volvo 240 station wagon. All the cars except the Volvo are flattened. Texas asserted, and Volvo admitted, that the ad was a phony. The roof of the Volvo station wagon was reinforced with lumber and steel, while structural roof pillars in the other cars had been cut or weakened. The company paid a $316,250 settlement to the state, an additional $150,000 fine to the FTC,

---

44. Rosden and Rosden, *The Law of Advertising.*
45. Kertz and Ohanian, "Recent Trends," 603.

and fired the agency that had handled its $40 million advertising account for the past 23 years. In 1991 the California attorney general brought a false advertising suit against Life Alert Emergency Response, a company that used television advertising to promote a medical alert system for the sick and the elderly ("Help! I've fallen and I can't get up"). In the late 1990s, Connecticut, West Virginia, Florida, New York and several other states aggressively pursued American Family Publishers, the magazine sweepstakes company, charging that the firm's promotions were blatantly false. New York won an $800,000 settlement from the company in August of 1998.[46]

In May 2003, the U.S. Supreme Court ruled on a case involving state regulation of telemarketing when it held that, "consistent with our precedent and First Amendment jurisprudence, States may maintain fraud actions (see pages 359–360 regarding fraud) when fundraisers make false or misleading representations designed to deceive donors about how their donations will be used."[47] The court wrote that while "the First Amendment protects the right to engage in charitable solicitation," it does not provide "a blanket exemption from fraud liability for a fundraiser who intentionally misleads in calls for donations." In this case, the Illinois attorney general had filed a fraud complaint against two telemarketing firms alleging they misrepresented during phone calls to potential donors how donations would be spent and, in particular, what percentage of money donated would actually go to the charity in question. The telemarketers, in contrast, claimed the fraud claims were barred by the First Amendment since the Supreme Court had previously held that statutes categorically banning all solicitations when fund-raising fees exceeded a specified level or percentage of donated money were unconstitutional. The court, however, distinguished those earlier cases because Illinois' case did not involve such a statute but instead was an individual fraud action against the telemarketing firms based on specific misrepresentations of fact.

FEDERAL REGULATION

A variety of federal agencies are empowered to enforce consumer protection laws. The Federal Trade Commission (FTC) is the primary agent of the government, but clearly not the only agent. Beginning in the 1990s the Food and Drug Administration (FDA) began an aggressive campaign against a variety of companies to force them to change their labeling and promotional practices. For example, the FDA

- told Procter & Gamble to stop calling its Citrus Hill Fresh Choice orange juice "fresh-squeezed," because it was made from concentrate, not fresh-squeezed oranges.
- ordered Ragu to stop promoting its bottled pasta sauces as "fresh" when they weren't.
- barred the maker of Mrs. Fields cookies from advertising its Chocolite and Semi-Sweet Classic brands as "low-fat," because the snacks contained almost twice the fat allowed by the law in "low-fat" cookies.

46. Rohde, "Sweepstakes in Agreement."
47. *Illinois* v. *Telemarketing Associates, Inc.,* 123 S. Ct. 1829, 1842 (2003).

■ began more closely scrutinizing video news releases and advertising prepared by pharmaceutical companies and broadcast by many networks and local television stations. A 1999 study by the FDA revealed that several drug companies made false or misleading statements in the releases and in TV advertising for prescription drugs.

■ forced the makers of Relenza, a flu medication, to stop exaggerating the effectiveness of the drug. The agency said the product does not cure the flu, as the ads implied, but cuts the duration of the symptoms of the illness.

The FTC was created by Congress in 1914 to police unfair methods of business competition. The agency was to make certain that Company A did not engage in practices that gave it an unfair advantage over its competitor, Company B. And, of course, an unfair advantage may be gained through the use of false or misleading advertising. As originally conceived, the FTC was not supposed to worry about the impact of advertising on consumers, only competitors. During the 1920s, however, the FTC substantially enlarged its mission in an effort to try to protect consumers as well. This effort was suddenly stopped in 1931 when the Supreme Court ruled that the FTC had illegally enlarged its jurisdiction and that it could only attempt to regulate advertising that unfairly affected the advertiser's competitor.[48]

In 1938 Congress adopted the Wheeler-Lea Amendment to the Trade Commission Act, which gave the FTC the power to proceed against all unfair and deceptive acts or practices in commerce, regardless of whether they affect competition. Since that time the commission has developed into one of the nation's largest independent regulatory agencies. In addition to policing false advertising, the FTC is charged with enforcing the nation's antitrust laws and several federal statutes such as the Truth in Lending Law and the Fair Credit Reporting Act. The five members of the commission are appointed by the president and confirmed by the Senate for a term of seven years. No more than three of the commissioners can be from the same political party. A chairperson, one of the five commissioners, is appointed by the president. Although the agency is located in Washington, D.C., it has 11 regional offices throughout the nation.

The history of the agency reveals that it has often been swept by the political winds of the time. For years it was known as the "Little Gray Lady on Pennsylvania Avenue" because of its timid performance. During the late 1960s and 1970s, in an era of consumer concern, the FTC showed new muscle and attacked some of the nation's largest advertisers, such as Coca-Cola and ITT Continental Baking. In the 1980s the FTC reflected the spirit of deregulation that ran throughout Washington, D.C., as Ronald Reagan entered the White House.

In the 1990s the agency renewed its aggressive efforts, instituting false advertising actions against several national advertisers, including Kraft General Foods, and bringing charges against a group of companies that were using program-length TV ads called infomercials to sell a variety of goods and services, including diet plans and treatments for cellulite buildup and baldness. By 2003 the gross revenue for television infomercials, including short-form spot ads, was more than $150 billion. The agency also brought a complaint against the tobacco industry that ultimately ended the career of Joe Camel and other cigarette advertising designed to appeal to children. On the antitrust front it blocked the merger of Office Depot and

---

48. *FTC* v. *Raladam,* 283 U.S. 643 (1931).

Staples, two large office supply retailers; stopped the purchase of Ingram Book Group, the nation's largest book wholesaler, by Barnes & Noble, the nation's largest book retailer; and prohibited H.J. Heinz from merging its baby food business with Beech-Nut, another large baby food maker.

The FTC also initiated in 2003 what would turn out to be one of its most popular and well-used programs—the National Do-Not-Call Registry that allows people to block the calls of telemarketers. The registry, however, would also prove controversial and contested. In particular, several telemarketing agencies filed lawsuits in 2003 against the FTC, alleging that it was beyond the scope of the FTC's jurisdiction to adopt the National Do-Not-Call Registry and claiming that the registry violated the First Amendment right of free speech of advertisers who use telemarketing.

In February 2004, the U.S. Court of Appeals for the 10th Circuit upheld the National Do-Not-Call Registry in *Mainstream Marketing Services, Inc.* v. *Federal Trade Commission.*[49] In concluding that the registry did not violate the First Amendment free speech rights of telemarketers, the appellate court applied the commercial speech doctrine and *Central Hudson* test (see pages 620–627). In a unanimous three-judge opinion, the appellate court wrote that

> the government has asserted substantial interests to be served by the do-not-call registry (privacy and consumer protection), the do-not-call registry will directly advance those interests by banning a substantial amount of unwanted telemarketing calls, and the regulation is narrowly tailored because its opt-in feature ensures that it does not restrict any speech directed at a willing listener. In other words, the do-not-call registry bears a reasonable fit with the purposes the government sought to advance. Therefore, it is consistent with the limits the First Amendment imposes on laws restricting commercial speech.

The FTC contended that the registry, which is a list containing the personal telephone numbers of telephone subscribers who have voluntarily indicated that they do not wish to receive unsolicited calls from commercial telemarketers, was necessary to reduce both intrusions upon consumer privacy in the home and the risk of fraudulent or abusive solicitations from telemarketers. The government had specifically limited the reach of the National Do-Not-Call Registry, which already had more than 50 million phone numbers by the time the appellate court issued its February 2004 opinion, only to telemarketing calls made by or on behalf of sellers of goods or services, and not to charitable or political fund-raising calls. The telemarketers, however, argued that the exemptions for political and charitable calls made the statute "underinclusive"—that to effectively serve the interests of protecting privacy and preventing fraud, the registry should also apply to political and charitable solicitations, not just to commercial sales calls. The appellate court, however, rejected the underinclusiveness argument, writing that "First Amendment challenges based on underinclusiveness face an uphill battle in the commercial speech context. As a general rule, the First Amendment does not require that the government regulate all aspects of a problem before it can make progress on any front." In other words, the government could focus its attention with the registry only on

---

49. 358 F. 3d 1228 (2004), *cert. denied,* 125 S. Ct. 47 (2004).

the problems caused by commercial sales calls without having to also sweep up and control problems caused by political and charitable calls.

The appellate court wrote that "four key aspects of the do-not-call registry convince us that it is consistent with First Amendment requirements." These aspects are as follows:

- The registry's application only to commercial sales calls—calls that, according to the court, "Congress, the FTC and the FCC have all determined to be most to blame for the problems the government is seeking to redress."
- The registry's targeting of "speech that invades the privacy of the home, a personal sanctuary that enjoys a unique status in our constitutional jurisprudence."
- The registry's nature as "an opt-in program that puts the choice of whether or not to restrict commercial calls entirely in the hands of consumers."
- The registry's ability to "materially further the government's interests in combating the danger of abusive telemarketing and preventing the invasion of consumer privacy, blocking a significant number of the calls that cause these problems."

The decision marked a victory for privacy advocates but can be seen as a blow to the free speech rights of telemarketers. In October 2004, the U.S. Supreme Court turned back a challenge to the appellate court's ruling, thus bringing an end (at least for the time being) to telemarketers' efforts to invoke free speech arguments to have the popular ban on unwanted phone solicitations declared unconstitutional.

The decision marked a victory for privacy advocates but can be seen as a blow to the free speech rights of telemarketers.

In late 2004, the FTC began its first civil lawsuit[50] enforcing the registry when it charged a Las Vegas company, the Braglia Marketing Group, with making more than 300,000 telemarketing calls to consumers on the national do-not-call list.[51] The FTC can mete out as much as $11,000 per infraction, which can add up quickly.

In early 2005, the FTC reached a settlement with the Braglia Marketing Group and its owners, Frank and Kate Braglia, for unlawfully calling hundreds of thousands of consumers who had placed their numbers on the registry. It was the first settlement reached by the FTC for violations of the do-not-call rules. Under the terms of the settlement, the defendants were banned from (1) ever owning more than 5 percent of a telemarketing operation; (2) directing a telemarketing operation; and (3) assuming responsibility for do-not-call compliance for a telemarketing operation. In addition, they were required to pay more than $526,000 in civil penalties, but that amount was reduced to $3,500 based upon their demonstrated inability to pay.

The settlement would prove to be just the first of many actions taken by the FTC to enforce the do-not-call rules. For instance, in July 2005, the FTC reached a settlement for $300,000 with Columbia House Company, a well-known direct marketer of home entertainment products such as DVDs and CDs, for violating federal law by calling existing or past subscribers of its home entertainment clubs after the subscribers had placed their telephone numbers on the National Do-Not-Call Registry, and after the subscribers had made specific requests to the company that they not be called. By September 2005, there were more than 105 million numbers on the National-Do-Not-Call Registry and it seemed clear that more actions in the future were inevitable as more people signed up for the service.

---

50. Complaint for Civil Penalties, Permanent Injunction, and Other Relief, *United States* v. *Braglia Marketing Group, LLC,* Case No. CV-S-04-1209-DWH-PAL (D. Nev. Aug. 30, 2004).

51. Davidson, "Feds Say Telemarketer Violated No-Call Rules."

To learn more about the National Do-Not-Call Registry, one can visit the FTC's Web site for the program at http://www.donotcall.gov.

REGULATING JUNK E-MAIL AND SPAM

One of the most pervasive and highly annoying forms of advertising today is on the Internet. Almost everyone who uses electronic mail is familiar with and has received unsolicited commercial advertising known as "spam." A 2005 survey conducted as part of the Pew Internet & American Life Project found that 67 percent of e-mail users consider spam to be unpleasant or annoying.[52] Without a filter or other form of protection on one's computer or e-mail system, spam can clutter an online mailbox. What's more, spam frequently takes the form of sexually explicit advertisements that may be both unwanted by, and offensive to, its recipients. On the other hand, to the extent that spam pertains to a lawful product and is neither false nor deceptive, it constitutes commercial speech that is protected by the First Amendment. Spam also represents an economically efficient and inexpensive way of marketing one's product or service.

To address the negative aspects of spam, Congress passed and President George W. Bush signed into law in 2003 a measure known as the CAN-SPAM Act.[53] The act's title represents a truly tortured acronym for a bill that was officially called the "Controlling the Assault of Non-Solicited Pornography and Marketing Act of 2003." The law took effect on January 1, 2004. It applies to "commercial electronic mail messages" that have as their "primary purpose" the "commercial advertisement or promotion of a commercial product or service."

In an excellent article on the CAN-SPAM Act,[54] attorneys Glenn B. Manishin and Stephanie A. Joyce identify five specific components of the law:

1. *False/Misleading Messages:* Commercial e-mail messages that include "materially false or misleading" header information or deceptive subject lines are prohibited.

2. *Functioning Return Address and Opt-Out Mechanism:* All commercial e-mail messages must contain either a functioning return address or an Internet-based reply "opt-out" mechanism for at least 30 days after transmission of a message.

3. *10-Day Prohibition Period:* Spam senders are barred from transmitting commercial e-mail messages to any recipient after 10 business days following the exercise by the recipient of his or her right to opt out of future commercial e-mail messages.

4. *Disclosure Requirements:* All commercial e-mail messages must disclose three specific items of content: (a) a clear and conspicuous identification of the message as an "advertisement or solicitation," (b) a notice of the "opt-out" mechanism, and (c) a "valid physical postal address." All commercial e-mail "that includes sexually oriented material" must also include a warning label on the subject line. To implement this provision, the FTC in May 2004 adopted a rule requiring

---

52. The organization's Web site can be found at http://www.pewinternet.org.
53. 15 U.S.C. § 7701 et seq. (2004).
54. Manishin and Joyce, "Current Spam Law & Policy."

spammers who send sexually oriented material to include the warning "SEXUALLY-EXPLICIT:" in the e-mail subject line or face fines for violations of federal law.[55] In addition, the matter in the spam e-mail message that is initially viewable when it is opened cannot include any sexually oriented material.

5. *Aggravated Violations:* The act proscribes as "aggravated violations," warranting additional civil and commercial penalties, (a) e-mail "harvesting" or the knowing use of harvested addresses, (b) the automated creation of multiple e-mail accounts used for commercial e-mail, and (c) the use of unauthorized relays for commercial e-mail messages.

The CAN-SPAM Act does not provide for a private legal cause of action or remedy for spam recipients. Instead, the Federal Trade Commission enforces the law. For instance, in November 2004, the FTC filed a complaint in federal court seeking to shut down an operation that used illegal spam to make deceptive claims about a magnetic, automotive fuel saver alternately called "FuelMAX" and "Super FuelMAX" that doesn't, in fact, save fuel. The FTC charged that the spam violates the CAN-SPAM Act. The FTC alleged that the spam contained the names of innocent third parties in the "from" or "reply to" fields—a practice known as spoofing—and did not contain a valid physical postal address.

In 2005, the FTC successfully used the CAN-SPAM Act to initially gain a temporary restraining order (and then a preliminary injunction) from a federal judge in Las Vegas, Nev., against a network of corporations and individuals that allegedly used spam to sell access to online pornography.[56] Among other things, the FTC contended that the defendants spammed hundreds of thousands of consumers without their consent, sending them sexually explicit or sexually suggestive e-mails that failed to include the required "SEXUALLY-EXPLICIT:" warning in the subject line of their sexually oriented messages, or failed to exclude the sexually oriented material from the initially viewable content of the messages. It marked the FTC's first law enforcement action targeting companies that spam consumers with sexually explicit e-mails in violation of the CAN-SPAM Act.

Also in 2005, the FTC contended that California-based Cleverlink Trading Limited and Real World Media, LLC, violated "nearly every provision of the CAN-SPAM Act" when they spammed millions of consumers with graphic sexual descriptions to drive traffic to their Web sites to "date lonely housewives."[57] Among other things, the FTC contended that the spam "contains misleading headers and deceptive subject lines. It does not contain a link to allow consumers to opt out of receiving future spam, does not contain a valid postal address, and

---

55. 16 C.F.R. 316 (2004).

56. *FTC* v. *Global Net Solutions, Inc.,* FTC File No. 042-3168, Civil Action No. CV-S-05-0002-PMP-LRL (D. Nev. 2005). The defendants included Global Net Solutions, based in Las Vegas, Nev.; Global Net Ventures, Ltd., based in London, England; Wedlake, Ltd., allegedly based in Riga, Latvia; Open Space Enterprises, Inc., based in Las Vegas; Southlake Group, Inc., based in Las Vegas; WTFRC, Inc., doing business as Reflected Networks, Inc., based in Las Vegas; Dustin Hamilton; Tobin Banks; Gregory Hamilton; Philip Doroff; and Paul Rose.

57. Press Release, "Spammer's Invitation to Date Lonely Housewives Halted by Court at FTC's Request," available at http://www.ftc.gov/opa/2005/05/housewives.htm. The FTC filed a lawsuit in the matter in federal court in Illinois. *FTC* v. *Cleverlink Trading Limited,* Case No. 05C 2889, File No. 042-3219 (N.D. Ill. 2005).

does not contain the disclosure, required by law, that it is sexually explicit. It also includes sexual materials in the initially viewable area of the e-mail, in violation of the FTC's Adult Labeling Rule."[58]

It is likely that there will be litigation over whether the CAN-SPAM Act violates the First Amendment protection of speech under the *Central Hudson* test and commercial speech doctrine (see pages 620–627). In addition, while the CAN-SPAM Act attempts to preempt state legislation on spam, an increasing number of states such as California and Virginia have drafted and are already enforcing their own laws against spam.[59] In April 2005, for instance, a judge in Loudoun County, Va., sentenced a 30-year-old North Carolina man named Jeremy Jaynes to nine years in prison for violating Virginia's anti-spam statute by "illegally flooding America Online accounts with tens of thousands of bulk e-mail advertisements."[60] Whether state laws like those in Virginia and California are valid will be left to courts to sort out in the near future. One of the first cases to address the issue of preemption was *White Buffalo Ventures* v. *University of Texas at Austin,* 420 F. 3d 366 (5th Cir. 2005), in which a federal appellate court held that a public university's internal anti-spam policy was not preempted by CAN-SPAM and that the university's anti-spam policy (referred to in the case as an anti-solicitation policy) was permissible under the *Central Hudson* commercial speech doctrine discussed earlier in this chapter. White Buffalo wanted to send unsolicited bulk commercial e-mails promoting its online dating services—one called "longhornsingles.com"—through the University of Texas' electronic mail system. White Buffalo contended that the university's anti-spam policy was preempted by the federal CAN-SPAM law and it sought an injunction prohibiting the university from enforcing its internal policy. The 5th Circuit Court of Appeals, however, rejected White Buffalo's argument in August 2005. In upholding the University of Texas' policy against spamming, the appellate court wrote that it was "unwilling to overrule the strong presumption against preemption."

Is the new federal law working? The answer is unclear. The Wall Street Journal reported in December 2004 that America Online had "seen a big decline in overall junk e-mail volume" in 2004, marking "a reversal of a five-year escalation in spam aimed at AOL members."[61] On the other hand, The New York Times reported in February 2005 that a "year after a sweeping federal anti-spam law went into effect, there is more junk e-mail on the Internet than ever."[62] According to The Times, "since the CAN-SPAM Act went into effect in January 2004, unsolicited junk e-mail on the Internet has come to total perhaps 80 percent or more of all e-mail sent, according to most measures. That is up from 50 percent to 60 percent of all e-mail before

---

58. Ibid.
59. In March 2005 a state court judge in Virginia threw out the conviction of a North Carolina woman named Jessica DeGroot on three felony charges of violating Virginia's anti-spam law. The judge concluded that "there was insufficient evidence that she flooded tens of thousands of America Online e-mail accounts with unsolicited bulk advertisements. But the judge upheld the conviction of the woman's brother [Jeremy D. Jaynes], who had been found guilty of the same crime." Brulliard, "Woman's Spam Conviction Thrown Out."
60. Brulliard, "Loudoun Judge Gives Spammer 9-Year Prison Term."
61. Richmond, "Canned Spam? AOL Notes Drop in Junk E-Mail."
62. Zeller, "Law Barring Junk E-Mail Allows a Flood Instead."

the law went into effect."[63] The long-term effects of anti-spam laws at both the federal and state level thus remain to be seen.

To increase the effectiveness of the CAN-SPAM Act, the FTC was considering a possible "bounty" system that would reward members of the public, whistle-blowers and so-called cybersleuths who track down spammers and provide high-value information about them. Such a reward system might help the FTC in overcoming three hurdles or difficulties that it identified in September 2004 in enforcing the Act:

- Identifying and locating the spammer
- Developing sufficient evidence to prove the spammer is legally responsible for sending the spam
- Obtaining a monetary award

In August 2005, the FTC released the results of a study of the practices of the top 100 "e-tailers," defined as companies that make significant use of the Internet to market their goods or services. The study involved the FTC creating its own e-mail accounts to test the e-tailers' practices, and it was designed to determine how well these companies were complying with CAN-SPAM's opt-out requirements. In a press release available on its Web site, the FTC reported "a high rate of compliance with the CAN-SPAM opt-out provisions. All of the e-tailers who sent e-mail to the FTC accounts provided clear notice of recipients' right to opt out of receiving future mail and provided recipients with an opt-out mechanism." It also determined that 89 percent of the e-tailers surveyed honored all of the opt-out requests received by the FTC staff.

In November 2005, the FTC issued another report, this one finding that spammers, using automated collection technologies, were continuing to harvest e-mail addresses from public areas of the Internet. But the report also noted that Internet service providers' anti-spam technologies could block the vast majority of spam sent to these e-mail addresses. The study, in which the FTC created 150 new undercover e-mail accounts to test the practices of companies gathering e-mail addresses, concluded that consumers who post their e-mail addresses on Web sites can reduce the risk of having their e-mail address harvested by masking their addresses. Masking entails the alteration of an e-mail address to make it understandable to the recipient but confusing to automated harvesting software.

In addition to tackling the problem of spam, the federal government is becoming increasingly involved in taking on another new and pesky form of advertising—unsolicited commercial facsimile messages. In July 2005, President George W. Bush signed into law the Junk Fax Prevention Act of 2005, which revises the Telephone Consumer Protection Act of 1991. Specifically, the Junk Fax Prevention Act of 2005 bans unsolicited advertisement faxes unless there is an "established business relationship" between the sender and recipient, known as an EBR exemption. If such an EBR exists, the express consent of the recipient is not necessary before a commercial fax may be sent. The Junk Fax Prevention Act of 2005 also imposes an opt-out provision requirement somewhat akin to that in the CAN-SPAM Act. In particular, the first page or cover sheet of all unsolicited fax ads must include a cost-free, opt-out provision allowing the recipient to be removed from the distribution list. The Federal Communications Commission is charged with investigating complaints and enforcing the new law.

63. Ibid.

SUMMARY   Self-regulation by the advertising industry has increased in recent years, especially with the growth of comparative advertising. The National Advertising Division and the National Advertising Review Board, divisions within the Better Business Bureau, are the primary agents for this self-regulation. Such regulation is geared toward satisfying the interests of advertisers rather than consumers, however. There has also been a rapid increase in lawsuits brought by advertisers against one another under Section 43(a) of the Lanham Act. An advertiser seeking redress under this federal law can seek to stop the misleading practice and/or win money damages. Again, this law provides little relief for consumers. Laws banning false advertising exist at both the state and local levels, but tend to be applied half-heartedly. The Federal Trade Commission remains the nation's most potent weapon against false or misleading advertising, but in the 1980s reflected the national political mood of getting government "off the backs of business" and took a passive approach to problems in advertising. The FTC became more vigorous in consumer protection in the late 1990s.

FEDERAL TRADE COMMISSION

One of the FTC's most important responsibilities is to ensure that Americans are not victimized by unfair, misleading or deceptive advertising. Through custom and practice, the agency has defined advertising as any action, method or device intended to draw the attention of the public to merchandise, to services, to persons and to organizations. Trading stamps, contests, freebies, premiums and even product labels are included in this definition, in addition to the more common categories of product and service advertising. At times a business has challenged the FTC by arguing that its particular exposition is not an advertisement but an essay or a statement of business philosophy. Rarely have these challenges been successful. Normally, what the FTC says is an advertisement is considered to be an advertisement for purposes of regulation.[64]

Does the FTC regulate all advertising? Legally, no, it cannot. But practically, it can regulate almost all advertising. Because the agency was created under the authority of Congress to regulate interstate commerce, products or services must be sold in interstate commerce or the advertising medium must be somehow affected by interstate commerce before the FTC can intervene. Although many products and services are sold locally only, nearly every conceivable advertising medium is somehow affected by or affects interstate commerce. All broadcasting stations are considered to affect interstate commerce. Most newspapers ship

Normally, what the FTC says is an advertisement is considered to be an advertisement for purposes of regulation.

64. The courts are not quite this consistent in defining advertising. Judges in both New York and California were asked recently whether statements taken from the text of a book and reprinted on promotional blurbs on the cover of the book were ads for the book or part of the text of the book. The publication involved was the "Beardstown Ladies' Common-Sense Investment Guide," a volume that contained highly exaggerated claims for the success of a particular investing scheme. All sides agreed that the false claims in the book were fully protected by the First Amendment, but the plaintiffs in both cases argued that when the claims were reprinted on the cover of the book (and the outside of a videotape cassette box) they were advertising or commercial speech and did not enjoy the full protection of the First Amendment. The court in California said the comments were commercial speech and not fully protected. The court in New York came to the opposite conclusion. See *Keimer* v. *Buena Vista Books,* 89 Cal. Rptr. 2d 781 (1999) and *Lacoff* v. *Buena Vista Publishing Inc.,* 705 N.Y.S. 2d 183 (2000).

at least a few copies across state lines. Even when a newspaper is not mailed across state lines, it is very likely that some of the news in the newspaper comes across state lines or that the paper on which the news is printed, the ink and type used to print the news, or parts of the printing machinery travel across state lines.

The FTC has consistently asserted jurisdiction over misleading or unfair practices on the Internet. In one case the agency brought a successful lawsuit against an Internet company that used unsolicited e-mails to try to convince Web users to buy billboards and banners on Web sites. "The rules for advertising by e-mail are the same as the rules for advertising through regular mail; don't mislead or lie to consumers or the FTC will come after you," said Jodie Bernstein, director of the agency's Bureau of Consumer Protection.[65] In May 2000 the commission issued a working paper in which it reiterated that all consumer protection guidelines it has promulgated apply to advertising and sales on the Internet. The paper focused on disclosures that must be contained on an Internet advertisement in order to prevent the ad from being misleading.[66] About one year later the agency issued another paper that reminded Internet retailers that they are subject to the same truth-in-advertising requirements that traditional brick-and-mortar sellers must comply with.[67]

Despite such warnings, the Internet continues to be a major source of consumer complaints filed with the FTC and its "Consumer Sentinel" database.[68] The FTC, in a report released in February 2005, found that Internet-related complaints accounted for 53 percent of all reported fraud complaints filed in the calendar year 2004, with monetary losses of more than $265 million and a median loss of $214. Some 57 percent of the fraud complaints in which the company's initial method of contact with the consumer was recorded were based on Internet solicitations: 35 percent via e-mail and 22 percent on the World Wide Web. The pie chart below indicates the overall top complaint categories from 2004, based on a total of 635,173 complaints received by the FTC-maintained Consumer Sentinel database between January 1 and December 31, 2004. A quick look reveals that, of the more than 635,000 complaints received, 61 percent were for various forms of fraud and a whopping 39 percent were for identity theft.[69] Of the fraud complaints filed in 2004, Internet Auctions was the leading complaint category, accounting for 16 percent of all consumer complaints. This category was followed by Shop-at-Home/Catalog Sales (8%), Internet Services and Computer Complaints (6%), Foreign Money Offers (6%), Prizes/Sweepstakes and Lotteries (5%), Advance-Fee Loans and Credit Protection (3%), Business Opportunities and Work-at-Home Plans (2%), and Telephone Services (2%).

Some other requirements must be met before the FTC can act. It must be shown that the agency is acting in the public interest, which is really not too difficult since false advertising

65. *Federal Trade Commission* v. *Maher,* DC Md., No. WMN 98-495, 3/4/98.
66. 5 E.C.L.R. 491 (2000).
67. 6 E.C.L.R. 121 (2001).
68. Consumer Sentinel, which was developed by the FTC and launched in 1997, collects information about consumer fraud and identity theft from the FTC and over 150 other organizations and makes it available to law enforcement partners across the nation and throughout the world for use in their investigations. One can learn more about it on its Web site located at http://www.consumer.gov/sentinel/pubs/Top10Fraud2004.pdf.
69. Credit card fraud (28%) was the most common form of reported identity theft in 2004, followed by phone or utilities fraud (19%), bank fraud (18%), and employment fraud (13%).

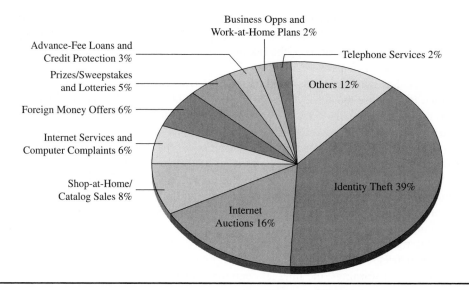

generally has an impact on the public. If the FTC says it is acting in the public interest, courts usually take its word for it.

Once it has been shown that the action meets the agency definition of "advertisement" and that it affects interstate commerce in some way, one final element must be present before FTC powers are invoked—the advertisement must be deceptive or untruthful. The standards currently used by the FTC to define deceptive advertising were outlined in 1983.[70] As cases proceed through the agency, minor tinkering with these standards can and does occur. It is an evolving policy. There are three parts to this deception policy.

FTC DEFINITION OF FALSE OR DECEPTIVE ADVERTISING

1. There must be a representation, omission or practice that is likely to mislead the consumer.
2. The act or practice must be considered from the perspective of a consumer who is acting reasonably.
3. The representation, omission or practice must be material.

FALSE ADVERTISING DEFINED

1. **There must be a representation, omission or practice that is likely to mislead the consumer.** The commission will consider the entire advertisement as well as all other elements of a transaction when making this determination. The issue is

---

70. FTC Policy Statement on Deceptive Acts and Practices, 4 Trade Reg. Rep. ¶13,205 at 20,919 (Oct. 4, 1983).

whether the act or practice is likely to mislead rather than whether it causes actual deception. In 1994, for example, the FTC ruled that health claims made by Häagen-Dazs about its frozen yogurts were false and misleading because many of the flavors were anything but "low fat" or "98 percent fat free." The commission also said that the company falsely claimed that its yogurt bars contained 100 calories and one gram of fat. Seven of the nine Häagen-Dazs flavors had 4 to 12 grams of fat per serving, while the Food and Drug Administration says "low fat" means 3 grams of fat or less. In addition, three of the eight frozen-bar flavors had more than 200 calories. The company said that each ad contained a disclaimer, in tiny print, that said the "98 percent fat free" referred only to certain flavors.[71]

The omission of important or material information in an advertisement can also be deceptive. For example, Beneficial Corporation, a finance company, advertised that it would provide a customer with an "instant tax refund" if the individual's tax return entitled him or her to a refund. But actually, what was unstated was that the customer had to first qualify for a loan, and there was nothing instant about the loan procedures. This omission was ruled to be deceptive by the FTC, and the agency ruling was upheld by a court of appeals.[72]

2. **The act or practice must be considered from the perspective of a consumer who is acting reasonably.** The test is whether the consumer's interpretation or reaction is reasonable. When advertisements or sales practices are targeted to a specific audience, such as those aimed at children, the elderly or the terminally ill, they will be viewed from the perspective of a reasonable member of that group. Also, advertising aimed at a special vocational group, such as physicians, will be evaluated from the perspective of a reasonable member of that group. A well-educated physician might be better able to understand a complicated pharmaceutical ad than the average individual can.

The advertiser is not responsible for every interpretation or behavior by a consumer. The law is not designed to protect the foolish or the "feeble minded," the commission has noted. "Some people, because of ignorance or incomprehension, may be misled by even a scrupulously honest claim," one commissioner noted. "Perhaps a few misguided souls believe, for example, that all Danish pastry is made in Denmark. Is it therefore an actionable deception to advertise Danish pastry when it is made in this country? Of course not," the commissioner noted.[73] When an advertisement conveys more than one meaning to a reasonable consumer, one of which is false, the seller is liable for the misleading interpretation. Here is a classic example: "Jones Garage will put a new motor in your car for only $350." What does this claim mean? One meaning is that the garage will sell you a new motor and install it for only $350. But an equally reasonable meaning is that for only $350 the garage will install a motor that you already own. If the second meaning is intended, the seller may very well be held responsible for the first meaning—which was not intended—as well.

---

71. Burros, "Minding the Store," B8.
72. *Beneficial Corporation* v. *FTC,* 542 F. 2d 611 (1976).
73. *In re Kirchner,* 63 F.T.C. 1282 (1963), aff'd. 337 F. 2d 751 (1964).

The commission will evaluate the entire advertisement when examining it for misrepresentation. Accurate information in the text may not remedy a false headline, because a reasonable consumer may only glance at the headline. If a television announcer proclaims that a watch is 100 percent waterproof, the advertiser cannot qualify this claim in a long printed message in small type that crawls across the bottom of the TV screen while the announcer tries to sell the product.[74] Nissan Motor Corporation agreed to stop its "Nissan Challenge" promotional advertising campaign. On its face the advertising said that Nissan would give consumers $100 if they bought a Honda Accord or Toyota Camry after test-driving a Nissan Stanza. But in order to get the $100 consumers had to meet several conditions, which were not prominently noted in the advertising. Consumers had to actually buy a Honda or Toyota, take delivery of it, and submit proof of purchase to Nissan within seven days of the test drive—but not on the same day as the test drive.[75] Similarly, an advertiser cannot correct a misrepresentation in an advertisement with point-of-sale information. A seller cannot advertise a vacuum cleaner as having a 100 percent money-back guarantee and then expect to qualify that claim in a tag that is attached to the product as it is displayed for sale in a store. Qualifying disclosures must be legible and understandable, the FTC has ruled.

"The commission generally will not bring advertising cases based on subjective claims (taste, feel, appearance, smell)," according to the 1983 guidelines. The agency says it believes the typical reasonable consumer does not take such claims seriously and thus they are unlikely to be deceptive. Such claims are referred to as **puffery** and include representations that a store sells "the most fashionable shoes in town" or a cola drink is "the most refreshing drink around."

Finally, the commission has stated that when consumers can easily evaluate the product or service, when it is inexpensive, and when it is frequently purchased, the commission will scrutinize the advertisement or representation in a less critical manner. "There is little incentive for sellers to misrepresent . . . in these circumstances since they normally would seek to encourage repeat purchases," a 1983 statement proclaims. That means the advertiser of small, dry cell batteries, a relatively inexpensive product purchased often by most consumers, will be given a bit more leeway in advertising than the advertiser of a $600 home generator.

3. **The representation, omission or practice must be material.** A material misrepresentation or practice is one that is likely to affect a consumer's choice of a product. In other words, according to the commission policy statement, "it is information that is important to the consumer." The FTC considers certain categories of information to be more important than others when deciding whether a claim is material. Express claims as to the attributes of a product are always considered material. Advertising claims that significantly involve health and safety are usually presumed to be material. Information pertaining to the "central characteristics of the product or service" are usually considered to be material. Information has also been found to be material where it concerns the purpose, efficacy, or cost of the product

---

74. *Giant Food, Inc.* v. *FTC,* 322 F. 2d 977 (1963).
75. "Nissan Unit Will Pull Ads."

or service. Claims about durability, performance, warranties or quality have also been considered material.

Demonstrations or mock-ups often become the subject of FTC inquiries, and the question of materiality is often raised. For many years a shaving cream manufacturer claimed that its product was so good that it could be used to shave sandpaper. In a TV demonstration, Rapid Shave was spread on sandpaper and then, a few moments later, the sand was shaved off. The demonstration was phony. What the demonstrator shaved was not sandpaper, but sand sprinkled on glass. The FTC argued that this advertisement was deceptive and that the claim that Rapid Shave could be used to shave sandpaper was a material representation. The Supreme Court agreed, despite the plea from Colgate-Palmolive that the product really could shave sandpaper if it was left on the paper long enough, but because the sand and the paper were the same color, a TV demonstration did not work. Hence the company had to use sand on glass.[76] The FTC found that two demonstrations used to advertise an immersion-style kitchen mixer in a 30-minute infomercial called "Amazing Discoveries: Magic Wand" were phony and hence misleading. The advertiser used a pineapple with the center core removed and precrushed to create the impression that Magic Wand could crush a whole fresh pineapple. The marketers also claimed Magic Wand would whip up skim milk, but they actually used a commercial dairy topping in their demonstration, the FTC said.[77]

But not all mock-ups or fake demonstrations are necessarily deceptive. Only those that are used to support a material product claim must be restricted. For example, plastic ice cubes may be substituted for the real thing in an advertisement for a soft drink because no claim about the quality of the ice cubes is involved.

Some lawyers who represent advertisers take the cynical view that an advertisement is deceptive when the FTC says it is, regardless of the content of policy statements or other official pronouncements. There is undoubtedly some truth to this argument. If an ad is ruled to be deceptive, what happens next? Let's now look at the means the FTC has at its disposal to control or correct false and deceptive advertising.

MEANS TO POLICE DECEPTIVE ADVERTISING

In dealing with false advertising, the FTC's greatest enemy is the time needed to bring an action against an advertiser. Since advertising campaigns are ephemeral, the FTC often has difficulty in catching up with the advertiser before the short-lived campaign has been replaced with something else. But if time is the greatest enemy, publicity is the FTC's strongest ally. Advertisers don't like the publicity that accompanies a charge of false advertising. A study by the commission of 122 false advertising cases acted upon between 1962 and 1985 revealed that the stock of companies charged usually dropped sharply after the charges were published. Bad publicity can cost a company millions of dollars. In addition, consumer reaction to the charges often results in lost sales as well.

---

76. *FTC v. Colgate-Palmolive Co.,* 380 U.S. 374 (1965).
77. Tewkesbury, "FTC Restricts Claims."

In addition to the informal sanction of publicity, the FTC has a wide range of remedies to deal with advertising. Let's briefly look at this arsenal.

FTC TOOLS OR REMEDIES TO STOP FALSE ADVERTISING

▮ Guides

▮ Voluntary compliance

▮ Consent agreement

▮ Litigated orders

▮ Substantiation

▮ Corrective advertising

▮ Injunctions

▮ Trade regulation rules

Guides

The FTC issues industry guides for a variety of products, services and marketing practices. These guides are policy statements that alert businesses to what the agency believes are permissible advertising claims or practices. Hundreds of such guides have been issued, including a guide on when the word "free" can and cannot be used in advertising, and guides for advertising private vocational schools, home study courses and environmental claims.

In July 1997 the FTC issued a statement that laid down principles by which it would evaluate the propriety of information collection and endorsement practices on Web sites used by children. The statement says, for example, that it is deceptive for a Web-site operator to represent that the personally identifiable information it collects from a child will be used for one purpose if the information will really be used for another purpose. The guide also says it is improper for Web-site operators to collect personally identifiable information about children and sell or disclose this information to third parties without the consent of the parents. In 1998, those guidelines were transformed into law after Congress passed the Child Online Privacy Protection Act (COPPA), which the FTC now actively enforces as the "COPPA Rule" to protect the privacy of children online.[78] For instance, in 2003 Mrs. Fields Cookies and Hershey Foods Corporation each agreed to settle FTC charges that their Web sites violated the COPPA by collecting personal information from children without first obtaining the proper parental consent. Mrs. Fields paid civil penalties of $100,000 and Hershey paid $85,000. In 2004, UMG Recordings and Bonzi Software settled FTC charges that they violated COPPA by knowingly collecting personal information from children online without first obtaining parental consent. UMG, an operator of several hundred music-related Web sites, paid civil penalties of $400,000, the largest civil penalty to date for a COPPA violation. According to

---

78. The FTC has information about the COPPA available on its Web site at http://www3.ftc.gov/privacy/privacyinitiatives/childrens.html.

the FTC, "UMG and Bonzi each violated the COPPA Rule when they failed to obtain verifiable parental consent before collecting extensive personal information from children under the age of 13. The companies each collected birth date information through their online registration processes, and thus had actual knowledge that they were collecting and maintaining personal information from thousands of children under the age of 13."[79] The COPPA Rule applies to operators of commercial Web sites and online services directed to children under the age of 13 and to general audience Web sites and online services that knowingly collect personal information from children under 13.

In November 1998 the agency issued a 26-page set of guidelines for advertising claims about dietary supplements. The guidelines address not only advertising claims made by the companies, but also claims that may be implied by advertising. The booklet contains 36 hypothetical advertising claims and explains how the law would apply to them. The dietary supplement industry earned nearly $12 billion in 1997, and many manufacturers have been accused of making extravagant claims about the efficacy of their products.[80]

Abuses still occur in this area despite the guidelines, and the FTC has been increasingly vigilant about taking action. For instance, it filed or settled 17 separate enforcement actions between December 2002 and July 2003 against parties engaged in false or misleading advertising of dietary supplements and other products deceptively marketed for their purported ability to treat or cure a wide variety of health conditions.[81] The FTC estimated these actions target products with a total of more than $1 billion in consumer sales. Given such concerns, the FTC introduced in December 2003 a new 18-page reference guide entitled "Red Flag: Bogus Weight Loss Claims" that was designed to help media outlets voluntarily screen out deceitful weight-loss advertisements. The FTC followed up its campaign against bogus weight-loss claims when, in November 2004, it launched "Operation Big Fat Lie," a nationwide law enforcement sweep against six companies making false and unsubstantiated weight-loss claims in national advertisements. The challenged ads ran in publications such as Cosmopolitan, USA Weekend and the San Francisco Chronicle. The products at issue included pills, powders, green tea, topical gels and diet patches. The FTC's sustained efforts against fraudulent weight-loss advertisements finally seemed to be paying off in 2005 when the FTC reported that year that the number of obviously false weight-loss claims in television, radio and print advertisements for dietary supplements, topical creams and diet patches appeared to have dropped from almost 50 percent in 2001 to just 15 percent in 2004.[82]

The guides don't have the force of law; in other words, a business that violates a provision of a guide is not automatically guilty of false advertising. The FTC will usually require an advertiser to substantiate claims that go beyond those permitted by the guides or may even bring a false advertising action against the business. The guides are of great benefit, however, to honest advertisers who seek to stay within the boundaries of what is allowable under the law.

79. FTC Press Release, "UMG Recordings, Inc. to Pay $400,000, Bonzi Software, Inc. to Pay $75,000 to Settle COPPA Civil Penalty Charges," available online at http://www.ftc.gov/opa/2004/02/bonziumg.htm.
80. Grady, "F.T.C. Guidelines Restrict Ad Claims."
81. The FTC documented this development on its Web site at http://www.ftc.gov/opa/2003/07/diethealth.htm.
82. "2004 Weight-Loss Advertising Survey."

Voluntary Compliance

Industry guides apply only to prospective advertising campaigns, events that have not yet occurred. The next remedy on the ladder is voluntary compliance and is used for advertising campaigns that are over or nearly over. Imagine that a company is nearing the end of an advertising campaign in which it has advertised that its mouthwash can prevent a consumer from getting a common cold. The FTC believes that the claim is deceptive. If the advertiser has had a good record in the past and if the offense is not too great, the company can voluntarily agree to terminate the advertisement and never use the claim again. In doing this, the advertiser makes no admission and the agency no determination that the claim is deceptive. There is just an agreement not to repeat that particular claim in future advertising campaigns. Such an agreement saves the advertiser considerable legal hassle, publicity and money, all especially desirable since the advertising campaign is over or almost over. This remedy is infrequently used.

Consent Agreement

The most commonly used FTC remedy is the consent agreement, or **consent order.** This is a written agreement between the commission and the advertiser in which the advertiser agrees to refrain from making specific product claims in future advertising. The advertiser admits no wrongdoing by signing such an order, so there is no liability involved. The consent agreement is merely a promise not to do something in the future. Sometimes the misleading statements are minor errors, but other times they represent a major attempt at deception. In 1996 the FTC won a consent agreement with the Remco Toys division of Azrak-Hamway International for the television advertising of its Steel Tec toy vehicle kits. The FTC said that the company misrepresented the number of toys that could be constructed from the kits and the kinds of things the toys could do. The toys, which cost between $9 and $40, were manipulated off-screen in the advertisements by hidden wires or tubes. Children who tried to play with the vehicles discovered that the toys did not perform as they had in the advertisements. Although the toy company continued to deny that its advertising was misleading, it nevertheless agreed to give customers who bought the toys a complete refund to avoid long and costly litigation with the FTC.[83] Here are some other examples of recent consent agreement settlements:

- In 2005 Tropicana Products, Inc. agreed to stop making claims, unless they can be substantiated in the future by reliable scientific evidence, that drinking two to three glasses each day of its "Healthy Heart" orange juice would produce dramatic effects on blood pressure and cholesterol and thereby reduce the risk of heart disease and stroke.[84]
- In 2003, the maker of a pill called Bloussant, which was claimed on television and in magazine ads to increase breast size by two cups in most women, agreed to settle with the FTC charges that it made false and unsubstantiated claims and to possess, in the future, scientific substantiation before making such claims again.

83. Collins, "Toy Maker to Give Refunds," C5.
84. Press Release, "FTC Puts the Squeeze on Tropicana's Orange Juice Claims," available at http://www.ftc.gov/opa/2005/06/tropicana.htm.

■ WebTV, a subsidiary of Microsoft, agreed to stop misrepresenting the capabilities of its enhanced TV system and promised to disclose to customers that many of them would incur long distance telephone charges while connected to the Internet via WebTV.

■ Jenny Craig Inc. agreed to terminate advertising that featured testimonial claims from customers who succeeded in losing weight unless these advertisements actually reflect the common results of Jenny Craig clients or explicitly state that the results portrayed are not typical.

■ Gerber Products Company agreed to stop claiming that four out of five pediatricians recommended Gerber baby food, since the study on which the company relied showed that only 12 percent of the pediatricians surveyed recommended Gerber.

Considerable pressure is placed on the advertiser to agree to a consent order. Refusing to sign the agreement will result in litigation and publicity. The publicity can do more harm to the advertiser than a monetary fine. Also, the time factor works in the advertiser's favor. Typically the advertising campaign is already over. A spokesperson for Häagen-Dazs said the company signed the consent agreement promising not to misrepresent the calorie or fat content of any of its products in the future "because we pulled the ads a year ago."[85]

Considerable pressure is placed on the advertiser to agree to a consent order.

What happens to an advertiser who signs a consent decree, then violates the provisions of the decree? In 1997 Mazda Motors of America signed an agreement to disclose far more clearly in its advertising important terms and conditions it imposed in leasing automobiles, including the up-front costs and the number, amount and timing of scheduled lease payments. While the company did improve disclosure in its advertising, it still spent too much time and space highlighting low monthly payments and insufficient time and space outlining the total lease cost, the government said. In October 1999 the FTC, working in conjunction with 24 states, levied a $5.25 million fine against the auto maker for failing to follow the stipulations it agreed to in the consent decree.[86]

Litigated Order

Sometimes an advertiser doesn't want to sign a consent agreement. It may believe that the advertising claim is truthful or may simply want to hold off any FTC ban on certain kinds of product claims. In this case the Federal Trade Commission can issue an order, usually called a **litigated order,** to stop the particular advertising claim. Staff attorneys at the FTC will issue a complaint against the advertiser, and a hearing will be held before an administrative law judge. The judge can uphold the complaint or reject it. In either case, the losing side can appeal to the federal trade commissioners for a final ruling. If the advertiser loses this final appeal before the commissioners, he or she can appeal the litigated order in federal court. Failure to abide by the provisions of a litigated order can result in the advertiser facing a severe civil penalty, as much as $10,000 per day. In the long-running (11 years) Geritol case, for example, the commission issued an order in 1965 prohibiting the J.B. Williams Company from implying in its advertising for Geritol that its product could be helpful to persons who complained that they

---

85. Burros, "Minding the Store," B8.
86. "Mazda Gets Hit with $5.25 Million in Fines."

were tired and run-down.[87] The commission contended that medical evidence demonstrated that Geritol, a vitamin-and-iron tonic, helps only a small percentage of people who are tired and that in most people tiredness is a symptom of ailments for which Geritol has no therapeutic value. The J.B. Williams Company violated the cease and desist order (at least, that is what the commission alleged) and in 1973 was fined more than $800,000. A court of appeals threw out the fine in 1974 and sent the case back to district court for a jury trial, which the advertisers had been denied the first time around.[88] The jury was to decide whether the Geritol advertisements did in fact violate the cease and desist order. At a second hearing in 1976, the FTC won a $280,000 judgment against the patent medicine manufacturer.

In 2000 the manufacturers of Bayer Aspirin agreed to pay a $1 million fine after the FTC charged that the company was falsely advertising that nearly all adults could prevent heart attacks and strokes by taking Bayer Aspirin. While aspirin can be a potent heart protector for some people, the agency said, it is not recommended for just anyone. There is little evidence that aspirin prevents a heart attack in someone who does not already have vascular disease, said a spokesperson for the American Heart Association. The drugmaker agreed to spend the $1 million to settle the case. The money was to be used for consumer education—including newspaper advertising and a consumer brochure—that was designed to clear up any misunderstanding about the effectiveness of the drug in preventing heart attacks and strokes.[89]

In September 2004, Chief Administrative Law Judge Stephen J. McGuire ordered the marketers of a device called the "Ab Force" belt to stop making claims that it caused or promoted weight, inches, and fat loss; caused or promoted well-defined abdominal muscles; or was an effective alternative to regular exercise.[90] The gizmo, which was marketed on infomercials (see page 637 discussing infomercials) by a New Jersey–based operation called Telebrands Corporation, is an electronic muscle stimulation (EMS) device that causes the muscles to contract involuntarily. Judge McGuire concluded that the "Ab Force" advertisements were "likely to mislead consumers, acting reasonably under the circumstances, in a material respect."

Substantiation

Advertising **substantiation** has been an important part of the FTC regulatory scheme since 1972. The basis of the program is simple: The commission asks advertisers to substantiate claims made in their advertisements. The FTC does not presume that the claims are false or misleading. The advertiser is simply asked to prove the claims are truthful. The substantiation process today involves panels of experts who scrutinize advertisements and target for documentation those claims that seem most suspect. The most recent commission policy statement on substantiation was issued in 1984. Under this policy, express substantiation claims, such as "doctors recommend" and "specific tests prove," require the level of proof advertised. Otherwise, advertisers will be expected to have at least a "reasonable basis" for claims in their advertising, wrote attorney Thomas J. McGrew in the Los Angeles Daily Journal.[91] The

---

87. *J.B. Williams* v. *FTC,* 381 F. 2d 884 (1967).
88. *U.S.* v. *Williams Co.,* 498 F. 2d 414 (1974).
89. Neergaard, "Bayer Rolls Back Ad Claims."
90. *In the Matter of Telebrands Corp.,* Initial Decision, Docket No. 9313 (Sept. 15, 2004).
91. McGrew, "Advertising Law."

degree of substantiation that will be deemed reasonable varies with "the type of claim, the product, the consequences of a false claim, the benefits of a truthful claim, the cost of developing substantiation . . . and the amount of substantiation experts in the field believe is reasonable," the policy statement said. Statements from satisfied customers usually are not sufficient to support health and safety claims requiring objective evaluation.

Corrective Advertising

Corrective advertising is a highly controversial scheme based on the premise that to merely stop an advertisement is in some instances insufficient. If the advertising campaign is successful and long running, a residue of misleading information remains in the mind of the public after the offensive advertisements have been removed. Under the corrective advertising scheme, the FTC forces the advertiser to inform the public that in the past it has not been honest or has been misleading. One commentator called the scheme "commercial hara-kiri."

The corrective advertising sanction was first used by the FTC in 1971 and was applied frequently during the heady consumer protection years of the 1970s. The agency has never outlined a hard-and-fast policy regarding when corrective advertising will be used. In response to a request from the Institute for Public Representation for such a policy statement, the FTC said corrective advertising may be applied:

> If a deceptive advertisement has played a substantial role in creating or reinforcing in the public's mind a false and material belief which lives on after the false advertising ceases, there is clear and continuing injury to competition, and to the consuming public as consumers continue to make purchasing decisions based on the false belief.

Since the early 1980s the corrective advertising sanction has been used sparingly by the agency. But it does still exist as a policy choice. In May 1999 the FTC ordered a giant pharmaceutical company, Novartis A.G., to run advertising correcting earlier statements that called its Doan's back-pain relievers superior to other analgesics. The agency said the company must spend $8 million on advertising messages that include the words, "Although Doan's is an effective pain reliever, there is no evidence that Doan's is more effective than other pain relievers for back pain." The company must make similar disclosures on its packaging for one year.[92]

Injunctions

When Congress passed the Trans-Alaska Pipeline Authorization Act in 1973, attached to that piece of legislation was a bill that authorized the FTC to seek an injunction to stop advertisements that it believed violated the law. Attorneys for the FTC can seek these restraining orders in federal court. An injunction is clearly a drastic remedy and one that the agency has said it will not use often. Spokespersons for the FTC have said that the agency will use the power only in those instances in which the advertising can cause harm, in those cases that contain a clear law violation, and in those cases in which there is no prospect that the advertising practice will end soon.

Attorneys for the FTC can seek these restraining orders in federal court.

92. "Novartis Is Ordered to Fix Doan's Ads."

For example, the FTC won a preliminary injunction against the National Commission on Egg Nutrition to block advertising claims that no scientific evidence exists linking egg consumption to a higher risk of heart disease. A lower court ruled that an injunction was too severe because it limited public debate on the cholesterol issue and damaged the advertisers financially. But a court of appeals reversed the lower-court ruling and granted the injunction.[93]

• In September 2004, the FTC reached a massive settlement, including a permanent injunction, in federal court with Kevin Trudeau, a prolific marketer who had either appeared in or produced hundreds of infomercials (see page 637 discussing infomercials). The settlement enjoined Trudeau from appearing in, producing, or disseminating future infomercials that advertise any type of product, service, or program to the public, except for truthful infomercials for informational publications.[94] Trudeau agreed to these prohibitions and to pay the FTC $2 million to settle charges that he falsely claimed that a coral calcium product called Coral Calcium Supreme can cure cancer and other serious diseases and that a purported analgesic called Biotape can permanently cure or relieve severe pain. In nationally televised infomercials, Trudeau had advertised that Coral Calcium Supreme, a dietary supplement purportedly made from Japanese marine coral, provided the same amount of bio-available calcium as two gallons of milk, could be absorbed into the body faster than ordinary calcium, and could cure illnesses such as cancer and heart disease. In another infomercial, Trudeau asserted that Biotape, an adhesive strip, provided permanent relief from severe pain, including debilitating back pain, and pain from arthritis. Lydia Parnes, acting director of the FTC's Bureau of Consumer Protection, said the permanent injunction "is meant to shut down an infomercial empire that has misled American consumers for years. Other habitual false advertisers should take a lesson; mend your ways or face serious consequences."

Trade Regulation Rules

In January 1975, President Ford signed the Magnuson-Moss Warranty–Federal Trade Commission Improvement Act, the most significant piece of trade regulation legislation since the Wheeler-Lea Amendment in 1938. The new law did many things, but basically it greatly enlarged both the power and the jurisdiction of the FTC. Until the bill was signed, the FTC was limited to dealing with unfair and deceptive practices that were "in commerce." The new law expanded the jurisdiction to practices "affecting commerce." The change of a single word gave the FTC broad new areas to regulate. The law also gave the agency important new power.

Three sections of the act expanded the remedies the FTC can use against deceptive advertising. First, the agency was given the power to issue trade regulation rules defining and outlawing unfair and deceptive acts or practices. The importance of this power alone cannot be overestimated. In the past the agency had to pursue deceptive advertisements one at a time. Imagine, for example, that four or five different breakfast cereals all advertise that they are good for children because they contain nine times the recommended daily allowance of vitamins and minerals. Medical experts argue that any vitamins in excess of 100 percent of the

93. *FTC* v. *National Commission on Egg Nutrition,* 570 F. 2d 158 (1977).
94. *FTC* v. *Trudeau,* Stipulated Final Order for Permanent Injunction and Settlement of Claims for
Monetary Relief, Case Nos. 03-C-3904 and 98-C-016 (N.D. Ill. 2004).

recommended daily allowance are useless; therefore, these advertisements are probably deceptive or misleading. In the past the FTC would have had to issue a complaint against each advertiser and in each case prove·that the statement was a violation of the law. Under the new rules, the agency can issue a trade regulation rule—as it had done for nutritional claims—that declares that claims of product superiority based on excessive dosage of vitamins and minerals are false and misleading. If advertisers make such claims, they are in violation of the law. All the commission must prove is that the advertiser had actual knowledge of the trade regulation rule, or "knowledge fairly implied from the objective circumstances."

The advantages of the **trade regulation rules,** or TRRs as they are called, are numerous. They speed up and simplify the process of enforcement. Advertisers can still litigate the question, challenge the trade regulation rule, seek an appeal in court, and so forth. In most cases they probably will not go to that expense. Trade regulation rules have had a great deterrent effect, as they comprehensively delimit what constitutes an illegal practice. In the past, after the commission issued a cease and desist order, businesses frequently attempted to undertake practices that fell just outside the narrow boundaries of the order. The TRRs are much broader and make it much harder for advertisers to skirt the limitations. Finally, via TRRs the FTC is able to deal with problems more evenhandedly. An entire industry can be treated similarly, and just one or two businesses are not picked out for complaint.

The second aspect of the law that improved FTC remedies allowed the FTC to seek civil penalties against anyone who knowingly violates the provisions of a litigated order, even if that person was not originally the subject of the order. To wit: Chemical company A sells a spray paint that is toxic if used in a closed area, but the product is advertised as being completely harmless. The FTC moves against the company and issues a cease and desist order stating that in the future the firm must not advertise the product as being completely harmless. Chemical company B also sells a spray paint that has the same toxicity and is advertised the same way. If it can be shown that company B was aware of the provisions of the order against company A and continued to advertise its product as being completely safe, B can be fined up to $10,000 per day for violating the order, even though the order is not directed against B.

The third section of the law gave the FTC the right to sue in federal court on behalf of consumers who have been victimized by practices that are in violation of a cease and desist order or by practices that are in violation of a TRR, a right that the agency has been reluctant to use.

SUMMARY

The Federal Trade Commission has the power to regulate virtually all advertising that is deceptive or misleading. To be deceptive an advertisement must contain a representation, omission or practice that is likely to mislead the consumer; the advertisement or practice must be considered from the perspective of a reasonable consumer; and the representation, omission or practice must be material. The FTC has many remedies to regulate deceptive or untruthful advertising:

1. Guides or advisory opinions that attempt to outline in advance what advertisers may say about a product

2. Voluntary agreements by advertisers to terminate a deceptive advertisement
3. Consent agreements or consent orders signed by advertisers promising to terminate a deceptive advertisement
4. Litigated orders to advertisers to terminate a particular advertising claim, failure to comply with which can result in severe penalty
5. Substantiation of advertisements, in which the advertiser must prove all claims made in an advertisement
6. Corrective advertising, in which an advertiser must admit in future advertisements that past advertisements have been incorrect
7. Injunctive power to immediately halt advertising campaigns that could cause harm to consumers
8. Trade regulation rules that can be issued to regulate advertising throughout an entire industry

THE REGULATORY PROCESS

To understand the importance of the regulatory process, students should be familiar with procedures followed in a deceptive advertising case, be aware of the kinds of advertising that can be considered deceptive, and be familiar with the defenses to a charge of deceptive advertising.

PROCEDURES

The FTC does not attempt to scrutinize every advertisement that is published or broadcast. Most cases come to the attention of the agency from letters written by either consumers or competitors. Today, an individual can file a complaint online from the FTC's Web site at http://www.ftc.gov. When a complaint is received, FTC staff attorneys examine it to see if it has merit. If they can find none, the case ends. If the staff members believe there is a provable violation, then a proposed complaint, a proposed consent agreement, and a memorandum are prepared for the commissioners. The commissioners then vote on whether to issue a complaint.

If the commissioners agree that the advertisement is in violation of the law, the advertiser is notified and given the opportunity to either sign the consent agreement that has been drafted or negotiate with the agency for a more favorable order. At this point one of three things can happen:

1. The advertiser can agree to sign the agreement, and the commissioners vote to accept this agreement. If this happens the order is published and made final in 60 days.
2. The advertiser can agree to sign the agreement, but the commissioners reject it.
3. The advertiser can refuse to sign the agreement.

If either of the latter two events occurs, a complaint is issued against the advertiser, and a hearing is scheduled before an administrative law judge. The judge works within the FTC and officiates at these hearings. The hearing is a lot like a trial, only more informal. If the judge believes that there is substantial evidence that the advertisement violates the law, he or she will issue an order telling the advertiser to stop this illegal practice (this is the litigated order). The judge also has the authority to dismiss the case. At this point either side can appeal to the commissioners to overturn the ruling of the judge.

If the commissioners agree that the advertisement is not misleading or deceptive, the case ends. But if the commissioners support an administrative law judge's ruling against an advertiser, the order becomes law after it is finalized by an appellate court. The advertiser may appeal this decision in a federal court.

It is difficult for courts to reverse an FTC ruling. There are only a handful of reasons that a judge can use to overturn the commission decision. The case goes to the court of appeals, and there is no new finding of fact: What the FTC says is fact, is fact. The following are all instances in which a court can overturn an FTC ruling: (1) "convincing evidence" that the agency made an error in the proceedings, (2) no evidence to support the commission's findings, (3) violation of the Constitution—for example, the agency did not provide due process of law, (4) the action goes beyond the agency's powers, (5) facts relied on in making the ruling are not supported by sufficient evidence, and (6) arbitrary or capricious acts by the commission. An appeal of an adverse ruling by a circuit court can be taken to the Supreme Court, but only if certiorari is granted.

There are only a handful of reasons that a judge can use to overturn the commission decision.

SPECIAL CASES OF DECEPTIVE ADVERTISING

A few special problems regarding deceptive advertising deserve special mention before we leave this topic.

Testimonials

The publication and broadcast of advertising of all kinds has escalated in recent years, but none faster than the growth of testimonial advertising. Whether the testimony comes from a celebrity like Bill Cosby, a race car driver, an organization like the National Football League, or simply an average consumer, product endorsements have grown dramatically in popularity. A dramatic increase in the broadcast of the 30-minute infomercials, which often feature celebrities, has resulted in even more testimonial advertising. For whatever reasons, advertisers believe (and they might be right) that for many people, a recommendation to buy a product by either a celebrity or a common person is highly persuasive. The Federal Trade Commission has issued "Guides Concerning Use of Endorsements and Testimonials in Advertising."[95] (See page 650 for more about FTC guides.) These guides don't have the force of law; the FTC would have to prove that an advertiser who failed to follow one of the guidelines violated the

95. 16 C.F.R. § 25 (1990).

federal false advertising statute. But they do clearly outline the parameters that guide the agency in scrutinizing testimonial advertising.

The FTC defines an endorsement or testimonial as an advertising message that consumers are likely to believe reflects the opinions, beliefs, findings or experience of a party other than the sponsoring advertiser. The endorsement can be communicated by a verbal message, demonstration, picture or likeness, signature, or other identifying personal characteristic or the seal of an organization.

The question of what is or is not an endorsement becomes more complicated each day, especially when an entertainer or celebrity is involved. The unknown announcer who reads a pitch for a soft drink or over-the-counter drug is surely not an endorser. What about a well-known performer with a recognizable voice who reads a script for a voice-over in a TV ad for a carmaker? No, not an endorser, just an actor making a living. Actors and actresses who actually appear as fictional characters in television or print ads are not considered endorsers, even though they may be recognizable as celebrities. But it is likely to be considered an endorsement when William Shatner (Captain James Kirk of the starship Enterprise for the uninitiated) promotes a Web site that markets discount airline tickets and hotel reservations, or when a well-known athlete touts a brand of candy bar.

In 2003, the FTC claimed that former baseball star Steve Garvey was more than just a paid actor when he was involved in two infomercials that allegedly made false and unsubstantiated claims for two weight-loss products called "Fat Trapper" and "Exercise in a Bottle." The two products together were part of the so-called Enforma System, and the two infomercials on which Garvey, the former Los Angeles Dodger, was involved aired about 48,000 times in the United States from December 1998 through May 2000. Between December 1998 and December 2000, sales of "Fat Trapper," "Fat Trapper Plus," and "Exercise in a Bottle" totaled more than $100 million. In making the infomercials, Garvey largely read from prepared scripts; he made only minor, nonsubstantive edits for his own speech patterns and vocabulary choices. Before shooting the infomercials, Garvey had tried the products and he reviewed two booklets on them containing information purporting to contain significant and relevant information substantiating claims made in the infomercials. In September 2004, a federal appellate court cleared Garvey of any civil liability in the matter, as either a direct participant in the making of false advertising claims or as an endorser of the product.[96] Judge Harry Pregerson wrote for a unanimous 9th U.S. Circuit Court of Appeals that "we find that the FTC has failed to show that Garvey was recklessly indifferent to the truth of his statements or was aware that fraud was highly probable and intentionally avoided the truth. . . . Garvey had firsthand anecdotal evidence of the efficacy of the Enforma System and had information that purported to present scientific bases for his claims." The court noted that "Garvey himself used the system and lost approximately eight pounds during a three-or-four-week period" and that his wife, "while using the Enforma System, lost approximately twenty-seven pounds between the filming of the first infomercial and the date the program was broadcast to the public." Ultimately, the court concluded that "the Garveys' weight loss is undisputed, and Garvey undoubtedly has firsthand knowledge of those facts. The endorsement claims—that he and his wife lost a certain number of pounds—clearly pass any substantiation

---

96. *FTC* v. *Garvey*, 383 F. 3d 891 (9th Cir. 2004).

requirement for celebrity endorsers." The appellate court's ruling clearing Garvey represents the highest court ruling on celebrity endorsements.

Although Garvey got off the hook as the celebrity pitchman for the products, things did not work out so well for the products themselves or their sellers. In early 2005 the FTC reached a settlement with Enforma Natural Products Inc. and several individual owners of "Fat Trapper" and "Exercise in a Bottle" that permanently enjoined them from ever advertising or marketing any weight-loss product, except exercise programs and equipment, and that required them to pay out $300,000 in consumer redress.[97] In addition, the settlement bans the continued use of the trademarks for "Fat Trapper," "Fat Trapper Plus," and "Exercise in a Bottle." The settlement came as a result of the FTC's allegations that the defendants violated the terms of an earlier May 2000 final order against them by continuing to make unsubstantiated and false claims regarding the purported weight-loss products. The FTC also secured a stipulated final order and settlement in February 2005 with the producers of the infomercials—a company called Modern Interactive Technology Inc. and its two principals, Mark Levine and David Richmond—that requires them to have "competent and reliable scientific evidence" for any and all future claims for dietary supplements and weight-loss products.[98]

Prior to 1932, when an individual received money for giving a testimonial, that fact had to be clearly stated in the advertisement. That is no longer the law. The government today believes that when a celebrity or expert endorses a product, consumers expect that person to have been paid for that testimony. But payment to a nonexpert or noncelebrity, the so-called average consumer, must be revealed if the promise of payment was made prior to the endorsement, or the consumer/endorser had reason to believe that a favorable endorsement might later result in payment, through the appearance in an advertisement for the product. Let's look at a hypothetical situation. Dr Pepper is seeking consumer endorsements for a new soda it has marketed. It takes these endorsements from letters it has received from satisfied customers. The soda drinkers gave the endorsement without any promise or hope of getting something in return. They can be paid for the use of their endorsements in advertising, and this payment does not have to be revealed. But if Dr Pepper seeks favorable consumer reactions at an in-store tasting of the new product and promises people who have not yet tasted the drink that if they give a good review to the new soda they may be paid to be in a television commercial, the fact that the endorsers were paid must be revealed in the advertisement. Even if the soda maker doesn't make a promise of payment but has a video camera recording customer reactions, this situation would meet the government standard that the consumer had reason to believe that a favorable review of the product could result in some future benefit. The entire thrust of these "Guides on Endorsements" is to assure the consumer that he or she is getting the honest opinions and beliefs of the endorser.

Experts who endorse products must have the expertise to evaluate the products. The government is especially concerned about endorsements of health and safety products. The identification of the expert must be accurate. The endorser of an automobile identified as an "engineer" must be an automotive engineer, not a chemical engineer. The FTC ruled that

97. Stipulated Final Order for Permanent Injunction and Settlement of Claims for Monetary Relief, *FTC* v. *Enforma Natural Products, Inc.,* Civil Action No. CV 00-04376-SVW (C.D. Cal. 2005).

98. Stipulated Final Order for Permanent Injunction and Settlement of Claims, *FTC* v. *Garvey et al.,* Civil Action No. CV 00-09358 GAF (C.D. Cal. 2005).

an expert endorsement by former astronaut Gordon Cooper of a product that supposedly increased automobile performance, reduced smog emission, and cleaned an engine was improper. Cooper's skill related to space missions; he did not have the education or training to qualify as an "expert" in the field of automobile engineering.[99]

A celebrity or expert endorser must be a bona fide user of a product at the time of the endorsement. This rule means the individual must use the product more than "now and then" or "once in a while." And endorsers must use a product because they like it and approve of it. The advertiser can continue to use the endorsement only so long as there is good reason to believe that the endorser still uses the product.

When an organization—like the National Football League—endorses a product, there must be evidence that the endorsement represents the collective judgment of the members of the organization, not just the judgment of the executive director or the management council of the group.

Celebrity endorsements must also reveal a material connection between endorsers and products if one exists.

Celebrity endorsements must also reveal a material connection between endorsers and products if one exists. Singer Pat Boone was fined by the FTC for failing to meet this rule in his endorsements of Acne-Statin, a skin-blemish medication. Cooga Mooga Corporation, owned and operated by Boone for the purpose of promoting the performer's business interests, was one of several companies marketing and promoting the skin medication. Boone received 25 cents for each $9 bottle sold. In this case Boone also implied that his four daughters had used the preparation successfully, which was not completely true, and that Acne-Statin was superior to other similar products, an expert evaluation he was not qualified to make.[100] This case was the first time a celebrity had been held directly responsible for deceptive endorsement. The singer paid a large fine and was ordered to pay partial restitution to persons who had bought the product. The link between a product and a celebrity endorser does not have to be as direct as the connection between Boone and Acne-Statin to require disclosure. Former astronaut Gordon Cooper was paid for his endorsement of the previously noted automotive product on the basis of the number of devices sold. The more products sold, the more money he received. The FTC ruled that this arrangement was a material connection between the product and the endorser and should have been revealed in the endorsements.[101]

An endorser cannot make any statement about a product that an advertiser cannot make. An advertiser cannot state that a cough syrup cures a cold; an endorser cannot say that either, even if he or she truly believes it.

Endorsements that claim to be from typical consumers must be made by consumers, not by actors playing the part of consumers. Note that most "man/woman on the street" testimonials never make the claim that the endorsers—who are normally actors—are typical consumers. That conclusion is one that advertisers hope we as viewers reach, but since no such claim is made, the ads are permissible. Finally, an endorsement concerning the efficacy of a product must represent the experience of a typical user. If a so-called baldness cure works on only one man in 500, the endorsement of the product by this person as a representative user would be clearly misleading.

99. In re *Leroy Gordon Cooper,* 94 F.T.C. 674 (1979).
100. In re *Cooga Mooga, Inc. and Charles E. Boone,* 92 F.T.C. 310 (1978).
101. In re *Leroy Gordon Cooper,* 94 F.T.C. 674 (1979).

Bait-and-Switch Advertising

One of the classic false advertising games is what is called **bait-and-switch advertising.** Here is the general idea. An appliance store advertises in the newspaper that it is selling a brand-new washing machine for $177. The advertisement is the bait to get customers into the store. When customers come to the store to grab up this bargain, the salesclerks are very honest about the advertised washer and say that it is a pile of junk (and it probably is!): It has no dials, it tears fine fabrics, it tends to leak, its motor is loud, and so forth. However, over in a corner is a really good buy, a snappy model that is on sale for $595. This high-pressure selling is the switch. If customers insist on buying the bait, chances are they will be told the machines have all been sold. The merchant had never intended to sell that model. The whole idea is to use the bait to lure into the store people who are in the market for washing machines, and then skillful, if not honest, salesclerks switch customers to a more costly model via high-pressure selling—convenient monthly payments and so forth.

Bait-and-switch advertising is illegal. Technically, the law says that it is deceptive to advertise goods or services with the intent not to sell them as advertised or to advertise goods and services with the intent not to supply reasonably expected public demand, unless limitation on the quantity is noted in the advertisement.

Bait-and-switch advertising is not the same as loss-leader advertising, legal in many places, in which a merchant offers to sell one item at below cost (the leader) in order to get customers into the store in the hope that they will then buy additional merchandise at regular cost. Supermarkets use this scheme and so do other retail outlets. Those states that outlawed this practice did so because of pressure from small merchants who cannot afford to sell anything at a loss and do not want to be put at a marketing disadvantage with high-volume sellers.

DEFENSES

The basic defense against any false advertising complaint is truth, that is, proving that a product does what the advertiser claims it does, that it is made where the advertiser says it is made, or that it is as beneficial as it is advertised to be. Although the burden is on the government to disprove the advertiser's claim, it is always helpful for an advertiser to offer proof to substantiate advertising copy.

Another angle that advertisers can pursue is to attack a different aspect of the government's case rather than try to prove the statement true. For example, an advertiser can argue that the deceptive statement is not material to the advertisement as a whole (that is, it will not influence the purchasing decision) or that the advertisement does not imply what the government thinks it implies. For example, to say, as Dry Ban did, that a deodorant "goes on dry" does not mean that it is dry when it is applied, merely that its application is drier than that of other antiperspirants.

The success rate in defending false advertising cases is not high. As with most legal problems, it is best to consult legal counsel before a problem arises and not after a complaint has been issued.

ADVERTISING AGENCY/PUBLISHER LIABILITY

What is the liability of the advertising agency that generates the ad or the medium that publishes or broadcasts it? The law in both regards is slowly changing. At one time neither the agency nor the publisher had much to fear. That is not the case now. Let's look at ad agency liability first.

At one time the ad agency could likely have avoided liability if it could show that it acted at all times under the direction and control of the client.[102] But today an agency might be held responsible if it can be shown that it was an active participant in the production of a false or misleading ad and that it knew or *should have known* that the advertisement was false and misleading.[103] This liability could result if the agency uses false and misleading data provided by the client or if it creates a false impression in the advertisement based on truthful data provided by the client.[104] It is the extent and nature of the agency's participation in the false campaign that will ultimately determine liability.

The liability of publishers is also changing.

The liability of publishers is also changing. Traditionally publishers have not been held responsible for the contents of their advertising. Courts, however, have re-examined this principle. In 1988 a U.S. District Court ruled that Soldier of Fortune magazine was liable in a wrongful death action because it had published an advertisement that led indirectly to a murder. In 1984 a man named John W. Hearn placed this advertisement in the personal services section of the magazine's classified advertising:

> Ex-Marine—67–69 Nam Vets—ex D.I.—weapons specialist—jungle warfare, pilot, M.E. high risk assignments U.S. or overseas.

A phone number accompanied the advertisement. Robert Black Jr. contacted Hearn and paid him $10,000 to kill his wife, Sandra Black. Hearn was caught and convicted of the crime and is now serving three life sentences in Florida for that murder and two other contract killings. Robert Black was convicted as well and was sentenced to die for his part in the slaying.

Sandra Black's mother and son sued the magazine, and in March 1988 a jury awarded the pair $9.4 million. The federal court ruled in this case that the First Amendment protection of commercial speech did not foreclose a simple negligence action by the survivors against the magazine.[105] But the 5th U.S. Circuit Court of Appeals threw out the decision, asserting that the ad placed by Hearn was simply too innocuous to punish the magazine for publishing it. "Given the pervasiveness of advertising in our society, and the important role it plays, we decline to impose on publishers the obligation to reject all ambiguous advertising for products or services that might pose a threat of harm," the court said.[106]

---

102. Kertz and Ohanian, "Recent Trends."
103. In re *American Home Products Corp.,* 98 F.T.C. 136 (1981).
104. In re *Merck & Co.,* 69 F.T.C. 526 (1966).
105. *Eimann* v. *Soldier of Fortune,* 680 F. Supp. 863 (1988).
106. *Eimann* v. *Soldier of Fortune,* 880 F. 2d 830 (1989).

Two years later, however, another federal trial court, looking at another classified ad in Soldier of Fortune, again found the magazine responsible. A gunman who killed one man and wounded another was hired on the basis of a classified ad in the magazine. This time the advertisement said:

> Gun for Hire: 37-year-old mercenary desires jobs. Vietnam Veteran. Discreet and very private. Bodyguard, courier, and other special skills. All jobs considered.

A telephone number and address followed. The U.S. district judge noted that in *Eimann,* the appellate court had ruled that the magazine was not liable because the advertisement was too innocuous or vague. Here, however, the ad was different: much less vague, according to the court. The phrases "Gun for Hire," "Discreet and very private," and "All jobs considered" certainly raise issues not found in the earlier ruling, the judge said. Whether a magazine should be held liable in this wrongful death action is a question properly left with the jury, the court said. The jury awarded the plaintiff $12.4 million, but the court reduced that amount to $2.4 million.[107]

In 1992 the 11th U.S. Circuit Court of Appeals upheld the lower-court ruling, saying that a publisher could be found liable for publishing "a commercial advertisement where the ad, on its face, and without the need for investigation, makes it apparent that there is a substantial danger of harm to the public."[108] The court granted $4.3 million in damages to the plaintiff. There have been no subsequent adverse decisions, but these rulings are a warning to publishers and broadcasters that it is always prudent to exercise care when accepting advertising.

SUMMARY

Complaints against advertisers are prepared by the FTC staff and approved by a vote of the commission. Administrative law judges can hold hearings, which are somewhat like trials, to determine whether the FTC charges are valid. A U.S. Court of Appeals can review all commission orders. Advertisers need to take special care when dealing with testimonials and endorsements. The law outlaws bait-and-switch advertising, in which customers are lured to a store with promises of low prices but then are pushed by salespersons to buy more expensive products. Although ad agencies and publishers/broadcasters are generally not held liable in cases of false or harmful advertising, there are signs that the law is changing.

107. *Braun* v. *Soldier of Fortune,* 757 F. Supp. 1325 (1991).
108. *Braun* v. *Soldier of Fortune,* 968 F. 2d 110 (1992).

BIBLIOGRAPHY ————————————————————————————————➤

"A Positive Agenda for Consumers: The FTC Year in Review." Federal Trade Commission, April 2003.

Brulliard, Karen. "Loudoun Judge Gives Spammer 9-Year Prison Term." *Washington Post,* 9 April 2005, B03.

———. "Woman's Spam Conviction Thrown Out." *Washington Post,* 2 March 2005, E01.

Burros, Marian. "Minding the Store on Food Claims." *The New York Times,* 23 November 1994, B8.

Cancelada, Gregory. "CBS and NBC Will Stop Running Some Miller Ads After Complaint by A-B." *St. Louis Post-Dispatch,* 18 December 2004, B03.

Collins, Glenn. " In Settlement, Toy Maker to Give Refunds." *The New York Times,* 13 February 1996, C5.

Cushman, John, Jr. "Judge Rules F.D.A. Has Right to Curb Tobacco as Drug." *The New York Times,* 26 April 1997, A1.

Davidson, Paul. "Feds Say Telemarketer Violated No-Call Rules." *USA Today,* 1 September 2004, 3B.

Daykin, Tom. "Networks Blow Whistle on Ads." *Milwaukee Journal Sentinel,* 6 January 2005, D3.

DeVore, P. Cameron. "Commercial Speech: 1988." Remarks to Communications Law 1988 Practicing Law Institute, New York City, 10 November 1988.

———. "Supreme Court Boots Commercial Speech." *First Amendment Law Letter,* Fall 1990, 5.

"Election Ad Law Struck Down." *The Washington Newspaper,* July 1998, 1.

Grady, Denise. "F.T.C. Guidelines Restrict Ad Claims for Supplements." *The New York Times,* 18 November 1998, A20.

Greenhouse, Linda. "Justices Strike Down Ban on Casino Gambling Ads." *The New York Times,* 15 June 1999, A1.

Howard, John A., and James Hulbert. *A Staff Report to the Federal Trade Commission.* Washington, D.C.: Federal Trade Commission, 1974.

Kertz, Consuelo L., and Roobina Ohanian. "Recent Trends in the Law of Endorsement Advertising." *Hofstra Law Review* 19 (1991): 603.

Kogan, Jay S. "Celebrity Endorsement: Recognition of a Duty." *John Marshall Law Review* 21 (1987): 47.

Labaton, Stephen. "The Regulatory Signals Shift." *The New York Times,* 6 June 2001, C1.

Manishin, Glenn B., and Stephanie A. Joyce. "Current Spam Law & Policy: An Overview and Update." *Computer & Internet Lawyer,* September 2004, 1.

Mann, Charles C., and Mark L. Plummer. "The Big Headache." *The Atlantic Monthly,* October 1988, 39.

"Mazda Gets Hit with $5.25 Million in Fines." *Seattle Post-Intelligencer,* 1 October 1999, B2.

McGrew, Thomas J. "Advertising Law: Inactive FTC, Activism in Courts." *Los Angeles Daily Journal,* 17 January 1985.

Morris, Brian. "Consumer Standing to Sue for False and Misleading Advertising under Section 43(a) of the Lanham Trademark Act." *Memphis State University Law Review* 17 (1987): 417.

Neergaard, Lauran. "Bayer Rolls Back Ad Claims of Benefits from Aspirin Use." *Seattle Post-Intelligencer,* 12 January 2000, A3.

"A Nissan Unit Will Pull Ads." *The New York Times,* 10 March 1993.

"Novartis Is Ordered to Fix Doan's Ads." *The New York Times,* 28 May 1999, C16.

Pompeo, Paul E. "To Tell the Truth: Comparative Advertising and Lanham Act Section 43(a)." *Catholic University Law Review* 36 (1987): 565.

Richmond, Riva. "AOL Notes Decline in Junk E-Mail, as Trend Reverses." *The Wall Street Journal,* 28 December 2004, D3.

Rohde, David. "Sweepstakes in Agreement to Reimburse New Yorkers." *The New York Times,* 25 August 1998, A16.

Rohrer, Daniel M., ed. *Mass Media, Freedom of Speech, and Advertising.* Dubuque: Kendall/Hunt, 1979.

Rosden, George E., and Peter E. Rosden. *The Law of Advertising.* New York: Matthew Bender, 1986.

Savage, David G. "Supreme Court Upholds Fees for Beef Ads." *Los Angeles Times,* 24 May 2005, A12.

Singdahlsen, Jeffrey P. "The Risk of Chill: A Cost of the Standards Governing the Regulation of False Advertising under Section 43(a) of the Lanham Act." *Virginia Law Review* 77 (1991): 339.

Tepper, Maury. "False Advertising Claims and the Revision of the Lanham Act: A Step in Which Direction?" *Cincinnati Law Review* 59 (1991): 957.

Tewkesbury, Don. "FTC Restricts Claims by Infomercial Producers." *Seattle Post-Intelligencer,* 8 July 1993.

Waltzer, Garrett J. "Monetary Relief for False Advertising Claims Arising under Section 43(a) of the Lanham Act." *UCLA Law Review* 34 (1987): 953.

Weber, Matthew G. "Media Liability for Publication of Advertising: When to Kill the Messenger." *Denver University Law Review* 68 (1991): 57.

"2004 Weight-Loss Advertising Survey: A Report from the Staff of the Federal Trade Commission." Federal Trade Commission, April 2005.

Zeller, Tom, Jr. "Law Barring Junk E-Mail Allows a Flood Instead." *The New York Times,* 1 February 2005, A1.

TELECOMMUNICATIONS REGULATION

There are literally volumes of federal rules that govern the operation of telecommunications in the United States. A substantial number of them focus exclusively on technical rules, for example, regulations on the height of broadcast towers or the power of transmitters. In this chapter we focus on two other kinds of rules: those that govern who can own and operate telecommunications facilities and those that regulate the content that is carried over these facilities. Both sets of rules clearly implicate the First Amendment, and there is a wealth of new material in this edition of the book on the regulation of "indecent" broadcast content by the Federal Communications Commission.

A PROLOGUE TO THE PRESENT

It is certainly easier to look at an institution like the law or government as it is now, without having it obscured by the haze of the past. But in the area of telecommunication regulation the past is an important prologue to the present. The past two decades witnessed a revolution in the governance of broadcasting and cablecasting, a revolution that is not yet over. These radical changes are highly controversial. Many people who have lived through these changes say the very soul of broadcasting has been irrevocably harmed. Other people, many of whom work in the industry, argue that the changes were long overdue. The changes were wrought by Congress and the Federal Communications Commission, under pressure from both the telecommunications industry and the federal courts. They are the result of a fundamental change in the way the industry is viewed, as less of a publicly oriented entity designed to serve society and more of a private business whose primary responsibilities lie with its customers (primarily advertisers) and its stockholders. An incremental but substantial redefinition of the meaning of the First Amendment spurred these developments. To understand telecommunications regulations today it is necessary to spend at least a few paragraphs discussing the development of both the telecommunications industry and the government rules that shaped it.

HISTORY OF REGULATION

The regulation of telecommunications in the United States dates from 1910, shortly after radio was developed. Congress passed a law that required all U.S. passenger ships to have a radio. Two years later the federal legislature adopted the **Radio Act of 1912,** which required that all radio transmitters be licensed by the federal government and that radio operators be licensed by the government as well. In the 1920s radio grew far faster than most observers had thought possible. There were millions of listeners and far too many stations. The electromagnetic spectrum, or the airwaves, through which radio signals travel is a finite medium. As a modern freeway can hold only so many vehicles, the airwaves can hold only so many radio signals. Too many cars on the highway cause accidents and gridlock. Too many radio signals meeting in the spectrum cause similar chaos. Signals overlap and block each other. To listeners the result is gibberish. Near the end of the 1920s a reluctant Congress was forced to act once again; it adopted the **Radio Act of 1927,** a comprehensive set of rules aimed at creating order from the problem caused by too many people trying to broadcast radio signals at the same time. The new law governed who could and could not broadcast, and when they could broadcast. But it focused on the content of radio programs as well. Both the licensing and the content regulations implicated the First Amendment. Radio broadcasting surely amounted to speech and press, rights guaranteed under the Bill of Rights. Surprisingly, the issue hardly arose. Three factors more than any other were responsible for the muted debate. Educators, labor and religious leaders, and others who saw broadcasting as primarily a noncommercial vehicle for the transmission of information and ideas, a medium much like the early printed press, raised questions about freedom of expression. But their queries were drowned out by the louder and more powerful voices of commercial broadcasters who were much more interested in seeing laws adopted that cleared away the existing broadcast cacophony and permitted them to get on with their money-making endeavors.[1] Hypothetical First Amendment problems were not a priority to these broadcasters. Second, the meaning of the First Amendment, the one we understand today, had evolved hardly at all by the 1920s. There was a constitutional guarantee of freedom of expression, all right, but few besides diligent constitutional scholars knew or cared about the dimensions of this guarantee. The courts were just beginning to interpret the First Amendment. Third, only a handful of broadcasters and listeners perceived of radio as anything other than a commercially based entertainment medium. There was no regular news on radio until later in the next decade. Movies did not enjoy First Amendment protection; neither did the circus. And radio seemed to be a lot more like those two phenomena than like newspapers, magazines or books.

The 1927 statute was substantially amended and revised seven years later when Congress adopted the **Federal Communications Act** in 1934. This law remains as the base for all telecommunications regulation today. It expanded the earlier statute to include telephones and the telegraph as well as radio. And it provided for the appointment of the Federal Communications Commission, or FCC, to regulate all these telecommunications media—the same FCC that some 70-plus years later is the bane of Eminem and Howard Stern's existence.

THE CHANGING PHILOSOPHY OF BROADCAST REGULATION

Even though the debate over First Amendment protection of broadcasting was never truly joined, a philosophy that justified a substantial regulation of broadcasting nevertheless existed. This philosophy was anchored by two seemingly immutable propositions. First, the broadcast spectrum is a limited transmission pathway. Not all who want to transmit radio signals can do so. Second, while private individuals might own the transmitters, the towers, the microphones and all the other paraphernalia that allow radio signals to be transmitted, the American people own the transmission path, the radio spectrum, through which the signals travel to the listener's radio set. As such, those who *use* the spectrum are bound to serve the needs of those who *own* the spectrum. So somebody had to decide who, among all those who sought to broadcast, should have that privilege. Rules were also needed to ensure that broadcasters met the needs of the spectrum owners. That is when the government stepped in, deciding who could and who could not broadcast, and establishing rules to ensure that those who

1. McChesney, "Battle for U.S. Airwaves."

did broadcast met their responsibilities to the people. The government called these responsibilities "meeting the public interest, convenience or necessity," or PICON, an acronym that became the code word to justify all the rules relating to broadcasting. And within PICON's critical concept of "public interest," the FCC traditionally has identified three major policy objectives that allegedly lead to its promotion:

- Competition
- Diversity
- Localism

Broadcasters who fulfilled the public interest mandate were permitted to use the airwaves to reap power and wealth; those who did not were punished by fines or loss of the privilege of broadcasting. Both Congress and the Federal Communications Commission fashioned a wide range of rules to ensure the fidelity of broadcasters between the late 1920s and the 1960s. Some of the issues that were dealt with were

- who could and could not broadcast, and how long a broadcast license could be held without being renewed;
- the number of broadcast properties and other media properties, like newspapers, a single individual or company could own;
- the responsibility of broadcasters to try to divine the needs and interests of the public they served;
- rules that required license holders to broadcast information about important community issues and to make certain that all sides of these issues were represented in the broadcasts;
- rules that ensured that political candidates would have access to radio and television stations to communicate with the voters; and
- rules that limited the number of commercial minutes that could be contained in each broadcast hour.

The thrust of these rules was simple. It was thought that the broadcast industry could best serve the nation if as many different individuals as possible owned the limited number of broadcast stations and if those who were permitted to broadcast provided a broad range of material to entertain, educate and inform the listeners and viewers. And the government, primarily the FCC, would ensure that these rules were followed.

But the two propositions that provided the underpinning for this regulatory philosophy turned out to be less immutable than first imagined, and the rationale for regulation began to unravel. True, the broadcast spectrum is limited. But new media forms, like cable television and the Internet, promised new pathways with unlimited transmission space. And the notion that broadcasters must serve the public interest began to erode under pressure from the new economic liberalism that grew in the last 25 years of the 20th century. The idea of serving the interests of the market as opposed to serving the needs of the public developed as a dominant theme in the industry. The large corporations that owned much of the telecommunications media argued that giving listeners and viewers what they wanted to hear and watch made more sense than giving them what the government thought they should hear and see. It was also more lucrative for station owners. So capitalism and market-driven theories were in; paternalism and PICON were put on the back burner. In addition, didn't the First Amendment bar just the sort of meddling that the government was undertaking with its myriads of regulations? Ultimately the regulators, courts, and even Congress bought into these ideas.

The incremental application of this new philosophy resulted in a general dismantling of broadcast regulations. These changes took place over the past 25 years. The most recent modifications were announced in the spring of 2003. The changes affected some rules relating to content, but most impacted regulations relating to the ownership of mass media properties. Rules regarding the number of radio and/or television stations a single broadcaster could own, rules limiting the ownership of a newspaper and broadcasting property in the same city by a single individual, and rules limiting the number of customers a multiple-system cable operator could serve were all relaxed. The length of time a broadcast license can be held without being renewed was substantially lengthened. Details about most of the modified rules are outlined in subsequent sections of this chapter. But a great many regulations have simply been abandoned. Included were the following:

- Rules that restricted the major television networks from owning and syndicating television programs
- Rules that required broadcasters to formally ascertain the needs and interests of listeners and viewers so they could devise programming that best served these needs
- Rules that required broadcasters to report all sides of important public controversies in their community, the so-called fairness doctrine
- Rules that indirectly limited the number of commercial minutes that could be broadcast every hour
- Rules that barred one individual from owning both a radio and television station in one of the top 50 markets
- Rules that limited the rates a cable television provider could charge subscribers
- Rules that prohibited a television station from owning a cable system and a television station in the same market, or vice versa
- Rules that prohibited a television network from owning another television network
- Rules that required television stations to provide free reply time for opponents of political candidates endorsed by the station, and for persons whose reputation or integrity was attacked by someone using the station
- Rules that prohibit a cable television system from carrying the signal of any broadcast station if the system owns a broadcast station in the same local market

THE *PROMETHEUS* DECISION

Many people think the law is nonpolitical, that it doesn't reflect the tensions that exist in a heterogeneous society. The law is simply the means to resolve disputes among competing interests. But remember the words of Justice Oliver Wendell Holmes quoted in Chapter 1 (see page 7). The law reflects the felt necessities of the times, the prevalent moral and political theories, intuitions of public policy, even the prejudices of judges, he wrote. Nowhere is this more true than in the regulation of telecommunications. And that is why it is important to understand what has happened with regard to these rules. For the debate and the disputes have not yet ended. In particular, the 3rd U.S. Circuit Court of Appeals in June 2004 issued a split 2-1 opinion that spanned more than 200 pages and dealt a major blow both to some of the FCC's measures to loosen media ownership rules and to the efforts of massive conglomerates seeking further ownership expansion across different media in local markets. The rules the FCC had adopted in 2003 (see page 680) were challenged by a number of citizen-activist groups, such as the aptly named Media Access Project, that were afraid of further consolidation of media ownership.

The case, *Prometheus Radio Project* v. *FCC,*[2] affirmed the power of the FCC to regulate media ownership. But, more important, it also held that "the Commission has not sufficiently justified its particular chosen numerical limits for local television ownership, local radio ownership, and cross-ownership of media within local markets." For instance, the appellate court held that while the FCC has the authority and power to repeal its nearly 30-year-old ban that prohibits common ownership of a full-service television broadcast station and a daily public newspaper in the same media community (known as the television/newspaper cross-ownership rule), the numerical limits that the FCC adopted in its place in 2003 on matters such as cross-ownership of newspapers, radio stations and television stations (see page 680) were not sufficiently justified by the FCC. The two-judge majority of the 3rd Circuit wrote:

> We have identified several provisions in which the Commission [FCC] falls short of its obligation to justify its decisions to retain, repeal, or modify its media ownership regulations with reasoned analysis. The Commission's derivation of new Cross-Media Limits, and its modification of the numerical limits on both television and radio station ownership in local markets, all have the same essential flaw: an unjustified assumption that media outlets of the same type make an equal contribution to diversity and competition in local markets.

The appellate court then instructed the FCC either to come up with additional justifications for its efforts to relax media ownership rules or to modify them. Until that time, the appellate court continued to stay the enforcement of the new rules (to put them on hold, as it were)—it previously had issued an emergency order in September 2003 preventing the FCC from enforcing the rules. As Bill Carter wrote in The New York Times, "frustration was the dominant emotion among media company executives" when they read the decision because "they will be stymied for some time in trying to take advantage of the relaxed FCC rules."[3] The now-enjoined 2003 rules, for instance, would have allowed a media conglomerate to own a daily newspaper, three TV stations, eight radio stations and a cable system in the same city.

The 2004 appellate court decision in *Prometheus Radio Project* v. *FCC* also frustrated then-FCC chairman Michael Powell, who told the Washington Post after the decision, "The court wants more explanation for the lines we drew. Yes, we failed to convince them on the first try. But we were not sort of way out of whack the way people portrayed it."[4]

The *Prometheus Radio Project* decision, however, did leave intact the 39 percent "national audience reach" limit (see page 680) on television ownership adopted by Congress in January 2004, thus allowing Viacom and News Corp., both of which already owned enough stations in 2004 to reach that cap, not to have to worry about selling off or divesting themselves of any stations. The term "national audience reach" is defined as the total number of television

---

2. 373 F. 3d 372 (3d Cir. 2004), *cert. denied,* 125 S. Ct. 2904 (2005).
3. Carter, "Media Ruling Merely Irritates Big Owners."
4. Ahrens, "Powell Calls Rejection of Media Rules a Disappointment."

households reached by a single entity's stations, with UHF stations attributed with only 50 percent of the television households reached (known as a "50 percent UHF discount"). In addition to this 39-percent rule for national audience reach remaining in effect in the realm of television, there continues to be no limit on the total number of radio stations that a single entity/licensee can own on a national basis.

In January 2005, shortly after Michael Powell announced that he would step down in March of that year as chairman of the FCC, the government also announced that it would not ask the U.S. Supreme Court to review the 3rd Circuit's ruling in *Prometheus Radio Project* v. *FCC*. Powell had fervently supported the now-enjoined 2003 rules that would have relaxed media ownership limits and encouraged further consolidation. Although the FCC and the Bush administration tossed in the towel on fighting for the 2003 rules, that did not entirely end the matter. Showing yet another layer of the political and economic complexities and machinations of the legal issues, the National Association of Broadcasters, the Tribune Co. (owner of newspapers such as the Chicago Tribune and the Los Angeles Times), News Corp.'s Fox, Viacom Inc.'s CBS and General Electric Co.'s NBC filed a joint petition asking the U.S. Supreme Court in 2005 to hear the case. They contended that the appellate court's 2004 decision in *Prometheus Radio Project* v. *FCC* abridged their First Amendment rights by restricting their capacity to engage in expression and limiting their ability to own both television stations and newspapers in the same market. Another petition was filed in 2005 by Sinclair Broadcast Group asking the Supreme Court to overturn the appellate court's decision.

In June 2005 the United States Supreme Court denied the petitions for certiorari and refused to hear the case, thus letting stand the appellate court's 2004 decision in *Prometheus Radio Project* v. *FCC*. The reaction to the high court's decision laid bare the raw politics behind the media ownership rules. In a very brief June 13, 2005, press release addressing the Supreme Court's decision, Republican FCC Chairman Kevin Martin stated, "I am now looking forward to working with all of my colleagues as we reevaluate our media ownership rules consistent with the Third Circuit's guidance and our statutory obligations." In stark contrast, Democratic Commissioner Jonathan Adelstein issued an effusive statement the same day, calling the high court's decision not to disturb the Third Circuit's ruling "a rare victory for the public over some of the most powerful corporations in America. The American public is concerned about concentration in the media, and our court system has rightly responded. The court's decision puts the issue of media consolidation right back in the FCC's hands and gives us an opportunity for a fresh start, so we better get it right this time. . . . We can't let a handful of media giants dominate the discourse in any community." It was anticipated that in 2006 the FCC would launch new proceedings evaluating its media ownership rules. In brief, the FCC now faces the daunting and politically tricky task of crafting new regulations that are consistent with the determinations of the appellate court's 2004 decision in *Prometheus Radio Project* v. *FCC*.

The reaction to the high court's decision laid bare the raw politics behind the media ownership rules.

But the effect of the 3rd Circuit's 2004 opinion restoring most of the old ownership rules was already being felt in 2005 before the Supreme Court even had a chance to deny the petitions for certiorari. This was particularly true when a federal judge in March 2005 in the case of *Ellis* v. *Tribune TV Co.* ordered the defendant media conglomerate to sell off a television station it owned in Waterbury, Conn.[5] The *Ellis* case centered on the FCC's television/newspaper cross-ownership rules—rules that had been relaxed by the FCC in 2003 but then

5. *Ellis* v. *Tribune TV Co.*, 363 F. Supp. 2d 121 (D. Conn. 2005).

were restored by the 3rd Circuit's 2004 ruling in *Prometheus Radio Project*. Those rules provide that the FCC shall not grant a license for a TV broadcast station to a company that either directly or indirectly operates or controls a daily newspaper in the same community or media market.[6] The legal trouble for the Tribune Co., which today owns major newspapers such as the Chicago Tribune and the Los Angeles Times, began in 2000 when it acquired the Hartford Courant newspaper in Connecticut. That acquisition came as part of a takeover by the Tribune Co. of the newspapers of another media giant, Times Mirror. Just before the Tribune Co. acquired the Courant, however, it was already managing and was applying with the FCC to acquire a television station, WTXX-TV Channel 20, in Waterbury, Conn., a town that falls within the same Hartford media community served by the Courant. In brief, the Tribune Co. was seeking to own both a television station (WTXX) and a daily newspaper (the Courant) in the same community, putting it in conflict with the television/newspaper cross-ownership rules. To address this situation, the FCC in 2001 issued an order granting the Tribune Co. a temporary, short-term waiver from the cross-ownership rules in order to allow it to resolve the conflict by selling off the WTXX television station in 2002. When this did not occur, however, and the Tribune Co. still owned both properties in 2003, a man named Neil Ellis, whose wife owns a small newspaper outside of Hartford, filed a lawsuit seeking to order compliance by the Tribune Co. with the earlier FCC order to divest itself of WTXX.[7] In March 2005, a federal district court judge sided with Ellis, found that the cross-ownership rules were violated and thus ordered Tribune to sell off WTXX. The FCC, however, came to the rescue of the Tribune Co. in April 2005 and granted it another short-term waiver and extension until April 2007 to sell off WTXX. But the news was not all good for the Tribune Co. at that time, as the FCC denied the company's request for a permanent waiver for WTXX from the cross-ownership rules.

There is another legal twist to the case of *Ellis* v. *Tribune TV Co.* that illustrates the effect of a very different FCC rule from the one on television/newspaper cross-ownership described above. In particular, before acquiring either WTXX or the Hartford Courant, Tribune already owned another television station, WTIC-TV, that served the greater Hartford media market. The proposed purchase by Tribune of station WTXX when it already owned station WTIC conflicted with the FCC's television duopoly rule. The television duopoly rule prohibits a single entity like Tribune from owning more than one television station in the same media market unless there are at least eight independently owned and operated full-power commercial and noncommercial educational television stations left after the proposed acquisition in that market (this is known as "the eight-voices test") and if at least one of the two stations for which joint ownership is proposed is not ranked in the market in the top four stations in audience ratings. The acquisition of WTXX by Tribune would have failed the eight-voices test. The FCC, however, granted Tribune a waiver from the television duopoly rule because the FCC considered WTXX to be a "failing station" with a small audience share and weak financial performance that might not otherwise survive. Tribune thus was able to avoid the television duopoly rule and could acquire WTXX despite already owning WTIC. Although the judge in *Ellis* v. *Tribune TV Co.* concluded that Tribune's ownership of both the WTIC television station and the Hartford Courant newspaper violated the television/newspaper

---

6. 47 C.F.R. § 73.3555(d)(3).
7. Tuohy and Moran, "Judge Orders Tribune to Sell WTXX-TV."

cross-ownership rule (just as the judge had found that the Tribune's ownership of WTXX and the Courant violated that rule), the FCC had earlier granted a waiver for Tribune with respect to the WTIC station from this rule until 2007 when its license was scheduled to come up for renewal. The issue of forcing the sale of WTIC, then, was not before the court in the *Ellis* case in 2005.

SUMMARY

Radio, the original electronic medium, was regulated almost from its inception. But until 1927 the regulation was minimal and failed to control the growing number of competitive broadcasters in a way that served the needs of the listeners. Congress passed comprehensive broadcasting rules in 1927, rules based on the assumption that because broadcasters used a valuable public resource, the radio spectrum or airwaves, they should be required to serve the public interest. This philosophy engendered the growth of broadcast regulation until the 1980s, when a competing philosophy constructed on free market economic theory began to dominate Congress and the government regulatory agencies. Under the new scheme, traditional market forces are seen as the best regulator of any industry. In the past 25 years, broadcasting and the telecommunications industry have seen a period of substantial deregulation, although the 2004 appellate court decision in *Prometheus Radio Project* v. *FCC* may have put a halt to that, at least when it comes to ownership issues. It was anticipated that the FCC would begin new hearings on its ownership rules in 2006.

BASIC BROADCAST REGULATION

FEDERAL COMMUNICATIONS COMMISSION

The 1934 Federal Communications Act provided that a seven-member **Federal Communications Commission (FCC)** regulate the broadcast industry. In 1982 Congress reduced the size of the commission to five members as an economy measure. Members of the FCC are appointed by the president, with the approval of the Senate, to serve a five-year term. One member is selected by the president to be chairperson. No more than a simple majority of the commission (three members) can be from the same political party. For instance, in March 2005 President George W. Bush named Harvard-educated attorney* and Republican Kevin J. Martin to chair the FCC, replacing outgoing Republican chair Michael K. Powell, who had held the top spot for four years. Senate confirmation is not required for the elevation of a seated commissioner like Martin to the chair position. Martin's original five-year term as an FCC commissioner began with his July 2001 appointment by President Bush, and thus his first term as both a commissioner and as chair ended on June 30, 2006. Martin's Republican credentials were clear: He served on the Bush-Cheney transition team and was deputy general counsel for the Bush campaign in 2000.

*Martin also holds a B.A. from the University of North Carolina at Chapel Hill and a master's degree in public policy from Duke University, suggesting his ability to keep cognitive dissonance in check when it comes to these rival schools. Which shade of blue he prefers is unclear.

Like all administrative agencies, the FCC is guided by broad congressional mandate—in this case the Federal Communications Act. The agency has the power to make rules and regulations within the broad framework of the act, and these regulations carry the force of the law. With regard to some matters, the 1934 law is very specific. For example, Section 315—the equal opportunity provision (or equal time rule)—details regulations concerning the use of the broadcast media by political candidates. But in other areas, Congress was eloquently vague. The mandate that broadcasters operate their stations in "the public interest, convenience or necessity" can mean almost anything a person wants it to mean.

Powers

States, counties and cities have no regulatory power over broadcasting stations.

Congress approved the 1934 law under the authority of the commerce clause of the U.S. Constitution. States, counties and cities have no regulatory power over broadcasting stations. The federal government has *pre-empted* the law in this area (state and local authorities have retained some jurisdiction to regulate cable television and other telecommunication industries such as common carriers). Under the 1927 act, the question had arisen whether this clause meant that the federal government lacked power to regulate broadcasters whose signals did not cross state lines, stations that were not engaged in interstate commerce. In 1933 in *FRC* v. *Nelson Brothers,*[8] the U.S. Supreme Court ruled that state lines did not divide radio waves and that national regulation of broadcasting was not only appropriate but also essential to the efficient use of radio facilities.

Some communications businesses—telephone and telegraph companies, for example—have been designated common carriers by the government. A common carrier must do business with any customer who wishes to use its service. Broadcasting stations are not common carriers. They may refuse to do business with whomever they please. In addition, the commission lacks the power to set rates for the sale of broadcasting time. Broadcasting is founded on the basis of free competition among holders of broadcast licenses.

The act makes it clear that although broadcasters may freely compete, they in no way assume ownership of a frequency or wavelength by virtue of using it for three years or for 300 years. When a license is granted, the broadcaster must sign a form in which any claim to the perpetual use of a particular frequency is waived.

Censorship Powers

Technically, the FCC lacks the power to censor broadcasters. Section 326 of the act states:

> Nothing in this act shall be understood or construed to give the commission the power of censorship over radio communications or signals transmitted by any radio station, or condition shall be promulgated or fixed by the commission which shall interfere with the right of free speech by means of radio communication.

In some instances the prohibition against censorship is applied literally, but the FCC can punish a broadcaster through a fine (called a forfeiture) or the refusal to renew a license if the

---

8. 289 U.S. 266 (1933).

broadcaster carries programming that in some way violates the law. The Supreme Court adopted this understanding of Section 326 in 1978 when it affirmed the agency's censure of radio station WBAI in New York for airing a monologue by comedian George Carlin that contained what the FCC said was indecent language.[9] Most people would call this censorship. Section 326, then, has limited meaning and is of limited value to broadcasters.

The commission has broad-ranging powers in dealing with American broadcasters. (These include the power to regulate the activities of the American broadcast networks. See *National Broadcasting Co. v. U.S.*)[10] Section 303 of the act outlines some of the basic responsibilities of the agency, which include classification of stations, determination of the power and technical facilities licensees must use, and specification of hours during the day and night that stations can broadcast. The FCC also regulates the location of stations, the area each station can serve, the assignment of frequency or wavelength, and even the designation of call letters. There are not many things that broadcasters can do without first seeking the approval or consent of the FCC.

The key powers held by the FCC, however, focus on licensing and renewal of licenses and the authority to regulate programming and program content. It is toward these powers that primary consideration is directed in the remainder of this chapter.

LICENSING

Licensing broadcasters is one of the most important functions of the FCC. In addition to getting a license for a new station, the broadcaster must also seek FCC approval for most operational changes, such as increasing power, changing the antenna height or location, selling the station, transferring ownership, and so forth. Broadcasting licenses are granted to radio and television stations for eight years.

An applicant for a broadcast license may seek a license to operate a new station or an existing station that he or she wishes to purchase. In either case the process is extremely complicated. Attorneys familiar with FCC rules guide the applicant throughout the process. Someone seeking a license for a new station, more and more a rarity as the broadcast spectrum is being filled up, must first obtain what is called a construction permit. Obtaining this permit is actually the biggest hurdle. If the permit is granted, if construction of the station conforms to technical requirements, and if the work is completed within the time specified by the permit, the license is routinely issued.

The prospective licensee must meet several qualifications:

1. The applicant must be a citizen of the United States. Companies with less than 25 percent foreign ownership also qualify.*
2. The applicant must have sufficient funds to build and operate the station for at least three months without earning any advertising revenue.

*The FCC in 1995 granted Rupert Murdoch, owner of the Fox Network and eight television stations, a waiver of this rule. While Murdoch is a naturalized U.S. citizen, News Corporation, Murdoch's parent company, which owns a 99 percent share in the broadcast properties, is an Australian company.

9. *FCC v. Pacifica Foundation,* 438 U.S. 726 (1978).
10. 319 U.S. 190 (1943).

3. The applicant must either possess or be able to hire people who possess the technical qualifications to operate a broadcasting station.

4. The applicant must be honest and open in dealing with the commission and must have good character. Making fraudulent statements on the application can doom the applicant to failure. The character matter relates to violation of FCC rules and regulations as well as felony convictions of the owners or managers.

Multiple Ownership Rules

The government has always placed a cap on the number of broadcast properties any single individual or company could own. As recently as 1984 that number was 21—seven TV, seven AM radio and seven FM radio stations. The rule represented classical libertarian First Amendment theory; that is, the more voices that are capable of speaking in the marketplace, the more likely truth will be discovered. These rules have been whittled away in the past quarter century under pressure from the industry and from Congress. In addition, the federal courts ruled that unless the government could show specifically how these rules served the public interest, they would have to be abandoned.[11] Simply arguing that a diversity of broadcast voices was better for the nation could not carry the day. The current rules, some of which are enjoined today due to the *Prometheus* decision, are as follows:

- A single company or individual may own television stations whose signals reach no more than 39 percent of the total national viewing audience, however many stations this might be. This rule is still in effect.
- There is no limit on the number of radio stations any single licensee can own. In 2005, one company, Clear Channel Communications, owned approximately 1,200 stations. This rule is still in effect.
- Ownership of both radio and television stations in a single market is limited, based on the number of stations in the market. If a market has more than 18 commercial and noncommercial television stations, a single licensee can own three stations, only one of which can be in the top four rated stations. In markets with more than five but less than 18 stations, a licensee can own two television stations, but only one can be in the top four. If there are five or fewer stations in a market, a licensee can own but one television station. Radio station rules follow a similar formula. A licensee can own eight stations in a market that has more than 45 stations; seven in a market with between 30 and 44 stations; six in a market with between 15 and 29 stations; and three in markets with less than 14 stations.
- Cross-ownership rules—the ownership of TV and radio stations and newspapers in the same market—are also guided by the number of media properties in the market. In markets with fewer than three television stations, no cross-ownership is permitted. In markets with between four and eight television stations, a licensee can own a daily newspaper, a TV station and half the normal number of radio stations permitted; or a daily newspaper, a full complement of radio stations, but no TV station; or two television stations, all the radio stations permitted under the law,

---

11. See *Prometheus Radio Project* v. *FCC,* 373 F. 3d 372 (3d Cir. 2004).

but no newspaper. There are no cross-ownership limits in markets with more than nine television stations, but the rules prescribe that no single licensee can own an "inordinate share" of the media in a community.

The government has also attempted to ensure racial and gender diversity in the ownership of telecommunications properties. The FCC, from time to time, has instituted numerous programs to try to make it easier for blacks, Hispanics and other ethnic minorities as well as women to own radio and television stations and hold jobs in broadcasting. The courts have viewed such efforts with suspicion for the most part. The Supreme Court in 1990 upheld the constitutionality of these preferential programs, with Justice William Brennan writing that the federal government has the power to devise what he called "benign race conscious" measures to the extent they serve important governmental objectives. Enhancing diversity in broadcast ownership was an important governmental objective, Brennan said.[12] But by 1995 many affirmative action programs in the United States were under attack. Not surprisingly, the high court reversed its earlier stance in a 1995 ruling and said that government set-aside programs that benefited minorities were illegal.[13] Two subsequent FCC plans designed to foster more diversity in broadcast hiring were also voided by federal court rulings. The first plan put station owners on notice that their hiring practices would be a factor when license renewal time rolled around. The appellate court said these rules failed to serve a compelling public interest.[14] A second set of rules simply set out initiatives that broadcasters should take to recruit more minorities and women as employees, but was not tied to license renewals. The agency said, however, it would investigate any owner who reported few or no employment applications from women or minorities. The court of appeals said this rule was "coercion" that ultimately created a race-based classification system that did not serve a compelling governmental interest and was unconstitutional.[15] In the fall of 2002 the FCC tried once again to increase racial diversity in broadcasting with a new set of rules that in effect required intensive recruiting for vacancies within a station and longer-term recruitment initiatives by broadcasters designed to inform all members of the community about employment opportunities in broadcasting. Substantial record-keeping requirements were included. These records are scrutinized by the government during the licensing and relicensing processes, but the new system appeared to many observers to be less "coercive" than the previous attempts. Data on minority ownership can be found on the FCC's Web site at http://www.fcc.gov/ownership/data.html.

Oftentimes more than one applicant seeks a single broadcast license. In the past the FCC used an elaborate formula that contained a variety of criteria to determine which applicant deserved to get the license. But in 1993 a federal court ruled that this so-called comparative-hearing process was capricious and arbitrary and had little relevance to whether the operation of a broadcasting station by a particular license applicant would serve the public interest.[16] While the FCC struggled to develop new criteria for its hearing process, Congress stepped in and told the agency that in the future it should award the license to the qualified applicant who was willing to pay the most money for it to the current owner. In other words, the agency

12. *Metro Broadcasting, Inc.* v. *FCC,* 497 U.S. 547 (1990).
13. *Adarand Constructors, Inc.* v. *Pena,* 515 U.S. 200 (1995).
14. Holmes, "Broadcasters Vow."
15. Labaton, "Court Rules Agency Erred."
16. *Bechtel* v. *Federal Communications Commission,* 10 F. 3d 875 (1993).

should use an auction system. And that is the way in which most licenses that are contested are awarded today.

A licensee doesn't have to pay the government for the license, but it must pay an annual licensing fee to hold the license. The fee is based on whether the license is for a television or radio station, and the size of the market served by the station. In 2003 the annual fee for a VHF television (channels two through 13) license in a major market was about $45,000. On the other hand, the annual cost of licensing an FM radio station in a small market was only about $500.

License Renewal

Broadcasting licenses must be renewed every eight years. The current renewal process is certainly not automatic, but under provisions of the 1996 Telecommunications Act, it is very close. Unless the license holder has seriously fouled up in the preceding eight years, the FCC will not even consider other applicants for the license. Under provisions of the law, Congress has instructed the FCC to renew a broadcaster's license as long as

1. the station has served the public interest, convenience and necessity;
2. the licensee has not committed any *serious* violations of the Communications Act or commission rules and regulations; and
3. the licensee has not committed any other violations of the Communications Act or the rules and regulations of the commission that, taken together, would constitute a pattern of abuse.

The act specifically states that the commission cannot even consider whether the public interest might be better served by granting the license to someone other than the license holder. If the commission determines that the license holder has in fact failed to meet the requirements listed here, the license renewal must be denied. Only after the renewal is denied can the commission consider other applicants for the license.

Only after the renewal is denied can the commission consider other applicants for the license.

What kinds of law violations is the FCC sensitive about? Stations that broadcast fraudulent advertising have been denied the renewal of their licenses.[17] The renewal of a license for a station that was used solely to promote the causes of its owner was denied.[18] If a station does not adequately supervise the programming it carries, its license may not be renewed.[19] Today, most nonrenewals result from the applicant lying on the renewal application. Federal courts have ruled that denial of a license renewal does not violate the First Amendment. Acknowledging that a First Amendment issue might arise when a licensee is stripped of the power to broadcast, the U.S. Court of Appeals for the District of Columbia Circuit nevertheless ruled 70 years ago:

> This does not mean that the government, through agencies established by Congress, may not refuse a renewal of license to one who has abused it to broadcast defamatory or untrue matter. In that case there is not a denial of freedom of speech, but merely the application of the regulatory power of Congress in a field within the scope of its legislative authority.[20]

17. *May Seed and Nursery,* 2 F.C.C. 559 (1936).
18. *Young People's Association for the Propagation of the Gospel,* 6 F.C.C. 178 (1936).
19. *Cosmopolitan Broadcasting Corp.,* 59 F.C.C. 2d 558 (1976).
20. *Trinity Methodist Church, South* v. *FRC,* 62 F. 2d 650 (1932).

The previous year another U.S. Court of Appeals judge had ruled that the commission had a perfect right to look at past programming practices of a renewal applicant to determine whether the license should be renewed. Invoking the biblical injunction "By their fruits ye shall know them," the court affirmed that past programming is a central issue in consideration of service in the public interest.[21]

The Public's Role

Although it is rare, a renewal applicant can also face a challenge from listeners and viewers. In particular, either a formal petition to deny or an informal objection to a radio or television license renewal application may be filed with the FCC after the filing of the license renewal application by a station. The last day for filing a petition to deny is one month before the license expiration date. The FCC provides details about the renewal process, including the filing of petitions to deny renewals and informal objections, on its Web site at http://www.fcc.gov/mb/video/renewal.html. Stations are required to maintain public inspection files that must be available for public review at any time during regular business hours and made available for printing or machine reproduction upon request made in person. Further information on public inspection files can be found on the FCC's Web site at http://www.fcc.gov/eb/broadcast/pif.html.

Recent FCC rulings have made it far more difficult for a citizen to challenge the renewal of a license. Because a station no longer is forced to keep many records that were at one time routine, it is often hard for a citizens' group to document its charges against the broadcaster. More important, however, the FCC has substantially lowered performance standards for radio and television stations. This move has sharply reduced the number of issues that a citizens' group might raise in challenging the renewal of the license.

SUMMARY

The five-member Federal Communications Commission has been established by law to regulate the broadcasting industry. The agency has the responsibility to supervise all over-the-air broadcasting as well as any other electronic communication that has an impact on over-the-air communications. Although the FCC is forbidden by law from censoring the content of broadcast programming, the agency nevertheless has considerable control over what is broadcast by radio and television. By licensing and relicensing broadcasting stations, the FCC can ensure that broadcasters meet certain standards, including programming standards.

Broadcast stations are licensed for eight years. To gain a license to broadcast, an applicant must meet several important criteria that have been established by Congress and by the FCC. When two or more persons seek the same license, the FCC uses an auction process to select who will get the license. The auction process replaces a comparative hearing process that was based on applicant merit. This latter process was costly and time-consuming, and courts ruled that at least one criterion used in the process was unenforceable. Listeners and viewers can challenge a renewal. Public participation in this process is relatively rare, and recent rule changes have made it even harder for citizens to mount an effective license challenge.

21. *KFKB Broadcasting Association* v. *FRC,* 47 F. 2d 670 (1931).

REGULATION OF PROGRAM CONTENT

SANCTIONS

Failure to abide by programming rules can cost a broadcast license at renewal time. But this sanction is rarely imposed by the FCC. The agency has a wide range of other kinds of sanctions, however, which are frequently levied against those who transgress the regulations (see boxed text).

**FCC REMEDIES AGAINST BROADCASTERS
FOR CONTENT VIOLATIONS**

1. Issue a warning notice.
2. Impose a monetary fine (a "forfeiture"; an increasingly common remedy).
3. Place conditions on renewal of a broadcast license.
4. Revoke a broadcaster's license entirely (very rarely used).

Broadcasters have a myriad of programming responsibilities that range from the very broad, such as serving the public interest in the community in which it is licensed, to the very small, such as airing a proper station break at prescribed times of the day or night. Like the rules related to licensing, rules related to program content are also evolving quickly in this new century. The FCC itself has made changes, but oftentimes it has been the courts that have insisted on the abandonment or modification of rules. Rules related to the broadcast of information and advertising of lotteries were deemed unconstitutional by the U.S. Supreme Court,[22] as noted on page 626 in Chapter 15.

Can the FCC control a broadcast station's format as part of its regulation of programming content?

Can the FCC control a broadcast station's format as part of its regulation of programming content? For many years the FCC resisted efforts by citizens' groups to force the agency to get involved when a radio station dropped one kind of music format—classical, for example—and adopted another format, such as rock. But listeners went to federal court, and the FCC was ordered in 1970 to *review* a format change by a station when the abandonment of a unique format produced community protests.[23] The U.S. Court of Appeals for the District of Columbia Circuit went one step further in 1974 and ordered the FCC to *hold a hearing* whenever a unique format was being abandoned by a radio station and persons in the community objected.[24] A unique format would be one that no other station in the market used. The loss of this format would deny the citizens in the community access to a particular kind of music or programming. Normally it has been supporters of classical music who have protested when a local station drops the classical format. But in Seattle in 1981, New Wave rock fans mounted a protest when the community's only (at that time) New Wave music station abandoned that format. Despite the earlier court rulings, the FCC continued to argue through the late 1970s

---

22. *Greater New Orleans Broadcasting Ass'n.* v. *United States,* 119 S. Ct. 1923 (1999).
23. *Citizens' Committee to Preserve the Voice of the Arts in Atlanta* v. *FCC,* 436 F. 2d 263 (1970).
24. *Citizens' Committee to Save WEFM* v. *FCC,* 506 F. 2d 246 (1974).

that the marketplace should determine the broadcaster's format; the government should not get involved. And in 1981 the Supreme Court of the United States supported the agency and overturned a lower federal court decision calling for a hearing on a format change. Justice Byron White, writing for the seven-person majority, stated, "We decline to overturn the commission's policy statement which prefers reliance on market forces to its own attempt to oversee format changes at the behest of disaffected listeners." Justice White warned the agency, however, to be alert to the consequences of its policies and stand ready to change its rules if necessary to serve the public interest more fully.[25]

REGULATION OF CHILDREN'S PROGRAMMING

There are two key aspects to the FCC's current regulation of children's television programming:

1. Limitations on commercials during programming targeting children
2. Requirements regarding educational programming that must be carried

With regard to limits on commercials, the FCC mandates that in an hour-long program aired primarily for an audience of children 12 years old and younger, advertisements must not exceed 10.5 minutes on the weekends and 12 minutes during the week. The commercial time limits, however, are not applicable to noncommercial educational stations that are prohibited from airing commercials. The FCC also bars what it calls "program-length commercials" targeting children. What does this term mean? When an advertisement for a product is aired in a program associated with that product, the entire program is counted as commercial time. An example is a cartoon program that airs a commercial for the dolls of its characters during the program broadcast. Children's programs must also be separated by either buffers or substantial pauses from commercials to help minors distinguish between shows and ads.

In terms of educational programming, the FCC today, under guidelines it adopted in 1996 to comply with the Children's Television Act of 1990, mandates that broadcasters carry a minimum of three hours per week (averaged over a six-month period in order to provide broadcasters with scheduling flexibility) of "core educational programming." Such programming must be specifically designed to serve the educational and informational needs of children ages 16 years and under. It must be

- at least 30 minutes long;
- aired between 7:00 a.m. and 10:00 p.m.; and
- a regularly scheduled weekly program not preempted more than 10 percent of the time.

Whether all stations are complying with the FCC's rules is up for debate. For instance, the Center for Digital Democracy and the United Church of Christ filed a petition in 2004 with the FCC asking it to deny the license renewals of two Washington, D.C., area stations, WDCA and WPXW.[26] Those two stations were among the first ones in the United States to apply for license renewals since the FCC adopted its children's television processing guidelines in 1996. The watchdog organizations contended that the stations should not be allowed to count shows such as "Miracle Pets" and the animated, action-oriented science fiction shows "Ace Lightning"

---

25. *FCC* v. *WNCN Listeners Guild,* 101 S. Ct. 1266 (1981).
26. Maynard, "FCC Is Asked to Revoke the Licenses."

and "Stargate Infinity" toward the core educational programming requirement. "Stargate Infinity," for instance, allegedly contains anti-social messages and depicts violent attacks.

In September 2004, the FCC adapted its rules on children's television programming to apply to digital television broadcasters. The new order, known as the Digital Kidvid Order, increases the amount of the core programming guideline proportionally to the increase in free video programming offered by the broadcaster on multicast channels. It also provides flexibility to broadcasters that multicast by permitting them the choice of whether to air core programming on a single channel or multiple channels, provided that at least three hours per week are shown on their main channel. Complete and current information on children's television programming rules and requirements can be found on the FCC's Web site at http://www.fcc.gov/cgb/consumerfacts/childtv.html.

OBSCENE, INDECENT AND PROFANE MATERIAL

The sale or distribution or publication of obscenity is illegal by virtue of a myriad of federal, state and local laws. Obscenity is not protected by the First Amendment, as noted in Chapter 13. Similarly, the broadcast of obscenity over television or radio is also illegal under the Federal Communications Act. But federal law also makes it illegal to broadcast what is called indecent material via radio and over-the-air television (cable is treated differently and will be discussed later in the chapter). The courts have more or less defined obscenity. The struggle to find a workable definition for indecency has been much more difficult.

The broadcast of obscenity over the airwaves has never been a serious problem. Indecency was not a problem either, until more recent times. In television the issue first reached national prominence in 1975 when ABC, CBS and NBC, with the cooperation of the National Association of Broadcasters and the FCC, instituted what they called "the family hour" in prime time.[27] Stations that subscribed to programming policies established by the NAB, and most of them did, were told to set aside the hours from 7 to 9 p.m. each evening for family viewing; programs with sexual overtones and excessive violence were taboo in this period. The result was a few months of silly self-censorship (e.g., the word "virgin" was cut from one program, and performers on programs starring Cher and Cloris Leachman were recostumed in a more modest fashion) before a federal court ruled that the constraints constituted a violation of the First Amendment because they had been motivated by the FCC.[28]

Until recently, over-the-air television, as opposed to cable channels like HBO or MTV which are governed by far more relaxed standards (see page 720), rarely generated indecency complaints because it sought to appeal to a large, heterogeneous audience. Radio stations, on the other hand, were more brazen and frequently subject to fines for broadcasting indecent material.* But TV broadcasters began to push vigorously at the legal boundaries in recent

---

*Infinity Broadcasting, for example, which owns and operates nearly 200 radio stations across America, was fined $27,500 in 2002 when the program hosts at WKRK-FM in Detroit invited listeners to call them and discuss their sexual practices.

27. Cowan, *See No Evil.*

28. *Writers Guild* v. *FCC,* 423 F. Supp. 1064 (1976). A U.S. Court of Appeals later overturned the lower-court ruling on the grounds that the U.S. District Court lacked jurisdiction in the case, that the issue should have first gone to the FCC for resolution. See *Writers Guild* v. *ABC,* 609 F. 2d 355 (1979). The networks made no effort to re-establish the policy.

years. When CBS telecast what many viewers described as a salacious Super Bowl halftime show in 2004 that included a very fleeting glimpse of singer Janet Jackson's breast, it ignited a firestorm of criticism that included angry congressional hearings. Mea culpas by industry officials did little to quiet the anger, and many observers agreed that the government would take some action to reduce the sexual openness on the small screen. Action against the Super Bowl broadcast would come later in September 2004 (see page 692). Before that, however, in June 2004, the FCC announced that it would raise the maximum fine for indecent material on broadcast television and radio from $27,500 per incident to $32,500, to adjust for inflation. But that paltry $5,000 increase paled in comparison to what Congress initially wanted to do to clean up the airwaves during a presidential election year and to prove to the public that it was serious about protecting children from indecent speech. The House of Representatives passed by a whopping 391 to 22 vote in March 2004 a bill dubbed the Broadcast Decency Enforcement Act of 2004, which called for increasing fines to $500,000 for a single violation, with repeat offenders subject to a loss of license. And in June 2004, the U.S. Senate passed by a 99-1 vote (the lone dissenter was Louisiana Democrat John Breaux) a measure (attached to a Defense Department bill) to increase the maximum fine for broadcasters airing indecent speech to $275,000 for a first offense, with a maximum of $3 million for each 24-hour period per station. With the House and Senate unable to agree on a measure by October 2004, however, a compromise bill was proposed in Congress that month that would allow the Federal Communications Commission to fine a station a maximum of $500,000 per violation, with a limit of $3 million for each 24-hour period for each *corporation,* rather than per *station* as it was under the Senate's earlier bill.[29] That change from "station" to "corporation" is very important given the number of stations owned by massive media conglomerates such as Viacom, News Corp. and Clear Channel. In addition, performers—not just broadcasters—could have been penalized under the measure.

Although none of the bills proposed in Congress in 2004 to raise fines for broadcast indecency ultimately became law, federal legislators did not give up and were back at it again in 2005. In particular, U.S. Senators Joe Lieberman (D.-Conn.) and Sam Brownback (R.-Kan.) introduced a bill called the Broadcast Decency Enforcement Act of 2005 designed to raise the FCC's maximum $32,500 fine 10-fold to a maximum penalty of $325,000 for each violation. The bill also proposed a cap of $3 million for any single indecent act aired by a network. In announcing the bill, Lieberman stated in an official press release, "In a media culture that increasingly pushes the envelope on sex and violence, the role of the FCC is to ensure that broadcasters do not cross that line of decency. This legislation gives the FCC more leverage to do its job by increasing the consequences of violating our broadcasting standards." A similar measure, dubbed the Broadcast Indecency Act of 2005, was introduced in the U.S. House of Representatives, where it was approved by an overwhelming 389-38 vote in February 2005. The House measure would allow fines of up to $500,000 for indecency violations. Neither bill had become law by the end of 2005, but the issue is likely to reappear in the future if there is a major indecency controversy on television or on the radio.

But proposals to increase the FCC's fines were not the only responses to the Janet Jackson Super Bowl incident. Many broadcasters responded in 2004 to the political pressures placed by Congress and the FCC by engaging in self-censorship—NBC, for example, eliminated

---

29. Lee, "Bill to Raise Indecency Fines."

"a glimpse of an 80-year-old patient's breast" from an episode of "ER,"[30] and several ABC affiliates in November 2004 chose not to carry the network's showing of Steven Spielberg's movie "Saving Private Ryan" because of its coarse language and intense violence[31]—and quickly settling indecency actions for massive amounts of money. For instance, Clear Channel Communications, the nation's largest radio chain with approximately 1,200 stations, paid the FCC a record figure of $1.75 million to settle a slew of pending indecency complaints filed by listeners against its stations, as well as $800,000 in outstanding fines, based on broadcasts by Howard Stern and other radio personalities. The desire to please the government and to avoid further legislative action was clear when Andrew Levin, executive vice president of Clear Channel, admitted that his company "didn't agree that all the complaints were legally indecent."[32] Just a few months before the settlement, Clear Channel voluntarily had pulled Howard Stern from its six stations that carried his syndicated show and it fired another controversial "shock jock" named Todd "Bubba the Love Sponge" Clem. Clear Channel already had paid the FCC, shortly after the 2004 Super Bowl controversy that launched the firestorm against indecency, a separate $755,000 fine for the Florida-based Clem's broadcasts. Stern would later announce in October 2004 that he was leaving broadcast radio and escaping the reach of both the FCC's fines and Clear Channel's self-censorship by moving in 2006 to Sirius Satellite Radio. Satellite radio currently is not subject to the FCC's indecency regulations, although some in Washington want to change that, as a bill introduced in the Senate in 2005 would direct the FCC to address violence and indecency on cable and satellite, not simply broadcast television and radio.* It is anticipated that other shock jocks will follow Stern's lead and move to satellite (in fact, shock jocks "Opie and Anthony" were already on XM Satellite Radio in late 2004, having abandoned over-the-air broadcasting after a major scrape with the FCC), with satellite radio becoming a last refuge, as it were, for scoundrels.

Satellite radio currently is not subject to the FCC's indecency regulations.

Some people also believed the real goal of companies such as Clear Channel in settling indecency disputes was a desire to have the government loosen rules on the number of local radio stations a single entity may own. The strategy, in other words, is that if conglomerates like Clear Channel can prove that they can police their own content, then they should be trusted to serve the public interest and, concomitantly, to own as many radio stations as they want. As Frank Ahrens wrote in the Washington Post about the record-setting Clear Channel settlement, "the deal is likely to be criticized by Democrats who draw links between the Republican-controlled FCC, the White House and Clear Channel. Executives at the San Antonio–based company have been large contributors to the campaigns of President Bush and other Republicans."[33] And journalist Travis Poling observed that "the bigger concern for broadcast companies is other big-money issues before the FCC, including loosening restrictions on the number of radio stations that can be owned in one market and determining when television stations must offer digital signals."[34]

---

*The bill, called the "Indecent and Gratuitous and Excessively Violent Programming Control Act of 2005," was introduced by Jay Rockefeller (D.-W.Va.) and Kay Bailey Hutchison (R.-Tex.) in March 2005.

30. Collins, "The Decency Debate."
31. Huff, "Fear Over 'Private' Parts."
32. Kerr, "FCC Gives Clear Channel a Stern Talking-To."
33. Ahrens, "Radio Giant in Record Indecency Settlement."
34. Poling, "Clear Channel Puts Indecency Issue Behind."

Source: © AP/Wide World Photos

The Supreme Court ruled in 1978 that it was not a violation of the First Amendment to bar indecency during certain times of the day from the airwaves. The high court upheld an FCC ruling that radio station WBAI in New York City had violated the law when it broadcast during the afternoon a recorded monologue by comedian George Carlin.[35] The monologue, called "Seven Dirty Words," was broadcast on the listener-supported station during a long discussion on the English language. The FCC said it was impermissible to broadcast "language that describes in terms patently offensive as measured by contemporary community standards for the broadcast medium, sexual or excretory activities and organs, *at times when there is a reasonable risk children may be in the audience*" [author emphasis]. The agency said it was unlikely children would be listening or watching after 10 p.m. and before 6 a.m., and it later designated this eight-hour block of time a safe harbor for the broadcast of adult material.

In the years following this high court ruling the FCC sought to refine its policies on indecent broadcasts. It was consistently challenged in court, but generally the agency's policy weathered these challenges.[36] Then in 2001 the commission published a new and fairly

A fleeting glimpse of Janet Jackson's right breast during the 2004 Super Bowl halftime show sparked an FCC crackdown on broadcast indecency. Jackson is shown here with singer Justin Timberlake.

35. *FCC* v. *Pacifica Foundation,* 438 U.S. 726 (1978).
36. *Action for Children's Television* v. *F.C.C.,* 58 F. 3d 654 (1995); *Action for Children's Television* v. *F.C.C. et al.,* U.S. Sup. Ct. No. 95-520, cert. den.; and *Pacifica Foundation* v. *F.C.C,* U.S. Sup. Ct. No. 95-509, cert. den.

comprehensive policy statement relating to the broadcast of indecent matter.[37] Here is a summary of this policy.

The commission's definition of indecency remains the standard: language or material that, in context, depicts or describes, in terms patently offensive as measured by contemporary community standards for the broadcast medium, sexual or excretory activities or organs. Before finding a broadcast indecent the commission must make two determinations. First, the broadcast material must fall within the subject matter scope of indecency; that is, it must depict or describe sexual or excretory activities. Second, it must be patently offensive as measured by contemporary community standards for the broadcast medium. The standards are not local and do not encompass any particular geographic area, the agency said. "Rather, the standard is that of an average broadcast viewer or listener," the policy statement said.

Although this definition of indecency and the two-step determination process remains intact today, the commission issued a controversial order in March 2004 that radically changes how the FCC interprets and applies its own standards. In particular, the FCC ruled that the use of the phrase "this is really, really fucking brilliant" by Bono, lead singer for the Irish rock group U2, during an acceptance speech at the 2003 Golden Globe Awards television program and broadcast by NBC outside of the FCC's safe-harbor time period, constituted "material in violation of the applicable indecency and profanity prohibitions."[38] The decision stunned many legal observers. Why? Because Bono's use of the word "fucking" was both isolated and fleeting—it was not repeated or dwelled upon, a factor that traditionally is important for the FCC in determining whether or not speech is patently offensive—and because it was not used in a sexual sense, but rather as a modifier for emphasis of how "brilliant" it was that U2 had won for Best Original Song. Furthermore, officials at NBC had no advance knowledge that Bono was going to use the expletive in question, and the network was able to "bleep" the language for its West Coast airing of the program (the program was aired live to the East Coast).

Despite these facts—and despite an earlier ruling in October 2003 by David H. Solomon, the chief of the FCC's Enforcement Bureau, that the broadcast was *not* indecent—the FCC reversed Solomon's decision and concluded that Bono's language, as used in context, was both indecent and profane. As to why the program was indecent, the FCC began its analysis by rearticulating its two-step process for indecency determinations, writing that "indecency findings involve at least two fundamental determinations. First, the material alleged to be indecent must fall within the subject matter scope of our indecency definition; that is, the material must describe or depict sexual or excretory organs or activities. . . . Second, the broadcast must be patently offensive as measured by contemporary community standards for the broadcast medium."

With respect to the first step, the FCC found that "given the core meaning of the 'F-Word,' any use of that word or a variation, in any context, inherently has a sexual connotation, and therefore falls within the first prong of our indecency definition." Turning to the second step

---

37. *In re Industry Guidelines on the Commission's Case Law Interpreting 18 U.S.C. §1464 and Enforcement Policies Regarding Broadcast Indecency,* FCC, File No. EB-00-1H-0089, 4/6/01.

38. *In the Matter of Complaints Against Various Broadcast Licensees Regarding Their Airing of the "Golden Globe Award" Program,* Memorandum Opinion and Order, File No. EB-03-IH-0110 (March 18, 2004).

of its indecency analysis—whether the broadcast of Bono's speech was patently offensive under contemporary community standards for the television medium—the FCC wrote:

> The "F-Word" is one of the most vulgar, graphic and explicit descriptions of sexual activity in the English language. Its use invariably invokes a coarse sexual image. The use of the "F-Word" here, on a nationally telecast awards ceremony, was shocking and gratuitous. In this regard, NBC does not claim that there was any political, scientific or other independent value of use of the word here, or any other factors to mitigate its offensiveness. If the Commission were routinely not to take action against isolated and gratuitous uses of such language on broadcasts when children were expected to be in the audience, this would likely lead to more widespread use of the offensive language.

The FCC thus concluded that the Golden Globes broadcast was indecent. Importantly, the commission suggested that NBC could have prevented the entire problem, writing that the network "and other licensees could have easily avoided the indecency violation here by delaying the broadcast for a period of time sufficient for them to effectively bleep the offending word." The FCC then added a new element to its indecency calculus, holding that the "ease with which broadcasters today can block even fleeting words in a live broadcast is an element in our decision to act upon a single and gratuitous use of a vulgar expletive." In addition, the commission wrote that "the mere fact that specific words or phrases are not sustained or repeated does not mandate a finding that material that is otherwise patently offensive to the broadcast medium is not indecent." What's more, the commission held that it made no difference whatsoever that NBC did not intend for the offensive language to occur.

The FCC did much more, however, than just hold the broadcast to be indecent; it also concluded that the broadcast was profane. Federal law provides: "Whoever utters any obscene, indecent, or *profane language* by means of radio communication shall be fined under this title or imprisoned not more than two years, or both."[39] Prior to the dispute over Bono's language during the Golden Globes ceremony, however, the FCC narrowly had limited the statutory meaning of the term "profane language" to "blasphemy or divine imprecation." It completely reversed course, however, in March 2004 and concluded that Bono's acceptance speech was profane. The FCC wrote:

> Broadcasters are on notice that the Commission in the future will not limit its definition of profane speech to only those words and phrases that contain an element of blasphemy or divine imprecation, but, depending on the context, will also consider under the definition of "profanity" the "F-Word" and those words (or variants thereof) that are as highly offensive as the "F-Word," to the extent such language is broadcast between 6 a.m. and 10 p.m. We will analyze other potentially profane words or phrases on a case-by-case basis.

In summary, the FCC's March 2004 opinion regarding Bono's acceptance speech suggests an aggressive and vigorous new approach by the commission in order to clean up language on the public airwaves. The FCC not only concluded that Bono's speech was indecent,

---

39. 18 U.S.C. § 1464 (2004).

but it also opened up a second avenue of attack, under the guise of profane language, for regulating broadcast content. In a separate statement to the FCC's opinion, then-FCC chairman Michael C. Powell wrote, "This sends a signal to the industry that the gratuitous use of such vulgar language on broadcast television will not be tolerated."

The signal may have been felt too severely, in some cases even affecting genuine news content and having a chilling effect on legitimate information. CBS-affiliated television stations, for instance, feared that "unless the Federal Communications Commission makes some exceptions in its crackdown on foul language, live news coverage may be an endangered."[40] The Los Angeles Times reported that "a CBS affiliate in Phoenix curtailed its live coverage of a memorial service for ex-football star Pat Tillman because of some mourners' language."[41] Tillman, a former safety for the NFL's Arizona Cardinals, had given up his athletic career and joined the army. He was killed in April 2004 near the Afghanistan-Pakistan border.

In September 2004, the FCC once again vigorously applied its indecency standard when it released a Notice of Apparent Liability (NAL) for a whopping aggregate sum of $550,000 against various television licensees concerning their February 1, 2004, broadcast of the Super Bowl XXXVIII halftime show.[42] The amount was, at the time, the largest indecency fine ever levied against a television broadcaster, namely CBS affiliates. The FCC focused its inquiry on Janet Jackson and Justin Timberlake's performance of the song "Rock Your Body." The raunchy duet infamously concluded with Timberlake's removal of a portion of Jackson's leather bustier, briefly exposing her breast to the camera, at the precise moment when Timberlake finished the song's lecherous last lyric, "gonna have you naked by the end of this song."

The FCC applied its two-step indecency analysis to this performance, considering first whether the broadcast described or depicted sexual or excretory organs or activities, and then, second, whether it was patently offensive as measured by contemporary community standards for the broadcast medium. The first step was easily satisfied, as the FCC wrote that the broadcast culminated in on-camera partial nudity with Jackson's exposed breast, thus constituting a depiction of a sexual organ. As to the second step—whether the broadcast was patently offensive—the FCC initially set forth three factors that it often considers to determine patent offensiveness:

1. The explicitness or graphic nature of the description
2. Whether the material dwells on or repeats at length descriptions of sexual or excretory organs or activities
3. Whether the material is used to shock, titillate or pander

Applying these three factors in a totality-of-the-circumstances approach in which they are weighed and balanced with each other, the FCC concluded that the broadcast was indeed patently offensive. It initially found that the videotape of the performance "leaves no doubt that the Jackson/Timberlake segment is both explicit and graphic. The joint performance by Ms. Jackson and Mr. Timberlake culminated in Mr. Timberlake pulling off part of Ms. Jackson's

40. Smith, "Profanity Rules Bother News Shows."
41. Ibid.
42. *In the Matter of Complaints Against Various Television Licensees Concerning Their February 1, 2004, Broadcast of the Super Bowl XXXVIII Halftime Show,* Notice of Apparent Liability for Forfeiture, File No. EB-04-IH-0011 (Sept. 22, 2004).

bustier and exposing her bare breast. CBS admits that the CBS Network Stations broadcast this material, including the image of Ms. Jackson's bared breast." The FCC then reasoned that the "nudity here was designed to pander to, titillate and shock the viewing audience. The fact that the exposure of Ms. Jackson's breast was brief is thus not dispositive."

> In determining the amount of the fine to mete out, the FCC wrote: Officials of CBS [the broadcast network for the Super Bowl] and MTV [which produced the halftime show] did have prior knowledge of, indeed were intricately involved in the planning process for, and tacitly approved, the sexually provocative nature of the Jackson/Timberlake segment. Moreover, they extensively promoted this aspect of the broadcast in a manner designed to pander, titillate and shock. Viacom [owner of both CBS and MTV] made a calculated and deliberate decision to air the Jackson/Timberlake segment containing material that would shock Super Bowl viewers, and to accurately promote it as such.

But the FCC did not stop there. It dialed up the rhetoric against Viacom in concluding its opinion:

> As the ultimate controlling entity of numerous television licensees, Viacom betrayed its trust, not only to the FCC arising from its obligation to operate its stations in the public interest and in a manner consistent with the Commission's rules, but to each parent who reasonably assumed that the national network broadcast of a major sporting event on a Sunday evening would not contain offensive sexual material unsuitable for children, the very class of viewers that the Commission's indecency rule was designed to protect. With its delivery into those homes of the Jackson/Timberlake duet, Viacom wrenched away from parents the ability to control the exposure of their children to the type of objectionable sexual material in which that performance culminated.

The Super Bowl decision did not mark the end of the FCC's crackdown on broadcast indecency in 2004. In fact, less than one month later, the commission issued a proposed fine totaling more than $1.18 million—more than double the amount of the Super Bowl fine, and a new record-level fine for indecency on a television program—against 169 Fox Television Network stations for airing an April 2003 episode of a reality-based program called "Married by America." The episode in question included scenes in which party-goers licked whipped cream from strippers' bodies in a sexually suggestive manner. Although the program electronically obscured any nudity, the FCC nonetheless held that the broadcast was indecent, in part because it believed that "the sexual nature of the scenes is inescapable, as the strippers attempt to lure party-goers into sexually compromising positions."[43] The FCC added that "merely obscuring (or "pixilating") sexual organs does not necessarily remove a broadcast from our indecency analysis." It wrote that "although the nudity was pixilated, even a child would have known that the strippers were topless and that sexual activity was being shown."

---

43. *In the Matter of Complaints Against Various Licensees Regarding Their Broadcast of the Fox Television Network Program "Married by America" on April 7, 2003,* Notice of Apparent Liability for Forfeiture, File No. EB-03-IH-0162 (Oct. 12, 2004).

The safe-harbor period today remains in effect from 10 p.m. to 6 a.m.

While the FCC began its vigorous new approach to both indecency and profanity in 2004 with decisions affecting the Golden Globes, the Super Bowl and "Married by America," one thing did not change: the so-called "safe harbor" time period when such content is protected from the FCC's regulation. The safe-harbor period today remains in effect from 10 p.m. to 6 a.m.—an eight-hour window during which both indecent and profane language may be broadcast. Obscene speech, however, falls completely outside the scope of First Amendment protection (see Chapter 13) and is not protected at any time of day. In other words, there is no safe-harbor period for obscenity on the public airwaves.

The bottom line from the indecency bloodbath of 2004 was that the FCC issued a record annual total of 12 Notices of Apparent Liability for Monetary Forfeiture—nine directed at radio shows and three targeting television programs—and proposed more than $7.9 million in fines.* That dollar amount is a whopping increase from the paltry $48,000 in FCC-proposed fines from 2000 against a total of only seven radio programs and none targeting television content.

About the only type of racy radio content, in fact, that apparently did feel the effects of the FCC in 2004 or 2005 was Spanish-language talk programming in cities like Los Angeles and Sacramento that may actually have grown more coarse. As the Sacramento Bee reported in April 2005, "detailed discussions of sex acts, profane outbursts and crude jokes have become commonplace on some Spanish-language talk shows" such as the syndicated program "El Cucuy de la Mañana" (the Morning Boogeyman).[44] The reason for the lax approach by the FCC may simply be a matter of numbers; the Los Angeles Times reported in 2004 that the commission has "only two Spanish-speaking investigators to deal with 705 Spanish radio and TV outlets in the U.S."[45] This comes despite the fact that nearly 10 percent of the radio listening in the top 100 markets is to Spanish-language stations.

Spanish-language radio aside, did the FCC continue to expand its aggressive approach to indecency in 2005? The answer is no, at least based on a number of rulings from early that year. For instance, in March 2005, the FCC concluded that a commercial featuring Desperate Housewives star Nicollette Sheridan that aired at the start of an ABC Monday Night Football broadcast was not indecent.[46] In the commercial, Sheridan was clothed in only a towel, which she dropped after being rebuffed by Philadelphia Eagles receiver Terrell Owens after Sheridan made a sexual advance toward the player in the Eagles' locker room. The camera showed Sheridan from the back only, nude from the waist up, and viewers could not see either her breasts or anything below the waist. In determining that the commercial was not indecent and, in particular, not patently offensive under its test for indecency, the FCC wrote:

> The Monday Night Football segment, although sexually suggestive, is not graphic or explicit. Owens is fully dressed throughout the segment, and, with the exception of a moment when her bare back is exposed to the audience,

---

*In addition to the amount of the 12 notices of apparent liability issued for 2004, this figure includes
(1) $952,500 from a consent decree settlement over indecency allegations with radio giant Clear Channel;
(2) $258,000 from a consent decree settlement over indecency allegations against Emmis radio; and
(3) $3,059,580 from a consent decree settlement over indecency allegations with Viacom.

44. Bazar, "Spanish Radio Gets Racier."
45. Gurza, "Television & Radio."
46. *In the Matter of Complaints Against Various Television Station Licensees Regarding the ABC Television Network's November 15, 2004, Broadcast of Monday Night Football,* Memorandum Opinion and Order, File No. EB-04-IH-0590 (Mar. 14, 2005).

Sheridan is at all times fully covered with a towel. No sexual or excretory organs are shown or described, and no sexual activities are explicitly depicted or described. . . . Although the scene apparently is intended to be titillating, it simply is not graphic or explicit enough to be indecent under our standard.

The FCC also rejected another complaint in 2005, this one filed by the American Family Association that claimed that an ABC broadcast of the award-winning World War II movie "Saving Private Ryan" was both indecent and profane.[47] In concluding that the broadcast was neither indecent nor profane, the FCC began by noting the chilling effect and self-censorship that had taken place at some ABC stations regarding the airing of the movie out of concern that the FCC's aggressive approach in 2004 to indecency would result in a fine. The FCC noted that "approximately 66 of a total of 225 affiliated with ABC declined to air the film, citing their uncertainty as to whether it contained indecent material, reportedly based, in part, on Commission indecency rulings." The film's dialogue contains a number of expletives that are repeated over and over, including variations of the same word ("fuck") that landed Bono and NBC in trouble. While the FCC once again found that this word has an inherently sexual meaning, it nonetheless found that, as used in the context of the movie "Saving Private Ryan," it was not patently offensive. The FCC wrote:

We do not find indecent every depiction or description of sexual or excretory organs or activities. Rather . . . we find material indecent only if it is patently offensive based on an examination of the material's explicit or graphic nature, whether it is dwelled upon or repeated, and whether it appears to pander or is intended to titillate or shock the audience. In connection with the third factor, we consider whether the material has any social, scientific or artistic value, as finding that material has such value may militate against finding that it was intended to pander, titillate or shock.

Applying this approach to the ABC broadcast of "Saving Private Ryan," the FCC found that, although the language was repeated and dwelled upon, "the complained-of material, in context, is not pandering and is not used to titillate or shock." This factor was key to its decision. The commission added that the language in question "is integral to the film's objective of conveying the horrors of war through the eyes of these soldiers, ordinary Americans placed in extraordinary situations. Deleting all of such language or inserting milder language . . . would have altered the nature of the artistic work and diminished the power, realism and immediacy of the film experience for viewers." The FCC's opinion rejecting the indecency and profanity complaints against the movie thus represents a major victory for the First Amendment rights of both broadcasters and their audiences—in particular the audience's right to receive and view important films.

A final thought on the subject of broadcast indecency is important here before moving on to the topic of broadcast violence in the next section (one will note, by the way, that the FCC's definition of indecency has *nothing* to do with violence, but only sex and excretory organs and activities). In particular, there is a lesson to be learned from the FCC's crackdown

---

47. *In the Matter of Complaints Against Various Television Licensees Regarding Their Broadcast on November 11, 2004, of the ABC Television Network's Presentation of the Film "Saving Private Ryan,"* Memorandum Opinion and Order, File No. EB-04-IH-0589 (Feb. 28, 2005).

One cannot overestimate the power of a small but very vocal and well-organized minority to influence the decisions of the FCC.

in 2004, and that lesson is this: One cannot overestimate the power of a small but very vocal and well-organized minority to influence the decisions of the FCC. According to official documents on the FCC's Web site (http://www.fcc.gov), the commission received only 111 total complaints in 2000 about allegedly indecent content and a slightly higher 346 complaints in 2001. But then, at that point, the numbers ratchet up significantly and dramatically, first to 13,922 in 2002, then to 202,032 in 2003, and, finally, to a whopping 1,405,419 complaints regarding allegedly indecent content in 2004. Why the sudden increase? Was the general public simply fed up with broadcast content? It turns out that in 2003 and 2004, more than 98 percent of those complaints (excluding ones filed about the Super Bowl halftime show in 2004) were filed by just one single organization: the Parents Television Council (PTC). There was not, in other words, some massive outpouring of complaints from the general populace, but rather from one group with an agenda of censorship. In contrast, there was not a similar uprising of "free speech" organizations against either the PTC or the FCC. A secondary lesson, then, is this: One must fight for free speech rights and not take them for granted, lest minority interests like the PTC silence what the majority of the public want to watch.

What, then, does it take for a group like the PTC or an individual to file a complaint with the FCC alleging that particular broadcast material is indecent? Three things are required by the FCC before it will investigate a viewer or listener's complaint. In particular, so-called "complainants" must provide the FCC with

1. the date and time of the broadcast in question;
2. the call sign and letters of the station that aired the content; and
3. a significant excerpt of the program.

The first requirement is important because, if the broadcast occurred during the safe-harbor period of 10:00 p.m. to 6:00 a.m., then any complaint for indecent content or profane language will be dismissed. That eight-hour window is when indecent and profane content (although not obscene speech) is protected from the FCC's wrath.

The second requirement is important because the FCC must know the particular station—the particular broadcast licensee—that carried the content. That station will, in turn, be named and investigated by the FCC.

Finally, the third requirement—that a significant excerpt of the program be provided to the FCC by the complainant—can be satisfied in several different ways. For instance, the complaining viewer may provide a full or partial tape or transcript of not only *what* was said but the *context* in which it was said. It is not enough for the complainant simply to state that "there was a broadcast involving sexual dialogue." That won't cut it. More details showing what was actually said (the precise language used or images shown) and the context in which it was said are key. Today it is easy for a group like the PTC to file a complaint online. The FCC accepts e-mail complaints online at fccinfo@fcc.gov.

What should one expect for the short-term future of broadcast indecency regulation? The answer lies largely in the approach and direction of the FCC chairman. In March 2005, Republican Kevin J. Martin was appointed by President George W. Bush to chair the FCC through June 2006, replacing Michael K. Powell, son of Colin Powell. Martin, as Daily Variety put it, "has consistently pushed for the agency to be more aggressive on indecency."[48] Media

48. Triplett, "TV Decency Proponent to Top FCC."

reporter Frank Ahrens of the Washington Post speculated that "the FCC under Martin is likely to be more active on indecency than under Powell. . . . Martin often said that indecency fines proposed in the past year were too low, and he called for broadcasters to be fined for each utterance or depiction of indecent material within a program."[49] The Parents Television Council certainly was happy with Martin's elevation to the FCC chair position, calling him "a stalwart leader on the issue of indecency." Some feared Martin would even attempt to stretch broadcast indecency rules to apply to cable operators and cable channels. Shortly after taking over as head of the FCC Martin gave a speech in San Francisco to the National Cable & Telecommunications Association suggesting that cable television should "voluntarily step up" to develop a "family-friendly tier" of programming. Seemingly encouraging self-regulation over government regulation, Martin appeared to back away from foisting his own program on the cable industry when he stated, "At bottom the Commission is a creature of Congress. Congress will have to determine whether indecency rules should be applied to cable."

Regardless of the FCC's future approach, members of the broadcast community made it clear in May 2005 that they would fight back against groups like the Parents Television Council. That month Viacom (owner of CBS), News Corp. (owner of Fox) and NBC Universal banded together to create a coalition called TV Watch (www.televisionwatch.org) that encourages parental control and responsibility over government regulation. TV Watch released a survey at the time showing that 91 percent of 1,000 adults sampled across the United States don't want their programming choices controlled by "the sensitivities of a few." Ultimately, 2005 proved to be a relatively quiet year—at least compared to 2004—with few high-profile indecency complaints filed.

VIOLENCE ON TELEVISION

The first thing to note in starting this section is that violent content is not included in the FCC's definition of indecency discussed in the last section. Broadcast indecency currently focuses only on sexual or excretory organs or activities, *not* on violent images or storylines. Parsed differently and more bluntly, violence and sex simply are not the same thing in the FCC's regulatory universe. That dichotomy, however, may not always remain in place. For instance, Senators David Rockefeller (D.-W.Va.) and Kay Bailey Hutchison (R.-Tex.) introduced a bill in 2005 called the "Indecent and Gratuitous and Excessively Violent Programming Control Act of 2005" that would bring violence within the concept and definition of indecency for the first time.[50] Although this bill failed to become law, other bills are likely to arise in the future as people increasingly foist blame and responsibility for real-life violence onto the media and media content.

Congress added new rules to the broad array of broadcast regulations when it adopted legislation in the Telecommunications Act of 1996 to regulate violence on television. The law required the manufacturers of television sets to include a microchip—nicknamed the V-chip—in television receivers manufactured after January 1, 2000. Sets with screens smaller than 13 inches are exempt from the regulation. This chip, along with a programming rating system imposed on

49. Ahrens, "FCC's New Standards-Bearer."
50. S. 616, 109th Cong. (2005). The wide-ranging bill also proposed a number of other changes including doubling the amount of required children's programming to six hours, up from the current three hours discussed earlier in this chapter.

broadcasters, permits viewers to block out violent television programming. The V-chip is activated by a signal contained in each television broadcast. The signal tells the receiver that a program with a certain rating is being transmitted. If the receiver is programmed to reject such a broadcast, reception of the show will be blocked. Two years after the law was passed, the broadcast industry, children's advocacy groups, the motion picture industry and the FCC agreed on a rating system. The system has two tiers. One is age-based and is designed to inform a viewer whether a particular program is suitable for children of a certain age. There are two ratings for children's programs:

TV-Y—approved for all children

TV-Y7—approved for children 7 or older

All other entertainment programs are rated at one of four levels (news programs and news magazine shows are exempt from the ratings):

TV-G—suitable for all ages; little or no violence, no strong language, and little or no sexual dialogue

TV-PG—parental guidance; may contain material that many parents would find unsuitable for younger children

TV-14—parent strongly cautioned; may contain material that many parents would find unsuitable for children 14 years of age and younger

TV-M—mature audience only; programs for adults, may be unsuitable for children under 17 years of age

The second tier of the system provides viewers with reasons for the age-based ratings. The descriptive letters attempt to summarize the content:

V—violence

S—sexual situations

L—coarse language

D—suggestive dialogue

FV—fantasy violence

Most over-the-air and cable broadcasters have adopted the system. A few have not. But the industry's acceptance of the V-chip ratings seems far more enthusiastic than that of television set owners. A study by the Henry J. Kaiser Family Foundation published in July 2001 showed that V-chip use was fairly low.[51] About 40 percent of American families had at that time at least one television set with a V-chip, but only about half of those families were aware the sets contained the blocking device. Of those who said they were aware, only about one-third said they had used the V-chip. The foundation concluded that of all parents surveyed, only about 7 percent actually used the new violence-blocking technology. This finding was despite the fact that most of the parents surveyed said they were still highly concerned about sex and violence on television.

---

51. Rutenberg, "Few Parents Use the V-Chip."

SUMMARY

The FCC has broad control over the content of broadcast programming. To enforce this control, the agency has a wide variety of sanctions, which include letters of reprimand, fine or forfeiture, and nonrenewal or revocation of broadcast licenses. Content regulations involve a wide range of broadcast programming. In the broadest sense, the broadcaster must program to meet the needs of the community. But programming rules also involve simple regulations, such as the requirement to present station identification at various times of the broadcast day.

The FCC has chosen not to attempt to control the selection of format by a broadcaster. Citizens groups have urged the FCC to hold hearings when a radio station drops one program format and adopts a new one. In the early 1970s federal courts supported these citizen protests, but in 1981 the U.S. Supreme Court ruled that the government need not get involved when a broadcaster decides to switch from one format to another. In the mid-1980s the FCC attempted to remove rules dictating programming standards for children's broadcasting. Congress resisted these changes and forced the agency to reinstate rules regarding both the number of commercial minutes permitted per hour in children's programming and minimum service standards for the younger viewers.

Federal law prohibits the broadcast of any obscene or indecent material. In 1978 the Supreme Court ruled that a radio or television station could be punished for broadcasting material that is not obscene but merely indecent. The court based its ruling on the premise that children might be present during the broadcast. In 2001 the FCC issued a comprehensive statement outlining its policies regarding indecent broadcasts. In 2004, the FCC began an all-out crackdown on indecent content. In 1996 Congress mandated that microchip circuitry be added to all new television sets that would allow parents to block the reception of programs rated as violent.

REGULATION OF POLITICAL PROGRAMMING

The guarantees of freedom of speech and freedom of the press were added to the Constitution in large measure to protect political debate in the nation from government interference. In recent years the courts and the FCC have voided two important content regulations that were related in many instances to political discussion, the fairness doctrine and rules that focused on personal attacks and political editorials. The fairness doctrine was generated by the FCC in the late 1940s and stipulated that all broadcasters had a responsibility to provide coverage of important public issues that arose in their communities. In providing such coverage the broadcasters had the additional obligation of ensuring that all significant viewpoints on these issues were represented. In the late 1980s the FCC said it would no longer enforce the fairness doctrine and a U.S. Court of Appeals subsequently ruled that the agency was within its rights to abandon the doctrine.[52] The personal attack rules stipulated that when broadcasters air what amounts to a personal attack on an individual or group, they must also notify the target of the broadcast attack and offer free time for the target to reply. The rules on political editorials

---

52. *Syracuse Peace Council* v. *FCC,* 867 F. 2d 654 (1989). See also *Arkansas AFL-CIO* v. *FCC,* 11 F. 3d 1430 (1993).

were similar. If a broadcaster endorsed a candidate for political office, the opposing candidate had to be notified about the endorsement and given an opportunity to respond. In October 2000 a U.S. Court of Appeals ordered the FCC to repeal these rules because of, among other reasons, First Amendment concerns.[53] Other rules remain, however. What follows is a summary of the two most important.

CANDIDATE ACCESS RULE

Broadcasters cannot completely block candidates for *federal* office from buying airtime on the station to promote their candidacies because of the existence of the **candidate access rule. Section 312** (a) (7) of the Federal Communications Act, adopted in 1971 by Congress, states that a broadcast license can be revoked for willful and repeated failure "to allow reasonable access to or to permit the purchase of reasonable amounts of time for the use of a broadcasting station by a legally qualified candidate for federal elective office on behalf of his candidacy." This statute applies only to candidates for federal office: presidents and vice presidents and U.S. senators and representatives.

Federal courts have provided important interpretations of this statute. Two cases stemmed from the 1980 presidential election campaign. The Carter-Mondale presidential committee sought to buy 30 minutes of time on all three networks in early December 1979 for President Jimmy Carter to announce that he would be a candidate for re-election and to present a film outlining Carter's record as president. The request was made in October 1979. NBC refused. ABC said it could not reach a decision on the question. CBS offered two five-minute segments, one at 10:55 p.m. and one during the day. Privately, all three networks were fearful of breaking into their prime-time entertainment schedules for a political broadcast. But publicly, the broadcasters argued that the political campaign had not yet started; it was too early to begin to carry political programming (the election was scheduled for November 1980).

The FCC ruled against the networks, the U.S. Court of Appeals for the District of Columbia Circuit ruled against the networks, and the U.S. Supreme Court ruled against the networks. The high court ruled in its 6-3 decision that a broadcaster could not institute an across-the-board policy rejecting all requests from federal candidates for airtime.[54] Chief Justice Burger wrote that once a political campaign begins, a broadcaster must give reasonable and good faith attention to access requests from legally qualified candidates.

> Such requests must be considered on an individualized basis, and broadcasters are required to tailor their responses to accommodate, as much as reasonably possible, a candidate's stated purpose in seeking air time. In responding to access requests, however, broadcasters may also give weight to such factors as the amount of time previously sold to the candidate, the disruptive impact on regular programming, and the likelihood of requests for time by rival candidates under the equal opportunities provision of Section 315 (a). These considerations may not be invoked as pretexts for denying access; to justify a negative response, broadcasters must cite a realistic danger of substantial program disruption—perhaps caused by insufficient notice to allow adjustments in the schedule—or of an excessive number of equal time requests.

53. *Radio-Television News Directors Association* v. *FCC,* 229 F. 3d 269 (2000).
54. *CBS* v. *FCC,* 453 U.S. 567 (1981).

Burger added that broadcasters must explain their reasons for refusing airtime or making limited counteroffers so the FCC can review these decisions if needed. Each of the networks had argued, however, that the 1980 presidential campaign had not really started. After all, the time period sought by Carter was 11 months prior to the election. In this case the networks should not be bound by Section 312, they asserted. The majority of the Supreme Court rejected this argument, noting the following evidence that the campaign had started:

1. Ten Republican candidates and two Democratic candidates had announced they were running for president.
2. The selection of delegates to the national political conventions had started in many states.
3. Many candidates were making speeches in an effort to raise money.
4. The Iowa caucuses to select convention delegates were scheduled for January, one month after the broadcast time sought by Carter.
5. Newspapers had been covering the national political campaign for at least two months.

Burger rejected the notion that Section 312 created a right of access to the media. None is created by this decision, he added. But a licensed broadcaster is "granted the free and exclusive use of a limited and valuable part of the public domain; when he accepts that franchise, it is burdened by enforceable public obligations."[55]

The Supreme Court's ruling means that a broadcaster cannot adopt an across-the-board policy of rejecting all requests for airtime. Each request must be considered individually and can be rejected only if the broadcaster can demonstrate good cause.

The Supreme Court's ruling means that a broadcaster cannot adopt an across-the-board policy of rejecting all requests for airtime.

Section 312 implies that the candidate can seek to buy time on a station or ask for free time. Does this mean a broadcast station must *give* a candidate for federal office free time if fulfilling such a request would not interfere substantially with the broadcast schedule or would not prompt requests for equal time from other candidates? The U.S. Court of Appeals for the District of Columbia Circuit answered no when that question was asked. On March 14, 1980, President Carter delivered a 30-minute speech on the economic condition of the nation. The speech was carried on all three networks. This was four days before the presidential primary in Illinois. Senator Ted Kennedy, who was also seeking the Democratic nomination for president, requested that the networks *give* him 30 minutes of airtime to respond to the president's speech. The networks said they would sell Kennedy the time but would not give it to him. Kennedy argued that they were obliged to provide him 30 minutes at no cost because of Section 312. The Court of Appeals supported the FCC's denial of Kennedy's request. The law does not confer upon a candidate the privilege of using a broadcaster's facilities without charge. Broadcasters may meet the demands of Section 312 by either giving the candidate free time or making time available for purchase, the court said. The networks had already given Kennedy's campaign considerable free time through its news coverage of the candidate.[56]

In September 1999 the FCC reversed a decision it had made five years earlier and ruled that federal candidates who seek to buy broadcasting time cannot be limited to buying only 30- and 60-second spots. In 1994, the FCC had ruled that broadcasters could refuse to sell the

55. *CBS v. FCC,* 453 U.S. 567 (1981).
56. *Kennedy for President Committee v. FCC,* 636 F. 2d 417 (1980).

longer spots. The 1999 ruling did not specify a length of time the candidates could buy, but the agency did note that five-minute spots might be better for the candidates.

Supporters of Section 312 see it as a means to permit candidates for federal office to use the important broadcast communication channels in this nation to talk to prospective voters. Opponents say Section 312 is government interference in broadcasters' operation of their business, and it can cause severe financial hardship if programming schedules are disrupted to facilitate political broadcasts.

When Congress adopted Section 312 in 1971, it also specified the highest rates that a broadcaster can charge a candidate for federal office for using station facilities. The general rule is that 45 days before a primary election and 60 days before a general election, the charge to a candidate cannot exceed the lowest rate the station charges its local advertisers for that particular time slot. At other times the rate must be "comparable" to what the station charges other advertisers. These rules contain other considerable details that are important but are too involved to outline here. Students who intend to enter broadcast sales should closely study Section 312 (a) (7) of 47 *United States Code.*

Although Section 312 applies only to candidates for federal office, a station that routinely denied candidates for state and local office reasonable access to communicate with voters would undoubtedly be sanctioned by the government. The FCC has interpreted Section 307 of the Communications Act, which outlines a licensee's public interest responsibilities, to bar any station from denying any candidate reasonable access simply to avoid obligations under the equal opportunity rules, which will be outlined next.

EQUAL OPPORTUNITY/EQUAL TIME RULE

Section 315 of the Communications Act outlines what are called the equal opportunity or **equal time rules.** These rules have been a part of the law since it was passed in 1934, although this section was substantially amended in 1959. The rules are quite simple. If a broadcasting station permits one legally qualified candidate for any elective public office to use its facilities, it must afford an equal opportunity for all other legally qualified candidates for the same office.

What does equal opportunity mean? It means equal time, equal facilities, and comparable costs. If John Smith buys one-half hour of television time on station WKTL to campaign for the office of mayor, other legally qualified candidates for that office must be allowed to purchase one-half hour of time as well. If Smith is able to use the station's equipment to prerecord his talk, other candidates must have the same opportunity. If the station charges Smith $100 for the one-half hour of time, the station must charge his opponents $100.

The station does not have to solicit appearances by the other candidates; it merely must give them the opportunity to use the facilities if they request such use within one week of Smith's appearance. Finally, Section 315 does not provide a right of access to any candidate to use a station's facilities. Section 315 only applies if the station first chooses to permit one candidate to appear on the station. However, remember the earlier discussion about requirements that exist under Section 312 and the general public interest standards that govern station operation.

Section 315 specifically bars the station from censoring material in broadcasts made by political candidates. And the courts interpret this provision quite strictly. In 1992 an Atlanta television station received many complaints when it aired a conservative congressional candidate's graphic anti-abortion spot in the early evening. So when Daniel Becker tried to buy an additional 30 minutes of airtime to show the video "Abortion in America—The Real Story" between 4 p.m. and 5 p.m. on Sunday following an NFL football telecast, the station claimed the highly graphic video was indecent and refused to show it in the afternoon. The station said it would broadcast the video after midnight when children were less likely to be in the audience. Becker claimed this violated both the candidate access rule (Section 312; see pages 700–702) and the equal opportunity rule as well as his First Amendment rights.

Both the FCC and a U.S. District Court sided with the station in the dispute,[57] but the District of Columbia U.S. Circuit Court of Appeals reversed these rulings. In September 1996 the court said that permitting a broadcaster to schedule the airing of political spots based on the content of the spot violates both Section 312 and the no-censorship provisions of Section 315. A rigid policy of refusing to provide access during prime-time hours would be "unreasonable," the court said, and would deny the candidate access to time periods with the greatest audience potential. This policy forces the candidate to choose between the content in the advertisement and the composition of the audience, the court added. "This self-censorship must surely frustrate the full and unrestricted discussion of political issues envisioned by Congress."[58]

Use of the Airwaves

Under Section 315 if one candidate gets the use of a broadcast facility, his or her opponents get to use the facility as well. What is a "use" under the law? Any presentation or appearance that features a candidate's voice or image is regarded as a "use" by the FCC. It is not a use if, for example, in a political advertisement an announcer simply recites the candidate's record or his or her position on an issue. Similarly, it is not a use if the candidate's voice or image is used by an opponent in one of his or her ads. But short of these exceptions most other appearances count, including appearances on TV entertainment programs like a situation comedy, guest shots on an entertainment talk show like the David Letterman program, and even appearances in televised feature films. In the spring of 2003 the scheduled appearance by Mayor John F. Street of Philadelphia on the CBS television crime drama "Hack" was canceled by the network when it was learned that Street was in the midst of a campaign for re-election. The network said the appearance might trigger provisions of Section 315 and force the Philadelphia CBS affiliate to give his opponents equal television exposure.[59] And when Arnold Schwarzenegger became a candidate for governor in the 2003 California recall election, television stations in that state were forced to stop showing his movies, or face requests from the 134 other candidates on the ballot for equal time.

In 1959 Congress amended Section 315 and carved out four rather broad exceptions to the meaning of the term "use." Since 1959 the FCC has liberally interpreted these exceptions to broaden them even more. The following appearances by a candidate do not constitute a use under the law. That is, an opponent cannot use one of these appearances as a justification for equal time from the station.

57. *Gillett Communications of Atlanta, Inc.* v. *Becker,* 807 F. Supp. 757 (1992).
58. *Becker* v. *FCC,* 1 E.P.L.R. 580 (1996).
59. "Pennsylvania: Mayor Cut from TV Show."

Source: © Zade Rosenthal/20th Century Fox/Kobal Collection

During the 2003 California recall election, TV stations in the state could not telecast movies like "Predator" in which Arnold Schwarzenegger, a candidate for governor, appeared, without triggering the equal opportunity rule.

APPEARANCES BY A POLITICAL CANDIDATE THAT ARE NOT GOVERNED BY EQUAL OPPORTUNITY RULE

▌ Appearance in a bona fide newscast

▌ Appearance in a bona fide news interview show

▌ Appearance in the spot news coverage of a bona fide news event

▌ Incidental appearance in a news documentary

---

1. **The appearance by a candidate in a bona fide or legitimate newscast does not constitute use of the facility in the eyes of the law.** Section 315 will not be triggered. The FCC has ruled that appearances by political candidates on ABC's "Good Morning America," NBC's "Today" and CBS's "Early Show" are exempt from provisions of Section 315, as are interview shows such as "Oprah Winfrey," "The View" and "Montel Williams." The agency considers all programs bona fide newscasts. The FCC ruled that an appearance in a news clip broadcast as a part of the program "McLaughlin Group" constitutes an appearance in a newscast.[60] But

---

60. *Telecommunications Research and Action Center* v. *FCC*, 26 F. 3d 185 (1994).

a candidate appearance during the panel discussion part of the program would not fall under the newscast exemption. If the newscaster or reporter who reads the news is a candidate for public office, this exemption does not apply to that candidacy. In an unusual case, TV reporter William Branch, a general assignment reporter for KOVR-TV in Sacramento, announced he was a candidate for town council in a nearby community. The station told him he would have to take an unpaid leave of absence if he chose to run for office because it could not afford to give his opponent free time equal to the time Branch appeared in the newscasts. Branch sought help from the FCC, arguing that his appearances in a bona fide newscast would not trigger Section 315. The FCC disagreed and a U.S. Court of Appeals supported the regulatory agency. "When a broadcaster's employees are sent out to cover a news story involving other persons . . . the bona fide news event is the activity engaged in by those other persons, not the work done by the employees covering the event," the three-judge panel ruled. Branch argued that this ruling extinguished his right to hold public office. The court disagreed; the ruling simply says the station will have to provide equal time for opposing candidates if the reporter is a candidate.[61]

2. **The appearance of a candidate in a bona fide news interview program does not constitute a use.** The FCC has defined a bona fide news interview program as one that is regularly scheduled, within the journalistic control of the producers, and is produced as a newsworthy and good faith journalistic exercise, not an attempt to advance a particular candidacy. An appearance on "Meet the Press," which is a bona fide regularly scheduled news interview show, is not use of a broadcasting facility. But an appearance on "Meet the Candidates," a public affairs show created by a television station for the express purpose of interviewing candidates prior to an election, is use because it is not a bona fide news interview show. The show was created especially for the election campaign by the station and is not broadcast when electioneering is not in progress.

3. **The appearance of a candidate in the spot news coverage of a bona fide news event is not use.** When candidate Smith is interviewed at the scene of a warehouse fire about the problems of arson in the city, this is not use in terms of Section 315. Political conventions are considered bona fide news events; therefore an appearance by a candidate at the convention can be broadcast without invoking Section 315.

4. **The appearance of a candidate in a news documentary is not a use if the appearance is incidental to the presentation of the subject of the program.** Imagine that during a 2008 election campaign for a U.S. Senate seat from Washington, a Seattle television station broadcasts a documentary on the 1991 Persian Gulf War and the role played by a particular U.S. Air Force unit that before the war was stationed at an air base in the state. One segment focuses on the wartime experiences of Luis Sanchez, a fighter pilot who was shot down over Iraq during the war but managed to elude the enemy for 10 days before reaching safety in Saudi Arabia. Sanchez is a candidate for the Senate seat. Would his appearance in

---

61. *Branch* v. *FCC*, 824 F. 2d 37 (1987).

this documentary trigger Section 315? Would the TV station be required to give time to his opponent? No. Because Sanchez's appearance focuses exclusively on his experiences during the war and not his political candidacy, his appearance in the documentary is regarded as an incidental appearance.

Debates between political candidates are considered bona fide news events, and the broadcast of these events will not initiate use of Section 315. This is true even if the broadcaster sponsors the debate, according to a 1984 ruling by the FCC. Prior to this ruling, an outside third party had to sponsor the debate before it was considered a news event. In both 1976 and 1980, for example, the League of Women Voters sponsored presidential debates that included only the candidates from the Democratic and Republican parties. Feminist Sonia Johnson, who ran for president with the Citizens Party in 1984, challenged this FCC policy after she was not permitted to take part in the nationally televised debates. She argued that exclusion from the debates effectively excluded her from winning the election and denied voters who were sympathetic to her cause, but who were unacquainted with her, the opportunity to vote for her. A U.S. Court of Appeals disagreed, ruling that Johnson did not enjoy a right under any federal law to be included in the televised debates.[62] By 1988 there was little pretense of outside sponsorship of the debates.

In 1996 the major television networks gave free time to Bill Clinton and Bob Dole to air their statements about major issues in the campaign. CBS and NBC did this within the scope of their evening newscasts and were not required to give time to other presidential candidates. ABC, PBS and Fox aired the short statements at other times, and the FCC declared that such telecasts were on-the-spot coverage of bona fide news events and exempted the three networks from obligations under Section 315.

Press conferences held by political candidates are also normally considered bona fide news events and are exempt from the provisions of Section 315. A press conference held by President Jimmy Carter in February 1980, several months after he announced he was a candidate for re-election, was broadcast live by all the television networks. Carter's opponent for the Democratic nomination, Ted Kennedy, sought time from the television networks under the equal opportunity rule. The networks said no. The FCC agreed with the broadcasters; the press conference was a bona fide news event. The agency had ruled in 1975 that all press conferences featuring political candidates were exempt from Section 315 as news events. Kennedy appealed the ruling to the U.S. Court of Appeals for the District of Columbia Circuit and lost. The court said that to determine if the coverage of a news conference can be considered spot coverage of a bona fide news event, three criteria must be examined:

1. Was the press conference broadcast live? Coverage of spot news should be live coverage.
2. Was there any evidence of favoritism on the part of the broadcaster? Did the station just carry Carter's press conferences and ignore his opponent's conferences?
3. Finally, did the broadcaster make a good faith judgment that the news conference was a bona fide news event?

62. *Johnson* v. *FCC*, 829 F. 2d 157 (1987).

In this case the press conference was carried live, the networks had covered Kennedy press conferences, and it was obvious that a determination had been made by the broadcasters that this was an important news event.[63]

Legally Qualified Candidates

The FCC has attempted to define who is and who is not a legally qualified candidate as precisely as possible (see boxed text).

A LEGALLY QUALIFIED CANDIDATE IS ANY PERSON

- who publicly announces that he or she is a candidate for nomination or election to any local, county, state or federal office, *and*
- who meets the qualifications prescribed by law for that office, *and*
- who qualifies for a place on the ballot or is eligible to be voted for by sticker or write-in methods, *and*
- who was duly nominated by a political party that is commonly known and regarded as such or makes a substantial showing that he or she is a bona fide candidate.

The first requirement is clear; the candidate must say he or she is a candidate. The second requirement means that the individual must be qualified to hold the office. There is an age requirement for most elective offices. Residency requirements usually apply to legislative offices: A woman can't run for Congress in Arkansas' 1st District if she lives in the 2nd District. Only natural-born citizens qualify as candidates for president. The third requirement speaks for itself; the person's name must either appear on the ballot, or the individual must be an eligible write-in or sticker candidate. The last requirement is the most confusing. What is a substantial showing? What is a political party, "commonly known and regarded as such"? The FCC will answer a broadcaster's inquiries regarding matters such as these.

In primary elections, Section 315 applies to intraparty elections, not interparty elections. In a primary election Democrats run against Democrats, Republicans run against Republicans, Libertarians run against Libertarians. If there is an appearance by a Democrat, the other Democratic candidates for the same office must be afforded an equal opportunity. The station does not have to give Republicans or Libertarians or even independents the opportunity to make an appearance. During general elections, Section 315 applies across party lines since at this point all candidates are running against each other for the same office.

In primary elections, Section 315 applies to intraparty elections, not interparty elections.

Whereas only an appearance by the candidate himself or herself can trigger Section 315, appearances by supporters of the candidate trigger another regulation called the **Zapple Rule.** This rule was formulated by the FCC in response to a letter from Nicholas Zapple, who was a staff member on the Senate Subcommittee on Communications. This rule states that if

---

63. *Kennedy for President Committee* v. *FCC,* 636 F. 2d 432 (1980).

a broadcaster permits the supporter of a candidate to make an appearance on the station, then the station must provide an equal opportunity for an appearance by supporters of other legally qualified candidates for the same office. In the FCC's 1972 "Report Regarding the Handling of Political Broadcasts," the agency outlined the Zapple Rule in this way:

> The commission held in "Zapple" that when a licensee sells time to sup-porters or spokesmen of a candidate during an election campaign who urge the candidate's election, discuss the campaign issues, or criticize an oppo-nent then the licensee must afford comparable time to the spokesmen for an opponent. Known as the quasi-equal opportunity or political party corollary to the fairness doctrine, the "Zapple" doctrine is based on the equal oppor-tunity requirement of Section 315 of the Communications Act; accordingly, free reply time need not be afforded to respond to a paid program.

Two last points need to be made about Section 315. First, since broadcasters are not per-mitted to censor the remarks of a political candidate, they are immune from libel suits based on those remarks. In 1959 the Supreme Court ruled that because stations cannot control what candidates say over the air, they should not be held responsible for the remarks. The candi-date, however, can still be sued.[64] Second, ballot issues like school bond levies, initiatives and referendums do not fall under Section 315. Do these rules apply to the Internet? No Supreme Court or federal appellate court ruling has focused specifically on that question. But clearly, since the Supreme Court ruled in 1997[65] that communication on the Internet enjoys the same First Amendment protection as communication in the printed press, it would seem highly improbable that the candidate access rule, the equal opportunity rule or any broadcast regula-tion could be applied to the Internet.

SUMMARY

Several rules govern political broadcasts carried by radio and television broadcasters. Sec-tion 312 of the Federal Communications Act states that broadcasters cannot have an across-the-board policy rejecting all paid and nonpaid appearances by candidates for federal office. A candidate's request must be evaluated and can be rejected only if it could cause serious disruption of program schedules or might prompt an excessive number of equal-time requests. Although this rule applies only to requests from candidates for federal office, the govern-ment's mandate that broadcasters operate their stations in the public interest may very well include similar standards for the treatment by broadcasters of requests for access to air time from state and local candidates.

Section 315 states that if a broadcaster provides one candidate for office with the oppor-tunity to use a station's broadcast facilities, all other legally qualified candidates for the same office must be given the same opportunity. The use of the station's facilities includes all appearances on the station with the exception of the following:

1. Bona fide newscasts
2. Bona fide news interview programs

---

64. *Farmers Educational and Cooperative Union of America* v. *WDAY,* 360 U.S. 525 (1959).
65. *Reno* v. *American Civil Liberties Union,* 117 S. Ct. 2329 (1997).

3. Spot news coverage

4. Incidental appearance in a news documentary

Candidate press conferences and debates between candidates are considered spot news events. During primary elections, Section 315 applies only to candidates from the same political party running against each other to win the party's nomination to run in the general election.

NEWS AND PUBLIC AFFAIRS

While the FCC has been quite willing to impose content regulations on entertainment programming, the agency has purposely steered away from making similar rules regarding broadcast news. The violence ratings do not apply to television news, for example. The agency reinforced this position in May 1998 when it rejected a petition to strip four Denver television station licenses on the grounds that the news programs on the stations are heavily saturated with violent content. A group called Media Watch asked the FCC to deny the station's license renewals because the news programming contained "toxic" levels of television violence, which in turn leads to "fear, disrespect, imitative behavior, desensitization and increased violent behavior." The agency responded by saying that "journalistic or editorial discretion in the presentation of news and public information is the core concept of the First Amendment free press guarantee."[66]

The agency treats claims of the falsification of broadcast news in a similar fashion. Distortion or falsification of real news programs is rare and normally condemned by those in the industry. The FCC has a rule against such distortion, but it is quite specific and poses a high hurdle for those who wish to make a complaint against a broadcast. Only those distortions or stagings that are deliberately intended to slant or mislead violate the FCC regulation. Any allegation that a story was deliberately distorted must be supported by extrinsic evidence—for example, independent witnesses who can testify they saw the staging. Also, the distortion must involve a significant part of the story being reported, not an incidental or minor part of the news report. The FCC has refused to investigate "inaccurate embellishments concerning peripheral aspects of news reports or attempts at window dressing which concerned the manner of presenting the news, as long as the essential facts of the news stories to which these presentational devices were related were broadcast in an accurate manner."[67]

The FCC usually has the last word in such falsification matters, but in August 1998 the U.S. Court of Appeals for the District of Columbia Circuit overturned an FCC decision exonerating CBS in a charge of news distortion and told the agency to re-examine the complaint. In 1994 the CBS newsmagazine show "60 Minutes" broadcast a segment highly critical of life in post-communist Ukraine entitled "The Ugly Face of Freedom." Complaints were filed by Alexander Serafyn, an American of Ukrainian ancestry. Among other charges, Serafyn

---

66. Brooke, "F.C.C. Supports TV News."
67. *Galloway* v. *FCC,* 7878 F. 2d 16 (1985).

claimed that the program had broadcast quotes out of context, mistranslated words to paint a dark picture of life in the former Soviet republic, and refused the help of a Ukrainian professor of history who could have given the report needed context and perspective. Other viewers complained about the program as well. When the FCC rejected his complaints, Serafyn appealed. A unanimous ruling by a three-judge panel reversed the FCC decision, finding that the agency had acted arbitrarily and capriciously when it denied Serafyn's claims. The judges acknowledged that each complaint taken separately might not be sufficient to prove a claim of distortion, but the FCC must reconsider all the claims taken as a whole in determining whether the broadcast had distorted the news.[68]

PAYOLA, PUNDITS AND PROPAGANDA

In 2005 conservative columnist and television pundit Armstrong Williams created a firestorm of controversy when it was revealed by USA Today that he was paid more than $200,000 by the U.S. Department of Education to praise and promote the No Child Left Behind Act on his nationally syndicated television show and to urge other black journalists to do the same.[69] The act was a centerpiece of the Bush administration's education policy in its first term, and the Department of Education needed support for it from the African-American community and thus employed Williams, who is black, to take up its cause. The situation raised obvious ethical concerns in journalism circles: Williams had crossed the line from being a conservative commentator to an undisclosed paid spokesperson and lapdog for the Bush administration. The money from the Department of Education, which was funneled through a major public relations firm to a firm headed by Williams called the Graham Williams Group,* suggested a clear cash-for-commentary, quid pro quo situation. Journalists, of course, are supposed to be independent of conflicts of interest that may affect their news judgment. Shortly after the news broke about the Williams contract, it was disclosed that another conservative commentator and columnist, Maggie Gallagher, had a contract with the Department of Health and Human Services (HHS) to help promote President Bush's policies on marriage and strengthening of families.[70] As the Washington Post reported, Gallagher's responsibilities under the contract "included drafting a magazine article for the HHS official overseeing the initiative, writing brochures for the program and conducting a briefing for department officials."[71]

But the trouble with the Armstrong Williams affair went beyond the realm of media ethics to the arena of media law when the FCC, after receiving a reported 12,000 complaints, opened up an investigation in 2005 into whether his dealings violated federal laws against "payola." Payola typically refers to the illegal but well-established "pay-for-play" practice in which record company representatives pay off disc jockeys to play certain songs on the radio. For instance, in November 2005 Warner Music Group agreed to pay $5 million to settle payola allegations brought by New York Attorney General Eliot Spitzer that Warner gave

*In an interesting side note, the "Graham" in the Graham Williams Group is Stedman Graham, the longtime companion of Oprah Winfrey.

68. Kirtley, "Second Guessing News Judgment."
69. Toppo, "White House Paid Journalist."
70. Kurtz, "Writer Backing Bush Plan."
71. Ibid.

radio station employees gifts and other financial benefits to obtain airplay for songs. The Williams situation put a new twist on this by shifting the focus from pay-for-play to pay-for-commentary, sometimes called "plugola." Regardless of the name, payola regulations do not prohibit paid-for commentary, but rather require its disclosure and sponsorship identification. In other words, the laws concentrate on what amounts to undisclosed or covert advertising. Specifically, federal law requires broadcasters to reveal and disclose the fact that content has been broadcast in exchange for money, services or other valuable consideration.[72] This, in brief, is a sponsorship identification requirement, and it also is embraced in the FCC's own rules.[73] In addition, federal law mandates that when a business or individual pays someone else to include program matter in a broadcast, that payment must be disclosed prior to the broadcast to the station that will carry it.[74] What's more, both the person making the payment and the recipient are obligated to disclose it in order for the station to make and satisfy its sponsorship identification requirement. Violations of the laws are considered criminal offenses subject to both fines and imprisonment.

Payola regulations do not prohibit paid-for commentary, but rather require its disclosure and sponsorship identification.

In addition to the payola investigation opened by the FCC into the Williams affair, a complaint was filed with the commission in March 2005 by the Center for Media and Democracy[75] and a media reform group called Free Press to determine whether the Bush administration's use of government funds to produce video news releases (VNRs)—the broadcast equivalent to a press release that masquerades as news but really is in fact created by a public relations firm or government agency—violated federal laws. VNRs often involve video clips featuring a person who appears to be a news reporter covering a story, when in fact the person is really an actor hired by a public relations firm reading from a script. Many claim that VNRs, which are virtually indistinguishable today from real news clips, amount to fake news and press-release journalism, especially when local television stations run them unedited as if they really were news and fail to disclose their origin. The use of VNRs by local news outlets makes great economic—although certainly not ethical—sense for television stations trying to save money by laying off reporters; VNRs amount to free content and fill the place of stories that would otherwise need to be produced by salaried reporters and producers. In their complaint with the FCC, the Center for Media and Democracy and Free Press wrote:

> Local stations have broadcast these official news releases without properly identifying the source to the public. A VNR produced by the U.S. Department of Agriculture (USDA) aired on more than 160 broadcast stations without proper attribution. An official news report produced by Karen Ryan for the Department of Health and Human Services appeared on at least 40 stations, again, without identifying the source. Ms. Ryan also has produced similar reports for the White House Office of National Drug Control Policy. One was used by more than 300 stations.

Senators John Kerry (D.-Mass.) and Daniel Inouye (D.-Haw.) also sent letters in 2005 to the FCC requesting it to investigate whether the use of taxpayer dollars to fund the VNRs

72. 47 U.S.C. § 317 (2005).
73. 47 C.F.R. § 73.1212 (2004). The FCC now maintains a link on its Web site devoted to the topic of payola at http://ftp.fcc.gov/cgb/consumerfacts/PayolaRules.html.
74. 47 U.S.C. § 508 (2005).
75. Information about this group can be found on its Web site at http://www.prwatch.org.

violated federal laws.[76] In April 2005 the FCC responded and issued a "Public Notice" announcing that "whenever broadcast stations and cable operators air VNRs, licensees and operators generally must clearly disclose to members of their audiences the nature, source and sponsorship of the material that they are viewing. We will take appropriate enforcement action against entities that do not comply with these rules."[77] The Public Notice stressed that broadcasters and cable operators are required under FCC rules "to inform their audience, at the time of airing [of a VNR]: (1) that such matter is sponsored, paid for or furnished, either in whole or in part; and (2) by whom or on whose behalf such consideration was supplied." The questions now are (1) how many broadcasters actually will heed the FCC's warning that they must disclose VNRs when they use them? and (2) how many broadcasters will now simply stop using VNRs in the first place rather than disclose that they are running what amounts to fake news that amounts to a sales pitch of government policies?

The FCC, however, was not the only government agency investigating the blurring lines between news and propaganda.

The FCC, however, was not the only government agency investigating the blurring lines between news and propaganda. In 2004 and 2005, the General Accountability Office (GAO)[78] determined that prepackaged news stories in several VNRs funded by federal government agencies constituted "covert propaganda" in violation of federal law. In Particular, Congress has adopted an appropriations limitation each year in its fiscal appropriations acts that provides "no part of any appropriation . . . shall be used for publicity or propaganda purposes within the United States not heretofore authorized by the Congress." The legal problem is that Congress has never defined the critical phrase "publicity or propaganda." David M. Walker, chief of the GAO, wrote in 2005 that "while [government] agencies generally have the right to disseminate information about their policies and activities, agencies may not use appropriated funds to produce or distribute prepackaged news stories intended to be viewed by television audiences that conceal or do not clearly identify for the television viewing audience that the agency was the source of those materials." The GAO is commonly called the investigative arm of Congress or the congressional watchdog.

The Bush administration, however, alleges that VNRs do not constitute propaganda. It should be noted that the use of VNRs existed under the Clinton administration, although the Bush administration increased the practice. As The New York Times wrote in a 2005 expose on the subject:

> Under the Bush administration, the federal government has aggressively used a well-established tool of public relations: the prepackaged, ready-to-serve news report that major corporations have long distributed to TV stations to pitch everything from headache remedies to auto insurance. In all, at least 20 federal agencies, including the Defense Department and the Census Bureau, have made and distributed hundreds of television news segments in the past four years, records and interviews show.[79]

---

76. Triplett, "Orgs Seek FCC Review of Bush Vids." In addition, Senator Kerry and Senator Frank Lautenberg (D.-N.J.) introduced a bill in the Senate in April 2005 that would require that "VNRs produced, distributed or otherwise paid for by the federal government clearly identify the federal government as the source of such material."

77. *Public Notice,* MB Docket No. 05-171, FCC 05-84 (released Apr. 13, 2005).

78. The GAO's Web site can be found at http://www.gao.gov.

79. Barstow and Stein, "Under Bush, a New Age of Prepackaged News."

The bottom line is that both ethical and legal issues have been opened up by the use of contracts with commentators like Armstrong Williams and the creation of VNRs. The ethical issues are relatively easy to resolve: Journalists should be independent from conflicting interests and they should never ever disseminate fake news and propaganda. The legal issues, however, are much more complex. The General Accountability Office ultimately reached a legal conclusion in its own investigation of the Armstrong Williams incident. On September 30, 2005, Anthony H. Gamboa, general counsel for the GAO, sent a letter U.S. Senators Frank R. Lautenberg (D.-N.J.) and Edward M. Kennedy (D.-Mass.) providing the GAO's determination that "the Department [of Education] contracted for Armstrong Williams to comment regularly on the No Child Left Behind Act without assuring that the Department's role was disclosed to the targeted audiences. This violated the publicity or propaganda prohibition for fiscal year 2004 because it amounted to covert propaganda." The letter added that "the commentary obtained as a result of these contracts violated the publicity or propaganda prohibition because it was 'covert,' in that it did not disclose to the targeted audiences that it was sponsored by the Department and was paid for using appropriated funds." In a separate letter sent to the same two senators on the same date regarding the Department of Education's use of appropriated funds to hire public relations firm Ketchum, Inc., to produce and distribute a video news release regarding programs available under the No Child Left Behind Act of 2001, Gamboa wrote that the Department of Education's "use of appropriated funds to produce a prepackaged news story regarding Supplemental Educational Services that failed to inform the viewing audience of the government source violates the publicity or propaganda prohibition. As we have stated in previous opinions and as recently affirmed by Congress, to avoid a violation of the publicity or propaganda prohibition, an agency must inform the viewing public that the government is the source of the information disseminated." In a nutshell, the GAO determined that *both* the paid-for-commentary of Armstrong Williams and the government-funded production of VNRs in support of the No Child Left Behind Act were illegal.

On an important and final side note for all journalism students interested in doing investigative reporting, USA Today first learned about the Armstrong Williams matter simply by making a Freedom of Information Act request (see Chapter 9). One request tore open an entire issue worthy of both journalistic and legal study.

THE FIRST AMENDMENT

Broadcasting stations are not common carriers; that is, they have the right to refuse to do business with anyone they choose. During 1969 and 1970 two groups, the Democratic National Committee and a Washington, D.C., organization known as Business Executives Movement for Peace, sought to buy time from television stations and networks to solicit funds for their protest of the Vietnam War and to voice their objections to the way the war was being waged by the government. Broadcasters rebuffed these groups on the grounds that airing such controversial advertisements and programming would evoke the fairness doctrine, and they would then be obligated to ensure that all sides of the controversy were aired. Such action was a nuisance and could be costly. The broadcasters told the Democratic committee and the business executives that one of their basic policies was not to sell time to any individual or group seeking to set forth views on controversial issues.

When this policy was challenged before the FCC, the commission sided with the broadcasters, noting that it was up to each individual licensee to determine how best to fulfill fairness doctrine obligations. But the U.S. Court of Appeals for the District of Columbia Circuit reversed the FCC ruling, stating that the right of the public to receive information is deeply rooted in the First Amendment. A ban on editorial advertising, the court ruled, "leaves a paternalistic structure in which licensees and bureaucrats decide what issues are important, whether to fully cover them, and the format, time and style of coverage." This kind of system, the court ruled, is inimical to the First Amendment.[80]

> It may unsettle some of us to see an antiwar message or a political party message in the accustomed place of a soap or beer commercial. . . . We must not equate what is habitual with what is right or what is constitutional. A society already so saturated with commercialism can well afford another outlet for speech on public issues. All that we may lose is some of our apathy.

The victory of the business organization and the Democrats was short-lived, for by a 7-2 vote, the U.S. Supreme Court overturned the appellate court ruling. Stations have an absolute right to refuse to sell time for advertising dealing with political campaigns and controversial issues, the court ruled. To give the FCC the power over such advertising runs the risk of enlarging government control over the content of broadcast discussion of public issues.

In response to the argument that by permitting broadcasters to refuse such advertising, we place in their hands the power to decide what the people shall see or hear on important public issues, Justice Burger wrote:

"For better or worse, editing is what editors are for."

> For better or worse, editing is what editors are for; and editing is the selection and choice of material. That editors—newspaper or broadcast—can and do abuse this power is beyond doubt, but that is no reason to deny the discretion Congress provided. Calculated risks of abuse are taken in order to preserve high values.[81]

The court was badly fractured on this case, and Justices Brennan and Marshall dissented. Only two other justices—Stewart and Rehnquist—joined the chief justice in his opinion. The remainder joined in overturning the appeals court ruling, but for their own reasons.

Finally, the high court used the First Amendment to strike down a congressional statute forbidding all noncommercial educational broadcasting stations that receive money from the Corporation for Public Broadcasting from editorializing on any subject at all.[82] The ban on all editorials by every station that receives CPB funds was too broad and far exceeded what is necessary to protect against the risk of governmental interference or to prevent the public from assuming that editorials by public broadcasting stations represent the official views of government.

80. *In re Business Executives Movement for Peace* v. *FCC,* 450 F. 2d 642 (1971).
81. *CBS* v. *Democratic National Committee,* 412 U.S. 94 (1973).
82. *FCC* v. *League of Women Voters,* 468 U.S. 912 (1984).

SUMMARY

The government exercises limited control over the content of public affairs broadcasts. The FCC has thus far rejected all complaints that television news coverage was slanted or staged and has made it difficult for those who seek to pursue this cause with the agency. The Supreme Court has given broadcasters the right to determine whether to air specific editorial advertising and has struck down a statute that forbade public broadcasting stations from telecasting editorial opinions.

REGULATION OF NEW TECHNOLOGY

Over-the-air broadcasting has been the primary focus of government attempts to regulate the electronic communications media, but as new technologies have emerged, the Federal Communications Commission and the Congress have moved to pass rules to govern their operation as well. Cable television has been the subject of numerous FCC rule-making efforts and two comprehensive federal statutes. Rules regulating low-power television, multipoint distribution services, satellite master antenna television, and direct satellite broadcasting have also been promulgated. The deregulatory waves that have swept away many broadcast rules have also hit cable regulation. In March 2001 a federal court ordered the FCC to reconsider and justify rules that limited both the size and program content of cable systems. Congress had given the FCC the authority to limit the number of cable subscribers one multiple system operator could reach—30 percent of all cable subscribers—and to prevent a cable operator, like AOL Time Warner for example, from filling the cable package it offered subscribers with programs created only by its affiliated companies. Only 40 percent of the programming could be produced by affiliated companies. The U.S. Court of Appeals ruled that both rules implicated the First Amendment and could be sustained only if it was shown they advanced important government interests unrelated to the suppression of speech and did not impact or limit more speech than necessary to further those interests. The court said in imposing the rules that the FCC had not adequately justified the need for the 30 percent cap on subscribers or the 40 percent cap on programming.[83]

SATELLITE RADIO

Just as air-conditioning once was a fancy option on the automobile that now is taken for granted by many buyers, today a prized new option on a car or SUV is a satellite radio—something that likely will become a standard vehicle feature in the not-so-distant future. While free, over-the-air broadcast radio had a total listening universe of approximately 229 million listeners in early 2005, pay-subscription-based satellite radio was still in its infancy at the time. The two leading satellite radio companies, XM Satellite Radio Holdings and Sirius Satellite Radio Inc. had a combined total of about five million subscribers in the initial months of 2005. But the well-publicized leap of radio personality and self-anointed

---

83. Labaton and Fabrikant, "U.S. Court Ruling Lets Cable Giants." See also *Time Warner Entertainment Co. v. FCC,* 240 F. 3d 1126 (2001).

"King of All Media" Howard Stern to Sirius in January 2006 and the announcement of Stern's whopping $500 million, five-year deal in late 2004, after more than 15 years of syndication on broadcast radio by Infinity Broadcasting Corp., helped to spark rapid and dramatic growth for the future. For instance, Sirius added more than 300,000 new subscribers in the first quarter of 2005, compared with about 90,000 new subscribers for the same period a year before. And by September 2005, XM Satellite Radio had five million subscribers and Sirius Satellite Radio had more than two million subscribers, with each company expecting to add another million subscribers during the final three months of that year.

Howard Stern's switch to satellite radio is important for media law students to understand. While free, over-the-air radio broadcasting is subject to the FCC's rules governing indecency and profanity discussed earlier in this chapter, satellite radio is—at least at the time this book went to press—exempt from similar content-based rules. Thus shock jocks like Howard Stern on Sirius and the rival duo of Opie & Anthony on XM can freely use profanity and expletives at any time of the day on satellite radio with no need to fear the wrath of the FCC. While some in Congress want to change this situation so that the FCC can police satellite radio content just as it now does broadcast indecency, in the meantime there is the slight potential that satellite radio will develop into a verbal gutter, so to speak, where profane content thrives. This is not likely to be the case, however, because satellite radio companies typically offer subscribers more than 100 diverse and largely commercial-free channels. What's more, the content sweeps up far more than shock jocks. For instance, XM has a $650 million contract to carry major-league baseball games for more than a decade, while Sirius has a contract with the National Football League and NASCAR. In addition to inking a contract with Stern in 2004, Sirius also signed a four-year deal in 2005 with Martha Stewart Living Omnimedia Inc. for a 24-hour channel focusing on cooking, gardening, decorating and homemaking programs targeting women. Unlike many other satellite channels that are devoid of advertising content, Stewart's features commercials. The $30 million deal, signed less than two months after Stewart was released from prison, suggests that the domestic diva's criminal conviction for perjury didn't hurt her commercial marketability.

Although the FCC does not yet control indecent content on either satellite radio or cable television, it does regulate other aspects of the relatively new medium of satellite radio. For example, Sirius, which was founded in 1990 (two years before XM), had to apply to the FCC to launch its three current satellites that were operating by 2000. In addition, the FCC required Sirius and XM to develop a radio device that will work with the signals from both of the rival companies, thus perhaps avoiding the situation with movie-video content machines that led to the demise of the Sony Betamax and the proliferation of the VCR decades before. What the future holds for FCC regulation of satellite radio remains to be seen, but one can easily predict increased regulation and control by the government agency as this new medium waxes in popularity.

CABLE TELEVISION

Cable television first appeared in the late 1940s. At that time it was called community antenna television (CATV). In rural communities where television reception was poor because of distance or topography, entrepreneurs installed large antennas on hilltops to receive the incoming television signals and then transmitted these signals (for a small price) to local homeowners via coaxial cable. The FCC first asserted its jurisdiction of cable or CATV in the early 1960s. But the agency had to move tenuously at first because its right to regulate cable television was not clearly established. Cable is not broadcast; signals travel through wires, not the airwaves. There is no scarcity of spectrum space, that important factor that justifies government regulation of broadcasting. Cable is not a common carrier, as are telephone and telegraph. The FCC authority to regulate these point-to-point services does not establish its right to regulate cable. It took more than 20 years, with the adoption of the Cable Communications Policy Act of 1984, before FCC jurisdiction over cable was firmly established.

FEDERAL LEGISLATION REGULATING CABLE TELEVISION

Two federal laws provide the foundation of the regulation of cable television. The first measure, the comprehensive Cable Communications Policy Act of 1984, was a cable-friendly measure designed to foster the orderly growth of this new medium. Cable flourished under this law. By the 1990s nearly all American homes had access to cable television, and more than 60 percent of all Americans received their television via cable. But viewers, and then members of Congress, became angry at many heavy-handed policies adopted by the cable industry using the freedom it had been granted under the 1984 legislation. Viewers complained about escalating cable rates among other things. In 1992 Congress adopted the Cable Television Consumer Protection and Competition Act, a decidedly not cable-friendly measure that imposed rate regulations on most cable systems, directed the FCC to develop mandatory service standards for cable television, and greatly strengthened the competitive position of local, over-the-air television stations vis-à-vis cable. The 1984 law remains the basic regulatory measure. Its most important provisions are outlined on the following pages. It will be noted where the 1992 law has modified this legislation.

Viewers complained about escalating cable rates among other things.

The Cable Communications Policy Act of 1984 (hereafter Cable Act) was adopted after decades of crazy-quilt regulation at the federal, state and local levels. The act was needed because some state and local governments were attempting to assert increased control over an industry that had become increasingly national in scope. In the summer of 1988, in a decision regarding the right of the FCC to establish certain technical standards for cable television, the Supreme Court read the new Cable Act in an expansive fashion, giving the FCC assurances that its regulation of the medium would be supported under the law.[84]

Purpose of the Law

The purposes of this legislation are enumerated in Section 601 of the Cable Act itself. They are as follows:

1. To establish a national policy concerning cable communications
2. To establish franchise procedures and standards that encourage the growth and development of cable systems and that ensure that cable systems are responsive to the needs and interests of the local community

---

84. *New York City* v. *FCC,* 108 S. Ct. 1637 (1988).

3. To establish guidelines for the exercise of federal, state and local authority with respect to the regulation of cable systems
4. To ensure and encourage that cable communications provide the widest possible diversity of information sources and services to the public
5. To establish a process that protects cable operators against unfair denials of renewal by franchising authorities and that provides for an orderly process for consideration of renewal proposals

Jurisdiction and Franchises

The federal government has jurisdiction to regulate cable television, but has given local governments the power to impose a variety of obligations on cable operators. The local government is what is called the "franchising authority"; it is given the power to grant the cable system the right to operate in a particular area. This right is contained in a franchise agreement, which gives the cable operator the right to serve customers in a particular area in exchange for the promise to provide certain standards of service. Until about 15 years ago, this was an exclusive right. This means that only a single operator served a particular community. Cable companies often had to bid against one another to win this exclusive right. These exclusive agreements were challenged on constitutional grounds, but the Supreme Court did not outlaw their use.[85] Congress did, however, in 1992. Economics, even more than government policy, makes it unlikely that more than a single operator will serve the cable customers in a community. The cost of wiring a community is simply prohibitive without the promise of exclusivity. If, as some predict, the day comes when a single wire carries all telephone, television and Internet traffic in a community, and the use of that wire is open to anyone who seeks to send a signal, competition for cable customers within a city or even a neighborhood may become a reality.

The 1984 statute speaks of "services" and "facilities and equipment." "Services" generally means programming. "Facilities and equipment" refers to hardware of the system and the physical capabilities of the system, such as channel capacity, two-way or one-way, and so on. Local governments are generally barred from establishing requirements for service or programming but are given a wide latitude to establish standards for equipment and facilities. The local government can insist that a cable operator provide broad categories of programming to meet the needs of children, different ethnic groups, or others and can insist that the cable operator provide public access channels for citizens to use.

Rate regulation has consistently been a bone of contention between cable operators and government regulatory bodies, both federal and local. The 1984 and 1992 cable laws gave the FCC substantial power to control what cable companies charge their customers. The 1996 Telecommunications Act reversed this policy and immediately abolished the FCC's power to regulate the rates for small cable systems and ordered the agency to phase out rate regulation for larger systems by March 1999. The marketplace model was the justification for this change in policy, and supporters of deregulation argued that the delivery of television programming through telephone lines and by direct broadcast satellite (DBS) would force cable operators to keep their rates competitive. But the competition to cable did not develop.[86] The telephone companies lost interest in carrying television programming when they discovered

---

85. *Los Angeles* v. *Preferred Communications,* 476 U.S. 488 (1986).
86. Gomery, "Cable TV Rates" and Labaton, "Cable Rates Rising."

they could make more money providing homeowners and businesses with hookups to the Internet. And television viewers resisted direct broadcast satellite services because these providers were not permitted to transmit programming from local television stations. In 1999 Congress changed the law and required DBS operators whose systems carried even one local channel to carry all the local channels.[87] The satellite operators didn't like this, but their challenge of the law on First Amendment grounds failed.[88] The change actually spurred the growth of DBS home receiving systems, but this seemed to have little impact on higher-than-ever cable rates in most communities.

Must-Carry Rules

Historically the government required all cable operators to retransmit the signals of all local television stations. These requirements were called the "must-carry rules" and were instituted to protect local broadcasters. By the 1980s, when cable networks proliferated, many cable operators found the rules to be onerous because they required operators to carry local over-the-air stations in preference to the more attractive (and lucrative for them) cable networks. Despite the so-called lack of scarcity in cable at the time, most systems were limited to 36 channels. The must-carry rules were challenged, and in 1985 a U.S. Court of Appeals ruled them to be a violation of the First Amendment.[89] By forcing a cable operator to carry a local station, the government denied the cable operator his or her First Amendment rights to communicate some other kind of programming. In other words, the court saw the must-carry rules as a content-based regulation. Attempts by the government to recast the rules failed to win court approval.[90] The 1992 cable law attempted to strengthen the position of the local broadcaster and contained substantially modified must-carry rules. Under this law the local broadcaster could either insist that the cable operator retransmit the station's signal to subscribers or forbid the cable operator from retransmitting the signal unless he or she paid what is called a retransmission fee. The application of the must-carry provisions varied with the channel capacity of the cable system. Small systems with less than 12 channels, for example, only had to carry three local commercial stations and one noncommercial station. Larger cable systems had to carry most or all local stations. Independent local stations with limited popularity insisted on cable carriage; popular network-affiliated stations often sought the retransmission fee.

Congress justified the new rules with the argument that 60 percent of Americans receive their television signals via cable. The heart of the American broadcasting system has consistently been local broadcasting. If cable operators are free to refuse to carry local broadcasters on their cable systems, this action could cause serious harm to the local stations. Cable operators said this fear was groundless, that it would be imprudent of them to drop the retransmission of popular local stations. But many local stations are not that popular, the broadcasters said, and the cable operator earns substantially more revenue by carrying a cable channel than by retransmitting a local broadcast signal. Many of the less popular over-the-air channels could be abandoned and ultimately die.

---

87. The Satellite Home Viewer Improvement Act of 1999; see also Clausing, "Satellite TV Is Poised."
88. *Satellite Broadcasting and Communications Association* v. *Federal Communications Commission,* 275 F. 3d 337 (2001).
89. *Quincy Cable* v. *FCC,* 768 F. 2d 1434 (1985).
90. *Century Communications* v. *FCC,* 835 F. 2d 292 (1987).

Turner Broadcasting, which owned several cable channels that might be displaced by the addition of local channels to the limited cable mix, challenged the new rules and a protracted legal battle ensued.[91] In two separate decisions the Supreme Court ultimately approved the new rules. Opponents of the rules challenged them on the grounds that by forcing a cable operator to carry one channel rather than another, the government was imposing decisions regarding the content of cable television on a system operator and that this content regulation violated the First Amendment. Justice Anthony Kennedy agreed that the rules do impact content because they determine who is allowed to speak in a given cable market. "But they do so based only upon the manner in which the speakers transmit their messages to viewers, not upon the messages they carry," he said.[92] The justification for the rules—the protection of local over-the-air broadcasting, the promotion of a diversity of programming sources, and the maintenance of fair competition in the TV market—is sufficient, the court said, inasmuch as in the end the rules are content neutral.[93] The issue of carrying local signals has receded with the growth of the capacity of most cable systems, yet the competition among cable channels to gain access to cable systems is as heated as ever.

Programming and Freedom of Expression

The FCC has imposed on cable systems that originate programming many of the same content rules that govern over-the-air television. The equal time rules, the "lowest unit rate" rule for political advertising, the candidate access rules, the sponsor identification rule, and many others apply to cable-originated programs. Federal rules prohibit the broadcast of obscenity on over-the-air television; similar rules apply to cable. The FCC has also ruled that over-the-air broadcasters must limit their broadcast of indecent material to those hours when children are not likely to be in the television viewing audience, between 10 p.m. and 6 a.m. (see page 696). But Congress and the courts have, in the past, given cable television operators far greater leeway in the broadcast of indecency. Federal courts, for example, have consistently struck down attempts by the states to bar cable companies from transmitting indecent or adult programming but denied cable operators any right to censor programming.[94] The 1984 Cable Act required that every cable operator provide, on request from a subscriber, a lock box device that permits the subscriber to block out the reception of specific channels. The 1992 law contained hastily drafted provisions that *permitted* cable operators to prohibit indecent programming on the commercial leased-access channels and on the public access channels available to government and public schools. If the operator decided to permit indecent programming on the commercially leased channels, these signals had to be scrambled and subscribers could only view these channels by requesting access in writing 30 days in advance of the viewing. In 1993 these provisions were declared to be unconstitutional by the U.S. Court of Appeals for the District of Columbia Circuit because they restricted speech protected by the First Amendment.[95] But two years later the full court sitting en banc reversed this earlier ruling. Then the

---

91. *Turner Broadcasting System, Inc.* v. *FCC,* 819 F. Supp. 32 (1993).
92. *Turner Broadcasting System, Inc.* v. *FCC,* 114 S. Ct. 2445 (1994).
93. *Turner Broadcasting System, Inc.* v. *FCC,* 117 S. Ct. 1174 (1997).
94. See, for example, *Home Box Office* v. *Wilkinson,* 531 F. Supp. 987 (1982) and *Jones* v. *Wilkinson,* 800 F. 2d 989 (1986), aff'd. 480 U.S. 926 (1987).
95. *Alliance for Community Media* v. *FCC,* 10 F. 3d 812 (1993).

court ruled that the provisions that *permitted* the cable operator to ban indecent programming from the access channels didn't involve any action by the government. The censorship is the result of an action by the cable system operator, a private party. Hence there were no First Amendment implications to these provisions.[96] In June 1996 a badly splintered Supreme Court voided some of these new cable rules but sustained other portions of the law. The court sustained the portion of the law that allowed the cable operator to ban patently offensive programming from the leased-access channels but struck down the regulation that required cable operators to scramble such programming and force subscribers to ask for access in writing. This latter rule limited what subscribers could see and constituted an invasion of their privacy by forcing them to acknowledge in writing that they wanted to see such programming, the court said. At the same time, the high court struck down that portion of the law that gave cable operators the right to ban indecent programming from the government access channels. The court said there was no history of problems of the transmission of indecency on such channels and indicated a concern that conservative cable operators might try to control the kind of programming telecast on public access channels, traditionally the haven of nonprofit organizations who seek to communicate with the larger audience.[97] Several opinions were written in the case, with members of the court shifting from majority to minority status depending on the particular rule under consideration.

In December 1998 a special three-judge panel of the U.S. District Court for Delaware struck down Section 505 of the 1996 Communications Decency Act, which required the distributors of adult programming over cable television to completely scramble both the video and audio signals, regardless of whether customers requested the programming to be scrambled. The law was aimed at protecting children from what is called "signal bleed," or incomplete scrambling. When signal bleed occurs, viewers can see and hear portions of the scrambled program. Programming distributors who could not fulfill this obligation were told to confine the transmission of this adult programming to the hours between 10 p.m. and 6 a.m. Playboy Entertainment challenged the provision, arguing that cable operators who could not afford the expensive scrambling technology would simply stop carrying this kind of programming rather than risk violating the law. The court ruled that while the government had a legitimate interest in attempting to shield young people from the adult programming, Section 505 was not the least restrictive means to fulfill this interest. The court said another provision in the CDA, which requires cable operators to supply blocking devices to subscribers who want them to screen out such channels, accomplishes the same goal without substantially interfering with the program distributors' First Amendment rights.[98] Two years later the Supreme Court affirmed the lower-court decision by a 5-4 vote. Justice Anthony Kennedy wrote that because signal-scrambling technology is imperfect, the "only reasonable way for a substantial number of cable operators to comply with the letter of §505 is to 'time channel,' which silences protected speech for two-thirds of the day in every home in a cable service area, regardless of the presence or likely presence of children or the wishes of the viewer." This requirement is a significant restriction on First Amendment protected speech, he wrote. The capacity required

---

96. *Alliance for Community Media* v. *FCC,* 56 F. 3d 105 (1995).
97. *Denver Area Educational Telecommunications Consortium Inc.* v. *FCC; Alliance for Community Media* v. *FCC,* 1 E.P.L.R. 331 (1996); see also Greenhouse, "High Court Splits," A1.
98. *Playboy Entertainment Group, Inc.* v. *U.S.,* 30 F. Supp. 2d 702 (1998).

in cable systems to allow subscribers to block unwanted channels is a far narrower and less restrictive alternative that would still serve the government's interest.[99]

The Cable Act has established that third parties—that is, persons other than the cable operator or the local government—must have access to the cable system. Several means are provided for such access. The local franchising authorities are permitted to require that the cable operator provide public access and government and educational access channels. A public access channel is set aside for free public use on a nondiscriminatory, first-come, first-served basis. Neither the cable operator nor the government can censor what appears on such a channel. The franchising authority can prescribe limited (content-neutral) time, place and manner rules for the public access channel, such as deciding that the access channel will give each user 30 minutes of time or that persons must sign up three days before the date they wish to use the channel. But these are about the only limits. The government and educational channels are used either by schools or to broadcast public hearings or city council meetings. These channels are to be programmed as the government sees fit.

Commercial access channels must also be provided by the cable operator.

Commercial access channels must also be provided by the cable operator. The law provides that a certain number of channels must be set aside for use by "unaffiliated programmers" at reasonable rates. The cable operator cannot control the content of these programs. The number of channels that must be set aside for commercial access depends on the number of activated channels in the cable system. An activated channel is one that is being used or is available for use. Systems with fewer than 36 channels need not have any commercial access channels; those with 36 to 54 channels must set aside 10 percent of the channels for commercial access. Systems with more than 54 channels must reserve 15 percent of these channels for commercial access. The cable operator can set the price and conditions of use for these channels, so long as they are "reasonable." Costs cannot have anything to do with content; that is, a cable operator cannot charge someone who puts on a conservative talk show $100 per hour and someone who puts on a liberal talk show $500. However, the cable operator can set different rates for different categories of program; for example, news programs cost $50 per hour, movies $100 per hour.

SUMMARY

The power of the FCC to regulate cable television was a clouded issue for many years. Slowly but surely, the commission, with the permission of the courts, moved to regulate this new technology. In 1984 both the Supreme Court and Congress gave the FCC what seemed to be clear jurisdiction to set broad rules for governing cable television. But a subsequent Court of Appeals ruling has cast some doubt on all government regulation of cable.

The Cable Communications Policy Act of 1984 is a comprehensive measure setting policies and standards for the regulation of cable television. The 1992 Cable Television Consumer Protection and Competition Act made some modifications in the earlier law. Local governments are given the primary responsibility under this measure to regulate the cable systems in their communities. They may issue franchises, collect franchise fees, and renew franchises. The Cable Act also provides for the inclusion of public, government and commercial access channels.

---

99. *United States* v. *Playboy Entertainment Group Inc.,* 120 S. Ct. 1878 (2000); the FCC repealed these rules in November 2001.

BIBLIOGRAPHY ⟶

Ahrens, Frank. "FCC's New Standards-Bearer." *Washington Post,* 17 March 2005, E01.
———. "Powell Calls Rejection of Media Rules a Disappointment." *Washington Post,* 29 June 2004, E01.
———. "Radio Giant in Record Indecency Settlement." *Washington Post,* 9 June 2004, A1.
Andrews, Edmund. "Court Upholds a Ban on 'Indecent' Broadcast Programming." *The New York Times,* 1 July 1995, A9.
Barstow, David, and Robin Stein. "Under Bush, a New Age of Prepackaged News." *The New York Times,* 13 March 2005, A1.
Bazar, Emily. "Spanish Radio Gets Racier, but Few Listeners Complain." *Sacramento Bee,* 7 April 2005, A1.
Bernstein, Andrew A. "Access to Cable, Natural Monopoly, and the First Amendment." *Columbia Law Review* 86 (1986): 1663.
Blair, Jayson. "FCC Approves One Owner for New York Area TV Stations." *The New York Times,* 26 July 2001, C18.
Brooke, James. "The FCC Supports TV News as Free Speech." *The New York Times,* 3 May 1998, A13.
Brown, Rhonda. "Ad Hoc Access: The Regulation of Editorial Advertising on Television and Radio." *Yale Law and Policy Review* 6 (1998): 449.
Carter, Bill. "Media Ruling Merely Irritates Big Owners." *The New York Times,* 25 June 2004, C1.
Clausing, Jeri. "Satellite TV Is Poised for New Growth." *The New York Times,* 26 November 1999, C1.
Collins, Scott. "The Decency Debate; Pulled into a Very Wide Net: Unusual Suspects Have Joined the Censor's Target List, Making for Strange Bedfellows (Wait Can We Say That?)." *Los Angeles Times,* 28 March 2004, E26.
Cowan, Geoffrey. *See No Evil.* New York: Simon and Schuster, 1979.
Creech, Kenneth C. *Electronic Media Law and Regulation.* Boston: Focal Press, 1993.
Cys, Richard L., "Broadcaster License Auctions: A Replacement for Comparative Hearings." *WSAB Bulletin,* January 1998, 4.
"FCC Repeals Network Rule." *The New York Times,* 20 April 2001, C13.
Fogarty, Joseph R., and Marcia Spielholz. "FCC Cable Jurisdiction: From Zero to Plenary in Twenty-Five Years." *Federal Communications Law Journal* 37 (1979): 361.
Gomery, Douglas. "Cable TV Rates: Not a Pretty Picture." *American Journalism Review,* July/August 1998, 66.
Greenhouse, Linda. "High Court Splits on Indecency Law Cable TV." *The New York Times,* 29 June 1996, A1.
Gurza, Augstin. "Television & Radio; Can They Say That?" *Los Angeles Times,* 20 August 2004, E1.
Holmes, Steven. "Broadcasters Vow to Keep Affirmative Action." *The New York Times,* 30 August 1998, A12.
Huff, Richard. "Fear Over 'Private' Parts." *Daily News* (New York), 11 November 2004, 111.
Kerr, Jennifer. "FCC Gives Clear Channel a Stern Talking-To." *Chicago Sun-Times,* 10 June 2004, 56.

Kirtley, Jane. "Second Guessing News Judgment." *American Journalism Review,* October 1998, 86.

Kurtz, Howard. "Writer Backing Bush Plan Had Gotten Federal Contract." *Washington Post,* 26 January 2005, C1.

Labaton, Stephen. "Cable Rates Rising as Industry Nears End of Regulation." *The New York Times,* 3 March 1999, A1.

———. "Court Rules Agency Erred on Mandate for Minorities." *The New York Times,* 17 January 2001, A15.

———. "Media Companies Succeed in Easing Ownership Limits." *The New York Times,* 16 April 2001, A1.

———, and Geraldine Fabrikant. "U.S. Court Ruling Lets Cable Giants Widen Their Reach." *The New York Times,* 31 March 2001, A1.

Lee, Jennifer. "Bill to Raise Indecency Fines Is Reintroduced." *The New York Times,* 9 October 2004, C3.

Levi, Lili. "The Hard Case of Broadcast Indecency." *New York University Review of Law and Social Change* 20 (1992–93): 49.

Maynard, John. "FCC Is Asked to Revoke the Licenses of Two D.C. Stations." *Washington Post,* 2 September 2004, C7.

McChesney, Robert W. "Battle for U.S. Airwaves, 1928–1935." *Journal of Communication* 40 (Autumn 1990): 29.

Myerson, Michael. "The Cable Communications Policy Act of 1984: A Balancing Act on the Coaxial Wires." *Georgia Law Review* 19 (1985): 543.

Miflin, Lawrie. "Revisions in TV Ratings Called Imminent." *The New York Times,* 16 June 1997, B1.

———. "TV Ratings Accord Comes under Fire from Both Flanks." *The New York Times,* 11 July 1997, A1.

Pember, Don R. *Mass Media in America.* 6th ed. New York: Macmillan, 1992.

"Pennsylvania: Mayor Cut from TV Show." *The New York Times,* 8 April 2003, A17.

Poling, Travis. "Clear Channel Puts Indecency Issue Behind." *San Antonio Express-News,* 10 June 2004, 1E.

Powe, Lucas A. *American Broadcasting and the First Amendment.* Berkeley: University of California Press, 1982.

Rutenberg, Jim. "Few Parents Use the V-Chip, a Survey Shows." *The New York Times,* 25 July 2001, B1.

Smith, Lynn. "Profanity Rules Bother News Shows." *Los Angeles Times,* 6 May 2004, C1.

Toppo, Greg. "White House Paid Journalist to Promote Law." *USA Today,* 7 January 2005, 1A.

Triplett, William. "Orgs Seek FCC Review of Bush Vids." *Daily Variety,* 22 March 2005, 6.

———. "TV Decency Proponent to Top FCC." *Daily Variety,* 17 March 2005, 1.

Tuohy, Lynne, and John M. Moran. "Judge Orders Tribune to Sell WTXX-TV." *Hartford Courant,* 22 March 2005, B7.

GLOSSARY

A

absolute privilege An immunity from libel suits granted to government officials and others based on remarks uttered or written as part of their official duties.

absolutist theory The proposition that the First Amendment is an absolute, and that government may adopt no laws whatsoever that abridge freedom of expression.

actual damages Damages awarded to a plaintiff in a lawsuit based on proof of actual harm to the plaintiff.

actual malice A fault standard in libel law: knowledge before publication that the libelous material was false or reckless disregard of the truth or falsity of the libelous matter.

administrative agency An agency, created and funded by the Congress, whose members are appointed by the president and whose function is to administer specific legislation, such as law regulating broadcasting and advertising.

admonition to a jury Instructions from a judge to a trial jury to avoid talking to other persons about the trial they are hearing and to avoid news broadcasts and newspaper or magazine stories that discuss the case or issues in the case.

Alien and Sedition Acts of 1798 Laws adopted by the Federalist Congress aimed at stopping criticism of the national government by Republican or Jeffersonian editors and politicians.

amici curiae "Friends of the court"; persons who have no specific legal stake in a lawsuit but are allowed to appear on behalf of one of the parties in a case.

appellant The party who initiates or takes the appeal of a case from one court to another.

appellate court(s) A court that has both original and appellate jurisdiction; a court to which cases are removed for an appeal.

appellee The person in a case against whom the appeal is taken; that is, the party in the suit who is not making the appeal.

appropriation In the law of privacy, use of a person's name or likeness without consent for advertising or trade purposes.

arraignment The first official court appearance made by a criminal defendant at which he or she is formally charged with an offense and called on to plead guilty or not guilty to the charges contained in the state's indictment or information.

B

bait-and-switch advertising An illegal advertising strategy in which the seller baits customers by an advertisement with a low-priced model of a product but then switches customers who seek to buy the product to a much higher-priced model by telling them that the cheaper model does not work well or is no longer in stock.

bench-bar-press guidelines Informal agreements among lawyers, judges, police officials and journalists about what should and should not be published or broadcast about a criminal suspect or criminal case before a trial is held.

bond; bonding A large sum of money given by a publisher to a government to be held to ensure good behavior. Should the publisher violate a government rule, the bond is forfeited to the government, and the newspaper or magazine cannot be published again until a new bond is posted.

C

California Plan See Missouri Plan.

candidate access rule Section 312 of the Federal Communications Act, which forbids a broadcaster from instituting an across-the-board policy that denies all candidates for federal office the opportunity to use the station to further a political campaign.

case reporter(s) A book (or books) containing a chronological collection of the opinions rendered by a particular court for cases that were decided by the court.

challenge for cause The request by a litigant in a criminal or civil case that a juror be dismissed for a specific reason.

change of veniremen Drawing a jury from a distant community in order to find jurors who have heard little or nothing about a criminal case or criminal defendant.

change of venue Moving a trial to a distant community in order to find jurors who have not read or viewed prejudicial publicity about the defendant.

citation The reference to a legal opinion contained in a case reporter that gives the name, volume number and page number where the opinion can be found. The year the opinion was rendered is also included in the citation.

civil complaint A written statement of the plaintiff's legal grievance, which normally initiates a civil suit.

collateral bar rule A rule that bars someone who violates a court order from trying to defend this action by arguing that the court order was unconstitutional.

commercial speech doctrine The legal doctrine that states that truthful advertising for products and services that are not illegal is normally protected by the First Amendment to the U.S. Constitution.

common law Principles and rules of law that derive their authority not from legislation but from community usage and custom.

concurring opinion A written opinion by an appellate judge or justice in which the author agrees with the decision of the court but normally states reasons different from those in the court opinion as the basis for his or her decision.

consent A defense in both libel and invasion of privacy cases that provides that individuals who agree to the publication of a libelous story or the appropriation of their name cannot then maintain a lawsuit based on the libel or the appropriation.

consent order or decree A document in which an individual agrees to terminate a specific behavior, such as an advertising campaign, or to refrain from a specific action, such as making a certain advertising claim.

constitution A written outline of the organization of a government that provides for both the rights and responsibilities of various branches of the government and the limits of the power of the government.

contempt of court An act of disobedience or disrespect to a judge, which may be punished by a fine or jail sentence.

continuance The delay of a trial or hearing; that is, the trial is postponed.

copyright That body of law that protects the works created by writers, painters, photographers, performing artists, inventors and other persons who create intangible property.

copyright notice The words "Copyright ©2003 by Don R. Pember," for example, which indicate to a user that a work is copyrighted by the author or creator.

corrective advertising Rules established by the Federal Trade Commission that require an advertiser to correct the false impressions left by deceptive advertising in a certain percentage of future advertisements.

court's opinion The official opinion of an appellate court that states the reasons or rationale for a decision.

criminal libel A libel against the state, against the dead, or against a large, ill-defined group (such as a race) in which the state prosecutes the libel on behalf of the injured parties.

criminal prosecution; criminal action A legal action brought by the state against an individual or group of individuals for violating state criminal laws.

criminal syndicalism laws Laws that outlaw advocacy, planning, or processes aimed at establishing the control over industry by workers or trade unions.

D

damages Money awarded to the winning party in a civil lawsuit.

defamation Any communication that holds a person up to contempt, hatred, ridicule or scorn and lowers the reputation of the individual defamed.

defendant The person against whom relief or recovery is sought in a civil lawsuit; the individual against whom a state criminal action is brought.

demurrer An allegation made by the defendant in a lawsuit that even if the facts as stated by the plaintiff are true, they do not state a sufficient cause for action.

de novo New or fresh. In some instances a court of general jurisdiction will hear an appeal from a case from a lower court and simply retry the case. This is a de novo hearing.

dicta Remarks in a court opinion that do not speak directly to the legal point in question.

direct appeal The statutorily granted right of an aggrieved party to carry the appeal of a case to the U.S. Supreme Court. The high court can deny this right if the appeal lacks a substantial federal question.

dissenting opinion A written opinion by a judge or justice who disagrees with the appellate court's decision in a case.

E

en banc; sitting en banc A French term to describe all or most of the justices or judges of an appellate court sitting together to hear a case. This situation is the opposite of the more typical situation in which a small group (called a panel) of judges or justices in a particular court hears a case.

equal time rule Section 315 of the Federal Communications Act, which states that when broadcasters permit a legally qualified candidate for elective office to use their broadcasting facilities, all other legally qualified candidates for the same elective office must be given similar opportunity.

equity A system of jurisprudence, distinct from the common law, in which courts are empowered to decide cases on the basis of equity or fairness and are not bound by the rigid precedents that often exist in the common law.

Espionage Act A law adopted by Congress in 1917 that outlawed criticism of the U.S. government and its participation in World War I in Europe.

executive privilege An asserted common-law privilege of the president and other executives to keep presidential papers, records and other documents secret, even from Congress.

executive session A popular euphemism for a closed meeting held by a government body such as a city council or school board.

F

fair comment A libel defense that protects the publication of libelous opinion that focuses on the public activities of a person acting in a public sphere.

fair use A provision of the copyright law that permits a limited amount of copying of material that has been properly copyrighted.

false light That portion of privacy law that prohibits all publications or broadcasts that falsely portray an individual in an offensive manner.

Federal Communications Act The law, adopted in 1934, that is the foundation for the regulation of broadcasting in the United States.

Federal Communications Commission (FCC) A five-member body appointed by the president whose function is to administer the federal broadcasting and communications laws.

federal open-meetings law (Government in Sunshine Act) A federal law that requires approximately 50 federal agencies and bureaus to hold all their meetings in public, unless a subject under discussion is included within one of the 10 exemptions contained in the statute.

Federal Trade Commission A five-member body appointed by the president whose function is to administer the federal laws relating to advertising, antitrust and many other business matters.

fighting words doctrine A legal doctrine that permits prior censorship of words that create a clear and present danger of inciting an audience to disorder or violence.

FOIA See Freedom of Information Act.

Freedom of Information Act A federal law that mandates that all the records created and kept by federal agencies in the executive branch of government must be open for public inspection and copying, except those records that fall into one of nine exempted categories listed in the statute.

FTC See Federal Trade Commission.

G

gag order(s) A restrictive court order that prohibits all or some participants in a trial from speaking about a case or that stops publications and broadcasting stations from reporting on certain aspects of a case.

Government in Sunshine Act See federal open-meetings law.

grand jury A jury whose function is to determine whether sufficient evidence exists to issue an indictment or true bill charging an individual or individuals with a crime and to take such persons to trial. It is called a grand jury because it has more members than a petit, or trial, jury.

H

heckler's veto A situation that occurs when the audience's negative, adverse and sometimes violent reaction to the message conveyed by a peaceful speaker is allowed to control and silence the speaker. The duty, instead, should be on the government to protect the speaker rather than to allow a "veto" of the speech by the audience.

I

identification As used in a libel suit, the requirement that the plaintiff prove that at least one person believes that the subject of the libelous remarks is the plaintiff and not some other person.

impeachment A criminal proceeding against a public officer that is started by written "articles of impeachment" and followed by a trial. The House of Representatives, for example, can issue articles of impeachment against the president, who is then tried by the Senate.

indictment A written accusation issued by a grand jury charging that an individual or individuals have committed a specific crime and should be taken to trial.

information A written accusation issued by a public officer rather than by a grand jury charging that an individual or individuals have committed a specific crime and should be taken to trial.

intrusion An invasion of privacy committed when one individual intrudes upon or invades the solitude of another individual.

invasion of privacy A civil tort that emerged in the early 20th century and contains four distinct categories of legal wrongs: appropriation, intrusion, publication of private facts and false light.

J

judgment of the court The final ruling of a court, which determines the outcome of a lawsuit. It is different from the verdict, which is the decision of the jury in a trial.

judicial decree A judgment of a court of equity; a declaration of the court announcing the legal consequences of the facts found to be true by the court.

judicial instructions A statement (often written) made by a judge to the members of a jury informing them about the law (as distinguished from the facts) in a case.

judicial review The power of a court to declare void and unenforceable any statute, rule or

executive order that conflicts with an appropriate state constitution or the federal constitution.

jury A group of men and women called together in a trial court to determine the facts in a civil or criminal lawsuit. It is sometimes called a petit jury to distinguish it from a grand jury.

jury nullification The controversial power of a jury, despite its sworn duty under oath to apply a law as interpreted and instructed by a judge, to instead ignore (and thereby to "nullify") a law and decide a case according to its own conscience and sensibilities or, as the U.S. Supreme Court once put it, the ability of a jury to acquit "in the teeth of both law and facts."

L

legal brief(s); brief Written legal argument presented to the court by one or both parties in a lawsuit.

libel Published or broadcast communication that lowers the reputation of an individual by holding him or her up to contempt, ridicule or scorn.

licensing process The process by which a government gives a publisher or a broadcaster prior permission to print a newspaper or operate a broadcasting station. Revocation of a license can be used as punishment for failing to comply with the law or the wishes of the government. Licensing of the printed press in the United States ended in the 1720s.

litigant A party in a lawsuit; a participant in litigation.

litigated order An order issued by a government agency, like the FTC, requiring that a particular practice, such as a certain advertisement, be stopped.

M

memorandum order The announcement by an appellate court of a decision in a case that does not include a written opinion containing the rationale or reasons for the ruling.

misappropriation Taking what belongs to someone else and using it unfairly for one's own gain; for example, attempting to pass off a novel as part of a popular series of novels written and published by someone else. It is often called unfair competition.

Missouri Plan A system used in some states by which judges are appointed to the bench initially and then must stand for re-election on a ballot that permits citizens to vote to retain or not retain the judge.

N

National Advertising Division (NAD) of the Council of Better Business Bureaus An industry organization that evaluates and rules on the truthfulness of advertising claims. Complaints are normally brought to the NAD by competing advertisers.

National Advertising Review Board The appeals body of a two-tier system created by the advertising community in 1971 for self-regulation that works closely with the National Advertising Division, the investigative body, in affiliation with the Better Business Bureau.

negligence A fault standard in libel and other tort law. Negligent behavior is normally described as an act or action that a reasonably prudent person or a reasonable individual would not have committed. In libel law, courts often measure negligence by asking whether the allegedly libelous material was the work of a person who exercised reasonable care in preparation of the story.

neutral reportage An emerging libel defense or privilege that states that it is permissible to publish or broadcast an accurate account of information about a public figure from a reliable source even when the reporter doubts the truth of the libelous assertion. The defense is not widely accepted.

nonjusticiable matter An issue that is inappropriate for a court to decide because the jurists lack the knowledge to make the ruling, because another branch of government has the responsibility to answer such questions, or because a court order in the matter would not likely be enforceable or enforced.

O

open-meetings laws State and federal statutes that require that certain meetings of public agencies—normally in the executive branch of government—be open to the public and the press.

open-records laws State and federal statutes that require that certain records of public agencies—normally in the executive branch of government—be open for inspection and copying by the public and the press.

opinion The written statement issued by a court that explains the reasons for a judgment and states the rule of law in the case.

oral argument An oral presentation made to a judge or justices in which the litigants argue the merits of their case.

original jurisdiction Jurisdiction in the first instance, as distinguished from appellate jurisdiction. A court exercising original jurisdiction determines both the facts and the law in the case; courts exercising appellate jurisdiction may only rule on the law and the sufficiency of the facts as determined by a trial court.

P

per curiam opinion An unsigned court opinion. The author of the opinion is not known outside the court.

peremptory challenge A challenge without stated cause to remove a juror from a panel. Litigants are given a small number of such challenges in a lawsuit.

petitioner One who petitions a court to take an action; someone who starts a lawsuit, or carries an appeal to a higher court (appellant). This person is the opposite of a respondent, one who responds to a petition.

plaintiff An individual who initiates a civil lawsuit.

pleadings The written statements of the parties in a lawsuit that contain their allegations, denials and defenses.

precedent An established rule of law set by a previous case. Courts should follow precedent when it is advisable and possible.

presumed damages Damages a plaintiff can get without proof of injury or harm.

pretrial hearing A meeting prior to a criminal trial at which attorneys for the state and for the defense make arguments before a judge on evidentiary questions—for example, whether a confession made by the defendant should be admitted as evidence at the trial. This type of hearing is sometimes called a suppression hearing.

Printers' Ink statute A model law drafted in 1911 to control false or misleading advertising. Most states adopted some version of this model in the early 20th century. Such laws are largely ineffective because they are not normally enforced.

prior restraint Prepublication censorship that forbids publication or broadcast of certain objectionable material, as opposed to punishment of a perpetrator after the material has been published or broadcast.

Privacy Act A federal statute that forbids the disclosure of specific material held by federal agencies on the grounds that its release could invade the privacy of the subject of the report or document.

public figure The designation for a plaintiff in a libel suit who has voluntarily entered a public controversy in an effort to influence public opinion in order to generate a resolution of the issue.

public official The designation of a plaintiff in a libel suit who is an elected public officer or is an appointed public officer who has or appears to have considerable responsibility for or control over the conduct of governmental affairs.

publication In libel law, exposing an allegedly libelous statement to one person in addition to the subject of the libel.

publication of private information In privacy law, publicizing embarrassing private information about an individual that is not of legitimate public concern. More than one person must see or hear this information.

puffery Often expansive hyperbole about a product that does not contain factual claims of merit. Normally, puffery is permitted by the law (e.g., "This is the best-looking automobile on the market today").

punitive damages Money damages awarded to a plaintiff in a lawsuit aimed not to compensate for harm to the injured party but to punish the defendant for his or her illegal conduct.

Q

qualified privilege In libel law, the privilege of the reporter (or any person) to publish a fair and accurate report of the proceedings of a public meeting or public document and be immune from lawsuit for the publication of libel uttered at the meeting or contained in the document.

R

Radio Act of 1912 The first federal broadcast law, which imposed only minimal regulation on the fledgling broadcast industry. Radio

operators were required to have a license under this statute.

Radio Act of 1927 The first comprehensive national broadcast law, which provided the basic framework for the regulation of broadcast that was later adopted in the Federal Communications Act of 1934.

respondent The person who responds to a petition placed before a court by another person; the opposite of the petitioner. At the appellate level, the respondent is often called the appellee.

restrictive order A court order limiting the discussion of the facts in a criminal case both by participants in the case and by the press. See also gag order.

retraction In libel law, a statement published or broadcast that attempts to retract or correct previously published or broadcast libelous matter. A timely retraction will usually mitigate damages, and in some states that have retraction laws, plaintiffs must seek a retraction before beginning a lawsuit or they lose the opportunity to collect anything but special damages.

right of publicity An offshoot of privacy law that protects the right of persons to capitalize on their fame or notoriety for commercial or advertising purposes.

right of reply A little-used libel defense that declares as immune from a lawsuit a libelous remark made against an individual in reply to a previously published libelous remark made by that individual.

S

scienter Guilty knowledge. In many criminal prosecutions, the state must prove that the accused was aware of the nature of his or her behavior. In an obscenity case, for example, the state must normally show that the defendant was aware of the contents of the book he or she sold.

Section 312 See candidate access rule.

Section 315 See equal time rule.

Sedition Act of 1918 An amendment to the Espionage Act adopted in the midst of World War I that severely limited criticism of the government and criticism of U.S. participation in the European war.

seditious libel Libeling the government; criticizing the government or government officers. It is sometimes called sedition.

sequestration of the jury Separating the jury from the community during a trial. Usually a jury is lodged at a hotel and members are required to eat together. In general, sequestration means to keep jurors away from other persons. Exposure to news reports is also screened to shield jurors from information about the trial.

shield laws State statutes that permit reporters in some circumstances to shield the name of a confidential news source when questioned by a grand jury or in another legal forum.

single mistake rule In libel law, a rule that states that it is not libelous to accuse a professional person or business person of making a single mistake (e.g., "Dr. Pat Jones incorrectly diagnosed the patient's illness").

slander Oral defamation.

Smith Act A federal law adopted in 1940 that makes it illegal to advocate the violent overthrow of the government.

special damages Damages that can be awarded to a plaintiff in a lawsuit upon proof of specific monetary loss.

stare decisis "Let the decision stand." This concept is the operating principle in the common-law system and requires that judges follow precedent case law when making judgments.

statute of limitations A law that requires that a legal action must begin within a specified period of time (usually one to three years for a civil case) after the legal wrong was committed.

statutes Laws adopted by legislative bodies.

statutory construction The process undertaken by courts to interpret or construe the meaning of statutes.

subpoena A court document that requires a witness to appear and testify or to produce documents or papers pertinent to a pending controversy.

substantiation A Federal Trade Commission rule that requires an advertiser to prove the truth of advertising claims made about a product or service.

summary contempt power The power of a judge to find an individual guilty of a contempt of court and impose a sentence without giving the individual the benefit of a jury trial.

summary judgment A judgment granted to a party in a lawsuit when the pleadings and other materials in the case disclose no material issue of fact between the parties, making it possible for the case to be decided on the basis of the law by the court. A summary judgment avoids a costly jury trial.

summary jury trial An abbreviated jury trial where jurors hear arguments but no witnesses are called and little evidence is presented. The jurors can issue an informal verdict, which can be used as the basis for a settlement of the case, thus avoiding a full-blown and costly trial.

survival statute A statute that permits an heir to continue to maintain a lawsuit if the plaintiff died after the suit was filed but before it was resolved.

T

time, place and manner restrictions or rules Rules, when justified by a substantial government interest, that can regulate the time, place and manner of speaking or publishing and the distribution of printed material.

tort A civil wrong not based on a contract, against the person or property of another. Typical torts are libel, invasion of privacy, trespass and assault.

trade libel Product disparagement, and not considered true libel; disparaging a product as opposed to the manufacturer or maker of the product.

trade regulation rules Rules adopted by the Federal Trade Commission that prohibit specific advertising claims about an entire class of products. For example, makers of fruit drinks that contain less than 10 percent fruit juice cannot advertise these products as fruit juice.

trespass Unlawful entry on another person's land or property.

trial court(s) Normally the first court to hear a lawsuit. This court is the forum in which the facts are determined and the law is initially applied, as opposed to an appellate court, to which decisions are appealed.

U

unfair competition See misappropriation.

V

variable obscenity statutes A Supreme Court doctrine that permits states to prohibit the sale, distribution or exhibition of certain kinds of nonobscene matter to children, so long as these laws do not interfere with the accessibility of this material to adults.

verdict The decision of a trial jury based on the instructions given to it by the judge.

viewpoint-based discrimination The worst form of content-based regulation that exists when the government censors or regulates one particular viewpoint or side on a given topic or issue but does not censor or regulate another viewpoint or side on the same topic or issue. For instance, if the government censored pro-life speech on the topic of abortion but did not censor pro-choice speech on the topic of abortion, that would constitute viewpoint-based discrimination. Viewpoint-based discrimination by the government on speech is always unconstitutional.

voir dire A preliminary examination the court makes of persons chosen to serve as jurors in a trial. Persons can be challenged for cause or on the basis of a peremptory challenge by either side in the legal dispute.

W

warrant A written order, signed by a judge or magistrate, that may take many varieties, such as a search warrant that allows a law enforcement officer to search for and seize property or possessions that constitute evidence of the commission of a crime.

writ of certiorari A writ by which an appellant seeks the review of a case by the U.S. Supreme Court. When the writ is granted, the court will order the lower court to send up the record of the case for review.

Z

Zapple Rule A corollary to the equal time rule that states that when the supporters of a legally qualified candidate are given time on a radio or television broadcast, the supporters of all other legally qualified candidates for the same office must also be given equal opportunity.

INTERNET APPENDIX

As all college students today are well aware, the World Wide Web provides a vast amount of information that helps to make research for term papers, projects and theses both easier and more efficient. The same holds true for legal research projects like the kind that you might be asked to conduct for a course on mass media law.

The Web provides hundreds of sites replete with legal information. From the Web, you can access case law, federal and state codes and statutes, and law journals.

There are 16 important and excellent resources that we highly recommend. Those 16 sites are broken down here into four different categories: (1) First Amendment Advocacy Organizations; (2) Freedom of Information Resources; (3) General Starting Points for Legal Research; and (4) Government Resources Related to Law.

Take the time to explore each of these sites and find out what each has to offer. Rather than rely on descriptions that we might supply, you should visit each firsthand.

There are, of course, many other valuable online resources that you may want to consult. The following sites merely serve as points from which to begin your research.

FIRST AMENDMENT ADVOCACY ORGANIZATIONS

- First Amendment Center
  http://www.firstamendmentcenter.org
- Reporters Committee for Freedom of the Press
  http://www.rcfp.org
- Student Press Law Center
  http://www.splc.org
- National Coalition Against Censorship
  http://www.ncac.org

FREEDOM OF INFORMATION RESOURCES

- Citizen Access Project
  http://www.citizenaccess.org
- IRE's Freedom of Information Center
  http://www.ire.org/foi
- University of Missouri School of Journalism's Freedom of Information Center
  http://web.missouri.edu/~foiwww
- OpenTheGovernment.org
  http://www.openthegovernment.org

GENERAL STARTING POINTS FOR LEGAL RESEARCH

- American Bar Association's (ABA) Legal Technology Resource Center
  http://www.abanet.org/tech/ltrc/lawlink/home.html

- FindLaw—Internet Legal Resources
  http://www.findlaw.com
- Legal Information Institute, Cornell Law School
  http://www.law.cornell.edu
- Jurist Legal News and Research
  http://jurist.law.pitt.edu

GOVERNMENT RESOURCES

- Federal Communications Commission
  http://www.fcc.gov
- United States Federal Judiciary
  http://www.uscourts.gov
- United States Supreme Court Official Web Site
  http://www.supremecourtus.gov
- Federal Trade Commission
  http://www.ftc.gov

TABLE OF CASES

INDEX

Index

Index